Masterplots

Fourth Edition

Masterplots

Fourth Edition

Volume 2
The Big Sky—The Confidential Clerk

Editor
Laurence W. Mazzeno
Alvernia College

SALEM PRESS
Pasadena, California   Hackensack, New Jersey

Editor in Chief: Dawn P. Dawson

Editorial Director: Christina J. Moose	*Editorial Assistant:* Brett S. Weisberg
Development Editor: Tracy Irons-Georges	*Research Supervisor:* Jeffry Jensen
Project Editor: Desiree Dreeuws	*Research Assistant:* Keli Trousdale
Manuscript Editors: Constance Pollock,	*Production Editor:* Joyce I. Buchea
Judy Selhorst, Andy Perry	*Design and Graphics:* James Hutson
Acquisitions Editor: Mark Rehn	*Layout:* William Zimmerman

Cover photo: Johann Goethe (The Granger Collection, New York)

Library of Congress Cataloging-in-Publication Data

Masterplots / editor, Laurence W. Mazzeno. — 4th ed.
     v.   cm.
Includes bibliographical references and indexes.
ISBN 978-1-58765-568-5 (set : alk. paper) — ISBN 978-1-58765-570-8 (v. 2 : alk. paper)
1. Literature—Stories, plots, etc.   2. Literature—History and criticism.   I. Mazzeno, Laurence W.
PN44.M33 2010
809—dc22

2010033931

Fourth Edition
First Printing

Contents

Contents

Complete List of Titles

Volume 1

Volume 2

Contents lvii

Volume 3

Volume 4

Volume 5

Volume 6

Volume 7

Volume 8

Volume 9

Volume 10

Volume 11

Contents. cccxcix
Complete List of Titles. . . . . cdiii

Volume 12

Masterplots

Fourth Edition

The Big Sky

Author: A. B. Guthrie, Jr. (1901-1991)
First published: 1947
Type of work: Novel
Type of plot: Adventure
Time of plot: 1830-1843
Locale: Western United States

Principal characters:
BOONE CAUDILL, a mountain man
TEAL EYE, his Indian wife
JIM DEAKINS, his friend
DICK SUMMERS, an old hunter
JOURDONNAIS, a keelboat captain
POORDEVIL, a half-witted Blackfoot
ELISHA PEABODY, a Yankee speculator

The Story:

In 1830, Boone Caudill sets out alone for St. Louis and the West after a fight with his father. Taking his father's rifle with him, he heads for Louisville to get out of the state before his father can catch him. On the road, he meets Jim Deakins, an easygoing redhead, and the two decide to go west together. At Louisville, where the sheriff and Boone's father are waiting for the runaway, he and Jim are separated. Boone escapes by swimming the Ohio River to the Indiana shore.

When Boone is falsely accused of attempted theft and jailed, Jim, who followed him after their separation, steals the sheriff's keys and releases him. Together the boys continue west.

In St. Louis, they sign on as part of the crew of the keelboat *Mandan*. Most of the crew are French, as is the leader, Jourdonnais. The boat is headed for the country of the Blackfeet with a store of whiskey and other goods to trade for furs. Teal Eye, the young daughter of a Blackfoot chief, is also on board the ship. She was separated from her tribe for some time; Jourdonnais hopes to gain the friendship of the Indians by returning the young woman to them.

The keelboat moves slowly upstream by means of poles, a tow rope, and oars. Boone and Jim find a friend in Dick Summers, the hunter for the *Mandan*, whose job is to scout for Indians and keep the crew supplied with meat. He makes Boone and Jim his assistants. Jourdonnais is worried about getting to Blackfoot country before winter, and he works the crew hard. At last, they pass into the upper river beyond the mouth of the Platte River. All the greenhorns, including Boone and Jim, are initiated by being dunked in the river and having their heads shaved.

At last they are in buffalo country. Summers takes Boone with him to get some fresh meat. Attacked by a hunting party of Sioux, the white men escape unharmed, but Summers expects trouble from the hostile Indians farther along the line. A few days later, the *Mandan* is ambushed by a large Indian war party. Only the swivel gun on the deck of the boat saves the men from death.

Shortly before the *Mandan* arrives at Fort Union, two men try to sabotage the cargo. At Fort Union, Jourdonnais accuses the American Fur Company trader McKenzie of trying to stop him. McKenzie denies the charge, but he tries to argue Jourdonnais out of continuing upriver and offers to pay double value for the *Mandan*'s cargo. Jourdonnais refuses. At Fort Union, Boone meets his Uncle Zeb, an old-time mountain man. He predicts that the days of hunting and trapping in open country are nearly gone. Boone and Jim, however, do not believe him.

When the *Mandan* arrives in Blackfoot country, Teal Eye escapes. The crew begins to build a fort and trading post. One day, Indians attack and kill all but the three hunters: Boone, Jim, and Summers. For seven years these three hunt together, and Summers makes real mountain men out of the other two. In the spring of 1837, the three head for a rendezvous on the Seeds-Kee-Dee River, where they can sell their furs and gamble, drink, and fight with other mountain men. They take with them a half-witted Blackfoot named Poordevil.

At the rendezvous, Boone kills a man who said that he was going to take Poordevil's scalp. Then, after they have their fill of women and liquor, the three friends leave the camp. Summers, however, does not go hunting with them. No longer able to keep up the pace of the mountain men, he goes back to settle in Missouri. Boone, Jim, and Poordevil head up the Yellowstone toward Blackfoot country. The journey is Boone's idea. He knows that Teal Eye is now a grown woman. Her beauty remained in his memory all those years, and he wants her for his wife. On the way to Three Forks, Boone steals a horse from the Crow Indians and takes a Crow scalp, two actions that will help him make friends with the Blackfoot Indians.

They come upon a Blackfoot village ravaged by smallpox, but Boone refuses to stop until he is certain that Teal Eye is dead. At last he locates her. She is with a small band led by Red Horn, her brother, who sells her to Boone.

Life is good to Boone. For five years he lives happily among the Blackfoot Indians with Teal Eye as his wife. Jim lives in the Blackfoot camp also, but he often leaves for months at a time to go back down the Missouri. He craves companionship, while Boone enjoys living away from crowds. On one of his trips, Jim meets Elisha Peabody, a shrewd Yankee speculating upon the future prosperity of the Oregon Territory, who wants someone to show him a pass where wagons can cross the mountains. Jim and Boone contract to show him a suitable pass. Before Boone leaves, Teal Eye tells him that he will have a son when he returns.

The expedition has bad luck. Indians steal all the horses and wound Jim badly. Then snow falls, destroying all chances to get food. Finally, Boone is able to shoot some mountain goats. Jim recovers from his wound, and the party goes ahead on foot. Boone and Jim show Peabody the way across the mountains and into the Columbia Valley. It is spring when Boone returns to Teal Eye and his son.

The child, born blind, has a tinge of red in his hair. The baby's blindness brings a savage melancholy to Boone. Then some of the old Indians hint that the red hair shows the child is Jim's baby. Boone lays a trap to catch Jim with Teal Eye. Jim, suspecting nothing, finds Teal Eye alone in her lodge; he tries to comfort her about her child's blindness and the ugly mood of her husband. Boone mistakes the intent of Jim's conversation. Entering the lodge, he shoots Jim in the chest, killing him. He curses Teal Eye and leaves the Blackfoot camp. Then he heads back to Kentucky to see his mother before she dies.

In Kentucky, he finds his brother married and taking care of the farm. Boone grows restless. Slowly it comes to him that he was wrong about Jim and Teal Eye, for he notices that one of his brother's children has a tinge of red hair. His mother says that there is red hair in the family. When a neighbor girl insists that he marry her because he made love to her, Boone starts back to the West. He longs both for freedom and for Teal Eye.

In Missouri, he visits Summers, who now has a wife and a farm. Over their whiskey, Boone reveals to Summers that he killed Jim. He knows now that he made a mistake. Everything is spoiled for him—Teal Eye and all the West. The day of the mountain man is nearly over; farmers are going to Oregon. Without saying good-bye, he stumbles out into the night. Summers can see him weaving along the road for a short distance. Then the darkness swallows him, and he is gone.

Critical Evaluation:

In the tradition of James Fenimore Cooper's Leatherstocking romances, *The Big Sky* is distinguished among other fine historical novels for its realism and sharp insight into the psychology of the American Western pioneer. Like Cooper's adventure fiction, A. B. Guthrie's book explores the clash between two cultures: that of the retreating Indian tribes and that of the advancing Yankee frontiersmen. As the frontier expands westward, the Indians are forced to surrender their lands, their freedom, and their spiritual heritage. In the unequal struggle, the white pioneer, too, loses a portion of his heritage: a sense of idealism.

The "big sky" of Guthrie's title is the vast open land of the frontier, once teeming with wildlife, but slowly— even within the chronology of the novel, 1830 to 1843— changing, with the slaughter of buffalo, beaver, and other creatures of the forest and plains. In his descriptions of the land, its vegetation, and its animals, as well as of the rough frontiersmen, Guthrie has the eye of a naturalist; the smallest detail does not escape his attention. From *The Big Sky*, one learns how deer, elk, and mountain goats survive in the wilderness, how rivermen operate a keelboat, how fur hunters kill and strip game, and how mountain men endure the bitter Northern winters. Unlike many other adventure stories treating the West, Guthrie's novel is without sentimentality. For the hunters, traders, and marginal farmers of the outlying territories, life is hard and often brutal. In his realism, Guthrie does not gloss over the harsh truths of the time. Trapped in a winter storm without food, Beauchamp becomes a cannibal and devours his dead companion, Zenon. Boone Caudill murders his best friend, Jim Deakins, whom he wrongly suspects of fathering his son. Guthrie's treatment of the Indians is similarly unsentimental. The squaws who mate with the white hunters are described, for the most part, as dirty, complaisant whores; whole tribes, like the Piegans, are wiped out by smallpox; others are reduced to the condition of drunkards. Poordevil, the Blackfoot who accompanies Boone, Jim, Dick Summers, and the other trappers, is a hopeless alcoholic. Thus, to Guthrie, the clash between the two cultures brutalizes both the white people and the native Indians.

In his analysis of the characters' motivations, the author is also a tough-minded realist. His protagonist, Boone, is a violent, headstrong, mostly insensitive man whose redeeming virtue is his loyalty. Throughout most of his adventures, he trusts, with good reason, his longtime friend Jim. Yet, at the last, he kills Jim when he fears, mistakenly, that his friend has betrayed him. In a similar vengeful action, he abandons his beloved Indian wife, Teal Eye, when he suspects her of adultery. From these impulsive actions he brings about the ruin of his dreams. Guthrie once wrote that the theme of *The Big Sky* (paraphrasing Oscar Wilde) is that each man destroys the thing he loves best. Nevertheless, Boone's destructive impulse results as much from his early experiences as from his conscious will. Abused by his father, robbed by the clever rascal Jonathan Bedwell, cheated by the law, Boone has come to regard men warily, as objects of his revenge. His passions, too elemental to be curbed by reason, run their course, as in Greek tragedy. In a larger sense, however, his personal defeat is insignificant compared to the greater tragedy of the dwindling American frontier. Although Boone and his fellow frontiersmen love the land, they are at least partly responsible for ravaging it. By 1843, the year when the novel ends, much of the frontier still remained, but the pattern for its destruction had already been established. The "big sky," like the mountain men's idealistic ambitions, would henceforth be diminished.

Further Reading

Astro, Richard. "*The Big Sky* and the Limits of Wilderness Fiction." *Western American Literature* (Summer, 1974): 105-114. Astro maintains that *The Big Sky* fails as a nostalgic historical novel depicting the fall of a tragic hero. Boone Caudill, a one-dimensional character who is ignorant of the effect of time on historical details, cannot learn from friends or enemies, cannot gain wisdom, and symbolizes bankrupt primitivism.

Cracroft, Richard H. "*The Big Sky:* A. B. Guthrie's Use of Historical Sources." *Western American Literature* 6 (Fall, 1971): 163-176. Cracroft describes how Guthrie augments authenticity by writing into *The Big Sky* language, scenes, and incidents from works by Henry Marie Brackenridge, John Bradbury, Washington Irving, and George Frederick Ruxton, among others.

Erisman, Fred. *Reading A. B. Guthrie's "The Big Sky."* Boise, Idaho: Boise State University Press, 2000. A concise analysis of the novel. Includes bibliography.

Farr, William E., and William W. Bevis, eds. *Fifty Years After "The Big Sky": New Perspectives on the Fiction and Films of A. B. Guthrie, Jr.* Helena: Montana Historical Society Press, 2001. Reprints papers delivered at a 1997 conference commemorating the fiftieth year of *The Big Sky*'s publication. Includes pieces examining Guthrie's work and placing him within the broader context of the American West. Several pieces focus on *The Big Sky*, including essays about the female characters and the elements of classic myth and tragedy in the novel.

Ford, Thomas W. *A. B. Guthrie, Jr.* Boston: Twayne, 1981. Critical biography and introductory overview of Guthrie's work. Chapter 3 treats *The Big Sky* in terms of its plot, Guthrie's desire to present facts about mountain men and to convey his love of the West, the novel's landscape pictures, its themes of destructive violence and encroachment of civilization, its Calvinistic meditations, and its unadorned handling of time and space.

Gale, Robert L. "Guthrie's *The Big Sky*." *Explicator* 38 (Summer, 1980): 7-8. Sees Jim Deakins's offer of his own flesh to feed Boone Caudill and the goat's gift of blood to Boone as forming a Holy Eucharist which Boone ignorantly spurns, resulting in unsociability and natural desolation.

O'Connell, Nicholas. *At the Field's End: Interviews with Twenty-two Pacific Northwest Writers.* Seattle: University of Washington Press, 1998. This volume, an expanded edition of a book originally published in 1987, includes an interview with Guthrie, in which he discusses the influence of the region upon his writing and other aspects of his work.

Petersen, David. "A. B. Guthrie, Jr.: A Remembrance." In *Updating the Literary West*, sponsored by the Western Literature Association. Fort Worth: Texas Christian University Press, 1997. An overview of Guthrie's work.

Stewart, Donald C. "The Functions of Bird and Sky Imagery in Guthrie's *The Big Sky*." *Critique: Studies in Modern Fiction* 19, no. 2 (1977): 53-61. Presents interlocking bird and sky similes and metaphors as transforming a well-organized novel into coherent, imaginative art. Demonstrates how images individualize characters and actions, underline moods, and elucidate themes.

The Big Sleep

Author: Raymond Chandler (1888-1959)
First published: 1939
Type of work: Novel
Type of plot: Detective and mystery
Time of plot: 1930's
Locale: Los Angeles

Principal characters:
PHILIP MARLOWE, a private detective
GENERAL GUY STERNWOOD, a sick, old rich man who
　employs Marlowe
VIVIAN STERNWOOD (MRS. REGAN), Sternwood's immoral
　older daughter
CARMEN STERNWOOD, General Sternwood's lascivious
　younger daughter
EDDIE MARS, a casino operator and racketeer
ARTHUR GEIGER, a pornographer and blackmailer
BERNIE OHLS, an assistant district attorney and Marlowe's
　friend
CANINO, a paid killer

The Story:

A tough, cynical, independent, thirty-three-year-old private detective, Philip Marlowe, recommended by his friend, Assistant District Attorney Bernie Ohls, agrees to interview wealthy General Guy Sternwood at Sternwood's lush West Hollywood estate.

Old and dying, Sternwood hopes to salvage the last remnants of family pride nearly destroyed by his two immoral daughters. Sternwood hires Marlowe to thwart Arthur Geiger, a blackmailer. Ostensibly, Geiger is squeezing Sternwood over a gambling debt incurred by Sternwood's disturbed younger daughter, Carmen. Dim-witted, spoiled, and promiscuous, Carmen unsuccessfully throws herself at Marlowe when he first arrives at the estate, only to be disdainfully rejected.

Before leaving, Marlowe is summoned by the General's older daughter, Vivian (Mrs. Regan). A seductive, black-haired beauty, Vivian seeks to discover whether Marlowe was hired to locate her missing husband, Rusty Regan. Marlowe already knows from the General that Regan, a former bootlegger and Irish Republican Army officer, was Sternwood's companion and protector—the bright spot in his waning life. Unimpressed by Vivian's rich-bitch style, Marlowe, with his trademark insouciance, refuses to reveal his client's wishes. Vivian seems relieved, however, that Marlowe apparently is not looking for Rusty. Nonetheless, displeased by Marlowe's blunt talk and lack of servility, she haughtily dismisses him. The detective leaves feeling that he emerged from a decadent loony bin.

Marlowe begins his assignment by casing Geiger's bookstore and by tracking Geiger, who soon confirms his hunch that the bookstore fronts for the sale of pornography. On a rainy night, he next trails Geiger home. While Marlowe

watches, Carmen's Packard arrives and a woman enters the house.

Events then move swiftly. Light from a flashbulb is followed by a scream inside the house, which draws Marlowe closer. His knock on Geiger's door is followed by three shots. Someone pounds down Geiger's back stairs and there are sounds of a car starting. Breaking in, Marlowe finds Geiger dead. Virtually naked and obviously drugged, Carmen, babbling incoherently, appears, unaware of what happened. Marlowe bundles her home in her Packard and leaves her with a trusted maid. Quickly returning to the murder scene, Marlowe finds that Geiger's body is gone. Since the killer fled, it is apparent that someone else wants Geiger missing. Searching the house, Marlowe locates a notebook listing hundreds of potential blackmail victims, leaving the police plenty of suspects.

The following day, Marlowe accompanies Ohls while Vivian's Buick is dredged from the water. Inside is a murdered man Marlowe identifies as Owen Taylor, an ex-con who once ran off with Carmen, but who at the end of his imprisonment was retained as the Sternwoods' chauffeur. After this incident, Marlowe returns to Geiger's store in time to observe someone removing Geiger's books. Following the cargo, Marlowe discovers the recipient is Joe Brody, a hustler who earlier successfully blackmailed General Sternwood over Carmen.

Later at his office, Marlowe is unexpectedly met by Vivian. Troubled and apologetic, she displays a blackmail note including a pornographic photograph of Carmen accompanied by a demand for five thousand dollars. A woman phoned her, she reports, demanding payment that night or else the negative will be given to the scandal sheets. Not yet in possession of her inheritance, Vivian proposes that she get the money from Eddie Mars, a racketeer in whose casino she often gambles. Marlowe agrees. Vivian, meantime, discloses nothing about her Buick or her murdered chauffeur inside. She reveals, however, why Mars is likely (as he soon does) to lend her the money. Her missing husband, Rusty, it seems, ran off with Mona, Mars's missing wife.

Returning to Geiger's, Marlowe finds Carmen lurking about. Inside with Marlowe, she names Brody, her former blackmailer, as Geiger's killer. Mars and his goons then arrive, demanding to know why Marlowe is there. In their ensuing exchanges, Mars denies killing Geiger. Warned off by Mars, Marlowe then locates Brody and his girlfriend, Agnes, whom he scares by implying that the police might find Brody a prime suspect in Geiger's still undisclosed murder. Having shadowed Marlowe, Carmen suddenly breaks in and tries to kill Brody. Terrified, Brody surrenders the photos of Carmen to Marlowe, who promptly sends Carmen packing. Brody, called to the door moments afterward, is fatally shot. Marlowe catches the killer, a youth who was Geiger's homosexual lover and the person responsible for moving Geiger's corpse.

Marlowe delivers the photos to Sternwood's trusted servant and Brody's killer to the police. Though hassled by them, he maintains the integrity of his client, despite having withheld evidence. The same day, Sternwood offers to pay Marlowe to find Rusty, but Marlowe, refusing the money, decides to proceed unassigned. At home, Marlowe finds Carmen, naked, waiting to seduce him, and angrily ousts her. In the evening, ignoring Mars's warnings, he visits Mars's casino. In their tough exchanges Mars again denies killing anyone. Vivian, too, is present and winning heavily. As she leaves, Marlowe prevents one of Mars's thugs from robbing her of her winnings. While being escorted home, Vivian, aping Carmen, fails either to seduce Marlowe or to gain information.

New connections materialize when another hustler, Harry Jones, desperate for money to leave town with Brody's ex-girlfriend, Agnes, sells Marlowe vital evidence. Jones confirms that Vivian knows Canino, a Mars hitman, and that Canino knows where to locate Mars's wife. Subsequently checking Jones's story, Marlowe, hidden in Jones's office, witnesses Canino poisoning Jones.

With these leads, Marlowe uncovers Mona Mars's hideaway, but in the process a flat tire lands him in Canino's hands. Slugged, captured, and bound, Marlowe briefly is guarded by the beautiful blond, Mona, whom Marlowe persuades to release him, although he is still handcuffed. Reaching his car and a pistol, he kills Canino in an ensuing shootout, all of which he swiftly reports to the police.

Marlowe's evidence then allows him to solve key parts of the mystery. Since everyone knows of bad blood between

Mars and Regan, Mars, with Mona's connivance and Canino's aid, fakes Mona's disappearance to allay suspicions that Mars killed Regan. In the meantime, Mars, through Geiger, runs an elaborate blackmail scheme. First, he blackmails the ever-vulnerable Carmen. Later, after Vivian receives her millions, Mars plans to blackmail her, too. Vivian and Mars are aware that Carmen killed Rusty for refusing to sleep with her and that Vivian then persuaded Mars to dispose of Regan's body. In love with Carmen, and loathing what Geiger did to her, chauffeur Taylor shot Geiger. Marlowe never clarifies who killed Taylor. It is because Geiger's death ultimately threatens to lead to Mona's whereabouts that Canino poisons Jones.

Finally, employed officially by Sternwood to find Regan, Marlowe, agreeing to teach Carmen to shoot, cons her into trying to kill him on the site where Regan's body has been dumped. To save Sternwood's pride, Marlowe then remands Carmen to Vivian, urging that she seek help for her now psychotic sister. Mars, his blackmail scheme aborted, is questioned and released by the police. Although guilty, he neither directly blackmails nor kills anyone. Justice for Marlowe means honoring Sternwood's wishes. Sooner or later, after all, everyone succumbs to the big sleep—but not without first having dreamed, as Marlowe does, of the gorgeous Mona.

Critical Evaluation:

The Big Sleep is Raymond Chandler's first novel. Many critics have considered it a classic. Arguably it is the best of Chandler's seven novels, and unquestionably it ranks above the writing of Dashiell Hammett as among the finest examples of its genre in the twentieth century. As such, it proved extremely influential. Other mystery writers, such as Ross Macdonald, Robert B. Parker, and Mickey Spillane, acknowledged Chandler's influence. Mystery readers into the mid-1980's listed Chandler as their third favorite, just behind Sir Arthur Conan Doyle and Agatha Christie. In addition, writers such as Alistair Cooke and Bernard De Voto regarded Chandler as an important literary figure. Chandler may have been all the more respected and influential because of his ardent belief that fine mystery writing deserves full acceptance as respectable literature by the world of letters. Moreover, many critics believed that, when other writers elevated the value of style, Chandler doubtless merited a front rank.

In Philip Marlowe, *The Big Sleep*'s narrator, Chandler creates a new species of hard-boiled private detective whose character continues evolving in his subsequent novels. Previous private-eye fiction had been freighted with square-jawed heroes who resolved matters with guns and fists. Encased in a cynic's armor, Marlowe, however, beneath all, is a knight, his name itself drawn by Chandler from Sir Thomas Malory's fifteenth century tales of chivalry.

Marlowe is an honest man in a sleazy trade, which he plies amid the tacky superficialities of Los Angeles and Southern California, a sump where the American Dream is going bad. In a world of money worshipers, Marlowe reflects Chandler's own hatred of the rich and their decadent influences. A romantic at heart, like the reasonably honest cops he encounters, Marlowe has learned to strip his expectations about American justice to the bone. He asserts his independence, however, and remains loyal to his clients, pragmatically attending to his craft. Thus, he manages to bring forth justice of a sort.

Chandler's story making is affected by his gift for near-total recall. Marlowe, for instance, is constructed from characters in four of his early short stories. The private investigator's more distant predecessors in American literature include James Fenimore Cooper's Natty Bumppo, Mark Twain's Huckleberry Finn, and Ernest Hemingway's Nick Adams, all of whom, a Chandler biographer observed, believed in the incorruptibility of at least a part of the population. Chandler keeps the scenes in the novel's thirty-two brief chapters simple, acknowledging he had difficulty getting characters in and out of rooms. His plot, on the other hand, which also contains elements from previous work, is Byzantine. Indeed, *The Big Sleep* might well have been two stories, one of which ends when Marlowe decides to discover Regan's fate. Chandler's fresh stylistic verve, however, moves his complicated tale successfully.

Filled with social criticism, another Chandler first for mystery novels, *The Big Sleep* is also rich in the metaphors that lace its tough-guy talk and keen repartee. Chandler's metaphors reflect, as perceptive critics have noted, a mechanistic world measured in time, space, mass, and inertia. This world is described with comparisons of size, speed, impact, and balance. Moral absolutes are conspicuous by their absence. Critical of himself, Chandler, hence Marlowe, as *The Big Sleep* confirms, approaches life as an ambiguous mixture of the romantic and the realist. Marlowe lives almost existentially, taking independent action in regard to people and institutions, refining his own values, resisting temptations that would destroy his self-esteem, and taking responsibility for his actions—knowing that nobody cares.

Clifton K. Yearley

Further Reading

Chandler, Raymond. *Raymond Chandler Speaking*. Edited by Dorothy Gardiner and Katherine Walker. Berkeley: University of California Press, 1997. Chandler speaks on a range of subjects, including his life, the mystery novel in general, his mystery novels in particular, the craft of writing, his character Philip Marlowe, and cats. Includes a chronology.

Durham, Philip. *Down These Mean Streets a Man Must Go: Raymond Chandler's Knight*. Chapel Hill: University of North Carolina Press, 1963. An outstanding study of Chandler's work, including *The Big Sleep*.

Freeman, Judith. *The Long Embrace: Raymond Chandler and the Woman He Loved*. New York: Pantheon Books, 2007. Freeman believed that Chandler's life was a greater mystery than his novels, so she set out on a journey to learn more about the author. She traveled to the almost two dozen Southern California houses and apartments where he and his wife lived and uncovered information about Chandler's wife Cissy, who played a crucial role in his understanding of women and of himself. Freeman's research resulted in a book that illuminates Chandler's personality and psyche.

Gross, Miriam, ed. *The World of Raymond Chandler*. London: Weidenfeld & Nicolson, 1977. A superb collection of critical essays on Chandler's work by writers and scholars who provide ample discussion of *The Big Sleep*.

Hiney, Tom. *Raymond Chandler: A Biography*. New York: Atlantic Monthly Press, 1997. A brief biography of Chandler that discusses his education in England, his relationship to Los Angeles, and the plots and characters of his most important detective novels and stories.

MacShane, Frank. *The Life of Raymond Chandler*. New York: E. P. Dutton, 1976. This is one of the best biographies of Chandler's character, as well as an informed analysis of his writings. Mentioned throughout, *The Big Sleep* is the subject of chapter 4.

Marling, William. *Raymond Chandler*. Boston: Twayne, 1986. An excellent critical survey of Chandler's life and writings. Although there are many references to *The Big Sleep*, chapter 5 is devoted entirely to the novel.

Speir, Jerry. *Raymond Chandler*. New York: Frederick Ungar, 1981. A thoughtful survey that contains frequent comments on *The Big Sleep*.

Widdicombe, Toby. *A Reader's Guide to Raymond Chandler*. Westport, Conn.: Greenwood Press, 2001. An alphabetical listing of Chandler's works, characters, places, allusions, and major topics. The appendixes contain information on Chandler's screenwriting, other writers' adaptations of Chandler, and the portrayal of the character of Philip Marlowe on film, television, and radio.

The Biglow Papers

Author: James Russell Lowell (1819-1891)
First published: first series, 1848; second series, 1867
Type of work: Poetry

Principal characters:
HOSEA BIGLOW, the Yankee author of the poems in *The Biglow Papers*
BIRDOFREDUM SAWIN, his correspondent, a Massachusetts militiaman (first series), an adopted Rebel (second series)
HOMER WILBUR, parson of the First Church of Jaalam, author of the editorial comments in *The Biglow Papers*

The Biglow Papers is political satire and, as such, cannot be understood or appreciated until the reader is acquainted, first, with the policies and ideas being satirized and, second, with the conditions of publication. In short, like all satire, it must be seen in historical perspective before it can be evaluated.

There are two series of *The Biglow Papers*. The first is an attack, from the Whig-Abolitionist point of view, on the Mexican War and the policies of President James Polk and the proslavery forces that authorized it; the second—all but the last paper—is an attack, from the Northern Republican point of view, on the rebellious, slaveholding South, the Democrats, and the interventionist policies of England during the first years of the American Civil War; the last paper is a condemnation of the "retrograde movement" of President Andrew Johnson.

The history of the papers is rather complex. In one sense, it dates back to 1840 and the beginning of James Russell Lowell's relationship with Maria White, who became his wife in 1844, for it was this visionary and forceful young woman who first converted him to the abolitionist cause. In any case, by the time of the outbreak of the Mexican War in 1846, Lowell had identified himself with the movement by contributions to the *National Anti-Slavery Standard*, which he edited for a short time. Such a radical position was more in keeping with the spirit of the Emersonians than with that of the aloof Brahmins with whom Lowell was allied by birth, and the strong influence of his wife's personality and ideals may be inferred from the fact that Lowell grew more and more conservative in the years following her death. By the time of his own death he was once more a conservative, but, in the 1840's, his radical leanings brought him into the camp of those idealistic New Englanders who preached freedom vociferously (and at times effectively) and those shrewd and stubborn rural Yankees who supported them for more practical reasons. The first series of *The Biglow*

Papers arose from the interaction of these two elements. Abolitionist idealism gave it motivation; Yankee shrewdness gave it form.

The first Biglow paper appeared as a letter to the editor of the *Boston Courier*, a weekly Whig newspaper, in June of 1846. The letter was signed by one Ezekiel Biglow of Jaalam, Massachusetts, and its ostensible purpose was to introduce a poem by Mr. Biglow's son, Hosea. The important thing here was the poem, an attack, in the Yankee dialect, on the recruiting of the Massachusetts regiment for service in a war which the abolitionists and their sympathizers claimed was being fought only to extend the borders of slavery.

The response to this first letter prompted Lowell to continue the poetic exertions of young Mr. Biglow. "The success of my experiment," wrote Lowell later in the introduction to the second series, "soon began not only to astonish me, but to make me feel the responsibility of knowing I had in my hand a weapon instead of the mere fencing stick I had supposed." Lowell, clad in the rustic armor of Hosea Biglow, entered the fray with this newfound weapon eight more times in the following two years. Five of these dialect poems are direct political attacks on the war party group and their sympathizers, the Democrats and the Cotton-Whigs (as opposed to the Conscience-Whigs, who favored the war and were more or less tolerant of slavery), particularly those to be found in Biglow's—and Lowell's—own Bay State. The other three provide a more general satire of the progress of the war, of the ignorance, inefficiency, and immorality of those in command, and of the mistreatment of the Massachusetts enlisted man, both as soldier and as disabled veteran.

This general satire is presented through a new character, Birdofredum Sawin, whom Lowell introduces in his second letter to the *Courier*. Sawin is a ne'er-do-well Yankee from Jaalam who, succumbing to the blandishments of the recruiting officer, enlists as a private in the Massachusetts regiment. From Mexico, he writes back to Hosea, who turns his letter into the Eastern Massachusetts equivalent of iambic heptameter couplets. Birdofredum's complaints and caustic observations supply the material for Papers Two, Eight, and Nine. In the second paper, he is engaged in combat. In Papers Eight and Nine, he is released from service minus one eye and one arm; he still has two legs, though by this time one of them is wooden.

The third character of these papers does not come upon the scene until the poems were published in book form late in 1848. This character is the pastor of the First Church of Jaalam, the Reverend Homer Wilbur, who is presented as the editor of the volume. Lowell admitted eighteen years later that he needed a character who would present the more cautious side of the New England character, expressing simple common sense enlivened by conscience.

The pedantry and the long-winded self-centeredness of Wilbur adds much to the book—literally, for the learned churchman's remarks take up more space in the volume than do the nine original poems. His verbose expatiations do, undoubtedly, allow Lowell to express those more cautious elements of the Yankee character and to extend his satire by poking fun at the excessive and distracting paraphernalia that encumber learned works. Most amusing, perhaps, are the "Notices of an Independent Press" that Biglow admittedly wrote himself and included as the lengthy material at the beginning of the volume. Besides offering amusing material, Wilbur becomes eloquent in his own right in defense of freedom. For the most part, however, Lowell's imitation of pedantry is too realistic. Rather than acting as ballast, Wilbur almost causes the book to sink. In the end, this character's main contribution is that of making the poems, when they finally appear, more delightful because of their contrast to his wordy prose.

The addition of Wilbur was a sign of the innate conservative caution in Lowell's character as artist, critic, and political figure. This caution and conservatism betray themselves still more in the second series of *The Biglow Papers*. By the time the slavery question reached its climax, Lowell was no longer the outspoken young abolitionist radical of the 1840's. By then he had been for six years professor of belles-lettres at Harvard (having succeeded his friend Henry Wadsworth Longfellow to that chair in 1855), had founded and was still editor of the *Atlantic Monthly*, and, perhaps most important of all, had lost his wife, Maria White Lowell, and had remarried. Occasionally he is effective in the second series, especially in the letters from Birdofredum Sawin (who, after having been falsely imprisoned in the South for two years, marries a slaveholding widow and becomes a sympathizer with the Southern cause) and in the last part of

the second paper, an attack on England that ends with a piece bearing the title of "Jonathan to John."

In these he rises to the satirical heights of the original collection, but for the most part, as Lowell admitted, the papers of the second series are more studied, less spontaneous, more cautious, and less biting than those of the first. Even the quaintness of the old Yankee diction is intentionally diminished, excused by the claim that Hosea is being tutored by Parson Wilbur and is learning proper spelling and academic phraseology.

Lowell keeps the Yankee dialect to the last, but in the end his apparent need to defend its use is another indication of the dying out of his earlier satiric fire. The individual numbers of the second series were first printed in the *Atlantic Monthly*; when, in 1867, they were collected in book form, Lowell wrote a lengthy introduction for them. A brilliant contribution to linguistic knowledge, the preface is made concrete by Lowell's sensitive ear for dialect, and it is documented by his voluminous reading in English and American literature. Valuable as it is in its own right, however, it is still an apology, and, when satire is apologized for, it loses much of its force, much of its reason for being.

As a whole, however, despite this decreasing force, *The Biglow Papers* remains an important American literary monument. First, it is important historically as a vivid expression of public opinion in a particular section of the country during an especially critical stage in the health of the United States. Second, it is important in American literary history as one of the earliest examples of dialect writing and as the very earliest example of the Yankee dialect. Most of all, it is intrinsically important as an outspoken example of independent thought, of that Yankee independence, outspokenness, and ironic humor that are a part of national tradition.

Further Reading

Arms, George. *The Fields Were Green: A New View of Bryant, Whittier, Holmes, Lowell, and Longfellow, with a Selection of Their Poems*. Stanford, Calif.: Stanford University Press, 1948. Places Lowell and his production in the context of the best popular poetry of the times. Downgrades *The Biglow Papers* in comparison to Lowell's other poetry.

Broaddus, Dorothy C. *Genteel Rhetoric: Writing High Culture in Nineteenth-Century Boston*. Columbia: University of South Carolina Press, 1999. Lowell and other writers living in Boston in the mid-nineteenth century shared a belief that an American writer should be moral, educated, appreciative of fine art and literature, and conduct himself with genteel bearing and good manners. Broaddus discusses the life and work of these writers and describes how this vision of gentility was altered by the reality of the abolitionist movement and the Civil War.

Butler, Leslie. *Critical Americans: Victorian Intellectuals and Transatlantic Liberal Reform.* Chapel Hill: University of North Carolina Press, 2007. Recounts how Lowell and three of his friends—writers George William Curtis, Thomas Wentworth Higginson, and Charles Eliot Norton—worked with British intellectuals to promote progressive and cosmopolitan reform in the decades between the 1850's and 1890's.

Duberman, Martin. *James Russell Lowell.* Boston: Houghton Mifflin, 1966. Largely concerned with the objects of satire in *The Biglow Papers*: the recruiting of Massachusetts troops for the Mexican War, the institution of slavery, shoddy politicians, and American expansionism. Criticizes the poems for their prose interruptions, tiresome repetitions, and inconsistent tone and point of view.

McGlinchee, Claire. *James Russell Lowell.* New York: Twayne, 1967. Summarizes *The Biglow Papers*, stressing the youthful, zestful satire of the first series and the sagacious patriotism, vivified by the profuse use of Yankee dialect, expressed in the second series.

Rodríguez, J. Javier. "The U.S.-Mexican War in James Russell Lowell's *The Biglow Papers.*" *Arizona Quarterly* 63, no. 3 (Autumn, 2007): 1. Examines Lowell's complex depiction of the Mexican War, which ranges from American jingoism to a "suspicious self-criticality" and finally to a "feverishly self-aware angst that questions the validity of nations, language, knowledge, and truth itself."

Wagenknecht, Edward. *James Russell Lowell: Portrait of a Many-Sided Man.* New York: Oxford University Press, 1971. Relates *The Biglow Papers* to Lowell the writer and the man, including his love of tobacco, lack of interest in drama, fondness for both Latinate and colloquial diction, vast reading experience, and political beliefs.

Wortham, Thomas. "Introduction." In *James Russell Lowell's The Biglow Papers, First Series: A Critical Edition.* DeKalb: Northern Illinois University Press, 1977. Details the political background inspiring Lowell to start *The Biglow Papers* and accounts for the immense popularity of the work. Analyzes Lowell's skillful handling of characterization, his use of pervasive irony, and the poetic and narrative structure of the poems.

Billy Bathgate

Author: E. L. Doctorow (1931-   )
First published: 1989
Type of work: Novel
Type of plot: Historical realism
Time of plot: 1934-1935
Locale: Bronx, New York City, Onondaga, and Saratoga Springs, New York; Newark, New Jersey

Principal characters:
BILLY BATHGATE, a teenager living in the Bronx
MARY BEHAN, his mother
OTTO "ABBADABBA" BERMAN, numbers runner in the Schultz mob
DIXIE DAVIS, a lawyer working for the Schultz mob
THOMAS E. DEWEY, a public prosecutor
ARNOLD GARBAGE, an orphan friend of Billy
IRVING, Dutch Schulz's right-hand man
MICHAEL "MICKEY" O'HANLEY, a former prizefighter and a driver for Schultz
DREW "MRS." PRESTON, a society "girl" who has relationships with Dutch Schultz, Bo Weinberg, and Billy
REBECCA, an orphaned friend of Billy
LULU ROSENKRANTZ, an enforcer for the Schultz mob
DUTCH SCHULTZ (ARTHUR FLEGENHEIMER), a psychotic gangster and former bootlegger
BO WEINBERG, a hit man for the Schultz gang

The Story:

One summer day in the middle of the Great Depression, the fifteen-year-old Billy Bathgate and his friends are socializing in front of a warehouse in the Bronx. The building belongs to Arthur Flegenheimer, better known as Dutch Schultz, a local boy who became a gangster by bootlegging alcohol during Prohibition. Dutch and his associates park in front of the warehouse, and the gangster notices Billy juggling across the street. Dutch calls Billy over and gives him ten dollars, saying he is a capable boy.

Billy parlays this brief introduction into a place, albeit a minor one, in Dutch's gang. He is taken under the wing of Otto "Abbadabba" Berman, the financial planner of the outfit, who makes Billy his protégé. Billy, a teen whose friends are orphans, whose father is missing, and whose mother is an eccentric, has experienced a difficult childhood. In addition to this background, the scarcity of money and opportunity helps motivate him to join the Schultz gang.

As he becomes more familiar with Dutch himself, Billy realizes that this initially glamorous figure is really a psychotic killer, capable of violent mood swings and outbursts of uncontrolled savagery. One day not long after Billy begins to associate with the mob, he witnesses Dutch beat a city inspector to death for little more than showing up at one of his establishments at the wrong time.

Dutch Schultz and his associates are in many ways past their prime by the time Billy meets them. A major player during the bootlegging days of the previous decade, by the mid-1930's Dutch has become an increasingly minor figure in New York's underworld. He is under indictment for tax evasion and is being sought by the Internal Revenue Service. Much of the story takes place in Onandaga, New York, the upstate venue that Schultz has finagled for his trial.

The Schultz gang moves to the small, economically depressed town of Onandaga and spends some weeks spreading largess and earning goodwill among the local population. Dutch has brought along his new girlfriend, Drew Preston, a socialite he took away from his hit man, Bo Weinberg, after killing him. During their residence, Drew poses as Billy's nanny, so the pair spends a lot of time together, a situation that leads them to begin a sexual relationship. This relationship places the couple in some danger if Dutch should find out. As the time for the trial to begin approaches, Dutch sends Billy and Drew to the horse races at Saratoga Springs to provide an excuse for them to leave town, reducing any distractions from the trial.

In Saratoga, Billy effects a reunion between Drew and her husband to protect her from Dutch, and he returns to the Bronx to await the outcome of the trial. As a result of the

goodwill he purchased in town, the jury acquits Dutch. He returns to New York City a free man.

When Dutch arrives back in New York, he discovers that the Sicilian mafia has assumed control of the city's organized crime structures and illegal trades. Dutch does not understand how this happened, and he is unwilling to tolerate the takeover. At the same time, district attorney and future presidential candidate Thomas Dewey begins to investigate Dutch's activities, forcing what is left of his gang to go into hiding. They move into a second-rate hotel in Newark, New Jersey.

Dutch asks Billy to run errands for him to maintain his declining connections in the city, while his associates are scattered or killed by the newly powerful mafia. Dutch and his closest associates meet nightly in a restaurant to eat and make their plans to regain the power they have lost. One night when Billy is in the restroom, all of the gang is murdered in the restaurant's back room. Billy escapes out the narrow bathroom window but only after he has been told the combination of the gang's safe back at the hotel. Loaded with a bag full of cash, Billy returns to the Bronx.

Billy is questioned by the Sicilians about Dutch's missing money but tells them nothing, emphasizing a naivete that is not entirely feigned. His deathbed vigil at Dutch's hospital room is his last act of loyalty to the man he has so ardently followed throughout the narrative.

Later, Billy discovers a barrel of cash in one of Dutch's warehouses and begins a business with one of his old orphan friends. The money also allows him to get a better apartment for his mother and himself. One day, a baby arrives, his child by Drew Preston and a harbinger of a future less violent than the past.

Critical Evaluation:

Through the historical realist novel *Billy Bathgate*, E. L. Doctorow delivers a fable of a young man's initiation into the world, his process of disillusion and education, against the background of a 1930's crime story. The novel begins in the middle of the story with a scene, both comic and sad, in which Bo Weinberg sits on a tugboat. The trousers of his evening dress are rolled up so that his feet can rest in a tub of cement, waiting for it to dry. Afterward, he will be thrown overboard. Billy witnesses this act of retribution and brutality, and it serves as a reader's introduction to the events that follow.

The novel contains a number of themes common to many of Doctorow's novels. One is the search for the absent father and the need for a mentor who will help the protagonist achieve success. The novel inverts the conventions of Horatio Alger's stories, in which luck and honest hard work allow the hero to succeed. Billy gains wealth, but it is wealth that he has not earned and that was amassed through others' criminal acts. As is true of *The Book of Daniel* (1971), *Loon Lake* (1980), and *World's Fair* (1985)—Doctorow's other books that treat the 1930's—*Billy Bathgate* uses a fable-like plot to explore the sources and pitfalls of success in America.

Additionally, the character of Billy acts as a surrogate for the writer. He is an observer, a shaper of the narrative, and the one who understands the larger issues that are obscure to the other characters. Through Billy, the novel explores the confluence of the literary and the historical. It examines the ways in which literature can present history and the ways in which history shapes literature.

Doctorow once observed that when Ernest Hemingway wrote a novel he would implant it in geography. It would be equally true to observe of Doctorow that when he writes a novel he implants it in history. *Billy Bathgate* is historical on several levels. It takes place during the Great Depression, when the United States was experiencing a catastrophic economic downturn and ordinary citizens lost their savings, jobs, and futures. Crime and criminals appeared less threatening, and many figures such as Dutch Schultz grabbed newspaper headlines and were treated as celebrities.

The novel is also historical in that it incorporates a number of traditional narrative types that rely on a first-person narrator who is subjected to a series of adventures. In some cases, as in the bildungsroman, these experiences provide a process of maturation during which a young person (usually a young man) learns about life through his encounters with older and wiser mentors. Charles Dickens's *Great Expectations* (1860-1861, serial; 1861, book) and Samuel Butler's *The Way of All Flesh* (1903) are examples of this kind of fiction. Sometimes, such works are also called apprenticeship novels after Goethe's *Wilhelm Meisters Lehrjahre* (1795-1796; *Wilhelm Meister's Apprenticeship*, 1824). In any case, the hero normally grows into a more responsible and engaged adult as a result of the experiences.

Billy Bathgate also employs elements of another historical first-person narrative called the picaresque novel, which traditionally involves a roguish character of questionable degree who experiences a series of events. However, unlike the bildungsroman, the picaresque novel tends to be episodic rather than developmental and the protagonist usually does not mature or change over its course. Billy Bathgate fulfills the role of the picaresque protagonist through his participation in the various scams and illegal machinations of the Dutch Schultz operation.

It is unclear just what Billy learns from his time with the Schultz gang and the psychotic ravings and seething silences

of Dutch. This issue of Billy learning is highlighted by a comic episode in which Dutch and Drew squabble over the pronunciation and meaning of the word "protégé." This episode may evoke Billy's search for a father in the guise of a mentor, emphasizing his need to learn to develop. That paternal search centers not only on Billy's relationship with Dutch but also on his relationship with Abbadabba Berman. Billy seems to respond to the teachings of Berman, who genuinely tries to help him learn something about life, even if that life is in the criminal world.

Historically, *Billy Bathgate* traces not only the decline of Dutch Schultz, one of New York's more prominent Jewish gangsters, but also the rise of the mafia, which would seize control of New York's crime structure from the more ethnically diverse mob of the 1930's. The presence that hovers over the span of the novel is this expanding power of a newer criminal organization, accompanied by the increasing legal pressures of Thomas Dewey's operation. Dutch Schultz is caught between the law and lawlessness, and his rise to power and wealth is compromised in many ways by the means by which he accumulated that wealth. Success is represented as a tenuous thing in American life, hard to achieve and easy to lose. Dutch Schultz, by remaining an individual entrepreneur, remains in rebellion against the corporate criminal world, and he pays for his refusal to be absorbed. In the modern world of commerce, criminal or not, there seems to be little place for eccentricity, personality, or rebelliousness.

Charles L. P. Silet

Further Reading

Bloom, Harold, ed. *E. L. Doctorow*. Philadelphia: Chelsea House, 2002. A general collection of essays on Doctorow covering the breadth of his work.

Doctorow, E. L. *Conversations with E. L. Doctorow*. Edited by Christopher D. Morris. Jackson: University Press of Mississippi, 1999. This collection of interviews with Doctorow covers his writing career. Chapter 3 focuses on *Billy Bathgate*.

Fowler, Douglas. *Understanding E. L. Doctorow*. Columbia: University of South Carolina Press, 1992. Puts forth an explication of Doctrow's major fiction.

Harter, Carol C., and James R. Thompson. *E. L. Doctorow*. Boston: Twayne, 1990. A concise general overview of Doctrow's work and career.

Levine, Paul. *E. L. Doctorow*. New York: Methuen, 1985. A short overview of Doctorow's life and writing.

Morris, Christopher D. *Models of Misrepresentation: On the*

Fiction of E. L. Doctorow. Jackson: University Press of Mississippi, 1991. Takes a broad approach to Doctorow's work. Chapter 10 focuses on *Billy Bathgate.*

Siegel, Ben, ed. *Critical Essays on E. L. Doctorow.* New York: G. K. Hall, 2000. This collection covers a variety of approaches to Doctorow's fiction.

Tokarczyk, Michelle M. *E. L. Doctorow's Skeptical Commit-*

ment. New York: Peter Lang, 2000. A generous discussion of the role of history in Doctorow's novels.

Williams, John. *Fiction as False Document: The Reception of E. L. Doctorow in the Postmodern Age.* Columbia, S.C.: Camden House, 1996. Applies a comprehensive, theoretical examination of Doctorow's novels with only a brief mention of *Billy Bathgate.*

Billy Budd, Foretopman

Author: Herman Melville (1819-1891)
First published: 1924
Type of work: Novel
Type of plot: Symbolic realism
Time of plot: 1797
Locale: Aboard a British man-of-war

Principal characters:
BILLY BUDD, a young British sailor
CAPTAIN VERE, commanding officer of HMS *Indomitable*
CLAGGART, master-at-arms aboard the *Indomitable*

The Story:

In 1797, the British merchant ship *Rights-of-Man*, named after the famous reply of Thomas Paine to Edmund Burke's criticism of the French Revolution, is close to home after a long voyage. As it nears England, the merchant vessel is stopped by a man-of-war, HMS *Indomitable*, and an officer from the warship goes aboard the *Rights-of-Man* to impress sailors for military service. This practice is necessary at the time to provide men to work the large number of ships that Britain has at sea for protection against the French.

The captain of the *Rights-of-Man* is relieved to have only one sailor taken from his ship, but he is unhappy because the man is his best sailor, Billy Budd. Billy is what his captain calls a peacemaker; because of his strength and good looks, he is a natural leader among the other sailors, and he uses his influence to keep them contented and hard at work. Billy seems utterly without guile, a man who tries to promote the welfare of the merchant ship because he likes peace and is willing to work hard to please his superiors. When informed that he is not to return to England but is to head for duty with the fleet in the Mediterranean Sea, he does not appear disturbed; he likes the sea, and he has no family ties. He is an orphan who was left as a tiny baby in a basket on the doorstep of a family in Bristol.

As the boat from the warship takes him away from the merchant ship, Billy calls farewell to the *Rights-of-Man* by name, a deed that greatly embarrasses the naval officer who

impressed him. The remark is unwittingly satirical of the treatment to which Billy is being subjected by the navy.

Once aboard the *Indomitable*, Billy quickly makes himself at home with the ship and the men with whom he serves in the foretop. As a result of his good personality and his willingness to work, he soon makes a place for himself with his messmates and also wins the regard of the officers under whom he serves.

At first, the master-at-arms, a petty officer named Claggart, seems particularly friendly to Billy, a fortunate circumstance, Billy thinks, for the master-at-arms is the equivalent of the chief of police aboard the warship. The young sailor is rather surprised, therefore, when he receives reprimands for slight breaches of conduct that are normally overlooked. The reprimands come from the ship's corporals who are Claggart's underlings. Since the reprimands indicate that something is wrong, Billy grows perturbed; he has a deadly fear of being the recipient of a flogging in public. He thinks he could never stand such treatment.

Anxious to discover what is wrong, Billy consults an old sailor, who tells him that Claggart is filled with animosity for the young man. The reason for the animosity is not known, and because the old man can give him no reason, Billy refuses to believe that the master-at-arms is his enemy. In fact, Claggart took a deep dislike to Billy on sight, however, and for no reason except a personal antipathy that the young man's appearance had generated. Sly as he is, Claggart keeps, or tries to keep, his feelings to himself. He operates through underlings against Billy.

Not long after he was warned by the old sailor, Billy spills a bowl of soup in the path of Claggart as he is inspecting the mess. Even then, Claggart smiles and pretends to treat the incident as a joke, for Billy did the deed accidentally. A few nights later, however, someone awakens Billy and tells him to go to a secluded spot in the ship. Billy goes and meets a sailor who tries to tempt him into joining a mutiny. The incident bothers Billy, who cannot understand why anyone would approach him as a possible conspirator. Such activity is not a part of his personality, and he is disgusted to find it in other men.

A few days later, the master-at-arms approaches the captain of the ship and reports that he and his men discovered that a mutiny is being fomented by Billy. Captain Vere, a very fair officer, reminds Claggart of the seriousness of the charge and warns the master-at-arms that bearing false witness in such a case calls for the death penalty. Claggart persists in his accusations, however, and Captain Vere stops the interview on deck, a place he thinks too public, and orders the master-at-arms and Billy to his cabin. There Captain Vere commands Claggart to repeat his accusations. When he does, Billy becomes emotionally so upset that he is tongue-tied. In utter frustration at being unable to reply to the infamous charges, Billy hits the master-at-arms. The petty officer is killed when he falls heavily to the floor.

Captain Vere is filled with consternation, for he, like everyone except the master-at-arms, likes Billy. After the surgeon pronounces the petty officer dead, the captain immediately convenes a court-martial to try Billy for assaulting and murdering a superior officer. England is at war, and two mutinies already occurred in the British navy that year, so action is to be taken immediately. The captain cannot overlook the offense.

The court-martial, acting under regulations, finds Billy guilty and sentences him to be hanged from a yardarm the following morning. Even under the circumstances of Claggart's death, there is no alternative. The only person who can testify that the charge of mutiny is false is the man who was killed.

All the ship's company are dismayed when informed of the sentence. Billy bears no animosity for the captain or for the officers who sentenced him to die. When he is placed beneath the yardarm the following morning, he calls out a blessing on Captain Vere, who, he realizes, had no other choice in the matter but to hang him. It is quite strange, too, that Billy's calm seems even to control his corpse. Unlike

most hanged men, he never twitches when hauled aloft by the neck. The surgeon's mate, when queried by his messmates, has no answer for this unique behavior.

Some months later, Captain Vere is wounded in action. In the last hours before his death, he is heard to murmur Billy's name over and over again. The common sailors do not forget the hanged man. For many years, the yardarm from which he was hanged is kept track of by sailors, who regard it almost as reverently as Christians might revere the Cross.

Critical Evaluation:

According to Harrison Hayford and Merton M. Sealts, the editors of the novel, Herman Melville began the novel in 1886, developed and revised it through several stages, and then left it unpublished when he died in 1891. The Hayford-Sealts text, published in 1962, differs considerably from earlier ones published in 1924 and 1948. Among the noteworthy differences is the change of name for the ship on which the action occurs, from *Indomitable* to *Bellipotent*. The symbolism of the latter name relates it to the emphasis that Melville places in the novel on war, human involvement in it, and the effects of war on the individual.

That Melville did not wish his readers to mistake the nature or the general intent of his novel is clear in his statement that Billy "is not presented as a conventional hero" and "that the story in which he is the main figure is no romance." The story is extremely simple. A young sailor on a British merchant ship is impressed for service on a British warship. He offers no resistance but accepts his new assignment with good will and attempts to be an ideal sailor. The ship's master-at-arms takes an immediate and unwarranted dislike to the sailor, plots to cause him trouble, and then accuses him to the captain of having plotted mutiny. The captain summons the sailor, asks him to defend himself, and sees him strike and accidentally kill his accuser. The captain imprisons him, convenes a court-martial, condemns him to death, and has him hanged. This plot is the vehicle for Melville's extended use of moral symbolism throughout the novel.

Billy Budd, Claggart, and Captain Vere are all clearly symbolic characters, and Melville brings out the symbolism through information supplied about their backgrounds, language used to describe them, and authorial comment of moral, theological, and philosophical import.

Melville employs a double symbolism for Billy: He is a Christ figure and a representation of innocent or Adamic man. Before Billy is removed from the merchant ship, the captain explains to the lieutenant from the warship that Billy has been most useful in quieting the "rat-pit of quarrels" that formerly infested his forecastle. "Not that he preached to them or said or did anything in particular; but a virtue went out of him, sugaring the sour ones." The captain's words echo Luke 6:19: "And the whole multitude sought to touch him: for there went virtue out of him, and healed them all." When the lieutenant is adamant about Billy's impressment, the captain's last words to him are, "you are going to take away my peacemaker." There is no mistaking the reference to the Prince of Peace. In describing Billy as he appears to the men and officers on the warship, Melville mentions "something in the mobile expression, and every chance attitude and movement, something suggestive of a mother eminently favored by Love and the Graces." An officer asks, "Who was your father?" and Billy answers, "God knows, sir." Though Billy explains that he was told he was a foundling, the hint has already been given of a divine paternity. Melville drops the Christ symbolism of Billy until the confrontation with Claggart when Billy, unable to reply to Captain Vere's request that he defend himself, shows in his face "an expression which was as a crucifixion to behold." At the hanging, Billy's last words are, "God bless Captain Vere!" and the reader recalls Christ's words on the Cross, "Father, forgive them; for they know not what they do." The symbolism continues with the hanging. Captain Vere gives a silent signal and "At the same moment it chanced that the vapory fleece hanging low in the East was shot through with a soft glory as of the fleece of the Lamb of God seen in mystical vision, and simultaneously therewith, watched by the wedged mass of upturned faces, Billy ascended; and, ascending, took the full rose of the dawn." In the final chapter, Melville adds that

> The spar from which the foretopman was suspended was for some few years kept trace of by the bluejackets . . . . To them a chip from it was as a piece of the Cross . . . . They recalled a fresh young image of the Handsome Sailor, that face never deformed by a sneer or subtler vile freak of the heart within. This impression of him was doubtless deepened by the fact that he was gone, and in a measure mysteriously gone.

Even in the verses that close the novel, with Billy's words, "They'll give me a nibble—bit o' biscuit ere I go./ Sure a messmate will reach me the last parting cup," one cannot miss the reference to the Last Supper.

Billy is Christlike, but he belongs to the human race. Melville repeatedly employs him as an archetype. Billy's complete innocence is first suggested in Melville's comment that "Billy in many respects was little more than a sort of upright barbarian, much such perhaps as Adam presumably might have been ere the urbane Serpent wriggled himself into his

company." Later, Captain Vere thinks of the handsome sailor as one "who in the nude might have posed for a statue of young Adam before the Fall." Innocence does not protect Billy. As Adam's human imperfection led to his fall, so an imperfection in Billy leads to his destruction. In times of stress, Billy stutters or is even speechless and, says Melville, "In this particular Billy was a striking instance that the arch interferer, the envious marplot of Eden, still has more or less to do with every human consignment to this planet of Earth."

The innocence that is his "blinder" causes Billy (or "Baby" as he is called) to fail to see and be on guard against the evil in Claggart, and his "vocal defect" deprives him of speech when he faces his false accuser. He strikes out as instinctively as a cornered animal, and his enemy dies. Billy does not intend to commit murder but, as Captain Vere tells his officers, "The prisoner's deed—with that alone we have to do." Billy does not live in an animal's instinctive world of nature. His life is bound by social law and particularly by naval law in a time of war. As Captain Vere explains, innocent Billy will be acquitted by God at "the last Assizes," but "We proceed under the law of the Mutiny Act." That act demands death for Billy's deed, and he dies in order that discipline may be maintained in the great navy that protects Britain against its enemies.

As Billy symbolizes innocent man, Claggart represents the spirit of evil, the foe of innocence. There is a mystery in Claggart's enmity toward harmless Billy. For, says Melville, "what can more partake of the mysterious than an antipathy spontaneous and profound such as is evoked in certain exceptional mortals by the mere aspect of some other mortal, however harmless he may be, if not called forth by this very harmlessness itself?" Claggart's evil nature is not acquired, "not engendered by vicious training or corrupting books or licentious living, but born with him and innate." He recognizes the good but is "powerless to be it." His energies are self-destructive; his nature is doomed to "act out to the end the part allotted to it." Although he destroys an innocent man, he is destroyed as well.

As Billy at one extreme is Christlike and childishly innocent and Claggart at the other is satanic, Captain Vere represents the kind of officer needed to preserve such an institution as the navy he serves. He is a man of balance, "mindful of the welfare of his men, but never tolerating an infraction of discipline; thoroughly versed in the science of his profession, and intrepid to the verge of temerity, though never injudiciously so." His reading tastes incline toward "books treating of actual men and events . . . history, biography, and unconventional writers like Montaigne, who, free from cant and convention, honestly and in the spirit of common sense philosophize upon realities." More intellectual than his fellow officers, he seems somewhat "pedantic" to them, and Melville hints that, in reporting Vere's long speech to his junior officers of the drumhead court, he has simplified the phrasing of the argument. Elsewhere, however, Captain Vere's speech is simple, brief, and direct.

Although Captain Vere is a thoughtful, reserved man, he is not without feeling. Quickly recognizing Billy's inability to speak when he has been ordered to defend himself, he soothingly says, "There is no hurry, my boy. Take your time, take your time." He is even capable of momentary vehemence as when he surprises the surgeon with the outburst, "Struck dead by an angel of God! Yet the angel must hang!" The captain quickly regains control. Melville does not report what Captain Vere says to Billy when he informs him privately of the death sentence, although Melville suggests that Captain Vere may have shown compassion by catching Billy "to his heart, even as Abraham may have caught young Isaac on the brink of resolutely offering him up." Captain Vere is seemingly overcome after Billy's last words, "God bless Captain Vere!" and the echo from the crew, since "either through stoic self-control or a sort of momentary paralysis induced by emotional shock," he stands "rigidly erect as a musket." The final view of a man whose heart balanced his mind is given in the report of Captain Vere's dying words, "Billy Budd, Billy Budd," spoken not in "the accents of remorse." Though capable of fatherly feeling toward an unfortunate young man, he causes to be carried out a sentence he believed was needed if the strength of order is to be maintained in the turmoil of war.

Although *Billy Budd, Foretopman* has occasionally been read as a veiled attack on the unjust treatment of a hapless man by an impersonal, authoritarian state, a close reading of the novel makes it seem more likely that Melville's intent was to show, especially through Captain Vere, that the protection of a state during a time of war must inevitably involve on occasion the sacrifice of an individual. Melville includes scattered satiric comments on the imperfections of men and organizations, but his overwhelmingly favorable portrait of Captain Vere as a principled and dedicated representative of the state leaves the reader with the final impression that Melville had at last become sadly resigned to the fact that imperfect people living in an imperfect world have no guarantee against suffering an unjust fate. That Billy uncomplainingly accepts his end, even asking God's blessing upon the man who is sending him to death, suggests that Melville, too, had become reconciled to the eternal coexistence of good and evil in the world.

"Critical Evaluation" by Henderson Kincheloe

Further Reading

Browne, Ray B. *Melville's Drive to Humanism*. West Lafayette, Ind.: Purdue University Press, 1971. The last chapter examines *Billy Budd, Foretopman* as a "provocative" and "disturbing" book that grew out of a balladlike story. Sees the novel as an assertion of a democratic "gospel" and of a humanistic perspective.

Chase, Richard. *Herman Melville: A Critical Study*. New York: Hafner Press, 1971. The last chapter, devoted to *Billy Budd, Foretopman*, calls Melville's final acceptance of life as tragic. Excellent analysis of the book's balance between action and philosophizing.

Delbanco, Andrew. *Melville: His World and Work*. New York: Knopf, 2005. Delbanco's critically acclaimed biography places Melville in his time, including information about the debate over slavery and details of life in 1840's New York. He also discusses the significance of Melville's works at the time they were published and in the twenty-first century.

Hove, Thomas. "Naturalist Psychology in *Billy Budd*." In *Herman Melville*, edited by Harold Bloom. New ed. New York: Bloom's Literary Criticism, 2008. Argues that *Billy Budd, Foretopman* presents a post-Darwinian naturalist ethics, in which deciding the appropriate course of action does not depend on "some accurate perception of truth but rather on interpretations of situations that can guide human energies toward desired ends."

Parker, Hershel. *Reading Billy Budd*. Evanston, Ill.: Northwestern University Press, 1991. A Melville scholar calls attention to, and demonstrates the largely unrealized potentialities of, the definitive edition of the novelist's celebrated last novel.

Scorza, Thomas J. *In the Time Before Steamships: "Billy Budd," the Limits of Politics, and Modernity*. DeKalb: Northern Illinois University Press, 1979. Approaches the "political dimension" of the novel. Argues that modern people find tragedy rather than glory in the limits of politics. Argues that Melville's analysis led him to see modern tragedy as the result of prideful rational philosophy.

Sedgwick, Eve Kosofsky. "*Billy Budd*: After the Homosexual." In *Epistemology of the Closet*. Updated ed. Berkeley: University of California Press, 2008. Argues that all of the characters in *Billy Budd, Foretopman* relate to one another based upon male desire and intimacy. Maintains that John Claggart is a homosexual, and examines this gender orientation in relation to his death.

Stafford, William T., ed. *Melville's "Billy Budd" and the Critics*. 2d ed. Belmont, Calif.: Wadsworth, 1968. Discussion of the text and early critical views. Treats themes of acceptance and resistance, spiritual autobiography, myth, art, social commentary, Christian and classical parallels, and the limits of human perception.

Vincent, Howard P., ed. *Twentieth Century Interpretations of Billy Budd: A Collection of Critical Essays.* Englewood Cliffs, N.J.: Prentice-Hall, 1971. Varied and excellent essays on innocence, irony, justice, tragedy, and acceptance

in *Billy Budd, Foretopman.* Part 2 gives the viewpoints of major critics.

Yannella, Donald, ed. *New Essays on Billy Budd.* New York: Cambridge University Press, 2002. Collection of essays, some of which explore *Billy Budd, Foretopman* and American labor unrest; religion, myth, and meaning in the novel; and the text's development and its ambiguities.

Biographia Literaria

Author: Samuel Taylor Coleridge (1772-1834)
First published: 1817
Type of work: Literary criticism

Samuel Taylor Coleridge's *Biographia Literaria* begins as an account of the major influences on the development of the author's philosophy and literary technique, but the total effect of the work is considerably less coherent than this plan would indicate. As he progresses, Coleridge apparently alters his purpose, and he discusses at considerable length intellectual problems of special interest to him and gives some of his standards of literary criticism, with comments on specific works. In his opening paragraph, he speaks of his work as "miscellaneous reflections," and such a description seems appropriate.

The loose, rambling structure of the *Biographia Literaria* accords well with the picture of Coleridge that has been handed down: that of a man with great intellectual and poetic gifts who lacked the self-discipline to produce the works of which he seemed capable. Charles Lamb and William Hazlitt both characterized him as an indefatigable and fascinating talker, full of ideas; this trait, too, plays its part in the creation of the *Biographia Literaria*, which is, in essence, a long conversation ranging widely over the worlds of poetry, drama, philosophy, and psychology. The lack of a tight organizational plan in no way prevents the book from being both readable and profound in its content; Coleridge's comments on the nature of the poetic imagination have never been surpassed, and his critique of William Wordsworth's work is still perhaps the most balanced and judicious assessment available, a model for all scholars who seek to form general views on the basis of close examination of individual texts.

In the opening chapter, Coleridge pays tribute to his most influential teacher, the Reverend James Bowyer of Christ's Hospital, who insisted that his students learn to think logically and use language precisely, in poetry as well as prose. Coleridge also discusses the poetry he preferred in the years when his literary tastes were being formed; he turned toward the "pre-Romantic" lyrics of minor writers rather than to the terse, epigrammatic intellectual poems of the best-known of the eighteenth century literary men, Alexander Pope and his followers. At an early stage, Coleridge developed sound critical principles, looking for works that gained in power through rereading and for words that seemed to express ideas better than any phrases substituted for them could. He quickly learned to distinguish between the virtues of works of original ideas and the faults of those that made their effect through novel phraseology. He confesses, however, that his critical judgment is better than his creative talent: His own early poems, though he thought highly of them when he wrote them, leave much to be desired.

The harshness of the critics of his time is a theme that recurs throughout Coleridge's biography. In his second chapter, he ponders the tendency of the public to side with the critics rather than with the poets, who are considered to be strange, irritable, even mad. The greatest writers—Geoffrey Chaucer, William Shakespeare, Edmund Spenser, and John Milton—seem to him unusually well balanced, and he suggests that the popular heresy results from the frustrations of the second-rate writer who pursues fame without real talent. These general comments are closely linked to Coleridge's sense of outrage at the vituperative attacks on him that issued regularly from the pages of the popular reviews, partly as a result of his association with Wordsworth and Robert Southey. The three poets were accused of trying to revolutionize, to vulgarize, poetry; they were avowedly interested in freeing poetry from the limitations of the eighteenth century poetic tradition. Coleridge denies that they deserved the abuses hurled at them.

After commenting on the works of Wordsworth and Southey, Coleridge turns to a number of philosophical problems that fascinate him, among them questions of perception, sensation, and the human thought processes. It is this section of the work that provides the greatest difficulty for the uninitiated reader, for Coleridge assumes considerable familiarity with the works of German philosophers and English psychologists and mystics. He surveys the theories of Thomas Hobbes, David Hartley, Aristotle, René Descartes, and others as they relate to problems of perception and of the development of thought through the association of ideas, and he assesses the influence of Immanuel Kant on his own philosophy.

Coleridge digresses from the complex history of his intellectual growth to describe his first literary venture into the commercial side of his world, his publication of a periodical called *The Watchman*. His attempts to secure subscriptions were ludicrous, and his project met with the failure that his friends had predicted; one of them had to pay Coleridge's printer to keep Coleridge out of debtors' prison.

One of the most important episodes of Coleridge's life was his 1798 trip to Germany, where he widened his knowledge of the literature and philosophy of that country. He returned to England to take a position with a newspaper, writing on literature and politics; he attacked Napoleon Bonaparte so vehemently that the French general actually sent out an order for his arrest while Coleridge was living in Italy as a correspondent for his paper. Coleridge evidently enjoyed his journalistic work, and he advises all would-be literary men to find some regular occupation rather than to devote all of their time to writing.

Returning to his philosophical discussion, Coleridge lists several of his major premises about truth and knowledge. He is particularly concerned about distinguishing between the essence of the subject, the perceiver, and of the object, that which is perceived. Related to this distinction is the nature of the imagination, which Coleridge divides into two parts. The primary imagination is the human power that perceives and recognizes objects; the secondary imagination acts on these initial perceptions to produce new thoughts: "It dissolves, diffuses, dissipates, in order to re-create."

Coleridge next turns to a presentation of his literary standards, referring especially to the *Lyrical Ballads* (1798), the revolutionary volume that contained much of Wordsworth's poetry and some of his own. He tries to define poetry, pointing out that it has as its "immediate object pleasure, not truth," and that it delights by the effect of the whole as well as of individual parts. In one of the book's most famous passages, he discusses the function of the poet who, by the power of his imagination, must bring unity of diversity, reconciling "sameness, with differences; of the general, with the concrete; the idea, with the image; the individual, with the representative; the sense of novelty and freshness, with old and familiar objects; a more than usual state of emotion, with more than usual order; judgment ever-awake and steady self-possession, with enthusiasm and feeling profound or vehement."

Coleridge applies these general tenets to specific works, analyzing Shakespeare's early poems *Venus and Adonis* (1593) and *The Rape of Lucrece* (1594) to determine what in them reveals genius and what is the result of the poet's immaturity. He praises particularly Shakespeare's musical language and his distance from his subject matter, saying, with reference to the latter point, that the average youthful writer is likely to concentrate on his own sensations and experiences. Shakespeare's greatness seems to him to lie, too, in the vividness of his imagery and in his "depth, and energy of thought."

Although he was closely associated with Wordsworth, Coleridge does not hesitate to indicate the points at which he differed from his colleague. He takes issue most strongly with Wordsworth's assertion that the speech of low and rustic life is the natural language of emotion and therefore best for poetry. Coleridge stresses rather the choice of a diction as universal as possible, not associated with class or region, and he says that it is this kind of language that Wordsworth has, in fact, used in almost all of his work. He argues that in the famous preface to the *Lyrical Ballads*, Wordsworth was, to a certain extent, exaggerating in order to make clear the advantages of natural, simple language over the empty poetic diction typical of the poetry of the time.

Coleridge's comments on Wordsworth lead him to an extended attack on the practices of the critical reviews, which published commentary on his friend's works that seemed to him both biased and absurd. He ridicules the tendency of anonymous reviewers to offer criticism without giving examples to support their assertions; they hardly seem to have read the works they lampoon. To counteract their ill-tempered, inconsistent judgments, he sets down his own views on Wordsworth's most serious flaws and outstanding talents. He criticizes Wordsworth's "inconstancy of the style," a tendency to shift from a lofty level to a commonplace one; his occasionally excessive attention to factual details of landscape or biography; his poor handling of dialogue in some poems; his "occasional prolixity, repetition, and an eddying instead of progression of thought" in a few passages; and, finally, his use of "thoughts and images too great for the subject."

With these defects in mind, Coleridge commends Wordsworth's work for the purity and appropriateness of its language, the freshness of the thoughts, the "sinewy strength and originality of single lines and paragraphs," the accuracy of the descriptions of nature, the pathos and human sympathy, and the imaginative power of the poet.

The major portion of the *Biographia Literaria* ends with a final assessment of Wordsworth's work; Coleridge thereupon adds a section of letters written to friends while he was traveling in Germany. The letters contain amusing accounts of his shipboard companions, a description of his meeting with the poet Friedrich Gottlieb Klopstock, and some of his literary opinions. To show how little his critical standards had changed, he also includes a long and devastating critique of a contemporary melodrama, Charles Robert Maturin's *Bertram: Or, The Castle of St. Aldobrand* (pr., pb. 1816). Coleridge's concluding chapter, as rambling in subject matter as the rest of the book, treats briefly the harsh critical reaction to his poem *Christabel* (1816), then turns to his affirmation of his Christian faith and his reasons for holding it. He makes no attempt to summarize his volume, which has presented a remarkably full portrait of his wide-ranging, questioning mind.

Further Reading

Barfield, Owen. *What Coleridge Thought.* Middletown, Conn.: Wesleyan University Press, 1971. A lucid exposition of Coleridge's philosophy, which is explained in its own terms rather than in its relations to other systems of thought. Emphasizes Coleridge's concept of "Polar Logic" and thoroughly discusses such key concepts as fancy and imagination, understanding and reason.

Christie, William. *Samuel Taylor Coleridge: A Literary Life.* New York: Palgrave Macmillan, 2006. Begins with a discussion of *Biographia Literaria*, describing Coleridge's attempt in that work to define and defend the literary culture of his time. Christie interprets Coleridge's life and work within the context of that culture.

Eilenberg, Susan. *Strange Power of Speech: Wordsworth, Coleridge, and Literary Possession.* New York: Oxford University Press, 1992. Chapters 6 and 7 are principally concerned with the *Biographia Literaria*. Includes extensive bibliographic notes and index.

Gravil, Richard, et al., eds. *Coleridge's Imagination: Essays in Memory of Pete Laver.* New York: Cambridge University Press, 1985. Fifteen collected essays treating one of the central aspects of Coleridge's thought. Jonathan Wordsworth's "'The Infinite I Am': Coleridge and the Ascent of Being" and Lucy Newlyn's "Radical Difference: Coleridge and Wordsworth, 1802" give particular attention to the *Biographia Literaria*.

Holmes, Richard. *Coleridge: Early Visions.* New York: Viking Press, 1990.

_____. *Coleridge: Darker Reflections.* London: HarperCollins, 1998. Two-volume biography; volume 1 covers Coleridge's life up to his departure for Malta in 1804, with the remainder of his life covered in volume 2. Well-researched, lively, and sympathetic to its subject. Fully captures Coleridge's brilliant, flawed, fascinating personality.

Newlyn, Lucy, ed. *The Cambridge Companion to Coleridge.* New York: Cambridge University Press, 2002. Collection of essays discussing Coleridge's life and the genres, themes, and topics of his works. Chapter 4 is devoted to an analysis of *Biographia Literaria*.

Richards, I. A. *Coleridge on Imagination.* New York: Harcourt, Brace, 1935. A landmark of Coleridge scholarship, still valuable despite its age. Richards, the father of the New Criticism, delves especially into Coleridge's anticipation of modern psychology.

Ruf, Frederick J. *Entangled Voices: Genre and the Religious Construction of the Self.* New York: Oxford University Press, 1997. Ruf focuses on the concepts of voice and genre, arguing that readers imagine different genres as the expression of different voices. In chapter 6, "Harmonized Chaos: The Mixed Voices of Coleridge's *Biographia Literaria*," he applies his theory to an interpretation of this book.

The Birds

Author: Aristophanes (c. 450-c. 385 B.C.E.)
First produced: Ornithes, 414 B.C.E. (English translation, 1824)
Type of work: Drama
Type of plot: Social satire
Time of plot: 431-404 B.C.E.
Locale: Athens and Nephelo-Coccygia, the city of the birds

Principal characters:
EUELPIDES, an Athenian
PISTHETAERUS, his friend
EPOPS, the hoopoe, formerly a man
THE BIRDS

The Story:

Euelpides and Pisthetaerus, two disgruntled citizens, want to escape from the pettiness of life in Athens. They buy a jay and a crow, which Philocrates, the bird seller, tells them can guide them to Epops, a bird not born of birds; from Epops they hope to learn of a land where they can live a peaceful life.

The jay and the crow guide the pair into the mountains and lead them to a shelter hidden among the rocks. They knock and shout for admittance. When Trochilus, Epops's servant, comes to the door, Euelpides and Pisthetaerus are prostrate with fear; they insist that they are birds, not men, a species the birds intensely dislike. Epops, a hoopoe with a triple crest, emerges from the shelter; he does not present a very colorful aspect, since he is molting. Epops informs the Athenians that he was once a man named Tereus, whom the gods transformed into a hoopoe.

When the Athenians reveal the purpose of their visit, Epops suggests that they move on to the Red Sea, but they say they are not interested in living in a seaport. Epops suggests several other places, but on one ground or another the pair rejects them all. The truth is that they want to stay among the birds and establish a city. Interested in this novel idea, Epops summons the birds, that they, too, might hear of the plan.

The birds swarm to the shelter from all directions until every species of Old World bird is represented at the gathering. The leader of the birds, fearful of all men, is dismayed when he learns that Epops talked with Euelpides and Pisthetaerus, and he incites all the birds to attack, threatening to tear the Athenians to pieces. To defend themselves, Euelpides and Pisthetaerus take up stewpots and other kitchen utensils. Epops rebukes the birds for their precipitous behavior. Finally, heeding his suggestion that perhaps they can profit from the plan of the two men, they settle down to listen. Epops assures the birds that Euelpides and Pisthetaerus have only the most honorable of intentions.

Pisthetaerus tells the birds that they are older than human beings. In fact, the feathered tribes were once sovereign over all creation, and even within the memory of people birds were known to have been supreme over the human race. For that reason, Pisthetaerus declares, birds are used as symbols of power and authority. The eagle, for example, is Zeus's symbol, the owl is Athena's symbol, and the hawk is Apollo's.

Seeing that the birds are interested in his words, Pisthetaerus propounds his plan: The birds are to build a wall around their realm, the air, so that communication between the gods and human beings will be cut off. Both gods and people will then have to recognize the supremacy of the birds. If human beings prove recalcitrant, the sparrows will devour their grain and crows will peck out the eyes of their livestock. If they accede, the birds will control insect plagues and help them store up earthly treasures.

The birds are delighted with his plan. Epops ushers the Athenians into his shelter, where the pair momentarily forget their project when they see Epops's wife, Procne, who bears an uncanny resemblance to a desirable young maiden. Meanwhile the leader of the birds speaks of humankind's great debt to the birds. Urging human beings to look upon the birds as the true gods, he invites them to join the birds and acquire wings.

Pisthetaerus, winged like a bird, organizes the building of the wall and arranges all negotiations with gods and human beings. As he prepares to make propitiatory offerings to the new gods, he is beset by opportunists who hear of the great project. An indigent poetaster offers to glorify the project in verse. A charlatan offers worthless prophecies. When Meton, a surveyor, offers to divide the realm of the air into the principal parts of a typical Greek city, Pisthetaerus thrashes him. An inspector and a dealer in decrees importune him and are likewise thrashed and dismissed. Annoyed by these money-seeking hangers-on, Pisthetaerus retreats into Epops's shelter to sacrifice a goat. The leader of the birds again sings the praises of his kind and tells how the birds are indispensable to the welfare of humankind.

The sacrifice is completed, and shortly thereafter the wall is finished. All the birds, using their various specialized organs, cooperate in the construction. Then a messenger reports that a winged goddess, sent by Zeus, penetrates into the bird kingdom in spite of the wall. Pisthetaerus issues a call to arms—the birds will war with the gods. When Iris, the goddess of the rainbow, makes her appearance, Pisthetaerus is enraged at the ineffectualness of his wall. Oblivious of the importance assumed by the birds under Pisthetaerus's influence, Iris declares that she is on her way to ask human beings to make a great sacrifice to the Olympian gods. When Pisthetaerus infers that the birds are now the only gods, Iris pities him for his presumption and warns him not to arouse the Olympians' ire.

A messenger who was sent as an emissary from the birds to human beings returns and presents Pisthetaerus with a gift, a golden chaplet. Apparently they are delighted with the idea of the bird city; thousands are eager to come there to acquire wings and to live a life of ease. Pleased and flattered, the birds welcome the human beings as they arrive.

First comes a man with thoughts of parricide, who believes that he will at last be free to murder his father. Pisthetaerus points out to him that the young bird might peck at his father, but that later it is his duty to administer to his father. He gives the youth wings and sends him off as a bird-soldier in order to make good use of his inclinations. Next a poet arrives and asks for wings so that he might gather inspiration for his verse from the upper air. Pisthetaerus gives him wings and directs him to organize a chorus of birds. An informer arrives and asks for wings, the better to practice his vicious profession; Pisthetaerus whips him and in despair removes the baskets of wings that were placed at the gate.

Prometheus, the friend of humankind, makes his appearance. Although he still fears the wrath of Zeus, he raises his mask and reports to Pisthetaerus, who recognizes him, that human beings no longer worship Zeus since the bird city, Nephelo-Coccygia, had been founded. He adds that Zeus is deeply concerned and will send a peace mission to the city; he is even prepared to offer to Pisthetaerus one of his maid-servants, Basileia, for his wife.

Poseidon, Heracles, and the barbarian god Triballus come upon Pisthetaerus as he is cooking a meal. Pisthetaerus, visibly impressed by their presence, greets them nonchalantly. They promise him plenty of warm weather and sufficient rain if he will drop his project. Their argument might have been more effective were they not so noticeably hungry. Pisthetaerus declares that he will invite them to dinner if they

promise to bring the scepter of Zeus to the birds. Heracles, almost famished, promises, but Poseidon is angered by Pisthetaerus's audacity. Pisthetaerus argues that it is to the advantage of the gods that the birds be supreme on earth since the birds, who are below the clouds, can keep an eye on humankind, while the gods, who are above the clouds, cannot. The birds can, in fact, mete out to men the justice of the gods. The envoys agree to this argument, but they balk when Pisthetaerus insists upon also having Basileia as his wife.

After a heated discussion, Pisthetaerus convinces Heracles, a natural son of Zeus, that he will receive nothing on the death of Zeus, and that Poseidon, as brother of Zeus, will get Heracles' share of Zeus's property. Heracles and Triballus prevail over Poseidon in the hot dispute that follows and Basileia is conceded after much argument. The envoys then sit down to dinner. Pisthetaerus, having received the scepter of Zeus, becomes not only the king of the birds but also the supreme deity.

Critical Evaluation:

First shown at the City Dionysia festival in 414 B.C.E., *The Birds*, although it only won second prize at the festival, is commonly regarded as Aristophanes' finest work. Richly imaginative and full of scintillating wit and lovely lyrical songs, *The Birds* is unquestionably a comic masterpiece. In it, Aristophanes takes a fantastic and amusing idea and quite literally soars into infinity with it. The entire play is a sustained and wonderful joke.

Some critics have concluded that this play satirizes the airy hopes of conquest that gripped Athens at the time the comedy was being written. In 415 B.C.E., a huge military expedition had sailed to subdue Sicily and establish an empire in the west. Two years later, the expedition was proved to have been a fiasco, but in the meantime Athens was rife with grand rumors and expectations. The grand, crazy scheme proposed in *The Birds* seems to convey some of the ebullience of the time. Aristophanes also uses the fantasy as a means of delivering several well-aimed kicks at contemporary figures, at Athens, and at human beings and gods in general. Nevertheless, later readers and audiences with no knowledge of its topical allusions can appreciate the work simply for its comedy and its beautiful language. The important facts are contained in the play itself.

In *The Birds*, Aristophanes adapts an idea he used earlier in *Nephelai* (423 B.C.E.; *The Clouds*, 1708), where Socrates explores the starry heavens in a basket. Debt-ridden, plagued by lawsuits in Athens, and seeking a restful retirement community, the hero, Pisthetaerus, conceives the ingenious idea of founding a kingdom in the sky. By organizing the birds to intercept the offerings made by human beings to the gods, he can starve the gods into submission. He can bring human beings to their knees by using the birds to control harvests and livestock. Elderly, quick-witted, and confident, Pisthetaerus is likable as well, a kind of supersalesman. He convinces the birds to collaborate with him and, by his through-the-looking-glass logic, he gains absolute mastery of the cosmos, winning a goddess, Zeus's former maidservant Basileia, for a bride in addition.

However, his true glory rests in the kingdom to which he gives birth—Nephelo-Coccygia, or Cloudcuckooland. It is the equivalent of the Big Rock Candy Mountain, a place where all one's dreams come true. This utopia is in harmony with nature, as represented by the birds, but it attracts idlers, parasites, and nuisances. Bad poets, a false prophet, a magistrate, a process server, an informer, a surveyor, and a sycophant flock to Cloudcuckooland, which gives Pisthetaerus the chance either to reform or to repel them. Even the gods are not really welcome. Pisthetaerus's own companion, Euelpides, leaves of his own accord, sick of being ordered about. The hero exercises his power mainly to exclude undesirables, with the result that when he is finished, his only comrades are the birds.

This rejection of human pests allows Aristophanes' satirical gift free play. The parasites in *The Birds* are the types the dramatist often lampooned, including representatives of the legal profession, fake seers, awful poets, toadies, cowards, pederasts, scientists, informers. Aristophanes is not just saying that without these types a community can be a paradise. He goes further than this. The birds, particularly the chorus, sing exquisitely beautiful and lyrically virtuosic songs that are vastly superior to anything the poets in the play invent. Almost all the birds have beautiful plumage, whereas by contrast the human beings are shabbily dressed. Moreover, whereas the birds are friendly once Pisthetaerus wins them over, the human beings are typically rapacious or looking for a handout. In short, the birds are altogether more desirable as companions than human beings. Even the gods come off poorly by comparison, for they are merely immortal "humans," full of greed and anxious to take advantage of their position.

The Birds is not completely misanthropic, for it pays ample tribute to the eternal human desire to achieve birdlike freedom and beauty. It suggests that human beings can best gain a utopia by their own wits and in friendly communion with nature. The stage called for in the play is singularly bleak, with a single bare tree and a rock, yet it is precisely here that Pisthetaerus founds his fabulous empire. It is a realm of sheer imagination, where anyone can erect castles in

the air, fashioned of daydreams and free of life's demands. This is the place where Pisthetaerus can find peace with friends of his own choosing, the kingdom where he can win out over the gods and his human foes alike. Imagination is the single area where a human being can enthrone himself as ruler of the universe. In a sense, *The Birds* is a dramatic hymn to schizophrenia. All the shackles of reality and of human limitation are in abeyance, while the play sails straight up into the wild blue yonder. It is escapist of course, but a daring, witty, songful, exhilarating kind of escape.

"Critical Evaluation" by James Weigel, Jr.

Further Reading

Dearden, C. W. *The Stage of Aristophanes*. London: Athlone Press, 1976. The work is an overview of Greek theatrical conventions that uses the plays of Aristophanes as models. It discusses form, staging, settings, the chorus, and the use of actors and masks. Each of the plays is discussed individually.

Dover, K. J. *Aristophanic Comedy*. Berkeley: University of California Press, 1972. Textual criticism of the plays of Aristophanes. Discusses *The Birds* as fantasy and as one of the few by the writer that does not point toward a didactic change in politics. Includes a discussion of the sexual humor of the time and the role of women in Greek society as reflected in the plays.

Ehrenberg, Victor. *The People of Aristophanes*. London: Methuen, 1974. Discussion of the creation of types as caricatures of Athenian society. An analysis of old Attic comedy from a sociological perspective.

Hall, Edith, and Amanda Wrigley, eds. *Aristophanes in Performance, 421 B.C.-A.D. 2007: Peace, Birds, and Frogs*. London: Legenda, 2007. A collection of papers originally delivered at a conference held in 2004. The papers discuss how Aristophanes' plays were staged at various times in England, South Africa, France, and Italy, and analyze specified performances of *The Birds*, *The Frogs*, and *Peace*.

Lord, Louis E. *Aristophanes: His Plays and His Influence*. New York: Cooper Square, 1963. Traces Aristophanes' influence on Athenian society as well as on later German, French, and English writers. Also presents an overview of Greek comedy as the origin and model for later sociological and political satire.

Rothwell, Kenneth S., Jr. "Aristophanes' *Birds* and the Rise of Civilization." In *Nature, Culture, and the Origins of Greek Comedy: A Study of Animal Choruses*. New York: Cambridge University Press, 2007. Rothwell's examination of animal choruses in ancient Greek comedies includes a detailed analysis of *The Birds*. He maintains that Aristophanes' inclusion of animal choruses in several of his plays may be a conscious revival of an earlier Greek tradition of animal representation.

Silk, M. S. *Aristophanes and the Definition of Comedy*. New York: Oxford University Press, 2002. Silk looks at Aristophanes not merely as an ancient Greek dramatist but as one of the world's great poets. He analyzes *The Birds* and the other plays to examine their language, style, lyric poetry, character, and structure.

Spatz, Lois. *Aristophanes*. Boston: Twayne, 1978. A discussion of the evolution of Greek plays and their religious connection to the festival of Dionysus. Presents each play chronologically and depicts the historical context in which it was created.

The Birth of Tragedy out of the Spirit of Music

Author: Friedrich Nietzsche (1844-1900)
First published: Die Geburt der Tragödie aus dem
  Geiste der Musik, 1872 (English translation, 1909)
Type of work: Philosophy

The 1872 publication of *The Birth of Tragedy out of the Spirit of Music*, a seminal work by Friedrich Nietzsche, includes the essay "Foreword to Richard Wagner." In the 1886 edition of the book (*Die Geburt der Tragödie: Oder, Griechenthum und Pessimismus*; "the birth of tragedy: or, Greek culture and pessimism") Nietzsche replaced this tribute to the German composer with "Attempt at a Self Critique," in which he rejects the creative direction of Wagner's operas.

The two introductory pieces to *The Birth of Tragedy*, the work's short title, recapitulate the development of Nietzsche's thought from an earlier, more romantic understanding of the central conceptual framework he offers in his contrast of the Apollonian and Dionysian categories. The first understanding emphasizes the potential for a new flourishing of tragedy in the arts of Germany, while the second understanding is framed with Nietzsche's more sober reversal of the values of optimism and pessimism. The spirit of music yields to the spirit of pessimism as the chief agent in the production of art through what Nietzsche terms a "transvaluation" of values.

The Birth of Tragedy itself is structured around an explanation of the rise of literature in Greek culture. The artistic impulse first manifests itself with the invention of the pantheon of Olympic gods, then with the parallel creations of the Apollonian epic and Dionysian lyric verse. These two forms are later united in Greek tragedy, which represents the acme of human thought and expression. This high point, Nietzsche argues, is followed by a decline from the time of Euripides to Socrates. Nietzsche then argues for the primacy of the arts over philosophy as the means for understanding human existence, and he closes with a foreshadowing of the possible rebirth of tragedy in his own contemporary German culture.

Elements of this last argument were soon used and abused by thinkers as well as tyrants, in particular Adolf Hitler and the Nazis, to claim an inherently superior status for German art and culture. Nietzsche, however, offers no such unambiguous nationalist agenda within *The Birth of Tragedy*; indeed, he explicitly states that the possibility for this union of Apollonian and Dionysian art exists within all cultures.

The Apollonian and the Dionysian offer perhaps the most significant challenges to an Aristotelian reading of Greek tragedy. In *The Birth of Tragedy*, the Apollonian aspect of creativity deals with image and representation, which Nietzsche terms the "plastic arts." Nietzsche links the Apollonian with the individual, the rational, and the male, and argues that this force creates a world of dreams. The Dionysian, in sharp contrast, arises from an original oneness of all being that precedes individuation. Nietzsche links it with the state of intoxication and with the female, and argues that this force creates a state of ecstasy. Late in the work, he employs the metaphor contained in the Greek term *pharmakos*, a word that means both "poison" and "medicine," to characterize the union between the Apollonian and the Dionysian. The Dionysian brings with it the knowledge of all human suffering and therefore has the potential to destroy those who can grasp that knowledge, but when the Dionysian is tempered with an Apollonian ordering in images, it becomes its own antidote.

In the work's opening argument, Nietzsche explains that

the Olympian gods function as a metaphor for the great variety of human experience and remain fundamentally amoral. As metaphor, Apollo, god of the plastic arts, rules the dream, and in dreams, all actions have meaning. The dreamer retains a sense of self while fully participating in an alternative reality. This Apollonian arena, Nietzsche asserts, comes purely from Greek culture.

Dionysos, god of music, on the other hand, enters the pantheon from an alien culture, which Nietzsche will later identify as Asian. The rituals for this god erase all sense of self, and thus all sense of rational causality. That force, called Dionysian by Nietzsche, exists in all cultures. He will later parallel the force with the folk culture of all groups. Dionysian intoxication transcends the boundaries between self and other and self and nature, and it even transcends language, replacing it with song and dance. In this Dionysian celebration, the division between artist and artwork is also erased, so that the singer or dancer becomes the work of art. When the two forces unite, the Apollonian becomes the translator for the Dionysian, bringing the ideal balance to human aesthetic expression.

After recounting the story of the encounter between King Midas and Silenos, one of the companions of Dionysos, Nietzsche moves into the background of Greek literature in the epic. In that story, Silenos tells Midas that the best fate a person can hope for would be either nonexistence or a quick death. Against just such wisdom, according to Nietzsche, the early Greeks had created a bulwark of gods. From this defensive bulwark is born the epic. Nietzsche describes Homeric epics as the pinnacle of purely Apollonian art, taking issue with the earlier definition of German author Friedrich Schiller of the epic as naïve. For Nietzsche, the triumph of the epic is the triumph of illusion, and it offers no meaningful response to the profound suffering expressed in the words of Silenos to Midas. To find such a response, Nietzsche returns to the Dionysian force.

Nietzsche then juxtaposes the development of lyric poetry to that of epic poetry, contrasting the lyric poet Archilochos to the epic poet Homer. Whereas the epic functions to defend humanity against the terror of the irrational, the lyric channels the Dionysian by drawing on the traditions of folk song, by combining melody with Apollonian image.

From just such lyric poetry, Nietzsche continues, the chorus of Greek theater is created. He sees the chorus as the sole original actor, and here he makes the significant connection between theater and the religious ceremonies carried out to honor Dionysos. His insight will be confirmed by later scholars, though Nietzsche himself does not attempt to give historical evidence for it. Seen as religious ritual, theater does not allow for distinctions between audience and actors, but rather becomes the site of transformation for all present and brings them into direct contact with the god.

The tragedies of Aeschylos and Sophocles inherit this power of effecting access to the Dionysian through the creation of an Apollonian representation. The suffering of the god Dionysos lies behind the suffering of characters such as Prometheus and Oedipus, and the story of the god's dismemberment at the hands of the Titans becomes the central metaphor for the fall into individuality from an original Oneness.

Euripides, Nietzsche continues, shows the waning of this union of the Apollonian with the Dionysian, because he drives the onlookers into a critical mode of thinking and reifies their role apart from the play itself. The exception to this can be seen in *The Bacchae*, which tells the story of Dionysos and his worshipers asserting their power over the ruler Pentheus. In telling the story of Dionysos, Nietzsche suggests, Euripides is forced to confront the Dionysian and recognize its power over the rational.

At this point, Nietzsche turns to Socrates and Plato, implicitly uniting the history of the arts with the history of philosophy, for he considers Socratic dialogue the logical next step in an increasingly fallen Apollonian literature. The Socratic dialogue represents the mistaken notion that reasoning through causality can give the philosopher access to what Nietzsche terms "the ground of Being." Only a perfectly balanced art, like Greek tragedy, writes Nietzsche, has that power.

Having established the role of music as Dionysian and thus a source of original unity, Nietzsche next addresses the question of whether that spirit of music that led to Greek tragedy in its highest form can reappear. He gives a brief exegesis of the nature of music that stresses its universality and its ability to connect human beings with suffering in a liberating rather than destructive bond. He then examines various kinds of general cultural types and the music they produce. His three categories for culture are Socratic-Alexandrian, artistic-Hellenistic, and tragic-Indian-Brahmanic. The first two cultures will fail to unify the Apollonian and the Dionysian. As an example, Nietzsche discusses the form of opera first produced in Italy. Italy is an Alexandrian culture in Nietzsche's eyes, and misses both the Apollonian goal of illusion and the Dionysian goal of ecstasy with its fatal invention of recitative. Such a talking style utterly destroys melody and, hence, kills the spirit of music.

Nietzsche does see hope in the early operas of Wagner, which draw on German folk culture and promise to reunite the German people with their original mythology. Nietzsche closes *The Birth of Tragedy* by reiterating the words of

Aeschylos, who had called on his fellow Athenians to sacrifice at the temple of the paired Apollo and Dionysos.

Amee Carmines

Further Reading

Hayman, Ronald. *Nietzsche: A Critical Life*. New York: Oxford University Press, 1980. Scholars consider Hayman's book one of the best biographies of Nietzsche. The book also links Nietzsche's life to his writings.

Kaufmann, Walter. *Nietzsche: Philosopher, Psychologist, Antichrist*. 4th ed. Princeton, N.J.: Princeton University Press, 1974. Kaufmann was largely responsible for the rehabilitation of Nietzsche's reputation after his ideas were co-opted by the Nazi Party in Germany to further its own nationalist agenda. Kaufmann also is one of the chief translators of Nietzsche.

Kemal, Selim, Ivan Gaskell, and Daniel W. Conway, eds. *Nietzsche, Philosophy, and the Arts*. New York: Cambridge University Press, 1998. This collection, working from a British perspective, provides readers with connections between philosophical concepts and literature as well as the other arts.

Magnus, Bernd, Stanley Stewart, and Jean-Pierre Mileur. *Nietzsche's Case: Philosophy as/and Literature*. New York: Routledge, 1993. Magnus offers a cogent reading of Nietzsche as a bridge between the fields of philosophy and literature, interpreting Nietzsche's own writings in literary terms.

Nehamas, Alexander. *Nietzsche: Life as Literature*. Cambridge, Mass.: Harvard University Press, 1985. Nehamas is one of the most important contemporary writers on Nietzsche. He brings a rich contextual understanding of the writers who were important to Nietzsche and of Nietzsche's own works.

Silk, M. S., and J. P Stern. *Nietzsche on Tragedy*. 1981. Reprint. New York: Cambridge University Press, 1999. Silk and Stern offer an extended reading of the philosopher's understanding of tragedy. This book places *The Birth of Tragedy* within the larger body of Nietzsche's work on tragedy.

Young, Julian. *Nietzsche's Philosophy of Art*. 1992. Reprint. New York: Cambridge University Press, 1999. Young treats the themes of tragedy and pessimism, demonstrating Nietzsche's argument that the arts balance these two potentially negative forces.

The Birthday Party

Author: Harold Pinter (1930-2008)
First produced: 1958; first published, 1959
Type of work: Drama
Type of plot: Absurdist
Time of plot: Mid-twentieth century
Locale: England

Principal characters:
PETEY BOLES, a man in his sixties
MEG BOLES, his wife, in her sixties
STANLEY WEBBER, their boarder, in his late thirties
LULU, a neighbor, in her twenties
GOLDBERG, a man in his fifties
McCANN, a man of thirty

The Story:

Petey Boles and his wife, Meg, are the proprietors of a dilapidated boardinghouse in a seaside town in England. One morning, as they are discussing the local news over breakfast, Petey mentions that two men approached him on the beach the previous night and asked him for a room. He says the men had agreed to drop by later that day to see if the room is available. Meg tells Petey that she will have the room ready if the men arrive.

When their only lodger, Stanley Webber, joins Petey and Meg for breakfast, he complains that he "didn't sleep at all."

As soon as Petey leaves for work as a deck chair attendant on the promenade, Meg begins her morning chores, telling Stanley about the two men who spoke to Petey. This news upset Stanley at first, but, after reflection, he dismisses the incident as a "false alarm."

When Lulu, a young neighbor, drops by to deliver a package, she questions Stanley about his morning activities and complains that his appearance makes her feel depressed. In response, Stanley first lies about what he did that morning, then asks her to "go away" with him, though they both agree that there is nowhere for them to go. Lulu calls Stanley "a bit of a washout" and leaves.

When two men named Goldberg and McCann arrive, Stanley avoids them by slipping out the back door. The men reminisce about "the golden days" and the "old school" and suggest that an informant provided important information regarding their "present job" which, according to Goldberg, is "quite distinct" from their "previous work." Meg tells them that if they take the room they can join the household in celebrating Stanley's birthday that night. She explains that he was formerly a pianist and that she hopes he will play at the party. She promises to invite Lulu and to wear her party dress, hoping that the party will improve Stanley's attitude; he was "down in the dumps lately." Goldberg and McCann decide to take the room and to attend the party.

As soon as they leave, Stanley returns and asks Meg about the men. When Meg tells him that they are the "ones that were coming," Stanley is visibly dejected. To cheer him up, Meg opens the package Lulu delivered. It contains a drum that Meg then gives to Stanley for his birthday present. Stanley slings the drum around his neck and marches around the room, beating the drum frantically.

That night, Stanley comes downstairs to find McCann "sitting at the table tearing a newspaper into five equal strips." Stanley tries to leave, but McCann stops him. When Stanley picks up the pieces of paper, McCann becomes violent and warns Stanley to leave the paper alone. Then Stanley tries to convince McCann that it is not his birthday, and the argument escalates into violence. When Goldberg joins McCann again, Stanley, desperate, claims that the room Meg promised the two men is not available, that it is taken, and that they will have to find lodging elsewhere. He tells them to "get out," but instead they begin to interrogate Stanley, alternating comically nonsensical statements with serious accusations, until their tirade becomes an existential inquisition questioning Stanley's identity. Finally, both men conclude that Stanley is dead.

The interrogation is interrupted by Meg, who brings Stanley his drum. As Meg begins toasting Stanley, Lulu joins the party, flirting with Goldberg, sitting on his lap, and embracing him. Meg then makes a play for McCann, and soon all of them are playing blindman's buff. Blindfolded, McCann stumbles around the room until he finds Stanley and removes his glasses. In turn, Stanley begins to strangle Meg, the lights go out, and, in the confusion, Stanley tries to rape Lulu. When McCann finally finds a flashlight, Stanley is backed up against the wall, giggling hysterically.

The next morning Petey, who missed the party, sits at the table as usual, reading his paper. Meg complains that the drum she bought for Stanley is broken, but she does not remember it being broken at the party. She tells Petey that the men are upstairs in Stanley's room "talking" and that the "big car" she sees in front of the house is probably Goldberg's.

When Goldberg comes downstairs, he informs Petey and Meg that he and McCann are taking Stanley with them because Stanley suffered a "nervous breakdown." McCann comes downstairs and explains that Stanley stopped talking and broke his glasses trying "to fit the eyeholes into his eyes."

McCann begins tearing strips of newspaper again, which so irritates Goldberg that he starts shouting for him to stop, and when McCann calls him "Simey" he becomes even more agitated, calming down only when McCann blows into his mouth. Lulu drops by and accuses Goldberg of seducing her after the party, but Goldberg counters that she wanted him to do it. Insulted, Lulu claims that she has a "pretty shrewd idea" about what is going on and leaves.

When Stanley is finally brought downstairs, he is dressed in a well-cut suit and a bowler hat. Goldberg and McCann begin another sequence of absurd statements regarding Stanley's situation, and by the time they finish, Stanley can respond only in unintelligible noises. Petey tries to stop them from taking Stanley, but Goldberg tells him they are delivering Stanley to "Monty" for "special treatment" and leave in a car with McCann and Stanley. While Petey resumes his breakfast, Meg insists that at the party that night she was "the belle of the ball" but is so confused that she still believes Stanley is upstairs in his room asleep.

Critical Evaluation:

The Birthday Party, which opened in 1958 to terrible reviews, was Harold Pinter's first full-length play. Neither the public nor the critics were aesthetically or culturally prepared for Pinter's style. Pinter's willful obscurity was often viewed as a breach of contract between the playwright and his audience, leaving many theatergoers feeling dissatisfied, cheated, or fooled, as if they missed something, while critics and scholars attacked Pinter for his frustrating dismissiveness regarding the meaning of his plays. Later, however, after the success of *The Caretaker* (1960), *The Birthday Party* was revived in London and became a commercial success. Subsequently, it was televised by the British Broadcasting Corporation (BBC) and, in 1968, it opened on Broadway. Along with *The Caretaker* and *The Homecoming* (1965), *The Birthday Party* is generally considered one of Pinter's most significant plays.

A lyrical dramatist, Pinter was impatient with epic plays involving multiple scene changes and large casts, preferring instead to use one set with a small cast. Pinter was also skeptical of "message" plays, which he believed were aesthetically compromised by social didacticism. Pinter explored the formal, structural properties of theater, developing meaning more by design than by plot or by characterization. Misunderstood by the general public and professional critics alike, Pinter was accused of intentionally teasing viewers into expecting revelations that were never delivered. Much of the confusion surrounding early public reaction to his work stems from the fact that his plays are neither clearly absurd nor clearly realistic; his style derives its distinctiveness from its quirky combination of elements from both schools. Pinter blends the authentic, mimetic behavior usually associated with realism, evoking a world the audience recognizes as the everyday world they inhabit, with the absurdist vision of a senseless, purposeless world to create, out of seemingly ordinary situations, symbolic overtones that both invite and frustrate interpretation. Frequently labeled an absurdist, Pinter distanced himself from any school of theater. He did, however, acknowledge the influence of Irish novelist and playwright Samuel Beckett. The lyrical dialogue, the meaningful silences, the intentional obscurity, the mordant humor, and the cryptic plots are all Beckettian techniques that Pinter assimilated into his own style.

The Birthday Party represented a turning point in Pinter's career. Not only did he prove he could sustain a full-length work but also he demonstrated an uncanny control of suspense, a sense of horror that is sustained throughout the play. *The Birthday Party* also marks a change in Pinter's approach to his material, from his cerebral, often abstract, early plays to plays that were less about ideas than they were about people. It was this shift in focus, from the philosophical concerns of the playwright to the human concerns of the characters, that assured Pinter his later critical and commercial success.

In the play, Stanley Webber is hiding from some unspecified event in his past that forced him into exile, isolated from the world outside the confines of his room. The uneventful, monotonous life at the house seems to be exactly what Stanley needs to maintain his isolation. The order of his routine provides him a measure of security against the contingent outside forces that he fears, while Petey and Meg Boles are like surrogate parents and Lulu is the girl next door.

Stanley's dream of infantile security turns to nightmare when McCann and Goldberg arrive to "do a job." The job, it appears, is to break down Stanley's defenses, both the tactical strategies he devises to hide from his past and the psychological barriers he erects against his own sense of guilt, until finally Stanley is unable to answer even the childish riddle of why the chicken crosses the road. A broken man, compliant, no longer able to speak, he is forced to accept his role as a sac-

rificial victim caught up in a fate he can no longer deny. In his refusal to act and in his withdrawal from the world, Stanley is not, as he hopes, free; he is still a man with a past that must be acknowledged. He is not excused from responsibility for this past simply because he is no longer either active or vital.

While the play is designed to suggest an open-ended set of possible allegorical interpretations—the forced socialization of a reclusive personality, a demand for conformity from a nonconformist, the abstract visiting of justice upon a man guilty of unnamed crimes, the persecution of an artist hounded and ruined by his critics—the significance of the play as drama is in the action itself. Dramatic tension is created and sustained during the play by Pinter's masterful handling of menacing surface details that defy simplistic symbolic interpretations. Of all the suggested meanings, the immediate situation is the most compelling: A man is discovered in hiding; hoodlums brutally reduce him through psychological techniques from a pianist to a babbling wreck, changing him from a man once capable of language and logic to a pliable creature capable of only nonsensical utterances. The inevitability of his dilemma, the hapless and innocent ineffectiveness of Petey and Meg, and the methodical brutality of Goldberg and McCann suggest a disturbing commentary on life concerning the existential suffering of a man desperately searching for certainty and comfort in the face of inexplicable destructive forces.

Jeff Johnson

Further Reading

Baker, William. *Harold Pinter*. London: Continuum, 2008. Brief critical biography examining the themes, patterns, relationships, and ideas that are common to Pinter's life and writings.

Billington, Michael. *Harold Pinter*. London: Faber & Faber, 2007. Critical biography focusing on literary analysis of Pinter's works. Discusses the major plays at length, providing information about their literary and biographical sources.

Bloom, Harold, ed. *Modern Critical Views: Harold Pinter*. New York: Chelsea House, 1987. An eclectic collection of essays by various critics. Offers comprehensive analysis of general themes as well as selected specific texts.

Burkman, Katherine H. *The Dramatic World of Harold Pinter: Its Basis in Ritual*. Columbus: Ohio State University Press, 1971. An analysis of Pinter's work viewed from the perspectives of Freudian, Marxist, and myth analysis. Heavy on theory with solid literary analysis of individual plays.

Esslin, Martin. *Pinter: The Playwright.* 6th exp. and rev. ed. London: Methuen, 2000. Comprehensive analytical survey of Pinter's writing career, offering critical commentary on all of his plays.

_____. *Theatre of the Absurd.* New York: Viking Penguin, 1987. Overview of the avant-garde and how the term relates to selected dramatic works. Includes an excellent discussion of Pinter's early work.

Gale, Stephen H., ed. *Harold Pinter: Critical Approaches.* Rutherford, N.J.: Fairleigh Dickinson University Press, 1986. A collection of essays by various critics on a wide range of Pinter's work. Places the material in the context of contemporary critical theories.

Merritt, Susan H. *Pinter in Play: Critical Strategies and the Plays of Harold Pinter.* Durham, N.C.: Duke University Press, 1990. Excellent discussion of current and past debates on critical theory as it relates to Pinter's work. Provides scrupulous textual examination.

Raby, Peter, ed. *The Cambridge Companion to Harold Pinter.* New York: Cambridge University Press, 2001. Collection of essays, including discussions of Pinter, politics, and postmodernism; Pinter and the critics; Pinter and the twentieth century theater; and a piece by director Peter Hall about directing Pinter's plays. The numerous references to *The Birthday Party* are listed in a separate index of Pinter's works.

The Black Arrow
A Tale of the Two Roses

Author: Robert Louis Stevenson (1850-1894)
First published: 1888
Type of work: Novel
Type of plot: Adventure
Time of plot: Fifteenth century
Locale: England

Principal characters:
SIR DANIEL BRACKLEY, a political turncoat
RICHARD "DICK" SHELTON, his ward
JOANNA SEDLEY, Lord Foxham's ward
SIR OLIVER OATES, Sir Daniel's clerk
ELLIS DUCKWORTH, an outlaw
LAWLESS, another outlaw and Dick's friend
RICHARD, duke of Gloucester

The Story:

One afternoon in the late springtime, the Moat House bell begins to ring. A messenger arrived with a message from Sir Daniel Brackley for Sir Oliver Oates, his clerk. When the peasants gather at the summons of the bell, they are told that as many armed men as can be spared from the defense of Moat House are to join Sir Daniel at Kettley, where a battle is to be fought between the armies of Lancaster and York. There is some grumbling at this order, for Sir Daniel is a faithless man who fights first on one side and then on the other. He added to his own lands by securing the wardships of children left orphans in those troubled times, and it is whispered that he murdered good Sir Harry Shelton to make himself the guardian of young Dick Shelton and the lord of the Moat House estates.

As guardian, Sir Daniel plans to marry Dick to the orphaned heiress of Kettley, Joanna Sedley. He rides there to take charge of the girl. Dick, knowing nothing of these plans, remains behind as one of the garrison of the manor. Old Nick

Appleyard, a veteran of Agincourt, grumbles at the weakness of the defense in a country overrun by stragglers from warring armies and insists that Moat House lies open to attack. His prophecy comes true. While he stands talking to Dick and Bennet Hatch, Sir Daniel's bailiff, a black arrow whirs out of the woods and strikes Nick between the shoulder blades. A message on the shaft indicates that John Amend-All, a mysterious outlaw, kills old Nick.

Sir Oliver trembles when he reads the message on the arrow. Shortly afterward, he is further disturbed by a message pinned on the church door, announcing that John Amend-All will kill Sir Daniel, Sir Oliver, and Hatch. Dick learns from the message that the outlaw accuses Sir Oliver of killing Sir Harry, Dick's father; but Sir Oliver swears that he had no part in the knight's death. Dick decides to remain quiet until he learns more about the matter and in the meantime to act in all fairness to Sir Daniel.

It is decided that Hatch should remain to guard Moat

House while the outlaws are in the neighborhood. Dick rides off with ten men-at-arms to find Sir Daniel. He carries a letter from Sir Oliver telling of John Amend-All's threats.

At Kettley, Sir Daniel awaits the outcome of a battle already in progress, for he intends to join the winning side at the last minute. Sir Daniel is also upset by the outlaw's threats, and he orders Dick to return to Moat House with a letter for Sir Oliver. He and his men leave to join the fighting; but not before he roundly curses his luck because Joanna, whom he held hostage, escaped in boy's clothing. He orders a party of men-at-arms to search for the girl and then to proceed to Moat House and strengthen the defenses there.

On his return journey, Dick meets Joanna, still dressed as a boy, who tells him that her name is John Matcham. Dick, unaware that she is Sir Daniel's prisoner, promises to help her reach the abbey at Holywood. As they hurry on, they come upon a camp of the outlaws led by Ellis Duckworth, another man ruined by Sir Daniel. Running from the outlaws, they see the party of Sir Daniel's retainers shot down one by one. The cannonading Dick hears in the distance convinces him that the soldiers of Lancaster are faring badly in the day's battle. Not knowing on which side Sir Daniel declares himself, he wonders whether his guardian is among the victors or the vanquished.

Dick and his companion sleep in the forest that night. The next morning, a detachment of Sir Daniel's men sweep by in disorderly rout. Soon afterward, they see a hooded leper in the woods. The man is Sir Daniel, attempting to make his way back to Moat House in disguise. He is dismayed when he hears that the outlaws killed a party of his men-at-arms. When the three arrive at Moat House, Sir Daniel accuses Dick of distrust. He claims innocence in the death of Dick's father and forces Sir Oliver to do the same. Another black arrow is shot through a window into a room in which the three are talking. Sir Daniel gives orders to defend Moat House against attack. Dick is placed under close watch in a room over the chapel, and he is not allowed to see his friend John Matcham.

That night, when John Matcham comes secretly to the room over the chapel, Dick learns that the companion of his adventures in the forest is really Joanna, the girl to whom Sir Daniel betrothed him. Warned that he is in danger, Dick escapes into the forest. There, he finds Duckworth, who promises him that Sir Daniel will be destroyed.

Meanwhile, the war goes in favor of Lancaster, and Sir Daniel's fortunes rise with those of the house he follows. The town of Shoreby is full of Lancastrians all of that summer and fall, and there Sir Daniel has his own house for his family and followers. Joanna is not with him; she is kept in a lonely house by the sea under the care of the wife of Hatch. Dick and an outlaw companion, Lawless, go to the town, and while reconnoitering Joanna's hiding place, Dick encounters Lord Foxham, enemy of Sir Daniel and Joanna's legal guardian. Lord Foxham promises that if Joanna can be rescued she will become Dick's bride. The two men attempt a rescue by sea in a stolen boat, but a storm almost sinks their boat, and Lord Foxham is injured when the party attempts to land.

That winter, Dick and his faithful companion, Lawless, return to Shoreby. Disguised as priests, they enter Sir Daniel's house and are there protected by Alicia Risingham, Joanna's friend and the niece of a powerful Lancastrian lord. When Dick and Joanna meet, she tells him that the following day she is to marry Lord Shoreby against her will. An alarm is given when Dick is forced to kill one of Lord Shoreby's spies. Still in the disguise of a priest, he is taken to Sir Oliver, who promises not to betray Dick if he will remain quietly in the church until after the wedding of Joanna and Lord Shoreby. During the night, Lawless finds Dick and gives him the message that Duckworth returned and will prevent the marriage.

As the wedding procession enters the church, three archers discharge their black arrows from a gallery. Lord Shoreby falls, two of the arrows in his body. Sir Daniel is wounded in the arm. Sir Oliver denounces Dick and Lawless, and they are taken before the Earl of Risingham. Aided by Joanna and Alicia, Dick argues his cause with such vigor, however, that the earl agrees to protect him from Sir Daniel's anger. Later, learning from Dick that Sir Daniel is secretly plotting with the Yorkist leaders, the earl sets him and Lawless free.

Dick makes his escape from Sir Daniel's men only to be captured by the old seaman whose skiff he stole on the night he and Lord Foxham attempted to rescue Joanna from Sir Daniel. It takes him half the night to escape the angry seaman and his friends. In the morning he is in time to meet, at Lord Foxham's request, young Richard of York, duke of Gloucester. On his arrival at the meeting place, he finds the duke attacked by bandits. He saves Richard's life and later fights with the duke in the battle of Shoreby, in which the army of Lancaster is defeated. He is knighted for his bravery in the fight. Afterward, when Richard is giving out honors, Dick claims as his portion only the freedom of the old seaman whose boat he stole.

Pursuing Sir Daniel, Dick rescues Joanna and takes her to Holywood. The next morning, he encounters Sir Daniel in the forest near the abbey. Dick is willing to let his enemy escape, but Ellis Duckworth, lurking nearby, kills the faithless knight. Dick asks the outlaw to spare the life of Sir Oliver.

Dick and Joanna are married. They live quietly at Moat

House, withdrawn from the bloody disputes of the houses of Lancaster and York. Both the old seaman and Lawless are cared for in their old age, and Lawless finally takes orders and dies a friar.

Critical Evaluation:

Robert Louis Stevenson has often been discussed as a children's author, and to some extent this description is justified. Many of his works can be enjoyed by children, and some of them were written with such an audience in mind. *The Black Arrow* was serialized in *Young Folks*, a magazine intended for boys, in 1888, five years after Stevenson's success with *Treasure Island*, which had been written for the same publication.

These novels are also part of a very old tradition of historical romance, dating back at least as far as Sir Thomas Malory and his *Le Morte d'Arthur* (1485). Closer to Stevenson's own time, Sir Walter Scott wrote *Ivanhoe* in 1819, and the two authors are often compared. In his handling of characters and motives, Stevenson clearly broke with the traditions of historical romance.

The Black Arrow is set in the fifteenth century, during the War of the Roses, a civil war among the British aristocracy. This setting presents an author with problems in terms of motivation. Unlike the many stories of Robin Hood, or the adventures of heroes battling ferocious monsters, there is no clear delineation between good and evil in this novel. The various noblemen of the rival houses of York and Lancaster are all ruthless, out for their own advantage. There is never the slightest suggestion that one branch of the royal family is morally superior to the other.

Dick Shelton, the young hero of *The Black Arrow*, begins by being completely uncertain of which side he will support in the war. His guardian, Sir Daniel, also wavers, determined to wait until the last minute and to join the winning side. When Dick becomes convinced that his guardian conspired in the murder of his father, he casts his lot with the side opposing his guardian; the choice is a matter of Sir Daniel's badness, not the side's goodness. Sir Daniel decides to join the Lancasters and Dick joins up with the Fellowship of the Black Arrow, who are Daniel's enemies and are siding with the House of York.

When Dick meets a major leader of that faction, he is suddenly catapulted to great importance in the war, because that leader, Richard, duke of Gloucester (later to become King Richard III), has a superstitious tendency to support anyone who shares his first name. Richard is obviously a cruel, almost inhuman individual, and Dick finds it very hard to reconcile his own feelings with his support of such a leader.

The members of the Fellowship of the Black Arrow are also far from pleasant. They are bandits, but not the sort of romantic bandits found in stories of Robin Hood. They steal from people of all classes, for their own gain, and are quite willing to commit murder if necessary. This causes Dick's final dilemma, and the one that forces him to lose all interest in the adventure in which he has taken part.

At the end of the novel, Dick has the chance to do away with his wicked guardian but decides to spare his guardian's life. Ellis Duckworth, the chief of the Fellowship of the Black Arrow, kills Sir Daniel instead. Dick marries Joanna, the woman his guardian wanted him to marry (a break with tradition, certainly), and retires from the war.

The Black Arrow works as an exciting adventure story, but it leaves something to be desired as a historical romance. There are certainly villains, including Sir Daniel and Duke Richard, but they are on different sides of the dispute. More important, Dick is not the romantic hero readers expect in such stories. He makes mistakes, he can never seem to make up his mind, and he "lives happily ever after" without resolving any of his problems.

The Black Arrow is somewhat difficult for a modern reader, because the language is deliberately archaic. A greater difficulty is that Stevenson was working within the framework of Victorian morality. Sex was practically nonexistent in most writings of the time, and violence was relatively tame. The story was written for a children's magazine, which meant that even by Victorian standards, it had to be especially clean. As a result, passionate love scenes and delightfully gory executions are not to be found in the book.

Stevenson was a great writer in this genre, perhaps the last. The term "romance" has changed its meaning over time and now almost always refers to a formulaic love story rather than to an adventure story. Apart from books intended for children, there are few stories about knights in shining armor being written today, and actual history has largely been replaced by fantasy in adventure stories.

The Black Arrow should not be dismissed because it is children's literature. Like many books for children, this story must be considered within a greater context. Presenting readers with a hero who has difficulty in deciding where his loyalties lie, and villains who seem willing to join whatever side is winning, Stevenson provides a realistic vision of humanity. Dick, Sir Daniel, and even Richard Crookback are more human than Ivanhoe or Robin Hood. The heroes of *The Black Arrow* are not perfect. Readers can therefore identify with them in a personal way.

"Critical Evaluation" by Marc Goldstein

Further Reading

Ambrosini, Richard, and Richard Dury, eds. *Robert Louis Stevenson: Writer of Boundaries*. Madison: University of Wisconsin Press, 2006. Collection of essays examining all of Stevenson's work; references to *The Black Arrow* are listed in the index.

Calder, Jenni. *Robert Louis Stevenson: A Life Study*. New York: Oxford University Press, 1980. Discusses Stevenson's works and how they were influenced by circumstances in his life, with an emphasis on the works, rather than on the author's life. Includes analyses of many of Stevenson's novels.

Green, Martin. *Dreams of Adventure, Deeds of Empire*. New York: Basic Books, 1979. A discussion of the genre of romantic adventure in English literature, particularly focusing on the nineteenth century. An excellent source for placing works such as *The Black Arrow* in their literary context.

Harman, Claire. *Myself and the Other Fellow: A Life of Robert Louis Stevenson*. New York: HarperCollins, 2005. A substantial biography of Stevenson, covering the writer's early family life, his writing and travels, and his curious but successful marriage. Includes bibliography and index.

Jones, William B., Jr., ed. *Robert Louis Stevenson Reconsidered: New Critical Perspectives*. Jefferson, N.C.: McFarland, 2003. Collection of essays providing critical overviews of Stevenson's fiction, as well as specific analyses of individual works.

Kiely, Robert. *Robert Louis Stevenson and the Fiction of Adventure*. Cambridge, Mass.: Harvard University Press, 1964. A discussion of Stevenson's adventure stories, their antecedents in English literature, and their effects on later works. Particular emphasis is placed on *Treasure Island* and *The Black Arrow*.

McLynn, Frank J. *Robert Louis Stevenson: A Biography*. London: Hutchinson University Library, 1993. A highly detailed biography of the author, covering his life from early childhood to his death in Samoa in 1894. Emphasizes Stevenson's extensive travels and their influence on his work.

Pope-Hennessy, James. *Robert Louis Stevenson*. London: Jonathan Cape, 1974. A biography, including a detailed discussion of the times and places in which Stevenson's works were written and the circumstances that inspired them. Includes many illustrations.

Black Boy
A Record of Childhood and Youth

Author: Richard Wright (1908-1960)
First published: 1945
Type of work: Autobiography

Principal characters:
RICHARD WRIGHT, the narrator
ELLA, his mother
NATHAN, his father
MARGARET and RICHARD WILSON, Richard's grandparents
AUNT MAGGIE and UNCLE HOSKINS, Ella's sister and her husband
CLARK and JODY, Richard's aunt and uncle
ROSS, a member of the Communist Party

The Story:

Richard Wright was a bored and frustrated young boy growing up in Natchez, Mississippi, in a household that he believed neither understood nor appreciated him. At the age of four, he demonstrated his boredom and frustration by setting his house on fire, thus incurring the wrath of his mother, Ella, who beat him into unconsciousness.

When the family moved to Memphis, Tennessee, Richard's father deserted the family, leaving them in poverty.

Richard's mother was forced to put her two sons in an orphanage, where they remained for six weeks before being reunited with their mother. They then moved to Elaine, Arkansas, to live with Ella's sister and her husband. En route to Arkansas, they stayed for a brief time in Jackson, Mississippi, with Ella's parents, Margaret and Richard Wilson. Margaret (called Granny), the matriarchal head of the house, was a stern ruler, intolerant of the love of fiction demonstrated by a schoolteacher who boarded with her. The school-teacher introduced fiction to Richard. From Granny's intolerance, Richard learned lessons about familial rigidity and cruelty that he carried with him throughout his youth.

When they arrived in Elaine, Arkansas, to stay with Aunt Maggie and Uncle Hoskins, it appeared that the Wrights' lives of constant mobility and poverty were over. They finally got the food they needed and the security they had lacked. This sustenance and stability were short-lived, however. Uncle Hoskins was murdered by whites who wanted his saloon, thus compelling the Wright family to leave. They fled to West Helena, a town near Elaine.

The mobility continued when Richard's mother suffered a stroke. Granny took her and the two boys back to Jackson, Mississippi. Even this move was temporary, because Granny could not afford to provide for the three Wrights. She sent Richard's brother to stay with their Aunt Maggie, who had moved to Detroit, and she sent Richard to Greenwood, Mississippi, to live with Uncle Clark and Aunt Jody. This sojourn in Richard's life was a miserable time for him because of his uncle's brutality. In the early 1920's, Richard returned to Jackson, Mississippi.

During his four years in Jackson, from 1921 to 1925, Wright went to two schools, graduating as valedictorian from Smith-Robinson Public School. Although this was his only formal education, he made the most of this brief schooling and immersed himself in all types of literature. He also published his first work, "The Voodoo of Hell's Half Acre," which appeared in the *Southern Register* in 1924.

Despite the fulfillment he discovered in literature, Richard's life in Jackson was painful because of the religious fanaticism of his grandmother and his Aunt Addie, who lived with them. When he could no longer tolerate those surroundings, Richard first got a job to earn money for his escape from Jackson, then stole money so that he would have enough support to go to Memphis, where he stayed for two years.

In 1927, Richard followed his dream to Chicago, what he envisioned as the promised land of the North. He arrived there looking for the freedom he had been denied in the South, and he believed he had found that freedom as well as solidarity with others in the John Reed Club, which was a Communist literary organization, and then in the Communist Party itself. This was only a momentary stop on his journey toward self-realization, however, for Richard learned that the Communist Party was not the organization he had thought it was. It wished to rob him of his individuality, his unique gifts as a writer, and his desire to be an individual who used words to create a new world. As he observed what the Communist Party did to people, including a man named Ross who was

tried as a traitor to the party, Wright realized that he needed to leave the party. Having learned that his calling was not to be a member of an organized group but to be a solitary individual whose strength was his identity as a wordsmith, he accepted his vocation. He was a writer.

Critical Evaluation:

When *Black Boy* was first published in 1945, it did not include Wright's conclusion, intended to be a critical part of the book. This section, published separately in 1977 under the title *American Hunger*, focuses on an important theme of the book—Richard's growth as a writer—and places the first part of the book—his challenging adventures en route to his acceptance of himself as a writer—within this context. The complete edition of the autobiography is now published as two parts, the first titled "Southern Night" and the second titled "The Horror and the Glory." In the concluding paragraph of this self-portrait, Wright announces his vocation as a writer and points, with hope, to the strength of his language:

> I would hurl words into this darkness and wait for an echo, and if an echo sounded, no matter how faintly, I would send other words to tell, to march, to fight, to create a sense of hunger for life that gnaws in us all, to keep alive in our hearts a sense of the inexpressibly human.

Quotations from the book of Job signal this theme, serving as epigraphs for the entire book and for the first part of the autobiography. The first quotation suggests the struggle that will characterize Richard's flight from the South to the North and his fight to find himself: "They meet with darkness in the daytime/ And they grope at noonday as in the night." The second quotation suggests that "Southern Night" will narrate the Job-like struggle Richard will endure as he moves from adventure to adventure, from home to home, from one stage of his childhood and youth to the next: "His strength shall be hunger-bitten/ And destruction shall be ready at his side." The subtitle of *Black Boy* captures this movement, for the book is indeed "A Record of Childhood and Youth" that is also a portrait of an artist as a young man.

This developing artist re-creates his childhood and youth through dialogue, the use of details, and the selection of symbolic scenes. All these techniques combine to demonstrate the ability of the child and youth to survive, to endure the challenges of his environment so that he can emerge from those surroundings a thoughtful, sensitive writer.

An example of Wright's effective use of dialogue is the conversation between Richard and a white woman whom Richard approaches about doing chores for her. The woman asks if he wants the job, and, learning that he does, poses what she believes is an important question: "Do you steal?" Richard bursts into a laugh and tells the woman that if he were a thief, he would never tell anyone. The woman is enraged by this response, and Richard realizes that he has made a terrible mistake, that he has demonstrated to the woman that he is "sassy," and that he must resume the mask that white people expect of blacks, the mask of respect and deference. Through the dialogue between the woman and Richard, the issue of black-white relations is revealed dramatically and without any need for editorial comment by the narrator.

The use of details also reveals thematic ideas, one of which is the paradoxical situation of destruction as a means of bringing about new growth. The detailed use of fire suggests this paradox, beginning with the opening scene in which Richard sets fire to the house, nearly destroying it and, more important, nearly destroying himself, because his mother had come close to killing him for his action. This act of potential destruction serves as a paradoxical opportunity for growth insofar as Richard learns, at the age of four, that his family is a destructive force in his life, one from which he must flee if he is to be free to pursue his dreams. He is reminded of this lesson at the end of the chapter, when he goes to see his father to request money so that he, his brother, and his mother can go to Arkansas. When Richard arrives at his father's house, he sees not only his father but also a strange woman with him, both sitting before a fire. Once again, detailed use of the image of fire reinforces the theme of destruction and its role in the education process. Richard sees the fire and understands that it represents the destructive force of his father, a force from which he must run if he is to mature.

Wright uses dialogue and details as techniques to plot the journey of his childhood and youth; symbolic scenes act as markers along the trip to self-knowledge. The opening scene and the conversation with the white woman who gives Richard a job doing chores for her are powerful markers. Another symbolic scene occurs in the second half of the self-portrait, when Richard describes his job in a medical research institute in a large, wealthy hospital in Chicago. On Saturday mornings, Richard assists a doctor in slitting the vocal cords of dogs, so that their howling will not disturb the hospital patients. Richard describes the sight of the dogs being rendered unconscious as the result of an injection, then having their vocal cords severed, and finally awakening and being unable to wail. Wright calls this "a symbol of silent suffering," clearly not confined to the canines.

As a book that gives testimony to the transformation of silent suffering into creative growth and as an autobiography that shows the development of a struggling artist who seeks to find words to describe that suffering, *Black Boy* is one of the most significant autobiographies created by an American, black or white. When it was first published in 1945, it was the fourth best-selling nonfiction title that year, and it has continued to be read, reviewed, and respected as a classic study of the growth of a young man and the environment in which he develops. It is both a portrait of an individual and a portrait of a culture, the two struggling with each other and meeting each other "with darkness in the daytime" to illustrate a way to survive, to endure, and to thrive.

Marjorie Smelstor

Further Reading

Andrews, William L., and Douglas Taylor, eds. *Richard Wright's "Black Boy" ("American Hunger"): A Casebook*. New York: Oxford University Press, 2003. Includes a 1945 interview with Wright and contemporary critical responses to *Black Boy* by W. E. B. Du Bois, Lionel Trilling, Mary McCarthy, and Ralph Ellison. The novel also is interpreted in eight modern essays, which include discussions of *Black Boy* as art, the novel's narrative design, and the politics of the book's "bad" language.

Bloom, Harold, ed. *Richard Wright's "Black Boy."* New York: Chelsea House, 2006. Compilation of critical essays about the novel, including discussions of Wright and the tradition of African American autobiography, a comparison of *Black Boy* and autobiographical works by Maya Angelou, and the novel's depiction of the South.

Fabre, Michel. *The Unfinished Quest of Richard Wright*. Translated by Isabel Barzun. Rev. ed. New York: William Morrow, 1973. A significant biography, with much useful information about Wright's literary works, including *Black Boy*.

Felgar, Robert. *Richard Wright*. Boston: Twayne, 1980. A useful introductory overview of Wright's life and works.

_____. *Student Companion to Richard Wright*. Westport, Conn.: Greenwood Press, 2000. Provides an overview of Wright's life and literary career and analyses of the plots, character development, themes, and other elements of his works. Chapter 5 is devoted to *Black Boy*.

_____. *Understanding Richard Wright's "Black Boy": A Student Casebook to Issues, Sources, and Historical Documents*. Westport, Conn.: Greenwood Press, 1998. Analyzes the dominant themes and structure of the novel. Provides primary source documents about the African American autobiographical tradition, the American dream of success and its deferment for blacks, and racism in the United States.

Mack, Richard, and Frank E. Moorer. *Richard Wright: A Collection of Critical Essays.* Englewood Cliffs, N.J.: Prentice Hall, 1984. A collection of essays examining the writer and his works, including a chronology of important dates in Wright's life.

Margolies, Edward. *The Art of Richard Wright.* Carbondale: Southern Illinois University Press, 1969. A general study, including a brief discussion of *Black Boy* as a film documentary.

Mitchell, Hayley, ed. *Readings on "Black Boy."* San Diego, Calif.: Greenhaven Press, 2000. Collection of essays in-terpreting the novel, including discussions of its narrative structure, the book as a twentieth century slave narrative, *Black Boy* as a metaphor for the birth of an artist, and the metaphor of the journey in the novel.

Wright, Richard. *Conversations with Richard Wright.* Edited by Kenneth Kinnamon and Michel Fabre. Jackson: University Press of Mississippi, 1993. Reprints about fifty interviews with Wright that originally appeared in American and European magazines and newspapers. Among other subjects, Wright discusses his politics, his craft, his individual works, and his exile in France.

Black Elk Speaks
Being the Life Story of a Holy Man of the Oglala Sioux

Authors: Black Elk (1863-1950) and John G. Neihardt (1881-1973)
First published: 1932
Type of work: Autobiography

Black Elk Speaks is the work of two collaborators: Black Elk, an Oglala Sioux holy man who tells his life story, and John G. Neihardt, a white man sensitive to American Indian culture, who interviewed Black Elk at the Pine Ridge Reservation in 1931 and fleshed out and gave artistic form to Black Elk's account. Black Elk tells the adventure story of a young Sioux boy as he grows into adulthood.

Black Elk had early memories of a father wounded in the Fetterman Fight against the Wasichus (white men), which at first seemed only like a bad dream that he did not understand. Then came a growing awareness of the white man and first seeing one when he was ten years old. His grandfather made him a bow and arrows when he was five years old, and with the other boys he had played at killing Wasichus. There were the times when an older man named Watanye took him hunting or down to a creek's woods to go fishing or told him funny stories like that of the misadventures of High Horse in his courtship of a chief's daughter. He had memories of playing pranks with the other boys—chopping off the top of the flagpole at Fort Robinson, teasing the people during a dance—and of endurance contests such as the breast dance, in which the boys burned sunflower seeds on their wrists and tried to keep them there without crying.

Black Elk's account includes memories of famous chiefs he had known: Red Cloud, who was too friendly with the white men; the defiant but always cautious Sitting Bull; and Black Elk's cousin, Crazy Horse, whom he idolized. Black Elk listened to the stories about Crazy Horse and how he became a great and daring warrior. He also heard about Crazy Horse's idiosyncrasies, but he especially remembered Crazy Horse's sense of humor. Crazy Horse sometimes teased him, and one time he invited him into his tent to eat with him.

The book is a rich source of information about Sioux customs. The psychologist Carl Jung called it a storehouse of anthropological data. Dances of various kinds were frequent, preceded by elaborate rituals. A comic dance was the heyoka ceremony, which involved considerable horseplay and clowns circulating throughout the crowd, provoking laughter. At the age of nine, Black Elk, with five other boys, went through the puberty rite of purification—his body and face painted yellow, a black stripe on either side of his nose, his hair tied up to look like a bear's ears, and eagle feathers on his head. Even the bison hunt, so necessary for the meat supply and survival, had a ritual that was preceded by the smoking of the sacred pipe and a prayer to the Great Spirit and

Mother Earth. The hunters attacked in a special order, with the soldier band first.

Black Elk's account documents events from much of the second half of the nineteenth century as witnessed by a young Indian boy. These include the series of battles in the Indian War and the sufferings of the Sioux as they were displaced from their lands by the white people. When Black Elk was eleven, tensions with the whites mounted as news arrived of the coming of Pahuska (literally, Long Hair, the name given to General George Custer). Many chiefs gathered in a council to discuss a strategy to deal with the whites, a gathering avoided by Crazy Horse and Sitting Bull, who were suspicious of any agreement with the whites. Black Elk's people did not hear of the subsequent attack on Crazy Horse's village for quite a while, but when they did, they joined the huge gathering of tribes on the Rosebud River. Chaos ensued when the Wasichus attacked, and Black Elk ran from place to place and even killed one of the soldiers.

Custer, eager to avenge the defeat on the Rosebud, decided to attack the Sioux at the Little Big Horn. Black Elk was not yet of age to fight. He watched with the women from the top of a hill, but all he could see was a cloud of dust. When it cleared, he rode down to where a vast army of Wasichus lay dead. He did not see Custer, and no one knew which of the corpses was his. When Black Elk saw a quivering soldier, he shot him with an arrow; he scalped another. He was not sorry, since the Wasichus came to kill them, but he got sick at the sight of so much blood and went home.

The victory did no good, however, and the Sioux began to travel the Black Road of suffering. Some went to the white agencies, but most tribes scattered in different directions, pursued by the soldiers. Sitting Bull and Gall went to Canada, but Crazy Horse stayed. Black Elk's tribe moved from one place to another, setting fire to the grass behind them to stave off pursuing soldiers. It was a hard winter. Most of their land was burned, and there were no bison. One day, when Black Elk was fourteen years old, Dull Knife came with what was left of his starving and freezing people. Black Elk's tribe gave them clothing but not much food because they themselves had only their frozen ponies to eat.

Then came the news of the arrest of Crazy Horse. Black Elk was in the crowd and could not see him, but he heard him struggle. When he heard that Crazy Horse was killed, all Black Elk could do was mourn with the others and watch the next morning as Crazy Horse's father and mother put the body on a drag and bore it away, nobody knew where. After that, Black Elk's tribe went to Canada for a while. When they returned home, they found the people in despair, but soon after they heard about the Messiah and his Ghost Dance, with

its mission for a spiritual revitalizing of the Indian nation and restoration of the old Indian culture. Because the Messiah seemed to promise the eventual defeat of the whites, the whites became alarmed and took the offensive again. Black Elk was a grown man when he heard that Sitting Bull was killed. The Messiah went to the soldiers at Wounded Knee to attempt conciliation. Black Elk, nearby at Pine Ridge, hearing that violence might occur, rode over and arrived to see the result of the Massacre at Wounded Knee: the land covered with the bodies of men, women, and children.

Black Elk Speaks, however, is primarily an account of a man's vision and what became of it. Black Elk first saw his vision when he was nine years old, lying in a coma for twelve days. In his vision he flew to a council of his grandfathers, where he was given a hoop representing his people. In its center was a flowering tree that promised they would flourish. The tree stood at the crossing of a red road, the road of good on which his nation would walk, and a black road, a road of troubles and war, on which he would also walk and where he would have the power to destroy his people's foes.

As a result of having seen the vision, Black Elk became a visionary seeker of salvation for his people. He was troubled because they were threatened not only by the destruction of their culture but also by their willingness to adopt the worst habits of their white conquerors. At intervals he sank back into the routines of Sioux life, but the vision recurred periodically throughout his life, for example, after the purification ceremony of puberty and again on his family's journey back from Canada, when he sat alone on a hillside. There, he experienced a strange foreboding that lingered until he returned home. When a medicine man urged him to tell others of his vision with a dance, he discovered he could heal the sick, and for three years he practiced curing. He felt, however, that his mission was greater than that: It was to save the nation's hoop.

When Buffalo Bill approached the tribe to recruit members for his Wild West Show, Black Elk joined. This, he concluded, was an opportunity to bring the whole world into the sacred hoop. His people had sunk back into selfish pursuits, everybody concerned only about himself. If the Wasichus had a better way, maybe his people should live that way. The travel with the show took him to many places, including into the presence of Queen Victoria, and although it was a happy time, he was in strange world. One night, he experienced another vision and returned to his people. Things there were even worse, however, and he lost his power. At first, he could hardly remember the vision, but when people came to him for help, the power returned. This was about the time when he heard of the Messiah, and for some time he believed that this was the answer to his vision. He soon discovered though, that it, too, was a mistake. At Wounded Knee, he found that his and the Messiah's vision of peace and unity was not to be. When Black Elk looked over the horror of Wounded Knee, he realized that something besides people had died in that bloody mud: a dream.

As the interview ended, Black Elk said to Neihardt: "He to whom a great vision was given is now a pitiful old man who has done nothing. His nation's hoop was there broken and scattered. There was no center any longer, and the sacred tree was dead." After the interview, Black Elk and Neihardt made a trip to Harney Peak in the Black Hills. Black Elk pointed out the spot where he had stood in his vision. He stopped, dressed and painted himself as he was in his vision, faced the west, held the sacred pipe before him in his right hand, and prayed to the Great Spirit: "The tree is withered. Maybe some little root of that tree still lives. Hear me that my people may once more go back into the sacred hoop and find the red road." The old man stood weeping in the drizzling rain, and then the sky cleared again.

Black Elk Speaks reflects Black Elk and Neihardt's affection for the Oglala Sioux and their sorrow for the Black Road the Sioux had to travel and for the way of life they lost. At the same time, the book promotes a genuine mysticism, a belief in the unity of all humankind under one great Being. It is about the failure to accomplish a mission but also about a hope that the mission could yet be accomplished.

Thomas Amherst Perry

Further Reading

Aly, Lucile F. *John G. Neihardt*. Boise, Idaho: Boise State University Press, 1976. Presents a synopsis of *Black Elk Speaks*, with emphasis on the vision, which Aly finds similar to apocalyptic visions in the Bible and to poems by William Blake.

Costello, Damian. *Black Elk: Colonialism and Lakota Catholicism*. Maryknoll, N.Y.: Orbis Books, 2005. Costello argues that Black Elk did not abandon his Lakota beliefs after converting to Catholicism; instead, he maintains, Catholicism empowered Black Elk to continue to challenge colonial threats to the Lakotas' way of life.

Dunsmore, Roger. "Nicholaus Black Elk: Holy Man in History." In *A Sender of Words*, edited by Vine Deloria, Jr. Salt Lake City, Utah: Howe Brothers, 1984. Concludes that Black Elk's life story and the wisdom of Oglala Sioux traditions are not merely a romantic longing for a lost way of life but the story of the responsibility imposed on those who have had a great vision.

Holler, Clyde, ed. *The Black Elk Reader*. Syracuse, N.Y.: Syracuse University Press, 2000. Collection of essays that provide literary, anthropological, and theological analyses of *Black Elk Speaks*. Some of the essays discuss *Black Elk Speaks* as testimonial literature, the use of Lakota tradition in the book, the role of horses in Black Elk's vision, and the relationship of Black Elk and John G. Neihardt.

Holloway, Brian R. *Interpreting the Legacy: John Neihardt and "Black Elk Speaks."* Boulder: University Press of Colorado, 2003. Holloway disagrees with scholars who maintain that Neihardt misappropriated and misinterpreted Black Elk's teachings. He demonstrates how Neihardt strove to faithfully re-create Black Elk's spiritual world and to convey that world to readers.

Rice, Julian. *Black Elk's Story: Distinguishing Its Lakota Purpose*. Albuquerque: University of New Mexico Press, 1991. Points out that Black Elk's story unfolds symbolically like sophisticated fiction, with an intuitive selection of details that create a coherent narrative. Black Elk draws on a wide range of religious metaphors, some of them Christian.

Whitney, Blair. *John G. Neihardt*. Boston: Twayne, 1976. Whitney concludes that *Black Elk Speaks* is a tragic book about a man who is too weak to implement his vision. The book's function is to preserve that vision for other men.

Black Lamb and Grey Falcon
A Journey Through Yugoslavia

Author: Rebecca West (1892-1983)
First published: 1941
Type of work: Travel writing

Black Lamb and Grey Falcon is a travelogue of epic sweep through the former Yugoslavia and its many cultural regions: Croatia, Dalmatia, Herzegovina, Bosnia, Serbia, Macedonia, Old Serbia, and Montenegro. Rebecca West re-creates the experience of her journey through culture and history, intertwining the near and distant past in a narrative that possesses something of the flavor of the great works of Marcel Proust. Her guide, the poet Constantine, speaks as the poetic imagination of the Yugoslav people in this cultural dialogue between Eastern and Western Europe.

The book begins with a prologue describing West's stay in a nursing home preparing for surgery. A nurse puzzles over why West is so disturbed about the assassination of Yugoslav king Alexander I (October 9, 1934). Was the king a friend of West? The question prompts West to think about how so many women are disconnected from world events and thus think only in terms of private, domestic matters; whereas men, preoccupied with public life, seldom give personal relationships the careful attention women do. Women and men, in other words, suffer from deficiencies that limit their capacities as human beings. In the broadest sense, then, *Black Lamb and Grey Falcon* is about West's exploration of her own humanity, using events in Yugoslavia as a prism to reveal the full spectrum of history that most people fail to perceive.

The author and her husband, Henry Andrews, enter Yugoslavia by railroad on the line that runs from Munich, Germany, to Zagreb, the capital of Croatia, formerly a province of Yugoslavia. Four German tourists share their train compartment and brag about the advantages Germany holds over the "barbaric" country they are entering.

In Zagreb, home of the Croats—who are southern Slavs—they meet Constantine, a Yugoslav poet and government official who had befriended West on her previous trip to the same country and who, this time, becomes their tour guide. In Zagreb, West and Andrews are surprised at the fierce arguments between Croats and Serbs (Serbia had been the largest Yugoslav province), while Constantine defends the central government in Belgrade (now in Serbia).

The country is also divided internally by religious beliefs. There are three main religious groups, the Roman Catholics, the Orthodox Catholics, and the Muslims. The last were either Turks who had remained in the country when the Serbs had driven out the Turkish regime more than a century before, or were Yugoslavs who had accepted Islam during the five centuries of Turkish occupation, especially in Bosnia-Herzegovina (another former province of Yugoslavia). West adopts Constantine's view that the Serbs must be the leading force in Yugoslavia and that the Croats harbor too much sympathy for Germany and Austria because Croatia was once part of the Austro-Hungarian Empire.

Although West finds parts of Croatia charming, especially the compact and beautiful Dubrovnik, which she calls "a city on a coin," she finds the Croats lacking in support of their native traditions and ungrateful in refusing to acknowledge the Serbian victories over the Turks and the Austro-Hungarian Empire, victories that led to the creation of a free and independent Yugoslavia.

At Sarajevo (a part of Bosnia-Herzegovina), West and Andrews meet Constantine's German wife, Gerda. She riles both West and Andrews because she is so contemptuous of the Yugoslavs and takes every opportunity to assert the superiority of German civilization. Gerda has no understanding of "process," by which West means a grasp of how history develops. Thus, Gerda becomes the symbol of a German mentality that justifies its invasion of Yugoslavia and other lands as the right of a superior people to dominate their inferiors.

The next phase of the journey is a rail trip to Belgrade, where the large supply of good food and the pleasant provincial air of the capital and its people impress West and Andrews. They also enjoy a stay at Lake Naum, on the southern edge of Yugoslavia near Greece and Albania. It is a wild and beautiful part of the country, despite the poverty of the land and its people. It is in episodes like this that West elaborates her view of Yugoslavia as a paradise on Earth, populated by a people who are close to the soil and to their own traditions in a way that other Westerners (like the British) no longer cherish.

From the Lake Naum area, they travel back part of the way to Belgrade on the railroad and then drive to Kotor on the Dalmatian coast. There Constantine and Gerda say farewell to West and Andrews. The author and her husband take a ship at Kotor and travel up the coast, returning to Zagreb by rail.

They visit the Plitvice Lakes on the way. The last leg of the journey is by rail from Zagreb to Budapest, Hungary.

In Budapest, the sadness of the plight of the Yugoslavs impresses West one last time. There she meets a university student who wants to write a paper about West's work. However, West believes the student will have a difficult time because her work is so diverse (biography, novels, travel writing, art criticism, and other forms of journalism and literature) that a unified view of her career would prove elusive. Like Yugoslavia, in other words, West is a congeries of contradictions, with sides of herself in conflict with one another.

In an epilogue written after the beginning of World War II, West reflects on how her country and the rest of Western Europe had failed to engage the forces of fascism that ultimately overwhelmed Yugoslavia. That country's history is vital, she believes, in understanding how the West ultimately defeated the reactionary forces of Islam. Western Europe is indebted to the Yugoslavs, especially the Serbs, which perhaps West's book will make clear to her compatriots.

The focus of *Black Lamb and Grey Falcon* is on the folk culture of the former Yugoslavia and the reactions and impressions of the narrator. The black lamb in the title refers to an incident in the book in which a lamb is sacrificed as part of an ancient religious custom; the grey falcon alludes to an old and popular Slavic folk song. Set in the years just prior to World War II, *Black Lamb and Grey Falcon* evokes the political attitudes of the period, somewhat sentimental expressions of the Marxist leanings of Constantine and the humanism of West and her husband, ironically counterpoised by history, with Nazism and Fascism nascent in the background.

West's style is elegant, witty, and rhetorically grand. Her first-person narrative permits frequent and delightful digressions into entertaining personal vignettes. The book is a compendium of intellectual and historical reactions to a personal experience, relayed through West's highly literate consciousness.

Critics have faulted *Black Lamb and Grey Falcon* for various errors and a pro-Serb bias, and it is true that West tended to take sides in her travels through Yugoslavia. However, she acknowledges that the Serbs could be overbearing and even murderous. Thus, she includes a scene in which her Serb driver, Dragutin, suggests the best way to deal with recalcitrant Croats is to kill them. Although Dragutin expresses his opinion in an offhand and even comic way, his words are chilling, foreshadowing the Balkan Wars of the 1990's, when the Serbs massacred thousands of Croats and Muslims. Even then, however, authoritative commentators on the Balkan Wars find West's book instructive and inspiring for its probing of the flaws that led to conflict among the southern Serbs.

The text of the book clearly reveals that West understood her failings. Her husband is often her foil, objecting to her sweeping interpretations of history and presenting an alternative to her romantic views that led her to identify so intensely with the Serbs and their noble quest to rid Yugoslavia of the repressive Ottoman Empire. Indeed, Andrews's presence in the book in the form of dialogues between husband and wife is crucial—not only as a corrective to West's biases but as a dramatic example of the conflict between men and women and how they view the world. For *Black Lamb and Grey Falcon* is also a feminist work, a profound mediation on the roles men and women adopt in society.

West's opinions are certainly open to challenge, but what makes her book a masterpiece is its brilliant portrayal of tensions between men and women; among ethnic, racial, and religious groups; and, ultimately, of the tensions in her own personality that make her view of the world so dynamic. She presents, in other words, a view of herself in the process of becoming herself. This self-conscious, introspective approach is also meant as a contrast to Gerda, a character critics have deplored because West makes her so prejudiced as to be incredible. For West, however, Gerda, is an allegorical figure, one who must be presented as West's opposite in order for the dialectical structure of the book to succeed.

West has often been credited (by Truman Capote and others) as having produced the first nonfiction novel because she takes actual events and people, set against the panoramic background of history, to create a deeply personal and fictive work, a narrative of interactions with different cultures and with world events.

Revised by Carl Rollyson

Further Reading

Deakin, Motley. *Rebecca West*. Boston: Twayne, 1980. A useful introduction to West's work. Addresses her roles as feminist, critic, journalist, historian, and novelist. Includes a selected bibliography, an index, and a chronology of West's life and career.

Glendinning, Victoria. *Rebecca West: A Biography*. New York: Knopf, 1987. Contains several pages on the sources and critical reception of *Black Lamb and Grey Falcon*, defending West's approach against the charges of her critics. Explores West's politics and provides a helpful discussion of her interpretation of Yugoslav history and the aftermath of World War II.

Lesinska, Zofia P. "Rebecca West's *Black Lamb and Grey Falcon: A Journey Through Yugoslavia*." In *Perspectives of Four Women Writers on the Second World War: Ger-*

trude Stein, Janet Flanner, Kay Boyle, and Rebecca West. New York: Peter Lang, 2002. Examines West's depictions of imperialism and ethnocentrism, as well as other elements of the book. Describes how she and the other three women presented a more feminist interpretation of World War II, without the emphasis on military battles and diplomacy that dominates the work of male historians.

Orel, Harold. *The Literary Achievement of Rebecca West.* New York: St. Martin's Press, 1986. Offers chapters on West's life and works, such as her literary criticism, political and philosophical works, novels, and *Black Lamb and Grey Falcon*. Contains useful notes, a bibliography, and an index.

Rollyson, Carl. *The Literary Legacy of Rebecca West.* New York: iUniverse, 2007. The first chronological treatment of West's literary career, treating *Black Lamb and Grey Falcon* and an integral work in a developing body of work rather than just as a stand-alone masterpiece.

_____. *Rebecca West: A Modern Sibyl.* New York: iUniverse, 2009. Rollyson explores the sources of *Black Lamb and Grey Falcon*, providing a new, comprehensive interpretation, surveying previous criticism and treating the book as a "self-correcting masterpiece."

_____. *Rebecca West and the God That Failed: Essays.* New York: iUniverse, 2005. Contains additional essays on *Black Lamb and Grey Falcon* and on West's politics in the light of the Balkan wars and other events since West's death in 1983.

Schweizer, Bernard. "*Black Lamb and Grey Falcon*: A Modern Female Epic." In *Rebecca West: Heroism, Rebellion, and the Female Epic*. Westport, Conn.: Greenwood Press, 2002. Assesses West's travel writings and novels, focusing on their reinvention of epic heroism from a feminist perspective. Discusses her spiritual and philosophical ideas.

West, Rebecca. *Rebecca West: A Celebration.* New York: Viking Press, 1977. A compilation of selections from West's major works. Samuel Hynes's introduction to this collection has proved to be one of the most influential pieces of criticism on West.

Wolfe, Peter. *Rebecca West: Artist and Thinker.* Carbondale: Southern Illinois University Press, 1971. Treats *Black Lamb and Grey Falcon* as West's most important work. Pays special attention to the book's style and structure and to how the influence of Saint Augustine colors much of West's writing.

Black Narcissus

Author: Rumer Godden (1907-1998)
First published: 1939
Type of work: Novel
Type of plot: Psychological
Time of plot: Early twentieth century
Locale: Mopu, India

Principal characters:
SISTER CLODAGH, a Roman Catholic sister superior
SISTER BLANCHE,
SISTER RUTH,
SISTER PHILLIPPA, and
SISTER ADELA, nuns under Clodagh's authority
THE REVEREND MOTHER DOROTHEA, Clodagh's superior
FATHER ROBERTS, an English priest
GENERAL TODA RAI, an Indian philanthropist
MR. DEAN, his agent
DILIP RAI, his nephew
ANGU AYAH, a palace caretaker
KANCHI, an orphan girl

The Story:

In October, a band of Anglo-Catholic nuns from the Order of the Servants of Mary set out by pony from Darjeeling for the rural highlands of India. There, they intend to found a school and clinic for women and children at Mopu Palace, which rests on land claimed by the British under colonial rule. By offering the palace rent-free, wealthy Indian general Toda Rai hopes to atone for the excesses of his late father, an impetuous ruler who kept courtesans on the remote estate.

Clodagh, the youngest sister superior in the order, heads the mission. Father Roberts and the Reverend Mother Dorothea advise her by letter.

Upon arrival, the nuns suffer altitude sickness, the chill of the incessant wind, and skepticism from those on whom they must depend. Mr. Dean, the English emissary who delivers supplies, servants, and advice, cautions that Mopu is no place for a nunnery, and he predicts that the nuns will take their leave by the next rainy season. Longtime Mopu caretaker Angu Ayah expects failure, too; earlier, the brothers of St. Peter abruptly abandoned their own St. Saviour's School at the palace.

Anxious for success, General Toda Rai pays otherwise indifferent villagers to attend the convent school and hospital before the nuns have unpacked. Mr. Dean foists Kanchi, a voluptuous orphan, into convent care. Later, Dilip Rai, the general's bejeweled nephew who is aiming to secure an English education at Cambridge University, requests lessons at the convent school. The nuns quickly assume their designated roles in the classrooms, dispensary, garden, kitchen, and chapel of the newly named Convent of St. Faith. Sister Ruth, however, resents being assigned minor duties.

By Christmas, the nuns, students, household workers, and an intoxicated Mr. Dean—by then, the object of Sister Ruth's untoward affections, although he is careful to avoid her—join St. Faith's holiday service and carol singing. After much discussion, the nuns decide to accept Mr. Dean's holiday gift of fleece-lined Tibetan boots for each of them; seemingly too personal and too unconventional an addition to their traditional garb, the boots are nevertheless practical in the frigid winter weather.

After the holiday, Sister Clodagh meets privately with Sister Ruth to discuss the latter's ailing health, erratic behavior, and obvious attraction to Mr. Dean. Ruth distrusts the sister superior, accuses her of bullying, and then weeps silently. Clodagh proposes that Ruth air her troubles in sealed correspondence to Mother Dorothea.

Later, Father Roberts pays a rare visit and finds the school well organized, but he finds the nuns curiously distracted. He worries about their isolation.

Gradually, convent routines and boundaries erode. Enraptured with the beauty of the mountains, Sister Phillippa neglects the prayer bell and the laundry. Sister Clodagh daydreams about Con, the Irish love she had expected to marry. Sister Ruth lapses into jealous outbursts. To safeguard her faith, Sister Phillippa transfers elsewhere. Her replacement, Sister Adela, objects to intrusions by Mr. Dean, Dilip Rau, and the Sunnyasi, a silent holy man living on convent grounds, ever staring at the Himalayas.

Spring at Mopu is marked by obsessive love, fatal mistakes, and exits. After Ayah beats Kanchi for stealing a vase, the girl disappears with Dilip Rai. Against advice, Sister Blanche gives medicine to a dying Indian baby; furious locals blame her for his death, and they shun St. Faith's.

Sister Ruth sneaks away from the convent to throw herself at Mr. Dean, who rejects her advances but fails to escort the madwoman home. While others search the river, tea fields, and factory for the missing nun, Ruth emerges from convent shadows to attack Clodagh. The two struggle on the terrace; Sister Ruth loses her footing and plunges over the railings. In the gulf below, her lifeless body is impaled on cut bamboo, speared through the chest.

Clodagh details all in a letter to Mother Dorothea, who recalls the nuns from their mission. Grieving and anxious to leave Mopu before the onset of the summer rains, they await General Toda Rai's farewell visit. Meanwhile, Dilip Rai avows his plan to keep, but never marry, Kanchi. Mr. Dean agrees to tend Sister Ruth's grave. Clodagh admits that she will be sent to another convent and given less responsibility. Finally, by late June, a disappointed Toda Rai manages to say good-bye.

As the nuns depart, a clap of thunder signals rain. Clodagh regrets that the oncoming deluge will wash away traces of their ill-fated time at Mopu, except for what may remain as village legend.

Critical Evaluation:

Houses in Rumer Godden's novels often function like characters. In *Black Narcissus*, the House of Women is a tainted link to the past, thwarting landlord Toda Rai's efforts to reform it by securing religious tenants with good intentions: "Sometimes it seemed to him that the house had a bad wild life of its own; the impression of its evil lingered." As residents, the nuns fight inherited battles between the forces of good and evil, wildness and order, and selflessness and narcissism—often within themselves. Biblical images and metaphors in their story make the battles seem truly primal: Ruth is snakelike, stealthy, and ready to strike; her death at Easter brings rebirth, or new humility and understanding, to proud Clodagh.

Shifts in time and streams of consciousness, stylistic hallmarks of Godden's work, arise in connection with two key characters in *Black Narcissus*. When Clodagh worries, the story shifts back in time. Specifically, flashbacks to romantic moments in Clodagh's past, or to early words of counsel from Mother Dorothea, reveal lingering doubts that the young leader dares not express. In flashbacks, Clodagh revisits her "secret unworthy reason" for entering the convent,

Reverend Mother's admonitions against haughtiness, and the decision to remain at Mopu in spite of imminent danger. Time oddities in her dreams also unsettle Clodagh: Con from her Irish past and Dilip Rai from her Indian present appear together, carrying mirrors and turning their backs on her.

Living in a small religious community from which she fears expulsion, Ruth struggles to contain her anger toward Clodagh: Clodagh is a browbeating rival who wants Mr. Dean for herself, who turns the other nuns into spies, and who even poisons Ruth's milk. As Ruth becomes more agitated, streams of consciousness in the narrative expose rampant envy and increasingly furtive urges to escape, seduce, and destroy—culminating in violence and Ruth's eerie, vampire-style death by bamboo spike. Like Clodagh's flashbacks, Ruth's disturbed streams of consciousness fuel the psychological intensity of the novel.

The theme of isolation pervades *Black Narcissus.* St. Faith's hilltop seclusion, as well as cancelled visits from clergy, leaves the nuns especially vulnerable to the dangers of isolation. Sister Adela, who attempts to fortify the convent with staunch English propriety, arrives late. Mr. Dean, the nuns' reluctant protector in India, cannot save them from themselves. In the isolation of Mopu, religious life implodes, and faith cannot stem tragedy. Not surprisingly, the most isolated among the nuns—problematic Ruth, whom no convent wants, who craves recognition but disdains the look and smell of every "little black brat" she must teach—becomes the most dangerous.

As the single Western male frequenting the convent, Mr. Dean is more than handyman, plumber, and construction supervisor. He speaks the native dialect, understands local customs and superstitions, and has influence with the villagers, so he also serves as cultural liaison, telling Clodagh what the nuns must do and not do among India's agrarian poor. Nevertheless, he remains a blunt, coarse, womanizing, and hard-drinking man who falls short of perfect. This is why, when Clodagh implies that Mr. Dean played a role in Ruth's death, he bursts out, "Why should I have done more? Why should you expect me to? I'm not infallible." In biblical terms, Mr. Dean is a flawed Adam, not God. Clodagh's demands of him, and perhaps of Ruth, make her seem culpable.

Black Narcissus is the name of the flowery London scent worn by Dilip Rai. It is also Sister Ruth's nickname for the preening Dilip Rai himself, who reminds Sister Clodagh of her lost love, Con. As a book title, *Black Narcissus* portends dark allure, self-involvement, and an incompatible mix of East and West. Why? Although Dilip Rai covets English scents and education, he ultimately reverts to the entitlements of his warrior ancestors. When his brother's death brings him greater fortune and privilege, Dilip Rai takes a concubine and stays put in the East. Similarly, after an entire youth of befriending and then courting Clodagh in Ireland, Con opts for solitary opportunity in the United States, driving his would-be wife eastward into a convent.

Moreover, according to some critics, the risky mix of East and West in *Black Narcissus* points to the inevitable end of the British Empire. Because colonialism is inherently unfair, the peaceful coexistence of English and Indian cultures under colonial rule is necessarily tentative. Indeed, despite the fine intentions of many Indian and English characters, *Black Narcissus* ends with death and separation, and the nuns are obliged to relinquish Mopu.

Internationally, Godden has been commended for authentic literary renderings of twentieth century British India, with its striking landscapes, exotic marketplaces, and timeless religious practices, along with racial and political tensions. Born in England, raised beside the Ganges River, and living intermittently in both India and England until late in life, Godden wrote some sixty works, including novels, short stories, biographies, screenplays, and children's books. Like *Black Narcissus*, a great many of them shed light on India in that distinct historical time. *Black Narcissus* was Godden's third novel and her first commercial success. It was adapted into an award-winning 1947 film, starring Deborah Kerr as Sister Clodagh.

Wendy Alison Lamb

Further Reading

Chisholm, Anne. *Rumer Godden: A Storyteller's Life.* New York: Greenwillow Books, 1999. A sympathetic biography attempting to explain how Godden shaped her own life circumstances, especially an idyllic childhood in India, into fictional tales.

Lassner, Phyllis. *Colonial Strangers: Women Writing at the End of the British Empire.* Piscataway, N.J.: Rutgers University Press, 2004. Lassner, who argues that "no place has been found" for Godden "in the postcolonial canon," makes a place beside Muriel Spark, Elspeth Huxley, and others, who wrote from and about outposts of the British Empire. Focuses on novels such as *Black Narcissus* to show Godden's Anglo-India as an "oppressively walled garden" for her female protagonists.

Lassner, Phyllis, and Lucy Le-Guilcher, eds. *Rumer Godden: International and Intermodern Storyteller.* Burlington, Vt.: Ashgate, 2009. Scholarly essays explore Godden's work. Includes a chapter on *Black Narcissus* looking at the novel in the context of "1930's mountain writing."

Another essay addresses Godden's incorporation of India as a literary landscape.

Macmillan, Margaret. *Women of the Raj: The Mothers, Wives, and Daughters of the British Empire in India.* New York: Random House, 2007. Draws on interviews, letters, and memoirs to describe life for women amid two cultures in India during the British colonial period.

Miller, Edmund. "Submission and Freedom: Five for Sorrow, Ten for Joy." *Renascence: Essays on Values in Literature* 54, no. 4 (Summer, 2002): 258-268. Miller points out the rarity of studies of Godden's works. He chooses one of her lesser known novels, one about religious life, to illustrate her narrative skill and her insight into the human psyche.

Rosenthal, Lynne M. *Rumer Godden Revisited.* New York: Twayne, 1996. Part of a reference series on English authors, this volume discusses Godden's scholarly contributions. Includes an annotated bibliography.

The Black Swan

Author: Thomas Mann (1875-1955)
First published: Die Betrogene, 1953 (English translation, 1954)
Type of work: Novella
Type of plot: Symbolism
Time of plot: 1920's
Locale: Düsseldorf, Germany

Principal characters:
FRAU ROSALIE VON TÜMMLER, a middle-aged widow
ANNA, her spinster daughter
EDUARD, her teenage son
KEN KEATON, a young American who tutors Eduard in English

The Story:

During the 1920's, Frau Rosalie von Tümmler is living in Düsseldorf with her unmarried daughter Anna and her teenage son Eduard. Widowed for more than a decade, Frau von Tümmler was the wife of a German lieutenant general who was killed in action in 1914. After his death, she retired to a small villa in Düsseldorf, partly because of the beautiful parks in which she could indulge her love for nature. She has many friends of her own age and older, and she believes her life quite happy. She has always been attractive to men, but as the time for her change of life nears, she and Anna are drawn closer to each other. Anna, who was always cut off from companions of her own age because of her clubfoot, is an abstract painter. Rosalie is often dismayed by her daughter's canvases of mathematical or symbolic designs, but she tries to understand what Anna is trying to express. On their walks together, they have many long talks on nature and art. Sometimes Rosalie complains that nature is cheating her by taking away her function as a woman while her body remains youthful and her mind as active as ever. Anna tries to convince her that body and soul will soon be brought into harmony by psychological changes following physical ones.

Rosalie is fifty years old when she hires Ken Keaton, a young American, to give Eduard lessons in English. Keaton is a veteran who chooses to live in Europe after the war. Like most expatriates of his generation, he speaks of his own country as a place of shoddy materialism, a land that in its pursuit of money loses all respect for the art of living. His interest in Rhineland history brings him to Düsseldorf, where he supports himself by tutoring the wives and children of the well-to-do.

Keaton brings a new spirit of youthfulness and vitality into the Tümmler household. Rosalie often listens outside her son's room to the snatches of conversation and the bursts of laughter she can hear from within; after a time, the young American is accepted as a friend of the family and soon thereafter Rosalie realizes that she is falling in love with the virile young man. Anna, watching what is happening, is greatly disturbed by this promise of her mother's autumnal romance, especially when Rosalie announces triumphantly that nature gave her a second period of physical flowering by renewing her fertile cycles. Rejoicing in what she believes a miracle of rejuvenation, Rosalie refuses to listen to her daughter's warnings.

Early in the spring, the Tümmlers and Keaton go on an outing to Holterhof Castle, a rococo structure not far from the city. Rosalie is pleased to show the young American the castle and the park, in which the spirit of earlier German culture was preserved. Keaton brings stale bread to feed the black swans on the castle lake. Rosalie takes some of the bread and nibbles at it playfully while one of the giant swans hisses indignantly for his dinner. In an alcove of the chilly, musty old castle, she throws her arms about the young man and embraces him. On the way home, she decides that she will give herself to Keaton without reserve.

That night, she is taken suddenly ill and rushed to the hospital, where an examination reveals that she is suffering from cancer. Nature plays on her the cruelest of jokes—the signs of renewed fertility were nothing more than the symptoms of coming death.

Critical Evaluation:

The Black Swan is a slight work that followed the vast, complicated novels of Thomas Mann's later period—such works as *Joseph und seine Brüder* (1933-1943; *Joseph and His Brothers*, 1948) and *Doktor Faustus* (1947; *Doctor Faustus*, 1948). Mann had previously worked successfully in the brief narrative form of the novella in *Tonio Kröger* (1903) and *Death in Venice* (1954). As he demonstrates in *The Black Swan* and the earlier stories, he does not need breadth to give his writing the effect of depth and insight.

In this work, there are reminiscences of *Death in Venice*, that wonderful short novel dealing with the dissolution of personality and with death in a plague-stricken pleasure resort on the Adriatic. *The Black Swan* presents on several planes of meaning the writer's favorite themes of life and death, body and soul, nature and spirit, art and decay, love and death. At the same time, his sense of ironic detachment and the deliberate parody of eighteenth century style make this one of the most puzzling books of his career.

The plot of *The Black Swan* is simple almost to the point of banality. However, by manipulating symbols and repeating key words and phrases that linger in the memory like motifs in music, Mann infuses multiple levels of meaning. In one sense, *The Black Swan* is a fable of one of the ways in which the creative spirit sometimes dies, in a late-flowering resurgence that is often no more than a prelude to death. The symbolism of death and decay also points to an interpretation of Rosalie as twentieth century Europe, an aging continent weakened by disease from within but finding in the symptoms of its corrupted state an urge to self-destructive vitality. Images of death are everywhere apparent in the novel: in the picture of the black swan stretching its wings and hissing for the stale crust that Rosalie withholds, in the decaying ancient castle moldering with dampness where Rosalie declares her love for the young American, in the corpse of the small animal that Rosalie and Anna find during one of their walks.

In *Tonio Kröger*, the leading character remarks that once an idea takes hold of him, he finds it all about him, so that he can even smell it. *The Black Swan* creates its atmosphere of

the charnel house in its sensuous effects. The novel begins as the story of a sentimental matron who loves nature, but the atmosphere surrounding the characters grows almost suffocating as the situation unfolds. What seems at first a light, playfully humorous parody of the eighteenth century sentimental story becomes a grotesque, almost diabolical fable when the reader realizes the contrast between the story being told and the manner of its telling. The book becomes a caricature and a brutal exposure of modern attitudes and failings. Perhaps Mann's intention was better illustrated in the original German title of the book—*Die Betrogene*, "the deceived." The novel is a study of deception and self-deception, of betrayal and death.

In spite of its disturbing and sometimes repellent details and somberness of vision, *The Black Swan* is a miniature work of art. Mann wrote it at an age when most writers are content with the place they have won by their performances in the past. Though the novel was written in a diminished tone, it probes deeply into areas of the strange and the perverse for its reflection of an age divided between the opposing forces of nature and the spirit.

Further Reading

Feuerlicht, Ignace. *Thomas Mann*. New York: Twayne, 1968. A brief treatment of *The Black Swan* in chapter 9 calls for a broader, more sympathetic reception. Views the story structurally as a novella—with its trademark turning point, dominant image, and strange occurrence—and not as a short story.

Kurzke, Hermann. *Thomas Mann: Life as a Work of Art, a Biography*. Translated by Leslie Willson. Princeton, N.J.: Princeton University Press, 2002. The English translation of a work that was celebrated upon its publication in Germany. Kurzke provides a balanced approach to Mann's life and work, and he addresses Mann's homosexuality and relationship to Judaism.

Latta, Alan. "The Reception of Thomas Mann's *Die Betrogene*: Tabus, Prejudices, and Tricks of the Trade." *Internationales Archiv für Sozialgeschichte der Deutschen Literatur* 12 (1987): 237-272. Painstakingly thorough study of the novella's reception, including detailed documentation.

_____. "The Reception of Thomas Mann's *Die Betrogene*: Part II, The Scholarly Reception." *Internationales Archiv für Sozialgeschichte der Deutschen Literatur* 18 (1993): 123-156. Latta demonstrates how the initial lack of understanding for the novella has been superseded by more open, thoughtful, and less taboo-determined interpretations.

Lehnert, Herbert, and Eva Wessell, eds. *A Companion to the Works of Thomas Mann*. Rochester, N.Y.: Camden House, 2004. A collection of essays about the range of Mann's work, including discussions of his late politics, the use of female identities and autobiographical impulses in his writings, and the chapter "The Gaze of Love, Longing, and Desire in Thomas Mann's *The Transposed Heads* and *The Black Swan*" by Jens Rieckmann.

Mundt, Hannelore. *Understanding Thomas Mann*. Columbia: University of South Carolina Press, 2004. Mundt discusses the themes, concerns, presentation, and meanings of many of Mann's works, using Mann's later published diaries as one of the sources for her analysis. *The Black Swan* is analyzed in chapter 12.

Robertson, Ritchie, ed. *The Cambridge Companion to Thomas Mann*. New York: Cambridge University Press, 2002. A collection of essays, some analyzing individual works and others discussing Mann's intellectual world, Mann and history, his literary techniques, and his representation of gender and sexuality. Includes bibliography and index.

Schoolfield, George C. "Thomas Mann's *Die Betrogene*." In *Thomas Mann*, edited by Harold Bloom. New York: Chelsea House, 1986. A scholarly, positive, and balanced treatment of the work, though it does not reflect the feminist concerns of later readings. Excellent on influences and the mythological background of the characters.

Straus, Nina Pelikan. Introduction to *The Black Swan*, by Thomas Mann, translated by Willard R. Trask. Berkeley: University of California Press, 1990. A female-centered, though not necessarily a feminist, positive reading of the novella. An excellent place to begin an in-depth interpretive study. Contains a brief description of earlier negative readings.

Black Thunder

Author: Arna Bontemps (1902-1973)
First published: 1936
Type of work: Novel
Type of plot: Historical realism
Time of plot: 1800
Locale: Henrico County, Virginia

Principal characters:
GABRIEL, a slave who leads a rebellion
JUBA, his girlfriend
THOMAS PROSSER, his cruel master
BUNDY, an old slave whom Prosser abuses
MOSELEY SHEPPARD, a slave owner, inherently decent
BEN and PHARAOH, Sheppard's slaves who betray the rebellious slaves
MINGO and MELODY, freed slaves

The Story:

In 1800, in Henrico County, Virginia, a slave rebellion grows out of Thomas Prosser's beating of his aging slave Bundy, whom he considers to be more of a liability than an asset. Bundy's main wish was to die free, but the beating results in his death. He dreamed of a rebellion like the Toussaint L'Ouverture uprising in Santo Domingo, which drew enough public support to succeed.

A group of French liberals in Richmond, espousing the ideals of the recent French Revolution, opposes slavery. Its members think that slave owners oppress both blacks and poor whites. These liberals, labeled Jacobins and revolutionaries, seek to enlighten Americans and bring about greater equality for oppressed groups throughout the world. Despite their high ideals, the Jacobins are too small a group to be effective in protecting the blacks, who are considered chat- tel, in their rebellion against involuntary servitude. The Jacobins do, however, circulate abolitionist ideas and ideals, as did Alexander Biddenhurst, a Philadelphia abolitionist who is making plans to smuggle black slaves to Canada and to freedom.

Following Bundy's death and funeral, Gabriel, another slave, solidifies plans for a rebellion to protest this senseless killing. Gabriel is a man of singular leadership and organizational ability, but he is limited in what he can do for the cause he espouses. Obsessed with a bedeviling dream of freedom, he always understands the odds against his succeeding. Despite these odds, he musters a rebellious army of eleven hundred blacks. They plan to overrun Richmond's arsenal and take control of that city, nearby Petersburg, and, eventually, Norfolk. Gabriel thinks that most slaves share his obsession, except for those who have been beaten down and co-opted to the point that their spirit and will are broken. Mingo, a freed slave, strongly supports the freeing of all slaves, saying that it is no good to be free if one's people, in his case his wife and children, still are slaves.

Gabriel believes that right will triumph in the end, although his chances of personally witnessing that triumph are remote. He has that unique sense of destiny that motivates great leaders and demands basic human rights for all people, regardless of race and social position. Although the dominant society is against his cause, Gabriel has the conviction that God and universal codes of human conduct are on his side and will eventually prevail.

Gabriel approaches his task of leading blacks to freedom fearlessly, yet matter-of-factly. His fight is futile, however, in part because unusually bad weather causes extensive flooding that makes it impossible for his full army to assemble. Recognizing a task he is called upon to do, he is determined to carry it out, regardless of what personal consequences might ensue. Gabriel is imbued not so much with a special stripe of courage as with a consuming zeal for the liberation of his people. At times, he is naïve in his belief that he can change the system.

The slave rebellion is suppressed. Ben and Pharaoh, two slaves belonging to Moseley Sheppard, are caught between loyalty to their owners and to their fellow slaves. After the rebellion erupts, Gabriel remains steadfast. Ben and Pharaoh, however, fearing for their lives if the rebellion fails, flee to Richmond in terror to report the uprising to the whites.

The result is crushing defeat and the hanging of countless innocent black slaves. Six weeks after the uprising, Gabriel is executed, going to the gallows convinced that his actions and his death are necessary steps toward the eventual liberation of his people. Thomas Prosser flogs Juba, Gabriel's girlfriend, who accompanied Gabriel throughout the rebellion, then sells her down the river.

Critical Evaluation:

Arna Bontemps's *Black Thunder* is often compared to William Styron's *The Confessions of Nat Turner* (1967), which focuses on a similar rebellion in Virginia. *Black Thunder*, which was called the best novel by an African American writer in its time, possesses a verity that is not consistently present in Styron's celebrated book, excellent though it is in its own right. Perhaps Bontemps succeeds more completely because, like his characters, he is an African American. He understands subtleties relating to the black experience to which persons of other races may not fully relate.

A notable characteristic of this novel is the dispassion of Bontemps's presentation. He never suggests that all slave owners are bogeymen or that all slaves or free blacks are saints. He writes with detachment, restraint, and balance, always permitting the facts to speak for themselves. This approach adds force to the topic that concerns Bontemps centrally. The telling of his tale, unbiased as it is, strikes with incredible force.

Bontemps presents his story in small segments, each dominated by a central character or event. This technique provides differing points of view and adds to the detachment with which the story unfolds. Segmenting the narrative also gives the reader a sense of immediacy as it is recounted.

Bontemps places slavery in an interesting social and historical perspective by including a report of the Virginia legislature that called for its members of Congress to promote federal legislation calling for the resettlement of all slaves in Louisiana as a means of ameliorating the racial problems that threatened the social structure of their state and of the South. He also writes about the Federalist press, which used the rebellion on which this story is based as a means of supporting a second term for President John Quincy Adams, citing the rebellion as something related to the radical social ideas of his opponent, Thomas Jefferson. By including this material, Bontemps conceptualizes the rebellion to an arena larger than the area in which it occurred, larger than Henrico County and its environs, larger, indeed, than Virginia or the South.

Bontemps's understanding of black folkways, many of them harking back to Africa, is apparent in *Black Thunder*. Bundy's funeral is pervaded with folkways relating to death and burial, such as roasting a pig and putting it on the grave. Still more telling is the fact that Bundy's spirit invades the being of one of his fellow slaves, which is in keeping with folklore conventions relating to one's departure from life.

In several instances, the rebels have long discussions about the stars and their meaning. Such an acceptance of signs and portents is well established in the traditions of African folklore. The rebels also attribute the success of the Toussaint rebellion in Santo Domingo to the fact that a hog was killed and its blood drunk before the uprising. Gabriel takes no part in this superstition, for which some of his followers later blame him.

A prediction of the death of one of the slaves is strengthened when the female house slaves shoo from the house a bird that has flown in. Birds are common harbingers of death in folk literature. In the course of the uprising, several of the slaves use charms as forms of protection, and countercharms against their oppressors.

A striking example of Bontemps's use of folklore has to do with "conjure-poisoning," which is akin to the use of voodoo in some African and Caribbean societies. Pharaoh, whose death has already been foretold by the bird in the house, is in a state of panic. He has betrayed his fellow slaves. After spreading the news of the rebellion among the white community, he falls sick, convinced that he is the victim of conjure-poisoning, a conviction that, added to his other pressures, quickly drives him mad.

These folk elements in *Black Thunder* lend a great deal to its authenticity. Such elements help readers to understand how the rebels could initially be galvanized into action as a group. Their belief in spirits, signs, portents, and conjuring all impose a unity upon the community of slaves who engage in the uprising.

By never deviating from his controlling theme, which concerns the basic need for living creatures to be free, Bontemps achieves a focus that results in a book of unique and remarkable credibility. Bontemps's presentation of Gabriel is psychologically convincing. If readers come away from the novel thinking that Gabriel is bigger than life, it is not because Bontemps has said that he is. Gabriel wins the trust of those who know him. Neither notably superstitious nor fervently religious, he is single-minded in his quest for freedom, which he realizes will not be likely to result in his personal freedom but that, over time, may result in the liberation of his people. It is only in this broader context that his actions, which are suicidal, make sense. He knows the risk, but he proceeds anyway. Psychologically, Gabriel is more like Martin Luther King, Jr., than any other major twentieth century African American leader, because King knew that he had embarked upon a course that was likely to prove fatal. Gabriel knows this, too, but he continues to strive for the good of his people.

R. Baird Shuman

Further Reading

Baker, Houston A., Jr. *Black Literature in America.* New York: McGraw-Hill, 1971. Places Bontemps within the broad context of twentieth century black literature. Asserts that Bontemps is more skilled as a poet than as a fiction writer. Clearly identifies significant symbols and images Bontemps used in his fiction.

Bone, Robert A. *The Negro Novel in America.* Rev. ed. New Haven, Conn.: Yale University Press, 1965. Argues that Bontemps is a transitional black writer whose work is rooted in the Harlem Renaissance and in the Depression era. Good discussion of the structure of *Black Thunder,* which Bone considers Bontemps's finest novel.

Bontemps, Arna. Introduction to *Black Thunder.* Boston: Beacon Press, 1968. In the introduction to this reprinted edition, Bontemps tries to place *Black Thunder* not only in the context of his own life but also in the context of the years of the Civil Rights movement, up to and including the assassination of Martin Luther King, Jr. An unusually frank and enlightening author's introduction.

Carlton-Alexander, Sandra. "Arna Bontemps: The Novelist Revisited." *College Language Association Journal* 34 (March, 1991): 317-330. An attempt to refocus critical attention on *Black Thunder.* Carlton-Alexander particularly examines some of the negative comments that have been made about the novel.

Davis, Arthur P. *From the Dark Tower: Afro-American Writers, 1900-1960.* Washington, D.C.: Howard University Press, 1974. Chapter on Bontemps deals insightfully with *Black Thunder* and several of his other novels, making thoughtful comparisons among them. Illuminates the psychological validity of Bontemps's characterizations.

Jones, Kirkland C. *Renaissance Man from Louisiana: A Biography of Arna Wendell Bontemps.* Westport, Conn.: Greenwood Press, 1992. The first full-length biography of Bontemps. An excellent source not only for information about the man himself but also for information about the background of his works, including *Black Thunder.* Includes a bibliographic essay that serves as a handy guide to primary and secondary material about Bontemps.

Scott, William. "'To Make Up the Hedge and Stand in the Gap': Arna Bontemps's *Black Thunder.*" *Callaloo* 27, no. 2 (Spring, 2004): 522-541. Analyzes *Black Thunder* to demonstrate how Bontemps's novel about the Gabriel Prosser slave revolt expresses Prosser's belief that in order to bridge the gap from the experience of slavery to an experience of freedom it was necessary to promise a passage from slavery to freedom.

Sundquist, Eric J. *The Hammers of Creation: Folk Culture in Modern African-American Fiction.* Athens: University of Georgia Press, 1992. Originally presented as a series of lectures, the three chapters in this book are more informally and more accessibly written than much modern literary criticism. The chapter on *Black Thunder* specifically focuses on Bontemps's use of folk culture and sources in his novel.

Wright, Richard. "A Tale of Courage." *Partisan Review and Anvil* 3 (February, 1936): 31. A very favorable review of *Black Thunder.* Wright argues that Bontemps's book marked a turning point in the African American novel. Of equal interest to those interested in either Bontemps or Wright.

Bleak House

Author: Charles Dickens (1812-1870)
First published: 1852-1853
Type of work: Novel
Type of plot: Social realism
Time of plot: Mid-nineteenth century
Locale: London, Lincolnshire, and Hertfordshire,
England

Principal characters:
JOHN JARNDYCE, the owner of Bleak House
RICHARD CARSTONE and ADA CLARE, his cousins
ESTHER SUMMERSON, his ward and companion to Ada
ALLAN WOODCOURT, a young physician
LADY DEDLOCK, Sir Leicester Dedlock's wife
TULKINGHORN, a solicitor
WILLIAM GUPPY, Tulkinghorn's clerk
SNAGSBY, a law-stationer
KROOK, the owner of a rag-and-bottle shop
JO, a young street sweeper

The Story:

The suit of *Jarndyce vs. Jarndyce* is a standing joke in the Court of Chancery. Beginning with a dispute as to how the trusts under a Jarndyce will are to be administered, the suit drags on, year after year, generation after generation, without settlement. The heirs, or would-be heirs, of suits such as *Jarndyce vs. Jarndyce* spend their lives waiting. Some, like Tom Jarndyce, blow out their brains. Others, like tiny Miss Flite, visit the court in daily expectation of some judgment that will settle the disputed estate and bring her the wealth of which she dreams.

Among those involved in the Jarndyce suit are John Jarndyce, grandnephew of Tom Jarndyce, who shot himself in a coffeehouse, and his two cousins, Richard Carstone and Ada Clare. John Jarndyce is the owner of Bleak House in Hertfordshire, a country place by no means as dreary as its name. His two young cousins live with him. He provides Esther Summerson as a companion for Ada. Esther suffered an unhappy childhood under the care of Miss Barbary, her stern godmother, and a servant, Mrs. Rachel. The two told the girl that her mother is a wicked woman who deserted her. Miss Barbary is now dead, and John Jarndyce is Esther's benefactor. Upon arriving in London on her way to Bleak House, Esther finds an ardent admirer in William Guppy, a clerk in the office of Kenge and Carboy, John Jarndyce's solicitors.

It is Guppy who first notices Esther's resemblance to Lady Dedlock, who is also tenuously connected to the Jarndyce suit. Sir Leicester and Lady Dedlock divide their time between their London home, where Lady Dedlock reigns over society, and Chesney Wold, their country estate in Lincolnshire. One day, when Lord Dedlock's solicitor, Tulkinghorn, is in the Dedlocks' London home, Lady Dedlock swoons at the sight of the handwriting on a legal document. Immediately suspicious, the lawyer traces the

handwriting to its source, the stationer Mr. Snagsby, who can tell him only that the paper was copied by a man named Nemo, a lodger in the house of the junk dealer Mr. Krook. When Mr. Tulkinghorn goes there, he finds Nemo dead of an overdose of opium. He is convinced that Nemo is not the dead man's real name, but he can learn nothing of the man's identity or connections.

Allan Woodcourt, a young surgeon called to minister to the dead Nemo, requests an inquest. One of the witnesses called is Jo, a crossing sweeper Nemo befriended. A short time later, Jo is found with two half crowns on his person. He explains that they were given to him by a lady he guided to the gate of the churchyard where Nemo is buried. Jo is arrested, and as a result of the cross-examination that follows, Mr. Guppy questions the wife of an oily preacher named Chadband and finds that the firm of Kenge and Carboy once had charge of a young lady with whose aunt Mrs. Chadband lived. Mrs. Chadband is the Mrs. Rachel of Esther's childhood. She reveals that Esther's real name is not Summerson but Hawdon.

The mystery surrounding Esther begins to clear. A French maid who left Lady Dedlock's service identifies her former mistress as the lady who gave two half crowns to the crossing sweeper. It is established that the man who called himself Nemo is Captain Hawdon. Years before, he and the present Lady Dedlock fell in love. Esther is their child, but Lady Dedlock's sister, Miss Barbary, angry at her sister's disgrace, took the child and moved to another part of the country. Esther's mother later married Lord Dedlock. She was afraid of exposure but also guiltily overjoyed that the child her unforgiving sister led her to believe dead is still alive.

Mr. Guppy informs Lady Dedlock that a packet of Captain Hawdon's letters is in the possession of the junk dealer,

Krook. Lady Dedlock asks Guppy to bring them to her, and the wily law clerk agrees, but on the night he is to obtain the letters the drunken Krook explodes of spontaneous combustion; presumably the letters burn with him.

In the meantime, Richard Carstone becomes completely obsessed by the Jarndyce case and abandons all efforts to establish his career. Living in the false hope that the Chancery suit will soon be settled, he spends the little money he has on an unscrupulous lawyer named Vholes. When John Jarndyce remonstrates, Richard thinks that his cousin's advice is prompted by selfish interests. Ada Clare is worried about Richard's behavior, but she remains loyal to him and secretly marries him so that her own small fortune might stand between Richard and his folly.

When Esther falls desperately ill of a fever, Lady Dedlock feels all of a mother's terror. When Esther gradually recovers, Lady Dedlock goes to Hertfordshire and reveals herself to her daughter. As a result of her illness, Esther loses her beauty and thus her resemblance to Lady Dedlock. John Jarndyce feels free for the first time to declare his love for her and asks her to marry him; she accepts.

Tulkinghorn is murdered, and several nights later, when she knows her secret is about to be revealed to her husband, Lady Dedlock flees. It is discovered that Tulkinghorn was murdered by the French maid through whom he learned of Lady Dedlock's connection with Jo. The maid attempted to blackmail the lawyer, and when he threatened her with imprisonment, she killed him. Inspector Bucket, who solves the mystery of the murder, also informs Lord Dedlock of his wife's past. The baronet, who previously suffered a stroke, tells the detective that his feelings for his wife are unaltered and that he will employ every means to bring her back. It is Esther, however, who finds her mother dead at the gate of the churchyard where Captain Hawdon is buried.

Among Krook's effects is a Jarndyce will made at a later date than the one disputed in the Chancery for so many years. It settles the question of the Jarndyce inheritance forever. Richard and Ada are declared the heirs, but the entire fortune was consumed in court costs. Richard does not long survive this final blow; he dies, leaving his wife and infant son in the care of John Jarndyce.

When John Jarndyce discovers that Esther's true love is young Doctor Woodcourt, he releases her from her promise to marry him and in his generosity brings the two lovers together. Before her wedding, John Jarndyce takes her to see a country house he bought in Yorkshire. He named it Bleak House, and it is his wedding present to the bride and groom. There Esther lives, happy in the love of her husband and her two daughters and in the lasting affection of John Jarndyce,

the proprietor of that other Bleak House that would always be her second home.

Critical Evaluation:

Bleak House was first published as a serial and appeared in book form in 1853 at the height of Charles Dickens's career. Preceded by *Martin Chuzzlewit* (1843-1844) and followed by *Hard Times* (1854), the work comes early in the group of Dickens's great novels of social analysis and protest. A major critical anatomy of mid-nineteenth century England, *Bleak House* shows some signs of concessions to audience taste in the use of pathos, melodrama, and a somewhat strident moralism. However, Dickens manages to weave out of these a controlled assessment of the corruption at the heart of his society.

At the center of the novel's intricate plot is the lawsuit of *Jarndyce vs. Jarndyce*. To this frame, Dickens adds an interlocking structure of subplots. On one level, the plot is a series of thin detective stories woven together so as to involve all strata of society. Character after fascinating character appears in episodes that are each of gripping interest; in Dickens's masterly resolution, no earlier action or detail remains extraneous.

The third-person narrator of most of *Bleak House* is a sharply ironic commentator on the political, social, and moral evils that abound in the book. There is no ambiguity in the narrator's stance toward the selfishness and irresponsibility he recounts (though he is not quite as sardonic or homiletic as the narrator of *Hard Times*), but this stern tone is both relieved and reinforced by the introduction of a second first-person narrator, Esther Summerson. While some critics consider the dual narration an aesthetic flaw, they concede that the two voices contribute different perspectives. Esther represents a sympathetic and morally responsible attitude that is rare in the world of *Bleak House*. She is a compassionate insider who represents a model that is, if sometimes sentimental, a corrective to the false values of society.

As the lawsuit of *Jarndyce vs. Jarndyce* lumbers to a close after years of litigation, a gallery of characters emerges, each revealing how the moral contagion spread. With his talent for caricature, Dickens creates memorable minor characters to people the corrupt world. There is Mr. Chadband, who is a preacher enamored of his own voice; Mrs. Pardiggle, who would feed the poor Puseyite tracts rather than bacon; Mr. Turveydrop, who is the model of deportment and little else; Mrs. Jellyby, who supports noble causes while neglecting her own children; and Mr. Skimpole, who is the model of unproductivity. Many of these characters betray the varieties of egoism and irresponsibility that leave society stagnant and infected. Perhaps the most striking is Krook, the junk dealer and small-scale surrogate of the Lord Chancellor, who dies of what Dickens calls spontaneous combustion. Krook is a microcosm of the self-destructive tendency of a diseased society.

Despite Dickens's talent for plot and character, *Bleak House* is primarily a novel of image and symbol. The first chapter insistently sets the moral tone as it repeats its images of fog and mud that surround the Court of Chancery and, by extension, all of English society. The fog, which captures all in a miasma from which there seems no escape, is a symbol of the Chancery, and the court itself, with its inert, irresponsible, and self-destructive wranglings, is a symbol of the calcified social and economic system strangling English life. The case of *Jarndyce vs. Jarndyce* is the model of the social canker. Characters sacrifice their lives to its endless wrangling, and in succumbing to the illusory hope of instant riches, they forfeit the opportunity to accept individual responsibility and make something of themselves. The conclusion of the suit is Dickens's ironic commentary on the futility of such vain hopes.

People and places in *Bleak House* so consistently have symbolic value that the novel occasionally verges on allegory. The cloudiness and rain that surround Chesney Wold symbolize the hopelessness of the nobility. Even the name of its inhabitants, Dedlock, is a sign of the moral deadlock and immobility of the ruling class. At the other end of the social spectrum, the dirty and disease-ridden part of town known as Tom-all-alone's is a symbol of the vulnerability and victimhood of the lowest classes. In a gloom of one sort or another, many characters act as detectives searching out the guilty secrets and hypocrisies that permeate this world.

On the more positive side is Bleak House itself, where the kindly John Jarndyce, who keeps aloof from involvement in the lawsuit, presides over a more orderly and benevolent demesne; but the contagion cannot be kept even from there, as is symbolized by the admirable John Jarndyce's periodic fits of depression and frustration, which he attributes to the east wind instead of the real cause, conditions in the world at large. Moreover, Ada and Richard bring the lawsuit into their uncle's house; Richard is another victim of the anachronistic system that destroys those who participate in it and feeds on the inertia, complacency, and hypocrisy of the whole society. Finally, when Esther contracts smallpox from Jo as a result of having been kind to him, Dickens is showing the interrelatedness of all levels of society. Jo is at the bottom but his misfortune becomes the misfortune of many as his contagion spreads through the social fabric. The implication is that the unfeeling society that creates Jo and Tom-all-alone's cannot protect itself from those victims.

Dickens offers no programmatic, revolutionary solution. If there is a solution, it is to be found in people such as John Jarndyce, Esther, and Allan Woodcourt. Jarndyce symbolizes the selflessness that is needed if injustice is to be rectified. Esther Summerson, as her name implies, is a bright antidote to the fog and rain. Her housekeeping keys are a sign of her commitment to domestic duties and an acceptance of responsibility. Woodcourt, too, is the kind of active individual society needs. The marriage of Esther and Woodcourt is a vindication of what they have to offer, as is John Jarndyce's generous acceptance of their love. The new Bleak House in which they live is full of the joy and the goodness that can reform society. The novel does not offer the easy optimism of radical political solutions, because it is only this revolution in the heart of humankind that Dickens believes can cure society.

"Critical Evaluation" by Edward E. Foster

Further Reading

Allen, Janice M., ed. *A Routledge Literary Sourcebook on Charles Dickens's "Bleak House."* New York: Routledge, 2004. Provides primary source documents, reviews, and essays designed to supplement the novel. Includes information placing the novel in its social, political, and literary context; a discussion of the book's critical history from its initial publication to the early twenty-first century; reprints of four reviews published in 1853; and several essays written between 1957 and 1999 that analyze and discuss various aspects of *Bleak House*.

Cain, Lynn. *Dickens, Family, Authorship: Psychoanalytic Perspectives on Kinship and Creativity.* Burlington, Vt.: Ashgate, 2008. Focuses on *Bleak House* and three other novels that Dickens wrote during the decade beginning in 1843, a period of feverish personal and professional activity. Cain argues that his representation of the family in these novels is a paradigm for his development as an author.

Hardy, Barbara. *Dickens and Creativity.* London: Continuum, 2008. Focuses on the workings of Dickens's creativity and imagination, which Hardy argues is at the heart of his self-awareness, subject matter, and narrative. *Bleak House* is discussed in chapter 4, "The Artist as Narrator in *Doctor Marigold, David Copperfield, Bleak House*, and *Great Expectations*," and in chapter 8, "Crises of Imagination in *Oliver Twist, A Christmas Carol, Dombey and Son, Bleak House, Hard Times*, and *The Lazy Tour of Two Idle Apprentices*."

Jordan, John O., ed. *The Cambridge Companion to Charles*

Dickens. New York: Cambridge University Press, 2001. Collection of essays with information about Dickens's life and times, analyses of his novels, and discussions of Dickens and language, gender, family, domestic ideology, the form of the novel, illustration, theater, and film.

Nelson, Harland S. *Charles Dickens.* Boston: Twayne, 1981. After four chapters of overview, Nelson uses *Bleak House* as a model to demonstrate how Dickens wrote all of his novels. This accessible guide includes plot summaries of other novels discussed.

Newsom, Robert. *Dickens on the Romantic Side of Familiar Things: "Bleak House" and the Novel Tradition.* New York: Columbia University Press, 1977. Discusses the implications of Dickens's comment in the novel's preface that he "purposely dwelt on the romantic side of familiar things."

Paroissien, David, ed. *A Companion to Charles Dickens.* Malden, Mass.: Blackwell, 2008. Collection of essays providing information about Dickens's life and work, including Dickens as a reformer, Christian, and journalist, and Dickens and gender, technology, America, and the uses of history. Also includes the essay *"Bleak House"* by Robert Tracy.

Shatto, Susan. *The Companion to "Bleak House."* Boston: Unwin Hyman, 1988. Lengthy but very useful to have while reading the novel. Detailed explanations, including allusions to earlier literature, definitions of unusual terms, and identifications of proper names from history—things Dickens's first readers would have known but which later readers will not understand.

Storey, Graham. *Charles Dickens, "Bleak House."* New York: Cambridge University Press, 1987. An excellent introduction, intended as a textbook. Focuses on the novel as a social commentary. Includes a chronology that pairs events from Dickens's career with dates from history and a guide to further reading.

Bless Me, Ultima

Author: Rudolfo Anaya (1937-   )
First published: 1972
Type of work: Novel
Type of plot: Bildungsroman
Time of plot: 1943
Locale: Rural New Mexico

Principal characters:
ANTONIO "TONY" JUAN MÁREZ Y LUNA, the narrator
GABRIEL MÁREZ, his father
MARIA LUNA, his mother
ULTIMA, the *curandera* who lives with Antonio's family
TENORIO TREMENTINA, her enemy
NARCISO, the town drunk, a good friend of the Márez family

The Story:

Tony dreams of his own birth. In the dream, his mother's brothers, the Lunas (*luna* means "moon"), bless him and offer him fruit, calling him a "man of the people." Then his brothers arrive on horseback. Shouting, shooting, and laughing, they smash the fruit and break up the gathering. They claim Antonio for the Márezes (*mar* means "sea"). Antonio senses that Ultima (*última* means "the last one"), who is present at the birth, is connected to his future.

Ultima comes to stay with the narrator's family the summer he is "almost seven." Antonio is living with his parents and sisters, Deborah and Theresa; his three older brothers are away in the war. Ultima is a *curandera*, or healer. One evening, Tony witnesses horrible violence. Lupito, whom people claim World War II made crazy, kills Chavez, the sheriff

of the town. Antonio secretly follows his father to town when his father goes to investigate the killing and, hiding on the river bank, sees the fugitive gunned down by a mob of pursuers. Narciso, the Márez family friend and peacemaker, pleads with the posse but cannot save Lupito. "'Bless me,'" Lupito says to Antonio as Lupito dies. Later, Antonio realizes that he was protected that night by Ultima's owl, who was always close by and who seems to carry the powerful spirit of the *curandera* and to watch over Antonio.

Antonio starts school in Guadalupe that fall. From his first teacher Miss Maestas he learns the magic of letters and how to write. He also experiences disorientation and humiliation in the English-only classroom. From Ultima, however, he learns equally important lessons, for example, about the healing power of the herbs and roots they gather as they walk along the river banks and about the spirits of the natural world. "I knew she held the secret of my destiny," he thinks. From his friends, Antonio learns about the golden carp that lives in the river surrounding the town and that will also form a part of this destiny. With his friend Cico he later sees the beautiful and sacred fish.

Antonio's three brothers—Andrew, Leon, and Eugene—return home, but not for long. The war gives them a taste for the larger world, and soon Leon and Eugene leave the family to work in it. Only Andrew remains.

Tony accompanies Ultima when she goes to El Puerto to heal Uncle Lucas, his mother's brother, who is sick from a curse laid on him by the witchlike daughters of Tenorio Trementina, a satanic saloonkeeper and barber. Ultima cures Lucas with her powerful folk medicines and puts a curse on the three witches; she thus earns the enmity of the evil Tenorio. When one of his daughters dies and the priest refuses her burial in holy ground, Tenorio begins his deadly campaign against the *curandera*.

Antonio enters third grade. Tenorio is still threatening Ultima, and Antonio witnesses a fight between him and Narciso, who is trying to protect her. When Narciso and Antonio try to save Ultima by enlisting the help of his brother Andrew, who is at that moment in the bordello, Antonio wonders whether through all his experiences so far—bad and good—he is already an adult. Andrew refuses to help, thus dishonoring the Márezes and leaving Narciso to fight a more powerful enemy.

Tenorio murders Narciso, and, for the second time, a dying man acts as if Antonio is a priest, for Narciso whispers, "Confess me," to Antonio before dying. Antonio hears his confession. After that terrible death, Antonio develops a fever and has one of his many dreams, each one of these visions seeming to teach him something or to show him the way through his childhood. Antonio learns magical powers from Ultima; he also goes through his catechism, and, at Easter that year, he makes his first confession and takes his First Communion. He is learning about the religion and culture of the Catholic Church and about the older, folk traditions represented by Ultima, his father, and the belief in the golden carp.

After school that summer Antonio accompanies Ultima to the house of Tellez, where a curse by Tenorio causes stones to rain down on his house. Ultima saves Tellez. Antonio's friend Cico warns him that he must choose between the church (the religion of his mother) and the lessons of Ultima and his father (which include belief in the power of the golden carp). After this conversation, Antonio's friend

Florence drowns, the third death Antonio personally witnesses.

When Tenorio's second daughter dies, he comes looking for Ultima, and Antonio runs ten miles to Guadalupe to warn her. This is his test of initiation. He cannot save her, however: Tenorio kills the owl (which was Ultima's spirit) and is shot and killed in turn by Antonio's Uncle Pedro, who redeems the Márez family after Andrew's refusal to help. Ultima dies, but Antonio becomes a man in the process of trying to save her. Ultima's lessons will stay with the young boy. He learns that he should embrace life and know that the spirit of the *curandera* will always watch over him.

Critical Evaluation:

Rudolfo Anaya's *Bless Me, Ultima* is one of the best novels of initiation in the Chicano tradition. The novel presents a powerful story of a young boy moving toward adulthood; Antonio's choices on that journey reveal the rich and diverse traditions of the Mexican Americans of the American Southwest. Ultima helps Antonio heal the split into which he is born, pulled as he is between the heritage of his father, who was a cowboy, and that of his mother, whose family members are farmers. This spiritual split between the Márez and Luna families, between the plains and the town, and between Ultima's magical folk religion and Catholicism is the central conflict of Antonio's childhood.

In the end, Antonio is not forced to choose between the two traditions of the horsemen and the farmers, but rather he blends them into a workable identity for himself. It also becomes clear, as a result of his association with Ultima and his use of words to influence the events of the novel, that he will use his gift for words, imagination, and learning to become not a priest but rather a writer. He achieves this fusion only through the aid of Ultima.

Ultima is a spiritual guide who teaches the young boy and directs him toward his future. Antonio will have to reach it himself, but Ultima points him in the right direction and protects him even after her death. Ultima not only helps Antonio reach adulthood but also teaches him a number of important lessons along the way—the healing arts of nature, for example, and the power of love. As Antonio says toward the end of his journey: "And that is what Ultima tried to teach me, that the tragic consequences of life can be overcome by the magical strength that resides in the human heart."

When Antonio looks back on his youth toward the end of the novel, he realizes what he gained from the adults in his life. From his mother he learned how close people are to the earth. From his father and Ultima he learned that "the greater immortality is in the freedom of man, and that freedom is best nourished by the noble expanse of land and air and pure, white sky." From these important lessons Antonio's adult self emerges.

Ultima helps Antonio to achieve his own identity; at the end of the novel, he directs his mother to take his sisters to their room. "It was the first time I had ever spoken to my mother as a man; she nodded and obeyed." Ultima also helps Antonio to heal the split in his own heritage; he can be a Catholic (as his mother wants) and a believer in the golden carp as well. Anaya's novel is important in the way it uses the literary and folk traditions of the American Southwest. The religious symbolism of the novel can be understood only in the context of that cultural geography, and Anaya taps a rich vein of southwestern folklore and history.

Characterization is rather two-dimensional, although the major characters (particularly Ultima) have shadings: For example, is she a *bruja* (witch), or just a healer? This question receives a somewhat noncommittal answer when she demonstrates that she is not a witch by walking through a door marked with a cross; however, the cross, made of needles, falls apart as she does so. The characterization works in terms of the point of view of the novel, which is that of a naïve young boy growing up in rural New Mexico.

Much more complex are the symbolic aspects of the novel. Antonio's dreams have a rich significance; they reflect and predict actions in the novel. They are, in the truest sense, revelations. Likewise, the literary symbolism of the novel—the importance of water, for example (the golden carp, the drowning) and of religious rituals (both Christian and native spiritual)—is complex and effective. A reading of the oppositions of the novel (Luna/Márez or moon/sea, female/male, agrarian/pastoral) points out its complexity and its final reconciliations. Anaya produced a novel of deep and subtle meaning, and one that reveals some of the rich literary traditions of the American Southwest.

David Peck

Further Reading

Bruce-Novoa, Juan. *Portraits of the Chicano Artist as a Young Man: The Making of the "Author" in Three Chicano Novels.* Albuquerque, N.Mex.: Pajarito Press, 1977. This important early analysis of *Bless Me, Ultima* reveals the novel to be "the apprenticeship of a writer who fulfills his training with Ultima by becoming a novelist, the author of his own text."

Calderón, Héctor. "Writing the Dreams of la Nueva México: Rudolfo A. Anaya's *Bless Me, Ultima* and the Southwest Literary Tradition." In *Narratives of Greater Mexico: Essays on Chicano Literary History, Genre, and Borders.* Austin: University of Texas Press, 2004. Calderón analyzes seven of Anaya's novels, including *Bless Me, Ultima*, describing how Anaya "puts to rest the fantasy of the Spanish Southwest and affirms the Mexican-mestizo origins of la Nueva México."

Dick, Bruce, and Silvio Sirias, eds. *Conversations with Rudolfo Anaya.* Jackson: University Press of Mississippi, 1998. Contains numerous interviews with Anaya, in which he discusses *Bless Me, Ultima* and his other works, Chicano literature and the Chicano movement, language, publishing, and writing, among many other subjects.

Fernández Olmos, Margarite. *Rudolfo A. Anaya: A Critical Companion.* Westport, Conn.: Greenwood Press, 1999. An introductory overview of Anaya's life and work, designed for students and general readers. Includes a brief biography, a chapter discussing Anaya and the Chicano literary tradition, and chapters focusing on analysis of individual works, including *Bless Me, Ultima.*

Fuse, Montye P. "Culture, Tradition, Family: Gender Roles in Rudolfo Anaya's *Bless Me, Ultima.*" In *Women in Literature: Reading Through the Lens of Gender*, edited by Jerilyn Fisher and Ellen S. Silber. Westport, Conn.: Greenwood Press, 2003. This book contains brief feminist analyses of ninety-six works of literature, including *Bless Me, Ultima.* It is useful for high school students and college undergraduates as well as for general readers interested in a feminist interpretation of a specific work.

Gonzalez-T., César A., ed. *Rudolfo A. Anaya: Focus on Criticism.* La Jolla, Calif.: Lalo Press, 1990. Includes useful essays on *Bless Me, Ultima* by Roberto Cantu, Jean Cazemajou, and others.

Kevane, Bridget A. "The Fiction of Rudolfo Anaya: *Bless Me, Ultima.*" In *Latino Literature in America.* Westport, Conn.: Greenwood Press, 2003. This discussion of the novel is included in Kevane's examination of works by eight Latino and Latina writers.

Lamadrid, Enrique R. "The Dynamics of Myth in the Creative Vision of Rudolfo Anaya." In *Paso por aquî: Critical Essays on the New Mexican Literary Tradition, 1542-1988*, edited by Erlinda Gonzales-Berry. Albuquerque: University of New Mexico Press, 1989. Shows the ways in which Anaya uses southwestern myth in his novel.

Saldívar, Ramón. "Romance, the Fantastic, and the Representation of History in Rudolfo Anaya and Ron Arias." In *Chicano Narrative: The Dialectics of Difference.* Madison: University of Wisconsin Press, 1990. Saldívar argues that Anaya's book "creates a uniquely palatable amalgamation of old and new world symbolic structures."

The Blind Assassin

Author: Margaret Atwood (1939-   )
First published: 2000
Type of work: Novel
Type of plot: Psychological realism
Time of plot: Early twentieth century to 1999
Locale: Port Ticonderoga and Toronto, Canada

Principal characters:
IRIS CHASE GRIFFEN, the narrator
LAURA CHASE, Iris's sister
RICHARD GRIFFEN, Iris's husband
WINIFRED GRIFFEN PRIOR, Iris's sister-in-law
ALEX THOMAS, Iris's lover
REENIE HINCKS, a Chase family servant
MYRA STURGESS, Reenie's daughter
AIMEE, Iris's daughter
SABRINA, Aimee's daughter

The Story:

Iris Chase Griffen, more than eighty years old and suffering from heart problems, begins writing the story of her life for her granddaughter Sabrina, whom she has not seen in years. She tells the story through flashbacks, with scenes from her present life mixed in. The story is not in chronological order.

Iris and her sister, Laura, grow up as the daughters of a wealthy button-factory owner in Port Ticonderoga, Canada. The family home, Avilion, is in decline from its grandest days. Iris's mother dies in childbirth when Iris is nine years old and Laura is six years old. Reenie Hincks, a family servant, cares for the two girls. Their father's business has increasing financial problems, which worsen with the Great Depression.

Iris and Laura are now teenagers, and their father's girlfriend introduces them to Alex Thomas, a young union organizer and socialist activist. Soon after they meet, the factory workers riot, and the factory burns. Alex is suspected of instigating the trouble, and Iris and Laura hide him in their attic from the authorities.

Soon, Iris's father explains to her that he expects Richard Griffen to propose to her and that he has already given his consent. Griffen, a wealthy industrialist from Toronto, is much older than Iris. Iris's father says the marriage is the only way to save the family business and ensure that Laura will be provided for. After the wedding, Richard and Iris spend several months in Europe on their honeymoon. By the time they return, Winifred Griffen Prior, Iris's new sister-in-law, had already decorated and furnished the new home Richard bought by telegram. Iris quickly learns that Winifred controls all of Richard's household affairs, although she does not live with the couple.

Laura telephones a few minutes after Iris arrives at her new home. She tells Iris that their father had died a week after

Iris left on her honeymoon. Laura had sent telegrams, and the news was in the papers. Richard explains that he did not tell Iris about the death because they would not have been able to return to the United States in time for the funeral; he did not want to spoil the trip for her. Iris goes to Avilion the next day and learns that her father died the day after the button factory was permanently closed. Iris feels that Richard betrayed her and her father because the two men had agreed that the marriage would save the factory.

Richard decides that Laura should live with him and Iris in Toronto. Laura, however, does not arrive by train when expected, so Richard informs the police. The papers learn that Laura is missing. Following up on a tip, Richard and Iris find Laura working at a carnival. After they take her to Toronto, Laura continues to resist the plans made for her. She openly dislikes Richard and is expelled from school.

Meanwhile, Iris sees Alex on a street in Toronto. They have an affair, and Iris becomes pregnant. They have a daughter, Aimee, and Iris sees in her Alex's features—dark hair and dark skin—confirming for Iris that Alex is Aimee's father. Alex later dies fighting in World War II, and Iris receives the telegram announcing his death because she had been listed as his next-of-kin.

One day while Iris is pregnant, Winifred and Richard tell Iris that Laura has "snapped." They send her to a mental institution, but Iris is not allowed to visit her. Winifred explains that Laura suffers from a delusion that she, too, is pregnant. Reenie, the Chase family servant, whom Richard has fired, works with the family lawyer to have Laura released from the institution. Iris finally sees her sister, and Laura explains that the doctors performed an abortion on her. She also says that she had made a bargain to protect Alex from Richard. Iris does not understand Laura's story and thinks that Laura must have gotten pregnant with Alex. Iris tells Laura that Alex is dead. She also explains that she had an affair with him, explaining why she got the telegram when he died.

When Laura hears that Alex is dead, she grabs Iris's purse and leaves the restaurant where they had been meeting. She takes Iris's car, and the next day, she drives off a bridge and dies. After Laura's death, Iris looks through some school notebooks Laura had left with her. Laura's notes reveal to her that Richard got Laura pregnant.

Wanting to memorialize her sister and to get revenge against Richard and Winifred, Iris writes and then publishes a novel, *The Blind Assassin*, but under Laura's name. Not until the end of the novel is it revealed that the book was written by Iris. The novel creates a renewed interest in Laura's death, which leads to an investigation of Bella Vista, the mental facility where she had been sent. The place is closed down, and when some correspondence between Richard and the director is made public, Richard's political aspirations are ruined. Richard soon commits suicide, and his body is found in the boat he refurbished and first sailed with Iris as a passenger.

Winifred has detectives follow Iris, and they catch her meeting a man in a motel. This enables Winifred to gain custody of Aimee. Aimee grows up, becomes a drug addict, and has a daughter named Sabrina. Aimee dies in an accident when Sabrina is still a little girl, giving Winifred custody of Sabrina as well.

Iris grows old in Port Ticonderoga, where Myra Sturgess, Reenie's daughter, and Myra's husband, Walter, check on her regularly and fix things around the house. Iris dies after she finishes writing her life story—her second novel—for her granddaughter Sabrina. Iris's obituary, written by Myra, says that her granddaughter will settle her affairs.

Critical Evaluation:

The structure of Margaret Atwood's *The Blind Assassin* accomplishes two goals: It makes the story a suspenseful read, and it builds the question of what constitutes truth into the novel's framework. By writing the story of her life for her granddaughter, Iris Chase Griffen disputes the versions of events that the novel's other characters believe are true. While the flashbacks that Iris uses to create the main thread of the story are primarily in chronological order, she saves the most surprising details for the end. In structuring the story in this way, she leads readers to the same false conclusions the characters reached, and later in the novel reveals that these conclusions are incorrect. Only in the last chapters does she explain that Laura was pregnant with Richard's baby and that she, not Laura, wrote the novel within the novel.

Iris's inclusion of newspaper clippings in her story cre-

ates the impression that she is conveying facts with them. Even in those clippings, however, the information turns out to be false or at least misleading. For example, the news story reporting Richard's death says that the boat in which his body was found was tied to the jetty. Iris reveals later that the boat was in the boathouse and that Winifred lied to the press because the truth sounded worse than her story. Even when the information in the clippings is accurate, it does not tell enough of the story to be meaningful. For example, a news clipping near the novel's beginning states that Laura's death was ruled accidental. While details of the news story may be accurate, the reader cannot understand why Laura committed suicide without reading the entire novel.

Besides the news clippings, the novel contains the book also called *The Blind Assassin*. At the beginning of the novel, the reader learns that Iris sent the book to a publisher shortly after Laura's death, leading to Laura becoming a revered and tragic literary figure. Only at the end of the novel does Iris reveal that she wrote the book itself. Describing her affair with Alex Thomas, it tells more about Iris's feelings and activities during the same time period than does the novel that contains it.

Even the novel attributed to Laura has stories within it. When the lovers in that novel meet, the man tells the woman installments of a story. A version of the story is published.

The stories within stories in *The Blind Assassin* suggest that there is always another story beneath the surface of what seems like the truth. Furthermore, words are not always the best source of information. Iris learns what Richard did to Laura from seeing some pictures that Laura colorized and from some notations in Laura's school notebooks that do not explicitly state their message.

Another major theme of the novel is the way in which social constraints limit and determine the actions that women can take. Iris is clear in her account that, as young women, she and her sister were powerless because of their gender. Iris has little choice in her marriage. Although she is led to believe that marrying Richard will allow her father to keep his business, she does not have even the power to sacrifice herself for her family. Richard closes the Chase factory soon after the wedding. In fact, Richard discounts Iris so much that he does not even notice when her baby has darker skin and hair than anyone in either of their families.

There is a power hierarchy among women, however. Winifred, who also relies on Richard for money, manages his household for him, and Iris is not even consulted about furniture.

Iris attributes her decision to publish the novel under Laura's name to the damage caused by the constraints that she faces. This novel within the novel provides a metaphor for what happens to her. In a story which a character in that novel tells, slave boys must weave rugs until they go blind. Then many of them become assassins, as their fingers are so nimble from the rug work that they can slit throats while their victims sleep. Like them, Iris becomes capable of hurting others because of the harm done to her. By publishing the novel under Laura's name, she ruins Richard's political career, and his suicide soon follows.

Writing can also have a redemptive effect, however. While Iris's first book destroys the family, she writes the second one to free her granddaughter from the pain that misinformation can cause. She wants Sabrina to understand that Richard was not her grandfather, and she was not related to Winifred.

Joan Hope

Further Reading

Bloom, Harold, ed. *Margaret Atwood*. Rev. ed. New York: Chelsea House, 2008. This collection features essays written by top Atwood scholars on major themes of her novels. Includes a brief biography, a chronology of Atwood's life, and an informative editor's introduction.

Cooke, Nathalie. *Margaret Atwood: A Critical Companion.* Westport, Conn.: Greenwood Press, 2004. Provides a brief biography, critical overview of Atwood's work, and a chapter devoted to *The Blind Assassin*. A general overview rather than a detailed analysis of particular themes.

Gorjup, Branko. *Margaret Atwood: Essays on Her Works.* Toronto, Ont.: Guernica, 2008. A collection of essays by literary scholars, examining major themes recurring in Atwood's novels.

Howells, Coral Ann. *The Cambridge Companion to Margaret Atwood.* New York: Cambridge University Press, 2006. Essays by various scholars are arranged thematically. Includes an essay that compares the theme of blindness in *The Blind Assassin* with this same theme in other novels by Atwood.

_____. *Margaret Atwood.* 2d ed. New York: Palgrave Macmillan, 2005. A detailed examination of *The Blind Assassin*. Includes both an overview of the novel and a scholarly analysis of the theme of negotiating with the dead.

McWilliams, Ellen. *Margaret Atwood and the Female Bildungsroman.* Burlington, Vt.: Ashgate, 2009. Focuses on the creation of women's self-identity and coming of age, with an analysis of these themes in *The Blind Assassin*.

Thomas, P. L. *Reading, Learning, Teaching Margaret Atwood.* New York: Peter Lang, 2007. *The Blind Assassin* is analyzed as an example of how Atwood creates mythologies about women. Geared to high school teachers but valuable to students as well, this book presents the major themes of Atwood's novels in an easily accessible style and format.

Wilson, Sharon Rose, ed. *Margaret Atwood's Textual Assassinations: Recent Poetry and Fiction.* Columbus: Ohio State University Press, 2003. A collection of scholarly essays that examine Atwood's work, with a focus on her writings published since the late 1980's. Includes discussion of *The Blind Assassin*.

Blindness

Author: José Saramago (1922-   )
First published: Ensaio sobre a cegueira, 1995 (English translation, 1997)
Type of work: Novel
Type of plot: Narrative realism
Time of plot: Twentieth century
Locale: A city in Portugal

Principal characters:
THE FIRST BLIND MAN
THE DOCTOR
THE DOCTOR'S WIFE
THE GUARDS

The Story:

A man sitting in his car at a traffic signal suddenly goes blind. He is helped by another man, who drives him home but then steals his car. Soon, more citizens of the city go blind. The blindness, characterized by victims seeing only a creamy whiteness, spreads through the city and quickly becomes endemic. As panic sweeps the general populace, the government takes action to isolate the blind in an asylum.

The quarantined persons are guarded by military troops

who facilitate the delivery of food and other necessities. More and more people become infected, and the social order, both inside and outside the asylum, starts to break down. As the numbers of quarantined people grow to unmanageable proportions, conditions become horrific. The asylum develops into a filthy place of horrible acts. The newly formed society of the blind becomes a place where criminals control the supply of food, demanding jewels and other valuables at first, then exchanging the meager food supply for sex.

The degenerating conditions within the asylum mirror the overall breakdown of society in the city. The soldiers guarding the internees become increasingly hostile. As one soldier after another becomes infected by the blindness as well, discipline in the ranks dissolves. The soldiers fire upon a group of blind internees who are waiting for food.

Seven internees band together as a way to survive the chaos within the asylum. The group is led by the wife of an ophthalmologist who has inexplicably escaped the blindness. She enters the asylum with her husband, feigning blindness and revealing to no one that she can see.

The group functions like a family, each member protecting another. The situation within the asylum becomes unbearable, and the group is desperate for a way out. With the help of the doctor's wife, who can find food and water, they succeed in escaping the asylum, only to find conditions in the city equally appalling. The breakdown within society is nearly complete. No government services are available. Police, schools, hospitals, and all other forms of collective governance are nonexistent. Violence is rampant. People live wherever they can find any form of shelter. Families are divided, and family members wander around the city, endlessly searching for each other. People distrust all others, and the fabric of the social order is completely destroyed.

The doctor and his wife slowly entice others to construct a new society, with a new form of existence. Little by little, the new family starts to build a new life. They find a home and start creating order within their group. Once a human-centered harmony is restored, the blindness starts to end; it ultimately disappears, as suddenly and inexplicably as it had begun.

Critical Evaluation:

As with all of José Saramago's fictional works, *Blindness* evolves like a present-day fable. The story begins with an event that marks the end of a fundamental concept of accepted reality, as the reader is confronted with a reality that is simultaneously absurd and plausible. The omnipresent and unnamed narrator describes fantastic and surreal scenes and

occurrences. With such settings, the reader is forced to confront the basis for human existence.

The novel also elicits many questions from the reader. Are humans dependent upon systems of order? Is modern society actually based upon a weak or shaky foundation of social interaction, a foundation that can disappear when challenged by relatively minor events? The characters struggle to find meaning, at precisely the moment of greatest social change.

Blindness explores the fragility of human societies. It mimics how one problem can lead to a complete breakdown of social systems. The reader is spectator to the consequences of blind power ambitions and their inevitable consequences. In the end, however, one of Saramago's literary traits comes into play: The new situation brings about a search for new ways of implementing the dignity of the human race. When forced to rely only upon each other, humans can and do reach out to one another. This new awareness of the importance of human dignity is revealed as almost spiritual in nature, and the novel contains hints of being an allegory about spiritual blindness and about humanity's lack of compassion for strangers. Saramago uses a more direct and secular analogy in the novel. Blindness here involves a misinterpretation between the signifier and the signified. That is, persons in positions of authority are misreading, or not "seeing," what is right before them.

The structure of *Blindness* is complex. The novel describes the most minor of settings and events in long sentences and paragraphs that often continue for pages at a time. Sentences are separated only by commas, and they lack colons, semicolons, hyphens, and quotation marks. It is often unclear who is speaking. Quotations are not separated by lines; instead, commas and capitalizations mark the first word of a new speaker. Saramago's style demands that readers pay close attention to who is, or who might be, speaking. Indeed, in *Blindness*, this style is most effective because it requires the reader to navigate speech without the usual visible clues. Characters are not named; instead, they are referred to in vague descriptive terms, such as "the doctor's wife."

Irony is employed, too. For example, the blind doctor is an eye doctor, an ophthalmologist, who is helpless just when he is needed most. The doctor's wife is the only one who can see, but she must hide this fact to be trusted by the others. She leads a group of internees in the asylum to sanity and, eventually, to safety, cohesiveness, and renewal. This inexactness of terminology reflects one of the author's major themes: the recurring mystery of life's impermanence.

Although Saramago rejects the use of proper nouns in many of his novels, in *Blindness* this anonymity reveals the impersonal nature of humankind in dealing with tragedy. The puzzling irony of the descriptive names of the characters illustrates the unimportance of individual identity: Saramago describes how the characters would be seen, but seen only by someone not blind. His characters include the girl with dark glasses, the boy with the squint, and the man with the black eye-patch.

The comical irony of characters who are described by their visible traits—which only the seeing can see—stands in stark contrast to the bleak and serious themes that Saramago presents in this work. Even more curious is the presence of the so-called dog of tears, named as such after licking away the tears of the doctor's wife after she leads the others out of the asylum and discovers that life in the city is equally devastated. Saramago has used anonymous dogs in other works, such as the special dog in *A jangada de pedra* (1986; *The Stone Raft*, 1994). In *Blindness*, however, the dog of tears seems to represent an occult reference to the suffering that accompanies human history. This canine has no real role in the novel; rather, the dog remains a presence, as if witnessing the collapse, suffering, and rebuilding of a society.

In the novel's epigraph, Saramago quotes from the fifth and final book of the Pentateuch: "If you can see, look. If you can look, observe." At the end of *Blindness*, when the citizens of the city begin to regain their vision, one character states, "I don't think we did go blind, I think we are blind, Blind but seeing, Blind people who can see, but do not see." With these words, Saramago is arguing that much of modern society's problems stem from indifference or apathy, that in many circumstances, humanity's problems are related more to human "blindness" to admitting obvious systemic failings.

Saramago is using disease, or a physical disability, to represent social and political ignorance in a crisis. This technique, the use of metaphor to symbolize the breakdown of social structure, is not new to literature. The analogy of the many failings of humankind to distinguish between "seeing" and "understanding" can be traced to one of the first Western philosophers, Plato. In his treatise *Politeia* (388-368 B.C.E.; *Republic*, 1701) he discusses the folly of humans seeing what is not there, or perhaps not seeing what is there. Plato describes a group of people sitting in a cave and positioned so that they cannot directly observe light from their fire. Using only their distorted view of light and shadow, they draw erroneous conclusions about the realities within the cave. The metaphor of blindness also can be compared to the H. G. Wells short story "The Country of the Blind" (1904), in which blindness represents individual struggles against conventionality within a repressive society. This idea of blindness is also similar to William Golding's use of the concept of childhood in his novel *Lord of the Flies* (1954). Golding illustrates the inability to recognize the not-so-obvious problems of society.

Paul Siegrist

Further Reading

Bloom, Harold. *José Saramago*. Philadelphia: Chelsea House, 2005. An extensive critical work on Saramago. Bloom finds Saramago to be one of the best living authors. Well written and informative. Includes a bibliography.

Frier, David Gibson. *The Novels of José Saramago: Echoes from the Past, Pathways into the Future*. Cardiff: University of Wales Press, 2007. A good critical analysis of Saramago's novels. Uses a European-based perspective of place and time. Includes a bibliography.

Hart, Stephen M., and Wen-chin Ouyang, eds. *A Companion to Magical Realism*. Rochester, N.Y.: Tamesis, 2005. A helpful guide to understanding Saramago's use of Magical Realism and to his unique style. Includes an extensive bibliography.

Rich, Mari, and Dimitri Cavalli. *Nobel Prize Winners: 1997-2001*. New York: H. W. Wilson, 2002. Saramago received the Nobel Prize in Literature in 1998. This collection of essays on late twentieth century prizewinners includes a look at Saramago's writing style.

Blindness and Insight
Essays in the Rhetoric of Contemporary Criticism

Author: Paul de Man (1919-1983)
First published: 1971; revised edition, 1983
Type of work: Literary criticism

The idea of this work's title, *Blindness and Insight*, is a paradoxical one. For Paul de Man, the qualities of blindness and insight are not polar opposites but qualities that strangely work together in exemplifying the mysteries of a complicated critical text. Often, de Man argues, critics will seem to have a blind spot and to willfully not notice aspects of a text that do not accord with the fixed ideas they bring to a text; and, he continues, these critics see some details of a literary work only to negate others. De Man does not suggest, however, that this "blindness" should be altered; instead, this blindness enables the critical insight in the first place. Insights are arrived at through the "cost" of blindness.

Blindness and Insight is de Man's first book, published when he was fifty-two years old. Like other influential works of literary criticism, such as Lionel Trilling's *The Liberal Imagination* (1950), *Blindness and Insight* is a book of essays, not written as a unified volume. Furthermore, some of the essays appeared in scholarly journals, and others in popular media such as *The New York Review of Books*. The essays have a wide following in critical and literary theory circles. Also, *Blindness and Insight*, in large measure, led to de Man's acceptance of a professorship at Yale. He finished his career there and soon became one of the most influential literary critics of the twentieth century.

For all the complexity of de Man's thought, *Blindness and Insight* is a peculiarly accessible book. De Man did not have a conventional academic career. When young in his native Belgium, he became involved in writing for literary journals that expressed a collaborationist viewpoint—a willingness to cooperate with the Nazis, who were then occupying Belgium. (This collaboration was discovered posthumously in 1988.) While in his mid-twenties, de Man emigrated to the United States and worked in a bookstore in New York. It was there that he met writer Mary McCarthy, who helped him get his first teaching position. He then did graduate work at Harvard, where he was a member of its Society of Fellows.

De Man, influenced by European philosophy and poetics, also knew of the then-dominant American critical and pedagogical method of New Criticism, which he learned from one of its finest exponents, Reuben A. Brower. New Criticism stressed the independence of the literary text from social, historical, or biographical contexts. De Man agreed with this foregrounding of literariness and its emphasis on close, attentive acts of reading what was actually on the page. He felt stymied, however, by the inertness of New Criticism, its tendency to be content with stable, well-rounded resolutions to intellectual questions.

In the essay "The Rhetoric of Blindness," de Man further explores the metaphor of blindness as insight. Although in general sympathy with philosopher and literary critic Jacques Derrida and his deconstructive theory, de Man diverges from him on one important point. Whereas Derrida considers the writings of Jean-Jacques Rousseau to be filled with a naïve exposition of the metaphysics of presence, of an undiluted and charismatic authenticity, de Man considers Rousseau's texts to be knowingly exposing their own literariness. This stress on the text's knowledge of its own instabilities is one of the major thrusts of a specifically de Manian turn in criticism.

With "Criticism and Crisis," de Man shows that he is the first literary critic practicing in the United States to be influenced by the deconstructive thought of Derrida, whom de Man had met the previous year at the famous Language of Criticism and the Sciences of Man conference convened by Richard Macksey and Eugenio Donato. Although de Man's emphasis—sober and directed toward acts of reading—was different from his French colleague—playful and oriented toward performances of writing—he quickly was established as the spearhead of American deconstruction.

In the book's several essays on individual critics, de Man is at times severely chastising, as when he argues that literary theorist Georg Lukács makes time into something simple and predicable that leads to a coarse view of history and ideology. At other times, de Man gently reveals ironies in a thinker he otherwise admires, such as Georges Poulet. He praises Maurice Blanchot and Ludwig Binswanger for their conscious interventions in the definition of an advanced mode of critical thought.

In "The Rhetoric of Temporality," irony comes near to being the master trope, or figurative strategy of language. Only if language covers up its truth through the distancing of irony does it have any chance of revealing truth; straightforward declaration only leads to calcified ideology, a mode of which Marxists would call false consciousness. De Man is less interested in specific instances of irony than in irony as a categorical literary stance, although one whose nature, situated as it is in the gap between intention and meaning, is never conclusively enumerated.

"Literary History and Literary Modernity" recasts the standard mid-twentieth century assumption that modernism represented something startlingly new and unprecedented. De Man argues that if there had been any sort of break or moment of critical transformation in the Western literary tradition, it came at the beginning of the Romantic era. Modernity's sense of linguistic self-consciousness and existential alienation was but an intensification or a recasting of the Romantic. More fundamentally, though, de Man sees literary history as the victor over literary modernity. Literary modernity tried to break out of history, to announce something new and unprecedented, both in terror and in triumph distinctively different from the past. De Man thought the past could never be entirely evaded, that traces of it would linger. He thought, too, that there was only one authentic experience of modernity: the aftermath of modernity's realization that the declarative break it sought would never be achieved. Still, de Man's posture is not a conservative rebuke of modernity; it is a demystified account of its real nature.

Modernity is not a fulfillment of the new, a cathartic surge into idyllic bliss of self-aggrandizing despair. Rather, modernity truly transpires when both the will to move forward and its paralytic failure are comprehended in one rich, simultaneous, contradictory gesture. Using the thought of Friedrich Nietzsche as an example of modernity, de Man differentiates between a genuine modernity that seeks to radically step beyond history from a contemporaneity that is merely faddish or current. De Man concludes the essay by notoriously remarking that "the bases for historical knowledge are written texts, even if they masquerade in the guise of wars and revolutions."

De Man was seeking to turn literary history from dry-as-dust recitations of facts and dates to a method much less annalistic and bibliographical and much more interpretive; he was reminding readers that even wars and revolutions are known through written texts, and that written texts often lay behind wars and revolutions. Though de Man's antihistorical language was no doubt employed to deliberate a certain strand of unreconstructed Marxism, the point behind that language is a reasonable one: What is known of history is mediated by structures and effects that are partly literary. This is the capstone to the redefinition of literariness as a sophisticated mode of textual self-awareness that preoccupies all the essays in *Blindness and Insight*.

Nicholas Birns

Further Reading

Culler, Jonathan. *The Literary in Theory*. Stanford, Calif.: Stanford University Press, 2007. This book by one of the great expositors of deconstruction and postmodernism in the United States focuses on the theoretical salience of what de Man famously called the linguistics of literariness.

Hoeveler, J. David, Jr. *The Postmodernist Turn: American Thought and Culture in the 1970's*. 1996. Reprint. Lanham, Md.: Rowman & Littlefield, 2004. Places de Man's thought in an American milieu from which it is too often excluded on account of its European origin.

McQuillan, Martin. *Paul de Man*. New York: Routledge, 2001. An accessible, balanced introduction to de Man's thought. One of the best books for the beginning student of de Man and his works. Part of the Routledge Critical Thinkers series.

Melville, Stephen W. *Philosophy Beside Itself: On Deconstruction and Modernism*. Minneapolis: University of Minnesota Press, 1986. Places de Man in the broader context of literary and philosophical thought in the twentieth century. Part of the Theory and History of Literature series.

Redfield, Marc, ed. *Legacies of Paul de Man*. New York: Fordham University Press, 2007. A look at whether—and if so, how—de Man's theories have survived the comparative eclipse of his reputation in the 1990's. Also includes fascinating appendices concerning de Man's teaching of literature at Yale in the 1970's.

Waters, Lindsay, and Wlad Godzich, eds. *Reading de Man Reading*. Minneapolis: University of Minnesota Press, 1989. This book of essays examines de Man's critical procedures and the vertiginous implications of his strategic acts of reading. Part of the Theory and History of Literature series.

Blithe Spirit
An Improbable Farce in Three Acts

Author: Noël Coward (1899-1973)
First produced: 1941; first published, 1941
Type of work: Drama
Type of plot: Comedy
Time of plot: Late 1930's
Locale: Kent, England

Principal characters:
CHARLES CONDOMINE, a novelist
RUTH, his wife
ELVIRA, his former wife, now deceased
MADAME ARCATI, a spiritualist medium and writer
EDITH, the Condomines' new maid
DOCTOR BRADMAN and MRS. BRADMAN, neighbors of the
     Condomines

The Story:

Charles and Ruth Condomine await three dinner guests, one of whom is the celebrated medium Madame Arcati, who is to hold a séance after dinner. The purpose of this séance—although Madame Arcati is not told this—is to allow Charles to gather background material for his new thriller, *The Unseen*. While waiting, Ruth attempts to teach the new maid, Edith, some discipline and decorum. Conversation turns to the subject of Charles's former wife, Elvira, who died of a heart attack brought on by a fit of uncontrollable laughter.

Ruth, who was also married before, claims that she does not mind in the least being thought less attractive than Elvira, although the manner in which she brings the subject up and Charles's determination to avoid making any such judgment suggest that she does mind. It seems that Ruth feels that she is still, in some sense, competing with her predecessor for her husband's affections. She suggests to Charles that he was dominated by women throughout his life and still remains under Elvira's spell. He denies this but says that if it were so then Ruth is obviously the one presently running his life.

When the Condomines' friends, the Bradmans, arrive, the discussion switches to the topic of Madame Arcati, whom all know only by sight and reputation. Charles is dismissive of her literary endeavors, which include fantasies for children and biographies of minor members of the royal families of Europe. Madame Arcati eventually arrives on her bicycle.

Before the séance begins, Madame Arcati puts the popular song "Always" on the gramophone because her spirit guide—a child named Daphne—likes music. The séance is rather chaotic to begin with, producing a good deal of table-rapping and an abundance of sarcastic remarks that begin to annoy the medium. Charles's mood undergoes a dramatic change, however, when he hears Elvira's voice speaking to him—a voice that, as becomes clear, no one else (except, of course, the audience) can hear. Madame Arcati faints, and when she regains consciousness everything seems normal.

As soon as Charles shows her to the door, the conversation between Ruth and the Bradmans becomes casual again. They are unable to see the ghost of Elvira enter the room and sit down.

When Charles returns he joins in the lighthearted conversation. Not until the Bradmans have gone does he move to a position from which Elvira is visible. Because Ruth is unable to see or hear Elvira, Charles's reaction to her presence and his subsequent dialogue with the ghost seems to be evidence of madness. Ruth soon stalks off to bed, leaving Charles to sleep in a chair.

When Charles awakens the next day he assumes that he was the victim of a hallucination. He almost makes his peace with Ruth when Elvira's ghost strolls in from the garden. As misunderstandings multiply once again, Charles prevails upon Elvira to prove she exists by moving various inanimate objects. As soon as Ruth is convinced, she summons Madame Arcati with a view to exorcising the ghost, but the medium is not at all certain whether this can be done.

The problem becomes urgent when Ruth becomes convinced that Elvira is trying to kill Charles in order to secure a permanent reunion on equal terms. Charles is initially skeptical about Elvira's murderous intentions, in spite of her constant sniping at Ruth. He is, however, forced to see the truth when one of Elvira's traps catches the wrong victim and kills Ruth instead of him.

At this point Elvira decides that perhaps she would be better off where she came from. Madame Arcati manages to locate a spell that might do the trick and tells her spirit guide that Mrs. Condomine now wishes to return. Because of her careless ambiguity, the Mrs. Condomine who "returns" is Ruth, brought back to earth exactly as Elvira was.

With two ghostly wives constantly bickering around and over him, Charles becomes increasingly desperate to exorcise both of them. He strenuously denies that it is the power of his desire—conscious or subconscious—that materialized the two ghosts. Nevertheless, it is necessary to identify the psychic power that is responsible in order to reverse the process. Madame Arcati sets out to determine how the psychic energy was provided. She conjures the deeply entranced Edith from her bed and mobilizes her newly revealed powers in the task of sending the ghosts back from where they came. They finally vanish, taunting Charles as they go. Their disappearance, however, is not absolute. The house remains subtly haunted, prone to mysterious rappings and movements of furniture that reveal that the wives, now invisible and inaudible even to Charles, are still present. Charles by now gains sufficient insight into the characters of both his wives that he no longer feels morally or emotionally bound to either one of them. He leaves the house—and them—bidding them a sarcastic farewell as he sets forth to live the rest of his life in splendid isolation from all womankind.

Critical Evaluation:

For two years before he wrote *Blithe Spirit*, Noël Coward had been involved in "war work." The British government, acutely aware of the fact that most of the public did not support the war, had recruited the literary establishment to the cause of building morale and disseminating propaganda. Coward had written the deeply sentimental and fervently patriotic *This Happy Breed* in 1939, which was first performed in 1942, and the unproduced *Time Remembered*. He had also undertaken a grueling schedule of personal appearances, which took him to Australia and New Zealand as well as continually back and forth across the Atlantic. When he got the chance for a holiday, he settled down to write a light comedy without any references to the war. *Blithe Spirit* is essentially a work of pure self-indulgence, written for the fun of it.

It may be that when writers are at their most self-indulgent and have no other intention than to please themselves they are most inclined to reveal something of themselves. On the surface, *Blithe Spirit* does not seem to differ much in style or substance from Coward's previous comedy, *Present Laughter* (written before *This Happy Breed* in early 1939 but likewise not produced until 1942). There, Coward used a protagonist who is an actor and unrepentant egomaniac as well as a writer, which would have enabled some "autobiographical" elements. Given that Coward was as openly homosexual as it was possible to be in his day—that is to say, it was no secret in the theatrical community—it does not seem that the theme of second marriages, which are often haunted by the ghosts of the former spouse, can have been of much relevance to him. Therefore, if there is any personal significance in *Blithe Spirit*, it is buried beneath the surface of glittering artifice.

The artifice of *Blithe Spirit* works to greatest effect in the character of Madame Arcati, who is a wonderful grotesque. Although she is clearly drawn from stereotypical images of spiritualist mediums, her idiosyncratic deviations from that stereotype provide a constant stream of amusing lines. Her insistence on traveling by bicycle, her observations on how various foods affect her psychic powers, her reasons for preferring a child to the more conventional Red Indian as a spirit guide, and so on, fuel the undercurrent of polite absurdity that sustains the pace of the play.

Even when she is not actually on stage, the other characters' remarks about Madame Arcati are essential to the flow of wit. When she is absent from the stage or from the conversation, the tempo is markedly different. Charles Condomine's dialogues with Elvira sparkle, but the only really funny scene that does not involve Madame Arcati is the one in which Charles's exchanges with Elvira are continually misinterpreted by Ruth, to whom Elvira is invisible and inaudible—a near-slapstick device that diverges sharply from Coward's usual method of raising laughs.

The mischievous Elvira, whose amorality is intensified rather than redeemed by her personal charms, is the kind of female character Coward loved to create. Her disregard for convention—which certainly warrants the description of "blithe"—is indicated in a fashion so subtle as to be sketchy, but any admirer of Coward's work would immediately recognize the precise tenor of her naughtiness. The same admirer might, however, have difficulty in recognizing Charles as another in the series of Cowardian alter egos who serve as his male protagonists. By comparison with Gary Essendine in *Present Laughter*, who is the epitome of the breezily appalling hams Coward loved to design and play, Charles is not merely restrained but positively ordinary. Ruth's role is largely that of playing sober foil to the mercurial Elvira, but she, too, is forced to exercise that sobriety with an uncommon restraint.

The relative quietness of the two leading players is counterbalanced by the fact that they are enmeshed in a structured plot. Many of Coward's characters had to be larger than life because they had to carry the plays forward by the sheer force of personality, but *Blithe Spirit* stands almost alone among Coward's comedies in having an element of mystery and narrative suspense. This is probably the reason that it has proved to be the most popular of all his plays with audiences, although connoisseurs often prefer *Private Lives* (1930). Significantly, when the play was filmed in 1945 the plot was considered so weak as to require a modified climax; the director evidently felt that Charles's casual farewell to his invisible spouses was disappointingly anticlimactic and added an extra "accident" to reunite the three of them beyond the grave. The fact that Coward felt that no such move was necessary or desirable in the play may provide the key to such personal significance as it has.

Coward spent his entire life performing in a calculatedly flamboyant manner that helped create the notion of "campness." His declared justification for this was, of course, that he was not just a man of the theater and a genius but a homosexual who was only permitted to acknowledge the fact within certain circles and thus forced to conduct his social life as a performance; his calculated exaggeration of that performance was, to some extent, a commentary on the absurdity of his situation. Of all the parts he wrote for himself, Charles Condomine is the least prone to exaggerated performance (Coward's "straight" parts were, of course, performances precisely because they pretended to set aside the kind of ostentation he employed in real life). The ending of Charles's story qualifies as a uniquely happy ending because his release from the various social pressures put upon him by his successive wives offers him the promise, or at least the possibility, of being able to stop performing altogether.

Charles is the one character Coward wrote for himself who is allowed the hope of being himself in being by himself. It was the kind of notion that the relentlessly gregarious Coward could probably never have contemplated had he not been temporarily surfeited with unusually onerous social responsibilities, but given the circumstances in which he conceived and wrote *Blithe Spirit* it is certainly understandable.

Brian Stableford

Further Reading

Gay, Frances. *Noël Coward*. London: Macmillan, 1987. A critical study of Coward's work. Discusses *Blithe Spirit* as a farcical comedy with "a darker dimension."

Hoare, Philip. *Noël Coward: A Biography.* New York: Simon & Schuster, 1995. Detailed biography, discussing, among many other topics, Coward's family background, drive to succeed, devotion to his mother, homosexual affairs, and how he transformed his life into his art.

Kaplan, Joel, and Sheila Stowell, eds. *Look Back in Pleasure: Noël Coward Reconsidered*. London: Methuen, 2000. Collection of essays and interviews assessing Coward's contribution to the British theater. Some of the essays examine Coward's transformation of British comedy, Coward and effeminacy, and "Cowardice, Decadence, and the Contemporary Theatre." A roundtable of actors, directors, and other participants discusses the challenges of staging Coward's plays in the twenty-first century.

Lahr, John. *Coward the Playwright*. London: Methuen, 1982. Reprint. Berkeley: University of California Press, 2002. The fullest and most detailed critical study of Coward's plays. *Blithe Spirit* is extensively discussed in the chapter "Ghosts in the Fun Machine."

Lesley, Cole. *The Life of Noël Coward*. London: Cape, 1976. A useful memoir by Coward's longtime secretary and companion.

Mander, Raymond, and Joe Mitchenson. *Theatrical Companion to Coward*. New York: Macmillan, 1957. A comprehensive and detailed reference work dealing with Coward's plays.

Morley, Sheridan. *A Talent to Amuse*. Garden City, N.Y.: Doubleday, 1969. Reprint. London: Haus, 2004. A sensitive and wide-ranging critical and biographical study.

O'Connor, Sean. *Straight Acting: Popular Gay Drama from Wilde to Rattigan*. London: Cassell, 1998. Focuses on the legacy of Oscar Wilde as both a playwright and a gay man by examining plays by Coward and other British dramatists. Places these playwrights' work within the context of twentieth century social history, describing the restrictions the writers endured in their personal lives and in their treatment of gay issues.

The Blithedale Romance

Author: Nathaniel Hawthorne (1804-1864)
First published: 1852
Type of work: Novel
Type of plot: Psychological realism
Time of plot: Mid-nineteenth century
Locale: Massachusetts

Principal characters:
MILES COVERDALE, a resident of Blithedale Community
ZENOBIA, a worldly woman
PRISCILLA MOODIE, a simple maiden
HOLLINGSWORTH, beloved of Zenobia and Priscilla
WESTERVELT, an evil conjurer
OLD MOODIE, Priscilla's father

The Story:

As Miles Coverdale prepares to journey to Blithedale, where he is to join in a project in community living, he is accosted by Old Moodie, a seedy ancient who seems reluctant to state his business. After much mysterious talk about having Coverdale do him a great favor, Old Moodie changes his mind and shuffles off without telling what it was that he wanted. It is April, but Coverdale and his companions arrive at Blithedale in a snowstorm. There they are greeted by a woman called Zenobia, a well-known magazine writer. Zenobia is a beautiful, worldly woman of wealth and position. At all times she wears a rare, exotic flower in her hair. Zenobia spends most of her energy fighting for "woman's place in the world."

On the evening of Coverdale's arrival, another of the principals arrives at Blithedale. He is Hollingsworth, a philanthropist and reformer. In fact, philanthropy is to him a never-ceasing effort to reform and change humanity. He brings with him Priscilla, a simple, poorly dressed, bewildered young girl. Priscilla goes at once to Zenobia and, falling at the proud woman's feet, never takes her eyes from that haughty face. There is no explanation for such behavior. Hollingsworth knows only that he was approached by Old Moodie and asked to take Priscilla to Blithedale. That is the request Old Moodie tried to make of Coverdale. Such is the community of Blithedale that the inhabitants make the girl welcome in spite of her strange behavior.

It is soon evident to Coverdale that Hollingsworth's impulse to philanthropy reaches such an extreme that the man is on the way to madness. Hollingsworth is convinced that the universe exists only in order for him to reform all criminals and wayward persons. The dream of his life is to construct a large edifice in which he can collect his criminal brothers and teach them to mend their ways before doom overtakes them. To Coverdale, he is a bore, but it is obvious that both Zenobia and Priscilla are in love with him. Priscilla blossoms as she reaps the benefits of good food and fresh air, and Zenobia views her, with evident but unspoken alarm, as a rival.

Hollingsworth seems to consider Priscilla his own special charge, and Coverdale fears the looks of thinly veiled hatred he frequently sees Zenobia cast toward the vulnerable young Priscilla, who is, ironically, devoted to Zenobia. When Old Moodie appears at Blithedale to inquire about Priscilla, Coverdale tries to persuade him to reveal the reason for his interest in the girl. The old man slips away without telling his story.

Shortly after this incident, Professor Westervelt comes to Blithedale to inquire about Zenobia and Priscilla. Coverdale sees Westervelt and Zenobia together and is sure that, even though Zenobia hates him now, she once loved and was made miserable by this evil man. Coverdale knows that all the pain that he sometimes sees in Zenobia's eyes must surely have come from this man. Coverdale believes also that there is still some bond between them.

After Westervelt's visit, Zenobia is short-tempered and more vehement than usual about the poor lot of women. She is so much in love with Hollingsworth that even the misery, or perhaps terror, caused by Westervelt does not deter her from literally worshiping at his feet. Hollingsworth, in his egotism, believes that women are placed on earth only to serve men, he being one, and so great is Zenobia's passion that she accepts his words without protest, not proclaiming her real thoughts in his presence. It is clear to Coverdale that Hollingsworth intends to use Zenobia's money to build the school for criminals of which he never ceases to talk. When Coverdale refuses to join him in this project, Hollingsworth becomes quite cool in his dealings with Coverdale.

Tiring of the life at Blithedale, Coverdale takes a vacation in town. He is greatly surprised when Zenobia, Priscilla, and Westervelt also arrive in the town shortly afterward. He calls on the ladies and is disturbed by the tension that is apparent. When he chides Zenobia about Priscilla and Hollingsworth, she warns him not to interfere lest he cause serious trouble. Priscilla does not know why she is there. She tells Coverdale that she is like a leaf blown about by the wind. She has no will of her own, only the will of Zenobia. Then Westervelt calls for the two women, and the three leave Coverdale standing as if they did not know he was there.

Determined to uncover the mystery surrounding the three, Coverdale seeks out Old Moodie and pries from him the story. Once Moodie was a wealthy and influential man until, through dishonest business practices, he was ruined. Then, leaving his wife and daughter, Zenobia, he wandered about in poverty and disgrace. His wife died and he married again. To them Priscilla was born, as different from his first child as it was possible to be. Zenobia was beautiful and proud, Priscilla plain and shy. Neighbors thought Priscilla had supernatural powers, but her kindness and her goodness made everyone love her.

Zenobia, after Moodie's disgrace, was reared by his brother; and since Moodie was believed dead, Zenobia, as the next heir, inherited her uncle's wealth. She grew up a wild and willful girl; it was whispered that she had made a secret marriage with an unprincipled man. No one, however, knew anything definite. Such were her beauty and wealth that no one criticized her. Moodie called her to his home and, not telling her who he was, cautioned her to be as kind as a sister to Priscilla.

During his vacation, Coverdale chances upon a magician's show in a nearby village. There he finds Hollingsworth in the audience and Westervelt on the stage. Westervelt produces a Veiled Lady, an ethereal creature whom he says will do his bidding. At the climax of the act, Hollingsworth arises from the audience and strides to the platform. He calls to the Veiled Lady to remove her veil, and Priscilla lifts her veil and flees into the arms of Hollingsworth with a cry of joy and love. She looks like one who has been saved from an evil fate.

Coverdale returns to Blithedale. There he witnesses a terrifying scene among Zenobia, Priscilla, and Hollingsworth. Hollingsworth admits his love for Priscilla to Zenobia. Zenobia reviles him and warns her half sister against the emptiness of his heart. She says she knows at last the complete egotism of the man and sees that he has deceived her only to get her fortune for his great project. After the lovers leave her, Zenobia sinks to the ground and weeps, and that night she drowns herself in the river flowing close by. Westervelt comes to view her dead body, but his only sorrow seems to be that he can no longer use Zenobia in his schemes.

After Zenobia's tragedy, Coverdale leaves Blithedale. Priscilla and Hollingsworth live quietly, he giving up his desire to reform criminals because he feels himself to be one—Zenobia's murderer. In his twilight years Coverdale confesses his real interest in these ill-fated people. He was from the first in love with Priscilla.

Critical Evaluation:

The self-conscious ironical tone of *The Blithedale Romance* is one of the first things that strikes the reader, and this tone is set by the first-person narrator, Miles Coverdale, an independently wealthy poet. In spite of his expressed desire to participate in the experimental paradise of Blithedale, Coverdale's implicit attitude is that of a dilettante, someone who loves his creature comforts but who, through boredom, is pursuing an idealistic alternative to his privileged artificial life. If Coverdale typifies those who, like Hawthorne, participated in the Brook Farm experiment of 1841, the reader can understand why the project failed.

Coverdale is essentially an observer of life. He is able to situate the socialistic experiment of Blithedale historically: It is a successor of the Puritan attempt to make one's principles the foundation of daily living. Coverdale notes that group living requires a sacrifice of individual development, and the prime leaders—Hollingsworth and Zenobia—are individualists incapable of such a sacrifice. Perhaps because of the first-person narrative mode, none of the three main characters described by Coverdale ever comes to life on the page.

Hollingsworth is the type of the single-minded philanthropist who has channeled all of his considerable energy into founding an institute for the reformation of criminals. This apparently selfless devotion endears him to the two female protagonists: the dark and sensual Zenobia and the pale and spiritual Priscilla.

Like true romantic heroines, Zenobia and Priscilla are initially shrouded in mystery. The proud, wealthy Zenobia chafes at the restrictions society places on her sex. Priscilla, on the other hand, a seamstress before coming to Blithedale, possesses an essentially dependent character, devoting herself first to Zenobia and later to Hollingsworth. According to their father, the impoverished Old Moodie, his daughter Zenobia represents the wealth and power that her father abused and lost through some unnamed crime, while Priscilla is the child of his poverty, a reclusive person who fills her imagination with her father's stories. Zenobia possesses many social qualities; Priscilla is rumored to be psychic.

Irony dominates the narration of *The Blithedale Romance*. For example, the judgmental narrator Coverdale finally acknowledges that if it is true, as he believes, that Hollingsworth's life is empty of human warmth because he cares only about his criminal project, so it is also true that Coverdale's own life is empty because he has no real interests beyond his own comfort. Ironically, Zenobia, a dominant personality who espouses the rights of women to receive equal treatment in society, is so devastated when Hollingsworth turns away from her to propose to the subservient, adoring Priscilla that she commits suicide. Again ironically, because of this suicide, Hollingsworth is so haunted by feelings of guilt he no longer pursues his great project of criminal reform and becomes a recluse devoted to converting one murderer, himself. Furthermore, the once powerful but now debilitated Hollingsworth is cared for by the weak Priscilla. Finally, Coverdale, who fills his narration with the wonders of Zenobia, admits in the final sentence of the novel he was in love with Priscilla all along.

Irony also envelops the account of the Blithedale experiment itself. These participants who aspire to improve the world are unable to handle their personal lives. Their condescension toward their managing farmer Silas Foster certainly undermines the professed sincerity of this democratic project. Ironically, Foster tells them that if they wish to succeed as farmers they must compete with more market-experienced farmers. Such competition seems a direct contradiction to their socialist goals. Coverdale, who like a true Transcendentalist rhapsodizes over communing with nature in his special treehouse, at the conclusion of the romance concedes nature is indifferent to the death of one of its noblest products, Zenobia.

In keeping with his practice of using characters as types, Nathaniel Hawthorne gives them names that suggest their symbolic role. Coverdale is a felicitous name for the narrator, who is adept at covering his personal feelings and motives while he attempts to uncover the hidden motives of others. Coverdale notes that Zenobia uses her exotic name like a mask. The name Zenobia recalls Queen Zenobia, a proud and capable ruler who ultimately fell victim to the all-too-male Roman Empire. The name Priscilla evokes the wan, enervated wraith who somehow inspires the love of Hollingsworth and Coverdale. The name Hollingsworth also reveals the person's character; he is hollow in worth, since the suicide of Zenobia effectively destroys his project and his spirit. When the protagonists meet by Eliot's pulpit, the name of the rock recalls the work of this idealistic Puritan apostle of the Indians; the irony is that his converts were massacred in King Philip's War. The name, therefore, effectively prophesies the unsuccessful conclusion of the idealistic experiment in improving the world. Old Moodie is called Fauntleroy in the fairy-tale-like narrative describing his fabulous wealth and power prior to his crime and flight. That name is the same as that of a well-known contemporary English forger. Hawthorne probably expected his readers to be able to identify Moodie's crime.

The most effective use of a name is the title of the work, apparently the name of the place. Any suggestions of the members to choose another name provoke objections; they feel Blithedale (happy valley) is appropriate. Madness, suicide, and depression soon find their way to Blithedale. Designating the work a romance in the title expresses Hawthorne's purpose of creating a work of mystery and fantasy, not a realistic work. The use of the word "romance" is ironic; the novel is all about disillusionment. The novel is filled with veilings and coverings; the author effectively shrouds his real-life adventure in utopian living at Brook Farm in 1841 in a fantasy of titanic star-crossed lovers. It remains for the reader to separate truth from fiction.

"Critical Evaluation" by Agnes A. Shields

Further Reading

Hawthorne, Nathaniel. *The Blithedale Romance*. Edited by Seymour Gross and Rosalie Murphy. New York: W. W. Norton, 1978. In addition to the text, this edition contains background information, sources, criticism, and bibliographies.

Johnson, Claudia D. *The Productive Tension of Hawthorne's Art*. Tuscaloosa: University of Alabama Press, 1981. Chapter 4 contends that Hawthorne attacks the romantic tendency toward artist-centered art in *The Blithedale Romance*. Includes bibliography.

Kaul, A. N., ed. *Hawthorne: A Collection of Essays*. Englewood Cliffs, N.J.: Prentice-Hall, 1966. Kaul's analysis of *The Blithedale Romance* identifies the author's theme as social regeneration. Includes chronology and bibliography.

Lee, A. Robert, ed. *Nathaniel Hawthorne: New Critical Essays*. New York: Barnes & Noble, 1982. Depicts Hawthorne as looking back to the Puritans and forward to modernist themes and concerns.

Millington, Richard H. *The Cambridge Companion to Nathaniel Hawthorne*. New York: Cambridge University Press, 2004. Collection of essays analyzing various aspects of Hawthorne's work, including discussions of Hawthorne and American masculinity, Hawthorne and the question of women, and "Sympathy and Reform in *The Blithedale Romance*" by Robert S. Levine.

Pearce, Roy Harvey, ed. *Hawthorne Centenary Essays*. Columbus: Ohio State University Press, 1964. Includes essays dealing with the reception of Hawthorne's work in the nineteenth century. Suggests that the author's complex, ambiguous feelings about the idealistic social experiment are evident in his work.

Pennell, Melissa McFarland. *Student Companion to Nathaniel Hawthorne*. Westport, Conn.: Greenwood Press, 1999. An introductory overview of Hawthorne's life and work designed for students and general readers. Includes a discussion of Hawthorne's contribution to American literature, analyses of his four major novels, a bibliography, and an index.

Person, Leland S. *The Cambridge Introduction to Nathaniel Hawthorne.* New York: Cambridge University Press, 2007. An accessible introduction to the author's life and works designed for students and general readers. It includes analysis of Hawthorne's fiction, with a separate chapter on *The Blithedale Romance.*

Weldon, Roberta. *Hawthorne, Gender, and Death: Christian-ity and its Discontents.* New York: Palgrave Macmillan, 2008. Weldon analyzes how Hawthorne depicts dying and his characters' reactions to death in *The Blithedale Romance* and other fictional works. Includes notes, bibliography, and index.

Wineapple, Brenda. *Hawthorne: A Life.* New York: Knopf, 2003. A meticulously researched, even-handed analysis of Hawthorne's often contradictory life which proposes that much of Hawthorne's fiction was autobiographical. Includes more than one hundred pages of notes, a bibliography, and an index.

Blonde

Author: Joyce Carol Oates (1938-   )
First published: 2000
Type of work: Novel
Type of plot: Narrative
Time of plot: June 1, 1926-August 5, 1962
Locale: Hollywood, New York City, and Maine

Principal characters:
NORMA JEANE MORTENSON, an actor, best known as Marilyn Monroe
GLADYS PEARL MORTENSON, Norma Jeane's mother
DELLA MONROE, Norma Jeane's grandmother
ELSIE PIRIG and WARREN PIRIG, her foster parents
SIDNEY HARING, her high school teacher
BUCHANAN "BUCKY" GLAZER, her first husband
OTTO ÖSE, a magazine photographer
CHARLIE "CASS" CHAPLIN, JR., her lover and friend
EDDY G., her lover and friend
THE EX-ATHLETE (JOE DIMAGGIO), her second husband
THE PLAYWRIGHT (ARTHUR MILLER), her third husband

The Story:

Norma Jeane, named for films stars Norma Talmadge and Jean Harlow, is born on June 1, 1926. Her unwed mother, Gladys Pearl (Monroe) Mortenson, works at The Studio. Unable to take care of her child, Gladys leaves her daughter with her own mother, Della Monroe. Grandmother Della is an alcoholic and abuses drugs, but she takes care of Norma Jeane the best she can. Gladys becomes ill from handling toxic chemicals at work. Mentally unstable, she is hospitalized in 1934, when Norma Jeane is eight years old. Also in 1934, Grandmother Della dies, forcing Norma Jeane to enter an orphans' home. In 1942, she is placed with foster parents Elsie and Warren Pirig in Los Angeles.

The Pirigs enroll Norma Jeane in Van Nuys High School, but she drops out of school during her sophomore year. When she is sixteen years old, she is encouraged by her foster parents to marry Bucky Glazer, a twenty-one-year-old high school graduate and local sports star. As World War II rages, Bucky joins the U.S. Merchant Marine and sets sail on *The Liberty.* Norma Jeane begins working at Radio Plane Aircraft.

In 1944, a U.S. military magazine photographer named Otto Öse takes photographs of Norma Jeane, marking the start of her career as a pinup model. Her photos are seen in *Stars & Stripes, Pageant,* and other publications. In 1945, she is named Miss Aluminum Products. She then establishes herself as a model and starts auditioning for film roles.

At the age of twenty-one, Norma Jeane gets her first part in a film. Early on, men take advantage of her beauty for profit. They even give her a new name—Marilyn Monroe. At about this time, Cass Chaplin, the son of actor-comedian Charles Chaplin, begins a romantic relationship with Monroe, also becoming her confidante. However, Cass is also the lover of Eddy G. The three are close-knit and begin calling themselves the Gemini. Monroe becomes pregnant but is not sure who the father is. She has an abortion rather than give up her career. Though Monroe leaves the "trio," Cass remains her friend, and he even ghost writes letters to her, from her father, to make her happy.

Although Monroe has only minor roles initially, she steals scenes in *The Asphalt Jungle* and *All About Eve* in 1950. Her first lead roles were in *Gentlemen Prefer Blondes* and *How to Marry a Millionaire*, both released in 1953. Comedies *Bus Stop* (1956) and *Some Like It Hot* (1959) are huge hits as well.

Monroe attracts the press, fans, and romantic interests, such as the Ex-Athlete (Joe DiMaggio). They marry in 1954, but because of her work schedule and his travel, the marriage does not last beyond one year. The Ex-Athlete is extremely jealous; he hires private security to watch her every move, even after the divorce. As her relationships unravel, it also gets harder for Monroe to look fresh and flawless. Her perfectionism on set causes her reputation to suffer. She takes pills to relax. She is late for filming, wrecking schedules and filming budgets.

The Studio has made millions from Monroe's talents while paying her a low salary. She finally gets a better contract. She studies with the Actors Studio in New York City and meets the Playwright (Arthur Miller). The Playwright, who is older than Monroe and is well established, leaves his wife to marry Monroe. They do not have children, in part because of Monroe's earlier abortions. (She also has a miscarriage.) Monroe and the Playwright divorce five years later. Monroe's last film, *The Misfits* (1961), had been written by the Playwright.

On August 5, 1962, Monroe is found dead in her bed at home, alone. It is not known how she died, but many speculate that she died either after overdosing on drugs or after having some sort of accident.

Critical Evaluation:

Joyce Carol Oates's *Blonde* fictionalizes the life of Norma Jean Baker from the time she was six years old. Synecdoche—the blending of multiple events into one or two events, based on facts—is used throughout the novel. Like an unfolding film script, the narrator takes the reader inside Norma Jeane's thoughts and the feelings of other characters to reveal the life of film star Marilyn Monroe.

At the outset, the third-person omniscient narrator sets the tone for story. Before long, a first-person ("I") narrator—Norma Jeane in her own words—enters the story. The third-person returns, accompanied by periodic "guest appearance"

omniscient narrators, such as the camera crew at one of Norma Jeane's early photo shoots. The guest narrators are cruel toward Monroe, objectifying her as a sexual object.

In *Blonde*, Oates reintroduces themes found in her other works. These themes include the potential for violence and its occurrence when least expected, the oppression and domination of girls and women, and the dichotomy between outward appearance and reality and deception and truth. Additionally, in *Blonde*, there is the foreboding of death.

Oates weaves into the novel a predestined fate to show how Norma Jeane's life was a struggle for survival. For example, Norma Jeane writes a poem in a high school notebook that her mother used to read to her, Emily Dickinson's "Because I Could Not Stop for Death." Fate works against the odds of resolving the actor's search for true love versus scripted, false love; against motherhood; against being reunited with her mother; and against a happy ending.

Readers witness vivid scenes in Norma Jeane's life in chronological order. All concrete details—names, dates, addresses—are gathered and presented as if from Hollywood magazine clippings of the day. Her happiest childhood memories are from driving around with her mother and looking at mansions of the stars in Beverly Hills.

Norma Jeane's thoughts and dreams are based on movie plots. The people who come and go in her life are compared to film stars. For example, her high school drama teacher, Sidney Haring, "looked like a weaker, less amiable Henry Fonda in *The Grapes of Wrath*." Visits to her mother are often accompanied by background music. Everyone—Mr. X, V, the Ex-Athlete, the Playwright—has a role in Norma Jeane's life, as in a script. The reader has to maintain a sense of distance to view these scenes, because they are so raw and shocking.

Substance abuse dominates Norma Jeane's life and the lives of the people who are closest to her, including Della, Gladys, and Cass. The novel also includes many references to others who died from drugs or alcohol. For example, actor Jeanne Eagels, a "hophead drug fiend," dies from overusing, and Aimee Semple McPherson, an evangelist, dies from an overdose. The substance abusers named in *Blonde*, not to mention the nameless bodies found along roadsides, are almost exclusively female. It is clear, also, that drugs and alcohol are tied to age, and aging is the enemy of women's success in the movies.

A macabre archetype named the Dark Prince shows up in various disguises in Norma Jeane's life. The Dark Prince character is a nod to a Rudolph Valentino film, suggesting a romantic and mysterious man who rescues the Princess (Norma Jeane). He is, in part, her missing father, who haunts her memory. He is also photographer Otto Öse as well as lovers and husbands. Norma Jeane often called husbands or lovers Daddy, a term of endearment possibly deriving from her strong desire to experience her father's love and attention.

Norma Jeane never stops yearning for a chance to meet her father. She hangs out at a Bel Air address in a borrowed car, on the eve of her twenty-third birthday, in the driveway of a man who might have been her mother's lover in 1925 (Mr. X). A security guard shoos Norma Jeane away. Her thoughts show a longing for love and acceptance, which always eluded her.

Norma Jeane, according to one character, "was the kind of girl who obeys . . . so if you're responsible, you take care what you tell her to do." She thus falls prey to a sexist Hollywood milieu. As Öse explains, "girls like you are luscious pieces of candy for whomever's got the dough to buy them." When in the middle of her first nude photo shoot, he says, she "obeyed" him "unquestioningly. . . . She might have been hypnotized."

On several occasions, Norma Jeane tries to educate herself or talk about complex issues; each time, she is dismissed by mentors and teachers, and her questioning is interpreted as disobedience. For example, with her first husband, Bucky Glazer, she brings up reading H. G. Wells's *War of the Worlds*; Bucky erroneously tells her that *War of the Worlds* was a radio show, and takes over the conversation. When she asks Öse about political theory or American collaboration in the death of Nazi victims, she is dismissed as "a joke." However, Öse would say later, "Her problem wasn't that she was a dumb blonde, it was she wasn't a blonde and she wasn't dumb." When Norma Jeane arrives at The Studio for an audition, she mentions Russian novelist Fyodor Dostoevski and is mocked by the director. However, he would later remark that he considered her to be

the first actress of the twenty or more he's auditioned for the role . . . who seems to have given the role any intelligent thought and who has actually read the entire script (or so she claims) and has formed some sort of judgment on it.

Isaac E. Shinn, Norma Jeane's first Hollywood agent, believed that Norma Jeane could have finished her education. However, he thought she had acting talent and potential for stardom, thus dissuading her from finishing her education and encouraging her toward being a star. Indeed, she could not shy away from the cameras. The photographer's camera had control over her, and that camera also symbolized destruction. During her first nude photo shoot, the third-person

narrator explains that "From the eye of Otto Öse's camera, as from the very eye of Death, *nobody hides*." This theme of hiding was illustrated well by Norma Jeane's lover Cass Chaplin, who said "being Charlie Chaplin's son was a curse that others stupidly wished to believe must be a blessing— 'Like it's a fairy tale, and I'm the King's son.'"

Hypnosis, dreams, and a film-like unreality thread through Oates's novel. Some of Norma Jeane's dreams are based on real events. Other threads in the story are a mouse and references to fate. The mouse motif symbolizes her low status in society: Mouse is her nickname at the orphans' home and she squeaks when she laughs, "like a mouse being killed." Doom is a pervasive plot element. For example, characters mention that Norma Jeane might hurt herself if she suffers a disappointment. Toward the end of her life, her internal monologue gets garbled, jumps back and forth in time. Shorter, disconnected fragments signal a breakdown of cohesive reality and a movement toward chaos and loss.

Blonde reveals the reality (versus the myths) of Norma Jeane's life. The best and worst of her life are fully disclosed, much like her famous nude calendar, and the novel shows how she moved beyond others' expectations. Oates chose a complex topic worthy of her writing style. *Blonde* provides a dense, full look at a complex life in the context of its time.

Jan Hall

Further Reading

Cologne-Brookes, Gavin. *Dark Eyes on America: The Novels of Joyce Carol Oates*. Baton Rouge: Louisiana State University Press, 2005. Presents analysis of selected significant works by Oates, with a focus on her philosophical and cultural worldviews. A valuable addition to studies of Oates's work.

Johnson, Greg, ed. *Joyce Carol Oates: Conversations*. Princeton, N.J.: Ontario Review Press, 2006. A collection of previously published interviews with Oates spanning the years 1970 to 2006. Topics covered include the author's thoughts on the art of fiction, her "lighter" side, and Marilyn Monroe, the subject of *Blonde*. Includes a brief chronology of Oates's life.

Oates, Joyce Carol. *The Journal of Joyce Carol Oates: 1973-1982*. Edited by Greg Johnson. New York: Ecco Press, 2007. A wide-ranging collection of thoughtful, reflective entries traces Oates's life through her move to Princeton University. Oates discusses the joys and frustrations of writing. Provides a record of her productivity as a writer as well as insight into her philosophical explorations and her views of the human condition.

Wagner, Linda, ed. *Critical Essays on Joyce Carol Oates.* Boston: G. K. Hall, 1979. A collection of twenty-eight reviews and essays that include discussions of particular works as well as analyses of Oates's general themes and stylistic considerations. Predates *Blonde,* but remains helpful for understanding Oates's literary style.

Wesley, Marilyn. *Refusal and Transgression in Joyce Carol Oates's Fiction.* Westport, Conn.: Greenwood Press, 1993. This feminist analysis focuses on the family as portrayed in Oates's fiction, before *Blonde* but relevant to this later novel. Contends that the young protagonists of many of Oates's stories and novels commit acts of transgression that serve as critiques of the American family.

York, R. A. *The Extension of Life: Fiction and History in the American Novel.* Madison, N.J.: Fairleigh Dickinson University Press, 2003. York examines the "complementary tendencies" in the fiction of American writers, including Oates, to document history while balancing creativity, to be true to facts while maintaining "self-conscious fabulation." Also examines works by Bernard Malamud, Saul Bellow, Truman Capote, Toni Morrison, Jane Smiley, Barbara Kingsolver, and others.

Blood Wedding

Author: Federico García Lorca (1898-1936)
First produced: *Bodas de sangre*, 1933; first published, 1935 (English translation, 1939)
Type of work: Drama
Type of plot: Tragedy
Time of plot: Early twentieth century
Locale: Spain

Principal characters:
THE BRIDEGROOM
THE BRIDEGROOM'S MOTHER
THE BRIDE
THE BRIDE'S FATHER
LEONARDO FELÍX, former suitor of the Bride
LEONARDO'S WIFE

The Story:

The Bridegroom's Mother is unhappy when she learns that her son wishes to be married to the woman he desires. In spite of her sorrow at losing him, she commands him to go buy fine presents for the Bride. The Bridegroom's Mother is also unhappy because the Bridegroom is her only surviving child. Her husband and her older son were killed many years before in fights with members of the Felíx family. Since then, the Bridegroom's Mother lived in fear that the only surviving man in her family, the Bridegroom, might also fall a victim to someone's knife or gun. She tells her son that she wishes he was born a girl, to sit in the house and knit instead of going out among men.

After the Bridegroom leaves the house to go buy gifts for the Bride, gifts to be presented when the parents meet, a neighbor stops to see his Mother. The neighbor tells the Bridegroom's Mother that there is bad blood in the Bride's veins, inherited from her mother. She also says that Leonardo, a member of the hated Felíx family and a cousin of the Bride, wooed the Bride unsuccessfully before his own marriage three years earlier. The Bridegroom's Mother grows uneasy at the news, but she determines to carry through her part in the marriage customs because her son is in love and because the Bride's Father owns rich vineyards comparable to those of her own family.

Meanwhile word of the proposed marriage reaches Leonardo, who still is in love with the Bride. In fact, he rides many miles to her house to see her whenever he has the chance. For some time both Leonardo's Wife and her mother realized that something was wrong. Leonardo is curt and sharp with his Wife for no reason at all, and he fails to take much notice of their child.

The next day the Bride's servant prepares her to meet with her father, the Bridegroom, and the Bridegroom's Mother in order to make plans for the wedding. The servant accuses the Bride of permitting Leonardo to visit late at night. The Bride, without denying the fact, merely indicates that she is not very happy at the prospect of marrying the Bridegroom.

After the arrival of the Bridegroom and his Mother, it is decided to have the wedding take place on the following Thursday, the Bride's twenty-second birthday. The Bride says that she will welcome the chance to shut out the world from her life and devote herself to the Bridegroom. A short time after the Bridegroom and his Mother depart, Leonardo's horse is heard neighing beneath the Bride's window.

The day of the wedding arrives, and early in the morning the servant begins to prepare the Bride for the ceremony. The Bride is not happy. When the servant begins to speak of the bliss that will soon be hers, the Bride commands the woman to be quiet. She even throws her wreath of orange blossoms to the ground.

A short time later the guests begin to arrive. The first to make his appearance is the Bride's cousin and former wooer, Leonardo. He and the Bride, despite the servant's pleas, have a talk in which bitter recriminations are flung back and forth. Neither wishes to be married to anyone else, but each blames the other for the unhappiness to which they are apparently doomed. Only the arrival of other guests breaks up the argument.

The guests having arrived, the party sets out for the church. Only the most vigorous language on the part of his Wife convinces Leonardo that he ought to ride in the cart with her, in order to keep up appearances. When the wedding ceremony is over, Leonardo and his Wife are the first guests to return to the Bride's Father's house. Leonardo drives like a madman.

Shortly after the guests gather at the house, the Bridegroom goes up quietly behind the Bride and puts his arms about her. She shrinks from his embrace. Complaining that she feels ill, she goes to her room to rest after asking the Bridegroom to leave her alone. As the wedding feast continues, some of the guests propose that the Bridegroom and the Bride dance together. The Bride, however, is nowhere to be found. Searchers discover that she and Leonardo rode away on his horse. The Bridegroom, furious at being so dishonored and filled with desire for revenge, organizes a posse of his relatives and immediately starts out after the fugitives. All day they search without finding the pair.

On into the night the Bridegroom continues his search and comes at last into the wood where the runaways stopped. The Bride, meanwhile, has a change of heart; refusing to give herself to Leonardo, she says that it is enough that she ran away with him. Leonardo, becoming angry, reminds her that it is she who went down the stairs first, who put a new bridle on the horse, and who even buckled on his spurs. Nevertheless, the Bride says she has enough. She does not want to stay with him, but she has no greater desire to return to her husband.

While they argue, the Bridegroom meets Death, disguised as a beggar woman. Death insists upon leading him to the place where he will find his escaped bride and her lover. By the light of the moon they search until they find the pair. When they meet, Leonardo and the Bridegroom fight, killing each other.

After they die, Death, still disguised as a beggar woman, goes back to spread the evil tidings. When she hears of her son's death, the Bridegroom's Mother takes the news stoically, not wanting her neighbors to see her overwhelming grief. Returning to her mother-in-law, the Bride is told to remain at the door without entering the room. The Bride tries to explain her actions, saying also that she comes so that the Bridegroom's Mother can kill her. No one pays any attention to the Bride's argument that neither Leonardo nor her husband ever slept with her.

The Bridegroom's Mother is joined in her lamentations by Leonardo's Wife when searchers carry in the bodies of the two men. The grief-stricken women, joined by the Bride, complain bitterly that an instrument as small as a knife can take away the lives of two such men, lives that were so much greater than the instrument that caused their deaths.

Critical Evaluation:

In the three plays—*Blood Wedding*, *Yerma* (1934), and *The House of Bernarda Alba* (1936)—that culminated his poetic and dramatic career, Federico García Lorca succeeded brilliantly where a host of modern poet-dramatists had failed; he created a true poetry of the theater. The twentieth century is dotted with half-successful attempts at poetic drama by playwrights who lacked the requisite verbal facility for writing poetry or by versifiers whose theatrical efforts are difficult to accomplish onstage. Even successful verse dramatists such as T. S. Eliot, Christopher Fry, and Archibald MacLeish offer self-consciously "poetic" and "literary" efforts that lack the impact or even the "poetry" of the best prose dramas of the period. García Lorca, who was both a great lyric poet and a practical man of the theater, fused all of the elements of the stage—language, movement, ritual, color, lighting, spectacle, and music—into a single dramatic presentation.

Much of the power of these plays comes from the way García Lorca combines a complex, sophisticated theatrical style with extremely simple dramatic situations. Although the original impulse for *Blood Wedding* came from a real incident, the basic plot—a bride stolen from her wedding by a lover—is a perennial one. Leonardo Felíx and the Bride are victims of their own uncontrollable emotions. He has a wife and child; she fervently desires the social and financial stability that marriage to the Bridegroom will bring. Since the entire society favors that match, they know that their passionate act will have fatal consequences. These logical and moral considerations, however, are irrelevant to them in the face of their powerful, passionate feelings.

García Lorca develops and expands the meanings of this tragedy with a dynamic synthesis of realistic, poetic, and symbolic theatrical devices. On the realistic level, he presents vivid, intense characterizations. The Bridegroom's Mother is an impressive, anguished woman who, having lost both husband and son, expects tragedy, but resolutely pursues the family destiny all the same. The Bridegroom is likable, sensitive, but hesitant, perhaps frightened by his pending marriage to a woman who is more strong-willed and passionate than he. The Bride's passion for Leonardo and clear disappointment at having lost him are evident from her first scene; her fervent desire for security and social respectability are doomed from the start and her troubled attempt to keep her emotions under control excites fear and pity in the audience. Leonardo—the only character in the play individualized by a name—is vital, volatile, frustrated, and overtly sexual; the intensity of his passion and the power of his attraction suggest energies and drives that are more than human. The Bride refers to him as "a dark river, choked with brush, that brought near me the undertone of its rushes and its whispered song."

All of this realistic characterization and conflict are then reinforced and extended by García Lorca's use of color, light, music, poetry, and symbolism. Even in the most realistic scenes there are patterns of imagery, both verbal and visual, that underscore the play's action. The Bridegroom's Mother broods over knives. Leonardo's mother-in-law sings a lullaby with images of "frozen horses" and "blood flowing like water." The Bride wears black. Leonardo identifies himself with his horse—a traditional symbol of sexual passion—and the Bridegroom is likened to "a dove/ with his breast a firebrand."

The masterful third act offers a full realization of García Lorca's stage poetry. The relative realism of the first two acts gives way to a stylized forest landscape, and symbolic figures replace "real" ones. The final violence is previewed by a "debate" between the Moon—a sexually ambiguous young man—and the Beggar Woman, an image of death. The Moon stands for the primal emotion that has driven the fated couple together; the Beggar Woman represents the inevitable consequence of that passion. The scene culminates with the last meeting between Leonardo and the Bride as the realistic and the symbolic fuse into a powerful acknowledgment of unbridled love, desperate loss, and heroic defiance. The play's finale, when the bodies of Leonardo and the Bridegroom are brought in to be mourned by a stage full of bereaved women, leaves the audience completely drained of emotion—a tragic catharsis reminiscent of the greatest classical dramas.

Further Reading

Bonaddio, Federico, ed. *A Companion to Federico García Lorca*. New York: Tamesis, 2007. An overview of García Lorca's life and work. The introduction provides a biography, while chapter 2 focuses on his plays. Three other chapters discuss the treatment of religion, politics, and gender and sexuality in his work. The references to *Blood Wedding* are listed in the index.

Crow, John A. *Federico García Lorca*. Berkeley: University of California Press, 1945. Examines the biographical, thematic, formalistic, and historical elements of García Lorca's poetry and drama. An excellent source for serious study.

Duran, Manuel, ed. *Lorca: A Collection of Critical Essays*. Englewood Cliffs, N.J.: Prentice-Hall, 1962. Extensive examination of the aspects of poetry and drama and how they complement each other in García Lorca's writings. Reveals how *Blood Wedding* is deeply rooted in Spanish folk and literary traditions, and analyzes the play in great detail.

Edwards, Gwynne. *Lorca: Living in the Theatre*. London: Peter Owen, 2003. Evaluates García Lorca's plays within the context of his private life and the political and social situation in Spain during the 1920's and 1930's. Chapter 3 is devoted to an analysis of *Blood Wedding*.

_____. *Lorca: The Theater Beneath the Sand*. Boston: Marion Boyars, 1980. Discussion of García Lorca's dramatic technique and innovation in the theater. Includes a thorough treatment of themes and characteristics and an intensive discussion of *Blood Wedding*. Excellent source for an understanding of García Lorca's scope, technique, and talent for dramatic expression.

Gibson, Ian. "Blood Wedding." In *Federico García Lorca: A Life*. New York: Pantheon Books, 1989. This chapter gives a historical and psychological discussion of the people of the Andalusia region of Spain. Analysis includes examination of the Spanish Fascist political response to the play and a discussion of the play as a timeless tragedy.

Honig, Edwin. *García Lorca*. Rev. ed. New York: New Directions, 1980. An excellent source for discussion of García Lorca's works. A critical guidebook of his life and work; treats in detail all of his available writings. Provides insight into how his poetry matured into full-scale drama.

Stone, Rob. *The Flamenco Tradition in the Works of Federico García Lorca and Carlos Saura: The Wounded Throat*. Lewiston, N.Y.: Edwin Mellen Press, 2004. Examines the elements of flamenco art in the poems and plays of García Lorca and the films of Saura. Stone maintains that both men used flamenco elements as a means of depicting marginalized and disenfranchised people. *Blood Wedding* and two other García Lorca plays are analyzed in chapter 5, while Saura's film adaptation of *Blood Wedding* is discussed in chapter 6.

The Bluest Eye

Author: Toni Morrison (1931-   )
First published: 1970
Type of work: Novel
Type of plot: Social realism
Time of plot: 1940-1941
Locale: Lorain, Ohio

Principal characters:
CLAUDIA MACTEER, a nine-year-old African American
FRIEDA MACTEER, Claudia's older sister
MRS. MACTEER, Claudia and Frieda's mother
PECOLA BREEDLOVE, friend of Claudia and Frieda
PAULINE BREEDLOVE, Pecola's mother
CHOLLY BREEDLOVE, Pecola's father
MAUREEN PEAL, a new girl in town
MR. HENRY, a boarder at the MacTeer home
MISS MARIE,
CHINA, and
POLAND, prostitutes living above the Breedloves
SOAPHEAD CHURCH, a psychic and spiritualist

The Story:

In the autumn of 1940, Claudia MacTeer, a nine-year-old African American child, begins the school year. The weather cools, and Claudia becomes ill. Her mother takes care of her, but Claudia does not understand that her mother's harsh words come from worry rather than anger. Claudia later remembers the pain she felt when her mother rubbed ointment on her to heal the illness; she also remembers the touch of soft hands (not connected to a real person) that comforted her in the night. Claudia reveals knowledge about the lives of the people around her family in the community of Lorain, Ohio. She and her older sister Frieda learn about life after hearing adult conversations.

The family is exposed to two boarders at their home: Mr. Henry and eleven-year-old Pecola Breedlove. The older girls become friends, but Claudia is different than the older children. Pecola and Frieda have reached a point in their lives where they appreciate and even adore film star Shirley Temple and white baby dolls. Claudia, on the other hand, hates what they represent. She complains about the gifts of hard white dolls given at Christmas and wishes that she could just have a day when she matters to someone. She dissects the dolls, searching for what makes them so appealing. She does not find an answer, and is reprimanded by adults.

Autumn also brings a description of Lorain, a small, depressed town where African Americans and poor whites live their lives. Housed in one particular building are a family of Roma (gypsies), a Hungarian baker, the Breedlove family, and prostitutes.

The Breedloves—Cholly, Pauline, Sammy, and Pecola—now live on the first floor in a poorly constructed apartment with poorly constructed furnishings. The family's ugliness comes to light, along with the way each family member lives with their respective physical deformity. Pecola yearns for blue eyes. Her desire for affection is divulged in her friendship with the three prostitutes—China, Poland, and Miss Marie—who live upstairs, and Miss Marie's life story is exposed.

Winter comes, bringing a new girl to the school. Claudia immediately shares her distinct dislike for Maureen Peal, the child of wealthy black parents. When Claudia, Frieda, and Maureen see Pecola being teased by a group of boys, Frieda steps in to protect her friend. Maureen's curiosity about the boys' taunting of Pecola opens a dialogue about the novelty of sexual changes. She treats Pecola, but not the MacTeer girls, to an ice cream cone, and then feels this gives her the right to ask Pecola questions about the taunts. When Pecola refuses to answer, Maureen's curious questions become jeers, and Pecola wilts. Claudia and Frieda chase Maureen away, calling her names, but Claudia becomes angry at Pecola's lack of backbone. The inquisitiveness about sexuality increases when the girls return home to find Mr. Henry entertaining prostitutes while their mother is out.

Winter also brings a new family to town. Contrasted to the hardworking MacTeer family and the dysfunctional Breedlove family is the oddity of an educated, sophisticated, untouchable, and Southern, light-skinned black woman. Geraldine is married to Louis, and they have a child named Junior. Geraldine has a well-kept home with nice furnishings, a supportive husband, and a son whom she does not know how to love. Geraldine's inability to do anything more than skim over the surface of life has left her son searching for emotion. Junior finds his outlet in cruelty. Unfortunately, his path intersects with that of Pecola.

As life for the girls passes into spring, more tragedies ensue. Mr. Henry touches Frieda's breasts, and Frieda's father attacks Mr. Henry in defense of his child. Frieda, again through hearing adult conversations, fears she has been damaged. Later, a childish misunderstanding leads Claudia and Frieda on a mission to get alcohol from Pecola, whose father is a known drunk. They find their friend waiting outside the home where her mother, Pauline, works. While they wait to help Pecola take the wash back to the dwelling, the white family's child comes into the kitchen. A pie is knocked off the counter. Though Pecola is the one burned by the hot juices, Pauline rebukes her and chases her away, then gently comforts the white child.

Spring also brings childhood memories to Pauline and Cholly Breedlove. Pauline remembers a childhood injury, the discovery that organization brings comfort, and her early married years. Early married life had been good, but loneliness, poverty, responsibility for her own family, and abuse had taken its toll. Pauline finds that working for a white family gives her the sense of belonging that she could not find with Cholly or her children. Cholly uses his history of being rejected as an excuse for his adult behavior. His story ends abruptly when he rapes eleven-year-old Pecola.

Soaphead Church advertises his services as a psychic, spiritualist, healer, and detective of sorts. His high opinion of himself does not take into account that he is a sexual predator. When Pecola comes to him asking for blue eyes, he tricks her. He then justifies his actions in a letter to God, expressing his superiority over the Creator.

It is now the beginning of summer. Claudia and Frieda learn through adult gossip that Pecola is pregnant with her own father's child. None of the adults want the baby to live, and Claudia longs for someone to care for the innocent life. She and Frieda decide to make a sacrifice to help the baby, so they bury the bike money they have been saving and plant marigold seeds, sure that the growth of the seeds will lead to the healthy development of Pecola's baby in God's eyes.

Next, Pecola is in conversation with an alternate personality that she had created while she was pregnant. Pecola believes that the baby has gained the blue eyes she herself so desired. As troubling as the split in Pecola's psyche, so too are the subtle hints that Cholly still rapes his daughter.

The baby dies, and Pecola is now a shadow, living in her own world. Claudia and Frieda fear their friend because they feel they have failed her in some unspoken way.

Critical Evaluation:

Toni Morrison, author, professor, editor, and speaker, has penned novels, works of nonfiction, children's books, and other works. In 1988, she won the Pulitzer Prize in fiction for her novel *Beloved*. Morrison's work has been instrumental in opening doors for a mainstream readership of African American literature. Her works are known for their exposure of racial issues through strong characterization, difficult themes, and varied points of view. *The Bluest Eye*, her first novel, is based on the memory of a childhood acquaintance's desire for blue eyes.

One of Morrison's common themes is community versus the individual. This theme confronts race issues through the consideration of the individual as other and the examination of a community's unwillingness to provide for or support the oppressed. Early in *The Bluest Eye*, Claudia MacTeer relates how she and her sister Frieda learn about their community.

> Their conversation is like a gently wicked dance: sound meets sound, curtsies, shimmies, and retires. . . . We do not, cannot, know the meanings of all their words, for we are nine and ten years old. So we watch their faces, their hands, their feet, and listen for truth in timbre.

In listening to this "dance," the girls learn how to behave, what to believe, and how to view the individuals in the community. Pecola's pregnancy, specifically, is related through this communal gossip.

Another community issue is intraracial tension. Maureen Peal, the wealthy light-skinned girl who temporarily befriends Pecola, and Geraldine, the light-skinned Southern mother of Junior, personify the issue of skin tone. Their denunciation of Pecola reflects the rejection of African Americans through white oppression.

Family is the strongest example of community in the novel. While the MacTeer family protects Frieda from Mr. Henry's advances, more important is the contrast between the MacTeer parents and the Breedlove parents. Claudia's father protects his child, while Cholly Breedlove is his daughter's predator.

Pauline and Cholly blame segregation from the broader community, because of poverty and racism, for their life choices. Furthermore, the community's lack of concern for Pecola or her baby is another example of a failure of responsibility. Many of the adults blame Pecola for her pregnancy, and only Claudia and Frieda seem to care about Pecola's baby. The cruelty of the women in the community extends to their condemnations of the baby.

> She [Pecola] be lucky if it don't live. Bound to be the ugliest thing walking. . . . Can't help but be. Ought to be a law: two ugly people doubling up like that to make more ugly. Be better off in the ground.

Claudia remembers that

we were embarrassed for Pecola, hurt for her, and finally we just felt sorry for her. . . . I believe our sorrow was the more intense because nobody else seemed to share it. . . . [W]e listened for the one who would say "Poor little girl," or "Poor baby," but there was only head-wagging where those words should have been.

At the end of the novel, Pecola is left wandering, both literally and symbolically, on the edges of the community that has rejected her.

One distinction between community and individual is self-hatred. Morrison explores this through Pecola's desire for blue eyes, through Claudia's hatred of blond-haired and blue-eyed white icons, and through the variety of characters. The Breedlove family member's self-hatred stems from their belief that they "were not relentlessly and aggressively ugly." Cholly, alone, is ugly because of his actions.

Another critical concern is the novel's narrative form. Morrison begins the novel with a passage from an old-fashioned elementary-school primer. This passage presents the typical white family as Dick and Jane, who live in a nice home, have solid parents, and enjoy life. Pieces of this primer are used as a contrast to start most chapters. Immediately following is a brief reminiscence from Claudia, providing basic thematic concerns. The rest of the novel is broken into the four seasons that pass as Pecola's story is revealed, intertwined with Claudia's observations. The chapters in each section vary in point of view: first-person, omniscient, and objective.

Claudia's chapters are always first-person, but in some chapters, she tells the story as a child. The chapters about Pecola also are often presented in first-person; however, she is further victimized because she is never the narrator. Instead, through the words of others, she is pitied (by Claudia), overlooked (by her mother), raped (by her father, Cholly), used and manipulated (by Soaphead), and objectified (by insanity).

Theresa L. Stowell

Further Reading

Eichelberger, Julia. *Prophets of Recognition: Ideology and the Individual in Novels by Ralph Ellison, Toni Morrison, Saul Bellow, and Eudora Welty.* Baton Rouge: Louisiana State University Press, 1999. Fascinating study that considers how Morrison's characters search for individual identity through a desire for or sometimes refutation of power. For undergraduate and graduate students. Includes a literature review.

Fultz, Lucille P. *Toni Morrison: Playing with Difference.* Urbana: University of Illinois Press, 2003. Examines Morrison's approach to differences (for example, black and white, male and female, wealth and poverty) in her intricate narratives.

Malmgren, Carl D. "Texts, Primers, and Voices in Toni Morrison's *The Bluest Eye*." *Critique* 41, no. 3 (Spring, 2000): 251-262. An insightful article that explores Morrison's use of the basic-reading-primer story of Dick and Jane as well as her varied narrative forms. Discusses the changing point of view used in the novel and how the narrators affect the outcome of the story.

O'Reilly, Andrea. *Toni Morrison and Motherhood: A Politics of the Heart.* Albany: State University of New York Press, 2004. Discusses Morrison's depiction of mothers and motherhood in her works. Considers how she addresses mothering and racism, sexism, and culture.

Pryse, Marjorie, and Hortense J. Spillers, eds. *Conjuring: Black Women, Fiction, and Literary Tradition.* Bloomington: Indiana University Press, 1985. A collection of essays about African American women's writing. Includes analyses of sexual assault, insanity, and silence in *The Bluest Eye*.

Sova, Dawn. *Literature Suppressed on Sexual Grounds.* New York: Facts On File, 2006. A collection of essays based on books, including *The Bluest Eye*, that have been censored because of their sexual content. Entries include publication information, summaries, and the background to each case of censorship. Includes a bibliography.

Stein, Karen F. *Reading, Learning, Teaching Toni Morrison.* New York: Peter Lang, 2009. An excellent primer for beginning studies of Morrison and her works. Includes a chapter on *The Bluest Eye* as well as an introductory chapter about the background to Morrison's fiction.

Tally, Justine, ed. *The Cambridge Companion to Toni Morrison.* New York: Cambridge University Press, 2007. An invaluable, comprehensive text covering the span of Morrison's work. The chapter on *The Bluest Eye* considers the novel alongside *Sula* (1973) as examples of the bildungsroman, or coming-of-age novel.

Wallowitz, Laraine. "Disrupting the Gaze That Condemns: Applying a Critical Literacy Perspective to Toni Morrison's *The Bluest Eye*." *NERA Journal* 43, no. 2 (2007): 36-42. Highlights the effect of the issues of the white gaze and oppression in the novel. Provides some background information on the type of criticism that will be helpful to general readers.

The Bohemians of the Latin Quarter

Author: Henri Murger (1822-1861)
First published: Scènes de la vie de Bohème, serial,
  1847-1849; book, 1851 (English translation, 1901)
Type of work: Novel
Type of plot: Sentimental
Time of plot: Mid-nineteenth century
Locale: Paris

Principal characters:
RODOLPHE, a poet
MARCEL, a painter
SCHAUNARD, a musician and painter
COLLINE, a philosopher
JACQUES, a sculptor
MIMI, Rodolphe's beloved
MUSETTE, Marcel's beloved
FRANCINE, Jacques's lover
PHEMIE, Schaunard's lover

The Story:

Alexander Schaunard, a poor musician and painter, is unable to pay the rent for his cold and windy top-floor room in the Latin Quarter of Paris. Eluding the porter who is on watch to keep Schaunard from moving his few pieces of furniture, the musician tries in vain to borrow money from his impecunious friends. Shortly after he leaves the tenement, Marcel, a painter, comes to take over the room Schaunard vacated. The painter has no furniture except his canvas flats, and he is pleased to find that his quarters contain Schaunard's table, chairs, bed, and piano.

Although Schaunard approaches all of his friends in alphabetical order, he is unable to borrow more than three of the seventy-five francs he needs to satisfy his landlord. At dinnertime, his stomach leads him to Mother Cadet's, famous for her rabbit stew. He arrives too late, however; his table companion, Colline, ordered the last stew of the evening. Colline, barricaded behind a pile of books, kindly offers to share the stew with Schaunard. Not to be outdone, Schaunard orders extra wine. Colline orders yet another bottle, Schaunard calls for a salad, and in conclusion Colline orders dessert. By the time they leave Mother Cadet's, they are well pleased with the world. Stopping by a café for coffee and liqueurs, they fall into conversation with Rodolphe, who, to judge by his clothes, can only be a poet.

Rodolphe soon becomes as expansive as they. Forgetting that he no longer has a room, Schaunard offers to take Colline and Rodolphe home with him, for the hour is late and they live at the far ends of Paris. As they reel into the house, the porter, too, forgets that Schaunard was dispossessed. The musician is a bit taken aback when he finds another key in his door, but the three make so much noise that Marcel opens the door to them and gladly accepts the supper they brought with them. Schaunard and Marcel decide to stay together, since the musician owns the furniture and the painter has paid the

rent. The other two are surprised to find themselves in a strange room the next morning. After another day and night of convivial treating, when all but Schaunard still have a few francs in their pockets, the four decide to meet daily.

One day, Marcel receives an invitation to dine with a patron of the arts. He is famished and yearns to go, but he realizes that he has no dress coat. Just then a stranger appears at the door asking for Schaunard, whom he wants to hire to paint his portrait. Marcel points to the caller's coat, and Schaunard, preparing to begin the painting, asks the man to doff his coat and put on a borrowed dressing gown because the picture, intended for the man's family, ought to be as informal as possible. Marcel appropriates the coat and goes to the dinner. Schaunard persuades his sitter to send out for a fine dinner and keeps the man entertained until Marcel returns.

One evening in Lent, Rodolphe is disturbed to find that everywhere he looks people and birds are pairing off. Schaunard tells him that he is in love with love and offers to find him a girl. Schaunard does produce a fresh, pleasing girl, but she refuses to stay with Rodolphe more than a few days. She does not understand his poetizing.

Lacking money for his rent, Rodolphe turns to his stovemaker uncle, who wants him to write a manual on stovemaking. Having learned that an advance to Rodolphe means that he will disappear until the money has been spent, the uncle keeps the young man locked up. The manual proves to be slow and boring work. Rodolphe strikes up an acquaintance with an actress on the floor below, and she promises to get his play produced. When a letter arrives with word that Rodolphe has won three hundred francs, the uncle refuses to let him go. Rodolphe makes a knotted rope out of his quilt and slides down to the actress's apartment. She provides a disguise for him, enabling him to leave the house. Later, she does have his play produced, but it brings the young writer neither fame nor fortune. Before long, his address, as he says, is Avenue St. Cloud, third tree as you go out of the Bois de Boulogne, fifth branch.

Mademoiselle Musette is a friend of Rodolphe, but she is never more than a friend, though neither knows why. When he asks leave to introduce Marcel, Musette invites them both to a party. She was just jilted by her lover, the councilor of state. On the day of her party, her creditors take her furniture from her rooms and put it in the courtyard to be sold the following morning. Unabashed, Musette has her party in the courtyard and invites all the tenants. They are still laughing and singing when the porters come to take the furniture away. It is such a successful party that Rodolphe and Marcel carry Musette off to the country for the day.

On their return to Paris, Rodolphe allows Marcel to take Musette home. Soon after he leaves her at her doorway, he feels a tap on his shoulder. There stands Musette, who tells him that she no longer has a key to her room and that it is after eleven o'clock at night. Calling her the goddess of mirth, Marcel takes her home with him. The next morning, he buys her a pot of flowers. She says that she will stay with him until the flowers fade. He is surprised at their continued freshness until the day he finds Musette watering them carefully.

M. Benoit is dunning Rodolphe for three quarters of rent, three pairs of shoes, and additional loans of money, for he is landlord, shoemaker, and moneylender all in one. Rodolphe walks the streets all day in the hope that providence will provide. When he returns, the room has already been rented to someone else, but the landlord allows Rodolphe to go upstairs to claim his papers. A young woman named Mimi is the new tenant. After one look at Rodolphe, she tells M. Benoit that she was expecting the gentleman.

On Christmas Eve, the four friends, accompanied by Mimi and Musette and Schaunard's Phemie, repair to the Café Momus, whose owner and wife have a weakness for the arts; relying on that weakness, the bohemians order a fine supper. In their high holiday spirits, they run up a huge bill before they draw lots to see who should be the one to speak diplomatically to the proprietor. Schaunard is having no success on that errand when a stranger, Barbemuche, asks to be introduced and offers to pay the bill. Schaunard suggests a game of billiards to settle the matter. Barbemuche has the good taste to lose the match, and the bohemians' dignity is saved.

Neither Mimi nor Musette can resist going off with other lovers. One time, Mimi and Rodolphe quietly agree to separate, but it is not long before Mimi comes to call, ostensibly to take away her belongings. Instead, she stays with Rodolphe again.

Jacques, a sculptor, and the dressmaker Francine are tenants in the same apartment building. They meet one evening when Francine's candle is extinguished by the wind and she comes to Jacques to relight it. In doing so, she also loses her key and the two play a lovers' game in looking for it (since Jacques, who finds it right away, has been so clever as to hide it quickly in his pocket). Francine, ill with tuberculosis and suffering terribly in the cold Paris winter, as a last request, asks Jacques for a muff to warm her hands. Jacques buys her the muff, but Francine dies the next day. Upon her death, Jacques is distraught, and although he recovers somewhat from the heartbreak, he becomes ill and dies not long after in a pauper's hospital.

Musette was said to alternate between blue broughams and omnibuses. While she is living with M. Maurice, she receives a letter from Marcel asking her to come for dinner, for the friends even have wood for a fire. She receives the note in a roundabout way but leaves the bewildered M. Maurice immediately. Because snow is beginning to fall, she stops at a friend's house and meets an interesting young man there. Five days later, she arrives at Marcel's room. The fire is dying out, and the food is gone. She stays one day before returning to M. Maurice with the announcement that she quarreled with Marcel. She tells M. Maurice that each of her loves is the verse of a song, but Marcel is the refrain.

The second time Mimi and Rodolphe separate, she goes to live with Paul, a young viscount. Meeting by chance on the street, Mimi and Rodolphe bow. The poet goes home and writes a long poem for Mimi, which so irritates the young nobleman that he puts Mimi out of his house.

On another Christmas Eve, as Marcel and Rodolphe try to forget their sorrows, Mimi comes back, so ill that a doctor insists that she be taken at once to a hospital. She is afraid to go, even though her friends try to encourage her with the hope that she will be well by spring. Rodolphe goes to see her on the first visiting day. Before the next day for calling, he hears that she is dead. A few days later, his correspondent admits that he was mistaken, that Mimi was moved to a different ward. Rodolphe hurries to the hospital, only to have his hopes shattered forever. Mimi, grieved because Rodolphe failed to appear for the expected visit, died that morning.

One year later, Rodolphe writes a book that is receiving much critical attention. Schaunard produces an album of songs. Colline marries well, and Marcel's pictures are accepted for the annual exhibit. Musette comes to spend a final night with Marcel before marrying the guardian of her last lover.

Critical Evaluation:

Henry Murger's *The Bohemians of the Latin Quarter*, which is also sometimes translated as *Scenes of Bohemian Life*, is not a literary masterpiece in the traditional sense, but it is a classic work. Murger, the son of a tailor/concierge and a man of little formal education, learned about writing from reading such popular nineteenth century French authors as Victor Hugo and Alfred de Musset, as well as from absorbing what he could from his associates.

Life in mid-nineteenth century Paris was a mixture of many elements. Louis-Philippe, who ruled from 1830 to 1848, had limited appreciation for the arts and literature, and the days of patronage for artists had faded. Murger's first literary attempts, mostly poetry and bits of prose, met with little success and he lived meagerly, experiencing firsthand the poverty, hunger, and illness that afflicted so many people in Paris. It was not until 1845, when he began to write the short episodes for the French publication *Le Corsaire*, a newspaper that was read avidly by the artist population of the Latin Quarter, that he began to gain a reputation. However, because the remuneration for one such article was a mere fifteen francs, his poverty continued.

By the end of 1846, more than two dozen of Murger's vignettes had been published in *Le Corsaire*, and he had established a small following. In 1849, Théodore Barrière, a successful Parisian theatrical producer, joined with Murger to produce a musical play, *La Vie de Bohème*, based on the experiences of Murger's characters. It was as a result of this play that Murger gained true recognition. His characters, positioned halfway between reality and fantasy, won the hearts of French readers who were tired of the drudgery of revolution and political strife.

In 1851, Murger published the combined episodes in book form. The value of *The Bohemians of the Latin Quarter* lies less in the work's literary style than in the fresh, unusual, expressive way in which Murger creates his characters and situations. Murger's scenes, which do not really constitute a novel, contrast the cruel realities of daily life defined by unrelieved material need with fantasies of wealth, comfort, and delightful suppers in the Latin Quarter. Probing social margins and testing society's rules of propriety, Murger's characters, not being able to afford other entertainment, turn facets of everyday life into art. Although poverty and its resultant hunger, illness, and desperation are never far from the surface, the book is filled with humorous scenes created by the characters themselves in their attempt to keep life bearable.

The Bohemians of the Latin Quarter is fundamentally an autobiographical work. Murger was born in the Latin Quarter, and it was there that he struggled to achieve literary success in his early adulthood. The Café Momus, where the bohemians meet, was a place Murger, too, frequented. His friends from that time, called the "Water-Drinkers," appear in his work as members of the "Bohemian Club." The Water-Drinkers were a group that included poets, a painter, a philosopher, and a sculptor, and Murger's fictional characters closely parallel them in their professions and personalities, though in some instances he combined the traits of different people to create a single character. The poet Rodolphe represents Murger himself, however, and his painter friend Marcel remains Marcel in the book.

Murger's first love, Marie Fonblanc, and his later beloved, Lucile Louvet, serve as models for Mimi, Musette, and Francine. It was Lucile's death that served as the model for the death of the character Mimi, which many consider the most poignant moment in the book. The women are categorized as "grisettes," poor young women of nineteenth century Paris who were unencumbered by middle-class restrictions. They were known for their gaiety, capriciousness, frugality, and fastidious lovemaking. Unwilling to sell their favors unless driven to it by need, they are portrayed as not promiscuous but valiant.

Murger depicts the picturesque details of everyday life in the Latin Quarter in a nonchalant and often conversational style that easily draws the readers into the lives of the characters. Readers feel a kinship with the youthful spirited artists, and they empathize with their pain as well as their delight. Certain recurrent themes unify the work, perhaps, most important, exposure to cold and hunger. Many of the episodes center around the characters' efforts either to alleviate their want or, if that is not possible, to find a way to forget about it. The freezing garret, snowy Parisian scenes, and Mimi's cold hands all arouse a longing for spring, the sun, or enough wood for a fire. The healing capacity of warmth becomes a familiar reference.

The term "bohemian" to refer to the carefree and impoverished lifestyle of the struggling artists of nineteenth century Paris did not exist at the time of Murger's writing. It was in fact this collection of sketches that, more than any other single work, forged the concept of "bohemian" artistic life, which within a few years became a permanent part of literary and social history. By the 1890's, Murger's play had been revived five times, and in 1896 in Turin, Italy, one of the most enduring operatic masterpieces, Giacomo Puccini's *La Bohème* (1896), which is based on Murger's book, was given its premiere. It is the pervading spirit of the youthful resilience that makes *The Bohemians of the Latin Quarter* a classic of French literature.

"Critical Evaluation" by Sandra C. McClain

Further Reading

Baldick, Robert. *The First Bohemian: The Life of Henry Murger.* London: Hamish Hamilton, 1961. Thorough biography of Murger, with an introduction giving background on the period and an extensive, although mostly French, bibliography. Offers biographical information about Murger and his literary career and discusses his style and the basis of characters and situations in his book.

Gluck, Mary. *Popular Bohemia: Modernism and Urban Culture in Nineteenth-Century Paris.* Cambridge, Mass.: Harvard University Press, 2005. Gluck's examination of the nineteenth century French artistic sensibility includes several references to Murger's "sentimental bohemia" that are listed in the index.

Josephs, Herbert. "Murger's Parisian Scenes and Puccini's *La Bohème.*" In *La Bohème,* by Henry Murger, translated by Elizabeth Ward Hughes. Salt Lake City: Peregrine Smith Books, 1988. Addresses specific aspects of Murger's writing, as well as the transformation of the novel into a libretto for Giacomo Puccini's opera.

Lewis, D. B. Wyndham. Introduction to *La Bohème,* by Henry Murger, translated by Elizabeth Ward Hughes. Salt Lake City: Peregrine Smith Books, 1988. Lewis's introduction to the first translation discusses the history of the book, aspects of Murger's style, and the value of his writing.

Moss, Arthur, and Evalyn Marvel. *The Legend of the Latin Quarter: Henry Murger and the Birth of Bohemia.* New York: Beechhurst Press, 1946. Gives an excellent overview and background information on *The Bohemians of the Latin Quarter.*

Seigel, Jerrold. *Bohemian Paris: Culture, Politics, and the Boundaries of Bourgeois Life, 1830-1930.* New York: Viking, 1986. Discusses the history of the concept of the bohemian lifestyle in Paris; includes background and specific discussion of Murger's writing and his influence; credits Murger with having defined bohemia in his writing.

Bonjour Tristesse

Author: Françoise Sagan (1935-2004)
First published: 1954 (English translation, 1955)
Type of work: Novel
Type of plot: Psychological
Time of plot: After World War II
Locale: French Riviera

Principal characters:
CECILE, a seventeen-year-old French girl
RAYMOND, her forty-year-old widowed father
ANNE LARSEN, a friend of Raymond's deceased wife whom Raymond decides to marry
ELSA MACKENBOURG, Raymond's young mistress
CYRIL, a young law student in love with Cecile

The Story:

On vacation in the south of France, Cecile and her youthful, philandering father Raymond are spending a leisurely, hedonistic summer in a rented villa. With them is Raymond's mistress of the moment, Elsa, a beautiful, red-haired woman almost half his age whom Cecile finds entertaining but rather simpleminded and nonthreatening to her companionable relationship with her father. The three of them spend lazy days swimming and lolling on the beach, and they dance and drink at the casinos into the nights. Cecile, over-indulged by her father, is enjoying being away from school, where she has flunked a couple of her exams. Raymond is unconcerned with her lack of interest in studying to retake her exams. He acts mostly oblivious to his responsibilities as a father and is more concerned with being his daughter's "friend" and "companion."

When the three vacationers have been at the villa for a while, Raymond announces that he has invited an old friend, Anne Larsen, to spend time with them at the villa. Anne was a good friend of Raymond's dead wife and has been part of their lives off and on during the fifteen years since Cecile's mother died. Cecile likes her, even though Anne's more conventional way of life and views on how a young girl should be raised differ considerably from the way her father is rearing her. When she learns that Anne will be staying at the villa, however, she has misgivings, especially since Elsa is also there.

When Anne arrives, Raymond acts pleased, Cecile is conflicted, and Elsa feels threatened. Elsa's reaction proves to be well founded, because it is soon obvious that Raymond is becoming very attached to Anne. Even Cecile admits that there is much to admire about Anne: She is not only beautiful but also cultured, intelligent, and an accomplished and successful fashion designer. She brings to the villa a more principled way of living and forces the others to a reluctant awareness of the shallowness of their lives.

Cecile begins to worry, however, when she notices that as her father gets closer to Anne, he is becoming more conventional in his habits. To take her mind off this troubling change, she diverts herself with a dalliance with a young law student named Cyril. Cyril has fallen in love with Cecile and even asks her to marry him. When Raymond tells his daughter, after several days, that he and Anne plan to marry, Cecile fluctuates between being pleased that Anne will be part of her family and worrying about Anne's effects on their family. Cecile believes that having to live Anne's kind of conventional life, "subjected to fixed habits," would destroy her father and Cecile as well. More afraid of losing the lifestyle she has grown accustomed to with her father than of adapting to a more settled way of life, Cecile decides she must prevent the marriage from taking place.

Cecile enlists both Cyril and Elsa in a plot to pretend they have become lovers. She believes that the rather vain Raymond will become jealous and try to seduce Elsa back to prove that he is youthful and attractive enough to get any woman he wants. Cyril goes along with the plan because he loves Cecile and wants to please her. Elsa does so because she thinks she can win over Raymond and convince him to marry her instead of Anne. Cecile manages to arrange for Raymond to see Elsa and Cyril at various times and places, looking as if they are in love. As Cecile suspects, Raymond becomes jealous. He not only still has some interest in Elsa but, even more, he needs to prove to himself that he is "not an old fogey." Thus, when he finally gets a chance to be alone with Elsa, he embraces and kisses her. Thanks to Cecile's manipulations, Anne sees them.

Stunned and hurt by Raymond's betrayal, Anne gets into her car and roars away from the villa, driving too fast and too recklessly. Cecile and Raymond try to stop her, but to no avail, and they wait nervously for her to return. Later that evening, they learn that Anne's car has gone off the road over a 150-foot bluff and she has died in the crash. It appears to have been an accident, but Cecile, knowing what she does of her plot to create a schism between Anne and Raymond and having seen Anne as she drove off in a fit of anguish, knows it could have been suicide.

For a month after Anne's funeral in Paris, Cecile and Raymond are desolate, Raymond because of his betrayal of Anne and Cecile because of the disastrous results of her immature scheme against Anne. After a while, though, both Cecile and Raymond drift back into their familiar and comfortable pre-Anne way of life.

Critical Evaluation:

Françoise Sagan, born Françoise Quoirez, was a child of a well-to-do family, educated at convent schools and at the Sorbonne. She failed her second-year examination to qualify for a higher academic degree at the Sorbonne, and in what she has suggested was an effort to placate her parents, she spent the summer writing *Bonjour Tristesse* ("Hello sadness"). She was only eighteen years old. The novel's seventeen-year-old heroine, Cecile, narrates the story, which has been praised for its mature style, its perceptiveness of human character, and Sagan's fine portrayal of an adolescent's emotional confusion. The brief, 125-page novel was a huge commercial success, with more than 810,000 copies sold in France by 1958 and more than one million copies sold in the United States. It has been translated into twenty languages and was awarded the prestigious Prix des Critiques. Sagan's lighter, escapist novel was a welcome change from the more profound, more philosophical or metaphysical writings of some of her literary predecessors. With this first and her subsequent novels, she was soon considered the spokesperson for a "particular brand of French upper-middle-class ennui."

Divided into two parts, the novel first introduces Cecile; her worldly, amoral father, Raymond; and his mistress Elsa in Part 1. Cecile as narrator reveals herself as simultaneously intelligent, sophisticated, and naïve. As is true of many self-absorbed teenagers, she is familiar with many aspects of grown-up behavior while naïvely unaware of what mature life is really all about—although she thinks she knows all she needs to know and has seen it all. When Anne Larsen comes on the scene, a surprising side of Cecile is revealed. Though no more self-absorbed than most, her exposure to one kind of grown-up living under her father's casual tutelage has caused her to be imprudent and selfish. She becomes manipulative and even perverse in her desire to reassert her position in her father's affections and, lacking that, to stop the marriage between Anne and her father.

Part 2 expands this newly revealed side of Cecile, showing her evolving into an even more conflicted personality. She changes from moment to moment, from being a child longing to win back or hold onto the favor of a beloved parent, or surrogate, as Anne has been to her in the past, to being a crafty schemer with no scruples. Her ambivalence toward all the other major characters keeps her in shifting states of disquiet. By the time Anne's tragic demise occurs, a reader has likely run the gamut of feeling about Cecile, from liking and disliking and being disappointed to feeling a vague optimism that she could turn out to be the person one hopes she is.

Cecile's characterization is so well drawn that this young girl with all her flaws is completely believable. She is the recognizable teenage girl, motivated by the love she has for her father and by the jealousy his relationship with Anne has provoked. Twenty-first century readers may not be as shocked with Cecile as were the readers of the 1950's. Most, however, will still be drawn to her typically teenage need to admire and even revere those adults important in her life, such as Anne, while she is still unable to resist an almost pathological desire to scandalize and even horrify them. Cecile flaunts her drinking, smoking, and sexual shenanigans with Cyril to encourage such reactions.

The novel features a deceptively simple structure, an attractive theme of an innocent in search of experience, and an artful portrayal of the decadence of a particular French social class, all delivered with irony and an easy narrative style. Sagan's narrator speaks from two points of view. Cecile tells her story after the events have occurred: At the beginning of Part 1, she says "That summer I was seventeen and perfectly happy." Cecile narrates the story, however, as if unaware of the events that will transpire. Sagan moves back and forth seamlessly between the unaware Cecile and the aware Cecile. Also, while the reader gets an intriguing insight into the psyche of an adolescent girl on the brink of womanhood, Cecile's and her father's lifestyle provides a fascinating view of an aspect of post-World War II French society.

Until Sagan produced several more of the forty-five novels she would write in her lifetime, many critics dismissed her as a superficial novelist. Her first-person narrative style and her youth seemed to confirm that she was not mature enough to write anything with any depth. However, her great success with *Bonjour Tristesse* and subsequent works lifted her into the pantheon of important modern French writers.

Bonjour Tristesse remains in print and, for a book more than half a century old, in reasonable demand.

Jane L. Ball

Further Reading

Brosman, Catherine, ed. "Françoise Sagan." In *French Novelists Since 1960*. Vol. 83 in *Dictionary of Literary Biography*. New Orleans: Tulane University/Gale Group, 1989. Provides biographical information and critical discussion of *Bonjour Tristesse* and others of Sagan's books.

Cismaru, Alfred. "Françoise Sagan: The Superficial Classic." *World Literature Today* 67 (Spring, 1993). Discusses Sagan's contribution to literature, including her own assessment of *Bonjour Tristesse* and some of her other works.

Hewitt, Nicholas, ed. *The Cambridge Companion to Modern French Culture*. New York: Cambridge University Press, 2003. Overview of French culture in the modern period; includes a section on post-World War II culture and identity and a section on French narrative fiction.

Lloyd, Heather. *Françoise Sagan: "Bonjour Tristesse."* Glasgow Introductory Guides to French Literature 35. Glasgow: French and German Publications, University of Glasgow, 1995. A brief overview of the novel, its themes and plot, and its critical context and reception.

Morello, Nathalie. *Françoise Sagan: "Bonjour Tristesse."* London: Grant and Cutler, 1998. An exploration of the novel that analyzes its structure and style, relevance to existentialism and feminism, and the character of Cecile.

Sagan, Françoise. *Reponses: The Autobiography of Françoise Sagan*. Translated by David Macey. Godalming, England: Black Sheep Books, 1979. Useful, among other things, for the author's discussion of the contemporary French writers who influenced her writing.

The Book of Evidence

Author: John Banville (1945-   )
First published: 1989
Type of work: Novel
Type of plot: Psychological
Time of plot: 1980's
Locale: Ireland

Principal characters:
FREDDIE MONTGOMERY, a mathematician, convicted of
    murder
DAPHNE, his wife
RANDOLPH, a drug dealer
AGUIRRE, a loan shark
CHARLIE FRENCH, Freddie's friend
DOLLY, Freddie's mother
JOANNE, her companion
HELMUT BEHRENS, an art connoisseur
ANNA BEHRENS, his daughter and Daphne's roommate
JOSEPHINE BELL, a servant who is killed by Freddie

The Story:

Freddie Montgomery, a former university lecturer in statistics, is in prison for murder, and he is ready to tell his story. He begins by describing the conditions of the prison he calls home, displaying in his tone a bravado that embraces his experience as a captured animal, a monster. He describes the noises and smells of prison but refuses to speak of the various kinds of darkness he and other prisoners face. This explicit refusal reveals the fear and uncertainty just beneath the controlled, analytical exterior Freddie generally presents.

Freddie introduces his wife, Daphne, and describes their life together, living in various places along the Mediterranean before returning to Ireland. He describes a life of modest luxury, and it becomes evident that they are living beyond their means. They make the acquaintance of a drug dealer named Randolph, and Freddie extorts a "loan" from him under the threat of revealing Randolph's criminal activities. Randolph gets the money from Aguirre, a loan shark. Freddie does not repay the loan, though, so he receives Randolph's ear in the mail—a threat from Aguirre. Freddie's wife and son are held as hostages, so Freddie returns to Ireland to raise money to pay Aguirre and secure his family's safety.

Eventually, Freddie goes to the home of his mother, Dolly, in Coolgrange, and engages in awkward conversation with her, a talk that escalates into fighting. He is surprised at the intimate nature of her relationship with her friend Joanne, after seeing them embrace and then finding them lying casually together on the bed. Dolly says that Joanne is like the son she never had. Freddie soon finds out, too, that his mother had sold some paintings that he had hoped to sell to raise money so that he could repay Aguirre. Dolly had sold the painting to Helmut Behrens, an art connoisseur, leading

Freddie to fly into a rage. Behrens, Freddie's father, and dealer and gallery owner Charlie French used to buy and sell paintings together.

Freddie leaves for Whitewater, the Behrens estate, to find out the fate of the paintings. His description of Whitewater shows his sensitivity to aesthetic stimuli, and he begins to describe in detail his love for the *Portrait of a Woman with Gloves*. From Behrens he learns that the paintings sold by his mother were of little value, and that they have been resold. Behrens had bought them from Dolly at an inflated price because of his admiration for her.

Nearly penniless and unable to return to Coolgrange, Freddie takes a room in town. The next day he hatches a half-baked plan to steal the painting that has captivated him. He buys twine, wrapping paper, rope, and a hammer, and rents a car for which he cannot pay.

Freddie returns to Whitewater to steal the painting, and it becomes evident that his interest in the work is not financial; rather, he is captivated by the picture in a kind of aesthetic obsession. He thinks about the picture's subject, its patron, and its artist, all those persons who had been involved in the circumstances of its creation. As his plan for stealing the painting falls apart, he compels a servant, Josephine Bell, to help him carry the framed work to his car. She is forced into the car, but she fights back. Freddie then beats her with a hammer. As he drives with her through the city, people assume that he is transporting an accident victim to the hospital. He drives Bell's body to the seaside and ditches his bloodstained jacket, the painting, the car, and his unfortunate victim.

Without money, clothes, or a plan, Freddie returns to the pub and meets up again with Charlie. He goes home with him and ends up staying with him for the next ten days or so. Freddie reads about the manhunt in the newspaper, and he is beginning to understand something about the life he had taken. He buys clothes with Charlie's credit cards and follows people around on the street, as if realizing for the first time the reality of other people. He drinks heavily. He also learns about Penelope, his father's former mistress, and learns that Charlie and Behrens were both attracted to his mother; he also finds out that Charlie had a relationship with her.

Charlie hosts a dinner party. Freddie serves as a butler and has a furtive sexual encounter with one of the guests. The police finally come for him, and he considers taking hostages. Instead, he goes with the police quietly.

Now in prison, Freddie receives a visit from his wife (whom Aguirre had released without payment). He learns that his son suffers from a developmental disability. He also learns that he has been cut out of his mother's will, but that his wife and son will live at Coolgrange as Joanne's guests. He reveals that the authorities have questions about Charlie, who made money on Freddie's father's paintings on at least two occasions. Finally, he appears to make some strides in his search for meaning.

Critical Evaluation:

In spite of its plot, John Banville's *The Book of Evidence* is no more an example of the crime or detective novel than is Fyodor Dostoevski's *Prestupleniye I nakazaniye* (1866; *Crime and Punishment*, 1886). Instead, *The Book of Evidence* uses the circumstances of Freddie Montgomery's painstaking reflection on his crime and incarceration to examine the question of truth.

As a former scientist and statistician, Freddie had explored and apparently already rejected the deceptive illusion of truth that science offers. He asserts early on that he had gravitated to science to make uncertainty more manageable. His overwhelming attraction to *Portrait of a Woman with Gloves*, the Dutch painting that leads him to theft and murder, can be understood as an abortive exploration into the attraction of artistic beauty. Freddie had always understood works of art only in terms of their monetary value.

It is only in the days following his crime that Freddie begins to take any interest in other people. He says at one point that he had killed Josephine Bell simply because he could. Elsewhere he attributes his crime to a failure of imagination, but it seems that the act of murder itself, or perhaps the series of events that preceded and followed it, unblock his imagination. While staying with Charlie French after the murder, he takes pleasure in following strangers on the street, indulging

in detailed speculation about them. It can be argued that his engagement with them is as superficial in its own way as his obsession with the painting, the subject and creator of which are lost and unknown to history. It can also be argued that his apparently benign interest in these nameless strangers, and the realization upon reading about his victim's humble life and bereaved mother that he has taken a human life as full and rich as his own, suggests a repentant breakthrough.

Early in the novel Freddie describes himself as an outsider, but near the end of the novel he appears to embrace humanity as he accepts his own guilt. The final lines of the novel bring this conclusion into question, however. Banville suggests that Freddie's confession is itself a construct, a web of lies. His sorrow over losing the community of men, which he never actually enjoyed, may or may not be sincere.

Another line of interpretation is suggested by Freddie's own sarcastic critique of Freudianism. He mocks the concept of the Oedipus complex as a too-easy explanation of his motivation, even as his emotional description of his father's death, during which he seems to reject the temptation to embroider it as he does everything else, underscores his complicated relationship with his family. He includes his mother and her companion in the list of women about whom he fantasizes, and perhaps more significant, he dreams of sitting with his father after having saved him from some life-threatening event in what appears to be a straightforward Freudian dream of wish fulfillment.

Even in these passages, though, it is never clear that Freddie's confession is sincere, because the ending casts doubt over the whole narrative. Still, the passages that deal with his father's death, his son's disability, and the acceptance of his separation from human society have the appearance, at least, of sincerity.

James S. Brown

Further Reading

D'hoker, Elke. *Visions of Alterity: Representation in the Works of John Banville*. New York: Rodopi, 2004. Provides readings of Banville's major novels, including *The Book of Evidence*, focusing on the relationship between the narrating self and the represented world.
Jackson, Tony E. "Science, Art, and the Shipwreck of Knowledge: The Novels of John Banville." *Contemporary Literature* 38, no. 3 (Autumn, 1997): 510-533. Considers the postmodern nature of knowledge and truth and their juxtaposition with the representation of everyday life in Banville's novels. Reads *The Book of Evidence* and

his other art novels as attempts to find truth in art after failing to do so in science, depicting the protagonist Freddie as a scientist engaging violently with art.

McMinn, Joseph. *The Supreme Fictions of John Banville.* New York: Manchester University Press, 1999. A survey of Banville's fiction focusing on the interrelationships between the novels and their postmodernist focus on the limitations of narrative. Addresses the chronological development of Banville's subjects and style.

McNamee, Brendan. *The Quest for God in the Novels of John Banville, 1973-2005: A Postmodern Spirituality.* Lewiston, N.Y.: Edwin Mellen Press, 2006. Discusses the tensions between realism and postmodernism in Banville's novels and shows how they form a bridge between mysticism and postmodernism.

Müller, Anja. "'You Have Been Framed': The Function of Ekphrasis for the Representation of Women in John Banville's Trilogy (*The Book of Evidence, Ghosts, Athena*)." *Studies in the Novel* 36, no. 2 (Summer, 2004): 185-205. A consideration of the role of ekphrasis (the imaginative verbal description of a work of art) in *The Book of Evidence* and two other novels, including analysis of the power dynamic inherent in the "framing" of female characters by the narrator.

The Book of Illusions

Author: Paul Auster (1947-   )
First published: 2002
Type of work: Novel
Type of plot: Narrative
Time of plot: 1930's and 1988
Locale: Vermont and New Mexico

Principal characters:
DAVID ZIMMER, a writer
HECTOR MANN, a silent-film comedian
FRIEDA SPELLING, Hector's wife
ALMA GRUND, Hector's biographer

The Story:

After his wife and children are killed in a plane crash, college teacher David Zimmer sinks into alcohol-fueled despair. Then, watching television one afternoon, he happens to see a clip from a silent comedy that makes him laugh. It is the first time he has laughed since he was widowed, and, although he does not feel able to resume his former life, he becomes fascinated by the comedian who made him laugh.

The actor in question is Hector Mann, a Latin American (though his origins are murky) who was famous for his moustache and his white suit. Mann made just twelve short films, right at the end of the silent era, before disappearing in mysterious circumstances in December, 1928. By chance, the twelve films he made have just been donated to various film archives in America and Europe, and Zimmer sets out to see them all. The quest quickly turns into a book, the first full-length critical study of Mann's work, which Zimmer publishes in 1988.

Within weeks of the book's publication, Zimmer receives a letter implying that Hector Mann is still alive. At first, Zimmer dismisses the letter as some sort of hoax, but eventually he returns home one night to find a young woman, Alma,

waiting for him. Zimmer is drunk, soaked from a heavy downpour, and shaken after a minor road accident, and he reacts badly when Alma tries to persuade him to come to New Mexico to meet Hector. At last, she pulls a gun on him, but Zimmer, convinced the gun is unloaded, takes it from her, points it at his own head, and pulls the trigger. Only then does he realize that the gun is fully loaded, but fortunately the safety catch is still on. This sobers him up, and Zimmer and Alma become lovers.

As they fly to New Mexico the next day, Alma tells Zimmer the story of Hector's life. In Hollywood, he was a famous ladies' man, but he had one longtime lover, the journalist Brigid O'Fallon. When he met and decided to marry the actress Dolores Saint John, he broke off his relationship with Brigid, not realizing that she was pregnant. Brigid, however, seemed to go insane and confronted Dolores, who shot her, apparently by accident. Hector helped Dolores bury the body, but, overcome by guilt, decided to walk away from the life he had known.

Hector changed his name, shaved off his trademark moustache, and for several years wandered from town to town taking menial jobs—including acting in pornography. He avoided relationships and instead spent his time reading as much as he could in an effort at self-education. Finally, Hector foiled a bank robbery and saved a girl the robber had taken hostage, though he was badly wounded in the process. The girl, Frieda Spelling, was the daughter of a wealthy family and recognized Hector. After she nursed him back to health, the two married. They built their own ranch in New Mexico, and there, following the death of their child, Hector resumed making movies on the condition that they never be seen by anyone else.

Alma is the daughter of Hector's cameraman. She reveals that Hector is now dying and Frieda is determined to destroy all the films once he has died. Alma, who is writing Hector's biography, is desperate to have someone else see the films before they are lost forever.

Immediately upon their arrival at the house, Zimmer is taken to meet Hector, who seems in good spirits. During the night, however, Hector dies. The next morning, Alma only has time to show Zimmer one of the films before Frieda starts to burn them. After that, Zimmer is told he must leave. He returns home to Vermont, expecting Alma to follow in a few days. Frieda, however, does not stop at burning just the films; she starts to destroy everything else relating to Hector's life after Hollywood, including the manuscript of Alma's biography. Alma reacts by hitting Frieda, who falls, bangs her head, and dies. Alma then commits suicide. Some years later, Zimmer writes the whole story on the condition that it is not published until after his death.

Critical Evaluation:

For a novel ostensibly about films, *The Book of Illusions* is remarkably bookish. Zimmer's book about Mann sets the plot in motion. When contacted by Alma, Zimmer is at work on a new translation of François-René de Chateaubriand's memoirs, from which he quotes extensively, and he discovers the same volume on Hector's shelves. During Hector's exile from Hollywood, he reads obsessively, and there are frequent references to other books throughout the novel. Alma is writing a biography of Hector. One of the late, unseen films is described as having no dialogue, only voice-over narration throughout, which is a very novelistic approach to film. The one late film of Hector's that Zimmer is able to watch, *The Inner Life of Martin Frost*, is about a novelist working on a new story. In the film, Martin Frost's most recent novel is called *Travels in the Scriptorium*, which is also the title of one of Hector Mann's unseen films and, curiously, is a title that Paul Auster also appropriated for a later novel of his own.

Likewise, Zimmer's narration is notable for how little visual detail he includes. Indeed, there are several passages where he comments on not noticing things. The one exception is Zimmer's descriptions of films (of which there are several lengthy examples in the novel): These are full of visual detail, such as the twitch of Hector's moustache, a sidelong glance, or the play of light in a scene.

The books and films quoted throughout the novel reflect the novel's action. This reflexivity is made explicit in Zimmer's account of Hector's penultimate silent comedy: Made at a time when Hector's producer was going bankrupt, cheating Hector out of money, and damaging Hector's future prospects, the film presents Hector as a successful businessman whose partner gives him a potion to make him invisible so the partner can steal from the company. Though rarely as overt as this example, every quotation from a book or description of a film amplifies the characters or comments on the plot in some fashion. The characters are aware of this: Alma, who has a strawberry birthmark on her face, recalls reading a short story by Nathaniel Hawthorne in which a chemist tries to remove the birthmark from his lover's face only to kill her in the process.

The theme that runs through so many of these quoted passages involves death in one form or another. The memoirs of Chateaubriand, which clearly mean much to both Zimmer and Hector, are given the title *Memoirs of a Dead Man* in Zimmer's translation, because Chateaubriand intended that they should not be published until after his death. This decision is echoed in Zimmer's own story, since readers are told at the very end of the book that Zimmer has given instructions that his account should not be published until after his death. These books also parallel the films that Hector makes at his New Mexico home, since he makes them with the explicit understanding that they will never be shown to an outside audience and will be destroyed upon his death.

Both Hector and Zimmer see themselves as dead men. So great is Zimmer's grief after the death of his wife that he comes close to killing himself on a number of occasions, most dramatically on the night he meets Alma, when he puts her gun to his head and pulls the trigger. This is not actually a suicide attempt, since Zimmer believes the gun is unloaded, but it does reflect how little his own life means to him. Again, there is an echo between Zimmer and Hector, since readers learn that, after fleeing Hollywood, Hector tried to kill himself on a number of occasions, including putting a gun to his head.

Other parallels run through the novel (Auster regularly uses coincidence in his work), as when Hector finds himself working for Brigid's father, who does not recognize him and in truth knows nothing about him. It is only when Brigid's sister falls in love with him that Hector decides he must move on. It is the parallels between David Zimmer in the modern portions of the story and Hector Mann in the portions of the story set in the past that are particularly notable. There are many such parallels, though the narrator Zimmer never notices them, or at least never makes reference to them. The most significant echo between Hector and Zimmer is that they are both men reborn—Hector almost literally so.

Hector is badly wounded when foiling the bank robbery and is symbolically brought back from the dead by Frieda. The two marry and move to a remote home in New Mexico, but it is only when their child dies in an accident that Hector returns to making films. This return represents a second rebirth, but a limited one. After behaving in a way that he saw as deserving of punishment when he helped Dolores bury Brigid, Hector swore off ever making movies again. He finds, however, that only by making films can he be whole. The compromise that Hector and Frieda reach is that, though they will make films, they will never be shown outside the family and they will be destroyed immediately upon Hector's death. (The question of art without an audience, of creation that can have no impact upon the world, is an issue that is raised obliquely in several of Auster's novels but, as here, is never directly addressed).

Zimmer, meanwhile, goes through a symbolic death following the accident that kills his family, a death from which he is raised by Alma. Again, there is a gun involved in the moment of rebirth, though this time it is not fired. Alma becomes Zimmer's Frieda, taking him away to New Mexico. Zimmer leaves his account of this whole episode to be published only after his death, making the book itself into a sort of rebirth of its narrator.

Paul Auster made an immediate impact with his first books, *The New York Trilogy* (1985-1986), an austere work that used postmodernist techniques to question conventional notions of what constitutes reality. His later works have rarely been as minimal, though they have tended to explore the same range of techniques and the same existential questions. They have also tended to become more humane, more emotionally involved, a trend that culminated in *The Book of Illusions* and *The Brooklyn Follies* (2006). Auster's novels following *The Brooklyn Follies* have tended to return to the postmodern austerity of his earliest work. *The Book of Illusions*, therefore, could be said to mark a turning point in Auster's career, and it is in some respects one of the best of his novels.

Paul Kincaid

Further Reading

Auster, Paul. *Hand to Mouth: A Chronicle of Early Failure.* New York: Henry Holt, 1997. An autobiography that is essential for understanding Auster's fiction and its relationship to his life experience.

Peacock, James. "Carrying the Burden of Representation: Paul Auster's *The Book of Illusions.*" *Journal of American Studies* 40, no. 1 (April, 2006): 53-70. Explores Auster's self-reflexive representation of representation in a novel that turns out to be the story of its own genesis, as well as an exploration of literary and cinematic representation in general.

Springer, Carsten. *A Paul Auster Sourcebook.* New York: Peter Lang, 2001. Compendium of information about the author's life and work.

Varvogli, Aliki. *The World That Is the Book: Paul Auster's Fiction.* Liverpool, England: Liverpool University Press, 2001. A study of Auster's work that places him in the context of earlier American writers.

The Book of Laughter and Forgetting

Author: Milan Kundera (1929-   )
First published: Le Livre du rire et de l'oubli, 1979
   (English translation, 1980)
Type of work: Novel
Type of plot: Political and psychological realism
Time of plot: 1948-1980
Locale: Czechoslovakia and France

Principal characters:
MIREK, a political dissident
ZDENA, his onetime mistress
MARKETA, a young woman
KAREL, her husband
EVA, Marketa and Karel's lover
MOTHER, Karel's mother
GABRIELLE, an American schoolgirl
MICHELLE, an American schoolgirl
MADAME RAPHAEL, their teacher
R., an editor
MILAN KUNDERA, the author
TAMINA, a Czech defector
BIBI, her friend
HUGO, a writer
KRISTYNA, a provincial woman
THE STUDENT, her boyfriend
KUNDERA'S FATHER, who loses his ability to speak as he
   slowly dies
JAN, a doctor
EDWIGE, his lover
PASSER, Jan's dying friend

The Story:

Lost Letters. Disregarding his friends' advice to destroy his diaries recording dissident political meetings, Mirek travels by car to meet Zdena. She is ugly, so he is ashamed that he had an affair with her twenty-five years earlier. He realizes that he is being followed by another car, most likely the secret police. Mirek asks Zdena to return his old love letters to him. She refuses. On the way back to his apartment, Mirek manages to elude the car following him. When he arrives home, he finds his apartment being searched by the police, who confiscate his diaries. Mirek is arrested and sentenced to jail for six years.

Mother. Marketa and her husband Karel ask his aging, nearly sightless mother to stay with them for a week. Mother refuses to leave on the day planned, insisting on staying another day. Eva arrives to stay with them that night, and Mother is told that Eva is Marketa's cousin. Marketa accuses Karel of infidelity, and they begin to fight, but Eva intervenes and smooths things over. As Mother is telling Karel that Eva reminds him of one of her old friends, Eva and Marketa emerge from their bath half-naked. After Mother retires for the evening, the three sleep together. Karel, thinking himself a superb tactician for having arranged the ménage à trois,

calls himself Bobby Fisher, after the chess master. In truth, his wife arranged that they sleep with his lover. The next morning at the train station, Karel invites his mother to move in with them, but she refuses.

The Angels. Gabrielle and Michelle discuss the play *Rhinocéros*, 1959 (English translation, 1959) by Eugène Ionesco, with Madame Raphael. The author, Milan Kundera, recalls that, after the Soviet invasion of Czechoslovakia in 1968, he lost his job and wrote under a pseudonym for a living. R., the editor of the magazine for whom Kundera wrote an astrology column, illegally covered up the fact that he was the author. Her boss requested that the "astrologer" write a personal astrological reading for him. Kundera, as a prank, predicted an awful future for the boss. Kundera then recalls that, in 1950, the French writer Paul Éluard, to show his solidarity to the communist movement, did not protest the unjust death sentence of his friend, the Czech artist Zavis Kalandra. Kundera imagined Éluard rising in the air while dancing with other communists. R. sent a letter to Kundera, informing him that it had been discovered that he was the author of the column. Kundera met with R., who had been fired from her job and was going to be interrogated by the police. After their class presentation on *Rhinocéros* is ridiculed by their class-mates, Gabrielle and Michelle ascend through the ceiling with Madame Raphael.

Lost Letters. Tamina and her husband defect from Czechoslovakia but leave behind their notebooks and letters to each other. Tamina's husband falls ill while abroad and dies. She wants to retrieve the notebooks to help preserve her memories of her husband and their life together. Bibi agrees to get the notebooks on her trip to Prague, but Bibi then cancels her trip. Tamina's brother, who still lives in Prague, is persuaded to get the notebooks, which her in-laws opened and read. Tamina has sex with Hugo, in part because he offers to travel to Prague to bring the notebooks back. While they make love, Tamina tries to remember her husband's image. After Hugo refuses to go to Czechoslovakia, Tamina resolves to forget her memories.

Litost. Kristyna travels to Prague from the countryside to see the student, who is embarrassed over her provincial dress and manners. Though invited to an important gathering of famous writers, the student declines so that he can be with Kristyna. She persuades him to attend, requesting that a famous poet sign his book for her. At the gathering, the student witnesses the drunken carousing of the poets, and the famous poet writes a personal message in his book for Kristyna. Upon his return, she refuses to have sex with him, ashamed to tell him directly that another pregnancy could kill her. The student interprets her vaguely worded excuse to mean that she will die from love. He finds this message inspiring. The next morning, she explains more fully, and he is dejected once he realizes his self-deception.

The Angels. Kundera's father, slowly dying, gradually loses the power of speech. Kundera recalls speaking with his father about his ideas on Ludwig van Beethoven's sonatas, which prompts Kundera's comments on the writing of the novel in terms of musical structure. Tamina is taken to an is-land inhabited only by children. She plays their games, but the children physically and sexually abuse her. She attempts to escape, but they capture her. Attempting to escape a sec-ond time, she swims into the water and drowns.

The Border. Jan reflects on his erotic life with Edwige, which loses meaning for him. Jan visits his dying friend Passer at a sanatorium, where they discuss their different views of the meaning of life. At Passer's funeral, the wind blows a mourner's hat into the open grave. As the mourners shovel some dirt into the pit and onto the hat, they struggle to restrain their inappropriate laughter. Afterward, at a group orgy, Jan is struck at the ridiculousness of the scene and is asked to leave when he laughs out loud. At a nude beach, Jan and Edwige discuss but misunderstand each other's interpre-tations of the myth of Daphnis and Chloë.

Critical Evaluation:

The Book of Laughter and Forgetting marked a new direc-tion in Milan Kundera's development as a novelist. The novel is a synthesis of the major themes and narrative techniques of his previous fiction, but its structure is radically different. *The Book of Laughter and Forgetting* is divided into seven sec-tions, most of which concern different characters (including Kundera) and different situations. The connections between the sections are primarily thematic and cluster around the shat-tering political and social impact of the Soviet invasion of Czechoslovakia, and the key words of the title. *The Book of Laughter and Forgetting* is, as Kundera writes in the novel, "a novel about laughter and forgetting, about forgetting and Prague, about Prague and the angels," but it is also a testimony to the tragedy of Soviet totalitarianism in Czechoslovakia.

The major theme of *The Book of Laughter and Forgetting* is the importance of memory to individual and collective lives. Kundera juxtaposes individual battles between mem-ory and forgetting with Czech culture's battle to retain its identity in the face of Soviet domination. Mirek, the main character in the first section, "Lost Letters," justifies keeping a written record of incriminating facts, names, and dates by saying, "the struggle of man against power is the struggle of memory against forgetting." For individuals such as Mirek and Tamina as well as for the Soviets in control of Czechoslo-vakia, "the past is full of life, eager to irritate us, provoke and insult us, tempt us to destroy or repaint it."

The novel's other major theme is the paradox of laugh-ter. Kundera distinguishes between skeptical, questioning laughter and self-righteous, joyful laughter throughout the novel. In a subsection entitled "On Two Kinds of Laughter," Kundera refers to these types of laughter as devils' and an-gels' laughter. He writes: "If there is too much uncontested meaning on earth (the reign of the angels), man collapses un-der the burden; if the world loses all its meaning (the reign of the demons), life is every bit as impossible." He complicates this relationship considerably, however, by asserting that "one and the same external phenomenon embraces two com-pletely contradictory internal attitudes." In the last section of *The Book of Laughter and Forgetting*, Kundera uses the met-aphor of the border to describe the instability of dualities in general. Although Kundera in *The Book of Laughter and Forgetting* portrays both extremes—fanaticism on one side and nihilism on the other—with distance, he is especially critical of angelic laughter, which he perceives as the laugh-ter of communist zealotry.

In *The Book of Laughter and Forgetting* erotic and sexual scenes play a dominant role. In every section of the novel, characters (though male characters profit more than female ones) learn something about themselves through failed sexual relations, but this self-knowledge is bitter and disillusioning. The two scenes of group sex in the novel are comically ridiculous, providing exaggerated examples with which to strip away any sense of human sexuality as essentially meaningful and life-affirming.

In terms of Kundera's development as a novelist, *The Book of Laughter and Forgetting* marks a breakthrough in Kundera's ideas about novelistic structure. Its formal discontinuity has led some critics to be reluctant to describe the book as a novel. John Updike is representative when he calls it "more than a collection of seven stories yet certainly no novel." Early in *The Book of Laughter and Forgetting*, Kundera gives the reader explicit advice on how to unify the book's disparate parts while outlining his new aesthetic ambitions for the novel: "This entire book is a novel in the form of variations. The individual parts follow each other like individual stretches of a journey leading toward a theme, a thought, a single situation, the sense of which fades into the distance."

Kundera's structural method in *The Book of Laughter and Forgetting* is based on an analogy with formal musical composition. References to music in *The Book of Laughter and Forgetting* and in Kundera's textual comments reflect his interest and early training in classical music. Each section of the novel contains very different kinds of discourse: autobiographical fragments, historical facts and anecdotes, philosophical reflection, and fantasy. In one section, for example, Kundera juxtaposes a dreamlike tale of Tamina on an island inhabited only by children, the story of Kundera's father's dying days, and mini-essays concerning the demolition of Czech monuments and history. The essays cover Czech leader Gustav Hasak ("the president of forgetting"), time in Franz Kafka's novels, Beethoven's use of theme and variation, and the inanity of popular music. All these reflections are unified in that they refer to the same theme: Communism makes everyone into children by promising the future in exchange for the past. This kind of juxtaposition of thematically related fragments is characteristic of the entire structure of *The Book of Laughter and Forgetting*, and the result is a tour de force of narrative skill that has established Kundera's reputation as a major writer.

Glen Brand

Further Reading

Banerjee, Maria Nemcova. *Terminal Paradox: The Novels of Milan Kundera*. New York: Grove Weidenfeld, 1990.

Thorough summary and discussion of the major themes of *The Book of Laughter and Forgetting*.

Bloom, Harold, ed. *Milan Kundera*. Philadelphia: Chelsea House, 2003. Collection of essays, including discussions of Kundera's use of sexuality, estrangement, and irony in his work, Kundera and kitsch, and "*The Book of Laughter and Forgetting*: Kundera's Narration Against Narration" by Ellen Pifer. Pearl K. Bell's essay, "The Real Avant-Garde," places Kundera in a tradition of dissident Eastern European writing and praises the originality of *The Book of Laughter and Forgetting*.

Frank, Søren. *Migration and Literature: Günter Grass, Milan Kundera, Salman Rushdie, and Jan Kjærstad*. New York: Palgrave Macmillan, 2008. Examines works by Kundera and three other authors, focusing on the theme of migration and the various strategies they use to describe the experience of exile and homelessness.

Miletic, Tijana. *European Literary Immigration into the French Language: Readings of Gary, Kristof, Kundera, and Semprun*. Amsterdam: Rodopi, 2008. Kundera, Romain Gary, Agota Kristof, and Jorge Semprun are twentieth century writers whose native language was not French, but who chose to write in this language. Applies linguistic, sociological, and psychoanalytic analyses to examine the common elements in their work.

Misurella, Fred. *Understanding Milan Kundera: Public Events, Private Affairs*. Columbia: University of South Carolina Press, 1993. Good discussion of the novel in the wider contexts of Kundera's thought, life, and career.

Petro, Peter, ed. *Critical Essays on Milan Kundera*. New York: G. K. Hall, 1999. Includes reviews of *The Book of Laughter and Forgetting* by novelist John Updike and Maria Nemcova Banerjee, several interviews with Kundera, and essays, including discussions of Kundera's Central Europe, the use of commedia dell'arte style in his novels, the slow pace of his novels, and "Genre and Paradigm in Milan Kundera's *The Book of Laughter and Forgetting*" by Herbert Eagle. David Lodge's essay, "Milan Kundera, and the Idea of the Author in Modern Criticism," compares the narrative technique of Kundera's first novel, *The Joke* (1967), to *The Book of Laughter and Forgetting*, calling the latter "a masterpiece of postmodernist fiction."

Updike, John. "Czech Angels." In *Hugging the Shore: Essays and Criticism*. New York: Vintage Books, 1984. An often-cited enthusiastic review/essay that focuses on the themes of forgetting and eroticism in the novel.

The Book of Songs

Author: Confucius (Kong Qiu, 551-479 B.C.E.)
First transcribed: Shi Jing, twelfth century B.C.E.
    (English translation, 1875)
Type of work: Poetry

The earliest repository of Chinese verse, *The Book of Songs,* contains 305 poems of folk and court origins. The court poems are more or less ceremonial in character, designed to be sung at sacrifices, to accompany the dances and feasts in honor of dynastic ancestors, or to adorn such formal occasions as receptions, banquets, chases, and archery contests. The folk songs comprise love lyrics of various kinds, epithalamiums, complaints, satires, elegies, and georgics.

Almost all the poems in *The Book of Songs* were composed in the pre-Confucian period of the Chou Dynasty (c. 1122-222 B.C.E.). In the ceremonial odes the wisdom and prowess of its founders—the kings Wen and Wu and the duke of Chou—are frequently recalled, although a few pieces, hardly of greater antiquity, celebrate the splendid achievements of even earlier dynasties, the Hsia and the Shang. According to a now-discredited tradition, Confucius was the compiler of this anthology and rejected nine-tenths of the three thousand poems then extant; but the canon must have been well fixed by his time, and diplomats and scholars even then knew the poems by heart, quoting them on every conceivable occasion to display their literary attainment or political sagacity. It is easy to see why the court poetry—so vital to the discharge of religious and state functions—should have been saved, but the early preservation of so much folk poetry is a more curious matter. In the absence of better explanation, one must accept the tradition that the Chou kings made a point of collecting the popular ballads of their many vassal states and using them as a political barometer to gauge the happiness or discontent of the populace. All the poems in *The Book of Songs* were meant to be sung, but the tunes were already lost by the time of the Han Dynasty (206 B.C.E.-220 C.E.).

The anthology, as it exists today, is divided into four sections: *kuo feng,* the smaller *ya,* the greater *ya,* and *sung.* While *kuo feng* are the folk songs of the vassal states and both *ya* and *sung* may be indifferently translated as odes, the divisions are hardly clean-cut. Many of the poems in the category of the smaller *ya* are apparently folk songs, and some of the greater *ya* poems are little differentiated from the religious and dynastic odes of the *sung* section. As documents of ancient China, the folk songs and courtly odes are of great historical and anthropological interest. To these, scholars owe the first mention of the sage kings and mythical heroes, the coherent presentation of the animistic beliefs of the early Chinese regarding ancestor worship and the adaptation of human labor to the cyclic changes in nature, the precise details of many religious and state rituals, and the intimate evocation of the life of a simple people of great emotional integrity: their courtships and marriages, their work on the farm, and their much-detested military service. On the strength of the love poems alone, the French Sinologist Marcel Granet reconstructed a fascinating picture of mating customs and fertility rites in the dawn of Chinese history.

Historical considerations aside, *The Book of Songs* is primarily poetry and should be read as such. Confucius once told his disciples,

> My children, why do you not study the Poetry? Poetry will stimulate your emotions, help you to be more observant, enlarge your sympathies, and moderate your resentment of injustice. It is useful at home in the service of one's father, abroad in the service of one's prince. Furthermore, it will widen your acquaintance with the names of birds, beasts, plants, and trees.

One is hardly surprised that Confucius attached great importance to *The Book of Songs* as a guide to good conduct and as a manual of useful information; in ancient Greece, the study of Homer was urged on similar grounds. The poetry, aside from its great social and ceremonial utility, also mentions by name about seventy kinds of plants, thirty kinds each of trees, beasts, and birds, ten kinds of fish, and twenty kinds of insects. The book is a virtual catalog of the more common flora and fauna of the Middle Kingdom. There are not many other sources for the study of ancient China in which such a variety of information is so readily available.

If one reads Confucius correctly, the key message in his little speech above attests his awareness of the humanizing influence of poetry, its power to regulate and refine emotions, to enlarge sympathy. To Confucius, *li* (ritual, etiquette), music, and poetry constitute an inseparable triad. While *li* is designed to bring out the best qualities of people in their everyday social intercourse as well as on the formal occasions of rejoicing and mourning, Confucius is also aware that there is an excess of emotion in people that cannot be rendered in terms of ritual or of etiquette. To him, therefore, *li* is the approximation of the ideal and poetry, the expression of the actual, although, as in much of *The Book of Songs*, poetry can be an integral part of a ritualistic occasion. Music is closely allied to ritual and poetry because it serves the dual function of supporting courteous behavior and facilitating the expression of one's true feelings.

To the modern reader, the more vital portion of *The Book of Songs* is surely the folk songs—160 *kuo feng* poems plus many others—because they speak the universal language of one's true feelings. These songs are quite simple in structure, a series of short rhymed stanzas. The basic unit is the four-word line, and the closing line of each stanza is usually a refrain. Within the simple structure of each poem, however, a little drama unfolds. As in all ballad poetry, the poet seldom speaks in person: The speaker may be a woman awaiting her lover by a ford (the wading of a creek or shallow river by a couple may be a symbol of marital engagement), or detaining her lover in bed while the dawn is breaking, or telling her story of woe after her husband has been pressed into military service or has deserted her. The speaker may be the lover who tosses and turns all night in bed thinking of his girl, who takes a walk by the eastern gate and sees women shining like clouds but still prefers his own choice, a modest woman of "plain cloth and gray kerchief." In other poems the speaker is the soldier who climbs a barren hill and acutely misses his kinsfolk; the exile who, seeing the yellow birds pecking in the fields, is seized with the sudden impulse to return home; the farmer who thinks of migrating to another state because the large rats in his fields remind him of the greater rapacity of the officials. This dramatic quality is one reason why the folk songs have a universal appeal and a perennial charm about them.

Another source of poetic appeal is the language. The diction of *The Book of Songs* has an archaic flavor that adds immeasurably to the meaning of the poems. The folk songs, especially, have retained a pristine quality because the simple emotions that they embody are clothed in a language beyond the contamination of modern idiom, beyond the corrosion of time. The language has another strength that is characteristic of Chinese poetry in general: its elliptical density. In a four-word line there is absolutely no room for decoration or for syntactical connectives; each word must have a maximal poetic weight and suggestiveness to merit inclusion.

To a student of English poetry long accustomed to its roses and nightingales, *The Book of Songs*, with its duck-

weed and dolichos, mulberry and date trees, magpies and orioles, cicadas and locusts, presents a distinctively new landscape. In almost every folk song, nature is an integral part of the human situation: The mulberry tree is shedding its leaves upon the ground and the woman thinks of her state of desertion; ripe plums are dropping from the tree and presently there will be only three left on the boughs, and the woman wonders if she will ever have a lover, because she, too, is ripe for love. The lovers, farmers, and soldiers in the folk songs are so physically close to nature, there is seldom any need to resort to simile or explicit metaphor. The strategy of correspondence, or objective correlative, is characteristic of *The Book of Songs*.

In view of the later development of Chinese poetry, the love songs and complaints appear especially important. Such conventional themes as the separation of husband and wife, the poverty of peasants, the evils of officialdom and war, and the appropriate moods induced by seasonal changes were all first embodied in *The Book of Songs*. The work has remained unsurpassed in its depiction of love. Whereas the later poets, with the exception of an exquisite few, adopt the mask of the forsaken or forlorn woman more or less as a literary convention, the Chinese women in *The Book of Songs* speak out unafraid in the spontaneity of the natural, unashamed womanhood. By contrast, Chinese women of subsequent history, confined in the home and disallowed the privilege of free social intercourse with men, appear sad and dull indeed.

Further Reading

Confucius. *The Book of Songs: The Ancient Classic of Poetry.* Translated by Arthur Waley, edited with additional translations by Joseph R. Allen. New York: Grove Press, 1996. Waley, a preeminent translator of East Asian literature, first translated *The Book of Songs* in 1937. This updated edition includes fifteen poems that were not included in the initial translation and restores the poems to their original order. It also contains a foreword in which Stephen Owens discusses the significance of the poems and a postface providing a literary history of the work.

Dobson, W. A. C. H. *The Language of "The Book of Songs."* Toronto, Ont.: University of Toronto Press, 1968. A grammar of the language of *The Book of Songs*, with useful discussions of the linguistic characteristics of each of its four divisions. Dobson argues that the poems derive from different periods.

Legge, James. *The She King.* Volume 4 of *The Chinese Classics.* Reprint. New York: Oxford University Press, 1961. Provides a rich source of materials for the critical reader who can excuse Christian interpretations for Chinese ideas and who can enjoy stories without needing strictly factual scholarship. Includes translation, notes, and history of the text.

Van Zoeren, Steven. *Poetry and Personality: Reading, Exegesis, and Hermeneutics in Traditional China*. Stanford, Calif.: Stanford University Press, 1991. Chronicles the principles for interpreting the text as they have changed over two thousand years, with a focus on the Mao school and the codes by which the text may have been written and read.

Yeh, Shan. *The Bell and the Drum: Shih Ching as Formulaic Poetry in an Oral Tradition*. Berkeley: University of California Press, 1974. Includes an index to references to the 305 poems. Argues that the work is poetry not because of originality but because of the totality of its cultural associations, which are contained in Chinese oral tradition and formulaic stock phrases.

Yu, Pauline. "The Book of Songs." In *Masterworks of Asian Literature in Comparative Perspective*, edited by Barbara Miller. Armonk, N.Y.: M. E. Sharpe, 1994. One of the best and simplest short discussions of the work. Includes topics for discussion and a view of translations of the text.

Book of Songs

Author: Heinrich Heine (1797-1856)
First published: Buch der Lieder, 1827 (English translation, 1856)
Type of work: Poetry

Although it is generally conceded that Heinrich Heine's finest poetry was not written until his last years, the *Book of Songs*, which assembles his entire lyrical output to the age of twenty-six, remains the core of his poetic work. The book gained immediate popularity and appeared in a new edition every other year for decades. German critical opinion of the period cited Heine for writing in the spirit and with the simple accents of German folk song, but he soon became a controversial figure. His merits are still fiercely disputed in German territories, much of the controversy centering on his later prose writings, in which the unquenchably poetic nature of his approach to religion and political philosophy yielded, along with chilling prophetic insights, considerable rhetorical muddle.

His own feelings toward Germany were intensely ambiguous. He later became, through his Paris exile, "a link that spanned the Rhine"; but the French influences that surrounded him in his first sixteen years (during which time the Rhineland was mostly under French military occupation or French civil rule) apparently had little effect. In his memoirs, he said that early school experiences imbued him with a permanent prejudice against French literature, and he went through a phase of nationalistic fervor that ended only when he discovered that he breathed more freely under the French than the Prussian regime; ultimately he denounced Gallophobia and German national egotism. "The Grenadiers," one of his earliest poems, expresses his boyish admiration for Napoleon—typically an admiration not for the deeds but only for the genius of the man. When Heine lived among the French, however, his admiration was chiefly directed toward their freedom from the idealism, prudery, and sentimentality that he deplored in the German philistines, at whose expense his satirical wit waxed especially brilliant.

In the North Sea cycle that closes his *Book of Songs*, Heine describes his deep love of Germany, a love that flourished in spite of the fact that Germany's "pleasant soil" was "encumbered with madness, hussars, and wretched verses." There are passages, especially in the early poems, in which he expresses identification with the German character, either lamenting the passing of old Germany's nobility and virtues or praising the oak that stands for the essential hardihood and "holiness" of the fatherland. There is, however, something in his love for Germany that resembles his commitment to the lost beloved, the false fair, the maiden with flowering beauty and decaying heart, and this constitutes his poetic stock in trade and is, in fact, almost his whole *Nibelungenhort*. Nevertheless, he considered himself from first to last a German, and his poetry is deeply rooted in the German Romantic movement. He liked to refer to himself as the last of the Romantics, marking the close of the old lyric school of the Germans, but he attacked the political, realist, engagé "Young Germany" group with much the same exuberance as he did the old "poesy" and regressive spiritualism.

Heine, experimenting in most of the modes of Romanticism but ultimately taking from the movement only what suited him, provided finally one of the paths by which the Romantic spirit was deflected toward Symbolism. Individual lyrics of the *Book of Songs* sometimes suffer from a facile outpouring of stock diction and sentiment, but here is poetry that from the beginning avoids either the heights or the depths of the abysmal absolute. Its dealings with the absolute are rather directed at maintaining a perilous equilibrium, buoyed by Heine's fresh, vigorous idiom, his delicate music, with its constant play of assonance, and his frequent ironic twists. Reacting to the artifice of eighteenth century diction, Heine sympathized with the Romantic interests in a return to the German folk tradition and a poetic approximation to the supposedly purer aesthetic impact of music. Nevertheless, in spite of the fact that some of his ballads ("The Lorelei," for example) were actually admitted into the canon of German folk song, Heine himself insisted of his poetry that it was only the form that was somewhat akin to the folk song; the subject matter was that of conventional society. Perhaps more important to Heine's poetry than the Romantic exaltation of the *Volk* was the concern, distinctive to the German Romantic school, with developing a rationale of the comic. This concern provided a sympathetic climate for Heine's particular form of mockery, itself partially a product of the satirical wit native to his Jewish cultural inheritance.

The Romantic movement was later to provide one of the most obvious targets for Heine's irony, and the lyrical preface to the third edition of the *Book of Songs* contains an implicit comment on that subject. It was Heine who once defined the German Romantic school as a return to the medieval poetry that sprang from the Catholicism in which men derived voluptuous pleasure from pain. The prefacing verses satirically summarize that pleasure as it finds expression in his own lyrics. It is the "old enchanted wood" through which the poet wanders, listening to the nightingale singing "of love and the keen ache of love." He comes to a gloomy castle before which lies a marble sphinx, half lion, half woman, which the song of the nightingale prompts him to kiss. The kiss awakens the statue, who proceeds to embrace him rapturously in return at the same time that she sinks her claws into him, kissing and rending simultaneously. As the poet submits to this "exquisite torture," the nightingale sings, "O wondrous sphinx, O love,/ Why this always distressing/ Mingling of death-like agony/ With every balm and blessing?" The whole effect involves the same burlesque by exaggeration that is operative at the end of the "Lyrical Intermezzo," in which Heine describes the enormity of the coffin that would be required for him to lower all his sorrows into the Rhine—a

facetious note not entirely confined to his earliest poems. On the whole, the *Book of Songs* contains Heine's exploration of the Romantic movement rather than his rejection of it, if only because it contains expressions of the sentimental attachments of various adolescent periods.

The first section, "Junge Leiden" ("sorrows of youth"), represents roughly Heine's *Sturm und Drang* period. It contains such characteristic pieces as "The Minnesingers" in which, with "word for sword," the singers engage in a tournament whose victor is the one who enters the fray with the deadliest wound. The section is subdivided into Dream Pictures, Songs, Romances, and Sonnets; the romantic decor of the poet's sensibility is rendered in its most studied garishness and most rollicking meter. Images include the enchanted garden and the graveyard vision; the wedding festivities and attendant corpse conjuring; the shining dream that turns to nightmare or to day-lit delusion; and Poor Peter, alias the clumsy knight, alias "King Heinrich"—a primordial Prufrock. Not all of the skeleton-rattling in this group is as delightful as that of "I came from my love's house." Here a minstrel sits on his crumbling tombstone and plays a delirious dance to arouse the graveyard's other inhabitants, and each tells how he came to be there—"How he fared, and was snared in love's mad and furious chase."

By the time of the "Lyrical Intermezzo" and the "Homecoming" sequence, which follow "Junge Leiden," Heine has largely abandoned his supernatural baggage in favor of a more natural imagery and a more personal, direct form of address:

> God knows where I'll find that silly
> Madcap of a girl again;
> I have searched this endless city,
> Wet and cursing in the rain. . . .

The imagery of sea, storm, seasonal change, and the like is never employed for its own richness, but for its directly evocative effect, as in the famous "Der Tod, das ist die kühle Nacht." Heine also proves himself capable of a restraint and lightness of touch in the most ageless tradition:

> The golden flame of summer
> Burns in your glowing cheek;
> But in your heart lies winter,
> Barren and cold and bleak.
> Soon it will change, my darling,
> Far sooner than you seek;
> Your heart will harbor summer,
> While winter lines your cheek.

In the "Lyrical Intermezzo," a subtle spring to autumn progression is threaded through the whole sequence.

Max Brod noted the remarkable cohesion revealed by assembling the whole of Heine's early poetry into a single book. The experiences of the hero of the poem sequences form a consistent whole in which the action develops with almost the progression of a verse novel. A biographical basis for these experiences is easy to establish, but it is detracting from its value to do so. Heine himself was extremely opposed to any biographical reading.

A unity less restricted to the theme of the rejected lover is attempted in the two North Sea cycles. Short, parallel sequences that exhibit a kind of symphonic development, they are often discounted as set pieces because they were written partly to escape the confines of a reputation for "lyrical, mordant, two-stanza" verse. They are not without rewarding moments, however, and their parallelism is curious and revealing. In the beginning the poet invokes the sea, the great symbol of inhuman immensity and constant change. In the poems that follow, the poet is actually at sea, witnessing and participating in various phenomena—storm, calm, seasickness, sunset, the progression of twilight, and night. There are also apostrophes to the ancient gods. Finally the poet comes to port, in the first sequence to the Peace of Christ, and in the final sequence, in a poem that parodies Christian metaphor throughout, to the haven of the wine cellar of Bremen. In a final burst of exuberance he writes, "Well, I have always declared/ That not among quite common people,/ Nay, but the best society going,/ Lived for ever the King of Heaven!"

Further Reading

Brod, Max. *Heinrich Heine: The Artist in Revolt*. Translated by Joseph Witriol. New York: New York University Press, 1957. An English version of Brod's 1934 biographical study, offering a post-Holocaust historical assessment. Emphasizes Heine's loneliness and restlessness as a Diaspora Jew, to which Brod paradoxically attributes the universality of his verse.

Perraudin, Michael. "Illusions Lost and Found: The Experiential World of Heine's *Buch der Lieder*." In *A Companion to the Works of Heinrich Heine*, edited by Roger F. Cook. Rochester, N.Y.: Camden House, 2002. Perraudin's analysis of *Book of Songs* is one of several essays in this collection that examine Heine's poetry. Other essays discuss the erotic elements in his work, his conception of history, and his relation to Jewish culture.

Phelan, Anthony. "From the Private Life of Everyman: Self-Presentation and Authenticity in *Buch der Lieder*." In *Reading Heinrich Heine*. New York: Cambridge University Press, 2007. Phelan provides detailed analyses of the *Book of Songs* and Heine's other poetic works. He emphasizes Heine's contributions to modernity.

Prawer, S. S. *Heine: Buch der Leider*. London: Edward Arnold, 1960. Stresses the significance of the doppelgänger motif in the *Book of Songs*, resulting in irony as Heine assumes various guises throughout the work. Prawer considers the collection's influence on German literature disastrous because Heine's imitators lacked his complexity.

Reeves, Nigel. *Heinrich Heine: Poetry and Politics*. London: Oxford University Press, 1974. Traces the apparently contradictory elements in Heine to a transitional historical context. Concludes that Heine's experiment with folk song failed largely because cultural refinement in Germany, with its subsequent loss of spontaneity and immediacy, was irreversible.

Sammons, Jeffrey L. *Heinrich Heine: The Elusive Poet*. New Haven, Conn.: Yale University Press, 1969. Argues that if Heine is taken seriously, the *Book of Songs* must not be dismissed, as many critics have done. Finds the work extraordinary in its concentration on a single theme and its revelation of the growth of a fictive persona.

Spencer, Hanna. *Heinrich Heine*. Boston: Twayne, 1982. Offers close analysis of most popular pieces in the *Book of Songs*, as well as a consideration of Heine's organization of the whole. Identifies a sudden change of mood, or *Stimmungsbrechung*, as the characteristic feature of the work.

Youens, Susan. *Heinrich Heine and the Lied*. New York: Cambridge University Press, 2007. Describes how nineteenth century composers, including Franz Schubert and Robert Schumann, used poems from the *Book of Songs* and Heine's other collections as the lyrics for their compositions. Examines the reasons for Heine's popularity with composers and how composers fashioned his poetry into new types of songs.

The Book of the City of Ladies

Author: Christine de Pizan (c. 1365-c. 1430)
First published: Le Livre de la cité des dames, 1405
  (*The Book of the City of Ladies: A Fifteenth-Century
  Defense of Women,* 1521, 1982)
Type of work: Biography
Type of plot: Allegory
Time of plot: Early fifteenth century
Locale: Paris and the City of Ladies

Principal characters:
CHRISTINE DE PIZAN, the narrator
LADY REASON, the first allegorical guide
LADY RECTITUDE, the second allegorical guide
LADY JUSTICE, the third allegorical guide

The Story:

Christine de Pizan is sitting in her study reading when her mother calls her to supper. The next day, as Christine resumes reading *The Lamentations of Mathéolus,* which slanders women's character, she reflects on the behavior of the female sex. While she is lost in thought, a vision of three ladies appears to her. They tell Christine that they come to correct the erroneous impressions that men created about women by helping her build a city where virtuous women will reside. They identify themselves as Lady Reason, Lady Rectitude, and Lady Justice.

Christine accepts their commission to build the City of Ladies by writing about worthy women. With Lady Reason's guidance, she places the foundations. Christine first asks Lady Reason why male authors malign women. Reason offers several explanations and affirms that these accounts of women's behavior are false. Christine inquires why women do not hold positions of governmental authority. Reason recounts the lives of several women who ruled after the death of their husbands, including Nicaula, empress of Ethiopia in antiquity, and French queens such as the Merovingian Fredegund and Blanche of Castile in the thirteenth century.

When Christine asks about women's strength, Reason tells how the ancient Assyrian Queen Semiramis led armies after her husband's death. Reason relates the feats of strength of the Amazons in ancient Greece and cites instances of other women from antiquity who acted with bravery. Lady Reason answers Christine's queries about learned women by mentioning two Roman poets, Cornifica and Proba, and the Greek poet Sappho. Other women, such as Manto, Medea, and Circe from Greek antiquity, excelled in magical sciences. Several women from ancient times, including Nicostrata, Minerva, Ceres, and Isis, discovered arts, sciences, and technologies. Women contributed to the arts and crafts of textiles and painting. To Christine's inquiry if women behave prudently, Lady Reason, explaining qualities of prudence

based on the biblical book of Proverbs, adduces the lives of the Romans Gaia Cirilla and Lavinia, Queen Dido of Carthage, and Queen Ops of Crete.

Lady Rectitude then assumes the guidance of Christine's work in completing the city walls and building edifices within the city. Rectitude instructs Christine on the wisdom of women by telling about the ten Sibyls and their gifts of prophecy. She cites several biblical women—among them Deborah, Elizabeth, and the Queen of Sheba—whose understanding made them prophetic. Other women, such as the Greek Cassandra and the Byzantine Antonia, had prophetic powers. When Christine asks why parents prefer sons to daughters, Lady Rectitude demonstrates that many daughters take care of their parents. The Roman virgin Claudine defended her father from attack, and another Roman woman nursed her imprisoned mother.

Rectitude announces that the buildings of the City of Ladies are complete and ready to be inhabited. In response to Christine's inquiries about women's role in marriage, Rectitude brings to the city Queen Hypsicratea, who shows such devotion to her husband that she accompanies him on military campaigns and into exile after his defeat. The city is filled with married women who counsel their spouses wisely and commemorate their deceased husbands. Of women who saved their people, Rectitude mentions Hebrew women such as Judith and Esther, the Sabine women of ancient Rome, and the Frankish queen Clotilda, who converted her husband Clovis to Christianity. Many women were noted for chastity, including the biblical Susanna and the Greek Penelope, wife of Ulysses. The Roman Lucretia tried to protect herself from rape. Women such as Griselda and the Roman empress Florence endured extreme hardships in remaining faithful to their husbands. Rectitude praises the virtues of French queens who are Christine's contemporaries, among them Queen Isabella, wife of Charles VI, and the duchesses of Berry, Orléans, and Burgundy.

Lady Justice takes up the task of completing the high towers and selecting their residents. The Virgin Mary becomes the queen of the City of Ladies. Justice leads in female martyrs for the Christian faith by recounting the acts of martyrdom of more than thirty saints. Christine finally declares that the city is complete and exhorts women to follow the virtuous examples of the residents of the City of Ladies.

Critical Evaluation:

Christine de Pizan is known as the first professional woman writer in France. She was Italian by birth, but her family moved to Paris when her father became court astrologer to King Charles V. Christine married a French notary, Estienne de Castel. His premature death left her a widow at the age of twenty-five, with responsibility for raising three children and caring for her mother.

Over her mother's objections, Christine's father encouraged her literary education, and she began to write to support herself. Initially, she composed verses that were popular with the French nobility. By dedicating her works to prominent individuals, Christine was able to acquire patrons in a male-dominated literary world.

Around 1400, after Christine developed a secure reputation, she expanded the range of topics about which she wrote. She began to pursue the problem of misogyny, addressing her defense of women in a number of literary arenas. Between 1401 and 1403, she participated in an epistolary debate on the *Roman de la rose*, a famous French literary work of the thirteenth century. She objected to its vulgar language and explicit misogyny. In the two allegorical prose works *The Book of the City of Ladies* and its sequel, *The Book of Three Virtues* (also known as the *Treasury of the City of the Ladies*), she attempted to correct the misogynistic views about women found in many works of literature by male authors.

The compositional structure of *The Book of the City of Ladies* is based on the allegory of building a city in which worthy women are to reside. The construction of the city is an image for Christine's writing about women. Her task is guided by the three female allegorical personifications of Reason, Rectitude, and Justice, who command her to "take the trowel of your pen" and "mix the mortar in your ink bottle" to build the City of Ladies.

The Book of the City of Ladies is divided into three sections or books. The first sets up the frame for the allegory by situating Christine in her study reading a misogynistic book. Her allegorical guides appear to her as she contemplates the implications of the depiction of women by male authors. With the aid of the personification of Reason, Chris-

tine narrates the lives of women who made positive contributions in various ways and thus lays both the allegorical foundation of the city and the literal foundation of her literary work.

In the second book, Rectitude becomes Christine's guide. The image of city building is continued as the city walls are finished, edifices are built, and the city is populated. Justice guides Christine's work in the third book, where the high towers are completed and inhabited by the Virgin Mary, the queen of the city, and by a host of female saints.

This framework provides a narrative scaffolding for a series of biographical sketches of women drawn from antiquity and from French history up to the time when Christine was writing, just after 1400. Christine arranges the lives of these women by topics introduced as queries to the allegorical guides. As Christine asks about subjects such as women's strength, their contributions to the sciences, and their faithfulness in marriage, Reason, Rectitude, and Justice illustrate women's conduct with examples drawn from particular women's lives. In effect, *The Book of the City of Ladies* is a collective biography of famous women united within the allegorical convention of building a city.

Christine drew on many sources to create *The Book of the City of Ladies*. The idea of an allegorical vision was used in such medieval literary works as Boethius's *De consolatione philosophiae* (c. 523; *The Consolation of Philosophy*; late ninth century), in which Lady Philosophy, who is similar to Reason, is his guide; Dante's *La divina commedia* (c. 1320; *The Divine Comedy*, 1802); and Guillaume de Lorris and Jean de Meung's *Le Roman de la rose* (thirteenth century; *The Romance of the Rose*, 1900) that Christine criticizes. The tripartite structure was also used frequently in medieval literature, for example in *The Divine Comedy*, which Christine acknowledges as one of her models. The image of a city was developed in one of the most influential works of early medieval theology, St. Augustine's *De civitate Dei* (412-427; *The City of God*, 1610).

The biographies of women for the most part come from stories that were retold many times from antiquity through the Middle Ages. Christine especially drew on the fourteenth century author Giovanni Boccaccio, who had written a collective *Concerning Famous Women* (c. 1361-1375). The saints' lives came from compendia such as Vincent of Beauvais' thirteenth century French encyclopedic history, *Speculum historiale*. This reliance on sources should not obscure the originality of Christine's composition. From a twenty-first century perspective, what seems like borrowing or compiling from other sources, drawing on traditional sources, was precisely what medieval writers were expected to do. It was not a question of inventing original material but rather of demonstrating what they could do with preexistent material.

Christine reworks her sources to emphasize women's positive qualities and contributions. As she recounts incidents in the lives of women, she recasts the narratives derived from Boccaccio, Ovid, and others. In her description of Queen Semiramis of Assyria, for example, she focuses on the queen's strength in military campaigns and governing her territories, while downplaying an incident of incest with her son. Christine's topical rearrangement of her material enables her to address such universal issues of concern as rape.

Feminist readings of *The Book of the City of Ladies* have criticized Christine for her conservative stance on the French political situation in the early fifteenth century, her acceptance of the social hierarchy, and her emphasis on female submissiveness to husbands. These criticisms fail to account for the historical context in which Christine wrote. Because her ability to support herself depended on patronage from the nobility, her criticism of the political and social order of her times had to be muted and contained within the prevalent code of conduct.

One of the few female voices in the Middle Ages to be expressed directly through writing, Christine de Pizan's *The Book of the City of Ladies* is an important literary achievement. Through the well-sustained allegorical structure and the subtle reworking of sources, Christine created a literary work that stands on its own merits and redresses the misogynistic imbalance created by the preponderance of male authors in the Middle Ages.

Karen Gould

Further Reading

Altmann, Barbara K., and Deborah L. McGrady, eds. *Christine de Pizan: A Casebook*. New York: Routledge, 2003. Collection of essays, including articles that place Christine within the context of late medieval France, French politics and theology, and critiques of her work. Part 2, "Building a Female Community," contains an analysis of *The Book of the City of Ladies* by Judith L. Kellogg and other feminist interpretations of Christine's life and work.

Birk, Bonnie A. *Christine de Pizan and Biblical Wisdom: A Feminist-Theological Point of View*. Milwaukee, Wis.: Marquette University Press, 2005. Examines how Christine used the religious traditions of her time to defend women against misogynist beliefs and attitudes. Chapter 5 focuses on *The Book of the City of Ladies*.

Brown-Grant, Rosalind. *Christine de Pizan and the Moral Defence of Women: Reading Beyond Gender*. New York: Cambridge University Press, 1999. Analyzes Christine's works to trace how her assault on misogynism evolved over the years, culminating in her defense of women in *The Book of the City of Ladies*.

Christine de Pizan. *The Book of the City of the Ladies*. Translated by Earl Jeffrey Richards. New York: Persea Books, 1982. A modern English translation of Christine de Pizan's book. Contains a substantial introduction to the work and helpful notes on the text.

Curnow, Maureen Cheney. "'La Pioche d'Inquisition': Legal-Judicial Content and Style in Christine de Pizan's *Livre de la cité des dames*." In *Reinterpreting Christine de Pizan*, edited by Earl Jeffrey Richards et al. Athens: University of Georgia Press, 1992. Curnow finds much evidence that the author's fourteen-year involvement in legal battles exposed her to a lexicon and style of argument which served her well in *The Book of the City of Ladies*.

Quilligan, Maureen. *The Allegory of Female Authority: Christine de Pizan's "Cité des dames."* Ithaca, N.Y.: Cornell University Press, 1991. Drawing on her extensive research in the field of medieval allegory, Quilligan goes through each part of the book offering an in-depth commentary which suggests Christine's purpose in choosing certain tales to include in the work, indicates sociopolitical views intimated in the text, and expresses Christine's ideas in terms of modern psychology. The author includes a defense of Christine against present-day detractor Sheila Delany and a discussion of *Le Livre des trois vertus* (*The Book of the Three Virtues*), also known as *The Treasure of the City of Ladies*, Christine's sequel to *The Book of the City of Ladies*.

Richards, Earl Jeffrey, ed. *Reinterpreting Christine de Pizan*. Athens: University of Georgia Press, 1992. A collection of essays about the literary works of Christine de Pizan, several of which focus on *The Book of the City of Ladies*.

Ulrich, Laurel Thatcher. *Well-Behaved Women Seldom Make History*. New York: Alfred A. Knopf, 2007. Christine de Pizan is one of the "misbehaving" women included in this study, which provides a feminist analysis of *The Book of the City of Ladies*.

Willard, Charity Cannon. *Christine de Pizan: Her Life and Works*. New York: Persea Books, 1984. An extensive biography that contains thorough summaries of Christine's works and documents her long and ardent involvement in the Quarrel of the Rose. The chapter entitled "A Feminine Utopia" examines the contents of *The Book of the City of Ladies*, its sources, and its relationship to the corpus of

Christine's works. Numerous manuscript illuminations are reproduced in black and white.

_____. "The Franco-Italian Professional Writer Christine de Pizan." In *Medieval Women Writers*, edited by Katharina M. Wilson. Athens: University of Georgia Press, 1984. A concise introduction to the life and works of Christine de Pizan, this essay by one of the leading authorities on Christine contains a brief summary and evaluation of the contents of *The Book of the City of Ladies*, twelve pages of abstracts from the 1982 English translation by Earl Jeffrey Richards, elucidating notes, and a substantial bibliography.

The Book of the Courtier

Author: Baldassare Castiglione (1478-1529)
First published: Il libro del cortegiano, 1528 (English translation, 1561)
Type of work: Didactic literature

Principal characters:
LADY ELISABETTA GONZAGA, duchess of Urbino
LADY EMILIA PIA, her witty friend and attendant
COUNT LEWIS (LUDOVICO) OF CANOSSA,
SIR FREDERICK (FEDERICO) FREGOSO,
LORD OCTAVIAN FREGOSO,
LORD JULIAN (GIULIANO) DE MEDICIS,
M. BERNARD BIBIENA,
LORD GASPAR PALLAVICIN, and
PIETRO BEMBO, Italian noblemen, courtiers to the duke of Urbino
FRANCESCO MARIA DELLA ROVERE, heir to the duke of Urbino

The Story:

The duchess, Elisabetta Gonzaga, asks the gentlemen of the court to choose a topic of conversation for the evening's entertainment. They settle on "what belongeth to the perfection of Courtiership." The resulting conversation, with digressions, addresses that topic. Lewis, count of Canossa, begins the discussion.

His ideal courtier must be, he says, nobly born, with a pleasant disposition, wit, and "a comely shape of person and countenance." Since his chief profession is to be a soldier, he needs training in all the skills that will make him an able warrior for his prince: riding, handling weapons of all sorts, wrestling, swimming, and other sports that increase strength and agility. The courtier also needs certain social talents, easy conversation, wit, the ability to dance, and, above all, a certain grace that makes all his activities seem effortless and unconscious.

The conversation turns to language, a burning issue in the Renaissance, when the vernaculars are struggling with Latin for supremacy. The count recommends that the courtier avoid using antiquated or unfamiliar words and that he take his vocabulary from those familiar Italian words "that have some grace in pronunciation." Sir Frederick Fregoso argues that the count depends too much on custom; the courtier should shun "vices of speech," even if they have been adopted by the multitude. The count concludes the argument by stating that it is the courtier's knowledge, rather than his diction, that will ultimately be important. The first evening's conversation ends with a brief consideration of the importance of a courtier's having some skills in music and art.

On the second night Sir Frederick Fregoso is instructed to discuss the proper times and places for the courtier to exercise those virtues that are essential for him. Frederick points out that most of all an ideal gentleman needs discretion to determine when to speak, when to be silent, and how to act so as to win praise and avoid envy. Fregoso recommends "little speaking, much doing, and not praising a man's own self in commendable deeds." He cites as a bad example an uncouth courtier who on one occasion entertains a lady with a description of his prowess with a two-handed sword and terrifies her with a demonstration of various strokes.

All courtiers are expected to be able to entertain ladies gracefully, and the ability to sing is a particularly valuable accomplishment. Sir Frederick notes that a gentleman needs the wisdom to recognize that time in his life when his age makes it ludicrous for him to perform in public; if such a man must sing, let him do it privately.

This point leads to a general consideration of the proper demeanor for the young and the old. Fregoso praises mildness, deference, and hesitancy on the part of the fledgling courtier, but he suggests that the more restrained older man should strive for a little liveliness. A golden mean is the ideal.

After a serious discussion of the value of friendship with loyal, honorable men, Sir Frederick turns, at the request of the cynical Lord Gaspar Pallavicin, to a consideration of court entertainments. In this area, too, Fregoso pleads for moderation; too great a concern with dice or cards can become a vice, and a man could waste the better part of his days in becoming a brilliant chess player. The best entertainment comes from a courtier's wit, as Castiglione shows by weaving into his narrative a number of anecdotes and "merry pranks." M. Bernard Bibiena, who tells many of the witty tales, cautions the company to be mindful of the time, the place, and the individuals in jesting; maliciousness and cruelty should have no part in court life.

The conversation then turns to the character of women, whose honor and trustworthiness are wittily attacked by Lord Gaspar and defended by the Lady Emilia. Lord Julian de Medicis is instructed to imagine an ideal court lady for the next evening's amusement. The position of women is eloquently defended in part 3; one of the gentlemen asserts that "no court, how great so-ever it be, can have any sightliness or brightness in it, or mirth without women, nor any Courtier can be gracious, pleasant or hardy, nor at any time undertake any gallant enterprise of Chivalry, unless he be stirred with the conversation and with the love and contentation of women."

Lord Julian wants for his ideal woman sweetness, tenderness, and womanliness, a pleasing disposition, noble birth, and a certain amount of beauty; she needs the same virtues of courage, loyalty, and discretion that the courtier requires, and her position, too, could be enhanced by pleasant conversation and modesty. She needs to avoid that common feminine failing, a fondness for gossiping about other women. The ladies, as well as the gentlemen, of the court need some skill in the arts, so that they can dance, sing, or play musical instruments with ease. Lord Julian says that the court lady should at least be acquainted with literature and philosophy.

Lord Gaspar, who has injected antifeminist sentiments throughout Lord Julian's discourse, scoffs at the notion of educated women and proclaims that the sex is an imperfection in nature. Lord Julian counters by enumerating those qualities in which he finds women superior to men and by relating stories of famous women in history.

Sir Frederick asks Lord Julian to consider what he thinks is most important for women: "what belongeth to the communication of love." The latter answers that a lady must first distinguish between true and false protestations of affection. A good Christian, he can approve only of love that can lead to marriage. To the objection that an aged, unattractive, or unfaithful husband might justify favors to a lover, Lord Julian replies: "If this mishap chance to the woman of the palace, that the hatred of her husband or the love of another bendeth her to love, I will have her to grant her lover nothing else but the mind; not at any time to make him any certain token of love, neither in word nor gesture, nor any other way that he may be fully assured of it."

The fourth part opens with a brief reflection on mortality. Castiglione relates the fates of members of the court of Urbino during the years between the nights he is describing and the time he completes his book. He turns then to the topic of the final evening's discussion, the courtier's role as adviser to his prince. Lord Octavian Fregoso points out that this role is often made difficult by the arrogance and pride of rulers, who consider that their power automatically brings wisdom. The courtier is obliged to lead his prince gently and subtly toward goodness, courage, justice, and temperance, mingling moral instruction with pleasure, one justification for the courtier's acquiring skills in the "polite arts." Lord Gaspar questions Fregoso's basic premise, that virtue can be taught, but the latter affirms his conviction that if moral virtues are innate, a man would never become evil. Morality is acquired, rather than inborn, and education is therefore of inestimable value.

The discussion shifts to government itself, and arguments about the relative value of the kingdom and of the commonwealth are weighed. The group concludes that the rule of the virtuous prince, a man attuned to both the active and the contemplative life, is best. Lord Octavian suggests that a council of the nobility and a lower advisory house, chosen from the citizens of the land, might increase the virtue and knowledge of the prince; such a government would combine the best aspects of monarchy, aristocracy, and the commonwealth.

Finally, Pietro Bembo discourses on Platonic love. The passions of youth are unfitting for the older courtier; he has to recognize that all love is, in fact, a yearning for beauty, and he must raise his thoughts from admiration of a single lovely woman to contemplate the idea of beauty. Purified of his human faults by this contemplation, he can reach "the high mansion place where the heavenly, amiable and right beauty dwelleth, which lieth hidden in the innermost secrets of

God." Bembo's discourse becomes more and more enraptured, and when he breaks off at last the others realize that it is daybreak. The courtiers and ladies disperse for the last time.

Critical Evaluation:

Baldassare Castiglione's *The Book of the Courtier* was one of the most widely read books in sixteenth century Europe. Noblemen and poets looked upon it as a portrait of the ideal man of the Renaissance, and such men as Sir Philip Sidney are said to have modeled themselves on Castiglione's imaginary courtier. There is, perhaps, no finer or more appealing picture of life in the Italian Renaissance than that in *The Book of the Courtier*. Castiglione had a brilliant dramatic gift that enabled him to bring to life his friends at Urbino and to express their ideals clearly and powerfully in natural, rapidly moving dialogue.

The Book of the Courtier became a handbook for the English gentleman. Queen Elizabeth's teacher, Roger Ascham, said a young man could learn more by reading the book than he would by spending three years in Italy. It seems ironic that Castiglione should find his most enthusiastic readers in England, for he distances himself from the original conversation in Urbino by pretending to have been in England at the time. His name appears in the dialogue only because he sends a glowing report about the education of Prince Henry, the future Henry VIII and the father of Elizabeth I.

Castiglione wrote *The Book of the Courtier* between 1508 and 1518. He kept adding to the text for another decade, during which it circulated among courts in the city states of what became Italy. Only when he got word of the circulation of an unauthorized copy did he finally prepare the text for publication. He presented specially bound volumes to surviving members of the group featured in the book. The group had gathered at the Palace of Urbino in March, 1507. The courtly ideal (or ideology) that Castiglione upheld was already dead in the Italian-speaking world, replaced by the power politics of the Medicis as described in *Il principe*, 1532 (*The Prince*, 1640) by Niccolò Machiavelli. Castiglione's son was forced to remove jokes about monks in order to keep later editions from being banned by the Catholic Church. Castiglione found an appreciative audience in England when Thomas Hoby translated the text.

Castiglione presents the book as an extended treatise for Alfonso Ariosto, a relative of the epic poet Ludovico Ariosto. In the opening of the first book, he addresses Alfonso directly, responding to his friend's request for an account of the ideal life at court. Rather than offer his own opinion, he says he is repeating what he heard about a famous exchange at Urbino. He says he is following classical tradition, and his closest model is Cicero's account of the ideal orator in *De oratore* (55 B.C.E.; *On Oratory*, 1742), also set as a dialogue in the past. Indeed, the courtier seems to be the Renaissance equivalent of the ancient Roman orator, a man of knowledge, influence, and eloquence. When Castiglione addresses Alfonso more briefly, at the outset of each succeeding book, he offers rhetorical proofs that public life is no worse in the Renaissance than it was in antiquity, that it has reached its recent perfection at the court of Duke Guidobaldo, and that it may again flourish at Urbino. Each major speaker gives a rhetorical declamation; together the speakers argue what a courtier should be, how he should act, how he should advise the prince, and what his female counterpart should be like.

The rules of the discussion that Lady Elisabetta proposes are the rules of rhetoric, as well as the rules of good manners, and everyone observes them. The rhetorical dimension of *The Book of the Courtier* was unmistakable to readers in the sixteenth century, when classical rhetoric was a central subject of education. Much of the dramatic interest, in what might easily have become a series of set speeches, derives from the rhetorical moves that the speakers make as they offer to be concise or beg each other to continue, as they challenge each other and reply to the challenges. Much of the pleasure that readers have had with the book is that of hearing genuine conversation among highly civilized people. Frederick Fregoso, who leads the discussion on the second evening, is especially concerned with metaphor, irony, and other figures of speech. It is not necessary, however, to know the names of all the rhetorical figures. It is enough to realize that Castiglione is not digressing or contradicting himself when he piles figure on figure and story on story; he is representing the twists and turns of a conversation.

Those twists and turns can be tiresome for modern readers who want to get on with the story. *The Book of the Courtier* is less a story about four evenings in Urbino than a book of stories about the courtly or courteous life. The chief method of proof that the various speakers use is the illustrative anecdote or exemplum, and there are even examples of good and bad practical jokes as the second evening draws to an uproarious end. Castiglione's model here may be *The Decameron* (1349-1351) by the great Italian storyteller Giovanni Boccaccio, a tale about people who tell tales. Castiglione's tales are in summary form, many of them no longer than a paragraph; they never use the street language that makes Boccaccio's tales so vivid, but they say much about the tellers. In the dedication to the bishop of Viseu, Castiglione rejects the comparison to Boccaccio that readers immediately made. His most fully realized characters, such as Emilia and Julian, nevertheless step out of the pages and live on their own. The advantage of a dialogue is that many points of view can be expressed, even if some are put down.

The villain in the piece is the sickly young Gaspar Pallavicin, who is thoroughly cynical about men and especially cynical about women. His views are barely tolerated, but they are forcefully expressed and belong to *The Book of the Courtier* as much as Bembo's encomium on love. Castiglione's *The Book of the Courtier* is inevitably paired with Machiavelli's *The Prince*, not only because the prince needs the courtier but also because idealism needs an antidote of realism. The Elizabethans saw the two works as poles apart. They coined the term "Machiavellian" to describe the rogues they feared in politics and cultivated the ideals of courtesy in the heroic courts of Sir Philip Sidney's *Arcadia* (1590, 1593, 1598) and Edmund Spenser's *The Faerie Queene* (1590, 1596).

"Critical Evaluation" by Thomas Willard

Further Reading

Berger, Harry, Jr. *The Absence of Grace: Sprezzatura and Suspicion in Two Renaissance Courtesy Books*. Stanford, Calif.: Stanford University Press, 2000. An analysis of *The Book of the Courtier* and Giovanni Della Casa's *Il Galateo*, focusing on how the authors depict the changing masculine identity in early modern Europe.

Burke, Peter. *The Fortunes of the Courtier: The European Recognition of Castiglione's Cortegiano*. University Park: Pennsylvania State University Press, 1995. Burke uses the European reception of Castiglione's *The Courtier* to illustrate historical and cultural shifts, particularly in the century following its first publication.

Castiglione, Baldassare. *The Book of the Courtier*. Translated and introduction by George Bull. New York: Penguin Books, 1967. Renders the Italian names more faithfully than Sir Thomas Hoby's classic translation. Includes a lively introduction, useful notes, and an index.

Finucci, Valeria. *The Lady Vanishes: Subjectivity and Representation in Castiglione and Ariosto*. Stanford, Calif.: Stanford University Press, 1992. A feminist and psychoanalytic perspective. Includes separate chapters on the discourse, the women, and the jokes in *The Book of the Courtier*. Draws comparisons to a popular epic of the same era.

Frye, Northrop. *Myth and Metaphor: Selected Essays, 1974-1988*. Edited by Robert D. Denham. Charlottesville: University Press of Virginia, 1990. Contains a lucid account of Castiglione's importance in Renaissance literature, written by one of the twentieth century's most influential literary critics.

Hanning, Robert W., and David Rosand, eds. *Castiglione: The Ideal and the Real in Renaissance Culture*. New Haven, Conn.: Yale University Press, 1983. Includes a chronology of Castiglione's life and essays on language, women, humanism, and Renaissance portraiture.

Kolsky, Stephen. *Courts and Courtiers in Renaissance Northern Italy*. Burlington, Vt.: Ashgate/Variorum, 2003. This study of the cultural renaissance in northern Italian courts during the late fifteenth and early sixteenth centuries begins with a discussion of *The Book of the Courier*, which Kolsky describes as "encapsulating" the period's sense of renewal. He then widens the perspective of Castiglione's text to address issues of biography, gender, and the role of the courtier as reflected in the lives and writings of other courtiers and patrons.

Rebhorn, Wayne A. *Courtly Performances: Masking and Festivity in Castiglione's "Book of the Courtier."* Detroit, Mich.: Wayne State University Press, 1978. Considers Castiglione's book from the perspective of courtly customs and entertainments.

Wiggins, Peter DeSa. *Donne, Castiglione, and the Poetry of Courtliness*. Bloomington: Indiana University Press, 2000. Examines the influence of Castiglione's book on English poet John Donne.

Woodhouse, John Robert. *Baldesar Castiglione: A Reassessment of "The Courtier."* Edinburgh: Edinburgh University Press, 1978. A new appraisal of Castiglione's work, emphasizing the artistic creation rather than the historical account.

The Book of the Dead

Author: Unknown
First transcribed: Papyrus Ani, 4500 B.C.E.-200 C.E.
(English translation, 1895, 1994 [authoritative edition])
Type of work: Religious philosophy

Principal characters:
OSIRIS, the judge and special god of the dead
ISIS, his sister goddess and mate
HORUS, twice-born, son of Osiris and Isis
ANUBIS, protector of dead; allotted destiny
SET, the principle of evil, murderer of Osiris
TEMU, spirit of creation; inspired Ptah
PTAH, author of creation; spoke First Word
RA, with Ptah, the principle of light; sun
NUT, sky goddess, great mother

The Story:

The god Temu, the spirit of creation, manifests first as Ptah and then as the word spoken by Ptah, which brings creation into existence. Ptah creates first himself, then the other gods, and finally creates Egypt, by speaking the divine words that make the gods aware of themselves; thus, all of creation exists as different aspects, or "faces," of Ptah, and of his words. Immediately after he speaks these first powerful magic words, while the earth and the waters of primordial chaos are still in the process of separating themselves, Ptah promises eternity to the dead who are not yet born. On that same day, the god Anubis, protector of the souls of the dead, allots to each person a destiny and holds all these fates in readiness.

For mortals, the immediate earthly manifestation of Ptah is Ra, the sun, and it is in this form that they most often contemplate the one God. Priests use many names to refer to the different faces of God; these names vary from place to place, but the names that the gods give themselves are hidden, because in their names lies their essence, and so their power. By a stratagem, Isis learns the hidden name of Ra and, with a power derived from his, becomes queen of the goddesses. Her power is illustrated by the story of her healing of her mate, the god Osiris.

Osiris is murdered by Set, his brother, who in his malice cuts the body of Osiris into pieces and scatters them across northern Africa. Isis, weeping, gathers these pieces together and rejoins them, and from the corpse conceives Horus, their son. Then she brings Osiris back to life, leads him before the gods, and brings him into new forms, with new powers. It is through this rebirth that Osiris becomes the principle of birth and rebirth. He is the fountainhead through which the earth receives life, from the first new life of sprouting corn and all the life it brings in its turn, to the rebirth in the afterlife of the pharaohs.

All the dead who receive the proper rites and who perform the sacred rituals are reborn in the afterlife as new forms of Osiris and share his glory. Like him, their bodies are made whole and perfect when they are resurrected in Osiris's name and in accordance with the prescribed formalities. The secrets of embalming, the processes and forms for charms and incantations and funereal rites, are given to mortals by Isis, who thus gives them a means of being reborn. As she recreates Osiris's body, so it is for the dead reborn in Osiris's name. As the dead approach Osiris in the afterlife, they recite the ritual incantations learned in life, and their impurities, manifestations of Set, fall away from them. Meanwhile the living, left to perform rites of ablution and purification, sprinkle cleansing water on the dead and make offerings. One after another the dead approach Osiris, and those who are justified are rejuvenated and are blessed by Isis and by Horus, who hold a special position within the hierarchy of immortals.

Horus, one of the greatest of the Egyptian panoply of gods, has as many as twenty different forms. In a sense he is one aspect of Osiris; in another sense he is an aspect of Ra. In most of his aspects, however, and perhaps because of his relationship to Ra, he is closely associated with light. In a battle with Set, Horus loses one eye, but pursues Set, the spirit of evil, and castrates him, making Set powerless. Horus is therefore especially revered by the dead, for by Horus's victory over the darkness of Set the dead can see to approach eternity, and by Horus's victory over the evil of Set the dead can be sanctified. Horus's face, in the aspect called Harmachis (translated as "Horus on the Horizon"), is immortalized as the face of the great Sphinx of Gizeh.

Horus leads the dead into the presence of Osiris and acts as intermediary for the dead during the process of judgment. Horus is especially suited for this role by virtue of his aspect as an avenger of his father and of the miraculous circumstances surrounding his conception. Making his petitions for the dead to his father in the presence of his mother, his pleas are granted. Then the dead make a special appeal to Osiris to restore the physical body and protect it from decay, as he renewed his own after it was dismembered by his brother Set.

The gods live in a paradise in the sky, and there the justified dead live with them. When Nut, the goddess of the sky, bends over forward and places her palms flat on the earth before her, her arms and legs form the pillars that uphold the sky. Across this sky pass the sun and moon, and through it sails the Celestial Boat, carrying the gods and the dead permitted to join them. Their souls arrive by ascending a ladder or by passing through a gap in the mountains. There they live in peace and serenity in the presence of the gods, renewed daily by the power of Osiris.

Critical Evaluation:

For five thousand years, those who lived along the Nile and across Northern Africa believed that when they died, they would be resurrected in body and spirit by the power of Osiris and would live forever in the presence of the majesty of the One God in all his different forms. Death was an untying of the knot that held the soul on the mortal plane and was more a cause for methodical care and preparation than for fear. The precepts on which the Egyptians built their convictions are recorded in what has come to be known, somewhat inaccurately, as *The Book of the Dead*.

The literal translation of the title by which the Egyptians referred to this remarkable work is "the book of coming forth by day." Its influences on Western culture have been significant, and various editions and forms of the book have been continuously available for study since long before the time of Cleopatra. Some "chapters" were inked on the sarcophagi of the pharaohs; others were carved into the stones of the secret and sacred chambers of the pyramids. Copies on papyrus of the spells, hymns, and incantations were buried with the dead for ready use in the trials that the departed soul would face in the netherworld. Whatever translation one reads, however, one finds that the book is a vehicle for profound feeling, from the weeping of Isis as she searches for the severed limbs of her beloved Osiris to the joy of the dead whose spirits awaken to a fresh northern breeze in the light from Ra.

Recorded editions exist in three forms; the earliest are the Pyramid texts, dating from 2400 B.C.E., hieroglyphics carved in the stones of the pyramids of the fifth, sixth, and eighth dynasty rulers. These texts are clearly derived from much older oral versions. Later, when coffins became shaped to conform to the body within, papyrus scrolls replaced the carvings or

inked symbols; gradually the use of hieratic script, a more abstract form of writing, replaced the earlier hieroglyphics. Finally, after the Roman conquest, scraps of spells or charms, their meanings largely forgotten, were written in contemporary script on small squares of papyrus and tossed into the coffins before they were sealed.

There is no authoritative version of the book, although a reasonably complete compilation appeared in German translation in 1842 and was widely available in English translation after 1895. The various chapters, of which there are now known to be more than three hundred, include hymns of adoration, charms, rituals of purification and passage, and devotional poems written over a period spanning five millennia. Copies were eventually mass produced by priests and scribes for sale to individuals for burial use, though the text was not standardized until the Ptolemaic period, which began in 322 B.C.E. Various "recensions," authoritative versions of which multiple and various editions exist, have been identified and studied extensively, but no comprehensive ancient version has been found to contain all of the chapters.

The influence this rich and vital book of scripture has had on other cultures is incalculable. The religion of Osiris was flourishing while the Israelites were captive in Egypt, and there can be little doubt that some of the images and symbols, as well as some of the more powerful precepts of faith and spirituality, were incorporated from the Egyptian cult of Osiris into the holy Hebrew writings that later formed the bases of the Talmud, the Qurʾān, and the Bible. Hymns to Ra and Osiris have much in common with the Psalms, both in image and theme. The image of King David dancing before God, for example, mirrors that of Seti I dancing before the assembled deities of the netherworld.

The most significant parallels, however, are in the coincident views on a single, all-powerful father/creator and on a redeemer, part man and part God, who will come to afford the souls of the sanctified resurrection and eternal life. All three of the major modern religions to originate in Northern Africa share these basic views; all three revere the power of ritual worship; all three believe in the existence of a paradise to which the justified dead may aspire, and all three have elaborate funereal procedures during which prayers are made to intercede for the departed souls. The Egyptian cult of Osiris significantly predates all three of the other main North African religions, and when the Romans introduced Christianity to the Egyptians they found fertile soil already prepared. Osiris and Horus, father and son, easily became identified with God and Christ, while the statues of Isis suckling Horus could be seen as Mary with the infant Jesus. Other parallels too numerous to mention may be noted.

The Book of the Dead is an affirmation of faith and joy. All such works are beautiful allegories reconciling seeming contradictions of light and darkness, good and evil, multiplicity and unity, and life and death. New generations of readers will bring new interpretations, but what is timeless will remain so, and *The Book of the Dead* will continue to be a subject of study.

Andrew B. Preslar

Further Reading

Budge, E. A. Wallis. *The Book of the Dead: The Papyrus of Ani in the British Museum—The Egyptian Text with Interlinear Transliteration and Translation*. Reprint. New York: Dover, 1967. An extensive introduction describes the gods, their roles, and their realms, along with the funeral ceremonies and their importance. Clear interpretations by chapter.

_____. *Egyptian Religion: Egyptian Ideas of the Future Life*. Reprint. London: Routledge & Kegan Paul, 1975. Explores conceptual and symbolic parallels between the beliefs of the Osirians and the modern Christians. Classification by subject imposes a degree of order on the diverse topics.

Černý, Jaroslav. *Ancient Egyptian Religion*. London: Hutchinson University Library, 1952. Černý describes Osirian beliefs in a style that is learned without being difficult. Includes a timetable matching dynastic periods with dates.

Champdor, Albert. *"The Book of the Dead," Based on the Ani, Hunefer, and Anhaï Papyri in the British National Museum*. Translated by Faubion Bowers. New York: Garrett, 1966. Arranges material chronologically, from creation to modern times. Champdor weaves interpretation with text to capture the substance and grandeur of the work. Extensive, beautiful illustrations provide visual context.

Dunand, Françoise, and Christian Zivie-Coche. "Death Will Come." In *Gods and Men in Egypt: 3000 B.C.E. to 395 B.C.E.* Translated from the French by David Lorton. Ithaca, N.Y.: Cornell University Press, 2004. There are numerous mentions of *The Book of the Dead* in this book about ancient Egyptian religion, but the majority of them are contained in this section that describes Egyptian ideas about death. The comprehensive index provides a listing of all of the references to the book.

Hornung, Erik. *Conceptions of God in Ancient Egypt: The One and the Many*. Translated by John Baines. Ithaca, N.Y.: Cornell University Press, 1971. An exhaustive treatment of the subject, in which Hornung outlines the Egyptian solution to the paradox of unity in multiplicity. Includes an invaluable chronology, a glossary of gods, and an index.

Schumann Antelme, Ruth, and Stéphane Rossini. *"Third Stage: The Book of the Dead*, Methods of Obtaining Immortality." In *Becoming Osiris: The Ancient Egyptian Death Experience*. Translated by Jon Graham. Rochester, Vt.: Inner Traditions, 1998. The authors describe the procedures set forth in *The Book of the Dead* and other practices that the ancient Egyptians believed were necessary for the human soul to attain immortality.

Book of the Duchess

Author: Geoffrey Chaucer (c. 1343-1400)
First published: c. 1370
Type of work: Poetry
Type of plot: Allegory
Time of plot: Indeterminate
Locale: Idealized dream landscape

Principal characters:
DREAMER, a dying man who has a vision
BLACK KNIGHT, a dying lover who has lost his beloved
WHITE, the beloved who has died

The Poem:

The Dreamer is lamenting his terrible loss, a loss which only one physician might heal. He lost his beloved lady, either through rejection or through death. In either case, the Dreamer is unable to sleep, fearful that death might come upon him. There seems to be no hope for him.

He decides to pass a lonely night by reading in a collection of tales, and there he finds the story of King Ceyx and Queen Alcyone. When Ceyx sailed away, his wife waited patiently yet eagerly for his return, but she was unaware that his ship was caught in a storm and all hands were lost. As the days went by, Alcyone began to despair, and, like the Dreamer, she was unable to sleep and finally prayed to Juno for relief. Juno sent a messenger to the god Morpheus, who inhabited Ceyx's drowned body and told Alcyone of his death. Alcyone died four days later of despair.

The Dreamer regrets Alcyone's pain but responds to the story of the god of sleep, Morpheus, and he imagines what rich gifts he will give to that god if only he will confer sleep upon him. In fact, his head begins to nod and he falls asleep over his book. He is instantly transported to a dream landscape. It is May; the flowers bloom, rivaling the stars in the sky in number. The fairies make their abode in the forest, and the whole place resembles a landscaped garden.

The Dreamer finds himself in a beautiful chamber filled with paintings and glazed windows that tell stories of love and romance. Then suddenly he is outside, watching the Emperor Octavian in a royal hunt. The hounds find the scent, but the hart is clever and escapes the dogs. The hunt is recalled, but the Dreamer, stationed by a tree, finds one of the young, untrained dogs coming up to him. He follows the whelp, which takes him deeper into the woods. The forest is beautiful, orderly, and full of deer.

There the Dreamer finds the Black Knight, who lies beneath a huge oak singing a song of sorrow over the death of his lady. In fact, his sorrow is so deep that, as the Dreamer watches, the Black Knight seems to be dying, the blood draining from all his limbs and leaving him green and pale. The Dreamer greets him, and though the Knight seems unaware of the Dreamer's presence at first, soon his courteous nature asserts itself and he greets the Dreamer gently. When the Dreamer offers to help bear his sorrow and asks the Knight to reveal its cause, the Knight is at first reluctant, but he then begins a diatribe against Fortune and its wiles. It is Fortune that has brought him low, he argues, by playing chess with him and stealing his lady.

The Dreamer does not seem to understand this image and encourages the Knight to stand firm against Fortune, arguing that no loss of a love should lead to this kind of woe. The Knight responds that the Dreamer does not understand how much he indeed lost, for, since his youth, he was wholly subject to love, and now that to which he devoted himself is destroyed.

The Black Knight tells how he first met his lady, dancing on a green with a company of ladies. She is by far the fairest, the most beautiful and courteous, the best in speech and manner, gentle, good, steadfast, and simple. She is faithful and temperate, unable to do wrong because she loves right so much. The Dreamer concludes that the Black Knight could not have bestowed his love on a better woman and asks to

hear of their first words together. The Black Knight confesses that for a long time he did not tell her of his love; he simply composed songs about her. His woe increased, however, and finally he approached her and swore his love. At first, she rejected him, and for a year he lived in despair until, gathering his courage, he approached her again. This time he was accepted because of his virtue, and for years they lived happily.

Then, the Knight moans, death took her. At that word, the Dreamer sees the hunters returning through the woods and the king riding homeward to a long castle with white walls. The Dreamer wakes up in his bed and resolves to put his dream into rhyme.

Critical Evaluation:

Geoffrey Chaucer is best known for his *The Canterbury Tales* (1387-1400). *Book of the Duchess* is one of his minor works, probably his first fully polished long poem. It is generally understood that the poem is meant to commemorate the death of Blanche, the duchess of Lancaster and the wife of John of Gaunt, one of Chaucer's patrons. If this is true, then the poem was probably meant not only to celebrate her physical and spiritual virtues but also to console John in some measure over the loss of his own beloved. The frequent references to the color white, including the principal woman's name, suggest that Chaucer was punning on the name Blanche.

If the poem is connected to a specific individual, it is still very much a genre poem. When Chaucer was writing this poem, he was heavily influenced by French poets who frequently used allegories in which a dreamer was suddenly transported to a beautiful, gardenlike setting, as though he had entered into a tapestry. There the lover learns something about the nature of love, usually by meeting a lover who has been rejected by his lady or who has suffered the lady's death. There are some indications, such as a reference to an eight-year illness, that Chaucer adds to these conventions specific references to the despair of John of Gaunt; nevertheless, he remains firmly within the convention of the dream allegory.

The story of *Book of the Duchess* is one of increasing woe and a search for consolation. The story begins with the Dreamer's own undefined loss and his suggestion that only one physician will help, suggesting that the physician is in fact his lady, who either will not or cannot help him. (The same image is later used to describe White.) His hopeless despair is so deep that he cannot sleep and fears that he will die.

In fact, the second story of loss suggests that this indeed might happen. The loss of King Ceyx is a mirror image of the loss of the Dreamer's lady, only here the despair does indeed drive Alcyone first to a lack of sleep, then to a telling dream, and then to death. The story has the potential of leading to a tragic conclusion for the Dreamer. However, this is a poem about consolation, and it does not end with tragedy. Some have gone so far as to suggest that Chaucer is using the story of Ceyx and Alcyone to encourage John of Gaunt to move past his grief, rather than to yield to it.

The third story of grief is that of the Black Knight and his lady, and the Dreamer learns of it as he encourages the Black Knight to tell of his lady, of their first meeting, and of his loss. Like the Dreamer, the Black Knight is physically devastated by his loss, and he can think of nothing else. In fact, it seems that for him to think of anything else would be a betrayal of his lady. The Dreamer leads him to the point of revealing the totality of his loss.

With this admission comes a vision of the return of the king to his white-walled castle set upon a rich hill, and, while the description may once again be a reference to John of Gaunt, it also suggests a heavenly vision, there lying the ultimate—and only—consolation. The recurring theme of each of the stories of loss is that "too little while our bliss lasts," that happiness is fleeting. The suggestion at the conclusion, however, is that, though this is true while on earth, it is not true in an eternal sense.

If the central issue of the poem is loss and consolation, it deals with that issue on several levels. The poem can be read as an idealized allegorical biography in which the Black Knight clearly represents John of Gaunt and White represents Blanche. The poem can also be read as an elegy meant principally to console John, encouraging him to keep intact his wife's memory but to move beyond his grief. (Certainly there is no other forum in which Chaucer, the son of a merchant, could have given advice like this to one of the most powerful men in England.) The poem can also be read as an examination of grief in which each of the characters represents an attitude toward loss: the Dreamer representing reason, the Black Knight symbolizing passion.

Chaucer does seem to suggest an inevitable progress in the ways characters respond to grief. Anxiousness leads to despair, leading to sleeplessness, leading, eventually, to sleep with troubled dreams that seem to accentuate the loss. When the Dreamer enters the dreamworld, it is hardly surprising that he comes upon a figure much like himself—not in terms of his social position but in terms of his psychological position. In his dream situation, the role of the Dreamer is suddenly reversed; whereas in the beginning of the poem, he was dying and in need of consolation, he is now the one to offer consolation to one who is also dying over the loss of a beloved.

The character of the Dreamer in this role has been variously interpreted. On one hand, he seems something of a dunce. He hears the Black Knight sing a song in which he laments the death of his beloved lady, yet later he seems unable to understand that the Black Knight is sorrowing over his lady's death. In fact, he gives him what appears to be callous advice, suggesting that the loss of a lady is not worth intemperate grief. Perhaps the Dreamer means well, but he is an inept comforter.

Yet, on the other hand, the Dreamer may be quite psychologically astute. In his apparent clumsiness, he leads the Black Knight into a recitation of joyful and happy memories—quite different from the Knight's initial moanings and groanings. At first, the Knight cannot make an open declaration of the cause of his grief, though he hints at it. Finally he is led to a point at which he declares his lady's death. Only at this point, when the words are stated boldly and accepted as true, does the Black Knight confront his own pain. As he confronts pain, so, too, does the Dreamer. It is then that consolation comes and the Dreamer awakes, for the dream is no longer necessary.

The poem is a recognition that this is a world of real pain and real loss. Such loss and pain lead to real sadness that cannot simply be wiped away; in fact, remembering a loved one, even though it may bring pain, is good and valid. Pain must be accepted rather than denied, for even though the long and white castle suggests a heavenly reunion, in this world it is only natural to feel grief in the face of inevitable loss.

Gary D. Schmidt

Further Reading

Boitani, Piero, and Jill Mann, eds. *The Cambridge Companion to Chaucer*. 2d ed. New York: Cambridge University Press, 2003. Collection of essays, including discussions of Chaucer's style, the literary structure of his works, the social and literary scene in England during his lifetime, and his French and Italian inheritances. Many of the essays analyze specific works, including "Old Books Brought to Life in Dreams: The *Book of the Duchess*, the *House of Fame*, the *Parliament of Fowls*" by Piero Boitani.

Bronson, Bertrand H. "*The Book of the Duchess* Re-Opened." In *Chaucer: Modern Essays in Criticism*, edited by Edward Wagenknecht. London: Oxford University Press, 1959. Bronson focuses on the apparent inconsistencies and ignorance of the narrator, arguing that these are not flaws but are actually built into the meaning and narrative structure of the poem.

Corsa, Helen Storm. *Chaucer: Poet of Mirth and Morality.* Toronto, Ont.: Forum House, 1970. In a chapter examining Chaucer's early work, Corsa argues that, though the occasion of *Book of the Duchess* is a sad one, the general tone is one of gladness and mirth.

Hieatt, Constance B. *The Realism of Dream Vision: The Poetic Exploitation of the Dream-Experience in Chaucer and His Contemporaries.* The Hague, the Netherlands: Mouton, 1967. Hieatt examines the ways in which Chaucer raises and uses reader expectations to create meaning in his dream visions.

Lawlor, John. "The Pattern of Consolation in *The Book of the Duchess.*" In *Chaucer Criticism,* edited by Richard J. Schoek and Jerome Taylor. Notre Dame, Ind.: University of Notre Dame Press, 1961. Lawlor examines the complex system of consolation which the narrator offers to the bereaved Black Knight, moving from apparent ignorance to assertion of his loss.

Lynch, Kathryn L. *Chaucer's Philosophical Visions.* Rochester, N.Y.: D. S. Brewer, 2000. Focuses on Chaucer's knowledge of and interest in late medieval English Scholasticism and other forms of philosophy, and how his works reflected his philosophical visions. Chapter 2 focuses on *Book of the Duchess.*

Millar, Robert P. *Chaucer Sources and Backgrounds.* New York: Oxford University Press, 1977. Millar supplies translations of the French and Latin sources that Chaucer used for his dream visions, though this book deals with the entire range of Chaucer's work.

Muscatine, Charles. *Chaucer and the French Tradition.* Berkeley: University of California Press, 1957. Muscatine focuses on the dream vision tradition from French literature and Chaucer's adaptations of those forms.

Robertson, D. W., Jr. "*The Book of the Duchess.*" In *Companion to Chaucer Studies,* edited by Beryl Rowland. New York: Oxford University Press, 1968. Robertson provides a general study of the background, thematic meanings, and critical understandings of *Book of the Duchess.*

Spearing, A. C. *Medieval Dream-Poetry.* New York: Cambridge University Press, 1976. In a chapter on *Book of the Duchess* within this general study of medieval dream visions, Spearing argues that, though the poem demonstrates many of the traditional elements of the dream vision, it differs from them in that it was written for a specific occasion and has a great deal of material not included in the actual vision. These differences affect the operation of the dream vision in terms of its overall meaning for the reader.

The Book of Theseus

Author: Giovanni Boccaccio (1313-1375)
First transcribed: Teseida, 1340-1341 (English translation, 1974)
Type of work: Poetry
Type of plot: Epic
Time of plot: Antiquity
Locale: Athens

Principal characters:
THESEUS, ruler of Athens
HIPPOLYTA, his wife
EMILIA, her sister
ACHATES, Theseus's kinsman
CREON, the leader against Theseus
ARCITES and PALAEMON, cousins and soldiers of Creon
PEIRITHOUS, a nobleman, friend to Theseus

The Story:

While Aegeus is king of Athens, the women of Scythia rebel against the men and elect Hippolyta queen. Theseus proposes to purge this sin and set sail with an army to fight the Amazons. When Theseus attacks the fortress of Queen Hippolyta, he receives a message from her saying that he should desist or he will be driven away. He in turn tells her that she must surrender or die. Hippolyta decides to surrender under a pact whereby she becomes Theseus's bride. After

the wedding, Theseus is struck by the beauty of Hippolyta's sister Emilia.

Two years later, Theseus, Hippolyta, and Emilia sail to Athens. On his return Theseus learns that Creon attacked Thebes and, hating the Greeks, prohibited the burial of the dead Thebans. Theseus vows to defeat Creon so that the dead men of the weeping Athenian women can have a proper burial. Theseus and his men follow the women to the scene of battle and confront Creon. After the warriors challenge one another, the two armies fight. During the battle Theseus encounters Creon and kills him. Creon's men flee to the mountains. Theseus then tells the women to collect the bodies of their men and burn them in proper ceremony.

Meanwhile, some Athenian soldiers find two wounded youths of Creon's army, Palaemon and Arcites, whose armor shows them to be of royal blood. When they are brought before Theseus, he has them taken as prisoners back to Athens. Several days after his triumphant return to Athens, Theseus summons Palaemon and Arcites and sentences them to eternal imprisonment in the palace, where, because of their station, they will be treated well.

On a day in the following spring, as Arcites is opening the window of his prison chamber, he sees Emilia in the garden below. He is so overwhelmed by her beauty that he believes her to be Venus. Arcites summons Palaemon; both immediately acknowledge their love for her. Emilia hears them and leaves, but every morning she returns and, because of her vanity, sings in the garden below their window. Each day the youths become more in love with her. In the autumn, however, she ceases her morning stroll, and Palaemon and Arcites become desperate.

At that time Theseus is visited by his friend Peirithous. When Theseus mentions his two prisoners to Peirithous, the visitor asks to see them. Peirithous, recognizing Arcites as an old friend, requests that Theseus release him. Arcites leaves Athens with great sadness, for he does not wish to leave his companion Palaemon in prison, nor does he want to lose his opportunity of seeing Emilia. Palaemon believes that Arcites is fortunate in being able to travel and alleviate his pain while he is forced to be confined.

Later, calling himself Pentheus, Arcites returns to Athens in disguise. He manages to obtain a position with Theseus and becomes his favorite servant. He is not able to keep his identity secret from Emilia, but she does not reveal what she knows and he is able to contain his desire for her by sleeping in a field three miles from the city. There he prays each night to Venus to encourage Emilia to love him. One morning, as Arcites returns to the palace from his abode, one of Palaemon's servants hears Arcites' lamentations and discovers his true identity. He returns to the prison and tells Palaemon that Pentheus is actually Arcites. This information enrages Palaemon. He decides to escape and win Emilia by armed force.

With the help of his servant, who intoxicates the guards, Palaemon escapes and goes to an inn. The next morning he arms himself and goes to the place where Arcites sleeps. After professing their love for Emilia, the kinsmen decide that a

sword fight will determine who should vie for her hand. They begin to fight savagely.

Theseus and Emilia, who are hunting with some companions, chance to pass the field where the battle is taking place, and Emilia summons Theseus to stop the fight. After Theseus confronts the youths, they inform him of their mutual love for Emilia. Believing that both men are qualified to be her husband, Theseus proposes a battle in the theater to decide who should have her hand. The conditions of the battle are that one year from that day the cousins will each bring one hundred chosen soldiers.

During the next year Arcites and Palaemon pass the time with lavish feasts, hunts, jousts, and finally with preparations for the battle. As the day approaches, great noblemen and warriors come to the city, elaborately dressed and armed. There is one last great feast for all the soldiers and nobility.

On the day before the battle Arcites and Palaemon pray to the gods. Arcites prays to Mars, promising that if he should be made victor, he will give great honor to Mars and his temples. To this plea, Mars gives a sign that the vow was heard. Palaemon, on the other hand, goes to the temple of Cytheraea, where he prays not for victory but for the hand of Emilia, and he, too, receives a sign. Emilia, not wishing harm to either suitor, prays to the goddess Diana, in whose temple she kindles two fires. She asks that the desires of the two lovers be quenched. If she has to accept one, however, she prays that it will be the lover who desires her more. She receives a sign that she will have one of the two, but that the outcome cannot yet be revealed.

The next day the spectators and soldiers gather in the great theater. Arcites and his men enter from the east, Palaemon and his men from the west. At the sound of the third call to battle, the fight begins, with many noblemen wounding one another. The sight of the battlefield wet with blood and so many men dying for her causes Emilia to wish that Theseus had let the two finish the fight in the grove. Shortly, the warriors become tired and perplexed, but Arcites, spurred on by Mars, fights more fiercely than ever, causing Emilia's affection to turn to him. Arcites, victorious, circles the field with his men.

Venus, who watched the battle with Mars, each concerned for their respective champions, tells Mars that his part is over, for he granted Arcites' prayer. She then directs Erinys to frighten Arcites' steed. The horse rears and Arcites falls, mortally wounded. Emilia and Palaemon are grief-stricken at the sight of the dying Arcites. A doctor is summoned and Arcites is carried to the palace and placed on a great bed. There he and Emilia are married by Theseus, and Palaemon is set free. Knowing that he will die with his love unconsummated, Arcites summons Palaemon and tells him that he should take Emilia. Emilia refuses to accept Palaemon. She tells Arcites that she will die a virgin.

After nine days of great suffering, Arcites dies, and Theseus orders a great funeral ceremony for the dead warrior. Later Palaemon has a temple built to Juno to contain Arcites' ashes. In it are represented all the adventures of Arcites' life. Emilia's grief for her dead husband causes her to become sickly, and it is therefore agreed that her lamentation should cease and that she will be wed to Palaemon. Theseus tells them that Arcites lived well and was mourned enough. Palaemon and Emilia are then married. A great feast is held for fifteen days to celebrate their wedding.

Critical Evaluation:

The Book of Theseus is an epic poem composed in Italian and written in stanzas of eight verses (octavos). The poem is divided into twelve cantos or books, the traditional number of books in classical epics. Boccaccio wrote this poem as the first epic in the Italian language, and the poem recounts the deeds of warriors. Boccaccio followed Dante Alighieri, who, a generation earlier with his *La divina commedia* (c. 1320; *The Divine Comedy*, 1802), established Italian as a legitimate vehicle for literary work of a serious intent, as opposed to the Middle Ages' established literary language, Latin.

The structure of *The Book of Theseus* is straightforward. Book 1 explores how Emilia came to be in Athens, and book 2 shows how Arcites and Palaemon arrived there—none of them being a native Athenian. The first six books lead up to the tournament fought between the two rivals for Emilia's love, and the second six books present the exploits of the contest and its aftermath. The work opens with the events surrounding the marriage of Theseus and Hippolyta, and it closes with the nuptials of Palaemon and Emilia.

Boccaccio's work reflects the literary influence of the "sweet new style," the poetic style popularized by Dante by which the Italian language was advanced as an avenue for the sophisticated expression of an emerging Italian culture. Boccaccio intended the work as a new type of vernacular literature, but much of it also reflects his medieval heritage. The romance epic was a well-established genre. Even though the principal figures of *The Book of Theseus* are ancient Greeks, they think and behave as medieval knights, demonstrating two medieval literary types. First, they strive for the courtly love of the unobtainable woman. As Arcites explains to Palaemon in book 5, Arcites can never expect to reveal his love for Emilia. Arcites is living in disguise as a servant to Theseus, someone customarily unworthy of Emilia's noble status. Palaemon, as an escaped prisoner and a former enemy of the Athenians, likewise cannot openly solicit her love.

Second, after Arcites' and Palaemon's passions for Emilia become known to Theseus, they engage in a medieval joust, a tournament involving them and their soldiers.

Theseus, the ruler of ancient Athens, is the namesake of the work, and he plays an important role. He is the force that moves the tale along, first by bringing all the participants together in Athens and then by supervising the unfolding of its various episodes. Books 1 and 2 establish Theseus as an ideal medieval knight. Twice he resolves to sacrifice himself in order to right a perceived wrong by marching off to war. In ensuing battles, he proves his soldierly competence, and afterward he demonstrates his generosity and wisdom. Readers might judge the other figures by his image.

The action of *The Book of Theseus* centers on the relationship between Arcites and Palaemon. Having proven their noble origins and knightly valor in book 2, they then individually seek the love of Emilia. Even though they compete directly for her and each attempts to defeat the other physically—even to death—they both also show concern and sympathy for each other. Arcites chooses not to slay Palaemon in the heat of battle while Palaemon lies unconscious, and Palaemon tends to Arcites' wounds after the tournament. The most poignant episode of their story occurs when Arcites, mortally wounded, wishes that his new bride, Emilia, should next marry Palaemon, and Palaemon resolves to follow through on Arcites' wish more out of love for him than for love of Emilia.

The Book of Theseus is much more than a simple story of two knights striving for the love of a lady. The travails of Arcites and Palaemon are an allegory for the tension between reason and passion. Arcites repeatedly offers prayers to Mars, the god of war. Palaemon is aided by Venus, the goddess of love and sexual appetite. Mars and Venus are participants in the action, and they are equal in degree to Arcites and Palaemon. They compete between themselves and at times involve themselves directly in the action of the human players. The two young men are their proxies, literally and metaphorically, as two competing impulses in human nature.

Emilia and Hippolyta demonstrate a traditional role for women in medieval romance epics; they also reflect medieval society's perspective on women. Both are major figures in the tale: Hippolyta is queen of the self-governing Amazons, and Emilia is the object of the desires of the two principal antagonists. Both women also serve the literary purposes of their corresponding male figures rather than having their own purposes. Hippolyta is the occasion for an illustration of Theseus's military skill, personal courage, and gentle benevolence. Emilia likewise exists to serve the literary purposes of male figures. Early in her youth (and in the work), she becomes aware of Arcites' and Palaemon's admiration of her beauty, but she never exhibits a voice of her own in their competition for her love. Theseus, with the full agreement of the two young men, declares that she will be the prize to the victor in their tournament. Emilia does not resist this plan, and she does not even reveal any preference between the two men.

Reflecting a familiarity with classical literature (from antiquity), Boccaccio uses the ancient Roman author Statius as an inspirational model. Boccaccio adapts the tale, according to his own words in the work, from the Byzantine (medieval Greek) heritage. Ancient epics were popular throughout the Middle Ages. Boccaccio frequently mentions stories and characters from ancient history and mythology. These references would have been readily recognized by Boccaccio's contemporaries. A modern reader may find these references esoteric, but they reinforce the story and increase its impact for readers.

According to Boccaccio's own words within *The Book of Theseus*, he intended this as a major epic to bolster the vernacular and culture of Italians. *The Book of Theseus* is narrative and epical, and the tale is entertaining, yet it did not achieve the renown for which Boccaccio hoped. A crucial reason was its lack of a distinctly Italian nature. The setting and the characters are, after all, Grecian.

"Critical Evaluation" by Alan Cottrell

Further Reading

Anderson, David. *Before the Knight's Tale: Imitation of Classical Epic in Boccaccio's "Teseida."* Philadelphia: University of Pennsylvania Press, 1988. A literary analysis. Anderson argues that Boccaccio's *Book of Theseus* is a creative imitation of the work of the classical writer Statius. Emphasizes Boccaccio's own sources of inspiration.

Boccaccio, Giovanni. *The Book of Theseus—Teseida delle Nozze d'Emilia.* Translated by Bernadette Marie McCoy. New York: Medieval Text Association, 1974. A translation of the work with an introduction. At the end of each of *The Book of Theseus*'s twelve books is a slightly abridged translation of Boccaccio's own marginal glosses to the text.

Branca, Vittore. *Boccaccio: The Man and His Works.* Translated by Richard Monges. New York: New York University Press, 1976. Authoritative biography of Boccaccio by a preeminent Italian scholar. Includes a specific discussion of the *The Book of Theseus*.

Branch, Eren Hostetter. "Rhetorical Structures and Strategies in Boccaccio's *Teseida.*" In *The Craft of Fiction: Essays in Medieval Poetics*, edited by Leigh A. Arrathoon. Rochester, Mich.: Solaris Press, 1984. Examines the various rhetorical devices employed by Boccaccio. Branch discusses the intellectual and stylistic traditions—for example, classical, Christian, and vernacular—into which Boccaccio's rhetorical devices fit.

Gittes, Tobias Foster. *Boccaccio's Naked Muse: Eros, Culture, and the Mythopoeic Imagination.* Toronto, Ont.: University of Toronto Press, 2008. Examines all of Boccaccio's works, including *The Book of Theseus*, to demonstrate how he used an innovative and coherent system of mythology in order to express his cultural experience and address the needs of his readers.

Hagedorn, Suzanne C. "Boccaccio's Teseo, Chaucer's Theseus: Duplicity and Desire." In *Abandoned Women: Rewriting the Classics in Dante, Boccaccio, and Chaucer.* Ann Arbor: University of Michigan Press, 2004. A feminist interpretation of medieval literature. Hagedorn's comparison of Boccaccio's and Geoffrey Chaucer's accounts of Theseus focuses on the authors' adaptation of classical tales about abandoned women.

Wallace, David. *Chaucer and the Early Writings of Boccaccio.* Woodbridge, Suffolk, England: D. S. Brewer, 1985. Examines the relationship between Boccaccio and Chaucer. Discusses *The Book of Theseus* in chapter 7.

The Border Trilogy

Author: Cormac McCarthy (1933-   )
First published: 1999; includes *All the Pretty Horses*,
    1992; *The Crossing*, 1994; *Cities of the Plain*, 1998
Type of work: Novels
Type of plot: Western
Time of plot: 1949-2002
Locale: Arizona, New Mexico, and Texas; Coahuila,
    Chihuahua, and Sonora, Mexico

Principal characters:
JOHN GRADY COLE, an accomplished horseman
LACEY RAWLINS, his friend
JIMMY BLEVINS, a waif
DON HECTOR ROCHA Y VILLARREAL, a ranch owner
ALEJANDRA, the don's beautiful daughter
DUEÑA ALFONSA, grandaunt and godmother to Alejandra
BILLY PARHAM, a sixteen-year-old
BOYD PARHAM, Billy's younger brother
THE GIRL, a waif
MAC McGOVERN, a ranch owner
MAGDALENA, a young Mexican prostitute

The Story:

It is 1949, outside San Angelo, Texas, and the death of John Grady Cole's grandfather causes his absentee mother to sell the family ranch. John Grady's poor, ill, vagabond father, who is also a gambler, cannot help the family.

John Grady and Lacey Rawlins, his friend, head for Mexico. The boys enjoy the old cowboy life without the cattle. They are followed by a skinny younger boy who calls himself Jimmy Blevins and claims ownership of the magnificent bay, or red-colored horse, he is riding. Although John Grady and Lacey doubt his story, they allow him to ride along anyway.

Jimmy exhibits his shooting skills and regales them with his stories. One day a norther, or strong storm with north winds, threatens, and Jimmy insists on trying to outride the storm; he hides in an arroyo wearing only his dirty underwear because he fears the fastenings of his clothes will draw lightning. The next day, John Grady and Lacey find Jimmy with only one boot and no horse. His clothes have washed away in the flood of the storm. John Grady consults the reluctant Lacey and then lends Jimmy a shirt. He and Jimmy ride double.

In Encantada, they spot Jimmy's pistol in a man's hip pocket and his horse in an old mud building. Rawlins argues that they should ride away before it is too late, but John Grady realizes that he cannot abandon Blevins, and Rawlins agrees to stay. Blevins says that he will not leave without his horse, saddle, and gun. The boys ride into town at daybreak but cannot locate the horse. Blevins vanishes into an open window of the stable and suddenly bursts through the fence on the galloping bay. They are hotly pursued until Blevins says that because his horse is faster, he should stay on the road and John Grady and Lacey should head cross country. With that, he is gone.

John Grady and Rawlins ride until they come to a huge ranch, La Purísima, and hire on as ranch hands. John Grady has exceptional skills with horses, and he makes a deal with Don Rocha to break and train his range stock. Rocha is impressed with John Grady and promotes him.

The boys also notice Rocha's beautiful equestrienne daughter, Alejandra. John Grady is invited by Alejandra's grandaunt, Dueña Alfonsa, to visit the house and play chess. Some days later, John Grady and Alejandra become lovers. The next day, officers appear at the house, but they soon leave. Don Rocha finds out about his daughter's activities and considers killing John Grady. Soon, however, John Grady is wakened and arrested by two officers tipped off by Rocha. He and Rawlins are handcuffed, returned to Encantada, and put into a small jail cell where Blevins is already incarcerated, his feet crippled from beatings. Two months after parting, Blevins had returned to the town to retrieve his pistol and ended up shooting three men, one of whom died. Though he likely acted in self-defense, Blevins is charged with murder. The boys are interrogated, brutalized, and taken away in a truck. At a stop, Blevins is removed from the truck and then shot. The boys end up in an old Saltillo prison, where the captain admits that, to save face, he fulfilled a contract on Blevins by the brother of Blevins's victim.

After much suffering in prison, John Grady secretly purchases a knife from inmates and kills a young would-be assassin. Wounded and scarred, he is set free along with Rawlins, paid out of prison by Alejandra's grandaunt. Rawlins promptly returns to San Angelo and John Grady returns to La Purísima, where Dueña Alfonsa tells him that because he is unlucky he will never be with Alejandra. He is given Rawlins's *grullo* horse. John Grady telephones

Alejandra, who sneaks out to meet him in Zacatecas. They spend a glorious day together but, devastated because her father is so angry at her, she cannot stay with him. They sadly part.

John Grady returns to Encantada, where he retrieves his, Rawlins's, and Blevins's horses and kidnaps the captain. In the mountains one night, he is awakened by three mysterious men who give him a serape, remove the captain's handcuffs, and take the captain away.

In early 1951, John Grady returns to Texas and searches vainly for the owner of Blevins's horse and identity. Finding neither, he is awarded the horse by a judge. He returns to San Angelo, delivers Rawlins's horse, and learns his own father has died. From a distance, he watches the funeral of the Mexican *abuela* who raised him, and he then rides west into a wild, fading world.

The Crossing opens in 1941, with sixteen-year-old Billy Parham observing the wolves running on the plain near his family's ranch, close by the Animas Peaks. One day, he and his brother, Boyd, meet an Indian boy who demands food. Billy complies, but though they agree to bring him coffee, they do not return from the house.

A wolf is killing calves on their range, so the boys and their father borrow traps and try to catch it. The wolf, a female who came up from Mexico after hunters had killed her mate, outsmarts them at every turn. However, she is more interested in finding other wolves than new hunting grounds. Billy asks an old man for help, and the old man tells him he must recognize the place where God sits and plans to destroy Creation, where fire is still in the earth. Billy sets a trap inside the dying embers of a vaquero campfire and catches the wolf. Upon finding her, treating her injured leg, and suffering much travail, he decides to lead her back to Mexico. He leaves, telling no one.

In Mexico, Billy is stopped by armed men who confiscate the wolf. She is taken to a festival, where she becomes the feature attraction. She is chained and forced to fight vicious dogs. Billy grasps her collar and demands her return, but guns are drawn in the crowd, so he steps away. With fresh dogs being readied for the fight, Billy shoots the wolf to spare her any more pain, and he exchanges his rifle for her corpse. He buries her and her unborn pups in the mountains.

Billy rides in the mountains for many weeks, then returns home to find the house splattered with blood, and empty. His parents had been murdered by a band of Indians, and six of their horses had been stolen. Billy takes Boyd away from his guardians, and they head to Mexico. In Bacerac, they find one of their family's horses and begin following leads on the others. They encounter a crying adolescent girl and take her along. Boyd becomes more and more protective of her. After encounters with a lapsed Mormon and an itinerant opera company, they lend the girl a horse so she can visit her family in Namiquipa.

During one struggle to find and keep the stolen horses, Boyd is shot during a chase and Billy races away with him on their dead father's horse. With the pursuers closing in, Billy spots a truck loaded with farm workers, who save Boyd by taking him along. Later, upon locating his brother, Billy gets a doctor and Boyd miraculously survives. Boyd is becoming a local legend and people are calling him man of the people.

Billy fetches the girl, whom Boyd is delighted to see, and a few days later the couple vanishes. They did not tell Billy they were leaving, so he begins his search for them, which lasts for weeks. He then returns to New Mexico to find the United States embroiled in World War II. He tries to enlist in the armed forces, but he is denied enlistment because he has a heart murmur. He drifts for some time before returning to Mexico.

Stories begin to surface that the girl is a notorious, beloved, and perhaps dead bandit, and that Billy's brother is an outlaw folk hero, also dead. Billy finds Boyd's grave, disinters him, takes him home, and buries him there. In the later years of World War II, Billy roams the Southwest.

It is 1952 as *Cities of the Plains* begins, and John Grady, Billy Parham, and Troy are working as cowboys on Mac McGovern's New Mexico ranch. The ranch is facing a takeover by the U.S. government. Returning from a trip, Billy and Troy see a truck with Mexican workers beside the road. Billy insists on helping the workers because he remembers such a group of workers had helped his late brother, Boyd. They are all vaqueros, or cowboys. Troy sleeps while Billy aids the workers, and then the two men drive on. Soon after, their windshield is destroyed when their car hits an enormous owl.

At a bordello in Juarez, John Grady glimpses a sixteen-year-old prostitute named Magdalena, and he cannot get her out of his mind. A spirited horse injures his foot, so he returns to the bordello but finds the girl gone.

Wolfenbarger, a wealthy ranch owner with an expensive filly, a gift for his daughter, sends the horse off to be trained at Mac's ranch. John Grady, though, can see right away that the filly is lame. He refuses to allow her to remain at the ranch. Wolfenbarger unsuccessfully tries to hire him away from Mac.

Returning again and again to Juarez to find Magdalena, John Grady pays to learn that she now works at a fancier brothel called White Lake. He finds her there, and they spend the night together. An old one-eyed woman takes care of the working girls and women, and Tiburcio serves as the brothel's manager. The owner, a pimp named Eduardo, notices John Grady's interest in Magdalena; Eduardo also is in love with her.

Though they rarely meet, John Grady and Magdalena soon fall in love. A blind musician tells John Grady that Magdalena does not belong among the human race. She fails to appear at a secret meeting planned with John Grady. When he goes to see her again, a waiter conveys a message from her, asking John Grady not to forget her.

Using dogs, the cowboys hunt a wild cat in the mountains. John Grady pawns his gun and returns to the bordello. Magdalena tells him that because of Eduardo, it is far too dangerous for them to meet. Mac and John Grady go to a horse auction and Mac tricks Wolfenbarger into buying an overpriced horse. At a bar, John Grady asks for Billy's assistance in taking Magdalena away from Mexico, and he admits that he loves and wants to marry her. Stunned, Billy says that John Grady is crazy, and flatly refuses to help.

Nevertheless, soon after, Billy bribes a bartender at the White Lake to see Eduardo, and Tiburcio the manager takes Billy to meet the pimp. When Billy tries to buy Magdalena, Eduardo says that the prostitutes do not want to leave and that Billy's friend, John Grady, has a skewed worldview. Both Eduardo and Billy acknowledge that John Grady is in danger, and Billy reports Eduardo's refusal to John Grady.

John Grady and Magdalena meet near the river, and he weeps as she tells him her life story. She agrees to marry him. He plans to fix an old, ruined adobe shelter to be their home. He sells his prized stallion to friends of Mac. He tells Mac everything, except that Magdalena is a prostitute, and Mac wants to meet her.

The cowboys realize that recent calf killings are the work of wild dogs, and they go after the pack with their own hunting dogs. A bloody battle ensues in the mountains, and the wild dogs are savagely killed. John Grady convinces Billy to help him search for pups of the pack, and they find them after tumbling a boulder; John Grady chooses one pup for himself.

John Grady's work has turned the ramshackle adobe hut into a welcoming home. The other cowboys begin to believe that he will indeed bring Magdalena across the border and marry her. The blind musician, however, refuses his request to be the girl's *padrino* because he believes Eduardo will kill her, and he does not want such responsibility.

John Grady and Magdalena meet once more and lay plans to sneak her into the United States. They part, and in the cab ride back to the White Lake, she has an epileptic seizure and is hospitalized. She escapes the hospital to return to the

brothel, and as she walks through Juarez barefoot and wearing little clothing, a woman offers her sanctuary, which she refuses. She reaches the brothel and leaves bloody footprints on its floor.

John Grady and Billy ride out and discuss the future of the cowboy life, the West, and the mystery that is Mexico. On Sunday, Magdalena carefully dresses with the help of the old one-eyed *criada*, Tiburcio's mother, who next tries to prevent her from leaving. The girl escapes and finds the cab arranged for her. However, the driver takes her to a lonely spot on the river where Tiburcio is waiting. He slits her throat, and she is later found in the river by weed cutters.

John Grady's search leads to Magdalena's body in the morgue. He returns to the little adobe house, then to the ranch house, and gets a knife. Billy, meanwhile, looks for John Grady in Juarez and finds Eduardo instead. Billy talks to the police but gets no help. John Grady returns to Mexico and provokes Eduardo into a knife fight. He kills Eduardo but is badly injured himself. He pays a young boy to contact the ranch for help, but the boy instead leads him to a crate on the street. He wakes to Billy's voice, asking him if he wants water. Billy leaves to get the water, and returns to find John Grady dead.

Critical Evaluation:

Cormac McCarthy amassed a devoted coterie of critics and readers decades before the publication of his breakout masterpiece *All the Pretty Horses*, but until then, he remained largely unknown, despite his Guggenheim Fellowship and grants from the MacArthur Foundation, the William Faulkner Foundation, and the American Academy of Arts and Letters. Widespread acclaim came when *All the Pretty Horses* won the National Book Award and National Book Critics Circle Award in 1992.

In McCarthy's *The Border Trilogy*, a complex world and its mythic characters evoke not only his own earlier works, such as the acclaimed *Blood Meridian: Or, The Evening Redness in the West* (1985), but also the works of writers such as William Faulkner, Mark Twain, Miguel de Cervantes, and William Shakespeare. McCarthy incorporates initiation narratives, heroes' journeys, history lessons, psychological portraits, and linguistic brilliance, making the trilogy challenging yet accessible as well as stunning and beloved.

McCarthy's main characters in the trilogy are remnants of a dying world—the Old West specifically and vast expanses generally. In each of these novels, society's encroachment is making open range and wild land valuable for housing developments and military installations while eradicating the age-old ways of animals and people. The boys grow into men who are increasingly lost, essentially evicted from the familiar country and existence in which and for which they were bred. This new reality is a catastrophe, out of which come not secure residents of the future but rootless anachronisms, picaros who can only wander and wonder at their fates.

Each boy heeds adventure's call, crosses threshold after threshold into the unknown (most notably the Rio Grande area), and journeys either destined or freely willed, graced along the way by gifts of knowledge, charity, joy, torment, and salvation. Each boy encounters mentors, sometimes blinded or one eyed, whose parables and talismans help him on the way; each boy also has animal companions. Archetypal elements such as night journeys, abductions, battles, and sacred bonds populate the tale, and both Billy Parham and John Grady Cole acquire tangible and intangible boons—horses, women, wisdom—with which they struggle to return despite dogged pursuits.

The boys receive mysterious assistance, such as from the "men of the country" who relieve Billy of the kidnapped captain. Deification occurs as Billy's brother, Boyd, is idealized as a folk hero in the Mexican countryside, and Billy and John Grady both become masters of two worlds. In the end, however, those worlds are fast disappearing, so one hero perishes and the other wanders; neither, in effect, returns home because "home" is no more. Furthermore, the separation from their fathers, both by distance and death, is left unresolved.

Despite vividness and narrative framing, the novels seem dreamlike and timeless. Histories and legends form much of the trilogy, reaching times before and beyond and adding layered perspectives to the main narrative. McCarthy weaves numerous historical events and incidents into the plot structure. Story motifs are pervasive, informed by the significance of dreams and the eternal dilemma of fate versus free will. In *Cities of the Plain*, the blind maestro speaks of human acts as "a vast and endless net" of irrevocable causes and effects, telling John Grady that "we are free to act upon only what is given [and that] each act . . . is itself an enslavement[,] for it voids every alternative and binds one ever more tightly into the constraints that make a life."

This theme is enhanced by Billy's latter-day meeting under an Arizona bridge with the tale spinner, who says that "all knowledge is a borrowing and every fact a debt. For each event is revealed to us only at the surrender of every alternative course." He continues,

[D]reams reveal the world also. . . . [O]ften the narrative is fugitive and difficult to recall [y]et it is . . . the life of the dream while the events themselves are often interchange-

able. The events of the waking world . . . are forced upon us. . . . It is we who assemble them into the story which is us.

Mary L. Otto Lang

Further Reading

Arnold, Edwin T., and Dianne C. Luce, eds. *A Cormac McCarthy Companion: "The Border Trilogy."* Jackson: University Press of Mississippi, 2001. Includes nine essays covering such topics as dreams and visions, allegory, warfare, gender, and the ethics and disappearance of the American West.

_____. *Perspectives on Cormac McCarthy*. Jackson: University Press of Mississippi, 1999. Seminal criticism that contains three essays on the trilogy, one on each novel, examining themes, structure, and interpretation. Also discusses *All the Pretty Horses* as a screenplay. Extensive bibliographies.

Bloom, Harold, ed. *Cormac McCarthy*. 2001. New ed. New York: Bloom's Literary Criticism, 2009. Essays examine several of McCarthy's works. The trilogy is featured in three essays that focus on interior spaces and violence.

Guillemin, Georg. *The Pastoral Vision of Cormac McCarthy*. College Station: Texas A&M University Press, 2004. Provides a context for McCarthy's vision that counterbalances critics who tend to see it only as violent, dark, and morbid. A scholarly work, yet accessible to all readers.

Hall, Wade, and Rick Wallach, eds. *Sacred Violence: A Reader's Companion to Cormac McCarthy*. Rev. ed. 2 vols. El Paso: Texas Western Press, 2002. Selected works from a 1993 McCarthy conference. Features essays on linguistics and language in the trilogy, John Grady Cole as hero, and other topics.

Jay, Ellis. *No Place for Home: Spatial Constraint and Character Flight in the Novels of Cormac McCarthy*. New York: Routledge, 2006. Analyzes the reasons so many of McCarthy's characters are restless, fleeing, wandering, on the road, or in quest of something.

Owens, Barcley. *Cormac McCarthy's Western Novels*. Tucson: University of Arizona Press, 2000. An accessible and informative work with connective chapters on myths and motifs in the trilogy and McCarthy's other Western novels.

Sanborn, Wallis R., III. *Animals in the Fiction of Cormac McCarthy*. Jefferson, N.C.: McFarland, 2006. A thorough, detailed, and thoughtful work that examines the roles of wolves, horses, and hunting in McCarthy's trilogy.

Boris Godunov

Author: Alexander Pushkin (1799-1837)

First produced: 1870; first published, 1831 (English translation, 1918)

Type of work: Drama

Type of plot: Historical

Time of plot: 1598-1605

Locale: Russia

Principal characters:

BORIS GODUNOV, the czar of Russia

FEODOR, his son

GRIGORY OTREPYEV, the pretender

MARYNA, Grigory's beloved

BASMANOV, a military leader

The Story:

Boris Godunov, a privy councilor, is a schemer. He plans the assassination of Czarevitch Dmitri so that the assassins are caught and promptly executed by a mob, so that no suspicion falls on Boris. He even orders the nobleman Shuisky to investigate the crime. Shuisky returns and tells with a straight face the version of the murder that Boris suggested to him.

When the people begin to clamor for Boris to become czar, Boris and his sister take refuge in a monastery, ostensibly to escape the pressure of the populace that acclaims him their ruler. With a great show of humility and hesitation, he finally accepts the great honor. In spite of his initial popular appeal, Boris proves to be a cruel ruler, binding the serfs more firmly than ever to their masters and crushing ruthlessly nobles who oppose him. There are a few, however, who do not forget that Boris murdered Dmitri.

Father Pimen is an old monk, a writer of chronicles. At night he writes his observations of Russia's troubled times, while a young monk named Grigory Otrepyev sleeps nearby. Grigory is troubled by grandiose dreams. It seems to him that he is mounting a great staircase from the top of which all Moscow is spread out before him. When he awakens, Father Pimen counsels him to forget the call of the world, for lust and power are illusory. Grigory scarcely listens, for he knows that in his youth Pimen was a soldier and had his fill of secular life.

When a wicked monk tempts Grigory by reminding him that he is the same age as the murdered Dmitri would have been, Grigory quickly resolves that he will indeed be Dmitri. To get support for his enterprise Grigory goes to Lithuania, and, so as to pass unnoticed through the country, he attaches himself to two beggar monks. Somehow Boris hears of the impostor's intentions. A description of Dmitri is broadcast, and the czar's agents are instructed to arrest him on sight. In a remote tavern, several officers come upon Grigory and his two companions. Grigory draws his dagger and flees.

Both the Lithuanians and the Poles are delighted to help Grigory march on Moscow. The Poles, especially, are eager to attack the hated Muscovites. As rumors of the impending rebellion spread, many Russians come into Poland to join the swelling ranks of Grigory's supporters. Before long, Grigory finds another powerful ally in a Jesuit priest who promises to throw the influence of Rome behind the pretender. Grigory at the head of a rebellious army in Poland is a real menace to Boris's throne and life.

However, Grigory, comfortably installed at an estate near the Russian border, lingers in Poland. He cannot bring himself to give orders to advance because Maryna, the daughter of the house, captures his heart. She is cold to him and finally asks him outright whether he is really Dmitri or an unfrocked monk, as some people are saying. When Grigory, unnerved by love, confesses that he is a baseborn monk, Maryna haughtily refuses to ally her noble blood with his. Stung by her actions, Grigory thereupon proudly declares that he will be czar, and if Maryna denounces him, he will use his power to punish her. Satisfied that he has an indomitable spirit, Maryna overlooks his birth and agrees to be his czarina.

The next morning, Grigory begins his conquering march, and for a while all goes well. Towns and villages join his campaign willingly, for the name of Dmitri is a powerful one. In Moscow, Boris is greatly perturbed and asks the patriarch to give his best counsel. He is told that Dmitri's grave is noted for its cures; the patriarch himself knows of an old man who was blind for many years before a visit to the tomb restored his sight. If Dmitri's remains are brought into the Kremlin and a miracle were to happen before all the people, Moscow will have proof that Dmitri is dead and the pretender is a fraud. Boris pales at the suggestion. Tactfully Shuisky proposes another course. Rather than appear to use religious means in a political quarrel, he will go before the people and denounce Grigory. Surely, when the people know the truth they will desert the baseborn monk who calls himself Dmitri.

For a time, events seem to favor Boris. Grigory is beaten back in several attacks on strongholds held by Boris's troops. Nevertheless, Grigory remains cheerful and confident, even after his forces are defeated.

Boris entrusts the command of his whole defense to Basmanov, an able leader though not of noble birth. Basmanov is gratified at the honor, for he has as little patience with the intrigues of the court as he does with the fickle loyalties of the mob. His conference with Boris is interrupted by the arrival of a delegation of foreign merchants. Boris hardly leaves the room before an alarm sounds; the czar is suddenly ill. Blood gushes from his mouth and ears.

Before his death, Boris formally names his son Feodor the next czar. As his life ebbs away, he advises Feodor to name Basmanov the military leader, to retain all the stately court procedures that give dignity to the government, and to preserve strictly the discipline of the Church. After the last rites are administered, Boris dies.

At army headquarters, Pushkin, a supporter of Grigory, has an interview with Basmanov. Pushkin admits that Grigory's army is only a rabble and that Cossacks and Poles alike are not to be trusted. If, however, Basmanov will declare for Grigory, the new czar will make him commander of all the Russian armies. At first, Basmanov hesitates, but Pushkin reminds him that even if Grigory is an impostor, the magic name of Dmitri is enough to ensure that Feodor has no chance of retaining his czardom. Basmanov, convinced, publicly leads his troops to Grigory's side.

Basmanov's defection spreads. The people of Moscow listen to Pushkin when he makes an inflammatory speech in the great square. As he reminds them of all they have suffered under Boris and of the justice of Dmitri's accession, the crowd shouts their allegiance to the false Dmitri. Impassioned, the mob surges into Boris's palace to seek out Feodor, who looks hopelessly out the window. Some in the crowd feel pity, but their voices are overruled. The boyars force their way inside, presumably to make Feodor swear allegiance to Dmitri. Out of the uproar comes screams. At last the door opens. One of the boyars makes an announcement: Feodor and his mother took poison. He saw the dead bodies. The boyar urges the people to acclaim Dmitri, but the people stand silent, speechless.

Critical Evaluation:

Alexander Pushkin began to work in earnest on *Boris Godunov* in November, 1824, and finished the play one year later. He was at the time turning away from Lord Byron as a literary model and toward William Shakespeare. The complexity and variety he found in Shakespeare's characters had a strong appeal for him, as did the English playwright's willingness to treat both history and tragedy with more freedom than had been allowed by the formal constraints of the French neoclassicism that had until then been the dominant influence on the Russian theater.

Boris Godunov consists of twenty-three loosely connected scenes. Of the dramatic unities (time, place, and action), Pushkin observes only the unity of action, and he casts the poetry in iambic pentameter, which is closer to natural speech than the hexameters of neoclassic drama, and intermixes poetry with prose. A large number of speaking characters are further augmented by crowd scenes. Though the play is a historical tragedy, Pushkin includes snatches of comedy. In short, Pushkin exhibits in *Boris Godunov* the romantic sensibility of his day in creating a poetic drama that places the arresting confusions of history above the theoretic requirements of art. Russian history in the early seventeenth century was somewhat confused, but Pushkin chose to set up several definite determinants. He took as the source for his play Nikolay Karamzin's *History of the Russian State* (1816-1829), which maintains that Boris Godunov was culpable in the death in 1591 of Dmitri, the half brother of the ruling czar, Feodor. There is in fact no clear evidence for this. Boris Godunov was first called to be czar after Feodor died in 1598, and initially he seems to have been a popular ruler. When the situation changed, however, people began to remember that Godunov had not been part of any ruling dynasty and that he had achieved power because, as Feodor's brother-in-law, he was strategically placed at a moment when Russia needed a ruler. This led many to suspect that he may have engineered his own rise to power by evil means.

Karamazin also claims that the false Dmitri was an ambitious monk with determination and ability but no legitimate claim to power. This put Pushkin in a difficult spot, for in order to remain faithful to his source, he could not develop a dramatic opposition of good and evil in his characters. A Boris Godunov who is a vicarious assassin and a Dmitri who is a crass impostor did not provide effective theater. Pushkin could, of course, have altered the historical premise, but that would have conflicted with his motive in writing the play, which was to record a critical epoch in Russia's past. Pushkin resolved his dilemma by finding the point in the story where history gives way to tragedy. He made his title character, Boris Godunov, a man who is capable and even in many ways honorable but in whose internal struggle between conscience and ambition, ambition has been the victor. Dmitri, on the other hand, is shown to possess few admirable traits so that in the conflict between the two ambitious men, Boris Godunov is the likeliest figure to be seen as a tragically flawed hero.

Another problem Pushkin had to surmount is the unexciting nature of Godunov's death. He resolved this difficulty by concluding the play with the death of Boris Godunov's children at the hands of Dmitri's agents. Having shown that Godunov is responsible for the death of the true Dmitri,

Pushkin implied a rough justice in showing Godunov's children being destroyed by the agency of the false Dmitri.

For the purposes of theater, history is more readily married to tragedy than to comedy. The dramatist must try to find in history patterns of human conduct that are somehow heroic, even if flawed. Shakespeare, Pushkin's model, often chose historical figures sufficiently remote in time or clouded in circumstance so that he could revise the past to fit a tragic mold. Plays treating more recent history could be shaped to gratify contemporary political sentiments. Boris Godunov, in many ways an excellent subject for dramatic treatment, posed a certain problem for Pushkin because it was Godunov's failure, as well as the failures of various pretenders (for eventually more than one man claimed to be Dmitri), that led to the emergence of the Romanov dynasty, which held power in Pushkin's lifetime. Insofar as the poet needed to write a play that would secure the approval of rulers in his own era, there was an advantage to showing both Boris Godunov and the pretender to possess great flaws.

The title character nevertheless exhibits enough of the qualities of a tragic hero to allow the audience's attention to center on Boris Godunov. The play is not exclusively a tragedy of ambition, but it is far more than a simple chronicle of history. Moreover, it proves a suitable record of a difficult moment in Russia's past.

"Critical Evaluation" by John Higby

Further Reading

Bayley, John. *Pushkin: A Comparative Commentary.* New York: Cambridge University Press, 1971. One of the best English-language studies of Pushkin. A long chapter on drama treats *Boris Godunov* in relation to William Shakespeare, the German poet Friedrich Schiller, and other writers.

Bethea, David M. *Realizing Metaphors: Alexander Pushkin and the Life of the Poet.* Madison: University of Wisconsin Press, 1998. Describes the relationship between Pushkin's life and his art and discusses why, more than two hundred years after his birth, his work remains relevant. Includes index and illustrations.

Binyon, T. J. *Pushkin: A Biography.* New York: Knopf, 2004. The winner of the Samuel Johnson prize for British nonfiction, this biography chronicles Pushkin's literary success alongside his personal failures. Binyon describes how the writer included small pieces of his life in *Eugene Onegin* and other works.

Briggs, A. D. P. *Alexander Pushkin.* New York: Barnes & Noble, 1983. In the chapter on drama, Briggs argues that Pushkin's success as a dramatist was limited, but his plays are more interesting than is sometimes allowed. Discusses such aspects of *Boris Godunov* as the work's historical background, Shakespearean influence, structure, characters, language, and poetry.

Clayton, J. Douglas. *Dimitry's Shade: A Reading of Alexander Pushkin's "Boris Godunov."* Evanston, Ill.: Northwestern University Press, 2004. Argues that the play signals Pushkin's emergence as a political conservative, demonstrated by the drama's defense of autocracy and its elements of orthodox religion.

Dunning, Chester, et al. *The Uncensored "Boris Godunov": The Case for Pushkin's Original Comedy, with Annotated Text and Translation.* Madison: University of Wisconsin Press, 2006. Contains the translated and annotated text of *Tsar Boris and Grishka Otrepiev* (1825), Pushkin's original comedic version of *Boris Godunov.* Includes essays analyzing the creation and fate of the comedy and the place of the comic play within Pushkin's canon and Russian literature.

Evdokimova, Svetlana. *Pushkin's Historical Imagination.* New Haven, Conn.: Yale University Press, 1999. An examination of Pushkin's fictional and nonfictional works on the subject of history, including *Boris Godunov.* Considers Pushkin's ideas on the relation between chance and necessity, the significance of great individuals, and historical truth.

Kahn, Andrew, ed. *The Cambridge Companion to Pushkin.* New York: Cambridge University Press, 2006. Collection of essays by Pushkin scholars discussing the writer's life and work in various genres; Pushkin and politics, history, and literary criticism; and Pushkin's position in Soviet and post-Soviet culture.

Sandler, Stephanie. *Distant Pleasures: Alexander Pushkin and the Writing of Exile.* Stanford, Calif.: Stanford University Press, 1989. Scholarly and subtle, this book is better suited to the serious student of Pushkin than to the general reader. *Boris Godunov* is discussed at considerable length.

Vickery, Walter N. *Alexander Pushkin Revisited.* Rev. ed. New York: Twayne, 1992. A brief but clear account of the historical circumstances leading to Boris Godunov's rule is useful to those not familiar with the background for Pushkin's play. Many of the established topics in the study of *Boris Godunov* are included.

The Borough
A Poem, in Twenty-four Letters

Author: George Crabbe (1754-1832)
First published: 1810
Type of work: Poetry

Principal characters:
PETER GRIMES, a fisherman
ELLEN ORFORD, a pauper
SWALLOW, a grasping lawyer
BLANEY, an inhabitant of the Alms-House
THE MAYOR OF THE BOROUGH
THE VICAR OF THE PARISH
A BURGESS, who writes the letters

George Crabbe was a writer of provincial background who made good in the capital by using his provincial material. His initial success in London with *The Library*, published in 1781, made it possible for the son of a fisherman and petty customs officer to enter the Church in 1782 and be given a respectable living as an Anglican clergyman. For a time he gave up poetry after publishing *The News-Paper* in 1785. His next publication, *Poems*, was not until 1807. In the decades between his two periods of composition, much changed in English poetry; Crabbe's continuation of his original style and matter makes it difficult to place him in the Romantic period.

He was really the last and best representative of the host of adventuring, provincial poetasters who flocked to London to make their fortunes in the eighteenth century—these included Thomas Chatterton, Oliver Goldsmith, David Mallet, and Samuel Johnson, to name but a few. This is to repeat a truism in Crabbe criticism—that Aldeburgh, where he was born, is all his material—but it also places Crabbe in literary history, shows his strength, and perhaps accounts for his durability. The most obvious manifestation of that is the initiation of the Aldeburgh Festival and Benjamin Britten's opera *Peter Grimes* (1945), derived from letter 22 of *The Borough*.

The Village, published in 1783, and *The Borough* contain and are contained by a seaside community in which the folk are at the mercy of the elements, their only salvation against bad times being native prudence. In their world, no help comes from the outside, only temptation and danger. Despite his absence from Aldeburgh after the age of twenty-six, Crabbe was unable to forget youthful privation and misery by adopting a tourist's attitude to provincial society and nature, an increasingly common mid-Victorian attitude of which Balmoral is the symbol. Few of his heroes and heroines have private incomes, and if caught in a storm at sea they are more likely to perish than to find themselves washed up on the sand.

Crabbe's realism was reinforced by parish duties; it is not the pessimism of which his mid-Victorian and Romantic critics accused him. Later readers appreciated the salt in his stories more than the sugar in the work of other poets, equipped with a less immediate experience of people and place, writing at the same time as Crabbe. His second importance in the history of English poetry is the fact that he casts a shadow beside the major figures of his second period and prepares the narrative form in English poetry for the genre work of Alfred, Lord Tennyson's *Enoch Arden, and Other Poems* (1864), Robert Browning's *Men and Women* (1855), and Thomas Hardy's local-color sketches in verse. In the early years of the nineteenth century Crabbe's work was paralleled in prose by Maria Edgeworth's Irish *Castle Rackrent* (1800) and John Galt's Scottish *Annals of the Parish* (1821), rather than the country novels of Jane Austen. All the foregoing is summed up in Crabbe's best-known line from *The Village*—"I paint the Cot, as Truth will paint it, and as Bards will not"—and illustrated in *The Borough*, the most unified of his works.

To "paint the Cot" Crabbe uses the pentameter couplet, a meter noted for its wit and music and not for the narrative use to which Crabbe put it; that *The Borough* is made up of twenty-four letters or "epistles" to some extent restricts the narrative and encourages general observation, conventional in the eighteenth century verse epistle. In place of wit and music, Crabbe relies on rugged and compact language that reflects that of his characters, especially that of the burgess who is supposed to be writing the letters. The most tiring feature of the succession of couplets is the regular placing of the caesura, which makes too obvious the antithesis and balance supporting the lines:

Then he began to reason and to feel
He could not dig nor had he learn'd to steal;
And should he beg as long as he might live,
He justly fear'd that nobody would give.

Crabbe arranges the letters in a certain order, precedes each with a curt prose argument, adds a long preface, and subscribes a brief envoi. After the "General Description" of letter 1, Crabbe arranges his aspects in the proper order, beginning with the most important person in the borough and its center, the vicar and his church, but concluding with the schools. His arrangement falls into two major divisions, the provident and the improvident, of the adult world, with the children bringing up the rear. The provident come under three headings or activities in order of importance: religion, work, and play. The improvident are divided into those in the almshouse and hospital and the poor outside parish relief, with a final letter on those in prisons. Seven of these letters narrate the miserable histories of those in or out of the almshouse. Within each of the three sections of the first division, Crabbe also observes a declining order of importance: After the church and the vicar are described, Crabbe turns to the "Sects and Professions of Religion," which he defends at length in his preface as a strong but essentially true picture of the "Calvinistic" and "Armenian" Methodists who so disturb the parson and his church, as Crabbe knew from bitter experience. The professions of law and physic are followed by the "Trades." The third section begins with "Amusements," followed in descending order by "Clubs and Social Meetings," "Inns," and "Players," which last leads straight down the path of destruction to the whole division on the improvident. The strength of this division is the seven narratives, but many readers prefer the first division for the extraordinarily vivid scenes briefly sketched there, especially in "Elections" and "Players." These include brief portraits such as that of the lawyer Swallow, who lives up to his name.

Crabbe's preface, like his arguments, outlines what is to come in each letter but also deals with the work as a whole. The whole scheme of *The Borough* is that Crabbe has apparently written to "an ideal friend," a burgess in an unnamed large seaport, asking him to describe his borough. The letters sometimes begin with a brief question that the correspondent answers. Crabbe admits that the resulting picture of the borough is uneven, but the envoi provides the answer:

Man's vice and crime I combat as I can, . . .
(The giant-Folly, the enchanter-Vice) . . . I point the
    powers of rhyme,
And, sparing criminals, attack the crime.

Here the country parson drops his mask and admits that he is preaching one of his regular sermons to encourage industry and thrift and to avoid the enticements of riches and city life. Most of the preface, including the long passage on the Methodists, is taken up with apologizing for the satire of religions, professions, and amusements in the first division and for the repetitious falls from fortune in the second. An exception is letter 20, "Ellen Orford," which ends in resigned piety. Crabbe's justification is that of "fidelity," that he did know such a person or instance, as when in letter 5 he cites a rich fisherman who never heard, until a friend told him, of the practice of lending money at interest, with this result:

Though blind so long to interest, all allow
That no man better understands it now: . . .
Stepping from post to post, he reach'd the chair,
And there he now reposes—that's the mayor.

Crabbe is the bard who will paint his borough "as Truth will paint it," and in the envoi to letter 24 he looks forward to his readers' reaction: "This is alikeness," may they all declare,/ "And I have seen him but I know not where. . . ."

It is sometimes difficult to see the "likeness" in the seven narratives of the poor and the almshouse because they all seem to decline with celerity into remorse and destitution. It may be, however, that time has removed such objects from what must have been Crabbe's daily observation both as a boy in Aldeburgh and as a country parson. Certainly the most surprising decline is that of Peter Grimes, which is at the same time the most convincing, partly because in this account Crabbe uses nature to much greater effect than in the other narratives. More than nature, society is his object, and especially the quirks of character and turns of fate in family histories well known to those who stay long in any place. If Crabbe seems to relish the misery and vice exhibited in the citizens of his borough, he is adopting what is often the provincial's revenge against his native town: a scarifying of its mean soul and low manners in gripping detail. This is not the whole effect of *The Borough*, but what there is marks it as a forerunner of that supremely provincial novel, James Joyce's *Ulysses* (1922).

Further Reading

Bareham, Tony. *George Crabbe*. London: Vision, 1977. Analyzes Crabbe's work against the backdrop of his life, emphasizing his experience as an ordained Anglican minister and a magistrate. Examines his position during turbulent times, when he became a voice for sane, rational, reliable English thought and custom. Includes frequent references to *The Borough*.

Blackburne, Neville. *The Restless Ocean*. Lavenham, England: Terence Dalton, 1972. An excellent biography. Identifies the various prejudices and influences underlying Crabbe's poetry. In chapter 10, Blackburne discusses *The Borough* as "the peak of Crabbe's poetic achievement." Includes illustrations and bibliography.

Chamberlain, Robert L. *George Crabbe*. New York: Twayne, 1965. Discusses the works in chronological order, showing Crabbe's development as a master of poetic diction and a superb creator of character. A twenty-page section of the book is devoted to *The Borough*. Includes an annotated bibliography and a helpful index.

Pollard, Arthur, comp. *Crabbe: The Critical Heritage*. London: Routledge & Kegan Paul, 1972. A collection of excerpts from reviews and essays dating 1780-1890. Includes eight contemporary reviews of *The Borough*. A separate index to the works indicates other critical comments. Pollard's introduction is an excellent starting point for any study of Crabbe.

Powell, Neil. *George Crabbe: An English Life, 1754-1832*. London: Pimlico, 2004. Comprehensive biography recounting the events of Crabbe's personal life and multifaceted career. Powell argues that Crabbe was an influence for later writers, such as Charles Dickens, George Eliot, Thomas Hardy, and twentieth century poet Philip Larkin.

Sigworth, Oliver. *Nature's Sternest Painter: Five Essays on the Poetry of George Crabbe*. Tucson: University of Arizona Press, 1965. Focuses on Crabbe's relationship to the eighteenth century and to the Romantic movement, his interest in nature, his use of narrative, and his reputation. Many comments about *The Borough* are scattered throughout. Bibliography.

Whitehead, Frank S. *George Crabbe: A Reappraisal*. Selinsgrove, Pa.: Susquehanna University Press, 1995. A thorough analysis of Crabbe's poetry. Whitehead traces the chronological development of Crabbe's work, describing how it reached its pinnacle in *Tales in Verse* (1812); chapter 5 provides a lengthy discussion of "Further Narrative Development in *The Borough*." Whitehead also examines Crabbe's relation to early Romantic poets, such as William Wordsworth and Samuel Taylor Coleridge, and provides a deconstructionist critique of Crabbe's verse.

The Bostonians

Author: Henry James (1843-1916)
First published: serial, 1885-1886; book, 1886
Type of work: Novel
Type of plot: Psychological realism
Time of plot: Early 1870's
Locale: Massachusetts and New York City

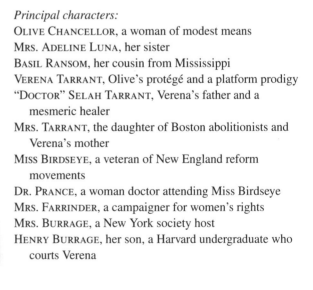

Principal characters:
OLIVE CHANCELLOR, a woman of modest means
MRS. ADELINE LUNA, her sister
BASIL RANSOM, her cousin from Mississippi
VERENA TARRANT, Olive's protégé and a platform prodigy
"DOCTOR" SELAH TARRANT, Verena's father and a mesmeric healer
MRS. TARRANT, the daughter of Boston abolitionists and Verena's mother
MISS BIRDSEYE, a veteran of New England reform movements
DR. PRANCE, a woman doctor attending Miss Birdseye
MRS. FARRINDER, a campaigner for women's rights
MRS. BURRAGE, a New York society host
HENRY BURRAGE, her son, a Harvard undergraduate who courts Verena

The Story:

Olive Chancellor, a Boston activist in the women's movement, is entertaining her cousin Basil Ransom, a Mississippian who lives in New York City. She invites him to join her at a gathering at the home of Miss Birdseye, a leader in the movement. Though he disagrees with the ideals of the feminists, Ransom accepts, partly out of curiosity and partly to meet Mrs. Farrinder, a national spokesperson for women's rights. At Miss Birdseye's, Ransom expresses his views on the movement to Dr. Prance, a woman who is successful in a traditionally male profession. Olive, becoming aware that Ransom opposes all she stands for, develops a strong animosity toward her cousin.

In attendance also at Miss Birdseye's are the Tarrants, a family supported by the father's lectures on mesmerism; the Tarrants claim that their daughter Verena has a special gift for oratory, and they persuade Miss Birdseye to let her speak to the group about the women's movement. Everyone is captivated by Verena's performance. Olive immediately recognizes that the young woman has a future as a public figure promoting women's rights. Ransom is smitten with Verena's beauty and charm. Both speak briefly to Verena after her performance.

Ransom is forced to return immediately to New York, but Olive goes to the Tarrants' home in Cambridge on the following day to try to persuade Verena to become active in the women's movement in Boston. The Tarrants are anxious to comply, Mr. Tarrant seeing this as a way to make money, and Mrs. Tarrant believing that it would provide an opportunity for her daughter to move into high society. Although Verena is being wooed by several young men, including the Harvard student Henry Burrage and the journalist Matthias Pardon, she agrees to collaborate with Olive. Over time, the two became inseparable, and Olive eventually enters into a financial arrangement with the Tarrants to permit Verena to live at the Chancellor home. There, Olive educates her protégé in feminist doctrine. Olive is insistent that Verena abandon all thoughts of marriage and devote her energies to the cause. After years of dominating women, she declares that "men must take *their* turn" as objects of domination and that "they must pay!"

During this time, Ransom is struggling to practice law in New York. He spends his spare time writing Carlylean tracts against modern times, but no one will publish them. He manages to make ends meet by working for Mrs. Luna, Olive's sister, who makes amorous advances that he consistently rejects. She is the first to recognize that Ransom is in love with Verena, whom she considers a sham.

Ransom decides to go back to Boston to woo Verena. Outside Olive's house, Ransom meets Miss Birdseye, who is under the impression that he supports the women's movement and therefore tells him that Verena is now staying with her parents in Cambridge. Ransom goes to see her, and though she rejects his advances, Verena nevertheless takes him on a tour of Harvard and agrees to keep the meeting secret from Olive.

Sometime later, after Ransom returns to New York, he receives an invitation to attend a meeting at the home of Mrs. Burrage, a socialite, who is sponsoring a public appearance by Verena. Basil attends, knowing that Verena arranged for the invitation. Before Verena's speech, he has an ugly encounter with Mrs. Luna, who accuses him of impropriety in his relationship with Verena. While she is in New York, Verena agrees to see Ransom socially. When he tries to persuade her to give up her work in the movement and marry him, Verena balks. She received an invitation to stay on in New York with the Burrage family, whose son, Henry, courted her in Cambridge and wants to marry her. Knowing that Olive has a special influence over Verena, Mrs. Burrage tries to convince her that such an arrangement would be good for women's rights, but Olive is not persuaded. When Verena insists that she cannot stay in New York, Olive takes her back to Boston.

Months later, Ransom travels to New England again, this time to Cape Cod, where Olive and Verena are staying together with Miss Birdseye and Dr. Prance. Olive is preparing Verena for a triumphant public engagement at Boston's Music Hall. Ransom once again ingratiates himself with Miss Birdseye and Dr. Prance, but though he stays with them for a month, he makes no headway against his cousin's dislike or in convincing Verena to marry him. Everyone is greatly saddened when Miss Birdseye, who was ailing, dies.

The party returns to Boston, where Miss Birdseye is buried. Little time is spent on mourning, however, as Verena's big night at the Music Hall approaches. Ransom is kept away from her. Olive even sends Verena into hiding so that he will not be able to divert her attention from her mission, and when he attempts to see her backstage at the Music Hall before her performance, he finds a policeman barring his way. He is finally able to see Verena in her dressing room, where he confronts Olive, Verena's parents, and Matthias Pardon and accuses them of expecting to profit in some way from Verena's newfound notoriety. Verena hesitates to go before the crowd in the Music Hall, and Basil senses that she is finally coming around to his way of thinking. He makes a final impassioned plea to her to abandon this scheme devised by others to use her talents for their ends. Finally persuaded,

Verena refuses to go on stage and leaves with Ransom to start a new life outside the spotlight and away from political wrangling.

"The Story" by Laurence W. Mazzeno

Critical Evaluation:

The Bostonians is the longest of Henry James's novels in an American setting, and in spite of his later dissatisfaction with its middle section or the high promise given to the unfinished *The Ivory Tower* (1917), it is his most important fictive statement on America. The name and setting of the novel are significant; two other American novels, *Washington Square* (1880) and *The Europeans* (1878), are set in New York City and Boston respectively, and though *The Bostonians* begins in Charles Street and ends in the Music Hall in Boston, its second half begins in New York, which James always claimed as his native city. James had difficulty selecting a title for the work, but when he had settled on *The Bostonians*, he knew it precisely suited the contents and his meaning.

The best commentary on the work is found in James's preface to the New York edition. James had several times tried to clarify a passage he had written in his life of Nathaniel Hawthorne, on what he believed that America offered and lacked with respect to writers. *The Bostonians* was James's attempt to write on a subject that was at once local and typical, a local manifestation of a national trait. James chose that distinguishing feature of American life, the American woman, whom he had earlier encapsulated in Isabel Archer and other heroines. The settings he chose were the Boston of the early 1870's and postabolitionist New York, with its atmosphere of exhausted triumph and its hectic pursuit of new reform movements, especially that of women's rights. James's general distaste for the reformers if not for their proposals may be sensed in his portraits in the novel.

The "Bostonians" may be variously identified as one, two, or more characters, but James uses the term only once to refer to Olive Chancellor and Verena Tarrant. Although James referred to Verena as the heroine, the true Bostonian is Olive, the embodiment of the clash between discrimination and undiscriminating action in Boston of the 1870's. Destined by nature and appearance to be what was called a New England Nun, she becomes a Boston battler in the very last paragraph of the novel, haranguing a capacity crowd in Boston's largest auditorium. She does so in place of Verena, who has been carried away by Basil Ransom. These three characters play out an ironic and psychologically penetrating form of the eternal triangle.

James seems to approve Verena's fate, largely because she is unawakened throughout almost the whole novel; she remains a pretty young girl with no mind, and James shows little interest in her. Ransom is a Mississippian trying to revive the family plantation by practicing law in New York; he does not have ideas (until he begins to write reactionary articles) but lives by a code: Everyone must do his or her work well in one's appointed station in life. When he tries to express this idea to Verena as they sit in Central Park, she is horrified and fascinated because there is no "progress" in his code. In the end, however, Ransom and Verena pair off as a fairly normal couple. What would become of Verena would have made a superb sequel to this work, but James did not know the South, and he treats it simply as the last reservoir of acceptable masculinity from which to pluck his hero.

Olive Chancellor is more of a known quantity for James. With no other family ties except those to her sister, comfortably settled in Charles Street, she has time, intelligence, taste, and money that she diffuses quietly through twenty committees and reform groups. She is the very portrait of a Boston lady; her tragic flaw is to allow her desire for real action to overrule her taste: She falls in love with Verena's sweet stream of humbug as Ransom falls in love with Verena's voice. This is not wholly Olive's fault, as is shown by the gallery of Bostonians introduced at the suffragist party in Miss Birdseye's tasteless apartment at the beginning of the novel. The two male Bostonians are a hack journalist and "Doctor" Selah Tarrant, a mesmeric healer and a fake not only to Ransom's eyes but also to those of Dr. Prance, a woman doctor who is active in her role as "new woman" and who has little time for talking about the subject. As the real and fake doctors are contrasted, so is Dr. Prance contrasted with the suffragist campaigner Mrs. Farrinder, who is not a Bostonian and who is also suspicious of Tarrant and Verena's "inspirational" views. Mrs. Farrinder's weak husband shows what men will amount to and what Ransom is fighting in the new regime; Mrs. Farrinder, in thinking that talk will achieve the revolution Dr. Prance quietly demonstrates, shows the possible and probable results of Olive's degeneration.

In addition, ranged about Olive in contrasting positions are three other Bostonians: Mrs. Luna, completely worldly and contemptuous of any womanly activity except that of the salon; Verena's mother, equally worldly but totally vulgar; and Miss Birdseye, James's favorite creation in the novel. At the age of eighty, she is still a compulsive reformer in a completely selfless and ineffectual manner that contrasts with the practical Dr. Prance and Mrs. Farrinder and with the worldly creatures of Boston and New York. She appears only three times in the novel: at the initial party that introduces most of the characters; when she plays the part of destiny in giving

Ransom Verena's Cambridge address; and at Olive's summer cottage at Marmion, where she dies happily, mistakenly believing that Verena has enlisted Ransom in the cause. She stands for Boston's true nature, which Olive ignores in trying to achieve a triumph through Verena.

In the second part of the novel, Olive compounds her failure of discrimination by accepting the invitation of Mrs. Burrage, a New York society host, to show off Verena in New York. Olive thinks she has triumphed in securing Verena's promise not to marry and in diverting young Henry Burrage's attentions from Verena, but she overreaches herself.

Verena is the fulcrum of the plot, and her affection first for Olive, then for Ransom, is reflected in the structure of the novel. The first twenty chapters contain Olive's dinner with Ransom, Miss Birdseye's party, Ransom's call on Olive and Verena the next morning, and some months later a tea party at the Tarrants for Olive and, as it turns out, Henry Burrage. This first half of the novel concentrates on Olive's developing affection for Verena. Verena, however, is incapable of decision or independent action, and in the second half of the novel, as Ransom takes center stage, she gradually falls under his influence.

Throughout the novel, the characteristic devices of James's late middle style are apparent: lengthening paragraphs, alternating direct and indirect colloquy, and the use of idiomatic terms to carry nuances of meaning. More obvious, especially in the dramatic close, is the growing dependence on set scenes to show the stages of the drama. Over all these is the play of James's irony and pity directed at the latter-day Bostonian Olive Chancellor, the local representation of a national type and the heroine of this distinctly American novel.

Further Reading

Bell, Millicent. "The Determinate Plot: *The Bostonians*." In *Meaning in Henry James*. Cambridge, Mass.: Harvard University Press, 1991. Bell compares *The Bostonians* with other James novels and argues that it serves as an ironic rejection of naturalism.

Bowen, Janet Wolf. "Architectural Envy: A Figure Is Nothing Without a Setting in Henry James's *The Bostonians*." *New England Quarterly* 65, no. 1 (March, 1992): 3-23. By focusing on the architectural imagery of *The Bostonians*, Bowen points out that the novel depicts conflicts between inner life and public persona.

Coulson, Victoria. *Henry James, Women, and Realism*. New York: Cambridge University Press, 2007. Examines James's important friendships with three women: his sister Alice James and the novelists Constance Fenimore Woolson and Edith Wharton. These three women writers and James shared what Coulson describes as an "ambivalent realism," or a cultural ambivalence about gender identity, and she examines how this idea is manifest in James's works, including *The Bostonians*.

Faderman, Lillian. "Female Same-Sex Relationships in Novels by Longfellow, Holmes, and James." *New England Quarterly* 51, no. 3 (September, 1978): 309-332. A feminist perspective on the novel that focuses on the contrasting treatment James gives to Verena's relationships with Basil and Olive.

Freedman, Jonathan, ed. *The Cambridge Companion to Henry James*. New York: Cambridge University Press, 1998. A collection of essays that provides extensive information on James's life and literary influences and describes his works and the characters in them. Sara Blair's essay "Realism, Culture, and the Place of the Literary: Henry James and *The Bostonians*" analyzes this novel.

Jacobson, Jacob. *Queer Desire in Henry James: The Politics of Erotics in "The Bostonians" and "The Princess Casamassima."* New York: Peter Lang, 2000. Analyzes the depiction of homosexual desire in what Jacobson describes as James's "most deliberately queer novels."

Jacobson, Marcia. "Popular Fiction and Henry James's Unpopular *Bostonians*." *Modern Philology* 73, no. 3 (February, 1976): 264-275. Focuses on the novel as a political work and examines it in the context of the social and political consequences of the Civil War and the emerging women's movement.

Stevens, Hugh. *Henry James and Sexuality*. New York: Cambridge University Press, 1998. A study of sexuality as it presents itself in James's work, including discussions of homosexuality and sex roles. Chapter 5 examines "queer plotting" in *The Bostonians*.

Wagenknecht, Edward. "Explorations: *The Bostonians*; *The Princess Casamassima*; *The Tragic Muse*; and *Reverberator*." In *The Novels of Henry James*. New York: Felix Ungar, 1983. This chapter, in a book which provides general background on James's life and works, places the novel in a biographical context.

Boswell's London Journal, 1762-1763

Author: James Boswell (1740-1795)
First published: 1950
Type of work: Diary

Principal personages:
JAMES BOSWELL, the author, a young Scotsman
SAMUEL JOHNSON, the great critic, lexicographer, essayist, and poet
WILLIAM TEMPLE, Boswell's friend, a sensible young law student
LORD EGLINTON, a wealthy young nobleman, another of Boswell's friends
THE HON. ANDREW ERSKINE, a Scotsman who befriends Boswell in London
LADY ANNE ERSKINE, his sister

James Boswell left his family at home near Edinburgh in the autumn of 1762 to spend the winter in London, where he hoped to obtain a commission in the Guards. He was convinced that the military life, which would allow him to live in the city he loved so much, would suit him far better than the legal profession chosen for him by his father, a noted Scottish jurist. He recorded the activities, the hopes, and the disappointments of this year in London in a diary, which he sent in regular installments to a young friend who remained in Scotland. This journal, which miraculously survived for two hundred years and came to light in the twentieth century, is a remarkably revealing document, for reticence was not one of Boswell's characteristics. The frankness of his account of his activities brings him vividly to life.

Boswell was only twenty-two when he traveled south into England. He passed his legal examinations, and his father at last grudgingly agreed to give his son an allowance to allow him to pursue the career he thought he wanted. Lord Auchinleck's decision proved to be a wise one, for, after months of discouragement, Boswell finally realized that he was not going to obtain the desired commission, even with the help of noble friends, and he agreed to take up law again, on the condition that he might travel on the Continent before he returned to Scotland to begin his practice.

These experiences were frustrating to Boswell, but they provide fascinating reading. The author's youth is evident in many of the actions and impressions he records. He went to the city to turn himself into a polished gentleman, and the pages of his diary are filled with resolutions for the improvement of his character and manners. At times this desire for sophistication manifested itself as a rather unattractive snobbery. Boswell records his disgust at the familiarity with which some of his Scottish friends treated him, at the provin-

cialism of their conversation, and at the lack of restraint in their manners. In these moods he overlooked the fact that these hospitable people, especially Captain Andrew Erskine and his sister, did much to alleviate his loneliness.

Boswell was, however, usually perceptive about his relationships. He knew that William Temple, an old comrade from university days and a reserved and studious young man, was a good influence on him and that Lord Eglinton, who introduced Boswell to various dissipations during his first trip to London in 1760, encouraged those vices for which his inclination was already too strong. Toward the end of the journal Boswell comments that Temple and Johnston, the Scottish friend to whom he was sending the diary, were those in whom he could confide his deepest feelings, while he feared to expose his sentiments to Erskine and Eglinton, though he valued their company for amusement. Boswell did, on occasion, lay himself open to their scorn with his sensitivity regarding his own dignity. He violently resented criticism of his writing, and he sent indignant letters to Lord Eglinton when he got the feeling that he was not treated with the civility to which he thought he was entitled. This overblown sense of his own importance was perhaps the hardest of Boswell's faults for him to recognize. It never occurred to him to doubt that courtiers, ladies, and distinguished literary figures would consider themselves privileged to make his acquaintance.

Boswell was, however, acutely aware of many of his other shortcomings. His daily memoranda constantly reminded him to correct them. His resolutions were short-lived. A vow of increased economy was sure to be followed by some extravagance, generally charitable but prodigal. Intense remorse over his profligate relations with women generally preceded new debauchery. Promised rejection of his more frivolous acquaintances often led only to renewed amity. His later works show him still at his youthful routine, repenting and renewing his wrongdoing with equal fervor.

He was often the victim of his essentially trusting nature, especially in his relations with women, as the first entries of his diary show in the account of his affair with Louisa, an actress. Anxious to see himself as a romantic hero, he trusted her protestations of affection, fidelity, and morality, lent her money, pursued her ardently, and as a reward spent five weeks in his rooms convalescing from the venereal disease with which she infected him.

For all Boswell's bravado and his apparent self-assurance, he suffered at times from a deep sense of melancholy and inferiority, probably the lingering result of a nervous disorder that struck him when he was in his late teens. He had a childish fear of ghosts, and in his darker fits, when he could not bear to sleep alone in his lodgings, he would seek refuge for the night with one of his friends. This melancholy strain in his personality may have been one of the things that drew Boswell close to the great lexicographer, critic, and essayist Samuel Johnson, whom he met for the first time during the winter of the time of the London journal. Johnson was himself subject to inexplicable terrors, and throughout his life he showed great compassion for this type of human weakness.

It is sometimes difficult to understand just what drew Boswell and Johnson together, but the account of their early acquaintance shows the appealing quality of Boswell's easygoing, candid nature, however brash it was at times. Boswell's hero-worship for Johnson, his anxiety to please, and his eagerness for the older man's counsel are also clearly evident. Johnson's attitude toward Boswell, as scholars have pointed out, was in many respects paternal. He responded warmly to both the adulation and the appeals for help, and he seemed to find Boswell's enthusiasm refreshing. His insistence on accompanying his young friend to Harwich to see him sail for his studies in the Netherlands provides touching testimony of the older man's affection.

Boswell's friendship with Johnson changed the character of the London journal to a degree. From the time of their meeting, Boswell recorded more and more about Johnson's opinions on life and literature and less about his own feelings, although the latter were never ignored. Boswell's widening interests tended to decrease his introspection.

The London journal is not simply jottings of the day's activities, but a conscious literary effort. Boswell likely composed the account several days at a time, basing the diary on sketchy memoranda, and this practice allowed him to build some dramatic suspense. His ability to capture the conversations of his day, the remarks of London citizens at Child's coffee house, and the discussions of Johnson and his circle

shows the gift for narration that makes the *Life of Johnson* a masterpiece. Spurred on by Johnson's praise of the practice of keeping a journal, Boswell strove with great diligence to improve the literary quality of the latter portions of his work. As a result the book presents a remarkably lively and accurate picture of life in Boswell's time.

Further Reading

Boswell, James. *The Heart of Boswell: Six Journals in One Volume.* Edited by Mark Harris. New York: McGraw-Hill, 1981. A compendium of Boswell's writings, along with various reviews, essays, and analyses that appeared in response to the 1950 publication of Frederick Albert Pottle's comprehensive edition of the London journal.

Finlayson, Iain. *The Moth and the Candle: A Life of James Boswell.* New York: St. Martin's Press, 1984. Exactingly researched, this illustrated volume draws on the letters between Boswell and his contemporaries and serves as an insightful factual counterpoint to Boswell's journal.

Ingram, Allan. *Boswell's Creative Gloom: A Study of Imagery and Melancholy in the Writings of James Boswell.* London: Macmillan, 1982. Combines literary criticism and psychoanalytic interpretation, exploring the process of thought and the method of creative expression employed by Boswell in his journal.

Larsen, Lyle, ed. *James Boswell: As His Contemporaries Saw Him.* Madison, N.J.: Fairleigh Dickinson University Press, 2008. Family, friends, rivals, eighteenth century literary critics, and others who knew Boswell give their opinion of the man and his work.

Martin, Peter. *A Life of James Boswell.* London: Weidenfeld & Nicolson, 1999. A readable and authoritative biography, in which Martin evaluates Boswell's literary achievements and skillfully re-creates the world in which he lived.

Pittock, Murray. *James Boswell.* Aberdeen, Scotland: AHRC Centre for Irish and Scottish Studies, 2007. A detailed examination of Boswell's published and unpublished works. Pittock demonstrates how Boswell deliberately wrote ambiguously about himself and the major events of his time; he discusses how Boswell's writing was influenced by his sympathies with Catholicism, Scotland, and Jacobitism.

Pottle, Frederick Albert. *Pride and Negligence: The History of the Boswell Papers.* New York: McGraw-Hill, 1982. Considered to be the most authentic account published of the loss, reacquisition, and publication of the missing Boswell papers. Informative on the factual accuracy of the London journal.

The Braggart Soldier

Author: Plautus (c. 254-184 B.C.E.)
First produced: Miles gloriosus, c. 205 B.C.E. (English
   translation, 1767)
Type of work: Drama
Type of plot: Comedy
Time of plot: Third century B.C.E.
Locale: Ephesus, in Asia Minor

Principal characters:
PYRGOPOLINICES, a braggart army captain
PLEUSICLES, a young Athenian
PERIPLECOMENUS, an old gentleman, Pleusicles' friend
SCELEDRUS, a servant of Pyrgopolinices
PALAESTRIO, another servant of Pyrgopolinices, former
   servant of Pleusicles
PHILOCOMASIUM, Pyrgopolinices' mistress
ACROTELEUTIUM, an Ephesian courtesan

The Story:

Pleusicles, a young Athenian, is in love with and is loved by Philocomasium, a young woman of Athens. While he is away on public business in another city, a captain of Ephesus, Pyrgopolinices, comes to Athens and, in order to get Philocomasium into his power, works his way into the confidence of her mother. As soon as the opportunity presents itself, he abducts the daughter and carries her off to his home in Ephesus.

News of the abduction of Philocomasium soon reaches Pleusicles' household, and Palaestrio, a faithful servant, immediately embarks for the city in which his master is staying, intending to tell him what happened. Unfortunately, however, Palaestrio's ship is taken by pirates; he is made captive and is presented by chance to Pyrgopolinices as a gift. In the captain's house, Palaestrio and Philocomasium recognize each other but tacitly agree to keep their acquaintance a secret.

Perceiving that the woman bears a violent hatred for Pyrgopolinices, Palaestrio privately writes to Pleusicles, suggesting that he come to Ephesus. When the young man arrives, he is hospitably entertained by Periplecomenus, an old gentleman who is a friend of Pleusicles' father and who happens to live in a house adjoining that of Pyrgopolinices. Since Philocomasium has a private room in the captain's house, a hole is made through the partition wall, enabling the two lovers to meet in the approving Periplecomenus's house.

One day Sceledrus, a dull-witted servant appointed to be the keeper of Philocomasium, is chasing a monkey along the roof of the captain's house when he happens to look through the skylight of the house next door and sees Pleusicles and Philocomasium at dalliance together. He is observed, however, and before he can report his discovery to the captain, Periplecomenus tells Palaestrio how matters stand. Palaestrio then develops an elaborate hoax to convince Sceledrus that he did not see what he thought he saw.

Philocomasium is to return immediately through the hole in the wall and pretend never to have left the captain's house. In addition, she is to make a reference at the proper time to a dream she had regarding the sudden advent in Ephesus of a pretended twin sister. This ruse is carried out before the ever more confused Sceledrus, Philocomasium first playing herself and then changing clothes, going through the hole to the other house, and playing her nonexistent twin sister. Sceledrus is slow in taking the bait, but at last he swallows it and becomes unshakably convinced that he did not see Philocomasium.

The danger of discovery temporarily averted, Palaestrio, Periplecomenus, and Pleusicles confer on how they might trick Pyrgopolinices into giving up Philocomasium and Palaestrio. The servant again formulates an elaborate ruse. Since the captain is ridiculously vain regarding his attractiveness to women as well as his pretended prowess in battle, it is decided that the plotters will use an Ephesian courtesan to undo him. Periplecomenus, a bachelor, is to hire her to pretend to be his wife but so infatuated with Pyrgopolinices that she is willing to divorce her aging husband for the captain's favor.

This plan is executed. Acroteleutium, chosen as the courtesan and using her maid and Palaestrio as go-betweens, sends the ring of her "husband" to the captain with word of her infatuation. Pyrgopolinices is immediately aroused, but as he is discussing the situation with Palaestrio, it occurs to him that he will be compelled to get rid of Philocomasium before he can take advantage of Acroteleutium's offer. When Palaestrio informs him that Philocomasium's mother and twin sister just arrived in Ephesus looking for her and that the captain can easily put her out and let her return to Athens with them, Pyrgopolinices eagerly accepts the suggestion. Overwhelmed by Palaestrio's flattery, he even agrees to let Philocomasium keep the gold and jewels he gave her.

When Pyrgopolinices goes in to tell her to leave, however, she feigns immense grief. Finally she agrees to leave quietly but only after he promises that she can take Palaestrio with her as well as the gold and jewelry. The captain, amazed at this sudden display of affection, attributes it to his irresistible masculine charm. When he returns to Palaestrio he is given to understand that Acroteleutium wants him to come to her in Periplecomenus's house. Although he is at first reluctant to do so for fear of the old man's wrath, he is told that Acroteleutium put out her "husband" and that the coast is clear.

At that moment Pleusicles, disguised as the master of a ship, appears and says he was sent to take Philocomasium and her effects to the ship where her mother and sister are waiting. Pyrgopolinices, overjoyed that the matter is being handled with such dispatch, sends Philocomasium and Palaestrio off as soon as he can manage it.

After their departure he hurries into Periplecomenus's house in expectation that Acroteleutium will be waiting for him. Much to his dismay, however, Periplecomenus and his servants are waiting instead, armed with rods and whips and intent on giving Pyrgopolinices the beating that a real husband would have inflicted under such circumstances. This punishment they accomplish with great alacrity, extorting from the captain, under threat of even more dire punishment, the promise that he will never retaliate against any of the persons involved.

When they are finished, Sceledrus comes up and crowns the captain's beating with the news that the ship's master is Philocomasium's lover and that he saw them kissing and embracing as soon as they were safely outside the city gate. Pyrgopolinices is overwhelmed with rage at the way he was tricked, but as Sceledrus and he enter the house the servant observes that the captain received only what he deserved.

Critical Evaluation:

Miles gloriosus, or *The Braggart Soldier*, provided the prototype of the vainglorious, cowardly soldier for many characters in later drama, not the least of whom is William Shakespeare's Falstaff. Pyrgopolinices' character, however, is not worked out with nearly the depth that Falstaff's is. Plautus tends in this play to fail to integrate character development with plot development: The action is frequently brought to a full stop while discussions take place that have little function other than to give the audience a notion of what the characters are like. Nevertheless, the action is ingeniously contrived. Even though the trickery seems in excess of that required by the situation, the tone of the play is suffi-

ciently light to prevent the audience from feeling any strong desire for verisimilitude.

The Braggart Soldier is one of Plautus's most successful and rollicking comedies. He adapted the play from a Greek original, and possibly he combined two different sources. This is probably an early work by Plautus, judging by the lack of variety in the meter and by the reference to Naevius, the poet and dramatist. The comedy was most likely very popular when it was first presented, because repeat performances were given.

In staging it must have resembled the American musical comedy, with song and dance used to enliven the dramatic action. Masks and Greek costumes may have been employed. The backdrop consisted of two adjoining houses, one belonging to Pyrgopolinices and the other to Periplecomenus. The play itself is rich in buffoonery, parody, punning, comic names, and verbal ingenuity. The action is lively, and the characters—stock types of farce—exhibit great energy in playing out their predestined roles. There is a unity of time as well as of place, since the action occurs in less than a day. Moreover, despite what many critics say, there is a unity of dramatic movement, not to mention suspense, in the way the play is constructed. The overall effect is one of exuberance carried to its utmost limits.

When Plautus wrote his plays during the early Roman Republic, Roman morality was still quite strict, and his audiences must have been titillated by the spectacle of lecherous generals, courtesans, rascally servants, and indolent lovers, all of whom were Greek. The Romans would never have allowed such characters to appear as Romans at that period, but the fact that they were Greeks must have added largely to their enjoyment. The theater, particularly the comic theater, has often served as a liberating force, a kind of psychic safety valve, by exposing private daydreams on the stage.

The Braggart Soldier is a comedy of deception with a highly intricate plot. Superficially it has two distinct sections: the duping of Sceledrus into thinking Philocomasium is two different women, and the duping of Pyrgopolinices into voluntarily releasing Philocomasium and Palaestrio. Both schemes are closely related, and the one follows from the other.

The opening scene, in which the vain, supremely boastful, and lewd captain appears with his toady, makes it clear that Pyrgopolinices is going to be the butt of the intrigue. Then the slave Palaestrio, in his prologue, explains he is going to play a trick on the slave Sceledrus in order to make Philocomasium's meetings with Pleusicles safer. Since Sceledrus has already seen the lovers together, the scheme becomes a matter of necessity. It takes a lot of elaborate guile to prove to the stupid, pigheaded Sceledrus that Philocomasium is two people. Even though he is intimidated by Palaestrio and Periplecomenus, he is never truly convinced of it. He says he is leaving until the trouble blows over, but in fact he sticks around and gets drunk, which poses a threat to the later scheme to trick Pyrgopolinices.

Having subdued Sceledrus into temporary silence, Palaestrio has to invent a plan for freeing himself and Philocomasium from the intolerable Pyrgopolinices. If his first deception fails, any new one would be impossible. The connection between the two schemes is further strengthened when Palaestrio incorporates the idea for the first (Philocomasium being twins) into the second. However, the crux of the new plan occurs to him in a supposedly irrelevant scene where old Periplecomenus pontificates on the joys of bachelorhood: Why not give Periplecomenus a fake wife infatuated with Pyrgopolinices?

The characters involved talk over this plan extensively, but the audience does not know how it will work until Philocomasium and Palaestrio are almost freed, which maintains suspense. Suspense is also maintained tactically when the audience learns that Sceledrus is getting drunk, when Palaestrio and Milphidippa nearly burst out laughing in Pyrgopolinices' face, when Philocomasium and Pleusicles almost begin making love before Pyrgopolinices' eyes, and when Palaestrio dangerously delays his escape in saying good-bye to Pyrgopolinices. All these things give excitement to the intrigue, making the audience forget how improbable it really is.

However, it is not enough to swindle Pyrgopolinices of his courtesan and his slave woman—he must be put in a position where retaliation becomes impossible. To do that he must be completely humiliated and deflated. Hence, the scheme by which he is enticed into Periplecomenus's house to rape the phony wife makes it possible for Periplecomenus to drag him in his underwear out into the street to be beaten and threatened with castration, the punishment for adultery. The threat is enough to get the desired result from the lascivious Pyrgopolinices, securing the safety of Palaestrio and Philocomasium. At the end Pyrgopolinices is left standing on the stage in his underwear, vanity collapsed, asking the audience to applaud. This conclusion is unique among comedies of deception in the way merry practical joking leads up to such a brutal, shaming finish.

This complex story revolves around a few simple elements of character—the colossal vanity and lust of Pyrgopolinices, the desire of Philocomasium to be free and reunited with her lover, and Palaestrio's ingenuity in securing their mutual freedom. In keeping with the martial nature of Pyrgopolinices' profession, the strategy against him is spoken of in military terms. Pyrgopolinices is one of a long line of cowardly, conceited, boastful, lecherous soldiers in the theater. Palaestrio, the wily slave, is the forerunner of the artful servant from Renaissance theater to the present.

"Critical Evaluation" by James Weigel, Jr.

Further Reading

Anderson, William S. *Barbarian Play: Plautus' Roman Comedy.* Toronto, Ont.: University of Toronto Press, 1993. A well-written scholarly work. In his discussion of *The Braggart Soldier*, Anderson suggests that in this play the quality of "heroic badness" is transferred from a conventional hero to the clever slaves who outwit their masters. Exhaustive bibliography.

Fraenkel, Eduard. *Plautine Elements in Plautus.* Translated by Tomas Drevikovsky and Frances Muecke. New York: Oxford University Press, 2007. This is the first English translation of a German study initially published in 1922. Fraenkel, an influential twentieth century classicist, provides an analytical overview of Plautus's plays, including their motifs of transformation and identification, mythological material, dialogue, and the predominance of the slave's role.

Hanson, J. A. S. "The Glorious Military." In *Roman Drama*, edited by T. A. Dorey and Donald R. Dudley. London: Routledge & Kegan Paul, 1965. Plautus's egotistical soldier is the most famous use of a military stereotype in Roman drama. This essay is an excellent examination of the subject.

Hunter, R. L. *The New Comedy of Greece and Rome.* New York: Cambridge University Press, 1985. The chapter on "Plots and Motifs: The Stereotyping of Comedy" explores the use of the comic soldier in Roman comedy. An index points to specific passages discussed. Detailed notes and bibliography.

Leigh, Matthew. *Comedy and the Rise of Rome.* New York: Oxford University Press, 2004. Analyzes the comedies of Plautus and Terence, placing them within the context of political and economic conditions in Rome during the third and second centuries B.C.E. Discusses how audiences of that time responded to these comedies.

Segal, Erich. *Roman Laughter: The Comedy of Plautus.* Cambridge, Mass.: Harvard University Press, 1968. Contains numerous references to the play, noted in the index to passages from Plautus, as well as useful comments on "military heroes" and relevant discussions of slaves. Extensive notes.

_____, ed. *Oxford Readings in Menander, Plautus, and Terence.* New York: Oxford University Press, 2001. Includes essays on Plautus and the public stage, the response of Plautus's audience, and traditions, theatrical improvisation, and mastery of comic language in his plays.

Slater, Niall W. *Plautus in Performance: The Theatre of the Mind.* Princeton, N.J.: Princeton University Press, 1985. Approaches Plautus's works from a different perspective. Some specific comments and notations about *The Braggart Soldier* suggest the subtleties that may be missed in a casual reading.

Brand

Author: Henrik Ibsen (1828-1906)
First produced: 1885; first published, 1866 (English translation, 1891)
Type of work: Drama
Type of plot: Social criticism
Time of plot: Nineteenth century
Locale: West coast of Norway

Principal characters:
BRAND, a priest
HIS MOTHER
AGNES, his wife
EINAR, a painter
THE MAYOR
THE DOCTOR
THE DEAN
THE SEXTON
THE SCHOOLMASTER
GERD, a Roma (Gypsy) girl

The Story:

Brand, a young priest, meets three types of people as he makes his way down the mountainside to the tumbledown church in his home valley. The first is a peasant who will not give his own life for his dying daughter. The second is Einar, a young painter returned from travel overseas, and Agnes, his betrothed, who are gaily on their way to the town of Agnes's parents. The third is a half-Roma girl named Gerd, who taunts him to climb up to her church of ice and snow. In the peasant, Einar and Agnes, and Gerd—the fainthearted, the lighthearted, and the uncontrolled—Brand sees exemplified the triple sickness of the world, and he vows to heaven to bring about its cure.

In the village, Brand gains the admiration of the crowd when he risks his life to aid a man. Later he sees Agnes sitting by the shore disturbed and uplifted by new powers awakening in her when she experiences a vision of God urging her to choose another path. He sees his aged mother, who offers him all her savings on condition that he preserve them for family use. Brand refuses and urges her to give up all her earthly possessions. The mother leaves unrepentant, unwilling that her lifetime savings should be scattered. By these encounters Brand is convinced that his mission lies close at hand in daily duties, even if he is unapplauded by the world.

Just as he is going to return to the village, Einar suddenly appears and demands that Agnes come back to him. Agnes, having seen her vision, refuses to go with Einar, even though Brand warns her it will be gray and sunless in his fissure between the mountains; he demands all or nothing.

Three years pass. Although success marks Brand's work, he realizes that, married to Agnes and blessed with her love and that of their son Alf, he has yet made no real sacrifices. The tests soon come. First his mother dies, still unrepentant. Then his child becomes ill, and the doctor advises them to leave their icy home or the child will die. When Brand agrees, the doctor points out that, in leaving, Brand will give the lie to his own stern attitude toward others. Agnes prepares to go, but Brand is plagued by indecision. Brand thinks that Agnes, as the child's mother, should make the decision. When Agnes says that she will abide by her husband's choice, Brand chooses the only way he thinks compatible with his beliefs, though he knows his decision means death for the child they love.

A year later, the mayor, with elections near, arrives to seek Brand's aid in building a house for the poor. When Brand says he himself is going to build a new church that will cost the people nothing, the mayor leaves.

Agnes feels that she must challenge her husband with what he demands of others, all or nothing. If she were to return to her old life, Agnes asks, would he choose her or his holy work? When she realizes that there can be only one answer, Agnes rejoices, knowing that for the husband she loves it is indeed all or nothing. Soon afterward she dies, leaving Brand alone.

A year and a half later the new church is complete and a great throng gathers for the consecration. The mayor and the dean congratulate Brand on his great accomplishment. Einar appears, emaciated. He has become a fanatic missionary, and he brushes aside as unimportant the news that Agnes and her child died; his only interest is the faith in which she died.

Einar leaves, but the encounter makes things clear to Brand. He exhorts the people to lead a new life. It was wrong, he says, to lure the spirit of God to their heart by building a larger church. There should be no compromise. It must be all or nothing. He waves them away from the church and locks the door.

When he calls the people to the greater Church of Life where every day is dedicated to God, they lift Brand on their shoulders. Up toward the mountains, he urges them. As the rain begins to fall, the sexton warns them they are on the way to the ice-church. The older ones complain of feeling faint and thirsty. Many cry out for a miracle. They feel the gift of prophecy is on Brand and call on him to speak. Uplifted, he tells them they are waging a war that will last all their lives; they will lose earthly wealth but gain faith and a crown of thorns. At this, the crowd cries out that they were misled, betrayed, and they are ready to stone and knife the priest.

Brand toils upward, followed far behind by a single figure, Gerd. He hears an invisible choir that mocks him, saying his work on earth is doomed. The apparition of Agnes appears, saying he can be reunited with his wife and son if he will blot out from his soul the three words that have characterized his old life: all or nothing. When Brand spurns the tempter, the phantom vanishes. Gerd, with her rifle, catches up with him. She sees that Brand's hands are pierced and torn, his brow marked with thorns. To Gerd he is the Lord, the Redeemer. Brand bids her go, but Gerd tells him to look up. Above him towers the ice-church. Brand weeps, feeling utterly forsaken. With his tears come sudden release. His fetters fall away, and he faces the future with renewed youth and radiant faith.

In the snow from the mountain heights, Gerd sees a mocking sprite, and she raises her rifle and shoots. With a terrible, thunderous roar, an avalanche sweeps down. As it is about to crush him, Brand calls out to God. Above the crashing thunder a voice proclaims that God is a god of love.

Critical Evaluation:

Immensely popular when first published, the verse drama *Brand*—a play in poetry—took the whole Scandinavian world by storm and launched Henrik Ibsen's European fame. Four editions appeared in the year of its publication; by 1889, the eleventh edition had appeared. Four translations were published in Germany between 1872 and 1882. Though not intended for the stage, the work's fourth act was played repeatedly (only in Sweden has the whole drama been performed). The play was written in Italy, where the author had exiled himself in protest against Norway's national shame in remaining neutral and failing to support Denmark in its war against invading Prussia. From Italy, Ibsen was able to catch in clearer perspective the strengths and weaknesses of his native land. The writing of *Brand* seemed to be a personal catharsis, and he was able thereafter to return to his northern home and produce in regular succession, almost every two years for the rest of his life, his original and stirring dramas. Though *Brand* is addressed to the people of Norway, it is universal in its appeal, depicting the never-ending and tragic struggle of the soul in its search for uncompromising truth.

Brand was written in the first phase of Ibsen's career, when his plays dealt mainly with historical themes, folklore, and romantic pageantry, and before the playwright turned to prose and social issues in the second phase of his career. *Brand* was the first of Ibsen's masterpieces, foreshadowing his best-known plays of social criticism. The play vitalized the Norwegian theater, which had been languishing under the shadow of the Danish theater in Copenhagen even after Norway's separation from Denmark in 1814. *Brand* thus has historical significance as well as artistic importance.

The play combines poetry and moral passion in a grim Norwegian landscape of jagged mountains, deep-fissured valleys, and cruel cold. The setting is an apt complement to the solemn, tragic atmosphere of the play and to the dour cynicism of many of Brand's parishioners and fellow villagers. Indeed, gloom pervades the play. At the beginning of the play, Einar and Agnes appear to Brand as symbols of lightheartedness that the priest deplores as evil. Soon after, Agnes breaks off her engagement to Einar to marry Brand and live a life of great sacrifice, which ends with her early death. Einar, too, subsequently forsakes his lighthearted ways and becomes a religious fanatic. It is the stern image of Brand, however, that dominates the play.

Brand is the tragedy of a supreme idealist misled by an image of holiness. His uncompromising attitude in his dealings with others—even with his wife and in matters relating to the survival of their son—reveals his conviction that the path to holiness is too narrow for concessions or backsliding.

Brand is so sure of his own judgment that even his mountain-climbing injuries appear as vindicating stigmata. Ironically, his epiphany is shattered by the rifle shot of Gerd, his one remaining follower and a social outcast. The manifestation of the transcendent mercy of God, however, just before the avalanche engulfs Brand and Gerd, is not a validation of his beliefs. Rather, Ibsen is showing that even the most pious and dedicated priest can do and be wrong and thus stand in need of the divine solace Brand had earlier exhorted his sinful parishioners to seek. *Brand* depicts the fate of a proud man whose ideals and idealism have blinded him to his own pride.

Further Reading

Bellquist, John E. "Ibsen's *Brand* and *Når vi døde vågner*: Tragedy, Romanticism, Apocalypse." *Scandinavian Studies* 55, no. 4 (Autumn, 1983): 345-370. A discussion of Brand's extreme idealism, which causes him to sacrifice the interests of his family members, as well as his own life and happiness. Bellquist regards Brand as a typical Aristotelian tragic hero.

Hurt, James. *Catiline's Dream: An Essay on Ibsen's Plays*. Urbana: University of Illinois Press, 1972. A survey of Ibsen's works. Contains a good discussion of Brand's spiritual struggles and the opposition between love and will as organizing principles in life.

Lyons, Charles R. *Henrik Ibsen: The Divided Consciousness*. Carbondale: Southern Illinois University Press, 1972. A volume with studies of seven Ibsen plays. The essay on *Brand* discusses the play's tension between the spiritual and the carnal.

McFarlane, James. *Ibsen and Meaning: Studies, Essays, and Prefaces, 1953-87*. Norwich, England: Norvik Press, 1989. Compares and contrasts *Brand* with another Ibsen play, *Peer Gynt*. Unlike the protagonist of *Brand*, McFarlane argues, Peer Gynt is a man who lives entirely in his illusions.

_____, ed. *The Cambridge Companion to Ibsen*. New York: Cambridge University Press, 1994. Collection of essays, including discussions of Ibsen's dramatic apprenticeship, historical drama, comedy, and realistic problem drama. The references to *Brand* are listed in the index.

Moi, Toril. *Henrik Ibsen and the Birth of Modernism: Art, Theater, Philosophy*. New York: Oxford University Press, 2006. A reevaluation of Ibsen, in which Moi refutes the traditional definition of Ibsen as a realistic and naturalistic playwright and describes him as an early modernist. References to *Brand* are listed in the index.

Robinson, Michael, ed. *Turning the Century: Centennial Essays on Ibsen*. Norwich, England: Norvik Press, 2006. Collection of the essays published in the journal *Scandinavica* during the past four decades, including discussions of Ibsen's style, language, and the reception of his plays in England.

Sohlich, Wolfgang. "Ibsen's *Brand*: Drama of the Fatherless Society." *Journal of Dramatic Theory and Criticism* 3, no. 2 (Spring, 1989): 87-105. A discussion of Brand's family relationships as a key to Ibsen's depiction of the social transformation at the time. The article relies heavily on the critical theory of the Frankfurt school.

Templeton, Joan. *Ibsen's Women*. New York: Cambridge University Press, 1997. Templeton examines the women characters in Ibsen's plays and their relationship to the women in the playwright's life and career. Chapter 4 includes an analysis of *Brand*.

Brave New World

Author: Aldous Huxley (1894-1963)
First published: 1932
Type of work: Novel
Type of plot: Dystopian
Time of plot: 632 years After Ford
Locale: London and New Mexico

Principal characters:
BERNARD MARX, an Alpha Plus citizen
LENINA CROWNE, a worker
JOHN, the Savage
MUSTAPHA MOND, a World Controller

The Story:

One day in the year 632 After Ford (A.F.), as time is reckoned in the brave new world, the director of the Central London Hatchery and Conditioning Centre takes a group of new students on a tour of the plant where human beings are turned out by mass production. The entire process, from the fertilization of the egg to the birth of the baby, is carried out by trained workers and machines. Each fertilized egg is placed in solution in a large bottle for scientific development into whatever class in society the human is intended. The students are told that scientists of the period developed the Bokanovsky Process, by means of which a fertilized egg is arrested in its growth. The egg responds by budding, and instead of one human being resulting, there will be from eight to ninety-six identical humans.

These Bokanovsky Groups are employed whenever large numbers of people are needed to perform identical tasks. Individuality is a thing of the past. The new society makes every effort to fulfill its motto—Community, Identity, Stability. After birth, the babies are further conditioned during their childhood for their predestined class in society. Alpha Plus Intellectuals and Epsilon Minus Morons are the two extremes of the scientific utopia.

Mustapha Mond, one of the World Controllers, joins the inspection party and lectures to the new students on the horrors and disgusting features of old-fashioned family life. To the great embarrassment of the students, he, in his position of authority, dares to use the forbidden words "mother" and "father"; he reminds the students that in 632 A.F., everyone belongs to everyone else.

Lenina Crowne, one of the workers in the Hatchery, takes an interest in Bernard Marx. Bernard is different—too much alcohol was put into his blood surrogate during his period in the prenatal bottle, and he has sensibilities similar to those possessed by people in the time of Henry Ford.

Lenina and Bernard go by rocket ship to New Mexico and visit the Savage Reservation, a wild tract where primitive forms of human life are preserved for scientific study. At the pueblo of Malpais, the couple see an Indian ceremonial dance in which a young man is whipped to propitiate the gods. Lenina is shocked and disgusted by the filth of the place and by the primitive aspects of all she sees.

The pair meet a white youth named John. The young man discloses to them that his mother, Linda, came to the reservation many years before on vacation with a man called Thomakin. The vacationers separated, and Thomakin returned alone to the brave new world. Linda, marooned in New Mexico, gave birth to a son and was slowly assimilated into the primitive society of the reservation. The boy educated himself with an old copy of William Shakespeare's plays that he found. Bernard is convinced that the boy is the son of the director of Hatcheries, who in his youth took a companion to New Mexico on vacation and returned without her. Bernard has enough human curiosity to wonder how this young savage would react to the scientific world. He invites John and his mother to return to London with him. John, at-tracted to Lenina and anxious to see the outside world, goes eagerly.

Upon Bernard's return, the director of Hatcheries publicly proposes to dismiss him from the Hatchery because of his unorthodoxy. Bernard produces Linda and John, the director's son. At the family reunion, during which such words as "mother" and "father" are used more than once, the director is shamed out of the plant. He later resigns his position.

Linda goes on a soma holiday, soma being a drug that induces euphoria and forgetfulness. John becomes the curiosity of London. He is appalled by all he sees—by the utter lack of any humanistic culture and by the scientific mass production of everything, including humans. Lenina tries to seduce him, but he is held back by his primitive morality.

John is called to attend the death of Linda, who took too much soma drug. Maddened by the callousness of people conditioned toward death, he instigates a mutiny of workers as they are being given their soma ration. He is arrested and taken by the police to Mond, with whom he has a long talk on the new civilization. Mond explains that beauty causes unhappiness and thus instability; therefore, humanistic endeavor is checked. Science is dominant. Art is stifled completely; science, even, is stifled at a certain point, and religion is restrained so that it cannot cause instability. With a genial sort of cynicism, Mond explains the reasons underlying all of the features of the brave new world. Despite Mond's persuasiveness, the Savage continues to champion tears, inconvenience, God, and poetry.

John moves into the country outside London to take up his old way of life. Sightseers come by the thousands to see him; he is pestered by reporters and television men. At the thought of Lenina, whom he still desires, John mortifies his flesh by whipping himself. Lenina visits John and is whipped by him in a frenzy of passion. When he realizes that he, too, has been caught up in the "orgyporgy," he hangs himself. Bernard's experiment fails. Human emotions can end only in tragedy in the brave new world.

Critical Evaluation:

Utopian—and dystopian (anti-utopian)—fiction is not really about the future; it is an indirect view of the present. The authors of such works begin with aspects of their own society that they like, dislike, desire, or fear, and by extrapolating them into a possible future, they demonstrate the likely consequences of such tendencies or pressures developed to extremes. If readers do not see their own society reflected in an exaggerated, distinctive, but recognizable form, it is unlikely that the projected world will offer more than amused distraction. *Brave New World* has endured as a classic of the genre because Aldous Huxley's vision not only was frighteningly believable when first presented but also has become more immediate since its initial appearance. Indeed, in *Brave New World Revisited* (1958), an extended expository gloss on the original, Huxley suggests that his only important prophetic error was the assumption that it would take six centuries to implement fully the brave new world; a scant twenty-six years after the novel's publication, Huxley revised his estimate of the time needed to less than a century.

The most disturbing aspect of *Brave New World* is the suspicion that many, perhaps most, people would like to live in such a society. After examining the modern Western world in general and America in the 1920's in particular, with its assembly-line techniques, its consumerism, its hedonistic tendencies, its emphasis on social conformity, and its worship of childhood and youth, Huxley projected his observations to their logical conclusions and then asked himself how a "sane" man would react to such an environment: the result was *Brave New World*.

Given modern industrial and scientific "progress," Huxley saw that the time would soon arrive when humanity would possess the knowledge and equipment to "solve" all of its material and social problems and achieve universal "happiness," but at a very high price—the sacrifice of freedom, individuality, truth, beauty, a sense of purpose, and the concept of God. The central question is this: How many people would really miss these things? Do they constitute enough of an intellectual, emotional, and moral force to alter the direction of modern society, and do they possess the requisite will, conviction, and energy to do so?

Compared to such earlier efforts as *Antic Hay* (1923), *Those Barren Leaves* (1925), and especially *Point Counter Point* (1928), *Brave New World* is a model of structural simplicity. The dynamics of a brave new world are presented in a long introductory tour of Huxley's futuristic society that takes up almost the first half of the book. Then a catalytic character, John the Savage, is introduced, who directly challenges the social system that has been described. This conflict leads to a confrontation between John, the representative of "sanity," and Mustapha Mond, who speaks for the brave new world. Their extended debate serves as the novel's ideological climax. The book ends as the Savage experiences the inevitable personal consequences of that debate.

The long opening sequence begins with assembly-line bottle births, in which the individual's potential is carefully regulated by a combination of genetic selection and chemical treatments and then follows the life cycle to show how all tastes, attitudes, and behavior patterns are adroitly controlled by incessant conditioning. The net result of the conditioning is a society that is totally and deliberately infantile. All activities are transitory, trivial, and mindless—promiscuity replaces passion, immediate sensory stimulation (feelies) replaces art, hallucinatory escape (soma) replaces personal growth.

At this point John the Savage enters the narrative. Reared among primitives by a mother who loves him in spite of her conditioning, John has known the beauty of great art, because of his reading of Shakespeare, and the pain of loneliness, having been ostracized by the natives because of his light skin and his mother's loose morals. Primed by Linda's nostalgic memories of her former life, the Savage is ready for contact with the outside world when Bernard Marx discovers him on the reservation and connives to use him in a revenge scheme against the director of the Hatcheries (John's natural father). At first, John is feted as an interesting freak, but, given his "primitive" moralism, a clash is inevitable. Reacting emotionally to the events surrounding Linda's death, John provokes a violent social disruption—the most serious crime in the brave new world—which leads to the discussion with Mustapha Mond, a World Controller.

In a bitterly funny way, this extended debate between John and Mond resembles the Grand Inquisitor passage in Fyodor Dostoevski's *Bratya Karamazov*, 1879-1880 (*The Brothers Karamazov*, 1912) and is the rhetorical center of the book. Like Dostoevski's Inquisitor, Mond justifies his social vision as the only one compatible with human happiness, and like his literary predecessor, he indicates that he, along with the other World Controllers, has taken the pain of life's ambiguities and indecisions upon his own shoulders in order to spare those less capable from having to endure such emotional and psychological pressures. The major difference between the Inquisitor's society and the brave new world is that Dostoevski's hero-villain had only a vision, but, with the aid of modern science and industry, the World Controllers have succeeded in making the vision a permanent reality—providing all distractions such as beauty, truth, art, purpose, God, and, ironically, science itself are suppressed. The Savage rejects Mond's world out of hand, for he demands the right to be unhappy, among other things.

Unfortunately, however, the brave new world cannot allow the Savage that right, nor, if it would, is he fully capable of exercising it. His designation as "savage" is ironical and true. He is civilized compared to the dehumanized infantilism of most brave new worlders, but he is also still the primitive. Shakespeare alone is not enough to equip him for the complexities of life. His upbringing among the pre-civilized natives, who practice a religion that is a form of fertility cult, has left him without the emotional and religious resources needed to face a brave new world on his own. Denied a chance to escape, the Savage tries to separate himself from its influence, but it follows him and exploits him as a quaint curiosity. Frustrated and guilt-ridden, he scourges himself and is horrified to discover that the brave new worlders can incorporate even his self-abasement into their system. Caught between the insanity of utopia and the lunacy of the primitive village, John reacts violently—first outwardly, by assaulting Lenina, and then inwardly, by killing himself.

It therefore remains for the other "rebellious" characters in the book to establish alternatives to the brave new world. In this aspect, perhaps, the book is artistically inferior to Huxley's previous works. One of the most impressive qualities in the novels that immediately preceded *Brave New World* is the way in which the author pursues and develops the qualities that he has given to his major characters. Unfortunately, in *Brave New World*, he does not fully develop the possibilities latent in his primary figures.

One of the sharpest ironies in *Brave New World* lies in the way Huxley carefully demonstrates that, in spite of mechanistic reproduction and incessant conditioning, individualistic traits and inclinations persist in the brave new world. As a result of alcohol in his prenatal blood surrogate, Bernard shows elements of nonconformity. As a result of an overdeveloped IQ, Helmholtz Watson is dissatisfied with his situation and longs to write a book, although he cannot imagine what he wants to say. Even Lenina Crowne has dangerous tendencies toward emotional involvement. However, Huxley largely fails to develop the potential of these deviations. After repeatedly showing Bernard's erratic attempts to conform to a society in which he feels essentially alienated, Huxley abandons him once the Savage enters the narrative. On the other hand, Watson's character is hardly explored at all; and after her failure to seduce John, Lenina is almost completely forgotten, except for her fleeting reappearance at the book's conclusion. Unlike the Savage, Bernard and Watson are allowed a chance to travel to an isolated community and experiment with individualism, but the reader never sees the results of their austere freedom.

Although the "positive" side of *Brave New World* is never developed and all of the artistic possibilities are not fully exploited, the novel remains a powerful, perceptive, and bitterly funny vision of modern society; but let readers fervently hope, along with the author, that the final importance of *Brave New World* does not come from its prophetic accuracy.

"Critical Evaluation" by Keith Neilson

Further Reading

Barfoot, C. C., ed. *Aldous Huxley: Between East and West*. Amsterdam: Rodopi, 2001. Collection of essays, including analyses of the themes of science and modernity in Huxley's interwar novels, utopian themes in his work, his views of nature, and his use of psychedelic drugs and mescaline.

Bloom, Harold, ed. *Aldous Huxley's "Brave New World."* Philadelphia: Chelsea House, 2003. Collection of essays by Huxley scholars that analyze the novel as both utopian and dystopian fiction and discuss its representation of technology, gender, and psychology and the world state.

Bowering, Peter. *Aldous Huxley: A Study of the Major Novels*. New York: Oxford University Press, 1969. Devotes a chapter to *Brave New World*, concentrating particularly on its themes of technological slavery and the limits of freedom. Includes substantial character analysis.

Firchow, Peter. *Aldous Huxley: Satirist and Novelist*. Minneapolis: University of Minnesota Press, 1972. Devotes most of chapter 5 to a discussion of *Brave New World* as a dystopian novel. Considers it as a satirical parable modeled on the Grand Inquisitor episode in *The Brothers Karamazov*.

Izzo, David Garrett, and Kim Kirkpatrick. *Huxley's "Brave New World": Essays*. Jefferson, N.C.: McFarland, 2008. The essays describe how Huxley's novel forecast many of the problems of capitalist society in the twenty-first century. Some of the essays discuss the anti-utopian ideals of the novel's rigid caste system, the novel's influence on philosophers Max Horkheimer and Theodor Adorno, and the novel's relationship to other works of dystopian fiction.

Meckier, Jerome. *Aldous Huxley: Modern Satirical Novelist of Ideas, a Collection of Essays*. Edited by Peter Firchow and Bernfried Nugel. London: Global, 2006. Collection of Meckier's essays written from 1966 through 2005 contains several discussions of *Brave New World*, including "Our Ford, Our Freud, and the Behaviorist Conspiracy in Huxley's *Brave New World*," "Aldous Huxley's Americanization of the *Brave New World* Typescript," and "*Brave New World* and the Anthropologists: Primitivism in A.F. 632."

_____, ed. *Critical Essays on Aldous Huxley*. New York: G. K. Hall, 1996. Includes thoughtful essays on Huxley's oeuvre, including "The Manuscript Revisions of *Brave New World*" by Donald Watt and "*Brave New World* and the Rationalization of Industry" by James Sexton.

Murray, Nicholas. *Aldous Huxley: A Biography*. New York: St. Martin's Press, 2003. Murray's 500-plus-page biography and intellectual history is a wide-ranging survey of Huxley's writing and his social, personal, and political life. The book stretches from Huxley's early satirical writing to his peace activism, and from his close relations and friendships with Hollywood filmmakers and other intellectuals to his fascination with spirituality and mysticism. Illustrations, bibliography, and index.

Nance, Guinevera. *Aldous Huxley.* New York: Continuum, 1988. Chapter 3 offers a critical summary and evaluation of *Brave New World*, considering its themes and paying particular attention to the moral implications of the Savage.

Watts, Harold H. *Aldous Huxley.* Boston: Twayne, 1969. One chapter discusses *Brave New World* as dystopian fiction, examining its themes, structures, and characterizations and considering its artistic value. A good general introduction to the novel.

Bread and Wine

Author: Ignazio Silone (1900-1978)
First published: Brot und Wein, 1936 (English
    translation, 1936; revised, 1962)
Type of work: Novel
Type of plot: Social realism
Time of plot: 1930's
Locale: Italy

Principal characters:
DON BENEDETTO, a liberal priest
PIETRO SPINA, a former pupil and a political agitator
BIANCHINA GIRASOLE, a peasant girl befriended by Spina
CRISTINA COLAMARTINI, Bianchina's schoolmate

The Story:

In the Italian village of Rocca dei Marsi, Don Benedetto, a former Catholic teacher, and his faithful sister, Marta, prepare to observe the don's seventy-fifth birthday. It is April, and war with the Abyssinians is in the making. Benedetto invites several of his old students to observe his anniversary with him. Three appear, and the group talks of old acquaintances. Most of Benedetto's students compromised the moral precepts that the high-minded old scholar taught them. Benedetto asks about Pietro Spina, his favorite pupil, and learns from his guests that the independent-minded Spina is a political agitator, a man without a country. It is rumored that Spina returned to Italy to carry on his work among the peasants.

One day Doctor Nunzio Sacca, one of those who was at the party, is summoned by a peasant to come to the aid of a sick man. Sacca, upon finding the man to be Spina, is filled with fear, but the sincerity and fervor of Spina make him ashamed. Spina, only in his thirties, used iodine to transform his features to those of an old man. Sacca administers to Spina and arranges for the agitator's convalescence in a nearby mountain village. Later, he furnishes Spina with clerical clothes. Disguised as a priest and calling himself Don Paolo Spada, Spina goes to the Hotel Girasole in Fossa, where he brings comfort to a young woman who is believed to be dying as the result of an abortion.

In the mountains, at Pietrasecca, Paolo—as Spina calls himself—stays at the inn of Matelena Ricotta. In his retreat, Paolo begins to have doubts concerning the value of the life he is leading, but the brutal existence of the peasants of Pietrasecca continue to spur him on in his desire to free the oppressed people.

Bianchina Girasole, the woman whom Paolo comforted at Fossa, appears, well and healthy. Attributing her survival to Paolo, she says that the man is surely a saint. Disowned by her family, Bianchina goes to Cristina Colamartini, a school friend who lives in Pietrasecca. The two women, discussing school days and old friends, conclude that most of their schoolmates took to ways of evil in one way or another. When Bianchina seduces Cristina's brother, Alberto, the Colamartinis are scandalized. Paolo lost his respect for Cristina, who shows only too plainly that her devotion to God excludes all reason and any humanity; she avows that a Colamartini can never marry a Girasole because of difference in caste.

Paolo begins to visit more frequently among the peasants. Soon he has a reputation as a wise and friendly priest. In his association with those simple people, he learns that no reformer can ever hope to be successful with them by use of abstractions; the peasants accept only facts, either good or bad. He leaves the valley. At Fossa, he again seeks out potential revolutionary elements. He speaks of revolution to Alberto and Bianchina, who move to Fossa, and to Pompeo, son of the local chemist. The youths are delighted. Paolo enlists Pompeo in the movement.

Paolo goes to Rome. There, in the church of Scala Santa, he discards his clerical dress to become Spina once again. In Rome, he finds an air of futility and despair. Romeo, his chief contact, tells him that peasant agitators do not have a chance for success. Spina explains that propaganda by words is not enough; success can be achieved only by living the truth to encourage the oppressed. Spina sees student demonstrations in favor of the leader and of the projected war. He talks to Uliva, who is completely disillusioned. Then he looks for Murica, a youth from his own district who, perhaps, can direct him to dependable peasants. Murica, however, returned to his home. Before Spina leaves Rome, he hears that an explosion killed Uliva in his apartment. The police learn that Uliva was preparing to blow up a church at a time when many high government officials were to be in it.

Back at the Hotel Girasole in Fossa, Spina, again disguised as Don Paolo, is sickened by the enthusiasm of the peasants for the success of the Abyssinian war. He sends Bianchina to Rocca to seek out Murica. During the prowar demonstrations, he goes about the village writing antiwar and antigovernment slogans on walls. Pompeo, who went to Rome, returns during the excitement and reveals that he was won over by the glory of the new war; he enlists for service in Africa. Paolo's charcoaled slogans soon have the village in an uproar. Pompeo, who suspects Paolo, announces publicly that he will disclose the culprit's identity, but Bianchina persuades the youth not to expose her beloved Paolo.

Paolo goes to visit his old schoolmaster, Don Benedetto, at Rocca. He appears before the venerable old priest as himself, not as Paolo, and the two men, although of different generations, agree that theirs is a common problem. They ask each other what has become of God in human affairs. They are not able to offer any solution to the problem, but they both agree that any compromise to one's belief is fatal not only to the individual but also to society.

Paolo gives Bianchina money and letters and sends her to Rome; he himself goes to Pietrasecca. There a young peasant brings him a letter from Don Benedetto. The messenger is Murica, the man he was seeking. When Spina reveals his true identity to Murica, the two men swear to collaborate. News of Murica's work with Paolo circulates in Pietrasecca, and Paolo finds himself playing the part of confessor to Pietraseccans. What they disclose to him disgusts him but at the same time convinces him more than ever that the peasants must be raised from their squalor. Paolo renews his acquain-

tance with Cristina, who was asked by Don Benedetto to give Paolo help whenever he needs it.

Don Benedetto is threatened because of his candid opinions. Called to officiate at a mass, he is poisoned when he drinks the sacramental wine. At the same time Paolo, who receives word that Romeo was arrested in Rome, goes to the Holy City, where he finds that Bianchina is a prostitute. She confesses her undying love for the priest. Paolo, now Spina, finds the underground movement in Rome in utter chaos after Romeo's arrest. Despairing, he returns to his home district, where he learns that Murica was arrested and killed by government authorities. He flees to Pietrasecca to destroy papers he left in the inn where he stayed during his convalescence. Learning that he is sought throughout the district, he flees into the snow-covered mountains. Cristina follows his trail in an attempt to take him food and warm clothing. Mists and deep snow hinder her progress. Night falls. Alone and exhausted, she makes the sign of the cross as hungry wolves close in upon her.

Critical Evaluation:

Ignazio Silone, Italy's chief novelist of the 1930's and 1940's, was attracted to communism in the 1920's, but by 1930 he became disillusioned with the party's hypocrisy and tyranny. *Bread and Wine*, his best novel, which was first published in German, is in part a study in political disillusionment. The novel reveals that reaction to social injustice is at the root of Silone's impulse to write fiction. He has said, "for me writing has not been, and never could be except in a few favored moments of peace, a serene aesthetic enjoyment, but rather the painful continuation of a struggle."

The central question in *Bread and Wine* is whether one can satisfy the demands of the soul and of social betterment at the same time. At the beginning of the novel, Pietro Spina is a full-fledged political propagandist and organizer for the Communists. He opposes the private ownership of land and he seems to believe that the world's wealth will eventually be shared equally. Forced to hide and rest in an out-of-the-way village in the garb of a priest, he begins to change his views. He asks himself whether he has not lost his sincerity in his wholehearted pursuit of party ideology. He asks whether he has not fled "the opportunism of a decadent church to fall into the Machiavellianism of a sect?" In his self-examination, the question of good faith is paramount. Political action in Silone's belief demands as much honesty and composure of soul as does a true religious vocation.

Two factors in particular contribute to Spina's change. The first is his assumption of the role of Don Paolo. As a priest, people come to him in trust, and his own instinctive love of truth and justice is, ironically, rekindled. The second has to do with the peasants he encounters and the region in which they live. The Abruzzi region is central in Silone's fiction. It is bleak and poverty-stricken, but its peasants are tough and basic. They and their land bring Spina back to the basic problems governing the individual's relationships with others.

Spina's problem can be put another way: As he becomes more and more influenced by his role as Don Paolo, he must not lose sight of Pietro Spina. He must keep Don Paolo and Spina together and integrated. His old schoolteacher Don Benedetto helps him here. Don Benedetto has moral authority and candor. His advice to Spina confirms him in his way. His death is a further sign to Spina that he must not back away from social problems. In his dialogues with Cristina Colamartini, Spina is also confirmed in his spiritual change. She, too, is sacrificed at the end of the novel. For Silone, such sacrifices are necessary to the pursuit of political justice and spiritual wholeness.

Two scenes in particular reveal Pietro's independence and help to define his rejection of party politics. In the first scene, Pietro refuses to follow the party line as enunciated by a character named Battipaglia. He points out that if he conforms to an edict in which he does not believe, he will be committing the same sin of which the Communists accuse the Fascists. The second scene follows directly after the first and is really a continuation of the argument begun in the first. Uliva, an old friend of Pietro, says he already foresees the corruption of their movement into orthodoxy and tyranny. The enthusiastic ideas they had as students have hardened into official doctrine. The party cannot stand any deviation, even if it leads to the truth. Uliva's disillusionment is great: "Against this pseudolife, weighed down by pitiless laws," he cries out, "the only weapon left to man's free will is antilife, the destruction of life itself." Later, he is killed in his apartment by a bomb that police evidence shows he meant for high government officials gathered in a church. This is his physical end, but he really was destroyed by the dialectical process. Between Battipaglia's cynical rigidity and Uliva's honest but misguided nihilism, Spina must find a way to perpetuate the cause. He succeeds because his faith cannot dry up and because he is able to pass on his belief to two or three others. The process of simple communion replaces the idea of the Communist state, and the revolutionary spirit is saved. Silone's communism is the primitive communism of early Christianity. Poverty is its badge of honesty, and its heroes are men who travel in disguise from place to place looking for kindred souls. They like to listen to peasants and simple people rather than to the learned.

In a scene that is repeated throughout Silone's work, Spina meets one such man and says he wants to talk with him. The man proves to be a deaf mute, but that does not prevent Spina from communicating with him. Indeed, it is the wordless nature of their communication that is important, for words can neither confuse nor betray them. Their spiritual communion is the most solid base on which to build a relationship. Spiritual communication is, Silone seems to be saying, the one thing absolutely necessary for successful political action, the only thing which should never be betrayed.

The humanistic basis of Silone's politics is stated most fully by Spina when he says to Uliva, "man doesn't really exist unless he's fighting against his own limits." At the end of *Bread and Wine*, the spirit of clandestine rebellion is abroad in the land. As in early Christian times, the history of martyrdoms and miracles has begun.

"Critical Evaluation" by Benjamin Nyce

Further Reading

Brown, Robert McAfee. "Ignazio Silone and the Pseudonyms of God." In *The Shapeless God: Essays on Modern Fiction*, edited by Harry J. Mooney, Jr., and Thomas F. Staley. Pittsburgh, Pa.: University of Pittsburgh Press, 1968. Notes the underlying Christian symbolism in this novel of failed revolution. Suggests that God is not dead but hidden, revealed not through religion but through sacrifice for others.

Holmes, Deborah. *Ignazio Silone in Exile: Writing and Antifascism in Switzerland, 1929-44*. Burlington, Vt.: Ashgate, 2005. Focuses on Silone's fifteen-year exile in Switzerland. Holmes discusses the influence of German antifascist émigres and Swiss socialists upon Silone's work, Silone's role in Zurich's intellectual community and the Swiss left-wing press, and the reception and rewriting of *Bread and Wine*.

Howe, Irving. "Silone: A Luminous Example." In *Decline of the New*. New York: Harcourt, Brace & World, 1970. Traces Pietro Spina's spiritual anguish and his ultimate rejection of Marxism in favor of the primitive Christianity of the Abruzzi peasants. Explores the possibility of modern heroism through contemplation rather than action.

Leake, Elizabeth. *The Reinvention of Ignazio Silone*. Toronto, Ont.: University of Toronto Press, 2003. In 1996, it was revealed that Silone, a hero among Italian liberals and a one-time high-ranking member of the Communist Party, had secretly supported the Italian Fascists. Leake reevaluates Silone's fiction from a psychoanalytic perspective, demonstrating how his novels reflect his struggles with this duplicity. *Bread and Wine* is discussed in chapter 4.

Lewis, R. W. B. "Ignazio Silone: The Politics of Charity." In *The Picaresque Saint: Representative Figures in Contemporary Fiction.* Philadelphia: J. B. Lippincott, 1959. Identifies Spina, with his alter ego Paolo Spada, as a picaresque saint, part hero and part rogue. Analyzes his encounters with other symbolic figures.

Paynter, Maria Nicolai. *Ignazio Silone: Beyond the Tragic Vision.* Buffalo, N.Y.: University of Toronto Press, 2000. Critical study focusing on the controversies surrounding Silone and his writing. Analyzes his intellectual and political convictions and assesses his development as a writer. Includes bibliography and index.

Pugliese, Stanislao G. *Bitter Spring: A Life of Ignazio Silone.* New York: Farrar, Straus and Giroux, 2009. A comprehensive and detailed account of Silone's life and work that addresses many of the misconceptions about Silone's political involvement. Describes how Silone's personal faith defied political and religious orthodoxies and was reflected in his fiction.

Scott, Nathan A., Jr. "Ignazio Silone: Novelist of the Revolutionary Sensibility." In *Rehearsals of Discomposure: Alienation and Reconciliation in Modern Literature.* New York: King's Crown Press, 1952. Characterizes *Bread and Wine* as a revolutionary novel, citing its disenchantment with all political parties. Examines the inevitable isolation of a revolutionary such as Spina.

Silone, Ignazio. *Bread and Wine.* Translated by Harvey Fergusson II, with an afterword by Marc Slonim. New York: Atheneum, 1962. Comments on significant changes in Silone's 1955 revision. Views the novel as a kind of ethical bildungsroman.

Sipe, A. W. Richard. "Will the Real Priest Please Stand Up: Ignazio Silone." In *The Serpent and the Dove: Celibacy in Literature and Life.* Westport, Conn.: Praeger, 2007. A study of religious celibacy, focusing on historic figures who were celibate, such as Mahatma Gandhi, and on literary accounts of celibacy, including the writings of Silone.

Break of Noon

Author: Paul Claudel (1868-1955)
First produced: Partage de midi, 1921; first published, 1906 (English translation, 1960)
Type of work: Drama
Type of plot: Problem
Time of plot: Early twentieth century
Locale: Far East

Principal characters:
FÉLICIEN DE CIZ, a French businessman
YSÉ, his wife
ALMARIC, a former lover
MESA, a disenchanted young man

The Story:

De Ciz and his wife, Ysé, are chatting one morning with their fellow passengers Almaric and Mesa on the forward deck of a liner on the Indian Ocean bound for the Far East from France. The married couple and their two children only recently embarked at Aden, and De Ciz, like Almaric, is traveling to China to seek new business opportunities. Mesa, a former seminarian, is returning to China where he previously achieved success as an influential customs official.

Ysé flirts with Mesa, teasing him about his gold rocking chair and extracting a promise that she might use it whenever she wishes. De Ciz and Ysé go below to attend to their luggage, and Almaric suggests to Mesa that Ysé has a romantic interest in him. Though Mesa protests that she is too vulgar and a brazen flirt, Almaric implies that the romantic interest might very well be mutual.

When De Ciz and Ysé return, De Ciz and Mesa go for a stroll. Ysé and Almaric reminisce about old times. By coincidence, they were lovers ten years earlier. They recall their affair with a regretful wistfulness. However, although Ysé does not particularly appreciate the life her husband provides for her, she insists that she loves him.

Almaric goes for a solitary smoke just as Mesa returns from his stroll. He finds Ysé alone, reclining in the rocking chair and reading a love story. Mesa tells Ysé that he knows she is attracted to him. She forces him to swear that he will not love her, thereby arousing his ardor. When Almaric and then De Ciz return with drinks for all, the four discuss their various prospects for making their fortunes in the Far East. In the glaring noon heat in the middle of the ocean they enjoy their drinks.

In Hong Kong, Mesa and Ysé arrange a rendezvous in an obscure corner of an old Chinese cemetery. Mesa, arriving early enough to get cold feet, leaves. Shortly afterward, Ysé and De Ciz arrive. They are arguing over his latest business deal, which requires that he leave her for a time. Despite her pleas that he take her with him, he leaves without her.

Mesa returns, unable to keep away from the rendezvous. Ysé tells him that De Ciz will be gone for one month but that Mesa should not come to see her during that time. Mesa finds her irresistible, even with her husband nearby. Ysé makes Mesa swear before a cross that she is no less desirable as a married woman, even though she is forbidden to him. She also tells him that he must help her become free of De Ciz, even if it means his death. Mesa balks at that, just as De Ciz unexpectedly returns. Ysé remains cool and leaves the two men discussing De Ciz's plans to undertake some shady dealings in Manila. Mesa encourages De Ciz to take a desk job in a customs house, which would require that De Ciz remain away from Ysé for several years. De Ciz, apparently unaware that Mesa is cuckolding him, agrees to accept the offer.

Some time later, Ysé and Almaric are hiding out in a ruined Confucian temple in a Chinese port where a bloody rebellion is raging. Almaric once again becomes Ysé's lover. Ysé left Mesa to save him from her, and she does not know where De Ciz or their children are. She and Almaric have with them the child she had with Mesa, a sickly child who dies shortly after.

Almaric sets a time bomb that will take their lives as well as the lives of the rampaging mob slaughtering any Europeans left in the city. As the sun begins to set, he and Ysé are philosophical at the thought that they will not survive the coming night. Almaric leaves Ysé to make the rounds of their hideaway when Mesa shows up at the door. She says nothing when he protests that he still loves her and that, because De Ciz is dead, they can now marry. When Almaric returns, Mesa announces that he comes to take Ysé and their child away. Almaric laughs in his face, but Mesa pulls a revolver, and, in the ensuing struggle, Mesa is knocked unconscious and his shoulder is dislocated.

Almaric finds a safe passage marker on Mesa's person. Thrilled that they will now be able to escape with their lives, Almaric goes off with Ysé. Soon, Mesa regains consciousness. Ysé, who accidentally misses the boat that would have meant her salvation, returns to comfort the injured Mesa. Knowing that they are soon going to die together, she apolo-

gizes to him for the pain she caused him, but she declares that none of it is her fault.

Critical Evaluation:

Paul Claudel, whose dramas have been compared to the works of Aeschylus and William Shakespeare, is regarded as one of the major writers of the first half of the twentieth century. A traditionalist in his religious beliefs after a life-altering conversion to Catholicism in 1886, he was nevertheless very much a product of and spokesperson for his time in his efforts to find themes and an idiom expressive of love and faith in contemporary terms.

The economy of action in *Break of Noon*, which many critics regard as Claudel's most realistic play (a second version debuted in 1948 and was published in 1949), makes clear that the work's drama resides in the internal moral and spiritual struggles of the characters. These struggles are broadly drawn. Mesa, who is generally equated with Claudel's alter ego in this somewhat autobiographical work, falls in love with a married woman, arranges for her husband's absence from the scene, and has a child by her, fully aware at all times that he is flirting with his own eternal damnation.

In the characters of De Ciz and Almaric, Claudel provides plausible foils to Mesa's highly refined spiritual sensibilities. The adventurous De Ciz is incapable of perceiving any action as right or wrong, good or evil. Almaric, on the other hand, is an atheist and recognizes wrongdoing only to the extent of reveling in it. Mesa, the former seminarian who confesses to a belief in God as the only significant other, is the most culpable of the play's characters because he believes in sin and then knowingly commits it.

Only Ysé seems capable of recognizing the limits of her own moral authority and tries to exercise that power effectively for the better. In the first act, Ysé forces Mesa to swear that he will not love her; in the second, she begs De Ciz to take her with him, and in the third, she leaves Mesa for his own good. With these actions, she is trying to do the right thing, although she knows that there is no solution to the problem posed by the desire between her and Mesa. Ysé is not sure that there is a God, but she believes in the real presence and power of the spirit more than Mesa does.

Mesa's fatal flaw is his inability to share either guilt or salvation with others, a result precisely of his belief in, and failed relationship with, God. By thinking that he is the only person with a spiritual relationship with God, he cuts himself off from the spiritual growth he could have realized through Ysé. The lesson Mesa should have learned is that others, for better or for worse, exist.

Ysé, as she tells him, is that embodiment of otherness that

is finally only self. Early in the play she reminds him of how two are made from one in the myth of Adam and Eve, and she tells Mesa bluntly that she is his soul. Mesa can only grow from this relationship, however, if he is prepared to make a full commitment, soul and body, to Ysé's soul and body. "And that's what you don't like, Mesa," Ysé tells him at the end, "to pay dearly for something." Ironically, he pays dearly nevertheless by failing to recognize the seed of salvation that even forbidden fruit must contain for it to be fully savored.

To achieve the combination of narrative economy and ambitious spiritual theme, Claudel uses symbolist techniques. A primary symbol is the passage of the day from mid-morning to midnight, which is already suggested in the title. The original French title, *Partage de midi*, is even more telling, however, for *partage* is a geological term denoting the separation of rainwater as it runs off a hill, in other words, a watershed. On the one side of the play's watershed, which occurs at the end of the first act, is light and life and youthful hopefulness; on the other side, the play descends into darkness, night, despair, and death. Only Mesa's raised hand is visible as the play ends, and the audience is left in the dark as to the significance of that gesture.

Another symbolic device is developed with the gold rocking chair, which in act 1 symbolizes the vainglory of Mesa's squandered spirituality, his selfish self-possession. In act 2, the omega-shaped entrance into an empty tomb portends the doom, both physical and moral, that looms over the lovers as well as signifies the contrary emblem of the redemption each is capable of achieving, Christ-like, through sacrifice of self. In act 3, it becomes what omega denotes, the last letter, the final note, or, as Ysé puts it, the pincers closing around them. No doubt, omega connotes as well the higher vision of the Gospels: divine judgment and, for the receptive heart, forgiveness. Because the audience cannot be certain what Mesa is reaching for—the stars, as Ysé has asked of him; the noon light that is gone; the desirable flesh that is still present; the otherness of God that eludes him, or that he eludes—the omega symbol remains ambiguous, as a good symbol must.

In the moral universe described in *Break of Noon*, there are a number of certainties: the necessity of choice, death, and the need to work out personal spiritual redemption through interrelationship with others. That redemption, however, remains only the promised grace.

Russell Elliott Murphy

Further Reading

Berchan, Richard. *The Inner Stage: An Essay on the Conflict of Vocations in the Early Works of Paul Claudel*. East Lansing: Michigan State University Press, 1966. Describes Claudel's early works, taking into consideration the conflicts caused by his being drawn to both a religious and a poetic vocation following his 1886 conversion to Roman Catholicism. *Break of Noon* is seen as a regression, intensified by personal experience, to earlier love-quest motifs.

Caranfa, Angelo. *Claudel: Beauty and Grace*. Lewisburg, Pa.: Bucknell University Press, 1989. Places Claudel in the twentieth century trend in French literature toward transcendent themes. The contrasts in *Break of Noon* between light and darkness, and the flesh and the spirit, exemplify the attempt to harmonize physical and spiritual impulses.

Fowlie, Wallace. Introduction to *Break of Noon*, by Paul Claudel. Chicago: Henry Regnery, 1960. Translator Fowlie's introduction to the play is informative and perceptive. He provides background to the 1948 production overseen by Claudel and discusses the work's place in Claudel's corpus.

Knapp, Bettina L. *Paul Claudel*. New York: Ungar, 1982. Provides a brief biography of Claudel and analyses of each of his plays, focusing on the religious themes in his drama.

Longstaffe, Moya. *Metamorphoses of Passion and the Heroic in French Literature: Corneille, Stendhal, Claudel*. Lewiston, N.Y.: Edwin Mellen Press, 1999. Maintains that the works of Claudel, Stendhal, and Pierre Corneille share a common aspiration for human dignity. Compares the writers' treatments of the ideal of the heroic and the relationship between men and women.

Breakfast at Tiffany's

Author: Truman Capote (1924-1984)
First published: 1958
Type of work: Novella
Type of plot: Psychological realism
Time of plot: 1943-1944 and 1957
Locale: Upper East Side, New York City

Principal characters:
HOLIDAY "HOLLY" GOLIGHTLY (LULAMAE BARNES), a
    Manhattan socialite
THE NARRATOR, a writer
FRED BARNES, Holly's brother, a soldier
DOC GOLIGHTLY, Holly's estranged husband
JOSÉ YBARRA-JAEGAR, a Brazilian millionaire, Holly's
    lover, and the father of her unborn child
SALVATORE "SALLY" TOMATO, an imprisoned drug kingpin
JOE BELL, a Manhattan bartender

The Story:

The narrator, an established writer, is summoned unexpectedly to a bar, an old haunt, where the bartender, Joe Bell, who shared the narrator's long-ago fascination with Holly Golightly, has received word about her: She passed through an African village just months earlier. Joe has a photo of an elegant wood carving made by one of the village artisans, and its profile is unmistakably that of Holly Golightly. The photo triggers the narrator's recollection of the tempestuous year he spent as Holly's neighbor in a Manhattan brownstone when he first arrived in New York as a struggling writer.

Everything about the young woman intrigued the narrator when he met her. Holly participated in the flamboyant night-life of New York's ritziest restaurants and nightclubs, escorted by a variety of rich and influential men. She exhibited an elegant goofiness and a casual sexiness. She was fond of a stray cat that she adopted but never named. Her background was mysterious, involving time spent in Hollywood as a promising starlet, and she would lapse into inexplicable bouts of melancholy. She was devoted to to brother, a soldier stationed overseas.

The narrator was particularly puzzled about Holly's source of income. She clearly had no problem securing money from the men she dated, but he could not tell whether or not she was a prostitute. She visited Sally Tomato, a notorious gangster, each Thursday in Sing Sing Prison and brought back cryptic messages about the weather to his lawyer in return for one hundred dollars. When Holly read some of the narrator's fiction, she tried to encourage her Hollywood friends to give his writing their attention, even though she disdained his writing because it lacked story and character and was too atmospheric and experimental.

Although she was a free spirit, marrying a rich man was Holly's preeminent ambition—she told the narrator that when she felt what she called "red meanies," a soul-deep anxiety about her life and its evident drift, she loved to roam among the swanky displays at Tiffany's jewelry store, where she felt safe and at home. She tested the possibility of marrying Rusty Trawler, a gay millionaire looking to secure a wife for appearance's sake, but when that fell through, she set her sights on José Ybarra-Jaegar, a rich Brazilian with ambitions to become Brazil's president. As he tells her story, however, it becomes clear that the narrator himself was falling under Holly's spell. When he received news that he had sold his first story, he shared the news first with Holly and they spent a romantic day celebrating.

In early spring, the writer had a chance encounter with a fiftyish stranger outside the brownstone. The man identified himself as Holly's husband, Doc Golightly, a veterinarian from Texas, and he told the stunned narrator about Holly's past: She and her brother had run away from an impoverished life with an abusive foster father in rural Texas. She had married Doc Golightly when she was only fourteen and had helped raise his children from a previous marriage for nearly three years, until one day she simply walked away. Doc had tracked down Holly, whom he knew as Lulamae Barnes, to give her a chance to return home—a chance she refused. She told him that their marriage was invalid because she was under age when it was conducted.

Soon after this encounter, Holly received the devastating news that her brother had been killed in action. Over the next several weeks, she decided in her grief to pursue marriage to José and the promise of a stable life in faraway exotic Brazil. She tried to teach herself Portuguese in preparation for such a life. In late September, she told the narrator that she was pregnant and would be leaving within days for Brazil. Seeing how badly he took the news, Holly offered to spend the day in Central Park riding horseback (she had loved horses growing up). When street kids spooked the narrator's horse, he lost control of the animal; Holly rescued him after a wild ride through Manhattan traffic.

When they returned to the narrator's apartment to recover, Holly was abruptly arrested and charged with criminal conspiracy. The weather reports she had been bringing back from Sing Sing were coded messages to help Tomato run his organization from behind bars. Within hours, Holly's photo was splashed across the newspapers. José decided his political ambitions could not withstand such a scandal. He flew to Brazil, leaving only a good-bye letter to Holly. Far more tragically, during the shuffle with the arresting officers and perhaps because of the excitement of riding the horses, Holly suffered a miscarriage.

Holly, however, was determined to go to Brazil and, despite the narrator's warning that she could face criminal charges, she convinced him to gather her belongings (including her cat) and meet her at Joe's bar before she was to depart for the airport. On the way to the airport, as they were driving through Spanish Harlem, Holly impulsively stopped the cab, opened the door, and simply left her cat on the street to demonstrate their independence from each other. Within a block, she relented and went back to try to find the cat, but to no avail. She left for the airport and for Rio only after the narrator promised he would find the cat—which he did. Weeks later, he saw the cat comfortably perched in the window of an apartment.

Save for a single postcard, the narrator reveals that he has never heard from Holly again. He can only hope that, like the cat, she has found a home.

Critical Evaluation:

Breakfast at Tiffany's is a frame narrative. That is, it is a tale told as a recollection years after the narrative's central events. Inevitably in such narratives, the ostensible subject of the memory—in this case the eccentric, charismatic socialite Holly Golightly—remains an impenetrable mystery, while the character of the narrator—in this case, a struggling writer mesmerized by the dazzling Holly—clearly emerges and becomes the central focus of the narrative.

Perhaps because the narrator is himself so taken by the mesmerizing character of Holly Golightly, many readers initially focus on Holly Golightly as the clear narrative center of the work. This reaction may be heightened by the tremendous impact the novel's 1961 film adaptation had on popular culture—the film was squarely centered on the elegant flightiness of Audrey Hepburn as Holly. As her allegorical name suggests, Holly embodies the reckless free spirit. Although the free spirit had been celebrated in American literature since Huck Finn, Truman Capote's creation shattered

conventional assumptions. Holly is a woman who is frank about her sexual appetites, who freely uses men to maintain her lifestyle, and who resists the traditional fulfillment of marriage and child-rearing.

A paradox, at once narcissistic and compassionate, willful and vulnerable, Holly Golightly defies imprisonment within social convention and the dreary responsibilities of family and marriage. Her relationship with her nameless pet cat, as well as her cavalier attitude toward her numerous escorts, suggests that loose sense of responsibility. The gifts Holly and the narrator exchange over their only Christmas together underscore this thematic tension: He gives her a medal of St. Christopher, the patron saint of safe traveling; she gives him an ornate bird cage on the condition that he never put anything living inside it.

Indeed, Holly is associated throughout the narrative with wild animals, most notably horses and birds. She disdains zoos. Capote is careful to avoid simplification: If Holly is a free spirit, she is also attracted by the capitalist enterprise. She relishes high living, she entertains men in exchange for money, she plots to marry money, and she is at home in Tiffany's, the epitome of lavish living. In the end, Holly Golightly's is a tragic narrative of a free spirit who both hungers for and resists a home, too wild for the humdrum of domestic living, too captivated by the lavish commodities of success for life in the margins.

What made Capote's novella a pioneering work was less the character of Holly Golightly and more the implications of her relationship with the narrator. At a time when American narratives did not forthrightly treat gay characters or investigate the nuances of gender roles, Capote created a narrative in which the construction of both gender and sexual identity served as thematic interest. Neither Holly nor the narrator is simply gay or simply straight. With her boyish hair and slender physique, her relationship with numerous women friends, and her provocative sexual comments, Holly, even as she pursues marriage, hints at several moments that she may be a lesbian. The narrator, a bachelor who is noticeably content to maintain an entirely platonic relationship with Holly and never pursues any other women and whose prose (like that of the early Capote) is delicate, atmospheric, and evocative, may or may not be gay.

Other characters—most notably Rusty Trawler, a millionaire Holly momentarily considers pursuing; Mag Wildwood, a loud, hard-drinking model who is Holly's roommate; and Joe Bell, the bartender who helps Holly escape New York—also exist suspended between clear gay and straight identities. Indeed, the rejection of such an either/or sense of sexual identity and gender roles marks the novella's achievement.

Breakfast at Tiffany's has been cited as a pioneering work in gay studies, as it suggests, well ahead of its time, that sexual identity and gender roles are themselves fluid constructions. They are conventional and fashioned, rather than predetermined, biological, or inevitable. Hence, the narrative uses several symbols of fluid or constructed identity, including acting (Holly is a former Hollywood starlet who still changes her hair color and hides behind garish sunglasses); fiction writing and the work of creating characters; masks (Holly and the narrator shoplift masks during the Halloween season); and, supremely, the logic of deception and the necessity of lying.

This sense of fluid reality is perhaps the novella's most sophisticated achievement. Although Capote himself disdained the emerging generation of postmodern writers intent on reexamining narrative form at the expense of exploring character and telling stories, *Breakfast at Tiffany's* shares the postmodern anxiety over the nature of reality itself. Capote carefully constructs a tale-within-a-tale-within-a-tale: Holly herself stays stubbornly mysterious, as her story is pieced out in recollections from other characters, and readers are ultimately in the hands of an unreliable narrator whose psychological profile affects the story he tells. Thus, *Breakfast at Tiffany's* ultimately tests the difference between reality and fiction, illustrating how people tend to impose readings on events and call them reality. This theme anticipates Capote's 1966 groundbreaking nonfiction novel, *In Cold Blood*.

As Holly's own agent surmises about her, she is a "real phony," and that paradox shapes a great deal of Capote's argument about reality. What one perceives to be true becomes what one believes to be real. In engaging a narrative voice-over that appears to be straightforward and even journalistic in its hard-boiled precision, careful readers must realize that every recollection is an angle of perception, that they are dealing with fallible memory and its construction of reality. When readers finish *Breakfast at Tiffany's*, they are no nearer to understanding Holly's complex emotional interior or her relationships with her brother, her husband, her lover, and the baby she loses. She is at once distant and near; like the photo of the African carving that bears a resemblance to her, the narrative necessarily remains thrice removed from its ostensible subject. That is the achievement of the novella—the more readers know, the less they understand; the closer they get to the truth, the farther away they are.

Joseph Dewey

Further Reading

Bloom, Harold, ed. *Truman Capote*. Philadelphia: Chelsea House, 2003. Compendium of significant essays on Capote. Gives context to *Breakfast at Tiffany's* by locating it in relation to the themes and stylistic innovations of Capote's larger body of work.

Clark, Gerald. *Capote: A Life*. 1988. Reprint. New York: Da Capo Press, 2005. Landmark exploration of Capote's life that provides a detailed analysis of *Breakfast at Tiffany's*, with attention to Capote's framing narrative and his interest in gender and sexual identity. Discusses Capote's significant issues with the Hollywood adaptation.

Garson, Helen S. "Never Love a Wild Thing: *Breakfast at Tiffany's*." In *Truman Capote*. New York: Ungar, 1980. Sees Holly as a complex woman-child, fragile, innocent, and unable to find the security of love and home. Important reading that investigates the frame and sees the device as critical to defining the story's bittersweet tone.

Hassan, Ihab. "Truman Capote: The Vanishing Image of Narcissus." In *Radical Innocence: Studies in the Contemporary American Novel*. Princeton, N.J.: Princeton University Press, 1961. Indispensable introduction to Capote's fiction. Sees Holly as representative of a new kind of American hero, an egocentric eccentric without stable identity or home, hungry only for experience but who must pay the price for nonconformity.

Nance, William L. *The Worlds of Truman Capote*. New York: Stein & Day, 1970. Highly regarded analysis of Capote. Sees Holly as Capote's alter ego, defiant, and unconventional, threatened by society and unable ultimately to find peace or to belong. Sees the novella as a transitional text between Capote's early moody gothic surrealism and his later experiments with journalistic realism.

Breakfast of Champions
Or, Goodbye Blue Monday

Author: Kurt Vonnegut (1922-2007)
First published: 1973
Type of work: Novel
Type of plot: Satire
Time of plot: 1970's
Locale: Midland City, United States

Principal characters:
DWAYNE HOOVER, a car dealer
FRANCINE PEFKO, Dwayne's secretary and lover
KILGORE TROUT, a science-fiction writer
BUNNY HOOVER, Dwayne's son
WAYNE HOOBLER, a former convict
FRED T. BARRY, a wealthy industrialist
RABO KARABEKIAN, a painter
BEATRICE KEEDSLER, a novelist
KURT VONNEGUT, a novelist

The Story:

Kilgore Trout is a largely obscure science-fiction writer living in Cohoes, New York. Although his work is widely published, it is used only as filler text in pornographic novels and magazines. No one, reader or fan, has ever acknowledged Trout for his writing. Trout himself can find copies of his fiction only by seeking them out in lurid sex shops.

One day in 1972, Trout receives a letter from Fred T. Barry, a wealthy industrialist from Midland City. Barry, strangely enough, has come across Trout's work and is an ardent fan. Barry uses his influence as chairperson of Midland City's arts commission to garner Trout an invitation to be the keynote speaker at the city's annual arts festival. A hermit for many years, Trout nonetheless takes Barry up on the opportunity to appear in Midland City, where he plans to use the festival as his chance to espouse to the reading public the highly unconventional views expressed in his stories.

Dwayne Hoover, a prosperous entrepreneur in Midland City, has no knowledge of Trout. Despite owning a lucrative car dealership and several other businesses in town, Dwayne is miserably unhappy and suffers from serious inner turmoil. His wife had recently committed suicide, and his son Bunny is estranged from him because Dwayne refuses to accept the young man's homosexuality. Dwayne also is involved in a torrid and less than fulfilling affair with his secretary, and he also is experiencing hallucinations, panic attacks, and other symptoms of an emotional breakdown.

Upon receiving word of his invitation to speak in Midland City, Trout, nearly penniless and devoid of all but the most rudimentary social skills, hitchhikes to nearby New York City, where he plans to thumb a ride to the Midwest with a long-haul trucker. Shortly after arriving, he finds a copy of his novel *Now It Can Be Told* in a pornography shop, but is promptly mugged. Having lost everything but the book and the ten-dollar bill he had stashed inside his trousers, he is forced to hit the road even earlier than he had anticipated.

In Midland City, Dwayne's symptoms continue to worsen. Unable to deal with people, he begins spending nights at the Holiday Inn near his car dealership. He devotes most of his day to driving aimlessly around town, listening to radio commercial jingles. One time while at the Holiday Inn, he becomes convinced that the asphalt under his feet is sinking deep into the ground as he walks across it. Shortly thereafter, he returns to the dealership to check up on things, only to find that he has developed echolalia—a rare condition that forces him to repeat the final words of those who speak to him.

Wayne Hoobler, a former convict, loiters around Dwayne's car dealership. Just released from a lengthy prison sentence, Hoobler is destitute and hopes to convince Dwayne to give him a job. He recognizes Dwayne's face from his car ads; Dwayne is the only person Hoobler knows outside prison because he has been locked up for most of his life. Because of his fragile emotional state, however, Dwayne barely notices Hoobler, even though Hoobler is determined to catch Dwayne's attention.

What does catch Dwayne's attention, however, is the allure of his secretary, Francine Pefko. Already involved in an affair with the doting Francine for several months, Dwayne stealthily calls her from his office and invites her for a rendezvous at the Holiday Inn. Sensing that her coworkers suspect that she is sleeping with Dwayne, she is reluctant to ask if one of them could cover her desk. Finding it impossible to not please Dwayne, she eventually succeeds in getting away from her desk.

During the ensuing encounter with Dwayne, Francine

makes an offhand remark about how nice it would be if Midland City had a Kentucky Fried Chicken fast-food restaurant. On the brink of insanity, Dwayne misinterprets her comment, thinking that she had attempted to blackmail him into buying her a lavish gift as compensation for her attention. Still suffering from echolalia, he mocks her repeatedly and causes her to become hysterical. A heated exchange occurs between the two, but as quickly as he had turned on Francine, Dwayne returns to being equally deferential. Unnerved but relieved, Francine returns to her usual passive self and pretends the exchange never happened.

In the meantime, Trout has been picked up by a series of traveling salespeople and truckers and is fast approaching Midland City. During the long hours on the road, he recalls the plots of several of the stories and novels he has written, giving his travel companions a sense of the quirky but highly insightful nature of his fiction. Finally, he reaches Midland City and checks into the Holiday Inn, the site of tomorrow's arts festival.

In the hotel's cocktail lounge, two other festival participants—Rabo Karabekian, an abstract expressionist painter, and Beatrice Keedsler, a novelist and member of one of Midland City's wealthiest families—commiserate about how horribly provincial and boring they find the city to be. Novelist Kurt Vonnegut is listening to them and claims, in writing, to be both their manipulator and their unobtrusive observer. Vonnegut finds their remarks about Midland City crass and distasteful, particularly because Karabekian has just received fifty thousand dollars from one of the city's wealthy benefactors for a painting consisting of nothing more than a piece of tape affixed to a painted canvas.

At the same time that Vonnegut is expressing his disdain for the two artists, Dwayne enters the lounge. Purely by chance, Dwayne encounters Trout. They start a conversation that ends with Dwayne asking him to explain "the secrets of life." Trout, taking this as an acknowledgment of his own literary genius, presents Dwayne with the copy of his novel *Now It Can Be Told* that he had purchased in New York. The book depicts human beings not as agents of free will but as mindless automatons. Inspired both by the novel's disturbing message and by his own intensifying dementia, Dwayne falls into a rage and attacks his son Bunny, the lounge's pianist. In his ensuing breakdown, Dwayne assaults not only Bunny but also Trout, Vonnegut, Pefko, Hoobler, and several onlookers.

Vonnegut and Trout, now in an ambulance, are being treated for their injuries. Ironically, they are treated alongside Dwayne, who is bound in a straitjacket and soon to be institutionalized.

Critical Evaluation:

Kurt Vonnegut, one of the most widely read and admired American novelists of the twentieth century, grew up in Indianapolis, Indiana. His legacy of stylistically innovative and thematically outspoken fiction has inspired generations of writers and fans in ways few other novelists can claim. The son of a prominent local architect and a mother who suffered from chronic schizophrenia, Vonnegut's childhood fostered a preoccupation with the age-old battle between normalcy and madness, themes that are pervasive in his works. In *Breakfast of Champions*, this conflict takes the form of an exploration of the dichotomy between American culture's obsession with neurosis and the fixation with maintaining the status quo that invariably feeds that neurosis.

An eclectic pastiche of science fiction, social satire, moral fable, humor, and experimental minimalism, the exact essence of Vonnegut's novel resists definitive description. Its plot, like the plot of its immediate predecessor, *Slaughterhouse-Five: Or, The Children's Crusade, a Duty-Dance with Death* (1969), defies conventional paraphrase. It seems nearly impossible to describe what "happens" in a Vonnegut novel without wavering between the sublime and the ridiculous. However, Vonnegut's method is deliberate. As with most postmodern writers, the nature of storytelling—with its plethora of devices, techniques, and machinations—is a central theme in his works. Even the structure of his narrative coincides closely with his principal concerns. Vonnegut's narratives borrow from almost every fiction-making approach imaginable, at times even expanding their parameters beyond the confines of the written word. Just as he does in *Slaughterhouse-Five*, Vonnegut, in *Breakfast of Champions*, incorporates several self-drawn illustrations to punctuate his ideas. At first glance, its pages look more like those of a children's book than a work of serious literary fiction, but it quickly becomes evident that the novel's content is far from juvenile.

Although Vonnegut presents his story in a fairly straightforward narrative sequence, the story does contain a number of distinct and innovative elements. The stories of Kilgore Trout and Dwayne Hoover run parallel, but they do not converge until the last plausible instant. Likewise, although it is common in modern fiction to have a first-person narrator, it is rare for that narrator to actually be the author or to play three roles simultaneously—character, narrator, and author. Most writers would balk at this unconventional device, fearing that it would destroy the suspension of belief that is crucial for most storytellers to maintain in their readers. Vonnegut, however, seems completely unconcerned with this literary convention. For the final third of *Breakfast of Champions*, he steps directly into the center of the novel's action. In the climactic cocktail lounge scene, Vonnegut becomes both narrator and character—he tells his readers that he not only is making up the story but also is taking the liberty of becoming one of its characters. The result for the reader is the rare experience of being entertained by a good story while simultaneously being fully aware that the story is entirely the construct of the author's imagination.

Because another of the novel's primary themes is the debate between free will and determinism as the driving force behind human behavior, Vonnegut's audacity in stepping into the center of his own work suggests that humans have a fundamental need to shape, or a need to believe they are shaping, their own destiny. Vonnegut not only manipulates his characters but also has no problem with his omnipresent hand, which determines their every move (much as readers want to believe they are the authors of the story that is human life). By contrast, Dwayne, whose belligerent tirade ends the book, seems little more than an automaton acting entirely on instinct. In the final chapter, Vonnegut finds himself in an ambulance, injured by one of his own characters—paradoxically, one who has both run amok and been allowed to run amok.

Hilarious yet ponderous, socially conscious yet nihilistic, minimalistic yet enthralling, *Breakfast of Champions* is a masterfully conceived study in contradictions. The novel also is exuberantly playful and sharply acerbic, and it stands as one of Vonnegut's most important works. Although it takes the form of a series of short vignettes padded by scores of cheeky illustrations, its ideas are far from fanciful or superficial. Indeed, *Breakfast of Champions* is widely considered to be one of the most innovative and significant novels of the late twentieth century.

Gregory D. Horn

Further Reading

Allen, William Rodney, ed. *Conversations with Kurt Vonnegut*. Jackson: University Press of Mississippi, 1988. One of the definitive sources on Vonnegut's personal insights into his literary themes and style and his aesthetic vision.

_____. *Understanding Kurt Vonnegut*. Columbia: University of South Carolina Press, 1991. A perceptive critical study of Vonnegut's fiction. Provides many valuable insights into his most important novels and short stories, including an extensive analysis of *Breakfast of Champions*.

Boon, Kevin A., ed. *At Millennium's End: New Essays on the Work of Kurt Vonnegut*. Albany: State University of New York Press, 2001. A diverse collection of essays on Vonnegut's fiction and broader cultural influence.

Broer, Lawrence R. *Sanity Plea: Schizophrenia in the Novels of Kurt Vonnegut*. 2d ed. Tuscaloosa: University of Alabama Press, 1994. One of the most significant and widely cited works on Vonnegut's fiction. Probes the depths of what Broer finds to be Vonnegut's most pervasive theme, schizophrenia.

Leeds, Marc. *The Vonnegut Encyclopedia: An Authorized Compendium*. Westport, Conn.: Greenwood Press, 1996. Ambitious both in scale and scope, this collection is especially useful as an introduction to Vonnegut's life, works, and aesthetic.

Marvin, Thomas F. *Kurt Vonnegut: A Critical Companion*. Westport, Conn.: Greenwood Press, 2002. A thorough and accessible overview of Vonnegut's major fiction, particularly *Breakfast of Champions* and *Slaughterhouse-Five*.

Reed, Peter J., and Marc Leeds, eds. *Vonnegut Chronicles: Interviews and Essays*. Westport, Conn.: Greenwood Press, 1996. A collection that includes three interviews with Vonnegut and eleven scholarly essays on his work. Among the topics that Vonnegut addresses in the interviews are postmodernism and experimental fiction. Includes a chronology, a bibliography, and an index.

Tomedi, John. *Kurt Vonnegut*. Philadelphia: Chelsea House, 2004. Presents an informative overall survey of Vonnegut's life and literary work, including his nonfiction.

Breathing Lessons

Author: Anne Tyler (1941-   )
First published: 1988
Type of work: Novel
Type of plot: Domestic realism
Time of plot: 1980's
Locale: Baltimore and Pennsylvania

Principal characters:
MAGGIE DALEY MORAN, a housewife and nursing home aide
IRA MORAN, her husband
JESSE MORAN, their son
DAISY MORAN, their daughter
FIONA STUCKEY MORAN, Jesse's former wife
LEROY MORAN, daughter of Jesse and Fiona
MR. OTIS, a traveler
LAMONT, Mr. Otis's nephew
SERENA GILL, Maggie's recently widowed friend

The Story:

Baltimore residents Maggie and Ira Moran are preparing to attend the funeral of Max Gill, husband of Maggie's school friend, Serena, in Deer Lick, Pennsylvania. Before the interstate drive can begin, Maggie, a nursing home aide who had turned down an opportunity to attend college, must retrieve the family car from the body shop. Deeply distracted by a caller on a radio talk show (whom she believes to be Fiona, former wife of her son Jesse) who is discussing her upcoming remarriage, Maggie smashes the left front fender of the newly repaired car as she departs from the garage. This unfortunate encounter with a Pepsi delivery truck foreshadows the randomness and impulse that characterize the rest of the day for the Morans.

Obsessed with the notion that Jesse and Fiona belong together and will reconcile given the right circumstances and encouragement, Maggie suggests to Ira that they drive to Cartwheel, Pennsylvania, after the funeral to pay a visit to their former daughter-in-law, who lives in this small town with her mother and her daughter, Leroy. Ira, who is a reticent and cynical counterpoint to Maggie's loquaciousness and unflinching optimism, is not at all in favor of adding this extra leg to the trip. His immediate concern as the drive begins is ascertaining the correct route to Deer Lick; a stop for directions at a diner provides Maggie with an opportunity to share her family foibles with the waitress behind the counter, yet another action upon which Ira frowns.

Max Gill's funeral turns out to be part high school reunion and part oldies revival concert. Maggie and Serena connect with several former schoolmates, and the program for the service features performances of several popular songs from 1956 that were sung at Max and Serena's wedding. Serena asks Maggie and Ira to reprise their duet of the tune "Love Is a Many-Splendored Thing"; Maggie is willing to do this, but

Ira refuses. A former male classmate of Maggie is asked to sing Ira's part. Despite being polar opposites in personality, sparks remain in the Moran marriage. Maggie and Ira become amorous in Serena's bedroom during the gathering after the service, in Serena's house; she catches them and asks them to leave.

On the road once again, Maggie pleads her case to make the trip to Cartwheel to see Fiona. Ira argues that whether or not Fiona is indeed remarrying, the notion of her getting back together with Jesse is a lost cause. The phrase "lost cause" constitutes Ira's impression of Jesse as well. A high school dropout who dreams of becoming a rock star (even after being faced with fatherhood outside marriage) and who struggles to find steady employment, Jesse is a major disappointment to Ira, whose own youthful aspirations of attending medical school were dashed in large part by his dependent father and sisters. Daisy, Jesse's younger sister, is more satisfactory to her parents. While it hurts Maggie that her daughter prefers the home of a better organized, more accomplished mother of a friend, Daisy is surpassing Jesse intellectually with her plans to attend college.

Back in the automobile, Ira and Maggie encounter a red Chevrolet that is weaving and stopping short in front of them. On impulse, Maggie shouts out to the driver, an elderly African American man, that the front left wheel of his car is falling off. Immediately after having done this, Maggie feels guilty and forces Ira to stop and assist the gentleman, Mr. Otis. Maggie awkwardly attempts to explain the comment, but Mr. Otis remains convinced that something is wrong with the wheel. With neither car equipped to repair a damaged tire, the Morans drive Mr. Otis to the garage where his nephew Lamont, a young divorced man, is employed. The testy exchange between Mr. Otis and Lamont, who expresses his criticism of the constant bickering between his uncle and aunt, parallels the intergenerational value conflicts that Maggie and Ira experience in their encounters with Jesse and Fiona.

With the day more than half-expended, and Cartwheel not too far away, Ira officially capitulates on the visit to Fiona. Maggie and Ira learn that their granddaughter, Leroy, is named well after all. Originally given a masculine first name because Jesse and Fiona were hoping to have a boy (a pregnancy that would have been terminated had it not been for Maggie's intercession), Leroy is now a tomboy, preferring a Frisbee and a baseball glove to girl's playthings. Fiona, who lacks the voice Maggie heard on talk radio, is studying to be a licensed practitioner of electrolysis. Remaining hopeful of engineering a reconciliation between Fiona and Jesse, Maggie exaggerates Jesse's response to their separation and divorce to the point that Fiona and Leroy agree to join Ira and Maggie on their return trip to Baltimore. At the right moment, Maggie phones Jesse to ensure his presence at dinner at 6:30 that evening.

Maggie's hopes for Jesse's family to be reunited come crashing down when her overstatement about Jesse is revealed as inaccurate. All chances of smoothing over this misstep are rendered impossible when the usually silent Ira speaks up and tells Fiona that Jesse has been having a physical relationship with a woman working at a nearby auto dealership. Jesse walks out, as do Fiona and Leroy, leaving their hastily packed suitcase behind.

Maggie finds some emotional and spiritual comfort in a nursing home resident's perceptions of the afterworld. She also reestablishes contact and reconciles with her friend, Serena. One final scheme that borders on the inappropriate is the plan Maggie shares with Ira to see if Fiona will allow Leroy to live with them during the school year so that she can attend school in the larger, presumably better quality, Baltimore school system. The following day, Ira and Maggie plan to drive Daisy to college.

Critical Evaluation:

Anne Tyler's *Breathing Lessons* won the 1989 Pulitzer Prize in fiction. While a handful of critics considered the book's subject matter ("twenty-four hours in the life of a marriage," as Tyler herself describes it) too mundane for this honor, the majority hailed the novel as most deserving of the award. Tyler may indeed focus on the regional (Baltimore and environs) and the ordinary in *Breathing Lessons* and her other novels, but her rich portraits of everyday people and events are grounded in universal themes that foster discussion long after her books are read. Like most of Tyler's

novels, *Breathing Lessons* leaves readers wanting more, questioning what the next Moran family adventure will encompass.

Whatever new events await the Morans, there is no doubt that Maggie will serve as a catalyst. Parts one and three of this tripartite novel are told from her perspective through a third-person narrator. (Part two, focusing primarily on the encounter with Mr. Otis, is presented from Ira's point of view, again through a third-person voice.) Maggie's energetic, positive, outgoing, and at times overly hopeful approach to life makes her one of Tyler's most unforgettable characters. While Maggie has been described by some scholars as antifeminist and a thoughtless schemer, her good heart, basic unselfishness, and love for those around her cannot be dismissed.

The modus operandi of Maggie's life, as perceived through Ira's perspective, is as follows: Maggie "refused to take her own life seriously . . . to believe it was a sort of practice life . . . to play around with as if they offered second and third chances to get it right." This suggests the potential for individuals to reinvent themselves through significant life changes, experienced with varying degrees of success by many Tyler protagonists, including Jeremy Pauling in *Celestial Navigation* (1974), Cordelia Grinstead in *Ladder of Years* (1995), and Maryam Yazdan in *Digging to America* (2006). Although Maggie does not take personal advantage of such an opportunity, the suggestion that she is aware of its presence allows her to join other Tyler characters on the thematic "second chance" continuum.

By the novel's denouement, readers learn that Daisy is likely to forge the type of career the rest of her immediate family lacks, and despite their basic differences of opinion on how life should be lived, Maggie and Ira demonstrate their lasting mutual love, understanding, and patience. However, an engaged reader may also come away from *Breathing Lessons* with a darker interpretation of the text. Maggie could be seen as acting out of an all-consuming, pathological loneliness; the young family of Jesse, Fiona, and Leroy has probably been irrevocably broken; and Ira is left to look back on a life of unfulfilled potential. Whether perceived as happy or sad, *Breathing Lessons* features talking points that transcend changing times.

In addition to her thematic treatment, Tyler must also be praised for her crafting of highly discussable characters, neither totally likeable nor completely reprehensible. Just as Maggie can be assessed through the proverbial "half-full" or "half-empty" glass, Ira is problematic. His quiet strength and illingness to take on family responsibilities without complaint are admirable, but readers could question his withdrawal from the parenting of Jesse. Having missed out on the education he coveted, Ira might be expected to figuratively (and maybe even literally) drag his son by his lengthy rock-star tresses to class; instead, Jesse is essentially given license to drop out of high school, with a shoulder-shrug response from Ira. Jesse joins a line of rebellious teenagers who populate Tyler's prose, such as those in *Searching for Caleb* (1975), *Back When We Were Grownups* (2001), and *The Amateur Marriage* (2004). Even though young characters play supporting roles in their respective novels, Tyler fashions them with such care and detail that readers might wonder how, and if (certainly in the case of Jesse), they will mature.

Through her thoughtful and insightful treatment of family matters, generational conflict, caring, and love, Tyler's *Breathing Lessons* provides substantive food for thought regarding the essentials of life. Hence, the novel's title could not be more fitting.

Cecilia Donohue

Further Reading

Bail, Paul. *Anne Tyler: A Critical Companion.* Westport, Conn.: Greenwood Press, 1998. A discussion of Tyler's literary influences, and analysis of twelve of her novels. Also addresses Tyler's approaches to plot, characters, themes, literary devices, historical settings, and narrative points of view as well as how the novels fit into southern regional literature, women's literature, and popular culture.

Carroll, Virginia Schaefer. "Wrestling with Change: Discourse Strategies in Anne Tyler." *Frontiers* 19, no. 1 (1998): 86-109. Analyzes the narratives of *Breathing Lessons* and *Ladder of Years* (1995), which have a common focus on female protagonists approaching midlife.

Croft, Robert W. *An Anne Tyler Companion.* Westport, Conn.: Greenwood Press, 1998. A comprehensive reference text on Tyler's early- and midcareer fiction. Includes biographical information; identification and discussion of key themes in Tyler's fiction; encyclopedic entries for story and novel titles, characters, themes, and recurring

motifs; bibliographies; and two appendices. The first appendix identifies geographic locales in Tyler's novels. The second, of likely interest to readers of *Breathing Lessons*, lists the songs mentioned in each of her novels.

Elfenbein, Anna Shannon. "Living Lesson: The Evolving Racial Norm in the Novels of Anne Tyler." *Southern Quarterly* 43, no. 1 (Fall, 2005): 63-79. Identifies *Breathing Lessons* as the first of Tyler's novels in which African American characters approach or share social and economic parity with white protagonists.

Koppel, Gene. "Maggie Moran, Anne Tyler's Madcap Heroine: A Game-Approach to *Breathing Lessons*." *Essays in Literature* 18, no. 2 (Fall, 1991): 276-287. Likens Maggie to *I Love Lucy*'s Lucy Ricardo on the basis of their penchants for scheming and game-playing, while arguing that Maggie's strong sense of responsibility is identified as essential to survival and fulfillment.

Salwak, Dale, ed. *Anne Tyler as Novelist.* Iowa City: University of Iowa Press, 1994. Compilation of essays on Tyler's novels through *Saint Maybe* (1991). *Breathing Lessons* is discussed in terms of its portrayal of Maggie, depictions of emotional dysfunction, wardrobe selections of female characters, the themes of memory and aging, connections between *Breathing Lessons* and other Tyler novels, and critical response.

Stephens, C. Ralph, ed. *The Fiction of Anne Tyler.* Jackson: University Press of Mississippi, 1990. Collection of essays on various works by Tyler, including *Breathing Lessons*. Particular attention is paid to the character of Maggie and the novel's perspective on gender and marital relations.

Town, Caren J. "'Three Meal a Day Aftermaths': Anne Tyler's Determined Adolescents." In *The New Southern Girl: Female Adolescence in the Works of Twelve Women Authors.* Jefferson, N.C.: McFarland, 2004. Discussion of the portrayal of adolescents in Tyler's works, part of a larger exploration of the depiction of teenage girls in the works of authors such as Tyler, Lee Smith, Jill McCorkle, and Dorothy Allison.

The Bride of Lammermoor

Author: Sir Walter Scott (1771-1832)
First published: 1819
Type of work: Novel
Type of plot: Gothic
Time of plot: Late seventeenth century
Locale: Scotland

Principal characters:
EDGAR, the master of Ravenswood
SIR WILLIAM ASHTON, Lord Keeper of Scotland
LUCY ASHTON, his daughter
LADY ASHTON, his wife
CALEB BALDERSTONE, Ravenswood's old servant
FRANK HAYSTON OF BUCKLAW, a young nobleman
THE MARQUIS OF A——, Ravenswood's powerful
    kinsman
ALICE, an old, blind tenant on the Ravenswood estate

The Story:

Sir William Ashton, the new master of the Ravenswood estate, is delighted to hear of the disturbances at the late Lord Ravenswood's funeral. He hopes that the brave stand of Edgar, the young and former master of Ravenswood, which made it possible for the previously prohibited Episcopal service to take place in Scotland, will put Edgar in disfavor with the Privy Council and prevent his attempt to reclaim his family's property. However, when the Lord Keeper and his daughter Lucy visit old Alice, a tenant on the estate, they are warned about the fierce Ravenswood blood and the family motto, I Bide My Time.

The Ashtons' first encounter with Edgar seems fortunate; he shoots a bull as it charges Sir William and Lucy, saving them from serious injury. The sheltered, romantic girl is fascinated by her proud rescuer, who leaves abruptly after he identifies himself. Her more practical father gratefully softens his report of the disturbances at Lord Ravenswood's funeral and asks several friends to help Edgar.

On the evening of the rescue, Edgar joins Bucklaw, the heir to a large fortune, and the adventurer-soldier Captain Craigengelt at a tavern where he tells them that he will not go with them to France. As he starts home, Bucklaw, who thinks himself insulted, challenges him to a duel. Edgar wins, gives his opponent his life, and invites him to Wolf's Crag, the lonely, sea-beaten tower that is the only property left to the last of the once-powerful Ravenswoods.

Old Caleb Balderstone does his best to welcome his master and his companion to Wolf's Crag in the style befitting the Ravenswood family, making ingenious excuses for the absence of whatever he is not able to procure from one of his many sources. The old man provides almost the only amusement for the two men, and Edgar thinks often of the girl he rescued. Deciding not to leave Scotland immediately, he writes to his kinsman, the Marquis of A——, for advice. The

marquis tells him to remain at Wolf's Crag and hints at political intrigue, but he offers no material assistance to supplement Caleb's meager findings.

One morning, Bucklaw persuades Edgar to join a hunting party that is passing by the castle. An ardent sportsman, Bucklaw brings down a deer, while his friend watches from a hillside. Edgar offers Wolf's Crag as shelter against an approaching storm for an elderly gentleman and a young girl who came to talk to him.

Poor Caleb's resourcefulness is taxed to its limit with guests to feed. When Bucklaw thoughtlessly brings the hunting party to the castle, Caleb closes the gate, saying that he never admits anyone while a Ravenswood dines. The old servant sends them to the village, where Bucklaw meets Captain Craigengelt again.

At Wolf's Crag, Edgar soon realizes that his guests are Sir William and Lucy; Sir William planned the hunt with the hope of securing an interview with Edgar. Lucy's fright at the storm and Caleb's comical excuses for the lack of food and elegant furnishings make relations between the two men less tense. When Edgar accompanies Sir William to his room after a feast of capon cleverly procured by Caleb, the older man offers his friendship and promises to try to settle certain unresolved questions about the estate in Edgar's favor.

An astute politician, Sir William heeds a warning that the Marquis of A—— is likely to rise in power, raising his young kinsman with him, and he fears the loss of his newly acquired estate. He feels that Edgar's goodwill might be valuable, and his ambitious wife's absence allows him to follow his inclination to be friendly. A staunch Whig, Lady Ashton is in London, where she is trying to give support to the falling fortunes of her party.

Although Edgar's pride and bitterness against the enemy of his father keeps him from trusting Sir William completely, the Lord Keeper has an unexpected advantage in the growing love between Edgar and Lucy. Anxious to assist the romance, he invites Edgar to accompany them to the castle where the young man once lived.

Edgar and Lucy go together to see old Alice, who prophesies that tragedy will be the result of this unnatural alliance of Ravenswood and Ashton. Edgar resolves to break off his relationship with Lucy, but at the Mermaiden Fountain, he asks her to marry him instead. They break a gold coin in token of their engagement but decide to keep their love a secret until Lucy's much-feared mother arrives.

Sir William correctly interprets the confusion of the pair when they return, but he overlooks it to tell them of the approaching visit of the Marquis of A—— to Ravenswood. He urges Edgar to stay to meet his kinsman.

Sir William's elaborate preparations for his distinguished guest leave Edgar and Lucy alone together much of the time, to the great disgust of Bucklaw, who inherited the adjoining property. He unfairly resents Edgar, thinking that he ordered Caleb to dismiss him summarily from Wolf's Crag. Bucklaw confides to his companion, Captain Craigengelt, that a cousin of his is intimate with Lady Ashton and made a match between himself and Lucy. He sends the captain to tell Lady Ashton of Edgar's presence and of the Marquis of A——'s impending visit. Bucklaw hopes that she will return and intervene on his behalf.

Lady Ashton is so upset by the news that she leaves for home immediately, arriving simultaneously with the marquis and striking fear into the hearts of her husband and daughter. She immediately sends Edgar a note ordering him to leave, thereby incurring the displeasure of his kinsman. She becomes still more furious when Lucy tells her of her engagement.

As Edgar passes the Mermaiden Fountain, traditionally a fateful spot for his family, he sees a white figure which he recognizes as old Alice or her ghost. When he goes to her cottage and finds her dead, he realizes that her appearance was her final warning to him.

The marquis joins his young cousin, who was helping with the funeral preparations, and reports that all his entreaties failed to make Lady Ashton tolerate the engagement. He asks Edgar to let him spend the night at Wolf's Crag, insisting over the young man's protests about the lack of comfort there. When the two approach the old castle, however, they see the tower windows aglow with flames. Later, after the people of Wolf's Hope provide a bountiful feast for the marquis and his retinue, Caleb confesses to Edgar that he set a few fires around the tower to preserve the honor of the family. Henceforth, he can explain the absence of any number of luxuries by saying that they were lost in the great conflagration.

Edgar goes to Edinburgh with his kinsmen, who quickly acquire their expected power when the Tories take over Queen Anne's government for a short time. In prospect of better fortunes, Edgar writes to Sir William and Lady Ashton asking permission to marry Lucy. Both answer negatively— the lady with insults and the gentleman in careful phrases, hopefully designed to win favor with the marquis. A brief note from Lucy warns her lover not to try to correspond with her; however, she promises fidelity. Edgar, unable to do anything else, goes to France for a year on a secret mission for the government.

Bucklaw, whose suit is approved by the Ashtons, requests an interview with Lucy and learns from Lady Ashton, who insists upon being present, that the girl agreed to marry him only on the condition that Edgar will release her from her engagement. Lucy writes to ask him to do so in a letter dictated by her mother, but Lady Ashton intercepts it, hoping that her daughter will give in if she receives no answer. Lucy confesses, however, that she sent a duplicate letter with the help of the minister and that she expects an answer before long.

She is not the same young woman with whom Edgar fell in love, for she is almost a prisoner of her mother for weeks. Unable to stand the constant persecution, she grows gloomy and ill. Lady Ashton hires an old woman as nurse for her, and at the mother's instigation, she fills the girl's wavering mind with mysterious tales and frightening legends about the Ravenswood family. Sir William, suspecting the reason for his daughter's increasing melancholy, dismisses the crone, but the damage is already done.

Edgar, who finally receives Lucy's request that their engagement be ended, comes to Ravenswood Castle to determine whether she wrote the letter of her own free will; he arrives just as she is signing her betrothal agreement with Bucklaw. Unable to speak, the girl indicates that she cannot stand against her parents' wishes, and she returns Edgar's half of the gold coin.

Lucy remains in a stupor after this encounter. Meanwhile, her mother continues making plans for the wedding. Old women outside the church on the marriage day prophesy that a funeral will soon follow this ceremony. Lucy's younger brother is horrified at the cold clamminess of the girl's hand. Later, she disappears during the bridal ball, and Lady Ashton sends the bridegroom after her. Horrible cries brings the whole party to the girl's apartment, where they find Bucklaw lying stabbed on the floor. After a search, Lucy is discovered sitting in the chimney, gibbering insanely. She dies the next evening, reaching vainly for the broken coin that once hung around her neck.

Bucklaw recovers, but Edgar, who appears silently at Lucy's funeral, perishes in quicksand near Wolf's Crag as he goes to fight a duel with Lucy's brother, who blames him for her death. Lady Ashton lives on, apparently without remorse for the horrors her pride had caused.

Critical Evaluation:

This novel of seventeenth century Scotland has a driving psychological as well as a political, a religious, and a social determinism. The conflict between Presbyterian (Lord Ashton and family) and Episcopalian (Edgar) is influential in the plot. So, to a lesser degree, is the political-social turmoil that involves disintegration of old-order Tory values before the energetic ambitions of the Whigs. Popular superstition thus thrives upon the inevitable confusion, disorder, and decay resulting from these changes. This power of the supernatural—manifest in omens, dreams, hidden fears, prophecies, visions, specters, and other phenomena—directs the thoughts and actions of both major and minor characters.

Sir Walter Scott, however, does not impose such superstitious paraphernalia directly upon the story; he employs them more subtly, so that they seem the result of psychological conflicts within the characters. The young master of Ravenswood, deprived of his castle and hereditary rights, can only, by submerging his proud loyalty, ally himself with the Ashtons, who usurped all he holds significant in life. In his own eyes, his sudden, almost unconscious love for Lucy Ashton, although a solace and partial fulfillment of loss, still demeans him. He knows he cannot betray the values of the past, yet he has within him youth and ardor, which force him into an engagement with Lucy. All the characters in the novel, and the reader as well, know that such an alliance will lead to doom. Old Alice tells him this, and Caleb Balderstone, Ravenswood's faithful, ingenious manservant, also warns him about the marriage. The apparition at Mermaiden's Fountain confirms Ravenswood's fears; even Lucy's passive affection and terror of her mother all underline the young man's own perception, but he remains psychologically divided, unable to free himself emotionally from what he realizes intellectually is a disastrous union.

The schism within young Ravenswood, a truly Byronic hero, finds its dark expression in the ugly prophecies of the village hags, the superstitious talk of the sexton, the mutterings of the peasants, and Henry Ashton's shooting of the raven near the betrothed couple at the well. However, step by step, Ravenswood almost seeks his fate, driven relentlessly by factors deep within his personality.

Lucy is equally torn. She loves Ravenswood but is paralyzed before the dominating force of her mother. She submits

to marriage with Bucklaw, but her divisive emotions drive her to murder, insanity, and death. Lord Ashton also has commendable motives in spite of his political chicanery, but he, like Lucy, is rendered ineffective by his wife's mastery.

To keep the novel from sinking into grotesque morbidity and gothic excess, Scott provides comic relief through specific character action. Caleb in his bizarre methods of replenishing the bare tables of Wolf's Crag and the rallying of all in the village to provide adequately for the marquis during his visit furnish this needed humor. Scott's sense of timing and his ability to tie supernatural elements to psychological divisions within personality manage to hold the novel together and to make it a controlled and well-structured work.

Further Reading

Brown, David. *Walter Scott and the Historical Imagination.* Boston: Routledge & Kegan Paul, 1979. A thorough discussion of Scott's tragic plot and comic subplot in *The Bride of Lammermoor.* Compares the novel to other Scott novels, focusing in particular on the similarities between *The Bride of Lammermoor* and *Guy Mannering.*

D'Arcy, Julian Meldon. *Subversive Scott: The Waverley Novels and Scottish Nationalism.* Reykjavík, Iceland: Vigdís Finnbogadóttir Institute of Foreign Languages, University of Iceland Press, 2005. Demonstrates how the novels contain dissonant elements, undetected manifestations of Scottish nationalism, and criticism of the United Kingdom and its imperial policy. Chapter 8 examines *The Bride of Lammermoor.*

Irvine, Robert P. "The State, the Domestic, and National Culture in the Waverley Novels." In *Enlightenment and Romance: Gender and Agency in Smollett and Scott.* New York: Peter Lang, 2000. Analyzes the fiction of Scott and Tobias Smollett within the context of the emergence of the social sciences and the dominance of novels written by female writers in the eighteenth century. Describes how the authors adapted the feminine romance and the domestic novel to assert control over the narrative structure of their novels.

Johnson, Edgar. *Sir Walter Scott: The Great Unknown.* 2 vols. New York: Macmillan, 1970. The standard biography of Scott. Regards the novel as a tragedy of character and fate—one in which the love affair is surrounded by an atmosphere of foreboding.

Kerr, James. *Fiction Against History: Scott as Storyteller.* New York: Cambridge University Press, 1989. Considers the most fascinating feature of the novel to be its merging of pessimistic historical narrative with complex love story. Notes how the novel is a lament for the decline of the feudal order and a critique of the new order. Emphasizes the way in which Scott deploys gothic elements to develop a historical lesson found often in the Waverley novels.

Lauber, John. *Sir Walter Scott.* Rev. ed. Boston: Twayne, 1989. An excellent introduction. Has a chronology of Scott's life, chapters on Scott's career, poetry, and fiction, and a selected bibliography. Refers to the novel as a book about oaths and omens, signs and warnings.

Lincoln, Andrew. "Liberal Dilemmas—Liberty or Alienation? *The Bride of Lammemoor* and *Redgauntlet.*" In *Walter Scott and Modernity.* Edinburgh: Edinburgh University Press, 2007. In his examination of Scott's novels and poems, Lincoln argues that these were not works of nostalgia; instead, Scott used the past as a means of exploring modernist moral, political, and social issues.

Milgate, Jane. *Walter Scott: The Making of the Novelist.* Toronto, Ont.: University of Toronto Press, 1984. Discusses the legend surrounding the novel's composition. Explores the importance of the dating of its action. Notes that the

novel depicts a particular historical moment, one with which both Ravenswood and Sir William Ashton are out of step.

Robertson, Fiona. *Legitimate Histories: Scott, Gothic, and the Authorities of Fiction.* New York: Oxford University Press, 1994. Analyzes Scott's Waverley novels within the context of eighteenth and nineteenth century gothic literature; examines the novels' critical reception. Devotes a chapter to *The Bride of Lammermoor.*

Shaw, Harry E., ed. *Critical Essays on Sir Walter Scott: The Waverley Novels.* New York: G. K. Hall, 1996. Collection of essays published between 1858 and 1996 about Scott's series of novels. Includes journalist Walter Bagehot's 1858 article about the Waverley novels and discussions of Scott's rationalism, storytelling and subversion of the literary form in his fiction, and what his work meant to Victorian readers. Bruce Beiderwell's essay "Death and Disappearance in *The Bride of Lammermoor*" examines this novel.

The Bride Price

Author: Buchi Emecheta (1944-   )
First published: 1976
Type of work: Novel
Type of plot: Social criticism
Time of plot: c. 1950-c. 1953
Locale: Lagos and Ibuza, Nigeria

Principal characters:
AKU-NNA, a teenage girl
NNA-NNDO, her brother
MA BLACKIE, their mother
CHIKE, a schoolmaster who becomes Aku-nna's husband
OKONKWO, Aku-nna's stepfather and Ma Blackie's second husband
OKOBOSHI, a young man who kidnaps Aku-nna for marriage

The Story:

Thirteen-year-old Aku-nna and her brother, Nna-nndo, two years younger, arrive home from school to find Aku-nna's father, Ezekiel Odia, unexpectedly standing in the middle of the family's one-room apartment. Obviously ill at ease, he tells his children that he is going to the hospital to have his foot examined. He had earlier injured his foot during service in World War II. He says that he will be back for the evening meal, adding that Aku-nna and Nna-nndo should remember always that they are his children.

Despite a patriarchal social structure in which daughters are devalued, Aku-nna feels a special bond with her father and knows that he, in turn, loves her. Her name means

"father's wealth," and Aku-nna has resolved to make a good marriage so that her bride price—the money paid to the family of the bride by that of the groom—will please him.

It is now evening, and Ezekiel has not returned from the hospital. More than three weeks later, the children realize that their father had died in the hospital. His funeral is a mixture of African and European traditions. Brother and sister are now in a serious plight: A family without a father is deemed one without a head or shelter, a family that does not exist. Aku-nna hears an aunt say that she will be married quickly so that her bride price may pay for her brother's schooling.

Before Ezekiel's death, Ma Blackie, his wife, had returned to her home town of Ibuza in the hope that indigenous practices could help restore her fertility and enable her to give him another son. Alarmed by rumors of her husband's ill health, she now decides to return to Lagos, where she learns of his death. Some weeks later, she, Aku-nna, and Nna-nndo take the only course of action open to them: They return to the mother's home town, the lack of a breadwinner making life in expensive Lagos impossible. The three arrive in Ibuza and happen to meet two young men on bicycles, one of whom is Chike, the handsome young headmaster of the local school. The ambition of Aku-nna—delicate, sensitive, and intelligent—is now to acquire enough education to become a teacher herself and thus help her mother. Chike, however, is not allowed to associate with the daughters of good families, so Aku-nna hopes Chike will at least be able to help her get the necessary certificate.

During the journey from Lagos to Ibuza, Aku-nna had noticed how the modern city had gradually given way to a more simple rural life. She comes to learn that Ibuza, in midwestern Nigeria, is much more traditional than Lagos. Okonkwo, Ezekiel's brother, marries Ma Blackie as his fourth wife, according to custom. She soon becomes pregnant and, therefore, happy. Okonkwo wishes to take the higher title of *Eze*, which will require an expensive sacrifice to the gods, and thinks that Aku-nna's bride price will help him attain this social ambition. Okonkwo is prepared to accept his stepdaughter's education for some time, as educated girls command a higher bride price, and he is determined that the money will come to him. Meanwhile, Ngbeke, his senior wife, jealously suggests to her sons that Ma Blackie will insist on keeping at least some of the money. She also suggests that Aku-nna, fourteen years old, physically undeveloped, and not yet menstruating, is an *ogbanje*, a living-dead person who is bound to die young, perhaps at the birth of her first child. To Ngbeke's sons' indignation, their mother also claims there is a special closeness between Aku-nna and Chike, who is not merely a foreigner to Ibuza but also the descendant of slaves.

Aku-nna and Chike are indeed falling in love. When Aku-nna is unable to concentrate in class due to her sense of isolation and consequent depression, Chike, disturbed by a growing attraction, loses his temper with her. He permits the weeping girl to leave the classroom and later follows her to a secluded part of the school grounds. He attempts to find out what is troubling her. Suddenly, Chike sees that she is menstruating. He asks her to keep her condition quiet until after her school examination. Later the same day, the two declare their love and, despite the barrier of custom, Aku-nna asks Chike to request her hand in marriage from her family.

It soon becomes clear that Aku-nna is marriageable. She had menstruated during a firewood-collecting expedition and could no longer hide the fact. Now, she is obliged to endure the crude attempts at love-play of Okoboshi, a spoiled youth lame from a snake bite. As part of a culturally sanctioned courtship tradition he grabs her breasts. The enraged Chike, who is present, knocks Okoboshi down. Soon, however, in another culturally accepted practice, Okoboshi's family has Aku-nna kidnapped with the intention of marrying her to him.

Confused and now a prisoner, Aku-nna knows that should she resist, custom permits Okoboshi to get help to have her held down while he consummates the marriage. Heartened by hearing Chike's distinctive whistle nearby, she resolves, at this defining moment in her life, to resist. Okoboshi approaches Aku-nna, who falsely tells him that she is not a virgin and that the descendant of a slave had repeatedly possessed her. Even if Okoboshi were to take her by force, rape her, and get her pregnant, he cannot be sure that he would be the father. Okoboshi punches Aku-nna in the face and, in the morning, arranges for her to be put to work carrying water.

Later in the day, when alone, she again hears Chike's whistling. He appears, and the two escape to a nearby village. Chike takes her to Ughelli, another town in the midwestern area, where he hopes to find a job. Chike and Aku-nna make love, and Chike realizes that Aku-nna is indeed a virgin. He says that the rumors to the contrary must be publicly denied. All Aku-nna asks is that her bride price be paid, for customary belief holds that a woman whose price is not paid will die in childbirth.

Aku-nna and Chike are married, and Aku-nna becomes pregnant. She is now sixteen years old but looks two years younger. She finds the pregnancy difficult. Meanwhile, her stepfather, Okonkwo, refuses the bride price offered by Chike's father, saying he will not marry his stepdaughter to a slave. Aku-nna dies giving birth to a girl. Her story is told to young girls in Ibuza to reinforce the cultural beliefs that a girl must accept the man chosen as her husband and that her bride price must be paid so that she will not die during childbirth.

Critical Evaluation:

The predecessors of Buchi Emecheta's *The Bride Price*, the novels *In the Ditch* (1972) and *Second-Class Citizen* (1974), narrate the lives of Nigerians living in London. If the obstacles Nigerian women find there include indigenous sexist attitudes on the part of their husbands, then both men and women struggle to live in a different culture, marginalized by British racist attitudes. Emecheta's third published novel, however, is set exclusively in Nigeria; indeed, most of the story takes place in provincial Ibuza, removed from the culturally pluralistic capital of Lagos. Although British law has circumscribed certain customs of the Ibo, the tribal grouping of *The Bride Price*, only one white person, the head of the local mission, actually appears in the novel, and does so briefly. The society whose virtues and vices are here depicted is relatively untouched by the West.

In the tradition of Nigerian writer Chinua Achebe's *Things Fall Apart* (1958), still the best-known African novel and also set among the Ibo, the third-person narrative voice carefully brings the reader to an understanding of and a respect for traditional culture—its assumptions and beliefs and the customs that flow from these beliefs. Like Achebe, Emecheta instructs the reader about the *chi*, or personal god, and about the *ogbanje*, or living dead. Also like Achebe, Emecheta quotes Ibo proverbs for the insight they provide into the culture that produced them and which they reflect. The narrative voice also omnisciently informs readers of the great strength of Ibo culture: The Ibo have what is called by psychologists "the group mind"; furthermore, in Ibo culture "a child is the child of the community" and Ibo young people have "that distinctive and good-humoured quality of ease which was the heritage of people who had long ago learned and absorbed the art of communal living." Ibo society works well on its own terms—after all, Aku-nna, her brother, and her mother are provided for on the death of their father and husband.

The strength and cohesion of the whole sometimes demand the subordination of the part. *The Bride Price* is a critique of traditional Ibo attitudes toward women. From the beginning of the novel, this point is clearly made. Aku-nna's father is careful not to show the love he feels for his daughter: He does not wish to be mocked for wanting to be her husband as well. Upon the death of her father, Aku-nna's educational ambitions are imperiled, leading her to face an unknown future. Her aunts try to console her with talk of the inevitability of women's lot: "This is the fate of us women. There is nothing we can do about it. We just have to learn to accept it." When Aku-nna arrives in Ibuza, she becomes a pawn in a complex game she does not understand, as Okonkwo, his senior wife, and their sons jockey to get possession of her bride price, the symbol of her virtual chattel status. Upon her attaining maturity, she is told by Okonkwo to discontinue her relationship with the man she loves. Finally, the Ibo still countenance the practice of kidnapping girls for marriage; and, in another culturally sanctioned practice, if a man who cannot afford a wife succeeds in cutting off a lock of a young woman's hair, that young woman is considered his wife to be.

The other obstacle separating Aku-nna and Chike in this romantic tale is the Ibo scorn for the descendants of slaves. The British outlawed the institution of slavery, but this has had little effect on the immemorial attitudes prevailing in the Nigerian interior, where the people of Ibuza still remember the days when slaves would be killed upon the death of their respective masters.

Aku-nna and Chike are both denied full human autonomy, the former because of her gender and the latter because of his caste. Ironically, the story of Aku-nna, who had felt it "unjust that she was not allowed a say in her own life" and who cried out against the "savage custom . . . that could be so heartless and make so many people unhappy," is made a warning to young girls against the very rebellion she had essayed.

M. D. Allen

Further Reading

Boostrom, Rebecca. "Nigerian Legal Concepts in Buchi Emecheta's *The Bride Price*." In *Emerging Perspectives on Buchi Emecheta*, edited by Marie Umeh. Trenton, N.J.: Africa World Press, 1996. A careful examination of customary Ibo law and British law and the social changes that had been already underway in 1950's Nigeria, the decade in which *The Bride Price* is set.

Cox, C. Brian, ed. *African Writers*. 2 vols. New York: Charles Scribner's Sons, 1997. This compilation on African writers includes a biographical and critical overview of Emecheta and her writings. Also includes a brief bibliography.

Emenyonu, Ernest N. "Technique and Language in Buchi Emecheta's *The Bride Price*, *The Slave Girl*, and *The Joys of Motherhood*." In *Emerging Perspectives on Buchi Emecheta*, edited by Marie Umeh. Trenton, N.J.: Africa World Press, 1996. A stylistic study of three of Emecheta's works, part of a larger collection exploring her career.

Fishburn, Katherine. *Reading Buchi Emecheta: Cross-Cultural Conversations*. Westport, Conn.: Greenwood Press, 1995. A more demanding postmodernist approach to Emecheta's work. For advanced readers with some knowledge of literary and cultural theories.

Katrak, Ketu H. "Womanhood/Motherhood: Variations on a Theme in Selected Novels of Buchi Emecheta." *Journal of Commonwealth Literature* 22, no. 1 (1987): 159-170. A thematic study of the biological and economic control of women displayed in Emecheta's fiction, including *The Bride Price*.

Taiwo, Oladele. *Female Novelists of Modern Africa*. New York: St. Martin's Press, 1984. This general study of African women novelists contains a short but good introduction to *The Bride Price* that also sketches out the novel's major themes.

Uraizee, Joya. "'They Who Are Beneath': Subaltern Voices in *The Conservationist, The Day in Shadow,* and *The Bride Price.*" In *This Is No Place for a Woman: Nadine Gordimer, Na Yantara Sahgal, Buchi Emecheta, and the Politics of Gender.* Trenton N.J.: Africa World Press, 2000. An ambitious use of the concept of subaltern con-

sciousness of literary critic Gayatri C. Spivak, a concept applied here to an examination of power relations in *The Bride Price.*

Uwakweh, Pauline Ada. "Carving a Niche: Visions of Gendered Childhood in Buchi Emecheta's *The Bride Price* and Tsitsi Dangarembga's *Nervous Conditions.*" *African Literature Today* 21 (1998): 9-21. A comparative essay arguing, in part, that gender identity, as evidenced in *The Bride Price*, is created by socialization.

The Bride's Tragedy and Death's Jest-Book

Author: Thomas Lovell Beddoes (1803-1849)
First produced: 1822, *The Bride's Tragedy* (first published, 1822); 1850, *Death's Jest-Book: Or, The Fool's Tragedy* (first published, 1850)
Type of work: Drama

Thomas Lovell Beddoes spent his life as a perpetual medical student, even after he qualified for his degree at universities in Germany and Switzerland; he ended his life by poison at the age of forty-five. Apart from two books of juvenile poems, Beddoes published only one work in his lifetime, *The Bride's Tragedy,* which became a best seller in London when he was a nineteen-year-old undergraduate at Oxford. Early success with this poetical drama suggested to him the notion of "reviving" the English drama, a desire shared by many English writers between the successes of John Dryden and William Butler Yeats or T. S. Eliot—witness the impossible verse dramas of William Wordsworth, Percy Bysshe Shelley, Robert Browning, Alfred, Lord Tennyson, and Thomas Hardy. The shadow of William Shakespeare and the Elizabethans stretched long across the centuries, but unlike the Elizabethans the great English poets had very little practical experience of the stage. Thus it is that Beddoes's two most complete works are verse dramas, *The Bride's Tragedy* and *Death's Jest-Book,* which he completed in the four years ending in 1828 and spent the rest of his life revising.

Beddoes enjoyed a competent income all his life and suffered no attachments. He seems to have spent his years on the Continent, between 1825 and 1848, as a graduate student and a political radical; a favorable rate of exchange and the reputation of a free Englishman made him a well-known figure among students and the secret police abroad. He seems to have been fortunate in his friends, especially his literary ex-

ecutor, Thomas Forbes Kelsall, but to have suffered a grand dyspepsia for life, of which he was thoroughly conscious:

> For death is more "a jest" than Life, you see
> Contempt grows quick from familiarity,
>   . . . Few, I know,
> Can bear to sit at my board when I show
> The wretchedness and folly of man's all
> And laugh myself right heartily.

Beddoes's long self-exile is perhaps the clearest indication of his malaise and the cause of his fragmentary work. He was unable to grasp the realities of life around him. A gentleman, a student, a foreigner, he sought an effective means of communication in a totally unrealistic medium, the poetic drama. Having little to say and no way of saying it, he turned ever inward, exploring his own melancholy and recording it in an outworn medium he acquired not from the stage but from books.

For all this perversity, eccentricity, and tragedy, however, no anthology of nineteenth century English poetry can afford to omit at least two of Beddoes's lyrics: "Old Adam, the carrion crow" from the final scene of *Death's Jest-Book* and "Dream-Pedlary" from "The Ivory Gate," the title of a collection of the poems written on the Continent. Remote as he was from the country of his speech, the events and literature of his time may have been preconditions of his unique tone, which escapes finer definition, as does that of his place in English literature. The situations of his lyrics are always slightly freakish, for it is the style that marks their individuality. Along with much conventional language there are turns in the lines that can only be crass or inspired phrasing: "And through every feather/ Leaked the wet weather...." The second line is ironic and realistic. This is the effect Beddoes was always trying to bring off, a *danse macabre* in polka time that forces his lines to try to outdo one another, often in a succession of compounds. When inspiration fails, crassness results. These terrible alternatives are more or less described in the words of Wolfram, which introduce the lyric:

> When I am sick o' mornings,
> With a horn-spoon tinkling my porridge-pot,
> 'Tis a brave ballad: but in Bacchanal night,
> O'er wine, red, black, or purple-bubbling wine,
> That takes a man by the brain and whirls him
>   round,
> By Bacchus' lip! I like a full-voiced fellow,
> A craggy-throated, fat-cheeked trumpeter,
> A barker, a moon-howler. . . .

There is more triumph than failure of these startling effects in the last poems of "The Ivory Gate," and the range is much larger. Beddoes can satirize Britannia from a penny: "O flattering likeness on a copper coin!/ Sit still upon your slave-raised cotton ball,/ With upright toasting fork and toothless cat." He concludes "Silenus in Proteus" with the wit, "I taught thee then, a little tumbling one,/ To suck the goatskin oftener than the goat?" "An Unfinished Draft," beginning "The snow falls by thousands into the sea," shows his lyric powers, as does the striking image in "The Phantom-Wooer": "Sweet and sweet is their poisoned note,/ The little snakes of silver throat, . . ."

Similarly, it is the lyrics in the verse dramas that are now best remembered. The larger effect Beddoes was trying for by constructing plot, character, and situation never quite comes off; the fault mainly lies in the plots of the dramas together with their settings and the distrait emotions of the speakers. The two brides of *The Bride's Tragedy* are Floribel and Olivia; the latter's brother, Orlando, has forced Floribel's wooer, Hesperus, to promise marriage to Olivia so that Orlando himself can wed Floribel. Hesperus decides that both shall be the "brides" of death. In act 3, he stabs Floribel when she keeps his tryst; as Olivia is preparing for her wedding to Hesperus his deed is discovered, and the duke orders his arrest at the marriage feast. When he is condemned to die, Olivia dies, too, and Floribel's mother (having poisoned

Hesperus with the scent of flowers at the place of execution) precedes Hesperus to the grave in a general holocaust that includes the fathers of Floribel and Hesperus. Most of the action takes place offstage, the characters making the most of the marvelous situations, such as a suicide's grave, for verbal arias that furiously imitate the clotted passages of witty exchange in the Elizabethan play. The play is effective from moment to moment, but as a whole it is impossible. Much the same can be said for *Death's Jest-Book* or "The Fool's Tragedy." Wolfram goes to the Holy Land to rescue Duke Melveric from the Saracens. The two fight over the love of Sibylla, and Melveric kills Wolfram, whose body is returned to Grussau accompanied by the duke, in the disguise of a friar, and Sibylla. There the duke finds his two sons, Adalmar and Athulf, plotting rebellion against the duke's governor, Thorwald, and fighting each other for the love of Thorwald's daughter. The rebellion is led by Isbrand, Wolfram's vengeful brother, who has substituted a clown, Mandrake, for Wolfram's corpse, so that when the duke, despairing of his present troubles, asks his African slave to raise the dead, first Mandrake, then Wolfram come from the sepulchre. The wedding of Adalmar and Thorwald's daughter is planned. Isbrand agrees to marry Sibylla; Athulf appears to commit suicide by drinking poison as the musicians, come to lead Thorwald's daughter to her marriage, sing the beautiful song, "We have bathed, where none have seen us." The scene ends with Athulf killing Adalmar. In the fifth act, the events are quite complicated, for the ghost of Wolfram is seeking revenge and the conspirators have decided to kill Isbrand. Sibylla dies but Athulf does not. The conspiracy first succeeds and then is overthrown. In the end, the duke loses both his sons, resigns his crown to Thorwald, and makes a marvelous final exit, going into the sepulchre with Wolfram. The play is saturated with echoes of Shakespeare, both in the language ("O Arab, Arab! Thou dost sell true drugs") and in the situation of a duke in disguise, and but for Beddoes's obvious gravity the situation would amount to a parody. Many of the situations and passages play on death, but apart from a soliloquy by Isbrand, the "Fool" of the subtitle, they do little more than weave around the subject. The soliloquy in act 5, scene 1, begins:

> How I despise
> All you mere men of muscle! It was ever
> My study to find out a way to godhead,
> And on reflection soon I found that first
> I was but half created; that a power
> Was wanting in my soul to be its soul,
> And this was mine to make.

This passage carries the ring of reality and makes it clear that Isbrand is a persona for Beddoes, one of the rare moments when he speaks recognizable truth. In the "Lines Written in Switzerland," after a passage that plays with the notion of truth, Beddoes again speaks out in what may well be his epitaph:

> Not in the popular playhouse, or full throng
> Of opera-gazers longing for deceit; . . .
> May verse like this e'er hope an eye to feed on't.
> But if there be, who, having laid the loved
> Where they may drop a tear in roses' cups,
> With half their hearts inhabit other worlds; . . .
> Such may perchance, with favorable mind,
> Follow my thought along its mountainous path.

Further Reading

Allard, James Robert. "The Body's Laws: Flesh, Souls, and Transgression in Beddoes's *Death's Jest-Book*." In *Romanticism, Medicine, and the Poet's Body*. Burlington, Vt.: Ashgate, 2007. Allard examines how English Romantic poetry was influenced by the professionalization of medicine in the nineteenth century. He focuses on the "poet-physician," a hybrid character appearing in the work of Beddoes and other medically trained poets.

Berns, Ute, and Michael Bradshaw, eds. *The Ashgate Research Companion to Thomas Lovell Beddoes*. Burlington, Vt.: Ashgate, 2007. Collection of thirteen essays providing a range of interpretations of Beddoes's work. The majority of essays analyze *Death's Jest-Book*, discussing its representation of the body and the state, performing genres, and nineteenth century medical theories and placing the drama within the context of German revolutionary discourse. Another essay compares *The Bride's Tragedy* to the myth of Cupid and Psyche.

Bradshaw, Michael. *Resurrection Songs: The Poetry of Thomas Lovell Beddoes*. Burlington, Vt.: Ashgate, 2001. Describes how the concept of resurrection influenced Beddoes's work. Bradshaw examines Beddoes's relationship to Renaissance and contemporary Romantic poets, the influence of his medical training on his work, his search for immortality, and the fragmentation of his writing.

Donner, H. W. *Thomas Lovell Beddoes*. Oxford, England: Basil Blackwell, 1935. Extensive critical examination of the writer's career that includes lengthy chapters on both *The Bride's Tragedy* and *Death's Jest-Book*. Discusses technical merits, sources, and themes for each verse drama.

Ford, Mark. "The Prince of Morticians: Thomas Lovell Beddoes." In *A Driftwood Altar: Essays and Reviews*. London: Waywiser, 2005. Ford, a twenty-first century British poet, discusses the work of Beddoes.

Frye, Northrop. "Yorick: The Romantic Macabre." In *A Study of English Romanticism*. New York: Random House, 1968. Extensive analysis of *Death's Jest-Book*, establishing its place in the Romantic canon and discussing Beddoes's handling of themes common to Romantic writers.

Snow, Royall H. *Thomas Lovell Beddoes: Eccentric and Poet*. New York: Covici, Friede, 1928. Scholarly investigation of the writer's life and works. Includes chapters on *The Bride's Tragedy* and *Death's Jest-Book*. Points out Beddoes's problem in meeting the requirements of the stage in both works, but acknowledges the author's ability to create powerful scenes.

Thompson, James R. *Thomas Lovell Beddoes*. Boston: Twayne, 1985. Introductory survey of the writer that contains a chapter on each play. Describes *The Bride's Tragedy* as a derivative of Jacobean drama. Claims that *Death's Jest-Book* is a satiric *danse macabre*. Explains why Beddoes chose drama as a form of artistic expression.

Wilner, Eleanor. *Gathering the Winds: Visionary Imagination and Radical Transformation of Self and Society*. Baltimore: Johns Hopkins University Press, 1975. Though somewhat eccentric in approach, this study provides significant insights into Beddoes's works and shows how his dramas may serve to counter typical notions of the Romantics' apocalyptic vision.

Brideshead Revisited
The Sacred and Profane Memories of Captain Charles Ryder

Author: Evelyn Waugh (1903-1966)
First published: 1945; revised, 1959
Type of work: Novel
Type of plot: Social realism
Time of plot: Twentieth century
Locale: England

Principal characters:
CHARLES RYDER, an architectural painter and the narrator
LORD MARCHMAIN, the owner of Brideshead
LADY MARCHMAIN, his wife
BRIDESHEAD (BRIDEY),
SEBASTIAN,
JULIA, and
CORDELIA, their children
CELIA, Charles Ryder's wife
ANTHONY BLANCHE and BOY MULCASTER, Oxford friends of Charles and Sebastian
REX MOTTRAM, Julia's husband
CARA, Lord Marchmain's mistress

The Story:

Captain Charles Ryder of the British Army and his company move to a new billet in the neighborhood of Brideshead, an old estate he often visited during his student days at Oxford. Brideshead is the home of the Marchmains, an old Catholic family. Following World War I, the Marquis of Marchmain went to live in Italy. There he met Cara, who became his mistress for life. Lady Marchmain, an ardent Catholic, and her four children, Brideshead, Sebastian, Julia, and Cordelia, remained in England. They lived either at Brideshead or at Marchmain House in London.

When Charles Ryder met Sebastian at Oxford, they soon became close friends. Among Sebastian's circle of friends were Boy Mulcaster and Anthony Blanche. With Charles's entrance into that group, his tastes became more expensive, and he ended his year with an overdrawn account of £550.

Just after returning home from school for vacation, Charles received a telegram announcing that Sebastian was injured. He rushed off to Brideshead, where he found Sebastian with a cracked bone in his ankle. While at Brideshead, Charles met some of Sebastian's family. Julia met him at the station and later Bridey, the eldest of the Marchmains, and Cordelia, the youngest, arrived. After a month, his ankle healed, Sebastian took Charles to Venice. There they spent the rest of their vacation with Lord Marchmain and Cara.

Early in the following school year, Charles met Lady Marchmain when she visited Sebastian at Oxford. Her famous charm immediately won Charles, and he promised to spend his Christmas vacation at Brideshead. During the first term, Sebastian, Charles, and Boy Mulcaster were invited to a London charity ball by Rex Mottram, a friend of Julia.

Bored, they left early and were later arrested for drunkenness and disorderly conduct. Rex obtained their release.

As a consequence of the escapade, Charles, Sebastian, and Boy were sent back to Oxford, and Mr. Samgrass, who was doing some literary work for Lady Marchmain, kept close watch on them for the rest of the term. Christmas at Brideshead was spoiled for almost everyone by the presence of Samgrass. Back at Oxford, Charles began to realize that Sebastian drank to escape his family. During the Easter vacation at Brideshead, Sebastian became quite drunk. Later, when Lady Marchmain went to Oxford to see Sebastian, he again became hopelessly drunk. Shortly afterward, he left Oxford. After a visit with his father in Venice, he was induced to travel in Europe under the guidance of Samgrass.

The next Christmas, Charles was invited to Brideshead to see Sebastian, who returned from his tour. Sebastian told Charles that during their travels Samgrass had completely controlled their expense money so as to prevent Sebastian from using any for drink. Before coming down to Brideshead, however, Sebastian managed to circumvent Samgrass and get liquor by pawning his valuables and by borrowing. He had enjoyed what he called a happy Christmas; he remembered practically nothing of it. Lady Marchmain tried to stop his drinking by locking up all the liquor, but her efforts proved useless. Instead of going on a scheduled hunt, Sebastian borrowed two pounds from Charles and got drunk. Charles left Brideshead in disgrace and went to Paris. Samgrass also was dismissed when the whole story of the tour came out. Rex was given permission to take Sebastian to a doctor in Zurich, but Sebastian slipped away from him in Paris.

Rex, a wealthy man with a big name in political and financial circles, wanted Julia not only for herself but also for the prestige and social position of the Marchmains. Julia became engaged to him despite her mother's protests but agreed to keep the engagement secret for a year. Lord Marchmain gave his complete approval. Rex, wanting a large church wedding, agreed to become a Catholic. Shortly before the wedding, however, Bridey informed Julia that Rex was married once before and was divorced for six years. They were married in a Protestant ceremony.

When Charles returned to England several years later, Julia told him that Lady Marchmain was dying. At her request, Charles traveled to Fez to find Sebastian. When he arrived, Kurt, Sebastian's roommate, told him that Sebastian was in a hospital. Charles stayed in Fez until Sebastian recovered. Meanwhile, word arrived that Lady Marchmain had died. Charles returned to London. There, Bridey gave Charles his first commission: to paint the Marchmain town house before it was torn down.

Charles spent the next ten years developing his art. He married Celia, Boy Mulcaster's sister, and they had two children, Johnjohn and Caroline, the daughter born while Charles was exploring Central American ruins. After two years of trekking about in the jungles, he went to New York, where his wife met him. On their way back to London, they met Julia, and she and Charles fell in love. In London and at Brideshead, they continued the affair they began on the ship.

Two years later, Bridey announced that he planned to marry Beryl Muspratt, a widow with three children. When Julia suggested inviting Beryl down to meet the family, Bridey informed her that Beryl would not come because Charles and Julia were living there in sin. Julia became hysterical. She told Charles that she wanted to marry him, and they both made arrangements to obtain divorces.

Cordelia, who was working with an ambulance corps in Spain, returned at the end of the fighting there and told them of her visit with Sebastian. Kurt was seized by the Germans and taken back to Germany, where Sebastian followed him. After Kurt hanged himself in a concentration camp, Sebastian returned to Morocco and gradually drifted along the coast until he arrived at Carthage. He tried to enter a monastery there but was refused. Following one of his drinking bouts, the monks found him lying unconscious outside the gate and took him in. He planned to stay there as an underporter for the rest of his life.

While Bridey was making arrangements to settle at Brideshead after his marriage, Lord Marchmain announced that he was returning to the estate to spend his remaining days. He did not arrive until after he had seen Bridey and Beryl honeymooning in Rome. Having taken a dislike to Beryl, Lord Marchmain decided that he would leave Brideshead to Julia and Charles. Before long, Lord Marchmain's health began to fail. His children and Cara, thinking that he should be taken back into the Catholic Church, brought Father Mackay to visit him, but he would not see the priest. When he was dying, however, and Julia again brought Father Mackay to his bedside, Lord Marchmain made the sign of the cross. That day Julia told Charles what he had known all along—that she could not marry him because to do so would be living in sin and without God.

Critical Evaluation:

Evelyn Waugh's official biographer, Christopher Sykes, asserts that the author relied upon metaphor to a greater extent in *Brideshead Revisited* than he had ever done before. Sykes further suggests that metaphor can be a perilous device. A principal characteristic of this novel is certainly its richness of language, yet some critics regard the language as the novel's chief sin. Foremost among these detractors is Edmund Wilson, who profusely praised Waugh's earlier novels and described him as the greatest comic genius since George Bernard Shaw. In his review of *Brideshead Revisited*, however, Wilson claimed that the novel tends toward romanticism and sentimentalism. Critics who consider the structure of the novel to be its greatest flaw argue that too much of the novel is devoted to the Oxford section and too little to Ryder's crucial love affair with Julia. Still others dislike the tone set by the protagonist and first-person narrator, Charles Ryder, who strikes them as smug and snobbish.

Despite the adverse criticism the work received—far more than was leveled at any of Waugh's previous novels—*Brideshead Revisited* was easily the most popular of Waugh's books. It was so popular in America that it brought the author downright celebrity, a level of attention that, in the role of curmudgeon that he played from his middle years until his death, he claimed not to enjoy.

Political aspects of *Brideshead Revisited* were controversial. Certainly Waugh's portrayal of the incompetent Lieutenant Hooper, who complains constantly about the army's inefficiency but cannot be trusted to perform the simplest task, was interpreted as hostility toward the working class. Indeed, Waugh has Ryder state that he considers Hooper the symbol of Young England, a typical product of the awful age of the Common Man. Controversial, too, was the fact that *Brideshead Revisited* was regarded as the first novel in which Roman Catholicism is at the heart of the narrative.

The far-from-ideal Marchmain family is certainly a curious device if, as some have charged, Waugh's novel is indeed an apologia for Catholicism. Lord Marchmain has been separated from his wife for many years and lives with his mistress in Venice. Lady Marchmain is lovely, kind, and good, but she is also enigmatic. Her saintliness makes her into a kind of vampire, who unintentionally sucks the lifeblood from her husband and second son. The eldest child, heir to Lord Marchmain's title, is Brideshead (Bridey), who is as stolid as his younger brother is charming, irresponsible, and doomed. Sebastian becomes a hopeless alcoholic. Perhaps Lady Marchmain is intended to represent God's demands on Sebastian and his father; the harder they struggle against those demands, the more complete becomes their ruin. Julia, who willfully marries the abominable Rex Mottram, later, when she falls in love with Ryder, decides she cannot marry him because of the Church's prohibition of divorce. Cordelia, the youngest, who is devout in a natural, unaffected way, is the most normal.

In book 2, the Marchmains submit severally to God's will. After Lady Marchmain's death, Lord Marchmain—in the most roundly condemned scene of the novel—returns and experiences in the opulent Chinese drawing room a deathbed reconciliation with the Catholic faith. Bridey marches pompously on, unimaginatively practicing his Catholicism to the letter and marrying a middle-aged widow whom no one in the family likes but to whom he is "ardently attracted." Sebastian, overwhelmed and ravaged by alcoholism, ends up living the austere life of a porter in a monastery near Carthage. Julia remains the wife of the unloved and unlovable Rex. Cordelia is destined for a life of service and self-abnegation. Ryder gains a faith but loses the woman he loves. It is not possible to say that any of these characters achieves "happiness"; if Waugh was writing about the Catholic life, at least he did not err on the side of glamorizing its earthly rewards.

The charges of romanticism laid against the book center on the way Waugh treats Ryder's Oxford days and his love affair with Julia. While Waugh sometimes employs metaphor recklessly in the serious sections of the book, he shows an admirable restraint in the comic sections. The passages featuring Ryder in conversation with his eccentric father are among the funniest Waugh ever wrote.

The significance of Waugh's shift to the first-person narrative can hardly be overemphasized. Every theme in *Brideshead Revisited* is implicit in the earlier novels, as is every prejudice and every antipathy of the author. It is as if Waugh is not directly associated with the ideas of his narrator until the narrator becomes a character in the novel. Then such is the power of suggestion in the first-person narrative that Ryder suddenly reveals himself to be very like Waugh.

It would be misleading to suggest that the adverse criticism of *Brideshead Revisited* resulted merely from personal disapproval of the author's attitudes. The criticism concentrates on two major areas of weakness in the novel—its structure and its tone—both of which were considered areas of great strength in the preceding novels. Negative response to the novel's structure must have stung, for Waugh had every right to be proud of his skill in architectonics. His 1960 revision of the novel attests the fact that he came to take this criticism seriously.

The problems with the novel's tone must finally be attributed to the first-person narrator. In *Brideshead Revisited*, Waugh does, however, succeed in creating a style that allows him to do more than merely criticize the modern world he has been humorously denouncing for a decade and a half. The snobbish but sensitive artist who narrates *Brideshead Revisited* makes explicit the social, political, and religious attitudes that are merely implicit in the earlier novels. Waugh proves that he can easily master the conventions of the realistic novel, and through the device of his first-person narrator, he proves that he is not limited to the point of view of the detached (or frequently sardonic) narrator.

Critical opinion remains quite mixed on this best known of Waugh's novels. Some influential critics have judged the book an artistic failure, and there is evidence to suggest that Waugh himself came to the same conclusion. If *Brideshead Revisited* is a failure, however, it must be considered one of literature's most magnificent failures.

"Critical Evaluation" by Patrick Adcock

Further Reading

Bényei, Tamás. *Acts of Attention: Figure and Narrative in Postwar British Novels.* New York: Peter Lang, 1999. A poststructuralist interpretation of *Brideshead Revisited* and four other post-World War II British novels. Focuses on their narrative themes, including remembering, seduction, desire, and initiation.

Cook, William J., Jr. *Masks, Modes, and Morals: The Art of Evelyn Waugh.* Rutherford, N.J.: Fairleigh Dickinson University Press, 1971. A valuable source because Cook analyzes the point of view employed in each of the novels. It is a commonplace observation that Waugh's style changed in midcareer, just before publication of *Brideshead Revisited*; Cook argues that the altered point of view accounts for the stylistic change.

Davis, Robert M. "Imagined Space in *Brideshead Revisited*." In *Evelyn Waugh: New Directions*, edited by Alain Blayac. New York: St. Martin's Press, 1992. Confronts the problem of a sometimes unlikable narrator who is at the center of the entire novel.

Lygon, Lady Dorothy. "Madresfield and Brideshead." In *Evelyn Waugh and His World*, edited by David Pryce-Jones. Boston: Little, Brown, 1973. An essay by one of Waugh's intimate friends. Discusses the country house that was the model for the fictional Brideshead.

Patey, Douglas Lane. *The Life of Evelyn Waugh: A Critical Biography*. Cambridge, Mass.: Blackwell, 1998. Examines Waugh's life within the context of his work, providing critical assessments of his novels and other writings. Chapter 6 is devoted to *Brideshead Revisited*, and there are other references to the novel in the index.

Quennell, Peter. "A Kingdom of Cokayne." In *Evelyn Waugh and His World*, edited by David Pryce-Jones. Boston: Little, Brown, 1973. A reminiscence of the Waugh whom the author knew at Oxford. Provides excellent background information for the Oxford segment of *Brideshead Revisited*.

Villa Flor, Carlos, and Robert Murray Davis, eds. *Waugh Without End: New Trends in Evelyn Waugh Studies*. New York: Peter Lang, 2005. Collection of papers presented at a 2003 symposium during the centenary of Waugh's birth. Includes discussions of Waugh and Catholicism, his depiction of the English gentleman, and homosexual themes in works by Waugh and E. M. Forester. Several other essays examine *Brideshead Revisited*.

Waugh, Alexander. *Fathers and Sons: The Autobiography of a Family*. London: Headline, 2004. Alexander Waugh, the grandson of Evelyn, chronicles four generations of his family, focusing on its father-son conflicts and its literary achievements. Includes illustrations, bibliography, and index.

Wilson, Edmund. "Splendors and Miseries of Evelyn Waugh." In *Critical Essays on Evelyn Waugh*, edited by James F. Carens. Boston: G. K. Hall, 1987. After having praised the young Waugh as a comic genius, Wilson here reflects his disappointment with *Brideshead Revisited*.

The Bridge

Author: Hart Crane (1899-1932)
First published: 1930
Type of work: Poetry

A serious student of poetry during the 1920's, Hart Crane saw himself as one whose poetry would celebrate rather than denigrate the modern experience. His was to be a poetry of hope in the future and in the poet's ability to transcend shortcomings. He sought to counteract the cultural despair that was typified, particularly, in T. S. Eliot's influential *The Waste Land* (1922), a poem that Crane described as "good, but so damned dead."

Crane consciously intended *The Bridge* to provide an antidote to the spiritual despair of modern life by holding up to its readers, as the emblem of the modern world's own inspiriting accomplishments, John Augustus Roebling's great technical achievement, the Brooklyn Bridge, which was completed in 1883. Crane had first essayed the long poem form in the three-part "For the Marriage of Faustus and Helen" (1923), which utilizes jazz rhythms and a wide range of classical, biblical, and historical allusions in its exhortation to his contemporaries to "unbind our throats of fear and pity."

The initial idea for *The Bridge* was the direct result of Crane's insight that the contemporary world was the product, and therefore more likely the fulfillment rather than the negation, of the world's previous effort toward understanding. By 1924, Crane had, for inspiration, taken up residence in the same Columbia Heights apartment that Roebling had occupied during the bridge's construction. By then, too, Crane's circle of literary friends, among them fellow poets and critics Gorham Munson, Waldo Frank, and Allen Tate, anticipated the completion of Crane's great modernist epic with much the same excitement as he continuously shared its progress with them.

A sudden spurt of productivity occurred when the banker and art patron Otto Kahn advanced Crane one thousand dollars, with the promise of an additional one thousand dollars, so that he might leave his job as an advertising copywriter to devote his full attention to *The Bridge*. During the summer of 1926, on the Isle of Pines, off Cuba, Crane composed nearly half of the fifteen individual pieces that constitute the completed poem, including, along with the first three sections, "Cutty Sark," "Three Songs," and the final section, "Atlantis"—in sum, much of the poem's most lyrical passages as well as its visionary heart.

The work then became bogged down as a result of Crane's philosophical doubts after his having read Oswald Spengler's *Der Untergang des Abendlandes* (1918, 1922; *The Decline of the West*, 1926, 1928). Crane joined the American expatriate scene in Paris from December, 1928, to July, 1929, but rather than the experience serving as a source of renewed inspiration, he gained a considerable notoriety by indulging in assorted debaucheries. Back in New York, he finally completed *The Bridge*, which was published in a limited edition in Paris by the Black Sun Press in January, 1930, and by Liveright in New York in March.

The finished work might appear at first to be no more than a series of loosely connected individual poems, disparate in tone, voice, and style from one another. In fact, however, *The Bridge* is orchestrated much like a symphony, in which a progressive series of interrelated lyrics creates a narrative sequence that achieves greater intensity of vision as history and common experience give way to the mythic quest for an overarching identity and purpose—hence Crane's ruling metaphor of a bridge.

In the opening poem "To Brooklyn Bridge," the reader begins at the foot of that noteworthy structure in Manhattan, from there to be transported, in vision, back in time to the deck of the *Santa Maria* as Columbus, unbeknown even to himself, approaches the discovery of a new world.

The hero and speaker of *The Bridge* identifies openly with a "bedlamite" who "speeds to thy parapets," the only difference being that the hero knows that he must not make any literal leap but wait for the visionary moment to descend. The madman and the poet are the same, nevertheless, in spirit. Both recognize, as Columbus, yet another visionary, does in the poem's next section, "Ave Maria," that there will always be "still one shore beyond desire."

Part 2, "Powhatan's Daughter," a section composed of five individual poems, duplicates the poem's structure thus far by beginning again in a contemporary setting in "Harbor Dawn" but then moving back through time, locating literary and other historical landmarks. "Van Winkle" returns to the earlier New Amsterdam of the original Dutch settlers. "The River" takes the reader into the heartland of the continent in a collage of nineteenth century American folklore. "The Dance" recalls the Native American culture embodied in Powhatan's daughter, Pocahontas of Jamestown. She and John Smith become an American Helen and Faustus, the representative wedding of European yearnings with a na-tive Indian wisdom. "Indiana," the closing poem of part 2, sends their spiritual descendant, young Larry, the son of pioneers, off to sea. America returns its new spirit to the Old World.

Part 3, "Cutty Sark," characterizes this uniquely American contribution as the settlers' capacity to subdue not only nature by mastering a continent but also time and space. This section celebrates the speedy clipper ships by which the early settlers' descendants spread American commerce, and so the pervading influences of American culture, everywhere. The seagoing "bridge" formed by those vessels takes to the air in part 4, "Cape Hatteras," an appropriate venue since it is not only a hazard for shipping but also the locale from which Wilbur and Orville Wright's heavier-than-air vessel took off in 1903.

In part 5, "Three Songs," there is a momentary lyric interlude in praise of the female, left behind in the closing section of "Powhatan's Daughter." Venus, Eve, and Magdalen, she is ultimately reincarnated in "Virginia" in both the fated Indian princess Pocahontas and the Judeo-Christian tradition's Mary.

A sort of quiescent domesticity is established as the energies that tamed a continent subside, and so part 6, "Quaker Hill," conveys, as the name implies (although the ghosts of Emily Dickinson and Isadora Duncan inhabit its pages), the placid suburban neatness of middle-class America. That surface quiet is deceptive, however, and part 7, "The Tunnel," is part 6's necessary companion piece, a descent, via the New York subway, into the sprawling urban nightmare that has also become, by Crane's time, another part of the American experience. There the reader meets another ghost from America's literary and mythic past, Edgar Allan Poe.

Naturally, this darkest hour is just before the visionary dawn, and this subway ride, for all its urban squalor and inchoate terror, stops in the Battery at the Brooklyn Bridge, site of Walt Whitman's old Brooklyn Ferry, and part 8, "Atlantis," concludes where the epic hero began, by rising out of the darkness of the urban nightmare into the bright nightlife of a modern city enlightened by the sight of the Brooklyn Bridge: "Through the bound cable strands, the arching path/ Upward, veering with light, the flight of strings. . . ." The hero-speaker has arrived back where he started, immeasurably wiser for the experience of spiritually living his nation's becoming. He hopes to see the fulfillment of the old European dream of Atlantis, the perfected human community. Columbus had, after all, sought a better world. The poet has already told the reader that there will always be that one shore beyond desire, and so the hero can only wonder if he has indeed reached the vision's source.

This concludes Crane's *The Bridge*, and there is perhaps no more sustained or ambitious a lyric undertaking from Crane's time. *The Bridge* has, nevertheless, generally been received as a flawed epic, grander in the scope of its design and of its central metaphor of America as the dynamic bridge between the past and the future than in the fulfillment of its execution. Crane later would comment, "So many true things have a way of coming out all the better without the strain to sum up the universe in one impressive little pellet."

Crane, committed to the visionary aspects of poetry, settled on an apotheosis of the American experience as a theme equal to his talents and ambitions. What Crane accomplishes, however, rather than a vision of America, is a vision of the poet as the dreamer who will not give up his dream, even if its realization is private or obscure. It is Crane's hero's recognition of these vulnerabilities, of the fact that he lets the world make a fool out of him, that realizes his heroism.

Crane apparently committed suicide by leaping into the Atlantic Ocean somewhere north of Cuba on April 24, 1932. Although he was only thirty-two, he thought himself a failure and a has-been. His poetic achievement fell far short of his aims, but his aims for his masterwork, *The Bridge*, were quite lofty. Its poetry continues to echo in the American experience.

Russell Elliott Murphy

Further Reading

Brunner, Edward. *Splendid Failure: Hart Crane and the Making of "The Bridge."* Champaign: University of Illinois Press, 1985. Despite its title, this work sets out to disprove the conventional wisdom that Crane's was a largely undisciplined and reckless talent. Brunner maintains that *The Bridge* is the culmination of Crane's continuing effort to hone his craft.

Clark, David R., ed. *Studies in "The Bridge."* Westerville, Ohio: Charles E. Merrill, 1970. A compilation of fourteen essays, providing a road map of critical responses to the poem virtually from the time of its publication to the 1960's. Most of the major commentators are represented.

Cole, Merrill. "Perversion's Permanent Target: Hart Crane and the Uses of Memory." In *The Other Orpheus: A Poetics of Modern Homosexuality.* New York: Routledge, 2003. Cole argues that male homoeroticism must be considered in order to attain a comprehensive understanding of modernism and male identity. He explores how homoeroticism functions in the work of Crane and other poets.

Crane, Hart. *The Letters of Hart Crane, 1916-1932.* Edited by Brom Weber. Berkeley: University of California Press, 1952. Crane was an astute critic of his own work and that of others. His letters offer many insights into *The Bridge*.

Fisher, Clive. *Hart Crane: A Life.* New Haven, Conn.: Yale University Press, 2002. Fisher's meticulously researched and detailed biography presents a vivid portrait of Crane's life and the times in which he lived.

Guy-Bray, Stephen. *Loving in Verse: Poetic Influence as Erotic.* Toronto, Ont.: University of Toronto Press, 2006. Focuses on Crane's use of his predecessor, Walt Whitman, to write *The Bridge*. Guy-Bray maintains that the poem depicts Crane and Whitman's relationship as that of a gay couple.

Mariani, Paul L. *The Broken Tower: A Life of Hart Crane.* New York: W. W. Norton, 1999. When this book first appeared, some critics hailed it as the first sympathetic account of Crane's homosexuality and the place of his gayness in his poetry. Mariani's biography also provides other previously unpublished insights into Crane's life and work.

Paul, Sherman. *Hart's Bridge.* Champaign: University of Illinois Press, 1972. The first book-length treatment of Crane's masterwork. *The Bridge* required Crane to achieve the maturity of vision and technique required of epic poetry.

Reed, Brian. *Hart Crane: After His Lights.* Tuscaloosa: University of Alabama Press, 2006. An examination of all of Crane's poetry from the perspective of poststructuralism and other developments in humanities scholarship since the mid-1990's. Includes analysis of the poems' composition, sources, and models, and measures Crane's influence on subsequent American poets, including the Black Mountain School and the Beats.

Tapper, Gordon A. *The Machine That Sings: Modernism, Hart Crane, and the Culture of the Body.* New York: Routledge, 2006. Examines Hart's poetry in relationship to the modernist preoccupation with the animal nature of the human body. Tapper argues that Hart represented the body as both a "surface inscribed by history" and a source for renewing one's animality. Chapters 2-4 are devoted to analysis of *The Bridge*.

The Bridge of San Luis Rey

Author: Thornton Wilder (1897-1975)
First published: 1927
Type of work: Novel
Type of plot: Philosophical realism
Time of plot: Early eighteenth century
Locale: Peru

Principal characters:
BROTHER JUNIPER, a Spanish friar
THE MARQUESA DE MONTEMAYOR, a lonely old woman
PEPITA, her maid
THE ABBESS MADRE MARÍA DEL PILAR, the director of the
    Convent of Santa María Rosa de las Rosas
UNCLE PIO, an actor-manager
LA PÉRICHOLE, an actress
MANUEL, a foundling
ESTEBAN, his brother

The Story:

On Friday, July 20, 1714, the bridge of San Luis Rey, the most famous bridge in Peru, collapses, hurling five travelers into the deep gorge below. Present at the time of the tragedy is Brother Juniper, who sees in the event a chance to prove, scientifically and accurately, the wisdom of that act of God. He spends all his time investigating the lives of the five who had died, and he publishes a book showing that God had a reason to send each one of them to his or her death at exactly that moment. The book is condemned by the church authorities, and Brother Juniper is burned at the stake. He went too far in explaining God's ways to humanity. Through a strange quirk of fate, one copy of the book is left undestroyed, and it falls into the hands of the author. From it, and from his own knowledge, he reconstructs the lives of the five persons.

The Marquesa de Montemayor was an ugly child and was still homely when she matured. Because of the wealth of her family, she was fortunately able to marry a noble husband, by whom she had a lovely daughter, Doña Clara. As she grew into a beautiful young woman, the Marquesa's daughter became more and more disgusted with her crude and unattractive mother, whose possessive and overexpressive love left Doña Clara cold and uncomfortable. The daughter finally married a man who took her to Spain. Separated from her one joy in life, the Marquesa became more eccentric than ever and spent her time writing long letters to her daughter in Spain. In order to free herself of some of her household cares, the Marquesa went to the Abbess Madre María del Pilar and asked for a girl from the Abbess's school to come and live with her, so Pepita, unhappy that her beloved teacher was sending her away from school, went to live with the Marquesa.

When the Marquesa learned by letter that Doña Clara was to have a child, she was filled with concern. She wore charms, bought candles for the saints, said prayers, and wrote all the advice she could discover to her daughter. As a last gesture, she took Pepita with her to pay a visit to a famous shrine from which she hoped her prayers would surely be heard. On the way, the Marquesa happened to read one of Pepita's letters to her old mistress, the Abbess. From the letter, the Marquesa learns just how heartless she was in her treatment of the girl, how thoughtless and egotistic. She realized that she was guilty of the worst kind of love toward her daughter, love that was sterile, self-seeking, and false. Aglow with her new understanding, she wrote a final letter to her daughter, telling her of the change in her heart, asking forgiveness, and showing in wonderful language the change that came over her. She resolved to change her life, to be kind to Pepita, to her household, to everyone. The next day she and Pepita, while crossing the bridge of San Luis Rey, fell to their deaths.

Esteban and Manuel were twin brothers who were left as children on the doorstep of the Abbess's school. She brought them up as well as she could, but the strange relationship between them was such that she could never make them talk much. When the boys were old enough, they left the school and took many kinds of jobs. At last they settled down as scribes, writing letters for the uncultured people of Lima. One day Manuel, called in to write some letters for La Périchole, fell in love with the charming actress. Never before did anything come between the brothers, because they were always sufficient in themselves. For his brother's sake, Manuel pretended that he cared little for the actress. Shortly afterward, he cut his leg on a piece of metal and became very sick. In his delirium, he let Esteban know that he really was in love with La Périchole. The infection grew worse and Manuel died.

Esteban was unable to do anything for weeks after his brother's death. He could not face life without him. The Abbess finally arranged for him to go on a trip with a sea captain who was about to sail around the world. The captain had lost his only daughter, and the Abbess believed he would understand Esteban's problem and try to help him. Esteban left to go aboard ship, but on the way, he fell with the others when the bridge broke.

In Spain, before he came to Peru, Uncle Pio found a young girl singing in a tavern. After years of his coaching and training, she became the most popular actress of the Spanish world. She was called La Périchole, and Uncle Pio's greatest pleasure was to tease her and anger her into giving consistently better performances. All went well until the viceroy took an interest in the vivacious and beautiful young actress. When she became his mistress, she began to feel that the stage was too low for her. After living as a lady and becoming prouder and prouder as time passed, she contracted small-pox. Her beauty was ruined, and she retired to a small farm outside town to live a life of misery over her lost loveliness.

Uncle Pio had a true affection for his former protégé and tried time and again to see her. One night, by a ruse, he got her to talk to him. She refused to let him help her, but she allowed him to take Jaime, her illegitimate son, so that he could be educated as a gentleman. The old man and the young boy set off for Lima. On the way, they came to the bridge and died in the fall when it collapsed.

At the cathedral in Lima, a great service is held for the victims. Everyone considers the incident an example of a true act of God, and many reasons are offered for the various deaths. Some months after the funeral, the Abbess is visited by Doña Clara, the Marquesa's daughter. Doña Clara finally learns what a wonderful woman her mother was. The last letter teaches the cynical daughter all that her mother so painfully learned. The daughter, too, learned to see life in a new way. La Périchole also comes to see the Abbess. She gives up bemoaning her own lost beauty, and she begins a lasting friendship with the Abbess. Nothing can positively be said about the reason for the deaths of those five people on the bridge. Too many events are changed by them; one cannot number them all. The old Abbess, however, believes that the true meaning of the disaster is the lesson of love for those who survive.

Critical Evaluation:

The Bridge of San Luis Rey marked the beginning of a key stage in Thornton Wilder's development and also revealed the essential dimensions of the artistic program he would follow. His first novel, *The Cabala* (1926), had viewed the decadent aristocracy of contemporary Rome through the eyes of a young American student. In the tradition of Henry James and Edith Wharton, the highly autobiographical work suffered by comparison and was not praised by the critics. *The Bridge of San Luis Rey*, however, which vividly evokes a forgotten era and a type of society utterly foreign to Wilder's experi-

ence, sold three hundred thousand copies in its first year and made its author a celebrity. This success confirmed Wilder's intention to make abundant use of historical materials, and he set his next novel, *The Woman of Andros* (1930), in postclassical Greece. *The Bridge of San Luis Rey* also served notice that a major philosophical and theological writer had entered the literary scene. The engaging simplicity of the book drew its readers toward problems no less recondite than those of the justice of God, the possibility of disinterested love, and the role of memory in human relationships. Wilder's subsequent works consistently returned to these themes.

The Christianity that inspires and informs *The Bridge of San Luis Rey* is existential and pessimistic. "Only one reader in a thousand notices that I have asserted a denial of the survival of identity after death," Wilder once remarked of the book. He also denied the value of the apologetic task that Brother Juniper undertakes. Even if human reason could scientifically demonstrate God's Providence—a proposition Wilder rejects—humanity would inevitably employ this knowledge in a self-aggrandizing manner. The inherent mystery of the divine intention is a check to human pride, and pride is Wilder's overriding concern, especially that pride which cloaks itself in the guise of unselfish love. If there is Providence, Wilder suggests, it most clearly operates as something that exposes the egoistic taint in all love and reveals to the lover his need to be forgiven both by the one he loves and by the social community.

Despite the ostensible importance of Brother Juniper, Uncle Pio, and Esteban, only Wilder's female characters develop sufficiently to gain awareness of the meaning of the novel's action. The Marquesa undergoes the clearest transformation. The maternal love that she cultivates so assiduously is neither spontaneous nor generous. Rather, the Marquesa craves her daughter's affection as an antidote to her own insecurity. Her imagination first magnifies the daughter's virtues and prestige; then, to assuage a deep self-loathing, she demands from her a meticulous and servile devotion. Although the Marquesa is aware of her manipulative impulses, she is nevertheless powerless to conquer them. She is not aware of how her distorted passion causes misery to those around her. The revelation of Pepita's agonized loneliness shames and humiliates her, but she thereby gains the strength to eliminate the element of tyranny in the love she bears for her daughter.

Because La Périchole (Camila) appears in each of the three tales, she is the novel's most real character. Her satirical attack on the Marquesa becomes ironic when, later on, her own ugliness and avarice also make her the object of gossip and scorn. Like the Marquesa, she does not believe herself to be intrinsically valuable. However, Uncle Pio, who first treats Camila as someone to dominate and in whom to take aesthetic delight, now loves her unconditionally. Her willingness to accept this fact and to express her love causes him to suffer and isolates her unnaturally from society. Such a painful yet liberating acceptance is made possible both by Pio's persistence and by La Périchole's love for Jaime. Her grief, and the possibility of disinterested love that it implies, moves her at last to present her disfigured self to society.

Even though her moral insight makes the Abbess the standard against which all in the novel are measured, she, too, must suffer and grow. Unlike the abstract and detached Brother Juniper, she makes herself vulnerable to the pains that love and service involve. Unlike the Marquesa, she does not demand instant expressions of servile devotion from those who love her. She does, however, yearn to have her work remembered, to gain that (in Wilder's view, illusory) immortality that comes to those who labor for great causes. Consequently, she manipulates Pepita much as Uncle Pio manipulates Camila. That Pepita dies lonely and forsaken reveals to the Abbess the results of her misguided passion. Her faith undergoes a purification when she confronts the fact that "Even memory is not necessary for love."

The episode of Esteban and Manuel does not fit neatly into the pattern Wilder generally establishes. Some critics have suggested that Wilder here means to deal with homosexual love. This view is partially refuted by the heterosexual activity of both youths and by Esteban's evident unwillingness to stand between Manuel and Camila. Does Esteban, however, unconsciously attempt to retain possession of his brother, communicating his feelings through the uncanny channels of sympathy that bind these twins? Even if this were so, there remains the fact that Manuel is also unable to conceive of a separation. The tale thus seems to constitute a digression, one that serves to underscore the enormous mystery and intensity of all relationships of love. It is linked to the central thematic pattern by Esteban's deep feelings for the Abbess, which enable him to reach out to another human being despite his tragic sorrow.

For Wilder, it is almost impossible for human beings to live serenely and faithfully knowing that their personalities will neither be remembered by society nor allowed to survive death in a hereafter. This prospect creates an anxiety that pervades all their efforts to love. They persistently use the beloved to prove themselves worthy and immortal. Then to love are added additional, degrading elements. People never realize, in the Abbess's words, that "the love will have been enough." Wilder's views could have led him to enormous

sentimentality, but, in truth, *The Bridge of San Luis Rey* is extraordinarily stark. It is sustained only by the single hope that "all those impulses of love return to the love that made them."

"Critical Evaluation" by Leslie E. Gerber

Further Reading

Anderson, M. Y. *"The Bridge of San Luis Rey": A Critical Commentary.* New York: American R. D. M., 1966. Provides concise background details on Wilder and effective commentary about the novel's plot structure, characterizations, and major themes.

Blank, Martin, Dalma Hunyadi Brunauer, and David Garrett Izzo, eds. *Thornton Wilder: New Essays.* West Cornwall, Conn.: Locust Hill Press, 1999. Collection of essays which discuss both the novels and plays. Some of the essays examine Wilder's legacy and achievement; Wilder's use of myth; point of view, human relatedness, and narrative technique in his novels; and his defense of the classical novel.

Bryer, Jackson R., ed. *Conversations with Thornton Wilder.* Jackson: University Press of Mississippi, 1992. A collection of interviews with Wilder, providing interesting perspectives on the man and his literary works. Includes index.

Burbank, Rex J. *Thornton Wilder.* New York: Twayne, 1961. An insightful introduction to Wilder and his writings. Explores the humanism of *The Bridge of San Luis Rey* and concludes that this novel, despite weaknesses, "has all the intellectual scope, depth of feeling, and complexity of character that make a mature and aesthetically satisfying vision."

Castronovo, David. *Thornton Wilder.* New York: Ungar, 1986. An excellent brief introduction to Wilder and his works. Sees *The Bridge of San Luis Rey* as a study "of isolation and chaos" which attempts to show how "to rise above the disasters of the modern world into a sustaining, if not always clear, spirituality."

Harrison, Gilbert A. *The Enthusiast: A Life of Thornton Wilder.* New Haven, Conn.: Ticknor and Fields, 1983. Includes important information about the writing of *The Bridge of San Luis Rey*, as well as emphasizing its purpose, reception, and contribution.

Konkle, Lincoln. *Thornton Wilder and the Puritan Narrative Tradition.* Columbia: University of Missouri Press, 2006. Wilder was the descendent of Puritans, and Konkle argues that the writer inherited the Puritans' worldview, particularly the Calvinist aesthetic, and drew upon it to create his novels and plays. Includes chronology, bibliography, and index.

The Bridge on the Drina

Author: Ivo Andrić (1892-1975)
First published: Na Drini ćuprija, 1945 (English translation, 1959)
Type of work: Novel
Type of plot: Historical realism
Time of plot: 1516-1914
Locale: Višegrad, Bosnia

Principal characters:
MEHMED PASHA SOKOLLI, a grand vizier
ABIDAGA, the first builder of the bridge
ALIHODJA MUTEVELIĆ, hodja and shopkeeper
LOTTE ZAHLER, an innkeeper
SALKO CORKAN, a Roma (Gypsy)

The Story:

The "blood tribute" is a most cruel practice of the Turkish rulers during the several hundred years of their occupation of the Balkans. It means taking young boys away from their parents and rearing them as the sultan's obedient servants, called janissaries. One of the boys, taken from a Serbian village called Sokolovici in Bosnia in 1516 when he is only ten years old, will later become Mehmed Pasha Sokolli and rise to the office of the grand vizier, the highest position a non-Turk can reach in the Ottoman Empire. In memory of his childhood, he decides to build a bridge across the Drina River by the town of Višegrad, the last place where he saw his mother when he was taken away and where he feels a sharp pain in his breast as the last memory of his home.

The building of the bridge begins in 1566. The first builder, Abidaga, is famous for his efficiency and the strict, at times cruel, methods of accomplishing his tasks. The bridge is built by slave labor conscripted from the nearby Serbian villages. The peasants resent having to work as slaves, and they see in the building of the bridge a sinister symbol of Turkish might. For that reason, they sabotage the bridge's progress, often destroying at night what is built during the day. To frighten the distrusting and rebellious populace into submission and obedience, Abidaga catches one of them, Radisav, and has him impaled on the site of the bridge. The excruciatingly painful process of his death lasts several days.

The bridge is finally completed in 1571, a beautiful structure of eleven arches rising above the turbulent Drina, with the *kapia*, an elevated fixture in the middle of the bridge where people can sit, as a focal point. A caravansary is also built next to the bridge for tired travelers. Thus begins the bridge's long influence on every aspect of life for the people on the shores as they finally resign themselves to the bridge, learning to like it because of its usefulness and its uncommon beauty. Mehmed Pasha is stabbed to death by a deranged dervish only a few years after the construction, without having seen the object of his dreams fully completed. As he is dying, he feels again a sharp pain in his breast. Although he accomplishes many other things as a vezir, his name in Bosnia will forever be remembered by this bridge.

Years and decades pass, life keeps changing, the floods come, and the Muslims, the Christians, and the Jews mingle, but the bridge survives everything, shining "clean, young and unalterable, strong and lovely in its perfection, stronger than all that time might bring and men imagine to do." As Serbia begins to rise against the Turks at the beginning of the nineteenth century, the bridge witnesses the beheading of two Serbs, Jelisije and Mile, at the *kapia* as a warning to the rebels—the first of many acts of intimidation and revenge. However, the bridge remains unchanged and unchangeable. The Turks withdraw gradually from Serbia between 1825 and 1850, cholera and plague visit the inhabitants on the shores, and the unquiet waters keep passing beneath the bridge's smooth and perfect arches, but nothing changes the bridge itself. It becomes a focal point of life in the town and surrounding villages. A beautiful young girl named Fata jumps from the *kapia* to her death during her wedding procession because her father is about to force her to marry a man whom she does not love. When Bosnia is placed under the Austrian protectorate, Alihodja Mutevelić, a shopkeeper, is nailed by his ear at the *kapia* by his town rival because he does not believe that the Austrians would come or that the people of Višegrad should resist them if they did.

The Austrian presence brings important changes in Višegrad and to the bridge as the new begins to replace the old. Trees are cut down and new ones planted, streets are repaired, drainage canals are dug, public buildings are constructed, permanent lighting is installed, and a railway is built. The caravansary is rebuilt into an army barracks, and the bridge itself seems to be forgotten. The *kapia*, however, continues to witness interesting events. For the first time, women are allowed to sit on it. Milan Glasicanin, an inveterate gambler, is cured of his vice by being challenged to gamble for his life by a mysterious gambling partner. Gregor Fedun, a young sentry from Galicia, commits suicide after having been tricked by two Serbian rebels, one of them a beautiful girl, into allowing them to cross the bridge. Salko Corkan, a powerful young Roma, dances precariously on the bridge railing and almost falls to his death after a drinking bout and the unsuccessful wooing of a girl. Lotte, a Galician Ashkenazi, builds a hotel next to the bridge, bringing a new aspect to life around the bridge.

The Austrian annexation of Bosnia in 1908 ushers in yet another new age and more changes. The bridge is mined in case a war with neighboring Serbia begins. The Serbian triumphs in the Balkan Wars bring new hopes for the Serbian population and fears for the Muslims. Most important, the new generation of young people gathers regularly around the *kapia* and holds endless discussions about the current events, reflecting a sharp rise in nationalistic feelings, as they defend their nationalist points of view. As Lotte's fortunes decline and the young Serbian teachers Zorka and Glasicanin dream of emigrating to America, the first bombs of World War I fall on the bridge. However, the bridge still stands between the two warring sides. When it is finally destroyed, it takes along Alihodja as a witness of the centuries-old history of the town, the people, and the bridge itself.

Critical Evaluation:

Ivo Andrić, a leading Yugoslav writer for four decades and the only Nobel Prize winner among the southern Slav writers, was always interested in his native Bosnia, and many of his works have Bosnia as a background. *The Bridge on the Drina* is a perfect example. The story of the bridge can be seen as a survey of Bosnian history between 1516 and 1914.

The story is completely historical. As a lifelong diplomat of the kingdom of Yugoslavia, Andrić was also an astute student of history, and he often studied historical facts and documents in preparation for the writing of his works. Even his doctoral thesis, "The Development of the Spiritual Life of Bosnia Under the Influence of Turkish Sovereignty" (1924), reveals his passion for history; it also served him well while writing this novel and other works. *The Bridge on the Drina* encompasses the entire period of the Turkish rule of the Balkans, mirroring the birth and death of the Ottoman occupation of Bosnia. It is a broadly conceived panorama of cultural changes brought about by the Turkish reign and of the multicultural and multireligious nation resulting from it. It also depicts the inevitable and multifaceted conflicts of the area. The novel is, therefore, a good source of general information about Bosnia, although not a substitute for a scholarly history.

On a personal level, *The Bridge on the Drina* serves its au-

thor as a tribute to his childhood. As a little boy, he was brought to Višegrad after the death of his father and left there by his mother to live with relatives. It is no wonder that the mentor of the bridge, Mehmed Pasha Sokolli, ordered the bridge built as a memory of his childhood. Thus, the story of the bridge embodies a return to one's roots and a monument to one's childhood.

Another symbolic connotation of the bridge lies in its long life, outlasting many generations and all the changes through the centuries since its construction. Andrić concludes no fewer than twelve chapters out of twenty-four with a short paragraph extolling the bridge as a symbol of the permanence of all life. Considering the constant changes taking place around the bridge, its permanence serves as a comforting and life-affirming value.

Andrić imparts yet another symbolic meaning to the bridge by calling it a thing of beauty, a reflection of humanity's age-old desire to create beauty and to enrich life. The inborn need of humanity to express itself in the arts found its fulfillment in the creation of this beautiful edifice that defies transience.

The final symbolic interpretation of the bridge lies in its spanning of the two shores, as if connecting two worlds, the east and the west, and the different nationalities, religions, and cultures of Bosnia. Himself a diplomat who saw the main key to success in the art of compromise, Andrić uses the metaphor of the bridge to underline the need for minimizing differences for the sake of living in harmony. The tragic events of Bosnia over the centuries clearly show what happens when this plea for harmony goes unheeded. In this sense, *The Bridge on the Drina* manifests an eerie mystical quality uncommon for a work of literature.

Andrić's narrative is characterized by a measured realistic style, reflecting the stoic firmness and beauty of the bridge. Nevertheless, beneath that calm exterior, life manifests itself in many forms and events are never static. As his translator, Lovett F. Edwards, notes, Andrić's style has "the sweep and surge of the sea, slow and yet profound, with occasional flashes of wit and irony." The novel is unusual in that it covers a long period of time, making it difficult to concentrate on character development. The episodic nature of narration, however, lends itself to the creation of individual pieces that stand by themselves. When put together, they create a remarkable mosaic, echoing the principal message of Andrić's entire philosophy that life is an incomprehensible miracle that is constantly being consumed and eroded, yet one that lasts and stands firmly like the bridge on the Drina.

Vasa D. Mihailovich

Further Reading

Bergman, Gun. *Turkisms in Ivo Andrić's "Na Drini ćuprija" Examined from the Point of View of Literary Style.* Uppsala, Sweden: Almqvist & Wiksell, 1969. The author examines the use of Turkisms in *The Bridge on the Drina* from both the linguistic and the literary point of view.

Goy, E. D. "The Work of Ivo Andrić." *Slavonic and East European Review* 41 (1963): 301-326. One of the best introductions to Andrić in English. Goy dwells on the main points in Andrić's life and creativity, specifying in each work its most important characteristics. In *The Bridge on the Drina*, for example, Andrić has solved the dilemma of existence through the beauty of creation.

Hawkesworth, Celia. *Ivo Andrić: Bridge Between East and West.* London: Athlone Press, 1984. An excellent overall portrait of Andrić the man and the writer. The author discusses in detail every important feature of his works, underlining the importance of *The Bridge on the Drina* as his seminal work.

Mihailovich, Vasa D. "The Reception of the Works of Ivo Andrić in the English-Speaking World." *Southeastern Europe* 9 (1982): 41-52. A survey of articles and reviews on Andrić in English through 1980. Useful for both beginners and established scholars.

Mukerji, Vanita Singh. *Ivo Andrić: A Critical Biography.* New York: McFarland, 1990. Another general introduction to Andrić. Not as significant and exhaustive as Hawkesworth's volume but still useful for finding out about the basic features of Andrić's works.

Vucinich, Wayne S., ed. *Ivo Andrić Revisited: The Bridge Still Stands.* Berkeley: University of California Press, 1995. Essays on Andrić and his times, his short stories, his view of Yugoslavia and of history, Bosnian identity in his work, and his handling of grief and shame, women, the folk tradition, and narrative voice. Includes notes and index but no bibliography. Vucinich's introduction is the place to begin a study of Andrić's role in the history of Yugoslavia and its literary traditions.

Wachtel, Andrew B. "Ivan Meštović, Ivo Andrić, and the Synthetic Yugoslav Culture of the Interwar Period." In *Yugoslavism: Histories of a Failed Idea, 1918-1992*, edited by Dejan Djokič. London: Hurst, 2003. The essay about Andrić is part of an examination of Yugoslavian history, from the country's creation in 1918 to its dissolution in the early 1990's. The book demonstrates how the concept of "Yugoslavia" differed at various times and was interpreted differently among the various Yugoslavian nations, leaders, and social groups.

A Brief History of Time
From the Big Bang to Black Holes

Author: Stephen Hawking (1942-   )
First published: 1988
Type of work: Science

Stephen Hawking's popularization of modern cosmology, *A Brief History of Time: From the Big Bang to Black Holes,* made publishing history (and the *Guinness Book of Records*) when it remained on the London *Times'* best-seller list for more than four years, much longer than any previous book. It was also extraordinarily successful in the United States and other countries and was translated into more than sixty languages. For a work dealing with abstruse astrophysical concepts to sell more than nine million copies was surprising, even to its author. Variously characterized as a landmark in scientific writing and the most popular scientific text of all time, it was also chosen as one of the one hundred most important books of the twentieth century, and a Cambridge Uni-

versity poll ranked it as the book "most likely" to have the same influence as Charles Darwin's *On the Origin of Species by Means of Natural Selection: Or, The Preservation of Favoured Races in the Struggle for Life* (1859).

Because of the phenomenal success of *A Brief History of Time*, Hawking published a series of corrected, updated, and expanded editions, including a tenth-anniversary edition and an illustrated edition with more than 240 photographs, diagrams, and computer-generated images. An abridged and simplified version was published in 2005. American film director Steven Spielberg, who had met Hawking, produced Errol Morris's successful documentary *A Brief History of Time*, released in 1991, which documented Hawking's life and accomplishments. The film's success led to the publication of a reader's companion to the film and book. The success of the companion in turn led to a six-part television miniseries, *Stephen Hawking's Universe*, first televised in 1997. In 2008, *The Illustrated A Brief History of Time* was combined with the illustrated version of Hawking's *The Universe in a Nutshell* (2001), demonstrating the book's continuing popularity.

Critics, scholars, and even Hawking's mother developed various explanations for the book's exceptional success. Hawking's publisher, who had warned him that every mathematical equation included in the text would halve the book's sales, felt that the absence of mathematics—with the exception of Albert Einstein's famous expression of the relationship between matter and energy—played a role in the book's popularity. Some commentators attributed the book's prodigious sales to the author's genuine talent for using similes, analogies, and humor to make complex mathematical and physical ideas understandable to lay readers. Others thought that, like Einstein, Hawking was able to communicate to ordinary readers his childlike wonder over the mysteries of the universe and the joy of discovering the solutions to some of these mysteries.

More controversially, a few critics admonished the book's publisher for exploiting Hawking's disabilities for commercial purposes. For most of his life, Hawking has suffered an increasingly debilitating case of amyotrophic lateral sclerosis, which requires him to use a wheelchair (as depicted on the front of the book's dust jacket). His mother responded that her son's ability to overcome his handicaps and become a very successful scientist and science popularizer served as an example of inspiration, not exploitation. Hawking himself has stated that he wrote the book, which took him over five years, to help provide for his family, especially for the education of his children.

In *A Brief History of Time*, Hawking tries to answer certain basic questions that nonscientists have about the universe. For example, how did it originate, how will it end, how is it structured, and is it finite or infinite? To communicate how modern scientists answer these questions, Hawking uses two fundamental theories: general relativity and quantum mechanics. General relativity is Einstein's theory, involving innovative ideas of space, time, matter, and gravity that enabled him and others to deepen their understanding of the large-scale structure of the universe. Quantum mechanics, developed by the German physicist Werner Heisenberg and others, enabled scientists to understand puzzling phenomena at the subatomic level. Like all theories, relativity and quantum mechanics are provisional. They are not even

consistent with each other. Nevertheless, they superseded the model of matter and the universe that had been formulated by Sir Isaac Newton, whose mathematical description of gravity as a mutual attractive force was able to account for the elliptical orbits of the planets and many other physical phenomena. Hawking, who, like Newton, was Lucasian Professor of Mathematics at Cambridge University, strongly identified with his predecessor's quest to determine the basic laws of the universe.

This quest for fundamentals also characterized the career of Einstein, who, after postulating that physical laws remained invariant in uniformly moving systems, rejected Newton's belief in absolute space, time, and simultaneity, because all three depend on the relative speed of an observer. Using the equivalence between gravity and acceleration, Einstein also formulated a general theory of relativity that applied even to nonuniformly moving systems, but, in what he later called the greatest blunder of his career, he modified his equations to account for what astronomers then assumed to be a static universe. However, in 1929, the American astronomer Edwin Hubble made observations that indicated that the universe is dynamic, or expanding. By extrapolating this expansion backward in time, other scientists formulated a theory of the universe's origin that was called the "big bang," in which a cosmic explosion of superdense matter about twelve billion years ago resulted in the cosmos observed today.

Hawking, using the mathematics of general relativity, proved that the universe had to have a beginning in what he termed a "singularity," an infinitesimally small point in space-time at which matter is compressed into an unimaginably dense state. In his book, Hawking discusses inflation, a theory describing the sudden expansion of this compressed matter within a fraction of a second of the universe's beginning. The way he discussed how credit should be assigned for certain aspects of this inflationary model proved seriously damaging to the reputation of a young scientist, and he changed the offending passage in the next edition of his book.

Because Hawking's most significant achievements have been in the field of black holes, he devotes the central chapters of his book to an investigation of them and their properties. He defines a black hole as a region of colossally compressed matter whose gravitational force is so strong that nothing, not even light particles, can escape it. When Hawking first began to study black holes, considerable uncertainty prevailed about their actual existence, but most astronomers came to agree with him that black holes exist not only in the Milky Way galaxy but in other galaxies as well. Observations made with the Hubble telescope indicate that extremely large black holes may exist at the centers of quasars, staggeringly distant objects that are many times brighter than all the stars in the Milky Way galaxy.

In the 1970's, Hawking began thinking about ways of distinguishing space-time points both within and outside a black hole. The boundary, or "event horizon," of a black hole designates the "point of no return" between this hole and the outside universe. By investigating this event horizon, Hawking found that "black holes ain't so black" (the title of one of his chapters). He then used quantum ideas to study the behavior of particles just outside the event horizon and made the surprising discovery that a black hole could emit subatomic particles. Now called "Hawking radiation," these ejected particles mean that black holes lose mass—large black holes very slowly, small black holes very rapidly. (Hawking also did important work on such "mini-black holes.") As a black hole loses matter and energy, its event horizon gradually contracts, leading to an important question about information and black holes. Hawking believed that when matter is compressed into a black hole, the result is the loss of all its information, such as mass, charge, and so on. Other scientists attacked this view, which Hawking continued to defend in later editions of his book, but in 2004 he finally admitted that he had been wrong. He was converted to the view that information about a black hole's matter can filter to the outside universe, perhaps through certain properties of Hawking radiation.

The final chapters of Hawking's book deal with the fate of the universe, which depends on which theory designed to unify general relativity and quantum mechanics turns out to produce the most accurate predictions. In one of these theories, the universe's history is analogous to the Earth's three-dimensional surface, which is finite in size but has no boundary. In a multidimensional model using the no-boundary condition, the story of the universe begins with a period of rapid expansion, with the density of matter varying from place to place. As time proceeds, the ultimate fate of this matter—continued expansion or eventual contraction—will be determined by the total amount of all kinds of matter and energy in the cosmos, including invisible or "dark" matter and hidden or "dark" energy, with the latter as the cause of the accelerating rate of the universe's expansion. Hawking favors a cosmos that is completely self-contained, with no boundaries and with no reference to anything outside it. In this view, he argues, God is not needed to give the universe its start, but other views of the universe, based on the unification of quantum and relativity theories, are possible. Hawking insists that any such theory, if it is discovered, should, at least in its basic thrust, be understandable by everyone. Humans will then know why the universe exists. He concludes his book with a sentence that has been often cited, criticized, and discussed: "If we find the answer to [this unification], it would be the ultimate triumph of human reason—for then we would know the mind of God."

The response of scientists, scholars, and the public to *A Brief History of Time* was overwhelmingly positive. Some scholars viewed the book as the culmination of a tradition of the popularization of physics and cosmology that had begun in the early twentieth century with Einstein and others. Nonscientists were willing to tackle the book's complex ideas because discoveries of human and especially nonhuman space exploration had made them curious about the universe, and the spectacular pictures from the Hubble space telescope kept this curiosity alive through the book's later editions (whose illustrated versions made use of these photographs). The book generated some controversy among scientists, atheists, and theists. Hawking responded to the scientific critiques by clarifying and correcting certain passages in later editions. Some atheists, bothered by Hawking's use of God in a scientific work, claimed he was using the Deity as a symbol or metaphor, since they knew he shared their atheism. Some religious reviewers found Hawking's analysis of theological arguments and the Bible less than enlightened. His religious views also played a role in the breakup of his marriage to Jane Wilde, who was a deeply committed Christian. This is ironic, since *A Brief History of Time* is dedicated to her. However, criticisms of the book and the troubles in Hawking's personal life did little to dampen the enthusiasm of succeeding generations of readers, who continued to find his guide to the cosmos congenial and enlightening.

Robert J. Paradowski

Further Reading

Ferris, Timothy. *The Whole Shebang: A State-of-the-Universe(s) Report*. New York: Simon & Schuster, 1997. The author, a prize-winning science popularizer, explains for general readers how scientists, including Hawking, envision the universe as a whole. He also surveys modern cosmological research and speculates on future trends. Extensive notes, glossary, and index.

Guth, Alan H. *The Inflationary Universe: The Quest for a New Theory of Cosmic Origins*. Reading, Mass.: Addison-Wesley, 1997. Just as Hawking analyzed Guth's ideas in *A Brief History of Time*, so Guth analyzes Hawking's views in this popular treatment of the second before the big bang, when the rapid inflation that started the universe began. Illustrated, with notes, glossary, and index.

Hawking, Stephen, assisted by Gene Stone. *Stephen Hawking's "A Brief History of Time": A Reader's Companion.* New York: Bantam Books, 1992. Expands the material covered by both book and film. Illustrated with photographs. Glossary and index.

Larsen, Kristine. *Stephen Hawking: A Biography.* Westport, Conn.: Greenwood Press, 2005. Explores for lay readers both the personal life and the scientific achievements of its subject. Notes at the ends of chapters, a helpful time line, and a glossary. Select bibliography and index.

Susskind, Leonard. *The Black Hole War: My Battle with Stephen Hawking to Make the World Safe for Quantum Mechanics.* New York: Little, Brown, 2008. The author wrote this book for a wide audience to explain why Hawking was wrong in stating that information is lost when black holes evaporate and that he is right in explaining, in agreement with classical and quantum physics, how some information is preserved. Glossary and index.

White, Michael, and John Gribbin. *Stephen Hawking: A Life in Science.* 1992. Rev. ed. Washington, D.C.: Joseph Henry Press, 2002. Details Hawking's life and work through the early twenty-first century. Some reviewers called this "the definitive portrait" of the person whom posterity will regard as the "new Einstein," an estimation denied by Hawking. References and index.

Brighton Rock

Author: Graham Greene (1904-1991)
First published: 1938
Type of work: Novel
Type of plot: Philosophical realism
Time of plot: Mid-1930's
Locale: Brighton, England

Principal characters:
PINKIE BROWN, a seventeen-year-old gangster
FRED HALE, a journalist, who is killed by Pinkie's gang
ROSE, a waitress who becomes Pinkie's wife
IDA ARNOLD, a London barmaid visiting Brighton on vacation
KITE, a former gang leader
SPICER and DALLOW, Pinkie's gangsters

The Story:

At the Brighton pier on a sunny Whitsun bank holiday, a terrified Fred Hale distributes his cards. Under the pseudonym Kolly Kibber, Hale places his cards along the route as part of his job as a newspaper promoter. Pinkie, the new leader of Kite's gang, begins to haunt Hale for being complicit in Kite's murder.

In a frantic search for comfort and protection, Hale links up with the affable London barmaid Ida Arnold, who is enjoying a relaxing holiday. Fearing for his life, Hale begs Ida to accompany him for the rest of the day, and she willingly accepts his invitation. Ida makes a quick trip to the ladies room; when she reappears, Hale is gone. He has been kidnapped. He is then murdered by Pinkie's gang.

To establish an alibi after Hale's murder, Pinkie's men continue to distribute Hale's cards along the pier. Gang member Spicer leaves a card at Snow's restaurant, and a waitress there, Rose, notices that a stranger is distributing Kibber's cards. Pinkie, in turn, sees Rose's concern. He then realizes that Rose could be an important witness against the gang in any future trial against them, and so he decides to befriend her.

Back in London after her brief holiday, Ida learns of Hale's death. She sees Hale's photograph in the newspaper and learns that the authorities have attributed his death to natural causes. Ida, who has "instincts," smells something "fishy" about the coroner's report and decides to do some investigating of her own. After interviewing a potential witness and attending Hale's cremation, Ida is still dissatisfied, and she vows to find justice for Hale.

In the meantime, Pinkie continues to curry favor with Rose. On a date at a local dance hall, Pinkie and Rose discuss religion and find they are both "Romans" (Catholics), albeit with different perspectives; Pinkie's mind is on Hell and Rose's is on Heaven.

Intent on unmasking the details of Hale's death, Ida takes a temporary room in Brighton. Following a racetrack tip that Hale had given her, Ida goes to the tracks to place a bet. Overhearing snippets of conversation that jog her memory of the day she met Hale, Ida begins to piece together Pinkie's complicity in Hale's disappearance. Further investigation leads her to Snow's restaurant and to Rose, who has seen the

Kibber impostor—Spicer. Talking to the frail and timid Rose awakens Ida's maternal instincts, and she vows to not only get Pinkie but also protect Rose.

Pinkie still courts Rose, fearing that she will put together the pieces of the puzzle and implicate his gang in Hale's murder. Although Rose is treated cruelly by Pinkie, she exhibits a growing devotion to him. Pinkie decides that he must marry Rose for his protection, knowing that a wife cannot testify against her husband. Witnessing Pinkie's wooing of the young and innocent Rose, Ida still shadows Rose to convince her that Pinkie is dangerous, but Rose staunchly defends Pinkie. When he learns of Ida's interference, and after his hastily conceived murder of Spicer, the frightened Pinkie puts his marriage plans into motion.

Pinkie meets Rose at her home in Nelson Place, the slum where she grew up, and the desolation and poverty remind Pinkie of his own miserable upbringing. Although Rose's parents "have a mood on," Pinkie is able to bargain with them for Rose's hand, finally "buying" her for fifteen guineas. When Ida later learns of the marriage, she redoubles her efforts to free Rose. After their wedding night at Pinkie's rented room, Pinkie leaves and Ida visits Rose. Rose, however, proves more resistant to Ida because Rose is now convinced she is carrying Pinkie's child.

When confronted with the prospect of a child, Pinkie realizes he cannot live the life he has made for himself and decides he must be free of Rose. To this end, he makes a suicide pact with Rose, who willingly decides to follow him to death and damnation. Pinkie, of course, plans to have Rose kill herself first, while he goes free.

To carry out the plan, Pinkie and Rose travel to the town of Peacehaven. With Ida, the police, and fellow gangster Dallow hot on their trail, Pinkie and Rose drive to a cliff overlooking the sea. Rose's will weakens as she puts a gun to her head, but Pinkie steadies her hand. As Rose hears footsteps, she throws down the gun. Pinkie, knowing he has been caught, retrieves a bottle of vitriol (sulfuric acid) from his pocket and threatens Dallow with it. A police baton breaks the bottle, splashing the acid in Pinkie's face. Shrinking in agony, Pinkie jumps off the cliff and falls into the sea below. The ignorant Ida returns Rose to Nelson Place, having saved her from eternal damnation with Pinkie, only to condemn Rose to a living hell with her detached and uncaring parents.

Critical Evaluation:

With a career spanning sixty years, Graham Greene was one of the most prolific writers of the twentieth century. A noted journalist, film and literary critic, and screenwriter, Greene was most famous for his twenty-seven fictional works, from the spy thrillers he dubbed "entertainments" to his serious psychological and philosophical novels. Greene, several times nominated for the Nobel Prize in Literature, is often hailed as the greatest novelist of the mid-twentieth century and is considered by many to be one of the greatest British novelists ever.

Within Greene's laudable body of work, *Brighton Rock* has repeatedly been singled out as his best novel. One of his harshest critics, Michael Sheldon, considers the book "audacious" and "brilliant"; another critic, Bernard Bergonzi, considers it Greene's "finest novel," and critic Harold Bloom says it is Greene's "most enduring work."

In matters of style, Greene is often regarded as a master. In *Brighton Rock*, he employs a free-ranging narrative voice that incorporates the authoritative third-person-omniscient point of view. Most critics cite his keen attention to realism, but hold their applause for his finely honed poetic sense. Whether comparing Rose's obstinacy in the face of Ida's meddling to a meeting of battleships gearing up for war, or comparing the snaking crowds at the Brighton pier to "a twisted piece of wire," Greene speaks the poetic language of metaphor.

Both in structure and theme, *Brighton Rock*'s focus is oppositional. Superficially, the novel deals with warring gangs at the Brighton racetracks. On a deeper thematic level, the book deals in the overarching antithetical themes of Christian good (salvation) versus evil (damnation) and the secular issues of right and wrong. Mirroring the oppositional theme of the novel, Greene's omniscient narrator frequently chooses the suitably oppositional language of oxymoron, describing Pinkie's face as a "young ancient poker face," painting Ida Arnold as a woman of "merciless compassion," and noting the slim comfort of Dallow's "friendly and oppressive hand."

Pinkie and Rose form the center of the theme of salvation and damnation. Many critics place Pinkie in the role of Satan incarnate, a character of unredeemable evil. Pinkie, a former choir boy fond of spouting Latinate religious phrases, is considered so emotionally damaged by his squalid upbringing and his mentoring by the ruthless gang leader Kite that even at the age of seventeen he is eternally damned. From his brutal murder of Hale to his depraved plan to do away with his young and innocent new wife, Rose, Pinkie's actions fall outside the considerations of even the most merciful God.

Following this same thread of good versus evil, many critics read Rose as innocence incarnate, the sixteen-year-old victim of an equally squalid and harsh upbringing who succumbs to Pinkie's lures because her romantic vision of life makes her easy prey. Although she ultimately hopes for salvation, to embrace damnation with Pinkie at her side gives her a sense of belonging that she has never felt. When she believes she is carrying Pinkie's offspring, she childishly sees herself as an incubator for an army of protectors for her beloved.

Within this mix of good and evil is Ida, the buxom, bold secular humanist who sees the world not in abstract terms of good and evil but in simple terms of right and wrong and justice and injustice. Even though she had known Hale only for a few hours at most, upon hearing of his death, her justice-seeking radar leads her back to Brighton, where she doggedly seeks the answer to Hale's death. Though some critics like Bergonzi see Ida as a sympathetic character, others, like Sheldon, see her as an "overbearing busybody" in love with the hunt, caring less for the people she is trying to save than with her own personal sense of satisfaction.

Because *Brighton Rock* is often considered a book with no answers to the moral questions of good and evil and right and wrong, it has been open to a variety of rich interpretations. For example, noted Greene critic Paul O'Prey views Pinkie from a different perspective. O'Prey, arguing against the early criticism of writer Evelyn Waugh, sees Pinkie as a lost and "alienated" soul whose "background of . . . misery and deprivation" and his painful loss of his father-figure Kite have led him down the wrong path, a path still open to ultimate salvation.

In this enigmatic text, there is room for alternative interpretations of Rose's character as well. Critic Bates Hoffer argues that Rose, despite her youth and virginity, is not a true innocent. She knows well the teachings of the Church but rather blithely chooses not to mind them. When she learns of the bottle of vitriol Pinkie carries with him, she responds not only in "horror" but also in "admiration." When Pinkie plots the double suicide, she seems more than willing to follow him into the ultimate mortal sin.

In the final assessment, *Brighton Rock* endures with critics and readers because it is an unsolvable puzzle. Is Pinkie damned or saved? Will Rose collapse or rebound from the horror she endures? Is Ida an avenging angel or a meddling interloper?

Karen Priest

Further Reading

Bergonzi, Bernard. *A Study in Greene: Graham Greene and the Art of the Novel*. New York: Oxford University Press, 2006. Examines all of Greene's novels, analyzing their language, structure, and recurring motifs. Argues that *Brighton Rock* was his masterpiece. Addresses Greene's Catholicism and how it informs his work, and offers a nontraditional view of Ida as a sympathetic character.

Gaston, Georg M. *The Pursuit of Salvation: A Critical Guide to the Novels of Graham Greene*. Troy, N.Y.: Whitston, 1984. A detailed work on Greene's major novels, assessing *Brighton Rock* as a theological thriller and providing an interesting window into Pinkie's internal motivation. Uniquely uncovers a common pattern in Greene's works, a movement that encourages the reader to see the characters in an increasingly sympathetic light.

Lewis, R. W. "The 'Trilogy.'" In *Modern Critical Views: Graham Greene*, edited by Harold Bloom. New York: Chelsea House, 1987. Focuses heavily on the oppositional factors in *Brighton Rock* and is the only source to address Greene's use of oxymoron. Offers an introduction by Bloom, who gives his assessment of Greene's works and career.

Miller, R. H. *Understanding Graham Greene*. Columbia: University of South Carolina Press, 1990. Focuses on Greene's entire body of work and offers an excellent and easily accessible overview of *Brighton Rock*. Cites *Brighton Rock* as a turning point in Greene's fiction and argues that its handling and themes point to the future direction of some of Greene's greatest works.

O'Prey, Paul. *A Reader's Guide to Graham Greene*. New York: Thames & Hudson, 1988. The perfect beginner's source for students of Greene's major novels, with a full bibliography. Rare among critics, O'Prey introduces the centrality of love in Greene's novels and makes an argument for Pinkie's potential for goodness.

Sherry, Norman. *The Life of Graham Greene*. 3 vols. New York: Viking Press, 1989-2004. This comprehensive, authoritative account of Greene's life was written with complete access to his papers and the full cooperation of his family members, friends, and the novelist himself.

Britannicus

Author: Jean Racine (1639-1699)
First produced: 1669; first published, 1670 (English
   translation, 1714)
Type of work: Drama
Type of plot: Tragedy
Time of plot: 55 C.E.
Locale: Rome, the palace of Néron

Principal characters:
BRITANNICUS, Claudius's son by the wife who preceded
   Agrippine
AGRIPPINE, Claudius's widow
NÉRON, Agrippine's son, Emperor of Rome
JUNIE, betrothed to Britannicus
NARCISSE, Britannicus's tutor
ALBINA, Agrippine's confidant
BURRHUS, Néron's tutor

The Story:

In the anteroom of the imperial palace Agrippine waits to speak with Néron, her son. The impatient nature of his character at last reveals itself in antagonistic behavior toward Britannicus, and Agrippine fears that she will next incur his disfavor. Albina is convinced of the emperor's continued loyalty to his mother. Agrippine feels that if Néron is indeed noble, the fact that she wins the throne for him will ensure his devotion; but if he is ignoble, the fact of his obligation will turn him against her.

On the previous night Néron abducted Junie, to whom Britannicus is betrothed, a deed possibly motivated by resentment against Agrippine, who begins to support Britannicus in an attempt to preserve her position in the future if Néron is to turn against her. Albina assures Agrippine that her public power and honor, at least, are not decreasing. Agrippine, however, needs the assurance of a more personal trust. She confides that once Néron turned her aside from the throne on which she customarily sits in the Senate. She is also denied all private audiences with him.

Agrippine, reproaching Burrhus for disloyalty to her, accuses him of attempting to gain power over Néron. Burrhus is convinced that his prime loyalty is to the emperor, who rules well by his own authority. Néron fears that Britannicus's children will inherit the throne if he marries Junie. Britannicus, distracted by his loss of Junie, complains of Néron's harshness. Agrippine sends him to the house of Pallas, the freedman, where she will meet him later. Britannicus tells Narcisse, who encourages him to join Agrippine, that he still wishes to claim the throne.

Néron decides to disregard his mother's reproaches, which he calls unjust, and to banish Pallas, the friend and adviser of Agrippine, who, he thinks, corrupts Britannicus. Narcisse assures him that Rome approves of his abduction of Junie, and Néron confesses that when he saw her he fell in love with her. He is convinced by Narcisse that Britannicus is devoted to Junie and that she probably loves him in return.

Narcisse insists that the love of Junie will be won by a sign of favor from the emperor. Narcisse advises Néron to divorce Octavia, Britannicus's sister, and marry Junie. Néron fears Agrippine's wrath if he does so; only when he avoids her completely does he dare defy her wishes, for in her presence he is powerless. Narcisse informs Néron that Britannicus still trusts him; he is therefore dispatched to bring Britannicus for a meeting with Junie. Junie asks Néron what her crime is and insists that Britannicus is the most suitable person for her to marry, as he is the only other descendant of Augustus Caesar at court. When Néron says that he himself will marry her, Junie, appalled, begs him not to disgrace Octavia by doing so. Finally she realizes that she can save Britannicus's life only by telling him, when they meet, that he is to leave Rome. Néron intends to listen to their conversation.

At their interview, Britannicus is bewildered by Junie's coldness toward him and by her praise of the emperor. When he leaves, Néron reappears, but Junie flees, weeping. Néron sends Narcisse to comfort Britannicus. Burrhus reports that Agrippine is angry at Néron, and he fears that she might plot against the emperor. When Néron refuses to listen to Burrhus as he begs him not to divorce Octavia, the tutor realizes that the emperor's true character is at last appearing.

Meanwhile, Agrippine plans to take Britannicus before the Roman army and to declare that she wronged him by exalting Néron to the throne. By this action she hopes to win their allegiance to Britannicus. Burrhus tells her that her scheme is impossible. Agrippine tells Albina that if Néron marries Junie and banishes Britannicus, her own power will end. That condition she can never accept. Although Britannicus does not trust her, she plans with his cooperation to prevent Néron's marriage to Junie.

Although Narcisse persuades Britannicus that Junie is faithless, she nevertheless manages to see him and insists that he flee to save his life. Accused of unfaithfulness, she explains that Néron was listening during their previous meeting. Britannicus falls at her feet in gratitude for her continued love. In this situation Néron comes upon them and demands from Britannicus the obedience that through fear he intends to extort from all Rome. Later Néron orders Britannicus arrested and Agrippine detained in the palace.

Burrhus advises Agrippine, before her audience with Néron, to be affectionate and even apologetic and to make no demands on him. Instead, she explains to him exactly how she procured the throne for him and reproaches him for his present behavior. Néron, infuriated by her continued claims on him, realizes that she made him emperor only for her own glory. Accused of being a plotter, Agrippine denies that she attempted to replace Néron with Britannicus; all she wants is for Junie to be allowed to choose her own husband and for her to see Néron when she wishes. When Néron appears to yield, Burrhus congratulates him. Néron merely deceives Agrippine, however; he still intends to punish Britannicus. Burrhus then implores him to continue his just reign and be reconciled with Britannicus. Néron, again wavering, decides to meet Britannicus.

Narcisse prepares poison for Britannicus, but Néron declares he will not now use it. Narcisse, counseling him against clemency, says that Agrippine already publicly boasts of her regained control. He also insinuates that Burrhus is not to be trusted. Néron decides to plan his future actions with Narcisse.

Britannicus informs Junie that he is to be reconciled with Néron and voices his conviction that she will be returned to him, but Junie, doubting Néron's sincerity, fears that Narcisse is deceiving them. Agrippine, on the other hand, believes that her words changed Néron completely and that her plans will be executed. Sometime after Britannicus leaves for his audience with Néron, Burrhus returns and informs the women that Narcisse poisoned Britannicus and that Néron, unmoved, watched him die. Appalled by Néron's callousness, Burrhus determines to leave Rome.

Although Néron declares that the death of Britannicus was inevitable, Junie flees from the palace. When Agrippine accuses Néron of murder, Narcisse attempts to explain that Britannicus was a traitor. Agrippine predicts that Néron has set the pattern for his reign. After a public disturbance, Albina informs the court that at the statue of Augustus, Junie pledged herself to become a priest of Vesta and that the crowd, to protect her, killed Narcisse. Agrippine and Burrhus go to Néron to try to console him in his despair.

Critical Evaluation:

Jean Racine's third play, *Andromaque* (1667; *Andromache*, 1674), established his mastery of the sentimental drama. In his fifth, *Britannicus*, he intended to prove his ability to write a Roman political tragedy to rival, and if possible surpass, the work of Pierre Corneille. The first performance was only moderately successful. Later its reputation improved after Louis XIV spoke highly of it. The play is constructed in keeping with Aristotle's unities, as was obligatory in seventeenth century French drama after the success of Corneille's neoclassic plays. The theme is Néron's first crime, which sets the pattern for the rest of his reign. Burrhus attempts to keep uppermost the good elements of Néron's character, while Narcisse, a supreme opportunist, works on the emperor's baser instincts. Although other plays by Racine have greater emotional insight and poetic beauty, *Britannicus* is a fine example of his command of verse and language and of his dramatic perception of the motivation of his characters.

Esteemed by many critics to be France's greatest composer of neoclassical tragedies, Racine was elected to the French Academy in 1673, after having established his concept of tragedy in *Bérénice* (1670; English translation, 1676). Racine's excellent education enabled him to brilliantly adapt Greek and Roman history to seventeenth century French plays; he composed eleven tragedies and one comedy in the style approved by the French Academy. Established in 1635, the French Academy had borrowed from Aristotle's *De poetica* (c. 334-323 B.C.E.; *Poetics*, 1705) to create the French neoclassical style, with its emphasis on reason, order, clarity, and the unities of time, place, and action. The observance of decorum and verisimilitude aided the spectator in empathizing with the characters who represented the universality of the human condition.

Racine surpassed in popularity his rival Corneille, who preferred to modify Roman tragedies into plots with exterior action. Racine showed his genius for creating inner drama, a genius that culminated with *Phèdre* (1677; *Phaedra*, 1701), his masterpiece taken from Euripides. After *Phaedra*'s success, he was named the king's historiographer. Racine wrote his last two plays, *Esther* (1689; English translation, 1715) and *Athalie* (1691; *Athaliah*, 1722), for Saint-Cyr's school, which was affiliated with Mme de Maintenon, in order to accommodate Louis XIV, who then appointed him to an advisory position.

After the success of *Andromache* in 1668, Racine responded to his rivals' criticism that he was incapable of treating subjects other than love by composing *Britannicus*. A principal theme of *Britannicus* is Agrippine's extreme domination of her son Néron and his destructive effort to extract himself from her powerful web. In fact, the French meaning of Agrippine's name refers to "gripping."

Agrippine's excessive attachment to the idea of controlling the thoughts and actions of her son Néron causes her to misinterpret situations. She tends to ascribe the wrong motives for her conduct. For example, Agrippine thinks her husband's murder was for her son's benefit.

Agrippine's obsessive will to control others prevents her from loving anyone; she therefore becomes the victim of her tragic flaw. Agrippine reveals her inhumane appetite for power through the treatment of her son. She tries to destroy him mentally and physically. First, she tries to place guilt upon him when she tells him that he owes her a debt because she stole and murdered for him. She also speaks of the wonderful past, when a younger Néron left all the matters of state to her.

Agrippine's second way to thwart her son's emotional development is to belittle him. She tells him that when he was still quite young, he exhibited unacceptable behavior and was noted for his anger, pride, and deceit. In order to break his spirit, his mother reinforces her negative attitude about his behavior by telling him that she kept his evil nature a secret. Agrippine then tries to have her son castrated; but Burrhus, Néron's tutor, tries to explain to her that since the people already revere her, she can release her control over her son. Burrhus's reasonable manner contrasts with her compulsive desire to dominate.

Agrippine's third attempt to cause her son's demise stems from jealousy. After her discovery of Néron's love for Junie, Agrippine, despite Burrhus's suggestion that she act in moderation, frantically summarizes her motherly sacrifices to secure her son's royal authority: her marriage to Claudius, her desire for Néron to be king, her consent from Claudius for Néron to marry Octavia, her insistence on Claudius's adoption of Néron, and her husband's murder. Disoriented, Agrippine accuses her son of deception and ingratitude. In order to subdue his mother's controlling behavior, Néron lies about allowing her to win in the affairs of state and in his personal life, declaring that he would become reconciled to Britannicus. Agrippine's reaction of excessive joy to Néron's pretended transformation contrasts with Junie's great sense of impending doom, producing a frightening atmosphere of suspense, which ends with the announcement of Britannicus's death. Agrippine is then able to see Néron as an individual rather than as a part of her own personality.

Burrhus, who advocates the stoic values of self-control and resignation, tries to teach Néron virtuous behavior, but Burrhus realizes he has misjudged the effectiveness of his teaching when Néron says that he will hug his rival in order to deceive him. Néron proceeds to erase the past from his mind and decides to gratify his present instincts. His next tutor, the evil Narcisse, encourages Néron to pursue his courtship of Junie despite her love for Britannicus. Narcisse is also instrumental in the murder of Britannicus. The evil character of Néron is further developed when he impassively observes Junie's pain at having to tell Britannicus she does not love him. Observing pain allows Néron to feel a sense of power. Néron experiences the same feelings of control as his mother.

On the other hand, Britannicus and Junie portray the concept of virtuous behavior, as does Burrhus. Britannicus serves in the plot as an object for Agrippine's machinations and a reason for Narcisse to be in the palace; he also thwarts Néron's plans because of his love for Junie. The conversation that takes place between Britannicus and Néron depicts this contrast in character. Néron's frantic insistence upon obedience reflects his feeling of weakness and leads to the evil poisoning of Britannicus.

Linked to the play's thematic exploration of good and evil are symbols. The palace, for example, is endowed with a past history and various chambers; it is a labyrinth, disorienting the characters. The personification of the palace as being able to sigh, hear, and see conveys a monstrous image of evil. The protagonists all meet their doom: Agrippine and Burrhus do not succeed in their endeavors; Britannicus and Narcisse die; Junie renounces the world; and Néron, unable to face reality, looks inward with despair.

"Critical Evaluation" by Linda Prewett Davis

Further Reading

Abraham, Claude. *Jean Racine.* Boston: Twayne, 1977. Introductory overview intended for the general reader; all quotations are in English. Gives a brief biographical sketch and discusses Racine's major works.

Butler, Philip. *Racine: A Study.* London: Heinemann, 1974. Introduction to Racine, with a section on how to read his works. Indicates the traditional approach to literary criticism as well as nontraditional approaches.

Campbell, John. *Questioning Racinian Tragedy.* Chapel Hill: University of North Carolina Press, 2005. Analyzes individual tragedies, including *Britannicus*, and questions if Racine's plays have common themes and techniques that constitute a unified concept of "Racinian tragedy."

Lapp, John C. *Aspects of Racinian Tragedy.* Toronto, Ont.: University of Toronto Press, 1955. Contains excellent thematic analyses. An informative account of Racine's dramatic art.

Racevskis, Roland. *Tragic Passages: Jean Racine's Art of the Threshold.* Lewisburg, Pa.: Bucknell University Press, 2008. Examines *Britannicus* and Racine's other secular tragedies, demonstrating how these works construct space, time, and identity. Argues that the characters in these plays are in various stages of limbo—suspended between the self and the other, onstage and offstage, life and death—and that the plays emphasize this predicament of being "in-between."

Turnell, Martin. *Jean Racine, Dramatist*. London: Hamish Hamilton, 1972. Shows how Racine may be considered the greatest French tragic dramatist. Gives an interesting analysis of Racine's imagery and an illuminating study of each of his plays.

Weinberg, Bernard. *The Art of Jean Racine*. Chicago: University of Chicago Press, 1963. Presents Racine's tragedies arranged chronologically in order to show how his dramatic art evolved. Refers to neoclassicism to explain Racine's plays.

Broad and Alien Is the World

Author: Ciro Alegría (1909-1967)
First published: El mundo es ancho y ajeno, 1941 (English translation, 1941)
Type of work: Novel
Type of plot: Social realism
Time of plot: 1912-1926
Locale: Peru

Principal characters:
ROSENDO MAQUIS, mayor of a community of Indians
DON AMENABAR, the tyrannical owner of a neighboring ranch
BISMARCK RUIZ, a rascal lawyer
CORREA ZAVALA, a lawyer friendly to the Indians
FIERO VASQUEZ, a highwayman friendly to the Indians
BENITO CASTRO, an Indian who has lived away from the village

The Story:

Rosendo Maquis is the mayor of Rumi, a small Indian town in the Peruvian uplands. The village is a communal organization, as it was for centuries. Its life is peaceful, for the Rumi Indians are an agricultural people. Rosendo's only troubles are personal. His wife is dying, and he is sent into the mountains to find herbs to be used in making medicine for the sick woman. On his way back to the village, he sees an evil omen in the passage of a snake across his path. Troubled times, he believes, lie ahead.

That same night, Rosendo's wife dies, and her death marks the beginning of many misfortunes for the mayor and his people. A few days later, it becomes known that Don Amenabar, whose ranch borders the Indian village, is filing suit to take away the best of the land belonging to Rumi. Rosendo and his selectmen saddle their horses and ride to the nearby town to get a lawyer to defend them. They hire Bismarck Ruiz, a man who has a poor reputation in the town because of his love affair with La Castelana, a notorious woman of very expensive tastes. In return for a large fee, Ruiz promises to win the suit for the Indians.

Life goes on as usual in the village during the days before the trial. There is a cattle roundup, to which Don Amenabar sends men to collect the cattle belonging to him. Although he does not pay the grazing fee, and the Indians know it would be futile to ask it of him, he charges them a high fee to redeem any cattle that accidentally wander onto his lands. The Indians are also busy building a school, for the commissioner of education of the province promised them a schoolmaster as soon as they have a hygienic place for the school to convene.

In an effort to learn what Don Amenabar is plotting against them, the Indians send one of their number to the ranch to sell baskets and woven mats. When Don Amenabar sees the Indian on his ranch, he orders his overseers to give the unlucky fellow a hundred lashes, a punishment that would kill many men.

Finally, the case comes to court. The Indians believe at first that they will win. Don Amenabar's men removed the stones marking the community boundaries, but the Indians returned them. The return, they believe, is indicative of their success. The case is soon over, however, thanks to a large number of perjuring witnesses who testify against the Indians by claiming that the people of Rumi encroached on Don Amenabar's land. Even the judge receives money and preferment from the rancher.

The Indians' lawyer immediately makes up a brief for an appeal to a higher court, but Don Amenabar's men, disguised as the followers of Fiero Vasquez, the outlaw, steal the mail-bag containing the documents as the mail carrier passes through a desolate part of the Andes. Don Amenabar does not want the authorities in Lima to hear of the affair because he wishes to send his son to the legislature and, eventually, to become a senator himself.

Correa Zavala, a young lawyer fired with zeal for the cause of the Peruvian Indians, takes up the villagers' case. It has become clear to the Indians that Ruiz is not helping them, and they have evidence that he is in the pay of Don Amenabar. The young lawyer makes up a long brief that includes many documents from the history of the village. These are sent to the capital with a guard of troops and Indians, for their loss will make it difficult to prove the village's legal existence as a community.

All is to no avail, however, for at last the day comes when the court order, enforced by troops, is delivered to the Indians. They are to leave the most fertile of their lands and move to what is left to them in the higher areas. When one of the village women goes to her lover, Vasquez, the notorious highwayman and bandit, he comes with his band of cutthroats to help the Indians drive off the people who are forcing them to leave. Rosendo refuses aid from the outlaws because he knows that resistance would be useless. His point is made when a villager is machine-gunned to death for daring to kill one of Don Amenabar's men with a rock.

Even in the highlands the Indians are not safe from Don Amenabar, who wants to make them slaves to work a mine that he owns on another piece of property. He resolves never to be satisfied until they are delivered into his hands. His men raid the Indians' cattle herds, even creeping up to the corrals in the village at night. At last, the prize bull of the village disappears. The Indians find the animal on Don Amenabar's ranch. In spite of the brand, Don Amenabar refuses to return the bull and orders Rosendo off the ranch. That same night the mayor returns, determined to regain the animal for his people. He finds the bull, but as he is leading the animal away, he is captured. Taken into town, Rosendo is jailed on a charge of thievery. At his trial, he is found guilty and sentenced to a long term in prison.

While Rosendo is in jail, Vasquez is captured and placed in the cell with Rosendo. Having plenty of resources to make bribes, the highwayman makes arrangements to break out of prison. When he escapes, Rosendo is blamed. The prison guards beat the old man so severely that he dies within a few hours.

Not long after the death of Rosendo, a young Indian he reared comes back to the village after an absence of many years. Benito Castro, a soldier and a gaucho, is quickly ac-

cepted as a leader by the Indians, who need the wisdom and aid of someone who was outside the mountain village. Under Castro's leadership, the people drain swampy meadows and rebuild their village in a better location in the highlands. Their relative prosperity, however, is short-lived, for Don Amenabar still plans to enslave them or drive them into hiding. At last, a large detachment of troops, augmented by men convinced that the Indians are mutinous against the government, attacks the village. In a long battle with the forces sent against them, the Indians are utterly defeated, their leaders are killed, and the village is destroyed. The few survivors, told by the dying Castro to save themselves, have no idea where they can go to seek a refuge in that harsh, lawless land.

Critical Evaluation:

Ciro Alegría's panoramic novel mirrors life in the Peruvian Andes early in the twentieth century. Its many themes include defense of the downtrodden, justice, injustice, the tragedy of human life, dishonest lawyers and courts, litigation over land boundaries, suffering, villainy and heroism, and racism.

The novel's power lies in its defense of the abused Indian populace of Rumi. The reader lives with Rumi's people throughout the story and identifies with them. Unforgettable is the noble old leader of Rumi, Rosendo Maquis, and his efforts, ideals, character, misfortunes, and death. Grave and good like the community of Rumi itself, Rosendo incarnates his people, who are idealized by Alegría. The dark night and demise of Rumi are ably painted by Alegría, giving the novel an epic reach. Besides its many regionalist qualities, moreover, *Broad and Alien Is the World* has a well-developed plot and generally convincing characterization that rank it as one of the better contributions to the literature of *indianismo*, which defends the Indian peoples of Latin America. The plot reaches a final crescendo with the destruction of Rumi and all that the recently murdered Rosendo stands for; but the noble Rosendo, his wife the pathetic Pascuala, black-clad Fiero Vasquez, and Benito Castro still live and stand out in the reader's memory.

Alegría's language is poetic, lively, and colorful. He uses standard Spanish laced with occasional regionalisms, including Quechua words, to good effect. Dialogue is authentic. The novel is also unwieldy, structurally chaotic, and lacking in careful planning (owing to its hasty composition; it was completed in a matter of months).

Geography is always a silent presence in the novel. At times, it is almost a dominant character, reflecting the fact of the importance of geography in Peru's culture. One sees the lofty Andean sierra with its crisp, thin air, its gaunt landscapes, sparse vegetation, and rocky soil, and pastel Rumi with its cobbled, wind-swept streets and huddled houses. Rumi's people grow potatoes and tend their llamas, but they chew coca to cope with hunger and the cold, and their chests are like those of pouter pigeons since the air has so little oxygen.

Alegría was born and reared on a hacienda in the same region in which he sets his novel. Although his parents were his first teachers, he later credited the whole Peruvian people with having molded him and caused him to understand their grief. An Indian wet nurse cradled him in her arms and taught him to walk; he played as a child with Indian children and later saw things that he could not forget. In *Broad and Alien Is the World*, thus, Alegría penetrates the Indian mind, revealing the native's feeling for the soil, his poverty, stoicism, dignity, superstition, and occasional lapsing into alcoholism or sexual license. Unfortunately, Alegría ladles out some crude propaganda in his lambasting of such types as white men, priests, and landowners. These stock, one-dimensional figures are reminiscent of Diego Rivera's murals with their pasty-faced, and evil whites, bloated priests, cruel-faced landowners, and clean-cut Indians. Thus, Don Amenabar, Bismarck Ruiz, and the cowardly, servile priest are not convincingly drawn. Alegría reveals unconscious prejudice in this respect, although his own family owned land and was Caucasian in appearance. As is often the case in Spanish American literature, the novel is inspired and sincerely motivated but betrays the fact that its author belongs to a privileged social class and has not been as truly a member of the working classes as, say, John Steinbeck, Jack London, or José Antonio Villarreal.

One of Alegría's great contributions is his pictorial depiction of rural Peruvian society. The reader experiences many social types and their folkways, traditions, mentality, society, and sorrows. In Rumi, readers see the kaleidoscopic results of four centuries of blending between Inca and Spaniard. One of the finest examples is the colorful sketch of Rumi's village meeting, with its touches of imagery wherein bronzed Indian faces mingle with lighter mestizos and an occasional white face, against a background of Inca and Spanish dress, manners, postures, and gestures. The novel is thus a storehouse of all that has happened to Peru, from the days of the Inca empire, through the dramatic conquest by the Spaniards, and the four ensuing centuries of racial and cultural blending. It is said that all of Alegría's works demonstrate a determination to create an original literature that not only interprets the Peruvian reality but also expresses contemporary Peru's peculiarities. He therefore draws the mestizo, whose heart is rooted in the Peruvian soil and in whose soul exists a harmonious mixture. A mestizo is the central personality in all of Alegría's novels, with the possible exception of *Broad and Alien Is the World*, and even in this work, the mestizo, Castro, inherits Rosendo's role and develops into the most significant personality of the latter part of the novel.

Broad and Alien Is the World is essentially a novel of the high sierra as other Spanish American novels are novels of the pampa, llanos, desert, jungle, or city. It nevertheless broadens the social and human conflict beyond the boundaries of the community of Rumi to Peru's coast and jungle—nowhere under the Peruvian flag is there a place that is not hostile to the Indian. Castro is regarded as an extremist agitator in Lima; one of Rosendo's sons is blinded by the explosion of a rubber ball in the eastern jungles; Calixto Paucar dies in a mine shaft; other emigrants from Rumi meet misfortune in many parts of the Peruvian Republic, demonstrating that, for the Indian at least, broad and alien is the world. Alegría's great achievement, thus, is that his masterpiece has undoubtedly helped to implement reform in favor of the mountain-dwelling Indians and mestizos of central Peru, for their lot has slowly but surely improved since the day when, while writing a scene for another novel concerning the expulsion of some Indians from their community, Alegría was struck with such force "by an intense gust of ideas and memories" that the inspiration for his masterpiece was born.

The novel is a veritable storehouse of Peruvian lore, giving as it does a detailed picture of the social structure of the Indian community, its innate dignity, its traditions, and its overwhelming tragedy. Alegría was exiled from Peru in 1934 because of his political views.

"Critical Evaluation" by William Freitas

Further Reading

Aldrich, Earl M., Jr. *The Modern Short Story in Peru*. Madison: University of Wisconsin Press, 1966. Historical survey introducing major writers, styles, and themes of the Peruvian short story of Alegría's day. Alegría's short-story production is analyzed within the context of the author's literary contributions.

Early, Eileen. *Joy in Exile: Ciro Alegría's Narrative Art*. Lanham, Md.: University Press of America, 1980. Survey of Alegría's short stories and novels. Traces Alegría's major literary motifs within the context of Peruvian literature.

Flores, Angel. "Ciro Alegría." *Spanish American Authors: The Twentieth Century*. New York: H. W. Wilson, 1992. Surveys Alegría's production, including bibliographical sources. Written primarily in Spanish. An excellent starting point for study of Alegría's works.

Foster, David William, and Virginia Ramos Foster, comps. and eds. "Alegría, Ciro." In *Modern Latin American Literature*. New York: Frederick Ungar, 1975. Excerpts from critical studies. A good introduction to Alegría's best-known works.

Gonzälez-Pérez, Armando. *Social Protest and Literary Merit in "Huasipungo" and "El mundo es ancho y ajeno."* Milwaukee: University of Wisconsin-Milwaukee, Center for Latin America, 1988. Alegría's two best-known novels are analyzed in terms of his ideological views. Alegría is presented as an influential intellectual who participated in social movements that promoted the advancement of the indigenous population.

Higgins, James. *A History of Peruvian Literature*. Wolfeboro, N.H.: F. Cairns, 1987. Higgins, a professor of Latin American literature who has written numerous books and articles about the literature of Peru, provides a lucid summary of Alegría's novels in this historical overview. Includes indexes and a bibliography.

Kokotovic, Misha. *The Colonial Divide in Peruvian Narrative: Conflict and Transformation*. Eastbourne, East Sussex, England.: Sussex Academic Press, 2005. Describes how the colonial divide between Peru's indigenous people and the descendants of Spanish conquerors is expressed in Peruvian literature. Includes an analysis of *Broad and Alien Is the World*.

The Broken Jug

Author: Heinrich von Kleist (1777-1811)
First produced: Der zerbrochene Krug, 1808; first published, 1811 (English translation, 1839)
Type of work: Drama
Type of plot: Farce
Time of plot: Late eighteenth century
Locale: A village in the Netherlands

Principal characters:
ADAM, the village judge
WALTER, a counselor-at-law
LICHT, the clerk of the court
MARTHE RULL, a villager
EVE, her daughter
RUPRECHT, Eve's suitor
BRIGITTE, Ruprecht's aunt
VEIT TUMPEL, Ruprecht's father

The Story:

Licht, clerk of the court of Huisum, a village near Utrecht in the Netherlands, appears in the courtroom one morning to prepare for the day's proceedings. He discovers Adam, the village judge, in a generally disreputable state, nursing a badly lacerated face and an injured leg. When he asks the judge how he came to be in such a condition, he receives a highly questionable story about an altercation with a clothesline and a goat. Licht, sensing that there was some philandering involved, hints as much to Adam, but the judge naturally denies the clerk's suggestions.

There are more important matters to discuss. A peasant passing through Holla, a neighboring village, hears that Counselor Walter, of the High Court at Utrecht, has inspected the courts in Holla and is preparing to come to Huisum on a tour of inspection this very day. This is serious business, particularly when Adam learns that in Holla both the clerk of the court and the judge were suspended because their affairs were not in order; the judge almost succeeded in killing himself when he tried to hang himself in his own barn. Needless to say, Adam's affairs are in no better shape than those of his unfortunate neighbors. Before he can get his clothes on and make an attempt to restore order, however, a servant comes to announce the arrival of Counselor Walter. Adam tries to defer immediate action by telling an even more unlikely story about his accident and begging that the inspection be delayed. Licht is calmer, however, and insists that Adam receive the counselor.

At the height of the chaos, Adam, discovering that he cannot find his wig, is informed by a spying servant girl that he came home without it after eleven o'clock the night before. He naturally denies this claim and tells the servant girl that she has lost her mind; he suddenly remembers that the cat kittened in his wig and therefore he cannot use it. The girl is sent to borrow a wig from the verger's wife, after being reminded not to mention the matter to the verger himself. Before the girl can return, Counselor Walter appears, expressing regrets that he was not able to announce himself in advance and assuring Adam and Licht that he knows matters will be only tolerably in order but that he expects little more. He then demands that the court proceedings get under way, just as the servant girl returns, bearing the calamitous news that she could not borrow a wig. Though it is highly irregular for a judge to sit without his wig, Counselor Walter insists that the petitions begin, wig or no wig.

When the doors open, Marthe Rull and her daughter Eve charge in, accompanied by Veit Tumpel and his son Ruprecht; all are in a high state of agitation over a broken pitcher. Marthe accuses Ruprecht, who is engaged to marry Eve, of breaking the pitcher, but Ruprecht denies doing so. Eve is having a mild case of hysterics because she is about to lose Ruprecht, who swears that he never wishes to see her again and keeps calling her a strumpet. Marthe vociferously demands that justice be done because she feels that Eve's good name was destroyed along with the pitcher.

In the middle of this confusion, Adam, wigless, appears in his robes to open his court; he is visibly shaken at the scene before him. Eve pleads with her mother to leave well enough alone, while Adam tries unsuccessfully to talk with Eve about a piece of paper. Counselor Walter finally insists that court begin. Marthe, brought to the stand, accuses Ruprecht of breaking the pitcher. He denies the charge and demands that she prove her accusation. Adam agrees completely with Marthe and tries to dismiss the case, but the counselor will not let him. The trial proceeds.

As the evidence is presented, it comes out that the pitcher was broken at eleven o'clock the night before. Marthe heard voices coming from Eve's room and rushed in to find the pitcher smashed, Eve in tears, and Ruprecht standing in the middle of the room. Ruprecht is the obvious suspect, but according to him a third party was present whom he cannot identify. According to Marthe, Eve, too, admitted that there was a third party in the room, but she refuses to identify him. When Ruprecht finally takes the stand, he testifies that he came to make a late call on Eve and found her near the gate to her house with another man. He watched until they went to Eve's room; then, overwhelmed by fury, he rushed after them and broke down the door, smashing the pitcher just as someone jumped out the window and got caught in the grapevine. He seized the door latch and beat the culprit over the head with it, in return receiving a handful of sand in the face. He thinks the man is the village cobbler, but he cannot be sure.

Adam is quite anxious to assign the blame to the cobbler and thereby prevent Eve from giving testimony, but his attempts are unsuccessful. When Eve takes the stand, she clears Ruprecht of smashing the pitcher but refuses to identify the third party.

There was, however, another participant in the evening's affair—Brigitte, Ruprecht's aunt. She appears in court with a wig that is identified as Adam's and a story of having seen the devil leave Eve's house around eleven o'clock the night before. She followed the tracks in the snow the next morning in order to find the devil's abode, and the tracks led to the judge's very door. Adam, declaring that this account has nothing to do with the case, proceeds to sentence Ruprecht.

The judge's decision prompts Eve to confess the whole story. It seems that Adam told Eve that Ruprecht would be drafted and sent to India but that he had the power to save Ruprecht from this fate; he forged a certificate that Eve went to her room to sign. He took the occasion to try to seduce her, at which time Ruprecht burst in, smashed the pitcher, and beat Adam, who jumped out the window. Before the whole story comes out, however, Adam runs off to escape a beating. The only person left unsatisfied is Marthe, who plans to take her pitcher to the High Court in Utrecht and demand justice.

Critical Evaluation:

Heinrich von Kleist wrote the one-act comedy *The Broken Jug* at the request of friends who had seen a French copper engraving entitled *La Cruche cassée*, which depicted a pair of lovers, a scolding older woman holding a broken jug, and a judge. In the original manuscript, Kleist also alluded to the influence of Sophocles' *Oidipous Tyrannos* (c. 429 B.C.E.; *Oedipus Tyrannus*, 1715). In both plays, the crime has already been committed and the audience knows the identity of the culprit. The action on the stage, therefore, consists of unraveling various past events for the purpose of naming this person. Johann Wolfgang von Goethe was the first to produce the play in 1808 in Weimar, where it proved a dismal failure. Goethe blamed the unkind reception on the play's slow action, not realizing that his own arbitrary division of the thirteen scenes into three acts had destroyed the unity of the work. Staging it after a long opera did not help matters, either. Perhaps the German playwright Friedrich Hebbel pronounced the most appropriate judgment on it after its 1850 Vienna production when he said that the only failure the play could have was that of its audience.

The Broken Jug derives its humor from the ridiculous situation involving a village judge holding court proceedings for a case in which he is guilty of the crime. The plaintiff, the defendants, and his superior all depend on him to preside over the case, yet all the while he himself and soon, too, the audience know full well that it is he who broke the jug. Judge Adam's ability effortlessly to tell outrageous lies is one important source of the play's comedy. Adam is a bald old man with a clubfoot who feels attracted to Marthe Rull's sweet, innocent daughter Eve. In creating a physically repulsive Adam, Kleist does not intend to provoke laughter at physical shortcomings. Rather, Adam's deformities are meant to symbolize his disgusting character and his decadence. Nevertheless, Adam's looks also arouse pity, for it is because of them that the audience realizes how all too human he is. His talent for inventing lies, which he uses to postpone the discovery of his complicity in the case, makes him into a stage clown putting on a show.

Kleist employs a colloquial language to re-create the realistic village scene. The characters use rough language with clever double meanings, thus creating a bawdy atmosphere. Their coarse sense of humor probably contributed to the lack of appreciation of the Weimar audience, which was used to seeing sentimental dramas.

Adam immediately wants to pronounce Ruprecht guilty, as he wants the potentially dangerous situation to end as soon as possible. The district judge, Counselor Walter, intervenes, however, to let the accused defend himself. As a higher official of the court he feels responsible for ensuring that the case is heard properly. Whenever Adam veers into irrelevant descriptions, Counselor Walter uses his authority to bring him back to the trial. Kleist thus creates an extended and very comical tug-of-war between Adam and his chief on the one hand, and Adam and the plaintiff, Marthe, on the other. A further source of merriment is that Marthe is more concerned about her jug than about her daughter's reputation. She pursues the culprit relentlessly, without considering that while doing so she may be destroying her daughter's good name. At the play's conclusion, Marthe is still pursuing the vain hope of recompense for her jug; she hardly seems to notice that her daughter and Ruprecht are reconciled.

In Eve, Kleist creates a strong, positive female character. She embodies his ideal of a sensitive woman who believes that trust is the ultimate component of a relationship. Because of her love for Ruprecht, she silently endures all kinds of aspersions on her character. Ruprecht's jealousy may make him disown her, but she staunchly refuses to expose Adam, as that would mean she would not get the medical certificate from him that is needed to save Ruprecht from military conscription. On the other hand, she cannot let Ruprecht appear as the culprit, because he will then be justified in believing that she was unfaithful to him. Only after Adam hurriedly pronounces a jail sentence for Ruprecht does Eve break her silence.

Kleist wrote one of the best German comedies and simultaneously presented a social critique of his time. The description of the village courtroom, with its leftover food and drinks strewn amid various documents, hardly resembles a place of justice. On the other hand, Adam's superior, Counselor Walter, is so bent on maintaining the dignity of the court that he refuses to pronounce Adam guilty even though he knows he committed the crime. It is more important for him to maintain respect for the authority residing in a judge's position than to uphold the truth. Instead of being jailed, Adam is therefore merely suspended; his ambitious clerk, Licht, is promoted to the level of judge. In Kleist's treatment, the theme that justice matters just as little to the people at the courthouse, who all have their individual concerns, becomes yet one more source of hilarity in *The Broken Jug*.

"Critical Evaluation" by Vibha Bakshi Gokhale

Further Reading

Doctorow, E. L. Foreword to *Plays by Heinrich von Kleist*, edited by Walter Hinderer. New York: Continuum, 1982. Doctorow discusses the farcical nature of *The Broken Jug*. The translation in this volume remains true to nineteenth century colloquial English, which imparts a rustic tone to the play.

Fischer, Bernd, ed. *A Companion to the Works of Heinrich von Kleist*. Columbia, S.C.: Camden House, 2003. Collection of essays analyzing various aspects of Kleist's work, including its themes of death, violence, and revenge and its challenge to Enlightenment Humanism.

Fordham, Kim. *Trials and Tribunals in the Dramas of Heinrich von Kleist*. New York: Peter Lang, 2007. Analyzes the various sorts of trials that occur in *The Broken Jug* and Kleist's other plays. Fordham demonstrates how these trials enable powerful people to manipulate the proceedings, seeking not truth and justice but their own version of order.

Greenberg, Martin, trans. *The Broken Jug*. In *Five Plays by Heinrich von Kleist*. New Haven, Conn.: Yale University Press, 1988. Excellent translation of *The Broken Jug* into colloquial English that successfully brings out the coarse and bawdy sense of humor of the original. The volume also contains a fine introduction to the plays.

Griffiths, Elystan. *Political Change and Human Emancipation in the Works of Heinrich von Kleist*. Rochester, N.Y.: Camden House, 2005. Griffiths demonstrates how Kleist's works offered a response to four major political and philosophical issues in late eighteenth and early nineteenth century Prussia: the relationship of national culture to the state; education and social reform; the theory and practice of war; and the administration and delivery of justice.

Maass, Joachim. *Kleist: A Biography*. Translated by Ralph Manheim. New York: Farrar, Straus and Giroux, 1983. A light treatment of the writer, written in an anecdotal, humorous style. Discusses the psychological torment of Kleist's characters. Presents a succinct analysis of Adam's corrupt but likable character.

McGlathery, James M. *Desire's Sway: The Plays and Stories of Heinrich von Kleist*. Detroit, Mich.: Wayne State University Press, 1983. Refers to *The Broken Jug* as a sexual comedy. Cleverly interprets Adam's various statements as expressions of his sexual fantasies.

Reeve, William C. *Kleist on Stage: 1804-1987*. Montreal: McGill-Queen's University Press, 1993. An excellent reference source for a history of productions of Kleist's plays. Gives an account of various interpretations of *The Broken Jug* and discusses the merits of actors who have played the part of Adam.

The Bronze Horseman

Author: Alexander Pushkin (1799-1837)
First published: *Medniy vsadnik*, 1837 (English translation, 1899)
Type of work: Poetry
Type of plot: Historical realism
Time of plot: 1703 and 1824
Locale: St. Petersburg, Russia

Principal characters:
PETER THE GREAT, czar of Russia, 1672-1725
THE BRONZE HORSEMAN, a statue of Peter
EVGENY, a clerk
PARASHA, the woman Evgeny loves

The Poem:

Peter the Great, astride his bronze horse, stands on the desolate Baltic shore on the northwest borders of his domain and gazes off into the distance. The very landscape around him seems unformed, unclear: the land soft and marshy, the sun shrouded in mist, the Finnish huts flimsy and temporary. Peter's design, however, is quite clear. Here, on the delta of the river Neva, out of nothing, he will build St. Petersburg, a fortress against the powerful Swedes, a new capital, a magnet to ships of all nations, a "window into Europe."

One hundred years passed, according to the narrator, and the city grew into a busy port, into a strategic fortress, and into a network of granite-faced rivers and canals lined with palaces, parks, and gardens, a metropolis whose power and elegance put dowdy old Moscow, the "dowager" capital, decidedly in the shade. It is all Peter's creation: the majesty of the architecture, the vast expanses of the city lit by the "white nights" of early summer, the sounds of winter—of sleighs and lavish balls—the sights and sounds of imperial troops on parade. Let the city flaunt its beauty, and let Peter's eternal sleep go undisturbed, says the narrator. However, there is a certain, terrible time and a sad story to be told.

On a dark November evening in 1824, a young man named Evgeny lies in his rented rooms in an unfashionable suburban quarter and listens to the rain and wind. He cannot sleep, and he thinks idly that it would be nice to have more brains and money or at least to have someone else's better luck. However, he does not bother mourning his more illustrious ancestors or envying them, either. Instead, his thoughts turn to his beloved Parasha, whom he hopes to marry one day. They will find a little place to live, and they will have children; a peaceful, humdrum life will go on until those children's children will, one day, bury him and faithful Parasha. Vaguely troubled by the storm, Evgeny falls asleep while the river rises and rises. By morning, it turns back on itself and, flowing upstream from the gulf, inundates the city.

Evgeny manages to save himself from the floodwaters by straddling one of a pair of stone lions on the portico of a nobleman's house. There he sits, pale, motionless, and trapped, as he watches the waves do their worst precisely where, far out toward the gulf, stands Parasha's house. He fears for her more than for himself. Not far away, its back toward him, the Horseman rises high above the waves.

Finally the Neva River begins to recede. Evgeny climbs down from his perch and finds a ferryman to take him to Parasha's island, where he finds familiar houses collapsed or wrenched off their foundations. Of Parasha's house and its inhabitants there is not a trace. The city begins to recover and go about its business, but Evgeny does not. He never returns to his rooms, and weeks stretch into months as he wanders the streets, oblivious to everything around him. He sleeps wherever he can find shelter, until one day, waking up on the quay near the stone lions that saved him, he recognizes where he is. His bewilderment seems to clear as he catches sight of the Horseman, and he walks round its base, muttering. He clenches his fists, whispering a furious threat. At that moment, it seems that the czar's face changes, and, as Evgeny turns to run, he hears the statue galloping after him, its ponderous hooves ringing on the city's cobblestones all night long.

From then on, he gives the Horseman wide berth, doffing his cap and lowering his eyes whenever he happens to be on that particular square. Not long after, Evgeny's body is found on a barren island in the river; he lies at the threshold of a small house wrecked and cast ashore by the flood, and that is where they bury him.

Critical Evaluation:

A poet who ranks with William Shakespeare, Johann Wolfgang von Goethe, and Dante Alighieri, Alexander Pushkin virtually created Russian literature. He was not the first Russian writer with talent or even genius, but he was the first (and some might say the only one) of such enormous range and brilliance, for he left models in lyric poetry, long narrative poems (the Russian *poèma*), drama, and fiction. Translated often but not always well, Pushkin is less known outside his homeland than the writers named above; the clarity and seeming simplicity of his style, its compactness and economy, its combination of unpredictability and inevitability makes him surprisingly difficult to translate. His place in his national literature is unique, and the Russian habit of referring to Pushkin in the present tense is not just literary convention, but rather a sense of him as a living presence, a continuing source of ideas and images. The characters seen in *The Bronze Horseman* and *Evgeny Onegin* (1823-1831), for example, have reappeared in various forms and guises in Russian literature ever since their creation, as has the idea of the artificial, "premeditated" city of St. Petersburg first evoked in Pushkin's poem.

Generally considered Pushkin's finest work, *The Bronze Horseman* was written in the autumn of 1833. It was not published until after Pushkin's death, and even then with some changes to pacify the censors, who, among other things, found the reference to a czar's statue as an idol disturbing. The work consists of an introduction and an exposition in two parts, a total of 481 lines of iambic tetrameter, freely rhymed. Though the shortest of Pushkin's serious narrative poems, it varies widely in style, tone, and tempo: Measured

and majestic passages with archaic or rhetorical vocabulary (as in parts of the introduction) give way to straightforward conversational speech and even a slightly flippant tone, seen in the choice of Evgeny's name (familiar and easy because Pushkin had used it in his great verse novel *Evgeny Onegin*) and his lineage (so similar to Pushkin's own), for example. The poet varies his rhyme scheme as well as his vocabulary, now speeding the action with couplets, now slowing it with quatrains and longer rhyming units. Violent similes and metaphors dominate in the description of the flood; jagged line breaks and a deliberately jumbled rhyme scheme that has nothing in common with anything preceding it depict Evgeny's increasing derangement and panic. Pushkin's deftness at modulating from one tone to another keeps his devices from overwhelming the story itself.

While the story is a model of straightforward simplicity, the poem is a tightly woven web of theme and reference, drawing in multiple historical, philosophical, and social strands so tightly that they are sometimes hard to separate. Pushkin drew on many sources: Polish poet Adam Mickiewicz's satiric indictment of Peter the Great and his city in his long poem *Forefathers' Eve* (1925-1946) is an immediate and important one, as were contemporary accounts of the disastrous flood. Pushkin had long been fascinated with Peter's life and times and had already written about them in his story of his great-grandfather, *The Negro of Peter the Great* (1828), and in his narrative poem *Poltava* (1828). There were personal complications as well. Pushkin's ancestors had been prominent and influential, but his own financial and social positions were precarious. Czar Nicholas I's "patronage" was a dubious honor, since it meant that the czar himself was Pushkin's personal censor. Then there were the Decembrists, conspirators who, in 1825, had attempted a palace coup d'état to overthrow the autocracy and to prevent Nicholas from ascending to the throne. The armed struggle resulting in their surrender took place in Senate Square, in the very shadow of Peter's statue; a number were hanged, and many more were exiled. Among them were some of Pushkin's closest friends. Though they are nowhere mentioned in the poem, no reader could fail to make the association between the place, the statue, and the revolt.

While differing in their interpretations of the poem, most commentators at least agree that the pattern is one of polarity, of seemingly irreconcilable opposites juxtaposed. Some of these pairings are specific to Russia, while others are universal: East versus West, the ongoing Russian preoccupation with national identity either inside or outside European culture, and the wisdom of Peter's forced Westernization of Russia. Peter's decision to "hack" out a window on Europe was an unresolved question in Pushkin's time and remains so in the post-Soviet era. That question involves yet other conflicting notions: Moscow versus St. Petersburg, religious tradition versus secular change, the organic versus the artificial. Unresolved, too, is the question of Russia's traditional preference for the strong hand that will impose order on a vast, chaotic land. What will that order bring, and what is its price? Is the Horseman reining in his steed on the edge of an abyss, or is he urging it on? Pushkin clearly celebrates Peter's— and Russia's—greatness in the introduction, but the fate of Evgeny does not bode well for the ordinary citizen, let alone the dissenter. What kind of overlord is it who will not brook even a ragged madman's muttered threat but descends from his pedestal to chase him down?

The question Pushkin poses about the relationship of the ruler to the ruled goes beyond Russia, as does the question of humankind's relationship to nature. Here, Peter indeed brings Cosmos out of Chaos, in lines that are deliberately suggestive of the blank formlessness of the world before creation. However, Peter builds in spite of the natural order, not in harmony with it, and his creation is vulnerable to destruction by the very elements he claims to have mastered—a point that his successor Alexander I briefly and poignantly makes before sending troops out to aid victims. At the same time, Alexander is portrayed as rueful, not ridiculous. The poet's irony is never facile or cheap—only tragic.

Russia versus Europe, state versus citizen, historical destiny versus individual fate, Peter's grand vision versus Evgeny's humble daydreams, humankind versus nature— these are some of the opposing principles Pushkin presents. He reconciles them poetically, creating a unified whole, but never resolves them. Just as the statue's pose is ambiguous, so is Pushkin's attitude, and it is quite deliberately so.

"Critical Evaluation" by Jane Ann Miller

Further Reading

Bayley, John. *Pushkin: A Comparative Study*. New York: Cambridge University Press, 1971. Analyzes Pushkin's work in the context of both Russian and European literature, with special attention given to William Shakespeare and the English poets. The chapter on Pushkin's narrative and historical poetry uses *The Bronze Horseman* as a standard of comparison both with Pushkin's own earlier poems, such as *Poltava*, and with Lord Byron's treatment of some of the same themes. Includes an extensive discussion of *The Bronze Horseman* in its own right.

Bethea, David M. *Realizing Metaphors: Alexander Pushkin and the Life of the Poet*. Madison: University of Wisconsin Press, 1998. Describes the relationship between Pushkin's life and his art and discusses why, more than two hundred years after his birth, his work remains relevant. Includes index and illustrations.

Binyon, T. J. *Pushkin: A Biography*. New York: Knopf, 2004. The winner of the Samuel Johnson prize for British nonfiction, this biography chronicles Pushkin's literary success alongside his personal failures. Binyon describes how the writer included small pieces of his life in *Eugene Onegin* and other works.

Briggs, A. D. P. *Alexander Pushkin: A Critical Study*. Totowa, N.J.: Barnes & Noble, 1983. A thorough introduction to Pushkin's work, with an entire chapter devoted to *The Bronze Horseman*. Briggs gives an overview of the poem's sources, themes, devices, including rhyming patterns, and structure.

Evdokimova, Svetlana. *Pushkin's Historical Imagination*. New Haven, Conn.: Yale University Press, 1999. An examination of Pushkin's fictional and nonfictional works on the subject of history, including *The Bronze Horseman*. Considers Pushkin's ideas on the relationship between chance and necessity, the significance of great individuals, and historical truth.

Kahn, Andrew. *Pushkin's "The Bronze Horseman."* London: Bristol Classical Press, 1998. Recounts the history of the poem's composition and discusses its form, themes, and critical reception.

_____, ed. *The Cambridge Companion to Pushkin*. New York: Cambridge University Press, 2006. Collection of essays by Pushkin scholars discussing the writer's life and work in various genres; Pushkin and politics, history, and literary criticism; and Pushkin's position in Soviet and post-Soviet culture.

Rosenshield, Gary. *Pushkin and the Genres of Madness: The Masterpieces of 1833*. Madison: University of Wisconsin Press, 2003. Analyzes *The Bronze Horseman* and other works written in 1833, when Pushkin began to describe both the creative and destructive aspects of madness. Examines how the poem confronts the legacy of Peter the Great.

Vickery, Walter N. *Alexander Pushkin*. Rev. ed. New York: Twayne, 1992. A revised edition of an earlier book by the same author, it incorporates new scholarship and is a brief but highly readable introduction to Pushkin's life and work. The section on *The Bronze Horseman* includes a synopsis, brief comments on style, and a discussion of major themes.

Brother Ass

Author: Eduardo Barrios (1884-1963)
First published: El hermano asno, 1922 (English
  translation, 1942)
Type of work: Novel
Type of plot: Psychological realism
Time of plot: Twentieth century
Locale: A rural town in Chile

Principal characters:
FRAY RUFINO, a friar with the reputation of a saint
FRAY LÁZARO, narrator and Fray Rufino's best friend
MARÍA MERCEDES, a friend of Fray Lázaro
GRACIA, María Mercedes' older sister

The Story:

Fray Lázaro is celebrating his seventh anniversary as a Franciscan friar. His major concern, that he never had a true call to the priesthood, leads him to write a diary. The diary focuses on his life and on the life of Fray Rufino, a friar who has earned the reputation of a saint.

Both men are under considerable stress because of life at the monastery. Fray Rufino trains cats and mice to eat from the same plate. The monks celebrate this event as a miracle. It soon becomes a curse, however, as the cats stop hunting mice, and rodents invade the monastery. As secret punishment for that "miracle," Fray Rufino begins to flagellate himself and maintains a heavy work schedule; he frequently takes upon himself the chores of his fellow friars.

Fray Rufino's reputation keeps growing outside the monastery. People from faraway places start coming to the monastery in order to meet the monk, whose miracles include cures of dying animals and the restoration of a blind woman's sight. Such personal attention creates in him a fear of losing his true Franciscan vocation to achieve total humility.

Fray Lázaro's fragile confidence in his religious calling suffers a great blow the day he sees in church a beautiful young woman who reminds him of a past love. To his surprise, the woman, María Mercedes, is the sister of Gracia, the former girlfriend, now a married woman living in town. Against his will, Fray Lázaro feels an attraction to María Mercedes, who appears to love him. Her constant visits cause him severe depression as he begins to debate whether he is in love. In desperation, and in order to stop seeing María Mercedes, Fray Lázaro pretends to be ill.

Suddenly Fray Rufino warns Fray Lázaro to be careful; Fray Rufino tells him that he can see that Fray Lázaro is losing his religious vocation. Fray Lázaro, surprised by the advice because he did not confide his secret to anyone, decides that Fray Rufino is right. That very day he will tell María Mercedes that they cannot see each other anymore. When he sees the young woman, however, he cannot resist her inno-

cence and beauty. He also experiences jealousy when he notices that a handsome young man has been trying to attract María Mercedes' attention. Fray Lázaro happily withdraws to the monastery when he realizes that María Mercedes does not respond to the young man's flirtation.

Fray Lázaro becomes more interested in Fray Rufino's well-being. He recognizes that something unusual is happening to Fray Rufino. His suspicions are confirmed one night when he discovers that Fray Rufino has increased his physical punishment to the point of crawling on his knees while carrying a heavy wooden cross. The crawling produces heavy bleeding in the weak old man. At last Fray Lázaro confronts Fray Rufino with the knowledge of the secret physical punishment. In turn, Fray Rufino confesses more terrible news: He says that an apparition, the ghost of a monk who claims to have come from Purgatory, visited him several times in order to warn him about his weaknesses as a monk. Fray Lázaro makes him promise to stop the intense punishment and to seek advice from higher religious authorities.

One day María Mercedes comes to mass accompanied for the first time by her sister Gracia. María Mercedes' aloofness toward Fray Lázaro makes him suspect that her family has discovered their relationship and forbidden her to speak to him. When María Mercedes speaks to Fray Lázaro, she confirms the monk's fears. She also insists upon seeing Fray Rufino. Fray Lázaro promises her a visit with Fray Rufino early the next morning.

Fray Lázaro arrives late for that meeting with Fray Rufino and María Mercedes. As he walks into the reception room, he is horrified by María Mercedes' screams for help as she is sexually attacked by Fray Rufino. In desperation, she manages to run away from Fray Rufino, who is screaming that he is not worthy of his saintly reputation. He also claims that the ghost of the monk makes him behave in such a brutal fashion. To avoid a scandal, Fray Lázaro assumes all guilt for the attack, and he is transferred to a monastery far from the town.

Critical Evaluation:

Eduardo Barrios was born in Valparaiso, Chile, the son of a Chilean father and a Peruvian mother. He lived in Peru and in various other countries of Latin America, where he traveled extensively and worked at odd jobs. He was a prolific writer of short stories, plays, and novels. Such versatility may have contributed to his careful, detailed literary style.

Brother Ass initiated in Latin America a literary trend that may be called the psychological novel. Within the realist mode focused on social critique, the psychological novel presents an analytical study of the human psyche by means of well-delineated characters, each of whom represents traits common to all people. The interaction and the clash of these types illustrate how human behavior works, including the ways in which people relate to each other in friendship. Psychological analysis such as this also includes a didactic approach to improvement of life in society at large. As a byproduct of the carefully orchestrated case study, the psychological novel offers a strong social comment on a particular problem in contemporary society.

In an analytical approach, Barrios's characters are important components of what could be viewed as a psychological behavior experiment, with close documentation of their reactions toward each other. Characters, therefore, stand as abstractions of the impact of strong personality traits when people find themselves together in society. The title, *Brother Ass*, incorporates the concept of human beings viewed as animals in their personal interaction. Life in a formal social setting, along with the rules and restrictions imposed by groups, clashes against people's animal-like feelings and emotions. That conflict reveals the metaphorical message: Each human being's struggle to keep "Brother Ass" under control constitutes the greatest challenge for all members of society.

The choice of setting, a Franciscan monastery in an isolated town, illustrates Barrios's intention to create a controlled environment for his psychological experiment. One could argue that Barrios's intentions are twofold. One is to show how characters behave when removed from society. The second is to show how, once isolated from civilized rules, characters reconstitute societal values. The odd, unexpected behavior of the characters and the surprising ending constitute Barrios's social comment.

Barrios moves away from examination of Latin American society as it was practiced by most of his contemporary realist fellow writers. Instead, Barrios attempts to achieve a universal message through contemplation of the human psyche and its function in the shaping of life within a social group. Unlike animals, human beings respond to one factor in particular that makes them relate to one another, making the social fabric of interpersonal relationships more apparent to the reader. Love and its opposite feeling, hatred, stand out as those forces that promote social cohesiveness. In *Brother Ass*, love is presented in three forms: fraternal, religious, and sexual. These loves, however, are interconnected, and their carefully maintained balance makes a well-rounded individual. Fraternal love makes people want to live together in a social group, as demonstrated by life at the monastery. The desire for companionship is the basic foundation of life in society. As demonstrated by the frantic behavior of Fray Lázaro and Fray Rufino, however, deprivation or overcommitment to the other two equally strong forms of love may result in a personal crisis.

In regard to sexual love, Barrios treats the roles of women in contemporary society in a new way. His contemporary fellow writers often take extreme positions in their representations of women. Either women represent evil vices (prostitution, for example) or they become ethereal beings, subjected to great stress from their immediate reality. In Barrios's novel, women protagonists, such as María Mercedes, are affected by the same strains in life that men are. María Mercedes shares with Fray Lázaro his doubt about his vocation for the religious because they both understand that such a choice opposes a natural desire for reproduction. Women, therefore, share equally with men the inherent human task of establishing themselves as members of a larger social group.

The function of yet another inherent human feeling is the ability to love a supernatural being, known in Western cultures as God. Barrios depicts love for a divine being as the most sublime expression because this loving relationship does not require physical reciprocity, yet he does not preach acceptance of the existence of God. Instead, he proposes life as observed by the Franciscan order as an example of simpler societal values. Life in a community with close attachment to nature is seen as a refreshing relief from the chaotic modern society at the beginning of the twentieth century. When life in the monastery loses its spiritual purpose, however (as happened to Fray Rufino), an existentialist crisis takes place.

Barrios's most important contribution to contemporary Latin American literature is his work with such modern psychological theories as Freudian psychoanalysis. Rather than bewildering his reader with macabre descriptions of situations in society, as most realist writers are doing, Barrios prefers a more in-depth critical analysis of the possible causes of those problems. His characters are also real, and they face psychological problems similar to those experienced by his readers.

Rafael Ocasio

Further Reading

Brown, James. "*El hermano asno*: When the Unreliable Narrator Meets the Unreliable Reader." *Hispania* 71, no. 4 (December, 1988): 798-805. Good study of the various modern literary techniques displayed in the novel. Stresses the relationship between the reader and the novel's narrator. Discusses the use of irony in the plot.

Foster, David William, and Virginia Ramos Foster. "Barrios, Eduardo." In *Modern Latin American Literature*, edited by David William Foster and Virginia Ramos Foster. New York: Frederick Ungar, 1975. A survey study of Barrios's work. Provides excerpts of critical studies by various critics. An excellent starting point to Barrios's works.

Souza, Raymond. "Indeterminacy of Meaning in *El hermano asno*." *Chasqui* 13, nos. 2/3 (February, May, 1984): 26-32. Good analysis of Barrios's literary craft and the treatment of rape as a literary motif. Focuses on women's issues.

Walker, John. *Gálvez, Barrios, and the Metaphysical Malaise. Symposium: A Quarterly Journal in Modern Foreign Literatures* 36, no. 4 (Winter, 1982/1983): 352-358. Comparative study of Barrios and novelist Manuel Gálvez. Both authors were interested in metaphysical subjects, and Walker stresses their interest in metaphysical issues as ways to improve contemporary society.

_____. *Metaphysics and Aesthetics in the Works of Eduardo Barrios*. London: Tamesis, 1983. Studies the relationship between Barrios's novel and his strong interest in metaphysics.

The Brothers

Author: Terence (c. 190-159 B.C.E.)
First produced: Adelphoe, 160 B.C.E.; first transcribed, 160 B.C.E. (English translation, 1598)
Type of work: Drama
Type of plot: Comedy
Time of plot: Second century B.C.E.
Locale: Athens

Principal characters:
MICIO, an aged Athenian
DEMEA, his brother
AESCHINUS, Demea's son, adopted by Micio
CTESIPHO, Demea's other son
SOSTRATA, an Athenian widow
PAMPHILA, Sostrata's daughter
SANNIO, a pimp and slave dealer
HEGIO, an old man of Athens

The Story:

Micio is an aging, easygoing Athenian bachelor whose strict and hardworking brother Demea permits him to adopt and rear Aeschinus, one of Demea's two sons. Unlike his brother, Micio is a permissive parent, choosing to let pass many of Aeschinus's small extravagances on the assumption that children are more likely to remain bound to their duty by ties of kindness than by those of fear.

Micio comes to wonder if his policy is the better. One day, shortly after Aeschinus tells him he is tired of the Athenian courtesans and wants to marry, Demea comes to Micio and informs him angrily that Aeschinus broke into a strange house, beat its master, and carried off a woman with whom he is infatuated. It is a shameful thing, Demea says, especially since Aeschinus has such a fine example of continence and industry in his brother Ctesipho, who dutifully spends his time working for Demea in the country. It is also shameful that Aeschinus was reared the way he was, Demea observes,

with Micio letting the youth go to the bad by failing to restrain his excesses.

After quarreling about their methods for rearing children, the two men part. Demea agrees not to interfere, and Micio, although confused and grieved by Aeschinus's apparent change of heart and failure to inform him of the escapade, determines to stand by his adopted son.

As it turns out, however, Demea's report of Aeschinus is correct only in outline. The house into which the young man broke belongs to Sannio, a pimp and slave dealer, and the woman carried off is a slave with whom, ironically, the model son Ctesipho fell in love but cannot afford to buy. Demea's restraint is more than Ctesipho can bear, and because he is afraid to indulge himself before his father, he chooses to do so behind his back. Aeschinus agrees to procure the woman for his brother but keeps his motives secret in order to protect his brother from Demea's wrath.

Sannio, furious at the treatment he received, hounds Aeschinus for the return of the slave. Sannio is soon to leave on a slave-trading expedition, so he has no time to prosecute the case in court; moreover, an obscure point of law creates the possibility that the slave might be declared free and that Sannio could lose his entire investment. In consequence, he finally consents to sell her for the price he paid for her.

Meanwhile, other complications arise. Long before the slave episode, Aeschinus fell in love with Pamphila, the daughter of Sostrata, a poor Athenian widow. Aeschinus promises to marry Pamphila and they anticipate this union, with the result that she is about to be delivered of his child. Then, while she is in labor, it is reported that he abducted the slave girl and is having an affair with her. The mother and daughter are, of course, extremely upset at Aeschinus's apparent faithlessness, and in despair Sostrata relates her dilemma to her only friend, Hegio, an impoverished old man who was her husband's friend and who is also a friend of Demea. Hegio, indignant, goes to Demea to demand that justice be done. Demea, having just heard that Ctesipho played some part in the abduction and assuming that Aeschinus seduced the model son into evil ways, is doubly furious at Hegio's news. Immediately he goes off hunting for Micio, only to be misdirected by one of Aeschinus's slaves, who is attempting to prevent the old man from discovering that Ctesipho and his mistress are both in Micio's house.

A short time later Hegio encounters Micio, who, having learned the truth regarding the abduction, promises to explain everything to Sostrata and Pamphila. As he is leaving the widow's house, he meets Aeschinus, who is himself coming to try to explain to the women the muddle in which he finds himself. Pretending ignorance of Aeschinus's situation, Micio mildly punishes the young man for his furtiveness by pretending to be at Sostrata's house as the representative of another suitor for Pamphila's hand; but when he sees the agony which the prospect of losing Pamphila produces in Aeschinus, Micio puts an end to his pretense and promises the grateful and repentant youth that he can marry Pamphila at once.

Demea, finally returning from the wild-goose chase that the servant sent him on, accosts Micio in front of his house. Although Micio calms his brother somewhat by telling him how matters really stand, Demea still retains his disapproval of Micio's parental leniency. The crisis occurs shortly afterward when Demea learns the full truth about Ctesipho—that the model son was a party to the abduction and that the whole affair was conceived and executed for his gratification. At first the knowledge nearly puts him out of his wits, but Micio gradually brings his brother to a perception of the fact that no

irreparable harm was done. Also, since Demea's strictness and severity ultimately did not succeed, perhaps leniency and generosity are most effective after all in dealing with children. Demea, realizing that his harshness made Ctesipho fearful and suspicious of his father, decides to try Micio's mode of conduct, and he surprises all who know him by his cheerful resignation. Indeed, he even goes so far as to have the wall between Micio's and Sostrata's houses torn down and to suggest, not without a certain malice, that the only truly generous thing Micio can do for Sostrata will be to marry her. At first Micio hesitates, but when the suggestion is vehemently seconded by Aeschinus, Micio at last gives in.

Demea also persuades Micio to free Syrus and his wife Phrygia, his slaves, and to give Hegio some property to support him in his old age. Then he turns to his sons and gives his consent to their amorous projects, asking only to be allowed in the future to check them when their youthful passions threaten to lead them astray. The young men submit willingly to his request.

Critical Evaluation:

The Brothers is one of Terence's most popular comedies, probably because it approaches in such a good-humored manner a subject that affects every member of a family. Responsible parents worry about the best way to bring up their children, and their offspring worry about how to live up to their parents' expectations.

Although both fathers love the young men for whom they are responsible, Demea and Micio could hardly differ more in their philosophies of child rearing. Demea believes in governing by fear, and Micio believes in governing by love. Ctesipho, raised by Demea's strict rules, was made to work hard, and, at least in his father's opinion, was kept away from temptation; Aeschinus, raised by Micio, was allowed total freedom, excused for his misdeeds, and easily forgiven.

As Micio explains his ideas in his opening monologue, his ideas seem extremely appealing, while Demea's ideas seem old-fashioned and unenlightened. By appearing to side with Micio, however, Terence is placing his audience off guard. In fact, neither brother has a foolproof solution to the problem of raising and educating the young. As the story progresses, it becomes evident how little the two fathers really know about their sons and how easily the fathers can be deceived.

When Terence looks at the outcomes of these two educational experiments, the young men have entered a critical time in their lives. They are old enough to get into serious trouble, but they are too young to govern their actions by reason. Each has become involved with a woman, and, as the customs of comedy dictate, these relationships have been concealed from the older generation. In fact, since one woman is a slave, and the other comes from a poor family, neither relationship seems likely to win parental approval.

Meanwhile, the fathers remain ignorant, not only of what the young men are doing but also of what their sons are really like. Demea thinks that he has created a boy in his own stern and upright image. He has no idea that Ctesipho is sneaking away whenever he can. Micio knows that Aeschinus is sowing his wild oats, but he cannot imagine that his son would ever fail to confide in him. It is doubly ironic, then, that Aeschinus not only deceives his father about seducing Pamphila but also admits to an involvement of which, in fact, he is innocent and then accepts his lenient father's forgiveness for it.

Even though *The Brothers* has a dual plot, as do all but one of Terence's plays, and though there are two love stories, this play is different from the other works because it does not focus on the love interest. The important pairings are not those of the lovers. The comparisons are between the two fathers; between the two sons, who, though so different in character, behave so much alike; and between the two fathers and sons.

Critics differ in their assessments of Micio and Demea. Some critics find Micio the more sympathetic of the two men, suggesting that his final punishment—losing money and property and acquiring an unwanted wife—is too harsh. Other critics agree with Demea that Micio is motivated not by true generosity but, instead, by laziness and a desire for popularity. These critics argue that he deserves what happens to him.

Another question is just how Terence wishes Demea to be viewed. If Demea actually chooses popularity over principle, he can hardly be respected. On the other hand, if he is merely tricking his brother in order to make a point, he goes too far. In either case, Demea seems to forfeit the sympathy of the audience. For some reason, however, Terence chooses him as the spokesman for moderation and, presumably, for the author.

There are, however, no problems of interpretation concerning the sons. Obviously, Ctesipho, the younger, is the weaker of the two, either by nature or perhaps because he has not been given a chance to make his own decisions. Certainly his willingness to let his brother take the blame for his own scheme does not say much for Demea's force-feeding of moral principles. Most audiences find Aeschinus much more appealing. He is loyal to his brother, and if he lacks the courage to face his imminent fatherhood, at least he cannot allow the woman he loves to be married to another.

The father-son relationships in *The Brothers* resemble each other because both of them are based on illusion on the part of the fathers and deception on the part of the sons. The relationships are also similar, however, because they are based on real affection. The fathers would not feel so strongly about their sons' conduct if they were not genuinely concerned about their future welfare. As for the sons, it seems unlikely that Ctesipho really dislikes his father, as Demea suggests in his bitterness. Although he does not appear in the last part of the play, Ctesipho previously shows no signs of callousness. It seems reasonable to assume that a youth so responsive to his brother's kindness also appreciates his father's efforts. As for Aeschinus, one need only look at his fourth-act soliloquy to ascertain the depth of his feeling for Micio. This speech may be as important a key to Terence's own attitude as Demea's final comments, which argue that in the rearing of children, the middle way between harshness and indulgence is best. It may be that even more important than commitment to any educational theory is children's assurance that they have their parents' unconditional love.

"Critical Evaluation" by Rosemary M. Canfield Reisman

Further Reading

Arnott, W. Geoffrey. *Menander, Plautus, Terence.* New York: Oxford University Press, 1975. After a short summary of Terence's environment and career, Arnott explores such major critical issues as Terence's "contamination" of his Greek sources, his use of innovation, and the quality of his work. The chapter on Plautus and Terence begins with a bibliographical essay.

Dutsch, Dorota M. *Feminine Discourse in Roman Comedy: On Echoes and Voices.* New York: Oxford University Press, 2008. Analyzes the dialogue of female characters in Terence's plays, noting its use of endearments, softness of speech, and emphasis on small problems. Questions whether Roman women actually spoke that way.

Forehand, Walter E. *Terence.* Boston: Twayne, 1985. Chapters on Terence's life, his literary career, and the theater of his day are followed by analyses of the plays. *The Brothers* is treated at length, with special attention given to its themes. Includes extensive notes, select bibliography, and index.

Goldberg, Sander M. *Understanding Terence.* Princeton, N.J.: Princeton University Press, 1986. Contains several references to *The Brothers*, discussing the implications of the education theme and the play's political significance. Topically organized and well indexed.

Leigh, Matthew. *Comedy and the Rise of Rome*. New York: Oxford University Press, 2004. Analyzes the comedies of Plautus and Terence, placing them within the context of political and economic conditions in Rome during the third and second centuries B.C.E. Discusses how audiences of that time responded to these comedies.

Sandbach, F. H. *The Comic Theatre of Greece and Rome*. London: Chatto & Windus, 1977. The chapter on Terence is an excellent starting point for study of the dramatist. Includes discussion of Terence's use of sources in *The Brothers*. The appendix features a useful glossary of Greek and Roman terms, as well as a brief bibliography.

Segal, Erich, ed. *Oxford Readings in Menander, Plautus, and Terence*. New York: Oxford University Press, 2001. Collection of essays examining comedies by Terence and other classical playwrights. The introduction describes how these plays are the foundations of modern comedy.

Sutton, Dana F. *Ancient Comedy: The War of the Generations*. New York: Twayne, 1993. Analyzes *The Brothers* and shows the unique quality of Terence's comedy, in contrast to that of Menander or Plautus. Agrees with Goldberg (above) that Terence lacks a spirit of fun but asserts that Terence's basic problem is philosophical. Includes bibliographical suggestions.

The Brothers Ashkenazi

Author: Israel Joshua Singer (1893-1944)

First published: Di brider Ashkenazi, 1936 (English translation, 1936)

Type of work: Novel

Type of plot: Historical realism

Time of plot: Late nineteenth and early twentieth centuries

Locale: Poland

Principal characters:

SIMCHA MEYER ASHKENAZI, an enterprising Jew

JACOB BUNIM, his twin brother

ABRAHAM, their father

DINAH, Simcha's wife

PEARL, Jacob's wife

GERTRUDE, the daughter of Simcha and Dinah

TEVYEH, a revolutionary weaver

NISSAN, a revolutionary

The Story:

Abraham is a pious Jew and a good businessman. General agent for the Huntze mills, he is greatly respected by the community. He always spends the Passover season with his beloved rabbi in a town some distance from Lodz. One year, his wife protests more than usual at being left alone because she expects to be confined soon. She knows the child will be a boy, for she feels stirrings on her right side. Abraham pays no attention to her.

When he returns, he finds two sons. The older by several minutes is Simcha; the younger is Jacob. Simcha is the smaller of the two and shows a meaner spirit. As they grow older, Jacob is the happy leader of neighborhood games, the favorite of all. Dinah, a neighbor girl, has worshiped him for years. Simcha seldom plays with anyone, and he has no stomach for even minor physical pain.

In school, however, Jacob is an amiable dunce, whereas Simcha is the scholar. Before long, Simcha is recognized as a genius. At an early age, he cites the Talmud and disputes with his teacher. When he is ten years old, he is sent to a more

learned rabbi, Nissan's father. His new teacher is more moral and uncompromising, and Simcha's glib smartness often leads him into disfavor. Moreover, here he has to take second place to Nissan.

Simcha keeps his leadership by running gambling games during class hours, and on holidays he leads his schoolmates into gambling houses. Simcha always wins, even from the professional gamblers. Nissan has no time for gambling, but his sin is even greater: He reads secular books on chemistry, astronomy, and economics. When Simcha betrays him and his father casts him out, Nissan becomes an apprentice weaver.

Because of Simcha's growing reputation for acuity, a marriage broker is able to arrange an advantageous engagement. At the age of thirteen, Dinah and Simcha are betrothed. Dinah is miserable. She is blonde and educated in languages; Simcha is unprepossessing and educated only in the Talmudic discipline. The marriage, which takes place several years later, is never a happy one, for Dinah never forgets Jacob.

Simcha, with a clever head for figures, keeps the accounts at the mill belonging to his easygoing father-in-law. By convincing the older man to sign promissory notes, Simcha soon becomes a partner. Although the family resents Simcha's hard dealing, he is grimly intent on making money. By shrewdness and trickery, he becomes sole owner of the mill in a short time. His father-in-law's mill, however, is only a handloom establishment; Simcha sets his sights higher.

The biggest steam mill in Lodz is owned by a crusty German named Huntze. Simcha's father is general agent, and the mill has a high reputation. Huntze's profligate sons want a title in the family, but old Huntze will not spend the money for one. Wily Simcha lends great sums to the Huntze boys, enough to buy a title and more. When their father dies, the sons recognize the debt by appointing Simcha their agent. Abraham is dismissed and thereafter counts his older son among the dead.

Jacob marries Pearl, the anemic daughter of the great Eisen household in Warsaw. Pearl saw Jacob at Simcha's wedding and fell in love with the ebullient younger brother. Jacob easily sheds his Jewish ways and becomes Europeanized. Because Pearl is sickly, she cannot keep up with her vigorous husband, and Jacob spends much time in Lodz. Eventually, to Simcha's chagrin, Jacob is made agent for the Flederbaum mills, a rival establishment.

When a depression comes, Simcha adulterates his goods to keep going and then decides to cut wages. Under the leadership of Tevyeh, a fanatic, and Nissan, now a well-educated weaver, the men strike. Simcha resists for a long time and then breaks the strike by bribing the police to arrest Nissan and Tevyeh. The two are sentenced to exile in Siberia.

By paying close attention to sales and by sweating his labor, Simcha makes money. He travels to the East and increases his market enormously. He is recognized as the merchant prince of Lodz. During the Russo-Japanese War, he makes great profits by selling to the military. Throughout these years, the trade union movement grows, however, and Nissan, back in Lodz, becomes a highly placed official in the revolutionary society. When the workers strike again, the unionists are too strong for Simcha, and his factory stays closed for months. This time the strike is broken only by military action, which turns into a pogrom against the Jews. Nissan is again sent to prison.

To increase his holdings and to get sufficient capital to buy the entire ownership of the Huntze mills, Simcha divorces Dinah and marries a rich widow. Jacob, matching his brother's affluence by becoming the lover of one of the Flederbaum girls after Pearl divorces him, is made director of the rival mill. Simcha's daughter Gertrude, a headstrong

modern young woman, wills Jacob to fall in love with her. He marries her because she reminds him of Dinah.

When World War I breaks out, Simcha moves his factory to Petrograd and so misses the German occupation of Lodz. Russia goes through a revolution, however, and the workers come to power. Once again, Nissan meets Simcha, but this time Nissan is the master, and his party confiscates Simcha's property. When the ruined Simcha tries to get out of Russia, he is betrayed by a fellow Jew, arrested, and jailed.

Back in Lodz, Jacob still maintains some position in the community, and Simcha's second wife manages to hold on to some wealth. Jacob goes to Russia and by judicious bribery frees his brother, who is now a broken man. When the two brothers attempt to reenter Poland, anti-Jewish feeling is strong. The border guards force Simcha to dance and grovel and shout a repudiation of his religion and race. Refusing to truckle, Jacob strikes a captain. Jacob is shot to death, but Simcha is permitted to live.

Simcha apathetically stays for a time with his wife, his divorced wife Dinah, his daughter Gertrude, and his granddaughter. Gradually, his cunning returns. He makes a trip to England and arranges for a substantial loan to rebuild his looted factory. He induces his long-forgotten son to come back from France. Ignatz brings his French wife with him. Simcha suspects darkly that she is not even Jewish, but he does not inquire. When the postwar depression strikes, Simcha is reviled by his fellow merchants for bringing in English capital. Commercially, Lodz is almost dead when Simcha dies.

Critical Evaluation:

At first glance, Israel Joshua Singer's *The Brothers Ashkenazi* appears to have many of the qualities typical of the historical fiction of writers such as Sir Walter Scott and Alexandre Dumas, who intermingle the lives of fictional characters with those of real personages, usually during periods when important events are affecting the future of a region or a nation. Seen in that light, the novel is a study of what happens to individuals when they are forced to act in response to, or in an attempt to influence, larger historical forces. Such a description could be misleading, however, since Singer's work is not simply a historical novel. Rather, it is a novel about history, a study of the way the historical process affects, or fails to affect, the lives of the Jewish people. Singer contrasts the prevalent view of world history, which is often described as a linear process, with that of Jewish history, which Singer represents as being cyclical. Anita Norich has said that in *The Brothers Ashkenazi* Singer tries "to come to terms not only with the tension between Jewish society and the Jew but also between Jewish society and its broader environment," thus highlighting "the similarity of Jewish experience in every age."

The lives of the brothers Jacob and Simcha Ashkenazi mirror the linear notion of history. Though radically different in temperament, both prosper in the city of Lodz, which is itself undergoing a renaissance as a result of the influx of foreigners who bring with them technological improvements. Whereas Jacob succeeds by looks and luck, Simcha relies on his cunning and his renunciation of traditional Jewish and family values to manipulate others to his advantage. In fact, Simcha is almost a stereotype of the Jew as he has been viewed by Gentiles throughout history, one who takes advantage of others' misfortunes, including those of close relations. Trying to distance himself from his heritage and become accepted by the non-Jewish community where he sees the opportunity to make his fortune, Simcha engages in a conscious attempt to achieve assimilation, a phenomenon rejected by more conservative Jews for centuries. He glibly changes his name to the more Germanic "Max" and, with almost equal ease, puts aside his wife when he learns that he can gain monetary and social advantage by taking a Russian bride.

What both Jacob and Simcha learn is that regardless of their actions, it is their fate to be Jews. When both are threatened by the Russian guards during World War I, they learn that their social status is no shield for anti-Semitism. Jacob is heroic in accepting his fate; he dies celebrating his Jewishness. Max, on the other hand, denies his heritage and escapes death but then finds little solace upon his return to Lodz, where he cannot avoid his lineage. His final, poignant scene in the novel shows him near death, sitting under a portrait of a satyr (the symbol of pagan pursuits of pleasure), reading from an old Hebrew Bible the words of the writer of Ecclesiastes about the vanity of human wishes.

Singer's lesson is not intended simply as a critique of Simcha. Readers are to understand that the novelist is making a comment on a much larger issue, the fact that there is no safe place for Jews in the larger world. Certainly Max is intended as a symbol of the fate of Jews who, no matter how hard they try, find that assimilation is a pipedream. For Singer, the Jewish heritage is both a blessing and a curse.

Singer reinforces his message through effective use of symbolism. The presence of the portrait of the satyr over the dying Simcha is only one example of his inclusion of signs that provide silent commentary on the significance of his protagonist's futile struggle. Even more telling are references to Mephistopheles, repeated throughout the novel at key points when Max has made some further attempt to pro-

mote himself at the expense of his own people. Max is a Faustian figure, willing to sell his soul for personal enhancement; like Faust, his fate is sealed, for anyone who gives in to temptation of this magnitude is doomed.

Adding to the symbolic resonance of the novel is Singer's representation of the city of Lodz and its inhabitants. The rise and fall of the Ashkenazi brothers are paralleled in the history of the city. Lodz stands in the novel as a symbol of the fate of the Jews when they interact with the outside world. The sleepy village undergoes a false renaissance when outside forces introduce the marvels of technology, but the city's prosperity quickly disappears when manufacturing ceases to be profitable; the collapse of industry returns Lodz to its former state, wiser perhaps for its experience but no better off than it was before the Germans brought their machinery and modern methods of production. Singer suggests, so it is with the Jews. They may interact with the forces of history, but they will never be able to achieve permanent benefit from them. They will always be outsiders. For Singer, that represents strength as well as struggle, for that which is permanent in Jewish heritage will always permit the Jews to transcend sorrow to achieve both personal and social dignity.

"Critical Evaluation" by Laurence W. Mazzeno

Further Reading

Epstein, John. "A Yiddish Novel with Tolstoyan Sweep." *The Wall Street Journal*, February 7, 2009. A favorable review of *The Brothers Ashkenazi*, which Epstein describes as the "best Russian novel ever written in Yiddish."

Horn, Dara. "Imagination as a Group Effort: What the Singer Siblings Reveal About Creativity in Families." *Forward*, June 25, 2004, p. 82. Analyzes the childhoods and literary careers of Israel Joshua Singer and his siblings, Isaac Bashevis Singer and Esther Kreitman, all of whom were Yiddish novelists. Describes how their success as artists depended upon their relationships to each other.

Howe, Irving. Introduction to *The Brothers Ashkenazi*, by Israel Joshua Singer. New York: Atheneum, 1980. Provides an assessment of the work as a historical novel and relates it to other examples of the genre. Argues that Singer adopted the Marxist notion that the sweep of history determines the lives and actions of individuals.

_____. *World of Our Fathers*. New York: Harcourt Brace Jovanovich, 1976. Links Singer with Scholem Asch as being Yiddish writers who achieved fame by writing in the tradition of European novelists of the nineteenth and twentieth centuries. Compares his techniques in *The Brothers Ashkenazi* with those used by Thomas Mann.

Norich, Anita. *The Homeless Imagination in the Fiction of Israel Joshua Singer*. Bloomington: Indiana University Press, 1991. Focuses on the cultural dimensions of Singer's writing. Offers a sensitive reading of *The Brothers Ashkenazi* and discusses the tensions Singer creates by contrasting the "extraordinary changes of the period he is depicting" with the static nature of the Jewish fate.

Schulz, Max F. "The Family Chronicle as Paradigm of History in *The Brothers Ashkenazi* and *The Family Moskat*." In *The Achievement of Isaac Bashevis Singer*, edited by Marcia Allentuck. Carbondale: Southern Illinois University Press, 1969. Compares Singer's novel to one by his more famous brother, Isaac Bashevis Singer, showing how each adapts the conventions of the family epic to the demands of a public attuned to the complexities of the historical process.

Sinclair, Claire. *The Brothers Singer*. London: Allison & Busby, 1983. Extensive analysis of major characters in *The Brothers Ashkenazi*. Pays special attention to the political and historical dimensions of the work.

The Brothers Karamazov

Author: Fyodor Dostoevski (1821-1881)
First published: Bratya Karamazovy, 1879-1880 (English translation, 1912)
Type of work: Novel
Type of plot: Psychological realism
Time of plot: Nineteenth century
Locale: Russia

Principal characters:
FYODOR KARAMAZOV, a profligate businessman
DMITRI, his sensual oldest son
IVAN, his atheistic, intellectual son
ALEXEY or ALYOSHA, his youngest son
GRUSHENKA, a young woman loved by Fyodor and Dmitri
SMERDYAKOV, an epileptic servant of Fyodor
ZOSSIMA, an aged priest
KATERINA, betrothed to Dmitri

The Story:

In the middle of the nineteenth century in Skotoprigonyevski, a town in the Russian provinces, Fyodor Karamazov fathers three sons, the eldest, Dmitri, by his first wife, and the other two, Ivan and Alexey, by his second. Fyodor, a good businessman but a scoundrel by nature, abandons the children after their mothers die. A family servant, Grigory, sees that they are placed in the care of relatives.

Dmitri grows up believing he will receive a legacy from his mother's estate. He serves in the army, where he develops wild ways. Becoming a wastrel, he goes to his father and asks for the money that he believes is due him. Ivan, morose but not timid, goes from a gymnasium to a college in Moscow. Poverty forces him to teach and to contribute articles to periodicals, and he achieves modest fame when he publishes an article on the position of the ecclesiastical courts. Alexey, or Alyosha, the youngest son, a boy of a dreamy, retiring nature, enters a local monastery, where he becomes the pupil of a famous Orthodox Church elder, Zossima. When Alyosha asks his father's permission to become a monk, Fyodor, to whom nothing is sacred, scoffs but gives his sanction.

When the brothers all reach manhood, their paths cross in the town of their birth. Dmitri returns to collect his legacy. Ivan, a professed atheist, returns home for financial reasons.

At a meeting of the father and sons at the monastery, Fyodor shames his sons by behaving like a fool in the presence of the revered Zossima. Dmitri, who arrives late, is accused by Fyodor of wanting the legacy money in order to entertain a local adventuress to whom he himself is attracted. Dmitri, who is betrothed at this time to Katerina, a colonel's daughter whom he rescued from shame, rages at his father, saying that the old man is a great sinner and in no position to judge others. Zossima falls down before Dmitri, hitting his head on the floor, and his fall is believed to be a portent of an evil that will befall the oldest son. Realizing that the Karamazovs are sensualists, Zossima advises Alyosha to leave the monastery and go into the world at Zossima's death. There is further dissension among the Karamazovs because of Ivan's love for Katerina, the betrothed of Dmitri.

Marfa, the wife of Grigory, Fyodor's faithful servant, gives birth to a deformed child. The night that Marfa's deformed baby dies, Lizaveta, a girl of the town, also dies after giving birth to a son. The child, called Smerdyakov, is taken in by Grigory and Marfa and is accepted as a servant in the household of Fyodor, whom everyone in the district believes is the child's true father.

Dmitri confesses his wild ways to Alyosha. He opens his heart to his brother and tells how he spent three thousand rubles of Katerina's money in an orgy with Grushenka, a local woman of questionable character with whom he fell passionately in love. Desperate for the money to repay Katerina, Dmitri asks Alyosha to secure it for him from Fyodor.

Alyosha finds Fyodor and Ivan at the table, attended by the servant, Smerdyakov, who is an epileptic. Entering suddenly in search of Grushenka, Dmitri attacks his father. Alyosha goes to Katerina's house, where he finds Katerina trying to bribe Grushenka into abandoning her interest in Dmitri. Grushenka, however, cannot be compromised. Upon his return to the monastery, Alyosha finds Zossima dying. He returns to Fyodor, to discover his father afraid of both Dmitri and Ivan. Ivan wants Dmitri to marry Grushenka so that he himself can marry Katerina. Fyodor wants to marry Grushenka. The father refuses to give Alyosha any money for Dmitri.

Spurned by Dmitri, Katerina dedicates her life to watching over him, although she feels a true love for Ivan. Ivan, seeing that Katerina is pledged to torture herself for life, nobly approves of her decision.

Later, in an inn, Ivan discloses to Alyosha that he believes in God but that he cannot accept God's world. The young men discuss the dual nature of humankind. Ivan discloses that he hates Smerdyakov, who is caught between the wild passions of Dmitri and Fyodor and who, out of fear, works for the interests of each against the other.

The dying Zossima revives long enough to converse once more with his devoted disciples. When he dies, a miracle is expected. In the place of a miracle, however, his body rapidly decomposes, delighting certain of the monks who are anxious that the institution of the elders in the Orthodox Church be discredited. They argue that the decomposition of his body proves his teachings were false.

In his disappointment at the turn of events at the monastery, Alyosha is persuaded to visit Grushenka, who wishes to seduce him. He finds Grushenka prepared to escape the madness of the Karamazovs by running off with a former lover. The saintly Alyosha sees good in Grushenka; she, for her part, finds him an understanding soul.

Dmitri, eager to pay his debt to Katerina, makes various fruitless attempts to borrow the money. Mad with jealousy when he learns that Grushenka is not at her home, he goes to

Fyodor's house to see if she is there. He finds no Grushenka, but he seriously injures old Grigory with a pestle with which he intended to kill his father. Discovering that Grushenka fled to another man, he arms himself and goes in pursuit. He finds Grushenka with two Poles in an inn at another village. The young woman welcomes Dmitri and professes undying love for him alone. During a drunken orgy of the lovers, the police appear and charge Dmitri with the murder of his father, who was found robbed and dead in his house. Blood on Dmitri's clothing, his possession of a large sum of money, and passionate statements he made against Fyodor are all evidence against him. Dmitri repeatedly protests his innocence, claiming that the money he spent on his latest orgy is half of Katerina's rubles. He saved the money to ensure his future in the event that Grushenka accepts him, but the testimony of witnesses makes his case seem hopeless. He is taken into custody and placed in the town jail to await trial.

Grushenka falls sick after the arrest of Dmitri, and she and Dmitri are plagued with jealousy of each other. As the result of a strange dream, Dmitri begins to look upon himself as an innocent man destined to suffer for the crimes of humanity. Ivan and Katerina, in the meantime, work on a scheme whereby Dmitri might escape to America.

Before the trial, Ivan interviews Smerdyakov three times. The servant once told Ivan that he is able to feign an epileptic fit; such a fit is Smerdyakov's alibi in the search for the murderer of Fyodor. The third interview ends when Smerdyakov confesses to the murder, insisting, however, that he has been the instrument of Ivan, who by certain words and actions led the servant to believe that the death of Fyodor would be a blessing for everyone in his household. Smerdyakov, depending on a guilt complex in the soul of Ivan, murders his master at a time when all the evidence will point directly to Dmitri. He believes that Ivan will protect him and provide him with a comfortable living. At the end of the third interview, he gives the stolen money to Ivan, who returns to his rooms and falls ill with fever and delirium, during which he is haunted by a realistic specter of the devil that resides in his soul. That same night, Smerdyakov hangs himself.

The Karamazov case attracts widespread attention throughout Russia, and many notables attend the trial. The prosecution builds up what seems to be a strong case against Dmitri, but the defense, a city lawyer, refutes the evidence piece by piece. Doctors declare Dmitri to be abnormal; in the end, however, they cannot agree. Katerina has her revenge by revealing to the court a letter Dmitri wrote to her, in which he declares his intention of killing his father to get the money he owes her. Ivan, still in a fever, testifies that Smerdyakov confessed to the murder. Ivan gives the money to the court, but he negates his testimony when he loses control of himself and tells the court of the visits of his private devil.

Despite the defense counsel's eloquent plea in Dmitri's behalf, the jury returns a verdict of guilty amid a tremendous hubbub in the courtroom. Katerina is haunted by guilt because she revealed Dmitri's letter; furthermore, she believes that she is responsible for the jealousy of the two brothers. She leaves Ivan's bedside and goes to the hospital where Dmitri, also ill of a fever, is taken. Alyosha and Grushenka are present at their interview, when Katerina begs Dmitri for his forgiveness.

Later, Alyosha leaves Dmitri in the care of Grushenka and goes to the funeral of a schoolboy friend. Filled with pity and compassion for the sorrow of death and the misery of life, Alyosha gently admonishes the mourners, most of them schoolmates of the dead boy, to live for goodness and to love the world. He himself is preparing to go with Dmitri to Siberia, for he is ready to sacrifice his own life for innocence and truth.

Critical Evaluation:

Fyodor Mikhailovich Dostoevski's budding literary career was interrupted in 1849 by a nine-year exile in Siberia and Asian Russia for political subversion, a charge never fully substantiated. When he resumed his career, at the age of thirty-eight, he began to work at a frenetic pace—as novelist, journalist, and editor—a pace that he maintained until his death, only one year after the publication of *The Brothers Karamazov*. Dostoevski was an inveterate gambler, frequently indulging in gambling binges of up to two weeks in duration; when his gambling debts mounted and his other creditors became insistent, he wrote, in a furiously intense burst of energy, to pay his bills. In addition, other catastrophes punctuated his hectic life. His first wife died; he began to have epileptic seizures; he got into further trouble with the government; he found it impossible to resist beautiful women. Woven through all this were his epiphanic flights of imagination, which culminated in his superb novels and the agonized soul searching of a man deeply concerned with truth, peace of mind, and religious faith. Indeed, the turbulence of Dostoevski's life never really subsided, although he did enjoy a relative calm of sorts during the last few years of his life under the careful ministrations of his second wife. That turbulence is reflected in Dostoevski's novels, particularly *The Brothers Karamazov*, his last novel and presumably the most mature expression of his style and his thought.

Like the other novels, *The Brothers Karamazov* is a psychological novel: Less emphasis is placed on plot, action,

and setting (although Dostoevski is a master craftsman at all three) than on emotions and thoughts. In fact, Dostoevski's psychological insights are so sharp that Sigmund Freud selected *The Brothers Karamazov* as one of the three greatest works in world literature. The other two he picked were *Oidipous Tyrannos* (c. 429 B.C.E.; *Oedipus Tyrannus*, 1715) and *Hamlet, Prince of Denmark* (pr. c. 1600-1601, pb. 1603). All three involve a death of a father and an intergenerational love triangle. Moreover, Freud's essay on *The Brothers Karamazov*, "Dostoevsky and Parricide," is considered a classic in psychology and literary criticism. In it, Freud gives a thorough explanation of the strong Oedipal theme in the novel, which echoes, according to Freud, Dostoevski's own unresolved Oedipal conflicts. In this Freudian age, it is most difficult not to cast Dmitri's hostility toward Fyodor in any other light. Each son resents his father in his own fashion and for his own reasons. All three legitimate sons, however, have less reason to despise Fyodor than his illegitimate son, Smerdyakov, does. All four sons have some justification—stemming largely from greed or vengeance—for wanting Fyodor dead.

It is evident, then, that the story proceeds from something more profound than plot. The loose structure of the novel, however, is offset by its intensity. It is frequently lurid, but Dostoevski never avoids a difficult question; he amalgamates thinking and feeling in a carefully planned interplay between the two. One of the consequences of this technique is an early foreshadowing of events that later come to pass—the creation of an atmosphere of premonition, as it were. There is, for example, frequent and early mention of patricide, especially in the scenes between Ivan and Smerdyakov, revealing a pathological obsession that besets both father and sons. Furthermore, the selection of details and their accretion contribute not only to the novel's verisimilitude but also to its psychological depth and profundity. Even so seemingly trivial a matter as numerous references to time sequence—all of them accurate—indicates Dostoevski's meticulous orchestration of his characters' emotions. However, these techniques serve only to enhance a novel whose impact ultimately derives from its head-on confrontation with the larger issues of human existence.

In *The Brothers Karamazov*, Dostoevski's search for truth leads him to the question, "What is the nature of humanity?" The answer takes shape in the characterization of three of the brothers. Dmitri is dominated by sensuality; Ivan prizes the intellectual; Alyosha represents spirituality, although his asceticism sometimes clashes with his incipient sensuality. Together, the three personalities (together with the evil, twisted, and victimized Smerdyakov) are symbolic of humanity. Another question, "Is there a God?" is less easily answered because neither "The Grand Inquisitor" story nor "The Devil: Ivan's Nightmare" definitively resolves the matter. Likewise, the question of humanity's relationship to God remains nebulous for the same reasons, Father Zossima notwithstanding. The questions about one's relationship to another and one's relationship to society, however, are more concretely dealt with: Hostility, fear, and resentment, commingled with morbid curiosity, characterize the relationship of one to another, appearing to mirror the same qualities in the relationship of the individual to society. Thus, when Dostoevski poses the question "Does humanity have free will?" the tentative answer is that free will, if it exists at all, is very limited. One can hardly see one's destiny, much less exert substantial control over it, as Dmitri, among others, so tragically learns. Finally, Dostoevski wonders whether human intellect is capable of development or change; but since the entire novel is an exposition of the predestined Karamazov family, the answer is a foregone conclusion. These deeply felt philosophical considerations permeate the book without dwarfing its characters. Indeed, what can diminish the operatic rages and the petty buffoonery of Fyodor, the screaming frustrations of Dmitri, the barely repressed seething indignation of Ivan, and the incredible shock of Alyosha's losing his spiritual innocence? Thus, philosophy and psychology go hand in hand in *The Brothers Karamazov* to shape a tale of immense emotional range and profound philosophical depth. *The Brothers Karamazov* is one of the masterpieces of the world's literature.

"Critical Evaluation" by Joanne G. Kashdan

Further Reading

Belknap, Robert L. *The Genesis of "The Brothers Karamazov": The Aesthetics, Ideology, and Psychology of Text Making.* Evanston, Ill.: Northwestern University Press, 1990. Considers the reading and experiences of Dostoevski that appear in the novel. A study of the mind behind the book.

Bloom, Harold, ed. *Fyodor Dostoevsky's "The Brothers Karamazov."* New York: Chelsea House, 1988. Selection of critical interpretations of the novel. Essays printed in chronological sequence from 1971 to 1977. Includes an extended chronology of Dostoevski.

Jackson, Robert Louis, ed. *A New Word on "The Brothers Karamazov."* Evanston, Ill.: Northwestern University Press, 2004. Collection of essays providing a range of interpretations, including discussions of the novel today

and tomorrow, Dostoevski and the limits of realism, and the novel's characters.

Leatherbarrow, William J. *Fyodor Dostoyevsky—The Brothers Karamazov.* New York: Cambridge University Press, 1992. Provides background for understanding, including historical, intellectual, and cultural influences. Discusses the major themes of the novel.

_____, ed. *The Cambridge Companion to Dostoevskii.* New York: Cambridge University Press, 2006. Collection of essays that examine the author's life and works, discussing his relationship to Russian folk heritage, money, the intelligentsia, psychology, religion, the family, and science, among other topics. Includes a chronology and a bibliography.

McReynolds, Susan. *Redemption and the Merchant God: Dostoevsky's Economy of Salvation and Antisemitism.* Evanston, Ill.: Northwestern University Press, 2008. McReynolds argues that readers cannot fully understand Dostoevski's writings without understanding his obsession with the Jews. She analyzes not only the elements of anti-Semitism in his works but also examines his views of the Crucifixion, Resurrection, morality, and other aspects of Christian doctrine.

Miller, Robin Feuer. *Dostoevsky's Unfinished Journey.* New Haven, Conn.: Yale University Press, 2007. Miller examines Dostoevski's works from numerous perspectives, analyzing the themes of conversion and healing in his fiction, questioning his literary influence, and comparing *The Brothers Karamazov* to Charles Robert Maturin's gothic novel *Melmoth the Wander.*

Scanlan, James P. *Dostoevsky the Thinker: A Philosophical Study.* Ithaca, N.Y.: Cornell University Press, 2002. Scanlan analyzes Dostoevski's novels, essays, letters, and notebooks in order to provide a comprehensive account of his philosophy, examining the weakness as well as the strength of Dostoevski's ideas. He concludes that Dostoevski's thought was shaped by anthropocentrism—a struggle to define the very essence of humanity.

Straus, Nina Pelikan. *Dostoevsky and the Woman Question: Rereadings at the End of a Century.* New York: St. Martin's Press, 1994. Straus argues that Dostoevski's compulsion to depict men's cruelties to women is an important part of his vision and metaphysics. She maintains that Dostoevski attacks masculine notions of autonomy and that his works evolve toward "the death of the patriarchy." Chapter 7 is devoted to a discussion of *The Brothers Karamazov.*

Terras, Victor. *A Karamazov Companion: Commentary on the Genesis, Language, and Style of Dostoevsky's Novel.*

Madison: University of Wisconsin Press, 1981. Reprint. 2002. Discusses the moral and religious philosophy that underlies the text, the use of language and symbolism, subtexts, and relevant myths.

Williams, Rowan. *Dostoevsky: Language, Faith, and Fiction*. Waco, Tex.: Baylor University Press, 2008. Examines the speech, fiction, metaphor, and iconography in four novels, including *The Brothers Karamazov*. Williams maintains that the style and goals of Dostoevski's fiction is inseparable from his religious commitments.

Brown Girl, Brownstones

Author: Paule Marshall (Valenza Pauline Burke, 1929-   )
First published: 1959
Type of work: Novel
Type of plot: Bildungsroman
Time of plot: 1939-1947
Locale: Brooklyn, New York

Principal characters:
SELINA BOYCE, the protagonist
SILLA BOYCE, her mother
DEIGHTON BOYCE, her father
INA BOYCE, her shy and traditional sister
BERYL CHALLENOR, her best friend while growing up
RACHEL FINE, her best and first close white friend at college
CLIVE SPRINGER, a would-be artist and Selina's first lover

The Story:

The brownstone in which the ten-year-old Selina Boyce resides with her family is a dusty memorial to the generations of white families now being replaced by brown West Indians. Selina dreams about the house's past and then turns her attention to a photograph of her own family before she was born. She tries to understand how her mother, Silla, changed from the shy and pretty young woman in the picture to the hard and aggressive mother she associates with darkness and winter. In contrast, Deighton, Selina's summery father, with his teasing smile and carefree attitudes, has not changed in the slightest from the man in the photograph. Just thinking about her father makes Selina feel warm and loved.

Deighton inherits a piece of land in Barbados, and Silla plots to get it away from him to buy the brownstone in which they currently live. She succeeds in selling the land but needs Deighton's signature to cash the check. Pretending defeat, he literally seduces her into trusting him and then spends the money on extravagant presents for each member of the family. However, his moment of triumph, able to walk into fancy stores and be treated with respect because of the cash in his hand, is short lived. The Bajan community mocks and rejects him, he ends up maimed by a machine at the factory where he works, and in his weakened state he is recruited to join a religious cult run by Father Peace.

Selina visits her father at his retreat but cannot help but acknowledge his utter emasculation. Silla, infuriated by

Deighton's abandonment of his family, tips off the immigration authorities to his illegal status and has him deported. He apparently commits suicide by jumping off the boat taking him back to Barbados. In the meantime, Silla, by working several jobs and mastering the powerful machines that contributed to Deighton's demise, is able to buy the brownstone after all.

In the aftermath of both World War II and the family war, Selina becomes a young woman in her first year of college. After a year of mourning, Selina finally agrees to visit her childhood friend Beryl. She finds herself torn between envy at her friend's ordered and privileged life and scorn for the degree to which she has let herself be molded by her parents' desires rather than her own.

Selina's own mother, now the proud owner of a solid piece of property, has joined the new Barbadian Association created to help support the growing middle-class community. Silla has kicked out longtime tenants to charge higher rents, and she is studying to be a nurse at night school. Selina finds her a bitter and lonely woman driven by a single-minded pursuit of ever-greater material success despite their already relatively comfortable circumstances.

Selina agrees to visit the Barbadian Association but is shocked by its refusal to allow African Americans to join. As she walks out in disgust, she meets Clive, a young artist who shares her disapproval. He seduces her that evening.

Selina gives in to Clive's caresses as if to prove she is indeed her father's daughter and not the respectable young lady her mother demands that she be. Ultimately, Clive will prove a disappointment; like Deighton, he seems to lack the drive and discipline that would allow him to make something of his artistic talent and is unwilling to rebel against his own mother despite Selina's requests.

A successful student, Selina joins a college dance club, where she becomes close friends with Rachel Fine, who seems to understand her yearnings in a way Beryl could not. Chosen to dance the lead birth-to-death cycle in the club's recital, Selina is triumphant in her performance and feels at the height of her powers. Soon, however, that triumph is undercut by the condescension and racist comments of another friend's mother.

Selina runs to Clive for comfort, only to have him reject her plans to flee to Barbados, as he acknowledges his own weakness and inertia in the face of her energy and enthusiasm. The novel ends as she learns to see her mother in all her complexity, to appreciate her love, and to recognize the trace of that promising young woman in the photograph behind the cold and wintry façade. Mother and daughter both pay tribute to their shared kinship: The very determination that sent Silla at age eighteen to seek her fortune in a new world will now lead Selina to set out on her own journey, perhaps beginning with a return to the country of her parents' birth.

Critical Evaluation:

Brown Girl, Brownstones features two interrelated story lines. The main plot traces Selina's development from a ten-year-old girl who takes her beloved father's side in the family quarrels into a mature young woman who comes to appreciate her mother's power and self-sacrifice. This story line plays out in the context of her parents' ongoing conflict over their competing visions and values as Barbadian (Bajan) immigrants in America.

After establishing the relationship between Selina's parents, Paule Marshall turns to Selina's friendship with Beryl and to the intimacy they share as prepubescent girls trying to understand their changing bodies and lives. The novel also sets up a contrast between Selina and her older, less rebellious sister, who will grow up and marry a nice, young Bajan man exactly as her family and community expect her to do.

The major theme of *Brown Girl, Brownstones* is the American Dream and the price immigrants pay when they pursue it single-mindedly or get caught up in its easy seductions. Silla Boyce, as she sits alone at night running her sewing machine because she cannot sleep, is an impressive, almost tragic figure who sacrifices love and happiness for material success. Deighton Boyce, in contrast, wants to get ahead without cost or effort. Typically, he skips practicing his musical scales and the introductory chapters of his accounting book in the mistaken belief that success is his for the asking. The novel, while critiquing American capitalism, expresses admiration for the successes of the hardworking West Indian community.

Community is itself a significant theme in the novel. The Bajan community is portrayed as a nurturing and supportive one despite Selina's rebellion against its conservative values and narrow-mindedness. Above all, it is a wonderfully vital linguistic community. Marshall has often spoken of growing up listening to her mother's friends, these "kitchen poets" cursing and commenting on the world around them in voices rich with metaphors culled from their earlier lives in Barbados. She has described their special idiom as a blend of the standard British English taught in West Indian schools, Bajan rhythms and syntax, and favorite biblical and African sayings.

Selina's coming-of-age story seems almost secondary given Marshall's powerful rendering of the above themes. Nonetheless, Selina's struggles to establish her own identity frame the novel's opening and closing sections. Some female readers respond powerfully to the psychological analysis of her sexual awakening; her rebellion against inherited values; her movement from a simplistic to a more complex understanding of her parents, friends, and community; and the maturation of her sense of self and agency. On the novel's last page, as she sets out on her unknown journey, Selina throws off some but not all of the bangles that would define her as a Bajan young woman and restrict her freedom to reinvent herself.

Finally, the novel is about time and place. Marshall's Brooklyn is vividly rendered with recognizable landmarks and streets. The historical context, including the opportunities that emerged during World War II for members of immigrant communities, is accurately established. The novel also deals with ethnicity and race. For example, it contrasts the experiences of African Americans and West Indians, as well as contrasting the overt and violent acts of racism experienced by older characters with the subtler prejudices encountered by Selina and her friends. Selina ultimately must learn firsthand that race trumps ethnicity in the eyes of white Americans, that the color of her skin masks her individuality behind a veil of blackness she cannot escape.

Brown Girl, Brownstones was a critical success but a commercial failure when it was first published in 1959. The novel was highly praised for its rich and colorful language and the complexity of Marshall's characterizations, especially those of Silla and Deighton Boyce. The novel may not have received the full attention it merited partly because it was ahead of its time—the Civil Rights movement was in its infancy, and minority and women writers remained largely invisible to the literary establishment. The year 1959 did see the highly acclaimed Broadway production of Lorraine Hansberry's *A Raisin in the Sun* (pr., pb. 1959), which has important thematic similarities to Marshall's novel but with the important difference that its protagonist is an adult African American male rather than a young West Indian girl.

It was also not clear where the novel belonged within the literary marketplace—was it an immigrant novel, a feminist novel, an African American novel, or a classic bildungsroman, albeit with a black, female protagonist? When reissued by the Feminist Press in 1981, *Brown Girl, Brownstones* was immediately embraced by the feminist literary community, and it continued to be this press's best-selling novel.

In 1999, on the fortieth anniversary of the novel's original publication, Howard University dedicated its annual literary conference to *Brown Girl, Brownstones*. The conference celebrated the work's pioneering role in the history of African American and Caribbean writing and its important position as a link between an earlier generation of women writers—including Zora Neale Hurston, Ann Petry, and Gwendolyn Brooks—and the later generation that included Toni Morrison, Alice Walker, Jamaica Kincaid, and Audre Lorde, women whose work Marshall seemed to prefigure. Though still less well known than those later writers, Marshall won her fair share of literary honors, and in 1992 she received a MacArthur Fellowship, the so-called genius award. She has published several additional novels and collections of short stories, as well as a memoir, *Triangular Road* (2009).

Jane Missner Barstow

Further Reading

Cobb, Michael L. "Irreverent Authority: Religious Apostrophe and the Fiction of Blackness in Paule Marshall's *Brown Girl, Brownstones*." *University of Toronto Quarterly* 72, no. 2 (Spring, 2003): 631-648. Analyzes the role of religion as a source of rhetoric in the novel. Argues that religion fails to empower Deighton, it offers only dead metaphors to Selina, and the biblical imagery Silla so loves is wielded for political rather than religious purposes.

DeLamotte, Eugenia C. *Journeys of Freedom: The Fiction of Paule Marshall*. Philadelphia: University of Pennsylvania Press, 1998. Interesting analysis of Marshall's work that sees all her major protagonists as silenced by their ex-

perience of an oppression rooted in nationality, race, class, or gender. To overcome their sense of alienation and achieve wholeness, Selina and other Marshall characters must develop their own voices and use them to speak powerfully.

Denniston, Dorothy Hamer. *The Fiction of Paule Marshall: Reconstructions of History, Culture, and Gender*. Knoxville: University of Tennessee Press, 1995. One of the first two full-length studies of Marshall's work. Provides important historical and cultural context for her fiction, especially in terms of gender roles. Of particular interest is its analysis of how Caribbean women, including Silla, have used storytelling to transmit and sustain African cultural practices and values.

Hathaway, Heather. *Caribbean Waves: Relocating Claude McKay and Paule Marshall*. Bloomington: Indiana University Press, 1999. Argues that these two writers need to be understood interculturally and not within the limitations of African American or Caribbean perspectives. Contrasts the interconnectedness one finds in the fiction of Marshall, a second-generation immigrant at home in both Barbados and Brooklyn, with the alienation that marks the life and work of the first-generation Jamaican McKay.

Japtok, Martin. "Paule Marshall's *Brown Girl, Brownstones*: Reconciling Ethnicity and Individualism." *African American Review* 32, no. 2 (Summer, 1998): 305-316. Sees the novel as both a critique and a celebration of the Barbadian community. Selina discovers that her ethnicity is inescapable despite her insistence on individual identity. Ultimately, her experience of racism leads her to understand if not accept her mother's materialism as self-protection against failure and prejudice.

MacLeod, Lewis. "'You ain no real-real Bajan man': Patriarchal Performance and Feminist Discourse in Paule Marshall's *Brown Girl, Brownstones*." *Ariel* 37, nos. 2/3 (April-July, 2006): 169-187. Sees the novel as focused on gender reversals rather than as a critique of patriarchy. Deighton is ostracized by the Bajan community for his failure to repress his feminine, maternal side, while Silla is lauded for her success in the role of a traditional family patriarch.

Pettis, Joyce. *Toward Wholeness in Paule Marshall's Fiction*. Charlottesville: University Press of Virginia, 1995. One of the first two full-length studies of Marshall's work. Offers a straightforward analysis of her female characters, including Selina Boyce, in terms of their fragmented personalities that can only be healed and made spiritually whole through reconciliation with their families and ethnic communities.

The Browning Version

Author: Terence Rattigan (1911-1977)
First produced: 1948; first published, 1949
Type of work: Drama
Type of plot: Problem
Time of plot: The first half of the twentieth century
Locale: The south of England

Principal characters:
JOHN TAPLOW, a student
FRANK HUNTER, a science master
ANDREW CROCKER-HARRIS, a classics master
MILLIE CROCKER-HARRIS, his wife
DR. FROBISHER, the headmaster
PETER GILBERT, Crocker-Harris's successor
MRS. GILBERT, his wife

The Story:

John Taplow, who is about sixteen years old and in the lower fifth form of an English public school, appears at the flat of Andrew Crocker-Harris for an end-of-term tutorial in the hope of being advanced to the upper fifth. Seeing a box of chocolates, he helps himself to two pieces, eats one, and then, either out of conscience or fear of being caught, replaces the other.

Shortly thereafter, Frank Hunter arrives, and in the course of the conversation between the two it becomes clear that Crocker-Harris is retiring because of ill health. Known for his strict discipline, students dub him the "Crock" and "Himmler of the lower fifth." Hunter, on the other hand, enjoys easy rapport with students, as can be seen in Taplow's readiness to share confidences with him. While they wait for the "Crock" to appear, Hunter instructs Taplow in a proper golf swing. Taplow admits that, although like most students he had his share of fun at Crocker-Harris's expense, he does have sympathy for him.

Taplow is in the midst of mimicking the classics master when Millie Crocker-Harris enters and overhears the mimicry. She dispatches Taplow on an errand to the druggist for Crocker-Harris's heart medicine so that she can be alone with Hunter, with whom she is having an affair.

Crocker-Harris appears, only to find that Taplow is not there. When Taplow returns, Millie leaves to prepare dinner, and Hunter leaves pupil and master to their work on a translation of Aeschylus's *Agamemnon* (458 B.C.E.). As with the earlier incident with the chocolates, Taplow's schoolboyish nervousness emerges in the form of a thoughtless comment about the master's inability to pass his love for the Greek play on to the boys. Frightened by his own audacity, Taplow attempts to make amends by encouraging Crocker-Harris to talk about the rhymed translation he made of the play at the age of eighteen. Then, overcome by emotion for the first time in years, Crocker-Harris cuts short the session and abruptly dismisses Taplow.

The next visitor, Dr. Frobisher, adds to Crocker-Harris's long-repressed sense of failure as a teacher when he informs him that the board voted to deny him a pension. In an attempt to be considerate, he requests that Crocker-Harris precede, rather than follow, a more popular master, whom the students will noisily applaud. When told about the denial of a pension, Millie is visibly annoyed and wonders how they will manage on the reduced salary her husband will receive in his new position at a crammer's school.

Dr. Frobisher's departure is followed by the arrival of Crocker-Harris's successor, Peter Gilbert, who comes with his wife to look over the quarters that are to be their new home. The Gilberts seem to be headed for the same kind of life as their predecessors. Mrs. Gilbert is as materialistic as Millie and, like Millie, brought money to her marriage.

After the Gilberts leave, Taplow reappears unexpectedly, bringing a gift for Crocker-Harris, a secondhand copy of Robert Browning's translation of *Agamemnon* that Taplow inscribed with a Greek line from the play, translated roughly as "God from afar looks graciously upon a gentle master." The emotional strain on Crocker-Harris is obvious, but his delight in the gift is cut short when Millie taunts him cruelly by telling him that Taplow earlier mimicked him; she adds that the gift is probably only a bribe for a passing grade.

Hunter faces Millie with the truth that both realized all along, that their affair is a purely physical one. He tells her that he intends to end their affair, partly because of her cruelty to her husband. He also tells her that he will not visit her at her parents' home in the summer as they planned.

Hunter then insists on telling the classics master the truth about his relationship with Millie, only to be informed that Crocker-Harris knew of the affair since its inception and that Millie is the one who told him. Hunter mentions that he is only the last of Millie's several affairs over the years. As Taplow did earlier, Hunter attempts to make amends to Crocker-Harris, telling him of Taplow's liking for him and insisting that Taplow's gift of the Browning version of *Agamemnon* is a genuine gesture. He promises to visit Crocker-Harris in the fall in his new home, even naming the specific date on which he will come. Crocker-Harris seems tentative in his acceptance of Hunter's offer but expresses his recovered dignity by granting Taplow his advancement and by accepting Hunter's offer of a visit. Most important, however, he phones Dr. Frobisher to inform him that he will, after all, as is his due as the older of the two retirees, speak after the popular younger retiree at the commencement ceremony, for, as he notes, "occasionally an anticlimax can be surprisingly effective." Having made that decision, he sits down to dinner, saying to Millie that they must not let their dinner get cold.

Critical Evaluation:

As one of two short companion plays, *The Browning Version* rapidly gained favor as one of Terrence Rattigan's best plays. Coming from the same tradition as James Hilton's famous schoolmaster, Mr. Chips, the figure of the "Crock" became almost as well known to English audiences as Hilton's schoolmaster. An award-winning Oxford University graduate, Crocker-Harris comes to his career at a public school with great enthusiasm about teaching the classics, especially *Agamemnon*. Gradually habit has taken over, however, and he develops into a strict disciplinarian no longer able to communicate his enthusiasm to students.

Crocker-Harris's marriage to a woman whose family provides her with an annuity is loveless from the start. He describes himself as having been unable to give his wife the type of sexual love that she requires. Their relationship soon turns to hatred. The play is about the failures of a career and a marriage, with both failures attributed to the conflict between private need and public behavior, a major theme in all of Rattigan's plays. The destructive disguising of inner feelings with outward decorum is an English character trait Rattigan has dubbed the "vice Anglais." Thus Crocker-Harris aptly describes his uncontrollable burst of emotion at Taplow's gift as the muscular twitchings of a corpse.

The fast-moving events on this last day of the school term serve to revive that living corpse. Crocker-Harris's emotional reaction to Taplow's gift, his confession to Gilbert of his initial excitement about teaching, and his admission to Hunter that he has known all along about his wife's infidelities, in conjunction with the denial of a pension and being forced to take a teaching position at an inferior school, free him from the emotional prison erected by the years of habitual responses to his wife, students, and colleagues. Hard truths emerge from Rattigan's diagnosis of his schoolmas-

ter's life. Both Millie and her replacement, Mrs. Gilbert, seem spiritually vacuous, and Dr. Frobisher has realized success at the expense of compassion. Only Taplow and Hunter display compassion.

Criticized by some for its sentimentality, the drama is seen by others as a hard, if sympathetic, view of a failed life that offers hope of recovery. Crocker-Harris is at the end able to look back on the mockery of the students and to advise Gilbert that even a single success can atone for many failures. To Millie and Hunter, he is able, for the first time in his married life, openly to acknowledge the failure of his marriage. To Dr. Frobisher, he courageously insists on speaking after, rather than before, a more popular retiree at the commencement exercises.

The play is much more tightly concentrated than most of Rattigan's other plays. The conversations among Taplow, Hunter, and Millie serve to introduce the schoolmaster before he makes his first entrance. All the characters impel the action of the play, which consists of Crocker-Harris's emotional reserve cracking in a series of confrontations with Taplow, Hunter, Frobisher, Gilbert, and Millie. The action of the play spans a twenty-four-hour period, occurs in one location, and consists of a tightly knit sequence of entrances and exits that lead inevitably to the conclusion. These are the unities of time, place, and action about which Aristotle wrote in his *De poetica* (c. 334-323 B.C.E.; *Poetics*, 1705).

In fact, the play's concentration resembles that of Sophocles' *Oidipous Tyrannos* (c. 429 B.C.E.; *Oedipus Tyrannus*, 1715), in which, one after another, important characters from Oedipus's life put together the pieces of his past. He must confront that past before he can know himself. Unlike Oedipus, however, Crocker-Harris has known his past all along, and it merely remains for him to acknowledge that past openly and to deal with what is left of his career and of his marriage. The marital plot in *The Browning Version* actually resembles that in *Agamemnon*. Both plays are about deceived husbands, though again, like Oedipus, Agamemnon discovers the pieces of his past, whereas Crocker-Harris has lived with the knowledge of his past during his eighteen years at the public school.

Susan Rusinko

Further Reading

Darlow, Michael, and Gillian Hodson. *Terence Rattigan: The Man and His Work*. London: Quartet Books, 1979. Reprint. 1999. This biography by the award-winning film and television director Michael Darlow and the film and television researcher Gillian Hodson is the definitive source of information about Rattigan's life and art. Contains photographs and concludes with a bibliography, an index, a valuable appendix of original casts and directors in important British and American stage productions, and a list of principal film and television productions.

O'Connor, Sean. *Straight Acting: Popular Gay Drama from Wilde to Rattigan*. London: Cassell, 1998. Describes the influence of Oscar Wilde on Rattigan and other British gay male playwrights. Places these playwrights' lives and work within the context of twentieth century social history, describing the restrictions the writers endured in their personal lives and in their treatment of gay issues.

Rusinko, Susan. *Terence Rattigan*. Boston: Twayne, 1983. A chronological treatment of Rattigan's plays, with one chapter devoted to his radio, television, and many film plays. Includes a chronology, biographical chapter, footnotes, bibliography, and index.

Smith, Kay Nolte. "Terence Rattigan." *Objectivist* 10 (March, 1971): 9-15. Defends Rattigan against accusations of mediocrity and provides a useful overview of Rattigan's

plays, including an assessment of *The Browning Version* as his finest work.

Taylor, John Russell. "Terence Rattigan." In *The Rise and Fall of the Well-Made Play*. New York: Hill and Wang, 1967. Places Rattigan as the last of a group of dramatists in the tradition of well-made English plays that went out of fashion in the 1950's.

Wansell, Geoffrey. *Terence Rattigan*. London: Fourth Estate, 1995. Wansell makes use of newly discovered archival material and extensive interviews to create this comprehensive and appreciative biography. Depicts how Rattigan was conflicted by his desire to be a commercial success and a serious dramatist.

Young, Bertram A. *The Rattigan Version: Sir Terence Rattigan and the Theatre of Character*. London: Hamish Hamilton, 1986. A memoirist more than a biographer or literary critic, Young creates a portrait of Rattigan and his times drawn from his many years as theater critic for *Punch* and *The Financial Times*. Contains photos, a selected list of play openings, and an index.

Brut

Author: Layamon (fl. c. 1200)
First published: c. 1205
Type of work: Poetry
Type of plot: Arthurian and medieval romance
Time of plot: Twelfth century B.C.E.-682 C.E.

For Layamon, the history of the British people begins—on the authority of Geoffrey of Monmouth—with the fall of Troy. The flight of Aeneas and his father and son to the Italian peninsula, where he establishes a Roman kingdom, is recalled from *The Aeneid*. Layamon then follows medieval Celtic tradition in telling of a great-grandson of Aeneas who, exiled from Italy, goes to Greece to unite and free the scattered Trojan people, whom he takes to the British Isles. He names them, in fact, after himself, for his name is Brutus—the "Brut" of the title. Landing in Britain, Brutus and his people find the island populated by giants, whom they defeat and slay.

The remaining 16,095 lines of *Brut* is an episodic succession of chronicles of the descendants of Brutus, some told in more detail than others. The nearly eighty kings from Brutus to Julius Caesar's invasion in 55 B.C.E. cannot be substantiated historically, but many of them are well remembered in later treatments of prehistoric British legend. For example,

Gorboduc, remembered tragically for dividing his kingdom among his sons and watching it disintegrate in civil war is celebrated in the pre-Shakespearean tragedy that bears his name. The Leir (Lear) of Shakespeare's tragedy is also described in some detail in *Brut*.

By the time Caesar's arrival brings Layamon's account into historical view, the poet is nearly one-quarter into his narrative (line 3588). From this point, historical and mythical figures alternate, including mythic figures like Old King Coel of the nursery rhyme (lines 5415-5503) and the historical arrival of the Germanic tribes, the Angles, Saxons, and Jutes, under Hengest and Horsa (lines 6880-8346, dated by Bede at 449 C.E.). In the middle of the Anglo-Saxon episode, the wizard Merlin makes his appearance, and the Arthurian segment of *Brut*—the most popular part of the poem, and for more than a century the only part in print—finally begins.

Merlin first appears in *Brut* as a boy, being bullied by

other boys. He soon, however, shows his skill at prophecy, first for the Saxon king Vortigern, then for the Briton's Aurelius and his brother Uther. Merlin predicts the birth of Arthur, and arranges it by transforming Uther into the shape of his counselor, Gorlois, so that he can sleep with Gorlois's wife, Igrene. When Arthur is born of that union, elves attend him, giving him magical gifts.

Arthur becomes king and draws the greatest knights to his court from all over the world. Since each is the best in his own land, the knights at Arthur's table begin quarreling over pride of place during the Yuletide feast. Consequently, Arthur has a Cornish carpenter build a round table that can seat sixteen hundred knights with equal dignity, yet a table that can be taken down and carried to any of Arthur's castles.

After many military successes against Saxons in England and Germany, fellow Bretons in France, and even the Roman Empire, Arthur is brought down by his nephew, Modred, in a final battle in which both Arthur and Modred are fatally wounded. As he is dying, however, Arthur tells of the elvish queen Argante, who will come for him and take him away to the isle of Avalon, where he will be healed and will await his return when the Britons need him most. Indeed, a ship appears and two splendid ladies carry him away. The remaining two thousand lines of *Brut* detail the reigns of British and Saxon kings, down to Cadwalader, a historic figure who died in 682 C.E.

All that is known about *Brut*'s author, Layamon—also spelled "Lawman" and "Laweman"—is what he says in the preface to the work. The identification of the author at a time when most written works were anonymous may strike the modern reader as odd, but as Rosamund Allen points out in the notes to her modern translation of *Brut*, Layamon is merely presenting an Aristotelian preface, which begins by identifying the "efficient cause" of the work. This efficient cause is what is now called the author. Next, Layamon reports the work's "material cause," the three sources for his history: the ecclesiastical history of Saint Bede the Venerable, an unnamed book by Alcuin and Augustine, and the *Roman de Brut* of poet Wace.

Layamon, however, did not use Bede's history; the second unnamed work is thought by most modern scholars to be a mistaken identification of *Historia regum Britanniae* (c. 1136; *History of the Kings of Britain*, 1718) by Geoffrey of Monmouth. The third book, which was Wace's Norman French versification of Geoffrey's book, was Layamon's almost exclusive source for *Brut*. Although *Brut* has been called virtually a paraphrase of Wace's romance, it is nearly twice as long. The near-doubling comes not from additional material, but rather from added or invented detail.

Nevertheless, there are key incidents in the English *Brut* that first appeared in print with Layamon, though many incidents come from French or Breton oral traditions. Many of the best-known elements of the Arthurian legends are first found in Layamon's *Brut*. Two of them, Arthur's birth and his death, involve supernatural elements that are likely to have origins in Celtic myth. At Arthur's birth, Layamon reports, *alven* (elves) appear with three gifts for the future king: might in battle, kingship, and long life. Elves appear also in his passing, as the dying Arthur tells Constantine, "And ich wülle varen to Avalun to vairest alre maidene,/ To Argante, there quene, alven swithe sceone;/ And heo scal mine wunden makien alle i-sunde" ("And I will fare to Avalon to fairest of all maidens,/ To Argante, the queen, elf most beautiful;/ And she shall make my wounds all sound").

The poetic line used by Layamon is in itself remarkable, being a bridge between Old English alliterative verse and the French-influenced rhyming verse of Middle English poetry. In the three lines above, for example, readers see something akin to the Old English pattern of two half-lines, each with two strong stresses, bound by alliteration. In Layamon's alliterative lines, such as the first quoted above, there actually seems to be an irregular number of syllables, but the two halves of the line are bound by the alliterative pairs *varen* (fare, or travel) and *vairest* (fairest). In the other two lines, however, the half-lines are bound by rhyme, *quene/sceone* and *wunden/i-sunde*.

Some commentators have found in the ensuing lines, describing the British belief in Arthur's return, a contemporary reference to Arthur of Brittany, thus dating the composition of the poem to the turn of the twelfth century. Richard I had named the son, Arthur, of his brother, Geoffrey, the heir to the throne. If Layamon had written the Arthurian passages before 1203, then, he may have intended the "return of Arthur" to reflect this latter-day member of the royal family. Strengthening this reading is that Layamon did not say merely that "Arthur would return," but instead that "an Arthur sculde yete cum," or "*an* Arthur was still to come."

Many of Layamon's earliest readers (and critics) were historians, and so the assessment of his work centered on the unreliable nature of his work as history. However, history in the modern sense of the word—an objective chronicle of real events—was far from Layamon's intention. Like his primary source, Wace's *Roman de Brut*, Layamon's *Brut* is intended to be a romance, an adventure tale about knights and the marvels they encounter. Layamon describes British kings encountering mermaids (line 664), giants (902-966), dragons (7952-7976), and even a Nessie-like sea monster, not in Scotland's Loch Ness but in Loch Lomond (10848-10852). Allen points out that Layamon employs even more of the romance themes and motifs than does Wace, who had called his work a *roman*.

Despite knowing Layamon only by what he writes in his preface, it is quite striking that readers have a name for him at all, given that he is an author of the twelfth or thirteenth century. His name itself also tells a great deal: It simply means "law man" or "man of law," which does not necessarily mean he was a lawyer or a judge (though "judge" was one of the meanings of the word "lawman" in the thirteenth century), for *laue* could also mean "national custom," an interest certainly reflected by Layamon's history of British heroes. The narrative, however, does show a particular interest in the laws, and Layamon has a recurring phrase for selected kings, telling the reader that they "made good laws." However, even if his name were a mere professional epithet, it must be treated as a personal name, for Layamon ends his preface by asking the reader to pray for him.

Though he may have had an interest in the law (or national custom), Layamon describes himself as a priest in the church at Areley, near Redstone, on the River Severn. This places him on the Welsh border, where he could not escape contact with oral traditions (or written ones that do not survive) about Arthur and other ancient Britons. An illuminated capital on the first page of one of the two manuscripts shows Layamon in the habit of a Benedictine monk. In one manuscript he calls himself the son of Leouenath, but in the other he gives his father's name as Leucais. His main reason for mentioning the name is, he says, to invite prayer for him.

Though many of the accounts of successive reigns in *Brut* are by their very nature tedious, Layamon has an eye for a good story. He gives readers the human element of British history in this romanticized version of English chronicles.

John R. Holmes

Further Reading

Allen, Rosamund. *Brut*. London: J. M. Dent, 1992. A complete translation of the poem, with a twenty-one-page introduction, a thorough bibliography, and fifty-eight pages of explanatory notes.

Everett, Dorothy. "La amon and the Earliest Middle English Alliterative Verse." In *Essays on Middle English Literature*, edited by Patricia Kean. Oxford, England: Clarendon Press, 1959. Demonstrates *Brut*'s relation to the earlier Old English poetic tradition, not only in verse form but also in theme and subject.

LeSaux, Françoise. *Layamon's "Brut": The Poem and Its Sources*. Arthurian Studies 19. Cambridge, England: D. S. Brewer, 1989. A source study contrasting Layamon's work with the Latin prose of Geoffrey of Monmouth and the Norman verse of Wace, showing that *Brut* was much more a simple translation of Wace's poem than previous scholars believed.

Lewis, C. S. "The Genesis of a Medieval Book." In *Studies in Medieval and Renaissance Literature*, edited by W. Hooper. New York: Cambridge University Press, 1969. Argues that Layamon supplements his three named sources with Welsh poetic tradition, and that such composition is typical of medieval authors.

Loomis, Roger S. "Layamon's *Brut*." In *Arthurian Literature in the Middle Ages*. Oxford, England: Clarendon Press, 1959. Accounts for Layamon's near-doubling of the length of Wace's poem (his major source), without expanding the story, by extensive use of simile, epic formulas, elaborations, and the expansion of the Arthurian story.

Tiller, Kenneth J. *Lazamon's "Brut" and the Anglo-Norman Vision of History*. Chicago: University of Chicago Press, 2007. Explores medieval concepts of translation and asserts that Layamon had viewed history as a form of translation.

Buddenbrooks

Author: Thomas Mann (1875-1955)
First published: Buddenbrooks: Verfall einer Familie,
    1901 (English translation, 1924)
Type of work: Novel
Type of plot: Social realism
Time of plot: Nineteenth century
Locale: Germany

Principal characters:
JEAN BUDDENBROOK, the head of a German business house
FRAU BUDDENBROOK, Jean's wife
ANTONIE (TONY), their daughter
CHRISTIAN and TOM, their sons
HERR GRÜNLICH, Tony's first husband
ERICA, the daughter of Tony and Grünlich
GERDA, Tom's wife
HANNO, the son of Tom and Gerda
HERR PERMANEDER, Tony's second husband

The Story:

In the year 1875, the Buddenbrook family is flourishing. Johann maintains intact the business and wealth he has inherited from his father, and the Buddenbrook name is held in high esteem. Johann's oldest son, Jean, inherits the business when old Johann dies. Antonie (Tony), Jean's daughter who is born in the family home on Mengstrasse, has aristocratic tendencies by nature and by temperament. The next child is Tom, followed by Christian, who from birth seems somewhat peculiar. Tom displays an early interest in the Buddenbrook business, but Christian seems indifferent to all family responsibilities.

Tony grows into a beautiful woman. When Herr Grünlich, obviously interested in Tony, comes to call on the family, Jean investigates his financial status. The headstrong Tony despises Grünlich and his obsequious manner. Going to a nearby seaside resort on the Baltic Sea to avoid meeting him when he calls again, she falls in love with a young medical student named Morten. When they learn of this, Tony's parents hurriedly bring her home. Tony, raised to feel a sense of her family duty, is unable to ignore their arguments in favor of Grünlich when he asks for her hand. Once the wedding date is set, Grünlich receives a promise of a dowry of eighty thousand marks. Grünlich takes his twenty-year-old bride to the country and refuses to allow her to call on any of her city friends. Although she complains about this in her letters to her parents, Tony resigns herself to obeying her husband's wishes.

Tom holds an important position in the business, which continues to amass money for the Buddenbrook family. Christian's early distaste for business and his ill health give him the privilege of going to South America. When Grünlich finds his establishment floundering, his creditors urge him to apply to his father-in-law for help. Only then does Jean discover Grünlich's motive for marrying Tony: The Budden-

brook reputation placed Grünlich's already failing credit on a sounder basis, but only temporarily so. Actually, Grünlich is hoping that Jean's concern for Tony will help him avoid financial failure. Tony assures her father that she hates Grünlich but that she does not wish to endure the hardships that bankruptcy will entail. Jean brings Tony and his granddaughter, Erica Grünlich, back to the Buddenbrook home. The divorce, based on Grünlich's fraudulent handling of Tony's dowry, goes through easily.

Jean loves his family dearly and firmly believes in the greatness of the Buddenbrook heritage. Tony is once again happy in her father's home, although she bears her sorrows so that everyone will notice. She grows quite close to her brother Tom and takes pride in his development and in the progress of the Buddenbrook firm.

Christian fails in his enterprises in South America and when he returns home his father gives him a job in the firm and an office, which Christian avoids as much as possible. His manners are still peculiar and his health poor. Serious Tom is able to handle the business as well as Jean, and he remains attached to family customs. When Jean dies and leaves the business to Tom, Tony believes that the family lost its strongest tie. Tom, too, is greatly affected by his father's death, but the responsibility of following in his father's footsteps becomes his principal goal.

Because Christian cannot adjust to Buddenbrook interests, the ever-patient Tom sends him to Munich for his health. Reports from Munich that he is seen often in the company of a notoriously loose actress distress the family. Then Tom makes a satisfactory marriage with the daughter of a wealthy businessman. Gerda, whose dowry is added to the Buddenbrook fortune, is an attractive woman who loves music. Once again, parties are held at the Buddenbrook mansion on Mengstrasse.

Tony returns from a trip hoping that a new acquaintance, Herr Permaneder, will call, and soon he does. He is a successful beer merchant in Munich. Tom and Frau Buddenbrook think that Permaneder, in spite of his crude manners and strange dialect, will make a satisfactory husband for Tony. Fortified with her second, smaller dowry, Tony goes to Munich as Frau Permaneder. She sends Erica off to boarding school.

Soon, however, Tony is once again writing passionate appeals to her family and complaining of her married life. When Permaneder betrays her by making love to a servant, she comes home. Tom protests against a second divorce, but Tony insists. She is surprised to learn that her husband will not fight the proceedings, that he believes the marriage was a mistake, and that he will return the dowry, which he does not need.

Tom and Gerda produce a son to carry on the family name. Little Johann, or Hanno, as he is called, inherits his mother's love for music, but he is pale and sickly from birth. Tom tries to instill in his son a love for the family business, but Hanno is too shy to respond to his father.

After the death of Frau Buddenbrook, Christian, Tony, and Tom haggle over the inheritance. Christian demands his share outright, but Tom, as administrator of the estate, refuses to take it out of the business. Christian thereupon quarrels bitterly with Tom, all the pent-up feeling of the past years vent in a torrent of abuse against what he considers to be Tom's cold, mercenary actions.

Tom is not mercenary; he merely works hard and faithfully. Despite his efforts, however, the business begins to decline because of larger economic changes. Now suffering from poor health, Tom believes that sickly Christian, who refuses to take on any responsibility, will outlive him.

Tony finds a fine husband for her daughter, but, like hers, the marriage of Erica and Herr Weinschenk ends in disaster when Weinschenk is caught indulging in foul business practices and sent to prison for three years. Accustomed to public scandal, Tony bears the new hardship with forbearance. Erica also adopts her mother's attitude.

Tom dies suddenly. He falls in the snow and is brought to his bed, where he dies a few hours later, babbling incoherently. His loss means more to Tony than to any of the others. Christian, arriving from Munich for the funeral, is too concerned over his own suffering to show grief over the death of his brother. Gerda, too, feels deep sorrow, for her marriage with Tom was a true love match.

After the will is read, Christian returns to Munich to marry the woman he was unable to marry when he was under Tom's financial control. Soon afterward, Christian's wife writes to Tony that his illness poisoned his mind and that she placed Christian in an institution. Life at the Buddenbrook home continues. Little Hanno never gains much strength. Thin and sickly at fifteen years old, he dies during a typhoid epidemic.

He was the last of the Buddenbrooks. From the days of the first Johann, whose elegance and power produced a fine business and a healthy, vigorous lineage, to the last pitiably small generation, which died with Hanno, the Buddenbrook family decayed.

Critical Evaluation:

Buddenbrooks, Thomas Mann's first novel, was a great and immediate success, and it is still one of his most popular works. Though not as complex or problematic as his later novels, it develops most of the major themes that occupied him throughout his career. The work originally had been planned as a novella about the boy Hanno Buddenbrook, but in assembling the material, Mann found himself tracing the story back four generations. Thus the novel became a family chronicle with a broad social milieu. This type of novel was rare in German literature, which tended to concentrate on the bildungsroman, which traces the growth of a single character. *Buddenbrooks* further departs from that tradition in reversing the emphasis on growth and development to concentrate on decay and decadence. This fascination with the conflict between the life force and the death wish, especially as it appears in the artist type, represents a typical aspect of Mann's work. Mann's artist figures are the product of robust bourgeois stock, families whose drive for work and achievement has led to prosperity and comfort. As the family attains greater refinement and sensitivity, however, the life force slackens. At this stage, the artist figure appears, estranged from the bourgeois world and its values and curiously drawn toward disease and death. It is no accident that several of Mann's works take place in sanatoriums, or that typhus, syphilis, and tuberculosis figure prominently in his work.

This theme is important not only to Mann the writer but also to Mann the human being. Indeed, *Buddenbrooks* is the most thoroughly autobiographical of his novels. Every character in it can be traced to an actual prototype. Certainly the people of Mann's hometown, Lübeck, were shocked when the novel appeared and protested what amounted to an invasion of privacy. The streets and houses of the town, the nearby seashore and countryside were all easily identifiable, and the Buddenbrooks could easily be identified as the Mann family. Mann was an artist, working in words rather than in music, and he rejected the values of his family, a middle-class career, and the expectations of his community. He had left Lübeck for Italy, where, in fact, he began to write the chronicle of the Buddenbrook family, and the stuff of the novel was intensely personal to him. Indeed, he drew largely on family documents and stories. Despite these autobiographical aspects, however, Mann carefully structures the work so that the process of family decay proceeds in a clear and almost inevitable movement, by stages through the four generations, gathering momentum and expressing itself simultaneously in the business fortunes and the physical characteristics, mannerisms, and psychological makeup of the four eldest sons of their respective generations: Johann, Jean, Tom, and Hanno.

At each stage there is both a descent and an ascent. Vitality and physical vigor decline and the business skills atrophy, as evidenced by the steadily declining capital. This external decline, reflected even in such details as increasing susceptibility to tooth decay, is, however, counterbalanced by an increase in sensitivity, an inclination toward art and metaphysics, and an increasingly active interior life. Johann may indeed play the flute—a necessary social grace for the eighteenth century gentleman—but he is not given to introspection. He lives to a ripe old age, and although he is an honest man, he has no scruples about the validity of running a business and making a profit; he also has a sure sense of the economic situation of his time and shows sound judgment in his investments. His son Jean is already far more concerned with moral principles, and business is no longer for him a natural drive but a responsibility. His health suffers and his life is shorter, but his capacity for artistic enjoyment and religious emotion is greater. A tension between inner and outer begins to manifest itself, which becomes even more evident in Tom. In him, refinement becomes elegance, and an inclination for the exotic manifests itself in his choice of a wife. However, the strain of preserving the exterior forms—a new house, social position, and the fortunes of the business—shows in his weakened physical constitution and in his attraction, late in his short, forty-eight-year life, to the philosophy of Arthur Schopenhauer, in which he sees the possibility of his embattled individuality dissolving into an eternal impersonal spiritual existence. Hanno, the last of the Buddenbrooks, dies while he is still a boy, his life filled with pain but rich in inner creativity that is expressed in his Wagnerian flights of musical composition. For Mann, composer Richard Wagner was always linked with decadence and the death wish.

Many of the elements of this sequence recur in Mann's other works, especially his early works. It is also clear that Mann is absorbed by the psychological development of his figures. The novel dwells more and more intensely on the inner states of the later characters. Hanno, the starting point of Mann's conception, retains a disproportionately large share

of the novel's pages and remains one of Mann's most engaging and memorable creations. It is clear, however, that Mann, for all of his understanding and sympathy toward the artistically inclined temperaments of the declining Buddenbrook family, draws a clear line between that sympathy and his own allegiance. Not only does he dwell on the increasingly difficult lives and demeaning deaths of the later characters—as when the eloquent and self-possessed Tom collapses and dies in a pool of filth on the street, or when Hanno dies suddenly of typhus—but, in the case of Hanno, he also unequivocally attributes the death to a failure of the will to live. In one of the most remarkable chapters of the book, the narrator, who generally retains his omniscience in chronicling the fortunes of the family, describes the course of a typical case of typhus and raises it to a mythical encounter between life and death: At the crisis, victims may either exert their will to live and return or they can proceed on the path to self-dissolution in death. Hanno, whose music expresses this longing for release from the demands of life to which he is not equal, takes the latter course and dies. Here, any similarity between Mann and his characters ends. Although Mann as an artist felt himself estranged from the social world of the bourgeois, for him, unlike Hanno, art itself is the means by which he can retain his focus on life. *Buddenbrooks* may describe a family's loss of will to live, but in so doing, it affirms the writer's most profound love of life.

"Critical Evaluation" by Steven C. Schaber

Further Reading

Gay, Peter. "The Mutinous Patrician: Thomas Mann in *Buddenbrooks*." In *Savage Reprisals: "Bleak House," "Madame Bovary," "Buddenbrooks."* New York: W. W. Norton, 2002. Gay, an eminent historian, examines the relationship between realist novels and history, concluding that novels are not accurate historical accounts and present their own versions of reality. He describes *Buddenbrooks* as "an act of retribution," an expression of Mann's "animus against his privileged family history."

Heller, Erich. "Pessimism and Sensibility." In *Thomas Mann: The Ironic German*. 1958. Reprint. South Bend, Ind.: Regnery/Gateway, 1979. This classic study explains the philosophical influences on the novel. Heller finds nearly all the elements of Mann's later masterpieces already present in this first novel.

Kurzke, Hermann. *Thomas Mann: Life as a Work of Art, a Biography*. Translated by Leslie Willson. Princeton, N.J.: Princeton University Press, 2002. An English translation of a work that was celebrated upon its publication in Germany. Kurzke provides a balanced approach to Mann's life and work, and he addresses Mann's homosexuality and relationship to Judaism.

Lehnert, Herbert, and Eva Wessell, eds. *A Companion to the Works of Thomas Mann.* Rochester, N.Y.: Camden House, 2004. A collection of essays about the range of Mann's work, including discussions of his late politics, female identities, and autobiographical impulses in his writings, and "Thomas Mann's Beginnings and *Buddenbrooks*" by Herbert Lehnert.

Mundt, Hannelore. *Understanding Thomas Mann.* Columbia: University of South Carolina Press, 2004. Mundt discusses the themes, concerns, presentation, and meanings of many of Mann's works, using Mann's later published diaries as one of the sources for her analysis. Chapter 3 is devoted to *Buddenbrooks.*

Ridley, Hugh. *The Problematic Bourgeois: Twentieth-Century Criticism on Thomas Mann's "Buddenbrooks" and "The Magic Mountain."* Columbia, S.C.: Camden House, 1994. A study of the reception of these two major novels in both literary and political history. Places the works in the contexts of the debate over modernism and of psychological and philosophical criticism

_____. *Thomas Mann: "Buddenbrooks."* New York: Cambridge University Press, 1987. A basic, well-balanced, and useful introduction to all aspects of the novel. Especially good on psychological interpretation. Includes a brief bibliography.

Robertson, Ritchie, ed. *The Cambridge Companion to Thomas Mann.* New York: Cambridge University Press, 2002. A collection of essays, some analyzing individual works and others discussing Mann's intellectual world, Mann and history, his literary techniques, and his representation of gender and sexuality. Chapter 8 is an analysis of *Buddenbrooks.*

Speirs, Ronald. "Mann, *Buddenbrooks.*" In *Landmarks in the German Novel,* edited by Peter Hutchinson. New York: Peter Lang, 2007. An analysis of *Buddenbrooks,* including discussion of the book's significance in the development of the German novel from the eighteenth century through 1959.

Swales, Martin. *"Buddenbrooks": Family Life as the Mirror of Social Change.* Boston: Twayne, 1991. Perhaps one of the best available treatments for nonspecialists, this is a thorough overview of sources, criticism, and reception, followed by a balanced essayistic reading that emphasizes philosophical aspects. Includes a brief annotated bibliography of primary and secondary literature.

Bullet Park

Author: John Cheever (1912-1982)
First published: 1969
Type of work: Novel
Type of plot: Psychological realism
Time of plot: Mid-twentieth century
Locale: Suburban New York

Principal characters:
ELIOT NAILLES, an advertising executive
NELLIE NAILLES, his wife
TONY NAILLES, his son
PAUL HAMMER, the crazed would-be murderer of Eliot Nailles
SWAMI RUTUOLA, a mystic
GRETCHEN OXENCROFT, Hammer's mother

The Story:

Paul Hammer is shown around the village of Bullet Park by a real estate agent. The foibles and residents of Bullet Park, which is connected to New York City by a commuter railroad, are the subject of the real estate agent's babble. Little or nothing is learned about the mysterious Mr. Hammer, who is about to buy a house.

Eliot Nailles is introduced to Hammer and his wife at church. Nailles is mildly irritated by the priest's pun upon their names (Hammer and Nailles), which strikes him as having a kind of inevitability about it. The two most important people in Nailles's life are his wife, Nellie, and his son, Tony, whom he dearly loves but has trouble approaching. Though she has pretensions in the arts, Nellie, coming home from a disastrous day in New York, is shocked by the sexual crudity of a play and other threats to her sensibilities. For Nellie and Tony, Bullet Park is a sanctuary. Nailles wins for his family this sanctuary by setting off daily for the city on the 7:56 to write copy for a mouthwash, Spang.

One day Tony refuses to get out of bed. The doctor finds nothing wrong with him. A psychiatrist gives Nellie a moral lecture about the lack of values of her class. A somnambulist expert gives Tony a series of tests and submits a bill for five hundred dollars. Nailles is distraught and cannot understand what is wrong with his son.

Mr. and Mrs. Hammer invite the Nailles to a dinner party, though they have been no more than introduced. The evening is a disaster. Mrs. Nailles insults her husband and ridicules suburban life: "All you have to do is to get your clothes at Brooks, catch the train, and show up in church once a week and no one will ever ask a question about your identity."

That lack of identity appears to be illustrated a few days later when a man named Shinglehouse, a regular on the 7:56, commits suicide by throwing himself under an express train. Though the rhythm of life seems barely disturbed by the event, Nailles is deeply shaken. Returning home, he tries harder to communicate with Tony about what he feels, but Tony only sleeps. In his mind he reviews difficult episodes in his attempts to be a parent. Nailles remembers the time Tony was arrested for attacking a teacher who denied him the privilege of playing football. He recalls another time when Tony briefly disappeared overnight, staying with a Mrs. Hubbard, whom he had met in a bookstore. Later, Tony invited Mrs. Hubbard to dinner in a grotesque parody of social convention. Nailles further remembers the confrontation with his son that immediately preceded his son's taking to bed, in which he was told: "The only reason you love me . . . is because you can give me things."

Desperate to do something about Tony's strange illness, Nellie takes the advice of a former cleaning woman and looks up Swami Rutuola, who lives above a funeral parlor in Bullet Park. The Swami visits Tony, asks him to repeat "love" and "hope" hundreds of times, and, as if by magic, Tony will thereby be cured.

Hammer, writing in his journal, reveals his madness in his own words, and a long interpolated letter from his mother shows her madness as well. Hammer first becomes aware of Nailles by a small article in a dental journal announcing his promotion to the head of the mouthwash division of his company. From that moment, Hammer settles on Nailles as his target for assassination, though he will later focus on Tony as the best way of hurting the father.

Hammer's account reveals his life as a lonely drifter. He was born out of wedlock and was hidden away at school. Until he settles upon Nailles, he is wholly without purpose and almost entirely cut off from normal human contact. In one passage, for instance, he describes his travels about the world in terms of the furniture of his hotel rooms. His mother, Gretchen Oxencroft, lays out the entire conspiracy on one of his infrequent visits: Hammer should settle in a place like Bullet Park, fix upon an advertising executive like Nailles (who represents the shallowest aspects of modern culture), and then nail him to the door of Christ's church as a statement that will wake up the world. With a purpose in his life, Hammer follows the plan like the dedicated assassin he has become. His marriage is an emotionally meaningless event that becomes part of his disguise as he moves into Bullet Park.

Nailles sponsors Hammer as a member of the volunteer fire department and accompanies him on a fishing trip. Hammer settles upon Tony's death as the best way of injuring Nailles. As Tony works directing traffic at a neighborhood party, Hammer knocks him out and drags him off to church. Hammer, however, had told Swami Rutuola of the intended murder, and the Swami comes running to Nailles. With a chain saw, Nailles cuts through the door of the church and rescues his son from the altar where he was about to be sacrificed.

Critical Evaluation:

Bullet Park is John Cheever's third novel. His long and distinguished writing career was capped by many honors, including two National Book Awards, the Pulitzer Prize for Literature (1979), and the Edward McDowell Medal in the Arts (1979). Much of his work, including the first chapter of *Bullet Park*, appeared originally in the magazine *The New Yorker*. His subject matter centers largely on the suburban types of *Bullet Park*. His stature as a writer, however, is greater than that of a journalistic social satirist.

Bullet Park proved problematic to early reviewers, who were disappointed that it veered away from the satirical humor with which Cheever had become identified, told a preposterous story without narrative logic, and plunged without warning into absurdist melodrama. However, criticism over time has reclaimed the novel's reputation. Difficult and complex, *Bullet Park* is a fine and rewarding novel.

A comparison of its two major figures, Eliot Nailles and Paul Hammer, defines the conflicts that shape this apparently malformed story. The suburbanite Nailles carries his share of psychological baggage. He gets through the day anesthetized with drugs and alcohol. His son, Tony, resents him deeply. His wife, Nellie, seems to have lost her way. His prayers and his opinions are perfunctory and shallow. He is, moreover, an advertising executive for Spang mouthwash. Readers of Cheever know what to think of admen. Nailles's supposed lack of substance, judged from the article in the dental journal, induces Hammer to select him as his victim. Nailles proves to be more than a stereotype, however, in the way he understands his world. He is deeply committed to his wife and especially to his son. He earns a living in the hostile city to preserve the domicile where his wife and son retreat for protection, and where he returns with gratitude each evening. When the snapping turtle appears on the lawn, Nailles goes out to shoot it, just as primitive man defended his home against the woolly mammoth. Cheever nevertheless uses the expectation of the stereotype of the suburbs to shape his paradox. Nailles is the one who loves; he thereby possesses a generous share of goodness.

Hammer, on the other hand, parodies the defeated person of existential literature. Nellie, in a thematic echo, is reading the works of the French philosopher and novelist Albert Camus in her book club. Mersault, in Camus's *L'Étranger* (1942; *The Stranger*, 1946), for example, is so psychologically empty that he shoots an unknown person to demonstrate to himself that he has the will to make a choice. Reading Hammer's own words in his journal, the reader discovers his moral emptiness in the texture of the prose: "Have you ever waked on a summer morning to realize that this is the day when you will kill a man? . . . Hammer mowed his lawns that day. The imposture was thrilling. Look at Mr. Hammer cutting his grass. What a nice man Mr. Hammer must be." Some readers will recall the string of political murders of the 1960's committed by assassins with vague and forlorn motives. Hammer is equally evil, crazed, and alone.

Bullet Park contrasts the moral states of Nailles and Hammer, revealing them in images and in the texture of language. Although flawed and foolish, Nailles celebrates his humanity. He loves Tony with a love that continues to flow although he gets very little in return. He describes the scene in which he almost kills his son in anger on a miniature golf course when Tony declares that he is going to quit school: "I said that even if he wanted to be a poet he had to prepare himself to be a poet. So then I said to him what I've never said before. I said: 'I love you, Tony.'"

A third character is also important to the book. The narrator, especially in the early part of the story, provides the commentary and wit that make up the characteristic Cheever voice: "The diocesan bishop had suggested that churchgoers turn on their windshield wipers to communicate their faith in the resurrection of the dead and the life of the world to come." Such humor is brittle and risks silliness (in one of Cheever's stories, the zoning laws do not allow anyone to die; a body has to be removed to another place before a death certificate can be issued). Here that voice is carefully modulated to serve a purpose within the story. People generally are fool-

ish and limited, and Nailles is only one example. With love and hate such people blunder into good and evil, in one mixture or another. The suburbs prove to be as good a place as any to look for fulfilling love.

Bruce Olsen

Further Reading

Bailey, Blake. *Cheever: A Life*. New York: Alfred A. Knopf, 2009. Thoroughly researched account of Cheever's life and paradoxical character.

Bosha, Francis J., ed. *The Critical Response to John Cheever*. Westport, Conn.: Greenwood Press, 1994. A collection of previously published reviews and criticism of Cheever's fiction, beginning with the earliest reviews in 1943. Also contains several new essays written for this collection and an interview with Cheever conducted a year before his death. Includes reviews of *Bullet Park* and two essays about the novel. In "The Resurrection of *Bullet Park*: John Cheever's Curative Spell," Samuel Coale concludes that the novel arose from creative tensions within Cheever himself, which find expression in Cheever's journals. In "Witchcraft in *Bullet Park*," John Gardner maintains that *Bullet Park* is a first-rate novel and takes early reviewers to task for misunderstanding it.

Byrne, Michael D. *Dragons and Martinis: The Skewed Realism of John Cheever*. Edited by Dale Salwak and Paul David Seldis. San Bernardino, Calif.: Borgo Press, 1993. Analyzes the style of Cheever's fiction. Includes bibliographical references and an index.

Donaldson, Scott. *John Cheever: A Biography*. New York: Random House, 1988. Full, objective, sympathetic account of Cheever's life and work. Fairminded and richly detailed.

Hunt, George. *John Cheever: The Hobgoblin Company of Love*. Grand Rapids, Mich.: Wm. B. Eerdmans, 1983. Contains a chapter on *Bullet Park* that relates it to the time in which it was written and offers a strong defense of its value.

Meanor, Patrick. *John Cheever Revisited*. New York: Twayne, 1995. The first book-length study of Cheever to make use of his journals and letters published in the late 1980's and early 1990's. Focuses on how Cheever created a mythopoeic world in his novels and stories. Includes three chapters analyzing *Bullet Park*, the Wapshot novels, and Cheever's other novels.

Waldeland, Lynne. *John Cheever*. Boston: Twayne, 1979. Defends the style and plotting of *Bullet Park* as appropriate to its exploration of good and evil.

The Bulwark

Author: Theodore Dreiser (1871-1945)
First published: 1946
Type of work: Novel
Type of plot: Social realism
Time of plot: 1890 to the mid-1920's
Locale: Dukla and Philadelphia, Pennsylvania; New
    York City; Atlantic City, New Jersey

Principal characters:
SOLON BARNES, a Quaker banker
BENECIA (NÉE WALLIN), his wife
CYNTHIA BARNES, Solon's sister
RUFUS BARNES, Solon's father
HANNAH BARNES, Solon's mother
PHOEBE KIMBER, Hannah's sister
RHODA KIMBER and LAURA KIMBER, Phoebe's daughters
JUSTUS WALLIN, Benecia's father
ISOBEL, the oldest child of Solon and Benecia
ORVILLE, the second child of Solon and Benecia
DOROTHEA, the attractive third child of Solon and Benecia
ETTA, the fourth child of Solon and Benecia
VOLIDA LA PORTE, Etta's friend
HESTER WALLIN, Justus's sister
WILLARD KANE, an artist and Etta's lover
STEWART, the youngest child of Solon and Benecia
VICTOR BRUGE and LESTER JENNINGS, Stewart's friends
PSYCHE TANZER, a young girl

The Story:

Rufus Barnes is a farmer and tradesman living near Segookit, Maine. He and his wife, Hannah, are good Quakers. When Hannah's sister, Phoebe Kimber, living in Trenton, New Jersey, loses her husband, she asks Rufus to come to New Jersey to help settle her husband's affairs. Rufus, finding himself the executor of a rather large estate, does a thorough and competent job. In gratitude for his help and in hopes that he will move his family close to her, Phoebe offers Rufus one of her properties, an old, run-down, but elegant house in Dukla, Pennsylvania, just across the Delaware River from Trenton. Rufus is willing to restore the house and try to sell it, but Phoebe is eager to give the house to him. At last, Rufus agrees to take the house and move his family to Dukla. He and his wife restore the house with great taste and beauty.

Rufus and Hannah become somewhat more worldly in Dukla. Rufus goes into business, dealing in real estate, but he applies his Quaker principles to his business and helps the poor farmers make their land yield more profit so that he will not have to foreclose. Respected and prosperous, he and his wife still follow their faith and teach it carefully to their two children, Cynthia and Solon.

Solon Barnes cuts his leg with an ax. An incompetent doctor bungles the treatment, and for a time, they all fear that the boy might die. His mother prays devoutly, however, and

Solon recovers, an event that keeps the family strictly loyal to their faith.

Sent to school with their cousins, Laura and Rhoda (Phoebe's children), Cynthia and Solon begin to acquire more polish and knowledge of the world. At school, Solon meets Benecia Wallin, the daughter of a wealthy Quaker. Cynthia, Laura, Rhoda, and Benecia are all sent to a Quaker finishing school at Oakwold, but Solon chooses to remain at home and help his father in the real estate business.

Justus Wallin, Benecia's father, is impressed by the Barnes family. He admires the way Rufus and Solon conduct their business; he is impressed with Hannah's faith and her behavior at Quaker meetings. The families become friendly, and Justus asks Rufus and Solon to become the agents for his extensive holdings. Solon and Benecia fall in love. Justus finds a job for Solon in his Philadelphia bank and, although Solon starts at the bottom, it is clear that he has both the talent and the influence to rise quickly to the top. Solon and Benecia are married, to the delight of both families, in a Quaker ceremony.

The years pass. Solon and Benecia are happy and successful. Solon does well at the bank in Philadelphia; Benecia is a quiet, principled, and religious woman. After the death of Solon's parents, Solon and Benecia move into the house in Dukla. Although Solon occasionally experiences metaphysical doubts, he lives in complete adherence to the moral principles of the Quakers. He becomes a bulwark of the community, an honest and forthright man who does not approve of smoking, drinking, art, music, literature, or dancing. He and Benecia bring up their five children in accordance with these strict Quaker principles.

Each of the children reacts differently to this upbringing. The oldest daughter, Isobel, unattractive and unpopular in school, finds it difficult to make friends. She begins to read books and decides, against the ideas implanted by her parents, that she wants to avoid the Quaker finishing school and go to college. Solon manages to compromise and sends her to Llewellyn College for Women, a Quaker institution, where she remains to do postgraduate work. Orville, the older son, inherits Solon's severity, although not his kindness. Orville becomes interested in business at an early age, although his materialism is not tempered by any principle deeper than respectability. He marries a wealthy socialite and goes into her father's pottery business in Trenton. The third child, Dorothea, is the beauty of the family. She is taken up by her father's cousin Rhoda, who marries a wealthy doctor, one of Benecia's cousins, in the Wallin family. More worldly than the Barnes family, Rhoda gives elegant parties, approves of dancing, and soon Dorothea marries a wealthy and socially acceptable young man. None of these three children, however, overtly abandons the Quaker faith or causes their parents serious concern.

The fourth child, Etta, is more interesting. Sensitive, pretty, highly intelligent, she soon begins to read forbidden books. She becomes friendly with a young girl named Volida La Porte, who introduces her to French novels and gives her the idea of studying literature at the University of Wisconsin. When Solon insists that his daughter attend the Llewellyn College for Women, Etta runs away to a Wisconsin summer session after pawning her mother's jewels to provide the fare. Solon goes after her, and the two are reconciled. Etta acknowledges the theft and returns the jewels. In the meantime, old Hester Wallin, Justus's sister, dies and leaves Etta, as well as each of her sisters, a small income.

Solon allows Etta to remain in Wisconsin for the summer session. After she leaves the university, Etta moves to Greenwich Village to continue her studies. There she meets Willard Kane, an artist, and eventually has an affair with him, even though she realizes that he has no intention of jeopardizing his artistic career by marriage. The Barnes family knows of the affair—Orville discovers it—and they highly disapprove.

The youngest child, Stewart, is the wildest of all. He lacks the essential honesty of his brother and sisters. Spoiled by his cousin Rhoda, who takes him up, as she took up Dorothea, and sends him to a snobbish private school, Stewart is interested only in his conquests of lower-class girls on riotous trips to Atlantic City. With his friends Victor Bruge and Lester Jennings, Stewart picks up girls and takes them off for the weekend. He often steals money from his parents or from his brother to finance his escapades. His reckless life is paralleled by wild financial speculations in the business world that increasingly worry Solon. Solon's bank is involved in some questionable activities, but Solon, true to his religious principles, feels he cannot pull out of the situation without hurting others who depend on him. Similarly, he cannot abandon Stewart.

One weekend, Stewart's friend Bruge gives a young girl, Psyche, some of his mother's "drops" because Psyche will not yield to Bruge, and he believes the "drops" might make her comply. They do, but they also kill Psyche. The boys, frightened, leave her body on the road. The police soon apprehend them and charge them with rape and murder. Unable to face his family and feeling some vestiges of religious guilt, Stewart kills himself in jail.

The shock of Stewart's suicide causes Benecia to suffer a stroke. Etta leaves her lover and returns home shortly before her mother's death. She finds Solon greatly changed. In his despair, he loses his severity and no longer believes he has the right to judge others. Realizing that his concern with business and with strict standards cut him off from the kindness and light at the center of his faith, he learns to love all things, all creatures of nature. Etta, who often reads to him, finds herself more and more attracted to the central "Inner Light" of the Quaker belief. Always the most understanding child, she and her father develop a genuine closeness and affection for each other before Solon dies of cancer six months later. Etta, left alone and removed from the commercial contemporary world, becomes the embodiment of essential Quaker principles.

Critical Evaluation:

Theodore Dreiser devoted the last year of his life to completing *The Bulwark*, a project that he had started numerous times before then but never completed. The idea for the novel was given to him in 1912 by a young woman named Anna Tatum, who told Dreiser about her Quaker father. Despite having an early outline and draft of the novel and promising several publishers the work, Dreiser did not publish it during his lifetime; it was not published until 1946, a year after his death. While the novel is no longer in print and still receives only mixed reviews, *The Bulwark* is noteworthy not only because it is Dreiser's final, complete novel but also because its prose style marks a significant deviation from Dreiser's previous fiction. The novel also explores and resolves thematic issues raised in all of Dreiser's works.

Stylistically, Dreiser wrote *The Bulwark* in a simple and concise style, not a technique for which he is known. *The Bulwark* is also the shortest of Dreiser's eight novels, even though the plot follows the Barnes family for three generations. In some passages, the prose reads like a plot summary devoid of detail and dialogue, a mere outline of events. An example of this simple, direct prose is evidenced at the beginning of chapter 26, in which the births of Solon and Benecia's first three children are recounted in three brief paragraphs. In comparison to Dreiser's other novels, the syntax and diction are also streamlined. *The Bulwark* lacks the masses of detail, the complex diction, and the melodramatic pronouncements on life that can be found in Dreiser's other works. When Etta claims at the end of the novel that she is crying not for herself or for her father but for life, this denouement seems reserved when compared to the conclusion of *Sister Carrie* (1900). Dreiser's age and failing health may have contributed to this change in style. It should be noted, however, that the sparse style fits the austere Quaker characters.

While this simple style is unusual for Dreiser, it is the unique exploration of themes commonly found in Dreiser's work that especially marks this book as significant. *The Bulwark* is an anomaly in that it is Dreiser's only extended exploration of his favorite themes from the point of view of the older, nineteenth century generation. Solon and Solon's father, Rufus, represent this older generation, and their rigid religious beliefs result in a spiritual dilemma for Solon and his children. On the one hand, Solon is a Quaker who believes, and whose ancestors believed, in an agrarian, spiritual, stoic, self-sacrificing existence. On the other hand, Solon is a wealthy banker who must exist in a society concerned with money, consumer goods, and pleasure. In previous fiction, Dreiser showed sympathy for those who held the agrarian, spiritual ideal of the nineteenth century, but only in *The Bulwark* does Dreiser tell an extended tale from what would have been the older generation's point of view.

In *The Bulwark*, Dreiser is asking: What happens to a human being who is raised to believe in a Christian, agrarian world but who is placed in an urban, materialistic setting? Dreiser raises the same question in other novels. Carrie Meeber, in *Sister Carrie*, leaves her rural hometown of Columbia City, Wisconsin, for Chicago and New York. Clyde Griffiths, in *An American Tragedy* (1925), abandons the poverty and religion of his parents' mission to enter the wealthy environment of the Green-Davidson hotel. *The Bulwark* reenacts this same transplantation, but the story is told from the perspective of the older generation; the devout parent, Solon Barnes, reflects on his own failings and on his children's inability to live by Quaker values.

It is Solon's children, not Solon himself, who embody the consequences of the relocation from a rural farm in Maine to a mansion in Pennsylvania, from an isolated agrarian lifestyle to an urban, materialistic mode of existence. Each of Solon's five children, like characters in an allegory, represents a different response to this clash between the father's values and his or her own experiences. None can maintain the Quaker belief system. Isobel, the first daughter, is not beautiful, and in an increasingly materialistic society where appearance is as important as social position and devotion, she abandons both her father's religion and secular society to become a scholar. Orville, the first son, inherits his father's severity and work ethic, but he adopts his father's religion only as a means of maintaining good appearances. Dorothea, the second daughter, is beautiful and charming; she marries well, and high society becomes her domain. While not openly denouncing the Quaker faith, Dorothea and Orville, through their actions, have embraced material wealth and social success as their ideals. Etta, the third daughter, embodies one more reaction to her father's inflexible code; she embraces art and moves to Greenwich Village. Stewart, the youngest, is ironically named because he, in the Quaker sense, is the worst "steward." He rejects his father's religion, embracing a destructive life of hedonism.

Each child, in a crescendo of tragedy, symbolizes the possible consequences of attempting to maintain Quaker beliefs strictly in an increasingly secular environment. By the end of the novel, however, Etta and Solon, unlike the other characters, have changed. They gain a tragic vision, a vision that allows them to accept both the good and evil in life. They achieve this vision, not by abandoning their Quaker roots, but by adjusting their beliefs to new circumstances, by becoming more flexible, and by more closely associating themselves with the creative force found in nature.

After losing his son and his wife, Solon encounters a snake, a symbol of evil in Christianity. Nevertheless, Solon communes with the snake. Dreiser, like Solon, had a similar experience. Discovering a puff adder, Dreiser killed it, believing it to be poisonous. Later, learning it was not a dangerous snake and experiencing great guilt, Dreiser reassuringly spoke to the next puff adder he encountered, causing the snake to uncoil and retreat. Like Solon, Dreiser believes in a creative force, one that he associates with a divine plan that he observes in nature. Just as Solon finds peace through a resigned acceptance of life's beauty and pain, so Dreiser must have found peace by writing *The Bulwark*, a novel that resolves many of the philosophical questions with which he wrestled throughout his life.

"Critical Evaluation" by Roark Mulligan

Further Reading

Cassuto, Leonard, and Clare Virginia Eby, eds. *The Cambridge Companion to Theodore Dreiser*. New York: Cambridge University Press, 2004. A collection of twelve essays focusing on the novelist's examination of American conflicts between materialistic longings and traditional values. Includes essays on Dreiser's style, Dreiser and women, and Dreiser and the ideology of upward mobility. The references to *The Bulwark* are listed in the index.

Gerber, Philip L. *Theodore Dreiser Revisited*. New York: Twayne, 1992. Provides a good introduction to Dreiser's life and writing. Contains a cogent chapter on *The Bulwark*.

Gogol, Miriam, ed. *Theodore Dreiser: Beyond Naturalism*. New York: New York University Press, 1995. Ten essays interpret Dreiser from the perspectives of new historicism, poststructuralism, psychoanalysis, feminism, and other points of view. Gogol's introduction advances the argument that Dreiser was much more than a naturalist and deserves to be treated as a major author.

Hussman, Lawrence E., Jr. *Dreiser and His Fiction: A Twentieth-Century Quest*. Philadelphia: University of Pennsylvania Press, 1983. Hussman's thesis is that Dreiser's beliefs changed toward the end of his life and that his fiction reflects this change. Thus, *The Bulwark* becomes a final sign that Dreiser was more interested in spiritual matters.

Lehan, Richard. *Theodore Dreiser: His World and His Novels*. Carbondale: Southern Illinois University Press, 1969. Offers thoughtful insights into Dreiser's writing and thinking. Lehan notices a gradual shift in Dreiser's late fiction toward communism and nature, away from technology and capitalism.

Lingeman, Richard. *Theodore Dreiser: An American Journey, 1908-1945*. Vol. 2 in *Theodore Dreiser*. New York: G. P. Putnam's Sons, 1990. In the second volume of a two-volume biography, Lingeman recounts the events in Dreiser's life and analyzes Dreiser's fiction.

Loving, Jerome. *The Last Titan: A Life of Theodore Dreiser*. Berkeley: University of California Press, 2005. This engrossing survey of the author's life and work is a welcome addition to Dreiser scholarship. Focuses on Dreiser's work, including his journalism, discussing the writers who influenced him and his place within American literature.

Pizer, Donald. *The Novels of Theodore Dreiser: A Critical Study*. Minneapolis: University of Minnesota Press, 1976. Pizer is a recognized authority on Dreiser and naturalism. He offers a solid reading of *The Bulwark* and important background information on the novel.

A Burnt-Out Case

Author: Graham Greene (1904-1991)
First published: Utbränd, 1960 (English translation, 1961)
Type of work: Novel
Type of plot: Bildungsroman
Time of plot: Mid-twentieth century
Locale: The Congo

Principal characters:
QUERRY, a retired Catholic architect
DR. COLIN, a doctor
RYCKER, a factory manager
MARIE, Rycker's young wife
DEO GRATIAS, Querry's servant, a leper
PARKINSON, a journalist
FATHER THOMAS, a doubting priest

The Story:

Querry takes the long boat ride into the African jungle, traveling deeper and deeper into the Congo and escaping farther and farther from the misery of his life in Europe. When the boat reaches its ultimate point—a leper colony run by Catholic missionaries—Dr. Colin and the priests invite Querry to stay. Settling in at the colony, Querry asks only for solitude. "So you thought you could just come and die here?" Dr. Colin asks him. "Yes, that *was* in my mind," he responds. "But chiefly I wanted to be in an empty place, where no new building or woman would remind me that there was a time when I was alive, with a vocation and a capacity for love." Querry explains to Dr. Colin that he is figuratively like the lepers—the burnt-out cases—who lose their toes and fingers to the disease, but, once mutilated, no longer suffer pain. "The palsied suffer, their nerves feel, but I am one of the mutilated, doctor," Querry says. After a month at the leper colony, Querry offers to drive to Luc, the capital city, to pick up some medical equipment for Dr. Colin. While in the city, Querry is accosted by Rycker, who recognizes the famous architect from an old cover photo in *Time* magazine. After picking up the doctor's equipment, Querry agrees to spend the night at Rycker's house, near the palm oil factory that Rycker manages. At the house, Querry meets Rycker's childlike young wife, Marie, and witnesses firsthand the misery of her marriage to Rycker.

While Marie is preparing a drink for her guest, Rycker explains to Querry that he married a very young woman because women age rapidly in the tropics and he wanted a wife who will still be sexually attractive when he is an old man. He adds that young women are more easily trained and that he trained Marie to "know what a man needs." Rycker, who spent six years in the seminary, complains that Marie is ignorant of Catholic rituals and that she cannot understand his spiritual needs the way Querry can. Querry insists he no longer believes, but Rycker refuses to listen. Appalled by Rycker's insensitivity and disgusted by his hollow professions of faith, Querry leaves hurriedly the next morning.

For a time, Querry feels at ease only in the company of Dr. Colin. Dr. Colin respects Querry's need for peace and quiet, but Rycker, the failed priest, and Father Thomas, the doubting priest, refuse to respect Querry's privacy. Although Querry protests, they see him as the great Catholic architect, the famous builder of monuments to God, and they torment him with their spiritual problems. After two months at the leper colony, Querry feels more secure, and he begins the long journey back from his emotional breakdown. At Dr. Colin's urging, he begins to draw up plans for a new leper hospital. When his leper-servant, Deo Gratias, becomes lost in the jungle, he rescues him. Querry and Dr. Colin talk often about God—Dr. Colin happy in his atheism and Querry tormented by his half-belief.

Just as Querry is beginning to enjoy a rebirth of interest in life, he suffers a setback with the arrival of the journalist Parkinson. Just when Querry believes that he truly escaped his past, hidden in the jungle where few know or care that he once was famous, the journalist's arrival shatters this sense of security. Parkinson, a lonely and bitter man, knows he can achieve fame for himself by publishing the whereabouts of the famous architect. He digs up painful events of Querry's past, including the suicide of a mistress who killed herself for

Querry's love. He seeks out Rycker, who pretends intimacy with Querry and feeds Parkinson a pack of lies. Angered by Rycker's lies to Parkinson, Querry travels to Rycker's house, determined to confront him and convince him to stay away from the journalist. Arriving at Rycker's home, Querry finds Rycker ill in bed and Marie in a state of panic, fearing she is pregnant and knowing her husband wants no children. Touched by her helplessness and moved by her tears, Querry offers to take Marie to the doctor in Luc. That night in the hotel in Luc, Querry hears Marie crying in the room next door and goes in to comfort her. He tells her a story about a famous Catholic jeweler who lost his faith in God, a story that Marie quickly recognizes as the story of Querry's own life. In the morning, Marie sees the doctor, who tells her she will have to wait two days for her pregnancy test results.

That same morning at the hotel, Querry and Marie meet Parkinson, and they are soon joined by Rycker, who insists that Querry and Marie slept together the night before. Querry tries to convince Rycker of the truth, but Rycker refuses to believe him. Disgusted with Rycker once again, Querry promptly leaves Luc and returns to the colony. Three days later, the priests hold a party to celebrate the completion of the new hospital. Querry, Dr. Colin, and the priests toast their accomplishment with champagne. Querry feels warm and happy, planning his future there among his new friends.

His joy, however, is interrupted with the news that Marie is at the nearby convent school, exposing her pregnancy and falsely claiming that Querry is the father. No amount of coaxing on Querry's part can persuade the young woman to tell the truth. She stubbornly clings to her lie, perhaps for love of Querry, or perhaps seeing her chance to escape from Rycker. Though Dr. Colin and some of the priests believe in Querry's innocence, others do not, and Querry sadly prepares to leave the colony. That very night, however, Rycker shows up in a rage. As Querry attempts to pacify him, Rycker shoots and kills Querry in a fit of jealous passion.

Critical Evaluation:

Considered by many critics to be the greatest British writer of the twentieth century, Graham Greene was made a British Companion of Honour in 1966 and awarded the Order of Merit in 1986. In a literary career that spanned sixty years, he published twenty-five novels, dozens of short stories and plays, two autobiographies, and countless critical and journalistic pieces. Unlike many great writers, Greene enjoyed not only critical acclaim but also popular success. Many of his fictional works were made into films, and a great number were best sellers. Upon Greene's death in 1991, William Golding proclaimed him "the ultimate chronicler of twentieth-century man's consciousness and anxiety," and Sir Alec Guinness hailed him as "a great writer who spoke brilliantly to a whole generation."

During his long and varied career, Greene was a journalist, a film critic, and, for a time, a British spy. In 1926, he converted to Catholicism, and many of his works have Catholic themes. Important, also, to Greene's fiction were his endless travels throughout the world, often to places of political unrest. With the journalist's eye for character and detail, Greene exposed the dark side of political intrigue in places such as Papa Doc's Haiti and Vietnam at the start of the conflict between Vietnam and the United States. For Greene, external political and religious conflicts were a reflection of the greater conflict within the human soul. Greene's characters—particularly in his later novels—struggle to find their identity in a ravaged and alienating world and fight to find meaning in lives where none is apparent.

Like most of Greene's later novels, *A Burnt-Out Case* is strong on characterization, rich in symbolism, and heavy with irony. Greene's third-person omniscient narration offers readers insights into each character's motivation, making the characters seem authentic and compelling. Greene's skillful use of symbol and metaphor gives the story emotional and psychological depth, and his masterful use of irony lends the story poignancy and immediacy.

In *A Burnt-Out Case*, Greene develops the theme of the individual's search for identity and for meaning by using two controlling metaphors, the "journey" and the "burnt-out case." As the story opens with Querry's river voyage, the narrator refers to Querry as "the cabin passenger"—a nameless, faceless traveler on an unknown journey. On the trip, Querry speaks little, insulating himself from the other passengers and wallowing in his self-imposed isolation. The boat travels far down the river, deep into the jungle, stopping finally at the leper colony. On a literal level, the river voyage is simply Querry's means of escape from his sad and sordid past. On a metaphorical level, however, Querry is seeking death, trying to "bury" himself in the jungle. Like the leper who loses his extremities and suffers from numbness, Querry is numb to joy and pain and longs to withdraw from a world he finds meaningless.

When he arrives at the leper colony, Querry disembarks because the boat "goes no farther." Metaphorically, though, his journey has just begun. On the deeper symbolic level, Querry's river voyage is a journey of self-discovery. The farther he travels into the jungle, the deeper he delves into himself. With an irony characteristic of Greene's work, what Querry finds at the end of his journey is not the death he seeks but a symbolic rebirth he once thought impossible. Sur-

rounded by the peace and the safety of the colony, Querry begins to lose his fear of the world. Strengthened by his friendship with Dr. Colin and his affection for Deo Gratias, he begins to think of others before himself. Stirred by compassion for Marie Rycker, he travels the long road back to the world of the emotionally alive. Once burnt out, Querry eventually regains the ability to feel, to care, and to love. Once a stranger to himself and the world around him, Querry learns to find meaning in the human community. Traveling to the Congo, Querry wants to lose himself in darkness and anonymity; paradoxically, he finds himself and his life's meaning by doing so. Having lost the ability to feel, he seeks symbolic death and burial; paradoxically, he finds a rebirth of interest in life. In one of Greene's fine ironic twists, Querry finds literal death at the moment he is reborn into the world of those who feel and care.

Karen Priest

Further Reading

Bergonzi, Bernard. *A Study in Greene: Graham Greene and the Art of the Novel*. New York: Oxford University Press, 2006. Bergonzi examines all of Greene's novels, analyzing their language, structure, and recurring motifs. He argues that Greene's earliest work was his best, *Brighton Rock* was his masterpiece, and his novels published after the 1950's showed a marked decline in his abilities. Chapter 7 includes a discussion of *A Burnt-Out Case*, and other references to the novel are listed in the index.

Bloom, Harold, ed. *Graham Greene*. New York: Chelsea House, 1987. Contains critical essays on all the major novels, with three essays dedicated to *A Burnt-Out Case*. Contains a chronology of Greene's life and works and a brief bibliography.

Bosco, Mark. *Graham Greene's Catholic Imagination*. New York: Oxford University Press, 2005. Focuses on the elements of Catholic doctrine in Greene's novels. Bosco contradicts many critics, who maintain these elements only are present in Greene's early novels, demonstrating how the writer's religious faith is a pervasive aspect of all of his work.

Hoskins, Robert. *Graham Greene: An Approach to the Novels*. New York: Garland, 1999. An updated look at Greene's oeuvre with individual chapters providing analysis of several novels, including *A Burnt-Out Case*. Examines the protagonists of Greene's novels in the first and second phases of his career.

Kurismmootil, K. C. Joseph. *Heaven and Hell on Earth: An Appreciation of Five Novels of Graham Greene*. Chicago:

Loyola University Press, 1982. Kurismmootil sees *A Burnt-Out Case* as the last of Greene's religious novels and addresses the novel's "Christian insights." Offers good coverage of characterization. Includes a bibliography of Greene's works and Greene criticism.

Land, Stephen K. *The Human Imperative: A Study of the Novels of Graham Greene*. New York: AMS Press, 2008. A chronological consideration of all of Greene's work, demonstrating the common themes and character types in his fiction. Charts Greene's development as a writer.

O'Prey, Paul. *A Reader's Guide to Graham Greene*. New York: Thames and Hudson, 1988. An excellent source for discussion of Greene's major works. Analyzes plot, character, and theme and includes a bibliography of all of Greene's publications.

Roston, Murray. *Graham Greene's Narrative Strategies: A Study of the Major Novels*. New York: Palgrave Macmillan, 2006. Roston focuses on seven novels, including *A Burnt-Out Case*, to describe the narrative strategies Greene devised to deflect readers' hostility toward his advocacy of Catholicism and to create heroic characters at a time when the traditional hero was no longer a credible protagonist.

Sherry, Norman. *The Life of Graham Greene*. 3 vols. New York: Viking Press, 1989-2004. This three-volume biography is the most comprehensive and authoritative account of Greene's life yet published, written with complete access to his papers and the full cooperation of family, friends, and the novelist himself. Includes a generous collection of photographs, a bibliography, and an index.

Thomas, Brian. *An Underground Fate: The Idiom of Romance in the Later Novels of Graham Greene*. Athens: University of Georgia Press, 1988. An outstanding exploration of eight Greene novels in terms of the romance myth, in which the hero descends into the underworld but then emerges reborn and triumphant. Thomas's work is remarkable in its argument that Greene's later works end in hope rather than despair. Offers an extensive bibliography of criticism about Greene's works.

Bury My Heart at Wounded Knee
An Indian History of the American West

Author: Dee Brown (1908-2002)
First published: 1970
Type of work: History

The title of this book, a poetic line from Stephen Vincent Benét's "American Names," introduces Dee Brown's history of the Indians in the American West. Brown presents a factual as well as an emotional account of the relationship among the Indians, the American settlers, and the U.S. government. The massacre at Wounded Knee Creek in South Dakota on December 29, 1890, provides the backdrop for the narrative. In his introduction, Brown states the reason for his work. Thousands of accounts about life in the American West of the late nineteenth century were written. Stories are told of the traders, ranchers, wagon trains, gunfighters, and gold-seekers. Rarely is the voice of the Indian heard. The pre-European occupant of the land was classified only as a hindrance to the spreading of American civilization to the West Coast. In this book, Brown seeks to remedy the historical injustice done to the Native American. The author declares that the reader will not finish the book with a cheerful spirit but will come away with a better understanding of what the American Indian is and was. Punctuating the book throughout are photographs of and quotations from those whose story is being told.

The opening chapter of Brown's chronological account begins with the attitudes of different groups of Europeans toward the natives they encountered in America. Although Christopher Columbus expressed admiration for the natives of the West Indies, the Spanish were often brutal. The English, capable of brutality when the occasion called for it, usually tried subtler methods. Included in this chapter are the initial relationships between the Indians and the government of the United States. Brown relates early indignities against Indian leaders, including that of the skeleton of Black Hawk, a Sauk and Fox chief who resisted American expansion, being on display in the office of the governor of the Iowa Territory. Black Hawk was the grandfather of Jim Thorpe, an Olympic gold medal athlete in 1912.

The remaining chapters of *Bury My Heart at Wounded Knee* are a survey of the Western Indians, tribe by tribe, event by event, and leader by leader. The story begins with the Navajo of the Southwest, led by Manuelito. Like many later Indian leaders, Manuelito at first tried to be realistic and to accept the presence of Americans in their territory on reasonable terms. When those terms were violated by the Americans, the Navajo retaliated. The result was war that involved atrocities on both sides. Brown supports his narrative by direct quotes from participants in the conflict, such as a white soldier's account of a massacre of Navajos at Fort Wingate in New Mexico in September, 1861.

Brown next turns to Little Crow, a chief of the Santee Sioux in Minnesota. After many years of trying to adopt the white man's lifestyle and dress, even visiting President James Buchanan in Washington, Little Crow became disillusioned and angry during the summer of 1862. The result of that anger was Little Crow's War. The war ended with the Santee Sioux moving west to the Great Plains and with Little Crow's scalp and skull being put on display in St. Paul.

Chapter 4 begins with a meeting at Fort Laramie, Wyoming, in 1851. Leaders of the Cheyenne, Arapaho, Sioux, Crow, and several smaller tribes met with United States government representatives. The agreements made there permitted the building of roads and military posts in Indian territory, but no land was surrendered by the Indians. The Pikes Peak gold rush in 1858 resulted in the arrival of thousands of white prospectors, ranchers, and farmers to the lands of the Cheyenne and Arapaho. In spite of the loss of much land, the Indians remained peaceful until 1864. Black Kettle, the Cheyenne chief, heard about the experiences of the Navajo and the Sioux; he hoped to spare his people that suffering. War did break out in the spring of 1864, when soldiers attacked some Cheyenne on the South Platte River. The fighting ended in November with the well-planned Sand Creek Massacre of Black Kettle's Cheyenne by a United States Army force under the command of Colonel John M. Chivington.

In the next two chapters, Brown's account returns to the Sioux, centering on Red Cloud, chief of the Oglala Sioux. It describes the Powder River Invasion of the northern Great Plains by white gold-seekers, traders, and United States Army regiments in 1865. Red Cloud was trying to keep the area between the Black Hills of South Dakota and Big Horn Mountain in Montana as the domain of the Indians, including bands of Cheyenne and Arapaho as well as the Sioux. In

1866, the United States government began preparation for a road through the Powder River country into Montana. The result was Red Cloud's War (1866-1868), beginning with the Fetterman Massacre of a contingent of soldiers in an ambush in December, 1866. After two years of conflict, Red Cloud triumphantly signed a treaty at Fort Laramie, Wyoming, that closed the Powder River road. The exact terms of the treaty after ratification by the United States Senate were disputed, but it did result in several years of peace.

Chapter 7 continues in the recounting of the struggle of Black Kettle of the Cheyenne and other Indians of the central Great Plains against white occupation of their lands. This includes the great council at Medicine Lodge Creek in Kansas in October, 1867. Although Black Kettle could only bring a few Cheyenne, more than four thousand Kiowa, Comanche, and Arapaho were present to negotiate an honorable peace with the United States government. At this meeting, Ten Bears of the Comanche gave an eloquent appeal on behalf of the Indians. Brown later includes a quote from that speech. The saddest incident in this chapter is the death of Black Kettle, who survived the Sand Creek Massacre, in another massacre led by George Custer in November, 1868. This chapter also includes the infamous words of General Phil Sheridan: "The only good Indians I ever saw were dead," which over time became "The only good Indian is a dead Indian."

After discussing the visit to Washington by Red Cloud and other Sioux chiefs, and attempts to clarify terms of the Fort Laramie Treaty of 1868, Brown moves to the Southwest and Cochise with the Apache warriors. The story, now becoming all too familiar, begins with Cochise welcoming white soldiers to his territory, even allowing a mail route and a stage station to be established. False accusations by an army officer and attempted arrest in 1861 convinced Cochise that all whites had to be driven from Apache territory. After his father-in-law, Mangas Colorado, was murdered by soldiers while a prisoner, open war broke out. The Camp Grant Massacre of unarmed Apaches in 1871 revealed the futility of Cochise's efforts. Although other Apache chiefs remained on the warpath, Cochise made peace in 1872.

In Chapter 10, the scene moves to the West Coast and the Modoc leader, Captain Jack. The account begins with attempts at cooperation and ends with Captain Jack's being hanged in 1873. The next chapter, "The War to Save the Buffalo," is an excellent account of the last major effort by the Indians of the Great Plains to preserve their traditional life. Brown includes part of the emotional speech given at the Council of Medicine Lodge Creek in 1867 by Ten Bears, who best tells his own story: "I was born upon the prairie, where the wind blew free and there was nothing to break the light of the sun. I was born where there were no enclosures and where everything drew a free breath. I want to die there and not within walls." This chapter includes more accounts of abuse by Custer. The story of Quanah Parker, the Comanche war chief whose mother was captured as a small child and raised as a Comanche, is another highlight of the chapter.

Chapter 12 of Brown's chronology returns the reader to the Sioux in the Black Hills of South Dakota. Red Cloud is joined in this narrative by Sitting Bull, Crazy Horse, and other Sioux leaders. In 1874, after the discovery of gold, the Black Hills were invaded by white miners. The miners were followed by soldiers under Custer. The war that followed ended in July, 1876, with the death of Custer and his men in the Battle of the Little Bighorn River in Montana.

The next four chapters record the flight of Chief Joseph and his Nez Perce from their home in the Northwest, the final Cheyenne subordination, the troubles of the Poncas and Standing Bear, and the removal of the Utes from their Rocky Mountain homes to undesirable land in Utah. Chapter 17 is a good account of the last Apache resistance, first by Victorio, then by Geronimo. After years of violent rebellion, Victorio was killed by Mexican soldiers in 1880. Geronimo then led the opposition until his surrender in 1886, after which the once-fierce Apache were in subjection to the United States.

The last two chapters are a fitting conclusion to a fascinating and disturbing story. Brown describes the Ghost Dance, a ritual attributed to Wovoka, a Paiute from Nevada. The dance was supposed to bring back dead Indians and the buffalo and eliminate whites from Indian lands. Sitting Bull of the Sioux, after years of Canadian exile, imprisonment in the United States, and appearances as a feature in Buffalo Bill's Wild West Show, became an advocate of the Ghost Dance. Growing despair among the Sioux intensified interest in the dance and led to Sitting Bull's death on December 15, 1890.

In the confusion that followed Sitting Bull's death, one group of his followers joined Big Foot, also a Ghost Dance advocate. On December 28, Big Foot's group was taken into custody by the U.S. Army and forced to camp along Wounded Knee Creek in southwestern South Dakota. The next day, as the Sioux were being disarmed, a minor incident involving one deaf warrior led to the massacre of the Sioux by the soldiers. Of about 350 people in the group, 51 wounded were left to be taken to the Pine Ridge Sioux Agency.

Bury My Heart at Wounded Knee is a factual account that needs no artificial elaboration. The pages of history are opened to many examples of the United States' inhumanity. The wounded from Wounded Knee were taken to the Episcopal Mission at Pine Ridge. Above the pulpit, four days after Christmas, a sign declared, "Peace on Earth, Good Will to Men."

Glenn L. Swygart

Further Reading

Beal, Merrill. *"I Will Fight No More Forever": Chief Joseph and the Nez Perce War.* Seattle: University of Washington Press, 1963. Using the words of Chief Joseph, Beal makes the account of the Nez Perce in *Bury My Heart at Wounded Knee* easier to understand. Emphasizes Nez Perce efforts to live peacefully with white settlers. Includes photographs and sketches.

Brown, Dee. *Tepee Tales of the American Indian.* New York: Holt, Rinehart and Winston, 1979. Describes the culture and heritage of the Indians. Contains good illustrations by Louis Mofsie.

Fixico, Donald L. *"Bury My Heart at Wounded Knee* and the Indian Voice in Native Studies." *Journal of the West* 39, no. 1 (January, 2000): 7. Discusses how the book persuaded American citizens to pay greater attention to Native Americans and their history. Brown's book also encouraged the emergence of an Indian voice in academia and created a significant change in the study of Native Americans.

Hagen, Lyman B. *Dee Brown.* Boise, Idaho: Boise State University Press, 1990. Brief overview of Brown's life and work.

Hyde, George. *Red Cloud's Folk.* Norman: University of Oklahoma Press, 1937. Covers the history of the Sioux from 1650 to 1878. Provides background on the dominant tribe of *Bury My Heart at Wounded Knee,* including the history of Red Cloud's family.

Underhill, Ruth. *The Navajos.* Norman: University of Oklahoma Press, 1956. Covers the origin of the Navajo, the first tribe discussed in *Bury My Heart at Wounded Knee,* up to the time of publication. Includes good photographs, maps, and a bibliography.

Bus Stop

Author: William Inge (1913-1973)
First produced: 1955; first published, 1955
Type of work: Drama
Type of plot: Comedy
Time of plot: 1950's
Locale: Thirty miles west of Kansas City, Kansas

Principal characters:
GRACE HOYLARD, owner of a restaurant
ELMA DUCKWORTH, a young waitress
WILL MASTERS, the local sheriff
CHERIE, a singer from Kansas City
BO DECKER, a young cowboy from Montana
VIRGIL BLESSING, a ranch hand, and Bo's guardian and
    close friend
GERALD LYMAN, a former college professor
CARL, a bus driver

The Story:

The phones are out of order at a street-corner restaurant on a snowy early morning thirty miles from Kansas City. It is 1:00 A.M., and restaurant proprietor Grace Hoylard and her teenage waitress Elma Duckworth await the arrival of the Kansas City-to-Wichita bus. Will Masters, the local sheriff, comes in to tell Grace that the blizzard has closed the roads; the bus will need to stop at the restaurant until further notice. The bus arrives, and passengers enter the restaurant. They will be marooned together until just before sunrise.

Cherie, a young woman in flashy clothes and wearing too much makeup, asks Sheriff Will for protection from a cowboy who is still on the bus. Cherie claims that the cowboy had abducted her from her job as a singer at the Blue Dragon nightclub in Kansas City. Dr. Gerald Lyman, an alcoholic has-been college professor in his fifties, makes a connection with Elma. Carl, the bus driver, shares a flirtation with Grace at the counter. Cherie tells Elma about her job as a chanteuse, or nightclub singer, and about her family background. Carl and Will have a brief exchange that establishes some information about Lyman, then Carl announces he is going for a long walk, which Will finds hard to believe, given the blizzard. The look between Carl and Grace, however, reveals that something is up between them.

Lyman quotes poetry to Elma, and they converse about William Shakespeare with Cherie. The door to the restaurant swings open, revealing a young cowboy, Bo Decker, and his older friend, Virgil Blessing, who is carrying Bo's guitar case. Arguments ensue between Bo and Will about closing the door and between Bo and Cherie about her name—is it or is it not Cherry? Virgil tries to warn Bo not to antagonize the sheriff, but Bo is headstrong, launching into a tirade about his ranch and his prowess at the rodeo. He then orders food and sits at the counter to talk to Cherie. He hugs and kisses her roughly, which embarrasses Cherie, and demonstrates his ar-

rogance and lack of manners. Grace excuses herself to her apartment, complaining of a headache.

Lyman begins to tell Elma about his first wife, and Bo demands to know why Cherie's suitcase is hidden behind the counter; she tries to evade him. Will intercedes, allowing Cherie to tell Bo the truth: that she is not interested in him. Bo refuses to acknowledge this. He reveals that they have been "familiar" with each other, so, he reasons, she has to marry him; still she refuses. Will promises Cherie she will not have to go with Bo on the bus. Virgil takes Bo aside and tries to calm him down. Bo is bewildered that any woman would not love him.

Dr. Lyman tries to impress Elma with his vast learning and experience and arranges to meet her in Topeka the following day. Bo reveals to Virgil the loneliness he has been feeling. Cherie tells Elma about her life and begins to realize that marrying Bo might be a reasonable choice, despite her reluctance. Elma encourages the passengers to put on a floor show to pass the time. Virgil plays his guitar, and Dr. Lyman and Elma reenact the balcony scene from Shakespeare's *Romeo and Juliet* (pr. c. 1595-1596, pb. 1597), during which time Lyman, overcome with intoxication, passes out.

Cherie sings "That Old Black Magic," inflaming Bo's passion to the point that he lifts her off her feet. Will comes to her rescue by lunging at Bo, enabling Cherie to free herself. Bo and Will move outside to engage in fisticuffs, as Grace enters the restaurant in her dressing gown. Outside, Will finally subdues Bo, slapping handcuffs on him. Lyman wakes up long enough to go to the restroom, and Virgil convinces Cherie not to press charges. He reveals to her that she is the first woman Bo has ever made love to. Cherie seems to be touched by Bo's naïveté.

It is now early morning, around 5:00. Carl and Grace had spent time together in Grace's apartment upstairs. Will announces that the highway will soon be cleared. He then explains to Bo that a person does not have a right to get whatever he wants, until he earns it. At Will's urging, Bo apologizes to everyone, offering money to Cherie to return to Kansas City. Bo shows genuine humility, which softens Cherie's attitude toward him and leads her to decide to go with him to Montana. Virgil, knowing that Bo will be happy with Cherie and that he will be in their way, lies to Bo, telling him that he has taken another job.

Carl reveals to Grace that Lyman has been in trouble many times for getting involved with girls. Will teases Carl and Grace about their rendezvous, which embarrasses Grace in front of Elma, who later assures her not to worry about it. Lyman appears to feel remorse for his inappropriate attention to Elma and begs off their meeting in Topeka; he goes outside to the bus. Bo and Cherie bid everyone good-bye and leave happily. Grace sets about closing the restaurant as the bus pulls away. She sends Elma home and sends Virgil outside so she can go to bed. Virgil has no idea where he will go next. Grace takes one last look around the restaurant and turns off the lights.

"The Story" by R. Baird Shuman;
revised by Jill Stapleton-Bergeron

Critical Evaluation:

Bus Stop is an expanded version of William Inge's one-act play *People in the Wind* (pb. 1962), which enjoyed both popular and critical success, having more Broadway performances than any of his other plays. Critics praised his abilities to accurately capture the flavor of the American Midwest in his diction and multidimensional characters, who ache with loneliness, without sentimentality.

In interviews, Inge stated that he viewed the play as an experiment in which he could examine different kinds of love, from innocence to depravity, and thought of *Bus Stop* as a comedy. Bo's undisciplined, yet well-intended behavior creates most of the humor in the play, and this combination of homespun wit with the pathos of the characters likely accounts for the play's continuing popularity over time.

Like his earlier works, Inge examines themes of loneliness along with the connection between love and sex. Overt references to sexual activity include Carl and Grace's casual affair during the course of the play, Bo's reference to being "familiar" with Cherie, and the undercurrent of immorality in Dr. Lyman's advances toward Elma. With the sexually repressed climate of the 1950's, many critics of the time objected to the play's preoccupation with sex, most of which is omitted from the film version (for which Inge did not write

the screenplay). Biographer R. Baird Shuman argues that Inge's use of sex in the play is not crass, however, but rather an effective way to reveal the alienation humans experience in the search for genuine love and acceptance. Inge succeeds in underscoring his dialogue with a profound sense of loneliness and longing for love.

This search for love and authentic human connection constitutes the main theme of the play. All the characters, with the exception of Will, refer in some way to their own sense of isolation. Grace tells Elma in the first few moments of the play that without the restaurant, she would go crazy with loneliness, and despite his bravado, Bo confesses to Virgil that "in the last few months, I been so lonesome, I . . . I jest didn't know what t'do with m'self." Although the other characters do not make explicit reference to being alone, it is suggested in their situations. Cherie, separated from most of her family by a flood, wants to appear strong and independent, but her revelations to Elma about her future prospects show Cherie to be a lonely young woman looking for a man to truly love her and not use her as a sexual object. Elma suggests that if Cherie only loved Bo, it would not be so bad to go with him to Montana, but adds "If you don't love him, it'd be awfully lonely." Lyman, too selfish to submit himself to true love, has three failed marriages and an unsuccessful teaching career. Knowing his attraction to girls is inappropriate, he lives a forlorn existence, traveling from one place to another in an attempt to escape the authorities. He chooses to remain in a drunken state, unable to bear the pain of his own depravity but incapable or unwilling to make any changes in his character.

The dialogue never clearly establishes whether or not Carl is married, but driving a bus is certainly a solitary profession. Inge hints in the play that other bus drivers have told Carl that Grace may be "agreeable" and that he is taking advantage of her loneliness. In the play's final act, Grace seems happy to have an occasional fling with Carl without the burden of commitment. This echoes Grace's earlier line to Elma about the loneliness she felt in her marriage when she says "makin' love is *one* thing, and bein' lonesome is another." When Will makes it clear that Carl and Grace have spent some time upstairs together, however, Grace is embarrassed, fearing Elma might think worse of her. Grace justifies her actions by explaining that she is restless and has to have a man occasionally, "just to keep m'self from gettin' grouchy." Even Elma—young, smart, and curious—reveals her sadness in not having any boyfriends. The unspoken implication is that Elma does not have a date for the school prom or for a Saturday night movie.

Inge portrays Virgil, Bo's longtime friend and father figure, as the most tragic of all the characters. To care for Bo, he has given up his chances of finding someone to love, and at the end of the play is left completely alone—literally out in the cold. It is almost inconceivable that Grace, a warm and compassionate woman, would not offer Virgil the option of waiting inside for the next bus, but Inge carefully plots the play in such a way that Grace and Virgil have no contact until the end—she never had a chance to get to know him. She is exhausted and wants to go to bed, but cannot chance leaving the restaurant unlocked, so she is forced to put him out. Had Carl not been interested in Grace, the play might have ended with her taking Virgil in, which would have made a much tidier and happier ending for the play. Inge rejects the happy ending, however, bringing a more honest and sardonic tone to *Bus Stop* that resonates beneath the action of the play, raising it above the level of trivial romantic comedy.

Because *Bus Stop*, however well-crafted, is considered largely predictable, it did not win any major awards, and most critics do not consider Inge a great playwright, even though he garnered the Pulitzer Prize with his play *Picnic* (pr., pb. 1953). No one can dispute, however, the overwhelming popularity of *Bus Stop* in not only the 1950's but also the twenty-first century.

The humor and romance between Bo and Cherie take central focus in the play, but Inge's gifts as a playwright rest most comfortably in his use of subplots and his creation of intricate and distinctive minor characters who are shaped with such compassion for their frailties that audiences are immediately drawn to them. The heavier, more complicated relationships of the supporting characters give *Bus Stop* a deeper meaning that speaks directly to the human heart about loneliness and the infinite search for meaningful connections, which accounts for the play's longevity in American theater.

"Critical Evaluation" by Jill Stapleton-Bergeron

Further Reading

Adler, Thomas P. *American Drama, 1940-1960: A Critical History*. New York: Twayne, 1994. A solid overview of important post-World War II works and playwrights, providing information about Inge and his place as a dramatist among his peers.

Greenwald, Michael. "'[Our] Little Company of the Odd and the Lonely': Tennessee Williams' 'Personality' in the Plays of William Inge." In *The Influence of Tennessee Williams: Essays on Fifteen American Playwrights*, ed-ited by Philip C. Kolin. Jefferson, N.C.: McFarland, 2008. The essay on Inge discusses his relationship with Tennessee Williams and the possible impact that connection had on their respective works.

Inge, William. "Interview with William Inge." In *Behind the Scenes: Theatre and Film Interviews from the "Transatlantic Review,"* edited by Joseph F. McCrindle. New York: Holt, Rinehart and Winston, 1971. A seven-page interview with Inge that is searching and revealing. It provides valuable insights into Inge's major dramas, including *Bus Stop*.

Johnson, Jeff. *William Inge and the Subversion of Gender: Rewriting Stereotypes in the Plays, Novels, and Screenplays*. Jefferson, N.C.: McFarland, 2005. Examines Inge's depiction of gender, focusing on the patterns of gender-role reversals, which Inge uses for dramatic effect and to subvert social expectations. Includes an analysis of *Bus Stop*.

Kansas Quarterly 18, no. 4 (1986). This entire issue of *Kansas Quarterly* is devoted to Inge. The dozen articles cover most of his plays and both of his novels. Although no single article is devoted to *Bus Stop*, at least half of the articles provide some interpretive consideration of the play.

Leeson, Richard M. *William Inge: A Research and Production Sourcebook*. Westport, Conn.: Greenwood Press, 1994. Includes a discussion of Inge's life and career, as well as plot summaries, production histories, and critical overviews of his plays.

Shuman, R. Baird. *William Inge*. 2d ed. New York: Twayne, 1989. Offers a complete reevaluation of all of Inge's plays and his two novels. Includes a major interpretive section on *Bus Stop*.

Voss, Ralph F. *A Life of William Inge: The Strains of Triumph*. Lawrence: University Press of Kansas, 1989. Perhaps the most thorough critical biography of Inge. Voss's analytical considerations of all the plays are strong, and his comments on *Bus Stop* have particular merit.

Wertheim, Albert. "Dorothy's Friend in Kansas: The Gay Inflections of William Inge." In *Staging Desire: Queer Readings of American Theater History*, edited by Kim Marra and Robert A. Schanke. Ann Arbor: University of Michigan Press, 2002. Analyzes the depiction of sexuality in the work of Inge and other figures who made their mark in the American theater before 1969, the year the Stonewall Rebellion in New York City accelerated the gay and lesbian rights movement.

The Business of Fancydancing
Stories and Poems

Author: Sherman Alexie (1966-   )
First published: 1992
Type of work: Short fiction and poetry

The five short stories and forty poems that form Sherman Alexie's first published collection add a decidedly unique new voice to contemporary American literature. Alexie, a Spokane Coeur d'Alene American Indian, eloquently describes the challenges facing both reservation and urban American Indians in the final decade of the twentieth century.

The collection is divided into three sections: Distances, Evolution, and Crazy Horse Dreams. Alexie generally begins or ends each section with a prose piece. The poems are usually lyric and brief, though many are narrative and begin to introduce actual or prototype versions of characters whom Alexie later developed in the short stories published as *The Lone Ranger and Tonto Fistfight in Heaven* (1993) and in the novel *Reservation Blues* (1995). With *The Business of Fancydancing*, Alexie initiates his publishing of collections of mostly poems, but collections that also include significant prose poems and several short stories, all anchored on common controlling metaphors.

Alexie generally employs free verse, though he has notably employed medieval European poetic forms such as the villanelle and the sestina, as he does in "Spokane Tribal Celebration, September 1987." The sestina originated in medieval Provence, with six sextets and a final three-line envoy; the form uses the six terminal words of the first stanza in a specific and complex pattern in each succeeding stanza. The concluding envoy includes all six of the terminal words in the middle and ends of the three lines and generally includes a dedication to a patron.

In Alexie's use of the form, he describes the tribal celebration of the title, providing character Seymour's experience of the powwow as emblematic in certain ways of the experience as a whole. There is irony and resignation when Seymour is quoted as saying, "I/ don't have no brothers except this night/and the moon and this bottle of dreams." The allure and comfort of alcohol are noted with humor and despair as the narrator observes wryly, "the only time Indian men/ get close to the earth anymore is when Indian men/ pass out and hit the ground." In the concluding envoy, there is no dedication but only unanswered queries: "I/ wonder if I

and the other Indian men/ will drink all night long. If Seymour's dreams/ will keep him warm like a blanket, like a fire."

"Traveling," the initial short story that opens the section Distances, introduces the theme of traveling, across distances, toward an uncertain future across geography that is actual, even as it is mythic. Resigned yet still proud, the narrator bemoans "all the Indians in the bars drinking their culture or boarded up in their houses so much in love with cable television." The narcotic fix of drinking alcohol or of mindlessly, continuously watching television represents contemporary attempts gone awry in terms of sustainable cultural expression and practice.

The difficulty of language and communication across distances is embodied in different ways in this section as well. In "Translated from the American," a grandmother insists on speaking to her grandson in Salish, even though the son does not know his native language enough to teach it to the grandson. When he asks for his mother, the baby's grandmother, to speak the words in English so that they can understand the meaning, she responds, "It doesn't make any sense that way," articulating the linguistic argument that translation cannot always accurately embody the original meaning of a thought in another language. In tending to the needs of an elder with terminal cancer, the narrator confesses to having "dreamed you learned a new language/ after they took your vocal cords."

Aching with the need to communicate and to articulate, Alexie treats the composition of poetry as a personal vision quest to reconcile the distances that he perceives. He also articulates the difference, or distance, between certain mainstream American values and those commonly shared by Spokane and tribal peoples. "November 22, 1983" looks back on his parents' reaction two decades earlier to the news of U.S. president John F. Kennedy's assassination. The line "ain't no Indian loves Marilyn Monroe," for example, suggests cultural distance and difference of opinion in terms of what constitutes feminine beauty and desirability.

In "Special Delivery," the short story that heads the section Evolution, Thomas Builds-the-Fire allegedly holds reservation postmaster Eve Ford hostage "with the idea of a gun." The entire section is concerned thematically with the title notion of evolution—of cultures and peoples but especially of their languages. Thomas, as the reservation storyteller, knows profoundly the value of language and its metamorphic development over time, but he is marginalized and even ridiculed by his Spokane peers who make fun of him or—worse, given his identity as a storyteller—ignore him. Ironically, there is no clear or initial "Special Delivery" that Thomas receives—not Eve's attention or her love, not the respect or even attention of his Spokane brothers and sisters and cousins, and no responses to his letters to members of the U.S. Congress, to game show hosts, and to the president of the United States.

At the end of the story, what Thomas receives instead in a new-ceremony "special delivery" is a visit from his vision animal, limping to him on three legs to tell him "Thomas, you don't have a dream that will ever come true," thereby attributing to him the burdens of being a seer. In the title poem, Alexie provides a quick evolutionary summary that describes Buffalo Bill's arrival on the reservation to open a twenty-four-hour pawn shop across the street from the liquor store. In five brief stanzas, the Indians are said to pawn both traditional and contemporary items as well as their bodies and their skin. Buffalo Bill then converts the pawn shop into the Museum of Native American Cultures and "charges the Indians five bucks a head to enter."

In "Ceremonies," Seymour defines "Crazy Horse Dreams" as "the kind that don't come true," acknowledging both the personal and professional glorious failures that the Lakota mystic and warrior Crazy Horse experienced. Here and in subsequent works, Crazy Horse serves both as historical figure and continuing metaphor, representing not simply Indian failure but also a sense of visionary leadership and the creative possibility of different and better futures.

This well-meaning—but flawed and tasked—mysterious persona of nineteenth century American Indian culture and history is transposed into a number of contemporary situations: as a clerk at a 7-11 convenience store, working the graveyard shift, drinking free cola and smoking cigarettes from the store stock; as a 3 A.M. hitchhiker on the reservation; as a putative blood donor whose contribution is refused because "we've already taken too much of your blood/ and you won't be eligible/ to donate for another generation or two"; and as a Vietnam veteran who returns home, goes to the Breakaway Bar, and sells his medals for a dozen beers, which he subsequently drinks. Crazy Horse becomes, in effect, a modern-day coyote figure in the folk mythology of Alexie's work, bringing contradictions into examination and creating

situations and narratives that provide insights into how human life should be lived.

At the close of "No Drugs or Alcohol Allowed," the narrator asserts that although Crazy Horse was presumably killed years ago,

white people don't realize
he came back to life
and started his own cable television channel and began the reeducation
of all of us who spent so many years
skinless, driving our cars straight off cliffs directly into
the beginning of nowhere.

Alexie's treatment of Crazy Horse shows a belief in the sustaining power of the stories and people of the past. This treatment also shows an understanding that the cultural transmission of values will continue to occur principally through structures of popular and electronic culture rather than through traditional and folk culture.

Richard Sax

Further Reading

Bruce, Heather E., et al. *Sherman Alexie in the Classroom.* Urbana, Ill.: National Council of Teachers of English, 2008. The tenth volume in the High School Literature series provides insights into teaching Alexie's work. Includes discussions in chapters 1 and 4 about poems collected in *The Business of Fancydancing*.

Gillan, Jennifer. "Reservation Home Movies: Sherman Alexie's Poetry." *American Literature* 68, no. 1 (March, 1996): 91-110. Gillan notes how Alexie uses a flat poetic style to confront the complex and problematic legacy of American Indian identity within mainstream culture, both celebrating and critiquing various aspects of contemporary American Indian life.

Grassian, Daniel. *Understanding Sherman Alexie.* Columbia: University of South Carolina Press, 2005. The first book-length work offering commentary on Alexie's poetry and fiction, with ample attention to reviews and other published discussions of his writings. Provides biographical details as well as analysis and interpretation of the poetry and short stories through 2004.

James, Meredith K. *Literary and Cinematic Reservation in Selected Works of Native American Author Sherman Alexie.* Lewiston, N.Y.: Edwin Mellen Press, 2005. James discusses the concept "reservation of the mind" in the work of Alexie, with significant reference to other contemporary American Indian authors Louise Erdrich, N. Scott Momaday, and Leslie Marmon Silko. Also examines how Alexie conveys the effects of federal Indian policy and popular culture stereotypes of Indians on contemporary Indian life.

Lundquist, Suzanne Evertsen. *Native American Literatures: An Introduction*. New York: Continuum, 2004. The section on Alexie includes summaries of important critiques of his work that question his representation of American Indian cultural values and reservation life as well as issues of "hybridity" and "essentialism."

McFarland, Ron. "Sherman Alexie's Polemic Stories." *Studies in American Indian Literature* 9, no. 4 (Winter, 1997): 27-38. McFarland notes that Alexie's stories are voices of Indian America as well as comments upon it. Argues that Alexie is a narrative polemicist.

Bussy d'Ambois

Author: George Chapman (c. 1559-1634)
First produced: 1604; first published, 1607; revised, 1641
Type of work: Drama
Type of plot: Tragedy
Time of plot: Sixteenth century
Locale: Paris

Principal characters:
BUSSY D'AMBOIS, a soldier of fortune
HENRY III, king of France
MONSIEUR, the king's brother
THE DUKE OF GUISE
THE COUNT OF MONTSURRY
TAMYRA, his wife
A FRIAR

The Story:

In Paris, Bussy d'Ambois is a soldier and gentleman too poor to gain favor at the court. He meets Monsieur, brother of King Henry III, by appointment in a side street. Monsieur, chiding Bussy for his downcast countenance, reminds him that some of the greatest men in history have endured obscurity and exile before becoming renowned. Anxious to have ambitious and ruthless young men about him, Monsieur invites Bussy to be his man and to become a courtier. Later, Maffe, Monsieur's steward, comes to Bussy and, seeing the wretched state he is in, gives him only one hundred crowns of the thousand that Monsieur sent Bussy. Bussy, perceiving that Maffe is a proud scoundrel and knowing Monsieur's reputation for generosity, is able to talk Maffe out of the remaining nine hundred crowns. With the money in his possession, Bussy strikes Maffe in payment for his insubordination. Maffe hints that he will be avenged.

Monsieur introduces Bussy, dressed in fine new clothes, at court. As he is presented to various noble people of the court, he impresses them with his directness. The duke of Guise jealously notes that Bussy is being quite free with the duke's wife, Elenor, and suggests that Bussy not be so forward. Bussy, in conduct unlike that expected of a courtier, answers Guise sharply. Although warned by Monsieur, Bussy persists in dallying pleasantly with Elenor. Having offended Guise, Bussy also bluntly incurs the enmity of three courtiers, Barrisor, l'Anou, and Pyrrhot.

In the duel that follows, the three courtiers and two of Bussy's friends are killed; Bussy is the only survivor. He later goes to the court with Monsieur, who successfully wins a pardon for Bussy from King Henry. Bussy thanks the king and declares that he could not avoid defending his honor. Guise is deeply offended by the royal pardon Bussy receives.

Tamyra, Countess of Montsurry, meets Bussy and falls in love with him. At the same time, Monsieur, making every attempt to seduce the noblewoman, gives her a pearl necklace. Later, Tamyra enters a secret chamber in back of her bedchamber. A friar, in league with her, brings Bussy by a secret passageway to the chamber on the pretext that Bussy is to explain to Tamyra a false report that he killed Barrisor because the dead man was interested in the countess. The friar, after hinting of Tamyra's love for Bussy and cautioning him to be discreet, leaves Bussy and Tamyra together.

After Tamyra's passion for Bussy is consummated, she expresses a deep feeling of guilt and fears that she might be discovered. Bussy assures her that he will protect her from all dishonor. As he takes leave of her, again accompanied by the friar, she gives him the necklace Monsieur gave her. At day-break, Montsurry returns home to find his wife awake and fully clothed. She explains that she was not able to sleep while he was away on business. When he asks her to come to bed with him, she begs off, saying that the friar does not approve of making love by daylight.

Bussy, having become a great favorite of the king, declares to the court that he will be the king's own right arm in exposing sycophants, rascals, and any other unprincipled men in the realm. Grown heady with favor, he taunts Guise, who retorts that Bussy is the illegitimate son of a cardinal. The two men are ready to settle their grudge in a duel, but the king manages to reconcile them momentarily.

Monsieur realizes that he sponsored a man who cannot be manipulated. He and Guise plot Bussy's downfall by gaining the confidence of the serving-women of the chief ladies of the court. Pero, Tamyra's maid, discloses to Monsieur that her mistress gave herself to Bussy, but the servant is unable to reveal the identity of the person who acted as go-between in the illicit affair.

Bussy, at the height of his power in the court, reminds his patron of Monsieur's ambition to be king. He declares that he will assist Monsieur in everything short of actually killing King Henry. Monsieur asks Bussy for his honest opinion of him; Bussy says he will give it in return for Monsieur's opinion of Bussy. Monsieur thereupon declares that Bussy is a vain, pompous, ruthless, and inconsistent man. Bussy, in return, says that Monsieur is a liar, a gossip, and the fountainhead of all cruelty and violence in France. The two, having made their disclosures of each other's worth, go together to a banquet given by the king.

During the banquet, Monsieur suggests to Bussy that he pay court to Tamyra, who is reputed to be unapproachable. When Bussy pretends to have only the slightest acquaintance with her, Monsieur hints that he knows more than he will tell. The king, sensing that violence is in the offing, beckons to his favorite to join him, and he and Bussy leave the banquet hall.

Monsieur offers to show Montsurry a letter that will reveal to him the perfidy of his wife. The trusting Montsurry refuses to take the letter, but his suspicions are aroused. Tamyra, aided by Pero, is able to convince Montsurry that he has no cause to suspect his wife of faithlessness.

Later, Bussy and Tamyra meet in the secret chamber and Tamyra reveals to her lover that Monsieur knows of their meetings. The friar invokes spirits so that the two can foresee what the future might hold. Behemoth, the chief spirit invoked, re-creates an image of Monsieur, Guise, and Montsurry in conference. Monsieur and Guise, having convinced Montsurry of Tamyra's passion for Bussy, urges him

to force Tamyra to reveal the identity of the go-between so that Bussy might more easily be ambushed and killed. Pero comes to the conferring lords and gives Monsieur a letter written by Tamyra. Montsurry, utterly confused by that time, and not knowing whom to trust, stabs Pero. Behemoth forecasts a violent end for the friar, Tamyra, and Bussy unless they are able to act with the greatest wisdom.

Montsurry returns to his house and seizes Tamyra, who is in the company of the friar. Despite the friar's warning to him not to act with violence, Montsurry orders Tamyra to write her confession. She resists, whereupon he stabs her repeatedly. When she persists in her refusal to write, he places her on a rack. The friar, who leaves the scene of violence, returns with a sword and kills himself with it. Tamyra, tortured on the rack, confesses that the friar was the go-between. She writes to Bussy in her own blood that he is to come to her in the secret chamber.

Montsurry, disguised as the friar, brings hired murderers to his friends Monsieur and Guise; then he leaves them to lure Bussy to a carefully plotted doom. The ghost of the friar appears to Bussy and predicts a dire fate for him. When the ghost leaves, after declaring that it will meet Bussy in Tamyra's secret chamber, Bussy apprehensively invokes the spirit of the underworld. The spirit appears and tells him that the friar is really dead and that Bussy should not heed his next summons from Tamyra. Bussy wants to know who will deliver the summons. The spirit cannot answer because a stronger spirit, Fate, controlled by Monsieur and Guise, prevents that disclosure.

Montsurry, dressed as the friar, brings the letter written in blood to Bussy. Duped by the disguise and defying the malign predictions he heard, Bussy follows Montsurry back to Tamyra.

The ghost of the friar, meanwhile, appears to Tamyra and advises her to shout a warning to Bussy as he is brought into the secret room. When Bussy and Montsurry enter the chamber, she does indeed warn Bussy. As his enemies and the hired murderers close in on their victim, the ghost of the friar unnerves the murderers and Bussy is given time to collect himself. Having killed one of the murderers, he is about to kill Montsurry when he is shot down. Bussy, propping himself on his sword so that he might die in a defiant attitude, forgives those who brought him to his death. After Bussy's death, Montsurry banishes Tamyra, his unfaithful wife.

Critical Evaluation:

George Chapman, an acquaintance of Christopher Marlowe and Ben Jonson, was a jack-of-all-trades among Elizabethan writers, turning out poetry and translations as well as plays. His reputation was first established as a poet with his *The Shadow of Night* (1594) and *Ovid's Banquet of Sense* (1595), but his only poem much read today was begun by another man: When Marlowe's *Hero and Leander* (1598) was left unfinished at his death, Chapman completed the poem by adding the final four books.

By about 1595, Chapman had begun writing for the theater, supplying plays to Philip Henslowe's company of actors, the Lord Admiral's Men. Although a contemporary source cites Chapman as a tragic author, whatever works led to that opinion have been lost; some comedies, written by Chapman alone and in collaboration with John Marston and Ben Jonson, are all that survive of his early dramas. In 1599, he left the Lord Admiral's company but continued to write for the stage until 1614. He made popular translations of Homer's *Iliad* and *Odyssey*. He may have had financial troubles in his later years; he died in 1634.

Chapman wrote *Bussy d'Ambois* about 1604. Surprisingly, given the play's subject, it was probably first acted by Paul's Boys, a children's company. Paul's Boys was one of the then-popular groups of child actors, in this case an outgrowth of the choir school at St. Paul's Cathedral. The play exists in two printed versions, one produced in 1607 and a later one, printed in 1641, that is noticeably different. Most critics believe the 1641 version derived from a revision of the play made by Chapman himself. The play was extremely successful: It continued to be performed until the closing of the theaters in 1642. After the Restoration of Charles II, the play was revived, and its last performance is recorded in 1691.

Chapman's play is based on the career of Louis de Clermont, Sieur de Bussy d'Amboise, a minor courtier during the reign of Henry III of France. The historical Bussy was widely known in his time and seems to have been every bit the swaggering bravo who appears in Chapman's play. Known for his dueling, his poetry, and his love affairs, Bussy was murdered by a jealous husband when he was about thirty years old. One might wonder how meaningful tragedy could be made from such unpromising material, but Bussy d'Amboise's life furnished Chapman with a scarecrow on which to drape his philosophy.

In one respect, *Bussy d'Ambois* represents a decadent, rather cynical comment on the Renaissance individual whose ambition and self-confidence know no bounds. Having achieved status in a ruthless and utterly corrupt court, he offends at every hand and dallies with abandon in illicit love. What the quarto of 1607 refers to as *Bussy d'Ambois: A Tragedy* appears to be as much satire as tragedy. Even Bussy's determination, after he has been shot, to die while he supports himself on his sword seems comic in its futility, considering the despicable nature of his antagonists and his mistress.

On the other hand, Bussy embodies the Renaissance ideal of the man who, by virtue of his physical, mental, and moral powers, is a law unto himself. In this sense, Bussy is a relative of the heroes found in Marlowe's *Tamburlaine the Great* (1587) and *Doctor Faustus* (1588). Although not bent on evil, Bussy resembles William Shakespeare's Richard III, in that neither recognizes any moral force higher than himself, nor submits to anything but his own will. Just exactly what virtues Bussy possesses are not always clear. Indeed, what he calls his honor leads him to kill in a duel three men who have insulted him by snickering at the wrong time. That same honor does not prevent him from speaking bawdily to strange women at court or committing adultery when the opportunity presents itself. However, Bussy is steadfast in his belief that he owes obedience to no one, not even to the king, as he states to the king's face in the scene in which he is pardoned for dueling.

Chapman often seems to sacrifice the plausibility of the plot to show his hero flouting society: Bussy's lover succumbs to an overwhelming passion for him at first sight. This, in itself, is not so hard to believe, but that Bussy should have the same desire for her is harder to accept, because he ignores her a few scenes earlier at court. In the play's least convincing moment, this adulterous passion is approved by a friar, who then consents to act as their go-between. Clearly, who the characters are and the reasons for their actions are of less interest to Chapman than are illustrations of Bussy's independence of customary morality.

The play is skillfully constructed, the language at times poetic and compelling. The style of the play, however, is rhetorical in the extreme, with long passages of obscure philosophizing that often bring the action to a halt. When Chapman's contemporaries accused him of obscurity, he defended himself by claiming that the language was appropriate to the gravity and nobility of the subject. In some speeches, however, the grammar breaks down entirely. In view of these and similar difficulties, the taste of the audiences that made the play so popular for so long a time might be questioned.

The play, however, retains more than enough elements of the Elizabethan tragedy to satisfy those who desire action, and plenty of it. Duels and murder fill the stage. The betrayed husband tortures his wife; the friar drops dead, providing the requisite ghost at the end of the play; and, in a scene harking back to the miracle plays of the fifteenth century, a devil is raised by Bussy in an attempt to discover his enemies' plots. The final scene shows Bussy and the ghost holding off a pack of paid killers, when an assassin with more sense than superstition draws a pistol and shoots Bussy down. With action like this, a good part of the audience must have simply endured the moralizing in the knowledge that something exciting would soon happen.

"Critical Evaluation" by Walter E. Meyers

Further Reading

Bertheau, Gilles. "George Chapman's French Tragedies: Or, Machiavelli Beyond the Mirror." In *Representing France and the French in Early Modern English Drama*, edited by Jean-Christophe Mayer. Newark: University of Delaware Press, 2008. Collection of essays examining the role and significance of France in English Renaissance drama, including a discussion of Chapman's French tragedies.

Braunmuller, A. R. *Natural Fictions: George Chapman's Major Tragedies*. Newark: University of Delaware Press, 1992. Analyzes the style and historical sources of some of the tragedies Chapman wrote during the first decade of James I's reign. Chapter 1 is devoted to a discussion of *Bussy d'Ambois*.

Braunmuller, A. R., and Michael Hattaway, eds. *The Cambridge Companion to English Renaissance Drama*. New York: Cambridge University Press, 2003. Chapman's plays are discussed in several places in this collection of essays, and these references are listed in the index.

Burks, Deborah G. "'Break . . . All the Bounds of Manhood, Noblesse and Religion': George Chapman's *Bussy d'Ambois*." In *Horrid Spectacle: Violation in the Theater of Early Modern England*. Pittsburgh, Pa.: Duquesne University Press, 2003. Focuses on the onstage depiction of torture, murder, infidelity, and other forms of violation in *Bussy d'Ambois* and other works of the period.

Rees, Ennis. *The Tragedies of George Chapman*. Cambridge, Mass.: Harvard University Press, 1954. Rees interprets Bussy's view of himself as subjective; he argues that, given the protagonist's actions, the play must be read ironically. Demonstrates one of the interpretative extremes the play has provoked.

Taunton, Nina. *1590's Drama and Militarism: Portrayals of War in Marlowe, Chapman, and Shakespeare's "Henry V."* Burlington, Vt.: Ashgate, 2001. Examines how plays by Chapman, William Shakespeare, and Christopher Marlowe depicted the realities of war in the late Elizabethan period. Taunton focuses on Chapman's depictions of Henry IV and Charles, duke of Byron.

Wieler, John. *George Chapman: The Effect of Stoicism upon His Tragedies*. New York: King's Crown Press, 1949. Excellent introduction to the philosophical background of the play. Asserts the play should be read as a straightforward Christian tragedy; however one reads it, the influence of Stoicism appears throughout the play.

C

Cadastre

Author: Aimé Césaire (1913-2008)
First published: 1961 (English translation, 1973)
Type of work: Poetry

Cadastre was formed from elements of two earlier poetic collections: forty of the seventy-two poems published in *Soleil cou coupé* (1948; *Beheaded Sun*, 1983) and all ten of the poems in *Corps perdu* (1950; *Disembodied*, 1983)—the latter of which were illustrated with thirty-two engravings by Pablo Picasso. Increasingly conscious of the leadership role he was taking in Caribbean politics, poet Aimé Césaire revised his texts thoroughly to make them more accessible. He shortened many poems, removed obscure words and free-associative imagery, eliminated obscenity, and reduced the prominence of elitist elements that presented the poet as a visionary prophet or as a sacrificial victim whose death would help redeem his people. He also added references to the black struggle for freedom, opportunity, and justice in Africa and the United States.

Césaire was born to a middle-class family in Basse-Pointe, a small coastal town near the volcano Mont Pelé (which had erupted in 1902, destroying the city of Saint-Pierre), in the French overseas territory of Martinique, an island at the eastern edge of the Caribbean Sea. He moved to the capital, Fort-de-France, in 1924. A brilliant student, Césaire was sent to the famous Lycée Louis-le-Grand in Paris in 1931 to prepare for admission to the elite teacher-training institution, l'École Normale Supérieure. In Paris, he befriended artist Pablo Picasso and many of the French Surrealist poets.

In 1934, Césaire and the French Guyanese poet Léon-Gontran Damas founded *L'Étudiant noir* ("the black student"), a newspaper that helped unite black people from France, Africa, North and South America, and the French island colonies in the international negritude movement. Along with Damas and Césaire, the third major leader of that movement was Léopold Senghor, who became a famous poet and served as the first president of the newly independent nation of Sénégal from 1961 until 1980. At the literary salon of sisters Paulette Nardal and Jane Nardal, Césaire, Damas, and

Senghor met and were strongly influenced by the French-speaking poets of the Harlem Renaissance, notably Claude McKay, Jean Toomer, Langston Hughes, and Countee Cullen. The concluding chapter of McKay's novel *Banjo* (1928) advocated restoring black people's connections to their cultures of origin, thereby recovering a pride and self-respect crushed by centuries of slavery, prejudice, and white hatred.

Members of the negritude movement adopted one of two contrasting programs: either glorifying African precolonial history and values while accepting the benefits of assimilation to white European culture (a course favored by Senghor) or militantly denouncing white injustice and cruelty and insisting on black autonomy, equality, and civil rights within a white-dominated society (a course adopted by members of the Harlem Renaissance and by the Haitian Frantz Fanon). In the United States, black militancy split into separate tendencies that advocated either violent resistance (Malcolm X, before his trip to Africa) or peaceable advocacy and protest (Martin Luther King, Jr.).

A *cadastre* is an official, line-by-line record of the ownership of various pieces of land. For Césaire, a descendent of slaves displaced into the black diaspora, the title suggests the mental act of taking stock of one's situation, to try to decide where one belongs. As is revealed by the gradual, fascinating development of *Cadastre* from two earlier poetic collections, Césaire's poetry suggests that he felt torn between the two opposing strategies of negritude. For him, the strategies represented contrary vocations: either to pursue a cozy, Europeanized intellectual elitism as a world-class poet or to devote himself to a painful, often frustrating struggle in solidarity with his mainly poor, often illiterate black brothers from Martinique.

In principle, Césaire's message was consistently militant, but his medium—employing an enormously rich vocabulary, complicated syntax, and surrealistic images—remained inaccessible to most readers. Most people in Martinique were unequipped to understand his masterpiece, *Cahier d'un retour au pays natal* (1939, 1947, 1956; *Memorandum on My Martinique*, 1947; better known as *Return to My Native Land*, 1968), which announced his definitive return home in 1939. Until 1945, the island was ruled by Vichy government officials, who collaborated with Adolf Hitler. They tried to suppress Césaire's journal *Tropiques*, which advocated full independence for the French Caribbean colonies.

After liberation, Césaire represented Martinique in the French Chamber of Deputies from 1945 to 1993, while simultaneously serving as mayor of Fort-de-France until 2001. Because he realized that the great majority of those he represented wanted to remain a part of France, Césaire reluctantly accepted the dependent status of an overseas department (D.O.M.) in 1946. Later, however, he consistently advocated for independence, despite the serious economic and military weakness of Martinique. He was a communist until 1956, when he rejected the continued Stalinization of Soviet communism (as evidenced in the invasion of Hungary by tanks and the establishment of a puppet government there in 1956). He then founded his own, autonomous Parti Progressiste Martiniquais (1958). Its newspaper, *Le Progressiste*, was the major source of information about Césaire's political activities and positions. From 1978 until 1993, Césaire was also affiliated with but not integrated into the French Socialist Party.

Throughout *Cadastre*, Césaire's poems are characterized by long lines of variable length, without rhymes, inspired by earlier models such as the Bible and the works of Walt Whitman, Paul Claudel, and Saint-John Perse. This form suggests poetic freedom and creative energy. To compensate for the resulting irregularity, Césaire uses many verbal repetitions: sometimes of entire lines but more often of a word or phrase at the beginning of a series of lines (anaphora) or at the ends (epiphora). For example, anaphora appears in twenty-six of the forty-three lines of "Ex-voto pour un naufrage" ("Ex-voto for a Shipwreck"): The poem repeats *tam-tam* or *tam-tams* fourteen times, *je* five times, *Roi* four times, and *roulez* three times.

As he also does in *Return to My Native Land*, Césaire in *Cadastre* frequently adopts a sarcastic tone while seemingly accepting humiliation, oppression, and injustice for himself and his people. Bizarre, dehumanizing metaphors ("I am the king's sunshade") suggest the process of enslavement. The speaker implicitly associates himself with subhuman or monstrous beings. He continually alludes to physical or mental suffering, including dismemberment evoked by mentioning separate body parts—especially internal organs. Suggesting that the sleeping giant of the oppressed black

peoples has the potential to awake to violent rebellion, Césaire frequently refers to convulsive disturbances in nature—downpours, earthquakes, and volcanic eruptions—as well as human dreams of revenge.

Césaire deploys a rich vocabulary of the names of plants and animals from various continents, and of place names and heroes' names from throughout the lands of the black diaspora. These lands include Africa, from which tens of millions of slaves were taken, and the Americas, where they were forced to labor on plantations as chattels of whites and mulattoes, and the role of such lands in *Cadastre* reflects the poet's sense of solidarity with the international black community. Césaire's international vocabulary is evident in poems from *Beheaded Sun* that include "Mississipi" [sic], "Blues de la pluie" ("Raining Blues," Harlem), and "Ex-voto for a Shipwreck" (denouncing forced labor in the diamond mines of South Africa and praising the great Zulu warrior chief Chaka). "Depuis Akkad, depuis Elam, depuis Sumer" ("Since Akkad, Since Elam, Since Sumer") refers to ancient Babylonia, where captive slaves were known in 2,100 B.C.E., while "Ode à la Guinée" ("Ode to Guinea") pays tribute to the legendary African ancestral home of displaced slaves.

The poems of *Disembodied* denounce the oppression of black people in generalized terms. These include "Mot" ("Word") and the work's title poem, which both focus on the racial slur *nègre* as a concentrated emblem of white racism and cruelty. In the concluding "Dit d'errance" ("Lay of the Rover"), the poet takes on himself all the sufferings of his race, but in the four previous poems—"Disembodied," "Ton portrait" ("Your Portrait"), "Sommation" (Summation), and "Naissances" ("Births")—the poetic self fuses with nature, becoming transformed. Like a nature god, the poetic voice sends forth the river, the tides, and the ocean and then summons the entire Caribbean archipelago to gather around him. Time returns to free him, and he plants the magical tree that heralds a new world.

A. James Arnold has demonstrated at length that, during his reworking of the earlier collections to combine them in *Cadastre*, Césaire downplayed the European and Judeo-Christian elements of his extensive Parisian education, such as references to the Babylonian captivity of the Jews in Revelation 13-18, which disguised imperial Rome as Babylon, the Great Whore. "Disembodied" remains Césaire's strongest, most triumphant affirmation of negritude in the double sense of the power and beauty of African civilization and the undying resolve of members of the contemporary black diaspora to achieve autonomy.

Laurence M. Porter

Further Reading

Arnold, A. James. *Modernism and Negritude: The Poetry and Poetics of Aimé Césaire*. Cambridge, Mass.: Harvard University Press, 1981. One of the best, most comprehensive studies of Césaire's art and ideas, of the evolution of the collections of verse that became *Cadastre*, and of ways that the key poems in that work function as apocalyptic visions.

Césaire, Aimé. *Lost Body*. Introduced and translated by Clayton Eshleman and Annette Smith. New York: Braziller, 1986. Makes available, for the first time since the publication of a limited edition of 219 copies in 1950, the record of the collaboration between Césaire and Pablo Picasso, who contributed thirty-two engravings to accompany the ten poems. Césaire and Picasso were communist militants until 1956. Bilingual edition.

Hurley, E. Anthony. "Link and Lance: Aspects of Poetic Function in Césaire's *Cadastre*—An Analysis of Five Poems." *L'Esprit Créateur* 32, no. 1 (Spring, 1992): 54-68. Closely reads five of the poems collected in *Cadastre*

in order to draw conclusions about the "poeticness" of Césaire's poetry.

Scharfman, Ronnie Leah. *"Engagement" and the Language of the Subject in the Poetry of Aimé Césaire*. Gainesville: University Press of Florida, 1987. Provides sensitive close readings of three poems from the two parts of *Cadastre*: "Totem" from *Beheaded Sun* and "Word" and "Disembodied" from *Disembodied*. Scharfman's Lacanian psychoanalytical reading nuances Arnold's interpretation in terms of a conventional heroic-quest narrative, but at the cost of dissociating Césaire's poems from their social and historical context.

Suk, Jeannie. *Postcolonial Paradoxes in French Caribbean Writing: Césaire, Glissant, Condé*. New York: Oxford University Press, 2001. Reads Césaire and two other francophone Antilles writers as existing on the margins of postcolonialism and therefore useful for understanding what does and does not count as postcolonial, as well as the political and cultural meanings and uses of that term.

Cadmus

Author: Unknown
First published: Unknown
Type of work: Short fiction
Type of plot: Adventure
Time of plot: Antiquity
Locale: Greece

Principal characters:
CADMUS, the founder of Thebes
JUPITER, the king of the gods
MINERVA, the daughter of Jupiter
MARS, the god of war
HARMONIA, the wife of Cadmus

The Story:

Jupiter, in the form of a bull, carries away Europa, who is the daughter of Agenor, the king of Phenicia. When her handmaidens tell Agenor of the kidnapping, he commands his son Cadmus to look for Europa and not to return until he finds her. Cadmus searches for his sister for many years and in strange lands. Although he searches diligently, killing many monsters and endangering himself many times in his quest, he cannot find her. Afraid to return to his father, he consults the oracle of Apollo at Delphi and asks where he should settle. The oracle tells him that he will find a cow in a field, and that he should follow her, for she will lead him to a good land. Where the cow stops, Cadmus is to build a great city and call it Thebes.

When Cadmus soon thereafter sees a cow, he follows her.

Finally, the cow stops on the plain of Panope. To give thanks to the gods, Cadmus sends his slaves to find pure water for the sacrifice. In a dense grove, they find a wonderful clear spring, which is, however, guarded by a terrible dragon sacred to Mars. His scales shine like gold, his body is filled with a poisonous venom, and he has a triple tongue and three rows of huge, ragged teeth. The servants, thinking only to please their master, dip their pitchers in the water, whereupon all are instantly destroyed by the monster.

After waiting many hours for the return of his servants, Cadmus goes to the grove and finds the mangled bodies of his faithful slaves and, close by, the terrible monster of the spring. Cadmus throws a huge stone at the dragon, but the stone does not dent his shining scales. Then, he draws back his javelin and heaves it at the serpent. It goes through the scales and into the entrails. The monster, trying to draw out the weapon with his mouth, breaks the blade and leaves the point burning his flesh. He swells with rage as he advances toward the hero, and Cadmus retreats before him. Cadmus then throws his spear at the monster, and the weapon pins him against a tree until he dies.

As Cadmus stands gazing at the terrible creature, he hears the voice of the goddess Minerva telling him to sow the dragon's teeth in a field. Hardly has he done so when a warrior in armor springs up from each tooth. Cadmus starts toward the warriors, thinking he must slay them all or lose his own life, but again Minerva speaks to him and tells him not to strike. The warriors begin to do battle among themselves. All are slain but five, who then present themselves to Cadmus and say that they will serve him. Together with these five warriors, Cadmus builds the city of Thebes.

Jupiter gives Cadmus Harmonia, the daughter of Mars and Venus, to be his wife, and the gods come down from Olympus to honor the couple. Vulcan forges a brilliant necklace with his own hands and gives it to the bride. Four children are born, and for a time Cadmus and Harmonia live happily with their children. Yet doom hangs over Cadmus and his family for the killing of the serpent. Eventually, Mars avenges himself by causing all of Cadmus's children to perish.

In despair, Cadmus and Harmonia leave Thebes and go to the country of the Enchelians, who make Cadmus their king. However, Cadmus can find no peace because of Mars's curse on him. One day, he tells Harmonia that if a serpent were so dear to the gods he himself wishes to become a serpent. No sooner does he speak the words than he begins to grow scales and to change his form. When Harmonia beholds her husband turned into a serpent, she prays to the gods for a like fate. Both become serpents, but they continue to love human beings and never do injury to anyone.

Critical Evaluation:

The story of Cadmus follows a typical pattern of the Greek hero myth: The young man is sent on a quest (in this case to find his lost sister), receives instructions from a god to found a new city, proves himself by killing a dragon, and endures the hostility of a god, who kills all of his children. The Cadmus myth is somewhat unusual in its combination of elements from both Eastern and Western mythological traditions. This is reflected in the Phoenician connections of Cadmus's lineage and the probable derivation of his name from a Phoenician or Semitic word meaning "the one from the east."

Cadmus's search for his missing sister is reminiscent of other famous mythological quests, such as that of Jason for the Golden Fleece and Odysseus's attempt to return to his home and family. The success of the hero in these cases represents the return of order to a disordered home, city, and, by extension, world. The monsters and obstacles that have to be overcome in the process indicate the difficulties of restoring order.

The story of the building of Thebes is reminiscent of the stories of other cities, for example the founding of Rome by the Trojan exile Aeneas and the closely related tale of Ilus and his cow and the founding of Troy. In these two cases, the cow, a symbol of female fecundity, seems to represent the earth goddess. In all of these stories, the hero must subdue the local inhabitants and make the land safe for the new city. The foundation of a city is accompanied by violence and death, out of which new life arises: In the case of Thebes, Cadmus must first kill the dragon that guards a spring of clear water. The dragon, sacred to the god of war, Mars, also represents the primeval forces of the earth goddess. When Cadmus kills the creature and from its teeth harvests warriors, with whom he founds Thebes, this indicates that the earth has been tamed and is prepared to cooperate with the hero in the creation of a new city.

Mars's curse on Cadmus for killing the dragon is another stock element in mythology, similar to the curse on the house of Atreus. The persistence of the Theban curse is remarkable for extending all the way down to Oedipus and his descendants. Cadmus himself loses all of his children, suggesting once again that the foundation of a city involves much personal suffering and sacrifice for the founder. To a certain extent, Cadmus is reincarnated in his descendant Oedipus, who likewise consults the oracle of Apollo, is driven to leave his city because of a divine curse, and is fated to lose his children to violent deaths.

The marriage of Cadmus and Harmonia, daughter of Mars and Venus, is likewise an ill-starred affair: Harmonia is the product of an adulterous relationship (Venus is married to Vulcan) and, despite the fact that the wedding celebration is attended by all the Olympian gods, Vulcan's gift of a beautiful necklace to the bride brings bad fortune with it, and the harmony that Cadmus and his wife enjoy is short-lived. The marriage recalls that of Menelaus and Helen, which set in motion the events of the Trojan war. Like Helen, Harmonia is beautiful, but her beauty holds the seeds of destruction for the hero who marries her. It might be argued, of course, that Harmonia is an essentially positive figure, devoted to her husband and prepared to stay with him throughout all his vicissitudes. Some have seen an analogy with the marriage of Dushyanta and Sakuntala in Hindu mythology. Others view

Harmonia as a version of Pandora or Eve, the archetypal woman who brings trouble to man in patriarchal myths. The fact that Cadmus's children are all girls and that they all die unpleasant deaths tends to strengthen a negative association with women that underlies this legend.

The story of Cadmus closes with the metamorphosis that transforms Cadmus and Harmonia into serpents. This represents a reconciliation with Mars as well as with the earth goddess from whom serpents spring. The serpent generally occupies a significant place in Theban mythology: Tiresias the seer is changed from a man into a woman and back again when he encounters two serpents in the forest, and Dionysus, the new god whom Pentheus tries to keep out of the city, is often associated with snakes. The fearsome dragon of the beginning of the founding myth is eventually transformed into a beneficial entity, for Cadmus and Harmonia do no harm to human beings. After their deaths, Jupiter carries both of them to the Elysian fields in recognition of their self-sacrifice and devotion to the gods.

The myth of Cadmus is a complex patchwork of several mythological archetypes and of Eastern and Western influences. It has enduring literary value in its presentation of a hero driven by forces beyond his control and victimized by hostile deities. The hero is also a man who must reap what he sows, yet his sufferings and sacrifices are ultimately beneficial and necessary for the growth of civilization, for Cadmus is responsible for the foundation of one of the greatest of all Greek cities.

"Critical Evaluation" by David H. J. Larmour

Further Reading

Apollodorus. "Cadmos and the Foundation of Thebes." In *The Library of Greek Mythology*. Translated by Robin Hard. New York: Oxford University Press, 1997. Apollodorus recounts the story of Cadmus and other Theban mythology. This edition of his book contains an introduction discussing the sources and narrative tradition of Greek mythology.

Calasso, Roberto. *The Marriage of Cadmus and Harmony.* Translated by Tim Parks. New York: Knopf, 1993. An imaginative exploration of the Greek myth cycles, ending with a discussion of the Cadmus story in chapter 12. Offers an interpretation of the complex and troubled relationship between gods and humans.

Edwards, Ruth B. *Kadmos the Phoenician: A Study in Greek Legends and the Mycenaean Age.* Amsterdam: Adolf M. Hakkert, 1979. Discusses the origins of the Cadmus story and locates these myths in the context of the Mycenaean civilization.

Euripides. *The Adorers of Dionysus (The Bakchai).* Translated by James Morgan Pryse. Los Angeles: J. M. Pryse, 1925. This edition contains an interpretation of the myth of Cadmus that shows him as a man who devotes his soul to the quest for divine wisdom.

Fontenrose, Joseph. *Python: A Study of Delphic Myth and Its Origins.* Berkeley: University of California Press, 1959. A useful study of the mythological context in which the Cadmus story exists; there are many similarities between Cadmus's slaying of the dragon and Apollo's killing of the Python and between the foundation myths of Thebes and Delphi.

Graves, Robert. *The Greek Myths.* Combined ed. New York: Penguin Books, 1992. Graves's classic account of the Greeks myths, originally published in two volumes in 1955, discusses the myth of Cadmus.

Green, Roger L. *The Tale of Thebes.* New York: Cambridge University Press, 1977. Tells the Theban myths in a narrative, simplified format that is easily understandable to nonspecialists.

Caesar and Cleopatra

Author: George Bernard Shaw (1856-1950)
First produced: 1906; first published, 1901
Type of work: Drama
Type of plot: Comedy
Time of plot: October, 48 B.C.E.-March, 47 B.C.E.
Locale: Egypt

Principal characters:
JULIUS CAESAR
CLEOPATRA, the queen of Egypt
PTOLEMY DIONYSUS, her brother and husband, the king of Egypt
FTATATEETA, Cleopatra's nurse
BRITANNUS, a Briton, Caesar's secretary
RUFIO, a Roman officer
POTHINUS, the king's guardian
APOLLODORUS, a Sicilian

The Story:

Act 1. Caesar is alone at night in the Egyptian desert, apostrophizing a statue of the Sphinx. Caesar is startled when a young girl, Cleopatra, addresses him from the paws of the Sphinx. He climbs up to her, thinking he is dreaming. She is full of superstitions about cats and Nile water. She tells Caesar she is there because the Romans are coming to eat her people. Caesar sees that he is not dreaming and identifies himself to Cleopatra as a Roman. She is terror-stricken, but Caesar tells her that he will eat her unless she can show herself to him as a woman, not a girl. Cleopatra puts herself in the hands of this Roman and they move to her throne room. Caesar tries to persuade Cleopatra to act like a queen; Ftatateeta enters and begins to order Cleopatra about until the nurse is chased from the room. Caesar orders Cleopatra's servants to dress her in her royal robes. When Roman soldiers enter and salute Caesar, Cleopatra finally realizes who he is and, with a sob of relief, falls into his arms.

Act 2. The ten-year-old king Ptolemy is delivering a speech from the throne in Alexandria, prompted by his tutor and guardian. Caesar enters and demands taxes, then calls for Cleopatra. Rufio reminds Caesar that there is a Roman army of occupation in Egypt, commanded by Achillas and supporting the Egyptians, while Caesar has only four thousand men. Achillas and Pothinus suggest that they hold the upper hand, but when Roman troops enter, the Egyptians back off. Lucius Septimius and Pothinus remind Caesar that they decapitated Pompey to ingratiate themselves with Caesar, who is horrified to hear of the act. All the Egyptians but Ptolemy leave, and Rufio again protests against Caesar's clemency. Ptolemy is escorted out. Cleopatra and Caesar discuss how much Cleopatra has grown, and Caesar promises to send strong young Mark Antony to Cleopatra. A wounded Roman soldier enters to inform Caesar that the Roman army of occupation has come; Caesar orders that all the ships be burned

except those that are to carry the Romans to the lighthouse on an island in the harbor. As Caesar starts to arm himself, Pothinus enters, followed by Theodotus with the news that the great library in Alexandria is burning. After Pothinus and Theodotus leave, Cleopatra helps Caesar put on his armor and makes fun of his baldness. Caesar and Rufio leave to lead the troops to the Pharos.

Act 3. On a quay in front of Cleopatra's palace, Apollodorus, who brings carpets for Cleopatra to look at, argues with the Roman sentinel. Cleopatra wants to be rowed to the lighthouse, but the sentinel refuses to allow it. Cleopatra thereupon says she will make a present of a carpet to Caesar, and secretly she is rolled up in one and put in a boat that is sailing for the lighthouse that the Egyptians begin to attack. When Apollodorus enters with the carpet, which is unrolled and reveals Cleopatra, Caesar regards the young woman as a nuisance. The Egyptians cut off the Romans and are approaching. Several Roman ships approach, whereupon Apollodorus, Caesar, and Rufio dive into the sea to swim to them. Cleopatra is tossed into the sea as well and carried along.

Act 4. Six months later, Cleopatra and her serving women are discussing Caesar when Ftatateeta brings in Pothinus, who is now a prisoner of the Romans and wants to make a deal with Cleopatra. After Rufio and Caesar enter, Rufio brings Pothinus to talk to Caesar privately. Pothinus finally blurts out that Cleopatra wants Caesar out of the way so that she can rule alone. Cleopatra denies this, but Caesar knows it is true. When Pothinus leaves, Cleopatra orders Ftatateeta to kill him. Caesar, Rufio, and Apollodorus, just returned for a banquet, hear a terrible scream. Apollodorus, sent to investigate, reports that Pothinus was assassinated and that the city, in an uproar, is blaming Caesar. Cleopatra admits that she gave the order, but Caesar cannot make her understand that this is not his way of governing. Lucius Septimius approaches Caesar and tells him that the relief army under Mithridates is near. Realizing that the Egyptian army left to fight Mithridates, Caesar leaves, intending to meet Mithridates and fight the Egyptian army. When Rufio learns that Ftatateeta killed Pothinus, he kills her.

Act 5. Having won the battle, Caesar prepares to return to Rome. He appoints Rufio to be the Roman governor of Egypt, praises Britannus for his conduct in the battle, and leaves Apollodorus in charge of Egyptian art. Cleopatra, in mourning for Ftatateeta, pleads for revenge against Rufio, who admitted to killing Ftatateeta; since it was a justified slaying, Caesar denies Cleopatra's plea. He says that Cleopatra learned little from him but again promises to send her Mark Antony. Caesar boards the ship to a salute from the Roman soldiers. Cleopatra remains behind, saddened but content.

"The Story" by Gordon N. Bergquist

Critical Evaluation:

Ever since the publication in 1579 of *Parallel Lives*, Sir Thomas North's translation of Plutarch's *Bioi paralleloi* (c. 105-115), Cleopatra has been one of the great romantic figures of English literature. To be sure, Dante had briefly glimpsed her, "tossed on the blast," in Hell's Circle of the Lustful in his *Inferno* (c. 1320), but he had hurried on to give the famous story of Paolo and Francesca. It remained for William Shakespeare, in *Antony and Cleopatra* (pr. c. 1606-1607, pb. 1623), to make her immortal as "the serpent of old Nile," the epitome of the eternal and irresistible female. Even the neoclassic John Dryden, in 1678, still found her the archetype of an all-consuming passion, for whose sake Antony held "the world well lost."

As for Caesar, his imprint has been upon the European mind since 44 B.C.E. To Dante—who saw him in Limbo as "Caesar armed, with the falcon eyes"—he is the founder of the Roman empire, and his murder is so terrible an example of treachery to lords and benefactors that Cassius and Brutus, his assassins, are placed with Judas in the jaws of Satan in the lowest pit of Hell. To Shakespeare, he is a man who in spite of arrogance and a thinly disguised ambition for absolute power actually bestrode "the narrow world like a Colossus." These are the figures of world history and world legend whom George Bernard Shaw chose to bring together in a comedy.

So strongly has Shakespeare stamped his interpretation of Cleopatra on Western literary consciousness that Shaw's heroine inflicts a distinct shock when audiences meet a girl of sixteen, on a moonlit October night, crouched between the paws of the Sphinx in the desert where she has fled to escape the invading Romans. She is the typical schoolgirl: highstrung, giggly, impulsive, terrified of her nurse, ready to believe that Romans have trunks, tusks, tails, and seven arms, each carrying a hundred arrows. She has the instinctive cruelty of a child; after encountering Caesar—whom she does not recognize and who forces her nurse to cringe at her feet—she is eager to beat the nurse and can talk gleefully of poisoning slaves and cutting off her brother's head. Shaw has set his plot at the moment in history when Egypt is divided. Ptolemy Dionysus has driven Cleopatra from Alexandria, and while the two foes—Ptolemy represented by Pothinus and Cleopatra by Ftatateeta—are at swords' points, Egypt is ready to fall into the conqueror's hand. It is the familiar situation of an immensely old and decadent civilization at the mercy of a rising world power, represented by Caesar.

Audiences with memories of Caesar's commentaries on the Gallic War and Mark Antony's funeral oration receive another shock when Caesar appears. The conqueror of the world is presented as a middle-aged man, painfully conscious of his years, somewhat prosaic, very far indeed from "Caesar armed, with the falcon eyes." He is past fifty, and the fateful Ides of March is less than four years away. As most men of his age in any period of history would be, he is somewhat amused and yet wholly fascinated by the lovely child he has met under such strange circumstances. Since he is quite aware of his weakness for women, the audience begins to anticipate a romantic turn to the plot. Shaw was not, however, a romantic dramatist. When Caesar returns Cleopatra to her palace, reveals his identity, and forces her to abandon her childishness and to assume her position as queen, he is revealed as a man who is eminently practical, imperturbable in moments of danger, and endowed with the slightly cynical detachment of a superior mind surrounded by inferiors.

The outline that Shaw uses for his somewhat rambling plot is to be found in Plutarch's *Life of Caesar* and in Caesar's *Civil War*. Shaw follows his sources quite faithfully, except in inventing a meeting between Caesar and Cleopatra in the desert and calling for Pothinus to be killed by Ftatateeta at Cleopatra's instigation after Caesar has promised him safe conduct from the palace. There is also a possible debt to the almost forgotten drama *The False One*, written by John Fletcher and Philip Massinger around 1620, which deals with the same story. Certainly Shaw's blunt-spoken Rufio appears to be a reworking of that play's Sceva.

Shaw also adds two characters of his own to the story: the savage Ftatateeta, who is eventually killed by Rufio, and Britannus, Caesar's secretary. The latter is Shaw's picture of the eternal Englishman—conventional, easily shocked, unable to understand any customs but those of his own island. It is in characterization, rather than in plot, that the play excels, and it also excels through the element of surprise, created by the device of presenting familiar literary figures from new angles, for it is obvious that Shaw intends to rub some of the romantic gilding from them. Cleopatra, although under Caesar's influence she becomes a precocious adult, loses her girlish charm without becoming a particularly attractive woman. She never really loves Caesar, nor he her, for Shaw rearranges history in this aspect of their relationship, and her one thought is of the arrival of Antony, whom she has met before and never forgotten. She has a presentiment of her coming tragedy, yet, eternally childish, she is poised to run to meet it.

The critic James Hunker maintained that this drama "entitled [Shaw] to a free pass to that pantheon wherein our beloved Mark Twain sits enthroned." Yet this play is no *Connecticut Yankee in King Arthur's Court* (1889), which was based on a conviction of the vast progress achieved since the Middle Ages. It was Shaw's conviction that there had been no perceptible progress since Caesar's day. Caesar himself knew that history would continue to unroll an endless series of murders and wars, always disguised under high-sounding and noble names. He was a great man, not because he was "ahead of his age" but because he stood outside it and could rule with mercy and without revenge. Such a leader would be great in any period of history.

Further Reading

Compton, Louis. "*Caesar and Cleopatra*." In *Shaw the Dramatist*. Lincoln: University of Nebraska Press, 1969. Discusses the social, philosophical, and historical backgrounds of the play. Offers a clear and accessible presentation of Shaw's ideas and their sources in the nineteenth century intellectual tradition.

Dukore, Bernard F. "The Center and the Frame." In *Bernard Shaw, Playwright: Aspects of Shavian Drama*. Columbia: University of Missouri Press, 1973. Concentrates on the formal aspects of the play and discusses how certain key scenes contribute to the whole. Deals at length with the prologues, which are seldom played, and act 3, which Shaw had suggested could be omitted but which Dukore claims is important and even necessary.

_____. *Shaw's Theater*. Gainesville: University Press of Florida, 2000. Focuses on the performance of Shaw's plays and how *Caesar and Cleopatra* and other plays call attention to elements of the theater, such as the audience, characters directing other characters, and plays within plays. Includes a section on "Bernard Shaw, Director," and another section in which Shaw describes how a director should interpret *Pygmalion* for theatrical production.

Evans, T. F., ed. *Shaw: The Critical Heritage*. London: Routledge & Kegan Paul, 1976. A useful collection of generally brief early reviews and notices of Shaw's plays, including *Caesar and Cleopatra*. Interesting to compare these early reviews with later scholarly views.

Holroyd, Michael. *Bernard Shaw: The Search for Love*. New York: Random House, 1988. In this first volume of his standard and indispensable biography of Shaw, Holroyd relates Shaw's life and thought to his works.

Innes, Christopher, ed. *The Cambridge Companion to George Bernard Shaw*. New York: Cambridge University Press, 1998. Collection of scholarly essays examining Shaw's work, including discussions of Shaw's feminism, Shavian comedy and the shadow of Oscar Wilde, his "discussion plays," and his influence on modern theater. *Caesar and Cleopatra* is analyzed in Matthew H. Wikander's essay "Reinventing the History Play: *Caesar and Cleopatra, Saint Joan,* 'In Good King Charles's Golden Days.'"

Pagliaro, Harold E. *Relations Between the Sexes in the Plays of George Bernard Shaw*. Lewiston, N.Y.: Edwin Mellen Press, 2004. Demonstrates how the relationship between men and women is a key element in Shaw's plays. Notes a pattern in how Shaw depicts these relationships, including lovers destined by the "life force" to procreate; relations between fathers and daughters, and mothers and sons; and the sexuality of politically, intellectually, and emotionally strong men.

Whitman, Robert F. "Plays for Realists." In *Shaw and the Play of Ideas*. Ithaca, N.Y.: Cornell University Press, 1977. Discusses the play's conflict between the realist and the idealist. Caesar's grasp of reality makes him immune to the temptations of vengeance and to Cleopatra's sensuality; Caesar is the representative of the future.

Cain
A Mystery

Author: Lord Byron (1788-1824)
First published: 1821
Type of work: Drama
Type of plot: Tragedy
Time of plot: The period of Genesis
Locale: Outside Eden

Principal characters:
ADAM, the first man
EVE, the first woman
CAIN and
ABEL, their sons
ADAH, Cain's wife
ZILLAH, Abel's wife
LUCIFER, the fallen angel

The Story:

While Adam, Eve, Abel, Zillah, and Adah pray to God, Cain stands sullenly by and complains that he has nothing to pray for because he had lost immortality when Eve ate the fruit from the tree of knowledge. He cannot understand why, if knowledge and life are good, his mother's deed has been deemed a deadly sin. Abel, Adah, and Zillah urge him to cast off his melancholy and join them in tending the fields. Alone, Cain deplores his worldly toil. Tired of the repetitious replies to all his questions, replies that refuse to challenge God's will, he is no longer sure that God is good.

At the conception of this thought, Lucifer appears to explain that Cain's mortality is only a bodily limit. He will live forever even after death. Cain, driven by instinct to cling to life, at the same time despises it. Lucifer admits that he also is unhappy in spite of his immortality, which is a cursed thing in his fallen state. He launches into a bitter tirade against God, whom he describes as a tyrant sitting alone in his misery, creating new worlds because his eternity is otherwise expressionless and boring to him. Lucifer exults that his own condition is at least shared by others. These words echo Cain's own beliefs about the universe. Long has he pitied his relatives for toiling so hard for sustenance, as God had decreed when he banished Adam and Eve from the Garden of Eden.

Lucifer confesses that the beguiling snake had not been a disguise for himself; the snake was merely a snake. He predicts, however, that later generations of humanity will array the fall of Adam and Eve in a cloak of fable. Cain then asks his mentor to reveal the nature of death, which holds great terrors for Cain. Lucifer promises to teach Cain true knowledge if Cain will worship him. Cain, however, having refused to worship even God, will not worship any being. His refusal is, according to Lucifer, in itself a form of worship.

Adah asks Cain to leave with her, but Cain claims that he must stay with Lucifer, who speaks like a god. Adah reminds Cain that the lying serpent, too, had spoken so. Lucifer insists that the serpent had spoken truly when it had promised knowledge from the fruit of the forbidden tree; humanity's grief lies not in the serpent's so-called lie but in humanity's knowledge of evil. Lucifer says he will take Cain with him for an hour, time enough to show him the whole of life and death.

Traveling with Lucifer through the air, Cain, watching with ecstasy the beauty around him, insists upon viewing the mystery of death, which is uppermost in his mind. The travelers come at last to a place where no stars glitter, and all is dark and dreadful. As they enter Hades, Cain again voices his hatred of death, the end of all living things.

In the underworld, Cain sees beautiful and mighty shapes that, Lucifer explains, had inhabited the world and died by chaotic destruction in an age before Adam was created. When Lucifer taunts Cain with his inferiority compared to those other beings of an earlier age, Cain declares himself ready to stay in Hades forever. Lucifer confesses, however, that he has no power to allow anyone to remain in Hades. When he points out to Cain that the spirits of the former inhabitants of the earth had enjoyed a beautiful world, Cain says that Earth is still beautiful. His complaint is against human toil for what the earth bears, human failure to obtain knowledge, and the unmitigated human fear of death. Cain, bewailing the trade humanity has made of death for knowledge, asserts that humanity knows nothing. Lucifer replies that death is a certainty and, therefore, so are truth and knowledge. Cain thinks he has learned nothing new from his journey, but Lucifer informs him that he has at least discovered that there is a state beyond his own.

Lucifer and Cain discuss Cain's relative state of happiness in life, which, Cain asserts, is dependent upon his love for his family. Lucifer's hints that Abel, favored by the others and by God, cause Cain some jealousy. Cain then asks his guide to show him where he lives, or else God's dwelling place. It is reserved for those who died, Lucifer claims, to see either one or the other, not both. As Lucifer prepares to return his pupil to Earth, Cain complains that he has learned nothing. He has, Lucifer retorts, discovered that he is nothing. With a warning to distinguish between real good and evil and to seek his own spiritual attachment, Lucifer transports the mortal back to Earth.

Standing over their son Enoch, who is asleep under a tree, Adah and Cain discuss their ever-present sorrow: They must all die. When Adah states she would gladly die to save her parents, Cain agrees, only if his own death might save everyone else. Adah prophesies that such a gift might some day be rendered. Seeing the pair of altars Abel had erected for a sacrifice, Cain utters his first evil thought by muttering a denial that Abel is his brother.

Abel insists that Cain share in the sacrificial rites he is about to perform. While Cain impiously stands by, Abel kneels in eloquent prayer. Cain's prayer is a defiant challenge to the omnipotent to show his preference for one of the altars. His own offerings are scattered to the earth, while Abel's sacrifice burns in high flames toward the heavens. In anger, Cain attacks his brother's altar, and when Abel protests that he loves his God more than life, Cain strikes him a mortal blow.

Adam, Eve, Adah, and Zillah, rushing to the scene, accuse Cain of murdering his brother. Eve utters loud imprecations against her guilty son. Adam orders him to depart. Only Adah remains by his side. The Angel of the Lord then appears to confront Cain and ask the whereabouts of his brother. The angel predicts that henceforth Cain's hand will cultivate no growing things from the earth and that he will be a fugitive. Lest the person guilty of fratricide be the cause of another murder, the angel brands Cain with a mark on his forehead, to warn the beholder that to kill Cain would engender a sevenfold vengeance. Cain blames his evil deed upon Eve, who gave birth to him too soon after her banishment from Eden, when her own mind was still bitter over the lost paradise. Adah offers to share her husband's fate. Carrying their children with them, she and Cain travel eastward from Eden.

Critical Evaluation:

Lord Byron's *Cain* is subtitled *A Mystery*, but the mystery is not that of "who did it"; the story of Cain's murder of Abel is well known. It is a mystery, but one that is a type of drama that had been used in medieval times to illustrate stories from the Bible. Unlike medieval mystery plays, *Cain*, like Byron's *Manfred* (pb. 1817, pr. 1834), is a closet drama, meant to be read, not staged.

The story of Cain and Abel had intrigued Byron for years. When studying German as a boy, he had read Salomon

Gessner's *Der Tod Abels* (1758; "the death of Abel") and came to think of Abel as "dull." *Cain* has three acts, and the principal source is the fourth chapter of the book of Genesis. Byron's Cain, however, is different from the Cain of Genesis. The influence of the Romantic movement is reflected in Byron's Cain as he strives for independence and for understanding of a world he did not create.

Byron's play includes Adam, Eve, Abel, and Zillah, but as minor characters. To Cain, Adam has been "tamed down," and Eve has lost that intellectual curiosity that "made her thirst for knowledge." Abel is a simple shepherd boy, and Zillah, like Abel, is happy with her simple life. Cain is alienated from all of them and is deeply conflicted.

Cain cannot understand why he should be punished for something someone else did. In addition, he cannot grasp why a God who has the power for good should set up circumstances so that humankind would fail and, therefore, be forced from Paradise and sentenced to till the earth and be subject to death. As the family gathers to pray, it is evident that Cain is not taking part. When asked why he is not giving thanks to God, Cain replies that he has nothing for which to thank God. Unlike his family, he is not content with "what is." Byron has set Cain up as an outsider. He cannot be satisfied living outside Eden, and he questions the justice of being punished for a deed committed before he was born. He stands outside Eden, gazing at what should be his just inheritance, as the elder son. He reasons that God had deliberately tempted Adam and Eve, causing their fall, and he doubts God's actions.

Cain's doubt provokes the appearance of Lucifer, the fallen angel. The character of Lucifer is complex and serves as a catalyst for the tragedy of act 3. Byron's Lucifer is different from John Milton's fallen angel, Satan, in *Paradise Lost* (1667, 1674). Milton's Satan is gigantic and is more human in his physical deformity. Byron's Lucifer is less human and states he is not the serpent who had tempted Eve; however, he is, indeed, like Milton's persuasive Satan, and he feeds Cain's doubts by flattering Cain's wisdom. By articulating what Cain feels, he makes Cain believe he has found someone who understands him, unlike his family. However, when Lucifer asks Cain to worship him, Cain refuses. In act 2, however, Cain will demonstrate his trust by traveling with Lucifer as his guide.

It is in act 2 that Byron anticipates certain scientific discoveries, referring, for example, to the world as having been created ages before the world that was created by God in Genesis. In a letter to his friend and fellow poet Thomas Moore, dated September 19, 1821, Byron identifies the creatures that Cain sees in act 2, scene 2 as "rational Preadamites, beings endowed with a higher intelligence than man, but totally unlike him in form." The idea that there were beings on Earth before Adam was a common, although heretical, speculation in Byron's time. In the same letter to Moore, Byron explains that the prehistoric past that Cain describes, also in act 2, scene 2, was an idea he developed from the writing of Georges Cuvier. Byron writes that before the time described in Genesis, "the world has been destroyed three or four times, and was inhabited by mammoths, behemoths, and what not; but not by man." He believes humanity is a recent creation.

It is notable that Byron had turned to science to supplement Scripture. While looking at such beings, Lucifer, in *Cain*, points out Cain's nothingness, yet Lucifer reflects the Romantic worldview when he tells Cain to rely on his own mind and, if need be, defy the ways of God, rather than justify them to others. When Lucifer shows Cain the mightiness of a former world in comparison to Cain's Eden-excluded existence, he works toward undermining what remains of Cain's faith in an omnipotent God. He flatters Cain, yet lowers his self-esteem by showing Cain how nothingness is all humans can know. During their time together, Lucifer also attempts to make Cain jealous of his brother, noting that Abel's sacrifices to God are more acceptable.

A third important character developed by Byron in the play is Adah, Cain's sister and wife. Similar to her mother Eve, she is initially attracted by Lucifer. Cain tells Adah that Lucifer is a god, but she comes to realize that Lucifer only speaks like a god, as did the serpent that had beguiled Eve. Adah warns Cain against Lucifer and urges Cain to remain with her, stressing her love for him. Cain is torn between her love and the knowledge Lucifer offers; Cain, like his mother, rejects love. Adah offers him love and contentment, a way to accept life with its limits, but Cain wants more, to transcend his limitations by following Lucifer.

Adah, aware of the danger of Lucifer, shows integrity and strength against temptation. Cain, in act 2, is torn between her love and wanting to know more, so he follows Lucifer. He returns, not enlightened but diminished. When, in act 3 Cain sees his sleeping son Enoch and despairs that he, too, has been disinherited from Eden, Adah suggests that he cease mourning for Paradise and make another. Cain states it would be better to beat Enoch's head against the rocks than to live in such a dispossessed state.

When Abel encourages Cain to sacrifice to God with him, Cain asks Abel to make his sacrifice alone since "Jehovah loves thee well." However, Abel urges Cain to join him. Cain, as the tiller of the soil, offers fruits; Abel, as keeper of the flocks, offers a blood sacrifice. Abel kneels, but Cain stands, stating how God must love blood if he accepts Abel's offering. When Cain's gifts are rejected, and Abel's are accepted,

it appears that Abel has supplanted Cain. Cain strikes his brother in anger and to prevent the sacrifice of more lambs; he does not believe it to be a mortal blow. Cain deplores the bloody slaughter of a lamb, but, ironically, he sheds his brother's blood. Although Lucifer had tried to make Cain jealous of Abel, it was not jealousy of Abel that caused the blow, but anger that God had rejected his offering.

Byron's Cain is not a murderer; his fatal blow is an accident. He cannot believe he has killed his brother and states he would take Abel's place and die to "redeem him from the dust"; he fully recognizes the consequences of his act, a major departure from the biblical account. Another difference is Eve's cursing of her own son. Adam simply tells Cain to go away. At the beginning the play Cain feels alienated from his family, now they reject him. Adah, who represents the redemptive power of love, stands by him. She and their two children will accompany Cain eastward from Eden.

Cain is yet another of Byron's heroes, similar to Manfred and, to a lesser degree, Childe Harold. Outside Eden at the beginning of the play, Cain becomes an outcast from the new world established outside Eden by Adam and Eve, as he is expelled from what he has known. His dissatisfaction with the choices of his parents and his future is exacerbated once he has killed his brother. This terrible sin results in his exile. Unlike Manfred and Childe Harold, both of whom choose exile, exile is not Cain's choice. Byron's Cain is not evil; he is a person who uses his gift of reason to question why he was expelled from Paradise before he experienced it. As a Romantic (Byronic) rebel, he shows how one who is disillusioned may turn from good intentions to violence. He is tempted by flattery and made to feel inadequate. Ironically, Cain's act and its consequences echo the fate of his parents, but it is worse. Cain has become a murderer and is even more removed from the Paradise he once coveted.

"Critical Evaluation" by Dennis R. Dean;
revised by Marcia B. Dinneen

Further Reading

Chew, Samuel Claggett. *The Dramas of Lord Byron: A Critical Study.* New York: Russell & Russell, 1964. Despite its age, Chew's study remains one of the best places to begin any study of Byron and his writing for the theater.

Corbett, Martyn. *Byron and Tragedy.* New York: St. Martin's Press, 1988. The essay on Cain includes an in-depth analysis of the play.

Franklin, Caroline. *Byron.* New York: Routledge, 2007. A concise yet important criticism of the play that includes a descriptive list of further readings.

Gleckner, Robert, and Bernard Beatty, eds. *The Plays of Lord Byron: Critical Essays*. Liverpool, England: Liverpool University Press, 1997. Includes three essays on *Cain*: "Byron's *Cain* and the Antimythological Myth" by David Eggenschweiler, "Byron's Lapse into Orthodoxy: An Unorthodox Reading of *Cain*" by Wolf Z. Hirst, and "'In Caines Cynne': Byron and the Mark of Cain" by Daniel M. McVeigh.

Marchand, Leslie. *Byron: A Biography*. 3 vols. 1957. Reprint. New York: Knopf, 1967. Byron, one of the most autobiographical of all poets, led a fascinating life. In many instances, his works are largely an idealized version of his own experiences. Marchand's biography is considered the standard account of Byron's life and reliably illuminates autobiographical elements in *Cain*.

Richardson, Alan. "Byron and the Theatre." In *The Cambridge Companion to Byron*, edited by Drummond Bone. New York: Cambridge University Press, 2004. Richardson provides an overview of Byron's plays, including *Cain*.

Simpson, Michael. *Closet Performances: Political Exhibition and Prohibition in the Dramas of Byron and Shelley*. Stanford, Calif.: Stanford University Press, 1998. Examines the closet dramas that Byron and Percy Bysshe Shelley wrote between 1816 and 1823, when they were living in Italy. *Cain* is discussed in chapter 4.

Stabler, Jane, ed. *Palgrave Advances in Byron Studies*. New York: Palgrave Macmillan, 2007. Contains twelve scholarly essays interpreting Byron's work, including discussions of homosexuality, gender, history, popular culture, war, and psychoanalytic criticism.

Thorslev, Peter L. *The Byronic Hero: Types and Prototypes*. Minneapolis: University of Minnesota Press, 1962. Probably the most helpful book that a student confronting Byron for the first time can read. Thorslev describes seven well-known types of heroes in Romantic literature before turning specifically to those of Byron. Depictions of Cain in legend and literature are summarized; Byron's Cain is usefully compared with John Milton's Satan and Johann Wolfgang von Goethe's Faust.

The Caine Mutiny

Author: Herman Wouk (1915-   )
First published: 1951
Type of work: Novel
Type of plot: Bildungsroman
Time of plot: 1942-1945
Locale: New York City, San Francisco, and the Pacific Ocean

Principal characters:
WILLIE KEITH, a young Naval Reserve officer
TOM KEEFER, an intellectual and Keith's communications officer
CAPTAIN DE VREISS, Keith's first commanding officer on the *Caine*
STEVE MARYK, Keith's fellow officer
CAPTAIN PHILIP FRANCIS QUEEG, the *Caine*'s second captain and a focus of controversy
LIEUTENANT BARNEY GREENWALD, the mutineers' defense attorney
MAY WYNN (MARIE MINOTTI), Keith's girlfriend

The Story:

Wealthy and sheltered, Willie Keith graduates from Princeton. To avoid Army service, he enters the Navy Reserve Officers' Training Program shortly after Japan's attack on Pearl Harbor. A spoiled adolescent, his distinctions are limited to amusing friends by playing piano and inventing clever ditties. Straying from his social reservation, he also begins an infatuation with May Wynn (born Marie Minotti), a hardworking nightclub singer and the daughter of immigrants. In the first of *The Caine Mutiny*'s six parts, Keith passes into the bizarre world of the Navy, war, and authority. During the next three years, the once callow Ensign Keith acquires the skills of his trade, learns self-reliance, acquiesces to cabals against his superior, becomes a party to a mutiny, and ultimately captains the final voyage of the U.S.S. *Caine*.

At the outset, however, Keith has difficulty comprehending that there is "a right way, a wrong way, and the Navy way." Loaded with demerits for his blunders, unclear about the meaning of service or sacrifice, and close to expulsion, he survives his midshipman's training at Columbia University only by mustering a surprising amount of inner determination. Expecting a soft billet thereafter, he is dismayed by his assignment to the *Caine*, a lowly, World War I-era destroyer that was converted to a minesweeper.

Keith's first tour aboard the battle-scarred *Caine* is a study in mixed signals. Boarding ship as it is being refitted in San Francisco Bay, he meets the aspiring novelist-intellectual Tom Keefer, a communications officer and Keith's superior officer. Keefer immediately defines himself as a sneering, acerbic critic of the Navy. Keith also meets Steve Maryk, soon to be the ship's executive officer, who admires Captain De Vreiss. Having just adopted respect for Navy regulations, Keith, however, is appalled by De Vreiss's lax discipline and slovenly shipkeeping, despite Maryk's stress on De Vreiss's superb seamanship and the respect he enjoys among the weary crew. Keith's estimate of De Vreiss drops lower when Keith's failure to deliver an important message to De Vreiss leads him to reprimand Keith. Upon transfer of command from De Vreiss to Lieutenant Commander Philip Francis Queeg, Keith therefore feels relieved and hopeful.

In his mid-thirties, Queeg, though physically unimpressive, is a Naval Academy graduate and a believer in strict adherence to regulations. Behind Queeg is fourteen years at sea and extended combat duty, so to the officers things look promising under their new captain.

Part 3 chronicles the growing estrangement between Queeg and his officers. As the *Caine* alternates in the Pacific between training exercises, routine convoy duty, and then Keith's first combat during the Marianas invasion, her officers, led by Keefer, awaken to mounting evidence of Queeg's indecision, ineptitude in shiphandling, personal quirkiness, and preoccupation with minor disciplinary matters.

A series of episodes casts doubt on Queeg's fitness for command. Initially maneuvering his ship in harbor, he grazes another vessel and runs the *Caine* aground. Called to account by his superior, Queeg blames the accident on crewmen. Later, while the *Caine* conducts a target towing exercise, Queeg, busy reprimanding a seaman for a flapping shirttail, allows the *Caine* to turn full circle, sever a towline, and sink a valuable target. Again, Queeg puts blame elsewhere. Returning his ship to San Francisco for repairs, Queeg sequesters his officers' liquor rations and illegally tries smuggling them ashore for himself. The liquor is lost overboard by a boat party in Keith's charge, and Keith is blamed.

Worse is to come. Responsible for guiding landing craft to an invasion beachhead, Queeg, frightened, drops a yellow marker before the *Caine* reaches its designated turning point, abandoning troop-filled small craft under fire. Shortly afterward, he fails to aid another ship busy suppressing enemy artillery. Keith and others, in addition, observe Queeg's habit of seeking the safest place on the bridge during combat. For a minor infraction, Queeg deprives the crew of water for days. Theft of a gallon of Queeg's strawberries results in turning the *Caine* inside out in a fruitless search that continues even after the culprits are identified. Meanwhile, at Keefer's urging, Maryk begins a record of Queeg's behavior.

At last, convinced that Queeg is psychologically unbalanced, Maryk, citing Navy law and joined by Keith and others, relieves Queeg of command as the *Caine* threatens to founder in a typhoon. Subsequently charged with mutiny, Maryk (who accepts full responsibility), Keith, Keefer, and other officers are defended reluctantly by Lieutenant Barney Greenwald, an experienced lawyer. Greenwald, with ruthless brilliance, discredits the Navy's psychological experts who testify to Queeg's sanity and then leads Queeg to discredit himself thoroughly on the stand. Morally, however, it is a hollow victory. At the acquitted officers' celebratory party, Greenwald denounces them, damning Keefer in particular as the real cause of the mutiny and the person responsible for making Greenwald ruin Queeg.

Justice is done in the novel's final section. Queeg is reassigned to ignominious service as executive officer of a Navy depot in Kansas. Placed in command of the *Caine*, Keefer demonstrates cowardice when he leaps overboard, his manuscript in hand, after a Japanese kamikaze plane crashes into his ship. Keith, by then seasoned and commanding, becomes the last captain of the *Caine*, sailing her home to decommissioning and destruction, and, despite his mother's doubts, to renewed romance with May.

Critical Evaluation:

Retrospectively, many critics, even those not well disposed toward some of Herman Wouk's later writings, considered *The Caine Mutiny* his best work and one of the finest war novels to emerge from World War II. Wouk was awarded a Pulitzer Prize for it in 1952. Certainly the reading public affirmed this decision, for it became one of the best-selling novels published in the twentieth century. By 1960, sales in the United States exceeded three million copies and the novel had been translated into sixteen languages. In addition, adapted for theater, *The Caine Mutiny Court-Martial* became a hit play, and, buoyed by actor Humphrey Bogart's superb performance as Captain Queeg, the screen version of *The Caine Mutiny* earned multiple awards that presaged recognition of it as a film classic.

Although Wouk served several years in the Pacific during World War II as an officer aboard a minesweeper much like the *Caine*, his novel is not autobiographical. *The Caine Mutiny* certainly reflects elements of Joseph Conrad's *The Nigger of the Narcissus* (1897) and of Herman Melville's *Billy Budd, Foretopman* (1924) in the sense that both of these major literary works are stories of seamen trapped by implacable nature and unbending authority, of mutinies, and of trials. These similarities ought not, however, to obscure *The Caine Mutiny*'s differences from them.

Philosophically, Wouk's themes are conservative and moralistic. The moral lesson he emphasizes by following spoiled Willie Keith through his rite of passage to genuine maturity is that Keith's maturation has demanded sacrifice. Part of that sacrifice entails the acceptance of an almost unquestioning obedience to properly constituted authority, along with the assumption of responsibility for making decisions. Wouk stresses how Keith, Maryk, even Keefer in his own manner, and not the least Greenwald, eventually realize, first by observation and then by the experience of rising to command themselves, that Captains De Vriess and Queeg are subject to crushing pressures. These pressures in their instances are worsened by their extended wartime sea duty and combat. Ultimate authority, and the accountability that goes with it, cannot be shared, the lives of those in command are marked by loneliness and alienation. Their actions are open to constant denunciation and their peccadilloes to ridicule. Such burdens and circumstances alone, Wouk implies, entitle authority to strict obedience and to substantial respect. Although he is disturbed about Queeg's performance, Steve Maryk initially demonstrates this point when, after becoming the detested Queeg's executive officer, he refuses to participate further in his fellow officers' daily fulminations against their captain.

A Keith put through the rigors of a maturation process becomes Wouk's metaphor for America's coming-of-age, a consequence of its involvement in World War II. In a confessional deathbed letter from his father that Keith opens at sea, his father, indeed, compares Willie to his country, young, naïve, and spoiled but still possessing sufficient pioneer determination to create a better life.

Keith's search for a father figure constitutes another minor theme. Keith's father nominally has been a successful physician; his final letter burdens Keith with the disclosure of a life of high-minded dreams betrayed by wasted opportunities, concessions to social status, and many unnecessary compromises. Thus, an irresolute Keith, harboring his own dreams of literary scholarship, confronts a number of surrogate fathers: two of his training instructors, a kindly admiral who likes his piano playing, Captain De Vreiss, Maryk, Keefer, and, eventually Queeg.

There are other minor themes. *The Caine Mutiny* is full of tensions that existed during World War II between former civilians, often innately contemptuous of the seemingly arbitrary nature of military authority, and the disciplined, underpaid, and socially demeaned officers such as Queeg, who began their careers in the peacetime Navy. It is also difficult for reserve officers to cope with the entrenched Navy bureaucracy or with the Naval Academy's old boy network. It is also unusual for reservists to get respectful hearings for their ideas. Wouk remained a reserve officer long after 1945. Emphasizing the virtues of both regulars and reservists, he frequently called for their greater mutual understanding.

Stylistically, Wouk's third-person narrative moves his story swiftly and satisfactorily, sometimes with passion and often with humor, if without true distinction. His dialogue varies from touching and insightful to comic and clichéd. His exclusion of the obscenities that composed the bulk of servicemen's speech appeared timorous to many authors, an error to some editors, and unrealistic to readers. Furthermore, even Wouk's admirers criticized his handling of Keith's romance and his trite characterization of May Wynn. Yet despite such flaws, *The Caine Mutiny* appears destined for longevity. Wouk's skill ensures that characters such as Keith, Keefer, and certainly Queeg will remain memorable ones. More than good entertainment, the novel represents a fresh address, particularly for war novels, to sensitive social and moral issues.

Clifton K. Yearley

Further Reading

Ardolino, Frank. "Herman Wouk's *The Caine Mutiny*." *Explicator* 67, no. 1 (Fall, 2008): 39-43. Argues that many of the characters are guilty of the mutiny and the novel "demonstrates the difficulty of affixing individual guilt in a complex moral situation."

Beichman, Arnold W. *The Novelist as a Social Historian.* New Brunswick, N.J.: Transaction Books, 1984. Concentrates on Wouk's conservatism. There are useful observations on *The Caine Mutiny* and the questions it raises about authority versus individualism.

Darby, William. *Necessary American Fiction: Popular Literature of the 1950's.* Bowling Green, Ohio: Bowling Green State University Popular Press, 1987. An insightful analysis of how popular novels such as *The Caine Mutiny* reflect American values of the decade.

Gerard, Philip. "The Great American War Novels." *World*

and I 10 (June, 1995): 54-63. Notes that World War II was "the last public event that defined a generation of novelists," and examines many of these books, including *The Caine Mutiny.*

Jones, Peter G. *War and the Novelist.* Columbia: University of Missouri Press, 1976. Uses *The Caine Mutiny* as an example of how war novels deal with the problems of wartime military command.

Mazzeno, Laurence W. *Herman Wouk.* New York: Twayne, 1994. One of the best studies of Wouk and his writings. Chapter 3 is devoted entirely to *The Caine Mutiny.*

Shapiro, Edward S. "The Jew as Patriot: Herman Wouk and American Jewish Identity." In *We Are Many: Reflections on American Jewish History and Identity.* Syracuse, N.Y.: Syracuse University Press, 2005. This collection of Shapiro's previously published essays includes a retrospective review of Wouk's career. Shapiro argues persuasively that Wouk is concerned principally with defining American Jewish identity.

Shatzky, Joel, and Michael Taub, eds. *Contemporary Jewish-American Novelists: A Bio-Critical Sourcebook.* Westport, Conn.: Greenwood Press, 1997. Includes an entry on Wouk's life, major works, and themes, with an overview of his critical reception and a bibliography of primary and secondary sources.

Waldemeir, Joseph T. *American Novels of the Second World War.* The Hague, the Netherlands: Mouton, 1971. Emphasizes how *The Caine Mutiny,* among a minority of war novels, commends the subordination of civilian individualism to military authority.

Cakes and Ale
Or, The Skeleton in the Cupboard

Author: W. Somerset Maugham (1874-1965)
First published: 1930
Type of work: Novel
Type of plot: Social satire
Time of plot: Late 1920's
Locale: London and Kent, England

Principal characters:
ASHENDEN, a writer
ALROY KEAR, a popular novelist
EDWARD DRIFFIELD, a great Victorian author
ROSIE, Driffield's first wife
AMY, Driffield's second wife
GEORGE KEMP, Rosie's lover

The Story:

Alroy Kear, the most popular novelist of the day, arranges to have lunch with his friend Ashenden, another writer. Ashenden is fond of Kear, but he suspects that his invitation was extended for a purpose. He is right. Kear wants to talk about the late Edward Driffield, a famous English author of the past century. Kear has nothing but praise for the old man's books, but Ashenden says that he never thought Driffield exceptional. Kear enthusiastically tells how well he knew Driffield in his last years and says that he is still a friend of Driffield's widow, his second wife. Luncheon ends without a request for a favor. Ashenden is puzzled.

Returning to his room, Ashenden falls into a reverie. He recalls his first meeting with Driffield. Ashenden was then a boy, home for the holidays at Blackstable, a Kentish seacoast town, where he lived with his uncle, the local vicar. Ashenden met Driffield in the company of his uncle's curate, but the boy thought the writer a rather common person. He learned from his uncle that Driffield married a local barmaid after spending a wild youth away from home.

Two or three days after Ashenden lunches with Kear, he receives a note from Driffield's widow. She wishes him to visit her in Blackstable. Puzzled, Ashenden telephones Kear, who says that he will come to see him and explain the invitation.

Ashenden saw Mrs. Driffield only once. He went to her house with some other literary people several years before, while Driffield was still alive. Driffield married his second wife late in life, and she was his nurse. In the course of the visit, Ashenden was surprised to see old Driffield wink at him several times as if there were some joke between them. After that visit, Ashenden recalls how Driffield taught him to bicycle many years before. Driffield and his first wife, Rosie, took him with them on many excursions. He liked the

Driffields, but he was shocked to find how outspoken they were with those below and above them in social station.

One evening, Ashenden found Rosie visiting his uncle's cook, her childhood friend. After Rosie left, he saw her meet George Kemp, a local coal merchant. The couple walked out of town toward the open fields. Ashenden cannot imagine how Rosie could be unfaithful to her husband.

Ashenden went back to school. During the Christmas holiday, he often joined the Driffields for tea. Kemp was always there, but he and Rosie did not act like lovers. Driffield sang drinking songs, played the piano, and seldom talked about literature. When Ashenden returned to Blackstable the following summer, he heard that the Driffields had fled, leaving behind many unpaid bills. He was ashamed that he had ever been friendly with them.

Kear arrives at Ashenden's rooms and explains that he is planning to write Driffield's official biography. He wants Ashenden to contribute what he knows about the author's younger days. What Ashenden tells him is not satisfactory, for the biography should contain nothing to embarrass the widow. Kear insists that Ashenden write down what he remembers of Driffield and goes to Blackstable to visit Mrs. Driffield. Ashenden agrees.

Ashenden remembers how he met the Driffields again in London when he was a young medical student. By chance, he saw Rosie on the street; he was surprised that she was not ashamed to meet someone from Blackstable, and he promised to come to one of the Driffields' Saturday afternoon gatherings. Soon he became a regular visitor in their rooms. Since Driffield worked at night, Rosie often went out with her friends. Ashenden began to take her to shows. She was pleasant company, and he began to see that she was beautiful. One evening, he invited her to his room. She offered herself to him and remained for the night; after that night, Rosie visited his room regularly.

One day, Mrs. Barton Trafford, a literary woman who took Driffield under her care, invited Ashenden to tea. He learned from her that Rosie ran away with Kemp, her old lover from Blackstable. Ashenden was chagrined to learn that Rosie cared for another man more than she did for him.

Ashenden then lost touch with Driffield. He learned that the author divorced Rosie, who went to New York with Kemp. Mrs. Barton Trafford continued to care for Driffield as his fame grew. Then he caught pneumonia. He went to the country to convalesce and there married his nurse, the present Mrs. Driffield, whom Mrs. Trafford hired to look after him.

Ashenden goes down to Blackstable with Kear. They talk with Mrs. Driffield about her husband's early life. She and

Kear describe Rosie as promiscuous. Ashenden says that she is nothing of the sort. Good and generous, she cannot deny love to anyone, that is all. Ashenden knows this to be the truth, now that he can look back at his own past experience. The others disagree and dismiss the subject by saying that, after all, she is dead.

Rosie, however, is not dead. When Ashenden visits New York, she writes to him and asks him to call on her. He finds her now a wealthy widow; Kemp died several years before. She is an old woman who retains her love for living. They talk of old times, and Ashenden discovers that Driffield, too, understood her—even when she was being unfaithful to him.

Rosie says that she is too old to marry again; she had her fling at life. Ashenden asks her if Kemp is the only man she really loved; she says that it is true. Then Ashenden's eyes stray to a photograph of Kemp on the wall. It shows him with a waxed mustache; he is dressed in flashy clothes, carries a cane, and flourishes a cigar in one hand. Ashenden turns to Rosie and asks why she preferred Kemp to her other lovers. Her reply is simple: He was always the perfect gentleman.

Critical Evaluation:

Cakes and Ale is a characteristic Somerset Maugham novel, a combination of social satire, autobiography, and roman à clef. It is a masterfully structured story, told largely in retrospect, with the Maugham touch of the unanticipated ending. Like many of the author's plays, novels, and stories, it underscores his conviction that human morals are relative, rather than absolute.

The title is taken from William Shakespeare's *Twelfth Night: Or, What You Will* (pr. c. 1600-1602, pb. 1623), in which the happy libertine, Sir Toby Belch, upbraids the priggish, hypocritical Malvolio with the pronouncement: "Dost thou think, because thou art virtuous, there shall be no cakes and ale?" Sir Toby's question applies to all who would shape the world around them to fit a preconceived, narrow code of conduct and behavior in which joy and earthy pleasure play little or no part. Maugham's *Cakes and Ale* offers a response to Sir Toby's question. The novel is about the self-discovery that comes through a young man's awareness of joy and carnal passion. Maugham sees these elements of life as vitally important. To those for whom human nature is more a failing than a triumph, joy and passion are subsumed by respectability and conformity to arbitrary standards of social conduct. Initially, young Ashenden, the narrator and Maugham's persona, is a petty snob, one who without thought or consideration embraces the strictures and prejudices of class-obsessed Victorian England. To Ashenden and to those with whom he shares a certain stratum of society, outspoken and uninhibitedly good-natured working-class people are considered beneath any social interaction beyond the most rudimentary formal politeness—men such as George Kemp, the coal merchant, for example, whose friendly camaraderie serves only to demonstrate to young Ashenden that Kemp is a man "who doesn't seem to know his place." Rosie's intrinsic goodness and the love she offers—of a nature entirely different from anything Ashenden has previously experienced—break through his barriers and teach him how shallow his preconceptions of human nature are.

Maugham's social satire in the novel centers on the contemporary literary society of the late 1920's, taking to task, in particular, its often shallow and self-serving pretensions, as well as its subservience to contemporary trends of fashionable literature. Created for particular parody in this regard is the character of Alroy Kear, the popular novelist with a decided penchant for managing the commercial and public relations side of his career, undoubtedly to compensate for the limitations of his creative ability. At the behest of Amy Driffield, Kear has undertaken to create a literary icon. He is in the preliminary stages of writing the authorized biography of the late Edward Driffield, Amy's recently deceased husband and a highly acclaimed Victorian author. As Driffield's second wife, she has chosen as her task in life to be the "keeper of the flame," the curator of all that his life and work have become. She is determined to reconstruct—or at least censor—that life, with Kear's aid and compliance, into an acceptable portrait for public view, devoid of scandal and above reproach. Kear's motives, however, fall far short of scholarly interest and integrity. He envisions his work on Driffield, as he explains it to Ashenden, as "a sort of intimate life, with a lot of those little details that make people feel warm inside . . . woven into this a really exhaustive criticism of his literary work, not ponderous . . . although sympathetic"—in brief, an insubstantial formula biography tailored to the mass market.

The character of Kear is based on Hugh Walpole, a highly popular novelist of the late 1920's; Walpole is now relegated to the occasional footnote in English literary history. Edward Driffield is largely drawn from Thomas Hardy. Although for many years Maugham denied the roman à clef identification, in later years he admitted to the Kear-Walpole creation. Walpole, according to Maugham, was a man he found "easy to like but difficult to respect." Literary posterity has generally agreed with Maugham and has credited Walpole with being a man who made the most of a moderate talent, even to the point of parlaying it into a knighthood, in 1937, for his service to literature.

The Driffield-Hardy conception is largely creative conjecture based on contemporary gossip. Hardy was a widower who married a second time late in life; he lived until 1928. Driffield's novel, *The Cup of Life*, seems to be a composite drawn from the public outcry associated with two Hardy novels, *Tess of the D'Urbervilles* (1891) and *Jude the Obscure* (1895).

The enduring heart of the novel, however, is Rosie, the warm center in the otherwise dreary lives of the men of Blackstable. She is a generous and loving woman whose childlike amorality and *carpe diem* philosophy enable her to endure and survive her own hidden suffering (the loss of the daughter she had with Driffield). She is a woman, the mature Ashenden tells the incredulous and contemptuous Kear and Amy Driffield, who "gave herself as naturally as the sun gives heat or the flowers their perfume."

In intellectual circles in the 1920's, it was fashionable to be in revolt against all things Victorian. One of the immutable laws of Victorian fiction decreed that "a woman who falls may never rise." Lost virtue may never be supplanted by regained respectability. Hardy himself was subjected to considerable criticism for permitting Sue Bridehead, in *Jude the Obscure*, to return to her husband; she had been insufficiently punished after her long sojourn with Jude Fawley, despite the fact that her children had all died tragic deaths. Rosie, whose love is readily available to any man who will be made happy by it, remains triumphantly unrepentant into old age, living in relative prosperity, with no regrets. She is Somerset Maugham's literary prototype of the twentieth century liberated woman, a free spirit who lives her life unfettered by pointlessly repressive convention.

"Critical Evaluation" by Richard Keenan

Further Reading

Cordell, Richard. *Somerset Maugham, a Writer for all Seasons: A Biographical and Critical Study.* 2d ed. Bloomington: Indiana University Press, 1969. Thorough analysis of Maugham as a writer proficient in all genres of literature.

Curtis, Anthony. *The Pattern of Maugham: A Critical Portrait.* New York: Taplinger, 1974. Analysis of Maugham's more prominent works, with insights into the role of his insecurities and his frequent digressions in *Cakes and Ale* and other novels, when he offers personal commentary on the state of society and the world of arts and letters.

Curtis, Anthony, and John Whitehead, eds. *W. Somerset Maugham: The Critical Heritage.* London: Routledge & Kegan Paul, 1987. Particularly valuable for tracing the critical reception of *Cakes and Ale* since its initial publication. Contains contemporary reviews by noted literary figures, such as Ivor Brown, Evelyn Waugh, and Leslie Marchand.

Loss, Archie K. *W. Somerset Maugham*. New York: Frederick Ungar, 1987. An in-depth analysis of the roman à clef aspects of the novel, emphasizing Maugham's disparaging treatment of Hugh Walpole and Thomas Hardy.

Meyers, Jeffrey. *Somerset Maugham*. New York: Alfred A. Knopf, 2004. This biography emphasizes Maugham's "otherness," particularly his homosexuality. Unlike other critics who have dismissed Maugham's work, Meyers defends Maugham as a great writer who influenced George Orwell, V. S. Naipaul, and other authors.

Morgan, Ted. *Maugham*. New York: Simon & Schuster, 1980. A comprehensive overview of Maugham's life and career, with an extended discussion of the character of

Rosie in *Cakes and Ale*. Morgan emphasizes her pragmatic morality and adaptability in a socially repressive atmosphere.

Rogal, Samuel J. *A Companion to the Characters in the Fiction and Drama of W. Somerset Maugham*. Westport, Conn.: Greenwood Press, 1996. An alphabetical listing of the characters—animal and human, unnamed and named—in Maugham's fiction and drama. Each entry identifies the work in which a character appears and the character's role in the overall work.

_____. *A William Somerset Maugham Encyclopedia*. Westport, Conn.: Greenwood Press, 1997. Alphabetically arranged entries provide information on Maugham's writings, family members, friends, settings, and the historical, cultural, social, and political issues associated with his life and work. Includes bibliography and index.

Caleb Williams

Author: William Godwin (1756-1836)
First published: 1794, as *Things as They Are: Or, The Adventures of Caleb Williams*
Type of work: Novel
Type of plot: Detective and mystery
Time of plot: Eighteenth century
Locale: England

Principal characters:
CALEB WILLIAMS
FERDINANDO FALKLAND, Caleb's employer
COLLINS, Falkland's servant
BARNABAS TYRREL, Falkland's enemy
GINES, Caleb's enemy
EMILY MELVILE, Tyrrel's cousin

The Story:

Caleb Williams is engaged as secretary by Mr. Ferdinando Falkland, the wealthiest and most respected squire in the country. Falkland, although a considerate employer, is subject to fits of distemper that bewilder Caleb. These black moods are so contrary to his employer's usual gentle nature that Caleb soon investigates, asking Collins, a trusted servant of the household, about them and learning from him the story of Falkland's early life.

Studious and romantic in his youth, Falkland lived many years abroad before he returned to England to live on his ancestral estate. One of his neighbors was Barnabas Tyrrel, a man of proud, combative nature. When Falkland returned to his family estate, Tyrrel was the leading gentleman in the neighborhood. As a result of his graceful manners and warm intelligence, Falkland soon began to win the admiration of his neighbors. Tyrrel was jealous and showed his feelings by

speech and actions. Falkland tried to make peace, but the ill-tempered Tyrrel refused his proffered friendship.

Miss Emily Melvile, Tyrrel's cousin, occupied the position of a servant in his household. One night, she was trapped in a burning building, and Falkland saved her. Afterward, Emily could do nothing but praise her benefactor. Her gratitude annoyed her cousin, who planned to take revenge on Emily for her admiration of Falkland. He found one of his tenants, Grimes, a clumsy, ill-bred lout, to consent to marry Emily. When Emily refused to marry a man whom she could never love, Tyrrel confined her to her room. As part of the plot, Grimes helped Emily to escape and then attempted to seduce her. She was rescued from her plight by Falkland, who for the second time proved to be her savior. Further cruelties inflicted on her by Tyrrel finally killed her, and Tyrrel became an object of disgrace in the community.

One evening, Tyrrel attacked Falkland in a public meeting, and Falkland was deeply humiliated. That night, Tyrrel was found dead in the streets. Since the quarrel had been witnessed by so many people just before the murder, Falkland was called before a jury to explain his whereabouts during that fatal night. No one really believed Falkland guilty, but he was hurt by what he considered the disgrace of his being questioned. Although a former tenant was afterward arrested and hanged for the crime, Falkland never recovered his injured pride. He retired to his estate, where he became a moody and disconsolate recluse.

For a long time after learning these details, Caleb ponders the apparent unhappiness of his employer. Attempting to understand Falkland's morose personality, Caleb begins to wonder whether Falkland suffers from the unearned infamy that accompanies suspicion of murder or from a guilty conscience. Determined to solve the mystery, Caleb proceeds to talk to his master in an inquisitive way, to draw him out in matters concerning murder and justice. Caleb also looks for evidence that will prove Falkland guilty or innocent. Finally, the morose man becomes aware of his secretary's intent. Swearing Caleb to secrecy, Falkland confesses to the murder of Tyrrel and threatens Caleb with irreparable harm if he should ever betray his employer.

Falkland's mansion becomes a prison for Caleb, and he resolves to run away no matter what the consequences. When he escapes to an inn, he receives a letter ordering him to return to defend himself against a charge of theft. When Falkland produces some missing jewels and bank notes from Caleb's baggage, Caleb is sent to prison in disgrace. His only chance to prove his innocence is to disclose Falkland's motive, a thing no one will believe. Caleb spends many months in jail, confined in a dreary, filthy dungeon and bound with chains. Thomas, a servant of Falkland and a former neighbor of Caleb's father, visits Caleb in his cell. Perceiving Caleb in his miserable condition, Thomas can only wonder at English law that keeps a man so imprisoned while he waits many months for trial. Compassion forces Thomas to bring Caleb tools with which he can escape. At liberty once more, Caleb finds himself in a hostile world with no resources.

At first, he becomes an associate of thieves, but he leaves the gang after he makes an enemy of a man named Gines. When Caleb goes to London, hoping to hide there, Gines follows him, and soon Caleb is again caught and arrested. Falkland visits him and explains that he knows every move Caleb made since he escaped from prison. Falkland tells Caleb that although he will no longer prosecute him for theft, he will continue to make Caleb's life intolerable. Wherever Caleb goes, Gines follows and exposes Caleb's story to the community. Caleb tries to escape to Holland, but just as he is to land in that free country, Gines appears and stops him.

Caleb returns to England and charges Falkland with murder, asking the magistrate to call Falkland before the court. At first, the magistrate refuses to summon Falkland to reply to the charge, but Caleb insists upon his rights, and Falkland appears. The squire is terrible to behold; his haggard and ghostlike appearance shows that he has not long to live.

Caleb presses his charges in an attempt to save himself from a life of persecution and misery. So well does Caleb describe his miserable state and his desperate situation that the dying man is deeply touched. Demonstrating the kindness of character and the honesty for which Caleb had first admired him, Falkland admits his wrongdoings and clears Caleb's reputation. In a few days the sick man dies. Although remorseful, Caleb is determined to make a fresh start in life.

Critical Evaluation:

William Godwin titled his novel *Things As They Are: Or, The Adventures of Caleb Williams*, but it survives under the name of its hero. It is a novel of divided interests, as it was written to criticize society and to tell an adventure story. All the elements that contribute to Caleb's misery are the result of weaknesses in eighteenth century English laws, which permitted the wealthy landowners to hold power over poorer citizens.

Historians of the novel have always encountered great difficulty in categorizing Godwin's *Caleb Williams*. It has been called a great tragic novel, the first pursuit novel, a crime or mystery novel, a chase-and-capture adventure, a political thesis fiction, a gothic romance, a terror or sensation novel, even a sentimental tale. To some extent, it is all of these—and none of them. The novel has, like most enduring works of art, taken on many shapes and meanings as new readers interpret the narrative in terms of their own personal, cultural, and historical experiences.

Godwin had no doubts about his book's meaning or about the effect he hoped to achieve with it: "I will write a tale that shall constitute an epoch in the mind of the reader, that no one, after he has read it, shall ever be exactly the same man that he was before." Having achieved fame in 1793 with his powerful, influential, and controversial political treatise *An Enquiry Concerning Political Justice*, he sought a form in which to dramatize his ideas. At the most obvious level, then, *Caleb Williams* can be seen as a fictional gloss on Godwin's previous political masterpiece.

Caleb Williams, however, is no simple political tract. Godwin knew that he must first develop a narrative, in his words, "distinguished by a very powerful interest," if he expected readers to absorb and seriously consider his philosophical and social ideas, so he took the most exciting situation he could conceive, creating, as he said, "a series of adventures of flight and pursuit; the fugitive in perpetual apprehension of being overwhelmed with the worst calamities, and the pursuer, by his ingenuity and resources, keeping his victim in a state of the most fearful alarm." Having first decided on the outcome of his adventure, Godwin then worked backward, like a modern mystery story writer, to develop a sequence of events leading up to his climax. The result is a well-constructed narrative in which the three volumes are tightly connected, both structurally and thematically, the action developing logically and directly with ever-mounting tension to a powerful, even tragic, denouement.

In Godwin's words, Ferdinando Falkland has the ability to "alarm and harass his victim with an inextinguishable resolution never to allow him the least interval of peace and security," because of an unjust and fundamentally corrupt society. The worst villain is a legal system that gives too much power to the rich and victimizes the poor, all in the name of justice. Falkland fears Caleb's knowledge, because Falkland has committed the only crime that an aristocrat could commit in eighteenth century England—an injury to a social equal. Had Tyrrel been poor, the issue would never have been raised. Caleb's alleged crime—stealing from his master and accusing the master of conspiracy against him—arouses such extreme repugnance because it challenges the social hierarchy and the assumptions that support it.

The problem, however, is not one of simple, conscious tyranny. The rich and the poor are unaware of the injustice and cruelty that their social institutions foster. They have been conditioned by their environment to accept the system as necessary, proper, and even benevolent. It is not the willful malevolence of a few but society itself that distorts and dissipates the best qualities of men, regardless of their social class, although the poor suffer the most obvious physical oppression. Falkland is not an example of deliberate evil; he is a good man who, because of his social role, has accepted a system of attitudes and moral values that is destructive. His passion to conceal his crime and his persecution of Caleb are the results not of any fear of legal punishment but of his obsessive concern for his aristocratic honor. "Though I be the blackest of villains," he tells Caleb, "I will leave behind me a spotless and illustrious name. There is no crime so malignant, no scene of blood so horrible in which that object cannot engage me."

There are no human villains in this novel; social institutions are Godwin's targets. This explains the novel's strange ending, which seems to reverse all of the book's previous assumptions. Having finally succeeded in turning the law against his tormentor, Caleb realizes, as he faces a broken Falkland, that he, Caleb, is the real enemy. Falkland, for his part, admits his guilt and embraces Caleb; but, to Godwin, neither man is guilty. Both have been caught up in a series of causal circumstances created by their environment and resulting in their inevitable mutual destruction. Only when the environment can be altered to allow people's natural capacities to emerge, undistorted and unfettered by artificial, malevolent environmental conditioning, can such self-destruction be avoided and human potential realized.

Further Reading

Boulton, James T. *The Language of Politics in the Age of Wilkes and Burke*. London: Routledge & Kegan Paul, 1963. Discusses the "inexorable deliberateness" of Godwin's novel, the way he builds up a systematic chain and combination of events. Boulton maintains that Godwin's weakness is a lack of dramatic immediacy; too often Godwin speaks about psychological states rather than dramatizing them.

Carlson, Julie A. *England's First Family of Writers: Mary Wollstonecraft, William Godwin, Mary Shelley*. Baltimore: Johns Hopkins University Press, 2007. Examines Godwin's work within the context of writings by his wife Mary Wollstonecraft and his daughter Mary Wollstonecraft Shelley, demonstrating how their works engage in a "dialogue" with each other.

Clemit, Pamela. *The Godwinian Novel: The Rational Fictions of Godwin, Brockden Brown, Mary Shelley*. New York: Oxford University Press, 1993. Clemit argues that Godwin created a new school of British fiction, which influenced the work of Charles Brockden Brown and Godwin's daughter, Mary Wollstonecraft Shelley. Points out the links between Godwin's techniques of fiction and his radical political philosophy.

Godwin, William. *Things As They Are: Or, The Adventures of Caleb Williams*. Edited by Maurice Hindle. New York: Penguin Books, 1988. Hindle's introduction discusses the novel's origins, the politics and history informing its narrative, and its place in the genre. Includes notes, bibliography, and appendixes.

Graham, Kenneth W. *The Politics of Narrative: Ideology and Social Change in William Godwin's "Caleb Williams."* New York: AMS Press, 1990. Each chapter focuses on one facet of the novel and places the book within the context of the ideological battles of the 1790's. Includes examination of the novel as a radical critique of women's inequality, the law, prisons, and the court system; the book as a detective novel; the work's gothic elements; and Godwin's influence on other writers, including Lord Byron, Percy Bysshe Shelley, and Mary Wollstonecraft Shelley.

Kiely, Robert. *The Romantic Novel in England*. Cambridge, Mass.: Harvard University Press, 1972. Considers how Godwin's philosophy influences his novel and compares him to his contemporaries. Discusses his fascination with fantasy and romance writing.

Miyoshi, Masao. *The Divided Self: A Perspective on the Literature of the Victorians*. New York: New York University Press, 1969. Considers the novel as part of the gothic tradition. Analyzes Caleb's motivations for spying on

Falkland, discusses the differences between Godwin's novel and his great work of political philosophy, *Political Justice*, and addresses differences between the imaginative and discursive process.

Ousby, Ian. *Bloodhounds of Heaven: The Detective in English Fiction from Godwin to Doyle*. Cambridge, Mass.: Harvard University Press, 1976. Discusses the novel as the first work of English fiction to take a sustained interest in detection. Other critics have emphasized how the structure of the novel influenced later detective fiction, but Ousby points out that the main character, Caleb, is equally important because he is an original detective in the English novel.

Call It Sleep

Author: Henry Roth (1906-1995)
First published: 1934
Type of work: Novel
Type of plot: Bildungsroman
Time of plot: 1907-1913
Locale: Lower East Side, New York City

Principal characters:
DAVID SCHEARL, a young Jewish immigrant boy
GENYA, his mother
ALBERT, his father
JOE LUTER, a print shop foreman
BERTHA, Genya's sister and David's aunt
YUSSIE MINK, David's friend
ANNIE MINK, his sister
LEO DUGOVKA, another of David's friends
NATHAN STERNOWITZ, a widower and later Bertha's husband
POLLY and ESTHER, his daughters
RABBI YIDEL PANKOWER, David's teacher

The Story:

In 1907, David Schearl, about two years old, and his mother, Genya, are on a steamer leaving Ellis Island, the last leg of their journey to America. David's father, Albert, came to America earlier, and the family is now to be reunited. Albert displays a coldness, however, that is in marked contrast to the joy pervading other reunions taking place around him. His remarks to his wife and son are contemptuous and accusatory; because he does not want his boy to look like an immigrant, he snatches David's old-country hat off his head and hurls it into the river.

Like the other immigrants, the Schearls are people in an alien culture. Unlike most of the other families, however, there is a deep alienation in the family, particularly between father and son: David is the immigrant in life who must seek his own meanings in maturity.

By the time David is six years old, his attachment to his mother is important not only for the relationship between them but also for the shelter she provides him from his father's icy contempt. Where Genya is placid and beautiful, Albert is aloof, suspicious, gullible, and eaten away by a tragic pride. Albert is at war with the world. His great fear—partly based on an awareness of his own foreignness and partly based on a deeper insecurity—is of being laughed at, cheated, or made to look a fool. David's immature but meticulous consciousness records that Albert's foreman, Luter, flatters Albert only to be with Genya. He also experiences a repugnant sexual encounter with a neighborhood girl and a terrible thrashing by Albert. In the second book, David watches the courting of Aunt Bertha by the laconic Nathan Sternowitz and listens in confused fascination to his mother's account of an earlier love affair in Russia. Through these experiences, David becomes uneasily aware of sexuality, particularly of the disturbing fact that his mother is also a sexual being.

In the Hebrew school, the cheder, David's intellect is awakened by Rabbi Yidel Pankower, a tragicomic figure of classic proportions. David learns rapidly, but one afternoon he is puzzled by a verse from Isaiah in which Isaiah, seeing the Lord seated on a throne, is afraid; then a seraph touches a fiery coal to Isaiah's lips, and he hears God speak. David yearns to ask about that coal but is not given an opportunity to do so. At home, he asks his mother to explain God. He is brighter than day, she tells him, and he has all power.

On the first day of Passover there is no school, and David wanders toward the East River. He stares at the river, meditating on God's brightness. The experience is almost a mystical trance, but the dazzling contemplation is broken by three boys who taunt him. They tell him that he will see magic if he goes to the train tracks and drops a piece of scrap metal in the groove between the tracks. When David does so, there is a sudden blinding light that terrifies him. His child's mind connects the thought of God's power and light with the electric flash.

David sometimes does not get along with the rough boys of the neighborhood. One day, he discovers the roof of the flat as a place of refuge. From there, he sees a boy with blond hair flying a kite. Leo Dugovka, a confident and carefree boy, also owns skates. He is surprised to learn that David does not know anything about the Cross or the Mother and Child. David desperately wants Leo to like him.

The next day, David walks the long distance to Aunt Bertha's candy shop to see if she has any skates he can use. The living quarters behind the store are cramped, dark, and filthy. Bertha tells him to get Esther and Polly out of bed while she watches the store, but she has no skates. David thereupon goes to Leo's flat. There he is attracted to a picture of Jesus and to a rosary. When Leo hears about David's two cousins, he becomes interested in seeing them. The next day, Leo promises to give David the rosary if he will take him to see the girls. Though uncomfortable with the proposal, David agrees. Leo is successful with Esther, but they are caught by Polly, who tattles.

David is terrified at the thought he might be implicated. At cheder in the afternoon, he is nervous when he reads before a visiting rabbi. Bursting into tears, he entangles himself in hysterical lies fabricated out of the secret in his mother's past. He says that his mother is dead and that his father is a Gentile organist in Europe. When the puzzled rabbi goes to David's parents to try to clear up the matter, Nathan angrily

blames David for what happened to Esther. The rabbi learns that David lied, but mention of the organist arouses Albert's suspicion. He accuses his wife of unfaithfulness and believes David to be the child of another man. Genya cannot convince him that he is wrong.

When Bertha arrives, the adults argue violently. David, terrified, runs into the street. Images, recollections, and fears spin through his mind. Finding a steel milk-dipper, he desperately decides to produce God again at the tracks. At first, nothing happens when he inserts the dipper; then, he receives a terrific electric shock that knocks him out. The flash draws a crowd of anxious people, but David is not seriously hurt. Even his father seems somewhat relieved to find that he is all right. David reflects that soon it will be night and he can go to sleep and forget everything. In sleep, all the images of the past—sights, sounds, feelings—become vivid and alive. Life is painful and terrifying, but in sleep he triumphs.

Critical Evaluation:

When Henry Roth's first novel, *Call It Sleep*, appeared in 1934, its critical reception was predominantly positive. The novel sold fairly well, going through first and second editions totaling four thousand copies, a large number for the depths of the Depression. Yet the novel soon fell into obscurity. Then in 1964, the book was republished in hardcover and paperback, and its sales and critical reputation soared. *Call It Sleep* came to be recognized as a masterpiece and one of the great works of American literature. Not until 1994 did Roth publish his second novel, *A Star Shines over Mount Morris Park*, the first volume of a projected series of books to be entitled *Mercy of a Rude Stream*. Roth seems to have conceived this later series as a kind of continuation of *Call It Sleep*. Many critics argue that the long time between Roth's first and second novels resulted in part from his dismay that the public seemed to have forgotten his first book.

After 1964, critics began to praise *Call It Sleep* for being a tightly knit, stylistically excellent piece of literary art. Roth uses imagery to give the novel a kind of organic unity that points inexorably to its ending. Especially important are the images Roth associates with the titles of the four books of the novel, "Cellar," "Picture," "Coal," and "Rail." "Cellar" is associated with David Schearl's fear, initially, of the dark cellar in the tenement where he lives and ultimately of a series of things that include his violent father and sex.

"Picture" points to Genya's picture of cornflowers, which reminds her of her home in Austria. The picture represents her European past, especially her affair with a Christian before she meets Albert. Balancing Genya's picture is Albert's pair of bull's horns, which he associates with the cattle he tended in Eastern Europe and with the accusation that he watched passively while a bull gored his father to death. Significantly, he is bitterly unhappy with every job he has in America until he works as a milkman. The horns also represent his fear that he has been cuckolded and that David is not his biological child.

"Coal" refers to the physical object, the source of heat and power. For David, it represents what he does not have, power, and he associates it with the passage in Isaiah in which an angel touches coal to Isaiah's lips and gives him divine knowledge.

"Rail" is a reference to the third rail, which provides power to streetcars. David is tricked into touching a piece of scrap metal to the third rail, which creates a blinding light that he associates with the power of God. He tries to draw on that power near the end of the novel when he runs from his apartment in fear that his father will kill him. This time, David uses a milk ladle against the third rail, which connects his actions with his mother, who gives him milk, and his father, who delivers milk. Knocked unconscious and near death, he has a vision full of religious and sexual imagery. When the policeman who revives him carries him into his home, his father talks "in a dazed, unsteady voice," and David listens to "him falter and knew him shaken." In fact, David sees that his father, whom Genya has reassured that David is his son, is genuinely concerned about him. This suggestion of a reconciliation has important implications for David's future growth.

Stylistically, *Call It Sleep* is a triumph. Roth often enables his readers to enter David's mind by using a stream-of-consciousness technique reminiscent of James Joyce. Roth also draws on Sigmund Freud's theories about dreams and their relationship to waking life when he combines surrealistic or dreamlike episodes with highly realistic, tangible impressions of life on the Lower East Side of New York between 1907 and 1913.

In *Call It Sleep*, the reader becomes immersed in the sights, smells, and especially sounds of the Lower East Side. When Roth's Jewish characters speak Yiddish, their language is represented by lyrical English. When they speak English, however, Roth shows their strong accents and the difficulty they have making themselves understood. He also reproduces Italian, Irish, and Hungarian accents and the English dialect associated with the streets of New York that David and his young companions speak.

Central to the story is David's growing up. Not only is it remarkable that he survives in an atmosphere of violence, it is a miracle that he manages to grow in spite of all the things that conspire to thwart his growth. It is Roth's magnificent achievement that David's growth is believable. Although the novel gives an extraordinarily good picture of Jewish life in New York City during the first part of the twentieth century, it simultaneously tells a universal story of maturation and reconciliation.

"Critical Evaluation" by Richard Tuerk

Further Reading

Buelens, Gert. "The Multi-Voiced Basis of Henry Roth's Literary Success in *Call It Sleep*." In *Cultural Difference and the Literary Text: Pluralism and the Limits of Authenticity in North American Literatures*, edited by Winfried Siemerling and Katrin Schwenk. Iowa City: University of Iowa Press, 1996. Focuses on the novel's representation of different languages and voices, included in a study of multiculturalism in literature.

Dembo, L. S. *The Monological Jew: A Literary Study*. Madison: University of Wisconsin Press, 1988. Argues that Roth uses an imagist technique of perceiving reality: David senses but never understands life.

Farber, Frances D. "Encounters with an Alien Culture: Thematic Functions of Dialect in *Call It Sleep*." *Yiddish* 7 (1990): 49-56. Analyzes the way Roth masters the "cacophony" of street dialects of immigrants becoming acculturated in early twentieth century New York City and how he uses speech to show "young David's temptations and terrors."

Guttmann, Allen. *The Jewish Writer in America: Assimilation and the Crisis of Identity*. New York: Oxford University Press, 1971. Analyzes David's agony as representative of the experience of first-generation Jews as they take their place in American culture. Recognizes the novel's universality.

Kellman, Steven G. *Redemption: The Life of Henry Roth*. New York: W. W. Norton, 2005. Engaging, readable account of Roth, particularly good in examining the long interim between his novels. According to Kellman, Roth deliberately stopped writing because he did not want to confront his adolescent incest in his autobiographical fiction.

Lyons, Bonnie. *Henry Roth: The Man and His Work*. New York: Cooper Square, 1976. Discusses *Call It Sleep* in the context of Roth's life and shows that it is a unified work of art.

Sherman, Bernard. *The Invention of the Jew: Jewish-American Education Novels, 1916-1964*. New York: Thomas Yoseloff, 1969. Treats the book as primarily a Depression novel but recognizes that central to it is the maturing of a young mind.

Weber, Myles. *Consuming Silences: How We Read Authors Who Don't Publish*. Athens: University of Georgia Press, 2005. Roth figures prominently in this discussion of four American authors who stopped writing for long periods of time. Weber argues that for some writers the decision to defer authorship can be a smart career move.

Wirth-Nesher, Hana, ed. *New Essays on "Call It Sleep."* New York: Cambridge University Press, 1996. Collection of some of the most engaging and useful analyses. Includes an essay by literary critic Leslie Fielder on the "many myths" of Roth and analysis of "language, nostalgic mournfulness, and urban immigrant family romance" in the novel.

The Call of the Wild

Author: Jack London (1876-1916)
First published: 1903
Type of work: Novel
Type of plot: Adventure
Time of plot: 1897
Locale: Alaska

Principal characters:
BUCK, a dog
SPITZ, his enemy
JOHN THORNTON, his friend

The Story:

Buck is the undisputed leader of all the dogs on Judge Miller's estate in California. A crossbreed of St. Bernard and Scottish shepherd, he inherited the size of the first and the intelligence of the latter. Buck cannot know that the lust for gold hit the human beings of the country and that dogs of his breed are much in demand as sled dogs in the frozen North. Consequently, he is not suspicious when a workman on the estate takes him for a walk one night. The man takes Buck to the railroad station, where the dog hears the exchange of money. Then a rope is placed around his neck. When he struggles to get loose, the rope draws so tight that it shuts off his breath, and he loses consciousness.

He recovers in a baggage car. When the train reaches Seattle, Washington, Buck tries to break out of his cage while he is being unloaded. A man in a red shirt hits him with a club until he is senseless. After that, Buck knows that he can never win a fight against a club. He retains that knowledge for future use.

Buck is put in a pen with other dogs of his type. Each day, some of the dogs go away with strange men who come with money. One day, Buck is sold. Two French Canadians buy him and some other dogs and take them on board a ship sailing for Alaska. The men are fair, though harsh, masters, and Buck respects them. Life on the ship is not particularly enjoyable, but it is a paradise compared to what awaits Buck when the ship reaches Alaska. There he finds men and dogs

to be little more than savages, with no law but the law of force. The dogs fight like wolves, and when one is downed, the pack moves in for the kill. Buck watches one of his shipmates being torn to pieces after he loses a fight, and he never forgets the way one dog in particular, Spitz, watches sly-eyed as the loser is slashed to ribbons. Spitz is Buck's enemy from that time on.

Buck and the other dogs are harnessed to sleds on which the two French Canadians carry mail to prospectors in remote regions. It is a new kind of life to Buck but not an unpleasant one. The men treat the dogs well, and Buck is intelligent enough to learn quickly those things that make him a good sled dog. He learns to dig under the snow for a warm place to sleep and to keep the traces clear and thus make pulling easier. When he is hungry, he steals food. The instincts of his ancestors come to life in him as the sled goes farther and farther north. In some vague manner, he senses the great cunning of the wolves who have been his ancestors in the wilderness.

Buck's muscles grow firm and taut and his strength greater than ever. Yet his feet become sore, and he has to have moccasins. Occasionally, one of the dogs dies or is killed in a fight, and one female goes mad. The dogs no longer work as a team, and the two men are on guard constantly to prevent fights. One day Buck sees his chance; he attacks Spitz, the lead dog on the sled, and kills him. After that, Buck refuses to be harnessed until he is given the lead position. He proves his worth by whipping the rebellious dogs into shape, and he becomes the best lead dog that the men have ever seen. The sled makes record runs, and Buck is soon famous.

When they reach Skaguay, the two French Canadians have official orders to turn the team over to a Scottish half-breed. The sled is heavier and the weather bad on the trip back to Dawson. At night, Buck lies by the fire and dreams of his wild ancestors. He seems to hear a faraway call like a wolf's cry. After two days' rest in Dawson, the team starts back over the long trail to Skaguay. The dogs are almost exhausted. Some die and have to be replaced. When the team arrives again in Skaguay, the dogs expect to rest, but three days later, they are sold to two men and a woman who know nothing about dogs or sledding conditions in the northern wilderness. Buck and the other dogs start out again, so weary that it is an effort to move. Again and again, the gallant dogs stumble and fall and lie still until the sting of a whip brings them to their feet for a few miles. At last, even Buck gives up. The sled stops at the cabin of John Thornton, and when the men and the woman are ready to leave, Buck refuses to get up. One of the men beats Buck with a club and would have killed him, but Thornton intervenes, knocking the man down and ordering him and his companions to leave. They leave Buck with Thornton.

As Thornton nurses Buck back to health, a feeling of love and respect grows between them. When Thornton's partners return to the cabin, they understand this affection and do not attempt to use Buck for any of their heavy work. Twice, Buck saves Thornton's life and is glad that he can repay his friend. In Dawson, Buck wins more than a thousand dollars for Thornton on a wager, when the dog breaks loose a sled carrying a thousand-pound load from the ice. With the money won on the wager, Thornton and his partners go on a gold-hunting expedition. They travel far into eastern Alaska, where they find a stream yellow with gold. In his primitive mind, Buck begins to see a hairy man who hunts with a club. He hears the howling of the wolves. Sometimes he wanders off for three or four days at a time, but he always goes back to Thornton. At one time, he makes friends with a wolf that seems like a brother to Buck.

Once Buck chases and kills a great bull moose. On his way back to the camp, he senses that something is wrong. He finds several dogs lying dead along the trail. When he reaches the camp, he sees Indians dancing around the bodies of the dogs and Thornton's two partners. He follows Thornton's trail to the river, where he finds the body of his friend full of arrows. Buck is filled with such a rage that he attacks the band of Indians, killing some and scattering the others.

His last tie with humanity broken, he joins his brothers in the wild wolf packs. The Indians think him a ghost dog, for they seldom see more than his shadow, so quickly does he move. Had the Indians watched carefully, however, they could see him closely. Once each year, Buck returns to the river where Thornton died. There the dog stands on the bank and howls, one long, piercing cry that is the tribute of a savage beast to his human friend.

Critical Evaluation:

Jack London's adventure stories made him one of the most popular writers of his day. In works such as *The Call of the Wild*, *White Fang* (1906), and *Jerry of the Islands* (1917) London makes animals into compelling leading characters, as engaging and sympathetic as any human protagonists. London's animal stories do not anthropomorphize animals simply to play on the heartstrings of his audience. Some of his contemporaries criticized him for writing maudlin beast fables suitable only for children, but these critics misrepresented London's books and misunderstood his literary aims. London resisted the sentimental beast fables of his day, which personified animals to manipulate the reader's emotions. London's stories, instead, reflect more substantial scientific and philosophical issues. His goal is not to make animals appear human, but to emphasize the hereditary connection that humans have with animals.

London was heavily influenced by the works of Charles Darwin (*On the Origin of Species by Means of Natural Selection*, 1859, and *The Descent of Man and Selection in Relation to Sex*, 1871). In *The Call of the Wild*, Buck's experience follows Darwinian principles. He is molded by the changes in his environment, thriving because he possesses the necessary genetic gifts of strength and intelligence to adapt to his mutable circumstances. He is an example of a popular understanding of Darwin's theories: survival of the fittest. Although raised in the domestic ease of Judge Miller's estate, Buck learns quickly what it takes to endure the brutal world of dog-sledding—the "law of club and fang." When Buck first learns to steal food from one of his French Canadian masters, readers are told that this "theft marked Buck as fit to survive in the hostile Northland environment. It marked his adaptability, his capacity to adjust himself to changing conditions." *The Call of the Wild* also reflects London's admiration for the works of nineteenth century German philosopher Friedrich Nietzsche. In the North, might makes right, and Buck proves to be the animal equivalent of Nietzsche's superman, possessing physical and mental abilities superior to those of the other dogs.

Buck, however, does not experience only raw nature.

With John Thornton he returns to a more civilized existence. London's dog stories shuttle between the poles of the domesticated and the wild, of the civilized and the natural. *The Call of the Wild* begins in a domesticated environment and ends in the wild. (Conversely, *White Fang* begins in nature and ends in civilization.) Thornton's compassionate influence helps temper the savage ferocity Buck develops to survive in a crueler world. The wild instinct still remains. Buck's love for Thornton compels Buck to be obedient, loyal, and altruistic, but his wild half keeps calling to him. Buck's romp in the woods with the wolf that seems like a brother to him anticipates his complete surrender to nature when Thornton dies. In the end, Buck obeys the call of the wild.

The Call of the Wild suggests that the reader draw a corollary between the divided nature of Buck and that of every human being. Inspired by Darwin, London believed in the evolutionary continuity between animals and human beings. If human beings evolved from animals, then what exists on a lower level in animals must hold true on a higher level for human beings. London does not give Buck human qualities but suggests that animals and humans share common traits and experiences because of their evolutionary connection. Buck's vision of the short-legged, hairy man sleeping restlessly near the fire symbolizes the primitive beast lurking within all civilized beings. Being an animal, Buck can completely surrender to his primitive half. London seems to celebrate the primordial throughout the book, lauding the "surge of life" Buck experiences when he hunts down prey, the "ecstasy" of tasting living meat and warm blood. For human beings the rift between nature and civilization is much more complicated. People cannot and should not revert completely to their animalistic ancestry. In *White Fang*, for example, human beings dominated by their primitive halves are degenerates and criminals. London deals more directly with this human struggle in *The Sea-Wolf* (1904), suggesting that for humans a balance between the brutish and the civilized is best.

Readers can also see how *The Call of the Wild* reflects London's socialism. No single philosophical system satisfied London, so he accepted bits and pieces of many different, even contradictory ideas. When the ideas of Darwin or Nietzsche fell short in his estimation, those of Karl Marx seemed attractive. From a Marxist perspective, Buck can be interpreted as a representative of the oppressed, subject to the whims of cruel masters and their corrupt use of power. Under these brutal conditions Buck must do what he has to do to survive. He becomes a brute and a thief himself, struggling individually to fend for himself. Thornton's benevolent, more equitable treatment encourages socialistic values in Buck. He cooperates with the other dogs, becoming productive and working for the good of the group. Without Thornton's guidance Buck once again is left with his instinct for survival. Under corrupt power the Darwinian and Nietzschean principles of "survival of the fittest" and "might makes right" apply. Under such conditions, the primitive brute, the evolutionary residue of millions of generations, takes control out of necessity. With a less oppressive system, cooperation can flourish; the civilized half is nurtured and is able to contain the brute. Whether read as a demonstration of Darwinian ideas, an homage to Marxist socialism, or an engaging adventure, *The Call of the Wild* is considered by many critics to be the best of London's dog tales. The story of Buck is the most popular of London's many books.

"Critical Evaluation" by Heidi Kelchner

Further Reading

Auerbach, Jonathan. *Male Call: Becoming Jack London.* Durham, N.C.: Duke University Press, 1996. Auerbach reverses the trend of earlier London studies, emphasizing how London used his writing to reinvent himself. Above all, Auerbach argues, London wanted to become a successful author, and in that respect he shaped his life to suit his art. Chapter 3 focuses on *The Call of the Wild.*

Cassuto, Leonard, and Jeanne Campbell Reesman, eds. *Rereading Jack London.* Stanford, Calif.: Stanford University Press, 1996. Essays on London as "representative man," his commitment to authorship, his portrayal of American imperialism, his handling of power, gender, and ideological discourse, his relationship to social Darwinism, and his status as writer/hero.

Doctorow, E. L. *Jack London, Hemingway, and the Constitution: Selected Essays.* New York: Random House, 1993. Doctorow, a major American novelist, provides a long and thoughtful reflection on London's politics and fiction; Doctorow is sympathetic but also critical of London's example.

Johnson, Claudia D. *Understanding "The Call of the Wild": A Student Casebook to Issues, Sources, and Historical Documents.* Westport, Conn.: Greenwood Press, 2000. A collection of primary documents that provides background information about the novel, including the Yukon Gold Rush, sled dogs, and the wolf as myth, symbol, and issue in the novel. The primary sources include newspaper and journal accounts, advertisements, legislative materials, and firsthand accounts from prospectors who sought gold in Alaska.

Labor, Earle, and Jeanne Campbell Reesman. *Jack London.*

Rev. ed. Boston: Twayne, 1994. Analyzes the elements that went into the stories that London wrote. Recognizes London's use of mood and atmosphere. Discusses *The Call of the Wild* chapter by chapter.

London, Jack. *The Call of the Wild: Complete Text with Introduction, Historical Contexts, Critical Essays*. Edited by Earl J. Wilcox and Elizabeth H. Wilcox. Boston: Houghton Mifflin, 2004. In addition to the text of the novel, this edition includes excerpts from London's letters and some of his other fiction, early reviews of the novel, and critical essays assessing the work.

Perry, John. *Jack London: An American Myth*. Chicago: Nelson-Hall, 1981. Discusses the validity of London's works, including London's misleading depiction of wolves. Describes the accusations of plagiarism that haunted London.

Roden, Donald. *Jack London's "The Call of the Wild" and "White Fang."* New York: Simon & Schuster, 1965. Begins with a brief overview of Jack London's life and follows with an in-depth discussion of *The Call of the Wild*.

Stefoff, Rebecca. *Jack London: An American Original*. New York: Oxford University Press, 2002. Well-researched biography in which Stefoff describes London's life, beliefs, adventures, and writings, placing them within the social context of his times. Includes illustrations, bibliography, and index.

Walcutt, Charles Child. *Jack London*. Minneapolis: University of Minnesota Press, 1966. Gives a well-rounded overview of the life and works of Jack London. Covers the effect of Darwinism and the other philosophies that London studied on his works. Discusses the use of the dog's point of view in the story.

Camel Xiangzi

Author: Lao She (1899-1966)
First published: Luotuo Xiangzi, 1936-1937, serial; 1939, book (English translation, 1945)
Type of work: Novel
Type of plot: Naturalism
Time of plot: 1930's
Locale: Beijing, China

Principal characters:
XIANGZI, a rickshaw boy
HUNIU (TIGRESS), Xiangzi's wife
XIAO FUZI (JOY), a prostitute
LIU SI YE (FOURTH MASTER LIU), Tigress's father
MR. CAO, a professor
ER QIANZI, Joy's father, a drunkard
RUAN MING, a false revolutionary

The Story:

After Xiangzi's parents die, he goes to the city of Beijing, bringing with him a country boy's sturdiness and simplicity. He rents a rickshaw from Fourth Master Liu, who owns the Harmony Rickshaw-renting Yard, to make a living. Unlike the other rickshaw pullers, who are addicted to smoking, drinking, and visiting prostitutes, Xiangzi leads a decent, frugal life. His only dream is to have a rickshaw of his own. After three or four years of struggle and hardship, he saves enough money to buy a rickshaw, believing that the rickshaw will bring him freedom and independence. No sooner does he buy the rickshaw than he is drafted into the army, and his rickshaw is confiscated. Later Xiangzi escapes from the barracks during a night attack, taking with him three army camels. He sells the camels and gets back to Beijing, starting another round of saving money to buy himself a rickshaw. For his theft of the camels, he becomes known as Camel Xiangzi.

Xiangzi deposits the money he made from the sale of the camels at Fourth Master Liu's place and works even harder. One night Fourth Master Liu's daughter Tigress seduces him. Ashamed of himself, he leaves Liu's place to work as a private rickshaw puller for Mr. Cao. Even so, he is repeatedly bothered by Tigress, who pretends to be pregnant. Around the same time, Ruan Ming informs the police of Mr. Cao's socialist ideas as a revenge for Ruan Ming's academic failure under Mr. Cao. During the police raid of Mr. Cao's home, Xiangzi surrenders all his savings, including the camel-sale money he just got back from Tigress, to a secret policeman who is the former lieutenant Xiangzi waited on in the barracks. Tigress then takes advantage of Xiangzi's misfortune, tricking him into marriage. As a result, Fourth Master Liu disowns his daughter for her determination to marry a penniless coolie and looks down upon Xiangzi, believing that he married Tigress for money. Xiangzi and Tigress move to a slum.

Counting on her father's eventual forgiveness, Tigress lives an easy life on her savings. She treats Xiangzi as a plaything and forbids him to work pulling a rickshaw. Xiangzi becomes depressed. He is frustrated when Tigress accuses him of marrying her for her money. When Tigress learns that her father sold the Harmony Yard and went into hiding with all the money, she finally lets Xiangzi buy a rickshaw with the rest of her savings. Xiangzi hopes the rickshaw will enable him to assert his independence. He works furiously day and night. Then he catches a disease after pulling the rickshaw in a summer storm. His health is impaired. Worse still, he is constantly tortured by his wife's nagging. He can only seek solace from Joy, the neighboring woman who is supporting her drunken father and two little brothers on her meager earnings as a prostitute. Tigress is terribly jealous of the friendship between Xiangzi and Joy. The two women become reconciled when Tigress gains some understanding of Joy's plight and her forced prostitution. When Tigress gets pregnant, the prospect of being a father gives Xiangzi a new hope in life. Tigress eats excessively and does not exercise, resulting in her death when she gives birth to an oversized baby. After Tigress's death, Joy wants to marry Xiangzi. For fear of supporting her large family, Xiangzi turns her down but promises to come to her someday.

Xiangzi is forced to sell his rickshaw to pay for the funeral of his wife and son. After the loss of his second rickshaw, he loses faith in the value of hard work. He begins smoking and drinking, even contracting venereal disease from the mistress of a house where he works temporarily. He indulges himself shamelessly in dissipation and grows pugnacious. One day Fourth Master Liu happens to ride by in a rickshaw and asks about Tigress. Xiangzi says she is dead but refuses to tell Liu where she is buried. Depriving the old rich man of his only relative, Xiangzi feels that he won a spiritual victory. He has a sudden urge to recover his old self, "that unfettered, unburdened, decent, ambitious and hard-working Xiangzi." He believes that Mr. Cao and Joy will help him succeed in establishing a decent life. As expected, Mr. Cao offers him a job and even agrees to let Joy come and work. In high spirits Xiangzi goes in search of Joy. After a few days of inquiries, however, Xiangzi discovers that Joy hanged herself after being forced by economics to enter a low-class brothel. His mind goes blank and life suddenly loses its meaning. He does not return to Mr. Cao's family but instead degrades himself by becoming lazier, dirtier, and more shiftless day by day. He delights not only in the small gains of petty thievery but also in the monetary reward he receives for betrayal of a revolu-

tionary. He finally degenerates into an automaton, parading for a pittance in Beijing's endless wedding and funeral processions.

Critical Evaluation:

Camel Xiangzi was first published serially in *Yuzhou feng* (cosmic wind) from September, 1936, to May, 1937. It was first translated into English by Evan King in 1945. The first English version was titled *Rickshaw Boy*, an apt title that reveals the intimate relationship between Xiangzi and the rickshaw. To own a rickshaw of his own seems to Xiangzi to be a moderate and practical ambition. Like a white bird gliding above the dark crows, the dream of owning his own rickshaw keeps Xiangzi's hope alive. Xiangzi's dream also helps him to maintain moral integrity and drives him to seek beauty even in the manner of pulling a rickshaw. Xiangzi does not comprehend that in his unjust society any effort to accomplish an idealistic goal is a joke. The degree of Xiangzi's demoralization corresponds to his repeated deprivation of a rickshaw. Whenever he tries to pull himself up, the dream of keeping a rickshaw fades. The death of his dream reduces Xiangzi to a living dead man. Lao She conveys the importance of holding on to one's dream, even if it is delusional.

The title of the novel, *Camel Xiangzi*, conveys another important theme: the degradation of an individual. The theft of the camels marks Xiangzi's first spiritual lapse. Xiangzi has justification for his theft of the three army camels in the confiscation of his rickshaw, but his adultery with Tigress destroys his self-respect and leads to his subsequent moral downfall. According to the tenets of naturalism, and this novel may be considered naturalistic, Xiangzi's downfall is not his individual responsibility but that of the society. Lao She, for example, makes it a point in the novel to criticize individualism. The grandfather of Little Ma compares an individual to a helpless grasshopper caught and tied by a child and believes that only swarms of grasshoppers can defeat the victimizing hand. Lao She ends the novel by denouncing the degenerated Xiangzi as "a lost soul at the end of the road to individualism." Although *Camel Xiangzi* is the first novel to reveal Lao She's inclination toward socialism, his socialism should be called Confucian socialism. Mr. Cao, a mild socialist who provides a moral oasis in the society's desert of evil, has Confucian aesthetic taste and individual integrity. He upholds Lao She's ideal. The novel negates selfish individualism; Xiangzi's tragedy is also caused by his abandonment of positive individualism, or personal responsibility. He is defeated by relying on Mr. Cao and on Joy for his salvation.

Tigress and Joy are two unforgettable female characters.

They represent two traditional types in literature: the vicious scourge and the nursing angel. Tigress, ugly, seductive, and vampirish, threatens Xiangzi's independence, whereas Joy, pure and innocent although forced to be a prostitute, nurtures his spiritual and bodily wounds. Lao She's favor for Joy's meek sacrifice and loathing of Tigress's aggressiveness are obvious. Joy represents the traditional type of woman whose identity equals self-annihilation. Tigress, at least, pursues her own happiness and struggles for status and economic independence among men. Lao She's fiction very often reveals his phobia of assertive women as well as of young revolutionaries because of their self-interested motives. It was not surprising that he committed suicide at the beginning of the Cultural Revolution in 1966 after a humiliating confrontation with the Red Guards.

Camel Xiangzi is Lao She's masterpiece, praised by the eminent critic C. T. Hsia as "the finest modern Chinese novel before the second Sino-Japanese War." The first piece of realistic modern fiction introduced to the West from China, as *Rickshaw*, King's translation, it was an instant best seller. People all over the world enjoy *Camel Xiangzi*; Xiangzi's tragic fate speaks to everyone, and the rickshaw world is a microcosm of human society. *Camel Xiangzi* also demonstrates Lao She's sophisticated humor and mastery of the Beijing dialect. Although Lao She was influenced by English and American literature, his *Camel Xiangzi* is uniquely Chinese.

Qingyun Wu

Further Reading

Becker, Jasper. "The Strange Death of Lao She." In *City of Heavenly Tranquility: Beijing in the History of China.* New York: Oxford University Press, 2008. Written to coincide with the Olympic Games held in Beijing in 2008, Becker's book recounts the city's history and how this history was destroyed by China's rapid modernization and economic growth. Includes a chapter about the humiliation that led to Lao She's death during the Cultural Revolution.

Birch, Cyril. "Lao She: The Humorist in His Humor." *China Quarterly* 8 (1961): 51-55. An insightful discussion of Lao She's humor and Chaplinesque characterization.

Hsia, C. T. *A History of Modern Chinese Fiction.* 3d ed. Bloomington: Indiana University Press, 1999. Contains a survey of Lao She and his fiction. Lucid and comprehensive; an excellent introduction to a serious study of *Camel Xiangzi.*

Kao, George, ed. *Two Writers and the Cultural Revolution: Lao She and Chen Jo-hsi.* Hong Kong: Chinese University Press, 1980. Contains five pieces translated from Lao She's fiction as well as several critical essays. Sheds light on Lao She's life and literary career in England and America. Examines the cause of Lao She's suicide in 1966. Includes a brief summary of the Western reception of *Camel Xiangzi.*

Lau, Joseph. "Naturalism in Modern Chinese Fiction." *Literature East and West* 2 (1970): 148-160. Discusses the naturalist dimension of *Camel Xiangzi*, attributing Xiangzi's downfall to his social environment.

McGreal, Ian P., ed. "The Fictional Works of Lao She." In *Great Literature of the Eastern World: The Major Works of Prose, Poetry, and Drama from China, India, Japan, Korea and the Middle East.* New York: HarperCollins, 1996. Discusses Lao She's life and the major themes of his works. Provides a critical evaluation of his writings and bibliographies of his works in English translation and of secondary sources about him.

Towery, Britt. *Lao She, China's Master Storyteller.* Waco, Tex.: Tao Foundation, 1999. An introduction to Lao She's life and writings, designed for the general reader. Places his life and works within their historical and cultural context.

Vohra, Ranbir. *Lao She and the Chinese Revolution.* Cambridge, Mass.: East Asian Research Center, Harvard University, 1974. A chronological study of Lao She's life and works, with bibliography, notes, and index. Discusses Lao She's childhood and political development in the 1920's and his artistic maturity and theme of alienation in the 1930's. Analyzes Lao She's humor and treatment of women characters.

Wang, David Der-wei. *Fictional Realism in Twentieth-Century China: Mao Dun, Lao She, She Congwen.* New York: Columbia University Press, 1992. The fourth chapter is devoted to the study of Lao She's fiction. Deals with the formal structure of *Camel Xiangzi*, focusing on the melodramatic and farcical aspects of the story. A good study of Lao She.

Camille

Author: Alexandre Dumas, *fils* (1824-1895)
First produced: La Dame aux camélias, 1852; first
published, 1852 (English translation, 1856)
Type of work: Drama
Type of plot: Sentimental
Time of plot: Nineteenth century
Locale: France

Principal characters:
MARGUERITE "CAMILLE" GAUTIER, a woman of Paris
NANINE, her maid
COUNT DE VARVILLE, who desires Camille
ARMAND DUVAL, who loves her
M. DUVAL, Armand's father
MADAME PRUDENCE, Camille's friend

The Story:

Marguerite Gautier is a courtesan in the city of Paris. The symbol of her character is the camellia, pale and cold. She was once a needleworker who, while taking a rest cure in Bagneres, was befriended by a wealthy duke whose daughter she resembled. After the death of his daughter, the duke takes Marguerite back to Paris and introduces her into society. Somehow the story of Marguerite's past life is rumored on the boulevards, and society frowns upon her. She is respected only by a few friends who know that she longs for a true love and wishes to leave the frivolous life of Paris. She is heavily in debt for her losses at cards and has no money of her own to pay her creditors.

The Count de Varville, her latest admirer, offers to pay all of her debts if she will become his mistress. Before she gives her consent, however, she meets Armand Duval. Armand has nothing to offer her but his love. He is presented to Marguerite by her milliner, Madame Prudence, who pretends to be her friend but who is loyal to her only because Marguerite is generous with her money.

At first Marguerite scorns Armand's love, for although she longs for a simple life she thinks she could never actually live in poverty. Armand is persistent, and at last Marguerite loves him and tells him she will forsake her present friends and go away with him. She has a racking cough. Armand wants Marguerite to leave Paris and go to a quiet spot where she can rest and have fresh air.

Marguerite, Armand, and Nanine, her maid, move to a cottage in the country. For many weeks Armand is suspicious of Marguerite and fears she misses her former companions. Convinced at last of her true love, Armand loses his uneasiness and they are happy together. The garden flowers he grows replace the camellias she always wore in Paris.

Their happiness is brief. Armand's father calls on Marguerite and begs her to renounce his son. He knows her past reputation, and he believes that his son placed himself and his family in a disgraceful position. Marguerite will not listen to him, for she knows that Armand loves her and will not be

happy without her. Then Armand's father tells her that his daughter is betrothed to a man who threatens to break the engagement if Armand and Marguerite insist on remaining together. Moved by sympathy for the young girl, Marguerite promises Armand's father that she will send his son away. She knows that he will never leave her unless she betrays him, and she plans to tell him that she no longer loves him and is going to return to her former life. Armand's father knows then that she truly loves his son, and he promises that after her death, which she believes will be soon, he will tell Armand she renounced him only for the sake of his family.

Marguerite, knowing that she can never tell Armand the lie directly, writes a note declaring her dislike for the simple life he provided for her and her intention to return to de Varville in Paris. When Armand reads the letter, he swoons in his father's arms.

He leaves the cottage and then Paris and does not return for many weeks. Meanwhile Marguerite resumes her old life and spends all her time at the opera or playing cards with her former associates, always wearing a camellia in public. Count de Varville is her constant companion, but her heart is still with Armand. Her cough is much worse. Knowing she will soon die, she longs to see Armand once more.

When Marguerite and Armand meet at last, Armand insults her honor and that of the Count de Varville. He throws gold pieces on Marguerite, asserting they are the bait to catch and hold her kind, and he announces to the company present that the Count de Varville is a man of gold but not of honor. Challenged by de Varville, Armand wounds the count in a duel and leaves Paris. He returns only after his father, realizing the sacrifice Marguerite made, writes, telling him the true story of Marguerite's deception, and explaining that she left him only for the sake of his sister's honor and happiness.

By the time Armand reaches Paris, Marguerite is dying. Only Nanine and a few faithful friends remain with her. Madame Prudence remains because Marguerite, even in her poverty, shares what she has. Marguerite and Nanine move to a small and shabby flat, and there Armand finds them. He arrives to find Marguerite on her deathbed but wearing again the simple flowers he had once given her. He throws himself down beside her, declaring his undying love and begging for her forgiveness. The once beautiful Marguerite, now as wasted as the flowers she wears on her breast, dies in the arms of her true love.

Critical Evaluation:

Camille established the artistic reputation of Alexandre Dumas, *fils*. Although Dumas initially could not find a theater to produce *Camille* because of its scandalous subject, the play caused a sensation as soon as it was performed in Paris. It went on to become one of the most popular plays of the nineteenth century in Europe and in America; nothing Dumas later wrote ever matched its phenomenal success.

There are many reasons for the play's great appeal. First, the play presents an intimate and realistic view of a segment of French society that has long fascinated respectable folk— the demimonde of high-class courtesans and their many wealthy protectors. Audiences may take vicarious pleasure in a world of private boxes at the opera, fancy-dress balls, high-stakes gambling, late-night suppers of oysters and champagne, fabulous clothes, and dazzling jewelry. The younger Dumas knew this world quite well; he and his father amused themselves at least on its fringes. Moreover, he had the keen eye of a born social anthropologist, and he focused on the details of this life—its pleasures, costs, and self-deceptions— with rapt attention.

At the same time, *Camille*, unlike Dumas's later thesis plays, brims with romantic sentiments not to say sentimentality. Marguerite earns her livelihood as a courtesan and leads a dissipated life that is literally killing her, but she finds redemption through the power of true love. Vice and redemption appear in their most audience-pleasing forms. Marguerite renounces her glamorous life in Paris. Without a backward glance, she sells off her fine possessions to pay her debts and begin a new life with Armand. When she realizes that all her efforts to reform will not redeem her in the eyes of the world and that her reputation will harm Armand and his family, she sacrifices the love of her life, although it means making him hate her. She knows that she will soon die of consumption; she gives up those last few months of happiness and peace for his sake. The sharp contrast between the inspiring generosity of her actions and the world's harsh view of fallen women places Marguerite safely in romanticism's pantheon of the beautiful and the doomed—redeemed sinners who die as they are saved. The poignant irony of her situation appeals irresistibly to the romantically inclined.

Camille derives much of its power from the intensity of Dumas's deep emotional commitment to the subject. In 1844, at the age of twenty, he had met and fallen in love with Marie Duplessis, who became the model for Marguerite Gautier in both his play and his earlier novel of the same name (1848). Like Armand, he lured his beautiful demimondaine to simpler pleasures for a time, but she soon returned to her old life and died of tuberculosis not long after. In real life, Marie had nothing to do with Dumas's father (who was anything but a provincial prude), nor did she renounce her lover for the sake of his family, nor was he present at her deathbed. The idealized version of their affair that appears in his novel proved popular with French readers, although not nearly so popular as the dramatization a few years later.

A remarkably skillful piece of theatrical writing, especially for a first play, *Camille* resembles and differs from Dumas's later works. Even in this tender romantic drama, audiences can discern traces of the preachiness that would soon dominate his work in Marguerite's frustration with a society that countenanced a sexual double standard and refused to forgive women who had strayed from the path of middle-class virtue. In part, that theme reflects Dumas's life, for he remained devoted to his mother all his life, despite the prevailing condemnation of women who bore children out of wedlock as she had done. In his later plays, the moralism, while well intentioned, becomes overt and fairly predictable. In *Camille*, however, the message comes through much more subtly, as a result of the audience's sympathetic emotional response to the characters. His most affecting play was written from the heart, not the head.

The image of Camille has permeated Western culture as an emblem of redemptive, self-sacrificing, romantic love. At least six cinematic versions of the play exist, and, up through the 1930's, the play itself was performed frequently. After that, however, it almost disappeared from the stage, except in the form of Giuseppe Verdi's popular opera *La traviata* (1853). In part, this reflects the more internalized styles of acting that developed in the twentieth century, such as the realistic psychological approach of Konstantin Stanislavski. The visible tears, audible sobs, full-body shudders, and racking coughs popular with earlier audiences seem overdone today. Melodramatic climaxes, as when Armand throws his gambling winnings in Marguerite's face, now probably would produce laughter rather than a horrified gasp. Such extravagant gestures may work well in an opera house but seem out of scale with more modern theatrical expectations.

In a sense, *Camille* appears destined to become, at best, a museum piece. Yet Dumas's urgent passion shines through the old-fashioned dramatic structure, probably because of the total conviction with which he portrays the young lovers. Novelist Henry James called it "an astonishing piece of work" that evokes the extreme joys and sorrows of the springtime of life. As he put it, *Camille* abounds in "fresh perversity, fresh credulity, fresh passion, fresh pain." While the literary artifact may fade because of being too closely tied to the period of its creation, the story, the characters, and, above all, the passionate emotions remain vivid and powerful. Unlike its heroine, the play, in this sense, will surely survive.

"Critical Evaluation" by Susan Wladaver-Morgan

Further Reading

Auchincloss, Louis. "Dumas 'fils.'" *New Criterion*, November, 1996. Discusses how Dumas was a theatrical celebrity in his time, living a life that was very much different than the morality about which he preached.

Chandler, Frank Wadleigh. *The Contemporary Drama of France*. Boston: Little, Brown, 1979. Sees Dumas as an important precursor of early twentieth century French drama and insists that Dumas saw himself primarily as a realist.

Matthews, J. Brander. *French Dramatists of the Nineteenth Century*. 3d enlarged ed. New York: B. Blom, 1968. Presents Dumas in the context of his contemporaries; describes him as not part of any tradition but his own. Sees *Camille*'s treatment of a scandalous subject as neither poetic nor unpleasantly realistic. Instead, considers *Camille* to be merely vulgar melodrama, fit only for the opera house.

Maurois, André. *The Titans: A Three-Generation Biography of the Dumas*. Translated by Gerard Hopkins. New York: Harper, 1971. Lively literary biography of *Camille*'s playwright, his father, and his grandfather. Gives the flavor of their lives and times. Abundant use of personal letters, illustrations, and notes. Includes bibliography.

Schwarz, H. Stanley. *Alexandre Dumas, fils, Dramatist*. New York: B. Blom, 1971. Focuses on Dumas's place in nineteenth century French literature, comparing his work with that of Eugène Scribe and Honoré de Balzac. Provides descriptions of the plays' productions and detailed analysis of Dumas's ideas on social problems.

Cancer Ward

Author: Aleksandr Solzhenitsyn (1918-2008)
First published: Rakovy korpus, 1968 (English translation, 1968)
Type of work: Novel
Type of plot: Social realism
Time of plot: 1955-1956
Locale: An unnamed city based on Tashkent in Kazakhstan, Soviet Union

Principal characters:
OLEG FILIMONOVICH KOSTOGLOTOV, a political exile with stomach cancer
PAVEL NIKOLAYEVICH RUSANOV, a bureaucrat with a tumor on his neck
LYUDMILA AFANASYEVNA DONTSOVA, the head of the radiology department
VERA KORNILYEVNA GANGART, a radiotherapist who takes a special interest in Kostoglotov
VADIM ZATSYRKO, a geology scholar with cancer in his leg
ZOYA, a young nurse who is attracted to Kostoglotov
DYOMKA, a teenage cancer patient
ASYA, a teenage athlete and cancer patient

The Story:

In February, 1955, Pavel Nikolayevich Rusanov is admitted into the cancer ward of a Soviet hospital. His wife, upon examining conditions in the hospital, immediately tries to bribe one of the nurses to offer him superior care. Rusanov is a Communist Party official in charge of labor relations—a euphemism for being a government informer—and used to having privileges. He chooses this hospital rather than one in Moscow because his doctor, Lyudmila Afanasyevna Dontsova, insists that he receive treatment as quickly as possible for the large tumor on his neck. Dontsova, fifty years old and one of the older doctors, is the head of the radiology department at the hospital.

Rusanov quickly sizes up the other eight patients in the ominously named ward no. 13 and decides that they are his inferiors. He takes a particular dislike to Oleg Filimonovich Kostoglotov, a former labor camp inmate whom he nicknames Ogloyed, or "lout," even though the man appears to be an avid reader. Dyomka, a teenage student with cancer in his leg, also reveals that he enjoys reading, now that he has the time to do so. Kostoglotov tells him that education does not necessarily make a person smarter, but Dyomka disagrees.

Kostoglotov asks Zoya, an attractive young nurse, whether he might borrow one of her medical books. His doctors never told him what is wrong with him, and he wants to know. He was near death when he arrived at the hospital less than two weeks earlier, and six months prior to that, a doctor told him that he had less than three weeks to live. Once he discovers the type of cancer he has, he asks Dontsova whether he might get a year of peace rather than undergoing the radiation treatments that will make him sick and not necessarily cure him. Dontsova becomes attached to him, in part because she is writing a professional thesis on cancers similar to his; the hospital has too many difficult cases to allow her to take a leave to finish the thesis. She recognizes the danger of radiation treatment and sympathizes with Kostoglotov.

Dyomka meets Asya, a beautiful girl, in a recreation area shared by male and female patients. She is an athlete, and she tells Dyomka that she is in the hospital for a checkup. In her opinion, she says, it would be better for him to be dead than to have his leg amputated. Dyomka receives contrary advice from Vadim Zatsyrko, another patient. Zatsyrko studies intensely in the ward and wants to go back to his research on a geological theory about radiation. He knows that he has less than a year to live, but he wants to leave behind his method of finding ore deposits.

Rusanov learns from the newspaper that the entire Supreme Court of the Union was replaced, and he has a nightmare that the people he denounced were being called to the new Supreme Court. His wife earlier revealed that amnesty was granted to Rodichev, a former neighbor whom Rusanov and his wife denounced, partly to get a larger living space.

Kostoglotov becomes friends with Vera Kornilyevna Gangart, a radiotherapist who is about his age. He is taking a diluted poison made from a mushroom that grows on birch trees, a folk cure for his cancer. She persuades him to pour out the poison. Kostoglotov finds Gangart attractive, but he also pursues Zoya. He persuaded Zoya to kiss him, and she tells him that he is getting hormone therapy that will eventually render him impotent. She briefly withholds the hormone treatments. When he stops pursuing her, she becomes more distant.

Dontsova begins having pains in her stomach. Like many of the other medical personnel, she was exposed to more X rays than is safe; the doctors choose to operate the X-ray machines according to patients' needs rather than according to recommendations for their own exposure. She later visits Dormidont Tikhonovich Oreshchenkov, an older doctor who is allowed to have a private practice as a reward for saving the son of a local politician. She asks him to examine her, and they discuss the merits of a private system of medicine. Later, because the doctors at the cancer ward are uncertain of her diagnosis, they send her to Moscow. Were she a regular patient, they would cut her open to examine her, because that is less expensive and more expedient.

Asya comes to visit Dyomka, who decides to have his leg amputated. She looks like the other patients, disheveled and in an old dressing gown. She reveals that she has breast cancer and asks him to kiss the breast that will be removed; she wonders if anyone will ever like her, once it is gone.

Rusanov and Kostoglotov are discharged. Because his neck tumor shrinks, Rusanov believes that he is cured, but the doctors expect new tumors to grow and are not sure whether he will live a year. Gangart offers to let Kostoglotov stay briefly at her apartment; as a political exile, he is not allowed to stay in a hotel. Unless someone takes him in, he will have to sleep at the railway station. Zoya also invites him to stay with her. He travels around the city, trying various things that he did not experience before. He decides not to see Zoya again and goes to Gangart's apartment, but she is not home. Rather than wait for her or return later, he goes to the railroad station and writes letters to Dyomka, Zoya, and Gangart.

Critical Evaluation:

Like *Odin den' Ivana Denisovicha* (1962; novella; *One Day in the Life of Ivan Denisovich*, 1963), *V kruge pervom* (1968; *The First Circle*, 1968), and other works by Aleksandr Solzhenitsyn, *Cancer Ward* has a close connection to the author's life. Like Kostoglotov, he was diagnosed with cancer and had to find his own way to a hospital. Like Kostoglotov, he took a folk cure that may have kept him alive until he reached the hospital. Kostoglotov is most clearly the author's mouthpiece, although the other patients also express his views. Rusanov and a few minor characters present contradictory views and show, through citing examples, the flaws of the Soviet system.

On the surface, *Cancer Ward* is an examination of the patients, and to a lesser degree the doctors, in a cancer treatment ward of a Soviet hospital. The novel is far more about the characters than about the setting; the experience of cancer forces them to come to terms with their beliefs. The novel could be analyzed as a political allegory, but it is not apparent that Solzhenitsyn meant it to be read as such. Politics figures in the novel primarily because it was so much a part of Soviet life at the time, not because it is an overtly political novel.

Rusanov, a party bureaucrat introduced in the opening sections, sets the scene. The disparaging view of the hospital and of the other patients, coming from an obviously officious and snobbish man, induces the reader to sympathize with the other patients and defend the hospital.

Rusanov later fades into the background. When he is mentioned, it is to show his metamorphosis. Particularly telling is the section in which the technologist and supply agent Maxim Petrovich Chaly joins the ward. Rusanov becomes friends with Chaly, an operator in the black market who brings in numerous luxury food items, even though this is contrary to party principles; through Chaly, he comes to see the value of letting people act in their own best interests. He is still chagrined, however, when his son, acting as a government investigator, fails to charge a truck driver for losing a case of macaroni from his truck. The truck broke down in a snowstorm, and the man left it for his own safety; when he returned, the macaroni was gone. Rusanov believes that the man should have risked death to guard his cargo and that he should be punished for not having done so.

The political exile Kostoglotov is the novel's primary character. One of the patients reads an essay on the subject of what it means to be a human being, which starts a general discussion. Kostoglotov illustrates various aspects of that discussion in his own life. He clings to the hope offered by the folk cure from the birch tree mushroom, even though the cure is unproven and potentially dangerous. He struggles literally with the meaning of being a man; the hormone treatment recommended for him will render him impotent, and he desires, for a while, a sexual relationship with Zoya. He also discusses with Dr. Gangart the relative merits of living a few more months in peace against the option of undergoing treatment that will make him weaker and sicker, with only a hope of prolonging his life.

The setting of *Cancer Ward* is important. Facing death, the characters are free to rebel. Few of them, perhaps only Kostoglotov, would dare to express their opinions in front of Rusanov in any other setting. Although discussions focus on the meaning of life, they also touch on political principles. With the exception of Rusanov, the patients agree that personal choice is important; the question becomes how people should choose to live. Characters offer different interpretations of what gives meaning to life. Many give materialistic answers: One mentions his homeland, and another suggests

that creative work makes a worthwhile life. Only Dyomka mentions love.

Political subtexts do enter the story. The doctors argue that they have the right to prescribe treatment that potentially will save lives, even though the patient may prefer to die a peaceful death. Although this argument is a statement of medical principles, it also touches on political themes in the era of de-Stalinization. Rusanov reflects on the meaning of de-Stalinization in his life, wondering what the changes will mean for him as a denouncer of many people who may now be freed. His concern is narrow, but his view offers one of many interesting perspectives on a period of social upheaval.

A. J. Sobczak

Further Reading

Allaback, Steven. *Alexander Solzhenitsyn.* New York: Taplinger, 1978. The chapter on *Cancer Ward* focuses on various characters' journeys toward self-discovery and the degree to which they represent Soviet society. Offers brief comparisons with other works by the author.

Bloom, Harold, ed. *Aleksandr Solzhenitsyn.* Philadelphia: Chelsea House, 2001. A collection of critical essays, including comparisons of Solzhenitsyn's work with that of Leo Tolstoy and of Boris Pasternak, an analysis of the representation of detention in the works of Solzhenitsyn and Fyodor Dostoevski, and a discussion of Solzhenitsyn's experiences as a creative artist in a totalitarian state.

Burg, David, and George Feifer. *Solzhenitsyn.* Briarcliff Manor, N.Y.: Stein & Day, 1972. There are references to *Cancer Ward* throughout this biographical volume. Includes an index, a bibliography, and a brief chronology of the author's life.

Ericson, Edward E., Jr. *Solzhenitsyn and the Modern World.* Washington, D.C.: Regnery Gateway, 1993. Examines Solzhenitsyn in light of the collapse of Communism in Russia. Answers some of the common criticisms that are leveled at his writing.

Ericson, Edward E., and Alexis Klimoff. *The Soul and Barbed Wire: An Introduction to Solzhenitsyn.* Wilmington, Del.: ISI Books, 2008. Two major Solzhenitsyn scholars provide a detailed biography of the writer and analyses of his major fiction. Includes a chapter on *Cancer Ward*.

Kodjak, Andrej. *Alexander Solzhenitsyn.* Boston: Twayne, 1978. Several chapters describe the author's major works. The chapter on *Cancer Ward* highlights the use of dialogue to present various philosophies.

Mahoney, Daniel J. *Aleksandr Solzhenitsyn: The Ascent from*

Ideology. Lanham, Md.: Rowman & Littlefield, 2001. Focuses on Solzhenitsyn's political philosophy and its impact on twentieth century thinking. Analyzes Solzhenitsyn's writings to demonstrate how they represent the political condition of modern man.

Rothberg, Abraham. *Aleksandr Solzhenitsyn: The Major Novels.* Ithaca, N.Y.: Cornell University Press, 1971. Discusses *Cancer Ward*'s use of cancer as a metaphor for the problems of Soviet society and institutions. Describes major characters and the plot lines involving them and provides an overview of the novel's themes.

Scammell, Michael. *Solzhenitsyn: A Biography.* New York: W. W. Norton, 1984. An impressive text of more than a thousand pages, including notes and an extensive index. The chapter entitled "Cancer Ward" compares Solzhenitsyn's own hospitalization for cancer with that of Kostoglotov.

Thomas, D. M. *Alexander Solzhenitsyn: A Century in His Life.* New York: St. Martin's Press, 1998. A personal portrait of Solzhenitsyn, providing insights into his struggle with the Soviet authorities and his relationship with the two women who provided strong support for his efforts to expose the evils of the Communist regime. An imaginative, well-documented, and at times combative biography, which includes a discussion of Solzhenitsyn's return to Russia in 1994.

Candida

A Mystery

Author: George Bernard Shaw (1856-1950)
First produced: 1897; first published, 1898
Type of work: Drama
Type of plot: Comedy
Time of plot: 1894
Locale: London

Principal characters:
THE REVEREND JAMES MORELL, a Christian Socialist clergyman
CANDIDA MORELL, his intelligent, vivacious wife
EUGENE MARCHBANKS, a poet in love with Candida
MR. BURGESS, Candida's father
THE REVEREND ALEXANDER MILL, Morell's idealistic, admiring young curate
PROSERPINE "PROSSY" GARNETT, Morell's secretary

The Story:

Act 1. In his London home, the Reverend James Morell, a popular speaker for Christian Socialist causes, is arranging lecture dates with his secretary, Prossy, who is secretly in love with him. His curate, the Reverend Alexander Mill, enters and announces that Morell's father-in-law, Mr. Burgess, is coming to see him. While Morell briefly leaves the room, Mill and Prossy argue about Mill's tendency to idealize Morell and his wife, Candida. When Burgess enters, Mill leaves. Burgess has not seen Morell, whom he regards as a fool, for three years. Morell despises Burgess for being interested only in money and for paying low wages to his help. Morell was instrumental in getting the county council to turn down Burgess's bid for a construction contract. Burgess says that he changed his ways and now pays higher wages, but Morell suspects that Burgess only wants to bid on other contracts. Candida returns from a vacation with her children, accompanied by Eugene Marchbanks; Burgess, impressed to discover that he is the nephew of a peer, leaves, promising to return that afternoon. Candida, too, goes out, and Morell invites Marchbanks to stay for lunch. Marchbanks announces that it is incredible that Morell should think his marriage to Candida a happy one; he himself loves Candida, and he dares Morell to tell Candida what he said. Morell begins to get angry when Marchbanks asserts that Candida is too fine a spirit for a life with Morell. Saying that he will not tell Candida of their talk, Morell instructs the young man to leave. Candida returns and invites Marchbanks to stay for lunch.

Act 2. Later that same afternoon, Prossy berates Marchbanks for fiddling with her typewriter. Marchbanks talks poetically of love until Prossy, who is at first exasperated, admits that she, too, is in love. Burgess enters and asserts that Morell is mad. When Morell comes in with the news that Candida is cleaning the house and the lamps, Marchbanks is horrified to think that his idealized woman is getting her hands dirty doing mundane chores. This amuses Candida, who takes Marchbanks out to peel onions. Morell leaves to answer a telegram brought to him by Prossy, who tells Burgess that Marchbanks is mad. When Morell returns, Burgess complains that Prossy insulted him and goes out; that upsets Prossy, who also rushes out. Candida returns and begins to baby Morell. She tells him of "Prossy's complaint," and that women are in love with him and not with his preaching and ideas. Saying that Morell is spoiled with love and worship, she claims that Marchbanks is the one who needs love. Marchbanks, she says, is always right because he understands Morell and Prossy and her. She ends by telling Morell to trust in her love for him. Mill comes in with the news that the Guild of St. Matthew is very upset that Morell canceled his lecture. Candida says that they should all go to hear Morell, but her husband, resolved to put matters to the test, decides that he will give the lecture but that Candida and Marchbanks should stay at home together.

Act 3. Later that evening, when Candida and Marchbanks are alone by the fire, Marchbanks reads poetry to her until Candida tells Marchbanks she would rather talk. Marchbanks sits on the floor with his head against her knees. Candida wants him to speak of his real feelings and not to indulge in attitudes, but Marchbanks only repeats Candida's name over and over. She asks him if he is happy and if he wants anything more. Marchbanks replies that he is happy. When Morell enters and Candida leaves to talk to the maid, Morell and Marchbanks argue about their differing views of Candida; Marchbanks says that he loves Candida so much that he wants nothing more than the happiness of being in love. Then he becomes very excited and begs Morell to send for Candida so that she can choose between them. Candida comes back into the room, followed by Mill, Prossy, and Burgess, who return from a supper after the lecture. All are full of praise for Morell. Prossy drinks a bit too much champagne, and Morell tells Mill to see her home; Burgess, satisfied with having made contact for business purposes with a member of the County Council Works Committee, also leaves. When Morell tells Candida that Marchbanks is in love with her, Candida scolds them both. Morell finally says that Candida has to choose between them. He offers strength, honesty, ability, and industry. Marchbanks offers his weakness and desolation. When Candida says that she chooses the weaker of the two, Marchbanks immediately realizes that she means Morell. Candida explains that Morell

was spoiled from birth and needs support, whereas Marchbanks is a rebel and really self-sufficient. Candida kisses Marchbanks on the forehead and he leaves. Morell and Candida embrace.

"The Story" by Gordon N. Bergquist

Critical Evaluation:

Some of George Bernard Shaw's critics bring the twofold charge against him that his characters are too academic and lifeless, and that his plays are merely tracts for expressing Shaw's ideas on love, war, property, morals, and revolution. This charge is not, however, often leveled at *Candida*. Generally the harshest critics concede that this play is, aside from a few comments on socialism and corruption in government, free from really revolutionary ideas. In fact, in *Candida*, Shaw is saluting that old, established institution, marriage. Of course, as he salutes, he does wink at the audience.

Candida belongs to the group of his *Plays: Pleasant and Unpleasant* published in 1898. It was given its first public London production in 1904, after a private presentation in 1897, and went on to become one of the most popular plays in the Shaw repertory. It was an early favorite with Shaw himself, and he held on to it for some time before allowing its production, preferring to read it privately to his friends, who, it is said, would weep aloud at the more touching scenes.

Candida is put together in a masterly way and has a uniformity often lacking in some of Shaw's other works. Here is a play that gives an audience intensely comic scenes as well as moments of serious insights. Moreover, it is a very actable play. Candida is one of the great roles in twentieth century theater, that of the self-possessed woman who, as in many homes, subtly runs the household while appearing to be subservient to her husband. The Reverend James Mavor Morell is also an excellent role: the hearty Christian Socialist clergyman, the popular speaker always in demand, the unintimidated man who is happy and secure in his important position until a young, wild, seemingly effeminate friend of the family, the poet Eugene Marchbanks, threatens his security. The role of Marchbanks, the eighteen-year-old worshiper of Candida, has also been a favorite of many stage juveniles. As the boy who grows faint at the thought of Candida's peeling onions, who rants, raves, and whines over the thought that the earthly, boorish Morell is married to such a poetic delight and inspiration as Candida, Marchbanks bears striking resemblances to the young and ethereal Shelley; possibly he is a younger Shaw.

A resemblance between *Candida* and Henrik Ibsen's *Et dukkehjem* (1879; *A Doll's House*, 1880) is also evident, though in his play Shaw reverses Ibsen's situation. In Ibsen's play, Nora is the doll, but in *Candida* it is Morell, the likable, high-principled husband, who is the doll. As he eventually learns, it is his wife who is responsible for his success. When Candida is "forced" to choose between Marchbanks and Morell, she chooses Morell, the weaker of the two. This is, supposedly, Shaw's Virgin Mother play; certainly Candida plays the role of Morell's wife, mother, and sisters rolled into one. She is the one who arranges his affairs, who keeps him happy and content, and who peels his onions for him. Morell eventually comes to realize her true status, though later he might try to rationalize his way out of his paradoxical victory. Many regard this, a husband and wife coming to a fuller understanding of each other, as the central aspect of the play.

This aspect bears a certain resemblance to romantic drama, which may be the secret of the play's success among non-Shavian theatergoers. Shaw indulged in tirades against romanticism, but *Candida* is infused with romantic ideas and situations. Although Candida discovers a typical Shavian thought—that service and not necessarily contentment is the greatest triumph in life—the play, with its celebration of the wife-mother role, is romantic in comparison with other Shavian drama.

In the growing awareness between the husband and wife, Marchbanks serves as the catalyst who brings about the final result. Because of Marchbanks's poetic railings, Morell begins to wonder if he might actually be too commonplace for Candida. Yet when Morell is chosen and the poet spurned, Marchbanks leaves as a more mature being with a secret in his heart, and he seems quite eager to go out into the night. It may well be that Marchbanks realizes that mundane domesticity is not for him—his is a greater destiny. Candida reveals the average happy marriage to him, and he realizes there is no poetry in it. A poet must go out into the night and on to greater and more exalted triumphs.

The force of the concept that the man of genius is out of place in conventional society is somewhat weakened by the fact that Marchbanks's role is somewhat overdrawn. Through his excessive behavior, the conflict between Marchbanks and Morell fails to convince many readers and viewers; to some, there is no choice at all between the likable clergyman and the effeminate boy. Others, however, are willing to overlook this flaw and to ignore the charge that Candida, in the "choosing" scene, behaves in a most conceited fashion. Audiences have generally preferred simply to delight in the high comedy of *Candida*, its amusing situations, and the consistently witty, sparkling dialogue throughout. There is no doubt that its great popularity is due not only to its tight construction but also to the fact that *Candida* is Shaw's safest play.

Further Reading

Carpenter, Charles A. "Critical Comedies." In *Bernard Shaw and the Art of Destroying Ideals: The Early Plays*. Madison: University of Wisconsin Press, 1969. Treats *Candida* as a sentimental comedy and discusses the conflict of ideals in the play. Devotes much space to an analysis of Candida's character and to her ability to use sympathy to dominate the other characters in the play.

Compton, Louis. "*Candida*." In *Shaw the Dramatist*. Lincoln: University of Nebraska Press, 1969. Discusses the social, philosophical, and historical backgrounds of *Candida*. Offers a clear presentation of Shaw's ideas and their sources in the nineteenth century intellectual tradition.

Dukore, Bernard F. *Shaw's Theater*. Gainesville: University Press of Florida, 2000. Focuses on the performance of Shaw's plays and how his plays call attention to elements of the theater, such as the audience, characters directing other characters, and plays within plays. Includes a section on "Bernard Shaw, Director," and another section in which Shaw describes how a director should interpret *Pygmalion* for theatrical production.

Gahan, Peter. *Shaw Shadows: Rereading the Texts of Bernard Shaw*. Gainesville: University Press of Florida, 2004. Reexamines Shaw's work from the perspective of modern critical theory and argues that his writings anticipated many of the elements of poststructuralism. Includes an analysis of *Candida*.

Holroyd, Michael. *Bernard Shaw: The Search for Love*. New York: Random House, 1988. In this first volume of his standard and indispensable biography of Shaw, Holroyd relates Shaw's life and thought to his works.

Innes, Christopher, ed. *The Cambridge Companion to George Bernard Shaw*. New York: Cambridge University Press, 1998. Collection of scholarly essays examining Shaw's work, including discussions of Shaw's feminism, Shavian comedy and the shadow of Oscar Wilde, his "discussion plays," and his influence on modern theater. The references to *Candida* are listed in the index.

Merritt, James D. "Shaw and the Pre-Raphaelites." In *Shaw: Seven Critical Essays*, edited by Norman Rosenblood. Toronto, Ont.: University of Toronto Press, 1971. Focuses on the character of Marchbanks and on the various references in the play to art, which Merritt relates to the Pre-Raphaelites and the art-for-art's-sake movement of the 1890's.

Pagliaro, Harold E. *Relations Between the Sexes in the Plays of George Bernard Shaw*. Lewiston, N.Y.: Edwin Mellen Press, 2004. Demonstrates how the relationship between men and women is a key element in Shaw's plays. Notes a pattern in how Shaw depicts these relationships, including lovers destined by the "life force" to procreate; relations between fathers and daughters, and mothers and sons; and the sexuality of politically, intellectually, and emotionally strong men.

Stanton, Stephen. *A Casebook on Candida*. New York: Thomas Y. Crowell, 1962. Very useful as an introduction to the play. Contains not only the text of the play and its sources but also selected prefaces and notes by Shaw and a variety of brief interpretations and criticism.

Candide
Or, The Optimist

Author: Voltaire (1694-1778)
First published: Candide: Ou, L'Optimisme, 1759
   (*Candide: Or, All for the Best*, 1759)
Type of work: Novel
Type of plot: Social satire
Time of plot: Eighteenth century
Locale: Europe and South America

Principal characters:
CANDIDE, Baroness Thunder-ten-tronckh's illegitimate son
MADEMOISELLE CUNEGONDE, Baron Thunder-ten-tronckh's daughter
PANGLOSS, Candide's friend and tutor
CACAMBO, Candide's servant

The Story:

Candide, the illegitimate son of Baron Thunder-ten-tronckh's sister, is born in Westphalia. Dr. Pangloss, his tutor and a devout follower of Gottfried Wilhelm von Leibnitz, teaches him metaphysico-theologo-cosmolonigology and assures his pupil that this is the best of all possible worlds. Cunegonde, the daughter of the baron, kisses Candide one day behind a screen, whereupon Candide is expelled from the noble baron's household.

Impressed into the army of the king of Bulgaria, Candide deserts during a battle between the king of Bulgaria and the king of Abares. Later, he is befriended by James the Anabaptist. He also meets his old friend, Dr. Pangloss, now a beggar. James, Pangloss, and Candide start for Lisbon. Their ship is wrecked in a storm off the coast of Portugal. James is drowned, but Candide and Pangloss swim to shore just as an earthquake shakes the city. The rulers of Lisbon, both secular and religious, decide to punish the people whose wickedness brings about the earthquake, and Candide and Pangloss are among the accused. Pangloss is hanged, and Candide is thoroughly whipped.

He is still smarting from his wounds when an old woman accosts Candide and tells him to have courage and to follow her. She leads him to a house where he is fed and clothed. Then Cunegonde appears. Candide is amazed because Pangloss told him that Cunegonde is dead. Cunegonde relates what happened to her since she last saw Candide. She is being kept by a Jew and an Inquisitor, but she holds both men

at a distance. Candide kills the Jew and the Inquisitor when they come to see her.

Together with the old woman, Cunegonde and Candide flee to Cadiz, where they are robbed. In despair, they sail for Paraguay, where Candide hopes to enlist in the Spanish army then fighting the rebellious Jesuits. During the voyage, the old woman tells her story. They learn that she is the daughter of Pope Urban X and the princess of Palestrina.

The governor of Buenos Aires develops a great affection for Cunegonde and causes Candide to be accused of having committed robbery while still in Spain. Candide flees with his servant, Cacambo; Cunegonde and the old woman remain behind. When Candide decides to fight for the Jesuits, he learns that the commandant is Cunegonde's brother. The brother will not hear of his sister's marrying Candide. They quarrel, and Candide, fearing that he killed the brother, takes to the road with Cacambo once more. Shortly afterward, they are captured by the Oreillons, a tribe of savage Indians, but when Cacambo proves they are not Jesuits, the two are released. They travel on to Eldorado. There life is simple and perfect, but Candide is not happy because he misses Cunegonde.

At last he decides to take some of the useless jeweled pebbles and golden mud of Eldorado and return to Buenos Aires to search for Cunegonde. He and Cacambo start out with a hundred sheep laden with riches, but they lose all but two sheep. When Candide approaches a Dutch merchant and tries to arrange passage to Buenos Aires, the merchant sails away with all his money and treasures, leaving him behind. Cacambo then goes to Buenos Aires to find Cunegonde and take her to Venice to meet Candide. After many adventures, including a sea fight and the miraculous recovery of one of his lost sheep from a sinking ship, Candide arrives at Bordeaux. His intention is to go to Venice by way of Paris. Police arrest him in Paris, however, and Candide is forced to buy his freedom with diamonds. Later, he sails on a Dutch ship to Portsmouth, England, where he witnesses the execution of an English admiral. From Portsmouth he goes to Venice. There he finds no Cacambo and no Cunegonde. He does, however, meet Paquette, Cunegonde's waiting maid. Shortly afterward, Candide encounters Cacambo, who is now a slave and who informs him that Cunegonde is in Constantinople. In the Venetian galley that carries them to Constantinople, Candide finds Pangloss and Cunegonde's brother among the galley slaves. Pangloss relates that he miraculously escaped from his hanging in Lisbon because the bungling hangman was not able to tie a proper knot. Cunegonde's brother tells how he survived the wound that Candide thought fatal. Candide buys both men from the Venetians and gives them their freedom.

When the group arrives at Constantinople, Candide buys the old woman and Cunegonde from their masters and also purchases a little farm to which they all retire. There each has his or her own particular work to do. Candide decides that the best thing in the world is to cultivate one's garden.

Critical Evaluation:

Candide, Voltaire's tour de force, surpasses most other famous satires. Like Alexander Pope's *The Rape of the Lock* (1712, 1714), it takes a swipe at the pretentiousness of the upper classes; like George Orwell's *Animal Farm* (1945), it undercuts political systems; like Jonathan Swift's ambitious *Gulliver's Travels* (1726), it sheds sharp light on the grossness, cupidity, and stupidity of human beings, as well as on their crude and frequently cruel institutions. Voltaire's satire goes beyond human beings and their society, however, to examine the entire world in which they find themselves. Its thesis is contrived in explicit response to the Leibnitzian optimism that this is "the best of all possible worlds."

The existence of evil in the world has been a problem for human beings ever since they began to speculate about the nature of things. It is treated in the literature of the West at least as early as the book of Genesis, which attributes evil to human beings' disobedient nature. St. Augustine and, later, John Milton enlarged on this theory, claiming that God limited his own interference in the world when he created people

"sufficient to stand though free to fall." The book of Job in the Bible centers more specifically on the problem of suffering. Its answer is essentially no answer, a restriction to an overwhelming (some have said obscene) demonstration of God's power, which humbles Job into acceptance. A third century Persian philosopher, Mani, devised the theory that Earth is a field of dispute between two nearly matched powers—one of light, one of darkness—with human beings caught in the middle.

Most later explanations appear to be variations on these three approaches. The seventeenth century Frenchman Blaise Pascal believed, like the author of Job, that human vision cannot perceive the justice in God's overall plan. Gottfried Wilhelm von Leibniz developed this explanation further. In his *Theodicée*, published in 1710, he described a harmonious universe in which all events are linked into a chain of cause and effect, and in which apparent evil is compensated by some greater good that may not be evident to the limited human mind. The English poet Pope expressed similar views.

In his early life, Voltaire was generally optimistic. Beginning in 1752, however, his writings evidence growing pessimism. On November 1, 1755, an earthquake in Lisbon, Portugal, killed between thirty and forty thousand people. This catastrophe provided Voltaire with a perfect springboard for his skepticism about the basic goodness of the world. "If Pope had been at Lisbon," he wrote, "would he have dared to say *All is well*?" His fellow Frenchman Jean-Jacques Rousseau responded that human beings, not God, are to blame for evil, including earthquakes: Human beings bring misfortune upon themselves by congregating in cities instead of living naturally in the country.

Voltaire continues the debate in *Candide*, where he creates a young, impressionable protagonist and sets him upon an incredible string of adventures, many of which he drew from real life. Historical events include the Lisbon earthquake and subsequent *auto-da-fé*, the political chaos of Morocco, and the execution of an admiral (Voltaire had tried to intercede in just such a situation). Like such other wandering heroes as Gulliver and Huckleberry Finn, Candide is naïve. For a time, like a schoolboy, he reacts to such events as torture, war, and catastrophe by recalling the favorite sayings of his tutor, Pangloss, among them "Every effect has a cause" and "All is for the best in this best of all possible worlds." As horror piles on horror, however, his doubts increase. Pangloss reappears periodically to soothe his pupil with further examples of illogical logic, but harsh experience begins to have its effect.

Candide's visit to Eldorado, the famed lost city of the New World, is a high-water mark. Here all is placid and serene. People live in absolute harmony. Suffering and poverty are unknown. There is no greed, and the natives smile at Candide's interest in the gold and jewels that lie on the ground as "clay and pebbles." Eldorado is utopia. Because of his desire to regain his lost love, Cunegonde, Candide leaves Eldorado; having however seen a truly harmonious world, he can no longer accept cruelty, catastrophe, and suffering as necessary ingredients for a universal good.

In the final chapter, Candide and his little band, including Pangloss, his more recent friend, the pessimistic Martin, and Cunegonde, who has now grown old and ugly, settle on a small farm "till the company should meet with a more favorable destiny." There they become almost as distressed by boredom as previously they had been by disaster until two neighbors bring enlightenment to them. A dervish, questioned about the existence of evil, responds, "What signifies it whether there be evil or good? When his highness sends a ship to Egypt does he trouble his head whether the rats in the vessel are at their ease or not?" This echo of a metaphor that Voltaire had contrived as early as 1736 briefly asserts the notion that the world may in the view of the "divine architect" be excellent indeed, but it is not designed for human beings, the "mice" in the hold. The second neighbor, a contented old farmer, advises Candide's group of the value of labor, which "keeps off from us three great evils—idleness, vice, and want." For once, those philosophical opposites, Pangloss and Martin, agree; the little community settles down to work in earnest, each member doing his part with good will and deriving satisfaction therefrom.

Candide, although it is an attack on philosophical optimism, is not a pessimistic work. Its ending, with the hero remarking that "we must cultivate our garden," reminds the reader of the words of another realistic but hopeful man, Anton Chekhov, who was to observe more than a century later, "If everyone in the world did all he was capable of on his own plot of land, what a beautiful world it would be!"

"Critical Evaluation" by Sally Buckner

Further Reading

Aldridge, Alfred Owen. *Voltaire and the Century of Light.* Princeton, N.J.: Princeton University Press, 1975. A thoughtful study that describes Voltaire's extraordinarily diverse literary career. Compares *Candide* with Jonathan Swift's masterful satire *Gulliver's Travels*.

Besterman, Theodore. *Voltaire.* 3d ed. Chicago: University of Chicago Press, 1976. An admirable and reliable biography of Voltaire that focuses on his development as a writer. In the discussion of *Candide*, Besterman explains the moral and emotional transformation of the protagonist from an immature and selfish adolescent into a sensitive, responsible adult.

Cronk, Nicholas, ed. *The Cambridge Companion to Voltaire.* New York: Cambridge University Press, 2009. Collection of essays examining Voltaire's life, philosophy, and works. Includes discussions of Voltaire as a storyteller, Voltaire and authorship, Voltaire and the myth of England, and Philip Stewart's analysis of *Candide*.

Knapp, Bettina Liebowitz. *Voltaire Revisited.* New York: Twayne, 2000. An introductory overview of Voltaire that describes his life and devotes separate chapters to all of the genres of his works, including *Candide* and other philosophical tales. Includes bibliography and index.

Mason, Haydn Trevor. *Candide: Optimism Demolished.* New York: Twayne, 1992. A two-part study of the novel. The first part provides literary and historical context, including critical reception, while the second part offers a reading of the novel's view of history, philosophy, personality, structure, and form. Includes notes and an annotated bibliography.

_____. *Voltaire: A Biography.* Baltimore: Johns Hopkins University Press, 1981. The chapter on *Candide* describes the philosophical and ethical motivation for Voltaire's criticism of excessive optimism.

Pearson, Roger. *The Fables of Reason: A Study of Voltaire's "Contes philosophiques."* New York: Oxford University Press, 1993. An insightful literary study of Voltaire's use of satire, irony, and understatement in his many philosophical tales. The lengthy chapter on *Candide* includes an explanation for the appropriateness of viewing *Candide* as a tale about moral education and the search for human honesty.

_____. *Voltaire Almighty: A Life in Pursuit of Freedom.* London: Bloomsbury, 2005. A readable, compelling account of Voltaire's life, focusing on his love of liberty and how that passion informed his life and work. Includes bibliography, index, and illustrations.

Richter, Peyton, and Ilona Ricardo. *Voltaire.* Boston: Twayne, 1980. Excellent general study of Voltaire's life and career. Describes several different levels of satire in *Candide* and Voltaire's other major philosophical tales, including *Zadig* (1748) and *Micromégas* (1752). Includes a well-annotated bibliography of significant critical studies on his work.

Williams, David. *Voltaire: Candide.* London: Grant and Cutler, 1997. A thorough study guide to the seminal text, containing critical literature about the novel. Includes bibliographical references.

Cane

Author: Jean Toomer (1894-1967)
First published: 1923
Type of work: Poetry and short fiction
Type of plot: Experimental
Time of plot: Early twentieth century
Locale: Georgia, Washington, D.C., and Chicago

Principal characters:
KARINTHA, a beautiful young woman in Georgia
BECKY, a white woman with two black sons
ESTHER, who becomes obsessed with King Barlo
KING BARLO, a man whom Esther thinks is a prophet
LOUISA, an African American woman loved by two men
TOM BURWELL, a man who loves Louisa
BOB STONE, a white man who loves Louisa
RHOBERT, a man obsessed with home ownership
PAUL JOHNSON, a student in Chicago
BONA HALE, a student to whom Paul is attracted
RALPH KABNIS, a teacher from Washington, D.C.
FATHER JOHN, a former slave, living in Halsey's
    basement

The Story:

The title character of "Karintha" is a woman whose beauty captivates men, making her like "a growing thing ripened too soon." She has a child, whom she apparently kills, and she becomes a prostitute. Becky is a white woman cast out by the community because she has two black sons. Townspeople build her a cabin and take food to her, but never see her. The boys grow up, cause trouble, and leave, cursing people of both races. When Becky's chimney collapses, burying her, someone throws a Bible onto the rubble.

The title character of "Carma" has affairs when her husband is away; he finds out and accuses her. She takes a gun into the cane field. Hearing a shot, her husband gathers men and finds her. The men carry her home and search for a wound, waking her. Realizing that he is deceived by his wife again, her husband becomes irrational and cuts one of the searchers. He is sent to work on the chain gang.

"Fern" tells of a young woman whose eyes attract men. They want to do great things for her, but she tires of them. A northerner visiting relatives in Georgia meets Fern. During a walk, he holds her, but she breaks away, sings a pained song, then faints. He can think of nothing to do for her, and he goes back north.

"Esther" follows its title character for eighteen years. When she is nine, she sees King Barlo appear to go into a trance and talk about an African's coming to the United States to redeem people. Years after Barlo leaves town, Esther dreams of having a child who is rescued from a fire. At first, she dreams the child is conceived without the involvement of sex; when Esther imagines normal conception, the child becomes ugly like Barlo. Barlo returns when Esther is

twenty-seven years of age; she visits him, but he repulses her, making her feel empty.

Louisa, in "Blood-Burning Moon," works for the family of her white admirer, Bob Stone, who wishes she were his slave. Tom Burwell, a black laborer, also loves her. One night, Stone finds Burwell talking with Louisa and challenges him. When Stone draws a knife, Burwell kills him. White townspeople burn Burwell in an old factory under a full, red moon.

In "Reapers," the narrator watches workers sharpen scythes and sees a horse-pulled mower cut a rat, then continue mowing. "November Cotton Flower" describes misery caused by drought and boll weevils; the untimely beauty of a cotton flower blooming in November causes people to lose fear. In "Cotton Song," cotton rollers sing of making a path to God's throne. In "Georgia Dusk," sawmill workers sing while walking home through the cane, combining music of African heritage with Christian hymns.

"Seventh Street" describes a street in Washington, D.C., that shows the influence of Prohibition and World War I. "Rhobert" is about a man who suffers the burdens of home ownership. "Calling Jesus" is about a woman whose soul follows her like a dog throughout the city, finding her only in dreams of hay and cane.

In "Avey," a man loves Avey from childhood, although he finds her indolent. After returning to Washington, D.C., from school, he runs into her again, and they go to a park, where he talks and she falls asleep.

"Theater" tells the story of a dancer, Dorris, who senses the attraction of the cabaret manager's brother, John. John dreams of Dorris but believes the difference between them is too strong for a relationship, so he does not pursue her. His rejection causes her pain. Dan Moore, in "Box Seat," feels anger toward a society that will not let him be its savior. He loves Muriel, a teacher, but she cannot become involved with such an unrooted man. Dan follows her to a vaudeville show, during which two dwarves fight; then one sings and offers a bloody rose to Muriel, who rejects it. Dan rises, shouts, and storms out, angering a man who challenges him to a fight. By the time Dan gets outside, he forgets the man.

"Bona and Paul" tells of two students. Paul's dark complexion causes rumors that he is black; everyone else in the school is white. He becomes attracted to Bona, a southerner, and a friend invites them on a double date. Their attraction is mutual, and they leave the nightclub together. Paul stops to tell the doorman of their love, and Bona leaves.

In "Beehive," a man likens himself to a honey-drinking drone in a crowded hive, wishing he could fly to a farmyard flower. "Her Lips Are Copper Wire" uses urban electrical objects to describe a woman's sexuality. "Storm Ending" compares thunder to bell-like flowers. "Prayer" is about the soul's separation from body and mind and its paradoxical strength and frailty. "Harvest Song" describes a tired, thirsty, hungry reaper who distracts himself with pain.

"Kabnis" tells of Ralph Kabnis, a Washingtonian with southern roots, who comes to a small Georgia town to teach. Unable to sleep, he kills a noisy hen in the next room. The next day he goes to church, then talks with his friends Halsey and Layman about lynchings. Through the window comes a stone with a note telling the black man from the North to go home. Kabnis is terrified. That evening, Halsey and Layman bring moonshine to calm him. Hanby, the principal, fires him for drinking, and Halsey offers him a job in his blacksmith's shop. Lewis comes to Kabnis's cabin and says the note was meant for him, not Kabnis. Kabnis, Lewis, and some women accompany Halsey to his basement to visit a former slave they call Father John. The next morning, Kabnis and Carrie Kate, Halsey's sister, hear the old man say "sin" several times. He explains that the sin is white people's making the Bible lie. Kabnis replies with contempt, but Carrie seems uplifted and calms Kabnis.

Critical Evaluation:

Cane is a collection of stories, poems, and sketches in three sections. *Cane* appeared in 1923, receiving favorable reviews although it was not widely read. Rediscovered during the 1960's, it has become one of the best-known and most respected African American works. Oddly, Jean Toomer was only a fraction African American; his ancestry was so mixed that some laws considered him white.

Cane is important in African American literature no matter what Toomer's ethnic background was because it describes the black Southern rural experience, the black Northern urban experience, and intellectuals' attempts to understand the connection between the two. It also uses experimental techniques to portray traditional experiences.

The first section, set in rural and small-town Georgia, contains stories about women and men's attraction to them. The poems generally concern workers and landscape and often describe farm labor. Other poems in the first section are portraits. "Face" is a word picture of an old, sorrow-filled woman. "Portrait in Georgia" uses lynching imagery to describe a woman: "Hair—braided chestnut,/ coiled like a lyncher's rope. . . ." "Nullo" is a portrait of rural Georgia, describing pine needles falling.

Three poems do not fit in any of these categories: In "Song of the Son," the narrator realizes that all former slaves will soon be dead, but he will sing their song, as a tree grows from a seed; in "Evening Sun," the narrator speaks of love at nightfall; "Conversion" describes negatively Africans' conversion to Christianity in the Americas.

The second section, set in cities, primarily Washington, D.C., contains poetry, short stories, and cryptic word sketches. Many short stories in section two continue male-female relationship themes; some of the poems relate to city life, such as "Her Lips Are Copper Wire."

Toomer's word sketches combine the cryptic imagery of poetry with the flowing quality of prose. This is true especially in "Calling Jesus," in which someone comes in "soft as a cotton boll brushed against the milk-pod cheek of Christ." Similar descriptions appear in the short stories. In "Karintha," for example, the title character carries "beauty, perfect as dusk when the sun goes down."

In the short stories, the author often portrays people on society's fringes to reveal the society itself. Becky, the white woman with sons of mixed race, is exiled by both communities. Townspeople are torn between their Christian duty to help her—to bring her food, build her a cabin—and their antagonism toward the mixing of races. The reader knows Becky only through townspeople's reactions.

Toomer's poetry often combines two aspects of African American experience: work songs and spirituals. "Cotton Song," for example, begins like a work song: "Come, brother, come. Lets lift it." A later stanza brings in elements of the spiritual: "Weary sinner's bare feet trod,/ Softly, softly to the throne of God. . . ." Other poems are more traditional, such as "Song of the Son," in which the narrator promises to sing his slave ancestors' song when they are gone.

The final section of *Cane*, "Kabnis," is a story originally written as drama. "Kabnis" is the most problematic part of *Cane*, but it also is the story that pulls the book together. The African American experience is displacement. Slavery displaced Africans from their homeland; emancipation freed slaves but also often displaced them. To escape the horrors of Southern persecution, many African Americans moved to Northern cities, again displacing themselves. Those who stayed in the South lived a way of life that was ending, as factories replaced farming. Ralph Kabnis is one of those displaced persons. An educated man from Washington, D.C.—considered Northern by any Southerner—Kabnis returns to his ancestral land to teach. There, however, he is frightened and does not fit in. He loses his position and becomes a blacksmith's apprentice, despite his education. He is afraid that both white people and black will think he is uppity and attack him. When the ancient former slave reminds him of the sin of slavery, Kabnis refuses to identify with the pain of his ancestors. Only Carrie Kate, still rooted in her home, finds profundity in the old man's talk; only she can comfort Kabnis.

Much of *Cane* is beautiful; other parts are disturbing. Toomer offers little solace, for human relationships fail; religion is portrayed as a sham; and escape seems impossible. The beauty almost intensifies the pain.

M. Katherine Grimes

Further Reading

Benson, Brian Joseph, and Mabel Mayle Dillard. *Jean Toomer*. Boston: Twayne, 1980. Discusses Toomer's writing, especially *Cane*. Includes bibliography.

Bone, Robert. *Down Home: Origins of the Afro-American Short Story*. New York: Columbia University Press, 1988. A critical survey that stresses the debts of black writers to an oral tradition that Bone calls a "blues aesthetic." The chapter on Toomer reviews his entire career, including the important influences of Sherwood Anderson and Waldo Frank, and includes detailed analyses of three stories from *Cane*: "Fern," "Theater," and "Bona and Paul."

_____. *The Negro Novel in America*. Rev. ed. New Haven, Conn.: Yale University Press, 1965. A pioneering study of black writing from 1853 to the works of James Baldwin. Bone's chapter on the Harlem School remains valuable, particularly for his discussion of Toomer and *Cane*.

Durham, Frank, ed. *The Merrill Studies in "Cane."* Columbus, Ohio: Charles E. Merrill, 1971. Includes critical studies of *Cane* published from 1923 to 1969. Of special interest is Waldo Frank's foreword to the first edition of the novel. Many other useful studies are included, by such

people as Robert Bone, Arna Bontemps, and W. E. B. Du Bois. Of questionable purpose is Durham's grouping of the selections by each author's race, especially since his racial classifications are not always correct.

Fabre, Geneviève, and Michel Feith, eds. *Jean Toomer and the Harlem Renaissance*. New Brunswick, N.J.: Rutgers University Press, 2001. Collection of essays about *Cane*, including discussions of *Cane*, modernism, and race in interwar America; myth and belonging, and preaching and dreaming in *Cane*; race and visual arts in the works of Toomer and Georgia O'Keefe; and analyses of some of the stories.

Kerman, Cynthia Earl, and Richard Eldridge. *The Lives of Jean Toomer: A Hunger for Wholeness*. Baton Rouge: Louisiana State University Press, 1987. Contains a long chapter about *Cane*, discussing autobiographical elements, the circumstances of its writing, and other authors' reactions to the work.

McKay, Nellie Y. *Jean Toomer, Artist: A Study of His Literary Life and Work, 1894-1936*. Chapel Hill: University of North Carolina Press, 1984. A comprehensive and lucidly written study, benefiting from McKay's access to the collection of Toomer manuscripts and correspondence at Fisk University. The interpretation of Toomer's imagery, structure, and themes is convincing, and McKay makes the interesting suggestion of a link between *Cane* and James Joyce's novel *Ulysses* (1922).

O'Daniel, Therman B., ed. *Jean Toomer: A Critical Evaluation*. Washington, D.C.: Howard University Press, 1988. This lengthy work includes essays about influences on *Cane*, interpretations of the book, male-female relationships, female characters, and other elements, as well as about Toomer himself. Includes a useful bibliography.

Toomer, Jean. *Cane: An Authoritative Text, Backgrounds, Criticism*. Edited by Darwin T. Turner. New York: W. W. Norton, 1988. Edited by a leading scholar in the field of black literature and a major force in advancing the reputation of Jean Toomer. In addition to reprinting the text of *Cane*, this excellent book includes early assessments of the novel, correspondence about his work between Toomer and others, and a balanced selection of critical studies from 1958 to 1984.

Whalan, Mark. *Race, Manhood, and Modernism in America: The Short Story Cycles of Sherwood Anderson and Jean Toomer*. Knoxville: University of Tennessee Press, 2007. A comparison of *Cane* and Anderson's *Winesburg, Ohio*. Examines how Toomer aims to broaden the racial basis of American culture to conceive a new type of manhood.

Cannery Row

Author: John Steinbeck (1902-1968)
First published: 1945
Type of work: Novel
Type of plot: Comedy
Time of plot: 1930's
Locale: Monterey, California

Principal characters:
DOC, a marine biologist
MACK, a leader of street vagabonds
LEE CHONG, a grocer
FRANKIE, a mentally disabled child
HENRI THE PAINTER, an aspiring artist
SAM MALLOY and MRS. MALLOY, inhabitants of Cannery Row

The Story:

In 1930's Monterey, California, sits an abandoned structure near the noisy, smelly sardine factories and wharves that line the Cannery Row neighborhood along the Pacific Ocean waterfront. A good-natured vagrant named Mack, the leader of a gang of vagabonds who inhabit the structure and have named it the Palace Flophouse and Grill, persuades the men to give a party for Doc. Doc is a friendly marine biologist who operates the Western Biological Laboratory, a modest scientific enterprise.

Mack and his gang have no money for the proposed party for Doc, so they hatch a plan to gather the necessary resources. After first considering getting jobs, they unanimously dismiss that idea in favor of a more subtle plan that involves doing a supposed favor for Doc. Under Mack's leadership, the gang devises a scheme to approach Doc and offer its services in a frog-gathering operation. They would go into the countryside, collect as many frogs as possible, and then sell the amphibians to Doc at five cents each so he can embalm and retail them later as biological specimens. Lacking transportation, the men haggle out a deal with Lee Chong, a local grocer who is also their landlord, to borrow a dilapidated truck on the condition that they restore it into working order. After discussing the details with Chong, the men repair the truck and embark on a madcap frog-hunting expedition that forms one of the most amusing episodes in the novel.

Despite getting drunk along the way, trespassing on private property, and stealing wayward chickens from local ranchers, the gang succeeds in catching hundreds of frogs, an event that they mark as one of the most successful frog-catching expeditions in all history. The gang then returns in mock triumph to Cannery Row to celebrate their victory, yet they still lack the funds to throw their intended celebration. After approaching Chong, Mack works out another scheme in which he sells frogs to Chong as currency.

Many of the individuals who inhabit the Row have tragicomic stories. The debt-ridden Horace Abbeville commits suicide after deeding the building that eventually became Chong's grocery. Mr. and Mrs. Sam Malloy live destitute in an abandoned boiler that Mrs. Malloy attempts to decorate by gluing curtains to the windowless, iron interior. Then there is Frankie, a mentally challenged child who lurks around Doc's lab, and whose sweet-natured attempts to be helpful always run amok and alienate him from the community. Henri the Painter has a confused identity: His name is not Henri, he is not French, and he is not really a painter; he is afraid of the water, yet spends most of his time building and modifying a landlocked boat, moored safely in a pine grove far from the Pacific shore.

One bittersweet tale involves a man named Gay, a woman named Mary Talbot, and a boy, Joey. Gay moves in with Mack and the rest of the gang to escape his wife, who often beats him after he falls asleep. Mary has little money but compensates for it by staging elaborate teas for the cats in the neighborhood, and the young Joey is forced to endure the taunts of neighborhood children because his father committed suicide by ingesting rat poison.

While Mack and the gang are on another frog quest, Doc heads south to collect octopi in the La Jolla tide pools. He captures several specimens but is disturbed when he discovers the drowned body of a young girl among the rocks. Meanwhile, Mack and the gang are busily preparing for the party, which is attended by several residents of the Row. Unfortunately, long before Doc returns, things get out of hand and a fight breaks out among the revelers, leading to broken doors, shattered glass, spilled books, and the destruction of the packing case that holds all of the captured frogs. By the time Doc arrives, the frogs have escaped and his place is in shambles.

The failed party shames Mack and the gang, and a gloomy mood settles over the Row until the arrival of more benign events. The gang nurses a sick puppy, Darling, back to health, then Mack begins planning a second party to celebrate Doc's birthday. Word gets out about the party, and before long, nearly everybody on the Row is looking for presents to give Doc. Mack's surprise, however, comes as no surprise to Doc, who finds out about the party beforehand. Doc prudently removes all the breakable items in his home before the guests arrive.

The party is a raging success, even though Doc is forced to spend as much time making food and caring for his guests as he does celebrating the occasion. As part of the entertainment, Doc plays recordings of classical music and even reads translations of Sanskrit poetry, which moves the guests to a state of sweet sadness until the idyll is broken by a gang of tuna fishermen, who crash the party and ignite a large brawl. When the police arrive to break up the fight, order is restored and harmony returns, to the point that even the cops are persuaded to join the festivities.

The morning after, Doc awakens with music still ringing in his ears. He then washes himself, puts a record on the phonograph, picks up a copy of *Black Marigolds*, and, from the closing pages of the book, recites a final stanza of this life-affirming Sanskrit verse.

Critical Evaluation:

John Steinbeck, one of the most famous and productive American authors, produced twenty-nine novels, short-story collections, journals, films, memoirs, and play-novellas during his writing career. In 1962, he received the Nobel Prize in Literature. Steinbeck spent his youth in Salinas, then a small town in a fertile agricultural valley nestled between two mountain ranges, less than thirty miles from Monterey and the Pacific Ocean. His experiences there provided him with the raw material that would feed a lifetime of fiction about the land and people of central California.

After graduating from high school, Steinbeck enrolled at Stanford University in 1919. He studied intermittently until 1925, when he left the school without completing his degree. In the five years that followed, he supported himself with several jobs including manual laborer, caretaker at a resort in Lake Tahoe, and New York journalist. Along the way, he worked on his first novel, *Cup of Gold* (1929), an uneven allegorical tale about pirate Henry Morgan. After marrying, he moved to Pacific Grove and published the first of his California fictions, *The Pastures of Heaven* (1932) and *To a God Unknown* (1933), and began working on some of the short stories collected later in *The Long Valley* (1938).

By the time Steinbeck published *Cannery Row*, he had already sealed his reputation as a significant American writer with such books as *Of Mice and Men* (1937) and his masterpiece, *The Grapes of Wrath* (1939). Written as something of a diversion from the exhausting work he performed during World War II, when he wrote everything from press dispatches from North Africa to war propaganda such as *Bombs Away* (1942) and the antifascist novella *The Moon Is Down* (1942), Steinbeck conceived *Cannery Row* as a complex, experimental work with several layers of meaning. On the surface, the novel pays tribute to the colorful waterfront community of Monterey, but underneath the comic facade is a subtle, scientific examination of the interconnected lives of the many marginalized characters living there.

The main theme of the novel focuses on the need for human connection and on the consequences of alienation. Like the intercoastal areas Doc visits during his specimen-gathering trips along the Pacific shore, Monterey is a human tide pool, teeming with life, washed to the edges of the continent by the forces of American manifest destiny. However, what captures Steinbeck's imagination in this environment is not mainstream respectable folk such as bankers, lawyers, doctors, or businessmen. Instead, he trains his fictive gaze on the human flotsam found there—the down-and-out and the underdogs like Mack and his gang of misfits, prostitutes like Dora Flood, loners like Henri and Doc, and the marginalized, such as Lee Chong. All of these characters live on the fringes and lead their own lives of quiet desperation, yet they depend upon one another to survive.

To explore this theme, the book follows a loose, organic structure rather than the usual pattern of rising action, climax, and falling action found in many conventional plots. Critics such as Warren French have likened this pattern to a wave that grows slowly and gains momentum, then divides, re-forms, and ultimately disperses upon the shore. Accordingly, eighteen chapters trace plans for the party for Doc and describe the unsuccessful first party, the sadness that follows, the gradual rejuvenation of hope, and, finally, the celebration when the second party surges toward its successful conclusion.

In the remaining fourteen chapters, Steinbeck employs devices including parables and interpolated fables such as the one of the mysterious, solitary "Chinaman"; the story of Henri the Painter; and the tale of the energetic gopher in chapter 31, who symbolizes the idea of failed dreams and lost paradise. Like his human counterparts on the Row, the gopher follows his dreams to a plot of empty land, where he builds what he thinks will be his ideal home. Unfortunately, no women live there, and ultimately he is forced to abandon his imagined Eden for more dangerous environs across the road.

The character who resonates most strongly is Doc. Although he is often aloof and detached from others, he has the last word; it is for him the party is held. His is the spirit that most clearly reflects the elemental humanness of the Row. Something of a man for all seasons, he rises above the other characters truly because only he is the guardian of wisdom and keeper of the creative spirit. The other characters, such as Mack, Chong, and Dora, lack the type of transcendent vision Doc possesses. Doc is the linchpin that connects the lives on the Row, and through music, art, and science, he binds them all.

Rodney P. Rice

Further Reading

Astro, Richard. *John Steinbeck and Edward F. Ricketts: The Shaping of a Novelist*. Minneapolis: University of Minnesota Press, 1973. A biographical study of the relationship between Steinbeck and marine biologist Ed Ricketts, upon whom Steinbeck modeled Doc's character in *Cannery Row*. Contains an excellent examination of Steinbeck's philosophical beliefs, including his nonteleological and phalanx theories.

Beegel, Susan F., Susan Shillinglaw, and Wesley F. Tiffney, Jr. *Steinbeck and the Environment: Interdisciplinary Approaches*. Tuscaloosa: University of Alabama Press, 1997. Interdisciplinary exploration of how Steinbeck's preoccupation with ecology and marine biology influenced works such as *Cannery Row*.

Benson, Jackson. *The True Adventures of John Steinbeck, Writer*. New York: Viking Press, 1983. The definitive biography of Steinbeck. Still one of the most comprehensive examinations of Steinbeck's life and literature.

Bloom, Harold, ed. *John Steinbeck*. New ed. New York: Bloom's Literary Criticism, 2008. Collection of essays discussing various aspects of Steinbeck's work, including analysis of *Cannery Row* and his other novels.

Crisler, Jesse S., Joseph R. McElrath, Jr., and Susan Shillinglaw, eds. *John Steinbeck: The Contemporary Reviews*. New York: Cambridge University Press, 1996. A valuable resource for students interested in reading contemporary reviews of Steinbeck's major works, including *Cannery Row*.

French, Warren. *John Steinbeck's Fiction Revisited*. New York: Twayne, 1994. One of the best starting points for critically examining Steinbeck's work. Contains an excellent chapter on *Cannery Row* and outlines everything from Steinbeck's early works to his final novels.

Levant, Howard. *The Novels of John Steinbeck: A Critical Study*. Columbia: University of Missouri Press, 1974. Traces the structural and organizational technique Steinbeck uses in his novels. An accessible and insightful textual analysis.

Lundy, A. L. *Real Life on Cannery Row: Real People, Places, and Events That Inspired John Steinbeck*. Santa Monica, Calif.: Angel City Press, 2008. Discusses the memorable persons and moments that inspired the writing of *Cannery Row*. Examines the novel's characters and the "true stories behind fictional events." A good companion piece for students of Steinbeck. Includes a foreword by Thomas Steinbeck.

Simmonds, Roy S. *A Biographical and Critical Introduction of John Steinbeck*. Lewiston, N.Y.: E. Mellen Press, 2000. Charts Steinbeck's evolution as a writer from 1929 through 1968, discussing the themes of his works and the concepts and philosophies that influenced his depictions of human nature and the psyche. Interweaves details about his writings with accounts of his personal life.

Timmerman, John H. *John Steinbeck's Fiction: The Aesthetics of the Road Taken*. Norman: University of Oklahoma Press, 1986. Evaluates Steinbeck's artistic premises and guiding beliefs and appraises his work in the light of those beliefs. Includes useful background information about *Cannery Row*.

The Cannibal

Author: John Hawkes (1925-1998)
First published: 1949
Type of work: Novel
Type of plot: Allegory
Time of plot: Twentieth century
Locale: Germany

Principal characters:
ZIZENDORF, the narrator
MADAM STELLA SNOW, a singer, wife of Ernst
ERNST, Stella's husband
CROMWELL, an English Germanophile
JUTTA, Stella's sister

The Story:

Part 1—1945. In 1945, at the end of World War II, asylum inmates are released in the city of Spitzen-on-the-Dein in Germany. The Allied victors left only a few overseers. One of these, Leevey, an American Jew, patrols one-third of the country on his motorcycle and is about to travel through the city. Zizendorf, the editor of the town's newspaper, *The Crooked Zeitung*, is planning to kill Leevey, liberate Germany, and found a neo-Nazi state.

Zizendorf is the lover of Jutta, the wife of the previous editor, a Nazi soldier, who was lost in Siberia during the war. Jutta and her two children live in a room on the fifth floor of Madam Stella Snow's boardinghouse. Madam Snow is Jutta's older sister. Herr Stintz, the schoolteacher, lives on the fourth floor, the Census-Taker on the third. The roomer who lives on the second floor, the Duke, is out, following Jutta's son through the rubble of the city. Madam Snow lives on the first floor, consulting her tarot cards every day. Balamir, a former inmate of the asylum, is put to work by Madam Snow, unearthing furniture in the basement.

Madam Snow's son, who returns from the war physically disabled, lives with his wife in the moving-picture house, where, each day, he shows the same film to an empty theater. The Mayor, his memory obliterated, is too blind to tend the chronicles of history. He is haunted by dreams of Pastor Miller, an innocent man who was executed because of the Mayor's betrayal. In the newspaper office, drinking with the Census-Taker, Zizendorf thinks about the Mayor's situation while he waits to kill Leevey. He places a log across the road where Leevey will be passing through town. Jutta's son flees for his life from the duke, who is following him, as Jutta's daughter, Selvaggia, watches from her window.

Part 2—1914. Stella and Ernst are inspired by their parents with romantic dreams of conquest and heroism. Singing for the soldiers in the *Sportswelt Brauhaus*, Stella, "the sorceress, sent them boiling and held them up for joy." Herman Snow, proprietor of the *Sportswelt*, urges Ernst, his son, to win Stella, to become the conquering hero. When Cromwell takes Stella home from the *Sportswelt*, Ernst runs after them down

the "avenue of heroes." He appears at the side of the carriage, tells Stella he will come back, and flees to the university, where he duels with the Baron. Wounded in the groin, he goes to Stella's, and she welcomes him. World War I begins the next day. Stella witnesses her mother's death when an English airplane falls from the sky, sending a "splinter" into her body.

After her father, the old Prussian General, also dies, Stella marries Ernst. They go to the mountains on their honeymoon, where Ernst becomes obsessed with Christ. He begins to collect wooden crucifixes and longs for death. Cromwell comes to their hotel with news of the war. He tells Ernst "everything he did not want to know." When Stella and Ernst return to Spitzen-on-the-Dein, they find Germany on the verge of defeat. Herman Snow was a "bare shell of the man." Finding Ernst dying, unable to admit to this death, Herman roars: "He's not sick!" Just before he dies, Ernst expresses hatred for his father and "was reprieved from saintliness."

After her parents die during the early part of World War I, Jutta is placed in a nunnery. She fears the nuns, especially the Mother Superior, who crosses off from the human list each night the names of those who submitted to "the slovenly captivity of forgiveness." When the Mother Superior comes to Jutta's cell, Jutta tells her she has nothing to confess. Wasting away with disease, Jutta begins to recover when the Oberleutnant, director of the nunnery, becomes her lover. After using him to fulfill her needs, Jutta abandons the Oberleutnant to marry a man who becomes a Nazi soldier in World War II.

Part 3—1945. Zizendorf and two henchmen wait by the side of the road. The Duke follows Jutta's son into the theater. Zizendorf remembers the day the Allies set up their headquarters in Madam Snow's apartment and the Mayor betrayed Pastor Miller. Leevey fastens the red cloth about Miller's eyes. The Colonel gives Zizendorf the only rifle containing a live cartridge. The Duke faces the boy in the theater. Herr Stintz watches a light circle along the autobahn. Leevey speeds up to go past the town. When the Duke reaches out his hand, the boy does not move.

Leevey is killed immediately when his motorcycle hits the log. With his henchmen, Zizendorf takes Leevey's body to the swamp. They are watched by Herr Stintz and Salvaggia. Zizendorf knows someone sees them with Leevey. The Duke takes Jutta's son toward the asylum. When Zizendorf goes back to Jutta's room, Selvaggia tells him that she saw Leevey get killed. Zizendorf goes to Stintz's room and murders him. Then he sets up the press in Madam Snow's chicken coop and prints his "Indictment of the Allied Antagonists, and Proclamation of the German Liberation."

The Duke kills Jutta's son with his sword and dismembers him. He ties the organs and mutilated pieces in the boy's jacket. Zizendorf decides to make Madam Snow's house the National Headquarters. He thinks the Duke will make a good chancellor, and the Census-Taker can be secretary of state. Zizendorf and the Census-Taker go to kill the Mayor. The Duke comes to Madam Snow's apartment. When she reads Zizendorf's pamphlet, thrust under her door, tears of joy run down her cheeks. She goes to dine with the Duke. Zizendorf returns to Jutta's room and gets in bed with her. When her daughter opens the door, Zizendorf says "draw those blinds and go back to sleep." She does as she is told.

Critical Evaluation:

In *The Cannibal*, the cannibalistic processes of nature, including human nature, dominate life when institutions of order have been destroyed in war. These institutions, however, are also destructive in their efforts to repress or control the processes of life. Zizendorf's plan to assassinate Leevey and to establish a neo-Nazi state parallels the nationalistic dream of Germany in 1914 and the Nazi goals of the 1930's. Each past dream is destructive, resulting in war, and each is abortive, destroyed by the war it provokes.

The parallel expressions of the cannibalistic life force in nature, in human beings, and in institutions are implied when Stella wonders how cannibals "could bear, in only their feathers, this terrible sun." She sees them, "carrying victims high over their heads, as tall vengeful creatures who sang madly on their secret rock." Stella senses the "terrifying similarity" between the cannibalism of nature, represented by the "terrible sun," and the cannibalism of people. Their need to protect themselves from death by feeding off the life of others parallels the need of the visible world to perpetuate itself. The cannibals secure a rock, an enclave of order, to facilitate their feeding and to protect themselves from the natural world and from other cannibals. The cannibals and their rock parallel the world's nations and their institutions of protective-repressive order.

The disorder and the threats of destruction that con-

front Zizendorf and the other characters are mirrored for the reader in the apparent incoherence of the novel and in John Hawkes's focus on seemingly gratuitous horrors. The central enormity is the butchering of Jutta's son by the cannibalistic Duke. Hawkes's surrealistic style contributes a nightmare quality to the novel. Like a literal nightmare, the novel is also characterized by disruption of chronology, abrupt transition in place, and fragmentation of action. The narrative of the first and third sections is interrupted by the narrative of the second section. Similar interruptions occur within each section as Hawkes carries several actions forward simultaneously.

Confronted with these disruptions, the reader attempts to order his or her experience of the novel, just as Zizendorf attempts to impose order on his experience. The success of the reader's effort depends on the perception of parallels in image, statement, character, and action as well as the perception of historical parallels. Herman Snow is identified with Kaiser Wilhelm II, the ruler of Germany during World War I. His personal desires parallel the nationalistic aspirations of Germany in 1914. The historical counterpart to Ernst is Gavrilo Princep, the assassin of the Austrian archduke. Ernst's desire to win Stella for himself parallels the Serbian desire for independence. His appearance at the side of Stella's carriage corresponds to Princep's assassination of Archduke Francis Ferdinand, the act that began World War I.

After Stella and Ernst become disillusioned with dreams of conquest and heroism, they seek protection from life in the institution of religion. Belief in another world and in the immortality of souls parallels in the novel the illusion that human beings can create a paradise of protective order in this world. Both dreams are cannibalistic: The institutions of aggression destroy life; the institutions of religion deny life. After Ernst dies, Stella abandons religion. During World War II, she sides with the Nazis and sacrifices her son to war, just as Herman and the old general, Stella's father, are willing to sacrifice their children in 1914.

In 1914, Cromwell and Jutta are disillusioned with their parents' dreams. Cromwell is associated with technological power and dehumanizing order. He is the prototype of Zizendorf in the 1945 sections of the novel. Jutta is imaged as an architect. She worships people "in the abstract." Her concern with "angles and structures" associates her with Cromwell's "Technological Revolution" and, later, with Zizendorf's plans to "build the house" of his neo-Nazi state. It is Jutta whom Zizendorf takes as his mistress. In another parallel, Madam Snow nurses Balamir in the 1945 sections, just as she comforts Ernst on the first night of World War I. She abandons Balamir and accepts the Duke's invitation to dinner, just as she leaves the dead Ernst to side with the Nazis in World War II.

When the inmates of the "ordered institution," literally a madhouse symbolizing the Nazi state, are released at the end of World War II, the pattern begins again. Zizendorf believes he can succeed where those before him failed because his plans are founded on a disillusioned view of reality, on his recognition that "life is not the remarkable, the precious or necessary thing we think it is." Zizendorf is identified with both the Duke and Balamir. His disregard for other human lives parallels the Duke's cannibalism. Zizendorf's belief that he can succeed mirrors Balamir's illusion that he can rebuild the old Germany. Zizendorf fails to recognize that there is really no division between the Germany of 1914, the Germany of 1945, and his new state; there is only a continuity. One abortive system of destructive order spawns another.

Hawkes said that *The Cannibal* is in the future. Zizendorf writes that he has to leave the town—"a garden spot; all of our memories are there"—but he assures the reader: "I am waiting, and at the first opportunity I will, of course, return."

James Green

Further Reading

Berry, Eliot. *A Poetry of Force and Darkness: The Fiction of John Hawkes*. San Bernardino, Calif.: R. Reginald, the Borgo Press, 1979. Discusses the link between historical time and the unconscious in *The Cannibal* and finds repression the link between the sexual and the political in the novel.

Busch, Frederick. *Hawkes: A Guide to His Fictions*. Syracuse, N.Y.: Syracuse University Press, 1973. Presents a close analysis of the novels. Discusses Hawkes's style and social concern in *The Cannibal*. Examines animal imagery in relation to the theme of sterility and hopelessness.

Ferrari, Rita. *Innocence, Power, and the Novels of John Hawkes*. Philadelphia: University of Pennsylvania Press, 1996. Ferrari traces Hawkes's development as a novelist, analyzing his experiments with narrative voice and perspective, his representations of gender and identity, and his ideas about language, among other elements of his fiction. *The Cannibal* is examined in chapter 1.

Greiner, Donald J. *Comic Terror: The Novels of John Hawkes*. Memphis, Tenn.: Memphis State University Press, 1973. Analyzes Hawkes's comedy in terms of "black humor" and discusses his use of poetic techniques and concern for structural coherence.

Kuehl, John. *John Hawkes and the Craft of Conflict*. New Brunswick, N.J.: Rutgers University Press, 1975. Discusses the tension between Eros and Thanatos in Hawkes's novels in relation to setting, myth, structure, characterization, and narrative focus. Analyzes Hawkes's use of characters to represent ideas.

Marx, Lesley. *Crystals out of Chaos: John Hawkes and the Shapes of Apocalypse*. Madison, N.J.: Fairleigh Dickinson University Press, 1997. A novel-by-novel examination of Hawkes's fiction, chronologically tracing his development as a writer. *The Cannibal* is analyzed in chapter 1.

Reutlinger, D. P. "*The Cannibal*: The Reality of Victim." *Critique* 6, no. 2 (Fall, 1963): 30-37. Sees the characters as victims of romantic politics and discusses Hawkes's antirealistic art as a way of evoking sympathy through intellectual apprehension of horror.

Whelan, Michaele. *Navigating the Minefield: Hawkes's Narratives of Perversion*. New York: Peter Lang, 1998. Approaches Hawkes's fiction from the perspectives of psychoanalysis, gender representation, and narrative structure, focusing on his depiction of various types of deformation.

The Canterbury Tales

Author: Geoffrey Chaucer (c. 1343-1400)
First transcribed: 1387-1400
Type of work: Poetry
Type of plot: Romance, farce, and fable
Time of plot: Late fourteenth century
Locale: The pilgrimage road between London and
  Canterbury

Principal characters:
CHAUCER, the narrator
HARRY BAILLY, the Host
THE KNIGHT
ROBIN, the Miller
ALISON, a young woman
THE NUN'S PRIEST

The Poem:

One April, a group of pilgrims gathers at the Tabard Inn in Southwark, near London, to embark on a pilgrimage to the shrine of St. Thomas à Becket at Canterbury. After dinner, Harry Bailly, the host, proposes a storytelling competition on the journey. The host will judge, and the winner will receive a dinner at the Tabard Inn. The following morning, as the pilgrims depart, they draw lots to begin. The Knight draws the shortest lot and tells his tale.

In "The Knight's Tale," Duke Theseus returns to Athens victorious over the Amazons with their queen, Hippolyta, as his wife and with her sister Emily. They encounter women mourning because the Theban king, Creon, refuses burial for their husbands, who were killed besieging Thebes. Duke Theseus then conquers Thebes. He captures two knights, Palamon and Arcite, and imprisons them.

One May morning, both Palamon and Arcite fall in love with Emily when they see her walking in the garden. Duke Perotheus, a friend of Duke Theseus, negotiates Arcite's release on the condition that he never return to Athens. Arcite longs for Emily, however, so he disguises himself as a squire, calls himself Philostratus, and serves at the court of Duke Theseus. Meanwhile, Palamon escapes by sedating his jailer.

By chance, Palamon and Arcite meet in the woods outside Athens. Duke Theseus finds them as they battle over Emily. He decrees that Palamon and Arcite should return in a year to wage a tournament for Emily. Palamon and Arcite gather with their knights at the new stadium built by Duke Theseus. Palamon is defeated, but Arcite is mortally injured while riding in victory around the stadium. After mourning Arcite, Duke Theseus arrange for the marriage of Palamon and Emily.

After commending the Knight's story, Harry Bailly asks the Monk to continue, but Robin, the drunken Miller, insists on telling his bawdy tale next. In "The Miller's Tale," John, an older carpenter who is married to Alison, a pretty young woman, is afraid of her attractiveness to other men. Nicholas, a student who boards in their house, proposes a tryst with

Alison. Absalom, a parish clerk, also tries to court her. Nicholas contrives a plan to deceive the carpenter. He convinces the carpenter of an impending flood and instructs John to provide tubs and provisions for them. At night, when they retire to their tubs in the attic to await the deluge, the carpenter falls asleep and Nicholas steals away with Alison to her bedroom.

Meanwhile, Absalom woos Alison outside her room. In the darkness, he asks for a kiss. She sticks her backside out the window. He kisses her backside. Realizing that he has been duped, Absalom obtains a red-hot iron. Absalom returns and asks for another kiss. Nicholas, amazed at Absalom's foolishness and wishing to participate in the jest, sticks his backside out the window while Alison says it is she, and Absalom brands Nicholas with the iron. Nicholas's screams of pain awaken the carpenter, who falls to the ground and breaks his arm. Nicholas and Alison convince the neighbors that the carpenter is delusional about the flood.

Next, the Reeve, the Cook, and the Man of Law tell their stories. In "The Reeve's Tale," a reaction to "The Miller's Tale," Oswald the Reeve tells about a dishonest miller who robs two clerks. They retaliate against him by getting him drunk and taking advantage of his wife and daughter. "The Cook's Tale," a fragment of about fifty lines, tells of a young man done out of his inheritance by a wicked older brother. In "The Man of Law's Tale," Constance, daughter of a Roman emperor, marries first a sultan of Syria who is killed and then a king. Both mothers-in-law cause her to be accused of treachery, but ultimately she is reunited with her second husband.

The wife of Bath next offers her tale. She prefaces the story with a discourse on marriage, based on her experiences with five husbands. In "The Wife of Bath's Tale," a knight in King Arthur's court rapes a young woman. When he is sentenced to death, the queen intercedes and agrees to save the knight's life if he searches for a year to ascertain what women most desire. As he is about to return after an unsuccessful search, he encounters an ugly old woman. She agrees to tell him the answer if he will grant her next request. The knight agrees, is told what women want, and returns to court. When the knight reveals to the queen that women desire power, his answer is accepted. The old woman appears and demands that the knight marry her. The knight is reluctant but changes his mind after the old woman lectures him on the true character of nobility. After the marriage, the old woman is transformed, becoming young and beautiful.

The Friar, the Summoner, the Clerk, the Merchant, the Squire, the Franklin, the Physician, the Pardoner, the Shipman, the Prioress, the Monk, and even the narrator himself all tell their tales as the pilgrims continue toward Canterbury. "The Friar's Tale," directed by the Friar at the Summoner, paints a humiliating picture of a wicked summoner in cahoots with the devil whose scheme against a widow backfires, landing him in hell. The Summoner retaliates by telling "The Summoner's Tale," in which a greedy, hypocritical friar visits the home of Thomas, a villager. In "The Clerk's Tale," patient Griselda, the daughter of the poorest man in a poor village, is married to a marquis who tests the limits of her patience by subjecting her to endless indignities. In "The Merchant's Tale," a young woman, married to an old man who goes blind, carries on an affair practically under his nose until the god Pluto restores the old man's sight. Proserpine in turn gives the wife a good excuse for what the old man "sees" as his wife's infidelity.

"The Squire's Tale," an incomplete tale, tells of a king's daughter, Canacee, who is given a brass horse that can fly, a mirror with the power to foretell disaster, and a ring that enables its wearer to understand the language of birds. In "The Franklin's Tale," Dorigen, wed to Averagus, is loved by Aurelius, in whom she has no interest. She promises to be his lover if he can accomplish the near-impossible task of clearing away all the rocks on the seacoast. With a magician's help, Aurelius completes the task, but when he realizes Dorigen does not really want him, he releases her from her promise. In "The Physician's Tale," the Roman knight Virginius has a beautiful daughter Virginia, who is lusted after by a wicked judge, Apius. Apius schemes to get her under his power, and, when his success seems inevitable, Virginia tells her father she would rather die than become Apius's lover. When she swoons, her father cuts off her head.

In "The Pardoner's Tale," three blasphemous, lecherous revelers decide to seek out Death to destroy him. In their search, however, they find a cache of gold, which makes them turn on one another in their greed. They end up killing one another, thus meeting Death at last. In "The Shipman's Tale," a monk cuckolds a miserly merchant and then causes his wife to reveal her infidelity to her husband. In "The Prioress's Tale," a boy, delighted with the song "Alma Redemptoris,"

sings it so much that a group of Jews become incensed enough to hire someone to kill him. The killer tosses the body into a pit to hide it, but, miraculously, the dead boy begins to sing, and those searching for him find his body and the killers, who are quickly put to death.

"The Monk's Tale" actually combines several stories that tell of the fall from power or high station of Lucifer, Adam, Samson, Hercules, Nero, Julius Caesar, and several other men. Chaucer, the narrator, next begins "The Tale of Sir Thopas," a kind of parodied romance, but he is interrupted by the Host, who claims the doggerel Chaucer uses is downright silly and lewd. Instead, Chaucer tells the story of Melibee/Meliboeus, in which Melibee debates with his wife the best way to deal with one's enemies.

Because "The Monk's Tale" was a tragedy that has saddened the company, Harry Bailly asks the Nun's Priest to lighten their hearts with a merrier tale. In "The Nun's Priest's Tale," Chauntecleer is a vain rooster. One night, as Chauntecleer sleeps beside his favorite hen, Pertelote, he dreams about a fox. Pertelote does not believe in dreams and chides him for cowardice. Although Chauntecleer thinks dreams have veracity, he flies down into the yard the next morning. Sir Russel, the fox, arrives and flatters Chauntecleer into singing. The fox seizes Chauntecleer and runs into the woods. Chauntecleer advises the fox to eat him immediately. When the fox opens his mouth to reply, Chauntecleer escapes.

"The Nun's Priest's Tale" is followed by "The Second Nun's Tale," "The Canon's Yeoman's Tale," "The Manciple's Tale," and finally "The Parson's Tale," a long prose tract. "The Second Nun's Tale" recounts the life of the famous Roman martyr St. Cecilia. "The Canon's Yeoman's Tale" is a story of a swindling alchemist that serves to denounce the trickery involved in alchemy. "The Manciple's Tale," a variation on the traditional telltale bird story, tells of the crow, who once was white. After he tells his owner, Phoebus Apollo, that Apollo's wife has been unfaithful—and after Apollo slays her—the crow is turned black by the angry god. "The Parson's Tale," more a sermon than a story, is about penitence, various sins, and their remedies.

Critical Evaluation:

The Canterbury Tales, Geoffrey Chaucer's last major work, was written between the mid-1380's and his death in 1400, although some of the stories, such as "The Knight's Tale," were composed earlier. It is considered one of the greatest works of English literature. Most of the work is poetic, but a few of the tales are written in prose. In the twenty-four tales, Chaucer demonstrates mastery of almost every literary genre known in the Middle Ages. Various pilgrims tell tales of romance (the Knight, the Wife of Bath), farce (the Miller), and beast fable (the Nun's Priest). Although many of the stories were not new, Chaucer transformed the material with an originality that made the tales unique. He imbued his characters with vivacity by skillfully playing the general types of stereotyped social classes and occupations against specific details of individuals' appearance and mannerisms.

The tales begin with a general prologue that sets up the frame narrative of the pilgrimage. It provides the rationale for the stories and introduces the pilgrims. The concept of a story collection has antecedents in medieval literature, including *Decameron: O, Prencipe Galeotto* (1349-1351; *The Decameron*, 1620), written in the fourteenth century by the Italian Giovanni Boccaccio. The frame of telling stories on a pilgrimage, however, was unprecedented and creates the potential for interaction among the storytellers, which Chaucer exploits. The descriptions of the pilgrims show how well Chaucer combines the typical with the particular. While the "true, perfect, gentle knight" represents the ideal estate of medieval knighthood, the Wife of Bath, a middle-class textile maker, comes to life with more individual details about her appearance and her ability to laugh and gossip.

"The Knight's Tale" is a romance, a medieval literary genre in which the setting is the distant past, the protagonists are from the nobility, and the plot stems from deeds based on love and chivalry. The tale is set in ancient Athens, the principal characters are knights, and the plot unfolds from their contest to win the love of a noble lady. Although Boccaccio's *Teseida* (1340-1341; *The Book of Theseus*, 1974) provided the idea for this tale, Chaucer shortened and changed the emphasis of Boccaccio's narrative. He also introduced new elements, particularly about the role of fate, from diverse sources. Individual character development is subordinated to maintaining the conventions of the romance genre.

With the drunken Miller's outburst, Chaucer poses a dramatic contrast between "The Knight's Tale" and "The Miller's Tale." The fable told by the Miller is the exact opposite of the Knight's refined, noble romance. Characters in a fable typically are from a lower social class, as is the Miller. John, the husband in the tale, is a carpenter; his young wife, Alison, is a pretty but common damsel. Her suitors are the student Nicholas and the clerk Absalom. The action takes place in Chaucer's Oxford. The plot generates humor from sexual exploits, as Nicholas and Absalom vie for Alison's favors. Chaucer's inspiration for this tale came from similar themes characterizing medieval fabliaux. He created lively characters through their appearance and actions. For example, his lengthy description of Alison utilizes comparisons with animals ("skittish as a colt") to emphasize her playful attractiveness. Its

fast-moving plot, contemporaneous setting, and earthy characters make "The Miller's Tale" memorable.

With the Wife of Bath, Chaucer returns to the romance genre. The Wife of Bath prefaces her tale with a lengthy discourse on marriage, in which she recounts her life with her trials and triumphs over five different husbands. The prologue to her tale allows Chaucer to develop her garrulous character. This passage is famous for the Wife of Bath's diatribe against medieval misogyny.

In contrast, the tale about a knight at King Arthur's court is restrained. Its source is probably English folklore, but it follows the requirements of romance with its setting in Arthurian England and a plot based on a love quest. The tale deals with nobility, not only in the social position of its main characters—including the knight and King Arthur's queen—but also in the old woman's discussion of nobility's true nature. While the tale's point about a wife's dominion over her husband supports the Wife of Bath's position on marriage, its courtly setting and economical narration diminish the impact of its message when compared to the vivid discourse and opinions in the wife expresses in her prologue.

The Nun's Priest tells a beast fable, in which animal protagonists provide a human moral. The tale of the cock, Chauntecleer, and the fox, Sir Russel, was a well-known beast fable that Chaucer transformed for his purposes. First, he amplified the plot with an extended commentary on the nature of dreams that drew on varied literary sources. Second, the full description of Chauntecleer, "the courtly cock," and his animated conversations with his favorite hen, Pertelote, created characters more real than the humans within the story or even than the storyteller. Chaucer again used his literary talents to create a memorable and distinctive story.

These selections provide only a glimpse into the variety that makes *The Canterbury Tales* such an intriguing literary work. This variety also introduces a question about the unity of *The Canterbury Tales*. The issue of this unity is complex because Chaucer died before finishing the work, and the order of the tales, in part, results from editorial efforts made from the fifteenth through the twentieth centuries to impart unity to what in fact remains a fragment of the intended whole. Many crucial elements contribute to the artistic integrity of *The Canterbury Tales* as a complete concept. The frame of the pilgrimage is maintained throughout, and dialogue among the pilgrims links some of the tales, as in the transition between "The Knight's Tale" and "The Miller's Tale." Particular themes repeat themselves: "The Wife of Bath's Tale," for example, is part of a larger group of tales discussing marriage. In its entirety, *The Canterbury Tales* provides an infinite source for entertainment and enlightenment and remains as engrossing a work of English literature as when Chaucer first composed it.

Karen Gould; revised by Jane L. Ball

Further Reading

Bloom, Harold, ed. *Geoffrey Chaucer's "The Canterbury Tales."* New ed. New York: Bloom's Literary Criticism, 2008. Collection of essays analyzing the prologue and many of the individual tales.

Boitani, Piero, and Ji Mann, eds. *The Cambridge Companion to Chaucer.* 2d ed. New York: Cambridge University Press, 2003. Collection of essays on topics including Chaucer's style, the literary structure of his works, the social and literary scene in England during his lifetime, and his French and Italian inheritances. Also includes four essays examining the use of romance, comedy, pathos, exemplum, and fable in *The Canterbury Tales.*

Brown, Peter. *Chaucer at Work: The Making of "The Canterbury Tales."* New York: Longman, 1994. Designed as an introduction to *The Canterbury Tales*; includes questions for discussion to guide readers in thinking about the workings of Chaucer's literary method. A good place to start a study of *The Canterbury Tales.*

Cooper, Helen. *The Canterbury Tales.* New York: Oxford University Press, 1989. A complete reference for all basic points about the literary character of *The Canterbury Tales.*

Howard, Donald R. *The Idea of "The Canterbury Tales."* Berkeley: University of California Press, 1976. Discusses the concept of *The Canterbury Tales* in terms of style and form as an unfinished but complete literary work.

Patterson, Lee, ed. *Geoffrey Chaucer's "The Canterbury Tales": A Casebook.* New York: Oxford University Press, 2007. Ten essays explicate the prologue and the central themes of the most frequently taught tales. Designed for undergraduates and general readers.

Pearsall, Derek. *"The Canterbury Tales."* Winchester, Mass.: Allen & Unwin, 1985. Approaches *The Canterbury Tales* by genre of stories. Includes helpful discussions of the surviving manuscripts and the reception of *The Canterbury Tales* from 1400 through the twentieth century.

Rigby, S. H. *Chaucer in Context: Society, Allegory, and Gender.* New York: Manchester University Press, 1996. Rigby, a historian, examines and assesses the competing critical approaches that have been used to analyze *The Canterbury Tales.* Emphasizes the importance of viewing Chaucer within the historical, social, and political contexts of the writer's time.

Shoaf, R. Allen. *Chaucer's Body: The Anxiety of Circulation in "The Canterbury Tales."* Gainesville: University Press of Florida, 2001. Explores the representation of the body in the poem, particularly the images of disease, contamination, and social and sexual intercourse.

Wetherbee, Winthrop. *Geoffrey Chaucer: "The Canterbury Tales."* 2d ed. New York: Cambridge University Press, 2004. Places the poem within the context of the crisis in fourteenth century English society. Discusses its language, prologue, representation of women and of the courtly and material worlds, literary style, and reception. Designed for students and general readers.

Canto general

Author: Pablo Neruda (1904-1973)
First published: 1950 (English translation, 1991)
Type of work: Poetry

When Pablo Neruda succumbed to cancer in his sixty-ninth year, he left behind nine unpublished manuscripts: one prose memoir and eight collections of poetry. He had already earned world recognition as one of the most important and prolific poets of his generation. One of the works that had brought him recognition was *Canto general* (general song), which appeared almost exactly at the midpoint of his career. His poetic career spanned about five decades. *Canto general* is a work of immense scope and poetic ambition, and one that has been accomplished by few poets of any time or place.

The collection is divided into fifteen sections, each containing from a dozen to more than forty individual poems. The sheer immensity of the work may be intimidating to the uninitiated, but it is a fine place for readers new to Neruda to become acquainted with his work. It provides a compendium of the poet's wide range of interests and gathers in one volume the forms he regularly explored during periods throughout his career. Neruda's passionate interests in history, politics, and nature, and his stunning ability to show the sublime within the mundane are all present in *Canto general* in full working order.

Neruda's emotional and spiritual history and his evolution as a poetic thinker become entwined with the natural history and political evolution of the southern half of the American continent. "A Lamp on Earth," the opening section, begins with "Amor America (1400)." This poem, as do most in this section, operates much in the manner of Neruda's numerous odes. The book's first poem conjures the beauty and relative peace of America prior to the arrival of the conquistadores. The succeeding poems of the opening section sing respectively to "Vegetation," "Some Beasts," "The Birds Arrive," "The Rivers Come Forth," "Minerals," and, finally, "Man."

"A Lamp on Earth" is something of a contemporary *Popol Vuh*, the sequence of ancient Mayan creation myths. Neruda's work may be more accurately dubbed a re-creation myth. As in the Mayan vision, each separate element of the natural world is treated to its own individual tale of creation. The creation of the world is described as a series of smaller creations—landscape, vegetation, animals, minerals, people—all of which finally exist together as though by way of some godly experiment. The destruction of Mayan culture by the Spanish is detailed in the third section, which concentrates on a selection of names and places. Before moving into that cataclysmic period, however, Neruda inserts one of the most highly regarded works of his career, "The Heights of Macchu Picchu."

From the age of twenty-one until illness curtailed his ability to travel, Neruda served as diplomatic consul for his native Chile, living in a variety of nations throughout the world. In the years preceding "The Heights of Macchu Picchu," he had been acting consul to Spain, during the unfortunate time when fascism was gaining momentum. Neruda relinquished his post and returned to the Americas. Soon after, during the early 1940's, he traveled to the Andes and saw Macchu Picchu. His journey proved to be a revelatory one, forming the basis of one of his masterpieces.

"The Heights of Macchu Picchu" is a numbered sequence of twelve poems. Taken as an entity separate from the larger work, it is the product of classic poetic inspiration and indicates a turning point in Neruda's work. It is a richly imagistic chronicle of the rebirth of the poet's imagination and heart. The grave disillusion brought about by the tragedy of Spain leads to a renewal of Neruda's recognition of his need for political action. Neruda's renewal is told somewhat in the diction of a manifesto:

Rise up to be born with me, my brother.
Give me your hand from the deep
zone of your disseminated sorrow . . .
show me the stone on which you fell
and the wood on which you were crucified. . . .
Throughout the earth join all
the silent scattered lips
and from the depths speak to me all night long,
as if I were anchored to you. . . .
Hasten to my veins and to my mouth.
Speak through my words and my blood.

Neruda's outrage is arguably at its most eloquent in "The Heights of Macchu Picchu." The sequence is equally powerful either in or out of the context of *Canto general*.

His political anger finds an increasingly explicit enunciation in succeeding sections. The work launches into a broad historical epic. "The Conquistadors," another section, includes a series of lyric narrative poems that recall the exploits of Hernán Cortés and a selection of his lieutenants. There are also poems of lament, eulogizing and grieving for a lost way of life, and poems about several legendary native resistors.

"The Liberators" and "The Sand Betrayed," the fourth and fifth sections, tell of the political rebels and freedom fighters of the eighteenth and nineteenth centuries. Neruda invokes the reader to join his lamentations for the noble spirits of murdered figures such as José Miguel Carrera, a Chilean rebel of the nineteenth century. Carrera holds a particular place of honor in Neruda's esteem. Carrera's life and work are the focus of a sequence of seven poems within "The Liberators."

Neruda's homage to freedom fighters of the past does not, however, confine itself to those of his native country. Nor are these rebels always soldiers. There is Castro Alves, a Brazilian poet of the nineteenth century, whose voice Neruda assumes throughout the greater portion of one of the fourth section's most eloquent poems:

Castro Alves from Brazil, for whom did you sing?
"I sang for the slaves who sailed aboard the ships
like a dark cluster from the sea of wrath . . .
I sang in those days against the inferno . . .
I wanted man's deliverance from man . . .
My voice knocked on door closed until then
so that, fighting, Freedom might enter."

There are also tributes to Toussaint Louverture, the eighteenth century liberator of Haiti, the first Latin American nation to become independent; to Emiliano Zapata, the farmer who became an instrumental leader of the Mexican Revolution in the early twentieth century; and to Augusto César Sandino, leader of the war against U.S. military presence in Nicaragua.

Neruda's preferences for communism and freedom are explicit in these poems, and there is little to suggest any distinction in the poet's mind between the two. His communist ideals are rooted in a purer Marxist view than has been practiced in reality. For Neruda, freedom means self-rule, regardless of the method, even at mortal costs. More than to any political ideology, Neruda was committed to the notion of class equalization.

Canto general's historical and political poems do not follow a rigid pattern. Neruda's scheme suggests a thematic sense of structure. From "America, I Do Not Invoke Your Name in Vain," the sixth section, and through succeeding sections, the poems become more directly autobiographical. The titles often include dates, focusing on the late 1930's through the late 1940's, just before the book's initial publication in Mexico.

The latter sections of *Canto general* extend the concerns and poetics of "A Lamp on Earth." Nature is seen more often as an entity separate from politics and war. The settings are less likely to appear as battlefields or the hometowns of martyred rebels, but places for solitary reflection, where the poet's personal and aesthetic epiphanies meld with the natural essence of creation at large. Neruda turns more often to the concept of the ode, as in "Hymn and Homecoming," an intensely passionate song of praise to his native land, which appears in the book's seventh section, "Canto General de Chile." This section often returns to specific points of Chilean topography and wildlife. As in earlier sections, several pieces express the poet's admiration of the characteristics of individual species. The "Red-Breasted Meadowlark" and "House Wrens" are described in anthropomorphic terms in comparatively simple lyrics. The creatures Neruda invokes are a source of consolation, an answer to the disappointments dealt with elsewhere.

The seventh section opens with "Eternity," which takes a panoramic view of Neruda's native landscape. The poet conjures himself as a product of his region, becoming integrated with it in dreams. "Eternity" is followed by "Hymn and Homecoming," in which his sad return from Spain brings him to reexamine his country as a source of spiritual nourishment. This is the section in which Neruda takes the opportunity to describe the more personal and confessional facets of

the regeneration he writes of in "The Heights of Macchu Picchu."

Neruda specifically mentions numerous places and people high in his esteem throughout the poem. In the fourteenth section, "The Great Ocean," he turns to the lives of mariners and coastal communities. Nowhere is Neruda as openly autobiographical as in the book's closing section, "I Am." A smattering of all the book's formal and thematic components appears in closing, and the poet assumes a more prominent presence in the poems. Again, the land, nature, youth, and the passions for travel and common people are sung to by way of odes, reminiscences, laments, and confessions. Two of the poems, "The War" and "Love," examine Neruda's experience in Spain.

Having finished the writing at age forty-four, Neruda had turned forty-six by the time *Canto general* was published. The final poems begin to look at his life as an artist, expressing his state of mind over arriving at the completion of such a monumental work. The poem "I End Here" describes *Canto general* as having been "written on the run." Allowing Neruda his moment of self-deprecation, one cannot avoid the immensity and deeply passionate drive of *Canto general*, even considering the work as part of the canon of a poet known for producing immense and passionate volumes.

Canto general is remarkable for its employment of a free sense of form, an idiomatic eloquence, and its musicality, which owes much to the treasures of the ballad tradition in Spanish. Neruda won a Nobel Prize in Literature in 1971, and the wonder is why, with a body of work that includes *Canto general*, he did not win it sooner.

Jon Lavieri

Further Reading

Bloom, Harold, ed. *Pablo Neruda*. New York: Chelsea House, 1989. A collection of writings on various aspects of Neruda's work. Includes Federico García Lorca's "Introduction of Pablo Neruda to the School of Philosophy and Letters, Madrid."

Costa, René de. *The Poetry of Pablo Neruda*. Cambridge, Mass.: Harvard University Press, 1979. Analyzes themes and techniques in a selection of Neruda's main works. Among the best sources for a detailed study of *Canto general*.

Dawes, Greg. *Verses Against the Darkness: Pablo Neruda's Poetry and Politics*. Lewisburg, Pa.: Bucknell University Press, 2006. Analyzes Neruda's poetry from the perspectives of his aesthetic ideas and political beliefs. Argues that in the period from 1925 through 1954, Neruda became more sophisticated literarily and politically as he became more radicalized during the Spanish Civil War and World War II.

Duran, Manuel, and Margery Safir. *Earth Tones: The Poetry of Pablo Neruda.* Bloomington: Indiana University Press, 1981. A straightforward overview of Neruda's work, organized thematically.

Méndez-Ramírez, Hugo. *Neruda's Ekphrastic Experience: Mural Art and "Canto general."* Lewisburg, Pa.: Bucknell University Press, 1999. Defines the work as the textual equivalent of mural art, in which Neruda provides

linguistic description of the murals' human complexities.

Teitelboim, Volodia. *Neruda: An Intimate Biography.* Translated by Beverly J. DeLong-Tonelli. Austin: University of Texas Press, 1991. A Chilean novelist, politician, and close personal friend of Neruda provides an excellent and accessible understanding of Neruda's life. Highly recommended.

Wilson, Jason. *A Companion to Pablo Neruda: Evaluating Neruda's Poetry.* Rochester, N.Y.: Tamesis, 2008. Chronological analysis of Neruda's poetry, charting his artistic development and the unity of his work.

Cantos

Author: Ezra Pound (1885-1972)

First published: 1917-1969 (including *The Pisan Cantos,* 1948; *Section: Rock Drill,* 1955; *Thrones,* 1959; *Drafts and Fragments of Cantos CX-CXVII,* 1969; *A Draft of XXX Cantos,* 1930; *Eleven New Cantos,* 1934; *The Fifth Decade of Cantos,* 1937; *Cantos LII-LXXI,* 1940; all 117 collected in *The Cantos of Ezra Pound I-CXVII,* 1970)

Type of work: Poetry

Ezra Pound may be considered one of the most powerful, disturbing, and enigmatic literary figures of the twentieth century. Often his public persona overshadowed his interest in being a poet who would be remembered for his poetry, but part of that was due to Pound's own unflagging energies and ambitions as an editor, as a friend to writers in exile from America, and as the "foreign correspondent" for Harriet Monroe's 1912 publication *Poetry: A Magazine of Verse.* He was responsible for the final version of T. S. Eliot's *The Waste Land* (1922), he influenced William Carlos Williams, he was instrumental in getting James Joyce published, and he spent time with Ernest Hemingway in Italy. He was the guiding voice behind the Imagist movement in poetry early in the twentieth century, and his association with Benito Mussolini still stands in infamy. Pound's time in a temporary detention center in Pisa, Italy, still stands in infamy—and led to *The Pisan Cantos* (1948)—as does his later imprisonment in St. Elizabeths Hospital in Washington, D.C., from 1945 to 1970.

Many who attempt to analyze Pound's literary career are so struck by its richness that they miss the kernel at the core of his poetry: the *Cantos.* While Pound worked on other

types of poetry and poetic movements, his mind and his focus remained on the *Cantos,* which he conceived of as a twentieth century epic. Pound worked on the *Cantos* for nearly fifty years, weaving scores of subjects and themes into the longest important poetic work of the modern era. When he set out on his poetic odyssey, Pound conceived of his poem as a modern version of Dante Alighieri's *La divina commedia* (c. 1320; *The Divine Comedy,* 1802); his intention was to mirror Dante's epic organization into "inferno," "purgatory," and "heaven." Pound, following Dante, called the individual units of the epic cantos. Small press publications of parts of the *Cantos* appeared upon occasion, but the poem as a whole was not published until 1948. The publication date was, perhaps, meant to coincide with the availability of *The Pisan Cantos.*

After his release from St. Elizabeths, Pound returned to Italy, where he had about five years of peace. Some who visited him there related that he continued to work on his masterpiece, but there is little, if any, of that work remaining.

Pound's poem *Hugh Selwyn Mauberley* (1920), also considered a classic in the English language, is often discussed in reference to the style of the *Cantos*, although the *Cantos* are much more ambitious. In *Hugh Selwyn Mauberley*, Pound uses a rhetorical persona who reflects on a wide variety of experiences. In many similar ways, the first sixteen cantos use a reactive rhetorical narrator, and at times these two figures have similar interests—not surprising, since the poems began to be composed at about the same time.

There is another influence on Pound's work, that of Eliot's narrator in *The Waste Land*. The difference between Eliot and Pound is clear: Eliot presents a rhetoric rich in narrative, while Pound presents a rhetoric steeped in speculation, myth, and ancient history. Some critics see the first canto as a reflection on Odysseus, and they believe that the Odysseus references are broad rather than specific, but if readers follow the Odysseus beginning, they are able to become grounded in specific myth.

In the *Cantos*, Pound displays his knowledge and his ability to present it without introductions, borders, or transitions. The poem is as much instructive as it is reflective, and it is in part the breadth of Pound's knowledge that causes so much continued study of the *Cantos*. To as great a degree as may be possible in English or American poetry, this poem is about everything.

Many sections of the poetic discourse written in English are interrupted by quotations from Provençal, Italian, German, French, Latin, and Greek, not to mention Anglo-Saxon and Middle English. There are quotations from the prosy diplomatic correspondence of John Adams, phrases more than a century old and deader in intrinsic interest than that. There are quotations from the fiscal regulations of Leopold of Habsburg-Lorraine, who instituted solid financial conditions in Tuscany before the disaster of Napoleon Bonaparte's arrival. There are abundant references to historical and literary figures good and bad, Eastern and Western. There are references to many people, both well-known and obscure. These people include contemporaries familiar to Pound; through them he memorializes the literary crusades and battles of the first half of the twentieth century. Further, there are many pages adorned with the completely enigmatic ideograms that Pound derived from classical Chinese, which he uses to symbolize ideas that are important to him. Pound also translates some foreign-language sources, among which his translations of Japanese poems are considered exemplary.

All this is included and woven into a tight but anecdotal structure that Pound introduces and embroiders with great metrical variety and dexterity. His language varies from noble simplicity and elegance through imitations of the banality (with which people of all ages have conducted the affairs of the world) to the argot of the illiterate. A special interest appears in the section entitled *The Pisan Cantos*, in which Pound describes his life in a prison camp at Pisa, working on an installment of his masterwork.

Many of the sections of the poem are highly musical, and Pound is virtuosic in his use of forms, but he never forgets the lessons of his early villanelles and of his poem "Sestina: Altaforte," which some see in the *Cantos*, in smaller form. Pound also uses the technique of the theatrical mask, taken from Greek tragedy. His speakers are often half-revealed or not revealed at all. This adds a dramatic texture and a certain richness to the poem and, once again, satisfies Pound's need to say as much as possible, to be as allusive as possible.

Most versions of the *Cantos* rely heavily on footnotes to direct the reader elsewhere, often to moments or events in the poet's life. Just as often the footnotes fill in historical or mythological information. When reading the *Cantos*, it must be remembered that Pound is attempting to write an epic poem and that he is very aware of his ambition and the requirements for an epic. He does not follow these requirements, however, because they would not work—and that lesson is as important as any other lesson about this work.

To a great degree, the *Cantos* are Pound's reactions to and reflections of his own almost limitless reading and to his broad knowledge and curiosity about his world and the preceding worlds. There are references to influences noted elsewhere, to Homer, to Ovid, and to Remy de Gourmont. Contemporary literary figures and occasions in Paris and London, and his important meetings with William Butler Yeats in 1908 and later, are also included, as are earlier poems by Pound.

Strange and without many literary parallels in its lack of plan and in its preference for jumble rather than clarity, the continuing poem that is the *Cantos* is a record of the workings of a sophisticated and ingenious mind that conducted a decades-long war with a world out of joint. In this work, language is in decay, social life is ebbing, and the economic system is a center of rot. The *Cantos* represents a break with the going social order and the modes of literary expression grateful to that order. Pound, in a phrase he derives from the Chinese, must "make things new." The techniques of confusion, blending, and non sequitur in the poem are techniques of assault; indurated sensibility must be awakened, and new habits of direct, nonabstract apprehension must be set up. Pound gathers hints from Homer, Confucius, the Provençal poets, and countless other writers who managed to be "human." By tearing apart the tapestry of the conventionally viewed past and weaving the threads into a new pattern of his own, Pound assaults ingrained and complacent sensibilities.

Pound also startles conventional and unreflective moral tastes by expressing admiration for such "natural" monsters as Sigismundo Malatesta, whose evil was at least direct and not transmogrified into a neutral entry in a ledger. One must have, in the world of the *Cantos*, a considerable amount of sin; in "good" ages, unlike the poet's own, sin and virtue declare themselves for what they are and do not masquerade as something else.

Thus the organized confusion of the *Cantos* becomes the pattern of Pound's own outraged and crusading sensibility. What the poem expresses is always clear to that sensibility. If it is not clear to readers, then, according to the poet, so much the worse for them and their blindness. Such, at any rate, is the intransigent accent of many a canto.

Many critics consider the *Cantos* to be flawed, but even such critics marvel at what Pound accomplishes in an epic poem of the twentieth century. This poem shows what can be done within the poetic medium, and Pound will always be one of the great literary masters because of it.

Revised by John Jacob

Further Reading

Baumann, Walter. *A Rose in the Steel Dust: An Examination of the "Cantos" of Ezra Pound.* Coral Gables, Fla.: University of Miami Press, 1970. A revisionist examination of the *Cantos*, with a view toward the postindustrial age seen through Pound's extreme interest in Dante and the French Provençal troubadours.

Cookson, William. *A Guide to the "Cantos" of Ezra Pound.* Rev. and expanded ed. New York: Persea Books, 2001. Provides page-by-page commentary on the poems, explaining their allusions, translating their foreign phrases, and identifying quotations. Offers introductory background material for each canto and discusses how Pound's opinions about literature, history, and economics are reflected in these works.

Goodwin, K. L. *The Influence of Ezra Pound.* New York: Oxford University Press, 1976. Places Pound firmly in the pantheon of modern poets, largely because of his having attempted the epic poem the *Cantos*.

Kenner, Hugh. *The Poetry of Ezra Pound.* Norfolk, Conn.: New Directions, 1951. Kenner is one of the foremost authorities on Pound, his work, and his influence. Chapters are devoted to the *Cantos*, and Kenner explains how the sequence drew together common threads in all Pound's work.

Leary, Lewis, ed. *Motive and Method in the "Cantos" of Ezra Pound.* New York: Columbia University Press, 1954. Early treatment of the epic poem. Explores political statements, prosody, and technique in Pound's fusion of myth and personal statement.

Makin, Peter, ed. *Ezra Pound's "Cantos": A Casebook.* New York: Oxford University Press, 2006. A collection of key critical essays interpreting the *Cantos* as well as two interviews with Pound.

Nadel, Ira Bruce. *The Cambridge Introduction to Ezra Pound.* New York: Cambridge University Press, 2007. Introductory overview containing information about Pound's life, poetry, and prose, and the contexts and critical reception of his work. Devotes a chapter to an analysis of the *Cantos*.

_____, ed. *The Cambridge Companion to Ezra Pound.* New York: Cambridge University Press, 1999. Collection of essays examining Pound and the making of modernism; his politics, economics, and anti-Semitism; and his depiction of women and gender. Several of the essays focus on the *Cantos*.

Pratt, William. *Ezra Pound and the Making of Modernism.* New York: AMS Press, 2007. Describes Pound as the "mastermind" of modernism, tracing his involvement in and impact on the literary movement. Describes Pound's evolution as a poet and his significant influence on twentieth century American poetry.

Selby, Nick. *Poetics of Loss in the "Cantos" of Ezra Pound: From Modernism to Fascism.* Lewiston, N.Y.: E. Mellen Press, 2005. Describes how the *Cantos* reflect both Pound's modernist concepts of poetry and his advocacy of fascism.

Captain Blood
His Odyssey

Author: Rafael Sabatini (1875-1950)
First published: 1922
Type of work: Novel
Type of plot: Adventure
Time of plot: 1685-1689
Locale: Bridgewater, Somersetshire, England; the
islands of Barbados, Hispaniola, Tortuga, and
Jamaica; Maracaibo, Venezuela; Cartagena,
Colombia; the Caribbean Sea

Principal characters:
PETER BLOOD, a doctor practicing in Bridgewater
JEREMIAH PITT, a shipmaster
WILLIAM BISHOP, colonel of the Barbados Militia, later
    deputy governor of Jamaica
ARABELLA BISHOP, the colonel's niece
DON MIGUEL DE ESPINOSA Y VALDEZ, admiral of the
    Spanish fleet in the Caribbean
LORD JULIAN WADE, an emissary of the British
    government
BARON DE RIVAROL, admiral of the French fleet in the
    Caribbean

The Story:

The Irish-born Peter Blood has served in the Dutch and French navies, spent two years in a Spanish prison, and now enjoys the life of a doctor in southwestern England. Blood is skeptical of the rebellion being raised by the duke of Monmouth against King James II, yet when Jeremiah Pitt begs him to come to the aid of the wounded Lord Gildoy, who has been involved in the rebellion, he accedes. As a result, Blood is arrested for treason along with Pitt and the nobleman whose life he has saved.

Gildoy subsequently buys his freedom, but Blood and Pitt are found guilty by the notorious Lord Jeffreys. Before they can be executed, however, the British secretary of state directs that one thousand of the rebels taken prisoner be transported to the West Indies as slaves. Blood and Pitt are shipped to Bridgetown, on the island of Barbados, where they are bought by the militia's cruel Colonel Bishop to work on his sugarcane plantation. Bishop discovers, however, that it is more profitable to allow Blood to tend to the ills of the island's aristocracy. As a result of his status, Blood becomes acquainted with Arabella Bishop, the colonel's attractive niece.

When the Spanish ship *Cinco Llagas* attacks Bridgetown, Bishop's troops are unprepared and are defeated, but the attack provides Blood with an opportunity. While the Spanish are celebrating their victory ashore, Blood, Pitt, and a handful of fellow slaves overpower the ship's remaining crew. They also take prisoner its captain, Don Diego de Espinosa y Valdez, when he returns and confiscate the ransom that the Spanish have collected. Blood's men destroy the rest of the Spanish boats with cannon before they can reach the ship, but their greatest pleasure comes when Bishop himself rows out

expecting to recover the ransom. Forced to swim ashore as the ship sails away, the enraged colonel becomes Blood's sworn enemy.

Blood agrees to release Don Diego on the Dutch island of Curaçao, but the wily Spaniard steers them to a Spanish settlement on the island of Hispaniola instead. Blood avoids the trap, but Don Diego dies of fright at his hands, earning him the enmity of the Spanish captain's brother, Don Miguel de Espinosa y Valdez—the admiral of the Spanish fleet in the Caribbean. Blood now joins the many buccaneers on the island of Tortuga who operate under the protection of the island's French governor. He knows that joining these pirates will damn him in the eyes of Bishop's niece, but he has little choice. The only outward sign of Blood's regard for her is to rename his ship the *Arabella*.

Blood continues to thwart Bishop and Don Miguel, outwitting the latter during a raid on the Venezuelan port of Maracaibo. So notorious has Blood become that the British government decides to enlist him in its own cause by pardoning him, entrusting the task to Lord Julian Wade. Wade's ship is attacked by Don Miguel, and he is captured, along with Arabella Bishop, who is traveling on the same vessel. Blood rescues them both and accepts Wade's offer, but Arabella's misunderstanding of his character and deeds throws him into despair. He also realizes that accepting the pardon will cause him to fall into the clutches of Colonel Bishop, who has become deputy governor of Jamaica. Moreover, Blood's love for Arabella earns him the enmity of Wade, who has fallen in love with the young woman himself. Unwilling to place himself in the power of these men, Blood rejects his pardon and escapes.

When France declares war on Spain in 1688, Blood is approached by the French governor of Hispaniola with a commission. He accepts the offer only to discover that his new masters intend to make a foolhardy attack upon the Spanish colonial city of Cartagena. Thanks to Blood, the attack succeeds, but the leader of the expedition, the treacherous Baron de Rivarol, sails away with the Spanish treasure.

While pursuing de Rivarol, the *Arabella* encounters British lifeboats off the coast of Jamaica, and Blood learns extraordinary news from two of their passengers. Admiral van der Kuylen, the commander of the British fleet, and Lord Willoughby, the new British governor-general of the West Indies, explain that England has a new king and that the hated James II has fled to France. When de Rivarol learned that his country and England were at war, he attacked the British fleet. Meanwhile, rather than protecting Jamaica, Bishop is off searching for Blood on Tortuga.

The news suggests that salvation may be at hand, but Blood is intent on apprehending de Rivarol. In a fierce sea battle, the baron's ship sinks the *Arabella*, but Blood's crew boards the French ship and takes control, recovering the plunder taken from Cartagena and saving Jamaica from a French attack. In recognition, Willoughby appoints Blood deputy-governor of Jamaica. Realizing their mutual love, Blood and Arabella make amends, and the blundering Colonel Bishop is arrested upon his return from Tortuga.

Critical Evaluation:

Although it is fiction, *Captain Blood* is based firmly on historical events. The Monmouth Rebellion took place, but it came to an abrupt end with the Battle of Sedgemoor (early July, 1685), the battle in which Lord Gildoy is wounded. Rafael Sabatini based the opening scenes of his book on the diary of a real doctor named Henry Pitman who cared for some of the soldiers wounded in that battle. Pitman, too, was arrested and tried by Lord Chief Justice Jeffreys during what are remembered as the Bloody Assizes, and he too was sentenced to death—a fate he avoided only because he was transported to the West Indies as a slave.

Blood's subsequent career as a privateer was based loosely on the exploits of seventeenth century Welsh privateer Henry Morgan, as related by Alexandre Exquemelin in his famous *De Americaensche Zee-Roovers* (1678; *The Buccaneers of America*, 1684). Sabatini's narrative voice, however, claims to draw his material from the account of Blood's activities kept by Jeremiah Pitt, and he establishes an air of verisimilitude by noting the latitude and longitude of certain events as supposedly recorded by Pitt. Acknowledging the resemblance between Blood's career and Morgan's, Sabatini cleverly suggests—in a fiction within a fiction—that Morgan's chronicler must have had access to Pitt's account in compiling his own.

The shifting political alliances that Sabatini dramatizes as taking place in the Caribbean are accurate. The British colony of Barbados and the buccaneers' lair of Tortuga were much as the novelist depicts them, and buccaneers did attack Maracaibo and Cartagena, although Sabatini alters the details to suit his story. It is in his seemingly perfunctory treatment of such places that twenty-first century readers may find Sabatini disappointing, for he is more interested in analyzing character than in describing coastlines and pinpointing the location of cities and islands. Realizing that he is dealing with inherently dramatic, even sensational material, Sabatini writes in a restrained, coolly ironic style that generally increases its drama, although again modern readers may occasionally find his treatment to be offhanded. He handles set pieces such as sea battles and personal confrontations agilely but supplies only the most essential details. He employs nautical terms naturally but sparingly.

The greatest appeal of *Captain Blood*, and one of the reasons for its continued popularity, lies in its protagonist's predicament, that of an honorable man wronged and misunderstood even by the woman he loves. Acting under the dictates of his own personal code, Blood strives to maintain a modicum of honor by following the career of a privateer rather than a pirate. Privateers operated as commissioned agents of a government and were expected to attack only the ships and settlements of hostile nations, while pirates, who became more common in the eighteenth century, regarded all ships and men as potential prey. Blood derives bitter satisfaction from his recognition that Don Miguel and de Rivarol—ostensibly honorable representatives of their governments—behave more like pirates than he does.

After Blood's escape from Barbados, the novel's plot is for the most part episodic, but Sabatini treats every episode as an opportunity to dramatize Blood's predicament or to advance, however indirectly, the story of his ongoing struggles with Bishop and Don Miguel. Coincidence plays a large role in the novel, and, realizing perhaps that even the most forgiving readers may find his use of the device excessive, Sabatini elevates it to a kind of historical principle: "Life itself is little more than a series of coincidences. . . . Indeed, coincidence may be defined as the very tool used by Fate to shape the destinies of men and nations."

Peter Blood proved to be such an intriguing and successful protagonist that Sabatini added two collections of stories to his odyssey: *Captain Blood Returns* (1931; also published as *The Chronicles of Captain Blood*) and *The For-*

tunes of *Captain Blood* (1936). These are not so much sequels as episodes drawn from the same period covered in
the novel. Adding to the figure's popularity was the 1935
Michael Curtiz film adaptation of *Captain Blood*. Starring
Errol Flynn and featuring rousing music by noted composer
Erich Wolfgang Korngold, the film is a faithful adaptation
and reproduces the gallant and swashbuckling spirit of its
source.

Grove Koger

Further Reading

Adrian, Jack. Introduction to *The Fortunes of Casanova, and
Other Stories*, by Rafael Sabatini. New York: Oxford
University Press, 1994. Summary of Sabatini's life and
career, stressing the writer's central role in the revitaliza-
tion of historical fiction.
Cordingly, David. *Under the Black Flag: The Romance and
the Reality of Life Among the Pirates*. New York: Random
House, 1995. Thorough examination of piracy and priva-
teering around the world and their treatment in literature
and film. Illustrations, maps, glossary of sea terms, bibliography.

Cornwell, Bernard. Introduction to *Captain Blood: His Odyssey*, by Rafael Sabatini. New York: Norton, 2002. Appreciation by a fellow historical novelist of Sabatini and
his most famous work.
Fraser, George MacDonald. Introduction to *Captain Blood:
His Odyssey*, by Rafael Sabatini. Pleasantville, N.Y.:
Akadine Press, 1998. Analysis of the novel as history in
the form of romance and an examination of its perennial
appeal.
Hoppenstand, Gary. Introduction to *Captain Blood*, by Rafael
Sabatini. New York: Penguin, 2003. Wide-ranging consideration of the novel, its historical background and
antecedents, and its place within the development of popular fiction. Suggestions for further reading.
Knight, Jesse F. "Rafael Sabatini: The Swashbuckler as Serious Artist." *Romantist* 9/10 (1985): 1-22. Rare extended
survey of Sabatini's life and literary career. Illustrations,
bibliography of books and uncollected short stories, film-
ography.
Olcott, Charles S. *At the Home of Rafael Sabatini*. Boston:
Houghton Mifflin/Riverside Press, 1927. Short appreciation of Sabatini, including a biographical account in his
own words. Portraits, numerous photographs.

Captain Horatio Hornblower

Author: C. S. Forester (1899-1966)
First published: 1939; includes *Beat to Quarters*, 1937;
Ship of the Line, 1938; *Flying Colours*, 1938
Type of work: Novel
Type of plot: Historical
Time of plot: Early nineteenth century
Locale: Pacific Ocean, South America, the Mediterranean,
Spain, France, England, and the Atlantic Ocean

Principal characters:
CAPTAIN HORATIO HORNBLOWER, the captain of HMS
Lydia and HMS *Sutherland*
BUSH, the first lieutenant
BROWN, the captain's coxswain
DON JULIAN ALVARADO (EL SUPREMO), a rich plantation
owner in Central America
MARIA, Hornblower's wife
LADY BARBARA WELLESLEY, the sister of the duke of
Wellington
ADMIRAL LEIGHTON, Hornblower's immediate commander
and Lady Barbara's husband

The Story:

Captain Horatio Hornblower, the commander of the
thirty-six-gun frigate HMS *Lydia*, is sailing under sealed orders from England around the Horn to the Gulf of Fonseca on
the western shores of Spanish America. He was ordered to
form an alliance with Don Julian Alvarado, a large landowner, and assist in raising a rebellion against Spain. The

Lydia carries the necessary munitions with which to start the
revolution. In addition, Hornblower has fifty thousand guineas in gold, which he is to give for the support of the rebellion
only if the revolt threatens to fail without English gold to
back it. If he does otherwise, he will be court-martialed. His
orders also casually mention the presence in Pacific waters of

a fifty-gun Spanish ship called the *Natividad*, which he is ordered to take, sink, burn, or destroy at the first opportunity.

After the *Lydia* anchors in the Gulf of Fonseca, a small boat appears with emissaries from Don Julian, who now calls himself El Supremo. They tell Hornblower that El Supremo requires the captain's attendance. Hornblower is not pleased with the evidence of El Supremo's tyranny. What he observes makes him all the more cautious. He refuses to hand over to El Supremo the arms and ammunition until his ship takes on food and water. The ship is loaded with stores as rapidly as possible, and the operation is going forward when a lookout on the mountain announces the approach of the *Natividad*.

Deciding to try to capture the ship in the bay, Hornblower hides the *Lydia* behind an island as the *Natividad* approaches. At the moment of greatest advantage, Hornblower orders the ship to sail alongside the *Natividad* and rake its decks with grapeshot. The British sailors lash the two ships together and board the *Natividad*. El Supremo demands the captured ship as his own. Hornblower hesitates to turn over his prize to El Supremo, but if he is to fulfill his orders he dares not antagonize the dictator.

Hornblower sails away and shortly afterward learns that upon Napoleon's deposition of King Ferdinand, England is now an ally of Spain. He also receives further orders, one from his admiral and one from an Englishwoman in Panama, Lady Barbara Wellesley, the duke of Wellington's sister, who requests transportation to England. During this period, the *Lydia* meets and defeats the *Natividad*, now commanded by El Supremo. The long period together on board ship leads to a deep love between Lady Barbara and Hornblower, but the captain cannot bring himself to act on that love because of his wife, Maria, at home. Lady Barbara is carried safely to England.

Hornblower is next ordered to command HMS *Sutherland*, a seventy-four-gun battleship. He sails with the *Pluto* and the *Caligula* to protect a convoy of merchant ships as far as the latitude of North Africa. They then meet French privateers and drive them off. Before parting company with the merchantmen, Hornblower impresses sailors from the convoy. Sailing along the coast, he captures the *Amelie*, attacks the battery at Llanza, burns and destroys supply vessels, and shells two divisions of cavalry on a highway passing near the seashore.

Admiral Leighton, now the husband of Lady Barbara, orders Hornblower to join and take charge of Spanish forces at the siege of French-held Rosas, but the operation fails because the Spaniards do not cooperate. After his retreat, Hornblower meets the *Cassandra*, a British frigate, and he learns that four French ships are bearing down upon them.

Hornblower decides to fight, even though the odds are four to one, and he sends the *Cassandra* to seek the *Pluto* and the *Caligula*. The *Cassandra* comes back with a message to Hornblower to engage the enemy, an order that indicates the presence of the admiral's flagship. Hornblower engages the French ships one at a time. The fourth French ship, however, comes upon him as he is fighting a two-decker and forces him to surrender.

After his surrender, Hornblower and Bush are imprisoned at Rosas. Admiral Leighton sails into the bay with the *Pluto* and the *Caligula* and completes the destruction of the French squadron. Hornblower watches the battle from the walls and sees the *Sutherland*, which was beached, take fire as a raiding party of British seamen burns it to prevent its use by the French. He learns from a seaman that Admiral Leighton was injured by a flying splinter.

Colonel Caillard, Napoleon's aide, comes to Rosas to take Hornblower and the wounded Bush to Paris. Bush is seriously ill as a result of losing a foot in the battle; therefore, Hornblower requests a servant to attend Bush on the long journey. He selects Brown, the coxswain, because of his strength, his common sense, and his ability to adapt himself to every situation. In France, their stagecoach is halted by a snowstorm near Nevers. Hornblower notices a small boat moored to the bank of a river and, as he and Brown assist the French in trying to move the coach, he makes his plans for escape. He attacks Colonel Caillard, and Brown ties up the Frenchman and throws him into the bottom of the coach. They lift Bush out of the coach and carry him to the boat. The whole operation requires only six minutes.

In the dead of night, the fugitives make their way down the river; Hornblower rows while Brown bails the icy water from the boat. When the boat crashes against a rock, Hornblower, thinking he lost Bush and Brown, swims ashore in the darkness. Brown, however, brings Bush safely to shore. Shivering with cold, the three men make their way to a farmhouse nearby, where they announce themselves as prisoners of war and are admitted.

Throughout the winter, they remain as guests of its owner, Comte de Gracay, and his daughter-in-law. Brown makes an artificial foot for Bush, and, when Bush is able to get around well, he and Brown build a boat in which to travel down the Loire. In early summer, Hornblower disguises himself as a Dutch customs inspector. To complete his disguise, the comte gives him the ribbon of the Legion of Honor that was his son's. That decoration aids Hornblower in his escape.

When Hornblower and his two men arrive in the harbor at Nantes, Hornblower cleverly takes possession of the *Witch of Endor*, conscripting a group of prisoners to be the crew, and makes his way back to England. Upon his arrival, Hornblower is praised for his exploits, knighted, and whitewashed at a court-martial. His sickly wife died during his absence, and Lady Barbara became guardian of his young son. Hornblower goes to visit Lady Barbara and to see his son. Admiral Leighton died of wounds at Gibraltar, and Lady Barbara is now a widow. Hornblower realizes from the quiet warmth of her welcome that she is already his. He is grateful to life for having given him fame and fortune and Lady Barbara.

Critical Evaluation:

C. S. Forester's *Captain Horatio Hornblower*, composed of three short novels—*Beat to Quarters* (1937), *Ship of the Line* (1938), and *Flying Colours* (1938)—falls in the middle of a series that begins with the intrepid officer's sea apprenticeship and concludes with *Commodore Hornblower* (1945), *Lord Hornblower* (1946), and *Admiral Hornblower in the West Indies* (1958). For its broad scope and sustained vigor, the whole series has appropriately been described as a modern saga. While Forester's Hornblower stories lack the philosophical and moral dimension of the sea fiction of Joseph Conrad, Richard Henry Dana, and Herman Melville, they certainly are the equal of sea-adventure novels by Captain Frederick Marryat or James Fenimore Cooper. Forester's novels combine meticulous historical reconstruction with a flair for storytelling. In 1932, he began writing screenplays for Hollywood. Unlike many other distinguished novelists who either failed or were only moderately successful in adapting their skills to this medium, Forester excelled as a scriptwriter and thereby learned how to use certain cinematic techniques in his fiction. Lively and fast-paced, the Hornblower stories, in which each scene builds to a climax, are easy to visualize. They are also based on historical information. The celebrated battle scenes bristle with sharp, concrete details that capture the excitement of the moment, and in Forester's descriptions of English manners, customs, and topical interests during the early nineteenth century, the robust age comes alive.

A realist, Forester does not gloss over the unpleasant truths about warfare at sea or the rigors of nautical life. Early in *Captain Horatio Hornblower*, readers learn that Hankey, the previous surgeon attached to HMS *Lydia*, died of the complications of drink and syphilis. Hornblower must perform several grisly operations on his wounded men. After one battle in *Beat to Quarters*, he cuts out a great splinter of wood lodged in a seaman's chest. Forester does not spare his readers the terrible details of Hornblower's crude operation, in which he uses no anesthetic. In *Flying Colours*, Hornblower must relieve the gangrenous pressure on the stump of his friend Bush's amputated leg. Applying cold vinegar to the stump to reduce the inflammation, he opens, cleans, and then sews up the victim's wound. Many such similar scenes of grim realism impart a sense of truth to the plots. In *Beat to Quarters*, Hornblower sees a man horribly tortured by the cruel El Supremo for no reason but that the man is judged "one of the unenlightened." Hornblower also witnesses the aftermath of battle: "dirty bodies with blood and pus and vomit." Forester creates realistic touches not only in the stark scenes of battle but also in the smallest details. He describes how ships are loaded with provisions, how the officers and crew function in a hierarchy of responsibilities, and how the ships operate in calm or storm. At one point, Hornblower's friend Gailbraith describes a poem that he admires, "The Lay of the Last Minstrel," whose author is "an Edinburgh lawyer." Instead of identifying the author as Sir Walter Scott, Forester thus creates a sense of contemporaneity, for at the time of the action, Scott was not yet famous and might easily have been known primarily as a lawyer who dabbled in poetry.

In his characterization of Horatio Hornblower, Forester provides sharp, realistic details that make his hero seem human. Although he is high-minded, courageous, and capable, Hornblower is not without frailties. He is vain, sometimes squeamish, and—strange to say—naturally indolent. Near the beginning of *Beat to Quarters*, Hornblower views himself critically in a mirror, noting all of his physical liabilities as well as his strengths. He does not like his "rounded belly" and fears that he is growing bald. Several times in the book he reflects unhappily on his receding hairline. For a hero, he has a weak stomach for scenes of squalor or bloodshed. He must be shamed by Lady Barbara Wellesley before he allows her to dress the wounds of the injured. Furthermore, he is, by his own admission, lazy. After a battle involving the *Lydia*, Hornblower retires to his hammock to sleep. Although he feels "a prick of shame" that the other officers and men have to clean up the bodies and wreckage, he confesses to his physical limitations. Again, in *Flying Colours*, he wishes "to be idle and lazy." When his gentle wife, Maria, dies, he is plunged into grief; when he holds his child in his arms, he feels paternal elation; and when he courts Lady Barbara, he is an ardent yet awkward lover. Forester humanizes Hornblower, making him a man as well as a hero and thus a hero worthy of his victories.

Further Reading

Forester, C. S. *The Hornblower Companion*. Boston: Little, Brown, 1964. The fullest account Forester left of the creative processes that led to the inception of the Hornblower series. In two parts, the first a useful atlas of thirty annotated maps depicting events in the Hornblower saga, and the second the essay "Some Personal Notes," in which Forester explains how he came to write each novel.

_____. *Long Before Forty*. Boston: Little, Brown, 1968. Posthumously published autobiography that Forester completed before he began the Hornblower saga. An appendix contains "Some Personal Notes," the memoir he wrote for *The Hornblower Companion*.

Grainger, John D. "Who Was Hornblower?" *History Today* 49, no. 10 (October, 1999): 32. Describes the methods Forester used to create his fictional character; summarizes the plot of *The Commodore*, one of the novels featuring Hornblower; and delineates the similarities between Hornblower and the real-life Captain Sir Home Riggs Popham.

Parkinson, C. Northcote. *The Life and Times of Horatio Hornblower*. London: Joseph, 1970. A pseudobiography of Forester's fictional character by a trained naval historian. Parkinson's creative solutions to gaps in the Hornblower saga have little to do with Forester; however, his knowledge of British naval history helps place Hornblower's fictional adventures in a broader historical context.

Perrett, Bryan. *The Real Hornblower: The Life of Admiral of the Fleet, Sir James Alexander Gordon, GCB, Last Governor of the Royal Naval Hospital, Greenwich*. Annapolis, Md.: Naval Institute Press, 1997. Perrett argues that the character of Horatio Hornblower is modeled on Admiral James Gordon, a British naval hero who fought under the command of Admiral Horatio Nelson.

Sternlicht, Sanford. *C. S. Forester and the Hornblower Saga*. Rev. ed. Syracuse, N.Y.: Syracuse University Press, 1999. A revised edition of *C. S. Forester*, which was published in 1981. This book, an introduction to and overview of Forester's life and work, devotes a long chapter to the Hornblower saga. Using Forester's "Some Personal Notes" as his starting point, Sternlicht examines Hornblower as Forester's most fully realized "man alone." He suggests that the historical British naval hero Thomas Cochrane may have served as a model for Hornblower, and he discusses the significance of the Hornblower stories in bolstering British morale during World War II, when the "Captain" books first appeared.

Captains Courageous
A Story of the Grand Banks

Author: Rudyard Kipling (1865-1936)
First published: 1897
Type of work: Novel
Type of plot: Adventure
Time of plot: 1890's
Locale: Grand Banks of Newfoundland

Principal characters:
HARVEY CHEYNE, a spoiled young rich boy
DISKO TROOP, the owner and captain of the *We're Here*
DAN TROOP, his son
MR. CHEYNE, Harvey's father

The Story:

Harvey Cheyne is a rich, spoiled fifteen-year-old boy, bound for Europe aboard a swift ocean liner. He is so seasick that he hardly realizes it when a huge wave washes him over the rail of the ship into the sea. Luckily, he is picked up by a fisherman in a dory and put aboard the fishing schooner *We're Here*. The owner and captain of the boat, Disko Troop, is not pleased to have the boy aboard but tells him that he will pay him ten dollars a month and board until the schooner docks in Gloucester the following September. It is then the middle of May. Harvey insists that he be taken to New York immediately, asserting that his father will gladly pay for the trip, but the captain, doubting that Harvey's father is a millionaire, refuses to change his plans and hazard the profits of the fishing season. When Harvey becomes insulting, Disko promptly punches him in the nose to teach him manners.

The captain's son, Dan, is glad to have someone his own age aboard the fishing boat, and he soon becomes a friend of the castaway. Harvey's stories about mansions, private cars, and dinner parties fascinate him. Dan recognizes that Harvey is telling the truth and that he could not possibly make up so many details of a wealthy person's life.

Harvey begins to fit into the life aboard the schooner. All the fishermen take an interest in his nautical education, and Long Jack teaches him the names of the ropes and the various pieces of equipment. Harvey learns quickly, partly because he is a bright young lad and partly because Long Jack whips him with the end of a rope when he gives the wrong answers. He also learns how to swing the dories aboard when they are brought alongside with the day's catch, to help clean the cod and salt them away below the decks, and to stand watch at the wheel of the schooner as they move from one fishing ground on the Grand Banks to the next. Even Disko admits that the boy will be a good hand before they reach Gloucester in the fall.

Gradually, Harvey becomes accustomed to the sea. There are times of pleasure as well as of work. He enjoys listening while the other eight members of the crew talk and tell sea yarns in the evenings or on the days when it is too rough to lower the dories and go after cod. He discovers that the crew members come from all over the world. Disko and his son are from Gloucester, Long Jack is from Ireland, Manuel is Portuguese, Salters is a farmer, Pennsylvania is a former preacher who lost his family in the Johnstown flood, and the cook is a black man who was brought up in Nova Scotia and swears in Gaelic. These men fascinate Harvey, for they are so different from anyone he ever knew. What pleases the boy most is that they accept him on his own merits as a workman and a member of the crew and not as the heir to millions. Of all the crew, only Dan and the black cook believe Harvey's account of himself.

One day, a French brig hails the *We're Here*. Both vessels shorten sail, and Harvey and Long Jack are sent from the schooner to the brig to buy tobacco. Much to Harvey's chagrin, he discovers that the sailors on the French boat can hardly understand his schoolboy French but that they understand Long Jack's sign language perfectly.

The French brig figures in another of Harvey's adventures. He and Dan go aboard the ship at a later time to buy a knife that belonged to a deceased sailor. Dan buys the knife and gives it to Harvey, thinking it has added value because the Frenchman killed a man with it. While fishing from a dory several days later, Harvey feels a weight on his line and pulls in the Frenchman's corpse. The boys cut the line and throw the knife into the sea; it seems to them that the Frenchman returned to claim his knife.

Although they are the same age, Harvey is not nearly as handy on the schooner or in the dory as Dan, who grew up around fishing boats and fishermen, but Harvey surpasses Dan in the use of a sextant. His acquaintance with mathematics and his ability to use his knowledge seems enormous to the simple sailors. So impressed is Disko that he begins to teach Harvey what he knows about navigation.

Early in September, the *We're Here* joins the rest of the

fishing fleet at a submerged rock where the cod fishing is at its best, and the fishermen work around the clock to finish loading the holds with cod and halibut. The vessel that first fills its hold is not only honored by the rest of the fleet but also gets the highest price for the first cargo into port. For the past four years, the *We're Here* finished first, and it wins honors again the year Harvey is aboard. All canvas is set, the flag is hoisted, and the schooner makes the triumphant round of the fleet, picking up letters to be taken home. The homeward-bound men are the envy of all the other fishermen.

As soon as the *We're Here* docks at Gloucester, Harvey sends a telegram to his father informing him that he did not drown and is well and healthy. Mr. Cheyne wires back that he will take his private car and travel to Gloucester as quickly as he can leave California. Disko and the rest of the crew, except Dan and the black cook, are greatly surprised to discover that Harvey was telling the truth.

Mr. Cheyne and Harvey's mother are overjoyed to see their son, and their happiness is further increased when they observe how much good the work aboard the fishing schooner did him. It changed Harvey from a snobbish adolescent into a self-reliant young man who knows how to make a living with his hands and who values people for what they are rather than for the money they have. Mr. Cheyne, who built up a fortune after a childhood of poverty, is particularly glad to see his son's improvement.

Disko and the crew of the *We're Here* refuse to accept any reward for themselves. Dan is given the chance to become an officer on a fleet of fast freighters that Mr. Cheyne owns. The cook leaves the sea to become a bodyguard for Harvey. In later years, when Harvey controls the Cheyne interests, the man gets a great deal of satisfaction from reminding Dan, by then a mate on one of Harvey's ships, that he told the two boys years before that someday Harvey would be Dan's master.

Critical Evaluation:

Captains Courageous was written in 1896 while Rudyard Kipling was living in the forests of Vermont. The period during which Great Britain's poet laureate—who wrote during Britain's imperial heyday when "the sun never set" on an empire stretching "from palm to pine"—wrote a sea story while living in the North American woods is a little known phase of the writer's career. Kipling loved Vermont's forests, especially during the colorful Indian summer season, and he also deeply appreciated the vital kinship between the United States and Great Britain. He equated such "captains courageous" of the Grand Banks as Disko Troop with the pioneers who journeyed into the American-Canadian West (Daniel

Boone, George Vancouver, and Kit Carson as well as railroad magnates such as Mr. Cheyne) with Sir Francis Drake, Sir John Hawkins, Sir Martin Frobisher, Sir Walter Ralegh, Sir Philip Sidney, and other bold Elizabethan adventurers. He believed that the Elizabethan spirit of adventure and accomplishment survived in the modern fishing captains and railroad magnates and that they were blood brothers of the earlier Anglo-Saxon adventurers, displaying the same spirit of freedom, free enterprise, and bravery against odds.

Kipling lived for many years among Asian peoples, and he believed that people of his kind could never exist naturally and thus could never be more than a dissolving white drop in a colored ocean. Partly for that reason, Kipling experienced great relief to find himself in Vermont. It must, however, be conceded that in *Captains Courageous* Kipling reveals a certain typical respect for all sturdy breeds. The British poet implies that men and the civilizations they create need challenges, not security, and must maintain healthy folk instincts while rearing each generation of their own kind in hardiness. In *Captains Courageous*, the representatives of European, expansionist, seafaring races—British, French, German, Portuguese—who have braved the Grand Banks for centuries are favorably presented, as is the black cook. His nineteenth century racist belief in a white man's burden notwithstanding, Kipling sometimes praised members of other races such as the tough Sudanese.

The novel stresses traditional virtues such as those of Horatio Alger. Harvey Cheyne learns practical skills and escapes emasculating luxury. He also learns the salutary value of hard work, sweat, and plain living, and he returns to nature and healthy simplicity by capturing his self-reliance amid the sheer beauty of the high seas. The physical environment of sea and shore is thus a character in the story, and it has been pointed out that *Captains Courageous* concerns the environment more than it does the protagonist. Even the theme of the boy's conversion stems from environment, though it is also linked to individual will and hereditary character. The driving ambition of Harvey's father, Mr. Cheyne, parallels Kipling's eulogy of the redoubtable fishermen who brave cold storms and fogs off the Grand Banks to fish for cod in their small dories. A millionaire's son becomes a man through enduring hardships on a fishing boat and through sharing the lot of toiling fishermen from Massachusetts, Canada, Germany, and Portugal.

The pith of Kipling's story is found in Mr. Cheyne's conversation with the redeemed young Harvey when the father relates the story of his life—how he had to toil for everything he earned, how he fought Indians and border ruffians before the West was tamed, how he encountered deadly struggles against odds, and how he built his railroad empire. He stresses the progress that railroads represented, enabling families to cross the immense and mountainous continent without suffering for months in covered wagons, sometimes having to bury their children along the way, as they were forced to do before Mr. Cheyne built his railroads. Infused with the pride of his heritage, young Harvey returns to Gloucester, borrows money from his father, and invests it in fishing boats. Hiring some of the friends he made on his first fishing expedition, Harvey starts his own fishing empire in the true Anglo-American tradition of creative enterprise.

Kipling's familiarity with the sea is evident. His descriptions of life on a fishing vessel, of how fish are caught and processed, and of the abrupt tragedies that sometimes overtake the "captains courageous" are not superficial. He evidently familiarized himself with Gloucester accents and idioms, for they are reproduced with the dialectal skill for which Kipling is noted. Like so many Kipling works, *Captains Courageous* is easy for children to read, enjoy, and understand, but its meanings are subtle and its literary virtues considerable.

After experiencing personal troubles and an unfortunate lawsuit, Kipling left Vermont. It is interesting to note that shortly after this military poet wrote one of the better novels of North Atlantic sea literature, he composed his famous *Recessional* honoring Queen Victoria's Diamond Jubilee in London in 1897. On this august occasion, rather than vaunting Great Britain's military might, however, Kipling shocked Empire enthusiasts by worrying over the fact that England's regiments were shedding their blood over the entire earth and that Royal Navy ships were sinking on distant headland and dune. Fearing "lest we be one with Nineveh and Tyre," Kipling wrote "Lord God of hosts, be with us yet, be with us yet." With these words, he shed light on the beliefs underlying his reasons for having written *Captains Courageous*.

"Critical Evaluation" by William Freitas

Further Reading

Allen, Charles. *Kipling Sahib: India and the Making of Rudyard Kipling*. London: Little, Brown, 2007. A biography focusing on Kipling's life from his birth until 1889, including his thirteen years in India, which were the inspiration for much of his writing. Allen traces the experiences of Kipling's parents in India, the Indian culture into which Kipling was born, and the state of the country when he returned in 1882 to begin his literary career by working on a newspaper in Lahore.

Dillingham, William B. *Rudyard Kipling: Hell and Heroism.*

New York: Palgrave Macmillan, 2005. Dillingham maintains that other biographers and critics have neglected Kipling's deeply pessimistic worldview and his complex code of heroism. He focuses on these aspects of Kipling's personality to analyze the writer's life and some of his works, including a discussion of *Captains Courageous* in chapter 4.

Gross, John, ed. *Rudyard Kipling: The Man, His Work, and His World*. London: Weidenfeld & Nicolson, 1972. Presents interesting background on *Captains Courageous* based on earlier materials and sketches that Kipling developed in the book. Argues that different sections of the novel fail to mesh.

Kipling, Rudyard. *Something of Myself: For My Friends Known and Unknown*. London: Macmillan, 1964. Fascinating autobiography first published in 1932 that provides insight into Kipling's detailed preparations for writing, which included his boarding ships, preparing fish, and analyzing fishing charts and railway timetables.

Lycett, Andrew. *Rudyard Kipling*. London: Weidenfeld & Nicolson, 1999. Lycett's exhaustive biography provides insight into Kipling's life and work. Includes bibliographical references and index.

Mason, Philip. *Kipling: The Glass, the Shadow, and the Fire*. New York: Harper & Row, 1975. Studies Kipling's development as a man and an artist. Mason argues that the plot and characters of *Captains Courageous* are weak, but he praises the atmospheric portrayal of the fisherman's world on the ship, where hard physical work is in conflict with the natural power of the sea.

Moss, Robert. *Rudyard Kipling and the Fiction of Adolescence*. New York: St. Martin's Press, 1982. Good introduction discussing thematic contrast between the crew of *We're Here*, whose codes of behavior and values are based on years of tradition, and the self-centered world of Harvey and the new industrial age represented by his father. Concludes that Kipling admires values in both but finds the former more sympathetic.

Peck, John. *Maritime Fiction: Sailors and the Sea in British and American Novels, 1719-1917*. New York: Palgrave, 2001. This study of the sea and of national identity discusses *Captains Courageous*, which along with *Treasure Island* by Robert Louis Stevenson and *The Sea-Wolf* by Jack London are described as adventure stories.

Shahane, Vasant. *Rudyard Kipling: Activist and Artist*. Carbondale: Southern Illinois University Press, 1973. Excellent introductory study. Argues that *Captains Courageous* breaks traditional form and excels in observation and descriptive detail, which sweep the reader into the world of the sea, a microcosm of the larger world. Also analyzes Kipling's treatment of character, theme, and setting.

The Captain's Daughter

Author: Alexander Pushkin (1799-1837)
First published: Kapitanskaya dochka, 1836 (English translation, 1846)
Type of work: Novel
Type of plot: Historical
Time of plot: c. 1774
Locale: Russia

Principal characters:
PETER ANDREITCH GRINEFF, a young Russian officer
MARIA IVANOVNA, his sweetheart
ALEXEY IVANITCH SHVABRIN, Peter's fellow officer
SAVELITCH, Peter's servant
EMELYAN POUGATCHEFF, a rebel Cossack leader

The Story:

Although Peter Andreitch Grineff is registered as a sergeant in the Semenovsky regiment when he is very young, he is given leave to stay at home until he completes his studies. When he is nearly seventeen years old, his father decides that the time comes for him to begin his military career. With his parents' blessing, Peter sets out for distant Orenburg in the company of his faithful servant, Savelitch.

One night, the travelers put up at Simbirsk. There, while Savelitch goes to make some purchases, Peter is lured into playing billiards with a fellow soldier, Zourin, and quickly loses one hundred rubles. Toward evening of the following day, the young man and Savelitch find themselves on the snowy plain with a storm approaching. As darkness falls, the snow grows thicker, until finally the horses cannot find their way and the driver confesses that he is lost. They are rescued by another traveler, a man with such sensitive nostrils that he is able to scent smoke from a village some distance away and lead them to it. The three men and their guide spend the night in the village. The next morning, Peter presents his hareskin jacket to his poorly dressed rescuer. Savelitch warns Peter that the coat will probably be pawned for drink.

Late that day, the young man reaches Orenburg and presents himself to the general in command. The general decides that there is a danger that the dull life at Orenburg might lead the young man into a career of dissipation; therefore, he sends him to the Bailogorsk fortress garrison under Captain Mironoff.

The Bailogorsk fortress, on the edge of the Kirghis steppes, is nothing more than a village surrounded by a log fence. Its real commandant is not Captain Mironoff but his lady, Vassilissa Egorovna, a lively, firm woman who sees to the discipline of her husband's underlings as well as the running of her own household.

Peter quickly makes friends with a fellow officer, Alexey Shvabrin, who has been exiled to the steppes for fighting a duel. Peter spends much time with his captain's family and grows deeply attached to the couple and to their daughter, Maria Ivanovna. After he receives his commission, he finds military discipline so relaxed that he is able to indulge his literary tastes.

The quiet routine of Peter's life is interrupted by an unexpected quarrel with Shvabrin precipitated by his having shown his friend a love poem he wrote to Maria. Shvabrin criticizes the work severely, and when he makes derogatory remarks about Maria they quarrel and Peter finds himself challenged to a duel for having called him a liar. The next morning, they meet in a field to fight but are stopped because Vassilissa Egorovna learns of the duel. Peter and Shvabrin, although ostensibly reconciled, nevertheless intend to carry out their duel at the earliest opportunity. Discussing the quarrel with Maria, Peter learns that she once rejected Shvabrin.

Having assured themselves that they are not watched, Shvabrin and Peter fight their duel the following day. Wounded in the breast, Peter lies unconscious for five days after the fight. When he begins to recover, he asks Maria to marry him. Shvabrin is jailed. Peter's father writes to say that he disapproves of a match with Captain Mironoff's daughter and that he intends to have his son transferred from the fortress so that he might forget his foolish ideas. Savelitch denies having written a letter home, so Peter concludes that Shvabrin was the informer.

Life would have become unbearable for the young man after his father's letter arrived if Captain Mironoff had not one evening informed his officers that the Yaikian Cossacks, led by Emelyan Pougatcheff, who claims to be the dead Emperor Peter III, are rising and are sacking fortresses and committing outrages everywhere. The captain orders his men to keep on the alert and to ready the cannon.

The news of Pougatcheff's uprising quickly spreads through the garrison. Many of the Cossacks of the town side with the rebels, so Captain Mironoff does not know whom he can trust or who might betray him. It is not long before he receives an ultimatum from the leader of the Cossacks ordering him to surrender. The Mironoffs decide that Maria should be sent back to Orenburg, but the attack comes early the next morning before she leaves. Captain Mironoff and his officers make a valiant effort to defend the town, but with the aid of Cossack traitors inside the walls, Pougatcheff is soon master of the fortress.

Captain Mironoff and his aides are hanged. Shvabrin deserts to the rebels. Peter, at the intercession of old Savelitch, is spared by Pougatcheff. The townspeople and the garrison soldiers have no scruples about transferring their allegiance to the rebel leader. Vassilissa Egorovna is slain when she cries out against her husband's murderer.

When Pougatcheff and his followers ride off to inspect the fortress, Peter begins his search for Maria. To his great relief, he finds that she was hidden by the wife of the village priest and that Shvabrin, who knows her whereabouts, did not reveal her identity. He learns from Savelitch that the servant recognizes Pougatcheff as the man to whom he gave his hareskin coat months before. Later, the rebel leader sends for Peter and acknowledges his identity. He tries to persuade Peter to join the Cossacks but respects his wish to rejoin his own forces at Orenburg. The next day, Peter and his servant are given safe conduct, and Pougatcheff gives Peter a horse and a sheepskin coat for the journey.

Several days later, the Cossacks attack Orenburg. During a sally, Peter receives a disturbing message from one of the Bailogorsk Cossacks that Shvabrin is forcing Maria to marry him. Peter goes at once to the general and tries to persuade him to raise the siege and go to the rescue of the village. When the general refuses, Peter and Savelitch start out once more for the Bailogorsk fortress. Intercepted and taken before Pougatcheff, Peter persuades the rebel to give Maria safe conduct to Orenburg.

On the way, they meet a detachment of soldiers led by Captain Zourin, who persuades Peter to send Maria to Savelitch's family under his protection, while he himself remains with the troops in Orenburg. The siege of Orenburg is finally lifted, and the army begins its task of tracking down rebel units. Some months later, Peter finds himself near his own village and sets off alone to visit his parents' estate. Reaching his home, he finds the serfs in rebellion and his family and Maria captives. That day, Shvabrin swoops down upon them with his troops. He is about to have all of them except Maria hanged, when they are rescued by Zourin's men. The renegade is shot during the encounter and taken prisoner.

Peter's parents change their attitude toward the captain's daughter, and Peter is able to rejoin Captain Zourin with the expectation that he and Maria will be wed in a month. Then an order comes for his arrest. He is accused of having been in the pay of Pougatcheff, of spying for the rebel, and of having taken presents from him. The author of the accusations is the captive, Shvabrin. Though Peter easily can clear himself by summoning Maria as a witness, he decides not to drag her into the matter. He is sentenced to spend the rest of his life in exile in Siberia.

Maria, however, is not one to let matters stand. Leaving Peter's parents, she travels to St. Petersburg and goes to Tsarskoe Selo, where the court is located. Walking in the garden there one day, she meets a woman who declares that she goes to court on occasion and will be pleased to present her petition to the empress. Maria is summoned to the royal presence the same day and discovers that it is the empress herself to whom she spoke. Peter is pardoned, and soon afterward he and the captain's daughter are married.

Critical Evaluation:

The longest of Alexander Pushkin's completed prose tales, *The Captain's Daughter* is based on true events that Pushkin wrote as history in his 1834 *Istoria Pugachev* (*The History of the Pugachev Rebellion*, 1966). The most astonishing aspect of *The Captain's Daughter* is that, though written in 1836, it possesses a brisk, lean style more suggestive of the twentieth century than of the mid-nineteenth century. Pushkin wastes no words, yet his scenes are vivid, his characters fully fleshed and remarkably alive, and his tale recounted in a suspenseful and moving manner. The realistic first-person narration adds to the verisimilitude of the story. The entire story is seen through Peter's eyes, allowing the reader to share his enthusiasms, impetuousness, and fears, as well as his youthful ardor and romantic spirit. The naïve, romantic illusions of the young protagonist are described by the narrator in a thoroughly disarming and often humorous manner. A sense of the vitality of youth pervades the book.

Pushkin recounts action, such as the duel or the siege of the Bailogorsk fortress, in a vivid, well-paced manner. Throughout the novel, he writes with extraordinary vitality, bringing situations and characters to life in a few strokes. Sly humor is an integral part of the narrative. When the hero notes that his

French tutor was sent from Moscow with the yearly supply of wine and olive oil, readers know precisely where that unlucky tutor fit into the household. Many of the characters possess a humorous side to their nature. The ill-fated, henpecked captain and his talkative but kindly tyrant of a wife are both portrayed with a light touch. Old Savelitch, Peter's servant, is the truest comic figure in the novel; devoted to his young master, as earlier he had been to Peter's father, the old man would willingly sacrifice his life for Peter but never hesitates to talk back to Peter or to the rebel Cossack leader if he feels that he is in the right. Even Pougatcheff, the self-styled claimant to the throne, is presented with a great deal of humor; in a sense, he is the only character in the book who does not take himself completely seriously, and this, at least in part, is because he has an ironic realization of the precariousness of his existence.

Many scenes in the novel possess double-edged humor, from the absurd, aborted, and then completed duel between Peter and Shvabrin to the moment, in the middle of horror, when old Savelitch dares to present an itemized list of destroyed and stolen goods to the man who holds all of their lives in his hands. The deaths of the captain and his wife are handled with a certain grotesque humor. As in William Shakespeare's tragedies, humor serves to heighten the horror of such dramatic scenes as the fall of the fortress and the murders of the innocent at the hands of the rebels. At the same time, there are shockingly realistic portrayals of the duplicity of human nature, Shvabrin's traitorous villainy, the garrison's cowardice when they all throw down their arms in the face of the enemy, and the pettiness displayed by many of the minor characters. Despite the terrible events portrayed in the novel, the book is, however, not grim. It is a romantic tale of action and romance, with an appropriate happy ending. Even the conclusion, with its scenes of mistaken identity, possesses a charming humor. The brilliant construction of the novel, with its alternating light and dark scenes, sweeps readers along, never letting them be quite sure of where they are. Pushkin seems to delight in catching readers off guard, making them laugh and gasp with horror, and then hurling a piece of slapstick at them before they have recovered from the surprise. The scene of the captain's fat wife being dragged naked from her house to the gallows, screaming and shouting abuse at the Cossacks, is both funny and horrible. Shvabrin, completely despicable, is shown to be absurd as he struts and postures during his brief glory, and then, even more so, when he falls. Pushkin is extremely deft at showing both sides of human beings, the noble and the phony, the absurd and the courageous, the hateful and the loving.

The Russian land is an important part of this novel. The

vast spaces become another character, as the hero flies across them in sleds and carriages or on horseback. Pushkin carefully builds a sense of intense patriotic fervor throughout the narrative, culminating in the scenes with the empress. The empress is seen as the mother figure of all Russia, wise and warm, quick to understand and forgive and to come to the aid of her "children." Frequently in the course of the book, words and phrases refer to the Russian people as one large family; underlings call their masters and mistresses "Father" and "Mother," and the land is referred to as the great mother of them all. The empress and the land are inseparable. In the light of this powerful sentiment, the daring of Pougatcheff to attempt to usurp the throne becomes all the more shocking, as Pushkin intended, because to attack the throne is to attack all of Russia and to undermine the structure of the entire country.

The Captain's Daughter exerted a tremendous influence on Russian fiction; it showed novelists the possibilities of Russian themes and Russian settings, and, above all, it illustrated the narrative capabilities of the Russian language. Never before had Russian prose been used in fiction in such a lean, vigorous, and completely unpretentious manner. The perfection of the book was inspiring to the writers who followed. It can be said that the great period of Russian fiction begins with *The Captain's Daughter*. The other great influence on Russian fiction, Nikolai Gogol's *Myortvye dushi* (*Dead Souls*, 1887) did not appear until 1842. The great tragedy for Russian literature and the world is that the year after writing this novel, Pushkin was killed at the age of thirty-seven in a duel.

"Critical Evaluation" by Bruce D. Reeves

Further Reading

Bayley, John. *Pushkin: A Comparative Commentary.* New York: Cambridge University Press, 1971. A good introduction to Pushkin's work, with a particularly fine analysis of the later prose tales. Integrates biographical information with analysis of basic themes and structures of the major works. Discusses Pushkin's works in the context of European Romanticism.

Bethea, David M. *Realizing Metaphors: Alexander Pushkin and the Life of the Poet.* Madison: University of Wisconsin Press, 1998. Describes the relationship between Pushkin's life and his art and discusses why, more than two hundred years after his birth, his work remains relevant. Includes index and illustrations.

Binyon, T. J. *Pushkin: A Biography.* New York: Knopf, 2004.

The winner of the Samuel Johnson prize for British nonfiction, this biography chronicles Pushkin's literary success alongside his personal failures. Binyon describes how the writer included small pieces of his life in *Eugene Onegin* and other works.

Debreczeny, Paul. *The Other Pushkin: A Study of Alexander Pushkin's Prose Fiction.* Stanford, Calif.: Stanford University Press, 1983. A complete survey of Pushkin's prose, including a thorough study of *The Captain's Daughter.* Provides extensive notes on the contemporary context of the prose works, combined with detailed narrative analysis.

Driver, Sam. *Pushkin: Literature and Social Ideas.* New York: Columbia University Press, 1989. Considers Pushkin as an engaged social thinker rather than an alienated romantic poet. Traces the development of Pushkin's social ideas and his involvement in contemporary politics. Devotes considerable discussion to issues of censorship and to Pushkin's relationship with the czar as it is revealed in his prose.

Evdokimova, Svetlana. *Pushkin's Historical Imagination.* New Haven, Conn.: Yale University Press, 1999. An examination of Pushkin's fictional and nonfictional works on the subject of history, including *The Captain's Daughter.* Considers Pushkin's ideas on the relation between chance and necessity, the significance of great individuals, and historical truth.

Kahn, Andrew, ed. *The Cambridge Companion to Pushkin.* New York: Cambridge University Press, 2006. Collection of essays by Pushkin scholars discussing the writer's life and work in various genres; Pushkin and politics, history, and literary criticism; and Pushkin's position in Soviet and post-Soviet culture.

Richards, D. J., and C. R. S. Cockerell, eds. and trans. *Russian Views of Pushkin.* Oxford, England: Willem Meeuws, 1976. A wide-ranging collection of Russian essays about Pushkin's verse and prose spanning the nineteenth and twentieth centuries. Includes important discussions of his major works and covers contemporary social issues, narrative structure, and thematic organization.

Ryfa, Juras T., ed. *Collected Essays in Honor of the Bicentennial of Alexander Pushkin's Birth.* Lewiston, N.Y.: Edwin Mellen Press, 2000. A selection of scholarly essays devoted to various works by Pushkin and his influence on his literary descendants. Some of the essays discuss *Eugene Onegin* and *The Captain's Daughter* and compare Pushkin to Russian writers Leo Tolstoy and Anton Chekhov.

The Captives

Author: Plautus (c. 254-184 B.C.E.)
First produced: Captivi, second century C.E. (English
    translation, 1767)
Type of work: Drama
Type of plot: Farce
Time of plot: War between Aetolia and Elis
Locale: Aetolia

Principal characters:
HEGIO, a wealthy Aetolian
ERGASILUS, a parasite
PHILOCRATES, a wealthy Elian and prisoner of war
TYNDARUS, son of Hegio and Philocrates's slave
PHILOPOLEMUS, elder son of Hegio
ARISTOPHONTES, a prisoner of war and Philocrates's friend
STALAGMUS, a runaway slave

The Story:

Hegio is a wealthy Aetolian who many years before lost a son, Tyndarus, when a runaway slave named Stalagmus carried the boy off at the age of four years. Later, during a war with Elis, his other son, Philopolemus, is captured and made a slave by the Elians. In an effort to rescue Philopolemus, Hegio buys up prisoners of war captured by the Aetolian army, hoping to find a wealthy young Elian whom he could exchange for his own son. He spends a great deal of money without finding a suitable prisoner. Mourning his son's loss with him is a parasite, Ergasilus, a favorite of Hegio's son and the recipient of many free meals.

One day, entirely by accident, Hegio buys a pair of prisoners of whom one, unbeknownst to him, is the son stolen years before. Tyndarus is now the slave of Philocrates, a wealthy Elian prisoner. Philocrates and Tyndarus change clothing and names, hoping by that ruse to get Philocrates set free to return to Elis. The ruse works, for Hegio allows Philocrates to return to Elis and arranges for an exchange of his own son for Philocrates' "master." Shortly afterward, Hegio, while visiting at his brother's home, finds a slave there named Aristophontes, who claims to be a friend of Philocrates. To satisfy himself as to the identity of his hostage and to do a kindness to both prisoners, Hegio takes Aristophontes home with him. At Hegio's home, Aristophontes lays bare the ruse that was played on Hegio. At first, Tyndarus, still posing as Philocrates, tries to complete the plan by claiming that Aristophontes is mad, but Hegio soon becomes aware that Tyndarus is not Philocrates. In his anger, Hegio has Tyndarus, actually his own son but whom his father does not recognize, sent to the stone quarries, with orders that he is to be worked hard for the trick he played on his new owner.

The parasite Ergasilus, meanwhile, is going hungry in the absence of his patron, Philopolemus, although Hegio occasionally gives him a frugal meal. Ergasilus is the victim of a move on the part of the wealthy Aetolians to pay no attention to parasites, thus forcing those unwelcome individuals to earn an honest living in some way or other.

Elian Philocrates is an honest man who loves his slave Tyndarus, for the two were companions since childhood. Upon his return to Elis, therefore, he arranges for the exchange of Philopolemus in return for his own freedom. He also decides to go with Philopolemus to Aetolia to regain his slave Tyndarus. He promises, through the false Philocrates (Tyndarus), to pay a sum of money as bail for Tyndarus's return.

The first person to see Philocrates and Philopolemus is the parasite Ergasilus. Realizing that the news is money in his wallet and food in his stomach, he rushes off to tell Hegio the tidings. Overjoyed, Hegio promises to give Ergasilus his board for the rest of his life and, for one meal, to give Ergasilus free rein in the kitchens. While Ergasilus rushes to have a feast prepared, Hegio goes to the harbor to meet Philopolemus and the former prisoner, Philocrates. Hegio's joy knows no bounds when he embraces his son.

As soon as he returns to his house, Hegio sends for Tyndarus, whom he still does not recognize, and has him released to his master Philocrates, without demanding the payment he initially set for Tyndarus's freedom. While they are waiting for Tyndarus, Hegio questions Stalagmus, his former slave, who was recaptured at Elis and returned by Philocrates. Hegio hopes to discover what happened to Tyndarus. Stalagmus tells how he kidnapped Hegio's son and took him to Elis. There, he says, he sold the young boy to Philocrates' father. Philocrates then relates how the little boy was given to him as a companion and playfellow and later became his valet. By the time Tyndarus returns from the quarry, the riddle is solved. He is welcomed not as a slave but as a free man, the brother of Philopolemus and Hegio's son.

Tyndarus is overjoyed by his good fortune. Hegio, eager to punish Stalagmus for the kidnapping and to make amends to his long-lost son, gives the kidnapper over to Tyndarus to be punished. Tyndarus sends immediately for a blacksmith to strike off his chains, which are exceedingly heavy, and places them on Stalagmus; he promises that unworthy person a life of hard labor and harsh treatment. Stalagmus philosophically accepts his fate; he was born a slave, and he expects to die a slave.

Critical Evaluation:

Information about the life of Plautus survives primarily in the writings of other Latin writers, which suggests the impact of his theatrical success even on his contemporaries. His critical reputation remained high after his death. It is likely that the reason he was credited with more than one hundred plays is because his name was such a guarantee of popular success. How many plays he actually wrote remains a mystery; it is commonly agreed that twenty plays and a fragment of another are his. As a group, they represent the Plautine contribution to New Comedy, the most influential comedic formula to survive to this day. His earthiness was frowned upon at certain stages of Western history, such as the Middle Ages, when the more decorous works of his younger contemporary, Terence, were favored. During the Renaissance, in the rebirth of all things classical, Plautus came into his own again, however, and he inspired many of the greatest English dramatists, including William Shakespeare.

The Latin comedy of Plautus's time was based on the new Greek Comedy, whose best-known practitioner was the Greek dramatist Menander. *Comoediae palliatae* was the name given to the category of Roman plays based on Greek originals. Most of these have not survived, so what is known about Plautus's originality and contribution is sometimes a matter of conjecture. By the number of Roman references in his plays, however, it is clear that Plautus did not simply translate his Greek sources. A man who had to live by his words, he was evidently adept at writing what would please his Roman audiences. Still, the illusion that he was writing about another time and place was useful when he poked fun at Roman values.

The Captives has an unusual position among Plautus's works. It appears to have a highly moral tone and is almost tragic in some aspects. The prologue and epilogue seem intended to assure audiences that this play is different from the others, without the usual comic stereotypes.

Critics have pointed out that the play does toy with some traditional comic features, and they have identified several reversals. It is common in both Greek and Roman plays of the New Comedy, for example, to have a climactic recognition scene, when, for example, the children who have been lost or thought dead are revealed to their parents. At times, this section of the plot unravels the knotty problems that have prevented a young man from marrying the young woman he loves. The young woman is frequently of a lower class, perhaps a slave, and unfit for the young man of a higher class un-

til something happens to change that gap in social position. The young man, with the help of his clever servant, may manage to find the money to free the woman, or the woman may be revealed to have been of high birth or to have been stolen away from her family as an infant.

The Captives has these plot elements, but with a twist. The servant helping his master is actually a peer; the character who turns out to be of higher birth is not the young female character but the male servant. The love that is demonstrated in the play is not between a young man and young woman, but between two men.

Some critics have argued that Tyndarus's great love and sacrifice for his master shows the remnants of a more obviously homoerotic Greek original. If so, this change would be an excellent example of what Plautus could allow himself through the expediency of pretending that the setting was Greek. Yet Erich Segal has noted that the surviving examples of New Comedy seldom refer to homosexuality; moreover, a Roman audience steeped in the usual love plot could very well have welcomed this new twist to an old plot.

One feature of *The Captives* that is typical of Plautus is the character of Ergasilus. According to some scholars, Plautus tends to favor the underdog in his plays and is most successful in his portrayal of clever slaves. The parasite figure is not intrinsic to the plot, and the play has been criticized for such a superfluous role. Without Ergasilus, however, the play could barely be amusing. As is typical of a parasite, he moans about his stomach, setting up a nice comic counterpoint to the more serious themes of the play. The emphasis on Ergasilus's down-to-earth physicality is typical of comedy, which traditionally focuses on what is necessary for survival and shows less concern for how that survival is achieved.

The Captives is not considered the most perfectly constructed of Plautus's plays. The parasite is an intrusion on a logical plot, and there are other inconsistencies that have caused some critics to call the play a failure. One eighteenth century critic, however, called it the most beautiful play ever to come to the stage. It has also been one of the popular choices for study, because its high-minded themes of loyalty and sacrifice seem more suitable in an educational context than Plautus's more ribald plays. *The Captives* also exhibits some of the features that have made Plautus endure, among them comic, entertaining features of plot and language. As Segal has pointed out, Plautus's irrepressible high spirits may have seeped into the title itself: In the original, it is ambiguous, meaning "take prisoner" or "take in," leaving the audience to wonder just how far the joking goes.

"Critical Evaluation" by Shakuntala Jayaswal

Further Reading

Beacham, Richard C. *The Roman Theatre and Its Audience.* London: Routledge & Kegan Paul, 1991. Explains the physical aspects of Roman theater with illustrations and speculates on the nature of the ancient audience. Useful for production ideas.

Duckworth, George. *The Nature of Roman Comedy: A Study in Popular Entertainment.* 2d ed. Norman: University of Oklahoma Press, 1994. The classic study of Roman comedy. Provides a comprehensive introduction to Latin playwrights, including Plautus.

Fraenkel, Eduard. *Plautine Elements in Plautus.* Translated by Tomas Drevikovsky and Frances Muecke. New York: Oxford University Press, 2007. This is the first English translation of a German study initially published in 1922. Fraenkel, an influential twentieth century classicist, provides an analytical overview of Plautus's plays, including their motifs of transformation and identification, mythological material, dialogue, and the predominance of the slave's role.

Konstan, David. "*Captivi:* City-State and Nation." In *Roman Comedy.* Ithaca, N.Y.: Cornell University Press, 1983. Examines the plays of Plautus and Terence in the light of the ancient city-states' cultural system. This play is seen to bring up the question of Greek national identity.

Leigh, Matthew. *Comedy and the Rise of Rome.* New York: Oxford University Press, 2004. Analyzes the comedies of Plautus and Terence, placing them within the context of political and economic conditions in Rome during the third and second centuries B.C.E. Discusses how audiences of that time responded to these comedies.

McCarthy, Kathleen. *Slaves, Masters, and the Art of Authority in Plautine Comedy.* Princeton, N.J.: Princeton University Press, 2000. Analyzes four of Plautus's plays, including *The Captives,* focusing on audience reactions to the heroic trickster characters. McCarthy maintains that the plays derive their comedy from the conflict between their naturalistic and farcical elements.

Segal, Erich. *Roman Laughter: The Comedy of Plautus.* Cambridge, Mass.: Harvard University Press, 1968. Organized by topics rather than by plays, this book presents an argument about Plautus's comedy as a whole. An appendix includes a twenty-three-page discussion of *The Captives.*

_____, ed. *Oxford Readings in Menander, Plautus, and Terence.* New York: Oxford University Press, 2001. Includes essays on Plautus and the public stage, the response of Plautus's audience, and traditions, theatrical improvisation, and mastery of comic language in his plays.

The Caretaker

Author: Harold Pinter (1930-2008)
First produced: 1960; first published, 1960
Type of work: Drama
Type of plot: Psychological realism
Time of plot: Twentieth century
Locale: London

Principal characters:
MICK, a man in his late twenties
ASTON, his brother, a man in his early thirties
DAVIES, an old man

The Story:

Mick and his brother Aston live alone together in a West London house until one night Aston brings home Davies, who just left his job as a kitchen helper at a restaurant. The old man proves to be a violent, selfish bigot, uncharitable himself but quick to exploit the kindness of others. He tells Aston that "Blacks, Greeks, Poles" are "treating him like dirt" and that "nobody's got more rights than I have." He also vows to get revenge on another employee at the restaurant. In contrast to Davies' vulgar, abrasive, vengeful attitude, Aston's is quiet, gentle, and accommodating. In addition to offering Davies a bed for the night, he tries to give him a comfortable pair of shoes. Davies, ungrateful, refuses the shoes, claiming they do not fit. When Aston offers him money, however, Davies accepts it, insisting that he has to "get down to Sidcup," where he can get his papers and resume his true identity as Mac Davies, instead of living as he was under the assumed name of Bernard Jenkins.

Davies stays the night, and in the morning Aston complains that Davies made noises. When Aston suggests that perhaps Davies was dreaming, Davies counters by saying that he never dreams and becomes angry when Aston says the "jabbering" kept him from sleeping. Nevertheless, Aston suggests that Davies stay on longer if he wants and gives him a key to the room. Before going out to shop for a jigsaw, Aston recalls an encounter he had recently with a woman he met in a café, who offered "to have a look" at his body. Davies asks him for money, but Aston reminds him that he gave him some money the previous night.

Left alone, Davies begins to rummage through items scattered around the room and is surprised by Mick, who grabs him in a hammerlock and throws him on the floor, asking "What's the game?" and demanding to know Davies' real name. Davies lies, saying his name is Jenkins, and, as if to punish him for lying, Mick aggressively interrogates Davies, undercutting his confidence, confusing the old man, critiquing his motives, and questioning his racism, ethnocentrism, suspicions, and arrogance. Mick finally accuses Davies of being "a born fibber" and teases him by not giving him his trousers. He is interrupted, however, by Aston returning with a valise—Davies claimed he left his at the restaurant the previous night. When Aston hands Davies the bag, however, Mick grabs it and continues teasing Davies.

Once Mick finally gives Davies the bag, the old man is so startled and frightened that he staggers back and drops it. Mick then leaves Aston alone with Davies, who, shaken and angry, calls Mick "a real joker." He also complains that the bag Aston brought him is not his, and though the bag contains some clothes Aston bought him, Davies is indignant, rejecting the gear—except for a smoking jacket which he puts on, claiming that it is not "a bad piece of cloth."

When Aston suggests the old man can become the caretaker around the house, Davies becomes evasive, reciting a list of excuses. Later, Davies returns to the room alone in the dark. Frightened upon discovering that the lights are not working and thinking that he hears an intruder, he pulls a knife, but the intruder turns out to be Mick, who chases Davies around the room with a vacuum cleaner. After sparring mentally with Davies, Mick pretends to befriend him, offering him a sandwich. Once he gains Davies' trust, however, Mick again sets a trap for him. Suggesting that his brother is odd and lazy, Mick gets Davies to join in the criticism of Aston, calling him a "funny bloke." Mick then demands that Davies clarify his statement, confusing the old man. To compound Davies' confusion, Mick asks him to become the caretaker, provided that Davies can produce references. Davies again asserts that his references—his papers—can be verified only if he can get to Sidcup.

The next morning Aston complains again that Davies is making so much noise that Aston cannot sleep. Aston recalls being arrested for having hallucinations and being sent to a doctor, who tells him he would "do something" to his brain. Aston claims that he wrote to his mother, hoping to prevent the treatment, but his mother signed the forms and allowed the doctor to perform shock therapy on him. After the treatment, Aston says, his thoughts "had become very slow." He says that he suffers from headaches and that he learned to stay out of public places. He also admits that he would like to find the doctor who administered the treatment.

Two weeks later, Davies, alone in the house with Mick, begins to list a series of complaints against Aston. Aston is not talking to him, he is not being "straightforward," he will not provide him with a clock, and he will not let him sleep. By the time Aston joins the other two, Davies is conspiring against him with Mick. That night, awakened by Aston's complaints about the old man's noises, Davies loses his temper and yells that Aston is "half-off." When Aston makes a move toward Davies, the old man pulls his knife, convincing Aston that it is time for Davies to leave. Davies appeals to Mick for help, but Mick defends his brother's position. Smashing a bust of Buddha, Mick launches into a tirade against Davies' selfishness. When Aston notices the broken Buddha, Davies reverses himself against Mick and again appeals to Aston, hoping that Aston will allow him to stay at the house. This time, Aston refuses to help the old man, telling him he cannot stay because he makes "too much noise."

Critical Evaluation:

Pinter's second full-length play, *The Caretaker*, opened in London in 1960 and, after a twelve-month run, moved to Broadway, where it was acclaimed as a critical, if not commercial, success. *The Caretaker* has been described as Pinter's most naturalistic play. The British theater critic Kenneth Tynan called it "a play about people," which, in Pinter's case, marked a significant turn in his approach to theater. His early work, such as *The Room* (1957) and *The Dumb Waiter* (1959), was laden with symbolism and was heavily influenced by the absurdist theater of Irish playwright Samuel Beckett and Russian-born French playwright Eugène Ionesco. In *The Caretaker*, however, Pinter eschews latent meanings and focuses instead on the lives of the three characters, presenting the action realistically and in a naturalistic fashion. The setting, a cluttered room, has no overt symbolic significance. It is, as is often the case in Pinter's plays, a realistic vision of isolation and withdrawal. Nor does Pinter force any allegorical message into the story. The characters are readily identifiable as local people in ordinary circumstances.

Nevertheless, the play is anything but conventional. The characters seem unfinished, indeterminate, with no stable, verifiable stake in life. Davies, an inveterate liar, claims he has "papers" in Sidcup that will establish his identity, but it is never made clear exactly who he is, where he has been, or what the papers in Sidcup would prove. Aston, the benevolent brother who befriends Davies, recites a poetic soliloquy that describes his incarceration and treatment in a mental institution, but why he was committed is never established. He says only that, at some point in his life, he saw things too clearly and talked too much where he worked. His brother, Mick, who is more hostile to Davies, seems to improvise his past, whimsically concocting stories that confuse Davies while providing no real information regarding his identity. Their plans about the future are especially vague. Davies hopes to get his papers from Sidcup but makes no real effort to go. Aston hopes to build a shed, but the idea sounds more like a pipe dream than any project he could actually complete. Mick mentions several projects involving renovation and a van, but he is never specific; when he offers details, no conclusions can be drawn from what he says.

Another characteristically unconventional tactic Pinter uses in *The Caretaker*, giving it a quality of uncertainty that is a trademark of his plays, is the way the meager plot belies the psychological complexities of the characters as they strive to discover and maintain their separate identities. Aston finds Davies one night after the homeless tramp has been fired from his job and offers to share his living quarters with him. Davies is a self-righteous bigot, a cantankerous reprobate, ungrateful, untrustworthy, and exceedingly selfish. Aston, who is laconic, withdrawn, and passive to a fault, overlooks the old man's negative traits and tries, inexplicably, to make him comfortable, offering him money, a bed, and a key to the house. As soon as Aston leaves the room, however, Davies is assaulted by Mick, who was trying to develop Aston's interest in some projects, hoping to help him adjust after his treatment at the mental institution. Mick sees Davies as a manipulator trying to take advantage of Aston's condition. He immediately engages Davies in a series of verbal encounters that serve to disorient the old man and to protect Aston, realizing that Aston must reject Davies voluntarily to assure himself that he can deal independently with people and situations in his life. In the end, after talk of Davies becoming "caretaker" of the property, Aston sees through the tramp's machinations and tells him to leave.

The irony in the title of *The Caretaker* evolves from Davies' being offered a job as caretaker when, in fact, he is capable neither of caring for himself nor of expressing care for others. It is his rejection of basic human kindness, his need to manipulate instead of trust, and his choice of lies over honesty that finally result in his being rejected by the brothers. Cynically, the play suggests that the innocents of the world are at risk and that to survive without being threatened one must develop the defensive tactics that Aston is still learning, but that Mick has already mastered.

Jeff Johnson

Further Reading

Baker, William. *Harold Pinter.* London: Continuum, 2008. Brief critical biography examining the themes, patterns, relationships, and ideas that are common to Pinter's life and writings.

Billington, Michael. *Harold Pinter.* London: Faber & Faber, 2007. Critical biography focusing on literary analysis of Pinter's works. Discusses the major plays at length, providing information about their literary and biographical sources.

Bloom, Harold, ed. *Modern Critical Views: Harold Pinter.* New York: Chelsea House, 1987. An eclectic collection of essays by various critics. Comprehensive analyses of early and late writings and selected specific texts.

Burkman, Katherine H. *The Dramatic World of Harold Pinter: Its Basis in Ritual.* Columbus: Ohio State University Press, 1971. An analysis of Pinter's work viewed from the perspectives of Freudian, Marxist, and myth analyses. Heavy on theory with solid literary analyses of individual plays.

Esslin, Martin. *Pinter: The Playwright.* 6th exp. and rev. ed. London: Methuen, 2000. Precise and exhaustive critical study combining biographical details with critical analysis to identify sources of style and theme in Pinter's work. Written with the assistance of Pinter, it includes discussion of previously unpublished material.

Gale, Steven H., ed. *Harold Pinter: Critical Approaches.* Rutherford, N.J.: Fairleigh Dickinson University Press, 1986. A collection of essays by various critics on a wide range of Pinter's work. Places the material in the context of contemporary critical theories.

Merritt, Susan H. *Pinter in Play: Critical Strategies and the Plays of Harold Pinter.* Durham, N.C.: Duke University Press, 1990. Excellent discussion of current and past debates on critical theory as it relates to Pinter's work. Provides scrupulous textual examination.

Raby, Peter, ed. *The Cambridge Companion to Harold Pinter.* New York: Cambridge University Press, 2001. Collection of essays, including discussions of Pinter, politics, and postmodernism; Pinter and the critics; and Pinter and the twentieth century theater. A piece by director Peter Hall concerns the directing of Pinter's plays. The numerous references to *The Caretaker* are listed in a separate index of Pinter's works.

Carmen

Author: Prosper Mérimée (1803-1870)
First published: 1845; revised, 1847 (English translation, 1878)
Type of work: Novella
Type of plot: Psychological
Time of plot: Early nineteenth century
Locale: Spain

Principal characters:
DON JOSÉ, a soldier
CARMEN, a cigarette worker
GARCIA, Carmen's husband
LUCAS, a toreador

The Story:

Don José is a handsome, young cavalryman from Navarre. The son of a good Basque family, he has excellent chances of being quickly promoted and making his name as a soldier. A short time after arriving at his post in Seville, however, he happens to meet a beautiful, clever young Gypsy named Carmen. Don José falls in love with her at once and allows her to escape after she was taken into custody for attacking another worker with a knife in a cigarette factory.

One night, she persuades him to desert his post and go with her. He is punished by being ordered to stand guard. When she goes to him again, and again urges him to come with her, he refuses. They argue for more than an hour, until Don José, exhausted by his struggle between anger and love, succumbs to her. After he becomes her lover, she caresses him and ridicules him by turn. Carmen is independent, rebellious, and tormenting. The more fickle she is, the more madly Don José loves her.

One night, having agreed to a rendezvous with Carmen, he goes to her apartment. While they are together, a lieutenant who is also Carmen's lover enters. He and Don José begin to argue and swords flash. In the struggle, Don José kills the lieutenant after himself suffering a head wound. Carmen, who remained in the room throughout the fight, accuses Don José of being stupid. She goes out and returns a few minutes later with a cloak, which she tells him to wear, as he will be a hunted man. Don José's hopes for a brilliant career are shattered as a result of this impetuous act. His love leads him to murder, and he is doomed to live the life of an outlaw with a woman who is a pickpocket and a thief.

Carmen has many friends and acquaintances who are outlaws. Because Don José has no choice in the matter, he agrees to go with her to join a small band of smugglers and bandits for whom Carmen is a spy. By that time, a reward is posted for Don José's capture. He and Carmen set out and eventually find the smugglers. For a long time, Don José lives with them, throwing himself into his new, lawless life with such vigor and enthusiasm that he becomes known as a desperate

and ruthless bandit. All the time, however, he is deeply unhappy. By nature, he is kind and has nothing of the desperado in him. His wild life is not the type of existence he envisioned. Worst of all, he knows that Carmen is unfaithful to him, and he grows silent and sullen.

His anger and jealousy increase when he discovers that Garcia, the one-eyed leader of the gang, is Carmen's husband. By that time, the band is reduced in numbers. One day, while Carmen is absent, Don José kills Garcia. A fellow outlaw tells Don José that he was very stupid and that Garcia would have given Carmen to him for a few dollars. When Carmen returns, he informs her that she is a widow. The death of Garcia also means that there are only two of the band left on the eve of a dangerous raid they planned.

Don José and a smuggler named Dancaire organize a new band. Carmen continues to be useful to them. She goes to Granada, and there she meets a toreador named Lucas. Jealous of his rival, Don José asks her to live with him always, to abandon the life they are leading, and to go off with him to America. Carmen refuses, telling him that nobody ever successfully orders her to do anything, that she is a Gypsy, and that she reads in coffee grounds that she and Don José will end their lives together. Her words half convince Don José that there is no reason for him to worry.

A short time later, Carmen defies him again and goes to Cordova, where Lucas is appearing in a bullfight. Don José follows her, but he catches only a glimpse of her in the arena. Lucas is injured by a bull. Outside the arena, Don José meets Carmen. Once more he implores her to be his forever and to go with him to America, but she only laughs and jeers at him.

Don José goes to a monk and asks him to say a mass for a person who is in danger of death. He then returns to Carmen and tells her to follow him. She responds that she will go with him, even to her death, though she knows that he is about to kill her. Resigned to her fate, she tells him that she no longer loves him and that she will not love him any more even if Lucas does not love her. Their affair ends. In desperation,

Don José takes out his knife and kills her. With the same knife, he digs her grave and buries her in a grove of trees. Then he goes to the nearest constabulary post and surrenders. The monk says the mass for the repose of Carmen's soul.

Critical Evaluation:

Prosper Mérimée is one of a handful of French writers credited with inventing the *nouvelle*, something more than a short story but less than a novel. His first exercise in this genre was *Colomba* (1840), a much-acclaimed tale about a vendetta set in Corsica. *Carmen* may be seen as an attempt to repeat the success of the earlier story by mixing similar ingredients: an exotic and colorful setting; a central character who operates outside the law but with reference to some definite code of honor; and, of course, a bewitching femme fatale.

The thematic materials in *Carmen* are somewhat reminiscent of the gothic novels that flourished a generation before, novels that were often set in wild places haunted by colorful characters. The form of its plot and the manner of its narration are, however, very different from the florid excesses of gothic melodrama. The plot of *Carmen* is borrowed from the Abbé Prévost's *Histoire du chevalier des Grieux et de Manon Lescaut* (1731, 1733, 1753; *Manon Lescaut*, 1734, 1786), which tracks the moral decline of a supposedly honorable man who becomes infatuated with an altogether unsuitable woman. Mérimée's narrative style is laconic and rather clinical, full of anthropological asides regarding the customs and language of the Gypsies. Most of these asides, as Mérimée admits, are lifted from the early works of the English writer George Henry Borrow, author of *The Zincali: An Account of the Gypsies in Spain* (1841). The result of Mérimée's syncretic amalgamation is a work delicately suspended between realism and Romanticism, a kind of work that had not previously existed and that Mérimée made his own.

In *Manon Lescaut*'s account, a worthy man's descent into ruin is attributed to an oppressive, almost tangible force operating within a context defined by the author's Jesuitical Catholicism. *Carmen*, too, is marked by fatalism, but the fate that pursues Don José is no dark, oppressive one. His decline, which occurs over a series of dispirited failures, begins even before he meets Carmen, for he has fled his homeland after killing a man in a duel fought over a tennis match. When Carmen tempts him, Don José knows precisely where his duty lies, yet by capitulating again and again, he eventually becomes so casual in his immorality as to plot and execute the murder of Carmen's supposed husband on a whim rather than as an act of true desperation.

The only resistance Don José can raise against his temptress is displayed in the frame narrative, when he refuses to murder the archaeologist to whom he eventually tells his life story. He is restrained by the fact that the archaeologist previously saved him from being captured. This raises the doubt as to whether Don José is entirely reliable as a narrator or whether his matter-of-factness represents the state of mind instilled by the imminence of his execution. Most of the events he describes speak for themselves, however, and they make sense only if one accepts that they happened as casually as he describes them.

Don José's fatalism matches Carmen's, especially in the remarkable conclusion of the story, which differs sharply not only from that of *Manon Lescaut* but also from those of such nineteenth century recapitulations of that plot as *La Dame aux camélias* (1848; *Camille*, 1857) by Alexandre Dumas, *fils*. Carmen knows that Don José will kill her, but she refuses to save herself by lying, even though she built her entire career on conscienceless deception. In effect, she not only invites destruction but also insists on it, and she does so not out of principle or passion but out of a basic inability to care.

Those who know the story of Carmen only through Georges Bizet's famous 1875 opera of that name would hardly recognize the story, because the composer and his librettist carefully obliterated the very elements that make the story unique. Lucas the picador becomes a much more powerful figure in the opera so as to justify Carmen's desertion and Don José's jealousy. Yet the point of Mérimée's story is that the motivation for murder is so slight. In his story, Carmen is fickle and Don José weak, and that is all there is to it; their infatuation is not a grand passion of the kind whose erotic ecstasy might explain—perhaps even justify—acts of reckless violence. Carmen is certainly a femme fatale in the great tradition of French literary femmes fatales, but she has neither the secret capacity for honest passion that marks the tragic heroines of Romanticism nor the cold callousness of the antiheroines of the Decadent movement. She is a Gypsy (or perhaps, if one of her seeming lies is in fact the truth, a changeling adopted by Gypsies), and she has a different way of feeling as well as a different way of behaving.

The clinical tone of Mérimée's description of the doomed affair is no mere pastiche of scientific objectivity; it expresses an authentically scientific view of the mechanisms of human behavior. Unlike the Abbé Prévost, who might have been a bad Catholic but was nevertheless a Catholic through and through, Mérimée is an agnostic who clearly considers that the soul—if it exists at all—is an irrelevance, and that judgment is a purely human business. He does record that Carmen is sometimes described as a sorceress and a "child of Satan," and he even concedes her a measure of magical and prophetic power, but he never endorses the evaluation to the point of regarding her death as predestined damnation.

Mérimée's objectivity secures his place as an original writer despite his tendency to borrow all his plots and much of his local color from any sources that came conveniently to hand. *Carmen* embodies this attitude of mind and manner of execution most strikingly and forcefully, and that is one of the reasons for the work's enduring position as a literary landmark.

"Critical Evaluation" by Brian Stableford

Further Reading

Auchincloss, Louis. "Prosper Mérimée." In *Writers and Personality*. Columbia: University of South Carolina, 2005. Mérimée is one of the authors whom Auchincloss, himself a novelist, discusses in his examination of writers' personalities and how their temperaments, interests, and other personal traits are linked to their fiction.

Cogman, Peter. *Mérimée: "Colomba" and "Carmen."* London: Grant & Cutler, 1992. A detailed account of the two texts, paying particular attention to their use of the exotic and to their deployment of femmes fatales.

Gould, Evlyn. *The Fate of Carmen.* Baltimore: Johns Hopkins University Press, 1996. Examines the character of Carmen in Mérimée's novella and its subsequent adaptations, in which she is represented as a femme fatale, a liberated woman, or a pioneer warrior in the battle of the sexes.

Horrocks, Gillian. "A Semiotic Study of *Carmen.*" *Nottingham French Studies* 25 (1968): 60-72. A brief but interesting structuralist analysis of the story.

Mickelsen, David. "Travel, Transgression, and Possession in Mérimée's *Carmen.*" *Romantic Review* 87 (May, 1996): 329-344. Argues that the story should be viewed as an unequal meeting of cultures in which the central figure is not the Gypsy Carmen but the French narrator visiting Spain. Claims that examining the role of the narrator helps reveal the cultural imperatives operating within the story, especially its hidden colonialist stance.

Raitt, A. W. *Prosper Mérimée.* London: Eyre & Spottiswoode, 1970. A comprehensive study of the author's life and works. Includes a detailed discussion of *Carmen.*

Segal, Naomi. *Narcissus and Echo: Women in the French Récit.* New York: Manchester University Press, 1988. A feminist analysis that discusses *Manon Lescaut* and *Carmen* as classic instances of women being blamed by male narrators for their own shortcomings.

Tilby, Michael. "Language and Sexuality in Mérimée's *Carmen.*" *Forum for Modern Language Studies* 15 (1979): 255-263. An analysis of the way in which Mérimée employs his borrowings from George Henry Borrow to establish Carmen's alluring sexual exoticism.

Carmina

Author: Catullus (Gaius Valerius Catullus, c. 85- c. 54 B.C.E.)

First transcribed: c. 50 B.C.E. (English translation, 1893)

Type of work: Poetry

The 116 *carmina*, or poems, of the corpus of Catullus do not appear in chronological order, nor do they separate mythic narrative from creatively recounted personal experience. Though their numberings differ in various editions, it is generally the case that the short lyric poems, which number about forty, appear first. Four longer poems often appear next, though in differing arrangements. Two of these poems are marriage hymns (epithalamia); another retells the story of the wedding of Peleus and Thetis, the father and mother of Achilles; and another retells the story of Attis, the self-castrated priest of the Moon goddess Cybele.

The last part of the collection comprises elegies, often introduced by the mythic tale of the lock of Berenice. The extraordinary variety of the collection paired with the merging of autobiographical and mythic elements as well as sophisticated use of meters make Catullus a singularity of the ancient world; they also account for the inspiration the poet provides for the modern world.

Catullus wrote in the age of Julius Caesar, an age of political corruption and decadence presaging the final years of the Republic. The period parallels the Alexandrine movement in Greek literature, though the learned sophistication of Alexandrian literature makes its appearance only in the cosmological poetry of Lucretius (c. 99-55 B.C.E.) or the philosophic works of Cicero (106-43 B.C.E.). The poems of Catullus represent something new for a Roman audience: a melding of personal history and fiction as well as a coherent love theme merging all the emotions that love inspires—happiness, anger, frustration, and melancholy.

The lyric poems tracing the narrator's relationship to Lesbia likely are familiar to general readers. Lesbia is Catullus's pseudonym for his mistress, Clodia Metelli, the wife of a patrician. Lesbia had been infamous for her scandalous behavior and numerous lovers. After a self-deprecating dedication of the collection to his patron Cornelius, Catullus turns to admiration of Lesbia's sparrow because his mistress plays with it, feeds it, and holds it in her lap. The bird displaces the lover, and the lover marks the free access the bird enjoys. A mock elegy for the bird appears in the following poem. This poem also asks all Venuses and Cupids to mourn the sparrow that has just died, for it must make the journey to the realm of the dead.

A lyric poem often called "Phaselus" by readers of the Latin text records the swiftness of the narrator's sailing ship and enumerates the exotic locales it visits. The poem represents Catullus's bow to Alexandrian learned allusion; however, that his ship has grown slow with age and no longer sails allows a sensual implication. The emphasis on swiftness frequently links it to the carpe diem ("seize the day") theme of the Lesbia poem that suggests that the brevity of life requires thousands of kisses to confuse the evil-eye curse of those who would wish the lovers bad fortune.

A poem noting the inelegant, rustic mistress of Flavius suggests that were she not so inelegant, he would be more forthcoming about her to Catullus and could celebrate her. The only conclusion is that Flavius is in love with some diseased wench and is afraid to confess it. This poem compares with another Lesbia poem, which asks how many kisses from her would constitute sufficiency and surfeit. Alexandrian learned allusion appears again by suggesting that the number of grains of Libyan sand, or stars on a clear night, or stolen loves of men would be a reasonable approximation of the required number of kisses from Lesbia.

Soon thereafter, it appears that the romance with Lesbia has ended. Catullus is an excluded lover, literally locked out of his mistress's home. This poem is the oldest use of the *exclusus amator* ("excluded lover") theme in Latin literature. As often occurs in Catullus, the Latin uses wordplay in its suggestion that Catullus remain *obdura* ("firm" or "hard") in his resolution to resist any blandishments Lesbia may offer.

This wordplay often emerges in the homoerotic poems of Catullus, such as in the lyric to Asinius Marrucinus—*manu sinistra/ non belle uteris* ("your left hand/ you use not beautifully") and *tollis lintea neglegentiorum* ("you lift the napkins of the more careless people"). The subject is the brother of Asinius Pollio, a politician, patron of the arts, and himself a historian (though his history of the civil wars has not survived). Another homoerotic poem, this one more clearly so, is that written to the effeminate Thallus, in which the poet asks return of his cloak, Saetaban napkin, and tablets lest they become trophies.

The lyric to Sirmio, Catullus's villa at the southern end of the Lago di Garda, is a classic praise of love of home after long travels to distant lands. The farm personified welcomes the return of its master after his year on the staff of Gaius Memmius, the governor of Bithynia; the farm's waters laugh with joy at Catullus's return. A final bitter reference to Lesbia can be found in a lyric that appears soon after the lyric to Sirmio, in which Catullus asserts Lesbia is at a crossroads serving the lusts of high-minded descendants of Remus. This would make her a prostitute akin to the she-wolf that suckled the infant Romulus and Remus.

After about forty lyrics, the collection morphs into its long poems, one an epithalamium to Hymen. In this marriage hymn, the chorus of eager young men contrasts the chorus of modest young women in praise of the god of the wedding bed. There follows the Attis poem, its luridly sensational reference to the castrated priests of Cybele exemplifying the beginning of the exotic religious cults that would find an increasing number of adherents as imperial Rome continued to incorporate faraway territories.

References to Mount Ida, near Troy, offer transition to the Peleus and Thetis poem. Thetis can never become Jupiter's mistress because she will then give birth to a deity who will overthrow him. Jupiter finds the mortal Peleus as his substitute, and Achilles is their offspring. He will die in the Trojan War, the victim of Paris, son of Priam, the king of Troy. Because Priam was aware that Paris's theft of Helen would bring a war to Troy, he concealed Paris on Mount Ida as a shepherd, though to no avail.

Paradoxically, the poem that aptly sums up the entire collection is but two lines. It incorporates the two extremes of the poet's personality and of the collection's recurring themes: "I hate and I love. Perhaps you ask why I do this./ I do not know, but I know it to be so and I am tortured."

Robert J. Forman

Further Reading

Anconia, Ronnie. *Writing Passion: A Catullus Reader.* Wauconda, Ill.: Bolchazy-Carducci, 2004. Presents the text of forty-two poems of Catullus along with line-by-line commentary. The text is useful for the high school advanced-placement examination in Latin. Includes a bibliography and information on the social and historical background against which Catullus wrote his poems.

Dettmer, Helena. *Love by the Numbers: Form and Meaning in the Poetry of Catullus.* New York: Peter Lang, 1997. An examination of verse form and prosody and how the neoteric, or new, forms mesh with the Alexandrine movement.

Duff, J. Wight, and A. M. Duff. *A Literary History of Rome: From the Origins to the Close of the Golden Age.* 3d ed. New York: Barnes & Noble, 1967. Remains a standard survey of the poems and is especially valuable for its historical commentary on the relationship of the Alexandrine movement and the neoteric approach of Catullus.

Luck, Georg. *The Latin Love Elegy.* 1960. Reprint. Totowa, N.J.: Rowman & Littlefield, 1979. Though the extant Attis and Berenice poems by themselves would hardly indicate that Catullus was a major influence on the Latin love elegy, no less an elegiac poet than Propertius provides testimony that he was so. Reexamines Catullus's use of elegiac techniques in both the longer poems and the shorter poems.

Ross, David O., Jr. *Style and Tradition in Catullus.* Cambridge, Mass.: Harvard University Press, 1969. Separates and defines the stylistic character of the collection. Ross discerns three varieties (polymetric poems, long poems, and epigrams) and relates them internally as well as externally through their historical context.

Wiseman, T. P. *Catullus and His World: A Reappraisal.* Cambridge, Mass.: Cambridge University Press, 1985. An excellent reconstruction of the historical background against which Catullus wrote. Wiseman focuses on Palatine society and the place of the patrician Clodia, the mistress Catullus calls Lesbia.

Carrie

Author: Stephen King (1947-   )
First published: 1974
Type of work: Novel
Type of plot: Horror
Time of plot: 1979
Locale: Chamberlain, Maine

Principal characters:
CARIETTA "CARRIE" WHITE, a seventeen-year-old girl
MARGARET WHITE, Carrie's mother
SUSAN "SUE" SNELL, a classmate of Carrie
TOMMY ROSS, a classmate and Carrie's prom date
CHRIS HARGENSEN, a classmate
BILLY NOLAN, Chris's boyfriend
RITA DESJARDIN, a high school gym teacher

The Story:

Carrie White lives alone with her mother, Margaret, a domineering woman and a religious fanatic, in the small town of Chamberlain, Maine. Carrie's parents had left the local Baptist church many years before, because it was too liberal for them, and they never found any other church in the area that was up to their traditional standards. Carrie's father died in an industrial accident before Carrie was born, and her mother supplements the money from the insurance by working in a laundry.

Margaret conducts worship services for herself and Carrie on Sundays, Tuesdays, and Fridays. She makes Carrie wear homemade clothing and forbids her from wearing makeup. Margaret regards sex, even within a Christian marriage, to be inherently sinful, and she still feels guilty for submitting to her husband when they conceived Carrie.

Carrie is at the bottom of the pecking order in her high school. She is overweight, her face has pimples, and she has no friends or even friendly acquaintances. Carrie is quite different in another way, too, because she has the power of telekinesis, the ability to move objects by the force of her mind alone. When she was four years old, she had made stones fall like rain on her mother's house because her mother frightened her.

Carrie's power remains dormant until she has her first menstrual period. Unfortunately, she has her first period in the shower at high school. Because her mother had not educated her about menstruation, Carrie panics and believes she is bleeding to death. Led by classmate Chris Hargensen, the other girls scream "period" and "plug it up" and throw sanitary napkins at her. Rita Desjardin, the gym teacher, stops them and sends them to their next classes. She then realizes that Carrie does not understand what has happened. She cleans her up and sends her home, where her mother locks her in a closet. Margaret, believing Carrie's sinful thoughts had caused her to begin menstruating, feels her daughter needs to be punished.

Classmate Sue Snell was one of the girls who ridiculed Carrie in the shower room, but she later feels guilty. She tries to atone for her actions by persuading her boyfriend, Tommy Ross, to ask Carrie to the prom. Carrie has had a crush on Tommy for years, so she accepts his request.

Gym teacher Desjardin imposes a week's detention with calisthenics and running laps to punish the girls for the way they treated Carrie. Chris refuses to take her punishment, so she is suspended from school for three days and barred from the prom. Chris blames Carrie and plots her revenge after learning that Carrie is going to the prom with Tommy. The plan calls for her and her boyfriend, Billy Nolan, to douse Carrie with pig's blood.

Billy gets the blood by leading his gang to a nearby farm; he kills two pigs with a sledgehammer and another boy cuts their throats, filling two pails. The night before the prom, Billy sneaks into the gym with the buckets of blood, which he places on a beam above the spot where the king and queen of the prom will be crowned. He rigs up a system of ropes that will allow Chris to douse Carrie with blood, if she is elected prom queen. Chris rewards Billy by having sex with him for the first time. Meanwhile, Carrie has been practicing her telekinesis. Also, Tommy gradually comes to like Carrie.

Prom night has arrived, and Carrie is wearing a dress she made herself. She and Tommy are voted prom queen and king, most likely because Chris had asked her clique to vote for them. In the end, Carrie and Tommy win by one vote. At the moment they are crowned, Chris pulls the rope that knocks over the buckets of pig's blood. One of the buckets strikes Tommy and knocks him unconscious, Carrie is drenched in blood, and everyone in the gym erupts in laughter. Using her power, Carrie begins destroying the school and then sets fire to the town. Tommy, Chris, Billy, and more than four hundred others die.

Carrie returns home and is fatally stabbed by her mother, who believes she is obeying the biblical command not to suffer a witch to live. Carrie lives long enough to stop her mother's heart from beating.

Because she had not gone to the prom, Sue is one of the few surviving members of her class. She writes a book about her experience, *My Name Is Susan Snell*. The gym teacher, Desjardin, who chaperoned the prom, also survives, but leaves teaching.

Critical Evaluation:

While *Carrie* is the sixth novel Stephen King wrote, it is his first to be published. King had wanted to write a story using telekinesis as a premise ever since high school, when he read an article that speculated that poltergeist phenomena were really caused by the unconscious telekinetic powers of children. Telekinesis places *Carrie* into the science fiction branch of horror fiction, especially since the novel is several years in the future.

King also had wanted to write stories about two girls he knew in elementary and high school. The first girl was overweight and quiet, and wore the same clothes to school every day. After wearing a new set of clothes one day, she was hazed by other students so fiercely that she was driven to tears. As an adult, she committed suicide by hanging herself. The other girl King knew had lived alone with her mother, like Carrie in the novel. This girl had suffered from epilepsy and wore modest, old-fashioned clothes. She also died after graduating from high school, although by an epileptic seizure, not suicide. As a youth, King had been hired by this second girl's family to move some furniture. He observed a giant crucifix hanging over the couch, large enough to kill someone if it ever fell down. In *Carrie*, King places a similar crucifix in Carrie's home. King combined the girls' stories in developing *Carrie*.

To give the story an air of authenticity and to lengthen what was originally a twenty-five-thousand-word novella to the size of a novel, King had inserted a series of newspaper and magazine articles, book excerpts, official documents, and eyewitness testimonies into the narrative so that the plot device of telekinesis could be presented matter-of-factly and with a pseudoscientific justification. King even gives away the novel's ending in the first fifty pages. If readers ignore the telekinesis premise, they could read *Carrie* as a conventional young adult novel about teenage anxieties.

Although marketed by its publisher as a horror novel, *Carrie* also works as a story about a dysfunctional family, a common theme in King's fiction. King's father had deserted his family when King was a boy, and the father was never heard from again. Other King novels featuring dysfunctional families include *The Shining* (1977) and *'Salem's Lot* (1975).

King was overweight as a teenager, and he remembers his high school years as unhappy ones, full of misery and resentment. Although he worked on the school newspaper and played on the football team, he identified more with the high school outsiders than with the jocks, cheerleaders, and other popular types. The summer after graduating, he wrote the novel that was later published under his Richard Bachman pseudonym, *Rage* (1977). In that novel, the main character is a male high school student who brings a gun to school one day, shoots two teachers, and takes his classmates hostage. By the time King wrote *Carrie*, he had graduated from college and worked as a high school teacher for a few years, so he had gained both perspective and distance. Although he shows that a rigid caste system with the likes of Tommy, Susan, and Chris at the top and Carrie at the bottom exists in high school, he treats Tommy and Susan quite sympathetically; even Chris, the daughter of an attorney, is treated as other than a stereotype. King continued to use the concept of the high school outsider in *The Stand* (1978) and *Christine* (1983).

Carrie can also be interpreted as a modern version of the Cinderella story, with Carrie in the title role, her mother as the wicked stepmother, Sue as the fairy godmother, Chris and her clique as the cruel stepsisters, and Tommy as Prince Charming. The prom doubles as the ball at which Cinderella/Carrie's beauty is acknowledged. Carrie's full name, Carietta, starts with the same letter and has the same number of syllables as "Cinderella." Unfortunately for Carrie, Tommy, and the others, King's story has an unhappy ending.

King learned from H. P. Lovecraft that fantastic literature does not have to be set in faraway places, but that New England, for example, where King was born and raised, can provide a more than adequate setting. Not normally considered a regional writer, King nevertheless set *Carrie* and many of his other novels and short stories in small-town Maine.

Thomas R. Feller

Further Reading

Beahm, George. *Stephen King from A to Z: An Encyclopedia of His Life and Work.* Kansas City, Mo.: Andrews McMeel, 1998. This comprehensive biographical reference book on all things King includes an entry on *Carrie.*

Collings, Michael R. *Scaring Us to Death: The Impact of Stephen King on Popular Culture.* 2d rev. ed. San Bernardino, Calif.: Borgo Press, 1997. Examines King's influence on the rise of horror fiction in the United States and the effects of such fiction on society. Includes a bibliography and an index.

Gresh, Lois H., and Robert Weinberg. *The Science of Stephen King: From "Carrie" to "Cell"—The Terrifying Truth Behind the Horror Master's Fiction.* Hoboken, N.J.: John Wiley & Sons, 2007. A study of the science behind King's fiction, including an analysis of the theme of telekinesis in *Carrie.*

King, Stephen. Introduction to *Carrie.* New York: Simon & Schuster, 1999. King's introduction to the twenty-fifth-anniversary edition of the novel provides background information on how he came to write the story, the two girls Carrie is based upon, and his use of telekinesis in the work.

Reino, Joseph. *Stephen King: The First Decade.* Boston: Twayne, 1988. Book-by-book analysis, from *Carrie* to *Pet Sematary*, which attempts to show King's literary merits, stressing subtle characterization and nuances of symbolism and allusion. Includes a chronology and primary and secondary bibliographies.

Russell, Sharon A. *Revisiting Stephen King: A Critical Companion.* Westport, Conn.: Greenwood Press, 2002. Provides biographical information and a discussion of the horror genre before analyzing King's novels from 1996 through 2001. Includes a bibliography and an index.

Spignesi, Stephen J. *The Essential Stephen King: A Ranking of the Greatest Novels, Short Stories, Movies, and Other Creations of the World's Most Popular Writer.* Franklin Lakes, N.J.: New Page Books, 2001. A detailed volume by a King enthusiast that combines serious critical examination of the author's works with the readable commentary of an unabashed fan. Includes discussion of many of King's novels, including *Carrie.*

Wiater, Stanley, Christopher Golden, and Hank Wagner. *The Complete Stephen King Universe: A Guide to the Worlds of Stephen King.* Rev. ed. New York: St. Martin's Press, 2006. A comprehensive reference volume that explores King's work, including the common themes, places, and characters of his fiction. Features a biographical chronology, a bibliography, informative appendixes, and an index.

Cass Timberlane
A Novel of Husbands and Wives

Author: Sinclair Lewis (1885-1951)
First published: 1945
Type of work: Novel
Type of plot: Social realism
Time of plot: 1940's
Locale: Grand Republic, Minnesota

Principal characters:
CASS TIMBERLANE, a district judge
JINNY MARSHLAND TIMBERLANE, his wife
BRADD CRILEY, Jinny's lover

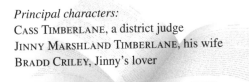

The Story:

After his divorce from his wife, Blanche, Judge Cass Timberlane continues to meet his old friends socially and to hold court in his usual honest and effective manner. It is not until Jinny Marshland appears in his court as witness in a routine case, however, that Cass once more begins to find his life interesting. Cass is forty-one years old and Jinny in her early twenties, so he tells himself that he is foolish to think of her in a romantic manner. In spite of his logical reasoning, Cass thinks more and more about Jinny. Within a few days of their first meeting, he arranges to see her again. Dignified Judge Cass Timberlane is falling in love.

He has no smooth romantic style. His friends think him stupid to become involved with a young woman of the working class. It seems strange to Cass that his friends would dare to criticize anyone. For example, there is Dr. Roy Drover, who openly makes love to any and every cheap woman he can, without bothering to conceal his infidelities from his wife. In the same class are Boone and Queenie Havock, both loud, brassy, and vulgar; Jay Laverick, a rich, lustful drunkard; and Bradd Criley, notorious for his affairs with the wives of his best friends.

Cass's friends are not the only ones opposed to the affair. Jinny's young radical friends think Cass a stuffy conservative. The only two people who are sympathetic with Cass are Chris Grau, who also wants to marry him, and Mrs. Higbee, his housekeeper.

What his friends think of Jinny does not matter; it is what Jinny will think of them that worries Cass at the time of their marriage. After the honeymoon, they live in his old family home, although Jinny prefers a new house in the country club section. They go out seldom, for they are happy enough to stay at home together. It is the first year of World War II, and Jinny finds work to do in various civic activities. Cass hopes that the work will keep her stimulated. When he notices that she is beginning to be bored by civic duties, he encourages her to accept a part in a little theater production. Later, he is sorry that he encouraged her, for the town begins to talk about Jinny and various male members of the cast, particularly Jay Laverick. When Cass speaks to her about the gossip, Jinny accuses him of being unreasonably jealous and then apologizes. Cass loves her more than ever.

Cass sells some property at an unexpectedly high price and buys the new house that Jinny desires in the country club district. While waiting for it to be finished, they take a trip to New York. At first, Jinny is enchanted with the size and brightness of the city, but soon she is bored by the unfriendliness of everyone she meets. After Bradd Criley arrives in New York and takes them under his wing, Jinny enjoys herself. Cass is not so happy.

Shortly after Cass and Jinny return home, they learn that Jinny is pregnant, but their happiness is marred by the knowledge that Jinny has diabetes. Roy Drover, her doctor, assures Cass that there is no cause for worry if Jinny follows her diet and gets plenty of rest. Bradd seems to amuse her, so Cass often invites him to the house.

Jinny goes through her delivery safely, but the baby dies. For many weeks afterward, she will see no one but Cass. Then, for no apparent reason, she wants to have a party almost every night. Cass tries to be patient with her, for he knows that she is still reacting to the death of the baby, and that the restrictions placed on her by her illness are irritating. When his friends once again warn him about allowing Jinny to see so much of Bradd, his patience wears thin; he almost orders Jinny to stop seeing Bradd, and he tells Bradd to stay away from Jinny. Later, Bradd apologizes to Cass and the three are friends once more.

After Bradd moves to New York, all tension between Jinny and Cass seems to disappear for a time. Then Jinny grows restless again and begins to talk of moving to a larger city. Although Cass prizes his judgeship and would hate to give it up, he is still willing to do anything for his wife. They take another trip to New York, where Cass hopes to find a partnership in an established law firm. They meet Bradd during their visit. Although he trusts his wife, Cass is relieved when Jinny tells him that she knows she would not really like living in New York and that she wants to go home. They leave hurriedly, without seeing Bradd again before their departure.

On their first night at home, Jinny tells Cass that she loves Bradd and that he became her lover while she was in New York. When Cass refuses to give her a divorce until she has ample time to consider her own wishes carefully, she goes back to New York to stay with Bradd's sister until Cass will free her. For Cass, the town, the house, his friends, and his work are now meaningless. He can think only of Jinny. Then he receives a telegram from her. After failing to follow her diet, she is desperately ill and she wants Cass. He flies to New York that night. He finds Jinny in a coma, but she awakens long enough to ask him to take her home.

After Jinny can be moved, Cass takes her to a seashore hotel and then home. He forgives her completely, but he warns her that she will have to work hard to win back their friends. They still have to make their own private adjustment. It is not until Bradd returns to Grand Republic that Jinny is able to see him as the charming philanderer that he really is. That night, she goes to Cass's room. He receives her as if she has never been away.

Critical Evaluation:

Published only five years before Sinclair Lewis's death, *Cass Timberlane* is one of two late works (the other being *Kingsblood Royal*, 1947) that compare favorably with his five major novels of the 1920's. As in earlier novels such as *Babbitt* (1922) and *Elmer Gantry* (1927), Lewis uses a memorable character to dramatize a particular social problem.

Lewis's subtitle, *A Novel of Husbands and Wives*, reveals the major theme and basic structural pattern of *Cass Timberlane*. The novel examines the institution of marriage through numerous comparisons and contrasts. Interrupting the main narrative of Cass and Jinny are fifteen brief accounts of other husbands and wives. Some are friends of the Timberlanes; others are residents of Grand Republic who have little or no connection with the main plot. In some cases, these accounts—labeled collectively "An Assemblage of Husbands and Wives"—are character sketches with little action. Others are narratives with economical but well-developed plots.

Among the marriages portrayed by Lewis, no more than five are successful. The others range from quietly desperate to violently destructive. For example, Nestor and Fanny Purdwin have been married for fifty years, but their time together has been as monotonous as the unvaried breakfasts of porridge they have eaten every morning for all those years.

Roy and Lillian Drover are considered one of the happiest couples in Grand Republic, but Roy is repeatedly unfaithful, Lillian considers suicide, and their two sons enjoy killing things. To escape from a truly vicious wife, Allan Cedar attempts suicide, but she defeats him even in this grim effort. In response to his marital problems, Vincent Osprey becomes a drunk and eventually succeeds in jumping to his death from a hotel window.

By recent standards, Lewis's depiction of sexuality is modest, but he documents the power of passion and displays a range of behaviors without resorting to graphic details. He alludes at times to the ideas of Sigmund Freud and Richard von Krafft-Ebing, and some of the accounts of husbands and wives sound like case studies of psychosexual problems. In George Hame's case, incestuous desire for his own daughter threatens his marriage. Sabine Grossenwahn is a nymphomaniac who spends part of her wedding night with a man other than her husband. Norton Trock calls his mother "sweetheart" from the age of three and later discovers that his homoerotic attraction to his chauffeur far surpasses the sexual allure of his wife.

Although these relationships are glimpsed in passing, that of the Timberlanes is developed in detail. The pairing of Jinny and Cass is not exactly a May-December romance, but at the ages of twenty-three and forty-one, respectively, they could almost be daughter and father. This disparity in age leads to two motifs in Lewis's main narrative. For the disillusioned older man, the romance leads to spiritual awakening. For the inexperienced younger woman, the courtship and subsequent marriage lead to education and maturing.

As the novel begins, Cass is clearly in a state of stagnation. After his divorce from Blanche, he is briefly a vagabond and an alcoholic. Now he is a responsible judge, but he battles sleep in the courtroom just as he struggles against lethargy in life. The dramatic appearance of Jinny Marshland as a witness in a minor case is the first step in his gradual reawakening. When he meets her young friends at the boardinghouse, he experiences the concerns of a new generation and a different social class.

In plotting Jinny's education, Lewis uses many standard devices, some of which parallel those used in developing the character of Carol Kennicott in *Main Street* (1920). By traveling away from her provincial environment, Jinny learns about her place in the larger world. Taking part in amateur theatrical productions enables her to explore new roles, on the stage and in real life. In hunting for a new house, she searches for a new identity. Suffering from diabetes, she plunges into a coma but awakens with a more mature vision of reality.

Although the main focus of *Cass Timberlane* is an examination of marriage, Lewis includes much incidental satire of provincial smugness and hypocrisy. He pokes fun at those who consider the *Reader's Digest* to be highly intellectual literature. At one point, Lewis includes a reference to his own novel *Main Street*, but the character who mentions this title to appear learned has never read it and thinks the author is Upton Sinclair. Lewis satirizes local organizations such as the Junior Chamber of Commerce, whose members routinely eat together at six o'clock, listen placidly to an invited speaker at seven-fifteen, and return home to their families by eight-thirty. In passages that recall *Babbitt*, Lewis portrays the local Rotarians as slightly higher in social rank but equally vacuous.

In this satire of Grand Republic, Lewis intends to point out the superficiality of an entire culture. Grand Republic sounds more like the name of a country than that of a city, and Lewis says that this midwestern metropolis is interchangeable with at least thirty other U.S. cities. The role of Cass in the context of satire of provincial narrowness is ambiguous. Like Lewis himself, Cass is both attracted to and repelled by the values and behavior of his hometown. This ambiguity is demonstrated best in Cass's attitude toward Bradd Criley. Bradd has been Cass's best friend since childhood but becomes Jinny's seducer. Cass condemns Bradd's immoral behavior but still treasures him as a friend. Cass similarly deplores the hypocrisy and shallowness of Grand Republic but continues to embrace those who blatantly display those qualities.

The conclusion of *Cass Timberlane* is somewhat contrived, but in the return to Grand Republic from New York City, Lewis proclaims the triumph of midwestern values over those of the effete East. At the same time, he suggests that the Timberlane marriage, having been tested in both the provincial town and the big city, can survive further trials and achieve success.

"Critical Evaluation" by Albert E. Wilhelm

Further Reading

Dooley, D. J. *The Art of Sinclair Lewis*. Lincoln: University of Nebraska Press, 1967. Reviews major criticism and considers arguments that the novel's contrived ending is more ironic than sentimental. Analyzes the contrapuntal effect of the brief accounts from "An Assemblage of Husbands and Wives."

Geismar, Maxwell. *The Last of the Provincials: The American Novel, 1915-1925*. Boston: Houghton Mifflin, 1949. Argues that *Cass Timberlane* displays Lewis's return to the values of his native Midwest. Asserts that Judge Timberlane is a true aristocrat, whose values are in contrast to corrupt East Coast values.

Grebstein, Sheldon Norman. *Sinclair Lewis*. New York: Twayne, 1962. Intelligent commentaries on Lewis's major novels, along with useful annotated bibliography. Praises the economical sketches in "An Assemblage of Husbands and Wives" as some of Lewis's best writing. Acknowledges that *Cass Timberlane* degenerates at times to soap opera, but argues that Lewis's aim is realism rather than satire.

Lingeman, Richard R. *Sinclair Lewis: Rebel from Main Street*. New York: Random House, 2002. A critical biography that includes analysis of Lewis's novels. Lingeman provides a detailed description of Lewis's unhappy life.

Schorer, Mark. *Sinclair Lewis: An American Life*. New York: McGraw-Hill, 1961. An authoritative biography. Points out parallels between Lewis's own life and that of Cass Timberlane; suggests that both were victims of a matriarchal complex. Sums up early reviews of the book, including comments by H. L. Mencken. Identifies similarities in structure with *Main Street*.

Wilson, Edmund. "Salute to an Old Landmark: Sinclair Lewis." *The New Yorker*, October 13, 1945. One of the most perceptive early reviews. Sees *Cass Timberlane* as significantly different from earlier Lewis novels in its treatment of midwestern values and of liberated young women.

The Castle

Author: Franz Kafka (1883-1924)
First published: Das Schloss, 1926 (English translation, 1930)
Type of work: Novel
Type of plot: Allegory
Time of plot: Early twentieth century
Locale: Europe

Principal characters:
K., a seeker and a land surveyor
FRIEDA, a barmaid
BARNABAS, a young man
OLGA and AMALIA, his sisters
ARTHUR and JEREMIAS, K.'s assistants

The Story:

It is late in the evening when K. arrives in the town that lies before the castle of Count Westwest. After his long walk through deep snow, K. wants to do nothing so much as to go to sleep. He goes to an inn and falls asleep by the fire, only to be awakened by a man wanting to see his permit to stay in the town. K. explains that he just arrived and comes at the count's request to be the new land surveyor. A telephone call to the castle establishes the fact that a land surveyor is expected, and K. is allowed to rest.

The next morning, K. decides to go to the castle to report for duty, although his assistants have not yet arrived. He sets off through the snowy streets toward the castle, which as he walks seems farther and farther away. He becomes tired and stops in a house for refreshment and directions. As he leaves, he sees two men coming from the castle. He tries to speak to them, but they refuse to stop. As evening approaches, K. gets a ride back to the inn in a sleigh.

At the inn, he meets the two men he saw, and they introduce themselves as Arthur and Jeremias and say they are his old assistants. They are not, but K. accepts them because he knows they came from the castle and therefore were sent to help him. Because the two men closely resemble each other, K. cannot tell them apart; therefore he calls both of them Arthur. He orders them to take him to the castle the next morning by sleigh. When they refuse, he telephones the castle. A voice tells him that he can never come to the castle. Shortly afterward, a messenger named Barnabas arrives with a letter from Klamm, a chief at the castle. K. is ordered to report to the mayor of the town.

K. arranges for a room at the inn. He asks to accompany Barnabas on a walk, to which Barnabas, a kind young man, agrees. He takes K. to his home to meet his two sisters, Olga and Amalia, and his sickly old mother and father. K. is ill at ease, however; it is Barnabas, not he, who comes home. When Olga leaves to get beer from a nearby inn, K. goes with her. At the inn, it is made clear to him that he will be welcome only in the bar, as the other rooms are reserved for the gentlemen from the castle.

In the bar, K. quickly makes friends with the barmaid, Frieda, who seems to wish to save him from Olga and her family. She hides K. under the counter. K. does not understand what is happening. He learns that Frieda is Klamm's mistress.

Frieda is determined to stay with K., if K. is willing. K. thinks he might as well marry her. He is determined to get to the castle and thinks his chances will improve if he marries the chief's former mistress. When Arthur and Jeremias enter the room and watch him and Frieda, K. sends them away. Frieda decides to go to the inn where K. is staying.

K. calls on the mayor, whom he finds sick in bed with gout. K. learns that a land surveyor was needed several years earlier but that nobody knows why K. comes now to fill the unnecessary post. When K. shows him Klamm's letter, the mayor says that it is not important. The mayor convinces K. that his coming to the town is the result of confusion. K. decides to remain and find work, so that he will become an accepted resident of the town.

K. returns to the inn to find Frieda made his room comfortable. The schoolmaster comes to offer K. the job of janitor at the school. At Frieda's insistence, K. accepts. That night, K., Frieda, and the two assistants move to the school to live there. The next morning, the assistants trick K. into so many arguments with the teachers that K. dismisses them both. After he finishes his day's work, he slips away and goes to Barnabas's house to see if there is a message for him from the castle.

Barnabas is not at home. Olga explains that her family is rejected by the town because Amalia refuses to become the mistress of one of the gentlemen of the castle, who wrote her a crude, obscene letter. Amalia destroys the letter; later the whole town will turn against them. K. is so interested in the story that he does not realize how late he is staying. When he finally prepares to leave, he sees that Jeremias is outside spying on him.

K. slips out the back way but then returns and asks Jeremias why he is there. The man sullenly replies that

Frieda sent him. She went back to her old job as barmaid and never wants to see K. again. Barnabas arrives with the news that one of the most important gentlemen of the castle is awaiting K. at the inn.

At the inn, K. learns that the gentleman went to sleep. As he stands in the corridor, he sees Frieda going down another corridor. He runs after her to explain why he stayed away so long and to ask her to come back to him. She seems about to relent when Jeremias comes up and persuades her to go with him. Frieda leaves K. forever. (At this point, the first edition of the novel ends. The remaining eighty or so pages were found among Kafka's papers and included in later editions.)

K. intrudes on a sleeping gentleman in a corridor of the pub, only to fall asleep himself in the corridor. After sleeping for twelve hours, he has a lengthy conversation with Pepi, the substitute barmaid, and criticizes the landlady for her old-fashioned clothing.

Critical Evaluation:

The fragmentary work *The Castle* was published posthumously, against Franz Kafka's instructions, by his friend Max Brod. Critics ever since have debated all aspects of it, from the textual problems to the interpretation of the highly suggestive symbolic structure. It is typical of Kafka's works that a final definition of his symbols is impossible; like dreams, they combine references to the everyday world with absurd fantasies and seemingly coherent mythic structure with a discontinuity that frustrates attempts to develop a rational interpretation. The images Kafka conjures are compelling, but they seem ultimately to stand for themselves and not for any symbolic message.

A knowledge of Kafka's circumstances in 1922 is germane to an understanding of *The Castle*. The author's tuberculosis was so advanced that he knew he had not long to live and also the manner of his death. Placed by disease in the position of an outsider, Kafka could for the first time view personal and professional concerns with detachment. His imminent death gave him the freedom to rise above manner and restraint and, through his novel's main character, K., to indulge his sense of humor with outrageous observations. K., who calls himself a land surveyor, takes a sharp look at his surroundings. Like Kafka himself, K., too, suffers from those paradoxical effects of advanced disease that leave a patient at once exhausted and impatient.

K.'s main counterpart in the novel is Frieda. Her name connotes *Frieden*, or peace, an irony because the couple has hardly a quiet moment together. Critics have seen in Frieda the fictional representation of Milena Jesenka-Polak, one of Kafka's translators, who professed to love Kafka but ulti-

mately would not leave her husband. The affair in the novel also reflects Kafka's lifelong attitude toward marriage: Although conditioned by society to feel that he should marry, he repeatedly broke off relationships when it became evident that they would interfere with his writing.

In *The Castle*, Kafka criticizes the roles imposed on men and women by the society of his time. Too often, women were perceived mainly as sexual objects and expected to be subservient to and dependent on men. Kafka chose to make his strongest female character in his novel a liberated woman. Set up by her parents (in a frilly blouse and garnet necklace) to attract a husband, Amalia instead repudiates the direct sexual advance of a "gentleman" from the castle. Amalia is portrayed as a capable and talented individual, a person who does not need affiliation with a man to realize her potential.

Just as Kafka criticizes the societal reduction of women to a secondary role, so, too, does he criticize the expectation that men automatically fulfill a dominant role. Using the device of satire, he represents all figures of male authority and the bureaucracies in which they operate as hopelessly and ludicrously inept, thus exposing the reverence in which they are held as all the more ridiculous. His first example is the most memorable: The mayor, who lets unorganized files accumulate, increases the disorder with every new and frantic search for information. Yet this is the man who solemnly assures K. that there is no possibility of error in the system. K. is not impressed and to the mayor's face calls it "ludicrous bungling."

While no such direct confrontation occurs with the more distant and respected "gentlemen" of the castle—mainly because K. during his one chance interview is overcome by sleep—these officials, too, are portrayed as being completely out of touch with the affairs of the village they purportedly control and influence. This is no idle criticism. Kafka, who held a doctorate in law and was a valued employee of an insurance company, knew what bureaucracies were like. By keeping the exact nature of the castle unspecific, Kafka uses that image to demystify arbitrary and illusory authority in all its forms. By having K. continually try to meet Klamm face to face, he shows that it is in the interests of the citizen to pierce the façade of authority.

K. in fact never does reach the castle. Perhaps it is enough that he has his say on important issues and thereby points the way for others to take. Kafka indicated to his friend and later executor of his estate, Brod, that had he finished the novel he would have had K. die of exhaustion without reaching the castle. Exhaustion is, in fact, a strong factor in the book. The entire four-hundred-page novel takes place in a winter landscape. The days are short, and the people are exhausted by the cold and spend much of their time sleeping indoors. In choosing this setting, Kafka draws on the literary convention of using winter as a metaphor for death.

The spiritual message of *The Castle* gains in impact by being merely suggested and allowed to continue independently of K.'s physical limitations. Where the mind is free, as it most certainly is in this dreamlike novel, a survey of the land yields new truths. Kafka shows that the castle is a jumble created by people themselves and in need of rearrangement.

Thomas Mann defined Kafka as a religious humorist. While Kafka's meaning perhaps eludes the attempts of critics to define it, his portrayal of the experiences of individual isolation and frustration and of the ambivalence toward the community and the vague forces that dominate the individual and human society remains compelling.

A critical reading of *The Castle* requires an evaluation of its various textual editions. As noted, when Kafka died in 1924, he left *The Castle* as an unfinished, handwritten manuscript. His executor, Max Brod, published an edition of *The Castle* in 1926 based on his editing of Kafka's manuscript and notes. This edition was beautifully translated into English by Edwin and Willa Muir in 1930. In 1982 a new critical edition of *The Castle* was published in German, edited by Sir Malcolm Pasley and based on the meticulous critical work of a team of international Kafka scholars. In contrast, Stroemfeld publishers aspired to publish a facsimile edition of Kafka's handwritten manuscripts for *The Castle*, as it already had for *Der Prozess* (1925; *The Trial*, 1937), to allow a more direct interface with Kafka's writings. In 1998, Schocken Books published a new English translation of *The Castle* by Mark Harmon, based on Pasley's German critical edition. In his translator's introduction, Harmon explains that he sought a more faithful rendering of Kafka's unique and often abrupt prose than the polished translation of the Muirs. Harmon's translation retains the sparse use of punctuation in Kafka's extraordinarily long sentences and paragraphs. It also retains Kafka's occasionally odd and startling word choice, tense, and grammatical structure. Most important, the German critical edition that Harmon translated numbers the chapters of *The Castle* differently, evoking an alternative flow to the narrative. Shocken's critical edition of *The Castle*, however, does not include the equivalent of volume two of the German Pasley edition, which annotated the choices and variations in Kafka's manuscripts.

"Critical Evaluation" by Jean M. Snook;
revised by Howard Bromberg

Further Reading

Boa, Elizabeth. *Kafka: Gender, Class, and Race in the Letters and Fictions.* New York: Oxford University Press, 1996. An excellent study focusing on the representation of gender in Kafka's works, including *The Castle*. Boa also examines Kafka's letters to his fiancé and to a Czech female journalist to understand his views of women.

Bridgwater, Patrick. *Kafka's Novels: An Interpretation.* Atlanta: Rodopi, 2003. A chapter-by-chapter analysis of *The Castle* and two other novels. Bridgwater focuses on Kafka's symbolic language, including his use of metaphors and of ambiguous words, describing how he uses this language to visualize "dreams and thoughts on the edge of sleep."

Calasso, Roberto. *K.* New York: Knopf, 2005. A scholarly study in which Calasso seeks to understand what Kafka's fiction is meant to signify. He also examines why K. and Josef K., the protagonists of *The Castle* and *The Trial*, respectively, are radically different from any other characters in the history of the novel.

Dowden, Stephen. *Kafka's Castle and the Critical Imagination.* Columbia, S.C.: Camden House, 1995. A study of the range of twentieth century interpretations of and reactions to *The Castle*.

Fickert, Kurt J. "Chapter IV: Castle and Burrow." In *Kafka's Doubles.* Bern, Switzerland: Peter Lang, 1979. A short but substantial work that provides new insights into Kafka's careful creative process. Interprets *The Castle* as the author's self-analysis.

Kraft, Herbert. "Being There Still: K., Land Surveyor, Stable-Hand." In *Someone Like K.: Kafka's Novels*, translated by R. J. Kavanagh. Würzburg, Germany: Königshausen & Neumann, 1991. A positive assessment of K. as the antitype. Since there is no mass resistance, individuals must stand alone, but they can be perceived to be powerful. K. knows what Amalia knows, but he also has the courage to act.

Krauss, Karoline. *Kafka's K. Versus "The Castle": The Self and the Other.* New York: Peter Lang, 1996. A good analysis of *The Castle*, in which Krauss argues that K.'s experiences in the castle enable him to undergo an existential maturation. Includes bibliographical references.

Neumeyer, Peter F., ed. *Twentieth Century Interpretations of "The Castle": A Collection of Critical Essays.* Englewood Cliffs, N.J.: Prentice-Hall, 1969. Part 1, "Interpretations," contains ten essays, while part 2 features shorter "View Points." A testimony to the astounding number of diverse and conflicting interpretations that *The Castle* has inspired.

Preece, Julian, ed. *The Cambridge Companion to Kafka.* New York: Cambridge University Press, 2002. Collection of essays about Kafka, including analyses of *The Trial* and *The Castle* and discussions of Kafka and Jewish folklore, gender, and popular culture.

Sheppard, Richard. *On Kafka's Castle: A Study.* London: Croom Helm, 1973. A close reading of the novel, which is in many aspects convincing, presents a bourgeois interpretation. Like the German critic Wilhelm Emrich, whose study of Kafka's writing appeared in English translation in 1968, Sheppard tends to take the viewpoint of the villagers and is critical of K. for not settling down with Frieda.

Spann, Meno. *"The Castle."* In *Franz Kafka.* Boston: Twayne, 1976. A lucidly written essay that places the novel in the context of Kafka's personal and literary development. Spann, one of the few critics receptive to Kafka's sense of humor, offers a convincing interpretation of *The Castle* as a satire on bureaucracy.

The Castle of Otranto

Author: Horace Walpole (1717-1797)
First published: 1765
Type of work: Novel
Type of plot: Gothic
Time of plot: Twelfth century
Locale: Italy

Principal characters:
MANFRED, the prince of Otranto
MATILDA, Manfred's daughter
CONRAD, Manfred's son
ISABELLA, Conrad's fiancé
FATHER JEROME, a priest
THEODORE, a young peasant and the true heir to Otranto

The Story:

Manfred, the prince of Otranto, plans to marry his fifteen-year-old son Conrad to Isabella, the daughter of the marquis of Vicenza. On the day of the wedding, however, a servant runs into the hall and informs the assembled company that a huge helmet has appeared mysteriously in the courtyard of the castle. When Count Manfred and his guests rush into the courtyard, they find Conrad crushed to death beneath a gigantic helmet adorned with waving black plumes. Theodore, a young peasant, declares the helmet is like that on a statue of Prince Alfonso the Good, which stands in the chapel. Another spectator shouts that the helmet is missing from the statue. Prince Manfred imprisons the young peasant as a magician and charges him with the murder of the heir to Otranto.

That evening, Manfred sends for Isabella. He informs her that he intends to divorce his wife so that he himself might marry her and have another male heir. Frightened, Isabella runs away and loses herself in the passages beneath the castle. There she encounters Theodore, who helps her to escape through an underground passage into a nearby church. Manfred, searching for the girl, accuses the young man of aiding her. As he is threatening Theodore, servants rush up to tell the prince of a giant who is sleeping in the great hall of the castle. When Manfred returns to the hall, the giant disappears.

The following morning, Father Jerome comes to inform Manfred and his wife that Isabella took sanctuary at the altar of his church. Sending his wife away, Manfred calls on the priest to help him divorce his wife and marry Isabella. Father Jerome refuses, warning Manfred that heaven will punish him for harboring such thoughts. The priest unthinkingly suggests Isabella might be in love with the handsome young peasant who aided in her escape.

Manfred, enraged at the possibility, confronts Theodore. Although the young man does not deny having aided the princess, he claims never to have seen her before. The frustrated Manfred orders him to the courtyard to be executed, and Father Jerome is called to give absolution to the condemned man; however, when the collar of the lad is loosened, the priest discovers a birthmark that proves the young peasant to be Father Jerome's son, born before the priest entered the Church. Manfred offers to stay the execution if the priest will deliver Isabella to him. At that moment, a trumpet sounds at the gates of the castle.

The trumpet signals the arrival of a herald from the Knight of the Gigantic Sabre, champion of Isabella's father, who is the rightful heir to Otranto. Greeting Manfred as a usurper, the herald demands either the immediate release of Isabella and Manfred's abdication or the satisfaction of mortal combat. Manfred invites the Knight of the Gigantic Sabre to the castle, hoping to get his permission to marry Isabella and keep the throne. The knight enters the castle with five hundred men at arms and a hundred more carrying one gigantic sword.

During the feast, the strange knight keeps silent and raises his visor only to pass food into his mouth. Later, Manfred broaches the question of marrying Isabella, telling the knight he wishes to marry again to ensure himself of an heir. Before he finishes, Father Jerome arrives with the news of Isabella's disappearance from the church. After everyone goes to look for Isabella, Manfred's daughter, Matilda, helps Theodore to escape from the castle.

In the forest, Theodore meets Isabella and promises to protect her. Shortly thereafter, they meet the Knight of the Gigantic Sabre. Fearing the knight means harm to Isabella, the young man overcomes him in combat. The knight, thinking he is about to die, reveals to Isabella that he is her father. They return together to the castle, where Isabella's father confides to her that he discovered the gigantic sword in the Holy Land. It is a miraculous weapon; on the blade is written that only the blood of Manfred can atone for the wrongs committed on the family of the true ruler of Otranto. When Manfred returns to the castle, he finds Theodore dressed in armor. It seems to Manfred that the young man resembles the prince whose throne Manfred usurped.

Manfred still hopes to wed Isabella, and he craftily wins her father's consent by allowing that nobleman's betrothal to Matilda. At that point, a nearby statue drips blood from its nose, an omen that disaster will follow the proposed marriages.

Manfred sees only two courses open to him. One is to surrender all claims to Otranto; the other is to proceed with his plan to marry Isabella. In either case, it appears that fate is against his success. A second appearance of the giant in the castle does not ease the anxiety he feels. When Isabella's father hears of the giant, he decides not to court disaster by marrying Matilda or by permitting Manfred to marry his daughter. His resolution is strengthened when a skeleton in the rags of a hermit exhorts him to renounce Matilda.

Hours later, Manfred is told that Theodore is in the chapel with a woman. Jealous, he goes to the chapel and stabs the woman, who is his own daughter Matilda. Over the body of Matilda, Theodore announces that he is the true ruler of Otranto. Suddenly, the giant form of the dead Prince Alfonso appears, proclaiming Theodore to be the true heir. Then he ascends to heaven, where he is received by St. Nicholas.

The truth becomes known that Theodore is the son of Father Jerome, when he was still prince of Falconara, and

Alfonso's daughter. Manfred confesses his usurpation, and he and his wife enter neighboring convents. Theodore marries Isabella and rules as the new prince of Otranto.

Critical Evaluation:

Horace Walpole's *The Castle of Otranto* is among the best-known, best-loved, and best-crafted novels of the gothic genre in English. It is also one of the first. Gothic fiction was representative of the late eighteenth century rejection of the rational, realistic creed of neoclassicism, which asserted the superiority of the familiar and contemporary for literary purposes. This reaction was but a phase of the revival of interest in the recondite past, an interest that focused on medieval life and manifested itself in pseudoscholarly antiquarianism, imitation Gothic castles, artificial ruins, balladry, and contrived narratives.

These narratives, permeated with fashionable melancholy, attempted to portray human conduct and sentiment with psychological realism while setting the action in remote and mysterious places and times. The emotional thrills of adventure provided the reader an escape from humdrum existence; hence, the villain was characteristically somber and restless, and the heroine—beautiful, innocent, young, and sensitively perceptive—waited dutifully to be rescued by a brave and courageous lover. The obligatory setting was a haunted castle, a cloister, or a ruined abbey, fortuitously furnished with underground passages, secret doors, and locked and unused rooms, and surrounded by wild and desolate landscape. The action inevitably included strange and deliberate crimes (often accompanied by rattling chains and other inexplicable phenomena), incidents of physical violence, and emotional anguish orchestrated with supernatural manifestations. A strong erotic element usually underscored the plot, and comic relief, following William Shakespeare's model, was confined to servants. In a bogus historical setting, chronologically and geographically remote, novels of mystery and passionate emotion depicted the trials and misfortunes of sentimental love with an overlay of ghosts, prescience, and preternatural forces, as well as the titillating horror of violence and crime.

The author of *The Castle of Otranto*, which stood at the very forefront of this gothic revival, seemed personally ideally suited to his book (rather than the more usual obverse). Walpole was a nobleman who was respected for his antiquarian scholarship, and he was a fussy bachelor in precarious health, unable to join his peers in hunting, tippling, and wenching. He escaped the demands of this world by psychologically and physically retreating into the past. He built himself a pseudo-Gothic retreat at Strawberry Hill, and there he displayed his collection of antiques and led an active fantasy life, imagining himself at one time a feudal lord and at another time a learned monk. One evening, he reportedly climbed his narrow Gothic staircase to his library so that he could dream—possibly with the aid of opium—of the romantic past.

The Castle of Otranto, spawned out of dreams, illustrates two major themes of the gothic genre. The story unites a baroque view of architecture and sentiment and a repudiation of neoclassical ideals of proportion, balance, and harmony. The physical appearance of the Castle of Otranto, therefore, is an exaggeration of genuine Gothic style, carrying the visual image to such excessive lengths that the structure bears hardly any resemblance to authentic examples of medieval Gothic architecture. Yet the effectiveness of the description in the novel is undeniable. Similarly, the emotional overreaction of the characters—in defiance of all neoclassical canons of moderation—serve to transcend the mundane realities of common life on the wings of fancy. In the very uncommon life of this story, Walpole sought to liberate imagination and allow it to rove freely in what he characterized as "the boundless realms of invention . . . creating more interesting situations." Simultaneously (and without any sense of contradiction), Walpole claimed to strive for naturalness and probability in his character development. Nevertheless, fanciful setting and untrammeled emotion were the hallmarks of his as well as many other gothic novels.

Walpole employs supernatural devices to create his interesting situations, and the totally immersed reader can become so wrapped up in the plot that inconsistencies escape notice. The plot is actually plausible, but the events that surround and to some extent precipitate it are more than a little suspect. The story opens with the ambiguous prophecy that "the castle and lordship of Otranto should pass from the present family, whenever the real owner should be grown too large to inhabit it." Intrigue thickens with Conrad's peculiar death and Manfred's frantic attempts to sire another heir. In due course, other supernatural manifestations intervene: Two menservants see a strange apparition, which also appears to Bianca, Matilda's maid. Manfred's reasonable objections notwithstanding, these events very nearly unseat his reason; but even as Manfred argues with Hippolita to annul their marriage so that he can marry Isabella and produce an heir, three drops of blood fall from the nose of the statue of Alfonso, the original prince of Otranto who won the principality through fraud and deceit. Manfred is thus given supernatural warning to desist from his wicked plan. He is still undeterred, but his intended father-in-law also sees an apparition when he goes to the chapel to pray for guidance. In the

end, after many such scenes of terror, violence, and bewilderment, the true heir of Otranto is unexpectedly discovered amid a thunderclap, a rattling of armor, and a disembodied pronouncement about legitimate succession.

Although in retrospect these contrivances may strain the credulity of today's reader, the chain of events is so engrossing that the reader's normal skepticism is effectively held at bay. It is only after the fact that the reader begins to examine the logic and question the veracity of Walpole's highly convincing tale. Therein lies the art of the story.

"Critical Evaluation" by Joanne G. Kashdan

Further Reading

Brown, Marshall. "Walpole: The Birth of *The Castle of Otranto*." In *The Gothic Text*. Stanford, Calif.: Stanford University Press, 2005. A history of the gothic novel, including a less-than-flattering analysis of *The Castle of Otranto*. Brown observes that, "When so poor a book spawns so long a line of fascinating, if slightly naughty, successors, distinctive questions arise about literary origins and creativity."

Day, William Patrick. *In the Circles of Fear and Desire: A Study of Gothic Fantasy*. Chicago: University of Chicago Press, 1985. A study of the themes and conventions of gothic fantasy from the publication of Walpole's novel through the twentieth century. Discusses Manfred as an example of the typical gothic male protagonist.

Heiland, Donna. "Patriarchal Narratives in the Work of Horace Walpole, Clara Reeve, and Sophia Lee." In *Gothic and Gender: An Introduction*. Malden, Mass.: Blackwell, 2004. A feminist examination of the themes in gothic literature, including *The Castle of Otranto*. In addition to the chapter about Walpole, there are other references to his novel that are listed in the index.

Kallich, Martin. *Horace Walpole*. New York: Twayne, 1971. Discusses the formal style and period-piece conventions of the novel. Suggests a reading of the story as a version of the Freudian family romance, with such Oedipal themes as desire for the mother, anger toward the father, and fear of punishment.

Sabor, Peter, ed. *Horace Walpole: The Critical Heritage*. London: Routledge & Kegan Paul, 1987. A valuable collection of reviews, introductions, contemporary discussions, and letters relating to Walpole's works. Includes eighteen items discussing *The Castle of Otranto*.

Varma, Devendra. *The Gothic Flame*. New York: Russell & Russell, 1966. A well-known history of the English gothic novel that discusses both the origins and the influences of the genre. Clarifies the various gothic conventions originated by *The Castle of Otranto*, particularly its surrealistic style and gothic hero.

Wall, Cynthia. "*The Castle of Otranto*: A Shakespeareo-Political Satire?" In *Historical Boundaries, Narrative Forms: Essays on British Literature in the Long Eighteenth Century in Honor of Everett Zimmerman*, edited by Lorna Clymer and Robert Mayer. Newark: University of Delaware Press, 2007. An unusual interpretation of the novel.

Watt, James. "Origins: Horace Walpole and *The Castle of Otranto*." In *Contesting the Gothic: Fiction, Genre, and Cultural Conflict, 1764-1832*. New York: Cambridge University Press, 1999. Charts the changing nature of gothic fiction from Walpole's novel to the works of Sir Walter Scott.

Wein, Toni. *British Identities, Heroic Nationalisms, and the Gothic Novel, 1764-1824*. New York: Palgrave, 2002. Argues that gothic fiction emerged in Britain during a time of upheaval that required the construction of a new national identity. Charts the historical and social developments that spurred the genre's development.

Castle Rackrent
An Hibernian Tale

Author: Maria Edgeworth (1768-1849)
First published: 1800, as *Castle Rackrent: An Hibernian Tale, Taken from Facts and from the Manners of Irish Squires, Before the Year 1782*
Type of work: Novel
Type of plot: Regional
Time of plot: Eighteenth century
Locale: Ireland

Principal characters:
HONEST THADY QUIRK, the narrator
SIR KIT RACKRENT, the owner of Castle Rackrent
SIR CONDY RACKRENT, Sir Kit's heir
ISABELLA, Condy's wife
JUDY QUIRK, Thady's niece
JASON, Thady's son

The Story:

After the death of Sir Patrick O'Shaughlin, his fine and generous master, Honest Thady Quirk finds himself working at Castle Rackrent for the heir, Sir Murtagh, a penny-pinching owner with a vicious temper. Lady Murtagh is also more interested in money than in the happiness of her tenants. After Sir Murtagh dies in a fit of temper, she strips Castle Rackrent of its treasures and goes to live in London. The estate passes to her husband's younger brother, Sir Kit Rackrent, a wild, carefree man. Finding the estate in debt and heavily mortgaged, Sir Kit goes to England to marry a rich wife who will repair the estate and bring a dowry for his support.

At last, Sir Kit comes back with a wealthy wife, a Jew he married while staying in Bath. It is soon apparent to Honest Thady that there is no love between the honeymooners. One serious difficulty arises over the presence of pig meat on the dinner table. Lady Kit insists that no such meat be served, but Sir Kit defies her orders. When the meat appears on the table, Lady Kit retires to her room, and her husband locks her in. She remains a prisoner for seven years. When she becomes very ill and appears to be dying, Sir Kit tries to influence her to leave her jewels to him, but she refuses. It is assumed she

will die shortly, and all eligible ladies in the neighborhood hope to become the next Lady Kit. Amid the controversy over his possible choice, Sir Kit is challenged and killed in a duel. Miraculously recovering from her illness, Lady Kit goes to London. The next heir is Sir Condy Rackrent, a distant cousin of Sir Kit.

Sir Condy Rackrent is a spendthrift but a good-natured master. Although the estate is more deeply in debt than ever, he makes no attempt to improve the condition of his holdings. Sir Condy soon begins a steadfast friendship with the family who lives on the neighboring estate. The youngest daughter, Isabella, takes a fancy to Sir Condy, but her father will not hear of a match between his family and the owner of Castle Rackrent. Sir Condy really loves Judy, the niece of Honest Thady. One day, in Thady's presence, Sir Condy tosses a coin to determine which girl he will marry. Judy loses, and soon after Sir Condy elopes with Isabella.

He expected that Isabella would bring some money to the estate, but she is disinherited by her father when she marries Sir Condy. While the newlyweds live in careless luxury, the house and grounds fall further into neglect, to the distress of the servants and tenants. Learning of a vacancy in the coming elections, Sir Condy decides to stand for Parliament. He wins the election, but too late to save himself from his creditors.

Honest Thady's son, Jason, a legal administrator, helps a neighbor buy up all Sir Condy's debts. With so much power in his hands, Jason scorns his own father. When Lady Condy learns that her husband's debtors are closing in on him, she complies with the demands of her family and returns to her father's house. Sir Condy writes a will, in which he leaves his wife all the land and five hundred pounds a year after his death. When Jason demands payment for the Rackrent debts, Sir Condy explains that he cannot make it because he gave an income of five hundred pounds a year to Lady Condy. Jason thereupon insists that Sir Condy sell Castle Rackrent and all the estates to satisfy his creditors. Having no other recourse, Sir Condy agrees. The five hundred a year is still guaranteed for Isabella. Thady is grief-stricken that his son maneuvered in this way against Sir Condy, and it causes a break between them. When Lady Condy's carriage is upset and she is nearly killed, Jason, assuming she will surely die, hurries to Sir Condy with a proposal that he sell him Lady Condy's yearly income. Sir Condy, needing the cash, complies with Jason's proposal.

Judy married, in the meantime, and her husband died. She pays a call on Sir Condy, who is staying at Thady's lodge. The old servant feels certain that Judy will now become Lady Rackrent, but Judy tells her uncle that there is no point in becoming a lady without a castle to accompany the title. She also hints that she might do better to marry Jason, who at least holds the lands. Thady tries to dissuade her from such a thought, but Judy is bent on acquiring a fortune.

Sir Condy, who long indulged in an excess of food and drink, suffers from gout. One night at a party, he drinks a large draught too quickly and dies a few days later. After Sir Condy's death, Jason and the now-recovered Lady Condy go to court over the title of the estate. Some say Jason will get the land, and others say Lady Condy will win. Thady can only guess the results of the suit.

Critical Evaluation:

Maria Edgeworth was famous in her day as the author of seven novels and as a writer interested in the education of children. She shared this interest with her father, Richard Lovell Edgeworth, an Irish landowner who settled his large family in Ireland in 1782 when Maria was at the impressionable age of fifteen. He was an intellectual and a believer in social and political reform. Throughout his life, Edgeworth deferred to his tastes, seeking not only his guidance but also his collaboration in much of her writing.

Castle Rackrent is the author's first novel, written sometime between 1797 and 1799 and published in 1800. It is a distinguished piece of work in several ways. A successful first novel, generally regarded as her best, it is also one of the few works in which her father had no part. The author herself declared that "it went to the press just as it was written."

In addition, *Castle Rackrent* holds a distinction in the history of the English novel as the first regional novel, a significance noted by Sir Walter Scott in the preface to his first historical novel, *Waverley* (1814), in which he stated his purpose of creating a Scottish milieu with the same degree of authenticity as "that which Miss Edgeworth so fortunately achieved for Ireland." In her own preface, Edgeworth takes pains to indicate the realistically Irish quality of the novel. Her first-person narrator, Thady Quirk, is a character based on her father's steward; he speaks in Irish idiom because "the authenticity of his story would have been more exposed to doubt if it were not told in his own characteristic manner." Moreover, the subject is peculiarly Irish: "Those who were acquainted with the manners of a certain class of the gentry of Ireland some years ago, will want no evidence of the truth of Honest Thady's narrative."

In the use of certain devices, Edgeworth anticipates the historical novel later developed by Scott—for example, in the historicity suggested by the early subtitle: "An Hibernian Tale, Taken from Facts, and from the Manners of Irish Squires, Before the Year 1782." More explicitly, Edgeworth assures her readers that "these are 'tales of other times'; . . . the manners depicted . . . are not those of the present age: the race of the Rackrents has long been extinct in Ireland." Similar to the kind of documentation Scott was to employ is her anecdotal glossary of Irish "terms and idiomatic phrases." The convention of the "true story," of course, is an eighteenth century legacy, and, like many eighteenth century novels, *Castle Rackrent* purports to be an original memoir for which the author is merely the editor.

The theme of the novel adumbrates Scott's characteristic theme, the conflict between a dying culture and one coming into being; the resemblance, however, stops there. Lacking historical events and personages, the Rackrent story is not too remote in time from the date of composition. Although the Rackrents indulge in gloriously absurd deeds—such as the sham wake staged by Sir Condy to spy on his own mourners—there are no heroic deeds in their past. The name Rackrent, referring to the exorbitant rents exacted by landlords from their tenants, reveals their main trait.

The novel is a satire on the Irish ruling class. With the sustained irony behind Thady's blind "partiality to the family in which he was bred and born," the author presents one Irish family's reprehensible history. Except for Sir Murtagh, who wastes his fortune in lawsuits, all the Rackrents ruin themselves and their estates through extravagance and dissipation. Whether they are squires in residence or absentee landlords dealing through agents "who grind the face of the poor," they increase the misery of the common Irish people. Concealed behind Thady's comical anecdotes is the judgment that the Rackrents represent the destructive arrogance and irresponsible stupidity of landowners who answer to no one except, eventually, moneylenders such as Thady's ruthless son Jason, who finally takes possession of the Rackrent estates.

The novel is centered on Thady himself, however, despite the title of the novel and Thady's own unwavering focus on the Rackrents, despite even several unforgettable comic episodes of Rackrent peccadilloes. His voice reveals his self-importance:

Having out of friendship for the family, upon whose estate, praised be Heaven! I and mine have lived rent free time out of mind, voluntarily undertaken to publish the Memoirs of the Rackrent Family, I think it my duty to say a few words, in the first place, concerning myself.

His self-importance is based on his illusions of living in the family's reflected grandeur and glory. If he lives by his professed loyalty, he acts on the example of his masters, exploiting his privileges as they do and just as blind to the inevitable outcome. Throughout the novel, for example, Thady boasts of various strategies to push forward "my son Jason," who acquires his first lease on Rackrent land because "I spoke a good word for my son, and gave out in the county that nobody need bid against us." As the opportunistic Thady comments, "Why shouldn't he as well as another?" Yet he complains bitterly of Jason grown rich that "he is a high gentleman, and never minds what poor Thady says, and having better than 1500 a-year, landed estate, looks down upon Honest Thady, but I wash my hands of his doings, and as I have lived so will I die, true and loyal to the family."

Thady's praise of the Rackrents is often coupled with his appreciation of money. When a new heir neglects Thady, the old man is hostile, but the first casual attention produces a characteristic response: "I loved him from that day to this, his voice was so like the family—and he threw me a guinea out of his waistcoat pocket." Another trait incompatible with honest devotion is Thady's evasive habit of silence at crucial moments, a silence very much at odds with his characteristic garrulity. There is a self-serving tone in the recurring motif, "I said nothing for fear of gaining myself ill will."

On the other hand, Thady's talkativeness, urged by vanity, contributes to the downfall of his favorite, Sir Condy, the last of the Rackrents. It is Thady's son who seizes the property, but it is Thady who made the young Condy his "white-headed boy" and fed his imagination with the disastrous "stories of the family and the blood from which he was sprung." He proudly takes credit for the adult Condy's unfortunate gambling habits, boasting, "I well remember teaching him to toss up for bog berries on my knee." The ultimate irony is that his teachings indirectly bring about Sir Condy's death; for the family legend of Sir Patrick's prodigious whiskey-drinking feat, which the last Rackrent fatally duplicates, is "the story that he learned from me when a child."

Torn between his son and his master and called by his niece an "unnatural fader," he confesses, "I could not upon my conscience tell which was wrong from the right." He is unaware, even as he explains it, that Rackrent rights derive from money just as Jason's pretensions do. Even the designation "ancient" is not appropriate for the Rackrents, since the estate came into "the family" in Thady's great-grandfather's time when Sir Patrick, by act of Parliament, took the surname to receive the property. Thady's dilemma is treated comically, but there is also pathos in the position in which he finds himself in the end: "I'm tired wishing for any thing in this world, after all I've seen it—but I'll say nothing; it would be a folly to be getting myself ill will in my old age."

Thady is a masterful characterization, requiring none of the apologies that Edgeworth as fictitious editor appends to his memoirs. However, those remarks serve the purpose not so much of the author of fiction but of the daughter of Richard Lovell Edgeworth when she offers her thoughts concerning a political resolution as her last word on the moral dilemma so convincingly portrayed in this short novel: "It is a problem of difficult solution to determine whether an Union will hasten or retard the amelioration of this country." Scott later praised her fictional Irish, England's "gay and kind-hearted neighbours," as having "done more towards completing the Union" than any subsequent legislation. Fortunately, Thady lives on as a fictional character, independent of the long-standing tumultuous relations between England and Ireland.

"Critical Evaluation" by Catherine E. Moore

Further Reading

Butler, Marilyn. *Maria Edgeworth: A Literary Biography.* London: Oxford University Press, 1972. The standard biography, eloquent and reflecting scrupulous research in Edgeworth family papers and correspondence. Includes information on the Edgeworth family's relationship with their retainers and tenants and on the reception of the novel.

Harden, Elizabeth. *Maria Edgeworth*. Boston: Twayne, 1984. A fine survey of Edgeworth's life and work that stresses her theme of "the education of the heart" through the various phases of her development. Close analysis of the narrative strategies of *Castle Rackrent*. Includes a useful annotated bibliography.

Hollingsworth, Brian. *Maria Edgeworth's Irish Writing*. New York: St. Martin's Press, 1997. Hollingsworth examines Edgeworth's Irish works, including *Castle Rackrent*, to explore her attitudes toward vernacular language and regionalism. Includes detailed notes and a bibliography.

Kaufman, Heidi, and Chris Fauske, eds. *An Uncomfortable Authority: Maria Edgeworth and Her Contexts*. Newark: University of Delaware Press, 2004. The editors have collected essays examining Edgeworth's works within various cultural and ideological contexts. Includes an analysis of *Castle Rackrent*.

Kowaleski-Wallace, Elizabeth. *Their Fathers' Daughters: Hannah More, Maria Edgeworth, and Patriarchal Complicity*. New York: Oxford University Press, 1991. Contains a substantial discussion of Edgeworth's life and works and her place in literary history, considered from the perspective of her place in the history of women's writing.

McCormack, W. J. *Ascendancy and Tradition in Anglo-Irish Literary History from 1789 to 1939*. New York: Oxford University Press, 1985. Contains a consideration of *Castle Rackrent* in the light of the ideological implications of its treatment of social class. A sophisticated contribution to the sociology of the Irish novel.

Nash, Julie. *Servants and Paternalism in the Works of Maria Edgeworth and Elizabeth Gaskell*. Burlington, Vt.: Ashgate, 2007. Examines the servant characters in Edgeworth's stories and novels, including *Castle Rackrent*, to show how her nostalgia for a traditional ruling class conflicted with her interest in radical new ideas about social equality.

_____, ed. *New Essays on Maria Edgeworth*. Burlington, Vt.: Ashgate, 2006. A collection of essays examining Edgeworth's work from a variety of perspectives, including analysis of *Castle Rackrent*.

Ó Gallchoir, Clíona. *Maria Edgeworth: Women, Enlightenment, and Nation*. Dublin: University College Dublin Press, 2005. A reassessment of Edgeworth's place in Irish literature that focuses on her views on gender and her depiction of Ireland from the 1790's until the aftermath of Catholic emancipation and parliamentary reform. Includes an analysis of Irish identity in *Castle Rackrent*.

Owens, Cóilín, ed. *Family Chronicles: Maria Edgeworth's Castle Rackrent*. Dublin: Wolfhound Press, 1987. A compilation of previously published critical views of *Castle Rackrent*, covering the work's genesis, its contexts, and some of its critical dimensions. Contains a full bibliography of other sources on the novel.

Cat and Mouse

Author: Günter Grass (1927-   )
First published: Katz und Maus, 1961 (English translation, 1963)
Type of work: Novella
Type of plot: Bildungsroman
Time of plot: World War II
Locale: Danzig, Germany

Principal characters:
PILENZ, the narrator
JOACHIM MAHLKE, his schoolmate
TULLA POKRIEFKE, a young girl
FATHER GUSEWSKI, a practical-minded priest
WALDEMAR KLOHSE, the headmaster of the boys' school, the Conradium

The Story:

Encouraged by his confessor, Pilenz writes down his recollections about the complicated cat-and-mouse relationship he had with Mahlke, his friend from school. He begins with a sunny day on the baseball field, when he set a cat on Mahlke's enormous Adam's apple; unable to resist, the cat scratched Mahlke, embarrassing him. Pilenz identifies himself with the "eternal cat" that will be Mahlke's undoing.

A group of boys that included Pilenz, Mahlke, Hotten Sontag, and Schilling spent their summers swimming around the abandoned wreck of a Polish minesweeper in the Danzig harbor. Mahlke went to a great deal of trouble to learn to swim, and soon he swam and dived better than any of the other boys. He often swam down into the minesweeper, bringing back a variety of objects, including a medallion of the Virgin Mary, a fire extinguisher, and a Victrola. Sometimes the boys were joined by Tulla Pokriefke, a girl who greatly admired Mahlke.

Because of his enormous Adam's apple, Mahlke wore a variety of objects around his neck, including the medallion and a screwdriver he brought up from the minesweeper. Once he even started a fashion trend by wearing yarn pom-poms as if they were a bow tie. These objects, according to Pilenz, did as much to draw attention to as they did to distract from Mahlke's Adam's apple.

One summer, Mahlke, exploring the insides of the minesweeper, found that he could reach a radio room that was not underwater. This became Mahlke's sanctuary, and he transported many of his treasures to the room, cleverly protecting them from water damage on the way. He took the Victrola and several records to his secret room, where he played music while the boys sunned themselves on top of the minesweeper.

Mahlke, a Roman Catholic, was remarkably devoted to the Virgin Mary, although he professed no faith in God or in Christ. This excessive devotion set him apart from the other boys, even from Pilenz, who was often an altar boy at the church Mahlke attended. Mahlke sometimes dreamed of being a clown when he grew up, and he was certainly very conscious of himself as a spectacle at school. With his odd looks, his religious fanaticism, and his collection of bizarre objects hanging from his neck, Mahlke was the object of alternating ridicule and admiration from his schoolmates.

The boys attended the Conradium, an elitist all-boys school run by the headmaster Klohse, a member of the National Socialist Party. After an alumnus of the school who was awarded the Iron Cross for his service in the air force came to speak to the student body, all of Mahlke's energy became focused on the Iron Cross. He began to dream of earning one for himself; the Iron Cross would be the perfect counterbalance to his Adam's apple.

Another speaker came, and although Mahlke did not want to go, Pilenz dragged him along. This speaker, although extremely boring, also had the Iron Cross around his neck; after the speech, in the school locker room, Mahlke stole the medal. He wore it to school under his shirt and tie. Eventually Mahlke confessed to headmaster Klohse, who expelled him from school.

For a while, Mahlke attended the nearby Horst Wessel School. He spent a summer in paramilitary training and then joined the army in an effort to gain his own Iron Cross. Eventually he succeeded in doing so and returned to Danzig in triumph. He expected that he, like other illustrious alumni, would be asked to give a speech at the Conradium. When he approached Klohse, however, his speech already written, Klohse refused to allow him to speak to the student body. Mahlke, frustrated, sought out Klohse near his home, confronted him, and slapped him in the face. Because of this, and because he overstayed his furlough from the army, Mahlke became a fugitive. When his old priest, Father Gusewski, was unable to help him, he turned to Pilenz for help.

Pilenz took advantage of Mahlke's total dependence on him. He refused to harbor him in his basement, instead suggesting that Mahlke hide in the old minesweeper. Even though it was not summertime, Mahlke and Pilenz rowed out to the minesweeper with two cans of pork and a can opener. When they arrived, Mahlke removed and carefully folded his uniform, put on the Iron Cross, and, wearing his old gym shorts from the Conradium, dived into the water with the tins. Pilenz, noticing that the can opener was left behind, pounded on the side of the minesweeper, shouting, "Can opener!" There was no response.

For years afterward, Pilenz searches for Mahlke among the clowns at circuses or at reunions for recipients of the Iron Cross. He never finds Mahlke and ultimately concludes that Mahlke, the eternal mouse, finally fell prey to the eternal cat, which Pilenz perceives as a combination of forces that include school, society, the army, and Pilenz himself.

"The Story" by Kelly C. Walter Carney

Critical Evaluation:

After World War II, the spiritual recovery of Germany lagged far behind its economic recovery, and nowhere was this lag more apparent than in the failure of German literature to regain the eminence it had attained before the war in the work of such authors as Heinrich and Thomas Mann, Franz Kafka, and Hermann Hesse. These writers and many others diagnosed the spiritual malaise of the society, which reached its culmination in the horrors of the Nazi regime. In the 1960's, the emergence of several writers of the first rank indicated a spiritual rebirth in Germany. Perhaps the most notable of these young writers, certainly the most heralded, was Günter Grass, whose first novel, *Die Blechtrommel* (1959; *The Tin Drum,* 1961), established him as a major figure in the postwar rehabilitation of German literature. In *Cat and Mouse,* his second novel, he reinforces his claim to that status by perceptively probing into what was continuing to ail the German spirit.

Although narrated in 1961 by an adult named Pilenz, who works as a secretary for a parish settlement house, *Cat and Mouse* is set in the years during World War II, when Pilenz was a teenager and schoolboy. Caught up in the dull round of secular life in postwar Germany and poignantly aware of a great spiritual emptiness in his world (he is a Catholic who has lost his belief in God), Pilenz feels compelled to tell the story of his boyhood friend Joachim Mahlke, who disappears, after deserting the army, by diving into a sunken minesweeper where they played as boys and where Mahlke has a secret retreat. Though fifteen years have elapsed since then, Pilenz has looked for Mahlke ever since and everywhere he can possibly appear; he has never given up hope that his friend will "resurface." *Cat and Mouse* is dedicated, as it were, to resuscitating the spirit of Mahlke and thereby to rediscovering a spiritual basis for German life and art.

The resuscitation—that is, Pilenz's writing of the novel—is a complicated matter. Time has dimmed and confused his memory, so his story is as much a reconstruction of the past as a recollection of it; it is as much the re-creation of Mahlke, and of that part of himself Mahlke represents, as it is memory. A self-conscious artist, Pilenz realizes that his story, written out of inner necessity, is like all art: a fusion of reality and imagination. What he remembers most vividly, providing him with a grip on the past and himself, is a boyhood scene in which he or one of his friends—he remembers it differently each time he returns to it—encouraged a black cat to pounce on Mahlke's mouse, that is, his Adam's apple, while he lay asleep. About this fablelike incident, Pilenz constructs his tale of how the beast of death eventually kills Mahlke's mouse. *Cat and Mouse* is a definition and revival of the spiritual qualities that were lost with Mahlke's disappearance, the dialogue of recollection being a way of making him reappear to the narrator and his public.

Endowed with an abnormally large and active Adam's apple and lacking physical grace, Mahlke is an unnoticed figure among the children of the neighborhood until at the age of fourteen he learns to swim. Thereafter, he is a moral force—leading them to the sunken boat, diving into dangerous depths, staying beneath the surface for long periods while collecting trophies, and being modest and considerate. He is not, however, nature's darling: Besides being clumsy in looks and manner, he never tans, and the cold water chills him blue and coarsens his skin. Furthermore, he has no interest in girls or in displays of virility. Rather, he is driven by self-consciousness to use the power with which he is blessed to hide his Adam's apple, to redeem his natural being and shortcomings. For that purpose, he devotes himself to self-transcending ideals, represented alternately by the Virgin Mother and military heroes. These provide him with religious idols before which he can kneel in purifying devotion.

Growing up audience-conscious, Mahlke originally wants to be a clown so that he can make people laugh and help them be happy, but the Catholic Church, the German state through its heroes and schools, and the war sap his faith and channel his power toward destructive ends. Eventually, he who had been called the Redeemer by a classmate caricaturist is refused recognition for his military exploits by the school that had taught him that heroes are made by slaughter in the name of the state, and he is led to betray his initial religious and humanistic impulses by the pressure of social and political circumstances. Frustrated in his aspiration to reveal the truth to schoolchildren, he is left with nothing in which to believe, with no honorable task to perform. His disappearance into the minesweeper comes as a final gesture of knowledge and repudiation, perhaps an awareness of his inability to hide his Adam's apple, certainly a recognition of the inability of his society to harbor his spiritual talents and aspirations or to acknowledge their source. His is the hero's dilemma: He is the victim of the contradictions between his inordinate desire to serve and the refusal of the common order to tolerate him and his idol.

The disappearance and absence of the heroic are what ails Germany in Günter Grass's diagnosis. It is not, however, the loss of the traditional heroes that he laments. What Grass resuscitates is the Christian-chivalric vision in which masculine power is bound in service to feminine tenderness, in which nature is tamed and saved from its inherent evil through devotion to purifying spiritual values, and in which the magnetism of love replaces domination by tyrannical force.

Mahlke's ultimate defeat hinges on the triviality of a medal stolen from a war hero at school, a circumstance that at first glance seems a narrative weakness but is actually the novel's strength. Though in places the novel is reminiscent of Franz Kafka's allegory and Thomas Mann's irony, the demoniac powers that haunt and doom the characters in the works of those writers are conspicuously absent in *Cat and Mouse*. Pilenz, though he cannot be sure he incited the cat to pounce on Mahlke's mouse, knows he is implicated in his disappearance and so writes out of guilt, using art as a vehicle to redeem his sin. Recognition of what he has lost, of how far he has fallen, implies a spiritual awakening sufficient for the first steps toward freedom from necessity and from the bondage of the past. Grass's fablelike story, with its blend of symbolism and irony with realism, expresses the power of the imagination to transform the "real." Only by forgetting enough of the past can Pilenz entertain ideals again; only by believing in the spiritual origins and power of art, as Mahlke believes in the Virgin Mother, is genuine art again possible. Lyric and comic as well as tragic, the novel expresses Grass's belief that the German spirit can again face its past, avoid possession by its demons, and be aware of the spiritual power and transcendent values necessary for a truly new and healthy life.

Further Reading

Cunliffe, W. Gordon. *Günter Grass*. New York: Twayne, 1969. Places Grass's work in its historical and political context. Includes a chapter on *Cat and Mouse*.

Grass, Günter. *Peeling the Onion*. London: Harvill Secker, 2007. Grass recounts the events of his life, including the revelation that he served in a Nazi combat unit during the last months of World War II. He describes how he turned people and events in his life into fiction.

Hayman, Ronald. *Günter Grass*. New York: Methuen, 1985. A survey of Grass's work that places *Cat and Mouse* in the context of Grass's aesthetic ideas and emphasizes the unreliable narrator. Compares the text to other works by German writers who have focused on the clown archetype.

Keele, Alan Frank. *Understanding Günter Grass*. Columbia: University of South Carolina Press, 1988. Examines *Cat and Mouse* primarily as a political allegory, drawing parallels between Mahlke and Germany, as well as between Pilenz and Grass himself.

Lawson, Richard H. *Günter Grass*. New York: Frederick Ungar, 1985. This survey of Grass's work includes a chapter on *Cat and Mouse* that discusses the text from a variety of perspectives. Includes a good discussion of the novella genre and traces the quest motif in the work.

Mews, Siegfried. *Günter Grass and His Critics: From "The Tin Drum" to "Crabwalk."* Rochester, N.Y.: Camden House, 2008. Mews concisely summarizes the reception to Grass's work that appeared in the popular press and scholarly journals between 1959 and 2005. Devotes a chapter to *Cat and Mouse*.

Preece, Julian. *"Cat and Mouse*: Is Pilenz Guilty?" In *The Life and Work of Günter Grass: Literature, History, Politics*. New York: Palgrave, 2001. Chronicles Grass's career, describing how his experiences, including his stint in a Nazi combat unit when he was a teenager, shaped his novels and political essays. Devotes a chapter to a discussion of *Cat and Mouse*.

Reddick, John. *The Danzig Trilogy of Günter Grass: A Study of "The Tin Drum," "Cat and Mouse," and "Dog Years."* London: Secker and Warburg, 1975. A good in-depth study of *Cat and Mouse* that examines the structure, imagery, setting, themes, and symbols of the work and relates it to the other elements of the Danzig trilogy.

Thomas, Noel L. *Günter Grass: "Katz und Maus."* Glasgow: University of Glasgow, French and German Publications, 1992. A fifty-six-page study guide to the book, designed for high school and undergraduate students.

Cat on a Hot Tin Roof

Author: Tennessee Williams (1911-1983)
First produced: 1955; first published, 1955
Type of work: Drama
Type of plot: Psychological realism
Time of plot: Mid-twentieth century
Locale: Mississippi

Principal characters:
BIG DADDY POLLITT, a plantation owner
BIG MAMA, his wife
BRICK and GOOPER, their sons
MAGGIE, Brick's wife
MAE, Gooper's wife

The Story:

The Pollitt family assembles to celebrate Big Daddy's sixty-fifth birthday. While Brick showers, Maggie describes the birthday dinner, telling how badly Gooper's five children behaved and how their mother, Mae, used them to impress Big Daddy. Brick comes out of the bathroom on crutches, having broken his ankle jumping hurdles.

Maggie informs Brick that a medical report arrived that day with the news that Big Daddy is dying of cancer. She also explains that Mae and Gooper want to send Brick to a hospital for alcoholics so that they can control Big Daddy's money. Maggie believes, however, that Big Daddy dislikes Gooper and his family and that he has a "lech" for her.

Maggie admits that she has become "catty" because Brick refuses to sleep with her and she is lonely. She does, however, intend to win back his love. After hinting that Brick's problems stem from someone named Skipper, she asks Brick to drink less. He replies that he needs to drink until he hears a "click" in his head that gives him peace. Maggie complains that her current situation makes her as tense as "a cat on a hot tin roof."

Big Mama enters to say how happy she is; she was told that Big Daddy has a spastic colon, not cancer. Brick retreats to the bathroom as she enters. After asking about Brick's drinking, Big Mama tells Maggie that sexual problems must be causing their marital troubles and childlessness.

When Big Mama leaves, Maggie again urges Brick to sleep with her; he suggests a divorce instead. Maggie returns to the subject of Big Daddy's cancer, explaining that the family will tell Big Mama the truth later. Then, ignoring Brick's anger, she recounts the story of Skipper, Brick's college friend whose homosexual love Brick cannot or will not return. Maggie says that she forced Skipper to face his feelings for Brick. To prove her wrong, Skipper tried to make love to her but could not. He later died of drink. Maggie reminds Brick that although Skipper is dead, she, Maggie, is alive and able to conceive a child. Brick asks how she plans to do that when he hates her.

At that moment, the family enters, bearing Big Daddy's birthday cake. Big Daddy becomes annoyed that others, especially Big Mama, appear to be trying to run his life. Since he no longer believes he is threatened by a terminal illness, he announces that he is resuming control of the family. Hurt, Big Mama realizes that Big Daddy never believed she loves him. When she tells him that she loves even his hatefulness, Big Daddy says to himself that it would be funny if that were true.

Eventually, the others drift out, leaving Brick and Big Daddy alone. Although he wants a serious discussion with Brick, Big Daddy talks instead about his trip to Europe. Brick wonders why communication is so difficult between him and Big Daddy. Big Daddy admits that he is afraid of cancer and that he is not ready to die. When Brick acknowledges his alcoholism, Big Daddy asks why he drinks. Because of disgust with the world's "mendacity," Brick answers, a reason Big Daddy does not accept. Most lives are based on lies, he says, and Brick must live with this fact. Big Daddy suggests that Brick is drinking because of guilt over Skipper's homosexuality and death. Brick angrily protests that he did not share Skipper's feelings or even discuss them; when Skipper tried to explain over the telephone, Brick hung up. That, then, is the real reason for Brick's drinking, Big Daddy says: Brick is disgusted with himself because he refused to face his friend's truth. Brick retaliates by telling Big

Daddy the truth about his cancer. Shattered, Big Daddy leaves, damning all liars as he goes.

In the original ending, the family and the doctor enter to tell Big Mama about Big Daddy's cancer. She at first refuses to believe them. Brick, meanwhile, goes to the balcony to drink, but he returns as Gooper tries to persuade Big Mama to sign legal control of the plantation over to him. Angrily, Big Mama refuses. As her final answer, she shouts Big Daddy's favorite word, "crap."

Big Mama then urges Brick to give Big Daddy a grandson. To everyone's surprise, Maggie announces that she is pregnant. Though Mae and Gooper disbelieve the news, they cannot disprove it and finally leave. At that moment, Brick hears the "click" in his head. Maggie refuses to allow him this escape and throws away his crutch, pointing out that she emptied the liquor cabinet. As she turns out the light, Maggie assures Brick that she does love him. Brick says to himself that it would be funny if that were true.

In the Broadway production ending, the family, after much preparation, tells Big Mama the truth about Big Daddy's cancer. While she tries to digest the news, Gooper explains why Big Mama should give him legal control of the estate. After dismissing Gooper's legal plans with Big Daddy's favorite word, "crap," Big Mama reminds Brick and Maggie that Big Daddy hopes they will have a son.

The loud talk brings Big Daddy back to the room. He relates a crude joke about a fornicating elephant, perhaps to remind Brick that sex is natural and necessary. Maggie then announces her pregnancy. Although Mae and Gooper refuse to believe her, Big Daddy professes to do so. When Brick and Maggie are at last alone, Maggie throws his liquor off the balcony while he watches with growing admiration. Finally, Brick and Maggie sit together on the bed as Maggie vows to use her love to help restore Brick to life.

Critical Evaluation:

As the author of *The Glass Menagerie* (1944), the Pulitzer Prize-winning *A Streetcar Named Desire* (1951), and many other plays, Tennessee Williams was one of the leading American dramatists of the twentieth century. Born in Mississippi, Williams used the South and southerners as a vehicle for exploring the confusing and even inexplicable minds and relationships of human beings. Although his plays have been criticized as too symbolic and theatrical, as well as philosophically murky, no one disputes his success in creating a gallery of memorable characters who grapple with some of humankind's most significant issues: love, sex, power, age, family, self-awareness, honesty, the past, dreams, and death.

At once tragic and comic, *Cat on a Hot Tin Roof*, which won the Pulitzer Prize in drama, examines the mysterious and even grotesque interconnections that define a family. The play also delineates the struggle of individuals within the family to define a self. On the surface, the play is realistic: The lapsed time of the story is equal to the time of performance; the characters are complex and human; the situation, a family birthday party, is ordinary. Yet despite the surface realism, the play can better be described as expressionistic. The set Williams calls for is dominated by a large bed and large liquor cabinet symbolizing sex and escape. The language is poetic, and the characters have nearly as many monologues as conversations. The action, too, is episodic and symbolic. The specific tensions of the Pollitt family are staged in a series of emblematic confrontations: husband and wife, youth and age, past and present, wealth and poverty, homosexuality and heterosexuality, truth and lies, love and hate, life and death.

Williams does not, however, allow the audience to choose one option over another or even to define each term clearly. Although he favors life and honesty, for example, he never promises that either is possible or even always desirable. Each side has its allure and validity. Big Daddy and Maggie are most directly associated with life and truth, yet both have important limitations. Maggie yearns for a child and vows to restore Brick to life; she insists that Brick must value her honesty if nothing else. In many respects, she is the healthiest and most appealing character in the play. In the end, though, she must pretend to be pregnant to affirm life, and that affirmation has as much to do with her need for financial security as with any real desire for children. Nor do the fertile Mae and Gooper represent a viable commitment to life: They have produced only rude, screeching "no-neck monsters" who function as a sort of Greek chorus of futility.

Big Daddy, in the words of Dylan Thomas that Williams uses as an epigram, does not "go gentle into that good night" of death; instead, he clings to life and to truth so fiercely that his energy overflows into the vulgarity and garrulity that make him larger than life. He refuses to allow Brick the refuge of drink and dissembling. Yet despite his powerful life force, Big Daddy is dying; his physical cancer mirrors the metaphorical corruption that touches the whole family and, by extension, the entire South. His dedication to honesty is complicated by his own lifelong "mendacity." Ironically, it is the self-destructive Brick, whose broken ankle symbolizes his broken spirit and who must rely on both literal and figurative crutches, who voices perhaps the most pertinent questions about honesty: "Who can face truth?" he asks Big Daddy. "Can you?"

Closely connected with the question of life are the topics of sex and homosexuality, which made *Cat on a Hot Tin Roof* controversial in the 1950's and 1960's but that had come to seem tame by the 1970's. In this play, Williams neither condemns nor explicitly approves of either homosexuality or heterosexuality. For the most part, he merely shows that society offers no livable place for homosexuals; he suggests, moreover, that sex of any kind is as likely to push people apart as it is to draw them together.

The two endings complicate the final effect of the play. Williams explained that he wrote the second version of act 3 at the request of Elia Kazan, who directed the 1955 Broadway production. Kazan wanted Maggie to be more sympathetic and Brick to be more obviously changed by his confrontation with Big Daddy in act 2. He also believed that Big Daddy was too important and dynamic a character to disappear after one act. Although the new ending offers slightly more hope for a reconciliation between Brick and Maggie, it is less consistent with the development of the first two acts. Williams's first version works better: Big Daddy, though certainly a powerful character, does not belong in act 3. His last words in act 2— "Christ—damn—all—lying sons of—lying bitches!! Lying! Dying! Lying!"—provide a more fitting thematic end to Big Daddy than his elephant story and his unconvincing acceptance of Maggie's pregnancy. The change in Brick is even less effective. Williams's reasons for initially resisting this change make sense: He did not "believe that any conversation, however revelatory, ever effects so immediate a change in the heart . . . of a person of Brick's state of spiritual disrepair."

Ultimately, *Cat on a Hot Tin Roof* presents, rather than corrects, several portraits of "spiritual disrepair." Although Williams may offer little hope of eventual repair, he does offer a sympathetic understanding of the human condition.

Kathleen R. Chamberlain

Further Reading

Bauer-Briski, Senata Karolina. *The Role of Sexuality in the Major Plays of Tennessee Williams*. New York: Peter Lang, 2002. Analyzes how sexuality is a dominant element in eight plays, including *Cat on a Hot Tin Roof*. Examines how the characters' behavior and relations with other characters are affected by their decisions to either express or repress their sexual inclinations.

Bloom, Harold, ed. *Tennessee Williams's "Cat on a Hot Tin Roof."* Philadelphia: Chelsea House, 2002. A collection of critical essays that includes discussions of the character of Brick Pollitt, homophobic discourse in Williams's work, and the play's debt to *Yerma* by Federico García Lorca.

Falk, Signi Lenea. *Tennessee Williams*. 2d ed. Boston: Twayne, 1985. A useful introduction to Williams and his works. Summarizes critical assessments of *Cat on a Hot Tin Roof*.

Hirsch, Foster. *A Portrait of the Artist: The Plays of Tennessee Williams*. Port Washington, N.Y.: Kennikat Press, 1979. An overview of Williams's work and career. Concludes that *Cat on a Hot Tin Roof* is "dishonest" but well-crafted.

Paller, Michael. *Gentlemen Callers: Tennessee Williams, Homosexuality, and Mid-Twentieth-Century Broadway Drama*. New York: Palgrave Macmillan, 2005. Charts the evolution of America's acknowledgment and acceptance of homosexuality by examining Williams's life and the plays he wrote from the 1940's through the 1970's. Describes how critics initially ignored his gay characters and how gay liberation activists in the 1970's reviled his work.

Spoto, Donald. *The Kindness of Strangers: The Life of Tennessee Williams*. Boston: Little, Brown, 1985. A thorough biography that includes critical commentary. Argues that *Cat on a Hot Tin Roof* is a deliberately ambiguous yet "compassionate" play.

Thompson, Judith J. *Tennessee Williams's Plays: Memory, Myth, and Symbol*. Rev. ed. New York: Peter Lang, 2002. Traces a pattern of mythic recollection in several of Williams's plays, including *Cat on a Hot Tin Roof*.

Tischler, Nancy M. *Student Companion to Tennessee Williams*. Westport, Conn.: Greenwood Press, 2000. Critical study of Williams's life, career, and works. Analyzes several plays, including *Cat on a Hot Tin Roof*, discussing their literary styles, their themes, and Williams's influences from poetry, film, religion, mythology, and personal experience.

Williams, Tennessee. *Cat on a Hot Tin Roof*. New York: New Directions, 1955. A useful edition that contains both versions of act 3 and commentary by Williams in which he explains why he wrote the second ending.

Catch-22

Author: Joseph Heller (1923-1999)
First published: 1961
Type of work: Novel
Type of plot: Metafiction
Time of plot: 1944
Locale: Rome and Pianosa, an island near Elba, Italy

Principal characters:
CAPTAIN JOHN YOSSARIAN, a United States Air Force bombardier
COLONEL CATHCART, the group commander
LIEUTENANT MILO MINDERBINDER, the mess officer, who turns black marketing into big business
CAPTAIN BLACK, the squadron intelligence officer
DOC DANEEKA, the flight surgeon
CLEVINGER,
ORR,
KID SAMPSON,
McWATT,
AARDVAARK (AARFY),
HUNGRY JOE, and
NATELY, pilots, bombardiers, and navigators of the 256th Squadron
NATELY'S WHORE, who blames Yossarian for Nately's death
GENERAL DREEDLE, the wing commander
GENERAL PECKEM, the commanding officer of Special Services
EX-PFC WINTERGREEN, a goldbrick who controls 27th Air Force Headquarters because he sorts, and unofficially censors, all the mail

The Story:

The events take place in Pianosa, a small Italian island where an Air Force bombing group is sweating out the closing months of World War II, and Rome, where the flyers go on leave to stage latter-day Roman orgies in a city filled with prostitutes. Men who behave like madmen are awarded medals. In a world of madmen at war, the maddest—or the sanest—of all is Captain John Yossarian, a bombardier of the 256th Squadron. Deciding that death in war is a matter of circumstance and having no wish to be victimized by any kind of circumstance, he tries by every means he can think of—including malingering, defiance, cowardice, and irrational behavior—to get out of the war. That is his resolve after the disastrous raid over Avignon, when Snowden, the radio-gunner, was shot almost in two, splashing his blood and entrails over Yossarian's uniform and teaching the bombardier the cold, simple fact of man's mortality. For some time after that, Yossarian refuses to wear any clothes, and when General Dreedle, the wing commander, arrives to award the bombardier a Distinguished Flying Cross for his heroism, military procedure is upset because Yossarian wears no uniform on which to pin the medal. Yossarian's logic of nonparticipation is so simple that everyone thinks him crazy, especially when he insists that "they" are trying to murder him. His insistence leads to an argument with Clevinger, who is bright and always has an excuse or an explanation for everything. When Clevinger wants to know who Yossarian thinks is trying to murder him, the bombardier says that all of "them" are, and Clevinger says that he has no idea who "they" can be.

Yossarian goes off to the hospital, complaining of a pain in his liver. If he has jaundice, the doctors will discharge him; if not, they will send him back to duty. Yossarian spends some of his time censoring the enlisted men's letters. On some, he signs Washington Irving's name as censor; on others, he crosses out the letter but adds loving messages signed with the chaplain's name. The hospital would be a good place to stay for the rest of the war were it not for a talkative Texan and a patient so cased in bandages that Yossarian wonders at times whether there is a real body inside. When he returns to his squadron, he learns that Colonel Cathcart, the group commander, raised the number of required missions to fifty. Meanwhile, Clevinger dips his plane into a cloud one day and never brings it out again. He and his plane simply vanish.

It is impossible for Yossarian to complete his tour of combat duty because Colonel Cathcart wants to get his picture in *The Saturday Evening Post* and to become a general. Consequently, he continues to increase the number of required missions for his outfit beyond those required by the 27th Air Force Headquarters. By the time he sets the number at eighty, Kraft, McWatt, Kid Sampson, and Nately are dead; Clevinger and Orr disappear; the chaplain is disgraced (he is accused of the Washington Irving forgeries); and Aarfy commits a brutal murder. Hungry Joe screams in his sleep night after night, and Yossarian continues looking for new ways to stay alive. It is impossible for him to be sent home on medical relief because of Catch-22. As Doc Daneeka, the medical officer, explains, he can ground anyone who is crazy, but anyone who wants to avoid combat duty is not crazy and therefore cannot be grounded. This is Catch-22, the inevitable loophole in the scheme of justice, the self-justification of authority, the irony of eternal circumstance. Catch-22 explains Colonel Cathcart, who continues to raise the number of missions and volunteer his men for every dangerous operation in the Mediterranean theater. Colonel Cathcart also plans to have prayers during every briefing session but gives up that idea when he learns that officers and enlisted men must pray to the same god. Catch-22 also explains the struggle for power between General Dreedle, who wants a fighting outfit, and General Peckem of Special Services, who wants to see tighter bombing patterns—they look better in aerial photographs—and issues a directive ordering all tents in the Mediterranean theater to be pitched with their fronts facing in the direction of the Washington Monument. It explains Captain Black, the intelligence officer, who compels the officers to sign a new loyalty oath each time they get their map cases, flak suits and parachutes, paychecks, haircuts, and meals in the mess. It explains, above all, Lieutenant Milo Mindbinder, the mess officer, who parlays petty black-market operations into an international syndicate in which every man, as he says, has a share. By the time his organization is on a paying basis, he is elected mayor of half a dozen Italian cities, vice shah of Oran, caliph of Baghdad, imam of Damascus, and sheik of Araby. Once he almost makes a mistake by cornering the market on Egyptian cotton, but after some judicious bribery, he unloads it on the United States government. The climax of his career comes when he rents his fleet of private planes to the Germans and from the Pianosa control tower directs the bombing and strafing of his own outfit. Men of public decency are outraged until Milo opens his books for public inspection and shows the profit he makes. Then everything is all right, for in this strange, mad world, patriotism and profit are indistinguishable; the world lives by Milo's motto, the claim that whatever is good for the syndicate is good for the nation.

Eventually, Yossarian takes off for neutral Sweden, three jumps ahead of the authorities and less than one jump ahead of Nately's whore, who for some reason blames him for her lover's death and tries to kill him. He spends the last night in Italy wandering alone through wartime Rome.

Critical Evaluation:

Catch-22 was the first of the post-World War II novels to convey the sense of war as so insane and so negligent of humane values that it can be treated only through exaggerated ridicule. One means whereby Joseph Heller suggests the ways in which war violates humanity is by violating the conventions of realistic fiction. The individual chapters are, for example, named after the different characters, although the character for whom a chapter is named may or may not be important in that chapter or anywhere else in the book. The chapters follow no evident plan; time in the novel is confused because there is no narrative line. Such structure as exists is based on recurrent references to specific situations. Only toward the end is there a progression in time from one chapter to the next.

The salient element that distinguishes *Catch-22* from more conventional war novels is its outrageous humor, much of it black and having to do with death and injury. In the late twentieth century, the term "metafiction" began to be applied to this kind of novel, suggesting a kind of fiction that does not pretend to portray reality and continually calls attention to its fictive nature. The cruel joke that gives the novel its title typifies its humor and the situation of the aviators. Each man is required to fly a certain number of missions against the Germans before he can be rotated home. Each time, however, a significant number of men approach that number, Colonel Cathcart, the commanding officer, raises the required number. Those in command are uniformly corrupt and have the power to force their subordinates to do whatever they wish; they plan dangerous missions, choose the most beautiful nurses, and make monetary profits from the war. The subordinate officers, led by Yossarian, have no choice but to act subversively to try to survive.

Many of the episodes of the novel reflect outrageous humor. There are many instances of wordplay, puns, and jokes the characters tell and play on one another, yet underlying the humor are always constant reminders of death and the grisly business of war. One of the threads that holds the novel together is found in the frequent references to a character named Snowden. His death is alluded to very early in the novel, and in the description of his funeral and burial midway through the book there is a description of an unnamed character who sits naked in a tree while the ceremony is performed. Later in the novel, it becomes clear that the naked man is Yossarian, who returned in shock from a mission, covered with Snowden's blood and flesh. He is so horrified by

Snowden's death that he cannot bear to wear anything, but he feels compelled to attend the funeral. Only very late in the novel is Snowden's death described in grisly detail, but with the same tone of outrageous humor. Snowden's death carries the novel's most overt message: "Man was matter, that was Snowden's secret. . . . The spirit gone, man is garbage." The novel's satiric targets include not only the mechanized destruction of modern war but also many aspects of civilian society in the postwar world that are linked, with satiric intent, with the war itself. Heller mocks the business ethic and the economic arrangements of American society in the sections dealing with the machinations of Milo Minderbinder; he savagely parodies the good-guy image of the typical American boy in the casual cruelty of Aarfy; he ridicules the scant attention paid to religion through his use of a chaplain, a good-hearted innocent whose ministrations have no effect on the problems of the men in the squadron; and he sees modern medicine only as it is used to patch up wounded men so as to return them to battle. Above all, Heller mocks the sheeplike way in which ordinary humans follow orders even when they know those orders will lead to their destruction and that those who give them are idiotic or stupid.

In the world Heller describes, values are of little account. Love is reduced to lustful sexual encounters in which women are barely human. The only absolutes in this world are human mortality and the corruption of the world, as depicted in the chapter "Eternal City," where the "holy" city of Rome is depicted in nightmarish terms as a kind of hell on earth. The choices in this world are few. The men may be killed at any time. They can take life as they find it, as most people do. They can try to fight against the forces that control them, knowing that their efforts are doomed. They can, if they are desperate enough, try to find a way out. Improbably, at the end of the novel, Yossarian chooses the last in imitation of his friend Orr. After accidentally killing his friend Kid Sampson, Orr manages to row from Italy through the Mediterranean Sea around the west coast of Europe and through the North Sea to a safe haven in neutral Sweden. This unbelievable journey is perhaps the novel's most bitter joke.

Catch-22 was a pioneering work of metafiction. Of Heller's later novels, only *God Knows* (1984) takes similar liberties with fact, and none of his subsequent works measures up to the high standard set by *Catch-22*. Most critics considered the book's sequel, *Closing Time* (1994), to be a distinct disappointment. *Catch-22* nevertheless deserves its continuing reputation as one of the four or five most memorable novels to come out of World War II.

"Critical Evaluation" by John M. Muste

Further Reading

Bloom, Harold, ed. *Joseph Heller's "Catch-22."* New ed. New York: Bloom's Literary Criticism, 2008. A collection of critical assessments of the novel, including pieces by respected writers and literary critics, such as Nelson Algren, Christopher Buckley, and Norman Podhoretz, and an introduction by Bloom.

Cacicedo, Alberto. "'You Must Remember This': Trauma and Memory in *Catch-22* and *Slaughterhouse-Five*." *Critique* 46, no. 4 (Summer, 2005): 357-368. A comparison of the novels by Heller and Kurt Vonnegut, focusing on the writers' ability to depict the horrors of World War II while creating a sense of indignation in readers that could result in ethical social action. Critics generally agree that Heller's novel was able to do this, while there is disagreement about the ethical engagement of Vonnegut's novel.

Craig, David M. *Tilting at Mortality: Narrative Strategies in Joseph Heller's Fiction.* Detroit, Mich.: Wayne State University Press, 1997. An examination of the ethical dimensions of Heller's work, linking his distinctive stylistic features to his preoccupation with questions of death, meaning, and identity. Includes separate chapters on each of Heller's first six novels.

Karl, Frederick R. *American Fiction 1940-1980: A Comprehensive History and Evaluation.* New York: Harper & Row, 1983. The judgment of an outstanding critic and biographer on forty years of American novels. Karl names *Catch-22* an outstanding product of its time.

Merrill, Robert. "The Structure and Meaning of *Catch-22*." *Studies in American Fiction* 14, no. 2 (August, 1986): 139-152. A detailed discussion of the effect of the novel's unusual structure on the message it conveys about society.

Potts, Stephen W. *Catch-22: Antiheroic Antinovel.* Boston: Twayne, 1989. The first single volume devoted exclusively to *Catch-22*. Discusses most of the major aspects of the novel.

_____. *From Here to Absurdity: The Moral Battlefields of Joseph Heller.* Rev. ed. San Bernardino, Calif.: Borgo Press, 1995. Comments on the place of *Catch-22* in the cultural climate of the 1960's and its reflection of counterculture attitudes.

Ruas, Charles. *Conversations with American Writers.* New York: Alfred A. Knopf, 1985. Contains a section on Heller in part 2 with a detailed interview on his life and intentions that focuses on *Catch-22*.

Woodson, Jon. *A Study of Joseph Heller's "Catch-22": Going Around Twice.* New York: Peter Lang, 2001. Uses the New Criticism and mythological criticism that Heller was familiar with to argue that *Catch-22* is in essence a retelling of the epic of Gilgamesh in much the same way that James Joyce's *Ulysses* is a retelling of Homer's *Odyssey*.

The Catcher in the Rye

Author: J. D. Salinger (1919-2010)
First published: 1951
Type of work: Novel
Type of plot: Social realism
Time of plot: Late 1940's
Locale: Pennsylvania and New York City

Principal characters:
HOLDEN CAULFIELD, a seventeen-year-old boy
PHOEBE CAULFIELD, his ten-year-old sister
MR. SPENCER, a prep school teacher
MR. ANTOLINI, a prep school teacher
ROBERT ACKLEY, a schoolmate
WARD STRADLATER, Holden's roommate
MAURICE, a hotel elevator operator

The Story:

Holden Caulfield is expelled from Pencey Prep, in Agerstown, Pennsylvania, just before Christmas. Before leaving his preparatory school, Holden says good-bye to Mr. Spencer, one of the Pencey teachers with whom he had good rapport, and has an altercation with his roommate, Ward Stradlater, and a dormitory neighbor, Robert Ackley. A disagreement over a composition Holden agreed to write for Stradlater and Holden's anger with Stradlater's treatment of the latter's weekend date, whom Holden knows and likes, precipitates a fight in which Holden is cut and bruised.

The Catcher in the Rye / SALINGER

Holden sets out by train to New York City. Since he is not expected at his home in the city for Christmas vacation for a few days, he decides to stop at a city hotel and contact some friends.

Holden tries to pick up some women in the hotel bar, takes in a show at Radio City Music Hall, and visits a local café. Upon returning to his hotel, he is approached by the elevator man, Maurice, who arranges for a prostitute to come to Holden's room. Holden prefers conversation to sex, however, and after he refuses to pay the woman for her services, Maurice arrives and beats Holden. After attending a play with a former girlfriend, Sally, Holden gets drunk in a bar and sits alone in Central Park, thinking, as he often does, about how lonely and depressed he is.

Finally, late at night, Holden goes home. His parents are out for the evening, and he spends some time talking with his ten-year-old sister, Phoebe, with whom he was always very close. Phoebe expresses her disappointment with Holden's being expelled from school, and brother and sister talk at length about what Holden truly believes in and what he will do with his life. Holden tells Phoebe of his idealistic vision of being a "catcher in the rye," protecting innocent children from disaster. He imagines children playing in a field of rye and himself catching them whenever they are in danger of falling over a cliff. He avoids seeing his parents on their return home and goes to see a former teacher, Mr. Antolini, from whom he intends to seek advice.

Mr. Antolini and his wife receive Holden warmly, and he is invited to spend the night. He listens carefully to Mr. Antolini's ideas on Holden's future. To Holden's shock and dismay, however, Mr. Antolini makes what Holden understands to be sexual advances, and he leaves the Antolini apartment hurriedly. He spends the rest of the night in Grand Central Station.

The next day, Holden visits Phoebe at her school and tells her of his plans to begin a new life in the West. Holden's story ends with his good-bye to Phoebe, but the novel's first and last chapters indicate that he has a nervous breakdown of sorts. He tells the story while in a hospital, apparently in California.

Critical Evaluation:

J. D. Salinger's *The Catcher in the Rye* has become, since its publication, an enduring classic of American literature. The novel is a favorite because of its humor, its mordant criticism of American middle-class society and its values, and the skill with which Salinger captures colloquial speech and vocabulary. *The Catcher in the Rye*, ironically enough, has received some criticism over the years because of its rough language, which Holden Caulfield cites to denounce. The novel's story is told in retrospect by the main character, Holden, apparently while staying in a psychiatric hospital in California.

What Holden tells is the story of his disenchantment with his life and the direction it is taking him. Throughout the novel, Holden speaks of his loneliness and depression; the story of a few days in his life indicates how sad and lonely his search for moral values is in a society in which he finds them sorely lacking. As the novel begins, Holden has been expelled, immediately before Christmas, from an exclusive preparatory school in Pennsylvania. He knows his parents will be angry with him, so he decides to spend a few days in New York City before going home. In New York, Holden endures several adventures before explaining to his only real friend, his sister, Phoebe, just what it is he believes in. This discovery of some moral identity does not, however, save Holden from hospitalization.

From the beginning of the novel, readers see Holden as the champion of the downtrodden: children, for example (whom he sees as essentially innocent, fragile, and uncomplicated), and those who have been persecuted by others. At the same time, Holden shows no patience for hypocrisy and self-delusion (except his own; readers need to keep in mind that the narrator is institutionalized), as seen in any number of his acquaintances. Holden's idealism does not spare even his own older brother, D. B., whom Holden accuses of prostituting his writing talent as a screenwriter in Hollywood. Holden admires courage, simplicity, and authenticity. He is preoccupied with the lack of justice in life, a point that leads him to defend a girl's honor in a fight with his Pencey roommate, Ward Stradlater, and results in another beating in New York, when Holden refuses to be cheated by a pandering hotel elevator operator. Moreover, Holden is devastated by the death of his younger brother, Allie, and it turns out that one of Holden's heroes is a former schoolmate named James Castle, who commits suicide rather than contradict his beliefs. In a well-known passage late in the novel, Holden sees obscene graffiti on the walls of Phoebe's school. He is enraged that someone would affront children in this way, and he manages to efface one set of obscenities. Later, however, he finds more such graffiti and depressedly comes to the conclusion that one can never erase all obscene scribblings from the walls of the world.

Salinger's novel takes its title from two key episodes that involve children. The first of these is Holden's chance observation of a little boy, who, with his parents, is strolling along a city street. Evidently, the happy boy is singing to himself, humming a song Holden calls "If a body catch a body coming through the rye." Holden is impressed with the fact that the boy is simply enjoying his own music, pleasing only himself in naïve artistic integrity.

Much later, when Holden spends an evening with Phoebe, he defends himself against his sister's charge of moral bankruptcy by indirectly alluding to the little boy. Holden tells Phoebe that he would like to be a "catcher in the rye," a man who watches over children, protecting them from falling from a cliff while they play. Holden's fantasy elaborates his obsession with innocence and his perhaps surprisingly traditional moral code.

It is important to realize that Holden's intention of making a new life for himself in the West places Holden Caulfield in a tradition of American literature in which young people seek out a better life away from the corruptions of civilization. Such characters seek to realize the American Dream and the ideals of justice, purity, and self-definition on the country's frontiers, away from cities. Unfortunately, Holden's move westward takes him only to a mental hospital; one wonders if this development is cruel irony or, perhaps, a real start on a new life for Holden.

Gordon Walters

Further Reading

Alsen, Eberhard. *A Reader's Guide to J. D. Salinger.* Westport, Conn.: Greenwood Press, 2003. Provides a biographical essay, pointing out the autobiographical elements in Salinger's works, and insightful analysis of *The Catcher in the Rye* and other works.

Bloom, Harold, ed. *J. D. Salinger.* New ed. New York: Bloom's Literary Criticism, 2008. Collection of essays, including several interpretations of *The Catcher in the Rye*, analyses of the novellas and short stories, and "Rhetoric, Sanity, and the Cold War: The Significance of Holden Caulfield's Testimony." Includes chronology, bibliography, and index.

_____. *J. D. Salinger's "The Catcher in the Rye."* New York: Chelsea House, 2007. A guide to the novel, featuring a biographical sketch of Salinger, a list of characters, summary and analysis, and essays providing critical interpretations. Includes an annotated bibliography and index.

Graham, Sarah. *J. D. Salinger's "The Catcher in the Rye."* New York: Routledge, 2007. Discusses the text and context of the novel and its critical history; contains new critical essays analyzing the book. Includes a list of books and Web resources providing additional information.

Grunwald, Henry Anatole, ed. *Salinger: A Critical and Personal Portrait.* New York: Harper & Row, 1962. Contains two important articles on *The Catcher in the Rye.* One deals with Holden Caulfield as an heir of Huck Finn; the other is a study of the novel's language.

Laser, Marvin, and Norman Fruman, eds. *Studies in J. D. Salinger: Reviews, Essays, and Critiques of "The Catcher in the Rye" and Other Fiction.* New York: Odyssey Press, 1963. Includes an intriguing essay by a German, Hans Bungert, another by a Russian writer, and one of the best structural interpretations of the novel, written by Carl F. Strauch.

Marsden, Malcolm M., ed. *If You Really Want to Know: A "Catcher" Casebook.* Glenview, Ill.: Scott, Foresman, 1963. Contains reviews that appeared after the novel's initial publication. Examines Holden from opposing points of view, as "saint or psychotic."

Pinsker, Sanford. *"The Catcher in the Rye": Innocence Under Pressure.* Boston: Twayne, 1993. A sustained study of the novel. Contains a helpful section on the body of critical literature about the novel.

Salzman, Jack, ed. *New Essays on "The Catcher in the Rye."* New York: Cambridge University Press, 1991. Provides an unusual sociological reading of the novel, as well as an essay that firmly places the book in American literary history.

Steinle, Pamela Hunt. *In Cold Fear: "The Catcher in the Rye" Censorship Controversies and Postwar American Character.* Columbus: Ohio State University Press, 2000. A study of the impact of the novel when it was released during an anxious period in American social and political history. Includes bibliography and index.

Catiline

Author: Ben Jonson (1573-1637)

First produced: 1611; first published, 1611, as *Catiline His
    Conspiracy*

Type of work: Drama

Type of plot: Political

Time of plot: First century B.C.E.

Locale: Ancient Rome

Principal characters:

CATILINE, the leader of a conspiracy against Rome

LENTULUS and CETHEGUS, his lieutenants

CURIUS, a conspirator and spy

CICERO, the defender of the state

CATO, the "voice of Rome"

JULIUS CAESAR, a shrewd politician and friend of the
    conspirators

FULVIA, a courtesan and spy

SEMPRONIA, a conspirator

AURELIA, Catiline's wife

The Story:

Under the sinister influence of Sulla's ghost, the reckless patrician Catiline organizes a conspiracy to overthrow the Roman Republic. The conspirators, among them the rash Cethegus and the outcast senators Lentulus and Curius, gather at Catiline's home. Catiline and his wife pander to the weaknesses of each and skillfully manipulate them without allowing them to realize that they are puppets. The conspirators conclude their meeting with a gruesome sacrament and pledge their faith by drinking the blood of a murdered slave.

The first step in their plan is to have Catiline elected as one of the two consuls. Success seems probable after four of the candidates withdraw in favor of Catiline. That leaves only two competitors in the race: Antonius, impecunious and lukewarm, and Cicero, a new man but a dangerous antagonist. A Chorus of Roman citizens gathers and discusses the uncertainty of the survival of great national powers, which often seem to carry in themselves seeds of their destruction: Luxuries and vices soften nations and leave them easy prey to their own malcontents or to alien invaders.

Fulvia, the profligate wife of an elderly fool, numbers among her lovers the conspirator Curius and, on a very casual basis, Julius Caesar. As she is interested in wealth, not romance, she forbids her servants to admit the down-at-heels Curius on future visits. She is being readied for her social day when Sempronia visits her, a politician well past the bloom of youth. Sempronia is an eager supporter of the patrician Catiline and a scorner of "that talker, Cicero," who presumes to be more learned and eloquent than the nobility. When Curius arrives to interrupt their gossip, Sempronia overrides Fulvia's objections, ushers him in, and makes great play of leaving the lovers alone. Fulvia's reception of Curius is so hostile that he becomes enraged and drops threats and hints of future greatness and power. Fulvia immediately shifts to the tactics of Delilah and wheedles information about the conspiracy from him.

The Chorus gathers before the election and prays for wisdom to choose consuls worthy of Rome's great past. Antonius and Cicero win the election, which shocks and infuriates Catiline and his party. Cato praises Cicero warmly, but Caesar and other sympathizers of Catiline regard the new consul with veiled hostility or open contempt. Catiline masks his fury in public, but in private he plans rebellion and civil war. Fulvia, partly because of self-interest and partly because of a vain dislike of playing second fiddle to Sempronia, carries information about the conspiracy to Cicero. He uses it to intimidate Curius, appealing to his greed and winning him as a spy. Fulvia serves the same purpose among the women conspirators. Alone, Cicero bemoans the low estate of Rome, which is reduced to dependence on such tools as Fulvia and Curius for safety. He strengthens his position still further by giving a province to Antonius.

Caesar shows Catiline favor and gives him advice, but he does not join the assemblage of conspirators. At the conspirators' next meeting, plans are laid for setting fire to the city at strategic points and starting local uprisings to be timed with an invasion from outside. The first move is to be the murder of Cicero that very night. The women conspirators enter with Catiline's wife, Aurelia. Under cover of their excited chatter, Curius whispers to Fulvia the plan to assassinate Cicero. She leaves the meeting and warns Cicero in time for him to gather protecting friends and impartial witnesses. Although the attempt on Cicero's life fails, the threat of civil violence terrifies senators and citizens. The Chorus expresses horror at the danger, which seems brought about by the city's guilt.

In the Senate, Cicero delivers an impassioned oration against Catiline and discloses detailed information about the conspiracy. Catiline thereupon loses control of himself, threatens Cicero and Rome, and leaves to join his army outside the city. Lentulus and Cethegus remain in charge of the internal organization of the conspirators. Cato warns Cicero of the danger from Caesar and other concealed supporters of Catiline, but Cicero chooses to avoid a break with them. He persuades the ambassadors from the Allobroges, who were approached by Catiline's men, to pretend to join the conspiracy and to secure incriminating documents. When the ambassadors are arrested, as prearranged, a conspirator taken with them turns state's evidence to save his life. With the evidence of the conspirator and the ambassadors, the Senate approves the arrest and execution of the conspirators remaining in Rome. Because Caesar tries to save their lives, he is accused by Curius, but Cicero chooses to pretend that this dangerous man is innocent, allowing him to remain alive and uncurbed.

After the execution of the conspirators, the leader of the Roman forces arrives and reports the defeat of Catiline and his "brave bad death" while leading his troops. Honored and rewarded by the Senate and the Roman people, Cicero pronounces thanks for Rome's rescue.

Critical Evaluation:

Ben Jonson's two tragedies based on Roman history, *Sejanus* (1603) and *Catiline* (1611), were critical failures when they were first presented, and they have remained the object of scholarly reservation, even of disapproval. *Catiline* in particular has been dissected for its rhetorical presentation, undramatic staging, and unsympathetic characters. In his essay on Ben Jonson, T. S. Eliot dismisses the play as "that deadly Pyrrhic victory of tragedy," and his judgment has been generally accepted.

To be fully appreciated, however, *Catiline* must be judged according to its author's intentions and his own self-imposed conventions, drawn largely from classical drama and Senecan closet drama, both genres that are very different from the more popular works of Elizabethan and Jacobean playwrights, including Jonson himself. In addition, it may well be that the real subject of *Catiline* is not the actual historical conspiracy that nearly overthrew the Roman Republic in 63 B.C.E. The real subject, instead, may be a broader topic: the state of England during Jonson's lifetime, politics in general, or even language as a means of human communication and control.

The immediate influences on the play are simple enough. Jonson intended to write a drama conforming to the strict considerations of classical drama; in particular, he is careful to exclude all violent action from the stage, so that battles and

deaths, including Catiline's, are reported but never seen. In this way, Jonson is working in the style and traditions of Senecan closet drama, where the language of the play takes precedence over action.

In addition, and as part of this adherence to the classical patterns, Jonson makes extensive use of a chorus, which comments upon the actions of other characters and which itself functions as a character. Unlike William Shakespeare's solitary chorus in *Henry V* (pr. c. 1598-1599, pb. 1600), Jonson's chorus is thought to be modeled on the classical Greek chorus, which consists of a group of characters who speak and act in unison.

As Eliot and others have long noted, the traditions and conventions of classical and Senecan drama were important influences on English playwrights during the Renaissance. When, however, presented in the severe, almost undiluted form Jonson employs in *Catiline*, those conventions run counter to the normal direction and impulse of English stagecraft. Unless *Catiline* is recognized as belonging to a different genre, the play cannot be appreciated or even understood. It is a meditation on the consequences of political actions rather than a presentation of the actions themselves.

In depicting those actions, Jonson drew upon ancient historical record, but he may also have been commenting on more recent events. In writing *Catiline*, Jonson was careful to remain close to his historical sources, most notably the Roman historian Sallust, whose *The Conspiracy of Catiline* (43-42 B.C.E.) is the fullest account of the conspiracy and its defeat. In addition, Jonson drew on a number of details from the historians Plutarch and Dio Cassius, including the hint that Julius Caesar was involved in the conspiracy. In particular, Jonson turned to the writings of Marcus Tullius Cicero, the consul at the time of the conspiracy, who was largely responsible, through his brilliant orations, for its exposure and defeat. Indeed, long passages of Jonson's play are simply paraphrases (or, more accurately, translations) of Cicero's *Orations Against Catiline* (60 B.C.E.).

Perhaps the outstanding example of this close dependence on original sources comes at the climax of the play, in the long speech in act 4 when Cicero reveals and denounces Catiline's conspiracy. The words here are taken almost verbatim from Cicero's own record. As Eliot and other critics have noted, however, what Jonson gains in historical accuracy is won at the expense of dramatic effectiveness. The audience sees and hears Catiline verbally rebuked in the Senate, but it is only told about his actual defeat and death on the battlefield.

Jonson's purpose in adhering so closely to the historical record, and his insistence on a strict classical form, may have been based on a desire to transcend the specifics of history and politics to reveal the underlying fundamental laws and principles and thereby to connect republican Rome and Jacobean England. Jonson presents these parallels either as specific instances or more general themes.

Some similarities have been noted between Jonson's presentation of the Catilinarian conspiracy and the Gunpowder Plot of 1605, in which Guy Fawkes and other Catholic dissidents attempted to kill King James I and the English Parliament. The explosion was timed to take place on November 5, and in his denunciation of Catiline during the play, Cicero thunders:

> I told too in this Senate that they purpose
> Was on the fifth, the kalends of November,
> T'have slaughter'd this whole order.

These lines, and repeated variants of the word "blow" in the dual sense of a sudden, violent overthrow and an explosion, suggest a deliberate connection between the ancient and the modern conspiracies.

Jonson's purpose in *Catiline* may well have been more general, however, serving to present an overview of the political processes in the abstract. During a period in which the political and social structures of England were being severely tested both by religious factionalism and dynastic change, there was an increased desire for stability and order. The villains in *Catiline* are those who seek to create disorder and to profit from it: Catiline himself, deeply ambitious, seeks to dominate Rome; Caesar, already aspiring to power, is implicated in the conspiracy but manages to escape censure; Fulvia, a courtesan and spy, mingles her own concerns with political intrigue. The common thread that links these figures is a desire for social and political revolution.

By contrast, Cicero, seen by many critics as the heroic protagonist of the play, is dedicated to upholding and defending the established principles of republican Rome. Although a "new man" himself (that is, not coming from a long-established patrician family), Cicero is more loyal to the traditions and principles of Roman life than is the patrician Catiline. Significantly, Cicero's victory is accomplished not on the battlefield but in the Senate chamber, and his victory is won by the power of language rather than by the strength of weapons.

Cicero's victory over Catiline through the mastery of language is central to both the content and the form of the play. As a Senecan closet drama, and as a play, *Catiline* is forced by convention to rely upon linguistic, rather than dramatic,

resources. It may well be, however, that Jonson was impelled to use the classical and Senecan models precisely because the subject matter of his drama, and the key events which it chronicles, are concerned with power and consequences of language itself and with its influence on human beings and their actions.

"Critical Evaluation" by Michael Witkoski

Further Reading

Barton, Anne. *Ben Jonson, Dramatist*. New York: Cambridge University Press, 1984. In a manner similar to T. S. Eliot but more extended in scope, Barton examines the play in terms of its relationship to Jonsonian comedy, especially in its use of the characters' names to define and describe their nature and roles.

Bloom, Harold, ed. *Ben Jonson*. Edgemont, Pa.: Chelsea House, 1987. Contains several perceptive essays on various aspects of *Catiline*.

De Luna, Barbara. *Jonson's Romish Plot: A Study of "Catiline" and Its Historical Context*. Oxford, England: Clarendon Press, 1967. Argues that the play was a retelling of the Gunpowder Plot of 1605. De Luna's most controversial conjecture is that Jonson himself may have been implicated in, or at least have had prior knowledge of, the plot.

Donaldson, Ian. *Jonson's Magic Houses: Essays in Interpretation*. New York: Oxford University Press, 1997. Donaldson, a Jonson scholar, provides new interpretations of Jonson's personality, work, and literary legacy.

Eliot, T. S. "Ben Jonson." In *Selected Essays*. Winchester, Mass.: Faber & Faber, 1932. First published in 1919, this essay asserts that *Catiline* failed primarily because Jonson could not place his theme, characters, and subject in the proper vehicle. Sees some parts of the play as similar to satiric comedy.

Harp, Richard, and Stanley Stewart, eds. *The Cambridge Companion to Ben Jonson*. New York: Cambridge University Press, 2000. Collection of essays about Jonson's life and career, including analyses of his comedies and late plays, a description of London and its theaters during Jonson's lifetime, and an evaluation of his critical heritage.

Loxley, James. *A Sourcebook*. New York: Routledge, 2002. An introductory overview of Jonson's life and work, particularly useful for students. Part 1 provides biographical information and places Jonson's life and work within the context of his times; part 2 discusses several works, including *Catiline*; and part 3 offers critical analysis of the themes in his plays, the style of his writing, and a comparison of his work to that of William Shakespeare.

McEvoy, Sean. *Ben Jonson, Renaissance Dramatist*. Edinburgh: Edinburgh University Press, 2008. McEvoy analyzes all of Jonson's plays, attributing their greatness to the playwright's commitment to the ideals of humanism

during a time of authoritarianism and rampant capitalism in England. Chapter 3 focuses on Jonson's Roman tragedies, *Catiline* and *Sejanus*.

Miles, Rosalind. *Ben Jonson: His Craft and Art*. New York: Barnes & Noble, 1990. A general study of Jonson's artistry. Includes an examination of *Catiline*.

Cat's Cradle

Author: Kurt Vonnegut (1922-2007)
First published: 1963
Type of work: Novel
Type of plot: Satire and science fiction
Time of plot: c. 1945-1963
Locale: Ilium, New York; Republic of San Lorenzo

Principal characters:
JOHN, the narrator, a freelance writer
FELIX HOENIKKER, deceased codeveloper of the atomic bomb
ANGELA, his daughter
FRANKLIN and NEWTON, his sons
BOKONON (LIONEL BOYD JOHNSON), a self-proclaimed holy man
EARL McCABE, self-proclaimed ruler of San Lorenzo
MIGUEL "PAPA" MONZANO, dictator of San Lorenzo
MONA AAMONS MONZANO, his adopted daughter
HORLICK MINTON, U.S. ambassador to San Lorenzo
H. LOWE CROSBY, an American businessperson
JULIAN CASTLE, an American millionaire
ASA BREED, a former colleague of Felix Hoenikker

The Story:

John, a cynical freelance writer, describes a journey that began with his attempt to write a book that he wants to call "The Day the World Ended." John's subject is the first atomic bomb dropped on Hiroshima, Japan, in World War II. His research leads him to Newton "Newt" Hoenikker, son of Dr. Felix Hoenikker, one of the bomb's chief scientists. Newt shares memories of his father, a brilliant physicist who had seemed completely detached from humanity.

John then travels to Ilium, New York, where Hoenikker had lived and worked, and interviews Dr. Asa Breed, a fellow scientist and former colleague of Hoenikker. Breed tells him about *ice-nine*, a theoretical project Hoenikker reportedly had been working on near the end of his life. Originally conceived as a way to keep soldiers from having to fight in mud, *ice-nine* rearranges the molecules of water so that it freezes, even in extreme heat.

Though Breed insists that *ice-nine* remains only a theory, it turns out that it actually exists. Hoenikker had been playing with a chip of *ice-nine* on the day he died, and his three chil-

dren divided the chip between them. John's investigations suggest that the Hoenikker siblings, all unpopular outcasts as children, have used the precious substance to buy themselves status and companionship. Gawky Angela has acquired a handsome husband; Newt, a "midget," had a brief liaison with Zinka, a Ukrainian dancer later revealed to be a spy; and Frank, a high school dropout whose only talent seems to be model making, becomes Major General Franklin Hoenikker, the minister of science and progress with the Republic of San Lorenzo.

Assigned to do a story about Julian Castle, a millionaire who had founded a free clinic in San Lorenzo, John flies to the island nation. On the airplane, he meets Angela and Newt Hoenikker; Horlick Minton, the U.S. ambassador to San Lorenzo, and his wife, Claire; and H. Lowe Crosby, a bicycle manufacturer who plans to start a factory in San Lorenzo, and his wife, Hazel, who takes a liking to John because they both are Indiana Hoosiers.

John tells his story from the perspective of Bokononism, a

frankly false religion invented by Lionel Boyd Johnson, a World War I veteran who, along with a U.S. Marines deserter named Earl McCabe, had been shipwrecked on the island of San Lorenzo. McCabe had set himself up as the island's ruler, and Johnson, known as Bokonon in island dialect, had styled himself a religious prophet. Although Bokononism is now outlawed on San Lorenzo, it is practiced by nearly everyone there, including Miguel "Papa" Monzano, the dictator who had replaced McCabe as ruler.

A central tenet of Bokononism is the formation of the *karass*, a group of seemingly unrelated people brought together by God to accomplish some purpose. At the center of the *karass* is the *wampeter*, the object that brings them together. John comes to believe that Felix Hoenikker's children, as well as the Crosbys, the Mintons, and Julian Castle, are members of Felix's *karass*, drawn together around the deadly *wampeter* called *ice-nine*.

Arriving on San Lorenzo, John and his companions are treated to a military display led by the aging ruler Monzano and Frank Hoenikker. Monzano is suffering from cancer, and he collapses during the greeting ceremony; he names Frank as his successor. Frank later meets in secret with John and offers him the presidency. John accepts, because he has become infatuated with beautiful Mona Aamons Monzano, the adopted daughter of Papa Monzano. A prophecy by Bokonon says that Mona will marry the next president of San Lorenzo. Mona agrees to marry John, but Frank feels they should ask for Papa Monzano's blessing before he dies. They all go to the presidential castle. Papa, dying in agony, says it does not matter who is president of San Lorenzo. He tells John to kill Bokonon, and to put his faith in science.

John's first day as president of San Lorenzo coincides with a national holiday, the Day of the Hundred Martyrs to Democracy, which memorializes the citizens of San Lorenzo who died during World War II. Just before the ceremony, John learns from a doctor that Papa had committed suicide by swallowing something from a vial he had worn around his neck. Papa's body is blue-white and frozen. John realizes that the vial must have contained *ice-nine*, but the doctor, not knowing what had happened, unwittingly touches his own tongue to the ice from Papa's body and immediately dies. John calls the Hoenikker children to show them the two bodies, and Frank admits he had given *ice-nine* to Papa to obtain a high-ranking job on San Lorenzo. John and Frank decide to conceal the truth about *ice-nine* and to burn the bodies after the ceremony.

At the ceremony, Ambassador Minton gives a speech about the futility of war, comparing San Lorenzo's martyrs to murdered children. As he concludes his speech, a spectacular air show begins. One airplane crashes into the cliffs at the foot of the presidential castle, triggering a cataclysmic rockslide. Part of the castle—and Papa's body—falls into the sea. Immediately, the sea freezes and the sky fills with deadly tornadoes. It is now, as Breed had predicted when denying the existence of *ice-nine*, the end of the world.

John and Mona survive by fleeing to a castle oubliette, or dungeon, that Papa had converted to a bomb shelter. When they emerge from the shelter, they find a valley filled with frozen corpses, people who had survived the first freeze and the storms only to commit suicide later by ingesting *ice-nine*. A note left at the scene says that the survivors had asked the holy man Bokonon what they should do, and he responded that because God is obviously trying to kill them, they should oblige and die. The note is signed by Bokonon. Mona, laughing at this absurd solution, touches the frozen ground, puts her finger to her lips, and dies.

In shock, John wanders away and is found by the Crosbys and Newt Hoenikker, who had survived, along with Frank, in a palace dungeon. John reveals that for the last six months, he had been living with a small group of survivors while writing his story. Only the ending of his story remains to be told. John feels he should climb to the top of Mt. McCabe, San Lorenzo's highest mountain, to leave some symbol there, but he is not sure what symbol would be right.

Driving through the ruins of San Lorenzo, John sees Bokonon, wearing a hotel bedspread. Bokonon tells John that he has written the final sentence in *The Books of Bokonon*, a sentence that seems to prophesy John's fate: to write a "history of human stupidity" and then climb to the top of Mt. McCabe, poison himself with *ice-nine*, and die thumbing his nose at an indifferent God.

Critical Evaluation:

An iconic American fiction writer, Kurt Vonnegut is a rarity in American letters: a cult figure known for his radical and experimental novels who also achieved widespread popularity. Vonnegut, a World War II veteran who survived the firebombing of Dresden, Germany, began writing short stories after the war while working as a publicist for General Electric.

Many of Vonnegut's early stories and novels contain science fiction, dystopian, and satirical elements; he questions developments of contemporary society, such as the trend toward mechanization, but also pokes fun at timeless human folly. *Cat's Cradle*, published just months after the Cuban Missile Crisis brought the United States and the Soviet Union to the brink of nuclear war, pulls together all these elements to form a quasi-realistic story that incorporates actual historical events, such as the development of the atomic bomb. In its mingling of science fiction and historical fact, *Cat's Cradle* presages *Slaughterhouse-Five* (1969), the novel most often acknowledged as Vonnegut's masterpiece.

Cat's Cradle begins with a telling line: "Call me Jonah." By styling himself Jonah, for the biblical prophet who was swallowed by a whale, Vonnegut explicitly connects his story to a biblical tale of disaster and redemption. The line also is an homage to Herman Melville's "Call me Ishmael," the famous beginning of *Moby Dick* (1851). John begins the novel explaining that he is trying to write a book about the figurative end of the world—the dropping of the atomic bomb. He ends the novel, ironically, by writing his own story as one of the few survivors of a far greater apocalypse.

Rather than ending in fire, the world in *Cat's Cradle* ends in ice. Whether by atomic fire or by the blue-white death of *ice-nine*, the result is the same: massive death and planetary devastation. While the destruction of the *Pequot* in *Moby Dick* is driven by Captain Ahab's obsessive hatred, the destruction of nearly all living beings in *Cat's Cradle* is perhaps more frightening because it arises from the seemingly innocent human traits of curiosity and playfulness. Felix Hoenikker, the scientist who engineers both the atomic bomb and *ice-nine*, is an absentminded tinkerer who "plays" with whatever happens to interest him at the time—atomic bombs, turtles, *ice-nine*—with no conception of the moral consequences of his inventions. The word "sin," applied to the atomic bomb by a scientific colleague, has no meaning for Hoenikker.

Rich in religious symbolism, *Cat's Cradle* is also a satirical critique of organized religion. Through his invention of Bokononism, a religion admittedly founded on lies, Vonnegut calls into question the many contradictory religions that claim to present the truth. However, the novel reaches beyond parody to an expression of Vonnegut's underlying humanism, for the only thing holy in this invented religion is humanity itself. Despite his self-admitted trickery, Bokonon becomes, perhaps against his will, a holy fool whose lies may be more helpful than the truths of science. The quotation from *The Books of Bokonon* that serves as an epigraph to *Cat's Cradle* advises people to live by the *foma*, or lies, which make them brave and kind, healthy and happy.

When John accepts the presidency of San Lorenzo, he contemplates reforms that include making Bokononism legal, but he soon realizes that the island's lack of resources makes poverty and misery inevitable. If Bokonon's lies, including the shared drama of his outlaw status, provide the islanders with escape, then why not allow them that escape? Religion may be the opiate of the people, Vonnegut seems to

suggest, yet its opposite—the soulless pragmatism represented by Felix Hoenikker's science—can lead only to emptiness and death.

Narrated entirely from John's point of view in 127 brief chapters, *Cat's Cradle* has a narrative simplicity that belies the complexity of its ideas. The novel does not challenge readers with the confusing time shifts of *Slaughterhouse-Five*. Instead, the story seems to amble along, as aimless as its narrator, a self-described hack. However, what seem to be amusing digressions, such as a visit to the hobby shop where young Frank Hoenikker had spent his time building model cities, turn out to be significant as the story progresses. In undeveloped San Lorenzo, Frank attempts to build a real-life version of his model city, yet what he builds is still no more than a model, a facade of progress. Without the humanizing influence of his mother, who had died early, Frank, like the rest of the Hoenikkers, had grown up warped, raised by a father who was interested in things and ideas, but not people.

The "cat's cradle" of the title, a child's string game, figures in one of the few interactions between Hoenikker and his younger son, Newt. Hoenikker's clumsy attempt to play with his son only terrifies the child and leaves him with a sense of emptiness that he later conveys through his dark, grotesque paintings. The image of the cat's cradle and others like it recur in the novel, underscoring Vonnegut's critique of science without soul, progress without compassion.

Kathryn Kulpa

Further Reading

Allen, William Rodney. *Understanding Kurt Vonnegut.* Columbia: University of South Carolina Press, 1991. This critical study gives special attention to Vonnegut's 1960's cycle of four strong novels—*Mother's Night, Cat's Cradle, God Bless You, Mr. Rosewater,* and *Slaughterhouse-Five*—showing Vonnegut's melding of science fiction, social criticism, and political satire.

Bloom, Harold, ed. *Kurt Vonnegut's "Cat's Cradle."* New York: Chelsea House, 2002. This collection includes sixteen critical essays from 1963 to 2000, offering different interpretations of *Cat's Cradle.*

Boon, Kevin A., ed. *At Millennium's End: New Essays on the Work of Kurt Vonnegut.* Albany: State University of New York Press, 2001. A diverse collection of essays on Vonnegut's fiction and broader cultural influence.

Davis, Todd S. *Kurt Vonnegut's Crusade: Or, How a Postmodern Harlequin Preached a New Kind of Humanism.* Albany: State University of New York Press, 2006. Analyzes Vonnegut's novels in the context of his humanism and his belief that authors should seek to be "agents of change" in society rather than live in artistic isolation.

Klinkowitz, Jerome. *The Vonnegut Effect.* Columbia: University of South Carolina Press, 2004. The "Vonnegut effect," as Klinkowitz defines it, is Vonnegut's unique ability to win wide popularity while experimenting with challenging fictional themes and structures. An accessible, admiring look at Vonnegut's evolution as a twentieth century writer.

Leeds, Marc. *The Vonnegut Encyclopedia: An Authorized Compendium.* Westport, Conn.: Greenwood Press, 1996. Ambitious in both scale and scope, this collection is espe-

cially useful as an introduction to Vonnegut's life, works, and aesthetic.

Marvin, Thomas F. *Kurt Vonnegut: A Critical Companion.* Westport, Conn.: Greenwood Press, 2002. This volume, suitable for upper-level high school and college students, offers close critical readings of Vonnegut's significant works, including *Cat's Cradle.*

Mustazza, Leonard. *Forever Pursuing Genesis: The Myth of Eden in the Novels of Kurt Vonnegut.* Lewisburg, Pa.: Bucknell University Press, 1990. This study of Vonnegut's fiction emphasizes his playful treatments of the myth of humankind's fall from innocence.

Cawdor

Author: Robinson Jeffers (1887-1962)
First published: 1928
Type of work: Poetry
Type of plot: Psychological realism
Time of plot: 1900
Locale: Carmel coast range, California

Principal characters:
CAWDOR, a farmer
HOOD CAWDOR, his son
GEORGE CAWDOR, another son
MICHAL CAWDOR, a daughter
MARTIAL, a neighbor
FERA, Martial's daughter
CONCHA ROSAS, Cawdor's Indian servant

The Poem:

In 1899 a terrible fire devastates many of the farms along the Carmel coast, but Cawdor's farm is untouched. Early one morning he sees two figures approaching his house: a young woman leading a blind old man. They are the Martials, who hold the land bordering his and with whom Cawdor has an old feud. Martial was blinded by the fire, his farm destroyed. His daughter Fera has only Cawdor to turn to for relief. Cawdor takes them in and sends his servant, Concha Rosas, to live in a hut. When the old man is well enough to walk around, Cawdor speaks of sending the two away unless Fera will marry him. She agrees.

Hood Cawdor leaves home after a fight with his father. On the night of the wedding he dreams that the old man died, and he decides to return to the farm to see if all is well. When he reaches a hill overlooking the farm, he camps and lights a fire. His sister Michal sees him and goes to tell him of their father's marriage. Cawdor receives his son in a friendly manner. For a wedding present, Hood gives Fera a lion skin.

Fera finds in Hood the same quality of hardness that drew her at first to Cawdor. She openly confesses to Hood that al-

though she loved his father when she married him, she no longer cares for him. She is jealous, too, of Concha Rosas, who was Cawdor's mistress before he married Fera, and whom he again seems to prefer to his wife. Disturbed by Fera's advances, Hood resolves to leave. After a prowling lion kills one of the farm dogs, he decides to stay, however, until he kills the animal. A terrible storm arises that prevents his hunting for several days.

Fera's father is dying. On the pretext that Martial wishes to talk to Hood, Fera calls him into the sick room. Openly, before her unconscious father, she confesses her passion. That night Fera asks Concha Rosas to watch with her by the old man's bedside. Toward morning Martial dies. Instead of summoning her husband, Fera goes to Hood's room, where Cawdor finds them. Fera tries to lull his suspicions by declaring that she tried to awaken him but could not, and so she went to rouse Hood.

The next morning the men dig a grave for the old man. Fera, who was watching them, calls Hood into the wood to help her pick laurels for the grave. Again she begs for his love. Suddenly he draws his knife and stabs himself deep in the thigh. Once more he was able to resist her. The funeral service for her father is short but painful. Afterward Fera finds her way home alone.

Desperate now, she covers herself with the lion skin Hood gave her and hides in the bushes. Hood shoots at her, his bullet entering her shoulder. He carries Fera to her room, where Cawdor attempts to set the bones that were fractured. Fera begs him to stop torturing her. Then, as if it were wrenched out of her because of the pain, she says that Hood seduced her by force. Her lie is a last resort to prevent Hood's leaving. Hood, however, already had left the farm and is camped once more on the top of the hill. There the infuriated father finds him. In the fight that follows Hood is pushed off the cliff, his body falling upon the rocks below. Cawdor meets Michal on his way down the cliff and tells her that Hood fled. Meanwhile Fera sends Concha Rosas from the room to get some water. Quickly she unfastens the strap around her arm and slings it over the head of the bed and around her neck. When Concha Rosas returns, Fera is almost dead. For many days she lies in bed, slowly recovering. Neither George Cawdor nor Michal will visit her. They hate her for what they know were false charges against Hood.

Cawdor is haunted by his secret sin. Fera tries to destroy him with her own death wish. She tells him the truth about Hood—how, rather than betray his father, he stabbed himself with his knife. Cawdor's grief is uncontrollable. When Fera taunts him, demanding that he kill her, his fingers fasten around her throat. When she begins to struggle, he releases her and runs into Hood's old room. There he thinks he sees Hood lying on the bed, and for a moment he imagines all that passed was a dream.

He is aroused when Fera comes to tell him that everyone knows he killed Hood, that soon the authorities are bound to hear of his crime. Again she urges him to seek the peace that death will bring. They are walking near her father's grave, with George and Michal nearby. Cawdor suddenly declares to them that their suspicions are correct, that he killed Hood, and that they are to send for the authorities. Then he reaches down and picks up a flint. Without warning, he thrusts it into his eyes. Then, patiently, he asks them to lead him back to the house, to wait for whatever fate his deed will merit. Fera follows him, weeping. Once again she feels that she failed. She tried to get Cawdor to kill her and then himself; instead, he showed the courage to face his crime and pay for it.

Critical Evaluation:

Robinson Jeffers, poet of the beautiful and often wild and harsh California coast, believed that the Big Sur, California, landscape in which he lived revealed the truth about both people and the rest of nature. That truth is that all existence is in a constant process of flux, driven by, in the case of inorganic nature, great physical and chemical forces, and, in the case of living beings, the desire to survive and to seek pleasure.

Sexuality is a source of pleasure for people. This pleasure is also the way in which nature survives and continues in the form of new life. People respond to some sexual acts with punishment because people are dependent on one another and on the survival of the social order. People must define some sexual activity as wrong and not only condemn it but also punish it.

Jeffers examines such sexual aberrations as incest in *Tamar* (1924) and loveless coupling in *The Roan Stallion* (1925). An obvious question is, can pain and misery be avoided by avoiding wrongful sex? In *Cawdor*, which Jeffers regarded as part of a trilogy that includes *Tamar* and *The Women at Point Sur* (1927), he investigates the same questions, and he concludes that sexuality is a trap from which there is no escape; even abstinence leads only to trouble and suffering.

Jeffers was well educated in the classics, and the Greek tragedies were his favorite form of literature. His model for the story of the house of Cawdor is Euripides' *Hippolytos* (428 B.C.E.). In that dramatic account of a myth, Theseus's son, Hippolytus, rejects the sexual advances of Aphrodite, the goddess of love, because he prefers, instead, Artemis, the goddess of the hunt. This relationship is doomed, however, because Artemis cherishes her virginity. Although Artemis's views would seem to be enough to punish Hippolytus, vengeful Aphrodite also clouds the mind of his stepmother, Phaedra, and causes her to fall in love with him. When Hippolytus rejects her, too, Phaedra sets Theseus against his son. Theseus has Poseidon send a sea monster to frighten Hippolytus's horses as the boy rides by the shore. He is thrown from his chariot and dragged to his death.

Jeffers was drawn to this story not only by the themes of sexuality and incest but also by the characters who are manipulated by forces they cannot control. The Greeks personified these forces as gods and goddesses; in the twentieth century, where Jeffers sets his story, people are not certain what to call these forces, but people are, nevertheless, at the mercy of them. The Greek myth is a good reference point.

In *Cawdor*, Fera Martial (whose name means "wild beast," a connection that is reinforced when she puts on the skin of the mountain lion that Hood gives her) plays the part of Phaedra, Cawdor plays the part of Theseus, and Hood plays the part of Hippolytus. Fera feels that her sexuality is wasted in the service of, on one hand, her much older husband and, on the other hand, her injured, disabled father. She reaches out to Hood, who stabs himself in the thigh as a gesture of self-condemnation for even considering betraying his father in a liaison with a woman who replaced his mother. He does not tell his father, however, what this woman did. Hood is trapped by his own sense of honor. He can neither yield to temptation nor inform his father of Fera's advances, lest he break the old man's heart. Like Othello, another possible model, Cawdor chooses to believe Fera's false reports. He attacks Hood, causing him to fall to his death. When Cawdor learns that he attacked and killed his son because of Fera's lies, he blinds himself in imitation of Oedipus; in this case, however, the sin is of father against son rather than son against father. Hood accidentally shoots Fera, mistaking her for a mountain lion while she wears the lion skin. All the major characters die or are wounded as a result of passion, whether the passion is acted upon or whether it is avoided.

Jeffers's description of Hood's self-mutilation, which he calls an "Attis-gesture," is an indication of another level of meaning. *Cawdor* is based not only on the Greek tragedies but also on the myths behind those tragedies. Attis destroys himself, but he merges into a larger reality by doing so, and he is reborn in a different form when spring returns. The idea that death is neither an end nor a gateway to immortality but, instead, is part of an ongoing cycle of reformation and synthesis appears in three passages: when old Martial dies, when Hood dies, and when George shoots the caged, broken-winged eagle that Michal keeps as a pet. In each section, Jeffers describes the dissolution of consciousness after death, as if death itself is not a final event but a process that continues after the one who dies is lost to the living. Critics consider the passage about the eagle's death one of Jeffers's best. Like many other artists, Jeffers uses the dream as a means of connection between the ordinary waking world and the larger process of which people are all a part; each of the "death dreams" grows more intense until the caged eagle's consciousness soars above the coast where its body has died. Cawdor blinding himself is only a small part of a great spectacle. The agony of the Cawdor family, which the rest of this long poem describes, becomes only a minor incident in the great evolving, revolving, and returning cycle of things, and then the eagle can "see" no more, as its consciousness merges into another type of life that no one—not the eagle, not Jeffers—can describe.

"Critical Evaluation" by Jim Baird

Further Reading

Brophy, Robert J. "*Cawdor.*" In *Robinson Jeffers: Myth, Ritual, and Symbolism in His Narrative Poems*. Hamden, Conn.: Archon Books, 1976. An analysis of *Cawdor* as a restatement of mythic themes and patterns, written by a major Jeffers scholar. Includes bibliography.

_____, ed. *Robinson Jeffers, Dimensions of a Poet*. New York: Fordham University Press, 1995. Collection of essays offering various interpretations of Jeffers's poetry. Includes discussions of Jeffers and the uses of history; Jeffers and the female archetype; his relationship to Carmel and Big Sur, California; his "versecraft of the sublime"; and his dialogue with poet Czesław Miłosz about nature and symbolic order.

Carpenter, Frederic I. "*Cawdor.*" In *Robinson Jeffers*. New York: Grosset & Dunlap, 1962. Analyzes *Cawdor* along with the rest of Jeffers's early long narratives as part of a chapter on Jeffers's early poetic career. Offers one of the best short introductions to all of Jeffers's work. Includes bibliography.

Coffin, Arthur B. "*Cawdor.*" In *Robinson Jeffers: Poet of Inhumanism*. Madison: University of Wisconsin Press, 1971. An examination of the poem by a critic who is primarily interested in the philosophical underpinnings of Jeffers's work, specifically such thinkers as Arthur Schopenhauer and Friedrich Nietzsche. Includes bibliography.

Houston, James D. "Necessary Ecstasy: An Afterword to *Cawdor.*" *Western American Literature* 19, no. 2 (Summer, 1984): 99-112. An analysis of the poem that links it to the California coast in which it is set.

McClintock, Scott. "The Poetics of Fission in Robinson Jeffers." *Clio* 37, no. 2 (Spring, 2008): 171-191. Analyzes the transformation of Jeffers's poetics from a metaphysical philosophy of inhumanism to his use of more violent imagery influenced by the development of nuclear weapons during the Cold War.

Zaller, Robert. "The Bloody Sire." In *The Cliffs of Solitude*. New York: Cambridge University Press, 1983. Treats *Cawdor* along with a number of Jeffers's other poems, particularly the other long narratives, from a psychological, specifically Freudian, perspective. Includes bibliography.

_____, ed. *Centennial Essays for Robinson Jeffers*. Newark: University of Delaware Press, 1991. Collection of nine essays analyzing Jeffers's work, including pieces by poets William Everson and Czesław Miłosz.

Cecilia
Or, Memoirs of an Heiress

Author: Fanny Burney (1752-1840)
First published: 1782
Type of work: Novel
Type of plot: Social realism
Time of plot: Eighteenth century
Locale: England

Principal characters:
CECILIA BEVERLEY, a beautiful and virtuous heiress
MR. HARREL, her profligate guardian
MR. BRIGGS, her miserly guardian
MR. DELVILE, a proud aristocrat and also a guardian
MRS. DELVILE, his wife
MORTIMER DELVILE, their son
MR. MONCKTON, Cecilia's unscrupulous counselor
MR. BELFIELD, a pleasing but unstable young man
HENRIETTA BELFIELD, his modest sister

The Story:

Cecilia Beverley, just short of her majority, is left ten thousand pounds by her father and an annual income of three thousand pounds by her uncle, the latter inheritance being restricted by the condition that her husband take her name. Until her coming of age, she is expected to live with one of her guardians, the fashionable spendthrift Mr. Harrel, husband of a girlhood friend. One who warns her against the evils of London is Mr. Monckton, her clever and unscrupulous counselor. His secret intention is to marry Cecilia; at present, however, he is prevented by the existence of an old and ill-tempered wife, whom he married for money.

The constant round of parties in London and the dissipation of the Harrels are repugnant to Cecilia. Kind but unimpressive Mr. Arnott, Mrs. Harrel's brother, falls hopelessly in love with the girl, but Harrel obviously intends her for his friend, insolent Sir Robert Floyer, whom Cecilia detests. After vainly begging Harrel to pay a bill, which Arnott finally pays, Cecilia becomes so disgusted with the Harrels' way of life that she decides to leave their household. However, she finds the abode of her miserly guardian, Mr. Briggs, so comfortless and is so repulsed by the pride and condescension of her third guardian, Mr. Delvile, that she decides to remain with the Harrels.

At a masquerade party, she is pursued by a man disguised as the devil. He is Monckton in disguise, attempting to keep others away from her. She is rescued first by a Don Quixote and later by a domino whose conversation pleases her greatly. At first, she believes the domino is Mr. Belfield, a young man she met before. Later, she is surprised to learn that Don Quixote was Belfield. Angered at Cecilia's courtesy to Belfield, Sir Robert insults him at the opera; a duel results, and Belfield is wounded. A young man, Mortimer Delvile, who is courteously attentive to Cecilia, proves to be the dom-

ino and the only son of her guardian. He is the pride and hope of his family, whose fortune he is to recoup by marriage. Cecilia visits his mother and is charmed by her graciousness and wit. She is disturbed, however, by the knowledge that she is universally believed to be betrothed to either Sir Robert or Belfield. Monckton, feeling that the Delviles are the only threat to him, attempts to destroy her friendship with them.

Cecilia meets and immediately likes Henrietta Belfield. When she visits her new friend, she finds Henrietta nursing her wounded brother, whom Mortimer wishes to aid. Seeing Cecilia there, Mortimer believes that she is in love with Belfield. Having been educated above his station, Belfield has grown to feel contempt for business. He is clever and pleasant but unable to settle down to anything. Although Cecilia refuses Sir Robert's proposal, she sees that Harrel is still bent on the marriage. Monckton's constant warnings against the Delviles disturbs her, for she is now in love with Mortimer. Knowing his father's pride, however, she determines to conquer her feelings.

Cecilia, who previously discharged some debts for Harrel, is now so alarmed by his threats of suicide that she pledges herself to a total of seven thousand additional pounds. Since Briggs will not advance the money, she is forced to borrow from a usurer.

Mortimer, learning that Cecilia loves neither Sir Robert nor Belfield, betrays his own love for her—and then avoids her. Cecilia discovers that Henrietta is in love with Mortimer. Mrs. Belfield, believing that Cecilia loves her son, constantly urges him to propose to her.

Cecilia lends another thousand pounds to Harrel, who is to escape his creditors by leaving the country. Meanwhile, his wife is to live with her brother until Cecilia's house is ready. Harrel shoots himself, however, leaving a note for Cecilia in which he reveals that her marriage to Sir Robert is to have canceled a gambling debt. Monckton discharges Cecilia's debt with the usurer; she is to repay him on coming of age. Against his wishes, she goes with the Delviles to their castle. Only Mrs. Delvile is agreeable there. The family is too proud to encourage visitors, and Mortimer still avoids Cecilia. Much later, during a thunderstorm in which he contracts a fever, he betrays his true emotions. Cecilia is puzzled and hurt; her emotions intensify when Mrs. Delvile, who has guessed the feelings of both Mortimer and Cecilia, lets Cecilia know that they are not for each other. Mortimer, before going away for his health, tells Cecilia that his family will never accept the change-of-name clause in the will.

Cecilia then goes to live with an old friend. There she is surprised to see Mortimer's dog, sent, she discovers later, as a joke, unknown to the Delviles. She speaks aloud of her love for its master and turns to discover Mortimer beside her. She agrees to a secret wedding, but Monckton, chosen as their confidant, persuades her of the wrongness of the act. Cecilia goes on to London with the intention of breaking off the match, but discovery makes her feel she is compromised, and she agrees to go through with the wedding. She cannot continue, however, after a disguised woman interrupts the ceremony. Later, Mrs. Delvile, whose family pride exceeds her love for Cecilia, makes her promise to give up Mortimer. She renounces him in a passionate scene during which Mrs. Delvile bursts a blood vessel. Cecilia consoles her misery by acts of charity that Monckton, feeling that she is squandering his money, tries in vain to prevent.

Finally of age, Cecilia goes to London with the Moncktons. There she discharges her debt to Monckton. Abused by Mr. Delvile, she is sure that someone slandered her. When Cecilia goes to visit Henrietta, Mr. Delvile sees her there. Having just heard Mrs. Belfield say that Cecilia loves her son, his suspicions of Cecilia's impurity are confirmed. Mrs. Harrel and Henrietta move with Cecilia into her new home. Mortimer comes to tell her that both his parents have agreed to a plan. If she will renounce her uncle's fortune, he will marry her, although she will have only the ten thousand pounds inherited from her father. Mr. Delvile knows, however, that she has already lost her father's money. Enraged at his father's treachery, Mortimer is determined to marry Cecilia, even though she is portionless. She agrees, but only if his mother will consent. Again, a secret wedding is planned, this time with Mrs. Delvile's approbation. They are married; Cecilia returns to her house, and Mortimer goes to inform his father.

A woman Cecilia befriends identifies Mrs. Monckton's companion as the person who had stopped the first wedding.

Mortimer is prevented from telling his father of the marriage by the scandals with which Delvile charges Cecilia. Upon learning that the slanderer is Monckton, Mortimer fights and wounds him and is forced to flee. The man who is to inherit Cecilia's fortune, since her husband did not take her name, demands his rights. Cecilia determines to join her husband. Mrs. Harrel takes Henrietta with her to Arnott's house. Cecilia hopes that Henrietta, as miserable in her hopeless love for Mortimer as Arnott is in his for Cecilia, will comfort and be comforted by him.

In London, Cecilia consults Belfield about her trip. Mrs. Belfield, hoping to get her son married to Cecilia, leaves them alone when Mortimer enters. The meeting seems to confirm his father's accusations, and he sends her to wait for him at his father's house. Mr. Delvile refuses to admit her. Wild with fear that Mortimer will fight a duel with Belfield, she begins a distracted search for her husband. Fevered, delirious, and alone, she is locked up by strangers. When Mortimer finds her, convinced of her purity by Belfield, she is too sick to know him.

After many days of uncertainty, Cecilia eventually recovers. Monckton also is out of danger and grudgingly admits that he deliberately lied to Mr. Delvile about Cecilia's moral character. Mr. Delvile then accepts her as his daughter. Mrs. Delvile recovers her health, and Mrs. Harrel marries again and resumes her life of careless frivolity. Arnott and Henrietta marry. With Mortimer's help, Belfield finally settles down to an army career. Monckton lives on in bitterness and misery. Impressed by Cecilia's unselfishness and sweetness, Mortimer's aunt wills her a fortune. Cecilia is then able to continue her charities, though never extravagantly. She does occasionally regret the loss of her own fortune but wisely recognizes that life cannot be absolutely perfect.

Critical Evaluation:

Following the phenomenal success of Burney's first novel, *Evelina: Or, The History of a Young Lady's Entrance into the World* (1778), *Cecilia: Or, Memoirs of an Heiress* shares thematic elements with its predecessor but demonstrates a marked shift in technique and style. Burney abandons the epistolary form of her first novel, adopting a third-person, omniscient narrative. This narrative approach provides a distant perspective that allows the author to delve into more diverse personal viewpoints and to cross various social boundaries. Critics have traditionally viewed this novel as flawed compared to Burney's earlier effort, but *Cecilia* was nevertheless admired by the great Samuel Johnson. Although the novel lacks the sentimental happy ending characteristic of eighteenth century fiction, thereby provoking much complaint among her readers, the novel was commercially highly successful. The novel's literary influence was considerable. Novelist William Godwin first parodied it and then tried to emulate it in *The Adventures of Caleb Williams: Or, Things as They Are* (1794); Jane Austen's classic novel *Pride and Prejudice* (1813) is also indebted to *Cecilia*.

The novel combines two major themes, those of romantic love and the destructive power of the love of money. These themes are interwoven in the major plot line and in the numerous subplots involving characters who come in and out of Cecilia's life. The tension of the novel derives from Cecilia's attempt to reconcile two impulses in her life: the desires to marry the man she loves and to have independence and meaningful work. The great irony of the novel is that to have one, she must surrender the other.

When Cecilia arrives in London, her country upbringing has prepared her to see through the sham of society, and she is aware that her well-attended reception springs more out of interest in her wealth than out of genuine regard for her personally. With a too trusting nature, at first Cecilia finds the frivolous nature of the upper classes merely amusing. When the flighty Miss Larolles, for example, recalls how a friend's fortunate illness allows her to attend a party in her place, Cecilia does not realize, as she later learns through the course of the novel, that such insensitivity can and often does lead to downright cruelty. As Cecilia gradually discovers the true nature of some of the people she trusts, Burney exposes the hypocrisy and materialism of London society in increasingly harsh terms.

Understandably, Cecilia is repeatedly disappointed by these people. Cecilia considers Mrs. Harrel an old and close friend and looks forward to living with her; however, Mrs. Harrel is entirely absorbed with her own vain pursuits, caught up in her husband's irresponsible insistence on living beyond their means and allowing him to take advantage of Cecilia, thus exhausting his ward's fortune. When Cecilia discovers the utter destitution of the family of Mr. Hill, a laborer whom Harrel refuses to pay, the young woman must face the extreme, tragic consequences of this reckless disregard for others. Mrs. Delvile, seemingly gracious and kind, withdraws her friendship upon learning of her son's interest in marrying Cecilia, whom she considers socially inferior. Mortimer listens to malicious gossip and jumps to conclusions about Cecilia's behavior regarding men and money. Furthermore, he weakly surrenders to his family's vain rejection of Cecilia as an appropriate bride. His careless actions lead to Cecilia's madness, homelessness, and complete isolation. Her trusted confidant, Mr. Monckton, turns out to be the one responsible for spreading the false rumors about Cecilia

and most deliberately sabotaging her happiness. Finally, none of Cecilia's guardians cares for her. One squanders her fortune, one advises her out of his own miserliness, and another considers her a nuisance and socially inadequate.

Society's obsession with wealth and related superficial concerns is at the root of all of this deceit. Mrs. Belfield, in educating her son to be part of the upper class, destroys him by distorting his values and ignores her other children, including Henrietta, the most loyal and noble character in the entire novel and Cecilia's only true friend. The Delviles' obsession with their family name, despite the fact that it has long ceased reflecting any real power or wealth, is the most frustrating example of the emptiness of society's values. Such vanity leads to much suffering and ultimately threatens to ruin the lives of Cecilia and Mortimer.

Although the plot contains an excess of coincidences, and the novel presents a number of minor characters who serve no plot function and who do not generate much interest, the novel does contain some memorable, well-crafted scenes. The masquerade ball intrigues, in which Cecilia makes mistakes about the identities of her disguised suitors, provide suspense and irony. The suicide of Harrel at Vauxhall is dramatic and affecting. His note, naming Cecilia's refusal to marry Sir Robert Floyer as the cause of his financial ruin, is a final revelation into the character of Cecilia's selfish guardian.

Although much of the dialogue is stilted and artificial and the authorial narrative intrusive, some of Burney's colorful characters emerge vividly. The miserly Mr. Briggs's speech is abbreviated, reflecting his stinginess, as if he does not want to waste words any more than he does money. Captain Aresby sprinkles his speech with French phrases self-consciously, a detail that allows Burney to provide humor to the novel as well as satirically expose such social pretenses.

Critical assessment of *Cecilia* diverges significantly. Some critics argue that *Cecilia* and subsequent works by Burney are inferior to *Evelina* and that Burney lost her spontaneity and abandoned her genuine voice as she yielded to the pressures of fame and the expectations of her readership. Others insist that Burney progressively improved, and that the later novels demonstrate a maturity and a growing sophistication of thought. This discrepancy can be attributed to the position of *Cecilia* in the development of the novel. Less conventional in theme as well as structure than *Evelina*, Burney's second novel is a product of some risk-taking. The unsatisfying, perhaps unconvincing, reconciliation of Cecilia with Mortimer and his mother, which ends the novel, and Cecilia's acceptance of human love as being by nature imperfect, do not correspond to those of any previous genre. The philosopher

Edmund Burke, who otherwise admired Burney's work, wished for either a happier or a more miserable ending to *Cecilia*, not the compromise with which it ends. Frances Burney insisted that her characterizations and her novel's conclusion are more realistic in their ambiguity. As Burney attempted to mirror a society she viewed with an increasingly mature and critical eye, such innovations were perhaps inevitable.

"Critical Evaluation" by Lou Thompson

Further Reading

Chisholm, Kate. *Fanny Burney: Her Life, 1752-1840.* London: Chatto & Windus, 1998. Biography that is partially based on the diaries that Burney kept from the age of sixteen, which offer a detailed description of life in Georgian England. Chisholm depicts Burney as a highly talented writer and places Burney's life and work within the context of her times.

Cutting-Gray, Joanne. *Woman as "Nobody" and the Novels of Fanny Burney.* Gainesville: University Press of Florida, 1992. Cutting-Gray detects significance in Burney's writing to "Nobody" in her diary and argues that the recurring theme of namelessness in Burney's work reflects the identity problems of eighteenth century women. Contains informative notes, a bibliography, and an index.

Daugherty, Tracy Edgar. *Narrative Techniques in the Novels of Fanny Burney.* New York: Peter Lang, 1989. A reexamination of the technical aspects of Burney's novels in the light of modern narrative theory. Daugherty considers point of view, plot, tempo, and characterization. He also evaluates Burney's novels within a broad context and objectively outlines the weaknesses as well as the strengths of *Cecilia.* A bibliography and an index are provided.

Epstein, Julia. *The Iron Pen: Frances Burney and the Politics of Women's Writing.* Madison: University of Wisconsin Press, 1989. Epstein's objective is to point out an overlooked theme in Burney's writing: the tension between the public, proper lady and the private, angry writer. The prominence of violence in the novels prefigures the direction of the novel toward the gothic, a genre dominated by women. Extensive notes and a selected but lengthy bibliography are included.

Harman, Claire. *Fanny Burney: A Biography.* New York: Alfred A. Knopf, 2001. An accessible and authoritative biography. Harman points out inconsistencies in Burney's memoirs, providing a more accurate account of the author's life and placing Burney within the broader context of her times.

Rogers, Katherine M. *Frances Burney: The World of "Female Difficulties."* New York: Harvester Wheatsheaf, 1990. Looks at *Cecilia* as social satire, as depicting an awkward blending of individuality and conformity, and as accepting and resisting society. Argues that Burney's intense depiction of the psychology of women is perhaps her greatest contribution to the development of the novel.

Sabor, Peter, ed. *The Cambridge Companion to Frances Burney.* New York: Cambridge University Press, 2007. Collection of essays covering Burney's life and work, including an essay discussing both *Cecilia* and *Evelina.* Other essays survey her critical reputation, political views, and Burney and gender issues.

Simons, Judy. *Fanny Burney.* New York: Barnes & Noble, 1987. Comprehensive study of Burney's works, including journals and plays. Argues that *Cecilia,* although lacking spontaneity, demonstrates a maturing of vision and incisive social criticism. Cecilia is not a typical eighteenth century heroine of sensibility, but a rationalist, a woman who wants independence.

Thaddeus, Janice Farrar. *Frances Burney: A Literary Life.* New York: St. Martin's Press, 2000. Scholarly account of Burney's life and career that greatly expands the reader's understanding of the novelist. Includes discussion of her four novels, as well as a genealogical table, notes, and index.

Zonitch, Barbara. *Familiar Violence: Gender and Social Upheaval in the Novels of Frances Burney.* Newark: University of Delaware Press, 1997. Devotes individual chapters to analysis of *Evelina* and Burney's other novels. Zonitch's introduction, "Social Transformations: The Crisis of the Aristocracy and the Status of Women," is especially useful to understanding Burney's place within eighteenth century English society.

Celestina

Author: Fernando de Rojas (c. 1465-1541)
First published: Comedia de Calisto y Melibea, 1499;
  revised edition, 1502, as *Tragicomedia de Calisto y
  Melibea* (English translation, 1631)
Type of work: Novel
Type of plot: Tragicomedy
Time of plot: Fifteenth century
Locale: Spain, probably Toledo

Principal characters:
CALISTO, a young nobleman
MELIBEA, his beloved
PLEBERIO, her father
ALISA, her mother
CELESTINA, a procurer
ELICIA and AREUSA, the girls in Celestina's house
SEMPRONIO and PÁRMENO, Calisto's servants

The Story:

One day, while pursuing his stray falcon, Calisto enters a strange garden where he sees and falls in love with a beautiful young woman named Melibea. His eagerness to take advantage of her gentle innocence shocks her, and she angrily drives him away. Calisto goes home desolate and ready to die; his only comfort is the melancholy tunes he plays on his lute. One of his servants, Sempronio, lets him suffer for a time before he suggests that his master seek the aid of Celestina, a procurer, with whose servant, Elicia, Sempronio is in love. At Calisto's command, the servant hurries to Celestina's house to summon the old bawd. He and the procurer agree to work together to cheat lovesick Calisto. The young nobleman has another servant, Pármeno, who once worked in Celestina's house. He tells his master of the bawd's evil reputation throughout the city and warns him against her.

Ignoring the warning, Calisto welcomes Celestina and offers her gold to act as a go-between in his suit. While he is upstairs getting the money for her, Celestina tries to win Pármeno to her side by assuring him that she is interested in his welfare because of her fondness for his mother. She also promises to help him in winning the affections of Areusa, whom he covets. Pármeno, knowing her tricks, is not entirely convinced.

Unable to control his impatience to make Melibea his own, Calisto sends Sempronio to hurry Celestina in her efforts. Refusing to consider Pármeno's suggestion that he court Melibea honorably instead of trusting a notorious go-between, he does, however, order his horse so that he can ride past her house. He rides away after further criticism of Pármeno for trying to cross his desires, harsh words that make the servant regret his decision to remain faithful to his young master.

When Sempronio arrives at Celestina's house, he finds her making a love charm. While she is busy, he and Elicia make love. Then Celestina, who weighed the threat to her life

from Melibea's father against the gold that a grateful Calisto will pay her, goes to talk to Melibea. Lucrecia, a servant in the household, sees the go-between coming and warns Melibea's mother against Celestina, but Alisa thinks the woman no more than a vendor of sewing materials, hair nets, and feminine makeup. Trustingly, she asks Celestina to stay with Melibea while she herself goes to visit a sick sister.

Celestina first tells Melibea that she comes on behalf of a sick man. After purposely confusing Melibea, she finally explains that all Calisto wants is a rope belt that was taken on pilgrimages to Rome and Jerusalem and a copy of a prayer by Saint Polonia, supposed to cure toothaches. Ashamed of what she thinks are unjust suspicions of the old bawd, Melibea gives her the rope girdle and promises to copy the charm so that it will be ready by the next day. Before she leaves the house, Celestina wins Lucrecia to her side by promising to sweeten the maid's breath and to make her a blond. Going to Calisto's house, the procurer boasts of her success, and the grateful lover promises her a new cloak. By that time, Pármeno decides to accept Celestina's offer and help her in her scheme. He suggests that he accompany her home. On the way he demands that she make arrangements to have him spend the night with Areusa. Celestina takes him to her house, where Areusa is in bed, and persuades the woman that Pármeno will comfort her during her sweetheart's absence.

The next day, while the servants are dining at Celestina's house, Lucrecia arrives with word that her mistress is ill and wishes to see the procurer. The bawd goes at once to Pleberio's house, where she discovers that Melibea's disease is lovesickness for Calisto. Celestina promises to cure the malady by having Calisto call at Melibea's door at midnight.

When she reports this latest development to Calisto, her news wins his regard so completely that he gives her a gold chain. Having no intention of dividing it with her partners, she refuses to agree when Sempronio and Pármeno demand their share. While they quarrel, she screams for the police. The servants silence her forever, but her screams are heard. Sempronio and Pármeno try to escape through a window but are injured in the fall. The authorities behead them on the spot.

In the meantime, Calisto goes to Pleberio's house, where he finds Melibea eagerly awaiting him. While the lovers talk through the door, his cowardly attendants, who are supposed to be guarding him, run away from imaginary enemies. The confusion awakens her parents, but Melibea explains that Lucrecia made the noise while she was getting a drink for her mistress.

The next morning, Calisto awakens happy, only to be saddened by news of Sempronio's and Pármeno's fate. The thought of seeing Melibea in her garden that night is enough to make him forget what happened, however, except for a fleeting thought that Celestina's bawdry is now punished. With another servant to carry a ladder, he goes that night to the garden and climbs over the wall. Melibea is waiting for him. When the time for parting comes, hours later, she laments the loss of her maidenhood. Calisto mourns only the shortness of their time together.

Grieved by the loss of their servant sweethearts, Elicia and Areusa are determined to avenge their deaths. By pretending to be in love with Sosia, another of Calisto's servants, Areusa learns that the lovers are meeting secretly each night in Pleberio's garden. Eager for her favors, Sosia is willing to join in the plot. Neither he nor the women are prepared for violence, however, and so they play up to a scoundrelly soldier and murderer named Centurio. Elicia, who takes over Celestina's house after the old bawd's death, has Areusa offer herself to Centurio if he will go into the garden and kill, or at least beat up, Calisto. At first the bully agrees, but prudent reconsideration convinces him that it will be unwise to meddle in the affair. Instead, he arranges to have several friends go to the garden and make a noisy but harmless commotion.

Meanwhile, Pleberio and Alisa talk over plans to marry off their daughter. Overhearing their conversation and conscience-stricken because she has spent every night of the past month with Calisto, Melibea almost confesses her wrongdoing to her unsuspecting parents. Once more Calisto goes to the garden with his servant and ladder and makes his way over the wall. A short time later, Centurio's friends arrive and pretend to get into a fight with Sosia in the street outside. Calisto is aroused by the disturbance. Despite Melibea's fears, he starts hastily over the wall to go to the aid of his servant.

He falls from the wall and is killed. Lucrecia, frightened by the vehemence of her mistress's sorrow, awakens Pleberio and Alisa. Meanwhile, Melibea climbs to the roof of the house. There she reflects upon the effect her actions will have on her parents. Her resolve to die unweakened by their pleadings, she compares herself to many parricides of antiquity, confesses her misdeeds, and bids them farewell. Then she leaps to her death. Pleberio carries her shattered body into the house, where he and Alisa sit alone in their grief.

Critical Evaluation:

Although written in dramatic form, with conventional division into acts, this work is regarded as a novel in dialogue because its excessive length and frequently shifting scenes make performance, without significant editing, impossible on any stage. In the 1499 version, the story consists of sixteen acts, which were increased to twenty-one in 1502, and at a considerably later date, to twenty-two. Some doubt has been cast upon the authenticity of certain of these additions. Although the work was published anonymously, Fernando de Rojas is generally accepted as the author, the chief evidence being an acrostic poem containing his name to which one of his early publishers first called attention, as well as several legal depositions made about 1525. The writer declared that he found the first act and amused himself by completing the story at the rate of an act a day during a two-week vacation at the University of Salamanca. Rojas was the mayor of Talavera as well as an educated lawyer who enjoyed the humanistic learning of the Renaissance.

The book has appeared in many editions and a number of translations. It was the first translation into English (originally translated as *The Spanish Bawd*, 1631) of any Spanish book, and it has had a tremendous influence upon all succeeding writing in Spain. Modern critics agree that *Celestina* is among the best novels in Spanish literature. Rojas demonstrates the tendency of Renaissance writers to refer to the texts of the ancient writers and to borrow subjects from ancient writers. The plot stems from an anonymous thirteenth century Latin poem, *Pamphilus* (the protagonist's name, which Rojas converted to Calisto), which is not readily available in English translation. The *Pamphilus* story was also incorporated as an episode in the *Libro de buen amor* by the "Archpriest of Hita," Juan Ruiz, in the fourteenth century. Rojas is known to have had access to both the original *Pamphilus* and the reduction in Juan Ruiz's *Libro de buen amor*, but Rojas greatly alters his source material. Classical literature also provides themes and motifs in the work. For example, there is an allusion to Pasiphae toward the beginning of the novel. This reference establishes desire as a principal theme of the work. According to Greek legend, Pasiphae mates with the minotaur because of lust. Pasiphae's daughter Phaedra is possessed with an illicit love like her mother, but Phaedra's passion is for her stepson. Rojas's portrayal of Phaedra's monstrous lust introduces Calisto's desire for Melibea. The idea of a cord leading Phaedra's future husband Theseus out of the labyrinth after he kills the minotaur, Phaedra's half brother, further suggests the confusion of the thread that Celestina uses to cause Melibea to be receptive to her message. To achieve this cooperation, Celestina invokes the god of Greek and Roman mythology Pluto, who rules the underworld, urging him to wrap himself in the thread so that Melibea may buy it and entangle her heart in it, thereby causing her to become imbued with a strong and cruel love for Calisto.

Celestina also shows a Renaissance scholar's appreciation for varieties of language. A lover in the Petrarchan style, Calisto declares himself to be unworthy of Melibea and delights in the sensual image of his beloved. She is, as one may expect, a voluptuous Renaissance beauty, with lustrous pure white skin; big green eyes highlighted by her long, thick lashes; red full lips; and shapely figure. Melibea incarnates the traditional, naïve, proud, and imprudent young woman sparked by Calisto's wild delirium. The two young lovers, representing the upper classes, use high, periodic speech and lace their expression of sensual desire with idealistic sentiment.

Deviating from the idealism of Calisto and Melibea, the proletarian characters present the themes of unsullied greed and desire. For example, Sempronio, Calisto's servant, connives with Celestina to profit monetarily from his master's passion. Sempronio introduces Calisto to Celestina, a witch shrewd in evil machinations, under the pretense that she may fix the affront to his master's honor, as well as to his ego, that occurs when Melibea initially rejects him in her garden. Celestina's great linguistic ability in the areas of persuasion and selling is linked to the devil. Frankness, superstition, and greed enable her to manipulate the other characters. Celestina's manipulative techniques are demonstrated in her dealings with the characters of both the upper and the lower classes. To convince Melibea to give Calisto her girdle and a prayer, Celestina skillfully uses psychology; the procurer makes Melibea feel sorry for her advanced age and for Calisto's toothache. Celestina uses popular speech and proverbs to persuade Pármeno, Calisto's other servant, to join Sempronio and her in extracting money from Calisto.

Celestina, not the somewhat unsympathetic lovers, is the main character of the novel. The novel's concentration upon surreptitious matchmaking and witchcraft is, at least in part, a reflection of the interests of the times. Rojas (a Jew converted to Christianity under the threat of immolation at the hands of the Holy Inquisition) is distinctly aware of the fate

of witches and other heretics. His portrait of Celestina is thus acutely sensitive and extraordinarily vivid.

Celestina has no religious identification; she could be Christian, Muslim, or Jew, for all three faiths coexisted in late medieval Spain. Her allegiance seems firmly rooted in the spirits of evil, judging from her imperious conjuration of the devil in act 3. Her affiliation with the occult is firmly established in the catalog of her pharmaceuticals detailed in acts 1, 3, and 7 and elsewhere. From her early sympathy for Areusa's abdominal cramps to her own susceptibility to fears of death, she remains a very human and humane criminal. Celestina truly recognizes the limitations of her powers, and in that recognition, she becomes a vulnerable, credible human being with relevance to her times and to any reader's own. Fernando de Rojas's creation of a dialogue novel, and of a character as singular as Celestina, became significant in the development of realism. The novel is a milestone in the development of literature. *Celestina* influenced the novel and drama in Spain and abroad.

Further Reading

Barbera, Raymond. "No puede creer que la tenga en su poder." *Romanic Review* 28, no. 1 (January, 1991): 105. A concise article in English that treats the relationship between the characters by developing the sentence that serves as the article's title. Describes the role of ambiguity in *Celestina*.

Burke, James F. *Vision, the Gaze, and the Function of the Senses in "Celestina."* University Park: Pennsylvania State University Press, 2000. Uses medieval theories about perception, including the belief that each individual was surrounded by an all-encompassing sensual field, to analyze the characters' actions.

Castells, Ricardo. *Fernando de Rojas and the Renaissance Vision: Phantasm, Melancholy, and Didacticism in "Celestina."* University Park: Pennsylvania State University Press, 2000. Seeks to resolve the illogical progression of *Celestina*'s plot by applying Renaissance concepts of dreams, phantoms, lovesickness, and melancholy to an analysis of the work.

Dunn, Peter. *Fernando de Rojas*. New York: Twayne, 1975. Provides a detailed summary of each act in *Celestina* followed by a helpful commentary. Acquaints the reader with literary evaluation by discussing the genre, antecedents, characters, and structure of the work.

Fontes, Manuel da Costa de. *The Art of Subversion in Inquisitorial Spain: Rojas and Delicado*. West Lafayette, Ind.: Purdue University Press, 2005. Writing during the height of the Inquisition, Spanish authors of Jewish extraction, such as Rojas and Francisco Delicado, could not openly express their doubts about Christianity. Fontes describes how *Celestina* and Delicado's *La Lozana andaluza* used superficial bawdiness and claims of morality to covertly denounce Christian dogma.

Gilman, Stephen. *The Spain of Fernando de Rojas*. Princeton, N.J.: Princeton University Press, 1972. Recounts the life of Rojas. Depicts the difficult circumstances that his Jewish family, converted to Catholicism, confronted in Spain.

Martin, June Hall. *Love's Fools: Aucassin, Troilus, Calisto, and the Parody of the Courtly Lover.* London: Tamesis Books, 1972. Explains the late medieval tradition of moralistic satire. Shows how Calisto exemplifies the parody of courtly love.

Simpson, Lesley Byrd. Introduction to *The Celestina*, by Fernando de Rojas. Berkeley: University of California Press, 1971. The introduction to this translation by Simpson situates the work in literary history. Gives a brief synopsis of the plot and a character analysis.

The Cenci
A Tragedy in Five Acts

Author: Percy Bysshe Shelley (1792-1822)
First produced: 1886; first published, 1819
Type of work: Drama
Type of plot: Tragedy
Time of plot: 1599
Locale: Rome and the Apennines

Principal characters:
COUNT FRANCESCO CENCI, a Roman nobleman
BEATRICE, his daughter
BERNARDO, his son
GIACOMO, another son
LUCRETIA, his wife and stepmother to his children
ORSINO, a priest once loved by Beatrice
OLIMPIO and MARZIO, assassins of Cenci
SAVELLA, a papal legate who discovers the murder of Cenci
CARDINAL CAMILLO, a merciful churchman

The Story:

Count Cenci is a cruel and brutal man whose greatest delight is to make people suffer. He sends two of his sons to Salamanca in the hope that they will starve. His daughter, Beatrice, was in love with Orsino, who enters the priesthood. She does not know where to turn for solace. Her father is worse than cruel to her, while her lover became a priest. Orsino promises to present to the pope a petition in which Beatrice begs relief from the sadistic abuses she and the rest of her family are suffering from her father. Beatrice tells Orsino of a banquet her father is giving that night in celebration of some news from Salamanca and says that she will give him the petition at that time. After they part, Orsino reveals his lust for her and resolves not to show the pope her petition, lest she be married by the pope's order and Orsino be left without a chance of winning her outside wedlock. He resolves also not to ask for special permission to marry lest he lose his own large income from the Church.

At the banquet that night, Cenci announces the purpose of his celebration: His two sons were killed by accident in Salamanca. Since they defied his tyranny, Cenci feels that this is well-deserved punishment. At first the guests cannot believe their ears. Beatrice boldly begs that the guests protect her, her stepmother, and her remaining two brothers from further cruelties at the hands of her father. Cenci, telling them she is insane, asks the guests to leave. Then he turns on his daughter, threatens her with a new cruelty, and orders her and his wife to accompany him to his castle in the Apennines on the following Monday.

At the Cenci palace, Beatrice discloses to her stepmother that Cenci committed a crime against her that she dare not name. Orsino comes to the women and proposes a plan for the assassination of Cenci. At the bridge on the way to the Apennines he will station two desperate killers who will be glad to murder Cenci. Giacomo enters to announce that he loaned his father his wife's dowry and was not able to recover it. In fact, Cenci suggests to Giacomo's wife that her husband is a wastrel who spent the money in riotous living. Orsino assures Giacomo that the pope, sympathizing with fathers, not children, will not restore his money. Egged on by Orsino, Beatrice and Giacomo conspire with him to murder their father.

Later Orsino comes to report to Giacomo that his father escaped from the plot and is safe within his castle in the Apennines. Giacomo then resolves to kill his father by his own hand, but Orsino says that he knows two men whom Cenci wronged who would be willing to rid the earth of their persecutor. At the castle in the Apennines, Cenci rages against the insolence of his daughter and confesses to Lucretia that he tried to corrupt the soul of Beatrice. While he is sleeping, the two murderers, Olimpio and Marzio, appear. Lucretia says she put a sleeping potion in Cenci's drink to make him sleep soundly. The two men are hesitant. Olimpio reports that he cannot kill an old man in his sleep. Marzio thinks he hears the ghost of his own dead father speaking through the lips of the sleeping Cenci. Beatrice snatches a dagger from them and crisd out that she will kill the fiend. Shamed into action, the assassins strangle Cenci and throw his body over the balustrade into the garden.

The papal legate, Savella, arrives with a warrant for the immediate execution of Cenci for his crimes. When Savella and his followers discover that Cenci is already dead, they begin an investigation. The guards seize Marzio, on whose person they find Orsino's note introducing the two murderers. Lucretia and Beatrice deny knowledge of the handwriting, but Savella arrests them to make them appear before the court in Rome. Giacomo, tricked by Orsino, falls into the hands of the Roman police. Orsino escapes in disguise.

Under torture, Marzio confesses, implicating the others. Threatened with torture herself, Beatrice swears to her purity and innocence, convincing Cardinal Camillo but not the judge. Marzio, confronted by her impassioned plea, denies that Beatrice is guilty of parricide. The judge sends him back to the wheel, but he dies with no further words. Camillo's pleas against further torture are futile, and Lucretia and Giacomo soon confess. Beatrice, to avoid torture, ceases denying her guilt. As they await execution, she reasserts her family leadership, comforting the others, even the distressed Camillo.

Critical Evaluation:

The Cenci is Percy Bysshe Shelley's poetic tragedy of the moral depravity that he believed tyranny fosters. It treats Shelley's favorite theme: the moral imagination as the faculty that awakens, through its capacity to empathize with others, sympathetic love, which defeats despotism. In this play, however, Shelley renounces his typical visionary ideal-

ism wherein love conquers unjust power. Instead, he presents the realism, as he sees it, of a world in which victims of absolute power have no recourse to mitigating moral sympathies. The drama, in blank verse, follows Elizabethan tragic form.

As did Shakespeare and other tragedians, Shelley took his plot from historical events. The sordid tale of the Cenci family in late sixteenth century Rome was a well-known legend through its many retellings. The story often is structured to represent a political struggle for liberty from feudal and papal tyranny. Converting history to art, Shelley minimizes the sensationalism of his source, emphasizing not the brutish details but the conflict between moral evil, which delights in the mental agony of its victims, and spiritual innocence, which can be violated by that evil. The play suggests that paternal tyranny succeeds only with the support of institutionalized powers of church and state. These powers were the causes, to Shelley, of a corrupt society. *The Cenci* is therefore a realistic representation of the same conflict that Shelley developed concurrently in the idealistic *Prometheus Unbound* (1820). Beatrice, the figure of defeated liberty erring tragically by seeking vengeance and perpetuating the cycle of violence, represents, mythically, a good that is helpless to overcome evil.

Dramatizing his revolutionary claim that power causes immoral abuse and only loving sympathy creates the conditions for justice, Shelley develops a rather bare historical account into fully motivated action. The tyranny of church and state produces the sadistic personal despot Francesco Cenci and the self-interested manipulator Orsino. The same unjust powers produce the weak, vacillating Giacomo; the helpless Lucretia; the broken-spirited Bernardo; the desperate hired killers; and the brutally victimized Beatrice. The kind Cardinal Camillo is Shelley's addition, for dramatic purposes, to history. The cardinal's fruitless appeals to Cenci show the limits of religion to convert diabolism, as his announcements of punishing fines enact Shelley's belief that the Church tolerated abuses to increase its wealth. Furthermore, Camillo's empathy for Beatrice balances the self-referential attitudes of Pope Clement VIII, who sees the murdered Cenci as another wronged father, justified in demanding total obedience. The dramatic contrast emphasizes Shelley's distinction between true empathy and sympathy, which extends only to others perceived as like oneself.

Unlike many closet dramas of the period, *The Cenci* was originally intended for stage production. Shelley sent detailed instructions to his friend Thomas Love Peacock concerning choices of actors for presentation at Covent Garden. He expected that the play's factual base would justify its content to the prudish and that its argument for liberty would appeal to revolutionary sympathies in England. However, he reckoned without the strength of idealistic literary taste and reactionary Tory censorship, which, missing the moral tragedy, decreed incest and parricide unfit subjects. The play was first produced in 1886, privately, by the Shelley Society. Since then, post-Victorian responses to several productions have affirmed that *The Cenci* is among the best verse dramas since Elizabethan times. Although the ascendancy of literary realism made the subject acceptable, it also made verse drama become less popular.

Apart from early censorship, the major critical question the play evokes concerns whether Beatrice's claims of innocence against the charge of conspiracy to murder her father are consistent with the character of a tragic protagonist, who, by classical standards, should assume responsibility for her actions. A related issue bears upon the larger question of tragedy in the modern world, in which human beings are often defined as helpless products of the circumstances that molded them instead of creatures who freely make their tragic choices. Since Shelley's revolutionary politics led him to define social evil as resulting from tyrannical power and to present character as formed by conditions that surround it, the question is whether Beatrice, as a brutalized victim, can possess tragic stature. Most post-Victorian critics and reviewers agreed that she can. Shelley carefully portrays her in the early acts as innocent and righteous, attempting every available solution for her family's protection from the fiendish paternal sadism that is known to church officials, including her former beloved, and to the social circle attending the banquet. All but the pope fear Cenci too much to check his despotism, and Shelley motivates the pope's inaction by the fines for Cenci's crimes that feed the Church coffers. When Beatrice's appeals fail and Cenci rapes her, his act temporarily deranges her natural nobility to a state of hysterical despair in which she chooses murder instead of believing, as Shelley did, that the act of another person cannot dishonor her. That she maintains her innocence to the papal court is consistent with the moral conflict between her goodness and Cenci's hatefully wanton will to corrupt. Her sense that she is a divine instrument ridding the world of monstrous evil is her tragic hubris. Shelley adds to the historical source Savella's sudden appearance with a warrant for Cenci's death, contrasting papal power with the family's helplessness. That Beatrice regains her self-possession and goes to her execution expressing loving care for Bernardo and Lucretia demonstrates her reassertion of a dignity that rises above her vengeful hysteria induced by her father's perverted violence. This self-possession is consistent with the character of a tragic heroine.

Some scholars conjectured that a biographical impulse underlies the parent-child conflict. Cenci's unpaternal avarice and tyranny toward his children echoes, one may argue, Shelley's experience with his father, Sir Timothy Shelley. Certainly Shelley's early experiences with a demanding father and an unaccepting society gave impetus to his works, which extol individual liberty of the spirit and argue for an end to social cruelties.

"Critical Evaluation" by Carolyn F. Dickinson

Further Reading

Behrendt, Stephen C. "Beatrice Cenci and the Tragic Myth of History." In *History & Myth: Essays on English Romantic Literature*, edited by Stephen C. Behrendt. Detroit, Mich.: Wayne State University Press, 1990. Argues that Beatrice's situation is like that of the English people in 1819. Shelley's play argues that the English needed to temper their urges toward violence to avoid self-destruction.

Cameron, Kenneth Neill. *Shelley: The Golden Years*. Cambridge, Mass.: Harvard University Press, 1974. Analyzes Shelley's transmutation of his source into *The Cenci*. Includes notes and bibliography.

Curran, Stuart. *Shelley's "Cenci": Scorpions Ringed with Fire*. Princeton, N.J.: Princeton University Press, 1970. Forms a basis for subsequent commentaries on the play, covering its historical context, Shelley's changes from his source, the play's critical reception, and its literary, philosophic, and mythic dimensions. Includes illustrations and notes.

Duffy, Cian. *Shelley and the Revolutionary Sublime*. New York: Cambridge University Press, 2005. Focuses on Shelley's fascination with sublime natural phenomena and how this interest influenced his writing and ideas about political and social reform.

Ferriss, Suzanne. "Reflection in a 'Many-Sided Mirror': Shelley's *The Cenci* Through the Post-Revolutionary Prism." *Nineteenth-Century Contexts* 15, no. 2 (1991): 161-170. Argues that Beatrice's succumbing to the urge toward vengeful violence is analogous to the French Revolution's descent to the Reign of Terror. Maintains that the play reflects Shelley's skepticism concerning the achievement of revolutionary ideals.

Henderson, Andrea K. "Incarnate Imagination and *The Cenci*." In *Romantic Identities: Varieties of Subjectivity, 1774-1830*. New York: Cambridge University Press, 1996. Describes the play's concept of selfhood, which is depicted as the relationship of an individual's external and inner being. Argues that the external being is expressed through masks, costumes, and other forms of theatricality, while the inner being is likened to the poetic concepts of imagination and beauty.

Morton, Timothy, ed. *The Cambridge Companion to Shelley.* New York: Cambridge University Press, 2006. Ten essays on various aspects of Shelley's life and work, including Shelley as a lyricist, dramatist, storyteller, political poet, and translator, and the literary reception of his writings. The references to *The Cenci* are listed in the index.

Reiman, Donald H. *Percy Bysshe Shelley.* New York: Twayne, 1969. Offers an excellent interpretive synopsis of the play, including an analysis of Beatrice as a tragic protagonist. Includes bibliography and notes.

Wasserman, Earl R. *Shelley: A Critical Reading.* Baltimore: Johns Hopkins University Press, 1971. The chapter on *The Cenci* discusses the play in full detail, focusing on Shelley's reference to the play's being based on "sad reality."

Ceremony

Author: Leslie Marmon Silko (1948-   )
First published: 1977
Type of work: Novel
Type of plot: Social realism
Time of plot: Just after World War II
Locale: Laguna, New Mexico

Principal characters:
TAYO, a Laguna Pueblo veteran of World War II
ROCKY, Tayo's cousin and best friend
JOSIAH, Tayo's beloved uncle
THE NIGHT SWAN, Josiah's lover
TS'EH, Tayo's lover
AUNTIE, Tayo's aunt who raises him
GRANDMA, Tayo's grandmother
KU'OOSH, a traditional Laguna healer
BETONIE, a nontraditional healer in Gallup
EMO, Tayo's war buddy

The Story:

Tayo and Rocky join the Army because Rocky wants to join and because they both want to travel. However, the young men did not plan on seeing the Philippine jungle and the death that occurs there. Tayo cannot bring himself to shoot Japanese soldiers because they all resemble his uncle Josiah. Rocky is killed, and as the rain pours down incessantly, Tayo curses it and begs for it to stop.

Back at Laguna, New Mexico, Tayo sees the result of his curse. The land is dry, and nothing is growing. Tayo is as sick as the land. He keeps throwing up and cannot eat. Tayo's family decides that he needs a healing ceremony, so the tribal healer, Ku'oosh, is called in to cure him. His ceremony, however, does not cure Tayo's sickness. Ku'oosh, knowing that Tayo needs a special ceremony, sends him to a medicine man named Betonie.

Betonie cures with elements from contemporary culture, such as old magazines and telephone books, as well as with native ceremonies. He explains Tayo's sickness to him. It is the witchery that is making Tayo sick, and it has the entire Native American population in its grip. The purpose of witchery is to prevent growth, and to grow is to survive. Betonie explains to Tayo that a new ceremony is needed and that he is a part of something much larger than his own sickness.

The Navajo medicine man makes a sand painting for Tayo to sit in to reorient him. When the ceremony is over, Betonie remarks that it is not yet complete. There are a pattern of stars, some speckled cattle, a mountain, and a woman whom Tayo has yet to encounter.

The speckled cattle are of Mexican origin, designed for the hard existence of northern New Mexico. Uncle Josiah bought them before he died, but when they were set loose to graze, they started south and kept moving, and neither Tayo nor Josiah can find them. Tayo realizes that part of his ceremony is to find these cattle.

He begins his search at the place where they last saw the cattle and soon meets a woman who lives in a nearby house. He ends up eating dinner and spending the night there. Later they make love. Tayo already had an experience like this one when, before the war, he went to the home of The Night

Swan, Josiah's lover, to tell her that Josiah could not make their appointment. After Tayo and The Night Swan made love, she said that he would remember this moment later.

While he is staying with the woman, he sees a pattern of stars in the north and decides to follow it. The search takes him to a mountain named for the swirling veils of clouds that cling to the peaks. On the mountain Tayo comes across the barbed wire of a ranch and finds the speckled cattle. He cuts the fence so they can escape toward Laguna. Two ranch hands catch Tayo but do not see the cattle in the distance. They are going to take him in but leave him when they see the tracks of a mountain lion. Still in search of the cattle, Tayo comes across a hunter with a freshly killed buck across his shoulders. The hunter suggests that Tayo's cattle are probably down in the draw by his house. Tayo follows the hunter down to the house and meets the hunter's wife, who is the same woman with whom he slept at the beginning of the search. The cattle are held in the woman's corral; they came down off the mountain the previous day. Tayo says good-bye to the woman and takes the cattle back to Laguna.

Upon returning, Tayo tells his grandmother that he is all right; the ceremony worked. He decides to stay with the cattle at the ranch rather than live among other people. There he again meets the woman, who this time calls herself Ts'eh, claiming that her Indian name is too long. They spend much time together, making love and talking. She teaches Tayo about plants and rain, and he is immersed in her love.

Ts'eh leaves and tells Tayo to remember everything she taught him. He takes a long walk and finds himself at the uranium mine. There he realizes the connection among all things of which Betonie spoke. He sees the mining and use of uranium as a sand painting created by witchery and used for destruction. In the production and release of the atomic bomb, from the first test explosion at Trinity site to the southeast to the top-secret laboratories in Los Alamos, the witchery joins everyone—Japanese, American, and Native American—into one clan united by one horrific fate. Tayo finally sees the pattern, the way all the stories fit together, and realizes that he is not crazy but is simply seeing things the way they truly are.

Critical Evaluation:

Leslie Marmon Silko's work is about the importance of stories, how they serve to orient one in the world and how they keep people and cultures alive. Her later work *Storyteller* (1981) is an attempt to weave together legends from Laguna mythology and lore, stories told by her family, her own short stories and poems, and her father's photographs of the Laguna area. The themes that are developed in *Ceremony*

regarding story and ritual are taken up in a different way in the labyrinthine and copious *Almanac of the Dead* (1991). In all of her work, however, Silko sees herself continuing what is essentially an oral tradition via the written word. The line breaks and spacing in *Storyteller* and in the verse portions of *Ceremony* are attempts to convey the pauses and stops in oral discourse, which is the way she heard these stories originally. Silko believes that stories are the lifeblood of a culture and can effect great changes in the world.

Ceremony is a multidimensional work in both form and content. The reader is immediately struck by the "interruptions" in the story. The opening pages of the novel are not prose, but verse, and speak of the mythological figure Thought-Woman "sitting in her room and whatever she thinks about appears." This figure, linked in the novel with the character Ts'eh, is associated with Grandmother Spider, a prominent figure in Laguna mythology; she is, in fact, the Creatrix herself. Versions of Laguna tales are woven into the narrative throughout the novel and parallel the story that Tayo is living. Silko's point is to show that which Tayo learns at the end of his ceremony, that "all the stories fit together— the old stories, the war stories, their stories—to become the story that was still being told."

Tayo is not so much finding himself as he is finding his place in the world. Native American writers and critics are careful to point out that finding one's place is a primary element of their culture and literature. Tayo is not the only sick one in this novel; Laguna society and the earth itself are out of sorts. Emo graphically depicts the attitude of the society when he remarks, "Look what is here for us, Look. Here's the Indians' mother earth! Old dried-up thing!" Tayo knows that Emo is wrong, but he feels disconnected from the earth as well. In fact Tayo blames himself for the drought that has made the earth an "old dried-up thing." He needs a ceremony that will restore his sense of place.

Women play a vital role in Tayo's ceremony. The encounter with The Night Swan foreshadows other ritualized encounters with women. Unlike his war buddies, who see women as conquests of war, Tayo experiences love and sex with the mysterious mountain woman, Ts'eh. Ts'eh is no doubt a shortened form of Ts'its'tsi'nako, or Thought-Woman, who begins the novel by thinking of a story. She appears in various forms but is always associated with Mount Taylor, which in Laguna is Tse'pina or Woman Veiled in Rain Clouds. She is the spirit of Mount Taylor and an extension of the earth itself. She is the feminine principle embodied and, thus, is Yellow Woman, Corn Woman, and other female figures from Laguna mythology. When Tayo makes love to these different expressions of Thought-Woman, he feels himself connected once again to a fertile and nurturing earth. He loses himself in the unity of all life and is no longer an invisible outcast; he has a place.

It is easy to see the importance of women in this novel, but an equal significance is given to language. In fact, the image of the web, Spider-Woman's web, appears throughout the novel. The spinning of the web is the spinning of tales, and these tales, if understood in the appropriate way, can effect healing for individuals, society, and the earth. On the first page of the novel, the spider is thinking of a story, and the reader is told the story she is thinking. The stories are "all we have to fight off illness and death." The stories connect everything in a web that is paradoxically both strong and fragile. When Ku'oosh first comes to offer a ceremony for Tayo, he remarks, "But you know, grandson, this world is fragile." The reader is informed that the word "fragile" is "filled with the intricacies of a continuing process" and "with a strength inherent in spider webs." Tayo realizes that even one person, acting inappropriately, can tear away the delicate web and injure the world. These descriptions of storytelling as a web of words offer a profound explanation of the nature of language in oral cultures. Silko, in writing the novel, is continuing to spin the web.

Few Native American writers have so provocatively and dramatically woven oral tradition into her work as Leslie Marmon Silko has done. Hers is a powerful voice that offers a tribal interpretation of contemporary American culture and values.

Gregory Salyer

Further Reading

Allen, Paula Gunn. "The Feminine Landscape of Leslie Marmon Silko's *Ceremony.*" In *Studies in American Indian Literature: Critical Essays and Course Designs*, edited by Allen. New York: Modern Language Association of America, 1983. A foundational essay, written by a Laguna Pueblo writer and critic, that articulates the importance of the feminine in Tayo's healing.

_____. *The Sacred Hoop: Recovering the Feminine in American Indian Traditions*. Boston: Beacon Press, 1992. Collection of seventeen essays that range from discussions of myths and symbols to contemporary literature, and from traditional family structure to American Indian feminism. Of particular interest is the essay devoted to *Ceremony*.

Chavkin, Allan, ed. *Leslie Marmon Silko's "Ceremony": A Casebook*. New York: Oxford University Press, 2002. Collection of essays interpreting Silko's novel from a variety of theoretical perspectives and providing background information on Native American culture. Some of the essays discuss animals and theme, circular design, and the function of landscape in the novel, while another compares Silko's work with that of Rudolfo Anaya. Includes an interview with Silko.

Coltelli, Laura. *Winged Words: American Indian Writers Speak*. Lincoln: University of Nebraska Press, 1990. A useful collection of interviews with major American Indian writers, including Silko. Includes a substantial discussion of *Ceremony*.

Fitz, Brewster E. *Silko: Writing Storyteller and Medicine Woman*. Norman: University of Oklahoma Press, 2004. An analysis of Silko's writing that focuses on the relationship between the written word and the oral storytelling tradition of her family and of Laguna culture.

Lincoln, Kenneth. *Native American Renaissance*. Berkeley: University of California Press, 1983. An excellent introduction to the writing of American Indians. Provides necessary background to understand key works. A thorough discussion of Silko's *Storyteller* and *Ceremony* is included.

Nelson, Robert M. *Leslie Marmon Silko's "Ceremony": The Recovery of Tradition*. New York: Peter Lang, 2008. Focuses on the Navajo and other Native American texts that form the backbone of Silko's novel, describing how she adapts and relates these texts to her narrative.

Salyer, Gregory. *Leslie Marmon Silko*. New York: Twayne, 1997. A critical study of Silko's work, describing how her fiction has been influenced by her Laguna background and by Native American stories. Includes a bibliography and an index.

Swan, Edith. "Laguna Symbolic Geography and Silko's *Ceremony*." *American Indian Quarterly* 12, no. 3 (Summer, 1988): 229-249. A thorough discussion of Laguna spiritual beliefs and symbols. Colors, animals, myths, and landscape are all explained in detail.

Teuton, Sean Kicummah. "Learning to Feel: Tribal Experience in Leslie Marmon Silko's *Ceremony*." In *Red Land, Red Power: Grounding Knowledge in the American Indian Novel*. Durham, N.C.: Duke University Press, 2008. Analyzes how *Ceremony* and other works of Native American literature from the late 1960's and the 1970's use historical memory and oral tradition to create a more "enabling knowledge" of the lives and possibilities of American Indians.

Ceremony in Lone Tree

Author: Wright Morris (1910-1998)
First published: 1960
Type of work: Novel
Type of plot: Psychological realism
Time of plot: Mid-twentieth century
Locale: Nebraska

Principal characters:
TOM SCANLON, an elderly man
LOIS MCKEE, his oldest daughter
WALTER MCKEE, Lois's husband
MAXINE MOMEYER, another daughter
BUD MOMEYER, Maxine's husband, a postal worker
LEE ROY MOMEYER, Bud's nephew, a high school boy
EDNA EWING, Tom's youngest daughter
"COLONEL" CLYDE EWING, Edna's husband, a wealthy
   Oklahoman
GORDON MCKEE, Walter's son
CALVIN MCKEE, Gordon's son
ETOILE MCKEE, Calvin's wife
GORDON BOYD, Walter's boyhood friend and hero
W. B. JENNINGS, a journalist and adventure story writer
"DAUGHTER," a hitchhiker whom Gordon Boyd picks up

The Story:

Tom Scanlon spends his life in the Lone Tree Hotel in Lone Tree, Nebraska, now a ghost town. The winter before he is ninety, his daughter Lois and her husband, Walter, take him on a trip to Mexico. There they run into Walter's old friend Gordon Boyd, who left Nebraska because he could not have Lois. Later, Walter writes to Boyd and invites him to a reunion in Lone Tree late in March, on Tom's ninetieth birthday.

After much soul-searching, Boyd leaves Acapulco in his dilapidated car and heads north. In a Nevada town, where tourists come to see nuclear bomb tests, Boyd offers a ride to a young, penniless girl. In Nebraska, after the car rolls into a ditch, Boyd and "Daughter" hop a passing freight train.

The members of Tom's family share several worries. One is the increasing violence around them. In Lincoln, Charlie Munger shot ten people, and Bud Momeyer's nephew, Lee Roy Momeyer, ran his car over two boys, killing them. Lois is concerned about her grandson Gordon McKee, who loves guns and likes to torment women. Even the friendly Bud has a sadistic streak; his hobby is shooting cats with a bow and arrow.

The women in the family also discuss the possibility of marriage between two cousins, the Momeyer girl, Etoile, and the older Gordon McKee's son, Calvin. Etoile's mother, Maxine, sees this as a chance for her daughter to catch a husband with money, but Etoile is primarily interested in sex. Calvin just wants to be free, like a cowboy. Calvin is busy planning a birthday surprise for Tom. Etoile will dress up like Tom's late wife Samantha, and the two of them will ride into Lone Tree in a mule-drawn buggy, just as in the old days.

Unable to get into high school at home, Lee Roy went to Lincoln, where he could stay with his uncle and take classes in shop and physical education. Lee Roy and Charlie Munger, who worked with him repairing cars, were regularly bullied by some boys at school. Enraged, Charlie started shooting people at random, and when the boys blocked his way once too often, Lee Roy gunned his car and ran into them.

Interested in the case, the journalist W. B. Jennings looks up Lee Roy's parents, but they say he needs to talk to Maxine and send him on to Lone Tree. On the freight train that goes in that direction, Jennings is joined by Boyd and "Daughter."

In Lone Tree, "Colonel" Clyde Ewing, his wife, Edna, and their valuable dog, Shiloh, are living in comfort in their huge trailer. The rest of the family camps out in the hotel. When Boyd arrives, he does not explain his relationship to "Daughter," but everyone is polite. The family also makes Jennings feel welcome. Maxine organizes things, cooks, and cries about being the family workhorse. Boyd keeps talking about the bomb.

At the dinner table, Walter and Boyd, who is Walter's hero, squabble about the past, and Walter calls Boyd a fool for ruining his life. When little Gordon wanders in with his grandfather's loaded pistol, Jennings manages to get first the ammunition, then the weapon, away from the child. Tom sleeps through all of this, but when Etoile appears in costume, he rises up, calling for Samantha. The Colonel is looking for Shiloh. Some time later, Bud goes out into the night with his bow and arrows.

The trip back to Lone Tree is more difficult than Calvin expects it to be. At one point, Etoile is thrown out of the buggy. When Calvin runs to her, she pulls him down onto the grass and persuades him to make love to her.

Boyd finds a 1927 newspaper, with a story announcing that Lindbergh is over the Atlantic, and broods about time. Lois thinks his notions were ridiculous. Her love is reserved for little Gordon; however, she is well aware that the child has an evil streak and enjoys making her suffer.

In the middle of the night, the buggy comes around the corner of the hotel, carrying Calvin and Etoile, entwined in each other's arms, and Bud with his trophy, the corpse of Shiloh. Lois shoots off her pistol, Tom starts toward the buggy and drops down dead, and Etoile keeps trying to announce that she and Calvin are married.

While the Colonel worries about his insurance and the rest of the family discusses what to do about their father, Calvin hitches up the mules to the covered wagon in which Tom was born. The Colonel and Edna drive off. Tom's corpse is loaded into the covered wagon; Boyd, "Daughter," Jennings, and Walter all climb on; and as Lone Tree vanishes in the dust behind them, Walter keeps urging Boyd to come back home to Nebraska.

Critical Evaluation:

Although for decades many critics have considered him one of America's most important writers, Wright Morris never attained the prominence he deserves. The reason may lie in the fact that much of his work is closely tied to a particular region of the United States, the rural Midwest, so some have misclassified Morris as a mere local-color writer. This myth should have been dispelled by his winning the National Book Award for *The Field of Vision* (1956). By this time, however, Morris was being accused of having too much to say rather than too little. In *Ceremony in Lone Tree*, Morris juggles multiple themes, complex characters, and rapid shifts in time and focus in a way that some readers find dizzying. Others, however, are exhilarated by their excursion into Morris's sometimes comic, sometimes nightmarish world, in which the only certainty is constant change.

The inevitability of change is emphasized in the first section of Morris's novel, entitled "The Scene." Tom Scanlon's home, Lone Tree, is a ghost town, with dusty, deserted streets and a hotel littered with dead flies. In contrast to Lone Tree, Walter's boyhood home, Polk, is still very much alive. It has green, tree-shaded avenues and even a new supermarket.

Polk also maintains its links with the historical past, represented by the Civil War cannon in the park, and with the personal past of Walter McKee and Gordon Boyd, who carved their initials on the cannon and who rode the sled which, although no longer used, still sits under the house where Boyd once lived. In some ways, Polk is changing; in other ways, it is unchanged. Significantly, Walter no longer lives there. He is a resident of Lincoln, where Maxine, Bud, and Etoile Momeyer also live, along with the killers, Lee Roy Momeyer and Charlie Munger.

Both Lone Tree, the ghost town, and Tom, who loves it and identifies himself with it, represent the Old West, both the reality and the illusion. Calvin McKee thinks of Tom as a Western hero, a cowboy who lived free and solitary, with just a horse and a gun for company. Threatened by Etoile's attractions and her mother's designs, Calvin goes west, as generations of restless men did before. In making Tom a hero of the frontier, however, Calvin ignores the realities of his great-grandfather's life. Even Tom's being born in a covered wagon, which was used to transport families, not individuals, indicates that the society of undomesticated men was already dying when Tom arrived on the scene. At least subconsciously, Calvin accepts this revised view of Tom's youth; when he re-creates it, he does not ride in on a horse, shooting a gun, but hitches mules to the covered wagon and puts Etoile, dressed as Tom's dead wife, on the seat beside him. Even Tom's funeral procession is certainly not what one would expect for a frontier hero. He is not laid to rest on the lone prairie, alone for eternity, but, with kinfolk and friends around him, he is loaded into the covered wagon to be taken to town.

Walter, too, finds that the person he always admired is not, after all, a hero. Gordon Boyd left Nebraska not because he was courageous, but because he was too weak to face reality, and he was drifting ever since. If he is to survive, he may have to accept Walter's generous offer, return home, and settle into a middle-class existence.

Such disillusionment is not the only result of the American male's continuing infatuation with the heroic ideal. The cowboy or the gunfighter is an individualist who makes his own rules, flees from the women who would trap him into domesticity, and, when pressed, speaks with his gun. When Calvin and Boyd act out this ideal, they do not endanger anyone but themselves, but not every hero is so harmless. Bud ventures forth to kill domestic animals, and little Gordon McKee has the same impulse in regard to human beings, especially women such as his doting grandmother.

In Charlie and Lee Roy, one can see how the Western ideal plays out in modern society. To be somebody, they believe, means to be feared, like a gunfighter in a Western movie. When such a hero encounters disrespect, he pulls out his gun, and his enemy either backs down or is killed. To Charlie, the obvious way to reestablish his worth is to shoot some people. Although Lee Roy's weapon is a car, not a gun, his will to kill heroically is the same as Charlie's.

In the myth, it is women who pose a threat to the hero; in *Ceremony in Lone Tree*, it is women who oppose the expression of the myth in the modern world. Ever since the murders in Lincoln, say Tom's daughters and daughters-in-law, they have lived in fear, and they do not like it. It is no accident that the other prevailing topic of conversation among these women is the possibility of getting Calvin married to Etoile. Instinctively, they seem to sense that the only way to disarm would-be Western heroes is to cajole them into domesticity. Otherwise, Morris suggests, by acting out their ideal, they may well destroy civilized society.

Rosemary M. Canfield Reisman

Further Reading

Crump, G. B. *The Novels of Wright Morris: A Critical Interpretation*. Lincoln: University of Nebraska Press, 1978. Argues that the primary theme of *Ceremony in Lone Tree* is the unhappy effects that the heroic ideal produces in individuals and in society. Crump's introductory discussion of earlier critical views is helpful. Includes an extensive bibliography.

Harper, Robert D. "Wright Morris's *Ceremony in Lone Tree*: A Picture of Life in Middle America." *Western American Literature* 11 (November, 1976): 199-213. In this exceptionally lucid essay, the novel is placed within the context of traditional American fiction. Unlike most of his con-

temporaries, Morris defines the hell of white, middle-class Americans.

Howard, Leon. *Wright Morris*. Minneapolis: University of Minnesota Press, 1968. A concise overview of Morris's work. In a brief discussion of *Ceremony at Lone Tree*, Howard points out how characters from earlier novels are fleshed out in this novel.

Knoll, Robert E., ed. *Conversations with Wright Morris: Critical Views and Responses*. Lincoln: University of Nebraska Press, 1977. This unusual volume contains essays about Morris written by four major critics and an informal conversation between each of the critics and the author. Also includes an essay by Morris, a biographical summary, and a bibliography.

Madden, David. *Wright Morris*. New York: Twayne, 1964. The chapter on *Ceremony in Lone Tree* explores the symbolic importance of the major characters, as they represent stages in the eternal process of change. Justifies Morris's characteristic ambiguity as an honest reflection of the human condition. Includes an annotated bibliography.

Pollak, Oliver B. "Wright Morris and the Jews." *Shofar: An Interdisciplinary Journal of Jewish Studies* 20, no. 4 (Summer, 2002): 18. Focuses on what Pollak calls the "Jewish motif" in Morris's works, delineating the references to Jewish issues in selected books. In *Ceremony in Lone Tree*, Tom Scanlon hears anti-Semitic broadcasts on the radio.

Wydeven, Joseph J. *Wright Morris Revisited*. New York: Twayne, 1998. A scholar who has written often about Morris updates Madden's study (above). Wydeven argues that Morris's works are about American dreamers who viewed the West as the place where they could fulfill their desires. Includes a portfolio of Morris's photographs.

The Chairs

Author: Eugène Ionesco (1909-1994)
First produced: Les Chaises, 1952; first published, 1954 (English translation, 1958, in *Four Plays by Ionesco*)
Type of work: Drama
Type of plot: Absurdist
Time of plot: Indeterminate
Locale: An island

Principal characters:
THE OLD MAN, aged ninety-five
THE OLD WOMAN, aged ninety-four
THE ORATOR, hired by the Old Man to speak, aged 45 to 50

The Story:

The Old Man and his wife, the Old Woman, live in a circular room in a tower in the middle of a circular island surrounded by nothing but a stagnant sea. The Old Man stands on a chair and peers out the window to look at the shadows of ships on the water, apparently waiting for someone, but the Old Woman scolds him to come down because she fears that he might fall and, besides, she tells him, it is early morning and thus dark out, so he cannot see the ships.

Reluctantly, the Old Man climbs down. The Old Woman begs him to entertain her by imitating the month of February, which he reticently does, and then she pleads with him to tell her once more the story of how they arrived on the island decades earlier. Reluctantly he agrees to, even though he told it and she heard it too many times before. When he mentions that by coming to this deserted isle he ruined his promising career, the Old Man begins to weep and moan like a child. The sun begins to rise.

The Old Woman, who calls him Semiramis, takes him on her lap and rocks him, as if he were a baby. She assures him that if they had remained in civilization, he could have been anything he wanted, even head orator. Even though the Old Man protests that he has too much difficulty in communicating to ever become a great speaker, he insists that he has something of such enormous importance to tell the world that he hired a professional orator and invited the most important people to come to the island that very day so that they will all hear what the Orator will say on the Old Man's behalf.

Afraid that the guests will tire them, the Old Woman says that he must call off this engagement. The Old Man wavers and begins to panic. Yet no sooner does he declare that it is too late to cancel than the doorbell rings. Nervously, the old couple prepare themselves. Slowly, the Old Man goes out of their tower room to the entry and, with the Old Woman following him, opens the door. The Lady they bring into their circular room is invisible. They usher the unseen woman into the room, greet and speak to her with extreme politeness, and offer her a chair. They even argue about what this invisible guest might mean by a particular remark and talk behind her back. As they sit beside her, they pause to listen to what the Lady is saying—none of which can really be heard.

Then, the bell rings again and the sounds of a boat pulling away from the island can be heard. The Old Man jumps up, orders his wife to bring in more chairs, and, excusing himself to the invisible lady, runs for the door. Just as the Old Woman returns with a chair, the Old Man comes back with another invisible guest, a colonel, to whom he presents his wife and also the invisible Lady, already seated. The Old Woman ad-

mires the colonel's uniform, and the Old Man asks him to sit down beside the Lady. The four of them—two visible and two not—become involved in a heated conversation. Once again, the doorbell sounds. The Old Man springs to his feet and runs for the door while the Old Woman races to find more chairs for these unseen guests.

More invisible people now arrive. The room soon begins to fill with chairs, and the light grows brighter and brighter. As more and more unseen guests come in, the Old Man and the Old Woman speak to them animatedly, entertaining them, sometimes individually, sometimes together. Outside they hear more boats docking on the island. As the doorbell continues to ring, the Old Man opens the door and the Old Woman goes for chairs. Finally, with the room completely packed with chairs and invisible guests, one more person arrives: the emperor himself. Deeply moved by his majesty's unseen presence, the Old Man tearfully introduces his wife and then explains that this moment is the high point of their long lives. They thank the emperor for gracing them with his presence on this special night when all will be revealed. The couple agree that they could not wish for anything more. Content now to lie eternally together in death, they unexpectedly jump from the window, both shouting "Long live the Emperor!"

Then, after a moment of silence, as the light in the room and through the windows suddenly dims, the Orator who was hired by the Old Man comes into the circular room. He faces the rows of empty chairs and begins to make sounds—not words, merely meaningless noises. He then tries to scrawl a message on the blackboard; he does not write words, just incomprehensible lines. He politely bows to the chairs and then leaves.

Now from the chairs come the sounds of people—laughter, murmurs, coughs—all the different noises that a theater audience might make. Gradually, these noises grow louder.

Critical Evaluation:

In Eugène Ionesco's plays, many ideas are presented very directly, through startling images that defy commonly accepted theatrical conventions. Setting, character, and story as they are usually understood are noticeably absent from *The Chairs*. The audience is asked to accept that the peculiar string of events it witnesses throughout the play is something that, presumably, has meaning.

Ionesco's dramas are absurd. In the context of theater, "absurd" does not simply mean "silly" or "ridiculous." Rather, absurdity refers to the perception that in the modern world, where people are cut off from their traditional ties, all actions become useless, senseless. The absurdity of the absurd play is a reflection of the absurdity of the world. The emphasis of many absurd plays is on the emotional content, or lack thereof, of the moment. Often, nothing appears to be occurring onstage, and characters seem shallow, puppetlike creatures, but amid the frightening lack of communication come waves of humor and terror. Rejecting the logic and reason of earlier writers, Ionesco offers an illogical and irrational drama that expresses the often mystifying feeling of senselessness that pervades the awareness of many modernists.

The Chairs very clearly concerns communication among human beings or perhaps the inevitable lack of communication. The Old Man, who spends his life on an isolated island, feels he must share the message of his life with others before he dies. He invites an audience of notables to hear what he has to tell them. Yet instead of experiencing the presence of other people, he and the Old Woman experience the absence of others. The "people" who come to this secluded island are invisible and mute. Similarly, the Orator whom the Old Man chooses to convey his message is incapable of presenting it, even if someone was there, because he can neither speak with any meaning nor write in intelligible signs. By the time the Orator begins his futile attempts, both the Old Man and the Old Woman kill themselves, convinced that they reached the high point of their long lives.

The old couple talk a great deal throughout the play, but very little of what they say makes any sense. The story that the Old Woman begs the Old Man to tell her, of their arrival on the island, seems circular, insignificant. Moreover, the Old Woman heard it so many times that she hardly even listens to what he says. Rather, she relates to the story as if it were a piece of music and seems more interested in the emotions that the Old Man's tale inspires rather than in gaining any meaning from the words.

Ionesco called *The Chairs* "a tragic farce," and indeed much of the play is extremely funny. The early scenes, for example, in which the Old Man and the Old Woman seem to shift from acting like old people to acting like small children, are especially humorous, and later in the play, with the arrivals of the unseen guests, the behavior of the old couple (who carefully observe all the social niceties with the invisible guests) amounts to high comedy. Nevertheless, the failure of the Old Man to communicate what he seems to believe is the essence of his life's experience, even amid the bizarre absurdities of the play, turns *The Chairs* toward tragedy.

Instead of providing any readily understandable answers, the tragic farce provokes many questions. Is communication between people possible? How much of what a speaker says is genuinely understood? Do writers actually make contact with their readers, whom they never meet? Perhaps most significant, what role does a theater audience play in a drama as it is in progress? Are spectators, who sit by silently in the darkened auditorium, in fact rather similar to the unseen, unheard guests who come to the old couple's island?

Since *The Chairs* premiered in 1952, it remains one of Ionesco's most respected and popular plays. Frequently revived all over the world, this play has contributed to Ionesco's reputation as a serious dramatist.

Kenneth Krauss

Further Reading

Bloom, Harold, ed. *Eugène Ionesco*. Philadelphia: Chelsea House, 2003. Collection of essays providing critical interpretations of Ionesco's plays, including *The Chairs*.

Coe, Richard N. *Ionesco: A Study of His Plays*. Rev. ed. London: Methuen, 1971. Presents a careful study of *The Chairs*, offering information about the early productions of this work and discussing how confused and delighted critics were by this cryptic play.

Cohn, Ruby. *From "Desire" to "Godot": Pocket Theater of Postwar Paris*. Berkeley: University of California Press, 1989. Has a chapter devoted to the first production of *The Chairs*, with much informative material about what the play means and has meant to those who have seen it. Provides a very solid discussion of how one might respond to this perplexing masterpiece.

Dobrez, L. A. C. *The Existential and Its Exits: Literary and Philosophical Perspectives on the Works of Beckett, Ionesco, Genet, and Pinter*. New York: St. Martin's Press, 1986. Emphasizing the philosophical aspects of absurdist theater, Dobrez explores Ionesco's most successful dramatic works, including *The Chairs*.

Esslin, Martin. *The Theatre of the Absurd*. 3d ed. rev. New York: Methuen, 2001. Long before other critics had a clue about what Ionesco's plays might mean, Esslin placed Ionesco in a group with other writers he called "absurdists." Esslin delivers an often moving interpretation of *The Chairs* and how Ionesco came to write it.

Gaensbauer, Deborah B. *Eugène Ionesco Revisited*. New York: Twayne, 1996. Reevaluation of Ionesco's life and work published two years after his death. Gaensbauer analyzes all of the plays and Ionesco's other writings, and she concludes that each work was a piece in a long autobiography in which Ionesco sought to understand himself and humankind.

Guicharnaud, Jacques. *Modern French Theatre: From Giraudoux to Genet*. New Haven, Conn.: Yale University Press,

1967. The chapter on Ionesco and his work uses *The Chairs* as a centerpiece. Long an admirer of the absurdist playwright, Guicharnaud looks into the texts of Ionesco's one-act dramas and finds much to explain.

Holland, Michael. *Ionesco: La Cantatrice chauve and Les Chaises*. London: Grant & Cutler, 2004. A concise introductory overview and survey of the plays' critical reception.

Chaka

Author: Thomas Mofolo (1876-1948)
First published: 1925 (English translation, 1931)
Type of work: Novel
Type of plot: Historical realism
Time of plot: Nineteenth century
Locale: Lesotho (Zululand), Africa

Principal characters:
CHAKA, a warlord and tribal king
SENZANGAKHONA, his father
NANDI, his mother
ISANUSI, a sorcerer
DINGISWAYO, a neighboring tribal king
NDLEBE and MALUNGA, agents of Isanusi
ZWIDE, a neighboring tribal king
NOLIWA, Chaka's favorite wife
NONGOGO, favorite and faithful servant to Chaka

The Story:

Senzangakhona, the tribal king, is without male children. He decides to marry again so that he can have a male offspring for the kingship. He is attracted to Nandi and, overcome by her beauty, takes her when they are not yet married, in violation of tribal law. She becomes pregnant, whereupon the two are married secretly. Chaka is born. The other wives are jealous of Nandi and her son Chaka, and they threaten to expose Senzangakhona for impregnating Nandi before marriage. In the meantime, other male heirs to the throne are born.

Senzangakhona banishes Nandi and Chaka to another village. At first, he sends them cattle and sheep to help, but when this is discovered by his wives he is forced to discontinue the presents. Chaka grows up lonely—an outcast from his father and from the other young boys, who torment him as an outsider. He learns early to fight and to seek and take vengeance.

Chaka's courage and boldness grow, as does his strength. He performs deeds of heroism that make him a favorite in the village rather than an outcast. He kills a lion that was terrorizing the people. Later, he kills a hyena as it dragged a girl away.

While bathing in the river, Chaka is visited by an ominous snake. The event foretells that Chaka is destined to greatness. His mother, having witnessed the event, tries to visit a sorcerer, but it is learned that the woman died after arranging for Chaka and Nandi to consult her own master in sorcery, Isanusi.

Chaka becomes the most likely successor to the tribal kingship, and a dispute arises with Mfokanzana, the chosen heir. Chaka is forced to flee the village after his father, Senzangakhona, arrives and orders Chaka killed.

Upon fleeing the village, Chaka meets the sorcerer Isanusi, who likes the young man and promises him that if he will obey in all things that he will one day inherit his father's kingship, which is rightfully his by birth. Chaka agrees. Isanusi makes several different kinds of medicine with which he strengthens Chaka and his resolve.

Chaka, who previously told his mother all things, does not report to her about his meeting with Isanusi. Chaka then, following Isanusi's instructions in all things, goes to the kingship of Dingiswayo, where he quickly becomes a hero and king's favorite by killing a madman. He helps Dingiswayo in battle, immediately becoming by far the best warrior in the tribe. Chaka likes warfare and determines that he wants to fight a war that has no end. Ndlebe and Malunga, sinister agents of Isanusi, appear mysteriously to assist Chaka in all things. Chaka lies to Dingiswayo about their origins, claiming that they are childhood friends. The two possess supernatural gifts that help Chaka in all things, particularly war, marriage, and tribal politics. Chaka falls in love with Noliwa, Dingiswayo's daughter, but he is afraid to take up the matter with the king. With the help of the two agents of evil, Ndlebe and Malunga, the marriage is eventually made. Noliwa is to be Chaka's favorite wife.

Senzangakhona dies, whereupon his son Mfokanzana claims the throne. Following the instructions of Ndlebe and Malunga, Chaka fights Mfokanzana and kills him, whereupon Chaka is installed as his father's successor. An old enemy of Dingiswayo, Zwide (king of a neighboring tribe), makes war against Dingiswayo and kills him. Chaka, after conquering Zwide, then becomes the new king of Dingiswayo's and Zwide's territories as well as that of his father.

Chaka, now with three kingships to his name, makes numerous reforms in his new, combined kingdom. His innovations assure that his warriors are the most fierce and feared in all of Africa. Chaka is visited by Isanusi, who promises him that he can become even more powerful and that he can control more land than he could ever see or people than he could ever visit—all if Chaka continues to follow Isanusi's orders. Chaka, lustful for power, agrees.

Chaka turns into a tyrant. He kills his own men without discretion, often killing even the most faithful of his own warriors for inconsequential reasons. The people come to fear him totally and want a new leader. Chaka responds by becoming more and more fierce, tyrannical, and arbitrary in controlling his growing kingdoms.

Chaka continues to follow Isanusi's instructions exactly. When he is told to make medicine for his warriors with blood from his son, he does so. When he is told to make more medicine with blood from his wife Noliwa, he kills her. Finally, Isanusi gives him the order to kill his mother Nandi, and Chaka carries out that command as well. Each time he acquires more land and people, becoming the greatest leader in all of African history.

Finally, Chaka becomes sick. In his illness he has numerous dreams in which he is visited by the ghosts of those he killed, particularly family members. When his own men come into his quarters with spears to stab him, he does not resist. He accepts his death with stoicism.

Critical Evaluation:

Published in 1925 in Sotho and in 1931 in English, *Chaka* was one of the first significant novels written by an African native to receive widespread attention and readership in Europe and in the United States. With this book, Thomas Mofolo provided the English-speaking world with a depiction of African life, culture, tradition, and mind-set before the coming of Europeans.

Unlike many African novels, *Chaka* is set in the eighteenth century, before the Europeans came. European forms of government and religion were not part of African life in the time in which the novel is set. Mofolo, himself educated by Christian missionaries, writes of a time previous to his own African existence, but he does so with a voice of authenticity and sincerity.

The story reveals much about human nature within a localized African setting. The soul-devouring nature of evil, the motive for revenge, the matters of love and war, the fall of a hero—all of these universal human stories are detailed in an African context.

As a result of circumstances of birth, Chaka is set apart from his family and his inheritance through no fault of his own. When he gives himself over to the evil of the sorcerer Isanusi, however, he morally takes things into his hands and assures his descent into evil. He slowly abandons all reason, love, and goodness in his life. He does so always for selfish reasons. In the beginning, it is reasonable and human that he would want to gain the throne that is rightfully his own and that he is denied. His descent into evil, however, begins with his pact with the sorcerer and is confirmed in his actions, which become increasingly selfish and despotic.

As Chaka descends morally yet rises in power, he becomes given to atrocities, even killing members of his own family. He murders the most faithful of his servants and warriors; it is suggested that he participates in cannibalism and unspeakable sexual acts. His greatest violation, however, is his lust for blood: The more people he kills, the more it is necessary for him to kill again to feel that his life has direction. He conquers and controls more of the world than he can ever even see, yet he remains dissatisfied.

In Christian terms, Mofolo is writing about a character who sells his soul to the devil. No Christian elements, however, enter the story. The coming of the whites is mentioned in only one instance, and their influence is totally absent in the work. Chaka is nevertheless comparable to other figures in literature who sell their souls, Christopher Marlowe's Dr. Faustus, for example. Chaka knows what he is doing when he is visited by Isanusi and enters into the agreement with him. Similarly, Isanusi knows exactly what he is doing and proceeds to tempt Chaka in his moral descent.

Mofolo records the story as history, making it read as factual biography. Elements of the supernatural, such as works carried out by Isanusi and his two agents Ndlebe and Malunga, are rendered in a matter-of-fact manner that never questions their credibility. The narrative itself is almost never interrupted with authorial intrusions. Nevertheless, the author is aware of the ignorance of Western readers (and twentieth century African readers) of the beliefs and culture of the eighteenth century Zulus. Accordingly, he weaves explanations and comments into the story.

The novel contains no preachy, moralistic attitude or outlook. It is clear to everyone that Chaka is evil long before his death. He dies, miserable not so much for his sins against human nature and whatever gods there be but because he cannot find pleasure in anything except blood and death. His own family and warriors kill him in his illness. He is too weakened to fight for himself, and he succumbs to death willingly.

Carl Singleton

Further Reading

Ayivor, Kwame. "Thomas Mopoku Mofolo's 'Inverted Epic Hero': A Reading of Mofolo's *Chaka* as an African Epic Folktale." *Research in African Literatures* 28, no. 1 (Spring, 1997): 49. Examines how Mofolo used the oral epic tradition to subvert traditional ideas of African heroism.

Dathorne, O. R. *The Black Mind: A History of African Literature*. Minneapolis: University of Minnesota Press, 1974. Discusses *Chaka* as a product of tradition and African oral history. Argues that the work is more than the mere debunking of myth about the Zulu leader.

Gerard, Albert S. *Four African Literatures: Xhosa, Sotho, Zulu, Amharic*. Berkeley: University of California Press, 1971. Gerard discusses *Chaka* within the context of Mofolo's Christian beliefs. Provides biographical information about Mofolo.

Hofmeyr, Isabel. "Portable Landscapes: Thomas Mofolo and John Bunyan in the Broad and the Narrow Way." In *Disputed Territories: Land, Culture, and Identity in Settler Societies*, edited by David Trigger and Gareth Griffiths. Hong Kong: Hong Kong University Press, 2003. Describes how Mofolo's first novel, *Moeti oa Bochabela* (1907; *The Traveler of the East*, 1934), draws on evangelical images of the Broad and Narrow Way and on Bunyan's *The Pilgrim's Progress* (1678, 1684). Provides an understanding of how Mofolo's religious beliefs influenced his work.

Ikonne, Chidi. "Thomas Mofolo's Narrator." In *Aspects of South African Literature*, edited by Christopher Heywood. London: Heinemann, 1976. Ikonne's criticism deals primarily with narrative techniques in the novel; he finds a "double narrative" running throughout.

Kunene, Daniel P. *Thomas Mofolo and the Emergence of Written Sesotho Prose*. Johannesburg: Ravan Press, 1989. Kunene, who has translated *Chaka*, provides a detailed history of Mofolo's manuscript of the novel and the historical forces that influenced Mofolo's writings.

Kunene, Mazisi. *Emperor Shaka the Great: A Zulu Epic*. London: Heinemann, 1979. Written as a narrative in poetry, this poem details biographical elements and stands in contrast to the novel.

Wauthier, Claude. *The Literature and Thought of Modern Africa: A Survey*. Translated by Shirley Kay. New York: Praeger, 1964. Discusses the historical figure, Shaka, in the light of Mofolo's literary creation. Gives particular attention to paganism in the novel and to the character of Isanusi.

The Changeling

Authors: Thomas Middleton (1580-1627) and William Rowley (c. 1585-1626)
First produced: 1622; first published, 1653
Type of work: Drama
Type of plot: Tragedy
Time of plot: Early seventeenth century
Locale: Alicante, a seaport on the east coast of Spain

Principal characters:
VERMANDERO, governor of the castle of Alicante
BEATRICE, his daughter
ALSEMERO, her suitor and later her husband
ALONZO DE PIRACQUO, another suitor of Beatrice
ALIBIUS, a jealous doctor
ISABELLA, his wife
ANTONIO, the changeling
DIAPHANTA, Beatrice's waiting-woman
DE FLORES, Vermandero's servant
JASPERINO, Alsemero's friend

The Story:

Alsemero, after glimpsing Beatrice at church, expresses to himself the hope that he can gain her hand in marriage. Outside, in the street, his musings are interrupted by Jasperino. To the latter's surprise, he learns that Alsemero, whose enthusiasm for travel is common knowledge, is reluctant to undertake a projected voyage to Malta. While they are talking, Beatrice enters, accompanied by Diaphanta, and the four talk in friendly fashion. The mood of Beatrice changes to anger, however, with the arrival of De Flores, her father's servant, to whom she has a seemingly unconquerable aversion. She makes no effort to hide her feelings from De Flores, who, nevertheless, remains unabashed and continues to follow her about.

Vermandero, Beatrice's father, passes by and meets Alsemero for the first time. He is pleased to learn that the young man is the son of an old friend of his, a battle companion now dead. To Alsemero he gives an invitation to visit the castle of which Vermandero is governor. The invitation is eagerly accepted, but Alsemero's pleasure turns to dismay when he learns of Vermandero's determination to wed Beatrice to Alonzo De Piracquo within the next seven days. As they start for the castle, Beatrice drops one of her gloves. In disdain she throws its mate after it rather than accept the glove from the hands of De Flores, who picks it up and offers it to her.

Meanwhile, in another part of Alicante, Alibius is giving instructions to his servant Lollio. Alibius, a doctor, makes Lollio promise to keep an eye on Isabella, the former's much younger wife. The doctor's establishment, which includes facilities for the care of madmen and fools, soon increases with the arrival of a new patient. Antonio, enamored of Isabella, chooses to pose as an idiot so that he can be near her. Lollio interrogates Antonio in an effort to establish his degree of stupidity, but Antonio cleverly parries the servant's questions.

With the help of Jasperino and Diaphanta, Beatrice and Alsemero communicate with each other and arrange a secret meeting. De Flores, coming to announce the arrival of Beatrice's suitor, Alonzo, is cruelly railed at, but he equally prolongs the interview to be in Beatrice's presence. His doggedness arouses in her a vague presentiment of evil, which is quickly dismissed when she rallies herself to face Alonzo. He and her father reluctantly agree to her request for a three-day postponement of the wedding. Her behavior prompts Alonzo's brother, Tomaso, to utter the warning that Beatrice is not in love, but Alonzo shrugs off any intimation that the marriage is not wise.

Beatrice and Alsemero confess their mutual affection. Beatrice, however, refuses her lover's offer to engage Alonzo in a duel because she fears that his death or punishment would be the result of such an affair. Instead, she suggests another scheme to get rid of Alonzo, with De Flores serving as a possible tool through whom to work her will. Seeking him out, she gains his consent to help her, but she does not know the price that he expects her to pay. Fate takes a hand in their plotting when Alonzo presently asks De Flores to guide him about the castle's obscure maze of passageways. De Flores cozens Alonzo into disarming himself, then kills him with a rapier previously hidden behind a door. Before disposing of the body, he cuts off a finger adorned by a diamond ring.

Back at the house of Alibius, Isabella complains to Lollio about the strict watch under which she is kept. Out of curiosity, she prevails upon him to let her visit the quarters reserved for the madmen and fools. There she meets Franciscus, who, like Antonio, is one of the gentlemen from the castle of Alicante with amorous designs upon Isabella. He manages to convey his feelings to her, and she reflects that, after all, a lady need not leave her home if she has any desire to stray from virtue. Lollio, infected by all this romantic intriguing, forgets his master's commission and makes advances to Isabella, but she repulses him.

De Flores, to prove that he did her bidding, brings the finger of the murdered Alonzo to Beatrice. Refusing her offer of gold, he threatens her with exposure for her part in the crime if she refuses to reward him with her love. Beatrice, twist and turn as she might, can find no avenue of escape from his relentless blackmail, and eventually she yields to his desires.

Vermandero misunderstands the sudden disappearance of Alonzo; angered, he allows his daughter to make a hasty marriage to Alsemero. Nevertheless, he begins to wonder about the prolonged absence from the castle of Antonio and Franciscus; they are sent for, to be questioned about Alonzo. A few hours before her wedding night, Beatrice begins to fear Alsemero's discovery that she is no longer a maid. Pleading timidity, she persuades Diaphanta, who is still a virgin, to act as her substitute in Alsemero's bed during the early part of the night. Diaphanta is far from displeased to be asked this favor, even without the gold with which her mistress promises to reward her.

Elaborate nuptial celebrations are planned for Beatrice and Alsemero. As part of the entertainment, Vermandero requests that Alibius rehearse some of his madmen and fools so that they might perform a weird dance for the amusement of the assembly. Alibius decides that he will let Isabella accompany him to the castle for that event. Meanwhile that lady, attracted to Antonio, disguises herself briefly as a madwoman to converse with him. Lollio plays a prank on Antonio and

Franciscus by pretending, to each, that Isabella will reward him for getting rid of the other.

Diaphanta, pretending to be Beatrice, amorously overstays her time with Alsemero, so that her impatient mistress becomes first dismayed, then suspicious, and at last vengeful. At the suggestion of De Flores, she agrees to Diaphanta's death. A fire is set, to create confusion and arouse Diaphanta from the marriage bed. The unfortunate young woman is followed to her own bedroom and slain by De Flores.

Franciscus and Antonio are apprehended and charged with the murder of Alonzo, since it is learned that they entered Alibius's house in disguise on the day of Alonzo's disappearance. Beatrice and De Flores finally bring about their own undoing, however, after Alsemero's discovery of their secret meetings makes him suspicious. Under his questioning, Beatrice breaks down and confesses. Although she pleads her love for him as an excuse for the crime, Alsemero, shocked, takes her and De Flores into custody. The pair are unwilling to face trial; De Flores gives Beatrice a fatal wound and then stabs himself, unrepentant to the last.

Critical Evaluation:

Written in 1622, toward the end of an extraordinarily rich period in English drama that produced a substantial body of the finest plays written in English, *The Changeling* is widely considered to be one of the best non-Shakespearean tragedies. The opening and closing scenes and the subplot are generally attributed to William Rowley, and the remainder of the play to Thomas Middleton. Of the two authors, Middleton was the more prolific. He wrote at least twenty-five plays alone or in collaboration with other playwrights, such as Thomas Dekker, John Webster, and Francis Beaumont. Middleton's output was varied, including comedies, tragicomedies, and masques. He is best known for his political satire, *A Game at Chess* (1624), and for his two great tragedies, *The Changeling* and *Women Beware Women* (c. 1621-1627). Rowley was well known in his own time as an actor of comedy roles. He also wrote at least eleven plays in collaboration with others and four plays unaided.

The word "changeling" has three definitions relevant to the play: a changeable person, a person surreptitiously exchanged for another, and an idiot. Various characters are associated with the different senses of the word, and the last few speeches of the closing scene point to many of these. Although the subplot of the play, with its fools and madmen, is tiresome and in poor taste according to twentieth century sensibilities, it provides some commentary on the main theme of the play. There is a shared imagery of change. Antonio and Francisco undergo transformation in their pursuit of love, as do Alsemero, Beatrice, and De Flores. Isabella, who remains true to her marriage vows in spite of temptation, provides a comparison to Beatrice's increasing immorality. The madness and folly observed in Alibius's institution form a grotesque reflection of the madness and folly of the outside world. In the play's development of the characters of Beatrice and De Flores, as well as in some fine passages of dramatic rhetoric, the play achieves great stature.

In the course of the play, Beatrice is transformed from an apparently pious, dutiful young woman into a damned soul, stabbed to death by her murderous lover. This process occurs with terrifying ease and speed. Her downfall begins with her passion for Alsemero and her desire to marry him rather than Alonzo. On the face of it this seems a reasonable wish. Beatrice does not reason, however; she does not consider or question the means she employs to achieve her ends. She is utterly self-centered, and this blinds her to the nature of the events she sets into motion. There is a willful irrationality about her initial loathing for De Flores and a selfish amorality in her determination to persuade her father to dismiss him. This is a foreshadowing of her later schemes. She is too intent on the gratification of her own desires to recognize that in instigating the murder of her unwanted fiancé, she participates in evil. When she realizes that the price she has to pay De Flores for his part in the crime is sexual surrender to him, she is horrified at the violation of her honor.

> Why, 'tis impossible thou canst be so wicked,
> Or shelter such a cunning cruelty,
> To make his death the murderer of my honor!

This "honor," the perception by others that her virtue is unsullied, remains, to her, a compelling value. The protection of this sham leads to the corruption and murder of Diaphanta. Beatrice's growing reliance, affinity, and then passion for De Flores are indicative of how she becomes accustomed to evil.

De Flores is a malcontent, resentful of his social status because he was born to a higher rank. His ugliness is an additional misfortune. Like Beatrice, he is motivated by passion, but unlike her, he acts in full consciousness of his own evil. He too puts his own desires above all other considerations. The moral values of the play clearly cast him as villainous. Not only does he commit murders but also he is clearly implicated in, although not wholly responsible for, Beatrice's downfall. In De Flores, as in Beatrice, there is a psychological complexity that allows the possibility for some measure of sympathy for him. He kills three times, but the first time is to win his beloved, the second to protect her honor, and the third because she has repudiated him. His loyalty to Beatrice makes him courageous and bold, as exemplified by his actions on the night of the fire. Having killed Beatrice, he kills himself, still glorying that she has been his: "I thank life for nothing/ But that pleasure; it was so sweet to me/ That I have drunk up all." De Flores speaks some of the finest lines in the play—for example, in act 3, scene 4—when he claims his reward from Beatrice. His speeches display a stark and unflinching clarity of vision expressed plainly and forcefully.

The typical themes of English Renaissance tragedies are intrigue, murder, revenge, and sexual desire. The characters of these plays are often types, sometimes caricatures. The Machiavellian villain, one who is consciously evil and who delights in it, is an example, and so is the irresponsible aristocratic girl. *The Changeling* is clearly a tragedy of its age. Beatrice and De Flores are developed beyond the standard heroine and villain types, with well-observed, subtle, and believable characteristics. The tragedy of these two characters, both driven by obsessive wills, is a tragedy of universal relevance. The dissatisfaction and the desire that drive De Flores to his destruction and the blind egocentricity of Beatrice are as familiar to contemporary audiences as they were to the original seventeenth century audience.

"Critical Evaluation" by Susan Henthorne

Further Reading

Bradbrook, M. C. *Themes and Conventions of Elizabethan Tragedy.* 2d ed. New York: Cambridge University Press, 1980. Analysis of the drama of the period, including its staging and conventions of plot and character. The chapter on Middleton finds him atypical in his simplicity of language and subtlety of implication.

Brittin, Norman A. *Thomas Middleton.* New York: Twayne, 1972. A good basic guide to Middleton's drama. Brittin claims that he is the most important writer of the Jacobean comedy of manners. Offers a sensitive analysis of *The Changeling* and a useful summary of critical assessments.

Chakravorty, Swapan. *Society and Politics in the Plays of Thomas Middleton.* New York: Oxford University Press, 1996. Reassesses the cultural significance of Middleton's plays, arguing that he was a pioneer of politically self-conscious theater. Chapter 7 is devoted to an analysis of *The Changeling.*

Farr, Dorothy M. *Thomas Middleton and the Drama of Realism.* New York: Harper & Row, 1973. Traces Middleton's development, initiated with the aid of William Rowley in *The Changeling*, toward a new form of tragic drama, which, Farr claims, is close to the modern theater.

Huebert, Ronald. "An Art That Has No Name: Thomas Middleton." In *The Performance of Pleasure in English Renaissance Drama.* New York: Palgrave Macmillan, 2003. Examines how English Renaissance dramatists, including Middleton, pursue and create pleasure, both the erotic pleasure presented onstage and the aesthetic pleasure experienced by readers and theatergoers.

Hutchings, Mark, and A. A. Bromham. *Middleton and His Collaborators.* Tavistock, England: Northcote, 2008. Examines Middleton's working relationships with several collaborators, including William Rowley, with whom he wrote *The Changeling*, and provides a detailed analysis of this play.

Jump, J. D. "Middleton's Tragic Comedies." In *The Pelican Guide to English Literature.* Vol 2. New York: Penguin Books, 1964. Focuses on two tragedies, *Women Beware Women* and *The Changeling*, with emphasis on the quality of the verse and the realism of the drama.

Mulryne, J. R. *Writers and Their Work: Thomas Middleton.* New York: Longman, 1979. Surveys the body of Middleton's work, including *The Changeling*. Includes a useful bibliography.

Taylor, Gary, and John Lavagnino, eds. *Thomas Middleton and Early Modern Textual Culture: A Companion to the Collected Works.* New York: Oxford University Press, 2007. This companion to a complete collection of Middleton's works contains numerous essays that place the writer in his literary and cultural context. Also provides introductory essays and textual notes for all of his writings.

The Changing Light at Sandover

Author: James Merrill (1926-1995)
First published: 1976-1982; includes "The Book of
  Ephraim," 1976, in *Divine Comedies*; *Mirabell:
  Books of Number*, 1978; *Scripts for the Pageant*,
  1980; *The Changing Light at Sandover* (complete
  poem), 1982
Type of work: Poetry

The Changing Light at Sandover is an assemblage of three previously published books of poetry by James Merrill to which is added a new poem, "Coda: The Higher Keys." The trilogy, as the first three books are commonly known, begins with the 1976 "The Book of Ephraim," which was originally the second half of Merrill's Pulitzer Prize-winning book of poems, *Divine Comedies*. The next section of *The Changing Light at Sandover* is "Mirabell: A Book of Numbers." For inclusion in *The Changing Light at Sandover*, Merrill retitled his National Book Award-winning *Mirabell: Books of Number*. In 1980, *Scripts for the Pageant*, the third part of the trilogy, was separately published. In 1982, these three books plus "Coda: The Higher Keys" were collected for the one-volume book of poetry, *The Changing Light at Sandover*. Of the four parts, only "The Book of Ephraim" stands alone as a complete book of verse; the others are interconnected by characters and themes.

The Changing Light at Sandover, regularly labeled as an epic poem, covers such diverse topics as the writing of poetry, the threat of nuclear war, the destruction of the environment, death and reincarnation, and the role of the arts in a technological world. Merrill's accomplishment in this book has led him to be compared with Dante Alighieri, William Butler Yeats, and Marcel Proust. As a poet, Merrill also represents the New Formalism movement in American poetry as he questions the balance between language and poetic form, as well as the effects of both on readers of poetry.

The trilogy begins with "The Book of Ephraim," which comes to represent the first step in the process of discovering the answers to essential questions about the relationships between reason and imagination, truth and fiction, power and impotence, and time and wisdom. The story told in this book begins in 1955 with Merrill, who is labeled "JM" in the poems, and his friend, David Jackson, "DJ," sitting down on a hot summer evening in Merrill's Stonington, Connecticut, home to ask questions of a homemade Ouija board. They use a blue and white willowware china teacup to spell out the answers received from the spirit world. As they start, the answers are disjointed as many spirits pass by; then, Ephraim, the spirit of a Greek Jew, born in 8 C.E. who died in 39 C.E., becomes their clearest and principal conductor through the world they have conjured up. With Ephraim, JM and DJ are taught that the people now on earth house souls, called patrons in his world, who are promoted in a celestial hierarchy based on the deeds of their earthly hosts. As the conversations progress (Ephraim's speeches shown in capital letters and unpunctuated lines), JM and DJ are able to speak with poets Wallace Stevens and W. H. Auden, friends and relatives of both men, and people from Ephraim's world. Ephraim also describes the organization of the universe.

"The Book of Ephraim" comprises twenty-six cantos, one for each letter of the alphabet, from "Admittedly" to "Zero Hour." Merrill employs iambic pentameter, both rhymed and unrhymed, and he uses the meter to write cantos in couplets, quatrains, strophes, and sonnets. The language of the poem is clear and vivid. Nearly every line alludes to other literary works, opera, art, travel, or friends of JM. For example, *The Arabian Nights' Entertainments* (first transcribed, fifteenth century), opera singer Kirsten Flagstad, composer Richard Wagner, and writers Thomas Mann, Virginia Woolf, and Isak Dinesen have their places next to Merrill's friends Hans Lodeizen, Maria Mitsotaki, and Maya Deren, among others. "The Book of Ephraim" is also marked by the poet's use of irony, wit, bluntness, and a plot structure of searching and accepting what is found.

"The Book of Ephraim" provides the exposition of the tone, ideas, and major figures that create the limited unity of *The Changing Light at Sandover*. In the "A" poem, the poet describes his mission to write a poem that will reveal the unities of past and present. The "B" poem yields setting and background, and the "C" poem introduces Ephraim. In the "D" poem, twelve real and imaginary people are listed as the *dramatis personae* of "The Book of Ephraim." In the "W" poem, JM converses with a fictional nephew, Wendell Pincus, about the poet's ability to transcend his own self when writing to create a literary work that is universally significant. Finally, the "Z" poem describes a break-in at the Stonington house. Although nothing is taken, the family's possessions are disturbed. The symbolism of intrusion of the unknown into their lives is captured here: "The threat remains, though of there still being/ A presence in our midst, unknown, unseen,/ Unscrupulous to take what he can get."

Supplementing the visits from Ephraim are two other plots in this first part of the trilogy: Merrill's incorporation of characters and partial story lines from his lost novel set in New Mexico and the poet's indication of how this book was written. Letter sections J, N, S, T, and X recount parts of Merrill's novel's plot as he rewrites how Leo Cade, a Vietnam veteran suspected of murdering a Vietnamese thought by his company to be a spy, falls under the influence of Eros, a sensual spirit, and how Joanna, an older woman with unclear motives, aims to seduce Matt Prentiss, a character reminiscent of DJ's father. Another character, Sergei Markovich, buys land from Rosamund Smith and is thought to parallel Merrill himself.

The third plot, on the writing of the poem, is described as the main activity of 1974. "The Book of Ephraim" spans about twenty years. The writing was completed mainly at Stonington, with trips to Greece and Italy. The Ouija board mentioned in the verse accompanied Merrill on these trips. The quests to define the differences between poetry and fiction and between the real and the imaginary give "The Book of Ephraim" its literary strengths as well as its complexity, as the fictional is designed to seem "real" by the confident, reliable voice of the poet.

"Mirabell: A Book of Numbers," the second book of the trilogy, is set in mid-1975 as Merrill and Jackson are residing in their second home, in Greece. Again, the Ouija board is with them. Their readings take them around the board's numbered sections, from zero to nine. The poems in this part are further subdivided into ten separately numbered units, so that "Mirabell" contains ninety individual poems. The predominant theme of this section of the book is death of those much loved and those loved little. The name Mirabell is given to the primary spirit-seeker by JM; Mirabell describes himself to JM and DJ as a peacock.

In "Mirabell," other spirits, which are again combinations of the real and the imaginary, play roles in the poet's journey to write a poem merging reason and imagination. In this section, the spirits of JM and DJ's guides, Mitsotaki and Auden, join the pair at the level of equals to explore cosmological and philosophical ideas. The spirits urge JM to write a poem about science. Much of the section is devoted to an examination of how ordinary people see and come to understand scientific concepts. It is here that the "science" themes of *The*

Changing Light at Sandover are addressed as the pair learn how "God B(iology)," described as "the accumulated intelligence of cells," operates through the "R/LAB" to conduct research into life, death, and reincarnation. Nature is presented as the powerful and constant force in the universe. Illustrations of the themes in this section include discussion of the biblical Fall of Man, the destruction of the lost civilization of Atlantis, and the retelling of the Faust legend. "The Book of Ephraim" weaves humor and irony into a loosely constructed plot; "Mirabell," in contrast, contains much more transcription (again all in capital letters and unpunctuated) with little interpretation to bring together ideas about science and pseudoscience and the role of the imaginary in the real.

"Mirabell" may be read as a representation of the raw materials from which poetry is made and as an assemblage of a variety of ideas, experiences, memories, and imaginings. In the course of this section, JM and DJ learn of the violent and destructive practices of civilization. As they try to acquire the keys to stopping these practices, the spirit guides are often silenced or punished by their bureaucracy, leaving large parts of the section unfocused and occasionally hard to follow. At the close of "Mirabell," the spirits awaiting rebirth are shown to be limited by their stage in the reincarnation process, so JM and DJ are made ready to meet the highest levels of the spirit world.

Scripts for the Pageant takes JM and DJ around the final section of the Ouija board, the "Yes," "&," and "No." "Yes" is a series of seven lyric poems, ten "lessons," and a commentary on "God B's" song spoken by the spirit of Auden. "&" features four titled lyric poems, five lessons, and five additional lyrics. "No" begins with ten lessons and ends with six lyric poems. In this last third of the trilogy, JM and DJ communicate directly with the archangels; God, Jesus, Buddha, and Muhammad; the Nine Muses of classical Greece; Akhenaton, Homer, Montezuma, Nefertiti, and Plato, collectively known as The Five; and a variety of poets and musicians. Ephraim and Mirabell are joined by a rather clumsy, comical spirit, Unice. Auden, Mitsotaki, George Cotzias (a biologist friend of Merrill), and Robert Morse (a musician friend and house guest at Stonington), whose recent deaths are recorded in *Scripts for the Pageant* along with those of DJ's parents, all have speaking parts.

In *Scripts for the Pageant*, the discussion of the poet's work continues and escalates as the mediums, JM and DJ, consider various elemental forces and how the self-destructive tendencies of humans might be stopped. By now, the writing of the poem of science has become known as V work, which refers to the number 5 (the halfway point in "Mirabell"), the Group of Five, and *vie*, which is the French word for "life."

"Mirabell" is based on opposition and the tension opposites create; *Scripts for the Pageant*, is focused on the attraction of opposites to stress how order can be brought from chaos.

As the part titles of *Scripts for the Pageant* underscore, there is no precise answer to the question of halting self-destruction: Individuals are shown as being only limitedly able to control their fates. In *Scripts for the Pageant*, the apparent limitations on JM's abilities to draw information out of the Ouija board become blurred as the lines between the known and the unknown are drawn. Morse's death and impending reincarnation are the narrative events that hold this third part of *The Changing Light at Sandover* together. The title is derived from the luminaries who cross the Ouija board stage and give long speeches on the nature of the universe. Among the outstanding literary features are the use of the *canzone* in the poem "Samos," which is found in the "No" section of *Scripts for the Pageant*. Yeats's *A Vision* (1925, 1937), Dante's *La divina commedia* (c. 1320; *The Divine Comedy*, 1802); John Milton's *Paradise Lost* (1667, 1674), and the poetry of Auden all provide models for the writing of *Scripts for the Pageant*. The magical realism of *The Changing Light at Sandover* is at its height as JM and DJ talk directly, through the board, to God. The insights they gain in this section allow them to set aside the limitations of the ordinary human, held back by fear, insecurity, and ignorance; this transcendence is symbolized in the breaking of the mirror, a recurring image in the poetry, in the poem "Finale."

"Coda: The Higher Keys" was written especially for the one-volume edition of *The Changing Light at Sandover*. This section contains thirteen lyrics. Like "The Book of Ephraim," "Coda: The Higher Keys" is narrative in its structure as JM learns, on the board, of Morse's reincarnation process. This section, set in Stonington in 1978, tells how DJ has painted a mural designed to fix in visual form the essence of the Ouija board personalities and what the two have learned in their manifold sessions. The body of the "Coda" has five poems titled "Ceremony" and they are numbered 1 through 5. These describe Morse's journey to a new life and the growing preparations for JM's reading of the poem the trilogy has led him to write. "The Ballroom at Sandover" completes *The Changing Light at Sandover* as Merrill imagines a return to his boyhood home, set here as "in the old ballroom of the Broken Home," so named because of the divorce of Merrill's parents when he was eleven. It is here that JM unveils the poem to the assembled and anxious spirits. When the poem is started, the spirits take their leaves of JM and DJ. The end of the poem begins with the first word of "The Book of Ephraim," "Admittedly," and it becomes clear to the reader

that *The Changing Light at Sandover* is constructed as its own complete world, a mirror of itself.

The Changing Light at Sandover is a complicated philosophical and personal poem that requires study for full appreciation of its intricacies. It is unique among American poetry, and among American poets Merrill has few rivals. His poetic compositions are consistently admired for their style, scope, and provocativeness. In *The Changing Light at Sandover*, Merrill asks readers to consider what they really know about life and death, human nature and self-destruction, the place of poetry in a technological and scientific world, and the differences between what is real and what is imaginary.

Beverly E. Schneller

Further Reading

Bauer, Mark. *This Composite Voice: The Role of W. B. Yeats in James Merrill's Poetry*. New York: Routledge, 2003. Examines Merrill's life and some of his writings to assess the influence of William Butler Yeats upon his poetry. Chapter 3 focuses on *The Changing Light at Sandover* and other references to this poem are listed in the index.

Gwiazda, Piotr. *James Merrill and W. H. Auden: Homosexuality and Poetic Influence*. New York: Palgrave Macmillan, 2007. Assess Auden's "gay" influence on Merrill's work. Chapter 2 focuses on *The Changing Light at Sandover*.

Labrie, Ross. *James Merrill*. Boston: Twayne, 1982. The first full-length reference book on Merrill. Provides an introductory overview of Merrill's life and an analysis of the poetry published before 1982.

Lehman, David, and Charles Berger, eds. *James Merrill: Essays in Criticism*. Ithaca, N.Y.: Cornell University Press, 1982. Collection of eleven essays ranging from analysis of unifying elements in Merrill's poetry to a memoir of the Ouija experiences by David Jackson. Two-thirds of the essays are on *The Changing Light at Sandover*.

Keniston, Ann. "Ghostly Projections: James Merrill's *The Changing Light at Sandover*." In *Overheard Voices: Address and Subjectivity in Postmodern American Poetry*. New York: Routledge, 2006. Examines forms of address, particularly the apostrophe, or the address of absent or inanimate others, in Merrill's poem.

McClatchy, J. D. "The Art of Poetry XXXI." *The Paris Review* 24 (Summer, 1982): 184-219. Poets Merrill and McClatchy discuss the genesis of the Ouija board's messages and their transformation into Merrill's verse. This frequently cited interview also features a photograph of the homemade board and sample transcripts from 1976.

Polito, Robert, comp. *A Reader's Guide to James Merrill's "The Changing Light at Sandover."* Ann Arbor: University of Michigan Press, 1994. Collection of reprinted and original reviews and essays about *The Changing Light at Sandover* and two volumes of poetry published prior to this epic.

Sastri, Reena. *James Merrill: Knowing Innocence.* New York: Routledge, 2007. Focuses on Merrill's handling of the theme of innocence in his poetry.

Shetley, Vernon. *After the Death of Poetry: Poetry and Audience in Contemporary America.* Durham, N.C.: Duke University Press, 1993. Chapter 3, "Public and Private in James Merrill's Work," includes a useful discussion of *The Changing Light at Sandover,* especially regarding the interpretation of "The Book of Ephraim."

Smith, Evans Lansing. *James Merrill: Postmodern Magus, Myth, and Poetics.* Iowa City: University of Iowa Press, 2008. Argues that the *nekyia,* or the circular Homeric narrative describing the descent into the underworld and reemergence in the same or similar place, gives form and meaning to all of Merrill's poetry. Chapter 9 provides an analysis of *The Changing Light at Sandover.*

Charles Demailly

Authors: Edmond de Goncourt (1822-1896) and Jules de Goncourt (1830-1870)
First published: Les Hommes de lettres, 1860, better known as *Charles Demailly,* 1868
Type of work: Novel
Type of plot: Naturalism
Time of plot: Mid-nineteenth century
Locale: Paris

Principal characters:
CHARLES DEMAILLY, a young author
MARTHE MANCE, an actress whom he marries
NACHETTE, a journalist and critic
COUTURAT, another journalist
REMONVILLE, a writer and Charles's friend
CHAVANNES, Charles's boyhood friend

The Story:

A new kind of literary world comes into being in Paris during the mid-nineteenth century—the world of the journals and little newspapers that thrive on gossip and superficial aesthetic criticism. By creating and catering to the shifting fads of the fashionable world through concentrating on personality, modishness, and sensationalism, they debase the public's taste.

Two young men among the writers for one of these journals, *Scandal,* are thoroughly immersed in this world. Nachette, a belligerent, clever man who fled his father's bad name in his home province, enjoys the power that he believes the journals possess to create or to ruin a reputation. Couturat, hiding behind a mask of innocence and gaiety, is a thorough opportunist. Also among the group is Charles Demailly, who dislikes the dilettantes and their trivial gossiping but seems unable to do anything more than observe them ironically as he accompanies them to cafés, salons, and balls.

After many illnesses as a child, Charles grew up a nervous and acutely sensitive young man. The heightened perceptivity of all his senses extends to an unusual awareness of emotional nuances in those around him, but at the same time it prevents him from finding satisfaction in real life. His search for perfection always meets his uncanny ability to perceive imperfection: Pleasure for him pales at the slightest false note. Even in writing, his real refuge, his hypersensitivity is a handicap, for his meticulously keen observation and his attention to detail almost preclude true depth and greatness.

A letter from his old friend Chavannes urges Charles to visit him in the country and to settle down to serious writing. Although Charles declines the invitation, he does go into seclusion to work on his novel. At last his book, *La Bourgeoisie,* is finished, but his friends at *Scandal,* irritated because he deserted them and jealous of his potential success, decide to do their best to prevent that success. Scarcely bothering to read the book, they ignore its attempt to convey psychological reality. Instead, they use the title as an excuse to generalize wittily on it as an inept social document. Full of anguish at these reviews, Charles wanders about the streets until he meets Boisroger, a poet who cares nothing for the superficialities of society. He recognizes the novel's worth and introduces Charles to a circle of men who are true artists in various fields. Charles is happy among these vivid, intelligent people, and he greatly admires their individualism and their informed opinions on art and literature.

Charles's uncle dies, leaving him feeling bereft. A discussion of the nature of love leads some of his friends to assert that the artist cannot be a true husband or lover; other men seek in love what the artist finds only in creation. These two factors predispose Charles to fall in love as a protest against the loneliness that his friends feel is unavoidable. At the theater, he sees a charming young ingénue, Marthe, and feels strongly attracted to her. At last he meets her at a masquerade ball; three months later, they are married.

For a time, they create a blissful world in which only they exist. Marthe delights Charles with her affection and endearing, childlike ways. Charles works secretly on a play whose heroine captures Marthe's coquettish innocence. Finding his hidden work, Marthe is enraptured by it because the role is so well suited to her. Charles is delighted by her appreciation. Failing to look beneath the surface, he assumes, in his idealization of her, that she is actually the character he created.

After Marthe reads an article by the now-fashionable Nachette that criticizes Charles's work, she suggests that he find a collaborator to help him with the play. Charles realizes that she cares only for his reputation and its effect on her own and not for his work. With that, he begins to see her as she really is: an insensitive chatterbox, full of false sentiment and other people's ideas. Marthe, too, tires of her sweet role. Now she tries another: the woman who despises her husband for the love he bears her and who delights in violent changes of mood and in being wholly self-absorbed.

When his distress at his disillusionment in his wife's character makes Charles ill, the couple go to a provincial spa so that he might recover. Charles rejoices in the placid beauty of the country, but Marthe, bored, poses as the martyred wife. Refusing to leave, she shows her pique in subtle ways. Her banality and insincerity further torture Charles, but the growing realization that she no longer loves him is even worse, for it threatens to destroy what remains of the image he created.

At a country fête, they meet the group from *Scandal*, and the visitors return to dine with them. Nachette stays on for a week. Shortly afterward, a mock play in which a sweet ingénue is held prisoner by a neurasthenic appears in *Scandal*. Charles is hurt, not by the silly play but by knowing that Marthe deliberately created the impression on which it is based.

After Charles grows well enough to return to Paris, events there combine to break him down again. He discovers that his wife borrowed money, ostensibly because he is a madman who never gives her any. In retaliation for his indignation at her falsehoods, she then announces that she is leaving her role in his play, which is in rehearsal. At length, trying to create a scene, she tells him that she loves Nachette. When he refuses to give her the opportunity for histrionics, she leaves.

She returns the next day, however, full of remorse, and almost succeeds in captivating Charles again with her winsome affection. For two weeks, she behaves as if they are again on their honeymoon. When she asks to have her role back, however, Charles refuses, saying truthfully that it is too late for any change before the opening night. At that, she breaks into a furious tirade, saying that she never loved him and that she spread stories to dishonor him. Overcome with anguish, Charles weeps. When she laughs at his tears, he runs into the street. Eventually, he regains enough self-control to return and to order her out of the house.

When Marthe leaves, she takes the letters Charles once wrote to her while gaily parodying some of his friends in the inner circle of artists into which he was welcomed. Although innocuous, the letters, when lifted out of context and changed slightly, look like malicious attempts to scoff at his friends. Marthe, unable to bear the thought that her husband's play might be a success without her, believes that if these influential gentlemen are offended, they might somehow contribute to its ruin.

Spitefully, she gives the letters to Nachette, who is engaged in a silent struggle with Couturat for control of *Scandal*. Nachette recognizes the sensational value but tells Marthe to leave him; she can do him no good, and her charms are wearing thin. Couturat, the opportunist, wins the paper, however, and sees in the letters, set up on the front page, an excuse to fire Nachette and establish himself as a good fellow. He sends one copy of the front page to Charles and burns the rest.

Charles's friend Chavannes brings the news that Charles suffered an attack when he saw the journal. At length, Charles, wraithlike but calm, appears to hear Couturat's supposedly profound apologies. To Charles, the knowledge that Marthe was behind the attempt to ruin him is intolerable. Loathing Paris, the theater, and life itself, he refuses to allow the performance of his play and withdraws to another part of the city. There, only his old nurse cares for him as he sinks into apathy and madness. Feeling his reason slipping away, he tries to write but can only scrawl his own name over and over.

Charles is taken to an asylum where treatment gradually restores him to health. When he is at last well enough to go outside, he rejoices at the prospects of a new life. He feels able to attend a small theater, but when he sees his wife on the stage—for Marthe descended to playing in second-rate theaters—madness overcomes him once more. After months of violence, he becomes calm again, but with the calmness of an idiot or a beast. So he lives, little more than a heap of flesh, to the end of his days.

Critical Evaluation:

Charles Demailly, one of the early novels of Edmond and Jules de Goncourt, describes the world of journalism in which they were enmeshed as well as the world of belles lettres to which they aspired. Although the theme of venal journalism was common in nineteenth century fiction, the thinly veiled portraits of their acquaintances were regarded as exposé. In addition to describing the offices of the journal *Scandal* in detail, the Goncourts present portraits of the journal's directors. They show how the lives of struggle, the wounded egos, and the disappointments create the acrimonious and insensitive journalistic character. At the journalists' café, the conversation is inelegant and witless. At the writers' café, Charles Demailly meets fictionalized versions of Théophile Gautier and Gustave Flaubert, and the conversation reflects an authenticity and shows up the shoddiness of the first group.

The journalists of *Scandal* epitomize the duplicity and emptiness of the world of Parisian letters. Couturat doggedly pursues his ambitions while laughing and punning; Malgras preaches duty and honor while obviously repressing evil instincts; and Bourniche is merely an imitator with no inner self. The journal pretends to be a responsible publication even while its journalists invent stories. The Goncourts believed that the low estate of journalism resulted from writing having been transformed into a trade. The world of journalism is merely a microcosm of a society given over to false values while maintaining an illusion of virtue. Charles, a true writer, dedicates himself to art as an antidote to the hypocrisy of the age. He is at ease among the literati with their personal integrity and, as the pages of his journal reveal, agrees with their elitist view of art.

The novel's second story line explores the interactions of artist and woman. The love affair between Charles and Marthe is based on the experience of a friend of the Goncourts, who told them of his wife's physical abuse and defamatory scheming. The brothers regarded women as "hysterical animals" lurking behind a façade of beauty and as morally bankrupt creatures of sensation. They made an exception of the women of the salons, whose attitudes reflected those of their male contemporaries. In their own lives, the brothers preferred women without education, titles, or

power. Although they recognized female beauty as inspiration, they theorized that celibacy is indispensable for the true artist. Adopting the deterministic point of view of naturalist novels, the Goncourts blamed the hypocritical upbringing of bourgeois women for their destructiveness.

Marthe meets Charles at a masked ball and appears in costume at various points throughout the novel, which emphasizes her ability to create a false identity. The reality behind the illusion is soon revealed. Although the honeymoon of Charles and Marthe seems idyllic, the Goncourts suggest that, however delightful, it is merely a lie. Marthe utterly lacks appreciation for art. Her ideal literature is formulaic and sensational. She encourages Charles to work with a hack collaborator to insure greater success and profit. Although Marthe's beauty initially inspires Charles's art, her scheming destroys him.

Charles's mental instability begins when he retreats from the exterior world to an inner one of fragmentary visions. In a complete reversal, the exterior world becomes illusion and the interior one of nightmarish reality. The Goncourts treat Charles's illness with clinical precision. Charles's doctor explains his illness as the weakness of a contemporary man with an overwrought nervous system. Motifs of the collapse of a decadent society pervade the end of the novel, and the beauty of nature is contrasted ironically with the horror of humanity.

The characters in *Charles Demailly* are representatives of traits the Goncourts wish to present rather than fully developed individuals. There is no explanation for Marthe's viciousness or for her reversal from love to villainy. Although the narrator suggests that she continues her role of a villainess from a play in which she stars, it is not developed within the story. Charles is never physically described and has no past, no family, no close friends; he exists in a vacuum. The dialogue, however, is successfully rendered with a combination of low and high discourse. The combinations of letters, diary entries, and plays taken from the newspaper contribute to the realistic detail assembled in the novel.

In the brothers' collaborations on their novels, Jules usually worked on the characters and dialogue while Edmond developed the architecture of the book. Like many of their works, *Charles Demailly* unfolds slowly in a succession of internally fragmented chapters, and the action culminates suddenly and explosively. The text oscillates between reality and fantasy. The fact that both brothers were artists is reflected in the attention they give to visual effect. As part of their "painterly writing," they frequently invent new words and combine unusual descriptive terms. In its emphasis on nuanced tone and gradations of light and color detached from a subject, their syntactical technique is comparable to that of the Impressionist painters. In general, the brothers favor abstraction as a means of creating visual effect.

Charles Demailly was greeted with little enthusiasm when it first appeared. Critics considered the integration of styles unsuccessful, the relation of events disordered and confused, and the attack on journalistic circles of which they were members personally offensive. Yet in its thematic coherence and stylistic invention, the semifictional depiction of the Goncourts' literary world stands out from other novels of the time. *Charles Demailly* realistically portrays the process of establishing a career as a writer, and it retains historical interest as a portrait of the literary scene of the period.

"Critical Evaluation" by Pamela Pavliscak

Further Reading

Ashley, Katherine. *Edmond de Goncourt and the Novel: Naturalism and Decadence*. Amsterdam: Rodopi, 2005. Ashley analyzes Edmond's four solo novels, arguing that these books deviated from the strict naturalistic style that characterized the novels he wrote with his brother. She places Edmond's work within the larger context of late nineteenth century fin de siècle literature.

Auerbach, Erich. *Mimesis: The Representation of Reality in Western Literature*. Translated by Willard Trask. New York: Doubleday, 1953. Auerbach considers the Goncourts, whom he classifies as second-tier writers, in the context of the naturalist school. Compares their novels with those of Émile Zola.

Baldick, Robert. *The Goncourts*. London: Bowes, 1960. Excellent survey that concentrates on biographical background to the novels. Analyzes *Charles Demailly* as a personal manifesto of the brothers' celibacy and misogyny.

Billy, Andre. *The Goncourt Brothers*. Translated by Margaret Shaw. New York: Horizon Press, 1960. The standard biography of the Goncourts. Discusses biographical events that are reflected in the novels and provides examples of contemporary reception.

Cordova, Sarah Davies. "Transformation—the Incursion of Modernity: *Charles Demailly*." In *Paris Dances: Textual Choreographies in the Nineteenth-Century French Novel*. San Francisco: International Scholars, 1999. Analyzes dance as a cultural activity in nineteenth century France and the role it played in the era's literature, including depictions of dance in *Charles Demailly*.

Grant, Richard B. *The Goncourt Brothers*. New York: Twayne, 1972. A chronological survey that integrates the authors' biographies with detailed stylistic and thematic analysis of their novels. Includes a detailed analysis of *Charles Demailly* and elaborates on the Goncourts' critique of the world of journalism.

Nelson, Brian, ed. *Naturalism in the European Novel: New Critical Perspectives*. New York: Berg, 1992. A collection of essays by prominent scholars on the naturalist schools in England, France, Germany, and Spain. Includes several important discussions of the Goncourts' role in the development of social documentary as a literary genre.

Charms

Author: Paul Valéry (1871-1945)
First published: *Charmes: Ou, Poèms*, 1922 (English translation, 1971)
Type of work: Poetry

Paul Valéry came rapidly to enduring prominence in French literature on the strength of his earliest work. His abstract poetry was widely noted for its unusually sensate quality, and he is arguably the most important figure in a transitional period of French poetry, forming a bridge from the prior Symbolist school to the subsequent Surrealist movement. Valéry was notably prolific not only as a poet but also as a philosopher and essayist who earned a firm reputation for dealing with a wide range of subject matter. Politics, science, the arts, and language were among the numerous concerns of his voluminous life's work. His greatest reputation, however, remains for his poetry, and he was deemed by some critics the greatest French poet of the twentieth century. *Charms* comprises poems written from 1917 through 1921, a period that proved to be significant in Valéry's artistic growth, and this volume is generally regarded as a seminal work.

The year *Charms* was published coincides with the death of Édouard Lebey, then director of the French press association and Valéry's employer since 1900. Having worked as Lebey's private secretary for more than twenty years, the poet's sudden state of unemployment caused him a brief period of serious concern as to how he would continue to earn a living. Trusting the encouragement and advice of friends as well as Gaston Gallimard, his publisher, Valéry seized this opportunity to begin earning his living solely from his literary work. This proved to be more easily accomplished than he first expected, as his reputation was on the rise. *Charms* did much to enhance the poet's popularity and reputation, containing some of his best-known and most highly regarded work, highly regarded by critics and by the poet himself.

Poetic form held a high degree of importance to Valéry, and the twenty-one poems gathered in *Charms* indicate the diversity of traditional structures he explored. The book's title is the French derivation of the Latin word *carmina*, meaning song, and it includes several odes and ballads that draw from English structures in addition to French. Valéry came to poetry during World War I, finding in it a welcome distraction from the daily pressures of that time of great stress and uncertainty. Even after the war, the period during which he wrote these poems, he continued to perceive the solitary reflection afforded the poet in the act of writing to be of higher intellectual value than the mundane or tedious demands of day-to-day living. Poetry was a vehicle Valéry used to separate himself from those aspects of life. He believed that the higher level of concentration necessary to follow a given structure allowed him to retreat that much further, which may explain his claim that form is of greater importance than content. The manifestation of this concept in *Charms* is an engaging sense of intimacy between the poet and his work, a sort of private circle, into which the reader enters upon entering the poems themselves.

Valéry adamantly refuted critics who attempted to apply overall conceptual interpretations to *Charms*, insisting that the poems were written at intervals spread too wide for this to have even been possible. One of his responses to critics was that any particular meaning in his poetry is that which the individual reader may take. His intention was to capture his reader with a more eclectic range of interests and frameworks to house them. There are a number of sonnets, although the styles range from Spenserian to Elizabethan to Italian. There are also several ballads, but again the styles and lengths vary considerably. The first and final poems of the collection are an unusual instance of poems appearing in the same form, both being regular odes.

As such, the thematic map of the work is as multidirectional as the structures of the poems themselves. The reader will find a reworking of the Narcissus myth, along with deeply symbolic meditations on a random array of temperaments and locations. Given Valéry's attachment to form, however, the collection draws a sense of cohesion by way of a conceptual thread. However secondary an element the poet believed content to be, his subjects are undoubtedly distinguished by the varying rhythms and tones that inform them.

The opening poem, entitled, appropriately enough, "Dawn," begins as a simple ode to the breaking of day: "at the rosy/ Apparition of the sun./ I step forth in my own mind/ Fully fledged with confidence." Four stanzas later, the images of the awakening physical world become increasingly laden with deeper spiritual implications: "These spiritual toils of theirs/ I break, and set out seeking/ Within my sensuous forest/ For the oracles of my song." From here, it is difficult not to see the poem as reinventing itself into a metaphor for poetic inspiration. The poet's physical world possesses a growing sense of sensuality, embodied within a female presence. This presence bears qualities of both mother and mistress. The poet becomes the "ravisher" of the dawning "world": "No wound however profound/ That is not to the ravisher/ A fecund wound." The act of creation is couched in an atmosphere of turbulence, but the closing stanza imagines the nurturing sense of peace awaiting the poet at the other end of his creative journey.

At the end of the book is "Palm," which shares its formal structure with "Dawn." These poems do overlap in their subject matter and were in fact a single poem until the author chose to separate them for their divergent handling of their material. Again, at the core of "Palm" is the matter of mental process, yet there is immediately a very different sense of movement. Palm trees require an extremely limited variation in climate to live. In the poem, the palm tree becomes a metaphor for constancy and intellectual patience, unlike the inner passions of the creative process. The poem emphasizes the palm's immobility, its slight swaying in the wind signifying the image of its rooted permanence: "It simulates the wisdom/ And the slumber of a sibyl." Here is a more direct statement than may be found in "Dawn." In general, "Palm" is less given to ambiguity than "Dawn," and the notion of the steadfast pursuit of wisdom at the poem's center is rather explicit.

"The Bee" is a sonnet with which Valéry makes a clear, simple statement on the nature of sensation: "A vivid and a clear-cut pain/ Is better than a drowsy torment." The poem is a direct address to the bee. The poet invites, actually welcomes, the bee's sting as a deliverance from the numbing effects of complacency: "let my senses be illumined/ By that tiniest golden alert/ For lack of which Love dies or sleeps!" To assume the poet means only romantic love would be to underestimate this work. It would not be a wholly inaccurate response, simply an incomplete one. In the word, "Love," Valéry really means to include a much more inclusive range of sensory and intellectual passions.

"The Footsteps," however, does bring out a more purely personal facet of the poet's work. The poem is baldly sentimental, dealing with romantic love in lyric simplicity that precludes ambiguous attachments. In juxtaposition to the more complex symbolism of the rest of the majority of the collection, this poem is bound to strike the reader as being deceptively simple. Considering Valéry's partiality to traditional form, however, it only seems fitting that this classically romantic lyric be included in such an eclectic collection.

Two of the most important pieces in the collection are those that later became regarded as the finest verses Valéry ever wrote; one considered so by the poet himself, the other considered so by critics. "Fragments of Narcissus" is an extended, three-part monologue in the voice of the mythical character named in the title. Though he never fully completed this poem, Valéry believed it was his best. It employs the Alexandrine line characteristic of classical narrative poetry. The story of Narcissus was of particular interest to Valéry, and this poem is not the only example of the appearance of this myth in his writing. In 1938, his "Cantata for Narcissus" would be set to music, but "Fragments of Narcissus" would remain his most successful use of the myth, regardless of its unfinished state. The poet claimed he never completed this work because of a lack of time. It would not be the only work on which he may have intended to spend more time but did not after its initial publication in a periodical. In this regard, Valéry brings credence to the axiom that poems are never finished, simply abandoned. The opening lines of the second section are among Valéry's best-known and most frequently cited lines.

> Fountain, my fountain, water coldly present,
> Sweet to the purely animal, compliant to humans
> Who self-tempered pursue death into the depths,
> To you all is dream, tranquil Sister of Fate!
> Barely does it alter an omen to recollection
> When, ceaselessly reflecting its fugitive face,
> At once the skies are ravished from your slumber!
> But pure as you may be of the beings you have seen
> Water where the years drift by like clouds,
> How many things, nevertheless, you must know,
> Stars, roses, seasons, bodies and their amours!

While many critics have agreed with the poet's opinion that "Fragments of Narcissus" was his best effort, at least as many have defended the same opinion of "The Graveyard by the Sea." This poem's setting derives from Séte, where Valéry spent time as a child. The graveyard's reappearance in the poem indicates the lasting importance of the setting in the shaping of the poet's imagination. Correspondingly, the poem itself is a meditation on meditation as well as on the nature of artistic and intellectual imagination.

The sea and cemeteries are settings that poets of every era since Homer have found conducive to poetic meditation. The combination of these atmospheres allows Valéry an advantageous standpoint from which to move through diverse levels of consciousness as they are informed by the poem's dual senses of location. In terms of form, this poem is arguably the one in which Valéry is at his best, as the form—six five-beat lines per stanza—is hardly noticeable as one becomes engaged by his seemingly effortless language. The vehicle comes into as perfect a harmony with the journey it accommodates as the poet may have ever achieved. Ironically, the cemetery featured in this poem is the one in which Valéry is buried.

What perhaps confounded critics the most was Valéry's assertion that the poems in *Charms* were written as exercises; he was experimenting with a greater diversity of forms than he did at any previous time. The considerable quality of these poems is what led critics to question the credibility of the author's claim. In all likelihood, the crux of the contention was semantic. Valéry was never overly fond of critics, to put it mildly, although it is certainly their valuable role to second-guess writers. Critics may feel the value of their work to be diminished when so much good attention has been expended on work the author casually passes off as "a collection of prosodic experiments" and not the product of some supposedly higher artistic goal. Had Valéry been a scientist, he would be forgiven his use of the word experiment. These experiments, however, were to signal a key turning point in the career of a poet who was later named the national poet of France.

Jon Lavieri

Further Reading

Anderson, Kirsteen. *Paul Valéry and the Voice of Desire.* Oxford, England: Legenda, 2000. Uses linguistics, psychoanalysis, and other modern theories to examine the power of voice as both image and theme in Valéry's work. Argues that his work is characterized by a tension between a "masculine" imagery and a repressed "feminine" dimension.

Gifford, Paul. *Paul Valéry: Charmes*. Glasgow: University of Glasgow, French and German Publications, 1995. An introductory overview of *Charms* designed for high school seniors and undergraduate students.

Gifford, Paul, and Brian Stimpson, eds. *Reading Paul Valéry: Universe in Mind*. New York: Cambridge University Press, 1998. Collection of essays providing various interpretations of Valéry's work. Includes discussion of Valéry's mythological models, negative philosophy, fascination with science, and poetics of practice and theory. References to *Charms* and its individual poems are listed in the index.

Grubbs, Henry A. *Paul Valéry*. New York: Twayne, 1968. A comprehensive overview of Valéry's life and work. *Charms* receives close attention in several sections. For readers new to Valéry, this is one of the best places to begin a detailed study.

Valéry, Paul. *The Art of Poetry*. Translated by Denise Folliot. Vol. 7 in *The Collected Works of Paul Valéry*, edited by Jackson Mathews. New York: Pantheon Books, 1958. Collection of essays, including one devoted specifically to *Charms*, in which Valéry discusses the original intentions at the base of his work. Provides information about the main points of contention between the poet and his critics.

Weiss, Ted, and Renee Weiss, comps. *Quarterly Review of Literature: Special Issues Retrospective*. Princeton, N.J.: Quarterly Review of Literature, 1976. From the publishers of one of America's foremost literary quarterlies, this issue presents chronological sequences of critical works on an eclectic variety of poets. There are six essays on Valéry, beginning with one by T. S. Eliot.

The Charterhouse of Parma

Author: Stendhal (1783-1842)
First published: La Chartreuse de Parme, 1839
(English translation, 1895)
Type of work: Novel
Type of plot: Historical
Time of plot: Early nineteenth century
Locale: Italy

Principal characters:
FABRIZIO DEL DONGO, a young adventurer
GINA PIETRANERA, his aunt
COUNT MOSCA, Gina's lover
MARIETTA, an actress, Fabrizio's first lover
CLELIA CONTI, Fabrizio's mistress

The Story:

Early in the nineteenth century, Fabrizio, son of the marchese del Dongo, grows up at his father's magnificent villa at Grianta on Lake Como. His father is a miserly fanatic who hates Napoleon and the French; his mother is a long-suffering creature cowed by her domineering husband. In his boyhood, Fabrizio is happiest when he leaves Grianta and visits his aunt, Gina Pietranera, at her home in Milan. Gina looks upon her handsome nephew as if he were her son.

When he is nearly seventeen years old, Fabrizio determines to join Napoleon. Both his aunt and his mother are shocked, but the boy stands firm. Fabrizio's father is too stingy to allow Fabrizio's mother or his aunt to give Fabrizio any money for his journey, but Gina sews some small diamonds in his coat. Under a false passport, Fabrizio makes his way to Paris as a seller of astrological instruments.

Following one of Napoleon's battalions out of Paris, Fabrizio is arrested and thrown into jail as a spy. His enthusiastic admiration for the emperor and his bad French are marks against him. Released from jail by the kindhearted wife of the turnkey, Fabrizio presses on, anxious to get into the fighting. Mounted on a horse he buys from a good-natured camp follower, he rides by accident into a group of hussars around Marshall Ney at the Battle of Waterloo. When a general's horse is shot, the hussars lift Fabrizio from the saddle, and the general commandeers his horse. Afoot, Fabrizio falls in with a band of French infantrymen and, in the retreat from Waterloo, kills a Prussian officer. Happy at being a real soldier, he throws down his gun and escapes.

Meanwhile, at home, Gina succumbs to the romantic advances of Count Mosca, prime minister of Parma. They make a convenient arrangement. Old Duke Sanseverina badly wants a diplomatic post. In return for Mosca's favor in giving him the post, he agrees to marry Gina and set her up as the duchess of Sanseverina. Then the duke leaves the country for good, and Mosca becomes Gina's accepted lover. It is a good thing for Fabrizio that his aunt has some influence. When he returns to Grianta, the gendarmes come to arrest him on a false passport charge. He is taken to Milan in his aunt's carriage. On the way, the party passes an older man and his younger daughter, also arrested but condemned to walk. Graciously Gina and Fabrizio take General Conti and his daughter Clelia into the carriage with them. At Milan, Fabrizio's difficulties are easily settled.

Gina is growing very fond of Fabrizio, who is a handsome youth, and she takes him with her to Parma to advance his fortune. There, upon the advice of Mosca, it is decided to send the young man to Naples to study for three years at the theological seminary. When he comes back, he will be given an appointment at court.

At the end of his studies, Fabrizio is a suave, worldly young monsignor, not yet committed to a life of piety despite his appointment as alternate for the archbishop. At the theater one night, the young cleric sees a graceful young actress named Marietta Valsera. His attention soon arouses the anger of a rascal called Giletti, Marietta's protector.

Fearing the consequences of this indiscretion, Mosca sends Fabrizio to the country for a while to supervise some archaeological excavations. While looking over the site, Fabrizio borrows a shotgun and walks down the road to look for rabbits. At that moment, a carriage drives by, with Marietta and Giletti inside. Thinking that Fabrizio intends to take Marietta, Giletti leaps from the carriage and rushes at Fabrizio with his dagger. In the fight, Fabrizio kills Giletti. The alarmed Marietta takes Fabrizio with her to Bologna. There his aunt's emissaries supply him with ample funds, and Fabrizio settles down to enjoy his lovely Marietta.

News of the affair reaches Parma. Political opponents of Mosca find an opportunity to strike at him through Gina, and they influence the prince to try the fugitive for murder. Fabrizio is tried in his absence and condemned to death or imprisonment as a galley slave.

Fabrizio soon tires of Marietta. Attracted by a young singer named Fausta, he follows her to Parma. There he is recognized and imprisoned. In spite of his influence, Mosca can do little for Gina's nephew, but Fabrizio is happy in jail, for Clelia, the daughter of his jailer, is the girl to whom Fabrizio offered a ride years previously. By means of alphabet cards, the two are soon holding long conversations.

Outside, Gina makes plans for Fabrizio's escape. With the help of a poet named Ferrante, she arranges to have ropes smuggled to her nephew. Clelia is to carry them in to Fabrizio. Fabrizio escapes from the tower and flees to Piedmont. At Parma, according to Gina's instructions,

Ferrante poisons the prince who condemned Fabrizio to imprisonment. In the resulting confusion, Gina and Fabrizio return to Parma, now governed by the new prince. Pardoned, he is named coadjutor by the archbishop. Later, he becomes archbishop and attracts great crowds with his preaching. In the meantime, Clelia marries a rich marchese. One day, moved by curiosity, she comes to hear Fabrizio preach. Her love finally leads her to take him for a lover. Every night he comes to her house. After their child is born, Fabrizio takes the baby to his own house, and Clelia visits her small son there. Fabrizio, however, is happy only a short time. The infant dies, and Clelia does not long survive her child. Saddened by her death, Fabrizio gives up his office and retires to the Charterhouse of Parma, a monastery on the river Po, where quiet meditation fills his days.

Critical Evaluation:

The Charterhouse of Parma, the second of Stendhal's great masterpieces, was written three years before his death. Written in its entirety over a seven-week period, the novel represents its author's return to his spiritual homeland of Italy. With its intensely beautiful landscapes and vividly detailed descriptive passages, the book is on one level a poetic hymn to the Italian spirit and land. On another level, it is the complicated story of the search of four people for happiness, a story rich in psychological revelations and social and historical insights. On whatever level *The Charterhouse of Parma* is read, it unfailingly impresses readers with its unmistakably magical quality and its pervasive atmosphere of happiness fraught with gentle melancholy and romantic yearning.

The Charterhouse of Parma has often been likened to a Mozart symphony; the important section at the beginning of the novel, in which the young Fabrizio runs away to join Napoleon's army, can easily be read as a musical prelude that contains the seeds of all the themes and action to follow. When Fabrizio, after a series of mishaps and near escapes, manages to find the scene of the Battle of Waterloo, it is already in progress. Instead of giving a panoramic, chronologically accurate account of the event, Stendhal fires a barrage of impressionistic detail at the reader, which leaves him or her overwhelmed and bewildered. The reader is as lost as Fabrizio, who, in his confusion, spends a whole day searching for the regiment from which he has been separated. He repeatedly stops soldiers and officers to ask them, amid smoke and grapeshot, where the battle is. Slowly, however, the individual, seemingly random details accumulate. Fleeing soldiers, deafening noise, a corpse trampled in the grass, the incessant cannon booming, fire, smoke, and infantry crowded so close that all sense of direction and movement is lost—these images gradually coalesce to produce a total effect of the horror of war remarkable in its vividness and realism. At the same time, this portion of the novel serves as prelude by showing the crucial aspects of Fabrizio's personality which are to be focal points in the narrative's later action. Against the grimness of the war backdrop, the figure of Fabrizio stands in happy contrast. He is youthful, fresh, and innocent; he has boundless enthusiasm and natural curiosity; he enjoys invincible high spirits and is filled with innate courage and grace. Furthermore, although he is still young, he retains throughout the narrative these essential qualities, which make him the ideal protagonist to search tirelessly for happiness through a multitude of loves and adventures.

Surrounding Fabrizio are the twin heroines of *The Charterhouse of Parma*, Clelia Conti and Gina Pietranera. The two women provide an important contrast in their respective characters: Clelia is young and innocent, pure and idealistic, religious and superstitious; Gina is mature and worldly, witty and intelligent, beautiful and passionate. The fourth major character, Count Mosca, combines within his character the qualities of a supreme diplomat and an ideal knight. Among these four men and women grow the three love relationships that are the focal point of the novel: the love of Gina for Fabrizio, of Count Mosca for Gina, and of Fabrizio for Clelia.

Stendhal's portrait of Gina is a triumph of characterization. Charming, stubborn, astute, devoted, erotic, and intelligent, Gina and her richly varied personality are revealed through her relationship with Count Mosca and, most crucially, through her love for Fabrizio. What begins as maternal affection for a small boy grows over the years into a love that is undefinable; Gina's feelings, which under acceptable circumstances would immediately flow into erotic channels, must be sublimated; she struggles to control her boundless energies, to guide them into outlets of devoted maternal concern and to disguise from herself all the while what she really feels. Ironically, Fabrizio is not genetically related to her, since a French soldier, rather than Gina's brother, is the hero's father; for all practical purposes, however, given their background and Fabrizio's attitude of boyish admiration for his aunt, any sexual relationship between the two would be psychologically incestuous.

The second love relationship in the book is that between Count Mosca and Gina. It is a one-sided affair insofar as the intensity of passion is all on the count's side; Gina feels a great affinity for Mosca and loves him in a certain fashion but not in the same way as he loves her. The count is a fascinating figure—intelligent, skilled in diplomacy, powerfully ambitious, warm, faithful, benevolent, yet capable of jealousy and anger. What draws Mosca and Gina together are their common wisdom tempered with skepticism, their basic love of humanity, and their fierce hatred of the petty tyrants who hold authority over the rest of humanity. In many ways, Stendhal wrote his own personality not only into Fabrizio but also into the gallant Mosca; it has been said that within him Stendhal "deposited, with his artist's curiosity, the residue of his knowledge and his disappointments—the supreme irony of a too ambitious ego which 'set its nets too high.'" Significantly, at the close of the novel, only Mosca is strong enough to survive the pain of loss and intense suffering.

The love Fabrizio and Clelia will later feel for each other is foreshadowed very early when Fabrizio gives twelve-year-old Clelia and her father a ride in his carriage. When the hero saves Count Conti, who is traveling in disguise, from exposure to the police, the little girl does not fully understand what is happening but suspects that the young man is somehow noble and admires him shyly from a distance. Years later, when they meet again as adults, their love blossoms slowly as they move through phases of the process which Stendhal called "crystallization." For Fabrizio, the feeling is new in its degree of intensity and joy; his love is so vehement that, at one point, it causes him to wish for death and to refuse help in escaping rather than to lose it. On Clelia's side, the reaction to love is more complex. She becomes increasingly passionate and demanding, yet purer in the sense that into her love for Fabrizio she pours her entire soul, concentrating in him all of her capacity for feeling. Her commitment is so total that she can feel compassion toward Gina; yet, simultaneously, jealousy taints her pity, and she leans toward hatred for the older woman. Her love allows her to sleep with Fabrizio after he has become a bishop and she is married, yet superstition makes her cling to her vow to meet him only in darkness and never see his face. The lovers' depth of emotion extends to their child so strongly that when the child Sandrino dies, his mother follows him shortly afterward, while his father retires to the Carthusian monastery that gives the novel its title.

Behind these four extraordinary figures is ranged a gallery of minor characters, the most memorable being those associated with the court in Parma. People are paraded before the reader's eyes in all of their vanity and pomposity to instruct the audience in the venality and pettiness of humanity. The Grand Duke Ranuce-Ernest IV leads this gallery of comic figures; in quick flashes, Stendhal reveals a man at once cruel and terrified to indulge his cruelty, proud of his power yet ashamed that it is not greater, affected and overbearing but inwardly filled with fear and indecision. While the main characters are used to show how humans can commit themselves wholly to love, through the minor characters, Stendhal ridicules, in a comic fashion reminiscent of the works of Molière, all the vices and follies of humankind.

"Critical Evaluation" by Nancy G. Ballard

Further Reading

Algazi, Lisa G. *Maternal Subjectivity in the Works of Stendhal.* Lewiston, N.Y.: Edwin Mellen Press, 2001. Examines Stendhal's depiction of maternal figures. Argues he was the first French writer who gave mothers the opportunity to be both maternal and sexual beings, challenging the traditional Madonna/whore dichotomy.

Alter, Robert, in collaboration with Carol Cosman. *A Lion for Love: A Critical Biography of Stendhal.* New York: Basic Books, 1979. Despite its relative brevity, this is one of the best biographies in English. Calls *The Charterhouse of Parma* the novel that Stendhal "had been gathering resources all his life to write" and skillfully relates the circumstances of its composition. Includes notes and illustrations, but no bibliography.

Bell, David F. *Circumstances: Chance in the Literary Text.* Lincoln: University of Nebraska Press, 1993. Examines the realistic writing of Stendhal and Honoré de Balzac. Devotes one chapter to an analysis of *The Charterhouse of Parma.* Includes notes, bibliography, and index.

Jefferson, Ann. *Stendhal: "La Chartreuse de Parme."* London: Grant & Cutler, 2003. Provides a summary of critical literature about the novel.

Manzini, Francesco. *Stendhal's Parallel Lives.* New York: Peter Lang, 2004. Examines the influence of Plutarch's *Parallel Lives* on the biographical sketches and "imaginary biographies" in *The Charterhouse of Parma* and other works by Stendhal. Demonstrates how Stendhal compares his themes and the lives of his characters to one another.

Talbot, Emile J. *Stendhal Revisited.* New York: Twayne, 1993. One of the best starting points for the beginning reader of Stendhal, providing a comprehensive introduction to his life and work. Includes a good annotated bibliography of secondary works.

Turnell, Martin. *The Novel in France.* New York: Vintage, 1958. A standard and highly acclaimed survey. Places Stendhal's three major novels in a tradition running from the seventeenth century through the early twentieth century. Turnell praises *The Charterhouse of Parma* for its "extraordinary poise and maturity."

Wood, Michael. *Stendhal.* Ithaca, N.Y.: Cornell University Press, 1971. An accessible study of Stendhal's major and some of his minor works. Wood is particularly good at identifying the many elements—personal, historical, social, and political—that contributed to the genesis of *The Charterhouse of Parma.*

Chéri

Author: Colette (1873-1954)
First published: 1920 (English translation, 1929)
Type of work: Novel
Type of plot: Psychological realism
Time of plot: c. 1910
Locale: Paris

Principal characters:
LÉONIE VALLON, called Léa de Lonval
FRÉDÉRIC PELOUX, called Chéri
MADAME PELOUX, Chéri's mother
EDMÉE, the woman Chéri married
MARIE-LAURE, Edmée's mother

The Story:

In the pink boudoir of Léa, a still lovely courtesan, Chéri, her handsome young lover, demands that she let him play with her valuable pearls. She discourages his mood, fearing that the removal of her pearls might cause him to notice that her neck is showing the wrinkles of age. Chéri curses his luncheon engagement with his mother. Léa gently and teasingly helps him in his erratic dressing. Although he becomes lazily

aroused at her touch, she manages to send him away to his luncheon.

Alone, Léa dresses with efficient care, choosing a white-brimmed hat for her visit to Madame Peloux. She eats a good lunch before joining Chéri at his mother's house. There she finds Madame Peloux loud-voiced, gossipy, and inquisitive. Also there are Marie-Laure, an elegant woman of forty years, and her quiet daughter Edmée, whose looks nearly equal her mother's. They leave as soon as Léa arrives, and the degree to which mother and son then relax disgusts Léa. Despite Chéri's careless manners, he still looks to her like a young god.

She remembers him as a very beautiful and lonely child who soon developed his mother's miserliness and her keen business sense. In his late adolescence, Chéri had been taken away by Léa to Normandy to feed him well and also to remove him from his dissipated life in Paris. Her offer to do so had been accepted with a kiss that had inflamed them both.

In Normandy, they had become lovers. Chéri was devoted to Léa for her passion and solicitude, and she to him for his youth, ardor, and faunlike freedom. At that point, Léa would still have been willing to abandon him because of the inconvenience he caused her; he was, in succession, taciturn and demonstrative, tender and spiteful. After they returned to Paris, however, Chéri still wanted Léa, and he became her established lover. He had remained with her for six years.

When Chéri returns to Léa after the luncheon party, he tells her that he is to marry Edmée. Since Léa has always known a marriage would be eventually arranged for Chéri, she does not outwardly react to this news. Chéri declares that his wife will influence him little and that she already adores him. Wounded by Léa's apparent lack of emotion, he declares that he would like her to hide herself in Normandy and grieve. He desperately wants to be her last lover.

In the few weeks before Chéri's marriage, he and Léa are very happy, though at times she is appalled at his heartlessness toward his future bride and realizes that by pampering him she has maintained in him the immaturity of a child. When Chéri chatters about his honeymoon, Léa reminds him that she will not be there. Chéri turns white and gives her great happiness by announcing ambiguously that for him she will always be there.

While visiting Madame Peloux during the honeymoon, Léa is suddenly overwhelmed by an ill-defined grief. Feeling ill, she returns home and goes to bed. When she realizes that for the first time she is really suffering from the loss of a great love, she flees from Paris, staying away for a year.

Chéri and Edmée live with Madame Peloux at Neuilly until their own house is finished. Chéri is also miserable and questions his mother about Léa's uninformative parting note. No one knows where she has gone. Sometimes he fights viciously with his young wife, who loves him and bores him. He becomes obsessed with plans for their house and gives many and contradictory orders for exotic decorations.

Edmée becomes so unhappy that at last she resorts to looking for love letters in Chéri's desk. When she accuses him of loving only Léa, weeping unrestrainedly, Chéri is un-

moved but interested; Léa had never cried. Edmée deeply offends Chéri when she suggests that their own lovemaking is not really love. Chéri explains that no man can tolerate such remarks. Their quarrels finally force Edmée to suggest a divorce. Chéri calmly rejects the suggestion because he knows that Edmée loves him and because divorce offers no real solution to his problem.

Chéri next goes to Léa's house, but her servants still have no news of her. In deep despair, he dines away from home for the first time. He stays in Paris, living a miserable and silent life with a young man who has frequently lived on his money before. He recovers the strength to act when at last the lamps in Léa's house are again lighted. Then, without seeing Léa, he buys jewels for his wife and returns home.

Léa does not wholly regret her exile, but she is distressed to discover how much the year had aged her. Only her eyes remain as lovely as before. Although a visit from Madame Peloux restores her spirit, she is hurt by the news she receives of Chéri, and she realizes that she is not free of her love for him. While out walking, she twice sees young men who she is convinced are Chéri. Realizing that she is not yet strong enough to meet him unexpectedly, she returns home. She changes her street clothes for a peach-colored robe and paces about her room while trying to face the fact that she is alone.

About midnight Chéri arrives, sullen and disheveled, and declares that he has returned to her. She quarrels with him for a time but at last is so completely disarmed by his pleas that she keeps him there. For the first time, that night, they declare to each other that they are in love.

In the morning, Léa, unknowingly watched by Chéri, makes wild plans for their departure together. She looks old to Chéri, and he feels exhausted. Unable to draw him into her plans, she bitterly denounces Edmée. He stops her by insisting that she is not being the fine and lovely woman he has always known. She tells him gently that their fate has been to love and then part. Although he knows how much he has hurt Léa, Chéri is unable to follow any course but return to his family. Léa begs him not to make Edmée miserable and tells Chéri how much she loves him. Having thus successfully sent him away, Léa catches her last sight of Chéri breathing in the air of the courtyard as if it were something that he could taste.

Critical Evaluation:

Colette is an enchantress when writing about the relations between the sexes. She has been criticized for being a writer whose main concern is the world of the superficial. Many of her characters are drawn from the world of the theater, the demimonde, and the arts, and many of her characters exist within the world of the cabaret and the brothel. Recent feminist theory has done much to portray Colette as a writer who wrote exquisitely about both sexes and who was especially adept at writing about the sensual natures of both men and women. In addition, she was one of the writers of her age who could see through the veil of patriarchal authority. While her characters have not always been able to free themselves of gender stereotypes, Colette's characters never indulge in self-pity or despair.

In *Chéri*, the interactions between the hopelessly young and beautiful Chéri and his much older lover, Léa, are defined along traditional gender lines. At the same time, these traditional gender divisions are subverted. Chéri, in his decision to marry Edmée, finds himself in the position of being bound to his young wife while still in love with Léa. For her part, Léa never betrays the dignity of her age. The marriage between Chéri and Edmée grieves Léa to the point that she leaves Paris for a year's travel in Europe, but she never reveals her sorrow to Chéri. In the end Chéri returns to declare his love for Léa; Léa maintains her superiority as the more experienced and comforting choice for Chéri.

Spoiled, petulant, and relying only on his beauty and social position, Chéri, not Léa, possesses the most superficial features of the two—traits, moreover, that are stereotyped as "female." Léa, on the other hand, as a woman of great dignity, experience, reserve, and strength, in a sense reinvents female identity by showing that she is not dominated by the need to have the fidelity and the attention of a man. While Léa's situation is not tragic—Colette was careful to respect the gaming and humorous side to interpersonal relationships—neither is it possible to condemn Léa on the grounds of superficiality. She makes her bid, withstands the indignity of rejection, and lives with her sorrow by maintaining a stance of remove, if not acceptance. In the end, she triumphs in character over a young man who can do nothing other than what he is told to do—and then only to his own destruction.

Chéri is a novel that gave Colette great satisfaction. It is also the first novel she wrote in the third person. Stylistically, the novel shows her at the apex of her craft. Written primarily in dialogue, *Chéri* captures the voices of its characters in haunting clarity. Chéri, the spoiled young man, sounds every bit the character that he is, and his mother's voice indicates the psychological origin for his haughty nature. Léa, on the other hand, is characterized by a carefully measured and precise choice of words. She teases Chéri, but always stopping short of hurting him. As the older woman, she is gentle, a source of great comfort to the young Chéri. In the novel, Colette explores the dichotomy of a relationship between unequal characters.

Colette practiced her skills in many earlier novels and stories before she wrote *Chéri*. Many critics consider her best work to have been written in her short stories, vignettes, and prose poems. In the stories as well as in the novels, Colette takes her experience as a cabaret dancer and courtesan as the primary material for her fiction. Her world was the amorphous and amoral world of pre-World War I French society. Her fiction captures its time.

Colette never made any secret of her bisexuality, and she lived openly with men and women. This is an important factor to consider when making any critical evaluation of her work because it explains her adeptness at entering the minds of both her male and female characters and drawing so closely on the feelings of both. In *Chéri*, this bisexual perspective allows her to explore—outside the stereotypes of her time—the variations on the traditional sexual roles of both men and women.

Colette is a consummate writer of short stories as well as novels. The "game of love" that is played out in *Chéri* was frequently explored by Colette, especially in her short fiction. It is important to keep in mind that Colette, a writer of the fin de siècle era, was also a contemporary of the author of psychoanalysis, Sigmund Freud. In her short stories and in her novels, Colette incorporates many Freudian ideas about sexual relations. She was especially capable, as a woman writer, of freeing her characters from the role of the "butt of the male joke" that Freud saw women as occupying in his conception of the joke, as recorded in *Der Witz und seine Beziehung zum Unbewussten* (1905; *Jokes and Their Relation to the Unconscious*, 1960). Freud posits woman as the butt of the male joke, that joke being obscenity. In Colette's writing, she often undermines this joke by reinstating a woman as a dominator of the joke structure. In *Chéri*, Léa, the butt of Chéri's joke of choosing a much younger woman as his wife, is vindicated by her dignity and resolve to abandon—however painful it may be for her—her pursuit of Chéri. In the novel *Chéri*, Colette reverses the traditional roles of sexual relations between a younger man and an older woman and ultimately reveals Léa, the woman, to be of much greater strength.

"Critical Evaluation" by Susan M. Rochette-Crawley

Further Reading

Cummins, Laurel. *Colette and the Conquest of Self.* Birmingham, Ala.: Summa, 2005. Focuses on the theme of the individual ascending to selfhood in Colette's works. Chapter 4 focuses on the treatment of love and self in *Chéri*.

Dormann, Geneviève. *Colette: A Passion for Life*. Translated by David Macey and Jane Brenton. New York: Abbeville Press, 1985. An excellent collection of photos and pictures from Colette's life, useful in understanding an author whose work is as autobiographical as hers. Contains some illustrations for an edition of *Chéri* by artist Marcel Vertès.

Francis, Claude, and Fernande Gontier. *Creating Colette*. 2 vols. South Royalton, Vt.: Steerforth Press, 1998-1999. A worthwhile and comprehensive biography. The first volume chronicles the first forty years of Colette's life and stresses the importance of her African ancestry and maternal family background in understanding her work. The second volume covers the years from 1912 until 1954. Includes bibliographical references and an index.

Lottman, Herbert. *Colette: A Life*. Boston: Little, Brown, 1991. A biography accounting for all Colette's major works. Provides a summary of the autobiographical content of *Chéri* and the conditions of its creation.

Marks, Elaine. *Colette*. New Brunswick, N.J.: Rutgers University Press, 1960. A critical biography that has remained authoritative over the years. Provides excellent close readings of *Chéri* and its sequels, which Marks terms "parables of experience."

Sarde, Michèle. *Colette: Free and Fettered*. Translated by Richard Miller. New York: William Morrow, 1980. A definitive biography. Provides a strong feminist perspective on Colette's life and work.

Southworth, Helen. *The Intersecting Realities and Fictions of Virginia Woolf and Colette*. Columbus: Ohio State University Press, 2004. Argues that although the two authors lived in different countries, there were similarities in their lives, their literary styles, and the themes of their works. Southworth places her two subjects within the context of a group of early twentieth century artists and writers and describes Woolf's contacts with France and Colette's connections with British and American writers.

Stewart, Joan Hinde. *Colette*. Updated. ed. New York: Twayne, 1996. Originally published in 1983, this edition offers a good introduction to Colette's work. Analyzes *Chéri* together with three works that continue its themes and use some of the same characters: *The Ripening Seed* (1923), *The Last of Chéri* (1926), and *The Break of Day* (1928). Stewart describes how Colette emerged as a writer, her apprenticeship years, the erotic nature of her novels, and her use of dialogue. Chronology, notes, annotated bibliography.

Ward Jouve, Nicole. *Colette*. Brighton, England: Harvester Press, 1987. A feminist analysis that addresses the question of "women's writing" in Colette's major works. *Chéri* illustrates an aspect of the power relationship between men and women.

The Cherokee Night

Author: Lynn Riggs (1899-1954)
First produced: 1936; first published, 1936
Type of work: Drama
Type of plot: Social realism
Time of plot: 1895-1931
Locale: Oklahoma

Principal characters:
VINEY JONES, a frontier schoolteacher
BEE NEWCOMB, a prostitute
HUTCH MOREE, a man of partial Cherokee ancestry
ART OSBURN, a man of partial Cherokee ancestry
GAR BREEDEN, a man of partial Cherokee ancestry
OLD MAN TALBERT, a traditional Cherokee
SARAH PICKARD, Viney's sister
MAISIE PICKARD, Sarah's daughter
KATE WHITETURKEY, an Osage Indian
GEORGE MOREE, Hutch's brother
CLABE WHITETURKEY, Kate's brother
JOHN GRAY-WOLF, a full-blooded Cherokee
EDGAR "SPENCH" BREEDEN, Gar's father
MARTHY BREEDEN, Gar's mother
FLOREY NEWCOMB, Bee's mother

The Story:

In the shadow of Claremore Mound, Oklahoma, a group of young people, all of whom are of mixed white and Cherokee ancestry, are having a frolicsome picnic one night in 1915. They quarrel among themselves, at first in a harmless fashion but later in a serious one. They verbally torment one another with insults and references to one another's personality flaws. Viney Jones, who was a schoolteacher, tells of keeping Hutch Moree, an oil hand, after school for his stuttering. Bee Newcomb is rightly accused of being a prostitute. Other insults are exchanged. Noises made by another person are then heard in the night. Directly, Old Man Talbert appears and informs the youth that he is collecting arrowheads, relics from the past with which he hopes to reestablish his own identity as an Indian, as well as to reestablish that of the part-Indians around him such as the members of the group. Talbert goes mad, recalling the long-gone greatness of the Cherokee and Osage Indians who once lived and fought on this very scene.

Some twelve years later, in the Rogers County Jail, Bee is hired by the sheriff to trick Art Osburn into confessing that he murdered his wife, a white woman much older than he with children of her own. The sheriff places Bee in the cell with Art, where she lies by claiming that she was put in jail for being drunk. She produces whiskey to help loosen Art's tongue. Shortly, thinking no one can hear what he says, Art confesses that he murdered his wife and that she did not drown as he claims. Art then discovers a tape recorder hidden in the cell by the sheriff, but it is too late. He attacks Bee, who is barely saved from his wrath. The sheriff then pays her for deceiving her fellow Indian.

In 1931, Viney decides to visit her sister Sarah Pickard, who lives on a run-down farm within sight of Claremore Mound. Sarah is the mother of Maisie, a young girl of seventeen years who recently married. The Pickard family is very poor and bordering on starvation. Viney, who hides and denies her Cherokee heritage, lives in town where she passes for white—evidently because of her husband's money. Viney offers some money to her sister, but out of pride Sarah rejects it. The two sisters quarrel bitterly; each accuses the other of being selfish and living a lie. As she exits the home, Sarah throws several coins at her sister and instructs her to use them to buy medicine. Maisie finds them and holds them gratefully.

The three youths—Gar Breeden, Hutch, and Art—as boys in 1906 are playing games in the absence of adults. In the woods in the summer, they seek out the location where an African American man was murdered by white men. The man was chased there after murdering another African American in a card game. The three boys search for blood and other evidence, and soon they find it. In so doing, they go into something of a frenzy, engaging in a war dance and even harming themselves to the point of bringing out their own blood.

A group of people, all of whom have varying amounts of Cherokee blood, are meeting in a small, primitive church for services in 1919. They sing and dance and chant in a fashion reminiscent of Indian war ceremonies. Into their midst and up the mountainside comes Gar, who is running from the white people for some unspecified reason. He turns to his Indian brothers to help him in his attempt to escape. They refuse, and rather than help him, they tie him to a tree so that he will be ready for the taking when the people who are chasing him arrive.

In 1919, George Moree comes to visit his brother Hutch after an absence of many years; Hutch is living with Kate Whiteturkey, a rich, eighteen-year-old, full-blooded Osage Indian. Evidently, the two are married. Kate somehow comes into money by denying her Indian heritage. Hutch, too, is living a white man's lifestyle, replete with ten silk shirts, six pairs of shoes, and a Studebaker car of his very own. Because of the differences in values, the two brothers verbally fight, and George leaves.

Gray-Wolf, one of the last purebred Cherokees and one of the last to know and hold somewhat to the traditions of his fathers, informs Gar (a very young boy) and Marthy Breeden (his mother) that the whites are after Edgar "Spench" Breeden for sundry acts of misconduct. Spench is chased to the cabin, where the conversation among the family members deals with Florey Newcomb, recently impregnated by Spench. (Florey later gives birth to Bee Newcomb.) Tinsley, a white man, arrives at the cabin to shoot Spench, but he is too late. Spench is already dead.

Critical Evaluation:

Structurally, Lynn Riggs's drama *The Cherokee Night* is actually a series of seven "mini-plays" that the playwright calls "scenes." Each of the seven scenes is populated with different characters, although some do appear in as many as three of these episodes. Each of the seven scenes has a different plot. These scenes are not directly or even indirectly connected to each other. Moreover, each scene is set in a different time, and the sequence is not chronological. An "experimental" play for the 1930's, Riggs's work was well ahead of its time. Consequently, this deserving and worthy work was not generally well received by critics and has been produced only infrequently.

Thematically, the play does succeed as a unified whole. Riggs's main point is revealed by the title *The Cherokee Night*. He depicts the disintegration of the Cherokee nation as it is slowly consumed by white people's religion, government, agriculture, industry, and way of life. Most of all, however, the Cherokee nation has disintegrated primarily through its loss of bloodline; all of the characters except Gray-Wolf are of mixed ancestry. They have not been assumed into the white society, but they have chosen to leave the old ways behind—all to their own destruction. Viney Jones, educated in the schools of the white people's culture, is given over to the white culture's ways because of money; Kate and Clabe Whiteturkey are similarly bribed. Gar and Spench Breeden have assumed all of the vices of white people: drunkenness, theft, laziness, and materialism. Bee Newcomb is a prostitute who will sell out her Cherokee brothers for money, and a small amount at that.

The play is also unified by setting. All seven scenes are either on or in the shadow of Claremore Mound, Oklahoma, at once a burial ground for the Cherokee and Osage and the location of many important battles, both between the two tribes and against the white people. Claremore Mound, an embodiment of the past and a shroud of American Indian graves and history, ominously and perpetually casts its shadow over all activities of the present generation of Cherokee and Osage.

The older generation of Indians is represented by two characters. Old Man Talbert collects arrowheads, artifacts which to him can magically work to resurrect the dignity and integrity of his heritage. He must do this to keep his heritage alive. To the younger people of mixed ancestry, however, they serve only as symbols of times gone by, a life that is no more, and a way of being which is meaningless. Similarly, John Gray-Wolf survives as something on the order of the last person of character. He fully understands the white people and knows what has happened to the younger generation of American Indians. They have taken on all of the evil characteristics of the pervasive white society while simultaneously abandoning all that is good about their own traditions and heritage. The result is that they are in the worst of circumstances—both materially and morally—by actions of their own design.

Lynn Riggs, himself part Cherokee, understood very well the fallacy of blaming whites for all that was wrong with American Indian society. The settlers took the land and killed the buffalo and so on, but such offenses did not deal the final death blow that produced the "Cherokee night." Even the miscegenation between American Indians and white people, though perhaps a contributing factor, is not the ultimate rea-

son that the Indian identity disintegrates into nothingness or, more correctly, transforms into decay and corruption. The Cherokees bring "night" upon themselves.

This theme, revealed primarily through characterization, singularly holds together the play as a statement of politics as well as of morality. The chronological order of the seven scenes, though clear to persons reading the script, is entirely perplexing to viewers. Similarly, it is confusing for one watching the play to determine who the various characters are at different ages of their lives; moreover, three or four of the main characters have different marital names or nicknames, or are variously identified by such titles as "young man." Doubtlessly, all of this is by design on the part of the writer. Riggs is concerned with thematics, not readily discernible consistencies in plot. Such design reinforces the idea of "Cherokee night" as the last whimper of Cherokee death.

Carl Singleton

Further Reading

Borowitz, Albert. "'Pore Jud Is Daid': Violence and Lawlessness in the Plays of Lynn Riggs." *Legal Studies Forum* 27, no. 1 (2003): 157. Analyzes the themes of violence and lawlessness in *Green Grow the Lilacs* and some of Riggs's other plays. Chronicles Riggs's early years and the external influences that are reflected in his depiction of violence. Examines the characters in his plays.

Braunlich, Phyllis Cole. "*The Cherokee Night* of R. Lynn Riggs." *Midwest Quarterly* 30 (Autumn, 1988): 45-59. One of the best critical discussions of the play. Examines characterization, experimentation in plot, and the main theme of the work itself: the disintegration of the Cherokee people.

_____. "The Oklahoma Plays of R. Lynn Riggs." *World Literature Today* 64, no. 3 (Summer, 1990): 390-394. Discusses *The Cherokee Night* as it relates to other plays written by Riggs during the same period. Finds this play to have a "dark mood" that makes for "haunting reading."

Scharine, Richard G. *From Class to Caste in American Drama: Political and Social Themes Since the 1930's.* New York: Greenwood Press, 1991. Discusses *The Cherokee Night* within the context of biculturalism produced by the miscegenation of white people and Cherokees. Explores the problems of assimilation into mainstream culture.

Sievers, Wieder David. *Freud on Broadway: A History of Psychoanalysis and the American Drama.* New York: Cooper Square, 1955. Provides something of a Jungian interpretation of the play, finding in it elements of racial memory which account for the basic conflicts of the work.

Sper, Felix. *From Native Roots*. Caldwell, Idaho: Caxton, 1948. Finding the play to be a "semifantasy," Sper argues that it basically applauds the cause of the American Indians: The Native Americans of mixed ancestry are taking a position against the white people's God, a position from which they cannot win.

Thunder, Juliette Little. "Mixedbloods and Bloodlust in *Cherokee Night*." *Midwest Quarterly* 43, no. 4 (Summer, 2002): 355. Discusses misconceptions and stereotyped depictions of Native Americans and mixed bloods in the play, including the racist notions of bloodlust.

Womack, Craig S. "Lynn Riggs as Code Talker: Toward a Queer Oklahomo Theory and the Radicalization of Native American Studies." In *Red on Red: Native American Literary Separatism*. Minneapolis: University of Minnesota Press, 1999. Womack argues that Native Americans have their own intellectual traditions, and these traditions should be the perspective from which to analyze Native American texts. He applies these standards to analyze *The Cherokee Night*, interpreting the work from the perspective of gay theory.

The Cherry Orchard

Author: Anton Chekhov (1860-1904)
First produced: Vishnyovy sad, 1904; first published, 1904 (English translation, 1908)
Type of work: Drama
Type of plot: Impressionistic realism
Time of plot: Early twentieth century
Locale: An estate in Russia

Principal characters:
MADAME RANEVSKAYA, a landowner
ANYA, her daughter
VARYA, her adopted daughter
GAEV, her brother
YASHA, a valet
DUNYASHA, a maid
FIERS, an old footman
LOPAKHIN, a merchant
CHARLOTTA, a governess
PISCHIN, a landowner
TROFIMOV, a student

The Story:

When Madame Ranevskaya's little son, Grischa, drowns only a year after the death of her husband, her grief is so overwhelming that she goes to Paris to forget, and she remains away for five years. The Easter before her return to her estate in Russia, she sends for her seventeen-year-old daughter Anya to join her. To pay the expenses of her trip and that of her daughter, Madame Ranevskaya is forced to sell her villa at Mentone, and she now has nothing left. She returns home to find that her whole estate, including a cherry orchard, which is so famous that it is mentioned in an encyclopedia, is to be sold at auction to pay her debts. Madame Ranevskaya is heartbroken, but her old friend Lopakhin, a merchant whose father was once a serf on her ancestral estate, proposes a way out. He says that if the cherry orchard is cut down and the land divided into lots for rental to summer cottagers, she will be able to realize an income of at least twenty-five thousand rubles a year.

Madame Ranevskaya cannot endure the thought that her childhood home with all its memories will be subjected to such a fate, and all the members of her family agree with her. Her brother Gaev, who remains behind to manage the estate, is convinced that there must be some other way out, but none of his ideas seem feasible. It will be fine, he thinks, if they all come in for a legacy, or if Anya can be wed to a rich man, or if their wealthy aunt can be persuaded to come to their aid. The aunt does not, however, entirely approve of Madame Ranevskaya, who, she believes, married beneath her.

The thought that Gaev himself might do something never occurs to him; he goes on playing billiards and munching candy as he did all his life. Others who make up the household have similar futile dreams. Varya, an adopted daughter, hopes that God might do something about the situation. Pischin, a neighboring landowner, who is saved financially when the railroad buys a part of his property, advises a policy of waiting for something to turn up.

Lopakhin, who struggled hard to attain his present position, is frankly puzzled at the family's stubborn attitude. He has no illusions about himself; in fact, he realizes that, compared with these smooth-tongued and well-mannered aristocrats, he is still only a peasant. He tries to improve himself intellectually, but he falls asleep over the books with which he is supposed to be familiar.

As he gazes at the old cherry orchard in the moonlight, the cherry orchard that seems so beautiful to Madame Ranevskaya, he cannot help thinking of his peasant ancestors, to whom every tree must have been a symbol of oppression. Trofimov, who is little Grischa's tutor, and who is more expressive than Lopakhin, tries to express this thought to Anya, with whom he is in love.

The cherry orchard is put up at auction. That evening, Madame Ranevskaya gives a ball in the old house, an act in keeping with the unrealistic attitude of her class in general. Even her aged servant, Fiers, supports her and remains loyal to her and her brother. Lopakhin arrives at the party with the news that he bought the estate for ninety thousand rubles above the mortgage. When he announces that he intends to cut down the orchard, Madame Ranevskaya begins to weep. She plans to return to Paris.

Others are equally affected by the sale of the cherry orchard. Gaev, on the basis of the transaction with Lopakhin, is offered a position in the bank at six thousand rubles a year, a position he will not keep because of his laziness. Madame Ranevskaya's servant, Yasha, is delighted over the sale because the trip to Paris for him means an escape from the boredom of Russian life. For Dunyasha, her maid, the sale means the collapse of her hopes of ever marrying Yasha and instead a lifelong bondage to Yephodov, a poor, ineffectual clerk. To Varya, Madame Ranevskaya's adopted daughter, it means a position as housekeeper on a nearby estate. To the landowner, Pischin, it is the confirmation of his philosophy. Investigators find valuable minerals on his land, and he is now able to pay his debt to Madame Ranevskaya and to look forward to another temporary period of affluence. Fiers alone is unaffected. Departure of the family is the end of this old servant's life, for whatever it was worth, but he is more concerned because Gaev, his master, wears his light overcoat instead of a fur coat as he escorts the mistress, Madame Ranevskaya, to the station.

Critical Evaluation:

The Cherry Orchard, Anton Chekhov's best-known play, was published in 1904, the year Chekhov died. The author's brief life had been a painful one. After an unhappy childhood he was forced, by his father's bankruptcy, to assume the responsibility of supporting his family. This he did by writing at the same time that he pursued a medical degree. By the time he earned his doctorate in 1884, his health was impaired by tuberculosis, which was to cut his life short at the age of forty-four. One might expect the final product of such an existence to reveal bitterness and rage. Instead, like most of Chekhov's work, *The Cherry Orchard* exemplifies his profound humanity.

The characters of *The Cherry Orchard* are not tragic in the usual sense of the word because they are incapable of any great heroic action. Chekhov shows them clearly in their frustrations, jealousies, and loves. Beyond his subtle characterizations, he catches in Madame Ranevskaya's household a picture of the end of an era, the passing of the semifeudal existence of Russian landowners on their country estates. Chekhov's fictional world is populated by persons who do not have the perception to understand their own lives, to communicate with those around them, or to bring their dreams to fruition. Most of the characters dream but only a few act. Madame Ranevskaya dreams that their estates will somehow be saved; her daughter, Anya, of a future without blemish; Fiers, the old valet, of the glories that used to be; Dunyasha, the maid, of becoming a fine lady; Trofimov, the student, of a magnificent new social order. Their predicament is summed up by Gaev, Madame Ranevskaya's somewhat unstable brother: "I keep thinking and racking my brains; I have many schemes, a great many, and that really means none." Only the merchant Lopakhin, the son of a serf, has the energy and will to make his dreams come true—but he does so with the single-mindedness of the ruthless manipulator he may well become.

The few characters who do not dream are perhaps even more pitiable than those who do. Yephodov, nicknamed two-and-twenty misfortunes because of his habitual bad luck, sees failure and despair everywhere. His only triumphant moments come when he fulfills his nickname. Charlotta, the governess, performs tricks to make others laugh because she herself is unable to laugh and views the future with empty eyes. Yasha, the young valet, a callous, self-centered cynic, is beyond dreams.

Only Varya, able to see her dreams for what they are, is realistic and fully human at the same time. Perhaps because she is the adopted daughter and unrelated to the ineffectual aristocrats, it is she who can look the future full in the face, who can see other characters—and accept them—for what they are. With the security of the estate crumbling, with prospects increasingly dim for her hoped-for marriage to Lopakhin, she finds salvation in work.

Madame Ranevskaya and her family have done nothing with their plot of land, which was once a grand and famous estate. Even the cherry orchard has become more dream than reality. Forty years before, the cherries made famous preserves, but the recipe has been forgotten. Lopakhin, the pragmatic merchant, points out, "The only thing remarkable about the orchard is that it's a very large one. There's a crop of cherries every alternate year, and then there's nothing to be done with them, no one buys them." Yet to the family the orchard continues to symbolize their former grandeur. When Lopakhin suggests that it should be cut down and the land developed into a summer resort, Gaev protests proudly, "This orchard is mentioned in the 'Encyclopaedia.'"

The Cherry Orchard, like Chekhov's other plays, is objectively written and may vary greatly in different productions. Madame Ranevskaya can be played as a dignified if somewhat inept woman caught in the vise of changing times, or as a silly lovesick female refusing to face truth. Lopakhin can be portrayed sympathetically—it is certainly easy to applaud his rise from menial to master of the estate—or as a villain, pretending to warn the family while knowing full well that they are incapable of action, gloating over his triumph, and heartlessly rejecting Varya. Trofimov has been interpreted as the perpetual student, given to long intellectual rumination and little else; after the 1917 Revolution, he was frequently portrayed as the spokesman for the new social order, a partisan of the common people.

Ambiguity is consistent with Chekhov's insistence that "to judge between good and bad, between successful and unsuccessful, would need the eye of God." The author himself chose not to play God but to be the eye of the camera, letting selected details speak for themselves. Madame Ranevskaya, exhorted by Trofimov to "face the truth," retorts, "What truth?" She and Chekhov are aware that there are many truths and that reality, like beauty, is frequently in the eye of the beholder.

Chekhov's friend Maxim Gorky once commented that "No one ever understood the tragic nature of life's trifles so clearly and intuitively as Chekhov did." Yet if Chekhov saw tragedy, he was also capable of recognizing the comedy in human experiments in living. "This was often the way with him," Gorky reported. "One moment he would be talking with warmth, gravity, and sincerity, and the next he would be laughing at himself and his own words"—as with himself, so with the remainder of humanity.

Chekhov saw life with double vision that encompassed the tragic and the comic almost simultaneously. It is accurate, therefore, that *The Cherry Orchard* is classified as tragicomedy. The comedy is evident in stretches of apparently meaningless dialogue (which makes *The Cherry Orchard* a precursor of the theater of the absurd much later in the century), and in the superficial behavior typical of a comedy of manners. The tragedy lies in the lack of communication—much is said, but little is heard, let alone understood—and in the blindness of the characters as they blunder through their lives, hardly ever fully aware of what is happening to them. In the final speech, Fiers, the ill, elderly valet, mutters words that echo as a coda to the entire play: "Life has slipped by as though I hadn't lived."

"Critical Evaluation" by Sally Buckner

Further Reading

Barricelli, Jean Pierre, ed. *Chekhov's Great Plays: A Critical Anthology.* New York: New York University Press, 1981. Seventeen essays that cover Chekhov's dramatic art and the individual plays. The essays on *The Cherry Orchard* include the editor's "Counterpoint of the Snapping String: Chekhov's *The Cherry Orchard*" and Francis Fergusson's "*The Cherry Orchard*: A Theater-Poem of the Suffering of Change."

Bunin, Ivan. *About Chekhov: The Unfinished Symphony.* Edited and translated from the Russian by Thomas Gaiton Marullo. Evanston, Ill.: Northwestern University Press, 2007. Bunin, a writer and Nobel laureate, began a biography of Chekhov but did not complete it before he died in 1953. Although incomplete, the book provides intimate details of Chekhov at work, in love, and in relationships with other Russian writers.

Gottlieb, Vera, and Paul Allain, eds. *The Cambridge Companion to Chekhov.* New York: Cambridge University Press, 2000. Collection of essays about Chekhov, including a biography, an essay placing his life and work within the context of Russian history, and a discussion of the playwright at the Moscow Art Theater. Also includes an interpretation of *The Cherry Orchard* by Edward Braun.

Kataev, Vladimir. *If Only We Could Know: An Interpretation of Chekhov.* Edited and translated from the Russian by Harvey Pitcher. Chicago: Ivan R. Dee, 2002. Kataev, a Russian scholar, offers interpretations of Chekhov's works, emphasizing the uniqueness and specificity of each character and incident. Includes the essay "'All of Us Are to Blame': *The Cherry Orchard*."

Loehlin, James N. *Chekhov: "The Cherry Orchard."* New York: Cambridge University Press, 2006. Chronicles the performance history of the play, beginning with its premiere at the Moscow Art Theater in 1904 and tracing its subsequent adaptations and reinterpretations.

Peace, Richard. *Chekhov: A Study of the Four Major Plays.* New Haven, Conn.: Yale University Press, 1983. A solid study of *Uncle Vanya* (1897), *Three Sisters* (1901), *The Seagull* (1896), and *The Cherry Orchard.* Excellent for basic information and knowledge about the plays.

Pitcher, Harvey. *The Chekhov Plays: A New Interpretation.* New York: Harper & Row, 1973. Offers bold new interpretations and nonstandard views, which make this study a valuable contribution to the understanding of Chekhov's plays. The chapter on *The Cherry Orchard* is particularly illuminating.

Rayfield, Donald. *Anton Chekhov: A Life.* New York: Henry Holt, 1998. Comprehensive biography, offering a wealth of detail about Chekhov's life and work.

_____. *"The Cherry Orchard": Catastrophe and Comedy.* New York: Twayne, 1994. A student guide to the play, offering information about Chekhov's life and the play's importance, critical reception, and literary and historical context. Rayfield provides a detailed analysis, arguing that *The Cherry Orchard* is best understood as the culmination of Chekhov's major plays, particularly *The Seagull* and *The Three Sisters.*

Valency, Maurice. *The Breaking String: The Plays of Anton Chekhov.* New York: Oxford University Press, 1966. One of the best treatments of Chekhov's plays. Valency analyzes Chekhov's approach to theater, and individually discusses all the plays, including *The Cherry Orchard.*

The Chevalier de Maison-Rouge

Authors: Alexandre Dumas, *père* (1802-1870) and Auguste Maquet (1813-1888)
First published: 1846 (English translation, 1846)
Type of work: Novel
Type of plot: Historical
Time of plot: 1793
Locale: Paris

Principal characters:
GENEVIÈVE DIXMER, a young woman of aristocratic birth
MAURICE LINDEY, an officer in the Civic Guard
LOUIS LORIN, his faithful friend
MONSIEUR DIXMER, a tanner and a Royalist conspirator
MORAND, his friend and the Chevalier of the Maison Rouge
MARIE ANTOINETTE, queen of France
SIMON, a cobbler
HÉLOÏSE TISON, an aide to the conspirators

The Story:

At the beginning of 1793, after the death of King Louis XVI on the guillotine, France is menaced at its borders by practically all of Europe. Internally, the political leadership is torn apart by dissensions between the Montagnards and the Girondins. One night in March, Maurice Lindey, a lieutenant in the Civic Guard, meets a group of enlisted volunteers who are taking a woman to the guardhouse because she has no pass permitting her to be out at that time. The woman implores the officer for his protection against these men, who show the effects of having drunk many toasts to their future victories. He decides to conduct her to the guardhouse himself, but she talks him into escorting her to her home.

Louis Lorin, Maurice's friend, tries to persuade the lieutenant to avoid involving himself with an unknown woman who is so afraid of the guardhouse and who might well be a *ci-devant*, an aristocrat. Maurice, however, is already in love with her; he is afraid only that she is returning from a lovers' tryst. He escorts her home, but she refuses to tell him her name. Once they arrive in the old Rue Saint Jacques, in the center of the tanneries with their horrible smell, she orders him to close his eyes, gives him a kiss, and, leaving a ring between his lips, disappears. The next morning, he receives a short note in which the woman gives him her thanks for his gallant conduct and says good-bye to him forever. He treasures this note with the ring.

Now that he has the lovely unknown woman on his mind he is not too upset to learn that the same night the Chevalier of the Maison Rouge, back in Paris, attempted a new conspiracy to free Marie Antoinette. The immediate consequence is that the Dauphin is taken away from the apartment where he is imprisoned with his mother, sister, and aunt. The boy is given to Simon, a shoemaker, to receive a so-called republican education.

On another evening, Maurice goes back to the same spot where the beautiful stranger vanished. When he begins reading all the names on the doors in the hope that love will prompt him to identify the right one, he is suddenly surrounded by seven men and thrown into an enclosed space with his hands tied and his eyes blindfolded. Behind the door he can hear the men deliberating to determine whether he is a spy and whether they should kill him. The name of Madame Dixmer is also mentioned. Maurice gathers from their talk that she is the wife of one of the men, apparently the manager of a large tannery. The men continue talking, emphasizing that Madame Dixmer must know nothing of this happening. Maurice wonders why a tanner would want to assassinate him.

Meanwhile, he succeeds in freeing himself from his bonds, and when the door is opened he jumps out, only to find himself in an enclosed garden where he finds no visible means of escape. He leaps through a window and finds himself in a room where a woman is reading. Dixmer follows him and orders the woman to step aside so that he can shoot the intruder. Instead, she stretches out her arms to protect him. Geneviève Dixmer is the unknown woman of his previous encounter. Dixmer offers his apologies, explaining that he is using prohibited acids in his tannery business and that his smugglers were afraid that Maurice is an informer. Maurice is asked to stay for dinner, where he meets Dixmer's business partner, Morand. At the end of the evening, he is invited to return.

One day in May, Maurice is on duty at the Temple—the apartment where Marie Antoinette is held—when Héloïse Tison comes to visit her mother, the prisoner's keeper. She is accompanied by a friend who is allowed to go upstairs. After they leave, a letter is discovered in Marie Antoinette's pocket, a note confirming the death of a friend. The handwriting is familiar to Maurice, and he wonders how Geneviève can have anything to do with the queen. The next day, Marie Antoinette asks to go to the top of the tower for a walk. After a while, turning to the east, she receives signals from a window. Maurice thinks he recognizes Geneviève and immediately goes to the Rue Saint Jacques, where he finds everyone very busy with a new dye. He is amused at his own suspicions.

While he believes that Geneviève feels esteem rather than real love for her husband, Maurice is growing more and more jealous of Morand, whom for no reason at all he suspects of being in love with her. One day he voices his jealousy; Geneviève pleads with him to remain her friend. On the following day, he receives a note from her asking him to send a letter to her husband giving any reason he might think of for stopping his visits. Once more he complies with her wish.

His action greatly upsets Dixmer and Morand, whose tannery business is only a cover to hide their conspiracies. Morand is the Chevalier of the Maison Rouge. After Geneviève refuses to write to Maurice or to invite him back to their home, Dixmer himself goes to see him. True to his promise, Maurice refuses to return. He becomes so lovesick that he cannot do anything until he receives a letter from Geneviève, in which, at her husband's insistence, she invites him to call once more. He has no suspicion that the conspirators have great need of him. They buy a house close to the Temple and work all night to connect its caves with a trapdoor leading into the prison yard.

When Geneviève expresses a desire to see the queen, Maurice asks her to come to the Temple on the following Thursday. He also invites Morand. When a flower seller offers them some carnations, Maurice buys a bouquet for Geneviève. Later, as the queen walks by on her way to the top of the tower, she admires the flowers, and Geneviève offers her the bouquet.

Simon, who hates Lorin and Maurice because they protect the Dauphin against his cruelty, picks up a flower that falls from the bouquet and discovers a note hidden inside; but the note is blown away by the wind. After Simon gives the affair great publicity, the flower seller is found, tried, and condemned to death. The Chevalier of the Maison Rouge is unsuccessful in his efforts to rescue her; she is executed immediately. The flower seller was Héloïse Tison. Her mother contributed to her doom by further substantiating Simon's accusations.

When the day set for the queen's escape arrives, Marie Antoinette asks to go into the yard for a walk. She is to sit by the trapdoor, then pretend to faint; during the confusion, she and her daughter and sister-in-law can be carried away through the tunnel. However, as they are entering the yard, the queen's little black dog jumps forward and barks toward the concealed tunnel. The conspirators are forced to retreat. The plot confirms Simon's earlier charge, so he becomes the man of the day. Maurice falls under suspicion, together with his friend Lorin.

Determined to save his friend, Lorin insists that he join

the expedition that is to arrest the man who bought the house to which the tunnel leads. Maurice accepts, only to learn that Dixmer is the man. He realizes that he is a mere instrument in the hands of his alleged friends. When he arrives at the house, Geneviève says that she truly loves him, and she promises to be his if he will let the Chevalier go free. He reveals the password to them, and the conspirators escape. The house is burned down. As Maurice runs everywhere desperately calling for Geneviève, Lorin realizes the woman's identity. He follows his friend through the city on a fruitless search for his love and finally takes him home after he has become completely exhausted. There they find Geneviève waiting for Maurice.

Maurice decides to leave France to take Geneviève away. She is left alone to pack her few belongings while Maurice goes to see Lorin. During his absence, her husband comes after her and forces her to go away with him.

In the meantime, Marie Antoinette is transferred to the Conciergerie. The Chevalier manages to be hired as a turnkey there, replacing the former turnkey, whom he bribed. Dixmer also has a plan for the queen's escape. His design is to introduce himself in the Conciergerie as a registrar. He hopes to get into Marie Antoinette's room with Geneviève and kill the two keepers. Geneviève will then persuade the queen to change clothes with her and leave with Dixmer.

The Chevalier of the Maison Rouge brings a small file into the queen's room with which she is supposed to cut the bars of her window. Meanwhile, he will keep the jailers busy at the other window. Unfortunately, the two attempts, taking place simultaneously, work against each other, and Geneviève is arrested.

After having searched all of Paris to find Geneviève again, Maurice goes to live with Lorin after narrowly missing arrest in his own quarters. He and Lorin are definitely marked as suspects.

It is not until Marie Antoinette's trial, at which he meets the Chevalier, that Maurice learns what has happened to Geneviève. He goes to the Revolutionary Tribunal every day in the hope of finding her there. Finally she is brought in, and Maurice is surprised to see Lorin brought in as well. The commissary who came to arrest Maurice arrested Lorin instead when Maurice was not to be found. Geneviève and Lorin are sentenced to death.

Maurice sees Dixmer in the audience. After the trial, he follows him and kills him during a quarrel. He takes a pass that Dixmer, to harass his wife and accuse her of adultery, secured for the purpose of entering the room where the prisoners are kept. Maurice runs to the waiting room and, handing the pass to Lorin, tells him he, Lorin, is now free. Lorin, how-

ever, refuses his friend's offer. Maurice is seized, and all three die on the scaffold.

Critical Evaluation:

The Chevalier de Maison-Rouge takes as its subject matter the so-called carnation conspiracy, the attempt by the Chevalier de Rougeville to rescue Marie Antoinette from prison following the French Revolution. As a novel, it is an excellent example of the ability of Alexandre Dumas, *père*, to interest and enthrall his readers when the ultimate result of the action is a foregone conclusion. The title of the novel is taken from La Maison Rouge which, under the monarchy of pre-Revolutionary times, was one of the companies of the King's Household Guard, so named because of the brilliant red cloak that was part of the uniform.

The carnation conspiracy is a relatively little-known incident that occurred in September, 1793, while the French queen Marie Antoinette was in prison awaiting execution. An officer in the Household Guard, the Chevalier de Rougeville, entered the queen's cell in disguise, escorted by a municipal officer named Michonis. De Rougeville caught the queen's attention and then dropped a carnation behind a stove in the room. The flower contained a note that detailed the plans for a conspiracy to rescue her from captivity. Unfortunately for the plotters, the action was observed by a gendarme, Gilbert, assigned to watch the queen. The incident was reported, and the revolutionary government, under the impression that there was a widespread plot in Paris to rescue the queen, took severe protective measures, including the arrest and imprisonment of everyone deemed by the officials to have had a part in the conspiracy. The queen's guard was replaced by a new and more numerous force, and a number of the people around her were placed in prison themselves. The harsh measures were effective and, as every student knows, the queen went to her execution as planned.

This footnote to history constitutes the framework on which Dumas chose to hang his plot. The author of a historical novel is certain to be somewhat hampered in his pattern making by the stubbornness of facts and events well-known to the reader and by the discrepancies of time and place. Yet in *The Chevalier de Maison-Rouge*, Dumas demonstrates small care for historical accuracy and the constraints of fact. At the same time, however, he exhibits a tremendous faculty for seizing the characters and situations that best render historical atmosphere. To write a good adventure story, an author must have rich materials with which he is naturally, and also by education, in sympathy. That these materials have been processed by other authors and are based on fact is of little consequence because adventure, not history, is the author's prime concern. In this novel, history provided the skeleton that depended on Dumas for life and development.

Dumas takes the reader into the open air of an extremely realistic world. His characters are active, not reflective. Their morality is that of the camp and field. Dumas never gloats over evil and shows no curiosity regarding vice and corruption. His heroes, Maurice Lindey and Louis Lorin, are moved by strong passions, their motives are universal and, as a rule, brave and honorable. Friendship, honor, and love are the trinity that governs their movements. In many respects, these two characters, like most of Dumas's protagonists, represent extensions of the author's own personality. Maurice is the romanticist and lover, an embodiment of the author, who goes from mistress to mistress, frequents the society of actresses, and tends to pattern himself upon the flamboyance of the romantic author Lord Byron. Lorin is the perfect gentleman and, like Dumas, the proponent of the virtues commonly found in aristocratic society.

Dumas's characterization, however, represents the most serious problem in the novel. Dumas was essentially aristocratic in temperament, and these qualities, when projected into the personalities of his protagonists—who ostensibly represent the post-Revolutionary common people—cause a serious contradiction in character delineation. Dumas's readers may wish simply to overlook such inconsistencies, concentrating instead on the action and adventure of the narrative.

The action and adventure of the narrative constitute the strength of Dumas's style in this as in the majority of his novels. The illusion of vitality comes across strongly to the reader. The author—a physically active man—reveled in his own physical exuberance and reveals this personal trait in the novel, especially in the two characters that are Dumas in disguise. In the era depicted in *The Chevalier de Maison-Rouge*, there was much material of a gruesome and painful character that could have found its way into Dumas's novel. The author, however, never dwells on the horrors of the torture chamber. He is all for the courage shown, not for the pain and cruelty inflicted and endured.

Accordingly, although his action scenes are not historical, Dumas is a master in depicting a duel or battle. The quarrel between Maurice and Dixmer, resulting in the mortal wound to Dixmer near the end of this novel, is an indication of that ability. The gusto of the novel's action scenes, however, is matched by the simplicity and yet the grandeur of his epic diction. Only such language is capable of portraying the enthusiasm of the protagonists, their loyalty, their courage, and the zest with which they approach a mystery or a beautiful woman.

On the other hand, *The Chevalier de Maison-Rouge* is not flawless, especially in terms of plot. The structure of the novel occasionally tends to be loose, and there are a number of inconsistencies in characterization. Yet, if judged in terms of the readers' reactions rather than according to codified mechanics, Dumas's novel has much unity and coherence.

"Critical Evaluation" by Stephen Hanson

Further Reading

Dumas, Alexandre, *père. The Road to Monte Cristo: A Condensation from "The Memoirs of Alexandre Dumas."* Translated by Jules Eckert Goodman. New York: Charles Scribner's Sons, 1956. An abridged translation of Dumas's memoirs that relate to his source material for his novels, including *The Chevalier de Maison-Rouge.*

Gorman, Herbert. *The Incredible Marquis, Alexandre Dumas.* New York: Farrar and Rinehart, 1929. Entertaining, popular biography of Dumas, *père* that chronicles the social circles in which he moved. Sheds light on biographical details of his life that enhance the readings of his novels.

Maurois, André. *The Titans, a Three-Generation Biography of the Dumas.* Translated by Gerard Hopkins. New York: Harper, 1957. An authoritative biography of Dumas, *père,* his father, and his son. Excellent bibliography. Approaches *The Chevalier de Maison Rouge* in a cursory fashion.

Poulosky, Laura J. *Severed Heads and Martyred Souls: Crime and Capital Punishment in French Romantic Literature.* New York: Peter Lang, 2003. Examines the depiction of capital punishment in the works of Dumas and other French Romantic authors.

Schopp, Claude. *Alexandre Dumas: Genius of Life.* Translated by A. J. Koch. New York: Franklin Watts, 1988. A biographical and critical approach to the life and works of Dumas, *père.* Discusses Dumas's adaptation of *The Chevalier de Maison-Rouge* into a drama called *Les Girondins* to pay his bills.

Stowe, Richard S. *Alexandre Dumas (père).* Boston: Twayne, 1976. An excellent starting point for an analysis of the life and works of Dumas, *père,* and one of the best sources in English. *The Chevalier de Maison Rouge* is analyzed in the chapter entitled "The Marie-Antoinette Romances," of which the novel is the fifth and final installment.

Chicago Poems

Author: Carl Sandburg (1878-1967)
First published: 1916
Type of work: Poetry

The publication of *Chicago Poems* created a furor characteristic of the introduction of material that is new both in subject matter and in style. The subject matter frightened and infuriated the conservatives, who insisted that Carl Sandburg's topics were vulgar, indecent, and scarcely poetic. The poetry itself could not be scanned in the conventional way, was very free verse, and could not be called poetically beautiful. Liberal critics and readers, however, such as Harriet Monroe, the editor of *Poetry: A Magazine of Verse* who had "discovered" Sandburg as she had also "discovered" Vachel Lindsay, were convinced that Sandburg might be the great democratic poet called for by Walt Whitman and that his style of writing, his Whitmanesque barbaric yawp, was not only his own particular voice in poetry but also exactly the correction that conventional poetry needed.

Even Monroe's first reaction to Sandburg's totally new kind of writing was unsympathetic, so different was Sandburg from even the unconventional poets of the day. When Sandburg first submitted "Chicago," the title piece in the later volume, and eight other poems to Monroe for publication in *Poetry*, her first response was one of shock. As she read on, shock turned to admiration. She published the poems and subsequently championed the author, defending him against the criticism leveled against him after the appearance of *Chicago Poems*.

The some one hundred fifty poems in the volume, although of the same style and content, differ rather sharply in quality. At their best they are powerful, harsh when covering harsh subjects, but astonishingly gentle when discussing gentle subjects. At their worst they are chopped-up prose, sometimes duller than spoken language.

In the title poem, "Chicago," Sandburg looks at the boisterous capital of the Midwest, and with great love and admiration catalogs Chicago's glories as well as its degradation; or rather, in recognizing its weaknesses and seeing through and beyond them, he arrives at its greatness: the muscular vitality, the momentum, the real life that he loves. He shows Chicago as the capital of the meatpacking industry, the great manufacturer of the Midwest, the crossroads of rail lines. All of these are its glory. He also sees it as the city of wicked people, of crooks and gunmen, of prostitutes. Chicago is fierce,

but it is a city of builders, proud of being sweaty, bareheaded, of destroying and rebuilding. Chicago, like the poet who sings its praises, is proud of being all these things.

The volume continues in this vein. Sandburg sees the city from its underbelly, the tenderloin, looking at it through the eyes of the men and women on the streets, the lost, the underprivileged, the exploited, the lonely, and the hated. In these poems he is, as he was called, the "mystical mobocrat." So comprehensive is his view that to read all the poems is to cover the whole seamy side of city life. Sandburg's feeling about these people and the conditions of their lives is not, however, one of despair. Although he sees the terror of poverty and lack of privilege, he believes in the happiness, the present, and the future of the poor of Chicago. His treatment of the people is optimistic and romantic.

"The Shovel Man" is a good example of this two-sided view of the same man. The laborer, as the poet sees him, is merely a person working with a shovel, a "dago," who works for very little money each day. This man's lot, however, is not discouraging and does not fill him with despair. For to an Italian woman back in Tuscany, he is a much greater success than one could imagine.

Another successful man, glad to be alive and doing what he does for a living, is the "Fish Crier," a Jew down on Maxwell Street, who with his sharp voice daily cries out his herring to customers. Far from unhappy, he is delighted that God created the world as great as it is.

This theme continues in the poem "Happiness." Sometimes there is a close approach to the mawkish and sentimental in Sandburg's sensibility. The democratic impulse sometimes carries him out of the realm of observation and common sense and into that of romanticized fantasy. In this poem Sandburg says he has asked professors and successful executives for the meaning of life, and they could not answer him, looking at him as though they felt he had meant to fool them. Then one Sunday afternoon he observes a group of Hungarians, with their beer and music, answering his philosophic question by unconsciously enjoying life merely by living it.

At times Sandburg quietly, in an undertone, states with telling effect the paradoxes and contradictions that exist in such a thriving city as Chicago, the city of the rich and the poor, the successful and the failures, the working and the jobless. In "Muckers," for example, he writes that twenty men are watching a group of men dig a ditch in preparation for new gas mains. Among the twenty are two distinctly different reactions. Ten men see the work as the sorriest drudgery, while the other ten wish desperately that they had the job.

The contrast in the ways of life in Chicago is furthered in "Child of the Romans." In this poem an Italian eats his noon meal of bread, bologna, and water beside the railroad track he is repairing. The poverty of his meal is spotlighted by the train that passes on the tracks he is repairing so that the ride on the train will be so smooth that nothing will disturb the wealthy passengers and their splendid living.

Another aspect of Chicago life, the lure of the city for the country woman, is brought out in the poem named simply "Mamie." The namesake of the poem comes from a small Indiana town, where she was bored and ached for the romance of the big city. Once in Chicago, however, working in a basement store, she continues to dream of another bigger and more romantic city where her dreams can be realized.

"Fellow Citizen" is another study of true happiness, in which Sandburg barks his belligerent democracy. The poet says he has associated with the best people in the best of clubs, with millionaires and mayors. The happiest man he knows is one who manufactures guitars and accordions. This man is happy because, in contrast with the rich and the powerful, he is not a money-grubber. He manufactures his accordions and guitars because he loves to, and he is so indifferent to money that he will scarcely mention price to someone who wants to buy his instruments. This man, says the poet, is the only person in Chicago for whom he ever held any jealousy.

There are other moods and other themes in this volume. Sandburg was familiar with the Imagist poets, their desire for simplicity and clarity, and although he disclaimed any influence from them, he did admit having been influenced by the Japanese poetry he had read. The section of his volume titled "Fogs and Fires" reveals characteristics of both types of verse.

"Nocturne in a Deserted Brickyard" is a gentle, hushed picture of a static moment of nature. Another quiet understatement is "Monotone." In "Monotone" the author is concerned with beauty and with what is beautiful. The monotone of the rain has this quality, as does the sun on the hills. Most beautiful of all, however, is a face that the poet knows, for it contains the aspects of beauty caught in all other bits of nature.

Perhaps one of the most deservedly popular of Sand-

burg's brief nature images is the six-line poem called "Fog." With compelling gentleness, the noise and violence of blustery Chicago is diminished to a single image in which fog steals catlike up to the city, looks over it for a moment, and then moves on.

Other themes are evident in the volume. One, the weakness of words in conveying strong emotion, is revealed in "Onion Days," a poem concerning the Giovannitti family caught in the iron grip of an exploiting millionaire named Jasper. Although they are wracked by economic necessity, there is a dignity about the Giovannittis, a simple goodness that, says Sandburg, no novelist or playwright could adequately express.

Another theme is the transitoriness of life, the ultimate disappearance of all. "Gone" tells the story of Chick Lorimer, a "wild girl" whom everybody loved, but who finally disappeared. Nobody has even the vaguest idea where she went.

"Murmurings in a Field Hospital," in the "War Poems," tells of a soldier longing for what is past: a singing woman in the garden, an old man telling stories to children, and his own past. This theme of the stupidity and uselessness of war constitutes many of Sandburg's powerful statements.

Early readers found *Chicago Poems* a work of tremendous impact; its voice was that of people talking and protesting in a manner never before attempted; its smell was of sweat, of the stockyards. Though Sandburg's ultimate status in the history of poetry has not yet been established, there can be no doubt that this volume was a powerful influence on the poetic revival during and after World War I.

Further Reading

Allen, Gay Wilson. *Carl Sandburg*. Minneapolis: University of Minnesota Press, 1972. Brief but useful introduction to Sandburg's poetry, with specific references to *Chicago Poems*.

Beyers, Chris. "Carl Sandburg's Unnatural Relations." *Essays in Literature* 22, no. 1 (Spring, 1995): 97-112. Discusses the critical interpretations of Sandburg's literary works, describing critics' emphasis on the influence of Sandburg's public life on his poetry. Examines the literary techniques used in Sandburg's poems.

Callahan, North. *Carl Sandburg: His Life and Works*. University Park: Pennsylvania State University Press, 1987. Overview of Sandburg's career, with sensitive readings of his poems. Chapters 5, 6, and 7 focus on Sandburg's Chicago experience and the poetry he produced during that period.

_____. *Carl Sandburg: Lincoln of Our Literature*. New

York: New York University Press, 1970. A critical biography of Sandburg that includes comment on his Chicago years.

Crowder, Richard. *Carl Sandburg*. New York: Twayne, 1964. One of the best general discussions of Sandburg's life and career. Relates how Harriet Monroe arranged for the publication of "Chicago" and other poems in *Poetry: A Magazine of Verse* in March, 1914, and the literary establishment's negative reaction to this unconventional poetry. Includes a useful chronology of Sandburg's life and a selected bibliography.

Marsh, John. "A Lost Art of Work: The Arts and Crafts Movement in Carl Sandburg's *Chicago Poems*." *American Literature* 79, no. 3 (September, 2007): 527-551. Describes how the poems reflect the influence of the Arts and Crafts movement. Analyzes "Fish Crier," "Fellow Citizens," "Skyscraper," and other poems that envision work as a form of art.

Niven, Penelope. *Carl Sandburg: A Biography*. New York: Charles Scribner's Sons, 1991. A first-rate critical biography of Sandburg that includes a section on "The Chicago Years" and the poet's creative work during that period. One of the best single works on Sandburg and his art.

Wooley, Lisa. "Carl Sandburg and Vachel Lindsay: Composite Voices of the Open Road." In *American Voices of the Chicago Renaissance*. DeKalb: Northern Illinois University Press, 2000. Describes how the two poets used language to convey simplicity, democracy, and Americanness—characteristics associated with Chicago's literary renaissance.

The Chickencoop Chinaman

Author: Frank Chin (1940-   )
First produced: 1972; first published, 1981, with *The Year of the Dragon*
Type of work: Drama
Type of plot: Comedy
Time of plot: Late 1960's
Locale: Oakland district of Pittsburgh, Pennsylvania

Principal characters:
TAM LUM, a Chinese American filmmaker
KENJI, a Japanese American research dentist
LEE, a Chinese American possibly passing for white
ROBBIE, Lee's son
CHARLEY POPCORN, a former boxing trainer who runs a porno house in Pittsburgh; Tam Lum has come to interview him for his latest movie project
THE LONE RANGER, a legendary hero of the Old West
TONTO, the Lone Ranger's American Indian companion
TOM, Lee's former husband and current fiancé

The Story:

Tam Lum, a Chinese American filmmaker and writer, goes to Pittsburgh to interview Charley Popcorn for a documentary film. Tam believes that Popcorn is the father of famous light-heavyweight boxing champion Ovaltine Jack Dancer. In Pittsburgh, Tam Lum stays with his childhood friend, "BlackJap" Kenji, a research dentist. Living in Kenji's apartment are Lee and her son Robbie. They are awaiting the arrival of Lee's latest fiancé, Tom, another Chinese American. Tom is currently at work on his latest book, a cookbook entitled *Soul on Rice* (a play on Eldridge Cleaver's *Soul on Ice*, 1967).

Lee accuses Tam, a caustic character, of hating his Chinese heritage, a charge that he immediately denies. She also accuses Kenji of being prejudiced against African Americans. Tam answers that this is untrue because he and Kenji at-

tend school with African Americans and Mexican Americans. If they do not dress and behave like the other students, they would be beaten every day. Now this antagonistic behavior toward African Americans and Latinos has become normal for them. Kenji joins the conversation, saying that he is not imitating African Americans. He lives with them and participates in their culture because he is as unsure of Japanese American culture as Tam is of Chinese American culture.

Although Tam pretends to hate everything that is part of the white culture, Lee reminds him that his former wife, Barbara, is white and that his children are biracial. She believes that his marriage to a white American is a further attempt to erase his Chinese identity.

Tam then declares that he does not like being part of the

"model minority." This designation is yet another stereotype, though a positive one. Tam sees Asians as the type of immigrant the United States wants: passive, hard-working, and highly educated. White Americans praise Tam for being Americanized and for the absence of juvenile delinquency in Chinatown. There is no delinquency, he explains, because there are no children. There are no children because there are no women. There are no women because the terms of the 1882 Chinese Exclusion Act prohibited the entry of Chinese women into the United States. Furthermore, under law, Chinese women born in the United States would lose their citizenship if they marry a man from China.

Tam has a strange dream that includes the Lone Ranger and Tonto. Tam is reminiscing about his childhood spent listening to popular radio programs, including "The Lone Ranger." He also reads about the Lone Ranger in the comic section of the Sunday newspapers. Tam, looking for the Chinese presence in American culture, identifies very strongly with the Lone Ranger. The only evidence of "Chineseness" that he finds in American culture is the Lone Ranger. Tam believes that the Lone Ranger wears a mask to hide his Asian identity by hiding his Asian eyes. In Tam's dream, while he is reminiscing about him, the Lone Ranger appears and shoots Tam in the hand, damaging his writing career.

The Lone Ranger can identify Tam only with the traditional Chinese occupation of launderer. He, like Kenji, associates Asian Americans with Helen Keller, claiming that she reminds him of the three Chinese monkeys that see no evil, hear no evil, and speak no evil. The Lone Ranger also reiterates the theory of Asian Americans as the model minority, fabled law-abiding citizens, and dubs them "honorary whites."

After Tam awakens, he and Kenji go to meet Charley Popcorn at the movie theater. Their Asian appearance surprises Popcorn; he expects them to be African American. He takes an immediate dislike to them, but not necessarily because of racial bias. Popcorn internalizes the American stereotype of Asians, although Popcorn explains his dislike of Asian Americans as coming from their treatment of African Americans.

Tam and Kenji return to the apartment with Tam symbolically carrying Popcorn on his back. Tom, Lee's fiancé, also arrives at the apartment. Tom tells the gathering that he is writing a book, not the Chinese cookbook, *Soul on Rice*, but a book on Chinese American identity. He apparently accepts the definition of others who make his group part of the model minority.

However, since Popcorn continues to deny fathering Ovaltine Jack Dancer, Tam decides to change his documentary to a straightforward professional boxing film. At the end of the play, Tam is in the kitchen wishing that his children knew and understood their history.

Critical Evaluation:

Frank Chin, essayist, novelist, short-story writer, and playwright, is probably the most prolific Chinese American writer of the late twentieth century. In *The Chickencoop Chinaman*, he brings together his ideas on the history and position of Chinese Americans in the society, history, and culture of the United States. In the first scene of *The Chickencoop Chinaman*, Chin establishes the play's themes: the absence of a Chinese American identity, the lack of respect for Asian women, and the emasculation of Asian American men by American culture. Chinese Americans, according to Chin, are not born. Instead, racists using various parts of the culture of the Western United States created them. He writes that Americans manufactured Chinese American identity in a chicken coop " . . . nylon and acrylic . . . a miracle synthetic!"

The chicken coop in the title refers to Chin's perception of Chinatown as a zoo or a dirty, noisy, foul-smelling place occupied by people who speak an unintelligible language. In many of his works, Chin depicts the Chinese of Chinatown as insects or frogs. He does not regard Chinatown as an ethnic enclave where the Chinese congregated to preserve their culture. Instead, Chin sees it as a product of American racism, of discriminatory housing laws.

The Chickencoop Chinaman depicts the cultural and historical dilemma of Tam Lum, who is insecure in his cultural identity and his place in American history and society. Chin uses Chinaman, an offensive term to some, because to him Chinese American suggests a split personality, half Chinese and half American; the phrase Chinese American also symbolizes assimilated Chinese Americans, not those who are aware of their history and culture.

The action takes place in Oakland, the mainly African American section of Pittsburgh, in the 1960's. This period was a time of protest against the inequities in American society. Chin uses this period because Asian Americans also began protesting their exclusion. He includes his frequently stated conviction that an Asian American sensibility cannot be found by imitating African Americans, although, in the play, Chin does recognize the groundbreaking efforts of African Americans in the Civil Rights movement.

Tam, who may be Chin's alter ego, is vitriolic about his Chinese American identity, insisting that Helen Keller is the metaphorical equivalent of Chinese Americans. Chinese Americans, like Keller, see no evil, hear no evil, and speak no evil about American racism. Keller overcame her disabilities not by rioting or protesting but by passively accepting them, becoming a model American citizen. Chinese Americans imitated Keller to overcome their racial impediments, becoming the model minority.

A Western hero, the Lone Ranger, is ironically the idol of Tam's youth. Searching for the presence of his group in American culture, Tam discovers the Lone Ranger. He is Tam's hero not only because the mask supposedly hid the Lone Ranger's Asian eyes, but because he applies Chinese color symbolism in wearing a red shirt for good luck and riding a white horse to bring death. The Lone Ranger, as a Westerner with a long history of anti-Chinese sentiment, arrogantly assigns Tam and all other Chinese Americans their place in American history as honorary whites. This assignment is unacceptable to Tam because the Chinese are an essential element of the history of the American West. Many Chinese Americans have ignored their history in the United States in their eagerness for acceptance.

Tom, Lee's fiancé, is the only character who accepts the designation model minority. He repeats the media hyperbole of Asians being the ethnic group with the lowest crime rate and highest education level.

Additionally, the emasculation and feminization of Chinese American males are favorite themes that Chin stresses in *The Chickencoop Chinaman*. The dominant culture has stereotyped Asian American men as effeminate. In the play, Chin seems to dramatize what he has written in his essays: that the stereotype of Chinese American men places them outside the John Wayne mold of white American masculinity. He adds that the dominant society considers African Americans and Latinos more masculine, therefore more threatening.

Chin classifies *The Chickencoop Chinaman* as a comedy. However, The *Chickencoop Chinaman* more appropriately fits the definition of a comedy of common sense. In this type of comedy, a character must maintain a careful balance between the theoretical standards of human conduct and the practical demands of society. Therefore, at the end of the play the conflict is unresolved because Tam has not maintained that balance. He is in the kitchen chopping green onions with a Chinese cleaver. He has rejected Cheerios, Aunt Jemima pancakes, and Chun King chop suey, all symbols of American culture. The issue of his identity is still unresolved. He is neither white American nor African American. He is something new, unique, a Chinaman.

Mary Young

Further Reading

Chin, Frank. "West Meets East: A Conversation with Frank Chin." Interview by Robert Murray Davis. *Amerasia Journal* 24, no. 1 (1998): 87. Among other topics, Chin discusses his life, his work, and the influence of his son upon his writing.

_____, et al. *Aiiieeee! An Anthology of Asian American Writers*. New York: Mentor, 1991. Contains act 1 of *The Chickencoop Chinaman* and some biographical information about Chin.

Davis, Robert Murray. "Frank Chin: Iconoclastic Icon." *Redneck Review of Literature* 23 (Fall, 1992): 75-78. A brief analysis of many of Chin's works, including *The Chickencoop Chinaman*.

Goshert, John Charles. *Frank Chin*. Boise, Idaho: Boise State University Press, 2002. A concise introduction to Chin, providing a biography and critical analysis of his work.

Kim, Daniel Y. *Writing Manhood in Black and Yellow: Ralph Ellison, Frank Chin, and the Literary Politics of Identity*. Stanford, Calif.: Stanford University Press, 2005. Analyzes the representation of Asian American and African American masculinity and race in the works of the two writers.

Kim, Elaine H. *Asian American Literature: An Introduction to the Writings and Their Social Context*. Philadelphia: Temple University Press, 1982. Contains a synopsis and an evaluation of many of Chin's works, including *The Chickencoop Chinaman*.

Li, David Leiwei. "The Formation of Frank Chin and Formations of Chinese-American Literature." In *Asian Americans: Comparative and Global Perspectives*, edited by Shirley Hune et al. Pullman: Washington State University Press, 1991. Explains Chin's reordering of Chinese American history and his application of that history to *The Chickencoop Chinaman*. Evaluates Chin's impact on Asian American literature.

McDonald, Dorothy Ritsuko. "An Introduction to Frank Chin's *The Chickencoop Chinaman* and *The Year of the Dragon*." In *Three American Literatures: Essays in Chicano, Native American, and Asian-American Literature for Teachers of American Literature*, edited by Houston A. Baker. New York: Modern Language Association of America, 1982. One of the best critical analyses of *The Chickencoop Chinaman* and *The Year of the Dragon* (1974).

Child of God

Author: Cormac McCarthy (1933-   )
First published: 1973
Type of work: Novel
Type of plot: Social realism
Time of plot: Early 1960's
Locale: Sevier County, Tennessee

Principal characters:
LESTER BALLARD, a young, solitary man
FATE TURNER, the high sheriff of Sevier County
JOHN GREER, an outsider who buys Ballard's house
REUBEL, a dumpkeeper, Ballard's drinking companion

The Story:

Under the supervision of Fate Turner, the high sheriff of Sevier County, a farm is being auctioned off for nonpayment of taxes. When the owner, Lester Ballard, threatens the auctioneer with a rifle, one of the men assembled at the auction hits Lester in the head with an ax and takes him away. From that time on, Lester has difficulty holding up his head. The blow might have affected his mind. Because of Lester's behavior, many local people are afraid to bid on the land, and it goes to John Greer, an outsider. Lester is determined to kill Greer.

Lester has no home and no way to support himself, without even enough money to buy whiskey; but he is not defeated. Deep in the woods he finds a deserted house, cleans it up, brings his few possessions to it, and moves in. He survives by stealing food and shooting game. He has no way, however, to fulfill his sexual needs. One night he relieves himself while watching a couple having intercourse in a car, but when they see him, they flee. Sometimes Lester visits Reubel, in hopes that one of his nine promiscuous daughters will help him, but they only laugh at him.

Lester has always been mean, but after he loses his farm, he seems to go crazy. It is inevitable that he will get in trouble. One fall morning, while he is hunting, Lester finds a woman lying on the ground, where she evidently passed out drunk. They fight; then Lester rips off the nightgown she is wearing and carries it away with him, leaving her naked. Later, the woman charges Lester with rape, and he is put in jail, where he spends nine rather pleasant days, eating his fill and enjoying the company of another inmate. After Lester is released, Fate warns him to stay out of Sevierville and out of trouble, predicting that if he does not change his attitude, Lester will end up murdering someone. Defiantly, Lester says that he does not care about the people of the town, or, he suggests, anyone else.

Lester still needs a woman. At a county fair, he shoots a rifle so well that he wins three stuffed animals and is chased away by the pitchman. Despite his skill and his trophies, the pretty girls in the crowd turn away from him. Lester goes home alone, carrying two toy bears and a tiger.

Hoping to win the favor of one of the girls in the area, Lester captures a live robin and, despite her mother's objections, gives it as a toy to the girl's retarded child. When the child chews off the bird's legs, the two women are annoyed and disgusted, and Lester leaves their house.

One December morning, Lester finds the solution to his frustrations. He happens upon a car in which a man and a woman are lying dead, victims of carbon monoxide poisoning. Lester's first thought is to take their money, their whiskey, and the woman's makeup. Then he has an inspiration. Returning to the scene of the accident, he carries off the woman's corpse. At his house, he puts her in the nightgown he had taken earlier from the drunk, and he hoists her body into the attic. Later, in Sevierville, he buys sexy clothing for his find, and from that time on, whenever he needs a woman, he brings the corpse down from the attic and uses it. Now Lester has money, as well as food and shelter, and even someone he can pretend is his wife. Since he hid the car and the man's body, Lester thinks he is secure. One night, however, the house catches fire and burns to the ground. Lester is able to save some possessions, including his stuffed animals, but the body in the attic is totally consumed.

Still undefeated, Lester makes his home in a cave. On one of his forays, he encounters Greer, but Lester makes no threats. In fact, he even denies that he is the man whose property Greer now owns. His revenge can wait; he has more pressing needs. Finding the girl with the retarded child alone in her house, he makes sexual advances to her. When she rejects him, he kills her and then burns down her house, with the child inside. Fate's prediction has come true; now Lester is a murderer.

When Lester is arrested, however, it is merely for setting fire to the house where he was living, and again he is released. Now Lester turns his attention to Greer. He takes pleasure in stealing eggs from the man he believes stole so much from him, and he spends most of his time hiding near Greer's house, watching him and brooding upon revenge. So far, Lester manages to cover his tracks. Even when Fate finds the car in which the couple died, he has no reason to connect Lester with the missing girl, and Lester remains free. Having given up on women who are alive, he now decides to procure dead ones. When he finds a couple parked in a pickup truck, he kills them both and takes the dead girl to his cave. Again, however, the cards seem to be stacked against him. In the spring floods, he loses not only the girl's body, but most of his possessions, even the stuffed animals. The little he has left, Lester drags farther up the mountain, depositing it in his new home, a sinkhole.

Then everything goes wrong. When Lester tries to kill Greer, he succeeds only in wounding him. Greer shoots back, and Lester awakens in the hospital with an arm missing. Certain that Lester is responsible for the other crimes, a mob seizes him, and to keep from being lynched, Lester admits his guilt and offers to take the men to the bodies. However, after he leads them into a cave, Lester gets away and makes his way safely back to the hospital. Judged insane, he is confined in a mental institution, where he dies of pneumonia. One spring day, a farmer's team disappears into a sinkhole, and, exploring the chamber below, the sheriff finds the bodies of seven women. At last Lester's victims can be properly buried.

Critical Evaluation:

Although Cormac McCarthy has not won the fame or attained the financial success of many of his contemporaries, his works have received high praise from critics and from other writers. Technically, he has even been called superior to William Faulkner, another Southern writer, who in 1949 won the Nobel Prize in Literature. McCarthy's skills with spoken and written language are evident in *Child of God*, in which he moves easily from the laconic, colorful dialogue of his Tennessee mountaineers to descriptive passages whose lyricism is as often inspired by junked cars and moldy mattresses as by the beauty of the natural setting.

McCarthy's handling of narrative is as brilliant as his use of language. *Child of God* is on one level the story of a single man, Lester Ballard, during a relatively brief period of time. The narrator also reaches far into the historic past to describe the misdeeds of Lester's distant ancestors and of a whole troubled society; McCarthy thus gives his novel intellectual depth and thematic complexity. Similarly, the references to Lester's history, whether they are presented through his dreams and reveries or through the narrator's vivid anecdotes, make Lester a more complicated character than might be assumed, given his appalling activities.

Lester's necrophilia, in particular, aroused the ire of some reviewers. Some who had praised McCarthy's previous work expressed disgust with *Child of God* and relegated its author to the ranks of those who peddle the grotesque with a Southern setting.

Other critics, however, have found much to interest them in *Child of God*. Some have even called the book a masterpiece. They point out that McCarthy is careful to emphasize Lester's humanity. One can understand the feelings of the boy who is abandoned by his mother, then deserted a second time when his father commits suicide, and of the man who is rejected whenever he reaches out to another human being. On a theological level, Lester's evil impulses can be explained by his being human. The question which must be asked is whether Fate's warnings constitute an offer of redemption, or whether, in Calvinistic terms, Lester was not born one of the elect but rather born damned.

Lester can also be viewed from a historical perspective. While murder, rape, and necrophilia would hardly have met the approval of any Jeffersonian democrat, it is true that Lester possesses many of the qualities that were admired on the frontier and that are still cherished by Americans with an agrarian leaning. He is an independent farmer, willing to fight to keep his land; when he is deprived of it, he remains independent, using his resourcefulness to live off the land. Clearly McCarthy does not intend to make of Lester a tragic hero; however, given the territorial imperative of an earlier time, it is not surprising that this man who makes his home in the wilderness sees the cars and trucks that invade his territory, and their inhabitants, as fair game. It could also be argued that although the way in which Lester expresses his territoriality is not acceptable in modern society, the impulse is simply another facet of human nature. After all, when Lester ventures outside his own area, as when he sells the watches he has acquired, he is mocked, cheated, and expelled by the community. McCarthy does not equate the territorial impulse with depravity, but like a good Southerner he seems to understand it. He may be suggesting that the territorial impulse is as basic to human beings as is their desire to do evil.

If the real theme of *Child of God* is human nature, the author leaves readers with more questions than answers. Aside from his technical virtuosity, McCarthy's creation of Lester Ballard, a character who is at once despicable, pitiable, tragic, doomed, and damned, should assure McCarthy's place in Southern literature.

Rosemary M. Canfield Reisman

Further Reading

Bartlett, Andrew. "From Voyeurism to Archaeology: Cormac McCarthy's *Child of God*." *Southern Literary Journal* 24 (Fall, 1991): 3-15. Argues that the real focus of

Child of God is not its sociopathic protagonist but the question of how he should be perceived. An incisive study of technique and theme.

Bell, Vereen M. *The Achievement of Cormac McCarthy.* Baton Rouge: Louisiana State University Press, 1988. This book-length study of McCarthy devotes one chapter to *Child of God* and also contains a helpful introduction.

Cant, John. *Cormac McCarthy and the Myth of American Exceptionalism.* New York: Routledge, 2008. An analysis of all of McCarthy's work to date, including a separate chapter on *Child of God.* Describes McCarthy as an iconoclast whose work deconstructs America's vision as a nation with an exceptional role in the world.

Ellis, Jay. *No Place for Home: Spatial Constraint and Character Flight in the Novels of Cormac McCarthy.* New York: Routledge, 2006. Examines nine of McCarthy's novels to determine "the relationship of ambivalent nostalgia for domesticity" to his descriptions of space. Chapter 3, "Unhousing a *Child of God*," focuses on this novel.

Grammar, John. "A Thing Against Which Time Will Not Prevail: Pastoral and History in Cormac McCarthy's South." *The Southern Quarterly* 30 (Summer, 1992): 19-30. An important essay, showing how one of the major themes in southern literature is basic to McCarthy's thought. Lester Ballard meets his doom because he is an anachronism.

Guillemin, Georg. *The Pastoral Vision of Cormac McCarthy.* College Station: Texas A&M University Press, 2004. Examines what Guillemin describes as the "ecopastoralism" in McCarthy's fiction. Guillemin argues that McCarthy's work does not express nostalgia for a lost pastoral world; instead, it is characterized by a radical and egalitarian land ethic. Chapter 1 contains an extensive discussion of *Child of God*, and there are other references to the novel listed in the index.

Holloway, David. *The Late Modernism of Cormac McCarthy.* Westport, Conn.: Greenwood Press, 2002. Holloway uses the ideas of several twentieth century Marxist political thinkers to analyze *Child of God* and seven other novels. He demonstrates how McCarthy resists postmodern narrative techniques and is more correctly defined as a modernist.

Lilley, James D., ed. *Cormac McCarthy: New Directions.* Albuquerque: University of New Mexico Press, 2002. Collection of essays analyzing McCarthy's works, including "The Case of Oblivion: Platonic Mythology in *Child of God*" by Dianne C. Luce.

Sanborn, Wallis R. III. "Bovines and Levity in *Child of God*." In *Animals in the Fiction of Cormac McCarthy.* Jefferson, N.C.: McFarland, 2006. Sanborn analyzes the role of animals in McCarthy's fiction, describing how they can be harbingers of death, figures of comic relief, or examples of harsh biological determinism.

Sullivan, Nell. "The Evolution of the Dead Girlfriend Motif in *Outer Dark* and *Child of God*." In *Myth, Legend, Dust: Critical Responses to Cormac McCarthy*, edited by Rick Wallach. New York: St. Martin's Press, 2000. An analysis of McCarthy's depiction of women, charting his work from the *Outer Dark* (1968) to *Child of God.* Sullivan argues that this transition marks the "crystallization" of the dead girlfriend motif in his mature fiction.

Childe Harold's Pilgrimage

Author: Lord Byron (1788-1824)
First published: 1812-1818
Type of work: Poetry
Type of plot: Picaresque
Time of plot: 1809-1818
Locale: Europe

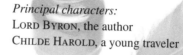

Principal characters:
LORD BYRON, the author
CHILDE HAROLD, a young traveler

The Poem:

In Canto 1, Bryon introduces Childe Harold, a young English nobleman who has been wasting his life with drinking, idleness, and making love to unsuitable women. The woman he does love he cannot have. Despondent, he leaves his family, his family home, his heritage. and his lands to travel, albeit with no clear destination. Perhaps, he thinks, he will find happiness and some meaning to his life once he leaves England.

Leaving, he sings a mournful song—the poem "Good Night"—bidding farewell to his homeland, to his parents, and to his wife and sons. Harold encourages the young page who accompanies him over the ocean not to be afraid. When Harold lands on the shore of Portugal, he finds himself moved in strange and unexpected ways. He begins exploring the land on horseback, moving aimlessly in search of his destiny, and he wanders into the mountains northeast of Lisbon, to Cintra, the site of the Convention that allowed the defeated French army to withdraw intact. Harold comments on the disgrace of this event. He makes many such comments on political events. He also reflects on the scenery, finding the land beautiful but the people dirty and immoral. Harold laments on the sorry state of these men and women who live in such a beautiful land. He continues into Spain.

In Spain, Harold is again thrilled by the magnificence of the scenery but appalled at the depths to which the civilization has fallen. His first real understanding of human cruelty occurs in Spain, where he watches a bullfight. He watches the cruelty of the humans tormenting the bull and the courage of the beast, who cannot understand why anyone would try to hurt it. The bullfight, as always, ends in the death of the bull but brings Harold no further in his quest to understand the meaning of his life.

Canto 2 shows Childe Harold's first change of heart when he travels through Albania into Greece, meeting a great many people of various nationalities and religions. He finds the Albanians to be barbaric by his standards but in some ways nobler than the more civilized people he has encountered thus far. His spirits begin to rise as he realizes that, whatever the situation of civilization, there is still great hope as he witnesses both the wonders of nature and the goodness of humankind. However, at the end of the canto, reflecting on death and loss, Harold decides to return home and confront what he had left behind.

In Canto 3, Harold again leaves England, embarking on a second Grand Tour. He travels to Belgium, the Rhine, Switzerland, and the Alps. Harold reflects on the child, Ada, he has left behind, yet he embraces the continuance of his journey. It is at this point that the fiction of Harold is replaced by the reality of Byron's own voice. This canto includes a description of Napoleon's defeat at Waterloo, as well as "Harold's" commentary on Napoleon. In Germany, along the banks of the Rhine, Harold finally feels a sense of hope and begins to see some meaning in the human condition. He continues on his journey, exalting in the beauty of the Swiss Alps and sites that remind him of the courage of the human spirit. Harold reflects on Rousseau and his life and work. The canto concludes with verses to his daughter.

Canto 4 is prefaced by a letter to Byron's friend John Hobhouse. Byron finally does away with the third-person narrator and speaks in the first person. He turns "from fiction to truth," telling his own story. The canto begins with Bryon's reflections while standing on the Bridge of Sighs in Venice. Bryon travels through the Italian countryside and the ancient cities that were once part of the Roman Empire. He comments on sites and on the people who lived there, average men, military leaders, and authors. His journey, like those of many pilgrims, ends in Rome. The stanzas on Rome constitute more than half of the canto. Finally, turning from cities and people, Bryon speaks about the ocean and declares his "task is done."

Critical Evaluation:

Lord Byron was one of the greatest poets of the Romantic Era of British literature. He was a rebel, a malcontent, and a traveler. While Byron was writing *Childe Harold's Pilgrimage*, he was himself traveling; he visited all of the places he described in the poem. When the first two cantos were published in 1812, he became an overnight sensation. The poem made Byron famous in Europe. It was favorably reviewed in the leading periodicals of the time and translated into many languages.

Childe Harold's Pilgrimage is a poetic journal, recording what Byron, as Harold, sees, learns, and feels as he travels. Immediacy is provided by the use of the present tense. The poem is subtitled *A Romaunt*, and it is a romance in the sense of a narrative of adventure. It was published in three sections, over a span of six years, and Byron wrote other works in between. Since the poem first appeared, critics have disagreed as to its meaning and whether it should be considered as two separate poems, or even three. The first two cantos (the equivalent of chapters in prose) were published together in 1812 and are as much a travelogue as they are the story of a pilgrimage. Byron interrupts his narrative regularly to make political and sociological comments about his own time. Canto 3 (pb. 1916) and Canto 4 (pb. 1918) are also travelogues with commentaries about Byron's present. The cantos vary in length, ranging from 93 stanzas in the first to 186 stanzas in the fourth. Contained within the cantos are additional lyric poems, such as "Good Night" in Stanza 13 and "To Inez" in Stanza 84 of Canto 1.

According to his preface to the first two cantos, Byron intended the poem to be a long narrative poem in the style (and even the meter) of Edmund Spenser, a sixteenth century English poet. Using ancient forms was an interest of the Romantic poets such as John Keats, who wrote "La Belle Dame Sans Merci" (1820) as a ballad, using archaic language. In

Childe Harold's Pilgrimage, the language of the first two cantos is deliberately archaic. Byron uses Middle English words such as "whilome" and "hight," and the very title is intended to lend a medieval flavor to the work: "Childe" was originally a term used to refer to a young man approaching knighthood. Consequently, it is an appropriate word to describe Harold, since a knight's duty is to go on quests.

Childe Harold's Pilgrimage is in the tradition of a romantic quest, a mission that will prove the hero's courage and test his moral values. However, Harold, a libertine and cynic, is no medieval knight. On one level, the poem tells the story of Harold's journey, but "pilgrimage" is probably an inappropriate word for this journey. Harold never searches for anything specific; rather, he runs away from his past and tries, in the process, to find some meaning in life.

Although the poem is written in Spenserian stanzas and uses archaic language, there is a visible change in the meter and language beginning with Canto 3. By this canto, much of the archaic language is gone, and the verse itself begins to flow more naturally. Finally, in Canto 4, the medieval language is almost entirely gone, replaced by the language that Byron spoke himself. Only a few outmoded words remain to preserve some of the flavor of the earlier sections and try to give some coherence to the whole.

Travelogues were popular literary forms in the early nineteenth century, but *Childe Harold's Pilgrimage* is more than a travelogue. It is like a diary in which Harold not only writes about places and people but also comments on the beauty of nature and human activities through history. The focus of these comments ranges from the creativity of ancient writers to a critique of the evolving political order in contemporary Europe. The poem includes reflections on nature and on social institutions, which are characteristic concerns of the Romantic poets. There are also powerful political messages, most of them having to do with the decadence Byron perceived in his own times as compared to the glorious past of ancient Greece and Rome. At a deeper level, Byron explores the question of human identity itself.

Many critics have insisted that, in Childe Harold, Byron was merely fictionalizing his own life. In his preface to the first two cantos, Byron insists that the narrator, Childe Harold, is fictitious. In the manuscript version of the cantos, however, the hero is named Childe Burun, an early form of Byron's family name. After reading the reviews of the poem, Bryon wrote the "Addition to the Preface" in 1813, affirming that Harold was a "fictitious personage." However, Byron and Harold have much in common. This becomes increasingly obvious in the third and fourth cantos. In his 1818 letter to Hobhouse, prefacing Canto 4, Byron finally states what

critics and readers have already surmised: that Childe Harold is Byron. In the introduction to Canto 4, Byron virtually disowns Harold, explaining that since almost everyone seems to assume that he is Byron's alter ego, there is no longer any point to keeping up the pretense.

It is essential to view *Childe Harold's Pilgrimage* in its historical context. When it was written, the French Revolution had failed and Napoleon had assumed the robes of emperor. These events deeply disappointed the idealistic Romantics, who had seen the French Revolution and Napoleon as beacons leading the way to a bright new era of Republican liberty, equality, and brotherhood. Although Byron and many of his contemporaries longed for bygone days, they also emphasized the dignity of humankind and the importance of equality. The rise of Napoleon, his subsequent fall, and the return of the French monarchy were tragedies, as was the destruction of many ancient works and the barbarism of the Reign of Terror. Canto 3, in the stanzas on Waterloo, reflects on that battle and questions whether the earth is "more free" because of Napoleon's defeat, or whether the defeat of one tyrant simply means a return to an older tyranny. Like other liberals, such as William Blake and Percy Bysshe Shelley, Byron was against any type of tyranny. Some critics see Canto 4 as a political poem and a plea that Italy, which during Bryon's time was a collection of states, be recognized as a cultural whole and throw off the tyranny of Austrian rule. Like other Romantic poets, Byron decries the unnaturalness of a people and a land subjected to an outside authority.

The influence of this poem on later literature has been great. There are no earlier or later versions of the specific tale, but its echoes are immense. In Childe Harold, the "Byronic hero" was born, a literary device that has lasted to the present day. The Byronic hero is essentially an antihero, alienated and rebellious. He is moody, passionate, and remorseful. Harold sees himself as a "wandering outlaw," and it is characteristic of this antihero that he needs to be forever traveling, trying to assuage his "deep hurt." The Byronic hero is full of guilt for past deeds yet is unrepentant. In Canto 1, the character of Harold is self-indulgent and judgmental, but he becomes more human and sympathetic to others as his pilgrimage continues. Harold is deeply affected by a series of losses at the end of Canto 2, reflecting Byron's own loss of his mother and two close friends, who died while he was traveling. Canto 3, which is the emotional center of the poem, provides a clear picture of the Bryonic hero. It begins with a heartfelt goodbye to his daughter Ada and England, as Harold once again departs into voluntary exile, echoing Byron's own final departure from England in 1816. Speaking more as Byron himself than as his character, he says goodbye to his daughter Augusta Ada, born a month before Bryon and his wife Annabella Milbanke separated. He never sees her again.

Canto 3 also includes stanzas describing the poet. Characteristic of Romantics such as Shelley, Bryon escapes into poetry. For him, writing is therapeutic, and in the poem his personal limitations are transcended. In creating the poem, the poet gains as he gives his ideas the physical form of words. As Harold, Byron sees himself as a rebel with little in common with humankind. He will not "yield dominion of his mind" to others, and he feels that he has little in common with others and can live his life "without mankind." Again, in the Romantic tradition, Harold finds companionship in nature; the mountains and the ocean are both friends and a home. Echoing Shelley, Bryon describes nature as speaking a language he can share and, like William Wordsworth, the hero finds solace and renewal in nature.

As a part of the Romantic tradition, Bryon creates a poet hero whose ultimate gift to humankind is the poem. Much like Shelley, Byron realizes how the poem itself can communicate his ideas beyond his lifetime. In Canto 3, stanzas 113 through 118, Bryon again restates the position of the hero, alone and apart from the world. He repeats that the poem is his gift to Ada, his lost "child of love," and prays, since she can never know him, that she might discover him through his words.

Ultimately, Byron's basic goal in *Childe Harold's Pilgrimage* is to explore the nature of humankind and humanity's relation to nature. The descriptions of natural and ancient architectural beauty are moving and are fine examples of Romantic poetry. Byron's long forays into social criticism are even more fascinating. For Harold (Byron), the poem chronicles a journey from despair to self-renewal.

Marc Goldstein; revised by Marcia B. Dinneen

Further Reading

Bone, Drummond, ed. *The Cambridge Companion to Byron*. New York: Cambridge University Press, 2004. This overview of Byron's life and work includes four essays, with each one discussing one of the four cantos of *Childe Harold's Pilgrimage*.

Crane, David. *The Kindness of Sisters*. New York: Alfred A. Knopf, 2003. A study of Byron's reputation after death, exploring bitter and conflicting accounts by the wife he divorced and the sister he seduced.

Franklin, Caroline. *Byron: A Literary Life*. New York: Routledge, 2007. Biography focusing on Byron as a professional writer, recounting the circumstances of his major poems' production. Includes numerous references to *Childe Harold's Pilgrimage*.

Gleckner, Robert F. *Byron and the Ruins of Paradise*. Baltimore: Johns Hopkins University Press, 1967. A critical discussion of Byron's viewpoint, as seen through his poetry. Byron's views of natural beauty and human failings are emphasized. Two chapters are dedicated to *Childe Harold's Pilgrimage*, an excellent example of how he expressed these opinions.

Jump, John D., ed. *Byron: A Symposium*. New York: Barnes & Noble, 1975. A collection of essays on Byron and his poetical works. "The Poet of Childe Harold," by Francis Berry, emphasizes the stylistic devices of *Childe Harold's Pilgrimage* and other works that Byron wrote during the same period and compares those device to those in the works of his contemporaries and of later writers.

Marchand, Leslie A. *Byron's Poetry: A Critical Introduction*. Boston: Houghton Mifflin, 1965. A general introduction to Byron's poetry, intended for students and general readers. Places Byron's work in the context of the literary tradition he followed, the works of his contemporaries, and the historical times in which he lived.

Rawes, Alan. *Byron's Poetic Experimentation: "Childe Harold," the Tales, and the Quest for Comedy*. Brookfield, Vt.: Ashgate, 2000. Traces the evolution of Byron's poetry over the course of the four cantos. Describes how the first two cantos were characterized by "sustained poetic experimentation" and how Byron subsequently sought to break free of the tragic idiom and write in a more comic mode.

Stabler, Jane, ed. *Palgrave Advances in Byron Studies*. New York: Palgrave Macmillan, 2007. Contains twelve scholarly essays interpreting Byron's work, including discussions of Byron in terms of homosexuality, gender, history, popular culture, war, and psychoanalytic criticism.

Thorslev, Peter L. *The Byronic Hero: Types and Prototypes*. Minneapolis: University of Minnesota Press, 1962. A study of the alienated antihero, common in Romantic poetry, that was essentially created by Byron, especially in *Childe Harold's Pilgrimage*. Emphasizes the historical background of Byron's times.

Children of a Lesser God

Author: Mark Medoff (1940-　　)
First produced: 1979; first published, 1980
Type of work: Drama
Type of plot: Psychological realism
Time of plot: Late 1970's
Locale: A state school for the hearing impaired

Principal characters:
JAMES LEEDS, a speech teacher in his thirties
SARAH NORMAN, deaf from birth, age twenty-six
MRS. NORMAN, her mother
ORIN DENNIS, a hearing-impaired student and campus activist
LYDIA, a hearing-impaired student
MR. FRANKLIN, the superintendent of the school

The Story:

James Leeds, a new speech teacher at a state school for the deaf, is working with Orin Dennis to improve his ability to pronounce English. The superintendent, Mr. Franklin, introduces James to Sarah Norman, a twenty-six-year-old deaf woman who does not read lips or use speech, preferring to communicate exclusively in American Sign Language (ASL). Even though James's charm intrigues her, she informs him, with deliberate rudeness, that speech therapy is a waste of time. Sarah's hearing mother, Mrs. Norman, chides James for trying to get Sarah to speak and read lips so that she can pass for a hearing person. James responds that he is only trying to help Sarah function in the hearing world.

In his next meeting with her, James tries reaching Sarah with humor. When she is not amused, James apologizes for using hearing idioms and promises to remember that she is deaf. She is skeptical but accepts his offer to go out for Italian food. In the restaurant James asks Sarah why she does not want speech therapy. She responds that ASL is just as good as English, but James counters that ASL is good only among the deaf. Sarah accuses him of wanting to be God, making her over in his own image. The next day, James discovers that Orin knows everything about his date with Sarah. Orin complains that deaf students do not want to be changed simply because hearing teachers want to change them. Orin vows that someday he will change the deaf education system.

Sarah and James are becoming attracted to each other. When Lydia, a teenage student, tries to join them by the duck pond, Sarah chases her away. James is oblivious to Lydia's infatuation with him. After Sarah leaves, Mr. Franklin appears from behind the trees and warns James that having sex with a student will lead to dismissal. James learns from Mrs. Norman that Sarah stopped trying to speak because she believes people will think she is retarded. James nevertheless tries again to convince Sarah to use her voice. Sarah retorts that the only successful "communication" she ever has with hearing boys is in bed. James realizes that he wants to com-

municate with her no matter what the language. He and Sarah begin an affair in her dorm room. Orin is outraged. He wants Sarah for his political agenda. Lydia is jealous and informs Mr. Franklin, who again threatens to terminate James, so James and Sarah decide to get married. She confides that she wants to become a teacher for the deaf and to have deaf children. Orin tries to tell Sarah, and Mr. Franklin tries to tell James, why their marriage cannot work. James proclaims that communication will cause no problems but immediately catches himself trying to censor the conversation for Sarah. He realizes he has no right to decide what she can and cannot "hear." The next day, alone, they are married. Sarah and James move into faculty housing and Sarah begins to enjoy life in the hearing world. When Orin visits her, he urges Sarah not to turn her back on the deaf and informs her that his lawyer is investigating injustices perpetrated by the school. Sarah is beginning to feel caught between the deaf and hearing worlds. Orin's lawyer decides to file a complaint with the Equal Employment Opportunity Commission because of the lack of deaf teachers at the school. Orin wants Sarah to join his cause because she is "pure deaf." He argues that deaf rights are more important than her marriage. When the lawyer arrives, Sarah and James decide to support Orin's complaint. During their meeting, Sarah realizes that James wants to change her into a hearing person, that Orin wants her to remain "pure deaf," and that the lawyer wants her to be angry about her deafness so that the commission will feel sorry for her. Orin and Sarah are both unhappy when they read the lawyer's brief because it is written from a hearing perspective. James suggests that the deaf protesters be allowed to speak for themselves, but Orin wants to speak for Sarah, too. Outraged by the hypocrisy, Sarah storms off to write her speech alone.

James finds Sarah and tries to make up with her. She asks him to watch her speech, but James is devastated when Sarah tells him he cannot interpret for her before the commission because she cannot say, through a hearing person, how she feels as a deaf person. Deeply hurt, James resorts to bitter accusations, finally goading Sarah into speaking—an eruption of passionate, unintelligible sounds that shocks and repulses him. Humiliated by James's reaction to her voice, she explodes in ASL and runs away.

Even without Sarah's testimony, Orin wins the grievance, but it is a hollow victory. When James finds Sarah at home with her mother, Sarah explains that she finally realizes that it is she who does not have the right to change him. She no longer wants deaf children, believing that people do not have the right to create others in their own image. James leaves, hoping that someday they might be able to help each other.

Critical Evaluation:

Children of a Lesser God followed William Gibson's *The Miracle Worker*, the last Broadway play to include a major deaf character, by twenty years. The two plays can be seen as metaphors for the deaf cultures of their time. In 1960, America was becoming aware of the deaf community, just as Helen Keller became aware of language. The intervening years brought the National Theatre for the Deaf, improved educational opportunities such as the National Technical Institute for the Deaf, the cultural attention of such groups as the American Theatre Association, which established the Program on Drama and Theatre by, with, and for the Handicapped, and civil rights legislation which included protection for individuals with challenging conditions. In 1980, deaf political activists, such as Orin in *Children of a Lesser God*, were beginning to have the impact that would lead to the 1988 Deaf President Now protest at Gallaudet University in Washington, D.C. Just as Sarah does in the play, the deaf community was demanding the right to represent and speak for itself.

Ostensibly a love story, one of *Children of a Lesser God*'s most significant contributions is the accurate portrayal of the complex issues facing the deaf community. Not all deaf people are the same. Two students are portrayed using residual hearing, reading lips, and having the ability to speak. Sarah, on the other hand, refuses to use her voice, wear a hearing aid, or read lips, preferring American Sign Language (ASL), the language of the manual deaf community. There is a hearing-impaired hierarchy; the hard-of-hearing think they're better than the "pure deaf." The goal of hearing teachers is to force deaf students to speak so they will be able to function in the hearing world, whether they want to or not. Several scenes in the play, such as the depiction of Sarah responding to music, are included merely to inform the audience about deafness.

Mark Medoff's recurring theme of self-discovery is developed primarily through the character of Sarah. In the be-

ginning, she proclaims that others do not have the right to re-create her in their image. She expresses her desire to have deaf children. Later she realizes that those around her want to re-create her for their own selfish purposes. James still wants her to function as a hearing person. Orin still wants to preserve her as a dependent "pure deaf" pawn in his political movement. The lawyer-activist still wants her to be an object of pity. In the end, Sarah's triumph is to recognize that oppressive trait within herself. She no longer wants to have deaf children, because not even she has the right to re-create someone in her own image.

When Medoff decided to write this play for deaf actress Phyllis Frelich, he did not realize he would have to devise a new literary technique to communicate to both the play's theatrical and reading audiences. Like the actress, the play's main character, Sarah Norman, communicates exclusively in ASL. The theater audience would not be able to understand her signing; the reader would not be able to understand a direct substitution of English words for ASL (English: "I have nothing; no hearing . . . no language . . . I have me alone." ASL: "Me have nothing. Me deafy . . . English, blow away . . . Think myself enough"). The reader's problem was solved when Medoff decided to write Sarah's lines in English, instructing theaters to use sign language experts to develop their own appropriate ASL. The translation problem for performance was solved by having another character, usually James, repeat in English everything that was signed. (Sarah [ASL]: "What I really want is pasta." James [speaking]: "What you really want is p-a—pasta. Now we're talking.") That Medoff was able to write this kind of double-speak without interfering with the natural flow or emotional build of the dialogue was remarkable. This device also succeeds because the story is told in flashback, as James's memory. Medoff uses a cinematic style of writing that blends one scene, one memory, with the next, without the need to stop the action to establish passage of time or locales. Some critics have labeled this a "feminist" play because the man who wants to help his wife becomes her oppressor. That argument can be made, but it is a rush to judgment, ignoring the author's intent and the richness of the play's depiction of deaf education and culture. If the gender of every character was reversed, the story would still be true, because it is a story of deafness and not one of feminism.

Gerald S. Argetsinger

Further Reading

Brustein, Robert. "Robert Brustein on Theater." *The New Republic*, June 7, 1980. Satirizes the play as part of a new genre, the politically correct "disability play." Argues that one cannot dislike such plays without being labeled "hearingist" or sexist.

Erben, Rudolf. *Mark Medoff*. Boise, Idaho: Boise State University Press, 1995. Provides a brief overview of Medoff's life and work.

Gill, Brendan. "Without Speech." *The New Yorker*, April 14, 1980. Proclaims *Children of a Lesser God* to be not only successful but also a work of art. Focuses on the honesty of a story that portrays a seemingly perfect union but is destroyed by ingrained flaws that the passion of the moment had at first minimalized.

Gladstein, Mimi Reisel. "Mark Medoff." In *Speaking on Stage: Interviews with Contemporary American Playwrights*, edited by Philip C. Kolin and Colby H. Kullman. Tuscaloosa: University of Alabama Press, 1996. Medoff is one of twenty-seven post-World War II American playwrights who discuss their work.

Guernsey, Otis L., Jr. *Curtain Times: The New York Theater, 1965-1987*. New York: Dodd, Mead, 1987. Focuses on the uniqueness of the point of view of a minority that does not want to become part of the mainstream.

Medoff, Mark. *The Dramaturgy of Mark Medoff: Five Plays Dealing with Deafness and Social Issues*. Compiled by Samuel J. Zachary. Lewiston, N.Y.: Edwin Mellen Press, 2004. Before the production of *Children of a Lesser God*, only a handful of plays featured deaf characters or dealt with the issues and culture of deaf people. Medoff has since written four other plays that deal in some way with deafness and were created for deaf actress Phyllis Frelich. In addition to the five playscripts, this volume includes an introduction by Medoff, in which he discusses the inspiration, writing, casting, production, performance, reception, and legacy of these plays; Frelich also offers her comments on the dramas.

Simon, John. "April on Broadway: Indoor Showers." *New York Magazine*, April 14, 1980. Describes the play's attempt to deal with weighty issues as shallow, falling short of melodrama, and functioning as mere soap opera. Simon cannot accept that James would become involved with the deeply troubled Sarah.

Weales, Gerald. "Belatedly, the Tonies." *Commonweal* 107, no. 18 (October 24, 1980): 595-596. Accuses the drama of being the standard didactic play with the hearing-impaired replacing blacks or homosexuals as the new misunderstood minority.

Wilson, Edwin. "Broadway: Two Openings and One Closing." *The Wall Street Journal*, April 1, 1980. Reprinted in *New York Theatre Critics' Reviews* 41, no. 6 (March 24, 1980): 303. Points out that the play is three stories: Sarah's life, the rights of deaf people, and the romance. Argues that the play is worthy of serious critical attention.

The Children of Herakles

Author: Euripides (c. 485-406 B.C.E.)
First transcribed: *Hērakleidai*, c. 430 B.C.E. (English translation, 1781)
Type of work: Drama
Type of plot: Tragedy
Time of plot: The age of legend
Locale: Before the temple of Zeus at Marathon

Principal characters:
IOLAUS, the aged friend of Herakles
COPREUS, the herald of Eurystheus
DEMOPHON, the king of Athens
MACARIA, Herakles' daughter
ALCMENE, Herakles' mother
EURYSTHEUS, the king of Argos

The Story:

Iolaus, the aged warrior friend of the dead Herakles, together with Alcmene and the Herakleidae, the children of Herakles, have for years been wandering over Greece seeking a refuge from Eurystheus, king of Argos. No city dares to take them in against the command of the powerful Argive ruler. At last the wanderers arrive in Athens. There, while resting at the temple of Zeus, they are immediately confronted by Copreus, the herald of Eurystheus, who demands that they proceed at once to Argos and submit to death by stoning. Iolaus staunchly refuses, and when Copreus seizes the children a violent conflict ensues and Iolaus is thrown to the ground.

The chorus of aged Athenians immediately summons their king, Demophon, who is warned by Copreus that his refusal to surrender the Herakleidae to the Argives will surely result in war. In response to Iolaus's plea, Demophon offers his protection on the grounds that the children of Herakles are gathered around the altar of Zeus, that they are bound to him by ties of kinship, and that the honor and freedom of Athens are at stake. Copreus sullenly departs, after warning that he will return with an army and punish Athens for its insolence. The grateful Iolaus praises the Athenians for their willingness to aid the helpless in an honest cause, but he refuses to leave the temple until the issue with Argos is settled.

The Argive host appears, led by Eurystheus himself. Demophon, who consults a variety of public and private oracles, comes to Iolaus with the news that victory depends upon the sacrifice of some royal maiden and that he cannot in good conscience slay his own daughter. When the distraught Iolaus offers to surrender himself to Eurystheus, Demophon points out that the Argive king desires only the children.

Macaria, daughter of Herakles, emerges from the temple to offer herself, insisting that she be chosen even after Iolaus proposes that the victim be selected by lot. After she is led away, a servant of Hyllus, son of Herakles, enters to announce that Hyllus arrives with an army to aid the Herakleidae. The elated Iolaus summons Alcmene from the temple to hear the good news. He is so overjoyed that in spite of his age he insists on donning armor and setting off to take part in the battle.

Later a servant brings Alcmene tidings of victory and describes how, after the cowardly Eurystheus refused single combat with Hyllus, the rejuvenated Iolaus plunged into the fray and took Eurystheus prisoner. Alcmene is astounded that Iolaus did not kill him on the spot. When guards bring the bound Eurystheus before her, she demands his immediate death.

The messenger of Demophon cautions her that such an act will violate Athenian custom, but the vengeful Alcmene swears that she herself will kill Eurystheus if necessary. The Argive king explains that he never had any personal quarrel with the Herakleidae and that he was forced to do as he did by the divine power of Hera, the deity of Argos. Nevertheless, he will not ask for mercy; in fact, since an old oracle predicted it, he is quite willing to submit to death if his body will be buried at Pallene, where in the future his spirit can protect his former enemies. The bloodthirsty Alcmene then demands that he be taken away from the city, slain, and cast to the dogs. Observing that, so long as Eurystheus is not killed within Athens, no stain of guilt will come upon the city, the chorus leads him away to be executed.

Critical Evaluation:

There is so much awkwardness in the structure of *The Children of Herakles* that critics have suggested that important scenes must be missing or that it was not intended as a tragedy but as a substitute for a satyr play. Another suggestion is that since *The Children of Herakles* was presented in the early years of the Peloponnesian War and glorifies the virtues of the Athenian city-state, Euripides depended upon the high patriotism of the play to carry it.

The Children of Herakles has been generally more criticized than praised. One critic sees it as "all in all the least attractive of Euripides' plays," although others have approved of its rapid pace, which moves inexorably toward the powerfully ironic, even satirical ending. The content of the play cannot be divorced form its political context: the Peloponnesian War between Athens and Sparta, which had just begun at the time it was produced, probably in 430 or 429 B.C.E. Eurystheus's promise to defend the city of Athens at the end of the play may be connected with the Spartan invasions of Athenian territory in 431 and 430 B.C.E. Likewise, the illegal execution of Spartan envoys at Athens in the winter of 430-429 B.C.E. may have inspired Euripides to explore the themes of supplication and refuge in a tragedy. These ambassadors were put to death without trial, in flagrant violation of the custom that such persons are not to be harmed.

The play draws upon the large body of myth surrounding Herakles, a hero whose career is marked by misfortune and subjection to the will of sundry gods and mortals. Persecuted by Hera and her agent Eurystheus, Herakles ended his life in agony on a funeral pyre. After his death, his children become the target of Eurystheus, who hunts them down with the same determination that drove him on against their father. Euripides fashions from these traditional elements a play about suppliants seeking asylum, which enables him to make pronouncements about Athenian policy in the war and about war in general.

Plays about suppliants are quite common in Greek drama. They tend to follow a pattern: The suppliants arrive seeking asylum, the pursuer attempts to seize them, the local authorities hear their appeal for sanctuary, a struggle ensues between the providers of asylum and the pursuer, and the suppliants are eventually saved. This pattern can also be seen in Aeschylus's *Hiketides*, 463? B.C.E. (*The Suppliants*, 1777), about the daughters of Danaus, or in Sophocles' *Oidipous epi Kolōnōi*, 401 B.C.E. (*Oedipus at Colonus*, 1729), in which the Athenians grant asylum to the outcast king of Thebes. In such stories, the city that provides asylum is rewarded by blessings.

The action of the play is fast and furious, giving an impression of the bustling city-state at war. Decisions are made rapidly, and there is always some new crisis looming. No character remains the center of attention for very long. The children of Herakles themselves, although they are named in the title, do not say anything; they are silent observers of the action throughout. They represent the helpless victims of war, whose voices are not heard and who are powerless to influence events.

The play turns on the issue of right versus might: Demophon takes a stand against the threats of Copreus and decides to protect the suppliants, whatever the cost may be. He does so partly out of duty to Zeus and partly because his father Theseus was indebted to Herakles. Moreover, the reputation of Athens as a free and honorable city has to be upheld. The treatment of the captured Eurystheus at the end of the play, however, undercuts the glorification of Athens: He is brought before Alcmene to be humiliated, physically abused, and sentenced to death. She has exchanged places with him and is now herself the incarnation of vengeful violence. Eurystheus, by contrast, seeks protection from Athens. The city that earlier took a brave stand against the pursuer to protect the pursued now abandons the suppliant to his fate. The speech that Eurystheus makes in his own defense reveals him to be courageous in the face of death, generous in his praise of Herakles, and even understanding of Alcmene's position. The chorus, who represents the Athenian state, urges Alcmene to let Eurystheus go, but is not prepared to stand in her way when she works out a means of killing him while ensuring that Athens suffers no harm from the murder. In other words, Athens acquiesces in an unjust act. It has failed the test when it comes to dealing with a prisoner of war, just as it did when it killed the Spartan envoys. In time of war, the poet seems to be saying, it is the spirit of Alcmene—vengeful, cruel, and irrational—that prevails. The play can thus be seen as a protest against the Peloponnesian war and a warning to Euripides' fellow Athenians that the war should be brought to an end as soon as possible.

The sacrifice of Macaria, demanded by the gods to ensure victory for Athens over Argos, recalls the sacrifices of Iphigeneia in Aeschylus's *Agamemnōn*, 458 B.C.E. (*Agamemnon*, 1777). It symbolizes the heroic gesture made by a noble soul in time of war. It is significant that women are the sacrificial victims in such stories: It is as if the killing of so many men on the battlefield requires a concomitant sacrifice by the women of the city. It is interesting therefore that the play also contains the miraculous rejuvenation of the male warrior Iolaus. Macaria's death also symbolizes the victimization of the innocent by war. The attention that Euripides

pays to the women Macaria and Alcmene in this play is typical of his work; it illustrates his concern with the subject of how men and women are to live harmoniously together in the same city.

The myth of the Return of the Children of Herakles provides a coda to the action of the play and also has some political ramifications. After the death of Eurystheus, the children made their way down through the Peloponnese, conquering Argos, Sparta, and other cities. The myth has been linked by some with the invasion of southern Greece by Dorian tribes in the prehistoric era. The aristocrats of the Peloponnese at any rate regarded themselves as descendants of Herakles, and so, when the king of Sparta led his army against Athens, he was marching against the city that had granted asylum to his ancestors. This is the kind of ironic twist that Euripides could well appreciate.

"Critical Evaluation" by David H. J. Larmour

Further Reading

Dumezil, Georges. *The Stakes of the Warrior.* Translated by David Weeks. Berkeley: University of California Press, 1983. Explains how the Herakles figure embodies attributes of both the monster-slayer and the monster itself. Provides a useful background against which to consider Euripides' tragedy.

Euripides. *The Children of Heracles.* With introduction, translation, and commentary by William Allan. Warminster, England: Aris & Phillips, 2001. The text of the play is written in Greek, with the English translation on the facing pages. The introduction discusses the play's structure, setting, staging, and the myth upon which it was based, and provides other details about the work's historical and literary context. The extensive commentary section clarifies allusions and references and provides other information to enhance understanding of the play.

_____. *Heraclidae.* Introduction and commentary by John Wilkins. New York: Oxford University Press, 1993. Suitable for more detailed study of the play.

Foley, Helene P. *Ritual Irony: Poetry and Sacrifice in Euripides.* Ithaca, N.Y.: Cornell University Press, 1985. An enlightening treatment of the issue of sacrifice in Euripides' plays. Provides a clearer understanding of the sacrificial elements in *The Children of Herakles.*

Mendelsohn, Daniel Adam. *Gender and the City in Euripides' Political Plays.* New York: Oxford University Press, 2002. Analyzes Athenian ideas of politics and the feminine as demonstrated in *Children of Herakles* and *The Suppliants.*

Morwood, James. *The Plays of Euripides*. Bristol, England: Bristol Classical, 2002. Morwood provides a concise overview of all of Euripides' plays, devoting a separate chapter to each one. He demonstrates how Euripides was constantly reinventing himself in his work.

Zuntz, Gunther. *The Political Plays of Euripides*. New York: Manchester University Press, 1955. A good account of the political elements found in many of Euripides' plays, which need to be taken into consideration by modern readers. Deals in detail with *The Children of Herakles*.

Children of the Game

Author: Jean Cocteau (1889-1963)
First published: Les Enfants terribles, 1929 (English translation, 1930)
Type of work: Novel
Type of plot: Psychological
Time of plot: Early twentieth century
Locale: Paris

Principal characters:
PAUL, a sensitive, imaginative boy
ELISABETH, his sister
GÉRARD, their friend
AGATHA, Gérard's wife and a friend of Paul and Elisabeth
MICHAEL, an American

The Story:

Paul and Elisabeth live with their paralyzed mother in an old quarter of Paris. They exist in a private, instinctual world, dissociated from adults by passivity, imagination, and secret, mysterious rites. One night, when the quarter is transformed by snow, Paul wanders among the snowballing groups in search of the school hero Dargelos, whom he worships. Dargelos, who possesses great charm, is both vicious and beautiful. As Paul moves toward him, Dargelos, perhaps accidentally, knocks him down with a stone-packed snowball. Although he injures Paul, he escapes immediate punishment but is later expelled from the school. Paul is taken home by Gérard, who loves Paul as much for his weakness as Paul loves Dargelos for his strength. Elisabeth is extremely angry with them when they reach Paul's home. Sixteen years old, two years older than Paul, she is utterly absorbed in her brother She is frequently transported by fury when he appears to be leaving her sphere of influence.

The three children go into the Room where Paul and Elisabeth eat, sleep, read, fight, and play the Game. The Room is the central fixture in their lives; the Game is their inner world. The Room exists in a chaos of boxes, clothes, papers, and books. Paul leaves it only for school and Elisabeth only to look after their mother or to buy magazines. Essentially the Game is daydreaming, a willed withdrawal to an imaginary world of submerged consciousness. After Elisabeth sends Gérard away, she undresses Paul and puts him to bed. Their doctor decides that Paul is unfit to return to school, a decision that plunges Paul into despair until he learns of Dargelos's expulsion. After that, school holds no interest for him.

The Room has hidden treasures, the artifacts of their unconscious minds—keys, marbles, aspirin bottles—and when Gérard tells Paul that Dargelos disappeared, a photograph of him dressed as Athalie is added to the collection. The mother dies suddenly. When Paul and Elisabeth see her, rigid and transfixed in her chair, staring forward, the image haunts them; it is the one they retain. The mother's nurse, Mariette, remains in the household, content to care for and love Paul and Elisabeth without altering them.

Now an accepted visitor in the Room, Gérard is aware of the almost tangible tension, expressed in fights, recriminations, and reconciliations, between the two siblings. When Paul is well enough, Elisabeth, surprisingly, accepts an invitation from Gérard's uncle to take a holiday by the sea. On the journey she watches Paul while he is sleeping and is disgusted by the air of weakness that his illness accentuates. She decides to remold him according to her own plans.

Once by the sea, they establish a Room as much like their own as possible. Paul gains strength under Elisabeth's tutelage, in part through stealing useless objects from local shops while on raids that she plans. Their booty forms a treasure imitating that in the Paris Room.

When they return to Paris, Elisabeth is suddenly aware that Paul outstripped her and that she is the subordinate party in their relationship. Paul spends his evenings wandering around Montmartre, watching girls, drinking, and finally meeting Gérard and bringing him home for the night. On these occasions, Elisabeth would use him as a means of tormenting Paul. The first time she succeeds in rousing her brother comes when she declares that she, too, will go into the world. Her position, she feels, is untenable, and she subsequently obtains work as a mannequin. This act enrages Paul, who declares that she is prostituting herself; she thinks the same about his nightly excursions.

At the dressmaker's establishment where she works, Elisabeth meets Agatha, an orphan whose drug-addicted parents committed suicide. For Agatha she feels, for the first time, warm affection, but Agatha's introduction to the Room precipitates the destruction of Paul and Elisabeth when Agatha becomes devoted to Paul. The photograph reveals a startling likeness between Dargelos and Agatha, and Paul enthralls her as he was in thrall to Dargelos. Agatha feels at home in the Room, but at the same time she recognizes the strange, dreamlike existence her friends lead.

As they mature, the Game fails to absorb Paul and Elisabeth completely. This situation so distresses Elisabeth that when she meets Michael, an American friend of Gérard, she transfers her dream life to him. Paul is excluded from this friendship with Michael, but his anger at learning of it evaporates when he discovers that Michael wants to marry Elisabeth and not, as he subconsciously feared, Agatha. Elisabeth does marry Michael, but true to Gérard's vision of her, the marriage is never consummated: Michael is killed while driving alone in his sports car a few hours after the wedding.

Elisabeth inherits his fortune and his Paris house, into which the four move. Lonely and disoriented in separate rooms, they gravitate to the Room that Paul finally establishes in the dining hall. Their lives move slowly to a climax from the moment that Paul realizes he is in love with Agatha. Afraid to tell each other of their love, they each tell Elisabeth. Terrified that Paul might leave her, Elisabeth moves tirelessly between them all one night to dissuade them from marrying. Lying, she tells Paul that it is Gérard whom Agatha loves, and she tells Agatha that Paul is too selfish ever to love anyone. She also convinces Gérard that by friendship he won Agatha's love and that it is his duty to marry her. Elisabeth is so dedicated to the idea of possessing Paul and so trusted by the others that she succeeds completely in her scheme.

A short time after his marriage to Agatha, Gérard meets Dargelos. The former schoolmate sends Paul a gift, part of his collection of poisons. Paul and Elisabeth were delighted with the present which, to Agatha's horror, is added to the treasure.

Weeks later, when Paris is again covered in snow, Elisabeth dreams that Paul is dead. She awakens to find Agatha at the door. Agatha is convinced that Paul killed himself;

she received a letter from him threatening suicide. They run to the Room and find Paul choking on poison fumes that fill the screened-in corner where he lies. Although he can barely speak, with Agatha he reconstructs Elisabeth's scheme. When he curses her, she feels that her heart dies. After admitting her guilt and jealousy, she snatches a revolver; by that violent act, she is able to regain their attention and thus to captivate Paul once more. Elisabeth works to charm him back into their world of the Room and the Game, far from Agatha, who seems less real to him than the snowstorm outside. The two women watch each other until Paul falls back exhausted. Thinking him dead, Elisabeth shoots herself. Crashing against the screens, she destroys the Room and lets in the enemy world. Paul sees visions of people playing with snowballs crowding the windows, watching as he dies. Theirs is the tragedy of outcasts who, unaware that they live on borrowed time, die fighting for their private existence.

Critical Evaluation:

Children of the Game is the most claustrophobic of all Jean Cocteau's works, although its intense concentration on the vagaries of love is matched by its later companion piece *Les Parents terribles* (1938; *Intimate Relations*, 1952). In Cocteau's fantasies based on myth or folklore—in the case of *La Belle et la bête* (1946; *Beauty and the Beast*, 1947)—love can play a redemptive role, rescuing characters from distortions of their inner being imposed by other forces. In his domestic dramas, however, love is a distortive affliction that leads to disaster.

Cocteau's film version of *Enfants Terribles* (released in 1950) was given a restrictive X rating in Britain because the censors deemed the relationship between Paul and Elisabeth to be implicitly incestuous. This is a misleading simplification of a more complicated and more problematic network of feelings. Although Paul initially leaves the Room only to go to school, while Elisabeth clings even more closely to its sanctuary, they broaden their horizons conspicuously as they grow to sexual maturity. The Game, which absorbs them completely in their childish innocence, is dramatically transformed as they struggle to come to terms with the greater game of the social world. The possessiveness reflected in Elisabeth's attempt to keep Paul and Agatha apart is not merely a simple desire to cling fast to what she and her brother always had. It also arises out of the fact that they both begin to yearn for something different, while fearing that what they want might be impossible to achieve. She reacts against her own impulses as well. The siblings are inextricably bound together but not by anything as straightforward as lust or sexual jealousy.

Paul's nemesis, Dargelos, is based on a real person of that name whom Cocteau encountered during his schooldays and to whom the author refers in several other works. Although he can hardly be said to figure large in *Children of the Game* as a character, Dargelos moves the two most important levers of the plot. Dargelos injures Paul with the stone hidden in the snowball; through this incident Gérard is drawn into the lives of Paul and Elisabeth, disrupting their privacy. Dargelos also provides the poison that Paul takes after Elisabeth convinces him that Agatha does not love him. Dargelos is tacitly present at the novel's end as well as its beginning, still armed with his deadly snowball. His cold cruelty brackets the entire tragedy in such a fashion as to suggest that if only he had looked with favor upon his acolyte, all might have been well. If, in fact, the reader decides that Agatha is only a substitute for the charismatic Dargelos, then Elisabeth might have a good reason to keep Paul and Agatha apart.

Through the actions and reactions of Gérard, the fascinated voyeur, Cocteau testifies to the fact that there is something precious in the Game, but not in the sense that it is some kind of small utopia. The Game provides Paul's and Elisabeth's lives with a fundamental structure that Gérard's lacks, but it is essentially something to fall back on when other projects fail. Wherever they go they can always return to the Room, or some simulacrum of it, to provide a safe haven for themselves—but that is all the Room is; it can never provide an answer to their inner needs.

There is a certain ironic paradox in the fact that the Game that Paul and Elisabeth play allows Paul to build up the strength he requires for his periodic ventures into the world beyond. He comes to appreciate this paradox when Elisabeth retaliates by moving outside herself, raising the possibility that when he next needs to recover from the personal disasters he constantly courts, she might not be there for him. The irony, of course, redoubles when Elisabeth's expedition to the outer world brings back Agatha, a much more dangerous invader than Gérard.

It is not easy to weigh Elisabeth's decision to marry Michael. Perhaps it is an authentic attempt to begin a new Game and move into a new Room, but its tragic interruption seals the fate of Elisabeth and of Paul in a relatively straightforward fashion. If Gérard's judgment of the matter is correct, however, her gesture is a feint that Michael's death merely serves to terminate in a relatively tidy fashion. If so, it is not entirely clear whether Elisabeth's halfhearted and doomed attempt to escape should be construed as a flight from Paul or as a flight from Agatha. To the extent that her subsequent determination to keep them apart is motivated by jealousy, it is not obvious which of them she is more jealous of—it is, after all, she who first becomes enamored of Agatha. Given Gerard's inherent ability to be manipulated, to him marrying Agatha cannot seem as definite a loss as allowing her to marry Paul.

If this interpretation is accepted, Elisabeth's emotions and motives are more complicated than she realizes, and certainly far more complicated than Gerard realizes. Her final attempt to rebuild the Room and restart the Game is clearly a matter of desperation rather than a constructive desire, and its failure is inevitable. The snow that conceals sharp stones ultimately blankets everything, banishing all the possible varieties of human warmth with evenhanded cruelty.

The Room is depicted throughout the novel as a prison, not so much because it embodies "the shadowy instincts of childhood" that are mentioned in the first few pages, but more because the world outside is full of sharp stones and subtle poisons. The apparent freedom of the world of adult relationships is spoiled by the lurking presence of Dargelos. He is the handsome and charming but ultimately treacherous object of desire. He is free, but the exercise of his freedom condemns others to their prisons and ultimately to death row.

"Critical Evaluation" by Brian Stableford

Further Reading

Brae, Germaine, and Margaret Guiton. *An Age of Fiction: The French Novel from Gide to Camus.* New Brunswick, N.J.: Rutgers University Press, 1957. Cocteau's novels are discussed on pages 140-148, where he is described as "a modern Daedalus."

Brown, Frederick. *An Impersonation of Angels: A Biography of Jean Cocteau.* New York: Viking, 1968. Like most studies of Cocteau, this concentrates more on his work for the cinema than on his novels. However, it does consider the relationship between the two versions of *Children of the Game.*

Centre Georges Pompidou. *Cocteau.* Paris: Centre Pompidou, 2003. A retrospective catalog compiled by the Centre Pompidou and the Montreal Museum that accompanied an exhibit of Cocteau's work displayed in 2003 and 2004. In addition to reproductions of the art works, the catalog includes seventeen essays on Cocteau's life and work, including discussions of the Cocteau image, Orphic self-portraits, and Cocteau and Dadaism.

Crosland, Margaret. *Jean Cocteau.* London: Peter Nevill, 1955. A biography and critical analysis. Discusses the novel version of *Children of the Game* on pages 166-169.

Fowlie, Wallace. *Jean Cocteau: The History of a Poet's Age.*

Bloomington: Indiana University Press, 1966. A sensitive study that includes a discussion of *Children of the Game*.

Lowe, Romana N. *The Fictional Female: Sacrificial Rituals and Spectacles of Writing in Baudelaire, Zola, and Cocteau*. New York: Peter Lang, 1997. Focuses on nineteenth and twentieth century French texts in which women were the sacrificial victims. Lowe traces structures and images of female sacrifice in the genres of poetry, novel, and theater with close readings of Charles Baudelaire, Émile Zola, and Cocteau.

Steegmuller, Francis. *Cocteau: A Biography*. London: Constable, 1986. A biography that is fuller than Crosland's and less florid than Brown's.

Williams, James S. *Jean Cocteau*. London: Reaktion Books, 2008. Biography chronicling the development of Cocteau's aesthetic and his work as a novelist, poet, dramatist, filmmaker, and designer. Williams concludes that Cocteau's oeuvre is characterized by a continual self-questioning.

The Children's Hour

Author: Lillian Hellman (1905-1984)
First produced: 1934; first published, 1934
Type of work: Drama
Type of plot: Problem
Time of plot: 1930's
Locale: Massachusetts

Principal characters:
KAREN WRIGHT, a cofounder of Wright-Dobie school
MARTHA DOBIE, a cofounder of Wright-Dobie school
MARY TILFORD, a student at the school
AMELIA TILFORD, Mary's grandmother, a patron of the school
LILY MORTAR, Martha Dobie's aunt
JOSEPH CARDIN, Karen's fiancé, the school doctor
ROSALIE WELLS, a student at the school

The Story:

In the living room of the Wright-Dobie private girls' school, seven girls aged twelve to fourteen conjugate Latin verbs and read aloud from William Shakespeare's *The Merchant of Venice* (pr. c. 1596-1597, pb. 1600). Fussily trying to teach the girls elocution, decorum, and sewing—all at once, to the girls' amusement—is school cofounder Martha Dobie's aging aunt, former actress Lily Mortar. Student Mary Tilford, tardy for the study session, explains that she was detained gathering April flowers for Lily. When grateful Lily sends "sweet" Mary for a vase for the flowers, Mary disdainfully sticks her tongue out at a classmate.

When twenty-eight-year-old Karen Wright enters, the girls' tone changes from amused tolerance of Lily to respect for Karen. Karen is clearly in charge. She quietly shows her disapproval for Lily's dramatics while demonstrating care for the girls, offering to repair Rosalie's poor haircut and inquiring about a bracelet lost by another student, Helen. Mary, returning with the vase and flowers, squirms under Karen's suspicion that Mary did not pick them but merely retrieved the bouquet from the garbage. Unhappy that Karen would destroy her excuse for missing the study session, Mary insists on her story. Karen, trying to break Mary's habit of lying, imposes punishment by grounding her. Mary, furious, threatens to complain of maltreatment to her grandmother, Amelia Tilford, a major school supporter. Mary then fakes a faint to avoid being sent to her room. Karen calmly picks her up and carries her away.

Cofounder and friend Martha Dobie discusses school problems with Karen, including what to do about Mary's bad influence on the other girls and how gently to rid themselves of Martha's outdated Aunt Lily. Clearly, Martha is struggling with another problem—Karen's impending marriage to school physician Joe Cardin. Karen tries to reassure her that they will be a threesome and that nothing will change at the school. When cheerful Joe arrives, he and Karen leave to examine Mary and her latest complaint.

In a heated argument, Martha persuades Aunt Lily to leave the school and return to Europe, the scene of Lily's pleasant acting memories. Hurt because she feels unwanted, Lily accuses Martha of harboring a lesbian attachment to Karen that aims to exclude all others, including Joe. Suddenly, both women realize that they were overheard by

Mary's roommates, hiding outside the room. Indignant, Lily leaves.

Joe enters, assuring Martha that Mary's health is fine. When Joe senses Martha's uneasiness about his marrying Karen, he promises Martha that the three will remain close friends. Karen, joining Joe and Martha, suspects that Mary's influence on her two roommates is responsible for their eavesdropping; to weaken Mary's control, she separates the girls' rooms. The adults leave. Furious, Mary smashes an ornament and threatens to blame her violence on her roommates. Next, she intimidates them into revealing Lily's accusation against Martha. Resenting the punishment for her earlier lie, Mary forces the girls to supply cash so she can flee to her grandmother and beg for sanctuary against Martha and Karen's "abuse."

Grandmother Tilford, at first determined to send Mary back to the school, gradually becomes convinced that the girl's fears are justified. Annoyed, then horrified, by Mary's whisperings about her schoolmistresses' "unnatural" behavior, she sends her granddaughter to bed. Immediately, she places a telephone call to Joe to come to her house after his hospital duties, then calls parents of other school boarders.

Several hours later, Rosalie joins Mary at Mrs. Tilford's for the night, wondering why several other girls suddenly are spending the night away from school at their parents' hasty requests. Mary blackmails Rosalie, who took Helen's bracelet, into supporting her secret about Karen and Martha's alleged unnatural relationship.

Alone with astounded Joe, Mrs. Tilford warns him not to marry Karen. Martha and Karen explode into the room, describing the chaos at school: Parents are snatching their daughters home because Amelia told them the two founders are lovers. Against Martha and Karen's furious denunciations and their threats of a libel suit, Mrs. Tilford calmly maintains her position of protecting young girls. She advises the young women to leave quietly.

Karen, Martha, and Joe realize that Mary is the source of the story, but Mrs. Tilford supports her granddaughter's accusations. Under Joe's interrogation, Mary repeats Lily's overheard accusation against Martha and embellishes it with concocted incidents about having seen the women behaving improperly together. Pinned down with inconsistencies in her story, such as peeking through a nonexistent keyhole, she then lies that Rosalie is in fact the one who saw them. Confused by her questioners and terrified by Mary's blackmail, Rosalie cries that she did, in fact, witness Karen and Martha kissing inappropriately.

Seven months later, in the dim, unkempt school living room, listless Martha and Karen refuse to answer the tele-

phone. They were reclusive for more than a week. Lily enters, relating her nomadic theater tour of several months. Her refusal to testify for her niece in court was crucial in Martha and Karen's loss of the libel suit against Mrs. Tilford. Bitter, Martha banishes Lily from the school.

Arriving with plans for the three to leave for Vienna to start a new life, Joe reports that he sold his practice. His slight hesitation when Karen kisses him is fatal to their relationship. Karen realizes that privately he will always wonder about the truth of the accusations against her and Martha. Tenderly, she sends him away to think for a few days, knowing he will probably never return.

After he leaves, the two women discuss the unfairness of Mary's lie. As she denies that her affection for Karen is unnatural, Martha quietly and slowly realizes that the charges are true, after all, and that she resented Karen's impending marriage because of jealousy, not because she feared for the school. In spite of Karen's protests, Martha confesses that she ruined their lives. She feels soiled. Karen thinks Martha is exhausted and gently sends her to lie down. Suddenly, a shot sounds in the next room. From upstairs, Lily dashes in, but both women realize that medical help for the suicidal Martha is too late. Mrs. Tilford arrives, admitting that she discovered Mary's blackmail scheme that forced Rosalie's support for the lie. Deeply remorseful, she apologizes and offered Karen financial reparation. Numbed, Karen provisionally accepts while bitterly sending her away. Karen is left utterly alone.

Critical Evaluation:

One of America's first and most successful female playwrights, Lillian Hellman began her dramatic career at the age of twenty-nine with *The Children's Hour*. With 691 performances, it was her longest-running play. A book reviewer and a reader for films and playscripts, Hellman read an account of an early nineteenth century Scottish trial, "The Great Drumsheugh Case," about a child's false accusations ruining reputations. This, Hellman's first play, contains nearly all the themes and dramatic devices used in her other eleven dramas. Hellman created many ambitious female characters who, by greedy overreaching, leave death and destruction in their wake. Mary Tilford's ruthless manipulation of her classmates and wealthy grandmother to wield power over them is echoed in many other Hellman characters who seek undeserved power or wealth. Amelia Tilford's family loyalty in believing her granddaughter's contrived distress (over her better judgment) leads to several deaths: of the girls' school, of Karen and Joe's relationship, and of Martha through her suicide. Other Hellman plays such as *The Little Foxes* (1939) trace how distorted family allegiances result in ethical compromise and devastation. Mrs. Tilford's belief at the end that money will relieve her conscience and Karen's pain demonstrates Hellman's harsh criticism of the wealthy classes and capitalism.

Traits found in all other Hellman plays make their debut here: a fast-moving plot using secrecy and increasing suspense, sparse detail about the past, and deftly drawn characters who speak everyday language. In her first play, Hellman introduces blackmail, a device that resurfaces in all her drama. Mary blackmails Rosalie, a petty thief, into supporting her story about Karen and Martha inappropriately kissing. This is an example of the terror inflicted on victims in other Hellman plays.

The play has been called dated because of its typical Hellman melodramatic style—obviously evil characters wreak havoc on clearly good or well-intentioned innocents before being discovered. Unlike in characteristic melodrama, however, the "evil" character in *The Children's Hour*, Mary, is not banished but is left in her grandmother's care. "Good" characters are not given clearly happy endings as in melodrama. Martha is dead; Karen is left without friendship, career, or marriage; and even Mrs. Tilford's remorseful recognition of her error comes too late. She also faces a bleak future in caring for her morally warped granddaughter. Mrs. Tilford's "good" sense of responsibility to the parents and children of the school results in the irresponsible destruction of the two school founders and an unwanted responsibility for Mary's future.

Some critics contend that the characters are flawed. For example, Mrs. Tilford is too intelligent to believe such a contrived story by a young girl. The girl's youth is one reason why the grandmother believes her: Mrs. Tilford cannot fathom that a young girl would make up so shocking an incident. Given Mrs. Tilford's privileged class, to change her mind after so strong a decision would be uncharacteristically humble.

In melodrama, a heroic man usually rescues victimized women. Here, Joe tries to rescue the two women with his plan to move to Vienna, but Karen takes control of their relationship by sensing Joe's unconscious doubt about the women's sexual past and pressuring him to articulate it. Unlike in melodrama, the lovers are not reconciled in the end: Joe's ultimate decision is left in doubt.

Although Mary is closer to a melodramatic villain with her intentional malice, her excuse of self-protection introduces a much more complex character. Mary believes that the two women discipline her because they dislike her. The young girl's parents are absent, and misbehavior by children to gain attention, even negative attention, is not uncommon.

The cycle of transgression-punishment-transgression does not necessarily have a clear beginning in the transgressor's perception.

The drama's last act has been criticized as anticlimactic: The lethargy of the two friends depletes the play's intensity for too long. Hellman realized after a few rehearsals that the last ten minutes should be cut, but because she could not find an appropriate alternative, she left the act alone.

The Children's Hour differs from other Hellman plays in its lesbian theme, which caused a sensation on Broadway. Today, the homosexuality might seem mild, tastefully handled, and ambiguous. The acts for which the women are ruined have been disproved for the audience, and Martha's sudden admission of harboring "unnatural" affections for Karen is not entirely convincing. The women have been isolated and disoriented by the months-long ordeal before Martha's guilt about her new self-evaluation drives her to suicide. With Karen's strong disagreement, Hellman leaves the truth unclear. By the time Martha shoots herself, however, the prejudice that caused her death seems more immoral than her socially unacceptable affections. Hellman declared in a 1952 interview that she considered the play's major theme to be not lesbianism but the power of lying.

Nancy A. Macky

Further Reading

Bigsby, C. W. E. *1900-1940.* Vol. 1 in *A Critical Introduction to Twentieth Century American Drama.* New York: Cambridge University Press, 1982. A chapter on Hellman evaluates *The Children's Hour*'s themes and explores its relationship to Hellman's life.

Falk, Doris. *Lillian Hellman.* New York: Frederick Ungar, 1978. A biographical study that includes summaries of Hellman's works and information about the composition, production, and reception of her plays.

Griffin, Alice, and Geraldine Thorsten. *Understanding Lillian Hellman.* Columbia: University of South Carolina Press, 1999. Examination of Hellman's major plays, discussing her style, concern for moral issues, and her influence on other American playwrights, including Tennessee Williams, Arthur Miller, and Marsha Norman. Chapter 2 focuses on *The Children's Hour.*

Horn, Barbara Lee. *Lillian Hellman: A Research and Production Sourcebook.* Westport, Conn.: Greenwood Press, 1998. Provides an overview of Hellman's life, and a plot summary, history, and critical overview of *The Children's Hour.* Includes bibliographies of works by and about Hellman.

Lederer, Katherine. *Lillian Hellman.* Boston: Twayne, 1979. This critical examination of Hellman's works includes a good discussion of her sources for *The Children's Hour,* as well as a biographical chronology and sketch and an annotated bibliography.

Martinson, Deborah. *Lillian Hellman: A Life with Foxes and Scoundrels.* New York: Counterpoint, 2005. Martinson recounts the events of Hellman's life, describes her galvanic, often acerbic personality, and provides information about the composition and production of her plays.

Reynolds, R. C. *Stage Left: The Development of the American Social Drama in the Thirties.* Troy, N.Y.: Whitston, 1986. Examines Hellman's literary world and the contribution made to it by *The Children's Hour.*

Rollyson, Carl. *Lillian Hellman: Her Legend and Her Legacy.* New York: St. Martin's Press, 1988. This literary biography offers a full account of the complex and elusive playwright. *The Children's Hour* receives extensive treatment. Contains many photographs of Hellman and her associates.

Wright, William. *Lillian Hellman: The Image, the Woman.* New York: Simon & Schuster, 1986. This readable popular biography is less concerned with analysis of Hellman's work than with a detailed narrative of her life. Contains an interesting selection of photographs.

The Chimeras

Author: Gérard de Nerval (1808-1855)
First published: Les Chimères, 1854 (English translation, 1965)
Type of work: Poetry

In the series of the twelve sonnets he grouped together under the title *The Chimeras*, Gérard de Nerval exploits ambiguities that resemble the creatures of his title. The chimera, a monster depicted in Greek mythology, is a hybrid creature combining elements of a lion, a goat, and a serpent. In its later derivation, the word refers to something fanciful or imaginary that does not exist. Nerval plays on both senses of the word: His poems recall mythic past times, and they also produce a somewhat fictitious portrait of Nerval himself.

Nerval separately titled each of the first six sonnets and the last but grouped the remaining five into a sonnet sequence entitled "Christ on the Mount of Olives." An analysis of the work, however, shows it to be composed of four parts, with the first and the last poems forming separate units. According to that model, the opening sonnet, "El Desdichado," presents the persona of Nerval himself. The next five sonnets, each bearing as title a name from antiquity (Myrtho, Horus, Antéros, Delfica, and Artémis), evoke the gods and goddesses of pre-Christian times. "Christ on the Mount of Olives" portrays the new leader, to whom the pagan gods must yield their power, in extremely human terms. Finally, "Vers dorés" (golden lines) returns to a perception of humanity in the present.

The autobiographical "El Desdichado" draws on Nerval's personal crisis of mental illness, seen here as a descent into Hell, and Nerval's identification of himself, through the lineage of his family, with heroes from French history. The linking of the poet's descent into Hell with that of the mythic musician, Orpheus, sets up a contrast of pagan and Christian referents within the poem, a dualism that leads to the poet's question concerning his own identity.

The opening quatrain introduces the complexity of the poem and Nerval's multiple perceptions of his own persona with a large number of separate references. In the first line, he describes himself as "somber and widowed," by implication separated from the woman he loves, as Orpheus was separated from Eurydice. In the second line, however, he is "the prince of Aquitaine at the abolished tower," a figure from a period of French history.

In the following lines the words "star" and "sun" are written in italics to emphasize the affinity of these similar objects. Their symbolic references, however, differ. When Nerval says "My *star* is dead," he seems to refer to the woman whose absence causes his widowed state. However, when his starry lute carries as a chivalric device "the *black sun* of *Melancholia*," he refers to the engraving by Albert Dürer in which an angel meditates sadly on the passing of time.

The second quatrain remains much more unified, as Nerval

cries out from the tomb in which he sees himself and desires the happiness he knew in the past on a trip to Italy. The symbolic flower (again italicized) that represents this experience anticipates the further flower imagery of "Artémis." Meanwhile, the rose growing together with grapevines, although it reflects a pattern of planting common in vineyards, parallels the combining of different elements in the rest of the poem.

The simple declarations in the quatrains become a question in the tercets, as multiple allusions reflect Nerval's confusion about his true identity as a character from pagan antiquity (Cupid or Phoebus) or from Christian France (Lusignan or Biron). In whichever guise he goes on the descent into Hell, to which he twice "crossed the Acheron river," he is in the process marked by a woman because his "forehead is still red from the queen's kiss." The identity of the woman remains ambiguous. Nerval, as Orpheus, sings alternately of "the saint" and "the fairy," mythic women who represent Christian and pagan cultures.

The ensuing five sonnets constitute an excursion through pagan antiquity. The first, "Myrtho," invokes the "divine enchantress" whose name recalls the myrtle plant and who is linked both with the Italian scene of "El Desdichado" and with the more distant "brightness of the Orient." The quatrains portray a seduction of the poet by the female spirit as muse. First he becomes drunk from the cup of wine she holds and worships the pagan Bacchus. Then he declares that "the Muse has made me a son of Greece." Perhaps Nerval means simply that he writes poetry based on Greek tradition, but, given Nerval's propensity for identifying himself with figures from the past, this claim to kinship can also be taken quite literally. The tercets in this poem refer to an eruption of Vesuvius that Nerval sees as having resulted from a French conquest of Naples. Such a conquest brings the Christian culture of France into direct confrontation with the pagan culture of antiquity still associated with southern Italy. Thus "the pale Hydrangea is united with green Myrtle" as the plants, like the rose and the vines of "El Desdichado," symbolize the fusion of unlike elements.

With "Horus," Nerval returns to his earliest point in history, to ancient Egypt where the male god, Kneph, attempts to dominate the female Isis. She denounces him, however, and observes that he is dying. She declares that "the eagle has already passed, and a new spirit is calling me." This new spirit is that of the Greek gods who would replace those of Egypt. Isis, dressed in new garments, is transformed into Cybele, but for such gods as Kneph, there is no future. This passing of the legacy of divine power parallels stories told of the coming of Christ, who would similarly eclipse the Greek gods.

The triumph of the new gods does not lead to an era of peace. In "Antéros," Nerval returns to the first-person narrative that he abandoned in "Horus" to describe himself as "descended from the line of Antaeus," a son of Neptune who gains his strength from the earth. He is an angry figure devoted to revenge, the force that "marked his forehead" just as the queen's kiss marked Nerval in "El Desdichado." Nerval claims that in this guise he again combines opposing forces, "the paleness of Abel" and the "redness of Cain." He resembles Abel in that he will be killed as the Greek gods yield to Jehovah, but he acts as Cain when he "plants the old dragon's teeth," a gesture through which Cadmus, in antiquity, was said to plant the seeds that would produce a crop of avenging warriors.

"Delfica" predicts the revenge of displaced gods. With another allusion to the dragon's teeth, Nerval affirms that "the Gods you weep for will return." The final tercet, however, sees the ancient sibyl "asleep under the arch of Constantine." For the moment, Christianity triumphs over pagan culture.

The imagery of "Artémis" is the most complex in *The Chimeras*. The rose, or hollyhock, held by the queen, could identify her with the queen in a deck of cards, thus justifying the sequence of thirteen in the first line, or with a figure of love or of death. There appear, however, to be two female figures in conflict. The white rose representing the Christian saint will fade because, as Nerval affirms in the last line, "the saint of the abyss" is stronger. This must be the Artémis of the title, Apollo's sister, noted in Greek tragedy for her conflict with Aphrodite.

After five sonnets devoted to pagan gods, the subsequent five-sonnet sequence turns to Christ as the exponent of the religion that replaced the old gods. Yet the Christ shown on the Mount of Olives is himself facing death. According to Christian belief, his death is the essential sacrifice for the redemption of humanity, but the Christ readers see here, with his "thin arms" and his despairing cry, is a very human figure. Power may have passed to him, but at this tragic moment, he seems about to lose it again.

Nerval did not create this humanized representation of Christ. In "Le Mont des Oliviers" (1844), Alfred de Vigny portrays Jesus in a similar state of despair. In both poems he is abandoned by his sleeping apostles, and in both he fears, as he does in Nerval's first sonnet, that "God no longer exists."

In the second and third sonnets, Nerval turns from the personal suffering of Christ to his attempt to ease human suffering. At first, Christ fails to find the reassuring presence of God in the vastness of the universe. Then, tormented by the harshness of his fate, he seeks God within himself. He sees his death not as a part of redemption but as the extinguishing of the last hope for religion. In the fourth sonnet, Christ desires death merely as an end to his personal suffering. Ironically, Judas appears as an ineffective figure, and the only one who can ease Christ's torment is Pontius Pilate, who condemns him.

The final sonnet of this sequence returns to figures from pagan mythology, comparing Christ with Icarus in his vain attempt to win heaven. Only "for a moment" Olympus totters toward the abyss. With the reference to Cybele, the goddess of resurrection, it appears that the old gods may survive. Their oracle, however, remains silent. The last line affirms that only the transcendent God understands the divine mystery.

Neither Christ nor the pagan gods can have the last word in Nerval's *The Chimeras*. After each religion comes and perishes, the work ends with "Vers dorés," in which a pantheistic spirit in nature dwarfs human understanding. This sonnet puts the flower imagery of "El Desdichado," "Myrtho," and "Artémis" in a new context. Animals, plants, and even stones contain souls that are hidden from human comprehension. This assertion leads Nerval to the view that humans must respect nature rather than putting it to "impious usage." Yet the power contained in nature may also be a threat to humanity. An eye hidden within a rock wall may be looking out, and all matter is capable of action. In the context of revenge established in some of the earlier sonnets, the nonhuman elements of the world may be ready for their own revenge.

Nerval's *The Chimeras* grew out of ambivalent feelings that haunted his life, but beyond that it crystallized a mood of religious incertitude prevalent in the nineteenth century. In the third sonnet of the sequence, Christ sees himself "between a dying world and another being born." Nerval's review of the past is also an attempt to foresee the future.

Dorothy M. Betz

Further Reading

Burwick, Frederick. *Poetic Madness and the Romantic Imagination*. University Park: Pennsylvania State University Press, 1996. Examines the concept of "poetic frenzy" as it was understood in the late eighteenth and nineteenth centuries. Analyzes the techniques Nerval used in *The Chimeras* to relate his visionary experiences.

Jones, Robert Emmet. *Gérard de Nerval*. New York: Twayne, 1974. This standard biography provides a chronology of Nerval's life and a selected bibliography. Chapter 2 on Nerval the poet analyzes the elements of his earlier works that contributed to *The Chimeras* and offers a partial interpretation of the work.

Knapp, Bettina L. *Gérard de Nerval: The Mystic's Dilemma*. University: University of Alabama Press, 1980. Offers an extensive consideration of Nerval's life and earlier work. Chapter 20 gives a line-by-line reading of the twelve sonnets of *The Chimeras*, incorporating paraphrases that amount to an analytical translation of the work.

Nerval, Gérard de. *Selected Writings of Gérard de Nerval*. Translated and edited by Geoffrey Wagner. Ann Arbor: University of Michigan Press, 1957. Contains an introduction that provides information on aspects of Nerval's life that influenced his poetry. Discusses *The Chimeras* in the context of Nerval's other work. Includes translations of the principal works, including all of *The Chimeras* except "Christ on the Mount of Olives."

Sowerby, Benn. *The Disinherited: The Life of Gérard de Nerval, 1808-1855*. London: P. Owen, 1973. This biography, with its convenient chronology of Nerval's life, focuses on events rather than Nerval's work. Includes some comments on *The Chimeras*, chiefly in the last chapter.

Winston, Phyllis Jane. *Nerval's Magic Alphabet*. New York: Peter Lang, 1989. Chapter 4 is devoted to *The Chimeras*, citing principally "Antéros" and "Delfica." Provides an intellectual context for the work but limited interpretation of the text.

Chita
A Memory of Last Island

Author: Lafcadio Hearn (1850-1904)
First published: 1888, serial; 1889, book
Type of work: Novel
Type of plot: Impressionistic realism
Time of plot: Nineteenth century
Locale: Barrier islands off the coast of Louisiana

Principal characters:
FELIU VIOSCA, a fisherman
CARMEN VIOSCA, his wife
CHITA, a foundling, adopted by the Vioscas
ADÈLE LA BRIERRE, Chita's birth mother
JULIEN LA BRIERRE, Chita's birth father

The Story:

Southward from New Orleans, one passes settlements of many nationalities and races. Beyond lie the islands of Grande Pass, Grande Terre, and Barataria, and farther south still is the modern resort of Grande Isle. On the northwest side of each island are signs of the incessant action of the wind and sea, for the trees all bend away from the water. The coast and island beaches all exhibit the evidence of hurricanes—broken tree trunks and skeletons of toppled buildings.

Forty miles west of Grande Isle lies desolate Last Island, once the most popular of the group, and a fashionable resort. Its hotel had been a two-story timber structure with many apartments, a dining room, and a ballroom. One night, years before, the sea destroyed the hotel. Thanks to a veteran ship's pilot, the narrator hears the story one evening on Grande Isle and relates it in turn.

It has been an unusually lovely summer, and the breathless charm of the season has lingered. One afternoon, however, the ocean begins to stir, and great waves hurl themselves over the beaches, suggesting that a hurricane is brewing. The wind rises. The steamer *Star* is due, but the residents of Last Island fear that it will not arrive. Nevertheless, Captain Abraham Smith has chosen to sail the *Star* to the island; he sees the storm rising as he approaches. The hotel guests, heedless of the approaching calamity, continue to dance until the water runs over their feet and the waves begin to buffet the building. Smith spends the night rescuing as many people as he can, but the destruction is total, and by daybreak countless corpses float on the stormy sea.

Fisherman Feliu Viosca and his wife, Carmen, live on a tiny island. On the night of the terrible storm, Carmen is awakened by the noise. Afraid, she rouses her husband, whose calmness comforts her, and he tells her to return to sleep. In her dreams, her dead child—dark-eyed Conchita—comes to her.

The next day, fishermen gather along the shore to see the wreckage and the floating bodies. A flash of yellow catches

Feliu's eye, and he strips and swims out toward a child, still alive, clinging to her drowned mother. Feliu manages to rescue the girl and swim back to shore. The half-drowned child is taken to Carmen, whose skillful hands and maternal instincts nurse the little girl into a warm, sound sleep. The girl's yellow hair had saved her, for it was the flash of sun on her tresses that had caught Feliu's eye.

Along with several other men, Captain Harris of New Orleans is sailing up and down the coast in search of the missing, the dead, or those still alive after the storm. Ten days after the rescue of the girl, Harris comes to Feliu's wharf. Hardly able to communicate with the men, Feliu tells them the story of his heroism but cautions them that if they wish to question the child, they must proceed gently, because she is not fully recovered from shock.

The child's Creole dialect is incomprehensible, until a Creole named Laroussel begins to question her. She tells him that although her Creole name is Zouzoune, her real name is Lili. Her mother was Adèle and her father was Julien. Realizing that the child's relatives may never be found, Harris decides to leave her with Feliu and Carmen, who promise to care for her. Meanwhile, near another island, a body has been recovered. Returned to New Orleans, it is identified as that of Adèle, the wife of Dr. Julien Raymond La Brierre and mother of Eulalie. The epitaph on Adèle's grave also announces the death of the doctor and Eulalie. However, the doctor had survived the storm, and six months later is dumfounded to read the epitaph.

The shock forces La Brierre to recall his past. He had grown up in New Orleans and, to please his father, had studied medicine in Paris. After his return to New Orleans, he had fallen in love and had been wounded in a duel with a rival named Laroussel. Following the death of his father and mother, the doctor had married Adèle, and their child Zouzoune was born.

Meanwhile, the child, now called Chita (for the deceased Conchita), has become a member of the Viosca family. She has gradually adapted herself to the ways of her foster parents and the lonely but fascinating life of the island.

Years later, La Brierre is practicing in New Orleans as a lonely and kindly physician. Then an elderly patient of his, named Edwards, goes to Viosca's island, which Captain Harris has recommended for the sick man's recovery. While there, Edwards suffers a stroke. La Brierre is summoned, but arrives too late to save his patient.

Before the doctor can set out for home, he, too, becomes ill. Carmen nurses him. In the vague consciousness that accompanies his malady, the doctor sees Chita, whose resemblance to his dead wife greatly excites him. In his delirium, he calls out to Zouzoune and Adèle, while Carmen tries to calm him. Reliving the horror of the hurricane that had taken Adèle and Zouzoune from him, the sick man dies.

Critical Evaluation:

Chita is based on actual events, and its origins lie in Lafcadio Hearn's residence in Louisiana in the 1870's and 1880's and his travels to the barrier islands off its coast in the Gulf of Mexico. It was at a dinner party in 1883 that New Orleans writer George Washington Cable told Hearn the story of Last Island's destruction in the great hurricane of August 10, 1856. According to that account, a girl belonging to a prominent Creole family had been rescued after the storm, was returned to her parents in New Orleans, and had subsequently been sent to a convent. By then, however, the girl had come to prefer the carefree life she had experienced on the coast, and she ran off to marry a fisherman and have numerous children.

Hearn was inspired by the barrier islands' wild beauty, and he actually wrote much of *Chita* during visits to Grand Isle in 1886 and 1887. He was able to supplement Cable's account with stories from New Orleans newspapers, learning, for instance, about the crucial role played by Captain Abraham Smith and his ship, the *Star.* Noted New Orleans doctor Rudolph Matas shared medical information with Hearn, and musician Henry Edward Krehbiel taught him about Creole music. Hearn went on to publish two sketches based on the material, "Torn Letters" and "The Post-Office," in the *New Orleans Times-Democrat* in 1884. The novel itself appeared in serial form in *Harper's Magazine* in April, 1888, and a revised version—dedicated to Matas—was published in book form the following year.

Hearn was a miniaturist rather than a natural novelist, and, as short as it is, *Chita* is one of his longest sustained works. However, it itself is divided into three sections, and each section includes myriad individual episodes, observations, and sensory details. The novel has been analyzed as a series of carefully structured musical "movements," but given the static effect of its style, it can also be interpreted as a kind of painting.

The nineteenth century art movement known as Impressionism, which emphasized individual brush strokes and the fleeting nature of light and color, had come into prominence in France during the period Hearn had lived in Louisiana. Although Hearn supplemented his modest writing income with woodcuts of typical New Orleans types, it is unclear whether he was aware of the French movement. Still, his literary style closely approximates the Impressionists' works. The effect is particularly obvious in the novel's opening section, in which Hearn paints an elaborate and extended word-picture of the Gulf Coast and its barrier islands: "Over the rim of the sea a bright cloud gently pushes up its head," runs one typical passage. "It rises; and others rise with it, to right and left—slowly at first; then more swiftly. All are brilliantly white and flocculent, like loose new cotton." Hearn's preference for the present tense, his short clauses and sentences, and even his use of punctuation (which is likely to strike modern readers as excessive)—all contribute to the shimmering effect.

Whatever Hearn's knowledge of French art, he was quite familiar with contemporary French literature. While in New Orleans, he had translated works by French authors Théophile Gautier and Pierre Loti, both of whom wrote of distant lands and amorous adventures. Hearn shared their fascination with the exotic and reveled in what he thought of as the strange life and landscape of Louisiana and the Gulf Coast. He also was drawn to marginalized groups, those people who stubbornly maintained a traditional way of life in the face of "progress." He also was drawn to the region's Creole culture—comprised, as he understood it, largely of French elements—finding a rich and vital subject. (Hearn would later move to Japan and write extensively about its traditional, and fast-disappearing, way of life.)

The evolutionary theories of English social philosopher Herbert Spencer would prove to be an important influence on the deterministic, even pessimistic American literary movement known as naturalism. Hearn's interest in Spencer (awakened by an acquaintance in New Orleans), however, led him in an entirely different direction, encouraging him to develop the more positive worldview he displays in *Chita*. It is this outlook that the girl acquires as she grows up with the Vioscas, memorizing "with novel delight much that was told her day by day concerning the nature surrounding her,—many secrets of the air, many of those signs of heaven which the dwellers in cities cannot comprehend."

Like the French writers he admired, Hearn was more concerned with description than with character development, and the individuals in his novel are scarcely more significant than the earth and the sky and the relentless waters of the gulf. Chita herself emerges as an important figure only in a few pages of the novel's final section. In Hearn's vision, each element of the novel (and the world) is a fragment of the greater whole.

Chita proved to be a critical and popular success. The novel was reprinted nearly one dozen times and appeared in a British edition in 1890. In subsequent decades, however, Hearn and his novel passed out of fashion. Twenty-first century readers may find its plot sketchy and overly sentimental, appreciating it instead as a poetic evocation of a vanishing culture. They may also appreciate it as an account of a vanishing landscape. "The sea is devouring the land," observes the novel's narrator in its opening section. "Many and many a mile of ground has yielded to the tireless charging of Ocean's cavalry." Vivid memories of the destruction wrought on the Gulf Coast by Hurricane Katrina in 2005, coupled with fears that erosion could destroy Louisiana's barrier islands by the end of the twenty-first century, make it possible to read *Chita* both in an ecological context and in a purely literary one.

"Critical Evaluation" by Grove Koger

Further Reading

Cott, Jonathan. *Wandering Ghost: The Odyssey of Lafcadio Hearn*. New York: Alfred A. Knopf, 1991. A biographical reader combining an affectionate account of Hearn's career with selections from his works. Cott maintains that although Hearn's depiction of the characters in *Chita* is overly sentimental, his poetic prose successfully imitates the sea's hypnotic tides and waves. Includes a chronological bibliography.

Gale, Robert L. *A Lafcadio Hearn Companion*. Westport, Conn.: Greenwood Press, 2002. Contains several hundred alphabetically arranged entries on Hearn's life, works, family members, and colleagues. Includes a chronology and a bibliography.

Hirakawa, Sukehiro, ed. *Lafcadio Hearn in International Perspectives*. Folkestone, England: Global Oriental, 2007. A collection of multicultural approaches to Hearn's life and writings, including discussions of his identity as an American writer, his treatment of the sea, and his depiction of mothers and motherhood. Includes a bibliography.

Humphries, Jefferson. Introduction to *Chita: A Memory of Last Island*. Jackson: University Press of Mississippi, 2003. A well-written analysis stressing Hearn's unusual background, the novel's origins, and the influence of contemporary French writers on Hearn's work. This edition also contains a preface and notes by Delia LaBarre.

Kunst, Arthur E. *Lafcadio Hearn*. New York: Twayne, 1969. A solid introductory critical study. Includes a detailed treatment of *Chita* and relates Hearn's poetic prose to structural elements of music. Includes a select bibliography.

Murray, Paul. *A Fantastic Journey: The Life and Literature of Lafcadio Hearn*. Ann Arbor: University of Michigan Press, 1997. Murray recounts the events of Hearn's life, including his writing and publication of *Chita*. Includes a bibliography.

Stevenson, Elizabeth. *The Grass Lark: A Study of Lafcadio Hearn*. New Brunswick, N.J.: Transaction Books, 1999. A thorough, beautifully written biography. Discusses *Chita* as a story of solitude, loneliness, and the sea. An updated edition of *Lafcadio Hearn* (1961), with a new introduction by the author. Includes a substantial bibliography.

The Chocolate War

Author: Robert Cormier (1925-2000)
First published: 1974
Type of work: Young adult fiction
Type of plot: Psychological
Time of plot: Early 1970's
Locale: Northeastern United States

Principal characters:
JERRY RENAULT, a freshman
ROLAND "GOOBER" GOUBERT, his friend
ARCHIE COSTELLO, assigner of the Vigils
OBIE, secretary of the Vigils
JOHN CARTER, president of the Vigils
BROTHER LEON, assistant headmaster
BROTHER EUGENE, a teacher
BROTHER JACQUES, a teacher
EMILE JANZA, a brute

The Story:

Jerry Renault, a skinny freshman at Trinity High School who lost his mother to cancer a year ago, tries out for the football team. He is brutally sacked, but he gets up afterward, and the coach tells him to come back the next day. Obie and Archie watch from the stands. Archie, the plotter of practical jokes for an underground group, the Vigils, must pick ten names and an assignment for each name. Obie, Archie's flunky, writes what Archie says: "Roland Goubert—Brother Eugene's Room; Jerry Renault—Chocolates."

Brother Leon, Trinity's assistant headmaster, has ordered twenty thousand boxes of chocolates for the school's annual fund-raiser, two times the normal order. He asks Archie for help with this endeavor, explaining that each student must sell fifty boxes. Archie enjoys seeing Brother Leon squirm but finally agrees that the Vigils will help.

The Vigils meet. Archie humiliates Goober, who is given the assignment to loosen every screw in Brother Eugene's classroom. Goober fearfully accepts the assignment. Then, Carter pulls out a small black box that contains six marbles—five white and one black. Archie must pick blindly. If the marble is white, the assignment remains with Goober. If black, Archie must carry out the assignment. Archie gets lucky.

The morning after Goober carries out his assignment, pandemonium breaks loose in Brother Eugene's room as the desks and chairs begin falling apart. Brother Eugene has a breakdown, and Goober feels guilty. After scrimmage that day, Jerry finds a letter taped to his locker door—a summons from the Vigils.

Brother Leon enjoys mentally torturing his students. In class, he reads their names from a list, asking each person if they will agree to sell fifty boxes of chocolates. Everyone says "Yes," until Brother Leon reaches Jerry, who says "No."

Brother Leon discovers why Jerry won't sell the choco-lates—it is a Vigils assignment. Jerry is to refuse to sell chocolates for ten days and then accept. After ten days, Brother Leon calls Jerry's name again. Jerry still refuses, and Leon is shocked. Jerry wants the battle between himself and Brother Leon to be over, but he cannot abide Brother Leon's cruelty. The words on a poster encourage Jerry: "Do I dare disturb the universe?"

Sales of the chocolates are down. Brother Leon blames Jerry. His refusal to sell candy has encouraged other boys to do the same. Goober, sensing trouble ahead, asks Jerry to cooperate with Brother Leon. Brother Leon orders Archie and the Vigils to sell more chocolates. Brother Leon threatens Archie, saying that if the sales go down, the Vigils go down.

The Vigils meet. Archie gives Jerry a new assignment—to sell the chocolates. Jerry refuses. Archie comes up with a campaign to make the candy sale more popular at school. His plan works. The Vigils sell chocolates for the other students. In class, Brother Leon continues to call Jerry's name and Jerry consistently says "No." The students turn against Jerry for his lack of school spirit. Goober becomes more worried about his friend. Jerry is beaten by Emile, the school bully, and five other boys. Jerry rides the bus home and goes to bed, keeping the attack hidden from his father.

Finally, only Jerry's fifty boxes of chocolates remain unsold. Archie goads Jerry into a boxing match with Emile on the athletic field at night. Jerry doesn't know the whole school will be watching. Archie sells raffle tickets for $1 each for a chance to win $100 plus chocolates. The night of the match, Jerry is upset, but his pride will not let him back down.

Before the fight, Obie and Carter carry the black box to an unsuspecting Archie. They tell him he has to draw two marbles, one for Jerry and one for Emile. Archie gets lucky and pulls a white marble. Then, he cheats on the second draw. The fight goes forward as planned.

The raffle tickets control the blows in the fight. Each student has written on his ticket who he wants to throw the punch. Most of the tickets are for Emile. Jerry takes a terrible beating. Brother Leon watches the fight from a distance. Suddenly, the lights go out in the stadium. Archie goes into the building and finds that Brother Jacques has turned them off. He rebukes Archie, but Brother Leon says "Boys will be boys." When the lights come on, most of the students have left. Goober cradles Jerry, who warns his friend to conform rather than disturb the universe. Obie calls an ambulance.

After everyone is gone, Archie and Obie sit in the stands. Obie says Brother Leon is a bastard for watching the fight and doing nothing. Archie reveals that he tipped Brother Leon off about the fight. Obie tells Archie that someday he will get what is coming to him.

Critical Evaluation:

"They murdered him." Thus begins *The Chocolate War*, a novel about evil and the abuse of power in a private boy's high school. Jerry Renault is not literally murdered that day, only tackled on the football field. However, by using that sentence, Robert Cormier sets an ominous tone for the book and hints at a grim ending.

The novel comprises thirty-nine chapters, each short but with significant impact. The author's writing has been called "cinematic" because the book's scenes are very tight and the dialogue is brief. Action and dialogue move the story along; there are no long, descriptive paragraphs. Cormier's career as a newspaper reporter and editor influenced his style. Journalists are trained to use the lead to draw readers in and to keep their sentences short. Cormier does not give away the ending, however. He draws readers in with little dramas, creating suspense with pacing and dialogue. "Rather than waiting for one big climax, I try to create a lot of little conflicts," Cormier explained, "a series of explosions as I go along."

The point of view changes from chapter to chapter. Some chapters are narrated from Jerry's perspective, while others are narrated from the perspectives of Obie and Archie. By shifting the point of view from one character to another, Cormier develops connections between a reader and every major character.

The metaphors and similes in the book are dark, comparing, for example, Brother Leon's breath to rancid bacon or a sunset to bleeding and spurting veins. Cormier draws upon his upbringing as a Roman Catholic for much of the symbolism: He describes goal posts that resemble empty crucifixes and names the bullies' group the Vigils in reference to the eve of a religious holiday.

The struggle of the individual against an evil system is a

major theme of the book. Cormier was a practicing and moral Catholic. Individual moral choices shape the lives of his characters, but he is interested in bigger issues than a freshman refusing to sell chocolate candy. He asks through his novel what responsibility each individual bears when faced with injustice. He portrays a choice between merely observing such injustice or, in the words of T. S. Eliot's "The Love Song of J. Alfred Prufrock" (1915) quoted on Jerry's poster, "disturb[ing] the universe."

Cormier's last editor, Karen Wojtyla, wrote, "He often places his characters at crossroads, exploring what happens depending upon which choice they make." *The Chocolate War* is about choosing defiance or conformity. Jerry chooses defiance, refusing to participate in the candy sale. The other students and Brother Jacques, by contrast, know of the Vigils but do nothing to stop or disband them. Cormier demonstrates the outcome of doing nothing. Someone gets hurt, and the evil Archie sits calmly on a bench, ironically wishing he had a chocolate bar.

Cormier ends the book the way it began, with the word "murder." Jerry is brutally beaten to the point of unconsciousness. He says to Goober, "Just remember what I told you. It's important. Otherwise, they murder you." Although Jerry does not die, his spirit is broken as he succumbs to the manipulations of Archie and Brother Leon. Jerry dared to disturb the universe, but he has lost.

The Chocolate War is historically significant in two ways. First, according to biographer Patty Campbell, "*The Chocolate War* initiated a new level of literary excellence in the fledgling genre of young adult fiction." Cormier created books for teens that were literature and paved the way for other writers in this genre to achieve literary recognition.

Second, Cormier's book represented new thinking regarding the types of books to which youth should be exposed. By rejecting the idea that endings must be happy and that the hero must prevail, Cormier opened the door to controversy, exposing teenagers to the real world. In this world, heroes can get hurt and they may not win in the end. This does not mean that the world is all bad or that Cormier was a pessimistic person. Cormier did his job as an author: He told a great story, with honesty, and created realistic characters with whom his readers could identify.

While there were objections and formal protests to the book because it contained violence, offensive language, and an upsetting ending, *The Chocolate War* has earned many honors since it was published. In 1974, the novel received a *New York Times* Outstanding Book of the Year Award and an American Library Association (ALA) Award for books for young adults. Margaret Sacco of Miami University of Ohio wrote, "It is considered the best young adult novel of all times by teachers, professors and librarians." The ALA named *The Chocolate War* one of the one hundred best books for teens written between 1966 and 2000.

Kat Kitts

Further Reading

Bagnall, Norma. "Realism: How Realistic Is It? A Look at *The Chocolate War.*" *Top of the News*, Winter, 1980, pp. 214-217. Asserts that Cormier's book is not realistic, since he depicts a totally evil world in which bad characters triumph. Emphasizes that the book teaches hopelessness because the protagonist cannot win.

Beckman, Wendy Hart. *Robert Cormier: Banned, Challenged, and Censored.* Berkeley Heights, N.J.: Enslow, 2008. Looks at the history of book banning and provides a time line from Plato on. Beckman explains terminology and lists some of the schools that have challenged *The Chocolate War* and had it removed from their libraries.

Campbell, Patricia. *Robert Cormier: Daring to Disturb the Universe.* New York: Delacorte Books, 2006. Presents a biography of Cormier and his contribution to young adult literature. Devotes one chapter to analyzing each of his major novels and novellas.

Carter, Betty, and Karen Harris. "Realism in Adolescent Fiction: In Defense of *The Chocolate War.*" *Top of the News*, Winter, 1980, pp. 283-285. Carter and Harris disagree with Norma Bagnall's criticism of Cormier's book. They see the book as raising large questions about the nature of tyranny and the responsibility of each individual.

Keeling, Kara. "The Misfortune of a Man Like Ourselves: Robert Cormier's *The Chocolate War* as Aristotelian Tragedy." *ALAN Review* 26, no. 2 (1999): 9-12. Discusses the reaction of students in Keeling's college class on adolescent literature to *The Chocolate War.* Contends that the book should be taught as tragedy, rather than realist fiction.

Veglahn, Nancy. "The Bland Face of Evil in the Novels of Robert Cormier." *Lion and the Unicorn* 12, no. 1 (June, 1988): 12-18. Cormier's victimizers hide behind a benevolent mask, but they are anything but bland. Veglahn compares the traits of the protagonists and the evil adult males in *The Chocolate War, Beyond the Chocolate War, I Am the Cheese, After the First Death,* and *The Bumblebee Flies Away.*

The Chosen

Author: Chaim Potok (1929-2002)
First published: 1967
Type of work: Novel
Type of plot: Bildungsroman and domestic realism
Time of plot: 1940's
Locale: Brooklyn, New York

Principal characters:
REUVEN MALTER, a teenage Orthodox Jew
DAVID MALTER, his father, a Talmudic scholar
DANNY SAUNDERS, a teenage Hasidic Jew
ISAAC SAUNDERS, his father, a Hasidic rabbi

The Story:

Two fifteen-year-old boys, growing up within five blocks of each other in the early 1940's, meet during a baseball game one Sunday in June. The game is an athletic competition between yeshivas, or Jewish parochial schools. The ensuing game takes on warlike proportions. One team is led by Danny Saunders, the eldest son of a prominent Hasidic rabbi, Reb Isaac Saunders, who had led his people out of Russia to the United States. This team, and all of Reb Saunders's followers, wear the traditional clothing, corresponding with Hasidism's founding in the eighteenth century: black hats or skullcaps, long black coats, and fringed prayer garments called tzitzits. Their long earlocks also set them apart.

The other team is led by Reuven Malter, son of widowed teacher and scholar David Malter. The marked difference between the two teams is exemplified by their respective coaches. Mr. Galanter, a gym teacher from the public school system, moonlights by teaching in Reuven's school. He wears modern clothing and is described as "fanatically addicted to professional baseball." Danny's team is escorted to the ball field by a coach who is a rabbi. Dressed in traditional black garb, he reads a book while the teams play ball. His sole advice to his team is "Remember why and for whom we play."

One of Reuven's teammates warns him "They're murderers." The truth of this observation becomes evident early in the game. Although the majority of Danny's teammates are unremarkable ballplayers, they play with a fierce intensity. During the game, one of Danny's hits strikes pitcher Reuven, shattering his glasses and injuring his left eye. Reuven is taken to the hospital and undergoes surgery to remove glass splinters. Reuven learns that, in addition to having a concussion, he faces the possibility of scar tissue causing blindness in that eye.

While in the hospital Reuven makes several friends. Two are fellow patients in the eye ward. Tony Savo, a professional boxer, had lost an eye because of a boxing injury. Billy Merrit, a young boy, had been blinded in a car accident. The most surprising new friend, however, is Danny. When Danny first visits Reuven in the hospital, Reuven notes that "he looked a little like the pictures I had seen of Abraham Lincoln before he grew the beard." Danny tries to apologize to Reuven, but Reuven orders him to leave.

Mr. Malter visits his son and, after learning how he treated Danny, reprimands Reuven, telling him that the Talmud commands listening and forgiveness when an apology is offered. During this visit, Reuven and his father also discuss the war in Europe, including the D day invasion by the Allied Powers. "It is the beginning of the end for Hitler and his madmen," Mr. Malter tells his son. The next day, Danny again visits. Reuven apologizes for his behavior, and the two talk civilly. Danny admits that he did not understand his feelings during the ball game. "I wanted to walk over to you and open your head with my bat," he says. Reuven observes that Danny "dressed like a Hasid, but he didn't sound like one."

During their first sustained conversation, Reuven learns of Danny's photographic mind and phenomenal intelligence. Danny can recite from memory virtually anything he has ever read. Reuven is both awed and disturbed by Danny's amazing ability, noting that "He did it coldly, mechanically . . . I had the feeling I was watching some sort of human machine at work."

The boys discuss their professional aspirations. Reuven plans to become a rabbi, although his father hopes he will become a mathematician. Danny is expected to become a rabbi because the position is an inherited one. He admits, however, that if he could choose otherwise, he would become a psychologist.

The hospital visits continue. Reuven's eye heals, and full vision returns. Sadly, his hospital mates do not fare as well.

Nothing could be done to help the boxer, Tony Savo, and the surgery to restore Billy's sight is unsuccessful. As Danny and Reuven's friendship develops, Danny is astonished to learn that he had already met Reuven's father.

On surreptitious visits to the public library, Danny approaches Mr. Malter. Without exchanging names, Danny asks him for book recommendations and Mr. Malter obliges. They often discuss Danny's reading. Mr. Malter knows he is dealing with the brilliant son of Rabbi Saunders and that nothing can stop Danny's quest for knowledge. He feels uneasy, however, knowing that Rabbi Saunders would not approve of Danny's reading.

Reuven is eventually introduced to Reb Saunders and to Danny's world. Reuven attends religious services in Reb Saunders's synagogue, which occupies one floor of the family home. While attending services, Reuven is drawn into an intense, public debate between Danny and his father. He and Danny pass the rabbi's strange test, though Reuven does not understand what has happened. His suspicions and distrust of Reb Saunders grow. Reuven is accepted by Reb Saunders, however, and he continues to visit and worship with the family. Reuven learns that Danny and his father never speak except when they discuss holy writings. This silence is mysterious to Reuven, and his resentment toward Reb Saunders grows. Danny does not understand the painful silence either; still, he trusts and respects his father.

The boys finish high school and continue their education at Hirsch College. Danny majors in psychology and Reuven studies philosophy with an emphasis in symbolic logic. They also continue their religious studies and gain the respect and admiration of professors and students alike.

A crisis in the friendship occurs following the end of the war and the subsequent movement to establish a secular Jewish nation. Reuven and his father support Zionism wholeheartedly, but Reb Saunders and his followers are vehemently opposed to it, claiming it would be a denial of the Torah and their hope in the coming Messiah. When Reb Saunders learns of Mr. Malter's avid, public support of Zionism, he forbids Danny from having any more contact with Reuven. A second silence begins. Danny's relationship with his father is still marked by silence, and the best friends can no longer communicate.

Danny obeys his father's wishes, although it causes both boys great pain. Reuven describes the silence as "ugly" and "black." The silence "leered, it was cancerous, it was death." Adding to Danny's misery is his disappointment with his college studies. His psychology professor stresses experimental psychology. Danny finds himself studying rats and experiments when he really wants to be studying Sigmund Freud and psychoanalysis. Reuven's pain is heightened when his father is hospitalized with a second heart attack.

One day in their third year of college, Danny surprisingly breaks the friends' two-year silence. Danny sits down at the lunch table at school and asks Reuven for some help with math. Reb Saunders had finally lifted the ban after the idea of a Jewish nation becomes real. Reuven resumes contact with the Saunders family and even attends Danny's sister's wedding. Reuven also learns that, in accordance with Hasidic custom, Danny's wife had been chosen for him since childhood.

Reb Saunders repeatedly asks Reuven to visit, but Reuven lets many months pass before honoring the request. Reuven's father is again disappointed to learn that his son has been unresponsive to another's wishes. He reminds his son, "when someone asks to speak to you, you must let him speak to you. You still have not learned that? You did not learn that from what happened between you and Danny?" He urges Reuven to support Danny in the inevitable confrontation with Reb Saunders. Danny has decided to reject the inherited position from his father and pursue graduate study at Columbia University to become a psychologist. Mr. Malter urges Reuven to help Danny plan how he will answer his father's questions.

Reuven visits the Saunders home during Passover and with Danny meets with Reb Saunders in his study. Reb Saunders speaks to Danny through Reuven, explaining how he himself had been raised in silence by his father. He speaks also of Danny's uncle, who had an exceptional mind but essentially no soul. In childhood, Danny had shown early signs of being like his uncle—restless, impatient, and disdainful of others with less intelligence. Reb Saunders knew that it was not enough to have a brilliant mind. His son's soul, that divine spark of God, must be cultivated. To develop his son's soul and prepare him to take on the suffering of his people, Reb Saunders had decided to raise Danny as he had been raised—in silence.

This discussion takes place during the Passover—the festival of freedom. Danny is in tears as his father releases him from the inherited position. Danny's brother, Levi, will become the tzadik, or "righteous one," thereby continuing the tradition. With a heavy but understanding heart, Reb Saunders accepts his son's wishes to become a psychologist, noting that "I have no more fear now. All his life he will be a tzaddik. He will be a tzaddik for the world. And the world needs a tzaddik." Reb Saunders asks his son for forgiveness: "A—a wiser father ... may have done differently. I am not ... wise."

Danny and Reuven graduate summa cum laude from Hirsch College. That September, as Danny prepares to move out of his family's home and into a rented room near Columbia University, he and Reuven once again discuss Danny's upbringing. Reuven learns that normal conversation has finally resumed between Danny and his father. Danny also tells Reuven that when Danny has a son of his own, he will consider raising him as he had been raised, "If I can't find another way."

"The Story" by Beverly J. Matiko

Critical Evaluation:

Chaim Potok's first novel, *The Chosen*, received the Edward Lewis Wallant Book Award (1967) and was nominated for the National Book Award (1968). On the surface, *The Chosen* seems to be a sentimental story about two Jewish boys coming of age at the end of World War II and becoming friends despite differences in devotion to their faith. On a deeper level, the novel is about conflict within relationships, between fathers and sons, between friends, and within orthodox Jewish life in the United States. In keeping with Orthodox tradition, the few female characters in the story are separated from the main drama, playing their supportive roles largely in the background as housekeepers, wives, sisters, or nurses.

The reader learns a great deal about Judaism through Reuven's memoirlike viewpoint, which includes scenes told mostly through indirect dialogue. The story also includes reflection and explanation, as Reuven recalls events as if he is sharing them with a modern listener, or reader. Still, the reader is drawn into Reuven's emotion as he moves from initially rejecting Danny's friendship to becoming Danny's confidant. As he comes to understand Danny, he grows to dislike Danny's tyrannical father on his friend's behalf.

This viewpoint serves to illustrate a metaphor of vision throughout the story. The story opens with Reuven nearly losing his sight when a baseball breaks his glasses during a ball game. The relief in the successful operation is pitted against the less fortunate result of eye surgery performed on two fellow patients; the surgery also leads Reuven to see the world in a new light. His world is no longer confined to his Jewish neighborhood. He learns to place his life within the context of world events, notably the end of World War II and what that war means for American Jews.

This larger vision is also expressed in Danny's personal struggle. Danny is driven to explore the world beyond his Hasidic roots. His brilliant mind is bored in his traditional studies, and he secretly spends free time at the public library, reading everything from the classics to Jewish history and Freudian psychology. As he reads he becomes more discontent with the future chosen for him by Hasidic law. He is to inherit leadership of his people. As he explores the broader world, his eyesight grows worse and he eventually must use eyeglasses during his college studies.

War is another metaphor woven through the story, a metaphor that points to conflict on many levels. The baseball game that brought Reuven and Danny together is an athletic competition between yeshivas. Reuven's yeshiva is very liberal, and Danny's Hasidic team turns the competition into a holy war for Hasidic superiority. Unlike many similar books about Jewish life, *The Chosen* does not create conflict between Jew and gentile but between two orthodox Jewish boys. They live at the extreme ends of their faith, but they both study the Talmud, follow Jewish custom, and struggle with Jewish identity in their stance on Zionism at the end of World War II. After Reuven's father becomes involved in the Zionist movement and makes a speech supporting the establishment of Israel as the new Jewish state, Reb Saunders forbids Danny or any of the Hasidic Jews to associate with Reuven. Conflict between students in regard to Zionism and Israel also causes problems at Hirsch College.

This rift within the Jewish community is a central point for another issue the novel addresses: silence. Reuven is confused by the strange relationship Danny has with his father, in which the two only speak to one another when they debate the Talmud on Shabbat, or the Sabbath. Danny wishes he could speak with his father but assumes his father's silence comes from his role as a spiritual leader. Reuven's father, however, is a scholar who tries to help Reuven understand Hasidic customs. Things get worse between Reuven and Danny when Danny's father uses Reuven as a means to speak to his own son. Reuven grows to resent this, though his own father encourages him to allow it as a true friend to Danny.

Eventually, Reuven becomes furious with Reb Saunders's treatment of Danny, as this same silence is forced upon the two friends because their fathers have different opinions about the creation of a Jewish state. Without Reuven, Danny has no one to speak with. Eventually, Danny becomes very ill, and Reuven's father has a serious heart attack. Just when the boys need each other most, they are forced apart, lonely and miserable. Eventually, violence in the newly created Jewish nation stuns everyone in the community, and Reb Saunders lifts the ban on communication between the boys. Still, Reuven cannot resolve his distaste for how Danny's father handled the issue. Finally, Reuven's father, still recovering from his heart attack, convinces Reuven that Reb Saunders is looking to him to help him communicate with his son.

Danny has by now decided to tell his father that he has no

intention of taking over the role of tzaddik and that he plans to study psychology instead. He expects his younger brother to become a spiritual leader, though he has not been groomed for the role. In an emotional scene, Reb Saunders explains to Reuven, and thus his son, the reason for the silence. He had feared that Danny's brilliance would supersede his compassion. He also had wanted to ensure that Danny would understand those he was meant to lead. The silence was intended to create suffering and understanding, ensuring that his son's soul was worthy of a tzaddik. Though Reuven believes this is cruel treatment, Danny's respect for his father provides understanding. Reb Saunders has accepted Danny's choices in life because he realizes that in pursuing psychology Danny will be a tzaddik to the world and not merely his community.

Potok's novel delivers a broad understanding of Judaism, of what it means to be a Jew in America, and of social, political, and religious history from around the world. In 1969, Potok published *The Promise*, a sequel to *The Chosen*, continuing the story of Danny and Reuven.

"Critical Evaluation" by Lisa A. Wroble

Further Reading
Abramson, Edward A. *Chaim Potok.* Boston: Twayne, 1986. The chapter about *The Chosen* discusses the Hasidic and Orthodox Jewish and non-Jewish worlds, the value of education, fathers and sons, and form and content.

Bloom, Harold, ed. *Chaim Potok's "The Chosen."* Philadelphia: Chelsea House, 2005. A student guide to the novel. Contains a biographical sketch of Potok, an account of the conditions under which the novel was written, a list of characters, plot summary and analysis, and critical opinion of the book. Includes an annotated bibliography.

Furman, Andrew. "Zionism in Chaim Potok's *The Chosen*, Messianic Complications and Current Crises." In *Israel Through the Jewish-American Imagination: A Survey of Jewish-American Literature on Israel, 1928-1995.* Albany: State University of New York Press, 1997. Furman analyzes *The Chosen* and works by seven other Jewish American authors to chart the evolution of American Jews' relationships with the state of Israel.

Shaked, Gershon. "Shadows of Identity: A Comparative Study of German Jewish and American Jewish Literature." In *What Is Jewish Literature?*, edited by Hana Wirth-Nesher. Philadelphia: Jewish Publication Society, 1994. Shaked briefly places *The Chosen* in the context of literature in which Jewish authors and their characters have a dual identity: Jewish as well as that of the country in which they live.

Sternlicht, Sanford. *Chaim Potok: A Critical Companion.* Westport, Conn.: Greenwood Press, 2000. A straightforward and useful guide to the novelist's works. Summarizes Potok's life, assesses his literary heritage and achievements, and devotes a chapter to an analysis of *The Chosen.*

Studies in American Jewish Literature 4 (1985). This special issue devoted to Potok includes several valuable critical essays, an interview with Potok conducted in 1981 by S. Lillian Kremer, and an autobiographical essay by Potok, "The First Eighteen Years." An indispensable source.

University of Pennsylvania, Jewish Studies Program. *Chaim Potok and Jewish-American Culture: Three Essays.* Philadelphia: Author, 2002. These essays, delivered at a memorial symposium for Potok, reappraise *The Chosen,* discuss "Potok and the Question of Jewish Writing," and examine how the author was a *Zwischenmensch,* or a person who negotiated between two cultures.

Walden, Daniel, ed. *Conversations with Chaim Potok.* Jackson: University Press of Mississippi, 2001. Reprints numerous interviews with Potok in which he discusses a range of topics, including his views on writing and other writers, his religious faith, and his novels.

Christabel

Author: Samuel Taylor Coleridge (1772-1834)
First published: 1816
Type of work: Poetry
Type of plot: Gothic
Time of plot: Middle Ages
Locale: Lake District, England

Principal characters:
CHRISTABEL, a young woman
SIR LEOLINE, her father, a wealthy baron and widower
GERALDINE, a young woman, who seems to be a vampire
BARD BRACY, a member of Sir Leoline's household

The Poem:

It is midnight at Langdale Hall, the English Lake District castle of Sir Leoline, and under an April full moon the baron's daughter Christabel passes through the gate and walks alone deep into the forest, eventually stopping to pray at an old oak tree for the well-being of the knight to whom she is betrothed. Hearing a moan, she goes to the other side of the tree and sees "a damsel bright,/ Drest in a silken robe of white . . . gems entangled in her hair." The stranger tells Christabel she is of noble birth, is named Geraldine, and was abducted by five warriors who left her beneath the oak, promising to return. Christabel assures Geraldine that her father will see that she is safely guided home and leads her to the castle and her bedchamber, where Christabel offers her guest wine made by Christabel's late mother (who "died the hour that [she] was born"). Seemingly sensing that the mother's spirit is present, Geraldine says

> "Off, old woman, off! This hour is mine—
> Though thou her guardian spirit be,
> Off, woman, off! 'tis given to me."

Restored by the wine, Geraldine assures her hostess, "All they who live in the upper sky,/ Do love you, holy Christa-

bel!" and she will attempt "to requite you well." Preparing for bed, Geraldine removes her clothes, and the narrator tantalizingly says

> Behold! Her bosom and half her side—
> A sight to dream of, not to tell!
> O shield her! Shield sweet Christabel!

Geraldine says nothing, but with a stricken look gets into bed, takes Christabel in her arms, and says

> "In the touch of this bosom there worketh a spell,
> Which is lord of thy utterance, Christabel!
> Thou knowest tonight, and wilt know tomorrow,
> This mark of my shame, this seal of my sorrow . . . "

Christabel will be unable to reveal to others this shameful mark. She sleeps that night with open eyes ("ah woe is me!" laments the narrator), whereas Geraldine "Seems to slumber still and mild,/ As a mother with her child." When Christabel awakens in the morning, smiling yet weeping, the narrator speculates hopefully that guardian spirits will look after her.

The second part of the poem begins with the daily morning tolling of the bell, which Bracy the bard says has been heard throughout the Lake District for years that span the lives of three sacristans. When Geraldine awakens, Christabel thinks her bedmate is fairer than she was the night before: "For she belike hath drunken deep/ Of all the blessedness of sleep!" She then says, "Sure I have sinned!" but under Geraldine's spell, she can only pray that Jesus might wash away any unknown transgressions. She introduces Geraldine to Sir Leoline, who at first welcomes her but, hearing her tale and father's name—Lord Roland de Vaux of Tryermaine—grows pale, recalling that he and Roland had been close friends when young but subsequently became estranged.

> They parted—ne-er to meet again!
> But never either found another
> To free the hollow heart from paining—
> They stood aloof, the scars remaining,
> Like cliffs which had been rent asunder.

Moved by recollections of past friendship and seeing in Geraldine a youthful Sir Roland, Sir Leoline vows to avenge those who wronged her. When he embraces Geraldine, she prolongs the closeness "with joyous look," and Christabel recalls her fearful vision of Geraldine the previous night.

> Again she saw that bosom old,
> Again she felt that bosom cold,
> And drew in her breath with a hissing sound.

Her father asks what ails her, but "so mighty was the spell" she cannot tell him.

Geraldine, feigning concern that she has offended Christabel, asks that she be sent home without delay, but the baron refuses. He orders Bracy to travel to Lord Roland's home, inform him his daughter is safe and that he should come to retrieve her. Bracy is also to say on his lord's behalf

> That I repent me of the day
> When I spake words of fierce disdain
> To Ronald de Vaux of Tryermaine!—
> For since that evil hour hath flown,
> Many a summer's sun hasth shone;
> Yet ne'er found I a friend again
> Like Roland de Vaux of Tryermaine.

Bracy, his voice faltering, asks of his master that "This day my journey should not be" because in a dream the previous night he found a dove called Christabel in distress in the forest with a snake coiled around its neck but awoke at that point (it was midnight) and vowed to search the forest this day "Lest aught unholy loiter there."

Ignoring his daughter, Leoline turns to Geraldine, addresses her as "Lord Roland's beauteous dove," says that he with her father will crush the snake, and kisses her forehead, at which time her eyes "shrunk up to a serpent's eye,/ And with somewhat of malice, and more of dread," she looks askance at Christabel, who stumbles and shudders with a hissing sound. Christabel begs her father "By my mother's soul" to send Geraldine away, although unable to tell him why, since she still is "O'ermastered by the mighty spell." Sir Leoline feels betrayed, thinking Christabel is jealous because of his obvious attraction to Geraldine. His "rage and pain" swell, his heart is "cleft with pane and rage," and he thinks his only child is dishonoring him in his old age. Turning to the "gentle minstrel bard," he reiterates his earlier order, turns away from his daughter, and leads forth "the lady Geraldine!"

Critical Evaluation:

Christabel was supposed to be one of Samuel Taylor Coleridge's contributions to the second edition of *Lyrical Ballads*, a joint project with William Wordsworth first published anonymously in 1798 that included *The Rime of the Ancient Mariner*, Coleridge's long ballad. He wrote the first part of *Christabel* in 1797, but by 1800, when an expanded, two-volume edition of *Lyrical Ballads* was published, he had completed only the second part of the poem. When the poem, still a fragment, finally was published 1816, Coleridge stated in a preface: "But as, in my very first conception of the tale, I had the whole present to my mind, with the wholeness, no less than the liveliness of a vision, I trust that I shall be able to embody in verse three parts yet to come, in the course of the present year." He never did, and this sentence subsequently was deleted from the preface.

Coleridge's reputation as a giant of English literature rests upon his literary criticism and just three poems—*The Rime of the Ancient Mariner*, *Christabel*, and *Kubla Khan* (1816)—only the first of which he completed. All epitomize the Romantic period's attraction to the remote (in time and place) and the mysterious (with supernatural and Gothic elements). Though *The Rime of the Ancient Mariner* (particularly in its early version) seems closer in poetic style than *Christabel* to the traditional English ballad, Coleridge in his preface to the latter says his meter is "founded on a new principle: namely, that of counting in each line the accents, not the syllables [which] may vary from seven to twelve, yet in line the accents will be found to be only four." Actually, much Anglo-Saxon and Middle English poetry was based on accent, with variation in the number of syllables per line, as in this poem, but since the 1500's English poetry had typically had a regular number of syllables per line, so Coleridge indeed was departing from prevailing practice. Compared to *The Rime of the Ancient Mariner*, the incomplete *Christabel*, follows more directly in traditions of the English ballad and the Gothic because of its native setting, folklore superstitions, overarching Christianity, and supernatural elements.

The opening stanzas of *Christabel* abound with familiar Gothic imagery, which focuses upon the unusual, the unnatural, and the un-Christian: a rooster crowing at midnight instead of at dawn, sleeping owls awakened, the tolling of a tower clock that rouses an old mastiff bitch, who may see his lady's shroud. There is a full moon, and when Christabel first encounters Geraldine in the forest, the stranger has a faint voice, is weary, and thinks she is under a trance. Further on, when they return to the castle and cross its moat, Geraldine faints, a sign that she either is possessed or is an evil creature of some sort, for such a person, according to lore, cannot freely enter a Christian household. To emphasize Geraldine's alien, un-Christian nature, the narrator describes how dying candles in the castle hall flare anew as she passes, a supposed indication of the presence of evil. In the bedchamber, a lamp chain in an angel's form sways as the women enter and casts its shadows on the walls, causing Geraldine to swoon. Meanwhile, the guest has demonized her hostess, it seems, because the narrator compares Christabel's eyes to those of a serpent, and on two occasions Christabel gives a snakelike hiss in her father's presence.

At the point at which the unfinished fragment breaks off, Geraldine is in control, largely as a result of Christabel's quixotic midnight adventure, about which there are unanswered questions. Christabel was concerned about her betrothed knight, who presumably was fighting for the king, and she wanted to pray for his safe return. Could she not have done so in her bedchamber? Why venture out alone into the forest? The castle as Coleridge presents seems a more than adequate Christian venue. Christabel's solitary quest for solace in prayer leads to unintended consequences, but Sir Leoline also is to blame for Geraldine's success, because he quickly becomes infatuated with her, is too credulous, and acts impetuously.

Throughout the poem, Coleridge tantalizes readers with hints of supernatural aspects of Geraldine's body and repeated descriptions of her rejuvenation through physical contact with Christabel and Sir Leoline. Geraldine is a vampire, or, more precisely, a lamia, a female of the species that

often is portrayed as a reluctant practitioner of her dark deeds. Vampires are malevolent creatures that need physical contact with humans to suck their blood to sustain themselves, and in the process their victims either become vampires or assume some of their traits. Absent the entire narrative, readers can only speculate about the true nature of Geraldine. She may be at the mercy of a malevolent power, herself a victim forced to prey on others. She may have committed a sin of some sort, for which her vampirism is punishment. More broadly, Coleridge may be using his narrative as a means of dealing with the problem of evil and its effect on good, and he may be showing that the two are inextricably intertwined (like the snake around the dove's neck in Bracy's dream). The heroine's name, starting with "Christ," could be emblematic and intended to heighten the adversarial tension of the narrative. On the other hand, Geraldine may simply be the "fatal woman" of Gothic literature (also the subject of "La Belle Dame Sans Merci," 1820, by John Keats), doomed to prey upon the innocent and unsuspecting. The poem has also given rise to psychosexual interpretations ever since it was published in 1816, some by critics who focus upon the ambivalence of the relationships among the principals and others who see it as a portrayal of lesbian love, albeit cloaked in medieval Gothic trappings. Without clear evidence of Coleridge's intentions for the unwritten parts (several scenarios have been proposed), uncertainty remains as to the fate of the residents of Langdale Hall and their mysterious visitor.

Gerald H. Strauss

Further Reading

Bate, Walter Jackson. *Samuel Taylor Coleridge*. New York: Macmillan, 1968. A comprehensive one-volume biography that has not lost its importance with the passage of time.

Holmes, Richard. *Coleridge: Early Visions*. New York: Viking Penguin, 1990. Focusing upon Coleridge's most productive years as a poet, this biography places "Christabel" in the context of the man's life.

House, Humphry. *Coleridge: The Clark Lectures, 1951-52*. London: Hart-Davis, 1953. A collection of six lectures, this small book provides extended analyses of the poetry, including a landmark discussion of "Christabel."

Magnuson, Paul. *Coleridge's Nightmare Poetry*. Charlottesville: University Press of Virginia, 1974. Looks closely at Coleridge's comments and textual revisions as a guide to interpreting his works.

Nethercot, Arthur H. *The Road to Tryermaine: A Study of*

the History, Background, and Purposes of Coleridge's
"Christabel." Chicago: University of Chicago Press, 1939.
A comprehensive study of the origins of the poem that is
patterned after *The Road to Xanadu*, the classic John
Livingston Lowes book on "Kubla Khan."
Paglia, Camille. "Christabel." In *Samuel Taylor Coleridge:
Modern Critical Views*, edited by Harold Bloom. New
York: Chelsea House, 1986. A psychoanalytic and femi-

nist analysis of the poem that offers fresh insight into the
work.
Taylor, Anya. *Erotic Coleridge: Women, Love, and the Law
Against Divorce*. New York: Palgrave Macmillan, 2005.
Reads Coleridge's representation of women in terms of
contemporary marriage and divorce law. Includes a chapter on "Christobel" that emphasizes its representation of
youthful vulnerability.

A Christmas Carol

Author: Charles Dickens (1812-1870)
First published: 1843
Type of work: Short fiction
Type of plot: Moral
Time of plot: Nineteenth century
Locale: London

Principal characters:
EBENEZER SCROOGE, a miser
JACOB MARLEY'S GHOST
BOB CRATCHIT, Scrooge's clerk
TINY TIM, Cratchit's son
SCROOGE'S NEPHEW

The Story:

Ebenezer Scrooge is a miser. Owner of a successful
countinghouse, he will have in his bleak office only the
smallest fire in the most bitter weather. For his clerk, Bob
Cratchit, he allows an even smaller fire. The weather seldom matters to Scrooge, who is always cold within, never
warm—even on Christmas Eve. As the time approaches for
closing the office on Christmas Eve, Scrooge's nephew stops
in to wish him a merry Christmas. Scrooge only sneers, for he
abhors sentiment and thinks only of one thing—money. To
him, Christmas is a time when people spend more money
than they should and find themselves a year older and no
richer.

Grudgingly, Scrooge allows Cratchit to have Christmas
Day off; that is the one concession to the holiday that he
makes, but he warns Cratchit to be at work earlier the day after Christmas. Scrooge leaves his office and goes home to his
rooms in a building in which he is the only tenant. They were
the rooms of Scrooge's partner, Jacob Marley, dead for seven
years. As he approaches his door, he sees Marley's face in
the knocker. It is a horrible sight. Marley is looking at
Scrooge with his eyes motionless, his ghostly spectacles on
his ghostly forehead. As Scrooge watches, the knocker resumes its usual form. Shaken by this vision, Scrooge enters
the hall and lights a candle; then he looks behind the door,
half expecting to see Marley's pigtail sticking out into the
hall. Satisfied, he double-locks the door. He prepares for bed

and sits for a time before the dying fire. Suddenly an unused
bell hanging in the room begins to ring, as does every bell in
the house.

Then from below comes the sound of heavy chains clanking. The cellar door flies open, and someone mounts the
stairs. Marley's ghost walks through Scrooge's door—
Marley, dressed as always, but with a heavy chain of cash
boxes, keys, padlocks, ledgers, deeds, and heavy purses
around his middle.

Marley's ghost sits down to talk to the frightened and bewildered Scrooge. Forcing Scrooge to admit that he believes
what he sees is real, Marley explains that in life he never did
any good for humankind and so in death he is condemned to
constant traveling with no rest and no relief from the torture
of remorse. The ghost says that Scrooge still has a chance to
save himself from Marley's fate. Scrooge will be visited by
three spirits who will show him the way to change. The first
spirit will appear the next day at the stroke of one. The next
will arrive on the second night and the last on the third. Drag-
ging his chain, the ghost disappears.

After Marley's ghost vanishes, Scrooge goes to bed, and
in spite of his nervousness, he falls asleep instantly. When he
awakens, it is still dark. The clock strikes twelve. He waits for
the stroke of one. As the sound of the bell dies away, his
bed curtains are pulled apart, and there stands a figure
with a childlike face, but with long, white hair and a strong,

well-formed body. The ghost introduces itself as the Ghost of Christmas Past, Scrooge's past. When the ghost invites Scrooge to go on a journey with him, Scrooge is unable to refuse.

They travel like the wind and stop first at Scrooge's birthplace. There Scrooge sees himself as a boy, neglected by his friends and left alone to find adventure in books. Next, he sees himself at school, where his sister comes to take him home for Christmas. Scrooge recalls his love for his sister, who died young. The ghost reminds him that she bore a son whom Scrooge neglects. Their next stop is the scene of Scrooge's apprenticeship, where everyone makes merry on Christmas Eve. Traveling on, they see a young girl weeping as she tells young Scrooge that she realizes he loves money more than he loves her. The ghost shows him the same girl, grown older but happy with her husband and children. Then the ghost returns Scrooge to his room, where he promptly falls asleep again.

When the Ghost of Christmas Present appears, he leads Scrooge through the city streets on Christmas morning. Their first stop is at the Cratchit home, where Bob appears with frail, crippled Tiny Tim on his shoulder. In the Cratchit home, a skimpy meal is a banquet. After dinner, Bob proposes a toast to Mr. Scrooge, even though it puts a temporary damper on the holiday gaiety. Then the ghost and Scrooge cross swiftly through the city where everyone pauses to wish one another a merry Christmas. As they look in on the home of Scrooge's nephew, gaiety prevails, and Scrooge is tempted to join in the games. There, too, a toast is proposed to Scrooge's health. As the clock begins to strike midnight, the ghost of Christmas Present fades away.

With the last stroke of twelve, Scrooge sees a black-shrouded phantom approaching him, the Ghost of Christmas Yet to Come. The phantom extends his hand and forces Scrooge to follow him until they come to a group of scavengers selling the belongings of the dead. One woman enters a dead man's room; she takes his bed curtains, bedding, and even the shirt in which he is to be buried. Scrooge sees a dead man with his face covered, but he refuses to lift the covering. Revisiting the Cratchits, he learns that Tiny Tim died.

After seeing his old countinghouse and his own neglected grave, Scrooge realizes that it was he who lay on the bed in the cold, stripped room with no one to mourn his death. Scrooge begs the spirit that it should not be so, vowing that he will change, that he will forever honor Christmas in his heart. He makes a desperate grasp for the phantom's hand and realizes that the ghost has shriveled away and dwindled into a bedpost. Scrooge bounds out of bed and thanks Jacob Marley's ghost for his chance to make amends. Dashing into

the street, he realizes that it is Christmas Day. His first act is to order the largest turkey available to be sent anonymously to the Cratchits. The day before, Scrooge ordered a man from his countinghouse for asking a contribution; now Scrooge gives him a large sum of money for the poor. Then he astounds his nephew by arriving at his house for Christmas dinner and by making himself the life of the party.

Scrooge never reverts to his old ways. He raises Bob's salary, improves conditions in his office, contributes generously to all charities, and becomes a second father to Tiny Tim. It is said of him thereafter that he truly knows how to keep Christmas well.

Critical Evaluation:

A Christmas Carol is one of Charles Dickens's best-known and most popular books. A century after it was written, it was still required reading at Christmas for many families. It has been made into films, plays, and parodies. As a result of this wide popularity, the book has come to be considered as a simplistic morality play, and its original intent is often forgotten.

As literature, *A Christmas Carol* is not easy to categorize. At one level, it is a ghost story, complete with clanking chains and foggy nights. It can also be viewed as a moral lesson about the true meaning of Christmas and the proper manner of treating fellow human beings. There is also a sociological element: Dickens had much to say about poverty, and the pitiful condition of the Cratchit family and especially the crippled Tiny Tim are set up as an indictment against an uncaring society. Another interesting aspect of the book is its psychological dimension.

Ebenezer Scrooge begins the story as a man obsessed by money, with apparently no feelings of humanity or interest in human society. He detests Christmas not because of any lack of Christian faith, but because Christmas is an interruption of business. Christmas is a time for emotions, which Scrooge has abjured. Christmas is used as a device for depicting Scrooge's attitudes toward people. The religious meaning of the holiday is relatively unimportant to the story, except in an indirect sense about Christian charity and love of one's neighbor.

It is important in this regard to consider that Dickens uses the terms "ghost" and "spirit" interchangeably in *A Christmas Carol*. The word "spirit" had several meanings in Dickens's time. The spirits that visit Scrooge on Christmas Eve are spirits in the supernatural, religious, and emotional senses.

Marley's ghost is the first visitor of the night and, interestingly, the only one that Scrooge is able to banish by his own willpower. Marley represents Scrooge's present state of mind, acting as a sort of mirror. He is also the only one of the four spirits that represents a human being. At the beginning of the story, Scrooge is still capable of ignoring human beings and can thus handle Marley's ghost with relative ease.

The Ghost of Christmas Past is a different case entirely. This spirit represents Scrooge's youth, and readers see scenes of a lonely boy, spending Christmas alone. Christmas Past represents memory, especially suppressed memory. As the second spirit departs, Scrooge has begun to understand that he has shut out the human race because he himself was excluded as a child.

The Ghost of Christmas Present represents the outside world, the world of joy and love that Scrooge has denied himself. Readers see the lives of other people at Christmas, including the Cratchits, who despite their poverty have hope and joy. Bob Cratchit has been treated as merely a faceless employee by Scrooge. At this stage of Scrooge's night, Bob becomes a symbol of a world that Scrooge can enter if he will allow himself to do so.

The final spirit, the Ghost of Christmas Yet to Come, is clearly Death, silent and hooded. It represents, however, a probable future, not a necessary one. When Scrooge awakens, he is immediately aware of the fact that he is capable of changing that future, of increasing happiness for other people, and thereby increasing his own happiness.

Scrooge ends the story by treating the Cratchits to a prize turkey, by joining his nephew's family in their Christmas celebration, and by joining children in their games out in the street. The last act is particularly important. By accepting the possibility of happiness, Scrooge has managed to redeem his own lost childhood and thereby becomes an adult.

There is some question as to how much Scrooge has really changed. He is still primarily interested in money. It is interesting that he decides to spread Christmas joy by sharing his wealth, as wealth is still central to his character. Even after his apparent changes, Scrooge is still basically a businessman, primarily interested in money; he is simply more willing to share that money.

Tiny Tim, a boy living in poverty and condemned to physical misery as well, is a very important device for showing the reader how callous Scrooge has become. The fact that Scrooge can ignore the existence of this pitiful little boy is central to his divorce from the human race. When he befriends the child, this is a clear sign that he has changed his ways.

A Christmas Carol is, above all, a story of the journey through life of a lonely man. Until the very end of the novel, the other characters exist only in Scrooge's visions and are no more real than the ghosts who show him those images. When the old miser begins to notice people, those people finally become real. The book is often dismissed as overly sentimental. Much better ghost stories have been written, and social commentary about Victorian England is sometimes difficult for contemporary readers to understand. Read as a psychological journey, however, *A Christmas Carol* is unique. It shows readers the innermost thoughts of an unhappy man, through the device of having him see himself in a series of supernatural mirrors.

"Critical Evaluation" by Marc Goldstein

Further Reading

Dickens, Charles. *A Christmas Carol*. Edited by Richard Kelly. Peterborough, Ont.: Broadview Press, 2003. In addition to the text of the novel, this edition includes appendixes with reviews of the book published upon its appearance in 1844; source material about child labor, education, and the workhouse and about Christmas in Victorian England; and a list of film, television, and radio adaptations of *A Christmas Carol*.

Donovan, Frank. *Dickens and Youth*. New York: Dodd, Mead, 1968. A discussion of Dickens's extensive use of children in his novels. *A Christmas Carol* is interpreted in detail from two perspectives: Scrooge's unhappy childhood is considered as the major cause for his present loneliness and misanthropy; and the children of Bob Cratchit, especially Tiny Tim, are examined as examples of innocents who are happy even when their circumstances are difficult.

Hardy, Barbara. *Dickens and Creativity*. London: Continuum, 2008. Focuses on the workings of Dickens's creativity and imagination, which Hardy argues are at the heart of his self-awareness, subject matter, and narrative. *A Christmas Carol* is discussed in chapter 3, "The Awareness of Art in *Sketches by Boz*, *Pickwick Papers*, *Oliver Twist*, *Barnaby Rudge*, *The Old Curiosity Shop*, *A Christmas Carol*, and *The Chimes*," and in chapter 8, "Crises of Imagination in *Oliver Twist*, *A Christmas Carol*, *Dombey and Son*, *Bleak House*, *Hard Times*, and *The Lazy Tour of Two Idle Apprentices*."

Jordan, John O., ed. *The Cambridge Companion to Charles Dickens*. New York: Cambridge University Press, 2001. Collection of essays with information about Dickens's life and times, analyses of his novels, and discussions of Dickens and language, gender, family, domestic ideology, the form of the novel, illustration, theater, and film.

Kaplan, Fred. *Dickens: A Biography*. New York: William

Morrow, 1988. A comprehensive biography of the author, with more than five hundred pages of text and more than one hundred illustrations. The focus is on Dickens's psychological makeup and how it affected his written works.

Paroissien, David, ed. *A Companion to Charles Dickens*. Malden, Mass.: Blackwell, 2008. Collection of essays providing information about Dickens's life and work, including Dickens as a reformer, Christian, and journalist, and Dickens and gender, technology, America, and the uses of history.

Prickett, Stephen. *Victorian Fantasy*. Bloomington: Indiana University Press, 1979. A study of fantasy writings in Victorian England. Chapter 2, "Christmas at Scrooge's," discusses the use of fantasy elements in *A Christmas Carol* and Dickens's other Christmas stories.

Slater, Michael, ed. *Dickens 1970*. Briarcliff Manor, N.Y.: Stein & Day, 1970. An anthology of essays on Dickens's works, on the occasion of the one hundredth anniversary of his death. Of particular interest is Angus Wilson's article "Dickens on Children and Childhood," which focuses on Tiny Tim as a symbol of innocence, hope, and faith.

Standiford, Les. *The Man Who Invented Christmas: How Charles Dickens's "A Christmas Carol" Rescued His Career and Revived Our Holiday Spirits*. New York: Crown, 2008. Recounts the circumstances that led Dickens to write *A Christmas Carol*, the novel's initial reception, and its continued popularity for its depiction of Christmas.

Stone, Harry. *Dickens and the Invisible World: Fairy Tales, Fantasy, and Novel-Making*. Bloomington: Indiana University Press, 1979. A treatment of Dickens's use of fantasy elements in his literary works. The fifth chapter focuses on five short works, including *A Christmas Carol*. The emphasis is on the emotions of the characters as reflected in their supernatural experiences.

Chronicles

Author: Jean Froissart (1337?-c. 1404)
First transcribed: Chroniques de France, d'Engleterre, d'Éscosse, de Bretaigne, d'Espaigne, d'Italie, de Flanders, et d'Alemaigne, 1373-1410 (English translation, 1523-1525)
Type of work: History

Jean Froissart, by being so much of his age, became a writer for all time. This unpriestly priest, this citizen celebrator of chivalry took such an intense joy in chronicling his times that he devoted an entire half century to traveling, interviewing, writing, and rewriting. He interviewed more than two hundred princes in various courts from Rome and the Pyrenees to Edinburgh, and with such zest that he was a favorite of the nobles on both sides in the Hundred Years' War. In his own time his works were widely copied and illuminated.

Although he recorded the Hundred Years' War on a colorful and unprecedented scale, he is not a reliable historian. Born in Valenciennes, now a city in France but at that time in the Low Country countship of Hainaut, Froissart was a Fleming who shifted his allegiance from one side of the conflict to the other, depending on the court that offered him patronage at the moment. Relying mostly on hearsay evidence from partisan observers, he never consulted official documents, many of which are still extant. As a result his history abounds in anachronisms, erroneous dates, garbled names, and impossible topography. Froissart was also, understandably, unaware that the fourteenth century marked the waning of the Middle Ages and that he was the last of the medieval innocents. The histories that follow his reflect a realism and disillusionment that are in startling contrast to Froissart's chivalric naïveté.

Froissart's purpose was clear: He wrote "in order that the honorable and noble adventures and feats of arms, done and achieved by the wars of France and England, should notably be registered and put in perpetual memory." His remarkable career was auspiciously launched in 1361, when he went to England as Queen Philippa's secretary and court historian. There he thoroughly ingratiated himself with the aristocracy and began a pro-English account of the wars from the time of Edward III in 1316 to the death of Richard II in 1399.

Curiously enough, he makes no mention of English poet Geoffrey Chaucer, a rival at court. Chaucer reciprocated the slight. After the queen's death in 1369, Froissart returned to Valenciennes, went into business, and completed book 1 of the *Chronicles* under the patronage of Robert of Namur, Philippa's nephew. A very large proportion of that version was directly plagiarized from his pro-English predecessor, Jehan (or Jean) le Bel, but Froissart's fame was such that Guy II de Chatillon, comte de Blois gave him first a prosperous living at Lestinnes and later a sinecure as a private chaplain. Under Guy's patronage Froissart traveled through France, making an especially fruitful trip in 1388 to Gaston de Foix in Orthez. During this period, he rewrote book 1 and completed books 2 and 3, adopting a pro-French perspective on the wars. "Let it not be said," he lies, "that I have corrupted this noble history through the favor accorded me by Count Guy de Blois, for whom I wrote it. No, indeed! For I will say nothing but the truth and keep a straight course without favoring one side or the other."

In 1397, Count Guy, a drunkard who had sold his patrimony, died. Froissart gained a new patron in the duke of Bavaria, who sent him again to England. Although Richard II, the new king, did not receive him cordially, it is interesting to note that the chronicles again took on a somewhat pro-English turn, whether subconsciously or by design, when Froissart retired to his hometown eighteen months later.

Froissart more than returned the favors of his patrons by immortalizing them as heroes and heroines of chivalry, and he took immense delight in doing so:

I have taken more pleasure in it than in anything else. The more I work on these things, the more they please me, for just as the gentle knights and squires love the calling of arms and perfect themselves by constant exercise, so I, by laboring in this matter, acquire skill and take pleasure in it.

What Froissart loved most was the resplendent panoply and pageantry of jousts and battle, and the *Chronicles* are really a pastiche of anecdotes, great and small. His knights are invariably "noble, courteous, bold, and enterprising" and his ladies are eternally noble, beautiful, and gentle. It is no wonder that Sir Walter Scott said of Froissart, "This is my master!"

The *Chronicles* abound in dramatic vignettes: the Black Prince graciously submissive to his own prisoner, King John; the duke of Brabant's envoy sick almost to death of the treachery he has unwittingly performed; King Henry IV meditatively feeding his falcons as he deliberates on the murder of deposed Richard; Gaston de Foix discovering a purse

of poison on his treacherous son's person and unwillingly killing him; the blind king of Bohemia found dead in battle surrounded by the bodies of loyal guardsmen. In these narratives Froissart's style occasionally soars above the conventional rhetoric of the medieval romance. Froissart can range from the crude language of peasants and soldiers to the lofty rhetoric of the bishop of St. Andrews. A knight storming battlements in Spain leans over the wall to see the defenders, "ugly as monkeys or bears devouring pears." The earl of Derby greets Pembroke after the Battle of Auberoche: "Welcome, cousin Pembroke, you have come just in time to sprinkle holy water on the dead!" "Where is that son of a Jew's whore?" demands de Trastamara before the murder of Don Carlos.

Perhaps one of the finest little dramas concerns Edward III's love game of chess with the countess whom he has rescued from a Scottish siege.

When the chessmen arrived, the King, who wished to leave some possession of his with the Countess, challenged her, saying: "My lady, what stakes will you play?" And the Countess replied: "And you, Sire?" Then the King placed on the table a very fine ring, set with a large ruby, which he was wearing on his finger. The Countess said: "Sire, Sire, I have no ring as valuable as that." "Lady," said the King, "put down such as you have, it is indeed good enough."

The countess, to please the king, takes from her finger a gold ring, which is not of great worth. Then they play at chess together, the countess playing as well as she can, in order that the king should not consider her too simple and ignorant, and the king makes wrong moves and does not play as well as he might. There is hardly a pause between the moves, but he looks so hard at the countess that she loses countenance and fumbles her game. When the king sees that she has lost a knight, a rook, or whatever it might be, he too loses to keep the countess in play.

Froissart is by no means always so delicately perceptive. He can describe in gruesome detail the dismemberment of Hugh Despencer, the heart thrown into the fire, the head sent to London, and the pieces of his quartered body carried off to be displayed in other cities—and then calmly proceed with the narrative of the queen's joyous arrival for feasting in London. One feels a bizarre sense of the grotesque when Froissart asserts matter-of-factly that Galeas Visconti murdered his uncle "by bleeding him in the neck, as they are wont to do in Lombardy when they wish to hasten a person's end." He laments when captives are killed because they would have brought a good ransom. There are dozens of accounts of towns sacked and women and children murdered, all related without the least trace of compassion. Perhaps this detachment is explained by the fact that in Froissart's time, violence, death, and murder were common, or by Froissart's evident commitment to the Boethian philosophy of the wheel of fortune, dramatically presented in one of the illuminated miniatures of an early manuscript.

Michel Eyquem de Montaigne, who was a touchstone of the Renaissance just as Froissart was of the Middle Ages, said of the *Chronicles* that they were the "crude and unshapen substance of history." If he meant that they lacked any profound philosophical perspective, he was right. The simplicity of Froissart's mind can be seen in his obtuse declaration that "Mankind is divided into three classes: the valiant who face the perils of war . . . , the people who talk of their successes and fortunes, and the clerks who write and record their great deeds." Froissart could report, without realizing the significance of his account, that French king John's Round Table of three hundred knights, who were to meet annually to tell their tales and have their heroism recorded, lasted only one year because all the knights perished.

Nevertheless, the *Chronicles* are rich in sheer entertainment value. Froissart's account of the blazing day when Charles VI went mad is illustrative. As the troupe rode along, a page accidentally struck another's helmet with his spear.

The King, who rode but afore them, with the noise suddenly started, and his heart trembled, and into his imagination ran the impression of the words of the man that stopped his horse in the forest of Mans, and it ran into his thought that his enemies ran after him to slay and destroy him, and with that abusion he fell out of his wit by feebleness of his head, and dashed his spurs to his horse and drew out the sword and turned to his pages, having no knowledge of any man, weening himself to be in a battle enclosed with his enemies, and lifted up his sword to strike, he cared not where, and cried and said: "On, on upon these traitors!"

Of greater horror are the descriptions of Sir Peter of Be'arn haunted by the ghost of a bear, or of the king of France at a marriage feast almost burned to death when five of his squires dressed in pitch-covered linen for an entertainment brush against a torchlight and are consumed in the flames.

Further Reading

Ainsworth, Peter F. *Jean Froissart and the Fabric of History: Truth, Myth, and Fiction in the "Chroniques."* New York: Oxford University Press, 1990. Examines Froissart's *Chronicles* as a literary work. Explores how Froissart crafted his historical subject matter in literary terms to attempt to reconcile the realities of war with the ideals of chivalry.

Coulton, G. G. *The Chronicler of European Chivalry.* London: The Studio, 1930. Relates Froissart's biography, using the *Chronicles* to provide information about his life. The illustrations of illuminations from two manuscripts of Froissart's *Chronicles* add vivacity to the events that Froissart recounts.

Froissart, Jean. *Chronicles.* Rev. ed. Selected, translated, and edited by Geoffrey Brereton. New York: Penguin Books, 1978. The most accessible English translation of Froissart's *Chronicles.* Contains a concise, informative introduction about Froissart, the composition of the *Chronicles,* and the manuscript versions of this work. Includes a helpful glossary, map, and index of persons.

Greene, Virginie, ed. *The Medieval Author in Medieval French Literature.* New York: Palgrave Macmillan, 2006. This collection of essays examining authorship of French medieval literature contains two essays focusing on Froissart: "The Experiencing Self and the Narrating Self in Medieval French Chronicles," by Sophie Marnette, and "Neutrality Affects: Froissart and the Practice of Historiographic Authorship," by Zrinka Stahuljak.

Maddox, Donald, and Sara Sturm-Maddox, eds. *Froissart Across the Genres.* Gainesville: University Press of Florida, 1998. Collection of essays analyzing Froissart's works, including several analyses of the *Chronicles.* Some of the other essays discuss Froissart and his contemporaries, Froissart and Geoffrey Chaucer, and the illustrations in book 1 of the *Chronicles.*

Palmer, J. J. N., ed. *Froissart: Historian.* Woodbridge, England: Boydell Press, 1981. A collection of essays by ten historians. Addresses aspects of Froissart's writings in the *Chronicles.* Evaluates his contribution as a source for modern historical study of the Hundred Years' War.

Shears, F. S. *Froissart, Chronicler and Poet.* 1930. Reprint. Folcroft, Pa.: Folcroft Library Editions, 1972. A literary biography of Froissart. Focuses on the *Chronicles* in the context of Froissart's life and experiences of English and French culture in the late fourteenth century.

The Chronicles of Narnia

Author: C. S. Lewis (1898-1963)

First published: 1950-1956; includes *The Lion, the Witch, and the Wardrobe*, 1950; *Prince Caspian*, 1951; *The Voyage of the Dawn Treader*, 1952; *The Silver Chair*, 1953; *The Horse and His Boy*, 1954; *The Magician's Nephew*, 1955; *The Last Battle*, 1956

Type of work: Novel

Type of plot: Fantasy

Time of plot: 1900-1950

Locale: England, Narnia, and other magical worlds

Principal characters:

ASLAN, a lion, the creator and deity of Narnia

DIGORY KIRKE, a child who goes to Narnia using a magic ring and grows up to be a professor

POLLY PLUMMER, Digory's friend

LUCY PEVENSIE,

PETER PEVENSIE,

SUSAN PEVENSIE, and

EDMUND PEVENSIE, four British siblings who come and go between Narnia and England, eventually becoming kings and queens of Narnia

JADIS, the White Witch

SHASTA (COR), a long lost prince of Archenland

BREE, Shasta's talking horse

PRINCE CASPIAN, a just ruler in Narnia who has to fight for his throne

PRINCE RILIAN, Caspian's son

EUSTACE SCRUBB, Pevensie cousin who transforms from annoying to heroic

JILL POLE, Eustace's school friend

REEPICHEEP, a heroic talking mouse

The Story:

The Magician's Nephew begins with Digory Kirke and Polly Plummer meeting in the yard of some London row houses. Digory is miserable because his mother is seriously ill. The two friends explore the attics of the connected houses, accidentally stumbling into Digory's horrible uncle Andrew's study. Uncle Andrew fancies himself a magician, and he gives Polly a magic yellow ring that transports her to a wood containing many tranquil pools. Digory is blackmailed into using a yellow ring to find his friend and give her a green ring that will bring her back.

While in the "wood between the worlds," the children discover that they can use the green rings to visit other worlds through different pools. They jump into a pool leading to a strangely quiet land called Charn. In the ruins of this apparently ancient place, they find motionless people dressed as royalty. Nearby is a bell with a sign that simultaneously warns and dares the children to ring it. Digory cannot resist, and when the bell sounds, one of the figures awakens.

The awakened figure is Jadis, a strikingly beautiful but terribly evil queen. The children escape from Jadis using the green rings, but they accidentally bring her with them. After a chaotic ruckus in London, they finally get Jadis back to the magical wood, but again they have brought uninvited guests:

Uncle Andrew, a cab driver, and his horse. They enter a pool hoping to get rid of Jadis in Charn but instead witness the beginning of a new world: Narnia. Aslan is singing the world into existence. Jadis throws a metal bar from a London lamppost at Aslan, but he doesn't even seem to notice that it hits him squarely in the head. The bar grows into a full sized lamppost.

Aslan gives the power of speech to some of the animals and tells Digory to obtain an apple from a magical tree. To get to the apple, Digory is to ride the cab driver's horse, which Aslan transforms into a flying and talking horse named Fledge. When Digory and Polly reach the apple tree, they find that Jadis has beaten them there. She has eaten an apple and now has eternal youth. She tries to convince Digory to steal an apple to give his dying mother, but Digory resists and returns to Aslan with the apple. Aslan tells Digory to plant the apple, which grows into a tree that will protect Narnia from evil for a time. He then gives Digory another apple, telling him he can use it to cure his mother. Aslan transports the cabby's wife to Narnia then crowns the couple the first king and queen of Narnia.

Aslan returns Digory, Polly, and the miserable Uncle Andrew to their own world, making Uncle Andrew forget everything that happened in Narnia. Digory gives his mother the apple, and she is healed. He and Polly bury the apple core and the magic rings. An apple tree grows from the core, and years later, Digory—grown into old Professor Kirke—uses the wood from the tree to make a wardrobe.

When *The Lion, The Witch, and The Wardrobe* begins, Peter, Susan, Edmund, and Lucy Pevensie have been sent to the country home of the eccentric Professor Kirke during World War II. Expecting their stay to be rather boring, they break up the monotony by playing games such as hide and seek. During one of the games, Lucy discovers Narnia through a wardrobe. While there, she meets a fawn named Mr. Tumnus near a lamppost. At first, Mr. Tumnus tries to hypnotize her and give her to the White Witch. He loses his nerve because he is surprised at how pleasant Lucy is, and he goes on to tell her all about the White Witch's reign, a time of perpetual winter without Christmas in the land. When Lucy returns, she excitedly tells her siblings about her discovery, but they don't believe her. She also realizes that while she spent hours in Narnia, no time at all has passed in her own world.

Later, Edmund makes his way into Narnia, where he meets the White Witch. She plies him with Turkish delight to secure a promise to turn his brothers and sisters over to her. The White Witch is worried about the presence of four humans in Narnia because of a prophecy that four humans will eventually become rulers in Narnia, ending her evil reign. Edmund falls under the witch's power.

Later, all four children enter Narnia and discover that the White Witch's police force of wolves has captured Mr. Tumnus. Soon, the children meet up with the Beavers, talking animals that tell the children about Aslan, a lion that is the rightful and just ruler of Narnia. During the visit at the Beaver's dam, Edmund sneaks out to notify the witch that his siblings are in Narnia. This time, he is offered no Turkish delight. Instead, he is mistreated and frightened by the lifelike statues displayed throughout the witch's courtyards. Edmund later learns that the White Witch turns innocent creatures into stone.

The other three Pevensie children rush to meet Aslan at the Stone Table. The White Witch's hold on Narnia is beginning to loosen, as is evidenced by the onset of spring. Also, Father Christmas visits Narnia for the first time in years, bringing special gifts for the children. Peter receives a sword and shield; Susan is given a bow, arrows, and a magic horn; Lucy gets a dagger and a vial of healing potion.

The children and Beavers reach Aslan's encampment after several close calls with the wolf police. There, they meet Aslan for the first time and are awestruck by his strength and majesty. The White Witch arrives with Edmund and her own army of hideous creatures. She bargains with Aslan privately. Aslan trades his own life for Edmund's. Edmund is then reconciled with his siblings.

Susan and Lucy follow Aslan that night, and witness the White Witch and her cohorts kill Aslan on the Stone Table. Soon after, Aslan comes back to life, more powerful than before. He takes Susan and Lucy on a joyful ride on his back, leaping through Narnia to reach the icy castle of the White Witch. There, he breathes new life into the statues. The group gathers strength as they head back to the battle site. There, a bloody conflict results in victory for Aslan's army. Lucy uses her healing potion to cure many of the injured, including Edmund.

The children are crowned kings and queens of Narnia, and they reign for many years in peace. *The Lion, the Witch, and the Wardrobe* ends with the Pevensies returning to the human world through the wardrobe portal. They are children again, and no time has passed in their world.

The Horse and His Boy is the story of Shasta and his talking horse, Bree. The story is set in Calormen. Shasta is miserable in his life as the adopted son of a cruel fisherman. When he overhears the fisherman offering to sell him as a slave, he and the horse decide to flee to Narnia. During the adventure across Calormen, Shasta and Bree meet Aravis and her horse Hwin. Aravis is of noble Calormene blood, and she is trying to escape an arranged marriage. At one point, Shasta is mistaken for Prince Corin of Archenland and the group discovers that an attack on Narnia is planned.

The four companions continue their trek across the desert, now pursued by the Calormene army and a huge lion. They find out later that the lion was Aslan, who chased them only to give them the strength to escape to Archenland, an ally of Narnia. While in Archenland, Shasta is recognized as Cor, the lost prince and heir to the throne of that country. This true identity explains why he was mistaken for Prince Corin, who is actually his younger twin. Shasta is restored to his rightful place and later marries Aravis.

In *Prince Caspian*, Peter, Susan, Lucy, and Edmund are suddenly transported to Narnia while waiting for their train to boarding school, approximately a year after their last trip. When the four children arrive this time, they find themselves near the ruins of a castle. They piece together that they are actually at Cair Paravel, where they once ruled as kings and queens. Since time does not work the same in Narnia as it does in their own world, they reason that at least a thousand years must have passed since their reign. They are amazed to find the gifts that they once received from Father Christmas, dusty but intact, in the castle keep. Only Susan's horn is missing.

Soon, the Pevensies see men throw something alive from a boat into the water that now surrounds Cair Paravel. The children rescue a dwarf named Trumpkin. Trumpkin updates the children on the happenings in Narnia over the centuries since they were last there, and they learn that talking animals and the Narnia of old have been relegated to the stuff of fairy tales. The wicked King Miraz, a Telmarine, has stolen the throne from the rightful heir, Prince Caspian, by murdering Caspian's father. Prince Caspian has fled under the advice of his kindly old teacher, Cornelius. Cornelius gave Caspian Queen Susan's horn, which has the power to summon help when it is sounded. It is revealed later that the blowing of Susan's horn was what called the four children to Narnia from the railway station.

Caspian has joined forces with the old Narnians, and they have set up a fortress at Aslan's How. Their army is not faring well when they decide to blow Susan's horn and send Trumpkin to Cair Paravel to meet help. Trumpkin and the four children meet with various misadventures on the way to Aslan's How, but first Lucy and later the others see Aslan leading their way. When they finally reach Caspian and the other Narnians, they discover a dwarf, a hag, and a werewolf who want to call upon the White Witch's power for aid. The three treacherous creatures are killed.

Peter and Miraz duel for victory, and Miraz loses. Two advisers to Miraz claim that the Narnians have stabbed their king while he was down, then they themselves stab him when no one is looking. A great battle ensues, and the Telmarines are defeated when the trees of the forest come to life and join forces with the other Narnians. Aslan creates a portal between the worlds. He returns the children to the railway station and offers the Telmarines the opportunity to return to the world from which their ancestors came.

In *The Voyage of the Dawn Treader*, Lucy and Edmund have been sent to stay with relatives in Cambridge. Their annoying cousin Eustace makes their stay miserable. They enjoy looking at a painting in one of the bedrooms because it reminds them of Narnia. Eustace says he hates the painting, but as they are looking at the picture of a ship, the waves begin to roll and all three children are drawn into the painting. Once in Narnia, they meet Caspian again, who is now sailing on a pretty ship called the *Dawn Treader* to find the seven lost lords who were banished years ago when Miraz murdered Caspian's father. Lucy and Edmund are thrilled to be joining the quest, but Eustace whines constantly. He especially hates the talking mouse, Reepicheep.

The first stop on the journey is the Lone Islands, where Caspian and the children are captured and sold as slaves. Caspian is sold to a kind gentleman who turns out to be the lost Lord Bern. Together, they rescue the others and overthrow the governor.

The next couple of weeks bring bad weather for the *Dawn Treader*. Eustace keeps a journal, where his private thoughts reveal that he is selfish and immature. After days of terrible storms, the ship docks at an unknown island, where Caspian hopes to rest and restock their stores. While the others are working to set the ship aright, Eustace gets lost in the mountainous lands. He witnesses the death of a very old dragon, then wanders into the dragon's cave for shelter. There, he finds treasure. He gathers as much as he can and puts a bracelet on his arm. He then falls asleep. When he awakens, he has transformed into a dragon.

Soon, Eustace returns to Caspian's worried crew as a dragon, and communicates to them that he has been enchanted. He is much nicer now, and has come to realize his previous character flaws. He helps by exploring the island and gathering provisions. Caspian notices that the diamond bracelet stuck on Eustace's arm bears the mark of the missing Lord Octesian.

After several days on Dragon Island, Aslan comes to Eustace. He peels off Eustace's dragon skin, turning him into a reformed boy. Eustace rejoins Caspian and the others, and they leave after surmising that the second lost lord, Octesian, might have been the old dragon that Eustace saw die.

After fighting off a sea serpent, the group lands on another island, where the water turns things into gold. They find the third lord, a solid gold corpse at the bottom of a clear pool. Next, they stop at an island that seems to be uninhabited. Lucy overhears invisible creatures planning to cut them off from the *Dawn Treader*. She rushes ahead to warn the others, and they discuss their options. As it turns out, the invisible creatures only want Lucy to go into a feared magician's house and break the invisibility spell that has been placed upon them. Lucy agrees.

Aslan appears and introduces Lucy to Coriakin, the magician that was so frightening to the invisible creatures. Lucy's spell has made the creatures, monopods, visible again. Lucy sees them sleeping with their single large feet in the air and compares them to mushrooms in appearance. They are simple creatures that Coriakin rules as gently as he can. Reepicheep shows the monopods how to use their single feet as rafts, and the group leaves, happy and rejuvenated.

The *Dawn Treader* sails into a cloud of dark mist and picks a stranger out of the sea. He tells them that the darkness is a place where dreams, including bad ones, come true. The frightened crewmembers nearly lose their minds in the darkness before an albatross leads them into the light. The stranger aboard the ship turns out to be the lost Lord Rhoop.

When the ship stops again, the sailors find a table set with a grand feast. At the table are three sleeping men with long beards. Caspian determines that they are the three remaining lost lords. A beautiful woman tells them to eat from Aslan's table, and after a bit of fearful hesitation, they do. They learn from the girl's father Ramandu, a resting star, that to break the enchantment of the sleeping lords, they must journey to the end of the world and leave one of their company. Reepicheep immediately volunteers. They let Lord Rhoop go to sleep among his old comrades and depart the island.

Next, Lucy watches tiny sea people in water so clear that she can see the shadow of the *Dawn Treader* moving along the bottom of the sea. Reepicheep jumps into the water and discovers that it is no longer salty, but sweet. Everyone drinks the magical water and understands it is a sign that the world's edge is near.

Caspian announces that he intends to go to the edge of the world with Reepicheep and tells the others to go back to Ramandu's island without him. No one agrees, and, after a vision from Aslan, a disappointed Caspian sends the three children and Reepicheep on in the lifeboat. They sail through white lilies until the boat hits ground, then Reepicheep goes on alone. Aslan magically sends the children back to their own world, where everyone notices that Eustace's character is much improved. The others make it back to Ramandu's island, and Caspian marries the old star's daughter.

The Silver Chair begins with Eustace Scrubb comforting his friend Jill Pole, who is crying because schoolmates have bullied her. Eustace tries to comfort her with stories about Narnia. The two call upon Aslan for help to escape jeering school children, then scramble through a door in the schoolyard wall into an unfamiliar place. Eustace falls off a high cliff, and Aslan blows him to Narnia. Then, Aslan tells Jill that they have been called to Narnia to rescue the missing Prince Rilian. He gives her four instructions that will guide her through the quest. He then blows her to Cair Paravel, where she joins Eustace in watching an ancient King Caspian departing to try one last time to find his missing son. Jill tells Eustace the first instruction from Aslan, which is to speak to the first person he knows in Narnia, but Eustace does not recognize Caspian until it is too late.

Talking owls tell Eustace and Jill about Rilian's disappearance. The prince had been out riding with his mother when a murderous green serpent killed her. Rilian vowed revenge and sought the snake. Instead, he met a mysterious woman who entranced and kidnapped him.

The froglike Puddleglum joins the children as a guide. Although a complete pessimist, Puddleglum is loyal and knowledgeable. The three follow Aslan's second instruction, which is to find the city of the ancient giants. On the way, they meet a beautiful lady and a silent knight. The lady tells them to visit Harfang, where they will be treated to comfort and good food. The children do not heed Puddleglum's warning that Harfang could be a trap.

Upon reaching Harfang, they are indeed treated with hospitality, but Aslan comes to Jill in a dream and warns her that they need to move on quickly. Jill sees writing in stone that says "under me." Aslan's third instruction had been to do what the writing on the stone advised. The group discovers that their giant hosts are preparing to eat them at a feast.

They escape and hide in a crevasse, which leads them to a whole world beneath the earth, filled with gnome-like creatures. They meet a handsome knight, the same one they had seen before. This time, he is not silent, but arrogant and quite strange. He tells them that he is under a spell, and the lady they had seen with him earlier is his savior from some evil enchantment. Each night, the knight states, he enters into a kind of mania, and only by being bound to a silver chair can he avoid destroying everything within his reach. He allows them to watch his attack, and during his delirium he calls upon them to release him in the name of Aslan. Aslan's final instruction was to do the first thing that someone asks them to do in his name. They release the knight, finding that he is the lost prince. Rilian destroys the silver chair and together, the children, Rilian, and Puddleglum slay the evil Queen of the Underworld, who is also the green serpent that murdered Rilian's mother.

After freeing all the creatures of the underworld, Rilian, Puddleglum, Eustace, and Jill return to the surface just in time for Rilian to say goodbye to his father, who dies happy. They go by magic to England, where Aslan and Rilian help Eustace and Jill frighten the bullies that had been pursuing them before the adventure began.

The Last Battle opens with an ape and a donkey finding a lion skin in the water. The ape, Shift, is a devious creature and convinces the donkey, Puzzle, to wear the lion skin and pose as Aslan. Puzzle feels uncomfortable with this plan, but Shift convinces him that it is Aslan's will.

Meanwhile, King Tirian of Narnia and a unicorn named Jewel have heard rumors that Aslan has appeared in Narnia again. The two feel joy at Aslan's supposed reappearance, but their joy turns to fear when a centaur tells them that the stars foretell evil. Not long after this announcement, they learn that Calormenes are felling talking trees and selling the wood for lumber. Tirian is enraged, but a river-rat tells him that Aslan himself has given orders for the trees to be cut down. Shift has joined forces with the Calormenes, and they have convinced many Narnians that Aslan has returned.

They are exploiting the creatures' faith in Aslan, forcing them into slave labor in his name.

Tirian and Jewel are taken prisoner after they defend a talking horse against a Calormene beating. When they arrive at the camp where the ape and his Calormene cohorts are set up, they refute the idea that Aslan and the Calormene god Tash are one and the same, an idea that has been disseminated by the deceivers. Tirian is tied to a tree, away from Jewel. From his place at the tree, he watches Shift present Puzzle as Aslan, and, although Tirian has never seen a real lion, he struggles with the idea that this awkward creature could be Aslan.

In utter desolation, Tirian calls out to the Narnian rulers of the past. In a dream, he sees seven of those rulers. When he awakens, Eustace and Jill arrive from their world, untie him and learn the status of Narnia. The three rescue Jewel, and Jill steals Puzzle. Although Tirian first wants to kill Puzzle for impersonating Aslan, Jill explains that Puzzle was an ignorant pawn in the situation. They meet a band of dwarfs being led by Calormenes. Tirian reveals Puzzle and the deception, but the dwarfs no longer want to follow Aslan or any god. Their new slogan is, "the dwarfs are for the dwarfs."

A dwarf named Poggin remains loyal to Tirian. He says that he has seen a cat named Ginger and the leader of the Calormenes privately discussing plans to continue to use Shift only as long as it takes to overthrow Narnia. While Poggin is talking, Tash, a great, dark creature that emanates evil, flies overhead. Poggin notes that the Calormenes should not have called upon evil if they did not want it to appear.

Based on the dwarfs' unfavorable reaction to the revelation about Puzzle, Tirian's group decides to meet the centaur, Roonwit, to join the army that they hope is coming from Cair Paravel. An eagle swoops in to tell them that Roonwit is dead, the castle at Cair Paravel has been taken, and the Narnian army is not coming.

Tirian thinks the children should return to the safety of their own world, but the children insist they would rather stay in Narnia. They point out that they could not get back to their own world even if they wanted to, since Aslan decides when they return. Jill and Eustace were standing on a railway platform right before they were transported to Narnia. They discuss the jerking motion they felt at the railway station immediately before their disappearance, and Eustace states that he thought it was the beginning of a railway accident.

The group heads back to Stable Hill, where they plan to reveal that Shift, Ginger, and the Calormenes have only been showing people a silly donkey dressed up as Aslan. When they arrive, they overhear Shift telling the crowd that a donkey has been impersonating Aslan and that the combination god called Tashlan is very angry. This enemy tactic circum-

vents any revelation they might have been able to make by showing off Puzzle.

The deceivers at Stable Hill offer anyone the chance to go into the building to see Aslan, and Ginger is the first to volunteer. Everyone is surprised when the cat comes screeching out of the stable, either a very good actor or genuinely scared witless. Right before their eyes, the cat transforms into an ordinary cat. This turn of events frightens the entire crowd, and the only other volunteer is a Calormene soldier named Emeth.

Tirian's group instigates a skirmish. Shift is thrown into the stable, and a blinding flash indicates a horrid fate for the ape. In the battle that follows, everyone eventually passes through the stable door. The evil god Tash, a vulture-like creature, eats the leader of the Calormenes, but each person meets a different fate. The true Narnians are met by the kings and queens of old and are welcomed into Aslan's country. The dwarfs sit in darkness, recognizing neither evil nor righteousness. Emeth is welcomed to Aslan's country because he was a good person, even though he did not know Aslan.

This is the end of Narnia. Aslan is there, and he calls the stars to him, and characters from the previous books join together to watch the world of Narnia end in darkness. As it turns out, there really was a railway accident back in Jill and Eustace's world, and—as far as their own world is concerned—all of the humans that have been friends to Narnia have perished in the accident, except Susan. Susan has apparently forgotten Narnia or has deemed her memories of the place childish games. Although Narnia is no more, Aslan's country will go on forever, and all of the good creatures of *The Chronicles of Narnia* will live eternally in great happiness together.

Critical Evaluation:

The Chronicles of Narnia is considered one of the most beloved works of children's literature. C.S. Lewis's novels explore serious themes in an easily read and delightful fairytale format. The seven books narrate the entire course of the history of the fantasy world of Narnia, beginning with its creation by Aslan and concluding when the world of Narnia comes to an end. Throughout that fictional and epic history, symbols and motifs abound.

The theme of good versus evil, with good always triumphing, certainly pervades these novels. Aslan, the great lion and deity, is the unambiguous symbol of righteousness. Jadis, or the White Witch, is equally clearly an evil presence. Lewis creates no questioning in the minds of readers as to which behaviors are good and right and which are unequivocally bad. He does, however, create good characters with flaws, characters who grow throughout the series, most notably Edmund and Eustace. While physical ugliness indicates evil in a character, certain personages, such as Jadis, are externally beautiful but wicked inside.

Critics have often pointed out the Christian allegory present throughout the series. There are many parallels between Aslan and Christ. Aslan is all-powerful, just, and loving. He dies to redeem Edmund's treachery, then comes back to life to save all. He creates and ends Narnia, bringing his followers to dwell with him in his country, which resembles representations of the Christian heaven. The faithful, such as the ever-loyal Lucy, often receive visions and spiritual rewards. Lewis, himself a converted agnostic, pointed out he did not write the books as pure allegory. Indeed, one of the most oft-quoted lines supporting the Christian theme occurs when, in *The Voyage of the Dawn Treader*, Aslan reassures Lucy that he is in her own world too: "But there I have another name. This was the very reason why you were brought to Narnia, that by knowing me here for a little, you may know me better there."

Mixed with the Christian symbolism of the novels are abundant images from other mythologies and cultural traditions. Many characters come directly from Greek and Roman mythology, including centaurs, fawns, nymphs, dryads, and even Bacchus. Dragons, giants, dwarves, werewolves, Father Christmas, and Father Time come from varied mythological sources and historical periods. Some critics have assessed this blending of various cultural folklores as inconsistent and anachronistic. However, Lewis proposes that time is unpredictable and relative by placing the two settings, England and Narnia, on different clocks altogether.

Nearly all of the novels contain a quest or journey toward growth. Digory finds the healing apple for his mother in *The Magician's Nephew*. In *The Horse and His Boy*, Shasta undergoes adventures until he reaches Archenland, where he becomes a king. Prince Caspian reaches the end of the earth and finds the seven lost lords in a sort of spiritual voyage. Eustace and Jill descend to the underworld to free a lost prince in *The Silver Chair*. In each journey, characters undergo a fundamental transformation: They come to a personal revelation and a renewed commitment to the power of good, embodied by Aslan. Further, some critics have commented that the series as a whole demonstrates the journey as literary device.

Faith and loyalty appear as important motifs. Characters that exhibit these traits are generally rewarded, as Lucy is in *Prince Caspian* when she follows Aslan despite the others' disbelief. That incident demonstrates the idea that only those who believe are able to see Aslan. In *The Last Battle*, the once revered Susan is excluded from Aslan's country because she no longer has faith that Narnia exists.

Some critics have pointed out that the books perpetuate stereotypes of females and Middle Eastern people. The strongest and most righteous characters are male, and people such as the Calormenes that have dark skin and wear turbans are depicted as evil. Others have excused Lewis of these stereotypes because they were typical of his time and upbringing. Regardless of the criticism, millions have read these children's classics and appreciated them for their entertainment value and inspirational qualities.

Valerie C. Brown

Further Reading

Bloom, Harold, ed. *C. S. Lewis's "The Chronicles of Narnia."* New York: Chelsea House, 2006. Collection of essays on the series by leading scholars addressing such topics as the representation of the environment and Lewis's concept of goodness.

Bowen, John P. *The Spirituality of Narnia: The Deeper Magic of C. S. Lewis.* Vancouver, B.C.: Regent College, 2007. Detailed exploration of Lewis's theology and of the relationship of *The Chronicles of Narnia* to other works of Christian fiction.

Downing, David. *Into the Wardrobe: C. S. Lewis and the Narnia Chronicles.* San Francisco: Jossey-Bass, 2005. Provides a detailed biographical analysis the relationship between Lewis's life and each of the books in the series.

Duriez, Colin. *A Field Guide to Narnia.* London: Inter-Varsity Press, 2004. Lists the characters, places, objects and events in Lewis's novels alphabetically. Comments on Narnia's influence on other fantasy authors and connects to themes present throughout Lewis's other works.

Jacobs, Alan. *The Narnian: The Life and Imagination of C. S. Lewis.* New York: HarperOne, 2005. Organizes Lewis's biography by themes rather than chronologically.

Ryken, Leland, and Marjorie Lamp Mead. *A Reader's Guide Through the Wardrobe: Exploring C. S. Lewis's Classic Story.* London: InterVarsity Press, 2005. Gives a basic look at the most popular of the Narnia books from Lewis's point of view, providing a clear description of his use of literary forms.

The Chrysanthemums

Author: John Steinbeck (1902-1968)
First published: 1937
Type of work: Short fiction
Type of plot: Symbolic realism
Time of plot: 1930's
Locale: Salinas Valley, California

Principal characters:
ELISA ALLEN, a housewife
HENRY ALLEN, her husband
A REPAIRMAN, a traveler seeking work

The Story:

Elisa Allen is at work in the garden on the grounds of a neat farm house she shares with her husband, Henry Allen. It is December, and there is no sunshine. Rather, a "high, gray-flannel" fog hovers over the mountains, causing the valley to seem covered like a lid on a pot. Henry's fall fieldwork is done, and now begins the time of waiting for rain to rejuvenate the ground. Elisa, however, is cutting back the old chrysanthemum stalks, inspecting the plants for pests, and transplanting sprouts for a new crop.

Elisa, who is thirty-five years old, has a slender and "strong" face with clear eyes. In her work clothes, she seems "heavy" because of their bulkiness. As she works, she is "over-eager, over-powerful," suggesting masculinity and more energy within her than the tasks at hand require. Even the house is "hard-swept" and the windows are "hard-polished." Occasionally, Elisa looks at the tractor shed, where her husband is talking business with two men.

Henry's voice startles Elisa, as he notes the new sprouts and compliments her on having a green thumb—which she acknowledges, believing that she has inherited planters' hands. Henry reveals that he has sold thirty of his three-year-old steers for a good price and suggests that they celebrate by going into Salinas for dinner and a movie. Perfunctorily, Elisa accepts the invitation, and he teasingly asks her if she would prefer to go to the fights.

Henry rounds up the steers, and Elisa transplants chrysanthemum sets. The sounds of squeaky wheels and the clop of hoofs cause her to look up. She sees a wagon drawn by a mismatched team. The driver is a tinker, or mender of household items. He is a large man with a stubble beard that, though partially gray, does not make him look old. He has dark, brooding eyes and calloused hands, and is wearing a wrinkled black suit with grease spots, and a worn hat. When asked for directions, Elisa suggests a faster way to the highway to Los Angeles, but the man volunteers that time is no concern; he travels from San Diego to Seattle and back annually, allowing himself six months each way. His apparent carefree attitude appeals to Elisa, who comments that his life must be a nice life to live.

The tinker calls attention to the crude lettering on the wagon that advertises his trade of mending pots and sharpening knives and scissors. He asks for work twice, but Elisa assures him that she has none. He appeals to her sympathy by saying that, with no work all day, he may not have an evening meal. Taking another approach, he asks Elisa about her plants. By noticing the flowers, he immediately causes her irritation to fade, leading her to eagerly tell him about the chrysanthemums that she takes pride in growing.

The tinker claims that a neighboring woman, also an avid gardener, has no chrysanthemums, and that she has asked him to be on the lookout for some seeds. He asks Elisa if he can take some of the sprouts to the woman. Delighted with having met someone who seems to show interest in her flowers, Elisa invites him into the yard while she prepares some sprouts for him. She gives directions for their care, adding that it is difficult to do so, for if one has "planting hands," they know what to do automatically. She wonders if he understands her. Now self-conscious, he agrees that perhaps he does understand, but only when he is in the wagon at night with the stars above. He tries to bring her back to matters at hand, that is, that he will not be able to eat if he cannot find work. Now feeling ashamed, she finds him some pots that she no longer uses.

While the tinker works, Elisa asks about life in the wagon and reiterates her wish to be able to live that way. He says, "It ain't the right kind of a life for a woman." She pays him fifty cents and reminds him that she, too, can repair pots and sharpen scissors. As he prepares to leave, she repeats her instructions for the plants. He has clearly forgotten about them, but then catches himself. The tinker starts down the road, and Elisa mouths the words "Good-bye, good-bye."

Once inside the house, Elisa scrubs her body with pumice and, dressing in her best clothes, lays out Henry's best suit and shoes. She then sits "primly and stiffly" on the porch, reflecting on what has taken place. When Henry comes out, she stiffens as he tells her how "nice" she looks. He blunders through, explaining what he means by "nice."

While traveling toward Salinas, Elisa sees a "dark speck" in the road and realizes that the tinker has discarded the chrysanthemums; he had been merely toying with her. She comments to Henry that dining out will be good, and he suggests that they should do so more often. Elisa asks if they can have wine with dinner and, after a bit, asks what goes on at the fights and if women ever go. Surprised, he offers to take her there is she really wants to. She declines, saying that having wine is enough. She then turns up her coat collar so Henry cannot see her weeping.

Critical Evaluation:

"The Chrysanthemums" has variously been praised as a masterpiece, one of the finest stories in American literature and a story that "seems almost perfect in form and style." In a realistic style rich with symbolism, John Steinbeck captures a sense of the 1930's in the United States in his depiction of the relationship between Elisa Allen and her husband, Henry.

Steinbeck was an immensely popular writer, but critics and scholars were not similarly enthused. Some questioned the decision to award him the Nobel Prize in Literature in 1962. The Swedish Academy, however, praised Steinbeck's concern with the ordinary life of the common person, and it felt that the stories collected in *The Long Valley* (1938), including "The Chrysanthemums," had paved the way for his masterpiece, *The Grapes of Wrath* (1939). The academy did not mention his works of the 1940's and 1950's, however, which were not well received by the critics. Most newspapers and periodicals responded to his award negatively or indifferently.

In "The Chrysanthemums," the image of weather figures importantly in the story's symbolism. For example, Elisa represses her femininity and her sexual desires in her marriage in a day in which women's submission was often the norm. Just as the fog, described as a "gray-flannel," has settled over the valley as if it were a lid on a pot, Elisa seems to be enclosed inside the fence that keeps animals from her garden. She feels emotionally enclosed as well. While Henry may love Elisa, he has little understanding of her needs as a woman.

The color yellow serves an important function in the story, too. The chrysanthemums are yellow, as are the willows near the river road. She notes, while waiting on the porch for Henry, "that under the high grey fog" the willows "seemed a thin band of sunshine." Her words suggest a ray of hope amid the gloom of gray.

Elisa also is a nurturing person, and because she is childless, she may be vicariously using this trait (of being nurturant) in producing the giant flowers and transplanting sprouts. Likewise, her brief encounter with the tinker arouses her feelings of sexuality, long stifled, and awakens in her the hope of fulfilling those impulses.

The point of view of the story is limited third person. As such, although Elisa knows what the tinker is saying when he inquires about the chrysanthemums, the reader is not told that he is insincere, that he is just using her. She knows also what Henry is saying when he says that she looks "nice," but she has to ask him what he means by the word.

Major themes related to frustration, limitation, and aesthetics are played out throughout the story as well. Even when Henry pays Elisa a compliment, he is inept and inadequate. Declaring her "strong enough to break a calf over [her] knee" does not appeal to her feminine side. The tinker, in showing even pretended interest in her gardening and in his poetic way of describing the chrysanthemums as looking like "a quick puff of colored smoke," flatters her. She removes her old hat and her bulky work clothes, which make her look masculine, and shakes "out her dark pretty hair," allowing her femininity to show.

After Elisa's sexual feelings are awakened by the tinker, she goes into the house to dress for her night out with Henry, but not before she tries to remove the guilt of her fantasized adultery with the tinker by scrubbing her body with pumice until she is red and scratched. She takes pains to look her best when she and Henry prepare to go into Salinas for dinner, hoping against hope that the romance she feels will spill over into their date.

While Elisa and Henry seem to respect, and probably love, one another, the nature of their relationship makes it impossible for Elisa to release her excessive energy other than through tending her plants and house. Henry does not possess the aesthetic sense that comes naturally to Elisa; he wishes that she would use her planters' hands in a more practical way—to grow apples as large as her flowers. As she works with the chrysanthemums, she is "over-eager, over-powerful." She is unable to release her pent-up feelings with Henry: she sits "prim and stiffly" on the porch, waiting for him to dress, and when he compliments her on her appearance, she "stiffens."

Elisa's momentary interest in the details of a boxing match suggests an identification with the male spectators at the fights; however, the image of the boxers fighting causes her to recoil, and she reasserts her femininity by again declining the offer to go to the fights, settling instead for the romantic touch, in her mind, of having wine with dinner. At the end, Elisa is a woman who has succumbed to the lot to which society, and marriage, has relegated her; hence, she sheds tears "like an old woman."

Victoria Price

Further Reading

Bloom, Harold, ed. *Bloom's Major Short Story Writers: John Steinbeck.* Broomall, Pa.: Chelsea House, 1999. Provides biographical information on Steinbeck as well as plot summaries, lists of characters, and critical essays on "The Chrysanthemums" and other works. Includes a secondary bibliography and an index.

Hayashi, Tetsumaro, ed. *Steinbeck's Short Stories in "The Long Valley": Essays in Criticism.* Muncie, Ind.: Steinbeck Research Institute, 1991. A collection of essays examining Steinbeck's short stories, including "The Chrysanthemums," in *The Long Valley.*

Parini, Jay. *John Steinbeck: A Biography.* New York: Henry Holt, 1995. One chapter in this biography of Steinbeck places *The Long Valley*, which opens with "The Chrysanthemums," in context with his other work. Considers "The Chrysanthemums" to be possibly his best story.

Schultz, Jeffrey, and Luchen Li. *John Steinbeck: A Literary Reference to His Life and Work.* New York: Facts On File, 2005. This reference collection features a biography of Steinbeck; synopses of his works; entries on the people, places, and topics associated with Steinbeck; and appendixes, including a chronology, a list of honors and awards, and lists of film, television, and theater productions featuring Steinbeck's work.

Simmonds, Roy. *A Biographical and Critical Introduction of John Steinbeck.* Lewiston, N.Y.: E. Mellen Press, 2000. Charts Steinbeck's evolution as a writer from 1929 through 1968, discussing the themes of his works and the concepts and philosophies that influenced his writing about human nature and the psyche. Interweaves details about his writings with accounts of his personal life.

Swisher, Clarice, Bruno Leone, and Scott Barbour, eds. *Readings on John Steinbeck.* San Diego, Calif.: Greenhaven Press, 1996. Of twenty-one essays in this anthology, "John Steinbeck's Authentic Characters" focuses on Elisa as one of his "characters with souls."

Timmerman, John H. *John Steinbeck's Fiction: The Aesthetics of the Road Taken.* Norman: University of Oklahoma Press, 1986. Evaluates Steinbeck's artistic premises and guiding beliefs and appraises his work in light of those beliefs. One chapter is devoted to Steinbeck's short stories. Timmerman, who argues that "The Chrysanthemums" is Steinbeck's most successful work of short fiction, also examines interpretations of the story and sources of tension in the work.

The Cid

Author: Pierre Corneille (1606-1684)
First produced: Le Cid, 1637; first published, 1637
 (English translation, 1637)
Type of work: Drama
Type of plot: Tragicomedy
Time of plot: Eleventh century
Locale: Seville, Spain

Principal characters:
DON FERNAND, the king of Castile
DOÑA URRAQUE, the infanta, daughter of Fernand
DON DIÈGUE, the father of Rodrigue
DON GOMÈS, the father of Chimène
DON RODRIGUE, the accepted suitor of Chimène
DON SANCHE, in love with Chimène
CHIMÈNE, the daughter of Don Gomès, in love with
 Rodrigue

The Story:

Because she is the princess royal, the infanta feels she cannot openly love Rodrigue, a nobleman of lower rank. She encourages, therefore, the growing attachment between Chimène and Rodrigue. Chimène asks her father, Don Gomès, to choose either Rodrigue or Sanche to be his son-in-law. She awaits the choice anxiously; her father is on his way to court and she will soon hear his decision. Don Gomès chooses Rodrigue without hesitation, chiefly because of the fame of Don Diègue, Rodrigue's father.

However, a complication soon arises at court. The king chooses Don Diègue as preceptor for his son, the heir apparent. Don Gomès believes that the choice is unjust. Don Diègue was the greatest warrior in Castile, but he is now old. Don Gomès considers himself the most valiant knight in the kingdom. In a bitter quarrel, Don Gomès unjustly accuses Don Diègue of gaining the king's favor through flattery and deceit. He believes that the prince needs a preceptor who will be a living example of the proper virtues, not a teacher who will dwell in the past. In the quarrel, Don Gomès slaps his older rival. Don Diègue, too feeble to draw his sword against Don Gomès, upbraids himself bitterly for having to accept the insult. His only recourse is to call on his young son to uphold the family honor.

Torn between love and duty, Rodrigue challenges Don Gomès to a duel. After some hesitation because of Rodrigue's youth and unproved valor, Don Gomès accepts the challenge of his daughter's suitor. To the surprise of the court, Rodrigue, the untried novice, kills the mightiest man in Castile, piercing with his sword the man whom he respected as his future father-in-law.

Chimène now feels herself in a desperate plight because her love for Rodrigue is mixed with hatred for the murderer of her father. She finally decides to avenge her father by seeking justice from the king. Since she has the right to petition the king, Don Fernand is forced to hear her pleas. In the scene at court, Don Diègue makes a strong plea in favor of his son, reminding the king that Rodrigue did only what honor forced him to do—uphold the family name.

The king is saved from the vexing decision when fierce Moors assault the walls of Seville. Chimène awaits the outcome of the battle with mixed emotions. The army of Castile returns in triumph, bringing as captives two Moorish kings. The man who inspired and led the Castilians by his audacity is Rodrigue. The grateful king gives the hero a new title, the Cid, a Moorish name meaning "lord." The infanta is wretched. Although her high position will not allow her to love Rodrigue, she can love the Cid, a high noble and the hero of Castile. She shows her nobility, however, by yielding to Chimène's prior right.

Chimène is still bound to seek redress. The king resolves to test her true feelings. When she enters the throne room, he tells her gravely that Rodrigue died from battle wounds. Chimène faints. The king advises her to follow the promptings of her heart and cease her quest for vengeance.

Still holding duty above love, however, Chimène insists on her feudal right of a champion. Sanche, hoping to win the favor of Chimène, offers to meet Rodrigue in mortal combat and avenge the death of Don Gomès. Chimène accepts him as her champion. The king decrees that Chimène must marry the victor. In private, Rodrigue comes to Chimène. Indignant at first, Chimène soon softens when she learns that Rodrigue resolves to let himself be killed because she wishes it. Again wavering between love and duty, Chimène begs him to defend himself as best he can.

Sanche goes bravely to meet Rodrigue, who easily disarms his opponent and shows his magnanimity by refusing to kill Chimène's champion. He sends his sword to Chimène in token of defeat. As soon as Chimène sees her champion approach with Rodrigue's sword in his hand, she immediately thinks that Rodrigue is dead. She runs in haste to the king and begs him to change his edict because she cannot bear to wed the slayer of her lover. When the king tells her the truth, that Rodrigue won, Don Diègue praises her for at last avowing openly her love. Still Chimène hesitates to take Rodrigue as her husband. The king understands her plight. He orders the Cid to lead an expedition against the Moors. The wise king knows that time will heal the breach between the lovers.

Critical Evaluation:

The neoclassical tragedies of seventeenth century France are especially in need of introductions for a modern audience, Pierre Corneille's *The Cid* only a little less than most. The Renaissance had seen, among other things, a growth of interest in the individual and in the self. This focusing of interest was in conflict with the medieval view, which perceived humanity more as members of a race than as individuals. The individual was perceived, to be sure, but perceived as a component of society, reproducing it and assuring its integrity by maintaining binding interrelationships with other members of society both alive and dead. In Corneille's time, the more romantic tenets of the Renaissance had been displaced by the neoclassical adoption of the life of reason and order within a cohesive community; and with this life there came, understandably, a high regard for honor.

Many readers do not easily understand the classical and neoclassical concern for "honor" because the twenty-first century is essentially a romantic one; its concerns are primarily for the immediate future and for those who are physically alive. These are the concerns of the individual. Romantic love, concerning itself as it does with the immediate future, is of extreme importance in the twenty-first century. Honor, however, is based not upon immediacy or subjectivity but upon loyalty to others (particularly those to whom one is related by blood ties, marriage, or a shared set of cultural traditions) and concern for the opinions of others. It is not merely a matter of respectfully but radically differing from one's peers on moral questions; one's peers are a part of oneself; to differ radically from them is to be out of order with oneself. The task then, in living a life of honor, is to live it so that others approve. For if others do not approve, no man or woman in such an age can approve of himself or herself.

This is the situation of *The Cid*. The infanta's dilemma is one of the keynotes of the play; she must choose between her romantic love for Rodrigue (to whom she is impelled by her feelings as an individual) and her honor (as demanded by her ties to her father and her attendant position in society). Love urges that she marry him, but honor insists that she not marry beneath her station. She chooses honor almost instinctively, even going so far as to take direct action to decrease her own romantic love; she brings Rodrigue and Chimène together so as to make him completely unavailable to herself as a lover. In act 5 she almost succumbs to love, thinking Rodrigue's newly won glories and title bring him nearly to her social station, but her lady-in-waiting (acting as her visible conscience on the stage) dissuades her. She goes on to aid in the final reconciliation of the principal pair.

Rodrigue and Chimène each face a similar choice. While the infanta's problem has a simpler (though not easier) solution, that of not declaring her love, Rodrigue cannot expect a loving response from the daughter of the man he has killed, and Chimène cannot give such a response. Both are acting in a typically honorable fashion, maintaining their fathers' reputations and forgoing their personal desires. To do less would be to make themselves less than human. Honor threatens the love affair of Chimène and Rodrigue, while love threatens the honor of the infanta.

It will seem to some readers that love wins out over honor in the end, the honorable scruples of the principal pair having been overcome by reason and circumstances. However, love and honor are actually synthesized, neither force canceling the other. The infanta's moral position, being above reproach, is perfect for her role as a proponent of marriage for the pair. Had she surrendered to her own emotion, she could not have been nearly so effective a spokesperson on the part of love for others. Add to this Elvira's chiding and, indeed, the king himself in the role of matchmaker, and it will be seen that Corneille is at some pains to overcome excessive preoccupation with honor, but only in such a way as to leave real honor intact and alive.

Until the denouement—Chimène's admission of her love—the heroine sees herself primarily as the daughter of Don Gomès; her admission of her feelings to the king and the resolution of the play are made possible by her being persuaded to see herself primarily as a member of the Castilian community. As a result of this shift in her perception of her role, she no longer sees Rodrigue as an enemy and begins to see the Moors in that capacity. As the principal bulwark against the common enemy, Rodrigue both lays the groundwork for this change in Chimène and is in a unique position to enjoy the benefits of it. Thus, while upholding the concept of honor in a humanly achievable form, the play uses a typically romantic process as the underpinnings of its plot: Thesis and antithesis (honor and love) are synthesized.

Critics have seen in this play certain basic similarities to William Shakespeare's *Romeo and Juliet* (pr. c. 1595-1596,

pb. 1597), foremost among which is the feud between the lovers' families. A more essential similarity, however, lies in the use of death by both dramatists as a threat to young love. Both Romeo and Rodrigue think of death (for themselves) as a solution to their problems, and both offer the solution with such alacrity as to give rise to speculations of a death wish on both their parts. Such speculations, however, have the distinct disadvantage of focusing attention entirely upon the characters, causing us to ignore the play's overall design. Death is not initially the preoccupation of either hero. Both want simply to marry the ladies they love. Death presents itself to them as a solution only when this desire becomes both undeniable and impossible to satisfy. This renders life impossible, and when life begins to seem impossible the natural impulse is to consign it to a state of nonexistence (the natural state for any impossibility). Death is the inevitable threat, but death becomes truly inevitable only when the character is convinced that life is indeed impossible, that there is no hope for change. Rodrigue repeatedly offers himself to Chimène for execution, believing there is no other solution.

Death, then, is not intrinsic to Rodrigue's character; it is a force from without, threatening a healthy love relationship with the ferocity of a tangible monster. There is a level at which most love comedies are fertility rites, celebrating and promoting the optimism and fecundity of a society. In such comedies the lovers' eventual wedding (or promise of one) affirms this social optimism. However, when optimism and fertility are seriously threatened by death, as they are in this play, a comedy is renamed as a tragicomedy. *The Cid* ends happily with the promise of a marriage, the protagonists having avoided death's many invasions into their happiness. Death's attempts, however, were persistent and were overcome by the slimmest of margins. *The Cid* is Corneille's first major play and is often considered his finest. His plays are often compared to those of his younger contemporary, Jean Racine. Both authors adhered strictly to the neoclassical unities (one action, one time, and one place), though Racine evidently worked more comfortably within those restrictions. Corneille reminds the reader throughout *The Cid* that the action occurs within one day but that the day is an unnaturally full one.

"Critical Evaluation" by John J. Brugaletta

Further Reading

Abraham, Claude. *Pierre Corneille*. New York: Twayne, 1972. Gives a short biographical sketch and discusses the structure, themes, and style in Corneille's plays. Shows the significance of *The Cid* in Corneille's works. Geared for the general reader, with all quotations in English.

Bénichou, Paul. *Man and Ethics: Studies in French Classicism.* Translated by Elizabeth Hughes. Garden City, N.Y.: Doubleday, 1971. Treats the social and moral conditions of life during the seventeenth century. Brilliantly considers the relation between aesthetic and moral values in literature.

Carlin, Claire L. *Women Reading Corneille: Feminist Psychocriticisms of "Le Cid."* New York: Peter Lang, 2000. Carlin surveys feminist psychoanalytic criticism of *The Cid* written during the past century. She concludes that play's enduring gender issues concern Chinéne and Rodrigue—whether their relationship is one of equality or dominance, whether she is as much of a hero as he is, and whether they will marry.

Cook, Albert Spaulding. *French Tragedy: The Power of Enactment.* Chicago: Swallow Press, 1981. Presents an interesting discussion concerning the style of the neoclassical play. The quotations are in both French and English.

Ekstein, Nina. *Corneille's Irony.* Charlottesville, Va.: Rookwood Press, 2007. A detailed examination of the use of irony in Corneille's plays, describing the different types of irony he employs and how it functions in specific plays.

Elmarsafy, Zid. "Freedom in Chains: Corneille and the Erotic Contract." In *Freedom, Slavery, and Absolutism: Corneille, Pascal, Racine.* Lewisburg, Pa.: Bucknell University Press, 2003. Argues that the works of Corneille and his two contemporaries depict a sovereign's absolute authority as the only form of government that can ensure freedom for its citizens.

Longstaffe, Moya. *Metamorphoses of Passion and the Heroic in French Literature: Corneille, Stendhal, Claudel.* Lewiston, N.Y. Edwin Mellen Press, 1999. Maintains that the works of Corneille, Paul Claudel, and Stendhal share a common aspiration for human dignity. Compares the writers' treatments of the ideal of the heroic and the relationship between men and women.

Margitic, Milorad R. *Cornelian Power Games: Variations on a Theme in Pierre Corneille's Theatre from "Mélite" to "Polyeucte."* Tübingen, Germany: Narr, 2002. Analyzes Corneille's first twelve plays, including *The Cid,* showing how each demonstrates a particular strategy of power. Margitic concludes that Corneille's universe is a highly manipulative and political place and his characters are complex and changing.

Moore, Will Grayburn. *The Classical Drama of France.* New York: Oxford University Press, 1971. Provides information about the form of the French neoclassical play. Explains the background of *The Cid.*

Yarrow, P. J. *Corneille.* New York: Macmillan, 1963. A general study of Corneille's plays that presents their structure and relates them to their epoch. An excellent treatment of *The Cid*'s importance in the development of seventeenth century French neoclassicism.

The Cider House Rules

Author: John Irving (1942-   )
First published: 1985
Type of work: Novel
Type of plot: Social realism and bildungsroman
Time of plot: 1920's-1954
Locale: St. Cloud's, Maine; Massachusetts

Principal characters:
WILBUR LARCH, a physician and the founder of St. Cloud's orphanage
HOMER WELLS, his apprentice, an orphan at St. Cloud's
CANDY KENDALL, a lobsterman's daughter
WALLY WORTHINGTON, the son of an apple-growing family
ANGEL WELLS, the secret son of Homer and Candy
ARTHUR ROSE, head of an apple-picking crew
ROSE ROSE, his daughter
FUZZY STONE and MELONY, orphans at St. Cloud's
MRS. GOODHALL, an orphanage board member

The Story:

The history of the orphanage in St. Cloud's begins with Wilbur Larch, a doctor from Maine whose experiences with poor and desperate women had convinced him that women have the right to a safe, legal abortion. As a young medical student, Dr. Larch had been sexually initiated by a prostitute, Mrs. Eames. He later meets her in the Boston hospital where he works. Her uterus is disintegrating from the effects of a drug she had taken to induce an abortion. Dr. Larch tries to save her, but she dies.

Eames's daughter, also pregnant, approaches Dr. Larch and asks him to give her a medical abortion. He considers her request but refuses. Later, she is found in front of the hospital, unconscious and burning with fever. Like her mother, she dies as a result of an illegal abortion. A note pinned to her dress, addressed to Dr. Larch, tells him to "shit or get off the pot." This is a turning point for Larch: He visits the office of a doctor who performs illegal abortions, sees the unsanitary conditions and the medical ignorance that women risk, and meets a girl who has been impregnated by her father. Larch offers to give her a safe, medical abortion.

Soon after he returns to Maine, Larch takes a position in the small town of St. Cloud's and establishes an orphanage that offers a judgment-free haven for women who need to terminate a pregnancy or find a home for their children. St. Cloud's becomes its own small kingdom, ruled by the benevolent but eccentric Dr. Larch, who devotes himself entirely to his medical work and the orphans he calls princes of Maine, kings of New England.

Despite his habit of sampling the ether used for surgeries, Larch is a competent doctor, and he manages to find homes for most of his orphans, with the exception of Homer Wells. After a series of failed adoptions, Larch decides to keep Homer at the orphanage and train him in medicine, in the hope that he will someday inherit Larch's place as a doctor. Homer is bright and willing to learn all that Larch can teach him, with one exception: After seeing an aborted fetus, Homer refuses to have anything to do with performing abortions.

By the end of his teenage years, Homer is a skilled obstetrician, though without formal education. He has delivered babies and saved a woman's life, but his knowledge of the world outside St. Cloud's is limited. He has a half-hearted sexual relationship with Melony, a tough, heavy-set orphan who makes Homer promise that he will never leave St. Cloud's without her. Homer breaks his promise when Candy Kendall, a lobsterman's daughter, and Wally Worthington, part of a wealthy apple-growing family, come to the orphanage, dazzling the orphans who imagine that the beautiful young couple have come to adopt someone. In fact, Candy, still in high school, has come for an abortion. When Candy and Wally leave, Homer leaves with them, ostensibly to pick up some apple trees Wally has offered to donate to the orphanage, but in reality, he wants to start a new life.

Homer is too old to be adopted, but he is taken in by Wally's family like a foster child. He learns how to grow ap-

ples and make cider at Ocean View, the family's apple orchard; he attends high school and learns the rules of dating and drive-in theaters. He dates a girl who works at the orchard, but he falls in love with Candy. His friendship with Wally keeps him from acting on this love, but there are hints that Candy is developing feelings for Homer as well.

Soon, the United States enters World War II, and Wally enlists in the Army Air Corps, leaving Homer (considered unfit for service due to an imaginary heart defect Dr. Larch claims he has) in charge of the apple orchard. When Wally is shot down in Burma and then missing in action for many months, Homer and Candy begin a secret love affair. However, as long as Wally's fate is unknown, they feel they cannot be together openly. Candy again becomes pregnant, and she returns with Homer to St. Cloud's, this time to give birth. They tell Candy's father and Wally's mother that they are doing volunteer work at the orphanage, and Homer devises a cover story that will allow them to return with their child: They will claim that they adopted one of the orphans. While Candy and Homer are at St. Cloud's, Wally returns, paralyzed but alive. Candy feels it would be disloyal to leave Wally after his injury. She marries him, and Homer, with his "adopted" son, returns to Ocean View to manage the orchard.

Melony, meanwhile, has left the orphanage in search of Homer, knowing only that he has gone to an apple orchard named Ocean View somewhere in Maine. She takes work in several apple orchards while looking for him. During the war, she works in a shipyard and eventually becomes an electrician. Always volatile and ready to fight, she finds a measure of stability in a lesbian relationship with coworker Lorna but never forgets her vow to find Homer. She now knows where he is, because she has seen a newspaper clipping about a wounded war veteran from Heart's Rock, Maine, who owns an apple orchard named Ocean View. When Lorna betrays Melony by getting pregnant during a brief encounter with a man, Melony decides the time has come to seek out her first betrayer. Fifteen years after Homer left St. Cloud's, Melony appears at the orchard.

Homer, Wally, and Candy live together at the orchard. Homer and Candy, whose now-teenage son, Angel, believes he is Homer's adopted child, suspect that Wally knows their secret, but no one speaks of it directly; the family structure, while nontraditional, seems to work. All of them, including Wally, love Angel, and Homer has learned to live with the deception. Melony's visit shakes his complacency. Homer had expected that Melony might attack him physically, but he is not prepared for the disappointment she expresses. She had expected great things of him, she tells Homer—had expected him to be a hero, like Dr. Larch—but instead, he is living a life of ordinary middle-class deception, sleeping with a disabled man's wife and lying to his own child.

Meanwhile, Dr. Larch and the nurses at the orphanage have been fighting attempts by some of the orphanage board members to replace Dr. Larch with a younger doctor. Knowing the board's conservative bent, Larch fears that his replacement would refuse to provide abortions to women and girls. Larch has put a plan in place to have Homer replace him, using the identity of Fuzzy Stone, an orphan who had died years ago. Larch devises a medical and missionary background for "Dr. Fuzzy Stone," whose forged letters make his antiabortion stance clear. For a while, Larch's plan seems doubtful. Homer has created a life for himself outside St. Cloud's, but Melony's harsh words make him question that life. Then, two things happen that lead Homer back to what seems to be his true home.

Rose Rose, the daughter of the apple pickers' foreman, Arthur Rose, becomes pregnant with her father's child. Homer calls the orphanage, seeking Larch's help, but learns Larch has died through an accidental overdose of ether. That night, Homer performs his first abortion. He tells his son the truth and leaves the orchard to begin his new life as Dr. Fuzzy Stone, head of the orphanage at St. Cloud's.

Critical Evaluation:

A sprawling social novel in the tradition of Charles Dickens and Thomas Hardy, *The Cider House Rules* is the story of a doctor who considers it his life's mission to provide women with safe abortions and the story of an orphaned boy who becomes the doctor's spiritual son. Along the way, author John Irving touches on issues of sexuality, drug addiction, women's rights, domestic violence, race, and class.

Like Dickens's David Copperfield, Irving's character Homer Wells is an orphan struggling to find his place in the world. For Homer, this place turns out to be the place he can be "of use." He grows up in St. Cloud's, a remote Maine orphanage where a woman facing an unplanned pregnancy can get a safe abortion, if she chooses, or can give birth knowing that her child will be raised in the orphanage until adopted. Even though Homer has been adopted several times, he always returns to St. Cloud's; the orphanage seems to be his true home.

The Cider House Rules, Irving's sixth novel, is considered one of his most celebrated and also one of his most controversial works. It attained the number one spot on *The New York Times* best-seller list, was widely reviewed, inspired a play and an Academy Award-winning 1999 motion picture, and has remained in print since its first publication in 1985. While some critics praise the book for its complex plot and

Dickensian scope, others find it excessively long and believe that the difficult topic of abortion is oversimplified.

At a time when many writers had been looking inward and focusing on experiments with narrative and prose style, Irving deliberately modeled his work after the nineteenth century novels of his own favorite writer, Dickens, who wrote of society and its ills. Irving borrows some Dickensian narrative techniques, such as a broad cast of characters and a complicated plot that sometimes relies on coincidence; he even uses one of Dickens's signature topics, orphans. In another nod to his favorite author, Irving has Dr. Wilbur Larch and Homer read Dickens's *David Copperfield* (1849-1850, serial; 1850, book) to the orphans as a bedtime story.

Irving, like Dickens, is critical of the rich, particularly those who ignore or dismiss the troubles of the poor. He also is critical of people who see life in terms of moral absolutes. In an early scene in the novel, a hospital colleague questions Larch about the note that reads "shit or get off the pot" that is found pinned to Mrs. Eames's dying daughter's dress. Larch says that the daughter is angry at him because he had refused to give her an abortion; the colleague self-righteously congratulates Larch for his stance. As he watches the young woman die from her botched abortion, Larch wonders why his refusal is considered a good thing. From that moment on, he offers women what they want—an orphan or an abortion—and refuses to judge others for their choices.

A sense of moral complexity, even ambiguity, underlies *The Cider House Rules*. The characters are multidimensional, and almost no one can be defined as unreservedly good or evil. Larch, by the law of his day a criminal and in the eyes of religion a sinner, is known to his orphanage staff as Saint Larch. Lonely and driven, he devotes his life to caring for unwanted children and to helping women in need. However, he also is an ether addict and at times seems inflexible in his desire to make Homer into his successor.

Homer is an essentially honest and decent character, yet he deceives his best friend and later lies to his own son. Homer is not opposed to lies when they serve a socially useful purpose. Unlike orphan Melony, who rages against Larch for keeping her parentage a secret, Homer accepts that there may be truths it is better not to know. When Wally is missing in Burma, Homer reflects on his fate and decides that if he knew Wally died in a horrible and painful way, he would keep this knowledge from those who loved Wally, to spare them suffering.

Arthur Rose, the orchard's crew leader, commits the unforgivable act of sexually abusing his daughter and getting her pregnant, but he is not a complete villain; he is capable of reflection and remorse. After his daughter stabs him and runs away, he claims before he dies that he had stabbed himself in an act of suicide; he does this to keep his daughter from being prosecuted for murder.

The only character who falls into complete caricature is Mrs. Goodhall, the self-righteous orphanage board member obsessed with replacing Larch. She is narrow-minded, is ostentatiously religious, and is constantly accusing others of sexual wrongdoing. Self-righteous judgment, Irving seems to suggest, is the only true sin.

The cider house rules of the novel's title comprise a list of rules tacked to a wall at Ocean View Orchards, rules that, throughout the novel, are both followed and broken. The rules at Ocean View are specific, concrete, and related mostly to safety. One such rule is that apple pickers should not sit on the cider-house roof, because they could fall. Homer notes that most of these rules are broken regularly. Rose, not the rules, controls the behavior of the African American pickers, and Rose follows his own set of rules. When the pickers speculate about the lights from a Ferris wheel visible from the roof, Homer tells them the Ferris wheel is at a carnival several towns away; Rose then claims that Homer is lying. Later, Rose asks Homer to take him to the carnival and, while there, is racially harassed by a young man in an incident that barely avoids violence. He tells Homer that it is better for the pickers not to know about the Ferris wheel; as black men in a racist society, they would be endangered if they visited the carnival.

Homer also learns the complex rules of sexuality when he double dates with Wally Worthington and Candy Kendall. Wally is expected to make certain sexual advances with his date, but other acts are forbidden. Accustomed to Melony's unbounded sexuality, Homer is confused by these rules, but he later realizes that they are designed to prevent unwanted pregnancy.

Abortion, the novel's central theme, has its own set of complex rules. During the time of the story, abortion is illegal in the United States. Despite this law, many women still seek abortions, and they remain available through a kind of underground network of sympathetic doctors and nurses, on one hand, and unscrupulous abortion providers like those who Larch finds "off Harrison" in Boston's South End.

Homer, too, has his own set of rules. His attitude toward abortion is complex, and it changes during the course of the novel. When he finds an aborted fetus at the hospital, he is horrified by what he sees—a dead human being. He then refuses to take part in any abortions. He later tells Larch that he believes abortions may be necessary in some circumstances and should be legal, but he still feels a personal objection to

them. It is only when Mr. Rose's daughter, Rose Rose, who is close to Homer and his son, faces an unwanted pregnancy that Homer is willing to break his own rules on abortion.

With its flawed but sympathetic characters, *The Cider House Rules* challenges moral absolutism. Rules, Irving's ending suggests, are made to be broken, or at minimum should be flexible enough to adapt to changing circumstances.

Kathryn Kulpa

Further Reading

Bloom, Harold, ed. *John Irving*. Philadelphia: Chelsea House, 2001. A collection of illuminating essays by noted scholars that address major aspects of Irving's work, from thematic content to style and structure. Discusses all of Irving's novels through 2000. Includes an informative editor's introduction, a chronology, and a bibliography.

Campbell, Josie P. *John Irving: A Critical Companion*. Westport, Conn.: Greenwood Press, 1998. This critical study includes a short biography of John Irving, a summary of his career, and chapters on each of his novels from 1968 to 1998, including *The Cider House Rules*. An accessible work, suitable for advanced high school students and college students.

Davis, Todd F., and Kenneth Womack. *The Critical Response to John Irving*. Westport, Conn.: Praeger, 2004. Discusses both positive and negative critical views of Irving's novels through *The Fourth Hand* (2001), and includes a discussion of his nonfiction works.

_____. "Saints, Sinners, and the Dickensian Novel: The Ethics of Storytelling in John Irving's *The Cider House Rules*." *Style* 32, no. 2 (Summer, 1998): 298-317. Discusses Irving's use of Dickensian narrative form and style in *The Cider House Rules*. This article is reprinted in Harold Bloom's *John Irving*.

Irving, John. *My Movie Business: A Memoir*. New York: Random House, 1999. Irving describes his experiences with the film adaptation of *The Cider House Rules* and the challenges of adapting a long novel to a screenplay.

Miller, Gabriel. *John Irving*. New York: Frederick Ungar, 1982. Covers Irving's career through *The Hotel New Hampshire* (1981). Includes a time line, a short biography, and an interview with the author.

Reilly, Edward C. *Understanding John Irving*. Columbia: University of South Carolina Press, 1991. Presents a concise exposition of Irving's work and situates the novels with regard to both British and Continental traditions.

Cinna

Author: Pierre Corneille (1606-1684)
First produced: Cinna: Ou, La Clémence d'Auguste, 1640;
    first published, 1643 (English translation, 1713)
Type of work: Drama
Type of plot: Tragedy
Time of plot: c. 10 C.E.
Locale: Rome

Principal characters:
AUGUSTUS, the emperor of Rome
LIVIA, his wife, the empress
CINNA, the grandson of Pompey
MAXIMUS, his friend and fellow conspirator
AMELIA, engaged to Cinna
FULVIA, her confidante and companion
EVANDER, Cinna's freedman
EUPHORBUS, Maximus's freedman

The Story:

Amelia, the daughter of Augustus's tutor, seeks revenge against Augustus for her father's death. She asks for vengeance as a provision of her marriage to Cinna, the grandson of Pompey, who was more deeply wronged by Augustus than Amelia. Her friend Fulvia believes that the plot against Augustus's life can be successful only if anger and hatred are not apparent, especially since Augustus holds Amelia in such high esteem that courtiers often ask her to act as an intermediary in affairs at court. The two women debate the worth of Augustus as compared to the cruelties exercised to establish him in his high position. Amelia thinks the winning of love through the destruction of a tyrant is worth all the risk involved, but self-glorification seems to Fulvia to be more of the impetus behind the plot than either love or desire for vengeance—a thought that almost causes Amelia to waver in deference to her endangered and beloved Cinna.

Cinna, however, believes the plot has an excellent chance of success. All the conspirators seem to him as desirous of vengeance and as eager for the rewards of love as he is, though their inspiration is the result of his oratorical eloquence in reciting his own as well as the historical grievances against the emperor. Cinna will, while bearing the sacrificial cup at the next day's ceremony of thanksgiving to the gods, stab Augustus to death. His friend Maximus will hold back the mob, while others will surround Cinna. Even though he proclaims that he cares not whether he lives or dies as long as honor is upheld—an honor not unlike that of Brutus and Cassius, the murderers of Julius Caesar, Amelia hastens to add—he believes that the people will then accept him as emperor. Evander, a freed servant of Cinna, brings news that Augustus wants to see both Cinna and Maximus, an event that upsets their plans and strikes fear into Amelia's heart. After the lovers swear to die for each other, Amelia retires to Livia's side, while Cinna goes to confront Augustus.

Augustus prefaces his remarks with a long history of human desire for the empty bauble of power and then asks the two young men to decide his fate, whether he should be the emperor or a private citizen. Both conspirators swear that Augustus, so much nobler than Julius Caesar, should remain supreme in power as the rightful ruler of a grateful empire. Although the sentiment redounds to Augustus's credit, neither feels it to be more than weakness to want a republic when a monarchy can be maintained. Augustus, however, is not convinced that five generations of struggle to eminence prove anything more than that the people want democracy. Cinna, disclaiming this idea, even citing his grandfather's claim on the throne as evidence, urges Augustus to name a successor who can carry on this Augustan age to posterity. Cinna is surprised to hear himself so named. Although Maximus wavers after such a noble act by their ruler, Cinna remains resolute in his bloody plan. He will kill Augustus, put his bloody hand in that of Amelia, and marry her on Augustus's tomb.

A short time later, Maximus reveals to his companion and confidant Euphorbus that he, too, loves Amelia; the freedman in turn urges his former master to kill Cinna and gain not only the girl but the emperor's gratitude. Maximus, after much argument, is repelled and yet intrigued by such a prospect. Just such a conflict exists in Cinna's breast as well; he loves the revenge but cannot feel true hatred for the object, so dear is his own person to Augustus. Maximus suggests that these sentiments are enfeebling, though he feels the justice of their cause. Cinna, alone with his conscience, reasons from cause to effect and decides to ask Amelia to release him from his promise of revenge.

Amelia greets her lover with rejoicing, for she, too, hears the news of Augustus's high regard for Cinna; she is, however, relentless in her desire for vengeance. When Cinna pleads with her to return not only his love but also that of Augustus, she replies that treason is the only answer to Augustus's tyranny. Finally, he agrees to her demands, though not without a commentary on female ruthlessness.

In the meantime, perhaps thinking to better his own low position, Euphorbus goes to Augustus with news of the plot against him. Augustus is more shocked at Cinna's treachery than at that of Maximus, who at least gave warning of his feelings, and he would have pardoned the latter had not Euphorbus lied and said that Maximus committed suicide. In a soliloquy, Augustus summarizes the pity of it all. Maximus proposes flight to Amelia as the best solution to a bad situation. When she spurns his love as traitorous to his friend, he in turn laments the counsel of Euphorbus.

Augustus summons Cinna and speaks of the leniency with which he allowed his traditional enemy to live as recompense for ancient wrongs. For this, he declares, Cinna plans to kill him at a religious ceremony in the capitol. The emperor then offers all to Cinna, even though, without the help of Augustus, the young man cannot succeed in his design. Cinna, unrepentant, refuses to give Augustus satisfaction over his death.

Amelia and Livia then resolve the conflict, the former taking the blame on herself, even begging to die with Cinna; the lovers quarrel over the seeming break in love and in honor. Maximus then hastens to reveal his betrayal, through Euphorbus, of the plot. These circumstances move Augustus to ask the friendship of those whom he most admires and loves. Amelia, the first to respond, is followed by the others, all moved by royal clemency. Livia commends her husband's generosity as a bright example to future rulers. Augustus humbly wishes it would be so and appoints the morrow as a day of joyous sacrifice, doubly so because of the plotters' remorse and the forgiveness of the man against whom they conspired.

Critical Evaluation:

Credited by many critics to have written the first play exemplifying the neoclassical style introduced into France in 1630, Pierre Corneille was received into the French Academy in 1647. His career was highly prolific, including thirty-two plays. Although he became a lawyer, the playwright won accolades at an early age for his versification in Latin and published poems entitled *Mélanges poétiques* in 1632. Corneille studied Aristotle, the Greek and Roman classics, and Spanish history, producing the neoclassical play *Le Cid* (1637), which defined the rules of seventeenth century French drama. Influenced by the precepts of both Aristotle and Horace concerning decorum, verisimilitude, and the unities of time, place, and action, Corneille brought reason, order, and clarity to French plays, combining realism with the marvelous by means of the elegant Alexandrine twelve-syllable line. After defining the neoclassical style with *Le Cid*, Corneille began his series of plays taken from Roman history; his first Roman tragedy was *Horace* (1640).

In the Roman tragedy *Cinna*, Corneille distinguishes himself by showing that a tragedy consisting of mental conflicts can be as theatrical as a drama involving exterior actions. *Cinna* illustrates one of the greatest contributions that Corneille gave to the development of neoclassical French tragedy: the establishment of abrupt changes of situation during the drama, changes designated as *coups de théâtre*. In act 1 of *Cinna*, Corneille establishes the conflict of the play as duty versus love. To be worthy of Amelia's love, Cinna has to fulfill her duty to avenge the death of her father through killing Emperor Augustus. Amelia ponders the threat to her lover's life upon achieving this duty, while Cinna plots enthusiastically with other conspirators to overthrow the tyrannical Augustus. The *coups de théâtre* occur when Cinna and Maximus are called to present themselves to the king. This concluding action cements the lovers' commitment to their duty and love, thus creating the suspense that Augustus might have already gained knowledge of the conspiracy. Corneille's implementation of abrupt changes of situation give interest to *Cinna* and provide the background for the irony of the play, in which the monstrous tyrant of act 1 is portrayed as a compassionate human being in the final act.

This humanization is foreshadowed by the play's subtitle, the mercy of Augustus, since it underscores the significance of the emperor's response to the assassination plot. Cinna's regeneration exemplifies the rule that a neoclassical play should take its background from a credible source. In fact, Corneille consulted several Roman sources, including Seneca's *De Clementia* (c. 55-56) and the works of Cassius Dio. Seneca's essay on mercy in *De Clementia* related the story of Augustus's discovery of the plot of Pompey's grandson Cinna upon whom Augustus had bestowed various favors; his wife Livia suggested that he use clemency to quell the conspiracy. This suggested the political theme of Corneille's *Cinna*, which involved the decision of the Romans to choose between anarchy or absolute monarchy. Augustus's first monologue to Cinna and Maximus reflects this indecisiveness: "Augustus, Rome, the State are in your hands. . . . You'll place all Europe, Asia, Africa under a monarch's or republic's rule." Corneille's use of dramatic irony is seen in Augustus's statement in that the emperor does not know that Cinna, Maximus, and Amelia have already devised a plot to kill him.

Corneille's condensation of the historical events in Roman history concerning the emperor's rise to power and the establishment of his absolute monarchy allowed the French author to emphasize Octavian's change of name to Augustus. This change of name, taken from the works of Cassius Dio, not only suggests that the sacred king merits respect but also links the political theme to the moral one. The moral theme refers to the evolution of Augustus's character, since the king could, in the end, reconcile himself with the conspirators because he ascertains that they are motivated by either love or jealousy. In fact, the plot could be reduced to the following formula: Maximus loves Amelia, who loves Cinna. The king's realization of this love triangle coupled with his wife's proposal to act out of clemency allows the monarch to develop morally in a way that is reminiscent of Seneca's three levels of moral ascendancy: pity, pardon, and clemency. At the beginning of the play, Augustus expresses pity for the fate of the people if he were to yield the throne to another monarch; Cinna hypocritically encourages the king to continue his reign. Then, after learning about the murder plot, Augustus offers Maximus an unmerited pardon out of sorrow over the whole situation, for Maximus has been tempted to arrange the death of his friend Cinna to marry Amelia. Finally, because of Livia's suggestion of clemency to resolve Cinna's participation in the treasonous situation, the play ends with the monarch's authority augmented. The positive result of Augustus's clemency is summarized by Cinna, who declares that the monarch's unparalleled action makes his own crime greater and Augustus's power more just. Hence, the emperor sees himself as the master of himself and of the world.

Augustus's act of clemency completes the theme of moral development as well as the political theme, since it allows the acceptance of the absolute monarchy. Corneille thus establishes in his plays a respect for the royal standard of conduct, a standard that the playwright termed "generosity."

Corneille's fast-moving, compact style and his observance of the unities of a single time, place, and action in *Cinna* prefigured Jean Racine's tragedies, which were written during the epoch of Louis XIV's absolute monarchy. Similar to Racine, Corneille based his action on psychological decisions, thus enabling *Cinna* to present a dramatic concentration that he rarely achieved in his other works.

"Critical Evaluation" by Linda Prewett Davis

Further Reading

Broome, J. H. *A Student's Guide to Corneille: Four Tragedies.* London: Heinemann Educational Books, 1971. Provides an introductory chapter about the scope of Corneille's works and his dramatic theory. Treats the subject, the scheme of the characters, the dramatic mechanism, and the themes. Gives an evaluation of possible interpretations of the tragedies.

Ekstein, Nina. *Corneille's Irony.* Charlottesville, Va.: Rook-wood Press, 2007. A detailed examination of the use of irony in Corneille's plays, describing the different types of irony he employs and how it functions in specific plays. Chapter 7 includes an analysis of *Cinna*.

Elmarsafy, Zid. "Freedom in Chains: Corneille and the Erotic Contract." In *Freedom, Slavery, and Absolutism: Corneille, Pascal, Racine.* Lewisburg, Pa.: Bucknell University Press, 2003. Argues that the works of Corneille and his two contemporaries depict a sovereign's absolute authority as the only form of government that can ensure freedom for its citizens.

Fogel, Herbert. *The Criticism of Cornelian Tragedy: A Study of Critical Writing from the Seventeenth to the Twentieth Century.* New York: Exposition Press, 1967. An excellent basic analysis of the history of Cornelian tragedy. Divided into four periods that designate marked contrasts or strict compliance with tradition.

Gossip, Christopher J. *Corneille: Cinna.* London: Grant & Cutler, 1998. A concise introductory overview and survey of the drama's critical reception.

Longstaffe, Moya. *Metamorphoses of Passion and the Heroic in French Literature: Corneille, Stendhal, Claudel.* Lewiston, N.Y.: Edwin Mellen Press, 1999. Maintains that the works of Corneille, Paul Claudel, and Stendhal share a common aspiration for human dignity. Compares the writers' treatments of the ideal of the heroic and the relationship between men and women.

Lough, John. *An Introduction to Seventeenth Century France.* New York: David McKay, 1969. An informative general depiction of seventeenth century France through the great literary works. Discusses the social and political history of the seventeenth century, including the absolutism of Louis XIV. Contains a section on the literary background, portraying the relationship between the writers and their public which influenced the development of language and literature.

Margitic, Milorad R. *Cornelian Power Games: Variations on a Theme in Pierre Corneille's Theatre from "Mélite" to "Polyeucte."* Tübingen, Germany: Narr, 2002. Analyzes Corneille's first twelve plays, including *Cinna*, showing how each demonstrates a particular strategy of power. Margitic concludes that Corneille's universe is a highly manipulative and political place and his characters are complex and changing.

Nelson, Robert J. *Corneille, His Heroes, and Their Worlds.* Philadelphia: University of Pennsylvania Press, 1963. Gives various analytical insights concerning Corneille's dramatic skills. Concentrates on the themes of the Cornelian hero and his world.

Cinq-Mars
Or, A Conspiracy Under Louis XIII

Author: Alfred de Vigny (1797-1863)
First published: Cinq-Mars: Ou, Une Conjuration sous Louis XIII, 1826 (English translation, 1847)
Type of work: Novel
Type of plot: Historical
Time of plot: Seventeenth century
Locale: France

Principal characters:
HENRI D'EFFIAT, the marquis of Cinq-Mars and a conspirator against Richelieu
CARDINAL RICHELIEU, France's minister of state
LOUIS XIII, the king of France
ANNE OF AUSTRIA, the queen of France
MARIE DE GONZAGA, beloved of Henri Cinq-Mars
FRANÇOIS AUGUST DE THOU, a fellow conspirator with Cinq-Mars

The Story:

One June day in 1639, at the château of Chaumont in Touraine, young Henri d'Effiat, the marquis of Cinq-Mars, takes leave of his family and sets out, at the request of Cardinal Richelieu, Louis XIII's chief minister, to join King Louis XIII's forces at the Siege of Perpignan. Shortly after he leaves, his mother's guest, Marshal Bassompierre, is placed under arrest at Richelieu's order and sent in chains toward Paris and the Bastille. Young Cinq-Mars tries to release the marshal, but the haughty old soldier refuses to be rescued. As if his flouting of the king's officers were not enough for one day, Cinq-Mars returns under cover of night to the château to bid good-bye to Marie de Gonzaga, the beautiful duchess of Mantua, who has been staying with Cinq-Mars's mother at the château. He returns to bid her farewell because the two, despite the differences of their stations, are very much in love.

Finally leaving Chaumont, Cinq-Mars, accompanied by a few servants, sets out for Loudun. Upon his arrival, he finds the town in turmoil because a local clergyman, a monk named Urbain Grandier, is on trial, accused of being a magician. Charges against the monk have been made by order of Richelieu, who wishes to do away with the independent cleric. The Abbé Quillet, Cinq-Mars's former tutor, has taken the clergyman's part and is about to leave Loudun in secret, fearful for his own life. At the execution of Grandier, Cinq-Mars discovers that officials in attendance, the man's assassins (for they are but that), have given him a red-hot cross to kiss. Cinq-Mars seizes the cross and with it strikes the face of the judge who condemned Grandier, thus earning the enmity of one of Richelieu's most trusted agents.

After the execution, Cinq-Mars hastens on his way to Perpignan. In the meantime, however, Cardinal Richelieu is making plans to use Cinq-Mars as a tool in undermining the authority of the king. The report of his agents about Cinq-Mars's actions with regard to the king's officers and

Richelieu's agents makes no difference to the cardinal, who believes he can shape the young man to his own ends.

Shortly after his arrival at Perpignan, Cinq-Mars is asked to represent the monarchists' side in a duel against a cardinalist sympathizer. Immediately after the duel, he finds himself in the thick of an attack on the walls of the besieged city, along with the members of the king's own guard. He behaves so valiantly in the struggle that the captain of the guard introduces Cinq-Mars to the king, much to the disgust of Cardinal Richelieu, who himself had planned to introduce Cinq-Mars to the monarch.

King Louis takes an immediate liking to Cinq-Mars, who has suffered a wound in the battle, and he makes the young man an officer in the royal guards. During the battle, Cinq-Mars had befriended the son of the judge he had struck with the cross at Loudun; the son, a bitter enemy of his father who hated all that his father and Richelieu represented, had approved of Cinq-Mars's actions. At Perpignan, Cinq-Mars had also renewed a friendship with a young aristocrat named de Thou, who was later to stand as close to him as a brother.

Two years pass, and Cinq-Mars has become the confidant of Louis XIII, has risen to become an important officer in the court, and is now the open and avowed enemy of Richelieu. He hates the minister of state for what he is doing to France; more important, however, is the fact that Cinq-Mars is ambitious to win for himself honors and posts that might allow him to marry Marie de Gonzaga, who, against her will, is being prepared to become the queen of Poland.

To accomplish his ends, Cinq-Mars has earned the king's confidence and has improved his influence with the nobility and the army. He also has gained the support of the duke de Bouillon, who has been estranged from the king by Richelieu. De Bouillon offers strong support, for he has his own army in southern France. Cinq-Mars also has gained the support of Gaston d'Orléans, the king's brother and another of Richelieu's enemies, and of Anne of Austria, the queen, who wishes to protect her children, including the future Louis XIV, from the hatred and ambitions of Richelieu. The success of the plan to depose the minister lies in gaining the king's support and in securing aid from Spain. Cinq-Mars and his fellow conspirators are forced to deal with Spain on their own initiative, for neither King Louis nor his queen can assume responsibility for bringing Spanish troops into France. In addition, Louis XIII has been under the influence of Cardinal Richelieu and his agents for so long that he has little mind of his own and knows almost nothing of the problems, great and small, that daily beset those who are guiding the kingdom of France in those turbulent years of the 1640's.

Taking his chances, Cinq-Mars signs a treaty with Spain and sends a copy, concealed in a hollow staff, via a trusted messenger to Spain. Then Cinq-Mars approaches King Louis and secures his royal permission to revolt against Richelieu, after convincing the king that the revolt will not be against the crown. Immediately afterward, as he is leaving the monarch's apartments, Cinq-Mars realizes that an agent of the cardinal is on his way to seek an audience with King Louis. All Cinq-Mars can do is hope that the king will honor the promise he has given the conspirators.

In order to ensure his union with Marie de Gonzaga, Cinq-Mars has the duchess and himself affianced by a clergyman, an act that is the equivalent of legal marriage. In so doing, however, Cinq-Mars reveals all his plans to the girl in the presence of the priest. Soon afterward, he learns that the priest is not his own agent but is instead a spy for Richelieu. Realizing that his plans are endangered, Cinq-Mars immediately travels to Perpignan, the designated scene of the revolt.

Richelieu has known all the time what is afoot and has made his plans. Having won over the armies, he knows he has nothing to fear in that quarter. He has also arranged for Marie de Gonzaga, in spite of her love for Cinq-Mars, to become queen of Poland. All Richelieu has left to do is to finish off Cinq-Mars and the other conspirators and prevent the treaty from reaching Spain.

The messenger carrying the treaty is intercepted in the Pyrenees by the cardinal's agents and is killed. In order to gain control of the conspirators, Richelieu pretends to resign his post as minister. King Louis realizes within a few hours that he does not know enough about the affairs of the kingdom to rule France. He calls back Richelieu and grants the minister's request to do as he pleases with the conspirators. Gaston d'Orléans is banished, while Cinq-Mars and de Thou are arrested at Narbonne, tried at Lyons by a secret court appointed by Richelieu, and beheaded. Marie de Gonzaga, pawn of the cardinal's political schemes, becomes queen of Poland.

Critical Evaluation:

Although critics have generally respected Alfred de Vigny's *Cinq-Mars* as one of the first important French historical novels, their judgments have varied wildly regarding its literary or artistic worth. Some of these critiques are that *Cinq-Mars* was Vigny's only mediocre work (his ranking as a poet has always been high), that Vigny did not know what he was doing, that he was ideologically confused, that the novel distorts history and truth, and that his plot lacks drama and his characters are flat.

Nevertheless, upon its publication in January, 1826, *Cinq-Mars* achieved popular success and subsequently went through more than a dozen editions. It was translated into English by William Hazlitt (not the famous critic and essayist, but his second son, a lawyer and a specialist in French translations) in 1847, and an American edition followed in 1889. Two other English translations were issued, one by W. Bellingham in 1851 and another, under the title *The Spider and the Fly*, by Madge Pemberton in 1925. As Edgar Allan Poe once pointed out, however, a book may prove exceedingly popular yet have no legitimate literary merit.

The reasons for the contrary critical evaluations of Vigny's *Cinq-Mars* are not difficult to imagine, given its controversial subject matter. Biases regarding politics, religion, and scientism, together with misunderstandings of Vigny's aim and of the generic tendencies of a prose romance, are the culprits. If Vigny's *Cinq-Mars* is to be judged fairly, Vigny's background and his political and moral positions must be understood and weighed in the balance. Likewise, his philosophy of history and his execution of his narrative must be considered in terms of his aim and the attributes found in the genre of the prose romance.

Vigny was born to a distinguished family of aristocrats dating from the ancien régime of prerevolutionary France. He did not regard the French Revolution of 1789-1799 as a progressive event but as a gross error caused by the centralization policy of the royal administration guided by Cardinal Richelieu. To Vigny, this policy, first, impoverished the majority of the rural nobility; second, contributed to the moral degeneracy of the few rich *gentilshommes champêtres* (country gentlemen) who were tempted to desert the land of their fathers and go to Versailles or Paris to purchase an appointment at court; and third, confused and unbalanced the social hierarchy because the state raised money by creating offices to be purchased by the increasingly rich bourgeoisie, who thereby had "nobility" conferred upon them.

Hence, Vigny was a royalist and a legitimist; that is, from a liberal point of view, he was a conservative and a reactionary. So was his mentor, Sir Walter Scott, whose adventures were his way of reacting against the effects of the Industrial Revolution in the region around Birmingham, England. Like Montesquieu, Vigny believed in the political balance of the three governing powers represented by the clergy, the nobility, and the common people. He was convinced that King Louis XIII and his first minister, Richelieu, were responsible for the gross errors that led to the French Revolution.

Therefore, Vigny intended his historical novel to be a thesis narrative, a feudal parable that would prove his moral conclusion. This narrative, however, is a romance and not a novel. That is, it tends toward divinity and the demoniac, dealing as it does with heroes and not with normal humans. The logic of this results in idealization on one hand and in demonization on the other, but it moves beyond the ideal to sink into the morass of the actual in a tragic and ironic conclusion. Armed with his didactic motivation, Vigny tends to allegorize his characterizations and even his settings to dramatize his characters appropriately. In thinking out his plot, his politics drove him to accept the feudal myth as true and forced him to face up to the problem of the relation of history to fiction. Attacked for his manipulation of history, he defensively included a manifesto-like preface, "Réflexions sur la vérité dans l'art" ("Thoughts on Truth in Art"), to the 1829 edition of *Cinq-Mars*, and it remained in place in subsequent editions.

In this preface, Vigny affirmed that the past existed only in the minds of living generations. History was a fabula and a romance originally created, true and experienced, by those who passed it on to later generations by word of mouth. Not knowing more than themselves and nature, there predictably were gaps in their accounts of the chain of events, which the imaginations of contemporary people would have to complete. What was true in fact ("le Vraie dans le fait") had to be complemented by the truth in art ("la Vérité dans l'art"); the first belonged to the narration of events, whereas the second belonged to the explanation of the events. This philosophy accounts for the liberties Vigny took with historical facts. To him, the value of history lay primarily in the moral lessons it taught.

These factors must be taken into consideration if a fair evaluation of the literary worth of *Cinq-Mars* is to be given. Vigny was an honest and sincere man who wrote in terms of his true feelings. *Cinq-Mars* is his protest against the destruction of the feudal aristocracy. Although a pessimist, he was strongly idealistic. In this light, his romance is much more interesting and exciting than has been reported by some critics in the past; indeed, it is eminently worthwhile.

"Critical Evaluation" by Richard P. Benton

Further Reading

Denommé, Robert T. "Alfred Victor de Vigny." In *The Romantic Century: Johann Wolfgang von Goethe to Alexander Pushkin*. Vol. 5 in *European Writers*, edited by Jacques Barzun and George Stade. New York: Charles Scribner's Sons, 1985. An excellent general account of Vigny and his work, including a fine discussion of *Cinq-Mars*.

Doolittle, James. *Alfred de Vigny*. New York: Twayne, 1967. Primarily a critical biography, with an acute and relatively balanced discussion of *Cinq-Mars*.

Jensen, Mark K. "The Relation of History to Literature in Vigny's Thought Before the Preface to *Cinq-Mars*." *French Forum* 18, no. 2 (May, 1993): 165-183. Shows that Vigny was strongly interested in writing about historical subjects—from his tragic dramas written from 1815 through 1817 (which he later destroyed) to the theoretical grounding of his position in the preface to *Cinq-Mars* in 1829.

Kushner, Eva. "Vigny's Vision of History." *Bulletin of the New York Public Library* 69 (1965): 609-617. A study of Vigny in the context of the historical consciousness of French Romanticism that shows him to have been "the most acutely curious inquirer" of all the Romantic writers.

Samuels, Maurice. "Scott Comes to France." In *The Spectacular Past: Popular History and the Novel in Nineteenth-Century France*. Ithaca, N.Y.: Cornell University Press, 2004. Examines the increasing interest in French history after the French Revolution, describing how the novel and other forms of popular entertainment sought to transform the nation's history. The chapter about Sir Walter Scott's influence on the French historical novel mentions *Cinq-Mars*.

Wakefield, David. *The French Romantics: Literature and the Visual Arts, 1800-1840*. London: Chaucer, 2007. Wakefield's study of the close relationship of literature and painting in the French Romantic period devotes a chapter to Vigny.

Wren, Keith. "A Suitable Case for Treatment: Ideological Confusion in Vigny's *Cinq-Mars*." *Forum for Modern Language Studies* 18, no. 4 (October, 1982): 335-350. Takes issue with Marxist interpretations that *Cinq-Mars* is a "straightforward threnody for the defunct second estate," the nobility. Argues that, on the contrary, the romance is ideologically confused and hence fails to demonstrate its thesis that the destruction of the nobility resulted in the collapse of the whole of society.

The City of God

Author: Saint Augustine (354-430)
First published: De civitate Dei, 413-427 C.E. (English translation, 1610)
Type of work: Religious philosophy

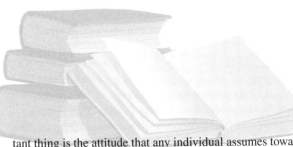

Saint Augustine is one of the most important theologians of the Christian church. He was born a Roman citizen in North Africa. Although he was trained as a classical scholar and was a teacher of rhetoric in Rome and Milan, he became a priest under the influence of Saint Ambrose in Milan and then served as bishop of Hippo in North Africa. His extensive writings include commentaries on books of the Bible, sermons, letters, and his famous autobiographical *Confessiones* (397-401; *Confessions*, 1620), which recounts his spiritual journey from his youth to his full acceptance of Christian beliefs during his years in Milan. Among these works, *The City of God* stands out as the most complete exposition of Saint Augustine's Christian theology.

Saint Augustine wrote *The City of God* during the later years of his life. The catalyst for writing *The City of God* was a key event in the history of the Roman Empire: the sack of Rome in 410 by the Visigoths, a barbarian Germanic tribe. This event shook the dwindling confidence of the civilized Roman Empire. The remaining pagan Romans blamed the Christian religion for this catastrophe, and Christians became insecure about their faith. In *The City of God*, Saint Augustine addresses these charges and fears.

The City of God is more than a defense of Christianity in response to a particular historical circumstance. Saint Augustine planned to write a work that set forth his worldview in its entirety, and *The City of God* fulfilled that goal. It is a lengthy work whose composition took about fifteen years. It contains twenty-two books, which can be divided into two thematic parts. The first ten books, books 1 through 10, are apologetic. Their primary purpose is to counter the accusations of pagans about Christianity, especially in view of the recent attack on Rome. In the second part, books 11 through 22, Augustine presents his view of Christian history and the history of salvation as epitomized in his account of the two cities, the heavenly and the earthly. Both parts contain sections that expressly refute pagan beliefs, and both parts develop Saint Augustine's ideas about the two cities.

Book 1 serves as a preamble because it confronts the immediate issues that the sack of Rome raised and it introduces the concept of the two cities. Augustine believed that disasters indiscriminately befall the good and the bad; the impor-

tant thing is the attitude that any individual assumes toward those circumstances. The true goal is the heavenly City of God, and its citizens, the righteous, are merely pilgrims as they sojourn through life in the earthly city.

Books 2 and 3 demonstrate that the pagan gods never protected the Romans. By surveying the numerous wars, internal conflicts, and natural disasters that Rome endured, Augustine reinforces the message that the Romans' pagan religion never prevented these calamities. Augustine then discusses the character of the Roman Empire and its rulers in books 4 and 5. He points out that God ordains the rise and fall of kingdoms and their rule by just or unjust rulers. Under God's omniscience, Roman power arose because of the virtues of Roman citizens and their leaders under Roman law, reaching its zenith under Christian emperors such as Constantine and Theodosius in the fourth century. In book 5, Augustine's description of the character of the just Christian ruler became a model of conduct, perhaps not always upheld perfectly, for Christian kings.

Books 6 and 7 turn from the politically oriented remarks about the Roman Empire to aspects of Roman religion. These passages provide an extensive catalog of the Roman gods. Augustine exposes the contradictions in the polytheistic Roman religion and demonstrates their lack of spiritual fulfillment, which, he argues, only the true Christian God can offer through the promise of eternal life. The first part concludes in books 8 through 10 by examining the claims of classical philosophy, particularly Platonism and its heir Neoplatonism. While Augustine acknowledges that philosophers articulated concepts about a transcendent one or god, the primary flaws in pagan philosophy are its acceptance of pagan beliefs, particularly in demon powers, and its inability to recognize Christ as the mediator between God and humanity.

The second major section, books 11 to 22, explains the origin, history, and ultimate end of the two cities. These twelve books can be subdivided into three groups of four books each. The first four, books 11 to 14, discuss the rise of the two cities from the Creation through the fall of Adam and Eve. The earthly city (sometimes called Babylon) came about from two events: the fall of angels and the fall of humanity. In both cases, willful behavior is the agency of bad deeds, not the essential nature of angels or humans, which is good. Books 12 and 13 refute a cyclical view of history in favor of a linear concept beginning with the Fall and proceeding toward the ultimate end of time in the Last Judgment. Book 14 summarizes the consequences of this situation in the formation of the two cities: the earthly city "seeks glory from men"; for the heavenly city (City of God or Jerusalem), God is "the greatest glory."

Augustine continues the history of the two cities in the next four books, 15 to 18. His account primarily covers biblical history from Adam's children Cain and Abel, who represent the two cities, through the advent of Christ. Particularly in book 18, biblical history is related to world history, including Assyria, Egypt, Greece, and Rome. The biblical narrative emphasizes prophecies about the coming of Christ, while the overview of world history takes additional opportunities to refute pagan beliefs.

With the coming of Christ, Augustine reaches his own age, and the last four books, 19 to 22, look toward the final destiny of the heavenly city. Book 19 is important because it contains most of Augustine's views about politics and society. Although true peace can be achieved only in the eternal City of God, he argues, society on earth can strive for peace and order through a well-administered state. The final three books deal with last things: the Last Judgment in book 20, the punishments of Hell in book 21, and the perfect harmony of God in Heaven for eternity in book 22. Thus, the two cities are a history of God's redemptive plan of salvation from the original Fall through the biblical history of God's people and other secular kingdoms until the final fruition of the City of God at the end of time. On Earth, in historical time, the course of the two cities is intertwined. While the citizens of the earthly city act out of self-interest, the citizens of the heavenly city think of themselves as transient pilgrims in this world, whose actions are guided only by the love of God. Their final reward will come not on Earth, but in the City of God, "the kingdom which has not end," where they will "rest and see, see and love, love and praise."

The City of God articulates most definitively the change from the humanistic viewpoint of classical philosophy to the God-centered outlook of the Christian Middle Ages. Throughout this work, Augustine challenges and refutes the belief systems of classical Roman culture, including the Roman religion, philosophy, and the political foundation of the Roman Empire. In its place, he puts forward the City of God, the eternal, heavenly city as the ultimate goal of righteous Christians. While it is a duty of citizens of the heavenly city to work for the greatest peace and order during their lifetime

spent in the earthly city, their ultimate concern is not with matters in this world but in the next world of the City of God.

In addition to this fundamental shift in perspective, from the Middle Ages to the present, *The City of God* was utilized often as a source of political ideas and to support particular political positions. Writing a treatise on political theory was not Augustine's purpose. In examining the character of the Roman Empire and its governance, however, particularly in the first part, and in confronting the reality of the earthly city in the second part, Augustine voices opinions on the way society should function. He believed in a separation between earthly political institutions, whose concern is social needs, and God's kingdom in heaven, whose concern is spiritual welfare and salvation. Even the Church as an institution of human agency is not to be equated with the heavenly city, and a Christian empire led by a Christian ruler is not God's agent on Earth. The most that can be expected of human government is the maintenance of an ordered and relatively harmonious society that will facilitate the journey of the citizens of the heavenly city in their pilgrimage through earthly life. Many of Augustine's comments on political matters, such as the discussion of the characteristics of the model Christian ruler in book 5, are designed as a guide to bring about this ideal of a peaceful existence in a troubled and tension-filled world.

One of Augustine's most original and influential contributions in *The City of God* was to articulate a new view of history. The idea of history in classical antiquity was primarily cyclical, and historical writing tended to be an accumulation of facts and observations. Augustine, in contrast, emphasized a linear and progressive view of history, which he develops in the second part of *The City of God*. The course of history begins with the Creation, but the defining event is the fall of humanity from God's grace. From that point, God's plan of redemption governs the course of history which proceeds to the final goal of the Last Judgment at the end of time. While *The City of God* was significant in redirecting the focus of the human viewpoint from the Earth-centered world of classical antiquity to the God-centered universe of the Middle Ages, the most enduring influence of *The City of God* in Western culture was the establishment of the progressive and developmental concept of history. This concept remains pervasive in interpreting the meaning of historical events.

Karen Gould

Further Reading

Battenhouse, Roy W., ed. *A Companion to the Study of St. Augustine*. New York: Oxford University Press, 1955. A collection of essays about Saint Augustine's life and works. Contains an essay by Edward R. Hardy, Jr., on *The City of God* and other essays that interpret the work within the context of Saint Augustine's thought.

Brown, Peter. *Augustine of Hippo*. New ed. Berkeley: University of California Press, 2000. One of the best biographical accounts of Saint Augustine, this book uses a chronological approach to reveal how his writings evolved during his lifetime. Heavily annotated.

_____. *Religion and Society in the Age of Augustine*. New York: Harper & Row, 1972. Places Saint Augustine in historical context.

Clark, Mary T. *Augustine*. Washington, D.C.: Georgetown University Press, 1994. A biographical sketch of the life of Saint Augustine, including his long search for truth that led to his conversion to Christianity. Evaluates many of his ideas. Gives an excellent summary of the nature and impact of *The City of God.*

Deane, Henry. *The Political and Social Philosophy of Saint Augustine*. New York: Columbia University Press, 1963. A treatment of the theological basis of Saint Augustine's belief about the "fallen man" or the idea of Original Sin and the resulting sinful nature of humanity. Also covers morality and justice, the state and order, the Church, heresy, and Saint Augustine's philosophy of history.

Dodaro, Robert. *Christ and the Just Society in the Thought of Augustine*. New York: Cambridge University Press, 2004. An analysis of Saint Augustine's ideas about politics and ethics, focusing on *The City of God* and other works in which he describes the relationship between Christ and the believers who accept Christ as the only source of the soul's virtue.

Elshtain, Jean Bethke. *Augustine and the Limits of Political Power*. Notre Dame, Ind.: University of Notre Dame Press, 1995. Demonstrates the relevancy of Saint Augustine's political theories to modern politics. Elshtain tries to adapt *The City of God* to twentieth century conditions; although some of the arguments are sound, Elshtain's conclusions are not entirely realistic.

Harrison, Carol. *Augustine: Christian Truth and Fractured Humanity*. New York: Oxford University Press, 2000. Examines the social and cultural conditions that shaped Saint Augustine's life.

Markus, R. A. *Saeculum: History and Society in the Theology of St. Augustine*. New York: Cambridge University Press, 1970. A study of *The City of God* that concentrates on Saint Augustine's concepts of history and the political place of society in history.

O'Daly, Gerard. *Augustine's "City of God": A Reader's Guide*. New York: Oxford University Press, 1999. Provides a detailed commentary on each part of the work; information on early fifth century politics, society, history, and literature; and *The City of God*'s place within Saint Augustine's oeuvre.

Van Oort, Johannes. *Jerusalem and Babylon: A Study into Augustine's "City of God" and the Sources of His Doctrine of the Two Cities*. New York: Brill, 1991. A complete study of *The City of God*, its compositional structure, the meaning of the two cities, and its character as an apologetic and theological work. The sources of Saint Augustine's ideas receive full examination.

Versfeld, Marthinus. *A Guide to "The City of God."* London: Sheed & Ward, 1958. A study of the second part of Saint Augustine's *The City of God*, interpreted from the perspective of moral philosophy.

The City of the Sun

Author: Tommaso Campanella (1568-1639)
First published: Civitas solis, 1623 (English translation, 1885)
Type of work: Novel
Type of plot: Utopian

Tommaso Campanella composed *The City of the Sun* in Italian in 1602, as *La Città del Sole*. It was not published until after he translated it, with significant changes, into Latin, the language of the learned during his time. The Italian version is generally regarded as truer to Campanella's thought.

The work is very much a product of its time and Campanella's life. The scientific worldview—that nature can be known by observing the things of this world—was developing, but the medieval view was still powerful. A member of the Dominican order and a learned man, Campanella had been trained in the medieval view that truth was largely to be sought through traditional logic and revelation, but he had reacted against too absolute a version of that view. As a result, Campanella suffered greatly for his religious and political ideas; he was imprisoned by the Inquisition. In this work, he offers a kind of order in which people like himself would have a real function.

The Englishman Thomas More had published, in 1516, his *De Optimo Reipublicae Statu, deque Nova Insula Utopia* (*Utopia*, 1551), a Renaissance version of Plato's *Politeia*, 388-366 B.C.E. (*Republic*, 1701). Their ideas of the perfect state underlie Campanella's. Although Campanella's subtitle is "a poetical dialogue," the work is a prose dialogue, in which a Genoese traveler, supposedly a sailor with Columbus, is questioned by a knight of the Order of Hospitalers of Saint John. The Genoese describes his visit to the City of the Sun, a utopian state which Campanella locates in, probably, Ceylon (Sri Lanka). The Hospitaler has little to say, his role being simply to feed questions to the Genoese. There are almost no critical responses to the traveler's assertions of what this utopia is or what it values.

The Genoese begins by describing the city itself, an ordered city built on a hill. It is defended by a series of seven great circular walls. On these walls are paintings, an early visual aid for purposes of teaching. Each circle is named after one of the planets, for astrology plays an important part in this utopia. (Campanella, an astrologer himself, regarded astrology as a science.) On the top of the hill, in the center of the city, is a magnificent temple, also designed to teach. Everything in the city is intended to teach, even if delightfully. Most of what is taught is useful knowledge and the values of the City of the Sun.

After the physical description, the Genoese speaks of the city's organization, in which everything is arranged so as to offer order, security, and companionship to all of its inhabitants. One can say that the impulse behind utopias is always the human need for community.

In both Campanella and Plato, the state absolutely controls the lives of all who live in it. To make the state more than just a tyranny, Plato developed the ideal of the philosopher-king, which was imitated by Campanella. That is, the man who is wise and knowledgeable should rule over, but in the interests of, those who are weaker and less able. There is an elite ruling class, but it is not hereditary, for a hereditary ruling class cannot guarantee ability and will soon decay.

The Genoese traveler admires the City of the Sun, where there is no poverty, almost no crime, and very little vice. Everyone serves the state and receives everything from the state. As there is no private ownership, no one can become rich, and no one is poor. Although some people receive honors for service to the community, including the right to wear better or distinctively marked clothing, they are not given private wealth. Most people dress alike. They live in dormitories; every six months, they are moved to new quarters. They eat communally; their food is simple and healthful. All the young, not just a few, must wait on the others. There is a slight inequality in that officials get better portions, but they can share these with other persons as a sign of honor. This healthy life enables the residents to live long lives, most to one hundred years of age, a few to two hundred.

Most of the people of the Sun, the Solarians, are presented as being happy with their existence, including the rules they must live by. They accept their officials, because these officials are the most knowledgeable and capable in their various fields. These men are not chosen by popularity or promises: Some are elected; the four top officials and some subordinates select the others. The only criterion is the ability to best fill the office. The four highest officials are self-selected, in that they agree to willingly step down if someone is found who knows their jobs better.

At the apex of the state and the state religion is a single man, called the "Sun" or the "Metaphysician," who must be almost universal in his knowledge. In Campanella's concept of the state, the secular and the religious should not be separated. The Solarians' religion is a kind of Christianity without Christ. They know about and honor Jesus, as they know about all other religions. The Hospitaler, listening to the Genoese (and no doubt with Campanella's approval), suggests that when the Solarians become Christian, their state truly will be the perfect state.

Under the Sun are three other major officials, "Power," "Wisdom," and "Love," each in charge of a major concern of the state. (One should note that these titles are attributes of God in Christianity.) These people need not know everything, but each must know well the matters entrusted to him.

"Power" is the war leader, chosen, like his subordinates, from the most courageous and able. He and his authority are necessary, because no state is safe in which individuals make their own decisions about what they should do in war. The neighboring states are continual threats, so the Solarians, even if they wish peace, will have to fight, but always defensively. Physical courage and ability are rewarded not by wealth or material goods, but by status and such symbols as a crown of oak leaves. Men and women are trained for war. The Genoese says that they would be trained for war even if they were not threatened, because such training keeps them from laziness. Idleness is a crime. The old and the infirm can serve, even in war, for if one is lame, that person still has eyes and can be a sentry.

"Wisdom" directs the sciences, as well as all practical matters. Practical life is of primary importance for all but the highest officials. The Solarians see labor as a communal activity, something everyone shares and from which everyone gains, not just a selected few. A craftsman is as important as anyone else. The Solarians laugh at the Europeans who esteem an idle upper class that is ignorant of crafts. The Solarians also honor agriculture, all going out to the fields in troops at the proper times, and value practical inventiveness. They are ahead of the Europeans in this regard: They have ships that move without oars or sails, and have even learned to fly.

Campanella suggests that love of labor can be taught. Although children are allowed to play, their play is physical so that their bodies are strengthened. The Solarians have no games that can be played sitting down. Children are observed so as to see what jobs they like and can do, so that workers fit and are happy with their jobs. The system is efficient and labor is not wasted on luxuries, so the Solarians work only four hours a day. As in war service, there is an equality of the sexes, although the heavier physical tasks are assigned to men.

The official "Love" is in charge of matters of sex. Sex in the City of the Sun is not for the pleasure of individuals. Like labor, it is a social matter. Although the delights of sex are admitted, its primary purpose must be procreation, because the Solarians believe that the state, to last, must be concerned with the kind of citizens that it has. Only the fit should have children. There is a certain sexual freedom, but sex is rather strictly controlled. Men and women may cohabit with many others, but chastity is valued up to a certain age, because restraint is thought to produce better children. Men and women come together only when the astrological signs are right, so as to ensure strong offspring. To keep balance, weak men are paired with strong women, so that the children will be fit. As the Solarians regard height, liveliness, and strength as beauty, there are no foolish unions based upon what Europeans imagine as beauty.

There is a paradox here. The Sun and other high officials, although necessarily capable of many practical things, spend most of their time in speculative thought, and so lack "animal spirits," that is, sexual drive. In order for them to father strong children, they must choose only the most vital, active women.

There are no families in the usual sense. Here is the basis of Solarian communism. The Genoese traveler explains that

the people of the Sun believe that when men set up families, with homes for their wives and children, egoism enters. The father wants to help his children, so he begins to acquire property. Therefore, to keep people from pursuing wealth, there are no permanent unions. The whole community becomes the family. That love that otherwise would be directed to a small group is directed toward the community. The Genoese remarks that the Solarians love their country in the way the ancient Romans did, giving up family, personal liberty, and life for the state.

Like Plato's state, Campanella's utopia is based upon a rather pessimistic concept of human nature. Human beings are capable of evil; therefore, to preserve the ideal community, the state must direct the fallible individual. There is crime, so there is punishment, even the death penalty, in this commonwealth, admittedly rare but necessary nevertheless.

Campanella's ideal state is not an egalitarian state, although that is supposedly because, without control by the wisest and the best, there is no order. Even if women get the same education as men, are apparently eligible for all offices, are almost equal to men in war, and, because there are no marriages, not controlled by one man, the state is still, in the end, patriarchal, for Campanella has only males in power.

L. L. Lee

Further Reading

Bonansea, Bernardino M. *Tommaso Campanella: Renaissance Pioneer of Modern Thought*. Washington, D.C.: Catholic University of America Press, 1969. A generally difficult book, but the chapter on *The City of the Sun* is quite clear and useful. Includes notes and an extensive bibliography.

Donno, Daniel J. Introduction to *La Città del Sole*. Berkeley: University of California Press, 1981. The introduction gives a sketch of Campanella's life and discusses the themes of *The City of the Sun*.

Eurich, Nell. *Science in Utopia: A Mighty Design*. Cambridge, Mass.: Harvard University Press, 1967. Examines Campanella's interest in and defense of science. This book's brief section on him is very helpful.

Headley, John M. *Tommaso Campanella and the Transformation of the World*. Princeton, N.J.: Princeton University Press, 1997. A biography and critical examination of Campanella's texts. Headley demonstrates how all of Campanella's intellectual pursuits were a means of imposing a distinctive order and direction upon the major forces of his time. There are numerous references to *The*

City of the Sun throughout the book and listed in the index; chapter 7 devotes sixteen pages to this work.

Malcolm, Noel. "The Crescent and *The City of the Sun*: Islam and the Renaissance Utopia of Tommaso Campanella." In *2003 Lectures*. New York: Oxford University Press, 2004. Malcolm argues that the "theme of Islam, the Ottoman system, and Ottoman power" is the essential "thread" that enables one to understand and interpret *The City of the Sun*.

Manuel, Frank E., and Fritzie P. Manuel. *Utopian Thought in the Western World*. Cambridge, Mass.: Belknap Press, 1979. An excellent chapter on Campanella and *The City of the Sun*. Notes, bibliography.

Negley, Glenn, and J. Max Patrick. *The Quest for Utopia: An Anthology of Imaginary Societies*. New York: Henry Schuman, 1952. Includes a partial translation of *The City of the Sun* and a short, insightful introduction.

Civil Disobedience

Author: Henry David Thoreau (1817-1862)
First published: 1849, as "Resistance to Civil Government"
Type of work: Social criticism

The long autobiographical essay most commonly known as "Civil Disobedience" was first published as "Resistance to Civil Government" in the magazine *Æsthetic Papers* in 1849. The essay appeared under its common title in *A Yankee in Canada, with Anti-slavery and Reform Papers* (1866), a collection of his works. The essay grew out of a series of lectures, "The Rights and Duties of the Individual in Relation to Government," which Thoreau delivered to the Concord Lyceum in 1848.

Two years before the Lyceum lectures, in midsummer 1846, Thoreau spent a night in jail because he had refused to pay six years of delinquent poll taxes. He argued that he could not pay funds that helped to support the U.S. government's war with Mexico, nor could he pay a government that still accepted slavery in its Southern states. Thoreau regarded the war as unjust and staunchly opposed slavery. Over his protests, one of his relatives paid his taxes, and Thoreau was released.

Thoreau's short stay behind bars helped inspire his great political essay. In it, he begins with an assertion of the desirability of limited government, subject to not only democratic will but also the conscience of the individual. The opening statement, "I heartily accept the motto, 'that government is best which governs least,'" establishes Thoreau as highly skeptical of political authority. He extends the criticisms of standing armies, which were often identified as instruments of tyranny in early American political thinking, to government itself, and argues that government is often an instrument of abuse against the people. Still, although Thoreau may be a philosophical anarchist, he specifically states that having no government at all will be practicable only when the people are prepared for such a situation, and he implies that, in his own day, they are not prepared. Nevertheless, he maintains that government is only an instrument through which people act, and that it should leave people alone as much as possible.

The laws passed by government, according to Thoreau, are only reflections of people, and he expresses no regard for law simply because it expresses the will or acceptance of a majority. Laws and government may be improved when they come from conscience, not when conscience follows laws or government. He asserts that the U.S. government does not merit his support because of the war on Mexico and the existence of slavery in the South. Given Thoreau's view of government, he does not believe that these injustices can be righted by the democratic means of voting, since voting simply expresses the acceptance of the will of a majority, not a dedication to the dictates of one's own conscience.

The commitment to justice does not mean that Thoreau believes he has an obligation to right the wrongs of the world. In fact, he explicitly states that no one has the duty to eradicate even the greatest of wrongs. He says that he was born to live in the world, not to make it a better place to live. However, he also claims that the wrongs of the world continue to exist because people are willing to support them. His obligation is to refuse to be a party to the wrongdoing, and not to participate in political procedures for change. Thoreau's essay, then, argues not for disobedience as a strategy of political engagement, but as an act of moral disengagement from politics.

Thoreau's disengagement should not be confused with inaction, though. Instead, it is a type of face-to-face action. When the conscientious person meets the agent of the state, in the form of the tax collector, that person can refuse to be a party to wrongdoing by refusing to pay taxes. Furthermore, the objector should recommend that the tax collector resign the official position and also refuse allegiance to the state. If the government imprisons the objector or confiscates property as a response, then that government, which is engaged in immoral actions, simply reaffirms the moral position of the objector outside the state. According to Thoreau, because money itself is issued by the state, a truly virtuous person would be likely to have little money or property and therefore will show little concern over any confiscation. Each act of refusal undermines governmental power, since this power exists only in obedience.

After the theoretical discussion of his views on the relationship between the individual and the state, Thoreau describes his own experiences directly. He discusses first how he had previously refused to pay taxes to support his family's church, which he himself did not attend. After someone else first paid that tax for him, he resolved the situation by giving local officials a written statement that he was not a member of the church and that he did not want to support any organization he had not voluntarily joined. He goes on to recount that he has paid no poll tax for six years.

He explains that his refusal to pay the poll tax led to his detention in jail for a night. In his mind, the walls between himself and his townspeople simply make him freer than the others, since he is acting in accord with his own thoughts. Thoreau's description of his time in jail reads more like an account of a vacation than a punishment. He describes arriving at the jail and finding the prisoners chatting in the doorway until the jailer announces that it is lockup time. His cell-mate had been accused of burning a barn, but Thoreau says that the man had probably just fallen asleep in the barn while drunk and accidentally set fire to it with his pipe.

Thoreau compares being in jail to traveling to a far country, both because it is a new place to him and because it gives him a new perspective on his own town. From the windows of the jail, he says that Concord, Massachusetts, seems as strange as a medieval land. When he leaves the jail, he sees his neighbors as foreigners, guided by odd prejudices rather than by reason.

Thoreau ends the essay by returning to his political philosophy. His refusal to pay the tax, he explains, is a refusal of allegiance to the government. In this way, he quietly declares war on the state. In the end, he returns to the beginning of the essay with remarks on the future of government. The progress from absolute to limited monarchy and from limited monarchy to democracy, can be carried further by moving toward the individual as an independent source from which all power and authority are derived.

The government of the United States arguably did not evolve in the direction Thoreau wished; it emerged from the American Civil War with a larger and more centralized political authority. The decades following Thoreau's essay also saw the rise of the modern corporation, which challenged his style of individualism, even if it eventually produced great material abundance. Slavery, one of the two provocations for Thoreau's act of refusal, did not end as a consequence of individual civil disobedience but as a result of the Civil War, which was led by officers of the Union and Confederacy who had learned military tactics in the war with Mexico. Still, Thoreau's ideal of principled refusal continues to inspire thinkers and activists, and his version of individual autonomy remains a part of the self-image and values of many Americans.

Carl L. Bankston III

Further Reading

Bedau, Hugo Adam, ed. *"Civil Disobedience" in Focus.* New York: Routledge, 1991. An examination of the philosophical arguments on civil disobedience. Part 1, covering the classic arguments, includes discussions of Plato on Socrates, Thoreau's essay, and the thinking of Martin Luther King, Jr. Helpful for examining Thoreau's thinking in terms of a broader tradition in political and social thought.

Cain, William E., ed. *A Historical Guide to Henry David Thoreau.* New York: Oxford University Press, 2000. A collection of essays on Thoreau's work, its influence, and his relation to his times. Readers interested in "Civil Disobedience" will want to look at the chapter "The Theory, Practice, and Influence of Thoreau's 'Civil Disobedience.'"

Milder, Robert. *Reimagining Thoreau.* 1994. Reprint. New York: Cambridge University Press, 2008. Although concerned mostly with Thoreau's *Walden: Or, Life in the Woods* (1854), this combined psychological and literary biography examines his complex relationship with the

Concord community. Sheds considerable light on the attitudes and motivations behind "Civil Disobedience."

Petrulionis, Sandra Harbart. *To Set This World Right: The Antislavery Movement in Thoreau's Concord.* Ithaca, N.Y.: Cornell University Press, 2006. An examination of the social setting behind Thoreau's opposition to slavery. Looks at the movement against slavery in Concord and discusses

the radicalism among Thoreau's neighbors. A useful book for placing Thoreau's thinking in its social context.

Tauber, Alfred I. *Henry David Thoreau and the Moral Agency of Knowing.* Berkeley: University of California Press, 2001. A philosophical account of Thoreau's life and work that explains both as attempts at achieving virtue through self-knowledge.

Civilization and Its Discontents

Author: Sigmund Freud (1856-1939)
First published: Das Unbehagen in der Kultur, 1930 (English translation, 1930)
Type of work: Psychology

Sigmund Freud's *Civilization and Its Discontents,* one of his last and most influential books, treats human misery in establishing ideas about repression and the place of humans in the world. The book's leading concepts can be traced back to Freud's earliest pronouncements on incest in his letters to Wilhelm Fliess from the late 1890's. A full analysis of the restrictions on the individual from external and internal forces that pave the way to civilization was not possible until Freud's investigations of ego-psychology had led him to his hypotheses on the superego in *Das Ich und das Es,* 1923 (*The Ego and the Id,* 1926). Only by clarifying the nature of the superego and the sense of guilt—which he later declared to be the maker of civilized humanity—could he begin to explore the clash of that sense of guilt with the aggressive instinct derived from the self-destructive death drive that he had first confronted in *Jenseits des Lustprinzips,* 1920 (*Beyond the Pleasure Principle,* 1922). Using the concepts of the superego, the sense of guilt, and the aggressive instinct, Freud formulated the main theme of *Civilization and Its Discontents*: the ineradicable antagonism between the demands of the individual's instincts and the restrictions of civilization.

The small book is divided into eight short chapters, each packed with complex ideas and analyses. Freud begins with a meditation on belief, discussing the "oceanic feeling"—a peculiar mood that he had found confirmed by many, in which the individual feels a sensation of "eternity," something limitless and unbounded, and of being one with the whole external world. Although Freud admits he has not discovered this feeling within himself, he uses the concept to discuss the

nursing infant who initially does not distinguish between his or her own ego and the external world. Because of internal pain and response from the external world to that pain, the infant begins the process of differentiating between what is internal (what belongs to the ego) and what is external (what emanates from the external world). In so doing, he or she arrives at the influence of the reality principle, which dominates further development, and the constructed ego, which will maintain sharp lines of demarcation toward the outside. The mature ego-feeling as separate and defined is, in fact, a shrunken residue of the all-embracing primary ego-feeling of infancy.

When this primary ego-feeling of undifferentiation persists alongside the sharply demarcated ego-feeling of maturity, the result is the "oceanic feeling." Freud explains that what is primitive in the mind is preserved alongside the transformed. To further elucidate this concept, he uses one of his most famous analogies: As in twenty-first century Rome, underneath which there are ancient cities, so in mental life everything is preserved and, given the appropriate circumstances, can be brought back to life.

In his critique of religion, Freud maintains that in childhood, there is no need as strong as the need for a father's protection. He traces the religious attitude in the adult back to the feeling of infantile helplessness. For the adult, likewise, a belief in God is the attempt to pacify the need for protection from the threatening dangers of the external world. The "oceanic feeling" becomes connected with religion because its recollection offers again the sense of protection and oneness and provides consolation for the imperiled ego. This throwback to infancy for consolation, Freud concludes, reveals that religion is patently infantile and foreign to reality.

Yet Freud concedes that life is hard, and that humans are faced with too many pains, disappointments, and impossible tasks. Humans therefore take palliative measures by drawing on the substitutive satisfactions offered by such deflections as art or intoxicating substances. Freud defines happiness as the absence of pain in combination with strong feelings of pleasure. In the quest for happiness, the purpose of life is the pleasure principle; however, all the rules of the universe run counter to it. Humans are threatened with suffering from three sources: the body, the external world, and the relations to others.

In opposition to the external world, humans have become members of a community within which individuals work for the good of all and for which the individuals attempt to control their instincts. The aim of the pleasure principle is not relinquished, but a measure of protection against suffering is secured by means of sublimating instincts. Work, both physical and intellectual, yields pleasure and provides security within the human community. Another method by which humans strive to gain pleasure is in loving and being loved, although it is in this state that humans are the most defenseless against suffering. Religion also offers a path to happiness and protection from suffering, but Freud sees it as doing so by restricting choice, decreasing the value of life, distorting the picture of the real world, and placing believers in a state of psychic infantilism that draws them into a mass delusion. Freud's critical analysis of religion seems particularly germane to the phenomenon of religious cults.

Freud goes on to suggest that happiness is so hard to achieve because of the superior power of nature, the feebleness of the human body, and the inadequacy of the artificial regulations that maintain relations in the family, state, and society. Civilization serves two purposes: to protect humans against nature and to regulate human relations. Some nevertheless argue that civilization is largely responsible for human misery. There are those, for example, who cannot tolerate the frustrations that society imposes in the service of cultural ideals. Civilization (like human activity) strives toward goals of utility and a measured yield of pleasure. Yet, because the power of the community is in opposition to the power of the individual, community is possible only when a majority is stronger than any separate individual. The final outcome of law is a sacrifice of the individual's instincts; members of a community restrict themselves in their possible satisfaction because justice demands that no one escape these restrictions. The struggle of humanity centers on the claim of the individual and the cultural claims of the group.

Using suppression and repression, civilization is built on a renunciation of instinct. If, however, a deprived instinct of satisfaction is not compensated, Freud warns, disorders will ensue.

Freud states that although Eros (love) and Ananke (necessity) are the driving forces of civilization, the tendency of civilization is to restrict sexual life (the vital drive of Eros) as it expands the culture unit. The founding of families made genital eroticism central while also restricting it; humans made themselves dependent on a chosen love-object and, in so doing, exposed themselves to extreme suffering. Since, moreover, a community requires a single kind of sexual life, it is necessarily intolerant of deviation from the norm, which leads to potentially serious injustices when deviation is judged as perversion. Freud maintains that humans are organisms with a bisexual disposition but that the sexual life of civilized humans is severely circumscribed by heterosexuality. Civilization summons up aim-inhibited libido to strengthen the communal bond through friendship, but for this to be fulfilled, sexual restrictions are unavoidable.

Freud goes on to insist that the golden rule ("Thou shalt love thy neighbor as thyself") cannot be recommended as reasonable. Humans are aggressive, not gentle, and one's neighbor is one who tempts, exploits, rapes, steals, humiliates, and even kills. Aggression is an instinctual disposition and forces civilization into a high expenditure of energy because instinctual passions are stronger than reason. It is, for example, possible to bind a number of people in love only as long as there are other people to receive their aggressiveness. The Jewish people, Freud observes, have served civilizations in this way for centuries. Civilization is a process in the service of Eros to combine individuals, families, races, peoples, and nations into greater unities, but the inclination to aggression constitutes the greatest impediment to such bonds. The evolution of civilization, the human species' struggle for life, is the struggle between Eros (life) and Thanatos (death).

Civilization inhibits aggressiveness that opposes it by sending that aggressiveness back where it came from—to the ego of the individual, where it is internalized as the superego. In the form of conscience or guilt, the superego then sets up an agency within the individual to disarm the dangerous desire for aggression. Threatened external unhappiness—loss of love or punishment by an external authority—is exchanged for a permanent internal unhappiness caused by the tension of guilt. Paradoxically, Freud points out, the instinctual renunciation imposed by the external world creates the conscience which then demands further instinctual renunciation. Remorse, he writes, presupposes that a conscience is already in place when a misdeed takes place.

The price paid for the advance in civilization is a loss of individual happiness through the heightening of guilt. The development of the individual is a product of the interaction of two urges, the urge toward happiness, called "egoistic," and the urge toward union with others in the community, called "altruistic." Because these two urges oppose each other, individual development and cultural development are in hostile and irreconcilable opposition. The cultural super-ego develops its ideals under the heading of ethics, but the commandment "Love thy neighbor as thyself" is an excellent example, notes Freud, of the unpsychological proceedings of that cultural superego. The commandment is impossible to fulfill, and those who follow it only put themselves at a disadvantage toward those who disregard it.

Freud is skeptical of the enthusiastic affirmation of civilization as the most precious possession of human beings. In conclusion, he offers no consolation, predictions, or even speculations but merely poses two fateful questions: To what extent will cultural development succeed in mastering the disturbances to communal life caused by the human instincts of aggression and self-destruction, and will immortal Eros make a sufficiently powerful effort to assert himself in the struggle with that equally powerful adversary, Death? *Civilization and Its Discontents* represents the summing up of a lifetime of reflection and invention from one of the twentieth century's greatest thinkers.

Janet Mason Ellerby

Further Reading

Bettelheim, Bruno. *Freud and Man's Soul*. London: Pimlico, 2001. Bettelheim argues that the erroneous translation of Freud's most important concepts has led readers to view his work as primarily scientific. In fact, Freud is always deeply personal in his appeals to humanity, and he writes not of what has been mistakenly translated as "mind" or "intellect" but of the soul (*die Seele*).

Elliott, Anthony, ed. *Freud 2000*. Cambridge, England: Polity Press, 1998. Essayists examine how Freud's theories apply to current issues in the social sciences and humanities.

Fromm, Erich. *Greatness and Limitations of Freud's Thought*. New York: New American Library, 1988. This is a critique of Freud by a dissenting psychoanalyst. Fromm believed that Freud exaggerated the role of sex in determining human behavior and that Freud's concept of love was narrow and self-serving.

Gay, Peter. *Freud: A Life for Our Time*. New York: Norton, 2006. In this important biography, Gay discusses in exhaustive detail the entire span of Freud's life, in the process revealing enough conundrums to pique the interest of any psychoanalyst. He devotes an entire chapter to *Civilization and Its Discontents*, including circumstances that precipitated the writing of the book, such as the horrors of World War I and the nature of the Jewish diaspora.

Grubrich-Simitis, Ilse. *Back to Freud's Texts: Making Silent Documents Speak*. Translated by Philip Slotkin. New Haven, Conn.: Yale University Press, 1996. This important contribution to the study of Freud offers understanding of the man as a writer as well as insight into Freud's creative process. The text details the history of Freud's German-language publications and examines key works.

Neu, Jerome, ed. *The Cambridge Companion to Freud*. New York: Cambridge University Press, 1991. Collection of essays analyzing various aspects of Freud's philosophy. Chapter 12, "Freud's Later Theory of Civilization: Changes and Implications" by John Deigh, focuses on *Civilization and Its Discontents*, and there are other references to the book listed in the index.

Parisi, Thomas. *"Civilization and Its Discontents": An Anthropology for the Future?* New York: Twayne, 1999. Discusses the central ideas of the book, including Freud and the unconscious, eros and death, and ethics and reason.

Ricoeur, Paul. *Freud and Philosophy: An Essay on Interpretation*. Translated by Denis Savage. New Haven, Conn.: Yale University Press, 1970. Ricoeur provides an unusual survey of Freudian thought, focusing on language and symbolism with an insightful reading of *Civilization and Its Discontents*, the primordial mutual hostility of human beings, and the cultural function of guilt.

Rieff, Philip. *Freud: The Mind of the Moralist*. 3d ed. Chicago: University of Chicago Press, 1979. Rieff provides clarity to one of the more difficult concepts of *Civilization and Its Discontents*: the relationship between civilization and its treacherous ally, neuroses. Rieff analyzes Freud's ambivalence toward repressive culture and his regard for health at the expense of culture.

Volosinov, V. N. *Freudianism: A Critical Sketch*. Translated by I. R. Titunik. Bloomington: Indiana University Press, 1987. Volosinov provides a useful chapter, "Freudian Philosophy of Culture," in which he elaborates on such central issues of *Civilization and Its Discontents* as social solidarity and cultural creativity.

Clarissa
Or, The History of a Young Lady

Author: Samuel Richardson (1689-1761)
First published: 1747-1748
Type of work: Novel
Type of plot: Sentimental
Time of plot: Early eighteenth century
Locale: England

Principal characters:
CLARISSA HARLOWE, a young woman of family and
   fortune
WILLIAM MORDEN, her cousin
ARABELLA, her older sister
JAMES, her older brother
ROBERT LOVELACE, her seducer
JOHN BELFORD, Lovelace's friend

The Story:

Robert Lovelace, a young Englishman of a noble family, is introduced into the Harlowe household by Clarissa's uncle, who wishes Lovelace to marry Clarissa's older sister, Arabella. The young man instead falls deeply in love with Clarissa, but he quickly learns that his suit is balked by Clarissa's brother and sister. James has disliked Lovelace since they were together at Oxford, and Arabella is offended because he spurns her in favor of Clarissa. Both are jealous of Clarissa because she was left a fortune by their grandfather.

Having convinced his mother and father that Lovelace is a profligate, James proposes that Clarissa marry Mr. Solmes, a rich, elderly man of little taste and no sensibility. When Solmes finds no favor in the eyes of Clarissa, her family assumes she is in love with Lovelace, despite her protestations to the contrary. Clarissa refuses to allow Solmes to visit with her in the parlor or to sit next to her when the family is together. Her father, outraged by her conduct, orders her to be more civil to the man he chose to be her husband. When she refuses, saying she would never marry any man against her will, not even Lovelace, her father confines her to her room.

Lovelace, partly out of love for her and partly in vengeance for the insults heaped upon him by the Harlowe family, resolves to abduct Clarissa from her family. He is greatly aided in this scheme by the domineering personalities of Mr. Harlowe and his son, who took away Clarissa's trusted maid and replaced her with a young woman who is impertinent and insolent to her mistress. They also refuse to let her see any of the family, even her mother. Clarissa's only trusted adviser is Miss Howe, a friend and correspondent who advises her to escape the house if she can, even if it means accepting Lovelace's aid and his proposal of marriage.

One evening, Lovelace slips into the garden where Clarissa is walking and entreats her to elope with him. After some protest, she agrees to go with him so as to escape her domineering father. Lovelace tells her she will be taken to the home of Lord ———, a kinsman of Lovelace, who will protect her until her cousin, Colonel Morden, can return to England and arrange for a reconciliation between Clarissa and her family. Lovelace does not keep his word, however, and takes her instead to a house of ill repute, where he introduces her to a woman he calls Mrs. Sinclair. Inventing reasons why he cannot take her to Lord M———'s house, he persuades the bewildered girl to pose temporarily as his wife. He tells Mrs. Sinclair that Clarissa is his wife with whom he cannot live until certain marriage settlements are arranged. Clarissa permits him to tell the lie, believing that it will prevent her father and her brother from discovering her whereabouts.

In Mrs. Sinclair's house, she is almost as much a prisoner as she was in her father's home. Meanwhile, her family disowns her and refuses to send her either money or clothes. Her father further declares that she is no longer his daughter and that he hopes she will have a miserable existence in both this world and the next. This state of affairs is distressing to Clarissa, who is now dependent upon Lovelace for her very existence. He takes advantage of the circumstances to press his love upon her without mentioning his earlier promises of marriage. Clarissa escapes and gets as far as Hampstead before Lovelace overtakes her. There, he has two women impersonate his cousins to convince Clarissa that she should return to her lodgings with them. Upon her return to Mrs. Sinclair's house, they fill her with drugs, after which Lovelace rapes her. A few days later, Clarissa receives a letter from Miss Howe in which she learns that she is in a house in which no woman of her station would be seen. Again, Clarissa tries to escape by calling for aid from a window. Lovelace finally promises to leave her unmolested until she can get aid from her cousin or from Miss Howe.

Lovelace leaves London for a few days to visit Lord ———, who is ill. While he is gone, Clarissa contrives to steal the clothes of a serving girl and escape from the house, but within a day or two, Mrs. Sinclair discovers Clarissa's whereabouts and has her arrested and imprisoned for debt. When John Belford, a friend of Lovelace, hears of the girl's plight, he rescues her by proving the debt a fraud. He finds shelter for Clarissa with a kindly glovemaker and his wife. Clarissa is worn out by her experiences, and her health declines, in spite of all that the apothecary and doctor secured by Belford do for her. She spends her time writing letters in an effort to secure a reconciliation with her family and to acquaint her friends with the true story of her plight. She refuses to have anything to do with Lovelace, who is by that time convinced that he loves her dearly. He wishes to marry her to make amends for the treatment she suffered at his hands, but she refuses his offer with gentle firmness.

Clarissa's friends do what they can to reunite her with her family. When her father and brother refuse to receive her, she goes to an undertaking establishment and brings a coffin that she fits as she wishes, including a plaque that gives the date of her birth as the day on which she left her father's house.

On his return to England, Colonel Morden tries to raise her spirits, but his efforts fail because he, too, is unable to effect any change in the attitude of the Harlowe family. He also has an interview with Lovelace and Lord ———. The nobleman and Lovelace assure him that their family thinks very highly of Clarissa. They wish her to marry Lovelace, and Lovelace wishes to marry her, but even her cousin is unable to persuade Clarissa to accept Lovelace as a husband.

When the Harlowe family finally realizes that Clarissa is determined to die, her father and brother lift their ban. Her sister is sorry she was cruel to Clarissa, and her mother is convinced that she failed in her duty toward her daughter. They all write to Clarissa, begging the girl's forgiveness and expressing their hope that she will recover quickly and be reunited with her family. Their letters arrive too late, for Clarissa died.

Clarissa's body is returned to her father's house, and she is interred in the family vault at the feet of the grandfather whose fortune had been one of the sources of her troubles. Lovelace, quite distracted by grief, is persuaded by Lord ——— to go to the Continent. There he meets Colonel Morden in France, and early one winter morning, Clarissa's cousin fights a duel with her betrayer. Lovelace is mortally wounded by a thrust through his body. As he dies, he expresses the hope that his death will expiate his crimes.

Critical Evaluation:

Few men would have seemed less likely than Samuel Richardson to be influential in the history of the novel. A suc-

cessful printer, he did not publish his first work until after he was fifty years old. Because of a reputation as an accomplished letter writer, he was encouraged to write a book of sample letters. Even before the publication of this volume, *Letters Written to and for Particular Friends, on the Most Important Occasions* (1741), he turned his epistolary talent to didactic purposes in fiction with the publication of *Pamela* (1740-1741), which was greeted with popular approval and critical disdain. By 1744, he had prepared a summary of his epistolary masterpiece, *Clarissa*. The massive novel was published in three installments between December, 1747, and December, 1748, and was subsequently printed in eight volumes. The length of the novel (about one million words) was probably not a great impediment for the more leisurely reading class of the mid-eighteenth century, but *Clarissa* eventually came to be read mostly in an abridged version by George Sherburn.

Richardson's main literary contribution is his mastery of the epistolary style. The use of letters as a means of narration has obvious drawbacks. Certainly the flow of the narrative is repeatedly interrupted, and it takes all the strength of the reader's will to suspend disbelief concerning the writing of thoughtful and informative letters by characters during periods of extraordinary stress. Conventions aside, it is difficult to sustain a continuous and progressive narrative in this form. The method frustrated Samuel Johnson, a friend of Richardson, who concluded that the work should be read for its sentiment. Richardson himself worried that his narrative technique had let his characters do too much in too short a period of time.

Richardson did, however, capitalize on the correlative advantages of the epistolary method. The immediacy of writing at the moment in which events are occurring is an excellent means of creating concerned attention in the reader. Moreover, Richardson's talent for dialogue transforms many of the lengthier letters into poignant scenes, and the text of each letter is most decorously cast in a style appropriate to the correspondent. There is the further advantage, especially in a didactic novel such as this, of multiple points of view that add complexity and sympathy to the interpretation of events. Letters are not simply presented but copied, sent, received, discussed, answered, intercepted, stolen, altered, and forged. The whole process of correspondence comes alive as Richardson blends theater, moral discourse, courtesy book, and romance into a compellingly tense analysis of contemporary morals and manners.

As the use of the epistolary style would suggest, action is less important to Richardson's fiction than reflection on the moral significance of the action. It may be that the author was familiar with the life of the gentry only through the theater. Nevertheless, despite an apparent ignorance of the occupations of a rich country family, the focus is so much on the tension of the situations and the meaning of actions that little is lost by the absence of sociological verisimilitude. Although Richardson occasionally presents dramatically vivid details, he usually is less interested in setting than in what Sherburn calls, in the contemporary eighteenth century terminology, a "distress."

The main theme of the novel, as described by Richardson on the title page, is "the distresses that may attend the misconduct both of parents and children in relation to marriage." There is no doubt that the motives of the Harlowes are crassly materialistic: to improve the already comfortable family fortune by forcing Clarissa to marry the suitable, but elderly, Solmes. There is a striking lack of tenderness and family feeling toward Clarissa, to whom they soften only after it is too late. Clarissa, for her part, is also strong-willed. As Richardson explains, "The principal of the two young Ladies is proposed as an exemplar of her Sex. Nor is it any objection to her being so, that she is not in all respects a perfect character."

At first, Clarissa is attracted by the roguish but fascinating Lovelace, who occasionally seems not entirely a bad fellow. At least he is the most vivid character in the novel. In his egocentrism and his love of intrigue he is inconsiderate and cruel to others, sins he does not recant until his sentimental dying breaths. After his assault on Clarissa, practicality seems to demand that Clarissa turn virtue into its own reward, as Pamela had done, by marrying her seducer. *Clarissa*, however, is a more complex novel than *Pamela*, and Clarissa and Lovelace have already shown a moral incompatibility that makes acquiescence by Clarissa impossible (despite the impassioned pleadings of Richardson's sentimental readers before the last third of the novel appeared).

At the heart of the incompatibility is Clarissa's rigid idealism. Although a gentle person, she is unreserved in her commitment to virtue and to, as Sherburn puts it, decorous behavior. She is not so much a puritan as a devotee of what is morally fit, and she carries her commitment to the grave. When her friend Miss Howe suggests that she take the expedient way out by marrying the ostensibly repentant Lovelace, Clarissa cannot give in. Her sense of propriety will not allow such moral and personal compromise. Nevertheless, it must be admitted that she is less interesting for her idealism than for the distressing situations and dilemmas her idealism occasions.

Despite its narrative improbabilities, *Clarissa* became a revered example not only of the epistolary novel but also of the refined novel of sentiment, and by the end of the century, the novel had been imitated and acclaimed both in England and on the Continent.

"Critical Evaluation" by Edward E. Foster

Further Reading

Blewitt, David, ed. *Passion and Virtue: Essays on the Novels of Samuel Richardson.* Toronto, Ont.: University of Toronto Press, 2001. A collection of essays examining various aspects of *Clarissa* and Richardson's other novels. Includes discussions of *Clarissa*'s "treasonable" correspondence, the passion of Clarissa Harlowe, *Clarissa* and Scripture, and the gnostic *Clarissa*.

Bueler, Lois E. *Clarissa's Plots.* Newark: University of Delaware Press, 1994. Examines the themes in the novel. Includes bibliographical references and an index.

Castle, Terry. *Clarissa's Ciphers: Meaning and Disruption in Richardson's "Clarissa."* Ithaca, N.Y.: Cornell University Press, 1982. An influential book that provides an interpretation from the perspectives of feminism and reader-response criticism. On the alleged textual incoherence in *Clarissa*, Castle asks: How can one expect coherence from a violated woman?

Doody, Margaret Anne. *A Natural Passion: A Study of the Novels of Samuel Richardson.* New York: Oxford University Press, 1974. Chapters 5 through 9 provide lively, informative, and authoritative discussion of themes and imagery in *Clarissa*. Doody's study is the source of much sympathetic interpretation of *Clarissa* and Richardson's other novels.

Goldberg, Rita. *Sex and Enlightenment: Women in Richardson and Diderot.* New York: Cambridge University Press, 1984. Highly intelligent discussion of *Clarissa* as a "mythic" book—a model for young women to follow. Examines the consequences to young women and their society of attempting to adhere to the prescribed model.

Hill, Christopher. "Clarissa Harlowe and Her Times." In *Samuel Richardson: A Collection of Critical Essays*, edited by John Carroll. Englewood Cliffs, N.J.: Prentice Hall, 1968. The seminal account of the social background of the novel. Includes examination of the economy, Puritanism, and the novel's attitudes toward the individual, the family, and marriage.

Lams, Victor J. *Anger, Guilt, and the Psychology of the Self in "Clarissa."* New York: Peter Lang, 1999. Focuses on Lovelace as a narcissistic personality and Clarissa's forced change of philosophical stance in reaction to his actions. Includes bibliography and index.

_____. *Clarissa's Narrators.* New York: Peter Lang, 2001.

Argues that the novel's structure consists of five movements resembling the acts in a play; these movements emerge from the round-robin transfer of three narrators. Includes bibliography and index.

Warner, William Beatty. *Reading Clarissa: The Struggles of*

Interpretation. New Haven, Conn.: Yale University Press, 1979. Uses a deconstructionist approach to question any supposed need to establish a single authoritative text to *Clarissa.* Argues for the aptness of the novel's conflicting texts. Maintains that Lovelace is the hero of the novel.

The Clayhanger Trilogy

Author: Arnold Bennett (1867-1931)
First published: 1910-1915; includes *Clayhanger*, 1910;
  Hilda Lessways, 1911; *These Twain*, 1915
Type of work: Novels
Type of plot: Domestic realism
Time of plot: 1870-1895
Locale: England

Principal characters:
EDWIN CLAYHANGER, a businessman
HILDA LESSWAYS, his wife
MAGGIE CLAYHANGER, Edwin's sister
MR. INGPEN, Edwin's friend
GEORGE CANNON, Hilda's first husband
DARIUS CLAYHANGER, Edwin's father

The Story:

In 1872, sixteen-year-old Edwin Clayhanger is forced to leave school to help his father in the Clayhanger printing shop. His father disregards Edwin's request that he be allowed to go to school and study to be an architect. Old Darius Clayhanger is a self-made man who rose from a boyhood in the workhouse to the position of affluence he holds in his Midlands community. Since he is a complete tyrant in the home, no one dares to cross him when he insists that his work be carried on by his only son.

Several years later, Darius builds a new house in a more affluent part of town. Edwin becomes friendly with the Orgreave family, who live next door. The elder Orgreave is an architect, with whom Edwin spends many hours discussing that profession. Unknown to Edwin, the oldest Orgreave daughter, Janet, falls in love with him. It is at the Orgreave home that Edwin meets Hilda Lessways, an orphan living in Brighton with the sister of a former employer, George Cannon, who wishes to marry her. Although she is attracted to Edwin, she returns to Brighton and soon after marries Cannon, giving him her small patrimony to invest for her.

By the time Hilda returns to visit the Orgreaves a year later she has learned about her husband's previous marriage, which makes her own marriage to him void. On this second visit, she admits to her love for Edwin and promises to marry him, for no one knows of her marriage at Brighton. Discovering that she is to have a baby, however, she returns to Brighton and writes to Janet to tell her she is married and to ask her to inform Edwin. Deeply hurt, he throws him-

self into his father's business, for his father becomes mentally ill.

Hilda bears her child and names him George Edwin, after his father and Edwin Clayhanger. She manages a rooming house owned by her husband's sister. Cannon, discovered by his first wife, is sentenced to serve a two-year prison term for bigamy. After his release, he is again imprisoned for ten years for passing a forged check. The money he imprudently invested for Hilda was lost when a hotel corporation, whose shares he bought, collapsed. Hilda is thereafter no longer financially independent.

After his father's death, Edwin and his sister Maggie continue to live alone in the Clayhanger house, and the printing business prospers and grows. Both Maggie and Edwin become settled in their habits, although many young women, including Janet, would gladly marry Edwin.

Edwin becomes quite fond of Hilda's son during the boy's visit with the Orgreaves. When George Edwin becomes ill with influenza, it is Edwin who sends for the doctor and notifies Hilda. Although neither speaks openly of his or her feelings, Hilda and Edwin feel their affection for each other return when they meet at the sick child's bedside. Edwin and Hilda met nine years ago. Once the boy recovers, he and his mother go back to Brighton, where Hilda struggles with the failing boardinghouse at Brighton.

Months later, when Edwin goes to see Hilda, he finds her penniless and about to be evicted. Edwin pays her bills, and Hilda tells him all that happened to her, explaining that her marriage was void and her child illegitimate. Edwin returns home but resolves to marry Hilda quietly in London. After marrying, they move into the Clayhanger house and Maggie goes to live with a maiden aunt. Edwin adopts Hilda's son and gives him the name of Clayhanger.

Edwin, having his own way for a long time, is accustomed to a certain routine in his home and to making his own decisions. Hilda has an equally strong personality, however, and Edwin believes that she is trying to make him conform too much to her own views and habits. Most of all he resents her attempts to influence him in business affairs, a realm he thinks solely his own.

A few months after Edwin and Hilda marry, the aunt with whom Maggie Clayhanger is living becomes seriously ill. During her last days, Mr. Ingpen, Edwin's business friend, is injured in a factory accident. At Ingpen's request, Edwin goes to his room to destroy some letters and pictures, so they will not be found if Ingpen dies in the hospital. Edwin finds there a woman sleeping who is Ingpen's mistress; her husband is incurably insane. Edwin is disturbed for his friend, but Ingpen laughs and says that the situation is best because he does not want to be trapped in a marriage.

When Edwin's aunt dies, her estate is left to the children of Edwin's younger sister, Clara. Edwin and Maggie are pleased, but Hilda thinks that she and Edwin should receive part of the estate. Her selfishness irks Edwin. He feels he is rich enough and that his nephews and nieces deserve the money. Nostalgically recalling his bachelor days, he begins to consider that a divorce might be the answer to his situation. The only bright ray in his life seems to be George Edwin, his stepson, who is studying architecture with the aid of John Orgreave. Edwin hopes that his adopted son might have the chance to become an architect.

On a visit to a nearby city, Hilda and Edwin are taken to inspect a prison. There they see Cannon. He is released soon afterward when he is found to be innocent of the forgery charge. When Cannon goes to Edwin without Hilda's knowledge, Edwin gives him money to go to America. Edwin never expects to see the money again, but he wants to get the man out of the country. He is also bothered by the fact that Hilda is in correspondence with Cannon's other wife.

The climax of Edwin's unhappiness with Hilda comes after she takes him to see a house in the country on Christmas Day. She tries to force him to buy it by diplomatic moves and conversations with their friends and family that will leave Edwin appearing foolish if he does not buy the house. After a violent argument, in which he accuses his wife of being grasping, underhanded, and dishonest, Edwin leaves the house in a rage. After a long walk in the cold winter night, he

realizes, however, that his marriage and his wife mean much to him. He realizes that he must make concessions and that they both must contend with having married so late in life, when their habits were already fixed. Finally he recalls his friend Ingpen, who is unable to marry the woman he loves. He goes back to the house to reconcile with Hilda. His faith in human nature is completely reestablished when he finds a check from America in the mail for the money he lent to Cannon.

Critical Evaluation:

Arnold Bennett completed *Clayhanger*, the first novel of the trilogy concerning the life apprenticeship of Edwin Clayhanger, on June 23, 1910, two years after the publication of *The Old Wives' Tale*. At the height of his creative powers and his critical reputation, Bennett ventured to write his most nearly autobiographical novel in a format popular with Edwardian readers. Compared to George Moore's *Confessions of a Young Man* (1888), Samuel Butler's *The Way of All Flesh* (1903), E. M. Forster's *The Longest Journey* (1907), and H. G. Wells's *Tono-Bungay* (1908), *Clayhanger* is a fairly typical bildungsroman, or "education novel." The representative hero of this genre is an inexperienced, often confused, but generally likable young man who, after learning from a series of valuable adventures, develops a better understanding about himself and about life. Typically, the hero comes to terms with his weaknesses and strengths, discovers a proper vocation for his talents, and begins to understand the meaning and limitations of romantic love.

Unlike the typical Erziehungsroman hero, whose education is completed at the end of the book, Edwin undergoes an extended apprenticeship from youth to middle age, testing the dreams and values of his young manhood against the often harsher realities of life itself. Indeed, in the novels that follow *Clayhanger*—*Hilda Lessways* and *These Twain*—Bennett alters some of the conventions familiar to the genre. With a relentlessly deterministic philosophy, he pursues the romantic follies of Edwin and teaches him, at the last, a bitter lesson about his restricted place in the world.

It was a lesson Bennett well understood, for his own early life resembled that of his protagonist. His father, Enoch Bennett, the Darius Clayhanger of the novel, was a Victorian tyrant who demanded absolute respect from his dreamy son, though he usually failed to get it. One theme of the novel that also appears in later twentieth century fiction is that of the quest of a son for his spiritual father. Edwin hates Darius and longs for the old man's death. However, he saves his father from financial ruin when, with astonishing presence of mind, he secures a cable to hoist a collapsing printing press; when

Darius dies of natural causes (a scene as harrowing as any deathbed drama in literature), the son is moved to thoughts not of vengeance but of pity. Other characters and locations in the novel are modeled after real people and places that Bennett knew intimately: Auntie Bourne becomes Auntie Clara Hamps, Absolom Wood becomes Osmond Orgreave, Cobridge becomes Bleakridge, and Waterloo Road becomes Trafalgar Road. Probably many characteristics of Marguerite Soule, Bennett's French wife, appear in Hilda Lessways. Above all, the trilogy is carefully crafted to simulate reality. Bennet reproduces all the details, trivia, and actual circumstances of life, and the reader has a sense both of place solidly rendered and of time remorselessly passing.

To be sure, time itself is a mysterious force, almost a metaphysical element of fate in the trilogy. Like such other twentieth century writers as Marcel Proust, James Joyce, Thomas and Heinrich Mann, and T. S. Eliot, Bennett is deeply concerned with both the nature and the effects of time. His characters develop, change, and mature to the slow rhythm of time, and they are ultimately destroyed by it. Whether with tantalizing deliberation (as time plays with old Mr. Shushion, its "obscene victim") or with sudden brutal finality (as time fells Darius), it is the sole absolute, the single truth around which all life appears to revolve as an illusion.

Counterpoised to time is the rhythm of life. In the wild sensual delight of Florence Simcox, the "clog-dancer" of the Midlands, Edwin first perceives the beauty of woman. At the "Dragon," where the Burseley Mutual Burial Club holds a "free-and-easy," he responds to the vital warmth of friendship; and with a single kiss from Hilda, a woman he both fears and loves, he is turned for the first time from a shy, fussy bachelor into a man of passion. For her part, Hilda ignores Edwin until he exclaims, in a moment of compassion and despair, "I'm ashamed of seeing my father lose his temper." In this moment of spiritual illumination, she begins to fall in love with him, touched by what she believes to be his confession of weakness. Brutalized throughout her life by men such as George Cannon, she senses that Edwin has the strength of his tenderness. Her judgment is flawed, however, because life conditions her to see Edwin not as he is but as she wants him to be. In addition, Edwin can never truly understand the real Hilda, who is not (as he believes) a woman of romantic mystery; yet the illusion of the moment becomes the pattern for life. For Bennett, it is the small moments of life that have the deepest effects on character. Magic is in the rhythm of life and its beauty, but the magic is terribly brief.

The last two novels of the trilogy, considerably less autobiographical than *Clayhanger*, show a decline in Bennett's emotional powers but complete his architectonic design.

Hilda Lessways is interesting from a technical point of view, because the novel describes Hilda's life in parallel with Edwin's. For each lover, the romantic partner is a projection of a dream, not the real person. Edwin and Hilda meet too late in their lives; their habits are formed, and they are incapable of change. Indeed, the very qualities they perceive in each other—willpower and assertiveness—are inimical to their happiness. In *These Twain*, Bennett details the inevitable results of their mismatch. Hilda becomes a shrew, and Edwin becomes a man very much like his father: intolerant, smug, and materialistic. His decision, at the end of the trilogy, to make the best of a marriage that lost its charm, is a triumph of practicality over romance. To Bennett, life at best is imperfect, but it is best lived without illusion.

"Critical Evaluation" by Leslie B. Mittleman

Further Reading

Anderson, Linda R. *Bennett, Wells and Conrad: Narrative in Transition*. London: Macmillan, 1988. Contains a chapter on the trilogy, which Anderson sees as the last novels in which Bennett managed to investigate his complicated relationship to his past honestly. Focuses on the theme of guilt and selfhood. Includes select bibliography and index.

Drabble, Margaret. *Arnold Bennett*. London: Weidenfeld & Nicolson, 1974. The most readable of the biographies on Bennett. Relates the complicated nexus that held Bennett to his past. Includes a detailed bibliography and index.

Hall, James. *Arnold Bennett: Primitivism and Taste*. Seattle: University of Washington Press, 1959. Contains a chapter on the *Clayhanger* novels, which Hall sees as the best example of the balance achieved between the two opposing forces of primitivism and taste. Includes select bibliography.

Hepburn, James, ed. *Arnold Bennett: The Critical Heritage*. Boston: Routledge & Kegan Paul, 1981. Includes a number of publication reviews of each of the *Clayhanger* novels as well as a general introduction, a select bibliography of critical material from the years 1904 to 1931, and an index.

Lucas, John. *Arnold Bennett: A Study of His Fiction*. London: Methuen, 1974. One of the best general introductions to Bennett. Includes a reasonably thorough discussion of the *Clayhanger* trilogy, which Lucas rates highly in Bennett's oeuvre.

McDonald, Peter D. "Playing the Field: Arnold Bennett as Novelist, Serialist, and Journalist." In *British Literary Culture and Publishing Practice, 1880-1914*. New York: Cambridge University Press, 1997. Examines the publishing careers of Bennett, Joseph Conrad, and Sir Arthur Conan Doyle to demonstrate the radical transformation of British literary culture in the years between 1880 and 1914.

Squillace, Robert. *Modernism, Modernity, and Arnold Bennett*. Lewisburg, Pa.: Bucknell University Press, 1997.

Squillace argues that Bennett saw more clearly than his contemporaries the emergence of the modern era, which transformed a male-dominated society to one open to all people regardless of class or gender. Detailed notes and a bibliography acknowledge the work of some of the best scholars.

Clear Light of Day

Author: Anita Desai (1937-   )
First published: 1980
Type of work: Novel
Type of plot: Domestic realism
Time of plot: 1930's-1940's and late 1960's or early 1970's
Locale: Old Delhi, India

Principal characters:
RAJA DAS, the oldest son in the Das family
BABA DAS, his autistic younger brother
BIM DAS, the older of the two Das daughters, caretaker of the family home and of Baba
TARA DAS, her younger sister
BAKUL, Tara's husband, a diplomat
HYDER ALI, a wealthy Muslim and a neighbor of the Das family
BENAZIR DAS, Hyder Ali's daughter and Raja's wife
AUNT MIRA, a penniless relative who reared the Das children

The Story:

In the late 1960's or early 1970's, Bim Das, an unmarried teacher, lives in her longtime family home in Old Delhi, India, with her autistic brother, Baba. Their sister Tara and her husband, Bakul, a diplomat, live in Washington, D.C. They come to Delhi for a brief visit on their way to their niece's wedding. As soon as their two teenage daughters join them, Tara and Bakul plan to go to Hyderabad to attend the wedding. The bride is a daughter of Raja, the oldest of the four Das children.

Bim insists that she will not attend the wedding; she no longer has anything to do with Raja. Bim expresses her resentment at being saddled with the house and with Baba while Tara and Raja live exciting lives. As they talk, the women hear the sound of Baba's phonograph, which he plays constantly. Bakul emerges from his room, eager to go into New Delhi to visit friends and family, and urges Tara to accompany him. However, though she no longer feels the same joy at being home as she did before Bim started to complain, Tara stays with her sister.

After Bim has finished teaching her class, she shows Tara a letter that Raja wrote to her after the death of his father-in-law, Hyder Ali, who left his property to Raja. Bim is still an-

gry because in the letter Raja made it clear that he was now her landlord, thus implying that he ranked above Bim. That night, Bim, Tara, and Bakul visit the Das family's longtime neighbors the Misras, but they leave after Mulk Misra, one of the grown sons of the family, gets drunk and becomes obnoxious.

In 1947, the Partition of India has resulted in sectarian strife. Hindu radicals at Raja's school pressure him to join their movement, but after he contracts tuberculosis and is confined to his home they leave him alone. In fact, although they are Hindus, the members of the Das family have always been friendly with their Muslim neighbor Hyder Ali, and he has taken a special interest in Raja. Hearing of his interest in Islamic culture, the scholarly Muslim has given Raja access to his library and has included him in his circle of friends. Raja has also grown fond of Hyder Ali's young daughter Benazir. One morning, Raja learns that the Hyder Alis have fled the city, and he is devastated.

The Das children's mother dies, and during Raja's illness their father is killed in a car accident. Aunt Mira, who has acted as mother and father to the children, becomes an alcoholic, goes mad, and eventually dies. The doctor who is attending Aunt Mira courts Bim and even takes her to meet his mother, but Bim finds him annoying, and his courtship goes nowhere. Through the Misras, Tara meets Bikul, a forceful young diplomat. Although she is only eighteen, they marry immediately and leave for his new post. After Raja becomes well again, he joins Hyder Ali in Hyderabad, marries Benazir, and becomes a successful businessman.

In the 1930's, the Das children are inseparable. After Baba's birth, their mother turns the care of her children over to her cousin, Aunt Mira. Aunt Mira persuades the family to buy a cow that falls into a well and drowns, but in most respects she is successful in making the children feel secure. For example, after Tara sees her father giving her mother an injection, it is Aunt Mira who explains that he is not trying to kill her but giving her the insulin that will keep her alive.

Inevitably, as they become older, the children grow apart. Raja starts avoiding females, including Bim, who had always thought of him as her best friend, and Bim takes out her resentment on Tara. Bim finds an outlet for her energy in school activities. By contrast, Tara loathes school. Her most vivid memories of her schooldays are seeing a rabid dog get shot and observing a teacher's heartbreak after her lover was chased away from the school. Tara also feels guilty because she ran away instead of trying to help when Bim was attacked by bees.

Years earlier, Tara notices that Bim, who once seemed so capable, has developed marked eccentricities. As they discuss the past, Bim dismisses the bee episode as unimportant but voices her resentment about being left to take care of Aunt Mira, Baba, the house, and the family's financial affairs. Bim's anger continues to grow until finally she terrifies Baba by threatening to desert him. Repentant, she realizes that she loves not just Baba but her whole family, including even Raja, whom she knows she must forgive. Her nieces, who have just arrived from America, are delighted with Bim and Baba, and after the wedding they look forward to spending several weeks with their aunt and uncle. After Bakul, Tara, and their daughters leave, Bim attends a party at the Misra home. This time, all goes well, and Bim finds new, positive meaning in the songs that Mulk's guru sings.

Critical Evaluation:

It is appropriate that the major influence on *Clear Light of Day*, which has been called Anita Desai's most complex novel, was the poetry of T. S. Eliot, the American British writer whose intricate works transformed the poetic traditions of the early twentieth century. Desai credits Eliot's *Four Quartets* (1943) with having inspired her to write her novel in four sections that, like Eliot's work, ignore chronology.

Clear Light of Day reflects the concept of time suggested in one of the epigraphs to the novel, in which Eliot defines the human experience as a series of dreamlike sequences in which people, places, and the individual all continually appear, vanish, and then reappear. Interestingly, though in that passage Eliot also mentions love, the implication in *Clear Light of Day* is that neither reason nor the will can cause one person to love another. Instead, love is influenced by seemingly random memories along with the inevitable fact of change.

In *Clear Light of Day*, Desai traces Bim's relationship with Raja as it alters through time. In the first section of the book, the adult Bim tells her younger sister Tara that she intends never to see Raja again. Later, she shows Tara a letter that Raja wrote years before; she presents it as providing a rational basis for her feelings. However, in the second part of the novel Desai shows how kind Bim is to Raja during his illness, when, without ever complaining, she takes the primary responsibility for his care. It seems almost unbelievable that within just a few years she would change so radically in her attitude toward her older brother.

In the section devoted to the Das siblings' childhood, it is evident that when they are very young the two oldest children do have a special bond. It is only when Raja becomes aware of the difference between males and females that he distances himself from Bim, and her sense of rejection is so painful that she deliberately inflicts pain on her sister. Years later, Raja's move to Hyderabad, his acceptance as a member of Hyder Ali's family, his preoccupation with his wife and children, and his financial success all contribute to Bim's growing hatred of her brother. However, she cannot admit, even to herself, that her feelings began in adolescence and that they have been fueled not only by a sense of injustice but also by envy and a desire for revenge. Thus, she fixes on the insult she read into his letter as a justification for her rejection of Raja. Ironically, it is only after the anger that she has cherished for so long has spent itself that she is able to take Raja back into her affections. The change that Eliot would probably have called redemptive, however, is portrayed as a purging of the emotions, achieved not through human effort or divine grace but as a result of the shifting patterns of the human experience.

Desai's brilliant application of profound philosophical concepts to the everyday lives of her characters would alone have justified the high praise *Clear Light of Day* received from reviewers. However, the work is also important as a feminist novel. Desai's approach to gender is subtle. She does not comment explicitly on the inequality between men and women in her culture; instead, she shows how a patriarchal society works or, rather, how it fails.

In one way or another, the women in Desai's novel are all victims of the patriarchal system. It is assumed that they will find both protection and fulfillment in being wives and mothers. However, marriage does not necessarily bring them either security or happiness. After being married at twelve, Mira finds herself at fifteen a widow and a slave to her husband's family. The two Misra girls are sent home because they cannot please their husbands, and, although at eighteen Tara appeals to Bakul by being helpless, as a woman in her thirties she must continue to defer to him to keep him happy.

Women are also victimized by being denied the educational opportunities that are open to men. In *Clear Light of Day*, it is assumed that boys will be sent to college while girls will remain home and prepare for their careers as wives and mothers. Thus, Raja takes his schooling for granted, while Bim has to work her way through college. The Misra girls, who are intelligent and would have liked to go to college, are married off instead. Having been denied an education, they have to work for a pittance to support their lazy, dissolute brothers. Although their elderly father tells Bim that it used to be different, that in the old days men knew that they must protect and cherish the women in their families, the old man's defense of the patriarchal system is negated by his proud assertion that, when he was their age, he was even worse than his sons.

In the end, despite her prickly personality, it is Bim who is the real protagonist of *Clear Light of Day*. Unlike Tara and Raja, Bim is determined to make her own way in the world. As a strong, independent woman who adheres to her own standards throughout the changes that time brings, she can serve as a model for the young girls she teaches and, by influencing them, she will change society.

Rosemary M. Canfield Reisman

Further Reading

Cronin, Richard. *Imagining India*. New York: St. Martin's Press, 1989. A chapter titled "The Quiet and the Loud: Anita Desai's India" comments on Desai's treatment of Indian life and culture in *Clear Light of Day*. Bibliography and index.

Daniels, Shouri. "Anita Desai's *Clear Light of Day*." *Chicago Review* 33, no. 1 (Summer, 1981): 107-112. Places emphasis on characterization and linguistic devices; discusses *Clear Light of Day* as a comedy of manners.

Desai, Anita. "Against the Current: An Interview with Anita Desai." Interview by Corinne Demas Bliss. *Massachusetts Review* 29, no. 3 (Fall, 1988): 521-537. Includes Desai's comments about T. S. Eliot's influence on *Clear Light of Day*.

Gupta, R. K. *The Novels of Anita Desai: A Feminist Perspective*. New Delhi: Atlantic, 2002. Focuses on the attempts of the married women in Desai's novels to attain self-respect and to command respect within the family without destroying their marriages. Selected bibliography and index.

Ho, Elaine Yee Lin. *Anita Desai*. Tavistock, England: Northcote House/British Council, 2006. A volume in the Writers and Their Work series. Discusses Desai's treatment of domestic life in India, the status of women in India, and the relationship between the home environment and the outside world. Bibliographical references and index.

Jussawalla, Feroza, and Reed Way Dasenbrock, eds. *Interviews with Writers of the Post-colonial World*. Jackson: University Press of Mississippi, 1992. In a revealing interview, Desai comments on the Western and non-Western influences upon her development as a novelist. Includes a brief profile, bibliography, and index.

Cligès
A Romance

Author: Chrétien de Troyes (c. 1150-c. 1190)
First published: Cligès: Ou, La Fausse Morte, c. 1164
   (English translation, 1912)
Type of work: Poetry
Type of plot: Romance
Time of plot: Sixth century
Locale: England, Brittany, Germany, and
   Constantinople

Principal characters:
ALEXANDER, the heir to the Greek Empire
SOREDAMORS, Sir Gawain's sister, King Arthur's niece
CLIGÈS, the son of Alexander and Soredamors
ALIS, Alexander's brother, later regent for Cligès
FENICE, a German princess, later empress of Greece
KING ARTHUR
QUEEN GUINEVERE
SIR GAWAIN, Cligès's uncle, a knight of King Arthur's
   court
THESSALA, a necromancer, Fenice's nurse
JOHN, an artisan in stone

The Poem:

Alexander, the older son of the emperor of Greece and Constantinople, scorns knighthood in his own country. Having heard of the famed King Arthur of Britain, the young prince is determined to emulate the brave and courteous knights of that monarch's court and to win knighthood by his own merits. Accordingly, he swears never to wear armor on his face or a helmet upon his head until King Arthur himself should place his knightly sword on him. At last he is allowed to have his own way, in spite of the disapproval of his father and his mother's grief at being separated from her son, and he sets sail at once for Britain. With him go twelve noble companions and a store of rich treasure.

When Alexander and his friends arrive at the royal court in Winchester, King Arthur and Queen Guinevere welcome them with gracious speech. All who see him are impressed by the young Greek, not only for his generosity but also for his strong character and handsome appearance. Sir Gawain, a knight of great prowess and the nephew of the king, takes him for his friend and companion, and King Arthur, about to make a journey into Brittany, includes the young man in his retinue. On the trip, Alexander and the damsel Soredamors, sister of Sir Gawain, fall deeply in love. Since each feels that such a love is hopeless, they do nothing but grow pale and sigh and tremble, so that Queen Guinevere, observing them, mistakes their lovesickness for the effects of the heaving sea.

King Arthur remains in Brittany through the summer, and during that time the young lovers are much perplexed and distressed by emotions they are unable to reveal to each other. At the beginning of October, messengers arrive with news that Count Angrès, who was entrusted with the rule of the kingdom during the king's absence, is raising an army and preparing to withstand King Arthur on his return. Angered by this traitorous deed, the king transports a great host across the channel and prepares to lay siege to London, where Count Angrès assembles his forces. Prince Alexander and his twelve companions are knighted while the king's army is encamped outside the city walls. Queen Guinevere's gift to the young knight is a white silk shirt on which Soredamors embroidered strands of her own hair, indistinguishable from the golden thread of the design.

When Count Angrès and his army slip away from the city under cover of night and retreat to the strong castle at Windsor, King Arthur and his troops pursue the traitors and besiege the fortress. During the siege Alexander displays great bravery and prowess. One night, while he attends the queen, Guinevere notices that the gold thread on his shirt is tarnishing but that the golden hair of Soredamors is as lustrous as ever. So the damsel's deed is disclosed, and Alexander rejoices to wear on his person a token of the lady to whom he vows undying devotion.

A short time later, Windsor Castle is taken through his wit and valor. He and several of his companions dressed in the armor of vanquished traitor knights and then went by a secret path into the fortress, where they killed many of the enemy and captured Count Angrès. For this deed Alexander is awarded a gold cup which the king promised to the most valiant of his knights. In the meantime, believing Alexander killed during the fighting inside the castle, Soredamors reveals her love for the young prince. After the battle, the knight receives three joys and honors as the reward for his valor: the town he captured, a kingdom in Wales, and, greatest of all, the hand of Soredamors. From this union is born a handsome son, Cligès.

Meanwhile, in Constantinople, the emperor dies without hearing again from his older son, and Alis, the younger heir, assumes the rule of the empire after receiving a report that Alexander died. Hearing that his brother took the crown, Alexander sets out to reclaim his kingdom, accompanied by his wife, his small son, and forty valiant knights from King Arthur's court. When Alis learns that his older brother is alive, an amicable arrangement is made whereby Alis will rule in name only and the affairs of the kingdom will be entrusted to Alexander. In addition, Alis promises never to marry or to have heirs, so that Cligès will in time reign over Greece and Constantinople. Before Cligès grows to adulthood, however, Alexander dies of a pestilence and Soredamors of grief.

Not long afterward, advisers begin to urge Alis to take a wife, with the result that the emperor is moved to break the oath made to his brother. The bride proposed is the daughter of the emperor of Germany, Princess Fenice, prophetically named for the phoenix bird. The princess previously was affianced to the duke of Saxony, however, and that incensed nobleman feels that he has a prior claim to her hand. While arrangements for the wedding are being made, Cligès and Fenice fall deeply in love. At about the same time, the duke of Saxony sends his nephew to proclaim that his uncle's claim to the princess will be defended against the Greeks. His defiant speech so angers Cligès that he challenges the young Saxon to trial by arms and, in the melee, unhorses him and routs his followers. By this time, although Fenice loves Cligès dearly, she prudently decides that she will not yield herself to either the uncle or the nephew, and, with the help of her nurse Thessala, a sorceress, she plans to remain a virgin. A potion served unwittingly to the bridegroom by his nephew makes it seem to the emperor that he possesses his bride, though he never does so in reality.

On the return trip to Constantinople, the nephew of the duke of Saxony sets an ambush for the travelers. When Cligès kills the treacherous knight and the duke offers a reward for Cligès's head, that resourceful young knight cuts off the head of an enemy and affects a disguise as his father did before him. Fenice is abducted, however, during the battle that follows. Overtaking her captors, Cligès kills all but one, who survives to carry to the duke news of what happened. The conflict ends when Cligès, inspired by his love for Fenice, defeats the duke in single combat. The lovers then part, Fenice going to Constantinople with her husband and Cligès traveling to England, there to fulfill his father's wish that he receive knighthood at the hands of King Arthur.

At a great tournament on the plain before Oxford, Cligès,

changing his armor each day, defeats King Arthur's most valiant knights and bears himself so bravely that he becomes the subject of much speculation concerning his origin and whereabouts, for the young warrior retires to his lodgings every night and keeps away from the feasting that follows each day's tourney. As the Black Knight, he defeats the mighty Sagremore; as the Green Knight, Sir Lancelot of the Lake; as the Vermilion Knight, Sir Perceval of Wales. On the fourth day, disguised as the White Knight, he would have defeated Sir Gawain, his uncle, had King Arthur not intervened. Then Cligès appears in his own person and at the royal banquet reveals his name and tells his story to the pleasure and astonishment of all. King Arthur and Sir Gawain, in particular, are delighted to find their young kinsman so brave in conduct, so pleasing in modesty and knightly courtesy.

On his return to Greece, Cligès learns that Fenice misses him as much as he desires her. Since their great love can no longer be denied, they are able, with the help of Thessala and an artful stonecutter, to devise a plan that will ensure their happiness. From the artisan, John, Cligès gets possession of a tower in which the builder constructed hidden chambers with secret entrances and exits. Thessala then concocts a potion that puts Fenice into a trance so deep that all except three skeptical physicians from Salerno believe her dead. The three doctors are slain by a mob of indignant women before they can restore Fenice to consciousness by acts of torture, and the body of the empress is placed, amid great mourning throughout the kingdom, in a sepulchre that John built. From there she is taken in secret by Cligès, restored to life, and hidden in one of the secret chambers of the tower.

There, for a year and two months, they are free to take their pleasure with each other as they please. At the end of that time, Fenice begins to pine for the out-of-doors, and John reveals a secret door that opens upon a walled garden filled with beautiful blooming trees and flowers. Cligès and Fenice have much joy in their hidden paradise until, one day, a hunter searching for his lost hawk climbs the wall and sees the lovers asleep in each other's arms. Although Cligès awakens and wounds the hunter, the man escapes to tell the emperor what he saw. Alis dispatches troops to the tower, but Cligès and Fenice have already fled. Arrested, John accuses the emperor of having tried to wrong Cligès by marrying and expecting to produce an heir; then the artisan reveals how Alis was tricked by the potion he drank on his wedding night, so that he never possessed his wife except in his dreams. The emperor swears that he can never again be happy until he takes his revenge for the shame and disgrace that was put upon him.

In the meantime, Cligès and Fenice, with Thessala's aid, elude their pursuers and enlist the aid of King Arthur, who promises to fill a thousand ships with knights and three thousand more with men-at-arms to help Cligès regain his rights. Before the mighty expedition can set sail, however, messengers arrive in Britain with word that Alis died of rage and grief because the lovers escaped him. With Fenice, Cligès returns to rule over Greece and Constantinople, and there the two live happily in love, as husband and wife, lover and mistress.

Since that time, however, every emperor, remembering the story of Fenice and her potions, has had little confidence in his empress and kept her closely guarded, attended by no man except one who was a eunuch since his boyhood.

Critical Evaluation:

Chrétien de Troyes' *Cligès*, like his later *Lancelot: Ou, Le Chevalier à la charrette* (c. 1168; *Lancelot: Or, The Knight of the Cart*, 1913), can be read as part of his analysis of and response to what scholars call "courtly love," though that is a modern, not a medieval, term. The twelfth century was the first point in recorded history in which the consensus did not hold amorous love in contempt. Both the Roman and the Germanic traditions regarded love as something that conflicted with higher passions—loyalty to Rome in the first instance, and to the king in the second. When political conditions in Europe settled down after the long period of anarchy ensuing from the collapse of the Roman Empire, the troubadours, or minstrels of southern France, began to express a new idea. Peace gave women a new prominence in society, and these minstrels were eager to make a profit from it. They began to write love songs that extolled ladies for their charm, wit, and beauty. It did not matter if she returned the emotion; what was important was the experience and the analysis of the emotion of desire itself. When the northern poets picked up the theme, it underwent a transformation. For such a love to be satisfactory, they argued, it must be mutual, and if it was mutual, it must be deserved on both parts. So, not only must the lady be charming, witty, and beautiful, but also must her lover (the knight, since the common people were not considered capable of fine emotion) be brave, courteous, and utterly devoted to pleasing the lady. Some regard as the ultimate expression of courtly love Tristan and Isolde, the story of the adulterous passion of Tristan, Cornwall's greatest knight, for Queen Isolde, the wife of his uncle.

Many have seen *Cligès* as a kind of anti-Tristan. The prologue indicates that Chrétien already wrote a romance "of King Mark and Isolde the Blonde," and he also makes a number of other references to the story. Cligès suggests to Fenice that they run away together, but she refuses. She does not want others to speak of them "as they do of Isolde the Blonde

and Tristan," for everyone will "blame our pleasures." Her solution is to feign her own death before the consummation of her marriage and to have Cligès hide her in an orchard. According to medieval custom, marriage was binding only if consummated, so technically they are not committing adultery. In addition, the potion Alis is given to convince him that he is taking his pleasure with Fenice parallels an episode in the Tristan legend. When Tristan takes Isolde to Cornwall to marry King Mark, Isolde's mother concocts a love potion so that the marriage should not be unhappy. Unfortunately, Tristan and Isolde drink the potion by mistake, beginning the whole affair. Rather than using a love potion—which seems rather an artificial excuse for falling in love—Cligès and Fenice fall in love because of their desirable qualities. It is, unlike Tristan and Isolde's, a genuine love naturally occurring. It is governed not by passion but by level-headedness, as Fenice's planning illustrates.

Another episode duplicating one in the Tristan legend is the deception of Alis. To preserve the illusion of her own virginity, Isolde has her maidservant, Brangane, stand in for her on the wedding night. Later, fearing that her servant will reveal the secret, Isolde plots to assassinate Brangane. For his romance, Chrétien designs the episode with the potion that gives Alis the illusion that he is sleeping with Fenice. This enables the author to avoid the rather uncomplimentary scene in which Isolde plots to have Brangane murdered. There are other parallels that help to clarify the similarity of the two stories. Cligès is Alis's nephew, just as Tristan is Mark's; Alexander and Soredamors (Cligès's parents) fall in love on board ship, as do Tristan and Isolde; and the orchard to which Fenice retires strongly resembles the idyllic paradise that Tristan and Isolde discover in the forest when they elope from the court. On the whole, however, the comparison is one of contrast rather than similarity.

In some ways, *Cligès* can be considered a manual for the perfect courtly love relationship. Both Alexander and Soredamors and Cligès and Fenice have the requisite personal characteristics for such a romance. However, the difference in their respective situations allows Chrétien the opportunity to test the theory of courtly love against two different sets of standards. Alexander and Soredamors are both unattached. The only obstacle between them is their own sense of inadequacy—which is, in truth, simply an appreciation for the excellence of the other's very great worth. Once recognized, their love follows a relatively simple path through courtship to marriage, and trouble arises only when they meet with political treachery in the form of Alis the usurper. When one passes to the next generation, however, one sees immediately that the author is eager to show a different situation in which courtly love can operate. The rules of southern courtly love required that the lady be unobtainable—preferably because married. This, of course, led to the idea that adultery was to be admired, a concept that Chrétien did not value. The question still persisted: What if married people fell in love? How could their love be resolved with moral conduct? The author's solution, of course, is that Fenice refrains from sleeping with Alis, but his allusions to the Tristan legend make it clear that the alternative is not something lovers should consider. The result of the morally correct conduct is a happy ending. Cligès and Fenice live happily ever after, reigning as emperor and empress of Constantinople until their extreme old age. The result of Tristan and Isolde's choice, however, is tragedy: the deaths of the hero and heroine. Here, Chrétien reveals one of the essential elements of medieval romance. It is the opposite of tragedy, for where tragedy concerns the results of making a morally bad choice, romance takes the potentially tragic situation and explores the alternative route: the morally good choice and its consequences.

"Critical Evaluation" by C. M. Adderley

Further Reading

Duggan, Joseph J. *The Romances of Chrétien de Troyes.* New Haven, Conn.: Yale University Press, 2001. Duggan's analysis focuses on the common characteristics of Chrétien's romances, such as the importance of kinship and genealogy, his art of narration, and his depiction of knighthood. Contains many references to *Cligès* that are listed in the index.

Frappier, Jean. "Chrétien de Troyes." In *Arthurian Literature in the Middle Ages*, edited by Roger Sherman Loomis. Oxford, England: Clarendon Press, 1959. This is a good starting point for a study of Chrétien de Troyes, dealing mainly with sources and characterization.

Haidu, Peter. *Aesthetic Distance in Chrétien de Troyes: Irony and Comedy in "Cligès" and "Perceval."* Geneva: Librairie Droz, 1968. An examination of the style and structure of two of Chrétien's romances. Haidu concludes that the major theme of *Cligès* is the difference between appearance and reality.

Lacy, Norris J., and Joan Tasker Grimbert, eds. *A Companion to Chrétien de Troyes.* New York: D. S. Brewer, 2005. Collection of essays, including discussions of Chrétien in history, his patrons, his literary background, the Arthurian legend before him, and the medieval reception and influence of his work. Also includes an analysis of *Cligès*, "*Cligès* and the Chansons: A Slave to Love" by Joan Tasker Grimbert.

Loomis, Roger Sherman. *Arthurian Tradition and Chrétien de Troyes.* New York: Columbia University Press, 1949. Loomis shows how most episodes in Chrétien's romances have their parallels in other Irish, Welsh, and Breton stories. Some of Loomis's work has been questioned, but he remains an acknowledged authority in the field.

Murray, K. Sarah-Jane. *From Plato to Lancelot: A Preface to Chrétien de Troyes.* Syracuse, N.Y.: Syracuse University Press, 2008. Murray argues that there were two intersecting sources for Chrétien's work: the works of Plato, Ovid, and other Greco-Roman writers and the Celtic myths and legends found in Irish monastic scholarship.

Noble, Peter S. *Love and Marriage in Chrétien de Troyes.* Cardiff: University of Wales Press, 1982. This book examines the theme of love and marriage in all of Chrétien's romances, concluding that he prefers in *Cligès* a more self-controlled love than that seen in the Tristan legend.

Polak, Lucie. *Chrétien de Troyes: "Cligès."* Critical Guides to French Texts 23. London: Grant and Cutler, 1982. This is one of the best critical studies on *Cligès*. Polak examines the themes of war and love, and she makes a detailed comparison of *Cligès* to the Tristan story. She points out that, according to Chrétien's epilogue, Fenice is not regarded with favor by posterity and argues that she was overly obsessed with appearing to be blameless.

Reichert, Michelle. *Between Courtly Literature and al-Andalus: Matière d'Orient and the Importance of Spain in the Romances of the Twelfth-Century Writer Chrétien de Troyes.* New York: Routledge, 2006. Reichert analyzes the references to Spain in Chrétien's romances, maintaining that these allusions occur at key moments and are often combined with linguistic "riddles" that suggest how the romances are to be read. Chapter 2 focuses on *Cligès*.

A Clockwork Orange

Author: Anthony Burgess (1917-1993)
First published: 1962
Type of work: Novel
Type of plot: Dystopian
Time of plot: Indeterminate
Locale: England

Principal characters:
ALEX, a violent young man
GEORGIE, a member of Alex's gang
PETE, another member of Alex's gang
DIM, the fourth gang member, later a policeman
PA, Alex's father
MUM, Alex's mother
F. ALEXANDER, a writer

The Story:

Alex, a young, English "ultra-violent" gang leader, leads his three "droogs" (or companions) in campaigns of robbery, mayhem, rape, and torture. Alex celebrates gratuitous cruelty and carnality, allowing nothing to get in the way of his impulses. After leaving the Korova Milkbar (the milk is spiked with various drugs) and ducking in and out of a pub, his gang beats up a "doddery starry schoolmaster type veck" (the gang members speak a dialect particular to their violent subculture) and destroys his books, assaults a man and woman while robbing their shop, and brutally thrashes a singing drunk. Spying a rival gang about to rape a girl, Alex, Georgie, Pete, and Dim, although outnumbered, go on the attack until the police break it up.

Their night is not yet over. In a stolen car they take a joyride into the country, wildly running over things. Stopping in a village, they attack a cottage occupied by a writer and his wife, whose educated accents drive them to even greater viciousness. They rape the wife and leave the husband permanently paralyzed. After returning to the Korova Milkbar, Alex bullies and insults Dim, who protests, with the support of Georgie and Pete. Alex's authority over the gang is faltering. At this point they quit for the night. For Alex, such an active evening requires music to make it complete. At Municipal Flatblock 18-A, where he lives with his parents, he enjoys terrible fantasies of violence as he listens to Mozart and Bach.

The next morning, his counselor sternly warns him that the police suspect him. Alex is undeterred. He lures two girls he meets at a record store back to his flat for an orgy of sex and Beethoven's Symphony No. 9. As he leaves the flatblock that evening, his gang intercepts him. Georgie asserts himself as the new leader, but Alex, in a quick display of ruthlessness, makes them back down. Alex nevertheless goes along with the robbery they planned. They force their way into the flat of a woman who calls the police and aggressively defends herself. Alex unintentionally kills her in the struggle.

On the way out, his companions betray him. Dim hits him with a chain, blinding him, and the police quickly arrest him. In two nights and a day, Alex participated in three gratuitous assaults on strangers, a rape, a murder, a gang fight, and statutory rape, all committed in a spirit of joyful anarchy.

Alex feels threatened in the overcrowded, hostile prison. Determined to win his early release by being a model prisoner, he attaches himself to the prison chaplain. His hopes turn to the Ludovico Technique, a conditioning procedure that reforms criminals by blocking their antisocial impulses. A prisoner is killed in Alex's cell, so he is put into the therapy program. Unwittingly, he becomes a pawn in a struggle between administrators eager to prove their new anticrime policies and the political opposition to those policies.

Alex undergoes the Ludovico Technique. After receiving an injection, he is forced to view films of street violence and rape. The drug and the images create in him a powerful aversion against even thoughts of violence. Beethoven's Symphony No. 9, his particular favorite, happens to be on a sound track, and he is conditioned against that as well. At the end of two weeks, he is displayed before the minister of the interior and other officials. Deliberately humiliated, he proves unable to defend himself.

Having been "cured" of his criminal nature, Alex is released. Though his therapy takes only two weeks, two years have elapsed since he entered prison. Meekly returning home to his Pa and Mum, he discovers that he is no longer welcome. The new boarder, Joe, declares that he is "more like a son to them than a lodger." Thoroughly rejected, he leaves the home of his parents. The old haunts, however, are no longer the same, and he begins to wish that he were dead or back in prison. In a highly improbable set of coincidences that suggest that the story is more fabulous than realistic, he runs into several of his victims. In the library he is recognized by the man he assaulted in the street and whose books he destroyed. The two policemen who come to his rescue are his old friend Dim and Billyboy, the former leader of a rival gang, who take him into the country and beat him. Alex, now victimized as he once victimized others, stumbles upon the cottage where he raped the woman and crippled the husband. The man recognizes Alex, from a picture in the paper, as the young man involved in the Ludovico Technique, which he opposes philosophically and politically. The man seizes upon Alex's deplorable condition to embarrass the government. He also realizes that Alex (who wore a mask during the attack) is the same person who crippled him and brutalized his wife.

As an appropriate punishment, Alex is locked in his room and subjected to an emotionally powerful symphony. Unable to stand it, he jumps from the window, intending suicide. Although Alex recovers, the conspiracy to make him a martyr succeeds. Alex is publicly celebrated as a victim of the reformers' inhumane policies. He is reconciled to his Mum and Pa, and his conditioning is reversed so that he can return to his old life.

Alex, however, is growing older and no longer feels the thrills of the ultra-violent. One evening he runs into his old friend Pete, who is now married, working respectably, and speaking standard English. Pete's wife laughs at Alex's language. Alex appears old to himself, out of it. Now eighteen, he envisions himself with a wife and son.

Critical Evaluation:

A Clockwork Orange is a dystopian novel, one that shows a seriously malfunctioning society. Dystopian stories contrast with the long tradition of visions of an ideal society, which began with Thomas More's *De Optimo Reipublicae Statu, deque Nova Insula* (1516; *Utopia*, 1551). After World War II, the dystopian novel, expressing a deeply pessimistic view of human nature and social possibility, became a literary staple. Probably the most famous example remains George Orwell's *Nineteen Eighty-Four* (1949).

A Clockwork Orange became Anthony Burgess's most popular novel in a long and varied literary career, but he protested what he believed to be its gross misinterpretation in an introduction to a new American edition (1988). In all earlier American editions the last chapter had been omitted, though it had always been present in the English and other versions. That last chapter gives a more hopeful view of Alex's life, describing him as eventually abandoning violence and yearning for marriage and fatherhood. The truncated American version, however, became the basis for Stanley Kubrick's film (1971) of the same name, which gave the story a brilliant visual and dramatic edge and was largely responsible for its popularity. The movie presented a starkly nihilistic world in which all institutions were corrupt and no hope was offered.

What Burgess intended to emphasize, as he points out in his introduction, is the necessity of free will and moral choice in the human makeup. Alex is a highly intelligent and articulate young man who chooses an evil life and later chooses to move away from it. Alex is a human creature only to the extent that he retains his free choice; when conditioned, he is reduced to nothing. Evil, the book argues, is a better condition than blankness. Alex is not given the usual excuses for being a criminal. He is not poor. His parents, however ineffectual, show concern. He demonstrates himself as a gifted natural leader. The title, derived from a Cockney expression, expresses what Burgess intended to emphasize: "A clockwork orange" is something that is "queer to the limit of queerness," something with its essential nature missing. In general imagistic terms, a clockwork orange applies to the conditioned Alex as well: Though he appears natural from the outside, he is thoroughly unnatural within.

Many readers, however, find that the author's professed interpretation of his book is not entirely convincing. Should the interpretation of the whole book be changed on the relatively slight evidence of the last chapter? The author's images of social disintegration and gang violence appear to be the novel's most compelling aspects and lead quite naturally to their visualization in the film and in the reader's imagination. Most American readers, at least, have attached their interpretation to what appears to be an uncompromising, nihilistic posture against all authority, attitudes that were popular in the 1960's and 1970's.

There is no such disagreement, however, about the novel's language. Alex's first-person narration, an elaborate patter filled with many Russian-derived words, gives the book a highly original and much-admired texture. The mock-Shakespearean cadence becomes part of Alex's aestheticism: "But where I itty now, O my brothers, is all on my oddy knocky, where you cannot go." Using more than two hundred distinct words and phrases, Alex speaks an apparently impenetrable dialect. Burgess's presentation is so skillful, however, that the attentive reader learns the vocabulary in the course of the narrative. If Alex's nightmare of "smecking malchicks doing the ultra-violent on a young ptitsa who was creeching away in her red red krovvy, her platties all razrezzed real horrorshow," is translated into "smiling guys viciously assaulting a young woman who was screaming while lying in her own blood, her clothes beautifully torn up," the masked violence becomes naked. Language both disguises and reveals. Its significance goes well beyond an external and superficial effect. The English, more than most other nationalities, are aware of dialect as a social identifier. In choosing his patois, Alex has declared who and what he is.

Language is a more important assertion of his identity than his oddly mannered clothes. Drawn into Alex's language, the reader enters his world of images and values, where there is no word for pity or compassion, and the familiar is brutally truncated ("father" and "mother" become "pee" and "em"). Language also creates an aesthetic of violence, celebrating the terrible and disgusting. The repetition of "O my brothers" is a grotesque irony in the middle of nonstop violence. Alex also learns that his chosen dialect has no lasting value. After two years, his patter is outdated, something laughable to the younger nadsats (teenagers) who already have expressions of their own.

Bruce Olsen

Further Reading

Biswell, Andrew. The Real Life of Anthony Burgess. London: Picador, 2005. A well-researched biography of Burgess that explores his personal life, including his heavy drinking and sexual promiscuity. A Clockwork Orange is also discussed, along with Burgess's common themes of corruption, sin, and the human capacity for evil.

Coale, Samuel. Anthony Burgess. New York: Frederick Ungar, 1981. A general discussion of Burgess's work, including an examination of the philosophical issues in A Clockwork Orange.

Lewis, Roger. Anthony Burgess: A Biography. London: Faber & Faber, 2002. This sprawling examination of Burgess's life is illuminating though sometimes chaotic. Instead of recounting the events of Burgess's life as a chronological narrative, Lewis presents a more stylized, psychodynamic interpretation of Burgess's personality and work.

Morris, Robert K. The Consolations of Ambiguity. Columbia: University of Missouri Press, 1971. Compares A Clockwork Orange to The Wanting Seed (1962), another of Burgess's dystopian novels.

Petix, Esther. "Linguistics, Mechanics, and Metaphysics: A Clockwork Orange." In Anthony Burgess, edited by Harold Bloom. New York: Chelsea House, 1987. Defines the author's dualistic worldview and relates it to the language and images of the novel.

Ray, Philip E. "Alex Before and After: A New Approach to Burgess's A Clockwork Orange." In Critical Essays on Anthony Burgess, edited by Geoffrey Aggeler. Boston: G. K. Hall, 1986. Argues that the three sections of the novel represent changes in Alex's inevitable development.

Tilton, John W. Cosmic Satire in the Contemporary Novel. Cranbury, N.J.: Bucknell University Press, 1977. Argues that the restoration of the last chapter greatly increases the depth of the novel.

Close Range
Wyoming Stories

Author: Annie Proulx (1935-   )
First published: 1999
Type of work: Short fiction
Type of plot: Psychological realism
Time of plot: Late nineteenth century to late twentieth century
Locale: Wyoming

The Stories:

Mero Corn, the main character of the opening story, "The Half-Skinned Steer," leaves his family's Wyoming ranch in 1936 and does not return for sixty years; he had received a phone call from his brother's wife, letting him know his brother Rollo died. Mero, who is now more than eighty years old, sets out on a four-day drive from Massachusetts.

The long drive shows Mero's age. He gets in a traffic accident after he enters the highway the wrong way. While talking to the police, he cannot, at first, remember where he is going. Interspersed with the story of his long trip is his recalling of a story about the curse of a half-skinned steer. In the story, a rancher has partially skinned a steer before stopping for dinner. When the rancher returns, the steer is gone. He had not killed the animal, only stunned it. He soon finds the steer struggling to walk away. The steer's evil glare leaves the rancher cursed forever.

Back on the road, Mero relies on his sixty-year-old memory of how to get to the family ranch. With ever-deepening snow, he veers off the road into a rocky field, and his car becomes permanently stuck. His only option appears to be a long, unprepared walk. As he starts down the road, he realizes something is trailing him—the half-skinned steer, with its cursing eye.

"The Mud Below" tells the story of how Diamond Felts becomes a rodeo bull-rider. For some spending money, Felts agrees to help out on a local ranch. After work, the rancher offers to let some local teenagers, including Felts, try to ride his bull. After a surprisingly successful ride, Felts is immediately excited by the challenge. Despite his mother's anger, he takes off to join the rodeo circuit. He begins to have success, until he injures his knee. While home recuperating, he continues to fight with his mother, a single parent, who takes him to see a former rodeo rider who had been permanently injured when kicked in the head. Felts runs off again, even more angry, and takes his temper out on everyone he meets. The story ends by revealing a source for all his violent and self-destructive behavior: He demands that his mother identify his father. He tells her that the man she names has denied parentage. In turn, she tells Felts that the man has lied, knowing full well what effect that lie would have on Felts.

The final story in the book is "Brokeback Mountain," which tells of the lifelong love between two Wyoming ranch hands, Jack Twist and Ennis del Mar. The two, neither more than twenty years old, meet in the summer of 1963 near Brokeback Mountain, where they had been hired to tend a herd of sheep together. Though neither young man wants to think or talk about it, they begin a passionate sexual relationship.

In the years that follow their work on the mountain, Ennis and Jack each follow the path of marriage, though they do so unhappily. The two men manage to get together every few years, under the guise of fishing or hunting trips. They talk about running off together, perhaps to Mexico or a hidden ranch somewhere, and dream of living as a couple. Their dream remains a dream, for they fear being killed if their relationship were in the open. Ennis remembers that at the age of nine, he had been shown by his father the dead body of a man tortured and murdered with a tire iron for living with another man.

After twenty years of spending some weekends together, Ennis discovers that Jack has died. His death is attributed to an accident with an exploding tire, but Ennis believes he had

been murdered. Ennis tries to fulfill Jack's wish of having his ashes scattered on Brokeback Mountain, but Jack's parents refuse. Ennis is allowed, however, to see Jack's old bedroom. In the closet, Ennis discovers Jack's keepsakes—two shirts, one worn by Ennis and the other by Jack while working together on Brokeback Mountain. Ennis asks if he can keep the shirts, and Jack's parents say yes.

Critical Evaluation:

Annie Proulx's *Close Range* is a collection of eleven short stories organized around life in Wyoming from the days of the earliest white settlers to the late twentieth century. The stories offer a bleak view of life. Though choices of genre and narrative tone can serve to distance a reader's ability to determine an overriding perspective, for the characters in these stories, finding a way to survive in the face of human misery and harsh, inhospitable landscapes is almost never accomplished in this book.

Proulx uses a variety of genres in this collection. As she notes in the book's foreword, some of the stories are derived from earlier folktales. "The Half-Skinned Steer," a reworking of an Icelandic folktale, tells of a rancher cursed for his mistreatment of an animal, a curse that seems to reach others in the book as well. A mock moral is in the story "55 Miles to the Gas Pump," a retelling of the Bluebeard folktale about the danger of opening forbidden doorways. The moral, "When you live a long way out you make your own fun," suggests that even murder can be explained away if the conditions are harsh enough.

Diamond Felts, in "The Mud Below," lives a life of rage because the man his mother identifies as his father has denied parentage. Felts uses, even rapes, the women around him, unable to form a close relationship. His father has abandoned him, and Felts cannot trust his mother, unable to determine who has lied to him. Mero Corn, in "The Half-Skinned Steer," distances himself from family for sixty years. He has grown up stubborn and independent and would rather trust a distant memory than accept offers of family help. The collection opens with an epigraph: "Reality's never been of much use out here," a statement that applies to family relationships throughout the book. The images of love lead at best to obsessive fascination, and are more than likely to lead to molestation, betrayal, and murder.

It is hard to find a loving voice in these stories, other than that of an object, a tractor, which "declares" its love to a character in "The Bunchgrass Edge of the World." The closest to a loving relationship between humans is in "Brokeback Mountain," but that story is also full of denial of reality. Both main characters try to present a false identity to the world, marrying, raising children, and having to lie to their families. They finally realize that they could have had a good life together, rather than two unhappy marriages, but all they really had was a life built around a memory of early, idyllic times on Brokeback Mountain.

Ennis suggests "if you can't fix it you got to stand it" as the only route to making one's way through the troubles of living. The narrator of the story offers an even bleaker belief of how life plays out: "Against its fixed mass the tragedies of people count for nothing although the signs of misadventure are everywhere."

Despite their dark view of life, Proulx's books have a wide range of readers. Her works have garnered for her many literary awards, including multiple O. Henry Awards for short stories, a Pulitzer Prize for fiction, a National Book Award, and a selection ("The Half-Skinned Steer") in the collections *The Best American Short Stories 1998* and *The Best American Short Stories of the Century*, edited by John Updike. Furthermore, a recent scholarly overview of woman writers from the start of American literature traces the canon to Proulx.

Brian L. Olson

Further Reading

Hunt, Alex, ed. *The Geographical Imagination of Annie Proulx: Rethinking Regionalism.* Lanham, Md.: Lexington Books, 2009. A discussion of how landscape, geography, and the "geographical imagination" figure across Proulx's works. Includes many articles examining Wyoming as a significant place in her stories.

Proulx, E. Annie. "Big Skies, Empty Places." *The New Yorker*, December 25, 2000. Proulx discusses how place, geography, and landscape influence her writings.

_____. Interview with Annie Proulx. *Paris Review*, no. 188 (Spring, 2009): 22-49. An interview with Proulx in a well-respected literary journal, discussing, among other things, the odd names of her characters.

Rebein, Robert. *Hicks, Tribes, and Dirty Realists: American Fiction After Postmodernism.* Lexington: University Press of Kentucky, 2001. Examines the works of Proulx, Dorothy Allison, Cormac McCarthy, Larry McMurtry, Louise Erdrich, and others and asserts that these authors' gritty realism has gained ascendency over metafiction in American writing.

Rood, Karen Lane. *Understanding Annie Proulx.* Columbia: University of South Carolina Press, 2001. Presents discussion of Proulx's novels and short fiction, including *Close Range.* Also includes an informative biographical chapter.

Showalter, Elaine. *A Jury of Her Peers: American Women Writers from Anne Bradstreet to Annie Proulx.* New York: Alfred A. Knopf, 2009. An overview and assessment of women writers, placing Proulx in a broad context.

Stacy, Jim, ed. *Reading "Brokeback Mountain": Essays on the Story and the Film.* Jefferson, N.C.: McFarland, 2007. A collection of fifteen essays that focuses on the short story "Brokeback Mountain" and on the award-winning film based on the story. Also includes essays on Proulx's style and her use of locale.

The Closed Garden

Author: Julien Green (1900-1998)
First published: Adrienne Mesurat, 1927 (English translation, 1928)
Type of work: Novel
Type of plot: Psychological realism
Time of plot: 1908
Locale: France

Principal characters:
ANTOINE MESURAT, a retired teacher
ADRIENNE, his daughter
GERMAINE, her disabled older sister
DR. DENIS MAURECOURT, a physician
MADAME LEGRAS, a neighbor

The Story:

Adrienne Mesurat lives with her father, a retired writing master, and Germaine, her disabled older sister, in a small, ugly villa in the country town of La Tour l'Eveque. The routine of the household is simple, for Antoine Mesurat lives only to indulge his own quiet tastes. Three meals a day, his morning and evening walks, his favorite newspaper, an occasional game of *trente-et-un*—these are his pleasures. In his tranquilly stubborn manner, he is a complete domestic tyrant, and the idea that his daughters might be unhappy with their lot never crosses his mind.

There was a time when callers came to the villa, for the Mesurats owned enough property to attract young men of the district. Old Mesurat, however, considers his daughters superior to the sons of provincial tradesmen and lawyers and laughs complacently at their proposals of marriage. Finally, the visits cease. In the uneventful round of Adrienne's days, the strange passerby in the street, the local gossip her father brings back from his walks, and the succession of tenants who each summer rent the Villa Louise on the corner become items for speculation and comment. Matters would have gone on indefinitely if Adrienne did not, in the summer of her seventeenth year, fall suddenly in love.

She is gathering flowers beside a country road when a carriage passes her. She sees in it a slight man of middle age, who half lifts his hat as the vehicle goes by. Adrienne recognizes him as Dr. Maurecourt, a recent arrival in the town. Because he notices her, a feeling of gratitude and adoration fills her. For the rest of the summer, she walks the same road every day, but the doctor never rides that way again.

At last, Adrienne hits upon another plan. Each night, after Germaine goes to her room and Mesurat settles in the parlor for his evening nap, she steals out of the house. From the corner on which the Villa Louise stands, she can see the front of the Maurecourt dwelling, and the sight of its lighted windows give her a deep feeling of happiness. Once she sees Maurecourt on the street. Later, she feels that she must see him again at any cost. One day, while cleaning, she discovers that she can also watch his house from the window of Germaine's room. As often as possible, she goes there and sits, hoping to see him enter or leave by his front door.

Germaine, surprising Adrienne in her bedroom, becomes suspicious. That night, the older sister is awake when Adrienne returns quietly from her evening vigil. Mesurat, informed of what happened, orders Adrienne to play cards with him after dinner the next day. Under her father's suspicious gaze, she plays badly. He becomes enraged and accuses her of stealing out nightly to meet a lover. From that time on, she is allowed to leave the house only when she goes walking with her father. Again she sees Maurecourt on the street. Thinking that if she were hurt he be called to attend her, she thrusts her arms through the windowpane. Her father and sister bandage her cuts, much to her despair.

Germaine's sickness grows worse. Refusing to acknowledge her serious condition, Mesurat insists that she get up for her meals. One morning, after he berates her at breakfast, Germaine confides her intention of leaving home, and she borrows five hundred francs from Adrienne's dower chest to

pay her fare to a convent hospital. Adrienne is glad to see her sister go; she hopes to occupy the room from which she can watch Maurecourt's house. Mesurat, surprised and furious, is puzzled about how Germaine arranged for her flight and where she secured money for her train fare.

In June, Madame Legras becomes the new tenant of Villa Louise. Adrienne and her father meet the summer visitor at a concert, and Madame Legras invites the young girl to visit. After Germaine's departure, Adrienne goes to see her new neighbor. Madame Legras is affable but prying. Confused by questions about a possible lover, Adrienne has a strange attack of dizziness.

That night, Mesurat angrily orders her to produce her dower box. Seeing that five hundred francs are missing, he accuses her of plotting with Germaine to outwit him. While he stands reviling her from the head of the stairs, Adrienne runs against him in the dark. He falls into the hall below. Dazed and frightened by her deed, Adrienne goes to bed.

The cook stumbles upon Mesurat's body the next morning, and Madame Legras, aroused by the disturbance, summons Maurecourt. Although there are some whispers that the old man's end might not be all it seems, the verdict is one of accidental death. Germaine does not return for the funeral. Before long, Adrienne, to her dismay, finds herself lonelier than ever. A feeling of lethargy possesses her much of the time. When the prioress writes asking for money in Germaine's name or lawyers send legal papers for her signature, she disregards them. Nothing seems to matter except the time she spent with Madame Legras, who assumed a protective attitude toward the young woman. At last, however, Adrienne begins to realize that Madame Legras suspects the truth about Mesurat's death, and her sly looks and pointed remarks seemed intended to lead the young woman into a trap.

One day, Adrienne decides to go to Montfort. There, walking the streets, she imagines that people are staring at her. She spends the night in Dreux, where a young workman accosts her. Later, frightened because she does not remember why she went away, she returns to La Tour l'Eveque after sending Maurecourt a card telling him of her unhappiness.

Shortly after her return, she collapses and has to be put to bed at Villa Louise. While undressing her, Madame Legras finds a love letter, which she gives to the doctor when he comes in response to her summons. That night, Adrienne awakens and goes back to her own home. Maurecourt goes to see her there the next day. When she confesses her love, he tells her that he is sick and soon to die. Overcome by his visit, she is barely able to rouse herself when Madame Legras appears and demands an immediate loan to pay some pressing debts. While she looks on helplessly, the woman empties the dower chest of its gold coins. Then she removes the watch and chain Adrienne is wearing and drops them into her purse.

A short time later, when the cook brings word that Madame Legras left town very suddenly, Adrienne realizes that the servant also knows her guilt. Dazed, she sits vacant-eyed when Maurecourt's sister calls to reproach her for her shameless behavior. At nightfall, she leaves the house and wanders toward the lighted square, where a party is in progress. Suddenly she turns and runs toward the dark countryside. Some peasants find her there a few hours later. She cannot tell them her name. She is mad.

Critical Evaluation:

Julien Green said that his novels allow glimpses of "great dark stirrings," which he believed to be the deepest part of the soul. Quietly, but inevitably, this novel probes the deepest aspects of Adrienne Mesurat's being. Green believed from the beginning of his literary career that a novelist is "like a scout commissioned to go and see what is happening in the depth of the soul," who then comes back to report what was observed. The writer never lives on the surface, but only inhabits the darkest regions. In his diary, Green observes: "The anguish and loneliness of my characters can almost always be reduced to what I think I called a manifold dread of living in this world." Although Green's characters rarely express ideas, his books hold a view of the world, a philosophy. *The Closed Garden* stands at the head of his works, both in form and in implied statement.

It has been said that the inspiration for *The Closed Garden* was a painting by Maurice Utrillo: The novel has the sunlit yet melancholy dullness readers find in many of Utrillo's street scenes. Green has also been compared with Emily Brontë for the intensity of his atmosphere and with Honoré de Balzac for his realistic rendering of French provincial life. These comparisons, however, are true only in part. Green is himself first of all, with his own powers and compelling insights.

The characters in *The Closed Garden* try to preserve their lives as they are, but nothing can stay the same. Even passivity is a choice, an action that must have consequences; and these consequences can force one forward to the destiny waiting at the end. Monotony can lead as inevitably as more colorful events to tragedy—and perhaps more inescapably. People can tangle themselves in tragic fates without realizing until too late (if ever) what happened. Green seems to imply in his tale that the inarticulate suffer as deeply as the more intelligent and sophisticated.

Adrienne Mesurat lives surrounded by quiet, but still deadly, selfishness. Her father thinks only of his own com-

fort, and her sister lives only for her illness. Adrienne is crushed beneath their wills—wretched and hardly knowing why. Green suggests that her condition is a metaphor for that of most of humanity. What happens when she wakes up and tries to break loose from her invisible bonds? Life does not have the happy ending of the fairy tale. There can be only one ending. It is not contrived tragedy: It emerges from the characters themselves. "The author creates characters," wrote Green, "and the characters create the plot."

The style of *The Closed Garden* is typical of Green's elusive, subtle manner. His prose is quiet and unobtrusive. André Gide commented about Green's books that the pencil seems never to leave the paper; the line is unbroken to the end. Green said that his intention in *The Closed Garden* and his other early works was to tell the story without ever allowing the reader to be "diverted by the style in which it was written, a sort of invisible style, good and strong, if possible, but not in any way noticeable." The complete effacement of the author is, for Green, one of the major requirements of literary perfection. He believed that it should be impossible for a reader to know what kind of person wrote the book. He wanted the characters to speak and to act for themselves and never be interfered with by the author's personality.

Green's premise is that, although Adrienne appears commonplace at first glance, she is as mysterious as any human being and just as alone. She breathes and moves in an atmosphere of solitude that gradually becomes oppressive. Green believed that most people never succeed in breaking down the barriers that separate them from the rest of humanity. Although people make constant contact with others, the communication is imperfect, at best. "When we are about to speak," wrote Green, "and reveal something about our inner life, who is in the mood to listen?" If one is heard, can the listener understand? This aloneness is the theme of *The Closed Garden* and of most of Green's fiction.

Green was born of American parents in Paris in 1900. While in his teens during World War I, he drove an ambulance and served in the French artillery. He studied music and art before turning to literature and achieving early recognition with his first novels. His elder sister, Anne, was also a novelist, although she wrote in English, while the body of his work is in French. He was a close friend of Gide and was influenced by the master's style. The fall of France in World War II forced Green's return to Virginia, where he previously attended college. During this time, he wrote his autobiographical *Memories of Happy Days* (1942), his only book composed in English. In 1942, Green entered the United States Army and worked with the Office of War Information. After the liberation of France in 1945, he returned to Paris.

A French critic spoke of Green as a "pure" writer, explaining that he never wrote a line except under absolute artistic compulsion. He lived and worked under rigid self-discipline, which ruled out all petty distractions. In 1939, after twenty years, Green returned to the Catholic faith. This is shown strikingly in the several volumes of his *Journal* (1938-2006). Critics compared his later novels favorably with those of François Mauriac and André Gide.

Green makes no sentimental appeals. He creates horror in books such as *The Closed Garden* by cumulative value, not by yielding to sensational effects. The realism of this novel is that of a nightmare. The lean style avoids decorations and seems to photograph the tragedy dispassionately. The emotion is concentrated and intense. Green maintains a firm control over the novel, avoiding the capriciousness and predictability of some of the later novels. His debt to the early United States writers Edgar Allan Poe and Nathaniel Hawthorne is evident in *The Closed Garden*. The carefully constructed prose and the moral concern that rule the story are especially reminiscent of Hawthorne. At times, Green seems to suggest that sexuality is apart from the rest of life and, because apart, evil. Certainly, Adrienne, as so many other of Green's characters, cannot cope with her own sexuality and is destroyed by it as much as by anything else. Green's characters seem to have a longing nostalgia for a peace and happiness that they never knew. Dreams and vague memories of bittersweet desires, however, are not enough, as Green artfully demonstrates. Green received many awards and prizes during his long career, and, in 1971, he became the first United States citizen to be elected to the French Academy.

"Critical Evaluation" by Bruce D. Reeves

Further Reading

Armbrecht, Thomas J. D. *At the Periphery of the Center: Sexuality and Literary Genre in the Works of Marguerite Yourcenar and Julien Green*. Amsterdam: Rodopi, 2007. Ambrecht compares the representation of homosexuality in the work of Green and Yourcenar, comparing their depiction of gay characters in their novels and plays. Includes bibliography.

Burne, Glenn S. *Julian Green*. New York: Twayne, 1972. Study of Green's literary achievement. Discusses the structure of *The Closed Garden*; comments on the development of the protagonist, a "solid young lady" who is subdued by fate.

Dunaway, John M. *The Metamorphoses of the Self: The Mystic, the Sensualist, and the Artist in the Works of Julien Green*. Lexington: University Press of Kentucky, 1978. Comments on the novel are included in a study that explores the biographical genesis of Green's major fiction.

O'Dwyer, Michael. *Julien Green: A Critical Study*. Portland, Oreg.: Four Courts Press, 1997. O'Dwyer provides a biographical introduction and a critical assessment of Green's novels, short stories, plays, autobiography, journals, and other writings. He highlights the importance of Green's American background for a full appreciation of his work. Includes a foreword by Green.

_____. "Julien Green: Expatrie et Sudiste." In *Exiles and Migrants: Crossing Thresholds in European Culture and Society*, edited by Anthony Coulson. Portland, Oreg.: Sussex Academic Press, 1997. Examines how Green's experience as an expatriate American southerner in France affected his work.

Reck, Rima Drell. *Literature and Responsibility: The French Novelist in the Twentieth Century*. Baton Rouge: Louisiana State University Press, 1969. Characterizes Green as an iconoclast whose impact on fiction was limited but important. Focuses on the sense of isolation the novelist evokes in *The Closed Garden*.

Stokes, Samuel. *Julian Green and the Thorn of Puritanism*. New York: King's Crown Press, 1955. Study of Green's novels, concentrating on the various intellectual influences that help explain the spiritual background of his work. Discusses Green's use of fiction to relate the lives of individuals to the society in which they live.

The Clouds

Author: Aristophanes (c. 450-c. 385 B.C.E.)
First produced: Nephelai, 423 B.C.E. (English translation, 1708)
Type of work: Drama
Type of plot: Social satire
Time of plot: Fifth century B.C.E.
Locale: Athens

Principal characters:
STREPSIADES, an Athenian gentleman
PHEIDIPPIDES, his son
SOCRATES, a Sophist philosopher

The Story:

Strepsiades, a rich gentleman of Athens, is plunged into poverty and debt by his profligate son, Pheidippides. Hounded by his son's creditors, Strepsiades ponders ways to prevent complete ruin. Hearing reports that the Sophists teach a new logic that can be used to confuse one's creditors and so get one out of debt, Strepsiades sees in the Sophist teachings a possible solution to his problem. He pleads with Pheidippides to enter the school of the Sophists and learn the new doctrines. When Pheidippides, more interested in horse racing than in learning, refuses to become a pupil, Strepsiades denounces his son as a wastrel and decides to enroll himself.

He goes to the Thoughtery or Thinking-School, which is the term used for the classroom of the Sophists, and asks to see Socrates, the philosopher. After Strepsiades explains his purpose, Socrates proceeds to demonstrate several logical conclusions of the new school. More certain than ever that the new logic will save him from ruin and disgrace, Strepsiades pleads until Socrates admits him to the Thoughtery.

Unfortunately, Strepsiades proves too old to master the Sophist technique in the classroom. Socrates then decides that Strepsiades can learn to do his thinking outdoors. When Socrates puts questions concerning poetry to Strepsiades, his answers show such complete ignorance that Socrates finally admits defeat and returns to the Thoughtery. Strepsiades, disgusted with his own efforts, decides that he will either make Pheidippides go to the Sophist school or turn him out of the house. Approached a second time by his father, Pheidippides again protests against enrolling in the school but finally yields to his father's demands. Strepsiades believes that all now will be well.

Some time afterward Strepsiades goes to learn what progress his son has made. Socrates assures him that Pheidippides has done well. At this news, Strepsiades feels sure that his plan was a good one and that the new logic, as learned by his son, will soon deliver him from his creditors. He asks Socrates to call Pheidippides from the classroom. When Pheidippides emerges, Strepsiades greets him between tears and

laughter and says it is fitting that he should be saved by the son who plunged him into debt.

He asks Pheidippides to demonstrate his new learning, and Strepsiades is amazed by the cunning of the new logic. At that moment one of Strepsiades' creditors appears to demand money that is owed him for a horse. Strepsiades, confident that the Sophist-taught Pheidippides can turn the tables on any creditor in the law court, refuses to pay, ignoring threats of court action. He treats a second creditor in the same way and goes home convinced that the new logic, as argued by Pheidippides, will save him in the pending lawsuits.

It becomes a different matter, however, when Pheidippides proceeds to demonstrate the Sophist teaching at home. Arguing that Strepsiades beat him often for his own good, Pheidippides buffets his father during a family argument and declares that he is beating Strepsiades for his own good. The old man protests, but with the new logic Pheidippides silences his protests and threatens to beat his mother on the same principle.

Strepsiades realizes that the Sophists can justify all manner of evil with their tricky logic. Thinking the teachings dangerous to the youth of Athens, he takes a torch and sets fire to the Thoughtery. As Socrates and the Sophist disciples scream their objection, the Thoughtery goes up in flames. Strepsiades watches it burn, certain that he is eliminating an evil.

Critical Evaluation:

The Clouds is one of the best known of Aristophanes' many comedies. In it, he attacks the use of logic to justify ridiculous or self-serving ends. Aristophanes rejects the Sophists, whom he considers irreverent and artificial, and he satirizes their teachings in *The Clouds*.

Largely because of its caricature of the philosopher Socrates, *The Clouds* is one of Aristophanes' best-known plays. The play's buffoonery and raillery are sometimes savage and biting. Through Socrates, Aristophanes satirizes the entire Sophist movement in education. Although the play won only third prize when it was presented in 423 B.C.E., a fact that vexed its author considerably, *The Clouds* must have given the Athenian audience moments of high entertainment.

Greek comedy is a mixture of song and dance, resembling satirical comic opera at least as much as it does a comedic play. Aristophanes' humor is bawdy and cutting. Stylistically, *The Clouds* follows a conventional structure known as Old Comedy. In Old Comedy, the prologue sets forth a problem and the comic idea by which it might be resolved. The play turns on one central satiric situation or conceit. In *The Clouds*, the problem is that Strepsiades has a mountain of debts incurred by his son, and the idea for the resolution is to send his son to learn the Sophist methods of argument. Failing that, he goes to learn from Socrates. The *parode*, or entrance song of the chorus, follows, in which Socrates' new divinities, the clouds, appear singing. Later, the playwright, Aristophanes, steps out and sings a *parabasis* on a theme of public interest, which tells the audience what a fine dramatist he is and how foolish the Athenians were to let Cleon have power. Next comes the *agon*, or debate, in which Right Logic and Wrong Logic, two characters, attack and defend sophistic teaching. Then a series of episodes follows in which the audience views the results of Strepsiades' original notion of sending his son to learn how to argue falsely. The episodes are often the funniest part of the comedy, as in this play. The *exode*, or final choral song, is unusually brief in *The Clouds* and occurs as Socrates' house is being burned. The plot hinges on Strepsiades' attempt to evade paying his creditors; but he is not wholly to blame, since his extravagant son, Pheidippides, incurred the debts.

The brunt of the satire, however, falls on the figure of Socrates (and through him the whole Sophist movement in Athenian education) rather than on Strepsiades. Plato's more famous representation of Socrates is quite different from that of Aristophanes. Aristophanes' portrait shows Socrates as completely amoral, a man who destroys traditional religion and morality and replaces these with nonsense supported by specious reasoning. A further discrepancy is that in *The Clouds* Socrates is farcically concerned with natural science, particularly astronomy and meteorology, but in Plato's works Socrates is concerned only with moral questions.

Some critics explain these divergences by saying that the comic Socrates is a composite figure of several Sophists, including Protagoras, the logic-twister; Anaxagoras, who was interested in natural phenomena; and Diogenes of Apollonia, who regarded air as the primal element. This view is inaccurate. The character of Socrates in *The Clouds* is meant to be Socrates, and there is enough agreement with Plato in this play to make the caricature ring true. Socrates did study the

natural sciences as a young man. Further, there are his ugliness, his poverty, his bare feet, his unorthodox religion, his penchant for homely analogies, his dialectical reasoning, his poking fun at the knowledge of the old, and, above all, his tremendous influence on young aristocrats. These are all subjected to farcical representation. Socrates was well known as a Sophist, even though he disclaimed the name. Furthermore, Aristophanes learned that if one intends to lambast some social ill one always picks the chief exponent of it. He invariably went for the chief figures—Cleon in politics, Euripides in tragedy, and Socrates in education.

Aristophanes, after all, was a conservative in every area of life. Born of landowners, he detested the way Athens was deteriorating in the Peloponnesian War, and he believed that the new spirit of radical experimentation was ruining the city. There is some justification for his assault on Socrates, for young idlers were learning his mode of dialectical logic and using it to prove that their immoral behavior was perfectly right, and that the gods were no longer to be feared. It is likely that these young men would have done as they pleased regardless of whether they had specious arguments, borrowed from serious thinkers, to support their actions. On the core of the matter, Socrates' own integrity, Aristophanes is completely wrong. It is likely that he came to realize this, because he lampooned Cleon and Euripides as long as they lived, and even after, but once he had written *The Clouds* he more or less gave up making Socrates the butt of his jokes.

It is interesting that the charges brought against Socrates a quarter of a century later, in 399 B.C.E., were identical to those that Aristophanes lodges against him in *The Clouds*. He was accused of corrupting the youth and of replacing the traditional gods with gods of his own making. Many of the jurors had seen Aristophanes' play and had been prejudiced by it.

James Weigel, Jr.

Further Reading

Aristophanes. *The Clouds*. Translated by William Arrowsmith with sketches by Thomas McClure. Ann Arbor: University of Michigan Press, 1962. Discusses the history of the play and how it was originally performed. Claims Aristophanes is exploiting Socrates as a convenient comic representative of sophistic corruption. Excellent notes and glossary.

Arnott, Peter. *An Introduction to the Greek Theatre*. London: Macmillan, 1959. Examines Aristophanes as a comic writer. Asserts the satire of *The Clouds* is lost to an audience with no understanding of sophistic philosophy.

Butler, James H. *The Theatre and Drama of Greece and Rome*. San Francisco: Chandler, 1972. Claims Aristophanes was the greatest master of Grecian Old Comedy. Says *The Clouds* shows the decadence of Athens as well as the Sophists who corrupted it. Places *The Clouds* in the context of Old Comedy.

Freydberg, Bernard. "*Clouds* and the Measuring of Logos." In *Philosophy and Comedy: Aristophanes, Logos, and Eros*. Bloomington: Indiana University Press, 2008. Freydberg analyzes the philosophical concepts in *The Clouds* and several other plays by Aristophanes.

Hadas, Moses. *A History of Greek Literature*. New York: Columbia University Press, 1953. Asserts that Aristophanes handles Socrates kindly compared to other Greek playwrights. Covers the history of *The Clouds*' production as well as modern audiences' reactions to the treatment of Socrates in the play.

O'Regan, Daphne Elizabeth. *Rhetoric, Comedy, and the Violence of Language in Aristophanes' "Clouds."* New York: Oxford University Press, 1992. O'Regan's analysis of *The Clouds* focuses on logos, or the power of reasoning, describing how that power is consistently defeated in the play when it is confronted by human desire.

Silk, M. S. *Aristophanes and the Definition of Comedy*. New York: Oxford University Press, 2002. Silk looks at Aristophanes not as merely an ancient Greek dramatist but also as one of the world's great poets. He analyzes *The Clouds* and the other plays to examine their language, style, lyric poetry, character, and structure.

Snell, Bruno. *Poetry and Society: The Role of Poetry in Ancient Greece*. Freeport, N.Y.: Books for Libraries Press, 1971. Claims Aristophanes sees most wise men as mere busybodies and fools, such as he portrays Socrates to be in *The Clouds*. Compares the play to other dramatic works.

Cloudsplitter

Author: Russell Banks (1940-   )
First published: 1998
Type of work: Novel
Type of plot: Historical realism
Time of plot: c. 1840-1859
Locale: North Elba, New York; Kansas; Harpers Ferry, Virginia

Principal characters:
JOHN BROWN, an abolitionist
OWEN and FRED, his sons
MISS PEABODY, a niece of writer Nathaniel Hawthorne

The Story:

As the twentieth century dawns, Owen Brown, the last survivor of the raid on Harpers Ferry, begins writing a series of letters to Oswald Garrison Villard, intended to help Villard with research for his biography of Brown's father, abolitionist John Brown. Owen never sends the letters.

John Brown is a sheep farmer in Ohio, where he has a reputation as an expert in fine wools, but he is a poor businessman, struggling to make ends meet by operating a tannery. At one point Brown and son Owen sail to England to try to negotiate a better deal from English wool merchants, but the trip is an expensive disaster. It is, however, a formative experience for Owen. On the boat, father and son meet Miss Peabody, who is the niece of writer Nathaniel Hawthorne. She is pregnant and unmarried. She urges Owen to reconsider his life by embracing a pragmatic philosophy rather than Puritan or Transcendentalist philosophies.

After his return from England, Brown moves his extensive family (he has seven children with his first wife and thirteen with his second) to a farm outside North Elba, New York. Tahawus Mountain overlooks the farm. Brown has been a passionate supporter of the abolitionist cause, and he makes his North Elba farm a stop on the Underground Railway for escaping slaves from the South. He soon becomes more actively involved in abolitionist politics, and when conflict flares in Kansas, he gathers several of his sons and sets out to fight.

At Pottawatomie, Brown is indecisive; son Owen instigates a massacre. Once again, at the Battle of Osawatomie, Brown proves to be an appallingly bad leader, sacrificing his favored son, Fred, in a needless and scrappy defeat. However, the battle transforms Brown into a national figure and a mythic hero, and from this moment events move with a tragic inevitability. The massacre at Pottawatomie puts an end to any possibility of compromise with the slavers. As soon as he returns from Kansas, Brown begins planning a raid on Harpers Ferry, which turns out to be as ill-conceived and as poorly executed as Brown's earlier military enterprises. Owen accompanies his father on the raid but is left to guard the camp outside the town, which it is hoped will be a staging post for liberated slaves. The raid goes disastrously wrong, and Owen is one of the very few to escape. The raid sets in motion events that will culminate in the American Civil War.

Critical Evaluation:

Russell Banks's *Cloudsplitter* is an epic novel that tells a familiar story, and the story sticks closely to the known facts. If it did not take much to retell the story of the novel, far more complex are the issues he raises in this novel.

Beginning around the mid-nineteenth century, and building on a Puritan and Transcendental tradition, American writers tended to espouse an extreme laissez-faire philosophy that surfaces in the figure of the lone hero, the competent man of so much American popular literature. This lone hero is Owen Wister's Virginian, the lone force for law and honor, who is in reality the protector of vested interests and the abuse of power (and more recently incarnated in Clint Eastwood's Dirty Harry). This lone hero also is the more liberal adventurer facing himself and the wilderness in Jack London's stories of Alaska, and is the rebellious vagabond of writers such as Henry Miller and Jack Kerouac.

From the left and right of the political spectrum, the lone hero displays the virtue of going it alone; of not being dependent on government resources, on society, on anyone else, for one's success. This staple of American fiction is a myth of the status quo, and much of American literature, of whatever stripe, has been a development of or an engagement with this myth. The novels that particularly address the American past, which remake its heroes and villains to suit a more modern mode, are among that form of American literature that is engaged in the business of mythologizing the United States.

Of all the heroes and villains who have emerged in this rethinking of the American past (and, hence, of the American present), one of the most ambiguous and most interesting is John Brown. Brown committed atrocities in Kansas yet pricked the conscience of the nation about slavery; he was foolhardy in his raid on Harpers Ferry, yet his foolhardiness, based on a belief in the rightness of his cause, in some way makes him admirable; he was a religious fanatic, yet he became a hero of the liberal cause; he was a failure at everything he did, yet he now stands for a people who worship success; and he was the trigger who would eventually unleash a cruel and divisive civil war, yet he wanted good. No wonder these contradictions have given rise to so many novels; John Brown is a perfect vehicle for mythologizing America.

In *Cloudsplitter*, Banks paints Brown's portrait through the eyes of his son, Owen Brown. Owen is the one who is split; he cannot share his father's beliefs but finds himself irresistibly drawn into all of his father's actions. Banks has written something that is determinedly not a hagiography, yet it is the creation of a mythic hero. John Brown is not just a force of nature (the mountain), he also is the measure by which one's own life must be judged. This, surely, is the role of the mythic hero, and although Owen himself does not believe the myth, he cannot help but witness it—and create it.

Like all mythic heroes, John Brown has his particular attributes; in *Cloudsplitter* (though it may seem paradoxical for one so closely associated with business failures and with the chaos of what is now called domestic terrorism), his attribute is order. He brings rightness to things. The Brown family, left to its own devices, sinks into apathy, disease, and disorder, until the Old Man, John Brown, arrives to set things straight. Brown is portrayed as more than a man; he is a force for order, for physical as well as social health. He even displays a supernatural aspect. For instance, at Osawatomie, John and Owen see a mirage that allows them to witness the killing of Fred Brown, John's son and Owen's brother.

Offset against this examination of a larger than life heroic age, the novel also presents a confrontation with the future. Part of this is inherent in the structure: Told from Owen's old age, events are witnessed in hindsight, seen from the turning point of the new American century and redolent with a sense of the future. A scene early in the book relates an elderly Owen hearing that his companions from the Harpers Ferry raid are to be reburied at John Brown's old farm at North Elba, New York. Owen travels by train across the country, walks the long road from the station to the farm, and stands silently during the ceremony, continuing to do so long after it has ended. During that long walk and during the ceremony, he had remained alone and apparently unnoticed, almost as if he were a ghost. It is a curiously haunted and haunting episode, loaded with significance—a supernatural visitation from America's past to America's future.

However, the novel features this sense of America coming up against the future. Miss Peabody expresses the notion that being a sinner is what it means to be modern and up to date. The new age is inevitably a lesser age, an age that cannot live up to its progenitors, just as Owen cannot live up to his father. Owen, reinventing himself at Miss Peabody's request, is leaving behind the Puritan and the Transcendental for a future that is pragmatic yet less significant than the past. Readers are forced to compare Owen to his father, because this is what Owen himself does, and from such comparisons readers see that John Brown is entirely of his age, yet he is the greater person for it. John Brown's moral certainty comes straight from the Puritan strand of American thought; Owen's more modern worries about the everyday application of morals are much more pragmatic.

The whole novel, therefore, becomes the story of Owen's struggle with the idea of his father. Owen sees his father's failures, as at Osawatomie, and yet the failures are what make his father great. He constantly chafes against his father's rule: John Brown is shown to be fiercely authoritarian, a hard man to like, yet Owen cannot break free as his older brothers, Jason and John, Jr., have done. Like Isaac (biblical echoes are, inevitably, profuse in this novel), Owen finds himself turning to his father for the rightness and the certainty he needs in his life. He sees the weaknesses in his father's plans for Harpers Ferry, but goes along anyway. At one point, Owen and his father attend a lecture by philosopher-writer Ralph Waldo Emerson on heroism. Owen recognizes that Emerson's words describe his father perfectly, and he wonders if the Old Man himself realizes this, too—though it is a characteristic of heroism that the hero does not recognize himself as heroic. Owen is right to recognize his father as a hero, the man who is larger than life and whose stature continues to grow in the novel, and beyond it. However, this great stature also refers obliquely to Owen, the hero of this novel, who does not realize he is heroic yet proves to be the moral shadow of his father for an age that does not need mythic heroes.

Cloudsplitter takes as its subject one of the archetypal figures of American history, a figure who has inspired numerous novels, yet Banks makes this novel a story not of great or terrible deeds, or of one strange, austere character. Rather, he makes it a story of a figure from the heroic age at large in an age of the shoddy, a story of a figure from myth in a rational age, a story of the product of Puritanism and Transcendentalism just at that point when America was turning to pragmatism. In other words, John Brown was made into a represen-

tative figure for a clash of philosophies, an aspect of the past when America had been turning to the future. If an epic is work that identifies a magical hero in whom the spirit of the age is given flesh, a work that recounts the story of how the past became the present, then *Cloudsplitter* has to be considered a great modern American epic.

Paul Kincaid

Further Reading

Banks, Russell. "In Response to James McPherson's Reading of *Cloudsplitter*." In *Novel History: Historians and Novelists Confront America's Past*, edited by Mark C. Carnes. New York: Simon & Schuster, 2001. Banks explains how he thinks novelists turn history into fiction. Written in response to a reading of *Cloudsplitter* in this same collection.

Hutchison, Anthony. "Representative Man: John Brown and the Politics of Redemption in Russell Banks's *Cloudsplitter*." *Journal of American Studies* 41, no. 1 (2006): 67-82. An examination of Banks's treatment of race, focusing on the centrality of race and racism in his fiction, including *Cloudsplitter*.

McPherson, James M. "Russell Banks's Fictional Portrait of John Brown." In *Novel History: Historians and Novelists Confront America's Past*, edited by Mark C. Carnes. New York: Simon & Schuster, 2001. A comparison of historical events as presented by Banks and actual historical events on record. Banks's response to this reading of *Cloudsplitter* is included in the same collection.

Niemi, Robert. *Russell Banks*. New York: Twayne, 1997. An introductory study, part of the reliable Twayne's American Authors series. This volume provides critical analyses of Banks's fiction and a brief biography, chronology, and annotated bibliography.

Trucks, Rob. *The Pleasure of Influence: Conversations with American Male Fiction Writers*. West Lafayette, Ind.: NotaBell Books, 2002. A collection of comprehensive interviews of American male writers of fiction, including Banks, who discuss their literary influences and their own works.

The Clown

Author: Heinrich Böll (1917-1985)
First published: Ansichten eines Clowns, 1963 (English
  translation, 1965)
Type of work: Novel
Type of plot: Psychological realism
Time of plot: 1945-1960
Locale: Bonn, Germany

Principal characters:
HANS SCHNIER, the protagonist, a professional clown
LEO SCHNIER, his brother
HENRIETTA SCHNIER, his dead sister
DR. and MRS. SCHNIER, his parents
MARIE DERKUM, his former lover
MONIKA SILVS,
KINKEL,
SOMMERWILD, and
HERIBERT ZÜPFNER, members of a Catholic group

The Story:

Hans Schnier, a professional clown, returns to Bonn, his hometown, after he injures his knee performing his act while drunk. When Schnier arrives in Bonn, he has little money (his last employer refused to pay his full fee), no savings, and little hope of future work. Only weeks before this injury, Schnier was a highly paid, well-regarded performer earning enough to live in luxury hotels with Marie Derkum, his lover and companion. When Marie leaves him to marry Heribert Züpfner, a Catholic official and a member of a religious group to which Marie belongs, Schnier ceases to care about the quality of his work as a clown. He stops practicing and starts to drink more, which causes his performances to decline rapidly.

From his Bonn apartment, Schnier calls friends and family members, hoping for monetary and emotional support. However, each of his actions, even his conversations, triggers painful memories. At first these flashbacks are brief recollections of Marie and her group of progressive Catholics, but the reveries increase in length. In one of his early flashbacks, Schnier remembers his sister affectionately; she often acted unconventionally, saying and doing what she felt. With her parents' encouragement, especially that of her mother, this sister was sent on antiaircraft duty in February, 1945, on a mission that killed her. Schnier blames his mother's nationalistic fervor for his sister's death, and when he calls his mother, her official tone and her greeting phrase—"Executive Committee of the Societies for the Reconciliation of Racial Differences"—angers Schnier and reminds him of his mother's zeal when sending her daughter off to save German soil from "Jewish Yankees." Although Schnier is calling his mother to ask for her support, he cruelly answers her greeting by saying, "I am a delegate of the Executive Committee of Jewish Yankees, just passing through—may I please speak to your daughter?" Mrs. Schnier is momentarily hurt, but she

recovers quickly and rebuffs her son with her severe, dogmatic manner.

After the conversation with his mother, Schnier thinks of Marie, and that triggers the memory of an event that occurred six years earlier and resulted in the consummation of their relationship. Hans was twenty-one and Marie nineteen when he went boldly to her room and slept with her. After this, Marie dropped out of school, and Schnier left his family to begin his career as a clown, but his career developed slowly and the two barely earned enough money to survive. They both wanted children, but Marie had a number of miscarriages. The final one occurred just before she left. Schnier's memories of his life with Marie were occasionally interrupted by speculations about Marie's present relationship with Züpfner, a relationship Schnier considered adulterous even though Marie and Züpfner are married.

Schnier calls other friends and relatives and holds unpleasant conversations with each. Although he wants money and psychological support from them, his manner ensures that even those who can help him do not. When he talks to Kinkel, a respected Catholic theologian and a member of the group to which Marie and Züpfner belong, Schnier blames Kinkel and the Catholic Church for his loss of Marie: "That much I have grasped of your metaphysics: What she is doing is fornication and adultery, and Prelate Sommerwild is acting the pimp." Schnier attacks Kinkel throughout their conversation, and he asserts that his relationship with Marie constitutes a marriage that Kinkel and others destroyed.

While waiting for friends to return his telephone calls, Schnier bathes and reads newspapers. This, too, causes him to remember Marie and her Catholic group. He recalls that at first he had refused to marry Marie because she insisted on a Catholic marriage that required him to swear that their children would be raised in the Catholic faith. Later, when he was willing to agree to these conditions, Marie refused to marry him because she did not accept his conversion as sincere. Schnier believed that his union with Marie constituted a marriage, whether condoned by the government and the church or not, but Marie needed Schnier's commitment to the church. When Schnier talks with Sommerwild, a Catholic priest who is a member of Marie's group, Schnier accuses him of having furthered Marie's marriage to Züpfner, claiming that the priest sent the couple to Rome "to make the whoring complete."

Still waiting for phone calls, Schnier is surprised by the unexpected appearance of his father, a wealthy German capitalist. The visit is awkward and unpleasant for both, since they had not seen each other for several years and never had a meaningful conversation. The two discuss many painful issues, but Schnier junior believes his father is playing a role that he cannot abandon even to help his son. Schnier junior refers to the needless hardships the family suffered and the fact that, despite their wealth, they never had enough food. Schnier also remembers that his father twice during the war showed compassion: once when Schnier was accused of "defeatism" and once when two women were accused of fraternizing with the enemy. The father agrees to pay his son a monthly stipend, but Schnier knows he will never receive it.

After his father leaves, Schnier reads in the evening paper that Herbert Kalick received a federal cross of merit for "his services in spreading democratic ideas among the young." This is the same Herbert Kalick who led the local Hitler youth group during World War II. It is Kalick who denounced Schnier as a "defeatist," and he is also responsible for the death of a young boy whom Kalick forced to carry a loaded bazooka.

Schnier attempts many times to contact his brother, Leo, who is in a Catholic seminary. Leo, who converted from Protestantism to Catholicism, renounced most worldly possessions and refuses to break the seminary's rules to help his brother. Schnier contacts Monika Silvs, a sympathetic member of the Catholic group who helped him in the past, but Sommerwild instructed her to avoid Schnier. When it becomes clear that he will receive no help or support, Schnier decides to sing, play the guitar, and beg at the train station. One March evening, Schnier walks to the train station and sits on the steps, singing a song about "Poor Pope John."

Critical Evaluation:

Nine years after writing *The Clown*, a work that exemplifies the themes and methods employed in his other novels, Heinrich Böll received the Nobel Prize in Literature. Böll

was a post-World War II German writer from a Catholic, pacifist family, a writer who fought in the war and was wounded four times before being captured and taken to an American prisoner-of-war camp, so his life and fiction encapsulate the religious, moral, and political dilemmas of post-World War II Germany. *The Clown* is the personal narrative of a single person, one individual, Hans Schnier, who is the clown of the title. In focusing on the character's idiosyncratic view of the world and in particular on his love for Marie, the novel explores the problems of all humans in twentieth century societies.

On a political level, the book recounts Hans's involvement with a Nazi youth group; his sister's death for the Nazi cause; his mother's anti-Semitic, pro-Nazi views; his own condemnation by another youth as a "defeatist"; and his father's tacit support of the Nazis. The focus of Böll's satire is on those hypocrites who blindly supported fascism as well as on those who impetuously shifted their allegiance after the war. Hans's mother, for example, an ardent Nazi supporter before 1945, afterward becomes the president of a society for the reconciliation of racial differences. Böll accurately depicts and attacks the erstwhile Nazis who attained positions of power in Germany during the 1960's, but on a more universal level the author satirizes all humans who heedlessly pledge allegiance to any political cause.

The Clown also explores a religious schism in German society. Hans is from a Protestant family, but Marie is an ardent Catholic and belongs to an influential and powerful Catholic group. The clown's brother abandons his family's Protestant religion and trains to be a Catholic priest in a seminary, a decision that hurts his parents. On one level, Böll examines the split between German Protestants and Catholics, but on another level he looks at a more universal question that parallels the political dilemma: To what extent should an individual blindly accept the doctrine of a religion? Marie accepts the teachings of her group and leaves the clown. Leo abandons his parents' faith to join the Catholic Church, but his decision appears no more thoughtful than had been his decision to enlist in the army. The religious and political themes ultimately reinforce the novel's discussion of marriage.

Who has the right to sanction a marriage? Hans learns that the state must issue a license before a church will perform the marriage. In his case, he would have had to sign a document swearing that he would raise his children in the Catholic Church. In opposition to these conventional, institutional definitions of marriage, the clown, Hans, advocates a monogamous, common-law definition that allows him to claim Marie as his wife. The issue of marriage moves the political and religious themes to a very personal level, forcing the reader to consider whether marriage is a private, personal commitment between two individuals or a public, religious matter.

These questions of politics, religion, and marriage are presented ironically through the eyes of Hans, whose interior monologue conveys his anger, suffering, headaches, depression, and grief. The reader can identify with him because in his suffering he exposes the failings of others, even though his persona as an alcoholic clown can elicit little empathy or compassion. His role as a clown symbolizes his inability to commit and to take life seriously, but despite his faults the clown represents the individual who locates morality and responsibility within himself and fears those who abdicate their responsibility to society at large. Through Hans, Böll explores the harm done by those who dogmatically accept the beliefs of political parties or organized religions. *The Clown* ultimately exhorts individuals to contemplate their relationship with authority and other human beings.

Roark Mulligan

Further Reading

Beck, Evelyn T. "A Feminist Critique of Böll's *Ansichten eines Clowns.*" *University of Dayton Review* 12 (Spring, 1976): 19-24. Beck analyzes Hans Schnier as a negative person who exploited Marie. Beck asserts that with Marie, Böll depicted a victim of male domination.

Böll, Heinrich. *What's to Become of the Boy? Or, Something to Do with Books.* Translated by Leila Vennewitz. New York: Knopf, 1984. Written just before his death, this is Böll's longest autobiographical work. In it, he reveals connections between his life and his novels.

Butler, Michael, ed. *The Narrative Fiction of Heinrich Böll: Social Conscience and Literary Achievement.* New York: Cambridge University Press, 1994. Analyzes Böll's recurring themes of love, morality, economic pressures, and organized religion and his emphasis on renewal and utopianism.

Conard, Robert C. *Heinrich Böll.* Boston: G. K. Hall, 1981. A good introduction to Böll's life and works.

_____. *Understanding Heinrich Böll.* Columbia: University of South Carolina Press, 1992. Includes a brief biography, a chronology, and a bibliography. In one chapter, Conard analyzes Böll's major novels, among them *The Clown.*

Finlay, Frank. *On the Rationality of Poetry: Heinrich Böll's Aesthetic Thinking.* Amsterdam: Rodopi, 1996. Discusses Böll's writings on literature, in which he defends the "rationality of poetry" and expresses his philosophy of aesthetics.

Reid, James Henderson. *Heinrich Böll: A German for His Time.* Oxford, England: Oswald Wolff, 1988. Reid's book explores the connections among Böll's fiction, his life, and his times.

Tachibana, Reiko. *Narrative as Counter-Memory: A Half-Century of Postwar Writing in Germany and Japan.* New York: State University of New York Press, 1998. Although this book does not discuss *The Clown,* it analyzes other fictional works in which Böll draws upon his personal memories to describe Germany's defeat in World War II and its subsequent occupation and reconstruction.

Zachau, Reinhard K. *Heinrich Böll: Forty Years of Criticism.* Columbia, S.C.: Camden House, 1994. Discusses critical approaches to Böll's work and evaluates Böll's influence on subsequent German literature.

The Cocktail Party

Author: T. S. Eliot (1888-1965)
First produced: 1949; first published, 1950
Type of work: Drama
Type of plot: Comedy of manners
Time of plot: Mid-twentieth century
Locale: London

Principal characters:
EDWARD CHAMBERLAYNE, a lawyer
LAVINIA, his wife
JULIA SHUTTLETHWAITE, a meddling woman
CELIA COPLESTONE, a sensitive young woman
PETER QUILPE, in love with Celia
ALEXANDER MACCOLGIE GIBBS, a meddling man
SIR HENRY HARCOURT-REILLY, initially unidentified

The Story:

The Chamberlaynes are giving a cocktail party in their London flat. The atmosphere is somewhat strained because Lavinia, the host, is not there, and Edward, her bumbling husband, hastily invents a sick aunt to account for her absence. As usual, Alex has an exotic story to tell, for he travels widely and knows everyone. Julia, a sharp-eyed and sharp-tongued family friend, misses the point of his tale and wonders why Alex and the Maharaja are up a tree. Julia usually misses the point of stories she hears.

The assembly demands that Julia give her inimitable imitation of Lady Klootz and the wedding cake. They have all heard the story before, except possibly Edward, who forgets stories, and an unidentified and unintroduced guest. Somehow Julia goes off on a family who has a harmless son, and the story never gets told. The harmless son is a fascinating person: He can hear the cries of bats. Then Peter tells of a scenario that he wrote and that, unfortunately, never was produced.

To Edward's relief, the guests prepare to leave. Only the stranger remains. He drinks gin with Edward for a while, and Edward is compelled to confide in him. Lavinia is not really at her aunt's house; she simply left with no explanation. The stranger points out that her leaving might be a blessing, since she is demanding and practical, but Edward is uneasy, without knowing exactly why he wants her back. The stranger promises that the erring wife will return within twenty-four hours if Edward will ask for no explanations. He warns also that both Lavinia and Edward might be greatly changed. The stranger, full of gin, breaks into song as he leaves the apartment.

Julia, returning for her glasses, has Peter in tow. The glasses are in Julia's bag all the time, and she departs again, leaving an agitated Peter behind. The young man wants to confide in Edward. He fell in love with Celia after attending many concerts with her, and she was very friendly. Lately, however, she is unresponsive. He asks if Edward will intercede for him. At this juncture, Alex comes gaily back. Edward is irritated. He asks Peter and Alex to lock the door when they leave so no one else will wander in. Alex archly goes to the kitchen, intent on whipping up a meal for the lone Edward. He succeeds in using up all the fresh eggs in some outlandish concoction.

At last, after answering the phone several times, Edward settles down in solitary comfort to play patience. Then the doorbell rings and in comes Celia. She divined that Lavinia left Edward, and now she thinks it would be a good time for Edward to seek a divorce so that he and Celia can marry. Edward agrees, but despite his repeated assurances of continued

love, Celia is uneasy, for she senses a change in him. Edward then confesses that Lavinia is coming back and that he almost wants her back. He scarcely knows why he does, for until his wife left he wanted only Celia. Celia is discomfited at her faint-hearted lover. When Julia returns once more, this time to invite Edward to dinner, Celia escapes into the kitchen. There, under pretext of getting a lunch for the lone Edward, she ruins Alex's concoction completely.

The next day, the stranger returns. Again he warns Edward that by wanting Lavinia to return he sets in motion forces beyond his control. When she returns, she will be a stranger and Edward will be a stranger to her. Edward made his choice, however, and will have to abide by it. After admonishing Edward to receive any visitors who might come, the mysterious stranger leaves by the back stairs.

Celia is the first to arrive. She comes at Julia's request, apparently in response to a telegram from Lavinia. While they are together, Celia has a chance to look at Edward carefully; he seems to her only a rather comic middle-aged man. She laughs now at her infatuation. Peter arrives in response to Alex's invitation. Alex also received a wire, ostensibly from Lavinia. He has time for some reproachful remarks to Celia and then announces he is leaving for Hollywood.

Lavinia arrives next, surprised to find Peter and Celia and disclaiming any knowledge of telegrams to Alex and Julia, with whose arrival the mystery deepens. At length the guests depart and Lavinia turns expectantly to Edward. He has little to say beyond reproaching her for her overbearing ways, and she twits him for being unable to make decisions. When she suggests that he is on the verge of a nervous breakdown, he is angered but interested in the possibility. He resolves stoutly not to visit any doctor Lavinia might recommend.

In Sir Henry's offices, preparations are being made to receive patients. The first is Edward, who is surprised to see that Sir Henry is his mysterious stranger. In the consultation, Edward reveals that he wants Lavinia back because she dominated him so long that he is incapable of existence without her. Sir Henry then brings in Lavinia, so that the whole problem can be threshed out.

During the conversation it is revealed that Lavinia left because of Edward's affair with Celia. Edward, somewhat shaken to learn that she knows of the affair, grows confident again when Lavinia confesses that she was infatuated with Peter. Sir Henry diagnoses their trouble as mutual fear: Edward is afraid he cannot make successful love to anyone, and Lavinia is afraid she is completely unlovable. The doctor assures them that they have every requirement for a successful life together. They have a mutual fear and hatred of each other, and both are quite mediocre people. They leave, moderately reconciled.

Julia arrives at the doctor's office to ask how successful her scheming was. It is she who induced Sir Henry to step in, and Alex abetted her. Celia also comes in for a consultation. She has vague feelings of guilt and sin and wants to take a rest cure. After talking with her, Sir Henry recognizes that she is an outstanding person, that her destiny calls her. He advises her to be at ease and do whatever she has to do.

Two years later, the Chamberlaynes are giving another cocktail party for many of the old crowd. They are smugly settled in their mediocrity and even make a pretense of being in love. To them, cocktail parties are their measure of social standing. Peter comes in hurriedly. He is a great success in America and now has money and renown of a sort. His destiny is a material one. Alex arrives next. He is just back from bearing the white man's burden on a tropical island. He reports Celia's death. Celia was a nurse on the island and was killed in a native rebellion. Her destiny called her to martyrdom for the love of humanity.

Critical Evaluation:

Ten years after T. S. Eliot presented *The Family Reunion* (1939) to mixed reviews, he completed his second verse drama, *The Cocktail Party*, which became more popular. In its first draft, sketched out in June, 1948, the play was in three scenes (or acts) with a projected epilogue and was tentatively titled "One-Eyed Riley." According to Elliott Martin Browne, producer of all Eliot's plays except *Sweeney Agonistes* (1932), the original draft with its revisions was based more closely than the completed work upon Euripides' *Alkēstis*, 438 B.C.E. (*Alcestis*, 1781). The "death" of Alcestis was to correspond with Lavinia's departure from Edward before the party begins in scene 1. The services performed by Heracles, who descends into Hades to restore to Admetus his sacrificing wife, were to parallel to some extent those of Sir Henry Harcourt-Reilly, the psychiatrist who later patches together the flawed Chamberlayne marriage. Celia Coplestone, whom Eliot later described as the major character of the play, is only a minor personality in the early drafts, and the roles of Julia Shuttlethwaite, Peter Quilpe, and Alexander MacColgie Gibbs (first called Alexander Farquhar-Gibbs) are unexpanded and mostly comic.

In the preliminary revisions of the manuscript, Alex does not appear between the party scene of the first act and the conclusion of the consulting-room scene, with its elaborate libation-ritual of the Guardians. That scene, however, was much more fully developed in the manuscripts. In the final version of *The Cocktail Party*, produced at the Edinburgh

Festival in August, 1949, the scene was simplified and its poetic values were sharpened; it was offered in its present form, in three acts, with act 1 in three fully developed scenes, act 2 in one scene (Sir Henry's office), and act 3 in a brief scene at the Chamberlaynes' London flat.

Because *The Cocktail Party* changed so markedly during the early stages of its writing, the parts, which separately are effective, do not perfectly cohere as a whole work of stagecraft. The play is both a comedy of manners, much like the social satires of the eighteenth century, and a theological—specifically Catholic—drama of salvation. The lighter parts, especially the entire first act and most of the last, resemble the witty, tart, urbane plays of Richard Sheridan or the sophisticated comedies of Oscar Wilde, W. Somerset Maugham, and even Noël Coward. The serious parts—also (*The Divine Comedy*, 1802) "comic" in the sense that Dante's epic may be called a *commedia*—resemble more closely the tragic farces of the novels of Evelyn Waugh. To satisfy the requirements of both light and serious comedy, Eliot's characters play two kinds of roles. The Julia of the first act is a meddlesome, scatterbrained old gossip, but in the second act, she is a sober and indeed sanctified Guardian of spiritual destiny. Alex in the first act is a bumbling froth, an incompetent who concocts outrageous dishes and pops in and out of the action, much to Edward's annoyance. Yet in the ritual scene at the end of act 2, he is another Guardian, perhaps even more mysterious than Julia, who has connections throughout the world—"even in California."

The most difficult character to understand, because of his double function in the play, is Sir Henry, the psychiatrist. In the first act, he is described simply as the Unidentified Guest. A secretive but enlightened visitor to the Chamberlayne party, he apparently understands the nature of the quarrel between Edward and Lavinia; pulls the strings, so to speak, to arrange for her return to her husband; yet never reveals his own position. A confessor figure, he is at the same time a drunken reveler. Before he departs, toward the end of the first scene, he sings a bawdy song (the verses in the play are quite decorous, but other stanzas are traditionally ribald). "One-Eyed Riley" may remind the audience of the fertility themes in *The Waste Land* (1922), or it may, as Eliot suggested, recall the heroic-absurd figure of Heracles from the Euripides play. Sir Henry is both savant and fool, gifted with insight but unsteady from too much gin.

The meaning of his actions is similarly ambiguous. In his professional activity as a psychiatrist, he becomes a parody of psychiatrists. Nobody lies on the analyst's couch but Sir Henry; he collects "information" about Lavinia and Edward, without their consent, as part of his investigation of their marital condition; and he prescribes, when necessary, a cure that may require the patient to visit a hotel or a sanatorium. The hotel, a halfway house or retreat between the sane and insane world, is Lavinia's first destination, before she returns to Edward. The sanatorium, still more mysterious, is intended to cure victims of illusion, unreality. Still other patients, like Celia, he urges to discover their own mental health by working out their proper salvation. No wonder Lavinia questions whether the psychiatrist is a devil or merely a practical joker. In fact, Sir Henry is called a devil several times in the play, but he more closely resembles a divine agent. Although he has no power to effect spiritual cures, he understands the maladies of human or spiritual deprivation and prescribes a course of action to remedy the problem. Those sick persons must, however, make a decision to reject or accept the psychiatrist's advice. Gifted with prescience, Sir Henry does not control the moral choices of his patients. They have free will, and although their destinies can be predicted, they must resolve whether to follow the example of Peter Quilpe, who chooses to go to Boltwell—earthly corruption—or Celia, who chooses martyrdom as a means of salvation.

Celia, the moral center of the play, is also a difficult person to understand. Unlike Sir Henry, she has no metaphysical function in the drama, but her character seems inconsistent. In the first scene of act 1, she is a vapid young socialite who presses Julia to finish her inane story about Lady Klootz's wedding cake. In the second scene, the audience discovers that Celia has been Edward's mistress. Disappointed when her faint-hearted lover tells her that he is quite comfortable in his relationship with Lavinia and awaits his wife's return, she comes to understand that he is mediocre and unworthy of her affections. In the third scene, she is further estranged from Edward but no longer annoyed with him. Rather, she dismisses him as an amusing little boy, ludicrous but not vexing. Like Peter, she announces her decision to go abroad. The audience is not fully prepared for the change in Celia's character in act 2, where she appears to be intense, introspective, almost visionary. In her consultation with Sir Henry, the most touching and poetically effective part of the play, she reveals unexpected resources of strength and integrity. She is weary of herself, not because others have failed her, but because she has failed the world. Guilt-ridden for no specific cause, she confesses to sin. Her psychiatrist-metaphysician suggests a spiritual cure for her guilt. She must discover her own redemption—one that will lead to a kind of crucifixion on an anthill, an absurd but (from Eliot's viewpoint) purposeful death.

Because Celia's death, announced by Alex in act 3, usually comes as a shock to the audience, it should be understood in the light of Eliot's theme. Although *The Cocktail Party* is superficially an elegant comedy of manners, it is a morality play. The theme of the play is that reality takes many guises. All of the characters attempt to approach the real—or what is real for their needs—but most continue to play out roles of illusion. Edward, a Prufrock-like lawyer, reconciles with his practical but unimaginative wife. At the end of the play, just as at the beginning, the Chamberlaynes prepare a cocktail party to amuse other bored, lonely people like themselves. Their reconciliation to the "building of the hearth," the commonplace but necessary compromises of domesticity, is satisfactory for each partner. Edward cannot love anyone, but at least he does not have to dissemble his frailty to Lavinia. She, for her part, is unlovable, but her vanity will not suffer any insult from a complaisant husband like Edward. So each is content, understanding no other destiny.

For the few elect souls such as Celia, reality is not a casual entertainment like a cocktail party but the narrow path of Christian service. Her martyrdom (and, presumably, sainthood) is earned at the cost of terrible suffering. In Eliot's first version of the play, her death was described even more terribly: She was a victim of devouring ants. The final version tones down most of the horror by alluding to a crucifixion "very near an ant-hill." Eliot's point, however, is to affirm, through the announcement of Celia's death, the reality of divine interference in a world of the commonplace. Similarly, the transformation of comic figures such as Sir Henry, Julia, and Alex into spiritual Guardians of humankind reminds the audience that the real world itself is illusion, the unseen world real. It is significant to remember that the Guardians' final blessing for Edward, Lavinia, and Celia is taken from the Buddha's deathbed exhortation to his followers: "Work out your salvation with diligence." That is the message of Eliot's play.

"Critical Evaluation" by Leslie B. Mittleman

Further Reading

Badenhausen, Richard. "T. S. Eliot Speaks the Body: The Privileging of Female Discourse in *Murder in the Cathedral* and *The Cocktail Party*." In *Gender, Desire, and Sexuality in T. S. Eliot*, edited by Cassandra Laity and Nancy K. Gish. New York: Cambridge University Press, 2004. This discussion of gender issues in the two plays is included in a collection of essays that examines the treatment of desire, homoeroticism, and feminism in Eliot's poetry, plays, and prose.

Gordon, Lyndall. *T. S. Eliot: An Imperfect Life.* New York:

W. W. Norton, 1999. An authoritative, thoroughly researched biography that concedes Eliot's many personal flaws as well as describing his poetic genius.

Jones, David E. *The Plays of T. S. Eliot*. London: Routledge & Kegan Paul, 1960. In chapter 5, Jones analyzes the play's relationship to its Greek model, Euripides' *Alcestis*, and explains the strengths of a verse drama that is easy to follow and yet profound.

Kari, Daven Michael. *T. S. Eliot's Dramatic Pilgrimage: A Progress in Craft as an Expression of Christian Perspective*. Lewiston, N.Y.: Edwin Mellen Press, 1990. Examines Eliot's steadily improving use of characterization, verse techniques, and stagecraft as an expression of his movement from ascetic to communal models of Christian faith. An innovative and readable critique.

Moody, A. David, ed. *The Cambridge Companion to T. S.*

Eliot. New York: Cambridge University Press, 1994. Collection of essays, including discussions of Eliot's life; Eliot as a philosopher, a social critic, and a product of America; and religion, literature, and society in Eliot's work. Also features the essay "Pereira and After: The Cures of Eliot's Theater" by Robin Grove.

Raine, Craig. *T. S. Eliot*. New York: Oxford University Press, 2006. In this examination of Eliot's work, Raine maintains that "the buried life," or the failure of feeling, is a consistent theme in the poetry and plays. Chapter 5 focuses on Eliot's plays.

Tydeman, William. *"Murder in the Cathedral" and "The Cocktail Party."* Houndmills, England: Macmillan, 1988. A simple and straightforward interpretation of the plays as dramas. A good choice for directors and actors wishing to perform the play.

Cold Comfort Farm

Author: Stella Gibbons (1902-1989)
First published: 1932
Type of work: Novel
Type of plot: Parody
Time of plot: Early twentieth century
Locale: London and Sussex, England

Principal characters:
FLORA POSTE, a young lady of excellent manners
ADA DOOM STARKADDER, her aunt
AMOS STARKADDER, Ada's son
JUDITH STARKADDER, Amos's wife
SETH and REUBEN, Amos and Judith's sons
ELFINE, their daughter

The Story:

Flora Poste's parents die when she is nineteen, leaving her an income of one hundred pounds a year. They provided her with an expensive education that did not prepare her to earn her living. She visits a friend near London to decide what to do and develops a warm relationship with her cousin, Charles Fairford. She writes to various relatives to ask if she might stay with them and chooses the Starkadders, an aunt and cousins who live at Cold Comfort Farm in Howling, Sussex. Charles promises to rescue Flora in his plane whenever living on the farm becomes too much for her.

Adam Lambsbreath, the ninety-year-old farmhand, meets Flora at the station. He tells Flora that a curse on Cold Comfort Farm prevents it from flourishing and any of the family from leaving. Flora suspects, however, that Mrs. Ada Doom Starkadder, her deceased mother's sister, is the real curse. Aunt Ada Doom stays in her room and rules the family with a

will of iron. She has not left the farm in twenty years. Appalled by the condition of the farm and by the many violent and brooding Starkadders, Flora determines to tidy up life at Cold Comfort Farm.

Flora glimpses her seventeen-year-old cousin, Elfine, who never attended school and spends most of her time wandering about the moors writing poetry. Flora hears Meriam, the hired girl, groaning while delivering her fourth illegitimate child by Seth. Conferring with Cousin Judith, Flora learns that Judith's husband, Amos, did a great, secret wrong to Flora's deceased father. Coarse and filled with lust for the land, Reuben is the only true farmer among the Starkadders. He suspects that Flora wants to take over the farm, but when she assures him that the farm is the last thing she wants, she wins him over. Seth makes suggestive advances to her, but Flora discovers that his great love in life is not women, as she has assumed, but "the talkies." Though exhausted by her interaction with these family members, Flora decides she must become acquainted with the other Starkadders.

Flora drops hints, but she is not invited to meet Aunt Ada Doom. Flora decides to work on Cousin Amos, a huge, rude, religious fanatic. She accompanies him to his sermon at the Church of the Quivering Brethren and twice proposes that he can do even more good by preaching throughout the country. Opposite the Majestic Cinema, Flora is reminded of Mr. Neck, a Hollywood producer she knows who will be flying to England in the spring to look for film actors.

Flora begins to worry about Elfine, who is apparently in love with Richard Hawk-Monitor, the scion of country gentry who live nearby. There is soon to be a ball in honor of Richard's twenty-first birthday, and Flora arranges an invitation for Elfine, with herself as chaperon. The Starkadders expect Elfine to marry Urk, a farm cousin. Flora secretly grooms the girl and gives her private instruction in good taste and deportment. Elfine makes a grand entrance at the ball. Before the night is over, Richard announces their engagement.

Satisfied with her night's work, Flora returns to Cold Comfort Farm with Elfine. They find the entire family, including Aunt Ada Doom, assembled downstairs for the annual counting, when the matriarch counts the Starkadders to see if anyone died. Flora announces Elfine's engagement, which causes Urk to fall into the sandwiches. Judith introduces Flora to Aunt Ada Doom, but the old woman only raves and thrashes. Amos announces to his mother that he broke her chain and will leave that night to spread the Lord's word abroad. Aunt Ada Doom grows wilder. Soon Urk drags Meriam out the door, bellowing that since he lost Elfine he will take Meriam.

The next afternoon, Flora discovers that Mr. Neck, her friend from Hollywood, has arrived. Flora introduces Seth, whom Mr. Neck recognizes as the sexually successful local bounder, a type of film actor who tends to be a big hit with women. Seth packs and leaves with the producer, accompanied by wild screams from Aunt Ada Doom. Letters arrive from Amos, who is off to America to preach and who leaves the farm to Reuben.

When Richard's mother decides to have the wedding reception at Cold Comfort Farm, Flora is dismayed. She installs the men's wives at the farm to prepare while she attends to Judith and Aunt Ada Doom. A luncheon for Judith with a Viennese psychoanalyst is arranged, and Judith drives off with Dr. Mudel for six months of treatment, looking quite content. Back in Howling, Flora brings her aunt's lunch upstairs and confers with her until late.

The day of the wedding dawns bright and beautiful. The remaining Starkadders watch the church ceremony with pleasure. At the farm, resplendent with garlands, lush gardens, and striped awnings, Aunt Ada Doom astonishes everyone by greeting guests in a black leather flying suit. Flora tries to discover the secret wrong done to her father, but Aunt Ada Doom does not have a chance to answer before the plane arrives to whisk her off to Paris. The honeymoon couple are next to fly off. Flora goes to the village to call Charles, who lands his plane at the farm three hours later. He and Flora fall into each other's arms, declare their love, and fly off to London together.

Critical Evaluation:

Stella Gibbons was a prolific writer who started out as a journalist after attending the University of London. For ten years she worked as a drama and literature critic, special reporter, and fashion writer. Later, she produced more than thirty novels and collections of poetry and short stories. In quality, none of them rivaled *Cold Comfort Farm*, her first published novel, which won the prestigious Femina Vie Heureuse prize in 1933 and became a popular classic of English literature. A member of the Royal Society of Literature, Gibbons was elected a fellow in 1950. She hated publicity and politics and spent the last thirty years of her life as a recluse.

Cold Comfort Farm is generally considered to be a parody of the type of novel that British authors such as Thomas Hardy, D. H. Lawrence, and Mary Webb wrote in the early twentieth century. Their novels are usually characterized by crude, uneducated characters; brooding landscapes; dark mysticism that includes a fatalistic view of life; and a pervasive atmosphere of violence, which occasionally erupts. Mary Webb's novel *Precious Bane* (1924) includes a semiliterate, harelipped heroine; a brother who murders his own mother; and a village of savage, superstitious people. Many of the characters of *Precious Bane* could have appeared in the pages of *Cold Comfort Farm*, yet while Webb's novel is tragic, Gibbons used her material to comic effect.

Gibbons sets the tone of *Cold Comfort Farm* in an opening letter to one Anthony Pookworthy, a fictional novelist. She tells him he has given her joy with his books, which are "records of intense spiritual struggles, staged in the wild setting of mere, berg, or fen. Your characters are ageless and elemental things, tossed like straws on the seas of passion." Yet Gibbons intends to write a book that is funny, for which she begs Pookworthy's forgiveness. The letter explains Gibbons's guidebook method of using asterisks to mark certain of the finer passages in the novel so that readers will be sure they are literature and not "flapdoodle." These marked passages are masterpieces of overwrought writing, full of long sentences teeming with lush adjectives and numerous clauses.

The vocabulary of *Cold Comfort Farm* adds to the novel's atmosphere, from the names of the characters, animals, and vegetation to the idiomatic country terms. Fourteen men live at the farm: Amos and his two sons, five distant cousins, two of Amos's half brothers, and four farmhands. The names include Urk, Ezra, Micah, Caraway, Harkaway, Luke, and Mark Dolour. Adam Lambsbreath is an ancient farmhand who enjoys a mystical connection to the beasts for which he cares: Graceless, Pointless, Feckless, and Aimless, the cows; Big Business, the bull; and Viper, the vicious carriage horse. One of Adam's tasks is to "cletter the dishes," and Reuben brags that he has "scranleted two hundred furrows." "Mommet" seems to be a word of endearment or disparagement (sometimes both at once). This vocabulary is typical of pastoral novels of the period, but here it is overdone and often incomprehensible to Flora Poste, the city cousin. Yet she finds her own speech lapsing into the same country idiom before she escapes from Cold Comfort Farm.

Part of the humor is Flora's ironic attitude toward the rough country ways of her cousins. She realizes that people of their temperament revel in misunderstandings, brooding, rows at mealtime, spying, skulking, and constant emotional turmoil. "Oh, they *did* enjoy themselves!" Flora concludes. By the end of the book she sees the family quietly enjoying a traditional wedding in an ordinary manner without violence, gloom, pride, or lechery, all due to her own good offices. Flora is, of course, herself a parody, with her reliance on her self-help books, *The Higher Common Sense* and *Pensees*, to which she frequently turns.

Geniuses and intellectuals—as exemplified by Mr. Mybug, a writer who stays in Howling while working on a revisionist biography of the Brontës—fare badly in this novel. Mybug's book is intended to prove that it was Branwell Brontë who wrote *Wuthering Heights* (1847) instead of Emily Brontë. Gibbons has much fun with this character, who is obsessed with sex and is later spied, drunk and dirty, trying to gate-crash Richard Hawk-Monitor's birthday ball.

Gibbons manages her large cast of characters well, integrating them into the many subplots involved in Flora's "tidying" of the Starkadders. The author tidies up her plot at the end with a literary device of deus ex machina, which in classic Greek drama ends a story by mechanically lowering a god onstage to resolve the plot (the term has come to mean any improbable device by which an author resolves the plot). In *Cold Comfort Farm* the deus ex machina is three airplanes that arrive to whisk off Aunt Ada Doom, the newly married Hawk-Monitors, and Flora. Here, Gibbons parodies the end of Thomas Hardy's *Tess of the d'Urbervilles* (1891).

Sheila Golburgh Johnson

Further Reading

Hammill, Faye. "*Cold Comfort Farm*, D. H. Lawrence, and English Literary Culture Between the Wars." *Modern Fiction Studies* 47, no. 4 (Winter, 2001): 831. Provides a plot summary of Gibbons's novel, critiques the literary and cultural contexts of the book, and analyzes Gibbons's use of pathetic fallacy.

_____. "'Literature or Just Sheer Flapdoodle?': Stella Gibbons's *Cold Comfort Farm*." In *Women, Celebrity, and Literary Culture Between the Wars*. Austin: University of Texas Press, 2007. Describes how Gibbons and other women writers of the 1920's and 1930's enjoyed fame and commercial success that affected the literary reception of their work. These writers' success caused critics to denigrate their work as "middlebrow," even though their work often challenged prevailing middle-class ideals and social discrimination.

Moorman, Charles. "Five Views of a Dragon." *Southern Quarterly* 16 (1978): 139-150. Moorman compares and contrasts five authors, including Gibbons, who write about Wales. Gibbons, the only one of the five who is not Welsh, sees the humor in Welsh extravagances.

Oliver, Reggie. *Out of the Woodshed: A Portrait of Stella Gibbons*. London: Bloomsbury, 1998. Comprehensive biography written by Gibbons's nephew, a playwright. Oliver describes how his aunt valued her religious beliefs and her desire to be a good wife and mother more highly than her literary career.

Vickers, Jackie. "Cold Comfort for Ethan Frome." *Notes and Queries* 40, no. 4 (December, 1993). A careful and balanced comparison of *Cold Comfort Farm* and Edith Wharton's *Ethan Frome* (1911). Traces some of the influences *Ethan Frome* may have had on Gibbons's work. Vickers also discusses the animal imagery in *Cold Comfort Farm*.

Cold Mountain

Author: Charles Frazier (1950-   )
First published: 1997
Type of work: Novel
Type of plot: Historical
Time of plot: 1864
Locale: North Carolina

Principal characters:
INMAN, a Confederate army deserter
ADA MONROE, his love
RUBY THEWES, Ada's friend and companion
STOBROD THEWES, her father, a Confederate army deserter
SOLOMON VEASEY, a preacher

The Story:

Inman lies in a Confederate hospital in Raleigh, North Carolina, recovering from a combat wound. He spends much time peering out a window. When well enough, he begins to explore the surroundings of the hospital, meeting a blind man he had seen through the window. The blind man observes that it is better to have been born blind than to lose sight after seeing the world. Inman decides to desert from the army and return to Cold Mountain and his beloved Ada.

Ada, the sole inhabitant of the Black Cove farm, struggles to feed herself. After her father died, Ada allowed Black Cove to fall into a general state of disrepair. She flirts with the idea of returning to Charleston but reasons that there is little point in doing so. Though educated, she was never taught farming, hunting, or any other survival skill. Through her neighbors, Ada meets a young drifter named Ruby, who agrees to help in the upkeep of Black Cove in exchange for a place to live.

Inman's journey progresses slowly because of his injury. During a stop at a general store, he is accosted by robbers, leading him to remember a Cherokee incantation called "To Destroy Life." Inman realizes that the journey home will be violent. After recalling his first introduction to Ada, Inman enlists the aid of a ferry girl to cross a river. While crossing, the robbers catch up and force Inman and the ferry girl into the water. Thanks to the girl's knowledge of the river, Inman makes it across and continues his journey west.

Back at Black Cove, Ada's indoctrination to manual labor commences under Ruby. Ruby surveys work that needs to be done and prioritizes tasks at hand. The two decide to trade some of Ada's possessions for food and supplies. After bartering Ada's piano, Ruby reveals to Ada that she had been abandoned as a child. She does not know her mother and had been left to fend for herself by her father, Stobrod.

Inman encounters a preacher named Veasey who is attempting to kill a woman he had made pregnant. Inman interferes and marches Veasey and the woman back to her home. He ties Veasey to a tree and leaves a note explaining why Veasey is tied up. Fearful of the Confederate Home Guard, Inman leaves the scene and makes camp with gypsies. Haunted by another memory of Ada, Inman dreams of her and makes a promise in his dream that he will never let her go.

Inman is reunited with Veasey, who has been exiled from his congregation. Veasey reveals himself to be little more than a man taken up with womanizing and thievery, and he gets into trouble with a prostitute. Inman and Veasey spend the night at the home of a lonely old man named Odell. Meanwhile, Ada and Ruby enter town and are told of how the Home Guard would rather kill outliers, or deserters, than return them to the army. On her return trip to the farm, Ada tells Ruby how her father had courted her mother for almost twenty years.

Inman and Veasey assist a man named Junior in removing a dead bull from a river. Afterward, Junior invites Inman and Veasey to his home. There, Junior's three daughters subdue and seduce Inman in an elaborate trap and hand Inman and Veasey over to the Home Guard. Later, the Home Guard decides to shoot them. Veasey is killed, but Inman survives. Inman feigns death and escapes, running into a slave who draws him a map to get home. Before Inman sets off, he stops by Junior's home and kills him.

Ada and Ruby, noting that their crops keep disappearing, set a trap to catch the culprit. Concerned that the thief might be human, Ada convinces Ruby to pad the trap. Ruby leaves to attend to matters in town, and Ada makes a scarecrow for the field. Afterward, Ada reminisces about the time she bade Inman farewell as he left for the war. Meanwhile, Inman follows the map and encounters an old goat-woman who feeds him and tends his wounds. At Black Cove farm, the trap Ruby set catches the culprit: her father, Stobrod, who has deserted the Confederate army and taken up the fiddle as his calling.

Inman next encounters a war widow named Sara. In exchange for food and shelter, Inman offers to help Sara butcher a hog for the winter. That night, Sara requests that Inman sleep next to her. The next morning, three federal soldiers arrive and pillage Sara's property. Inman hides as the soldiers leave with the hog. He follows and then kills them. Upon his return, he and Sara butcher the hog.

Stobrod returns to Black Cove with a companion, Pangle. Ruby, wary of assisting outliers, forces Stobrod to leave but agrees to leave food for him hidden at a predetermined spot. Later, as Inman continues through the mountains, Stobrod and Pangle are captured by the Home Guard and shot. A third outlier runs to Black Cove for help. Ada and Ruby set off into the mountains and find Pangle dead and Stobrod barely alive. The two women bury Pangle and move Stobrod to an abandoned American Indian village nearby.

While Ruby tends to her father, Ada hunts wild turkey and fires a shot. Inman, nearby, hears the shot and reunites with Ada. As Stobrod recovers, Inman and Ada decide that Inman will surrender to federal troops. That night, Ada and Inman make love.

On the way back to Black Cove, Inman insists that Ruby and Ada travel alone in case they are intercepted by the Home Guard; they are soon intercepted. Inman engages in a firefight as Stobrod escapes. Inman is mortally wounded. Ada arrives and holds Inman until he dies in her arms. Years later, Ada lives with Ruby, Stobrod, and her and Inman's daughter in Black Cove.

Critical Evaluation:

Cold Mountain is Charles Frazier's debut novel, based predominantly on stories of Frazier's ancestor William P. Inman that were passed down from generation to generation following the American Civil War. Though highly fictionalized, much of the novel is based on fact, including several of the battles and the political landscape of the late-war South.

The novel is, at its core, two separate coming-of-age stories that intersect into a single love story. The first coming-of-age story is that of Inman, whose journey not only is the physical journey from Raleigh to Cold Mountain but also is a spiritual one, as his character attempts to come to terms with the meaning of his life. While it is easy to claim that Ada, Inman's purported true love, is the reason for his being, Frazier takes great care to depict Inman as someone lost in purpose, even though Ada and Cold Mountain remain his ultimate goal. Though Inman does take his place as the soldier who no longer knows what is worth fighting for, his odyssey does not lead him to answer that question but rather the questions he asks along the way.

Religion and philosophy, while never directly addressed, criticized, or praised, present themselves throughout Inman's journey. Veasey, in particular, seems to represent a facet of religious thought that Inman does not accept. Indeed,

it is one Inman wholly rejects. He seems keen to discover religion anew, remembering with fondness the tales told to him by an old American Indian friend, Swimmer.

The second coming-of-age story is that of Ada, whose journey is unlike that of Inman in that it is not physical or overtly spiritual. Instead, Ada evolves from a life of leisure and education into a life of physical labor, survival, and an appreciation for natural things. Whereas Inman utilizes an internal catalyst in his journey—he simply wants to go home—Ada is forced to accept external influences, personified in the form of Ruby, who seems to represent Mother Nature and becomes both her teacher and her friend. There are clear hints of Henry David Thoreau's *Walden: Or, Life in the Woods* (1854) in Ada's transformation, and she ultimately finds joy in her shedding the materialism of her previous life.

Frazier balances these two stories with a rigid structure, alternating chapters featuring Inman and Ada until interjecting a chapter about Ruby's father, Stobrod. This chapter, "naught and grief," is the only part of the novel not directly experienced or narrated by either Inman or Ada. Nevertheless, the chapter is significant, for Frazier uses the change in narrative pattern to set up the novel's climax. Prior to "naught and grief," Frazier makes heavy use of flashbacks to fill in background details and to offer deeper characterization, particularly for the deceased Monroe, Ada's father. This rigidity in structure is also found in the supporting characters. Those whom Inman encounters are blatant in their attempts to either help him or impede him. Those characters Ada encounters, in a reflection of her own personal journey, gradually shift from assisting her to relying on her. While Frazier's supporting characters are used effectively, most remain little more than archetypes.

There is a great deal of symbolism in *Cold Mountain*, largely focusing on flora and fauna. Animals play an extremely large part in Inman's journey and include an encounter with a dead bull just prior to his arrest by the Home Guard, the slitting of a goat's neck to provide food, the slaughter of a pig following Inman's slaughter of the federal soldiers, and the mercy killing of a bear cub after Inman explains that he had promised to never again kill a bear. Birds are present in the novel as well. Owls, crows, peregrines, roosters, and countless other birds appear as signposts or memories in the book. Indeed, Inman takes the symbolism one step further and muses on the ability to fly.

Much of the novel deals with moral ambiguity inherent in war. While little of *Cold Mountain* deals with actual combat, except for a few of Inman's recollections, much is concerned with the effect the war has on those who are not directly involved in the fighting. Though clearly a Confederate tale,

Frazier takes great care in not depicting soldiers (on either side) strictly as villains; one notable exception involves Sara, the lonely widow who assists Inman late in his journey. The villainy in the story is reserved for the motivations of individual characters, usually that of the greedy or, in the case of the Home Guard, the bloodthirsty.

Complementing the coming-of-age stories of Inman and Ada is the ultimate theme of *Cold Mountain*: the perceived meaningless of the war. Both Inman and Ada are affected by this perception, with Ada initially disturbed by the war's interruption of her old way of life and Inman, who has never been a slaveholder, wondering why everyone is fighting each other. Admittedly pro-South at the start of the conflict, Inman comes to realize that the Civil War has devolved into an excuse for soldiers to kill each other. At one point he witnesses Confederate generals waxing poetic about warfare, leading to Inman's revulsion to war. Ironically, his pacifism never extends to the act of killing itself, and he remains pragmatically aware that he will kill to be able to return home. Ada, however, learns how to sustain life. It is perhaps for this reason that Inman's fate results in death and Ada's fate results, in the form of their child, in life.

Jeffrey K. Golden

Further Reading

Ashdown, Paul. "'Savage Satori': Fact and Fiction in Charles Frazier's *Cold Mountain*." In *Memory and Myth: The Civil War in Fiction and Film from "Uncle Tom's Cabin" to "Cold Mountain,"* edited by David B. Sachsman, S. Kittrell Rushing, and Roy Morris. West Lafayette, Ind.: Purdue University Press, 2007. This chapter on *Cold Mountain* is part of a collection exploring "creative responses to the Civil War" and the formation of "historical memories of the war into durable, ever-changing myths."

Garren, Terrell T. *The Secret of War: A Dramatic History of Civil War Crime in Western North Carolina*. Spartanburg, S.C.: Reprint Company, 2004. A historical novel similar to *Cold Mountain* that offers more historical detail. The protagonist had been assigned to the same army unit (Inman's) fictionalized by Frazier. An excellent historical and narrative companion to *Cold Mountain*.

Inscoe, John C., and Gordon B. McKinney. *The Heart of Confederate Appalachia: Western North Carolina in the Civil War*. Chapel Hill: University of North Carolina Press, 2000. A scholarly look at western North Carolina's disposition at various stages of the Civil War. Explains the confusing political landscape of the region in detail, affording a greater understanding of the seemingly sophisticated motivations of the characters found in Frazier's novel.

Peuser, Richard W., and Trevor K. Plante. "*Cold Mountain*'s Inman: Fact Versus Fiction." *Prologue Magazine* 36, no. 2 (Summer, 2004): 6-9. Military historians trace the journey of the historical William P. Inman during the Civil War. Offers clues about how Frazier distilled his research into a workable plot for *Cold Mountain*.

Trotter, William R. *Bushwackers! The Mountains*. Winston-Salem, N.C.: J. F. Blair, 1991. A factual account of the many skirmishes and incidents in the mountains of North Carolina during the American Civil War. Much of the background and setting that Frazier mentions in passing in *Cold Mountain* is greatly expanded upon in this book.

Yearns, Wilfred B., and John G. Barrett, eds. *North Carolina Civil War Documentary*. Chapel Hill: University of North Carolina Press, 2002. A collection of primary sources pertaining to North Carolina's involvement in the Civil War. Like *Cold Mountain*, this work is concerned less with the military aspect of the war and more with its effects on the home front.

Collected Poems

Author: Marianne Moore (1887-1972)
First published: 1951
Type of work: Poetry

Even after her poems had been published and critically acclaimed, Marianne Moore continued to revise them; sometimes she rejected them altogether. Between her first book, *Poems* (1921), and her last, *The Complete Poems of Mari-* anne Moore (1967, 1981), she published several other volumes of poetry. Typically, a new book was made up of substantially revised poems from the previous book together with a number of previously uncollected poems. *Collected*

Poems (1951), for example, begins with most of the poems from *Selected Poems* (1935), which in turn contains many of the poems from *Observations* (1924). *Collected Poems* also contains all but four poems from *What Are Years* (1941), a volume of previously uncollected work, and the six new poems from *Nevertheless* (1944), to which Moore added nine new titles "Hitherto Uncollected."

The Complete Poems of Marianne Moore, which claims to be the "Definitive Edition, with the Author's Final Revisions," contains a section headed "Collected Poems (1951)." This section omits the poem "Melanchthon" from the 1951 publication but contains two poems from *Observations*, "The Student" and "To a Prize Bird," which were originally omitted from *Collected Poems*; these poems were subsequently revised for *The Complete Poems of Marianne Moore*.

Confusing as all this seems, it is necessary for serious students of Moore's work to be aware that the different publications contain different collections of poems and that the poems themselves are likely to differ from collection to collection. Perhaps the most striking example of the changes undergone by a poem is "Poetry," which appears in *Poems* as a poem of thirty lines in five stanzas. In *Observations*, the poem is changed drastically in form and in length, retaining only phrases from the original. In *Collected Poems*, its form is restored to one resembling the original, but the poem itself is significantly different. In *The Complete Poems of Marianne Moore*, finally, it is reduced to three lines. It is important to note that all references here will be to *Collected Poems* as published in 1951.

In the poem "Silence," there is the passage "The deepest feeling always shows itself in silence;/ not in silence, but restraint." The word "restraint" implies reserve, discipline, control, and moderation, and indeed, restraint is one of the principal characteristics of Moore's poems. The overriding impression created by the book is that it consists of reasoned, intelligent discourse.

Some poems, such as "New York" and "Marriage," are free verse, but more frequently the forms of the poems show a concern for orderliness and control, with close attention to detail. Moore can be compared to her own description of an octopus: "Neatness of finish! Neatness of finish!/ Relentless accuracy is the nature of this octopus." She tends to use subtle, sometimes almost hidden metrical patterns. Poems such as "Peter" and "Bird Witted" have precise forms, repeated in each stanza; the forms are based on syllabic count but without regard to whether syllables are stressed or unstressed. It is unlikely that even a careful reader would be conscious of this type of form without actually counting syllables. Other syllabic forms, as in "Melanchthon," are more obviously

crafted. The syllabic counts in the short lines are quite noticeable, and there is a clearly visible repeated form in each stanza of two short lines followed by two long lines.

There is some use of end rhyme, as in "The Jerboa," but the rhyme is often unobtrusive. This can be because of uneven line length, as in "Those Various Scalpels" and "To a Steam Roller," or because the lines run on in such a way that a rhyming word is unstressed, as in "To Statecraft Embalmed." Sometimes, as in "The Fish," the rhyme is on unexpected words such as "an" or "the"; sometimes a word is broken up to rhyme just one syllable as when the first syllable of "accident" is rhymed with the word "lack": "ac/ cident—lack." Frequently, there is rhyme, partial rhyme, or assonance in random fashion over a number of lines. In "An Octopus" and "Sea Unicorns and Land Unicorns," such rhymes are easily apparent, but at times they are so concealed as to be virtually unnoticed, save possibly at an unconscious level.

Another area of restraint is in Moore's diction. Her tone can be conversational; often it is rather dry, with a cool formality. There is no hyperbole, no prettiness, little that is conventionally "poetic." A prominent feature of *Collected Poems* is a sizable section of notes at the end, citing the sources of her quotations and allusions, which in the poems are generally set off by quotation marks. This is more the practice of the essayist than the poet.

A part of Moore's educational background included undergraduate experience in a biology laboratory. Her scientific training in careful observation of phenomena and in careful deductions from observation provides the basis for many of her poems. Her interest in the natural world surfaces frequently. *Collected Poems* is peppered with animals, including cats, monkeys, elephants, birds, a snail, a woodweasel, and many others. Moore typically observes an animal's appearance and behavior, then sets her imagination the task of interpreting the meaning of the observed facts.

In "Peter," Moore observes a cat with close attention to detail: "the detached first claw on the/ foreleg, which corresponds/ to the thumb, retracted to its tip." The poem becomes an occasion to celebrate the cat's uninhibited naturalness. He spends his time doing as he pleases, unconstrained by the human world that surrounds him but does not impinge on his consciousness unless he chooses. The cat's behavior is contrasted to the complexity of the human world, and the poem arrives at the conclusion that such instinctive behavior is good: "to do less would be nothing but dishonesty." Observation of the cat has been used as a means to make a subtle, seemingly casual comment on moral issues such as selfishness, hypocrisy, and frankness.

"Melanchthon" shares with "Peter" a similar movement

from approval of animal nature to a broader moral statement. This time the focus of the poem is an elephant, who is also the narrator of the poem. The rhythm of the poem is slow and ponderous, evocative of the physical being of the subject, and the overall tone is serene, in keeping with the natural personality, which, unconcerned with intellectualizing its experience, basks in the sun, enjoying experience for its own sake. Like the river mud that encrusts the elephant's skin, the "patina of circumstance"—the accumulation of life's experiences—enriches and strengthens what is inside. It is the soul that is the true seat of power, which will "never/ be cut into/ by a wooden spear." The strength of the soul is inexplicable, and the center of spiritual poise is unknown, but recognition of the supreme importance of the spiritual world allows the individual an entirely new dimension of perception: "My ears are sensitized to more than the sound of/ the wind." This poem, less condensed and difficult than many in the book, deals with ideas central to Moore's moral world. To understand this poem can be an aid to understanding some of the others.

Naturalness is central not only to Moore's moral values but also to her aesthetic tastes. Artistic integrity is the theme of a number of poems. The much anthologized "Poetry" is a clear exposition of this theme, with its blunt, rather shocking opening statement: "I, too, dislike it: there are things that are important beyond all this fiddle." What emerges in the poem is that Moore dislikes "all this fiddle" rather than poetry itself, which can be genuine and natural. In "Picking and Choosing" and "In the Days of Prismatic Color," she tells the reader that she does not like the nonsense of poetry created by willful obscurity and lack of genuine feeling masked by heightened language: "the opaque allusion—the simulated flight// upward—accomplishes nothing."

The spiritual underpinning of Moore's moral world is also a part of her aesthetics. In "When I Buy Pictures," she states that all art must be "'lit with piercing glances into the life of things';/ it must acknowledge the spiritual forces which have made it." In "An Egyptian Pulled Glass Bottle in the Shape of a Fish," Moore contemplates an inanimate object in the way that she observes animals, using it as a concrete image from which to develop more abstract thoughts. The bottle is beautiful, pleasing to the eye, a work of art, yet its beauty is derived from more than its outward appearance. Its making required "patience," a moral quality, and it was made in response to "thirst," a need, so it is functional. This combination of elements invests the bottle with perfection that should be celebrated.

The poems in the "What Are Years" and "Nevertheless" sections of the book were written during World War II and are in many cases responses to that great crisis in the history

of civilization. The poems encompass such themes as courage, heroism, and endurance. The final poem in these sections, "In Distrust of Merits," is a direct and uncharacteristically emotional testimony to the poet's feelings of horror, outrage, and fear for the outcome. However, responsibility for the war lies, at least in part, with the individual: "There never was a war that was/ not inward; I must/ fight till I have conquered in myself what/ causes war, but I would not believe it." In other poems in these sections, contemplation of the ostrich, the mother mockingbird, and the nautilus leads to the understanding that naturalness includes a nurturing that requires courage and love and patience. "Elephants" illustrates strength hand-in-hand with philosophical resignation. In "The Pangolin," that unattractive animal is used, surprisingly, as an exemplar of physical grace which leads to contemplation of humans—flawed, ambiguous, and fearful, but the recipient of grace in the theological sense.

When *Collected Poems* was published, Moore's work had already attracted the attention and acclaim of such literary giants of her generation as Ezra Pound, T. S. Eliot, W. H. Auden, and William Carlos Williams. She was already the recipient of numerous awards when *Collected Poems* gained her additional accolades: the Bollingen Prize, the Pulitzer Prize, and the National Book Award. Moore's poetic voice is admired for its distinctive, even eccentric qualities, her vision for its acuity and its integrity. Her use of form is inventive, her craftsmanship is meticulous, and her subject matter displays a wide range of interest and knowledge. The poems are sometimes oblique, their meanings elusive, but they reward persistent and repeated readings.

Susan Henthorne

Further Reading

Costello, Bonnie. *Marianne Moore: Imaginary Possessions.* Cambridge, Mass.: Harvard University Press, 1981. Demonstrates how to read Moore's poems by investigating recurrent themes, images, and forms. Examines in detail individual lines and phrases, as well as whole poems.

Gregory, Elizabeth, ed. *The Critical Response to Marianne Moore.* Westport, Conn.: Praeger, 2003. Collection of more than seventy reviews and essays about Moore that were originally published between 1917 and 1975. Many of the pieces are by other poets, including Ezra Pound, W. H. Auden, T. S. Eliot, H. D., and Elizabeth Bishop.

Joyce, Elisabeth W. *Cultural Critique and Abstraction: Marianne Moore and the Avant-Garde.* Lewisburg, Pa.: Bucknell University Press, 1998. Places Moore's poetry within the avant-garde art movements of the early twentieth century, such as cubism, collage, Dadaism, and surrealism.

Kent, Kathryn R. *Making Girls into Women: American Women's Writing and the Rise of Lesbian Identity.* Durham, N.C.: Duke University Press, 2003. Analyzes literature written by American women in the late nineteenth and early twentieth centuries to trace the emergence of lesbian identity, which Kent maintains is rooted in white, middle-class culture. Two of the chapters focus on the poetry of Moore and Elizabeth Bishop.

Lentfoehr, Therese. *Marianne Moore: A Critical Essay.* Grand Rapids, Mich.: William M. Eerdmans, 1969. A lucid and sensitive analysis of Moore's work from a specifically Christian perspective. Without laboring the point, it concludes that there are religious meanings latent throughout Moore's poetry.

Nitchie, George W. *Marianne Moore: An Introduction to the Poetry.* New York: Columbia University Press, 1969. A useful introduction that traces the evolution of Moore's poetic voice and the complex history of the poems.

Praises the poet's originality and intelligence. Includes an interesting and varied "List of Works Consulted."

Schulman, Grace. *Marianne Moore: The Poetry of Engagement.* Urbana: University of Illinois Press, 1986. Analyzes the poetry by tracing the poet's thought processes. In many cases, this is achieved by relating the dialectic of the poems to the visual perception that inspired and informed them.

Tomlinson, Charles, ed. *Marianne Moore: A Collection of Critical Essays.* Englewood Cliffs, N.J.: Prentice-Hall, 1969. One of the best starting points for the serious student, this book provides an excellent, varied overview of the entirety of Moore's work. Contains essays by her contemporaries such as Ezra Pound and T. S. Eliot, as well as by later critics.

Zona, Kirstin Hotelling. *Marianne Moore, Elizabeth Bishop, and May Swenson: The Feminist Poetics of Self-Restraint.* Ann Arbor: University of Michigan Press, 2002. Examines how the three poets challenged feminist ideas about selfhood, autonomy, and sexual authenticity.

The Collector

Author: John Fowles (1926-2005)
First published: 1963
Type of work: Novel
Type of plot: Psychological realism
Time of plot: c. 1960
Locale: London and Sussex, England

Principal characters:
FREDERICK CLEGG, a butterfly collector
MIRANDA GREY, an art student

The Story:

Frederick Clegg, a government clerk in his middle twenties, wins seventy-three thousand pounds in the football pools, which enables him to act out his secret fantasy. Just as he collected butterflies in the past, he stalks and kidnaps Miranda Grey, an art student in her early twenties who is studying at the Slade School in London. Clegg recently purchased an expensive home in the Sussex countryside, with an underground room that he secured and prepared for his kidnapped guest, as he calls her.

When Miranda is chloroformed and taken to Clegg's house, she discovers that he made extensive preparations for her, including the purchase of clothing and other items. In the beginning he treats her deferentially, serving her the food she

wishes, and brings her anything she desires. It quickly becomes clear to Miranda that, although Clegg apparently is not interested in sex or violence, he does not plan to allow her to leave. The two, of approximately the same age but from very different worlds, become acquainted with each other.

Clegg, of working-class origin, resents his lower social position and did not have access to the privileged, artistic world that Miranda inhabited. In addition, his mental problems become more pronounced as his conversations with Miranda continue, just as her idealism and naïveté are revealed. Her naïveté is particularly evident when she believes he will make good on his promise to release her at the end of four weeks, for Clegg has no intention of doing this.

During the four weeks, more differences between the two emerge, particularly between her artistic, politically liberal worldview and Clegg's disturbed, repressed mind. In his spare time, Clegg is a butterfly collector who kills and photographs his collections, activities that Miranda abhors. She makes clear her disgust with his narrowness and lack of culture and usually criticizes him sharply. Clegg accepts her verbal abuse and continues to defer to her wishes, telling her he abducted her because he is in love with her.

Shortly before the four weeks are to end, Clegg purchases an expensive dress and diamond necklace for Miranda. They pretend to have a party, and he permits her to come upstairs into the house. She refuses his proposal of marriage, one that he specifies will be in name only, and afterward he makes it clear he will not release her as promised. She attempts to escape, but he catches her and again gives her chloroform to subdue her. While she is unconscious, Clegg removes all her clothing except for her underclothes and takes photographs, the first time he violates her physically since her arrival.

Several days later Miranda, after being taken upstairs by Clegg to bathe, strikes him in the shoulder and head with an ax he left lying around. The blow only slightly injures him, and he is able to bind, gag, and lock her up once again in the underground room. Miranda, desperate to be released, again asks to be taken upstairs for a bath. She then attempts to seduce Clegg. When he proves to be impotent, he lies and says that an army psychiatrist told him that he would never be able to perform the sexual act.

Clegg's response to his sexual failure is humiliation and rage, and he blames all his subsequent actions on Miranda's attempted seduction. He claims he no longer respects her, and when she asks to live in an upstairs bedroom he pretends to prepare it for her. He then asks permission to photograph her nude, which she angrily refuses. It is at this point that Clegg's anger and the depths of his perversion begin to surface as his earlier ostensible fondness for Miranda disappears. When she taunts him that he is "not a man," he binds and gags her, removes her clothing, and photographs her tied to her bed.

The next day, the cold she catches from Clegg worsens, and she tells him she has pneumonia. Although her temperature is 102 degrees and she is unable to eat, he refuses to take her symptoms seriously. As her condition worsens, Clegg begins to understand that she is very ill, but he cannot bring himself to get her medical attention. When he finally goes to a doctor's office to ask advice, he is overwhelmed by fear and paranoia, and right after this incident he is terrified when a policeman begins asking him questions.

After he returns to Miranda, it is clear that she is dying, but Clegg still refuses to get her any help. After her death he considers suicide but instead he buries her body, which he refers to as "the deceased," under the apple trees. Clegg then begins to follow another young woman and to dry out the underground room in preparation for another guest. The next experience, he promises himself, will be different because Marian, his next victim, will be someone he can teach, someone who will not place herself above him.

Critical Evaluation:

John Fowles's fiction met with a popular and commercial success that is unusual for a novelist who also received such serious critical attention. *The Collector*, his first novel, was followed by *The Magus* (1965; revised, 1977), *The French Lieutenant's Woman* (1969), *Daniel Martin* (1977), *Mantissa* (1982), and *A Maggot* (1985). The first three novels were made into successful films, and both the novel and the film versions of *The French Lieutenant's Woman* were critically praised. Fowles enjoyed experimenting with narrative technique, and with each new novel he attempted to find different forms and structures for his fiction.

In *The Collector*, Fowles tells the story from two points of view. Fred Clegg narrates the first half of the novel in an unimaginative, flat-footed style that underscores the horror and the realism of his tale. The second half of the novel is narrated by Miranda in the form of a journal she keeps during her captivity, which is found by Clegg after her death. Her voice, completely different from Clegg's, reveals her artistic, idealistic, and sometimes pretentious personality and gives the reader an entirely different perspective on the incidents recounted earlier by Clegg. Her journal entries end just before her death, when Clegg returns for a brief final section that recounts her death and burial and his ominous plans for the future.

Like many postwar British novels, *The Collector* focuses on issues of social class. Clegg's deprived background and lack of education stunted him emotionally, intellectually, and spiritually, just as Miranda's privileged upper-middle-class upbringing provided her with opportunities to develop herself personally and artistically. This is revealed in both the form and the content of their speech in the novel. Clegg, resentful and hesitant because of his social inferiority, is always bested verbally by Miranda, whose spirited assertiveness and self-confidence attract and later enrage him. Fowles said that Clegg's environment played a major role in shaping him, and that the relationship between Clegg and Miranda is representative of the problems of social class in England.

The difficulties between the two characters go much deeper than social class. *The Collector*, like so many of

Fowles's later novels, is profoundly concerned with the nature of power and its abuses. Fowles, who was at one time a collector of butterflies, talked at length about the connections among power, fascism, and collecting. Clegg's psychological problems are related to his desire for complete power over another person. Unable to have any kind of loving, living, interdependent relationship with Miranda, he forces her into an environment over which he has complete control and subjects her to a variety of humiliations.

After his inability to respond to her sexual overtures, he reduces her to the status of a pornographic photograph, a photograph he can pose and later view as a voyeur with no fear of its talking back to him. Just as collectors must kill their specimens to capture, mount, and preserve them, Miranda must eventually die so that Clegg's collection of her can be complete. His desire for power is rooted in his inability to connect with the world of free, living, protean human beings. Fowles, a strong believer in individualism and the individual's potential for growth and development, posits Clegg as emblematic of the person who can resort only to the abuses of power to feel anything at all.

The Collector also concerns another issue important to Fowles, the distinction between what he calls "The Many" and "The Few." Clegg is a representative of The Many, those dulled to the real significance of life by their lack of emotional and intellectual sensitivity and their need to acquire more and more material possessions. Having no aesthetic sense, Clegg is instead at the mercy of what he considers to be proper opinions and popular taste. His leaden, cliché-filled language reflects this, just as Miranda's quirky, fragmented, questioning verbal style identifies her with The Few, those who refuse to be compromised by bourgeois values and instead embody liberal-humanist, aesthetic ideals marked by tolerance, skepticism, and open-mindedness. Although Fowles accuses Miranda of being a "liberal-humanist snob" and he sometimes treats her ironically, she is indeed represented as a true alternative to the intellectual and emotional void that is Clegg.

In spite of the fact that *The Collector* is a starkly realistic novel, Fowles inserts references to William Shakespeare's play *The Tempest* (pr. 1611, pb. 1623) that help mitigate the intensely claustrophobic world that is created. In Shakespeare's play, Ferdinand is the young, handsome hero who falls in love with the beautiful young heroine Miranda. When Caliban, a monstrous creature, earlier unsuccessfully attempts to rape Miranda, he is prevented by her magician-father, Prospero. Clegg, who dislikes his real name, Fred, lies to Miranda that his name is Ferdinand, but she refers to him in her journal as Caliban. Unlike *The Tempest*, in which

Prospero is able to save his daughter, Fowles's novel has no magician, and Miranda's death is the prelude to another, perhaps more brutal, abduction. *The Collector* is an important novel about the nature of obsession and perversion.

Angela Hague

Further Reading

Acheson, James. *John Fowles*. New York: St. Martin's Press, 1998. An excellent introduction to Fowles's life and works, in which Acheson traces the development of his novels. Chapter 2 focuses on *The Collector*.

Foster, Thomas C. *Understanding John Fowles*. Columbia: University of South Carolina Press, 1994. An accessible critical introduction to Fowles's principal works, featuring analysis of *The Collector* and other novels. Includes an annotated bibliography.

Lenz, Brooke. *John Fowles: Visionary and Voyeur*. Amsterdam: Rodopi, 2008. A feminist analysis, in which Lenz demonstrates how Fowles progressively creates female characters who subvert male voyeurism and create alternative narratives. Chapter 1 focuses on *The Collector*.

Olshen, Barry N. *John Fowles*. New York: Frederick Ungar, 1978. Discusses the narrative structure of *The Collector* and focuses on issues of social class and opportunity. Olsen maintains that the most significant distinction in the novel is between life- and freedom-loving individuals and those who can only attempt to possess and destroy.

Reynolds, Margaret, and Jonathan Noakes. *John Fowles: The Essential Guide*. London: Vintage, 2003. A guide designed for students, teachers, and general readers, this volume contains an interview with Fowles and reading guides, reading activities, and information about contexts and comparisons. Includes complementary readings for three novels: *The Collector*, *The Magus*, and *The French Lieutenant's Woman*. Also includes a glossary and select bibliography.

Warburton, Eileen. *John Fowles: A Life in Two Worlds*. New York: Viking, 2004. A thorough, entertaining, and well-reviewed biography. Warburton was given full access to Fowles's journals and personal papers, and she presents many previously untold details of his life, most notably his thirty-seven-year love affair with his wife.

Wilson, Thomas M. *The Recurrent Green Universe of John Fowles*. New York: Rodopi, 2006. Described as a work of "ecocriticism," this book focuses on how Fowles's novels and other writings reflect his feelings and thoughts about the natural world. Includes a bibliography and index.

Wolfe, Peter. *John Fowles, Magus and Moralist*. Cranbury,

N.J.: Bucknell University Press, 1976. Excellent introduction to Fowles's philosophical and aesthetic ideas. Discusses *The Collector* specifically in the light of Fowles's attitudes about "collecting," the dichotomy between The Many and The Few, and the social and cultural milieu that produces a Frederick Clegg.

Woodcock, Bruce. *Male Mythologies: John Fowles and Masculinity.* Brighton, England: Harvester Press, 1984. Suggests that Clegg is "the prototype of masculinity," both perpetrator and victim of male power, and also the representative for the novelist himself, who can collect his characters and subject them to his own male fantasies.

Color of Darkness
Eleven Stories and a Novella

Author: James Purdy (1914-2009)
First published: 1957; includes *Sixty-three: Dream Palace*, 1956; "Color of Darkness," 1957; "Why Can't They Tell You Why?," 1957
Type of work: Short fiction
Type of plot: Psychological realism and gothic
Time of plot: Mid-twentieth century
Locale: Central United States

Principal characters:
BAXTER, a preteen boy
BAXTER'S FATHER
PAUL, a preteen boy
ETHEL, his mother
FENTON RIDDLEWAY, a young man
CLAIRE RIDDLEWAY, his younger brother

The Stories:

"Color of Darkness." A young boy named Baxter has a bizarre relationship with his often-absent father. Baxter wants to be close to his father, physically and emotionally, but his father admits that he does not know people, that he cannot even remember the color of his former wife's eyes or of Baxter's eyes. The boy accuses his father of always thinking about something else, and his father thinks of his son as an infant brother whom he does not know well.

Baxter's father, upset to learn that his son sleeps with a toy crocodile, buys him a puppy, but Baxter only likes the dog's misbehavior, such as when he soils the floor. One day, Baxter and his father argue over something that Baxter has in his mouth. It turns out to be his father's wedding ring, negligently cast aside. After being forced to spit out the ring, Baxter kicks his father in the groin and calls him a foul name.

"Why Can't They Tell You Why?" Paul, a young boy, finds a box of photographs of his long-dead father, whom Paul never knew. He stays home from school for several days, looking at the photographs. His mother, Ethel, who refuses to let her son call her Mama, criticizes Paul after hearing him tell his friend over the telephone that he is a "sick kid."

One day, a few months later, Ethel awakens to find that Paul is not in his cot. She goes to the kitchen to search for him—skeptically because Paul never eats anything, as far as she can tell. She finds him at the back stairs, sleeping protectively beside the photographs. She tries to take them from him, saying the photographs are the cause of his being sickly. She wants to punish him and says she will burn the photos. Paul pleadingly encircles her legs. She tells him not to touch her and then threatens him with mental incarceration. She takes him to the basement and tells him to throw the photographs into the blazing furnace. Paul refuses to do so and runs, but she catches him and is able to burn some of the photographs. Paul crouches over the remaining photographs and hisses at his mother, while blackness spews from his mouth.

"Sixty-three: Dream Palace." Fenton Riddleway, a young man who is twenty years old, and his sickly younger brother, Claire, move from rural West Virginia to the city after the death of their mother. They have nothing, so they take up residence in an abandoned slum dwelling, which has only one bed and is bug-infested. However, Fenton meets a writer who takes an interest in him and then introduces him to a wealthy, middle-age widow. The woman, Fenton realizes, likes him because he reminds her of her deceased husband, and Fenton knows that she will take him and his brother in if Claire agrees to go.

However, unlike Fenton, Claire is religious and refuses to go, saying it would be a rotten thing to do. Fenton argues, saying he has dreamed that he marries the rich woman and lives in a mansion and dresses grandly. Claire will have none of it, and even Fenton admits to something rotten about it all. Fenton is enraged at Claire, though, realizing that he cannot go without his little brother, or that, if he does, he will have no peace, knowing he has deserted Claire in the slums in the not-right house.

Fenton is outside one day and is picked up by a gay man on the way to a play. After the play, the man takes Fenton to a postperformance party with the cast, where Fenton drinks too much. The man attempts to molest him, but Fenton fights him and escapes. He returns to the old slum house and finds Claire dead. Fenton then recognizes that he killed Claire in his rage before leaving the house. Realizing now, too late, that Claire mattered much more to him than his own dream of gigolo prosperity, Fenton places Claire's body upstairs in the old house in an old chest.

Critical Evaluation:

James Purdy is probably the best twentieth century American fiction writer of limited reputation. Despite numerous novels and short stories of impeccable artistry, he has not received the acclaim that he deserves, at least partly because he is gay and African American, but also because of the unusual nature of his fiction, which is difficult to categorize. *Color of Darkness* is the first collection of that unusual fiction published in the United States, in 1957. The novella *Sixty-three: Dream Palace* and most of the stories in the collection were published previously in England.

Most fundamental to Purdy's writing is his obsession with and genius for portraying the evil inherent in human relationships, the incredible cruelty with which human beings often treat each other. This dark vision, akin to that of Nathaniel Hawthorne and Herman Melville in its psychological realism but also with elements of the gothic reminiscent of Edgar Allan Poe, whom Purdy admires, appears in incipient but often powerful form in *Color of Darkness*.

The title story, "Color of Darkness," astutely presents how emotional coldness, similar to the heart of stone that will not burn in Hawthorne's "Ethan Brand" (1850), can ruin a child. The father in "Color of Darkness" has no emotional tie to his son, Baxter, who is a virtual stranger. The son's evil traits (defiance, obscenity, violence) derive directly from his father's own inability to be a loving parent to his child. This inability to parent is effectively symbolized by Baxter's finding and fighting over his father's discarded wedding ring, the emblem of the marriage that should have provided Baxter with a two-parent family but which did not because of his parents' divorce.

This same theme of intrafamily cruelty and evil is also presented in "Why Can't They Tell You Why?," probably one of the most perfect short stories ever written. Baxter's mother, Ethel, is even more uncaring than the distant father in "Color of Darkness." Because she has lost her husband to death, and because she hates her child for his love for the dead husband—symbolized by the photographs—she tries to force the child to burn the photographs and thereby destroy the last thing that gives the boy a sense of love, of humanness. She verbally abuses him so that others can hear her do so, thereby destroying another level of his humanity, his sense of self-worth. She fails to properly mother in other ways, including by refusing to let Baxter touch her or to call her Mama. Thus, the child develops a lack of love for her, which increases her jealousy of his love of the photographs.

The story brilliantly depicts how a troubled, selfish, uncaring parent can reduce a child into a subhuman animal, epitomized by the child clutching the photographs and hissing at his mother while "thick black strings" spew from his mouth. At a time of increasingly numerous single-parent families, Purdy sounded the alarm and presented the most fundamental causes of divorce and emotional and physical neglect in these two stories, written in the 1950's.

Probably most emotionally powerful and tragic of all in *Color of Darkness* is the intrafamily cruelty in *Sixty-three: Dream Palace*. With the rundown slum residence as the ironic dream palace, where Fenton Riddleway conjures up his desperate plan to marry the rich widow and live as a dandy in her mansion (the imagined dream palace), Purdy develops Fenton's psychological dilemma in a manner worthy of the very best American writers. Because he is religious, Fenton's sickly little brother, Claire, will not stoop to the rottenness of participating in or benefiting from Fenton's selling of himself. Although he is not religious, Fenton knows that he will have no psychological peace if he leaves his sick younger brother in the slum house, infested with bugs and lacking food. Thus, Fenton's dream drives him to kill Claire, realizing later that he cannot live a life of degeneracy, as he had planned, and that Claire was all that really mattered to him. As in all great tragedy, this realization comes too late. Thus, the ultimate intrafamily evil, the killing of a sibling by another sibling, with its biblical overtones, is the powerful conclusion to Purdy's depiction of human evil.

John L. Grigsby

Further Reading

Canning, Richard. *Gay Fiction Speaks: Conversations with Gay Novelists*. New York: Columbia University Press, 2000. This book's extensive interview with Purdy focuses primarily on his identity as a gay novelist. Purdy also discusses his plays.

Chupack, Henry. *James Purdy*. Boston: Twayne, 1975. This solid introductory overview contains a biography, an introductory chapter on what Chupack terms the "Purdian trauma," and analyses of Purdy's works. Includes a bibliography and an index.

Highberg, Nels P., ed. *James Purdy: A Bibliography*. Columbus: Ohio State University Libraries, 1999. A comprehensive compilation of works by and about Purdy's fiction and poetry, including translations, adaptations, media recordings, and even dissertations and theses.

Hipkiss, Robert A. *Jack Kerouac: Prophet of the New Romanticism*. Lawrence: Regents Press of Kansas, 1976. Although primarily a study of Kerouac, included are insightful discussions of Purdy's works as comparative, including "Don't Call Me by My Right Name," "Why Can't They Tell You Why?," and *Sixty-three: Dream Palace* from *Color of Darkness*.

Nelson, Emmanuel S., ed. *Contemporary Gay American Novelists: A Bio-Bibliographical Critical Sourcebook*. Westport, Conn.: Greenwood Press, 1993. An inclusive collection of essays about fifty-seven gay American novelists that includes perceptive treatment of Purdy's major works.

Purdy, James. "Out with James Purdy: An Interview." Interview by Christopher Lane. *Critique* 40 (Fall, 1998): 71-89. Purdy discusses racial stereotypes, sexual fantasy, political correctness, religious fundamentalism, gay relationships, and the reasons he has been neglected by the literary establishment.

Sarotte, Georges-Michel. *Like a Brother, Like a Lover: Male Homosexuality in the American Novel and Theater from Herman Melville to James Baldwin*. New York: Doubleday, 1978. A detailed study of male homosexuality in American literature, including sections on Purdy and his writing.

Schwarzschild, Bettina. *The Not-Right House: Essays on James Purdy*. Columbia: University of Missouri Press, 1968. A short but perceptive study of Purdy's early works, including *Color of Darkness*.

Woodhouse, Reed. *Unlimited Embrace: A Canon of Gay Fiction, 1945-1995*. Amherst: University of Massachusetts Press, 1998. A comprehensive collection of essays on contemporary gay fiction, including the work of Purdy.

The Color Purple

Author: Alice Walker (1944-   )
First published: 1982
Type of work: Novel
Type of plot: Social realism
Time of plot: 1920's-1940's
Locale: Georgia, Tennessee, and Africa

Principal characters:
CELIE, the novel's narrator-protagonist
MR.——, Celie's husband
SHUG AVERY, Mr.——'s longtime mistress
NETTIE, Celie's younger sister
HARPO, Mr.——'s eldest son by a previous marriage
SOFIA, Harpo's wife

The Story:

Celie, a poor, barely literate black woman living in rural Georgia, is raped and impregnated by a man she assumes is her father when she is fourteen years old. A short time later, Celie's mother dies, and Pa, her stepfather, takes Celie's children away, removes her from school, and has her married to a poor farmer she called Mr.——. She becomes the stepmother of his four children by a previous marriage, and she becomes his slave. When his son, Harpo, asks him why he beats his wife, he says that he does it because she is his wife and because she is stubborn.

Far from rebelling against her treatment by Mr.——, Celie accepts her abuse and neglect. Having been called ugly and worthless so often by both her stepfather and her husband, Celie comes to accept their view of her. Whatever hope she possessed early in life is directed outward in two directions: toward God and toward her sister, Nettie. By writing letters to both, Celie asserts that she is still alive. Her real hope for life lies in Nettie, to whom she is very devoted and whom she helped escape when Mr.—— made advances to her and threatened to have someone marry her. While Celie believes that her own life is over, she hopes that Nettie—who has a similar intelligence and a love of learning—can escape; then she can live vicariously through Nettie. Nettie moves to Africa to become a missionary, and the sisters vow to write to each other; however, Mr.—— intercepts Nettie's letters for many years.

Harpo marries Sofia and, modeling his behavior after his father, attempts to dominate her in the same way his father dominated Celie. Sofia is too strong and independent, however, to submit to his abuse. Though she later feels guilty for having betrayed Sofia by telling Sofia's husband that if he wants to keep her in line he should beat her, Celie is actually jealous of Sofia's strength.

When Mr.—— brings his mistress, Shug Avery, home to be nursed through an illness, Shug joins him in mocking Celie's looks and submissive behavior. A growing closeness emerges between Celie and Shug, however; Shug is a strong, independent woman with a career as a blues singer. She teaches Celie many things: to stand up to Mr.——, to believe in her self-worth, to appreciate her own beauty, and to experience the joys of sexuality. Shug is the first person, besides the absent Nettie, to love Celie for who she is, and Shug and Celie band together to make Mr.—— end his abuse of Celie. With Shug's encouragement, Celie defies Mr.—— and eventually curses him when she discovers that he kept Nettie's letters from her. She leaves him, just as Sofia previously left Harpo.

Shug takes Celie to her home in Memphis, and Celie begins a business making men's trousers. Later, when Celie discovers that her stepfather left her and Nettie a house and a dry goods store in Georgia, she returns to Georgia as an independent woman.

Nettie's letters from Africa indicate that the relationship between African men and women parallels the relationship between men and women in the American South. Nettie's life in Africa is fulfilling and frustrating. Unlike Celie, she was able to escape the rural South, and she is educated by books and by the experience of a wider world. A sincerely religious person, she feels that she is doing important work as a missionary, but she is frustrated by her lack of success. Nettie, her family, and Celie's children have to return to the American South to find integration into a true community. Like Celie, Nettie is frustrated by her lack of communication with her sister, but she develops a meaningful relationship with Samuel, another missionary. She later marries him.

At the conclusion of the novel, Nettie, her husband, and Celie's long-lost children return to Georgia to live in the home that was left to Celie. The novel ends with a Fourth of July celebration that signifies the absorption of all the characters of the novel into a living, vital community.

Critical Evaluation:

The Color Purple won the American Book Award and the Pulitzer Prize in fiction in 1983. Alice Walker's novel is unique in its preoccupation with spiritual survival and with exploring the oppressions, insanities, loyalties, and triumphs of black women. Walker's major interest is whether or how change can occur in the lives of her black characters. All the characters except Nettie and Shug lead insular lives, unaware of what is occurring outside their own small neighborhood. They are particularly unaware of the larger social and political currents sweeping the world. Despite their isolation, however, they work through problems of racism, sexism, violence, and oppression to achieve a wholeness, both personal and communal.

In form and content, *The Color Purple* is a slave narrative, a life story of a former slave who has gained freedom through many trials and tribulations. Instead of black oppression by whites, however, in this novel there is black oppression by blacks. It is also a story by a black woman about black women. Women fight, support, love, and heal each other—and they grow together. The novel begins in abject despair and ends in intense joy. To discover how this transformation occurs, it is important to examine three aspects of the novel: the relationships between men and women; the relationships among women; and the relationships among people, God, and nature. At the beginning of the novel, alienation and separation are evident in all of these relationships, but by the conclusion of the novel, an integration exists among all elements of life. In terms of the relationship between men and women, no personal contact between the sexes is possible at the beginning of the novel, since the male feels that he must dominate the female through brutality.

The correspondence between Celie and Nettie is the novel's most basic example of the alienation of women from women. Sometimes the alienation is caused by the men, as when Mr.—— keeps Nettie's letters from Celie, but often it results from the attitudes of the women themselves. For the first half of the novel, the women are against one another, often because of jealousy, as when Shug mocks Celie and flaunts her relationship with Celie's husband. Walker presents numerous examples of women in competition with one another, frequently because of men, but, more important, because they have accepted the social code indicating that women define themselves by their relationship with the men in their lives.

The first indication that this separation between women

will be overcome occurs when the women surmount their jealousy and join together. Central to this development is the growing closeness of Celie and Shug. Shug teaches Celie much about herself: to stand up for herself to Mr.——, about her own beauty and her self-worth, and about the enjoyment of her own body. The love of Celie and Shug is perhaps the strongest bond in the novel; the relationship between Celie and her sister is also a strong bond.

While the men in the novel seem to have no part in the female community, which, in essence, exists in opposition to them, they, too, are working out their salvation. As a result of the way the women have opposed them, they reevaluate their own lives and they come to a greater sense of their own wholeness, as well as that of the women. They develop relationships with the women on a different and more fulfilling level. The weakness of the men results from their having followed the dictates of their fathers, rather than their having followed their own desires. Mr.——, for example, wants to marry Shug, but in the face of his father's opposition, he marries another woman and makes her miserable because she is not Shug. Harpo tries to model his relationship with Sofia on the relationship between his father and Celie. Ultimately, both men find a kind of salvation because the women stand up to them and because the men accept their own gentler side. The men, by the end of the novel, become complete human beings just as the women do; therefore, the men are ready for relationships with women. Near the end of the novel, Mr.—— is content to sew trousers alongside Celie. By the end of the novel, Celie and Mr.——, whom she at last calls Albert, find a companionship of sorts. Harpo is content doing housework and caring for the children while Sofia works outside the home. Each individual becomes worthy in his or her own eyes—and in the eyes of others. The separation between men and women is shattered, and fulfilling human relationships can develop.

Alienation is also present in Nettie's letters from Africa. The relationship between African men and women is presented as similar to that of men and women in the American South. The social structure of the Olinka tribe is rigidly patriarchal; the only roles available to women are those of wife and mother. At the same time, the women, who frequently share the same husband, band together in friendship. Nettie debunks the myth that Africa offers a kind of salvation for African Americans searching for identity.

In Walker's view, God and nature are inextricably intertwined; therefore, alienation from one implies alienation from the other. Celie writes to God for much of the novel, but she writes out of despair, not hope; she feels no sustaining connection with God. Through her conversations with Shug, she comes to believe that God is in nature and in the self, and that divinity is found by developing the self and by celebrating everything that exists as an integrated whole. Celie also comes to believe that joy can come even to her; she learns to celebrate life's pleasures, including the color purple.

That spirit of celebration is embodied in the conclusion of the novel. At the Fourth of July celebration, all the divisions between people—divisions that had plagued and tormented the characters throughout the novel—have been healed. The characters' level of consciousness has been raised, and the seeds of feminism and liberation have been planted.

Genevieve Slomski

Further Reading

Bloom, Harold, ed. *Alice Walker's "The Color Purple."* New ed. New York: Bloom's Literary Criticism, 2008. Collection of critical essays about the novel, including discussions of Celie's search for identity; Walker's revisioning of racial stereotypes; the treatment of comedy, race, gender, and nation in the novel; and the function of sewing, knitting, and quilting in the book.

Butler-Evans, Elliott. *Race, Gender, and Desire: Narrative Strategies in the Fiction of Toni Cade Bambara, Toni Morrison, and Alice Walker.* Philadelphia: Temple University Press, 1989. Insightful comparative study of the relationship between narrative technique and politics in three African American women writers. Includes bibliography.

Davis, Thadious M. "Alice Walker's Celebration of Self in Southern Generations." In *Women Writers of the Contemporary South*, edited by Peggy Whitman Prenshaw. Jackson: University Press of Mississippi, 1984. Focuses on themes and patterns apparent in Walker's work, from her poetry through *The Color Purple*. Shows Walker's need to resolve her intellectualism with her rural roots.

Dieke, Ikenna, ed. *Critical Essays on Alice Walker.* Westport, Conn.: Greenwood Press, 1999. Several of the essays focus on *The Color Purple*, including "Creating Generations: The Relationship Between Celie and Shug in Alice Walker's *The Color Purple*" by E. Ellen Barker, "*The Color Purple*: An Existential Novel" by Marc A. Christophe, and "Alice Walker's American Quilt: *The Color Purple* and American Literary Tradition" by Priscilla Leder.

Evans, Mari, ed. *Black Women Writers (1950-1980): A Critical Evaluation.* Garden City, N.J.: Anchor Press, 1984. Contains three excellent essays on the novels of Alice Walker and discusses her work in the context of African

American women's writing. "Alice Walker: The Black Woman Artist as Wayward" by Barbara Christian examines thematic patterns in Walker's work and points out issues inherent in the role of the black female artist, such as the need for change. "Alice Walker's Women: In Search of Some Peace of Mind" by Bettye J. Parker-Smith describes how Celie affirms herself and finds the strength she needs by discovering that God is within, that God is herself.

Gates, Henry Louis, Jr., and K. A. Appiah, eds. *Alice Walker: Critical Perspectives Past and Present.* New York: Amistad Press, 1993. A comprehensive and well-written collection of essays on Walker. Contains reviews, essays, and interviews. Includes chronology and bibliography.

Harris, Trudier. "From Victimization to Free Enterprise: Alice Walker's *The Color Purple.*" *Studies in American Fiction* 14 (Spring, 1986): 1-17. Focuses on the movement from domination to liberation in Walker's female characters.

Hite, Molly. *The Other Side of the Story: Structures and Strategies of Contemporary Feminist Narrative.* Ithaca, N.Y.: Cornell University Press, 1989. Discusses Walker's fiction as an attempt to create an opposing view to the dominant stories of culture. Analyzes her relationships to language and to narrative tradition.

Lauret, Maria. *Alice Walker.* New York: St. Martin's Press, 2000. A critical evaluation of Walker's life and work, with chapter 4 devoted to an analysis of *The Color Purple.* Demonstrates that Walker was influenced by Virginia Woolf and Carl Jung, among others, and discusses the epistolary format of *The Color Purple.*

Simcikova, Karla. *To Live Fully, Here and Now: The Healing Vision in the Works of Alice Walker.* Lanham, Md.: Lexington Books, 2007. Focuses on the "spiritual wisdom" in Walker's works, arguing that her spirituality goes beyond feminism and "womanism" to incorporate global awareness, concern for environmental devastation, and a belief in the unity of all people.

The Colossus, and Other Poems

Author: Sylvia Plath (1932-1963)
First published: 1960
Type of work: Poetry

Sylvia Plath's first book of poetry, *The Colossus, and Other Poems*, was generally well received as the clever first book of a promising young poet. The poems contain images and themes that Plath revisited in her writing, themes such as death, nature, the sea, water, and the parent-child relationship.

The Colossus, the only book of poetry Plath published during her lifetime, was published first in England in 1960, then in the United States in 1962. Some poems were omitted in the American edition for fear that their resemblance to the poetry of Theodore Roethke could cause legal problems. While Plath was influenced by Roethke, the poems in this collection are distinctly hers. Furthermore, some reviewers had undercut Plath's individual poetic achievements by drawing attention to her marriage to fellow poet Ted Hughes.

Plath's poetry, to take one particular example, examines the theme of death from many angles. In two poems in the first half of the collection, Plath contemplates dead bodies. In "Two Views of a Cadaver," the almost unrecognizably human corpses are contrasted with the two living lovers observing them, and the poem ends on a slightly hopeful note: There is life before inevitable death. Considering a mummified body in a museum in "All the Dead Dears," however, the poet's tone is bleaker, acknowledging that being alive implies eventual death. The poem's speaker feels a bond with the dead, another theme that reappears. In several poems, death is presented as a quiet, neutral place in contrast to the noise and disorder of life.

In three poems in the second half of the book, this idea of death is represented by images of dead animals. The two dead moles in "Blue Moles" have left behind the "fury," "war," and "battle-shouts" they struggled with in life, and are now "neutral as the stones." Their positioning is benignly described as a "family pose." In "Medallion," the poet describes a dead snake admiringly, as grinning and laughing, and notes that the snake's firelike colors are beautiful. She also depicts the snake as "pure" and "chaste." A crab's corpse is presented similarly in "Mussel Hunter at Rock Harbor," a long poem near the end of the book. Even though the crab's inner body has been washed away, its hard outer skeleton remains as a "relic." Its shell is "bleached" and "pallid," with the white colors suggesting a desirable purity and neutrality.

Water and the sea appear repeatedly in Plath's work. A more explicit wish for death appears in three poems about drowning. The first poem, "Lorelei," uses German mythological figures (similar to the Greek sirens) to symbolize the attractiveness that death can have: "They sing/ Of a world more full and clear/ Than can be." Another poem, "Suicide off Egg Rock," also depicts death's attractiveness, but couples it with the desperation of a suicidal man. He cannot stand the noises and smells of the public beach around him, or even the sound of his own pulse. As the poem progresses, his senses slowly recede, and the sea in which he drowns himself offers a "blank" and "forgetful" respite. In Plath's heavily autobiographical novel *The Bell Jar* (1963; written as Victoria Lucas), the main character contemplates committing suicide this way, but she cannot go through with it. Plath herself attempted suicide in 1953, and eventually did kill herself in 1963. Finally, in "Full Fathom Five," a daughter feels compelled to join her drowned father: "Father, this thick air is murderous./ I would breathe water." This poem foreshadows Plath's later themes, and its title comes from a line spoken by a character named Ariel in William Shakespeare's play *The Tempest* (pr. 1611, pb. 1623). Plath later wrote a poem titled "Ariel," which also was used as the title of her next book.

Other poems in *The Colossus* deal with the parent-child relationship. The title poem "The Colossus" is widely thought to refer to Plath's father, Otto Plath, who died when his daughter was eight years old. In a technique she commonly uses, Plath projects her thoughts about people close to her onto a larger-than-life image, in this case the Colossus of Rhodes, one of the Seven Wonders of the World. The speaker of this poem tends, mends, and listens to the giant statue to try to understand something of the unintelligible "barnyard" noises issuing from it. No connection is made, however; the poem's first line is "I shall never get you put together entirely." "The Beekeeper's Daughter" is a more literal attempt by the poet to get close to her father through his work. (Otto Plath had studied and written a book about bumblebees.) The mother-child relationship is addressed from the point of view of a child in "The Disquieting Muses" and from that of a pregnant mother in the book's first poem, "The Manor Garden." Both "The Disquieting Muses" and "The Beekeeper's Daughter" depict neglectful mothers, the first using an image of sinister godmother figures. These figures were partly inspired by the Giorgio de Chirico painting *The Disquieting Muses* (1916); other poems by Plath that refer to works of art include "Snakecharmer" (Henri Rousseau's *Snake Charmer*,

1907), "Two Views of a Cadaver" (Pieter Bruegel the Elder's *The Triumph of Death*, c. 1562), and "The Ghost's Leavetaking" (Paul Klee's *Fleeing Ghost*, 1929).

Nature is another major theme in *The Colossus*, but Plath does not portray nature as ideally or as gently as do many other poets. Plath's poems are filled with animals, plants, and landscapes that are dead or menacing, harsh, and indifferent. Even when a landscape appears calm and inviting, as in "Watercolor of Grantchester Meadows," danger lurks beneath the surface: The poem ends with an owl disrupting a tranquil domestic scene to kill a rat. Similarly, in "The Eye-Mote," a beautiful landscape is spoiled by the speaker's distorted vision. "Mushrooms" uses short lines, repetition, and words like "nudgers and shovers" to show how a quiet, insistent force can slowly overwhelm its surroundings. "Frog Autumn" highlights the decay that characterizes that season, while "Hardcastle Crags" emphasizes a particular landscape's harshness, reminding the reader that nature does not care if humans live or die. "Departure" and "Point Shirley" both depict houses, symbols of civilization, being eroded relentlessly by the sea. Though the title character in "The Hermit at Outermost House" has endured the corroding force of the sea, it has taken all his strength, and he is alone.

The poems in *The Colossus* were carefully selected to represent years of Plath's work, much of which had been published previously in magazines and journals. Together, they represent a more controlled poetry than Plath's next book, *Ariel* (1965), which is looser and more intense and which was somewhat overshadowed by her dramatic death. Almost every poem in *The Colossus* is written in some kind of form, whether traditional or improvised, or includes rhyme (often slant or off-rhymes). The most commonly used form is terza rima, three-line stanzas in which the first and third lines rhyme. An example of this form (using off-rhyme) is "Sow."

Plath's controlled approach to emotion in *The Colossus* is an example of learning the rules to break them successfully, which she does in later poems. She could not have written these later poems without preparing the groundwork in *The Colossus*.

Elizabeth M. Galoozis

Further Reading

Axelrod, Steven Gould. *Sylvia Plath: The Wound and the Cure of Words*. Baltimore: Johns Hopkins University Press, 1990. A literary biography blending biographical information with themes in Plath's work, including language, the mother-daughter bond, and death.

Bassnett, Susan. *Sylvia Plath: An Introduction to the Poetry.*

2d ed. New York: Palgrave Macmillan, 2005. Concentrates on close readings of Plath's texts, rather than on the cult of her personality and suicide. Chapters include "God, Nature, and Writing" and "Writing the Family."

Gil, Jo. *The Cambridge Introduction to Sylvia Plath*. New York: Cambridge University Press, 2008. A brief but comprehensive introduction to Plath's life and work. Includes chapters on *The Colossus*, the critical reception to her work, and analyses of the cultural contexts—including the domestic sphere and suburbia—in which she lived and wrote.

Kroll, Judith. *Chapters in a Mythology: The Poetry of Sylvia Plath*. 2d ed. Stroud, England: Sutton, 2007. First published in 1976, this book is one of the first to concentrate

on the complexity of Plath's work, rather than on the circumstances of her life and death. Discusses books and artwork that influenced Plath, including mythological and psychological sources.

Newman, Charles, ed. *The Art of Sylvia Plath: A Symposium*. Bloomington: Indiana University Press, 1970. A compilation of essays including an early assessment of *The Colossus*, an analysis of sea imagery in Plath's poetry, and a discussion of her use of form, rhythm, and metaphor. Includes a checklist of criticism and a bibliography.

Wagner-Martin, Linda. *Sylvia Plath: The Critical Heritage*. 2d ed. New York: Routledge, 1997. A collection of criticism on Plath and her work. Includes reviews of all editions of *The Colossus*.

The Comedy of Errors

Author: William Shakespeare (1564-1616)
First produced: c. 1592-1594; first published, 1623
Type of work: Drama
Type of plot: Farce
Time of plot: First century B.C.E.
Locale: Greece

Principal characters:
SOLINUS, duke of Ephesus
AEGEON, a merchant of Syracuse
ANTIPHOLUS OF EPHESUS and ANTIPHOLUS OF SYRACUSE, twin brothers, sons of Aegeon and Aemilia
DROMIO OF EPHESUS and DROMIO OF SYRACUSE, twin brothers, attendants of above twins
AEMILIA, Aegeon's wife
ADRIANA, wife to Antipholus of Ephesus
LUCIANA, Adriana's sister
A COURTESAN

The Story:

According to the laws of the lands of Ephesus and Syracuse, it is forbidden for a native of one land to journey to the other; the penalty for the crime is execution or the ransom of a thousand marks. Aegeon, a merchant of Syracuse who recently traveled to Ephesus, is to be put to death because he cannot raise the thousand marks. When Solinus, duke of Ephesus, hears Aegeon's story, he gives the merchant one more day to raise the money.

It is a sad and strange tale Aegeon tells. Many years earlier, he journeyed to Epidamnum. Shortly after his wife joined him there she delivered identical twin boys. Strangely enough, at the same time and in the same house, another woman bore identical twin boys. Because that woman and her husband were so poor that they could not provide for their children, they gave them to Aegeon and his wife Aemilia, to

be attendants to their two sons. On the way home to Syracuse, Aegeon and his family were shipwrecked. Aemilia and the two children with her were rescued by one ship, Aegeon and the other two by a different ship, and Aegeon did not see his wife and those two children again. When he reached eighteen years of age, Antipholus, the son reared by his father in Syracuse, grows eager to find his brother, so he and his attendant set out to find their twins. Aegeon comes to Ephesus to seek them.

Unknown to Aegeon, Antipholus and his attendant, Dromio, are just arrived in Ephesus. There a merchant of the city warns them to say that they come from somewhere other than Syracuse, lest they suffer the penalty already meted out to Aegeon. Antipholus, having sent Dromio to find lodging for them, is utterly bewildered when the servant returns and says that Antipholus's wife waits dinner for him. What happens is that the Dromio who returns to Antipholus is Dromio of Ephesus, servant and attendant to Antipholus of Ephesus. Antipholus of Syracuse gives his Dromio money to pay for lodging, and when he hears a tale of a wife about whom he knows nothing he thinks his servant tricked him and asks for the return of the money. Dromio of Ephesus was given no money, however, and when he professes no knowledge of the sum, Antipholus of Syracuse beats him soundly for dishonesty. Antipholus of Syracuse later hears that his money was delivered to the inn.

A short time later, the wife and sister-in-law of Antipholus of Ephesus meet Antipholus of Syracuse and, after berating him for refusing to come home to dinner, accuses him of unfaithfulness with another woman. Not understanding a word of what Adriana says, Antipholus of Syracuse goes to dinner in her home, where Dromio is assigned by her to guard the gate and allow no one to enter. Thus it is that Antipholus of Ephesus arrives at his home with his Dromio and is refused admittance. So incensed is he that he leaves his house and goes to an inn. There he dines with a courtesan and gives her the gifts he intended for his wife.

In the meantime, Antipholus of Syracuse, though almost believing that he must be the husband of Adriana, falls in love with her sister Luciana. When he tells her of his love, she calls him an unfaithful husband and begs him to remain true to his wife. Dromio of Syracuse is pursued by a kitchen maid whom he abhors but who mistakes him for the Dromio of Ephesus who loves her.

Even the townspeople and merchants are bewildered. A goldsmith delivers to Antipholus of Syracuse a chain meant for Antipholus of Ephesus and then tries to collect from the latter, who in turn states that he received no chain and accuses the merchant of trying to rob him.

Antipholus and Dromio of Syracuse decide to leave the seemingly mad town as soon as possible, and the servant is sent to book passage on the first ship leaving the city. Dromio of Syracuse brings back news of the sailing to Antipholus of Ephesus, who by that time is arrested for refusing to pay the merchant for the chain he did not receive. Antipholus of Ephesus, believing the servant to be his own, sends Dromio of Syracuse to his house to get money for his bail. Before Dromio of Syracuse returns with the money, however, Dromio of Ephesus comes to Antipholus of Ephesus, naturally without the desired money. Meanwhile, Dromio of Syracuse takes the money to Antipholus of Syracuse, who did not send for money and cannot understand what his servant is talking about. To make matters worse, the courtesan with whom Antipholus of Ephesus dined gave him a ring. Now

she approaches the other Antipholus and demands the ring. Knowing nothing about the ring, he angrily dismisses the woman, who decides to go to his house and tell his wife of his betrayal.

On his way to jail for the debt he does not owe, Antipholus of Ephesus meets his wife. Wild with rage, he accuses her of locking him out of his own house and of refusing him his own money for bail. She is so frightened that she asks the police first to make sure that he is securely bound and then to imprison him in their home so that she can care for him.

At the same time Antipholus and Dromio of Syracuse are making their way toward the ship that will carry them away from this mad city. Antipholus is wearing the gold chain. The merchant, meeting them, demands that Antipholus be arrested. To escape, Antipholus of Syracuse and his Dromio flee into an abbey. To the same abbey comes Aegeon, the duke, and the executioners, for Aegeon did not raise the money for his ransom. Adriana and Luciana also appear, demanding the release to them of Adriana's husband and his servant. Adriana, seeing the two men take refuge in the convent, thinks they are Antipholus and Dromio of Ephesus. At that instant a servant runs in to tell Adriana that her husband and Dromio escaped from the house and are now on the way to the abbey. Adriana does not believe the servant, for she herself saw her husband and Dromio enter the abbey. Then Antipholus and Dromio of Ephesus appear before the abbey. Aegeon thinks he recognizes the son and servant he is seeking, but they deny any knowledge of him. The confusion increases until the abbess brings from the convent Antipholus and Dromio of Syracuse, who instantly recognize Aegeon. Then all the mysteries are solved. Adriana is reunited with her husband, Antipholus of Ephesus, and his Dromio has the kitchen maid once more. Antipholus of Syracuse is free to make love to Luciana, and his Dromio, too, is freed. Still more surprising, the abbess turns out to be Aegeon's wife, the mother of the Antipholus twins. So the happy family is together again. Lastly, Antipholus of Ephesus pays his father's ransom and brings to an end all the errors of that unhappy day.

Critical Evaluation:

William Shakespeare was not always the master playwright that he became in his later life. When he first began writing plays, he did not have the mastery of plot, character, concept, and language for which he was to be universally praised. In 1592, he was a young playwright with a historical trilogy and a classical tragedy to his credit; he was just beginning to explore and perfect his craft. *The Comedy of Errors* is an early experiment with comedy, and his enthusiasm for the experiment is clear in his writing.

Shakespeare followed the example of most playwrights of the Elizabethan era by adapting other plays and sources to make his dramas. This in no way detracts from his genius because what he adapted he made distinctively his own.

Most of *The Comedy of Errors* derives from *Menaechmi* (pr. second century B.C.E.; *The Menaechmi*, 1595) by the classical Roman playwright Plautus, who lived from c. 254 B.C.E. to 184 B.C.E. Act 3, scene 1 of the play originates from another work by Plautus, *Amphitruo* (*Amphitryon*, 1694). Both of these plays concern mistaken identity, which Shakespeare adapted for the crux of his plot as well. Just as Shakespeare adapted Plautus, Plautus apparently drew from an unknown Greek playwright. It was said of Plautus that his special genius was for turning a Greek original into a typically Roman play with typically Roman characters. Similarly, Shakespeare, like Plautus, set the play in ancient Ephesus and used some of Plautus's situations, but Shakespeare's characters are typically and recognizably of Shakespeare's Elizabethan age.

Shakespeare changed the framework of the plot, making it much more romantic and accessible to popular tastes. In Shakespeare's version, the twins' father, Aegeon, is introduced in the middle of his search for his wife and other son, separated from him by shipwreck. This story line, demonstrating husbandly and paternal devotion, was appealing to the audience. Shakespeare then created the servant twins (Dromios) to add to the fun of the mistaken identity plot. In so doing he doubled the amount of action. He also introduced Luciana, sister of the wife of Antipholus of Ephesus, thus providing a love interest for Antipholus of Syracuse. Out of the Plautine cast of nine, Shakespeare retained six of the original characters and developed many more of his own.

In addition, Shakespeare changed the characters to fit the tastes of his audience. Plautus's twins are extremely one-dimensional characters. Both are self-centered, callous young men whose only interest is the gratification of their animal appetites. It is difficult to feel any sympathy or empathy for them. In Shakespeare's play, however, the twins are simply callow youths whose characters are not yet completely formed. They are not amoral, as are Plautus's twins. They are simply naïve.

The relationship between Shakespeare's Antipholus of Ephesus and his wife was much more appealing to Elizabethan audiences than that relationship, as depicted by Plautus, would have been. Shakespeare's Antipholus does not steal his wife's jewelry and gowns to give to a courtesan. In fact, he dines with the courtesan and gives her his wife's presents only out of revenge at being shut out of his house and being given the impression that his wife was entertaining another

man. There is a moral dimension to Shakespeare's play that is lacking in Plautus's.

Like Plautus's, Shakespeare's play is a farce, filled with fast-paced action and dialogue, peopled with eccentric characters, and developed by improbable, exaggerated situations. It is the most elementary of the comic arts—the comedy of situation, rather than the comedy of character or theme. Shakespeare's later comedies would develop the more difficult styles.

Even in this elementary comedy, Shakespeare shows talent enough to draw some basic characterization and suggest polarities of characters. The younger twin from Syracuse is, stereotypically, more timid than his arrogant older brother. Luciana is gentler and shyer than her sister. The eccentrics, the courtesan and Doctor Pinch, are each separately and strikingly developed.

Shakespeare's experiments with language and poetry betray his apprenticeship. There is a noticeable simplicity and repetition of diction. The play's accomplishment and fluency augur what the mature Shakespeare would later produce. The poetic passages of wooing that he created for the Syracuse twin and Luciana anticipate *Romeo and Juliet* (pr. c. 1595-1596, pb. 1597). Dromio of Ephesus's punning description of his twin's wife, the slattern Nell, in geographic terms, is a masterpiece of comic overstatement, as is the bawdy, double entendre that enriches the scene in which Ephesus is denied access to his home and wife. All of these touches are strokes of genius and wit.

Shakespeare's later romantic comedies are foreshadowed by the dignified characters of Aegeon and Aemilia: Their lifelong devotion and eventual reunion elevate the farce to a higher level of comedy. Their plot resolution not only incorporates the plot and subplots but also unites all the characters. This plot development anticipates the festive communion that is the goal of all of Shakespeare's later romantic comedies.

Shakespeare probably set out to write the perfect Roman-style play. It observes two of Aristotle's unities: It is set in one locale, and it takes place in the span of a day's time. Shakespeare added subplots, however, to complement and complicate the main plot. Plautus would never have broken the third unity. Shakespeare also handles his exposition tritely (Solinus asks Aegeon what brings him to Ephesus), and, as a result, the first act moves slowly. Once the playwright moves into the plot complications of act 2, the action and humor never slow until the conclusion.

The characters are shallowly developed, the plot is improbable, and the comedy is developed primarily through situation, but *The Comedy of Errors* has proved to be a play that delights audiences. Shakespeare wrote more thought-provoking plays than this one, plays that were more sensitive and profound, and plays peopled with better-developed characters, but *The Comedy of Errors* remains a fun romp, written in excellent pentameter.

"Critical Evaluation" by H. Alan Pickrell

Further Reading

Baldwin, Thomas Whitfield. *On the Compositional Genetics of "The Comedy of Errors."* Champaign: University of Illinois Press, 1965. Likens Shakespeare to the Dromios, awed by their change from the rural to the urban.

Berry, Ralph. *Shakespeare and the Awareness of the Audience.* New York: St. Martin's Press, 1985. Discusses the "dark underside" of the play, which enriches and complements the comedy. Argues that Aegeon may be more important to the plot structure than he seems to be.

Colie, Rosalie L. *Shakespeare's Living Art.* Princeton, N.J.: Princeton University Press, 1974. Sees Shakespeare's plays as experiments with the craft of writing plays. Discusses Shakespeare's improving on Plautus.

Dorsch, T. S., ed. Introduction to *The Comedy of Errors*, by William Shakespeare. New York: Cambridge University Press, 1988. This edition features a comprehensive introductory essay by Dorsch, with a brief look at the play's history, sources, characters, and plot.

Gay, Penny. *The Cambridge Introduction to Shakespeare's Comedies.* New York: Cambridge University Press, 2008. Concise introductory overview of Shakespearean comedy. Explains the theory and practice of comedy in Shake-speare's times. Includes a brief discussion of *The Comedy of Errors* in chapter 1.

Greenblatt, Stephen. *Will in the World: How Shakespeare Became Shakespeare.* New York: Norton, 2004. Critically acclaimed biography, in which Greenblatt finds new connections between Shakespeare's works and the Bard's life and engagement with Elizabethan society.

Leggatt, Alexander, ed. *The Cambridge Companion to Shakespearean Comedy.* New York: Cambridge University Press, 2002. Although none of the essays is specifically about *The Comedy of Errors*, there are numerous references to this play that are listed in the index. The essays about Roman comedy, forms of confusion, comedy and sex, and matters of state are particularly useful.

Miola, Robert S., ed. *"The Comedy of Errors": Critical Essays.* New York: Garland, 1997. A compilation of criticism published from 1836 through the late-1990's, including an essay by Samuel Taylor Coleridge and George Bernard Shaw's review of an 1895 production of *The Comedy of Errors.* Includes reviews of other productions, including a 1976 musical adaptation staged in Japan, a 1983 circus production, and a television adaptation. Some of the other essays discuss the play as a comedy of love; analyze the significance of food, misrecognition, and the uncanny in the play; and place the play within the context of the late 1580's and early 1590's.

Tillyard, E. M. W. *Shakespeare's Early Comedies.* New York: Barnes & Noble, 1965. Tillyard, one of the most noted of Shakespeare's commentators, points out that Shakespeare probably did not read the Roman original for the play; Tillyard focuses on a translated manuscript.

Commentaries

Author: Julius Caesar (100 B.C.E.-44 C.E.)
First transcribed: 52-51 B.C.E., 45 B.C.E.; includes
Commentarii de bello Gallico, 52-51 B.C.E.;
Commentarii de bello civili, 45 B.C.E. (English translation, 1609)
Type of work: History

Principal personages:
JULIUS CAESAR, the Roman governor and general in Gaul
VERCINGETORIX, the rebel leader of the Gauls
ARIOVISTUS, a chieftain of the Germanic tribes

In 59 B.C.E., after the Roman Empire had expanded north and west into the area now known as France and Germany, Julius Caesar, already famous as a general and administrator, was appointed to govern the Roman territories inhabited by the Gauls. Here a strong, active government was required, and from the start Caesar kept records of the events of his governorship. The record eventually came to be known as Caesar's *Commentaries* and to be regarded as an important record for posterity. Indeed, scholars and general readers have wished that Caesar had left a more complete record than he did. To expect a detailed history in the *Commentaries* is, however, to misunderstand the writer's purpose. His intention was not to write a definitive history of the period of the Gallic Wars but rather to put down in writing what he, the Roman general and administrator, considered most important.

No one can understand the *Commentaries* without having some concept of the flux of migration and its consequent pressures in Europe during the first century before Christ. The Gallic peoples were under pressure from the Germanic peoples across the Rhine River who coveted the rich lands of the Gauls and were, in their turn, under pressure from migrations still farther to the east. Rome faced a double threat from the Germanic tribes: They were pressing constantly southward (and would eventually invade and dismember the Roman Empire), and they threatened Rome indirectly by the unrest they created in Gaul. Being a man of action and a clear analyst of the situation confronting Rome, Caesar took war into the German territory.

In his *Commentaries*, he gives a chronological account of his activities in Gaul from the time of his succession to the governorship of Gallia Narbonensis in 59 B.C.E. to the end of the Gallic revolt led by Vercingetorix late in the same decade. During those years, Caesar and his Roman legions confronted first one group of tribes, then another. Most of the sections of the book carry such headings as "Campaign Against Ariovistus," "Expedition Against the Unelli," "First Expedition into Germany," and "Siege and Sack of Avaricum." Only two sections, the first section of book 1 and the second section of book 6, are not about actual battle operations or preparations. The former is a description of Gaul and its inhabitants; the latter is an account of customs of the Gauls and Germans.

In his comments about the Gauls, Caesar stirs the imagination and stimulates curiosity by giving only enough information to make the reader wish more had been written. An account of the druids' place in Gallic culture, for example, and of the religious rites at which the druids officiated would have been welcome. In other cases, however, Caesar taxes credulity, as in reporting certain kinds of animals as existing in the Hyrcanian Forest. One such animal, according to Caesar, was an elk captured by partly cutting trees against which the elk leaned to rest; because the animal had no joints in its legs, it could not rise once it was down. Caesar also reports a fabulous ox with but one horn growing from the middle of the forehead. Such reports resemble other natural histories of the period and do not detract from the value of the *Commentaries*, for in Caesar's time such reports were generally taken seriously.

Caesar's account of the Gallic Wars is a reminder that war has been a continual factor in human affairs. As one example of the fury and effectiveness of war in ancient times, Caesar comments at the end of his account of the battle with the Nervii:

> This battle being ended, and the name and nation of the Nervii almost reduced to annihilation, their old men, together with the boys and women whom we have stated had been collected together in the inlets and the marshes, when this battle had been reported to them, convinced that nothing was an obstacle to the conquerors, and nothing safe to the conquered, sent ambassadors to Caesar with the consent of all who survived, and surrendered themselves to him; and in recounting the calamity of their state, they said that their senators were reduced from six hundred to three; that of sixty thousand men who could bear arms, scarcely five hundred remained.

Another example of the character of these ancient wars is the siege of Avaricum, at which, according to Caesar, scarcely eight hundred people of all ages and both genders escaped the city when it was taken, out of a population of forty thousand; the rest were killed.

Caesar the Roman administrator is apparent throughout the *Commentaries*. He writes in an impersonal fashion, however, much as though he were preparing a favorable report to the Roman senate. Only rarely does an individual come through to the reader as a real personality. Even Caesar himself, whose name figures more largely than any other, remains an official and a general rather than emerging as a clearly visualized person. The Gallic and Germanic chieftains who oppose him are little more than names, and the same is true of the lieutenants who serve under him. The only outstanding exception to this general statement is the passage concerning Sextius Baculus, who, sick though he was, arose from his bed and saved the day for the Romans by rallying their forces when they were attacked in a camp at Aduatuca; he fought bravely until he was carried back to rest.

Of particular interest to English-speaking readers are those portions of the *Commentaries* that deal with Britain and Caesar's invasions of Britain. Caesar's account of the early history of that part of the world is the earliest of the Roman documents. Caesar tells of his first expedition, an abortive one, made in 55 B.C.E., and his second and more successful attempt the following year, an invasion that paved the way for the Roman occupation that lasted until the fifth century C.E. For his second invasion, he ordered a fleet of more than eight hundred vessels built and assembled, a logistical success noteworthy in any era of history. This fleet carried two thousand cavalrymen with their mounts and five Roman legions, each consisting at that time of about five thousand men.

Caesar was a remarkable man, one of the greatest in human history, in the sense that greatness may be defined as leaving an indelible mark on the pages of history. Few such men have lived; fewer still have left written records for posterity; and none has left a document to compare with Caesar's *Commentaries*. The book occupies a unique place in the written records of the Western world. In addition to its value as history, it deserves to be read as an example of a concise report presented with an idiosyncratic style and flavor.

Further Reading

Adcock, Frank E. *Caesar as a Man of Letters*. Hamden, Conn.: Archon, 1969. A brief biography that focuses exclusively on Caesar's literary style. Valuable as a supplement to other historical works that deal primarily with Caesar's military and political achievements.

Balsdon, John Percy Vyvian Dacre. *Julius Caesar and Rome*. Harmondsworth, England: Penguin, 1971. A political biography by one of the twentieth century's most influential Roman historians. Scholarly but accessible to the general reader, this work focuses more on Caesar's triumphs than on his literary works, but it reveals much about the background and origin of the *Commentaries*.

Batstone, William W., and Cynthia Damon. *Caesar's Civil War*. New York: Oxford University Press, 2006. Literary analysis of Caesar's commentary on the civil war, discussing his selection of material for the work, literary techniques, characterization, and structure and placing the work within the context of Roman history. Includes maps, a time line of Caesar's life and the events of the war, a glossary of technical terms, and a list of prominent Romans in Caesar's time.

Gelzer, Matthias. *Caesar: Politician and Statesman*. Translated by Peter Needham. Cambridge, Mass.: Harvard University Press, 2003. Unquestionably the most comprehensive and scholarly biography of Caesar available in English. Contains copious notes and an analysis of nearly every detail of Caesar's life and literary work.

Grant, Michael. *Caesar*. Chicago: Follett, 1975. An accurate account of Caesar and his *Commentaries*. Combines biographical information with literary analysis. Extensively illustrated and easy to read.

Kagan, Kimberly. *The Eye of Command*. Ann Arbor: University of Michigan Press, 2006. A response to *The Face of Battle* (1976), in which military historian Sir John Keegan emphasized the importance of soldiers' accounts of small-unit actions. Kagan refutes this theory, maintaining that the view of a commander offers more significant information about the major events of battle. She proves her thesis by analyzing Caesar's account of the Gallic Wars and the work of Roman military leader Ammianus Marcellinus.

Kahn, Arthur David. *The Education of Julius Caesar*. Norwalk, Conn.: Easton Press, 1993. Both a biography and a reconstruction of the educational forces that influenced Caesar's life. Useful both for its background on the literary style of the *Commentaries* and for its information on pedagogical values of Roman society in the first century B.C.E.

Yavetz, Zvi. *Julius Caesar and His Public Image*. London: Thames and Hudson, 1983. A detailed account of Caesar's use of propaganda, of which his published *Commentaries* were a major part.

Common Sense

Author: Thomas Paine (1737-1809)
First published: 1776
Type of work: Political philosophy

Common Sense, a sixty-seven-page pamphlet advocating complete separation of Great Britain's North American colonies from the parent country, is one of the most influential pieces of political writing ever published. It is also an important landmark in the history of literary development, representing the first major piece of political writing, in any language, to effectively reach the working classes. The pamphlet appeared in Philadelphia on January 10, 1776, at a critical juncture in the genesis of the American Revolution. A state of armed rebellion had existed in Massachusetts since

April, 1775. The Continental Congress, first convened in 1774 and reconvened in 1775, was meeting in Philadelphia. Many of its members, selected by colonial assemblies, were cautious in their approach to independence and believed a compromise was possible. Thomas Paine wrote on behalf of those who felt such caution did not reflect the will or best interests of most North Americans. *Common Sense* aimed to bring pressure to bear on indecisive politicians by galvanizing popular opinion in favor of complete separation backed by force of arms.

The pamphlet appeared at a particularly opportune moment. Its publication coincided with the arrival of George III's address to Parliament declaring the colonies to be in a state of rebellion and pledging to use military force to prevent separation. The resentment against the British monarchy that this communication fanned resonated with the strong antiking, antiaristocratic message of *Common Sense*.

The work comprises four chapters, with an introduction and appendix added in the second (February, 1776) edition. The first two chapters discuss the origins of government and the structure and function of the British monarchy, respectively. Chapter 3 focuses on the political situation in 1775-1776 and contains specific recommendations for recruiting soldiers, financing a war, and structuring a new government. Chapter 4 recapitulates the arguments of chapter 3, urging unity and continued armed resistance at a level sufficient to achieve victory.

In the first chapter, "On the Origin and Design of Government in General, with Concise Remarks on the English Constitution," Paine views government as a necessary evil, arising when people begin associating in larger social groups and require rules and authority to restrain their baser instincts. He envisions the original form of human government as republican, without hereditary distinctions, and views the British government of his day as the base remnant of two ancient tyrannies—monarchy and aristocracy—with some new republican materials grafted on in the form of the House of Commons. Any disposition to retain this fundamentally corrupt form of government, he warns, will hinder the formation of something better. The chapter was an argument against those who wanted more colonial autonomy but wished to retain ties to the Crown.

Chapter 2, "Of Monarchy and Hereditary Succession," begins with a commentary on the biblical stories of Gideon's refusal of the crown of Israel (Judges 8) and Samuel's anointing of Saul (I Samuel 8-10), emphasizing that Israel became a monarchy in imitation of its heathen neighbors and that the prophet Samuel warned the Israelites against crowning a king. It argues that, as bad as it is to vest absolute power in

one man under any circumstances, hereditary kingship is far worse because the representatives of the people no longer have any say in the succession.

Paine minces no words in his abuse of George III, calling him insolent, ignorant, and unfit. Britain's king, according to Paine, has no real function but devours the public wealth and controls the Commons by dispensing places. Paine points out that some would argue that a monarchy confers stability. In response, he asks: If this is the case, why has England been so frequently plagued by civil wars, while Switzerland and Holland, which have no king, have been peaceful by comparison? Chapter 2 is an argument both against retaining ties to the British crown and against founding a new American dynasty.

Chapter 3, "Thoughts on the Present State of American Affairs," emphasizes the universality of Paine's message and stresses the common cause of all the inhabitants of North America, "An eighth part of the habitable globe." This chapter speaks to those in the colonies who hope to spread the struggle to Canada and to the Spanish possessions in Louisiana and Florida. Paine argues that America is no longer a colony of Britain, since it is populated by "the persecuted lovers of liberty from every corner of Europe." At the time he wrote, colonial troops were besieging Quebec.

Paine argues that America does not need to retain ties with Britain to defend itself. Other European countries, he says, are hostile to America only because of its connection to Great Britain; they would become willing allies and trading partners in the event of independence. Americans, moreover, have a duty to their posterity to fight the war of independence to a successful conclusion, rather than negotiating a compromise. Otherwise, all the sacrifices they have already made will have been in vain.

Paine presents the outline of a proposed government for the new nation, with a single house of representatives and a rotating annual presidency. The president would be chosen by ballot from among the representatives of a given state (itself chosen by lot), and a three-fifths majority would be required to pass any law. Paine calls for freedom of religion and of property for all men. *Common Sense* makes no mention of slavery, but elsewhere Paine is on record as one of its earliest unequivocal opponents.

Chapter 4, "Of the Present Ability of America: With Some Miscellaneous Reflections," addresses the question of whether America can win the war. America, Paine says, has sufficient manpower. Although England is far more populous and has an enormous treasury, American men are better prepared to fight, and the country abounds in raw materials. While America has no navy, it has a thriving shipbuilding industry and could easily produce one. To pay the debt such a war will inevitably incur, Paine proposes selling unoccupied lands. He anticipates that petitions to foreign courts will produce aid, but only if the Continental Congress opts for total independence and does so quickly.

When *Common Sense* appeared in print, Paine, an Englishman, had been in America for two years and had established himself as editor of the *Pennsylvania Magazine*. The son of a Norfolk corset maker, he had unsuccessfully pursued a number of occupations in England before emigrating to avoid creditors. His working-class background, limited formal education, and Quaker heritage produced a more populist outlook than that of most contemporary political thinkers.

Paine experienced considerable difficulty finding a publisher for the first edition of one thousand copies. When he finally secured one, the pamphlet was an instant success. As a result of the absence of copyright laws, a rival publisher was able to offer a revised version, with commentaries on the king's address to Parliament, selling it for a shilling and paying Paine a royalty, which he donated to the colonial armed forces. *Common Sense* eventually sold in excess of 200,000 copies, making it the number one best seller of the eighteenth century. The absence of copyright protection in the colonies prevented Paine from realizing much income from these phenomenal sales.

The success of *Common Sense* was due in no small part to Paine's writing style and method of developing arguments. British North America was nearly unique in having a literate working-class population, a high proportion of whom were involved in the political process. Without their support, any independence movement would have been doomed to fail. Paine correctly identified the issues of most urgency to this audience and laid them out in a clear, straightforward manner, without referring to schools of political thought, obscure historical episodes, or the authority of ancient Greece and Rome. His main reference, other than current events, was the Bible, with which his readers were thoroughly familiar.

Paine's writing itself is a superb example of fitting the English language to subject and audience without rendering it a blunt and clumsy tool. The text abounds in vivid turns of phrase that have remained highly quotable. Even if it were not a key document in American history, *Common Sense* would deserve a place in the front rank of important books on the strength of its innovative expression alone.

The call for complete independence fell on willing ears. On July 4, 1776, the Continental Congress produced a document making Paine's sentiments and recommendations official policy for the rebellious colonies. The American War of Independence began in 1775, but the United States marks the issuance of the Declaration of Independence as its moment of birth.

Martha A. Sherwood

Further Reading

Canavan, Francis S. J. "Thomas Paine." In *History of Political Philosophy*, edited by Leo Strauss and Joseph Cropsey. 3d ed. Chicago: University of Chicago Press, 1987. A general assessment of Paine's political views.

Foner, Eric. *Tom Paine and Revolutionary America*. Rev. ed. New York: Oxford University Press, 2004. An essential work for understanding the historical background of *Common Sense*.

Larkin, Edward. *Thomas Paine and the Literature of Revolution*. New York: Cambridge University Press, 2005. Places Paine in the context of his contemporaries, providing a good overview of eighteenth century political discourse.

Nelson, Craig. *Thomas Paine: Enlightenment, Revolution, and the Birth of Modern Nations*. New York: Viking Press, 2006. Discusses the relationship of Paine to the Founding Fathers. Details *Common Sense*'s publication history.

Paine, Thomas. *Political Writings*. Edited by Bruce Kuklick. New York: Cambridge University Press, 2000. The bulk of this text comprises Paine's original works; also includes a good introduction and annotations. Part of the Cambridge Texts in the History of Political Thought series.

The Communist Manifesto

Authors: Karl Marx (1818-1883) and Friedrich Engels
(1820-1895)
First published: Manifest der Kommunistischen Partei,
1848 (English translation, 1850)
Type of work: Economics and politics

The Communist Manifesto is a masterpiece of political pamphleteering—a work intended to inspire people to action, even revolutionary action. It builds upon descriptions of true social evils and offers a simple diagnosis and simple, if violent, remedies. In conjunction with Karl Marx's subsequent writings, notably *Das Kapital* (1867, 1885, 1894; *Capital: A Critique of Political Economy,* 1886, 1907, 1909; better known as *Das Kapital*), it has inspired millions of people. Its rhetorical language is magnificent—if overblown and often misleading.

"A spectre is haunting Europe—the spectre of Communism." With this striking opening sentence, the manifesto connects with the incipient radical movement that inspired it. Marx and Friedrich Engels had participated in 1847 in the first international Congress of the League of the Just, which then changed its name to the Communist League. Marx and Engels were commissioned to prepare a statement of the aims and purposes of the movement, which became the manifesto. Within weeks, a series of revolutions had broken out in several European countries, but the Communist League was only a minor element in these developments.

"The history of all hitherto existing society is the history of class struggles." This sentence, which begins the substantive part of the manifesto, is at the heart of Marxist doctrine. According to the authors, society is becoming polarized into the "bourgeoisie" and the "proletariat." From its linguistic origins, the bourgeoisie are simply people who live in towns and cities. Marx and Engels co-opted this term and redefined it to mean "the class of modern capitalists, owners of the means of social production and employers of wage-labor." The bourgeoisie at the time was itself a revolutionary class, having staged successful revolutions against the aristocracy at the end of the last century in the United States and France.

In 1848, there were very few large manufacturing enterprises using mass production, such as cotton textile production and iron making. The owners of businesses were typically the managers as well. The other class, the proletariat, was "the class of modern wage-laborers who, having no means of production of their own, are reduced to selling their labor-power in order to live."

The audacity of Marx and Engels is clear from the fact that, in 1848, most people—even in Great Britain—did not fall into either of these two categories. The largest number were farmers, and there were large numbers in trade and service industries, including domestic servants. The manifesto brilliantly anticipated the advance of mechanized mass production, but that advance never went as far as Marx and Engels imagined. In many parts of Europe, wealthy landowners were still the politically dominant class. Nevertheless, antagonism between employers and workers was widespread.

Marx and Engels paid tribute to the economic and political impact of the bourgeoisie, which has played a revolutionary role, disrupting the business world with innovations such as steamships, railroads, and spinning and weaving machinery. The bourgeoisie has weakened the power of national boundaries, creating a world market and popularizing the notion of international free trade. The manifesto pays tribute to the fact that "the bourgeoisie, during its rule of scarce one hundred years, has created more massive and more colossal productive forces than have all preceding generations together." However, the process has been grossly unfair, characterized by brutal exploitation.

According to the manifesto, bourgeois society has reached the point where it is threatened by internal contradictions. Notable among these are the tendency toward periodic commercial crises—"an epidemic of over-production." Furthermore, mass production creates large masses of workers assembled in one place, readily able to communicate with one another and thus to organize. Work becomes simple and monotonous. Wages cannot rise above the level of bare subsistence. Working hours and work intensity are steadily increased. Large numbers of the middle class, including peasants, shopkeepers, and handicrafts makers, are forced into the proletariat because they cannot compete with modern technology and organization.

Marx and Engels predicted that economic evolution would intensify conflicts until "war breaks out into open revolution, and . . . the violent overthrow of the bourgeoisie lays the foundation for the sway of the proletariat." Strictly speaking, the manifesto is merely predicting revolution, but to many readers it was urging that it come about. According to the manifesto, the principal goals of the Communists are helping the proletariat achieve power and abolishing private property.

Once in power, the proletariat will use "despotic" means to take control of all capital under the central control of the state. Their goal will be to achieve rapid economic growth. More specifically, Marx and Engels predict or advocate abolishing private property in land and establishing central control of credit, as well as the means of communication and transportation. Public education will be free and universal. There will be "equal liability of all to labor. Establishment of industrial armies, especially for agriculture."

The distinction between the bourgeoisie and the proletariat lies in the ownership of the means of production by the former. When the proletariat has successfully abolished private property, the basis for class division will disappear. Since the state is an organization devoted to promoting the interests of the ruling class, it too will disappear.

The final sections of the manifesto indulge the authors' propensity to denounce rival intellectuals, especially "utopian socialists." The essay closes by affirming that communists' "ends can be attained only by the forcible overthrow of all existing social conditions. . . . The proletarians have nothing to lose but their chains. They have a world to win. Working men of all countries, unite!"

In his subsequent writings, Marx attempted to build an analytical foundation for the ideas in the manifesto. This included his labor theory of value, according to which labor is the source of all commodity value. Capitalists extract surplus value from commodities, keeping it for themselves, and pay the laborers who generate the value only a subsistence wage (this process of surplus value extraction is known as exploitation). Marx's concept of "surplus value" implied that property incomes served no useful function and were unjust—thus they could and should be abolished. *The Communist Manifesto* does not use the term "capitalism," nor does it refer explicitly to a "dictatorship of the proletariat." These terms appear in later writings.

It is not easy to determine how much responsibility Marx and Engels bear for the mass murders and other disasters associated with such self-proclaimed followers as Joseph Stalin, Mao Zedong, Kim Il-sung, and Pol Pot. In later years, Marx and Engels conceded that the working class could achieve its goals by peaceful means. Moreover, many of those supposed followers were attempting to establish communism in nations that had never experienced capitalism. This, according to Marx, would be impossible: Marx believed that capitalism is a necessary stage in world history, because it is the only economic system capable of producing the sheer abundance of goods necessary for communism to succeed.

Nonetheless, would-be revolutionaries such as Vladimir Lenin and Mao found the early ideas of Marx and Engels useful. Nominally communist regimes followed many of the specific programmatic suggestions in the manifesto. They sought a high rate of investment and economic growth. They used "despotic means" to seize control of productive property. They imposed central control of the media of communication, monopolizing newspapers, radio, television, and publishing in order to promote thought control and suppress political or intellectual opposition. Communist regimes relied extensively on forced labor to punish dissidents. Emphasis on revolution rationalized the Soviet seizure of Eastern Europe and the attempts to spread murderous dictatorship into South Korea. Most destructive was the emphasis by Marx and Engels on the evils of the bourgeoisie, inspiring campaigns of mass murder against "kulaks," "capitalist roaders," and the like.

Almost every substantive economic prediction advanced by Marx and Engels has failed to come about. The process of capitalist economic development brought about steady improvement in the incomes and working conditions of the working class, who have generally not revolted in capitalist societies. Meanwhile, the communist states instituted in precapitalist, feudal, or agrarian societies, such as Soviet Russia and China, have predictably failed, as communism without capitalist-produced surplus generated inefficiency and injustice. Marx and Engels were never able to understand agrarian societies; they spoke of "the idiocy of rural life." Their theory would hardly have predicted that discontented peasants would provide most of the muscle for the revolutions in Russia and China.

For many intellectuals, the most appealing feature of *The Communist Manifesto* has been its emphasis on social class and class conflict. However, polarization into two opposing classes did not occur—quite the contrary. Most people in developed economies identify as middle class, neither capitalists nor proletarians. Marx believed that the bourgeois ideology driving this sort of identification was doomed to self-destruct in the near future. The fact that it has only strengthened demonstrates either his incorrectness about class consciousness or his underestimation of the power of ideology. Social classes arise from many sources, moreover, including ethnic identity, religious affiliation, education, and occupation. Few people identify as a worker first and a member of a nation or religion or ethnic group second.

Many editions of *The Communist Manifesto* contain useful commentaries. The Centennial edition (1959) contains contemporary and subsequent prefaces by Marx and Engels, as well as fascinating prefaces by American communist Arnold Petersen. The Modern Library edition (*"Capital," "The Communist Manifesto," and other writings by Karl Marx*, 1932) has a valuable introduction by editor Max Eastman and an essay on Marxism by Lenin.

Paul B. Trescott

Further Reading

Cowling, Mark, ed. *"The Communist Manifesto": New Interpretations*. Edinburgh: Edinburgh University Press, 1998. Collection of essays looking back at the manifesto from the point of view of post-Cold War culture.

Desai, Meghnad. *Marx's Revenge: The Resurgence of Capitalism and the Death of Statist Socialism*. London: Verso, 2002. Grandiose, fascinating study of the interaction of ideas and economic systems, in which the later Marx emerges as a defender of capitalism.

Heilbroner, Robert. *The Worldly Philosophers*. 7th ed. New York: Simon & Schuster, 1999. This wildly popular history of economic thought examines Marx's life and work in chapter 6.

Schumpeter, Joseph, *Capitalism, Socialism, and Democracy*. New York: Harper & Brothers, 1942. After examining Marx's central ideas, Schumpeter interweaves them into the history of socialist and communist movements.

The Company of Women

Author: Mary Gordon (1949-   )
First published: 1980
Type of work: Novel
Type of plot: Social realism
Time of plot: 1963-1977
Locale: New York City and western New York State

Principal characters:
FELICITAS, the protagonist
CHARLOTTE, Felicitas's mother
FATHER CYPRIAN, a Roman Catholic priest
MARY ROSE,
ELIZABETH,
CLARE, and
MURIEL, friends of Father Cyprian
JOE, Mary Rose's friend
ROBERT, Felicitas's lover
SALLY and IRIS, Robert's other women
RICHARD, Robert's neighbor
LINDA, Felicitas's child
LEO BYRNE, Felicitas's husband

The Story:

Part 1, 1963. Fourteen-year-old Felicitas Maria Taylor travels with her mother, Charlotte, to Orano, in western New York State, to meet Elizabeth, Clare, Mary Rose, and Muriel for a summer retreat. Since meeting in 1932, the women made this retreat every year under the guidance of the Roman Catholic priest Father Cyprian, who conducts retreats for working women.

Felicitas believes she has to lie to her friends about how she spends her summer vacations because her friends are interested in "TV doctors" and will not understand the pleasure she has in being the center of attention for three of the four childless women and for Father Cyprian, who calls

Felicitas the group's "only hope." Of the women who follow "Cyp," as Charlotte calls him, only Muriel detests the child Felicitas and considers her a threat. The other women do not regard Muriel as one of them. She was excluded from Felicitas's baptism, when Charlotte's daughter was given not one but three godmothers—Mary Rose, Elizabeth, and Clare. Father Cyprian is the focus for the women, each of whom characterizes "Cyp" in a different way. For example, Charlotte is "down to earth," Clare a wealthy and genteel lady, Mary Rose the divorced and wronged woman, and Muriel "an extraordinary soul" who does not fit with the other women and whom

Father Cyprian always admonishes to fight against bitterness.

On a ride with Cyprian to inspect the family property that he recently acquired, thanks to Clare's generosity, the car goes out of control and Felicitas suffers a concussion. She shares a hospital room with another fourteen-year-old, Gidget, who is smart-mouthed and worldly. Although she despises the girl, Felicitas finds herself betraying her relationship with Father Cyprian and with the women by telling Gidget that the only reason she puts up with the constant attention from the adults is because her mother promises to buy her a car when she turns sixteen as long as she continues to come on the group vacations. Felicitas's guilt over this betrayal is increased by the loving attention that Father Cyprian and the women give to Gidget. When Felicitas is released from the hospital, she learns that Gidget is dying of Hodgkin's disease, but this knowledge does not soften her heart.

Each woman reflects on the gifts she gives to Felicitas while the child is in the hospital. Felicitas's favorite gift is a copy of Jane Austen's *Pride and Prejudice* (1813) given to her by Elizabeth. Her least favorite gift, a collection of inspirational religious pamphlets, comes from Muriel.

Part 2, 1969-1970. Felicitas transfers to Columbia University from the Catholic college she attended. She is very concerned about the Vietnam War and takes a political science class in addition to the Latin and Greek courses in which she is majoring. At first sight, Felicitas falls in love with her political science professor, Robert. He advises her to drop the class so that they can become lovers. Completely under his spell, Felicitas not only drops the course but also moves into Robert's "free love" household, where two of Robert's other women, Sally and Iris, live in an uneasy equilibrium. Sally, who hates Felicitas purely, has a son, Mao, by Robert but refuses to tell Robert that he is the father.

Felicitas finds herself very involved in training the dogs of Robert's neighbor, Richard, who spends most of his time in Robert's apartment. Felicitas gives the animals dog food, as opposed to the vegetarian meal they were getting, and within a week she house-trains them. During the time that Felicitas lives at Robert's apartment, Clare, Mary Rose, and Joe Seigel all visit her. They are all concerned about her, but only Joe has the worldly experience to see what is actually going on in the house. He warns Felicitas that men do not want what they can have easily, and he suggests that Felicitas move out.

Robert tires of Felicitas quickly and advises her to make love with other men. To please Robert, she sleeps with Richard, who falls in love with her. When Felicitas becomes pregnant, she cannot be sure who the father is. After seri-

ously considering abortion, Felicitas decides instead to have the baby. She takes the dogs, Ho, Che, and Jesus, from Richard's apartment and goes back to her mother's home.

Part 3, 1977. Felicitas, her mother, Clare, Muriel, and Elizabeth all go to live near Father Cyprian after learning of Felicitas's pregnancy. Father Cyprian, the women admit, was magnificent. When he learns of Felicitas's pregnancy, he says merely that perhaps the pregnancy saved her from greater sin. Each of the women builds a house near Father Cyprian's. On the way to Cyprian's, they rename the dogs Joe, Jay, and Peaches. Felicitas does not have any say in the matter of the move, which, she feels, is just as well.

When her child is born, she gives her the common name of "Linda" in the hope that she will have a "normal" upbringing. Several years later, Felicitas plans to marry a very quiet, slow man named Leo Byrne, who is close to the earth and its workings. Felicitas tries to give her daughter the most ordinary upbringing she can. By marrying Leo, she hopes to assure her girl an "ordinary childhood," something she thinks she herself missed.

Charlotte continues to work to maintain herself, her personality, and her equilibrium. She feels lucky to be near her daughter—"As if that explains it," she says at the end. Elizabeth is content to remain near her friends and Father Cyprian, to whom she is especially devoted; it seems that Felicitas's child gives her a sound reason to position herself closer to those she loves best. Muriel, who feels "inconvenienced" by the other women's descent on Cyprian, believes that eventually her own self will be lost in the vision of God and that she will die as the "first beloved of no soul." Clare's voice articulates the beauty of their surroundings. In her old age, she turns her attention to the house she built.

Father Cyprian, who has a heart attack and suffers from failing health, ends his days believing he was a failure as a priest. He feels that he was not true to the perfection of the Mass. He recalls his love for Felicitas and his feeling during the years of her rebellion "the bitterest of Jesus's sorrows," likening his intolerance to Christ's agony in Gethsemane.

Linda, in her childish understanding, knows that Cyprian will die. She knows death, she says, from having seen dead animals along the road, and she compares herself and her mother and grandmother to Cyprian: "We are not dying," she says.

Critical Evaluation:

Mary Gordon's second novel, *The Company of Women*, followed the first, widely acclaimed, *Final Payments* (1978). In both novels, Gordon deals with the theme of being the offspring of a deeply religious Roman Catholic family in a secularized American society. In both novels, daughters must come to grips not only with their strict religious upbringing but also with the issues of "choice"—whether to remain virginal, to use contraceptives, or to consider abortion.

In *The Company of Women*, Gordon sets up two spheres of womanhood, each centered on charismatic yet domineering males. In the early sections, the "company of women" centers on the austere and commanding figure of Father Cyprian, who sees the main character, the child Felicitas, as the group's only hope for the future. Father Cyprian's influence over Felicitas is broken by her youthful rebellion against his authority and, by extension, that of the Church. However, Felicitas leaves one "company of women" only to find herself in another, that of Sally and Iris around Robert.

The novel suggests that any company of women centered on a patriarchal male figure will succeed only insofar as the women form their own independent "company." It is the women who hold one another together in both "companies," and by holding together they attain a collective authority that enables them to survive the conditions under which they find themselves.

The main theme of the novel concerns the regaining of matriarchal strength. While the liaisons formed in consequence of the domination and direction, spiritual or carnal, of a single male personality consist initially of the women orbiting around that male, in the end it is the force of maternity that determines the lives of Felicitas, her mother, and her mother's friends. Linda is, as her mother puts it, the daughter of "one of two men who live very far away." While Linda has little knowledge of her paternity, she knows well who her mother and grandmother are. With the last words of the novel—Linda's "We are not dying"—Gordon indicates that matriarchy is, in the present age, a well-kept but powerful secret to longevity.

The use of varied narrative voices in the novel reveals the author's strength as a stylist. The earliest parts of the novel are written in a well-tempered but fairly omniscient voice. Much of the imagery is taken from the beauty of Roman Catholic ritual and relates to the women's adherence to Roman Catholic teachings. Later, in part 2, following Felicitas's rebellion, the narrative voice shifts to a sardonic yet subtly comic voice. In part 3, each one of the original "company of women" is allowed to speak. Cyprian's voice, which until this point was often the "last word," is superseded by the voice of the daughter, Linda.

An underlying theme of the novel—that the Old World seems to be crumbling under the impact of the New—is both played out and subverted in the novel. The Old World patriarchy, the novel makes clear, is near extinction. To a great ex-

tent, this failure of Old World values is encapsulated in Felicitas's rebellion, which is directed not so much against the Church but against the male-dominated government that sends young men to die in a senseless war.

Susan M. Rochette-Crawley

Further Reading

Bauman, Paul. "A Search for the 'Unfettered Self': Mary Gordon on Life and Literature." *Commonwealth* 118 (May 17, 1991): 327. Offers brief but highly useful comments.

Bennett, Alma. *Mary Gordon*. New York: Twayne, 1996. Introductory overview, with brief biography and chapters devoted to an analysis of each of Gordon's books published during the first twenty years of her career.

Detweiler, Robert. "Sisterhood and Sex: *Agnes of God*, *Mariette in Ecstasy*, and *The Company of Women*." In *Uncivil Rites: American Fiction, Religion, and the Public Sphere*. Urbana: University of Illinois Press, 1996. Examines Gordon's novel and two other Catholic-oriented works in which an impressionable young girl becomes enmeshed in the intricacies of sex and religion.

Gordon, Mary. *Conversations with Mary Gordon*. Edited by Alma Bennett. Jackson: University Press of Mississippi, 2002. Reprints previously published and broadcast interviews with Gordon, in which she discusses her life and work.

Gray, Francine du Plessix. "A Religious Romance." *The New York Times Book Review*, February 15, 1981. Gray focuses on the religious themes in *Final Payments* and in *The Company of Women* and notes Gordon's conclusion in both novels that friendship is the most important requirement for human happiness.

Kessler-Harris, Alice, and William McBrien, eds. *Faith of a (Woman) Writer*. New York: Greenwood Press, 1988. Susan Ward's chapter, "In Search of 'Ordinary Human Happiness': Rebellion and Affirmation in Mary Gordon's Novels," is a thoughtful, interesting study of the heroines of Gordon's first two novels.

Lardner, Susan. "No Medium." *The New Yorker*, April 6, 1981. In this review of *The Company of Women*, Lardner compares Gordon's second novel to her first, *Final Payments*, and notes that the overriding theme in both is the question of whether female self-sacrifice is a form of self-indulgence.

Pearlman, Mickey, ed. *American Women Writing Fiction: Memory, Identity, Family, Space*. Lexington: University Press of Kentucky, 1989. An interesting collection of essays, each followed by bibliographies. While John W. Mahon's essay on Gordon focuses on her third novel, it comments briefly on *The Company of Women*. Includes bibliographies of writings by and about Gordon.

Perry, Ruth. "Mary Gordon's Mothers." In *Narrating Mothers*, edited by Brenda O. Daly and Maureen T. Reddy. Knoxville: University of Tennessee Press, 1991. Perry explores the nature of what she calls the "motherlessness"

of the mothers in Gordon's fiction. The discussion centers primarily on *Men and Angels* (1985) but can be applied as well to *The Company of Women*.

Seabury, Marcia Bundy. "Of Belief and Unbelief: The Novels of Mary Gordon." *Christianity and Literature* 40, no. 1 (Autumn, 1990): 37-55. Seabury's analysis of the female protagonists in Gordon's first four novels and her critiques of other scholars' analyses are insightful.

The Compleat Angler
Or, The Contemplative Man's Recreation

Author: Izaak Walton (1593-1683)
First published: 1653
Type of work: Philosophy

The Compleat Angler is a practical guide to the art of angling, or fishing. The work has a nominal plot: Piscator (a fisherman), Venator (a hunter), and Auceps (a falconer) meet by chance and fall to discussing the merits of each man's preferred sport. Piscator's eloquent description of the joys and virtues of fishing convinces Venator to accompany him for several days of fishing. The bulk of the work, however, consists of practical advice to fishermen, as told by Piscator to Venator, about such topics as bait and fishing equipment, the habits of different kinds of fish, and methods of catching and cooking various fish.

The Compleat Angler was by no means the only fishing handbook of its day. It was certainly the most popular, however, and by the middle of the twentieth century, *The Compleat Angler* had been reprinted and translated nearly four hundred times. What sets *The Compleat Angler* apart from other practical handbooks and puts it firmly in the realm of literature is its delightful style that is technically polished and charming to read and its abundance of insight into human nature.

Being a fishing handbook, *The Compleat Angler* does not fit neatly into any traditional literary category. It at times was described as a pastoral (that is, an idealized description of country life), a georgic (a poem dealing with rural concerns, not usually as idealized as a pastoral), or an eclogue (a poetic dialogue between shepherds or other rural characters), and it was even credited with originating a category of its own, the "piscatory." The difficulty in categorizing *The Compleat Angler* and in separating the voluminous practical information

from its more "literary" aspects may be one of the reasons that the work historically suffered from critical neglect. From a critical point of view, however, *The Compleat Angler* is interesting for its structure (which owes much to plays and other dramatic pieces of its day), its witty and rhetorically complex style, and its political and historical underpinnings.

To understand fully the subtle themes of *The Compleat Angler*, it is necessary to understand the historical era in which Izaak Walton wrote. Walton published *The Compleat Angler* in 1653, when he was sixty years old, and when England was in social upheaval. Walton was alive at the time that Oliver Cromwell's army overthrew the monarchy and in 1649 executed King Charles I. The Puritan movement, with its austerity and religious fanaticism, was in full swing. Persecution of Anglican and Catholic believers was widespread. The struggle of the Royalists (supporters of the monarchy and the king's son Charles) against the theocratic rule of Cromwell and his successors would soon succeed, resulting in a hedonistic backlash against Puritanism during the Restoration. It was a time of social, religious, and political extremes.

Walton was not an extremist by nature. A successful merchant and biographer, Walton had during the course of his life befriended many leading Anglican thinkers, including John Donne and Richard Hooker. In the gentle, intelligent theology of these friends and colleagues, Walton saw an ideal "middle path" between the extremes of Puritan and of Royalist. One of the themes of *The Compleat Angler* centers on finding this ideal (and theologically based) compromise between two extremes of thought. Early in the work, Piscator and his student Venator encounter a hunter pursuing otters. Although Piscator and the hunter enjoy a pleasant enough exchange, Piscator later confides to Venator that he does not care much for the company of the hunter, because he swears excessively and is given to sacrilegious and lewd jests. Piscator is not a prude, however; he explains that he does not enjoy the company of serious and overly grave men, of "sowre complexion" and "anxious care," any more than he enjoys the company of the foul-mouthed hunter. Piscator describes the qualities of the type of company he prefers: "learned and humble, valiant, and inoffensive, vertuous, and communicable."

Walton's belief in the middle way is not confined simply to questions of personality, however; it encompasses a wider theological view. Piscator expounds at length on the relative virtues of the two traditional paths of religious life, the active and the contemplative. Piscator ultimately argues for a "via media" (middle way) that reconciles action and contemplation. What better emblem of the via media, he argues, than the art of angling: time spent peacefully enjoying nature but still accomplishing something worthwhile. Walton embraces a naturalistic theology that finds God through contemplation of his creation; Walton's praise of the countryside and of country life is often couched in religious terms. Walton's religious beliefs require action, too, and specifically acts of charity. The bounty of fish that Piscator catches allows him to make charitable offerings of food to poorer characters such as the group of beggars and the milkmaid and her mother.

While the opposing attractions of the active and contemplative lives are nothing new to literature or theology, for Walton and others of his day they had a special meaning. With the tensions inherent in the religious and political extremes of the English civil war and Restoration eras, many prominent men chose to retire from public life to a life of seclusion in the country rather than take sides with the Puritans or the Royalists. While Walton's religious views seemed to incline him to reject worldliness and involvement in political affairs, his active social conscience made him acutely aware that running from the pressing issues of the day was socially and politically irresponsible. Walton's paean to angling can thus be seen as a wider social and political analogy for the importance of reconciling quiet, unostentatious retirement with productive, benevolent activity.

The art of fishing has another religious significance for Piscator (and Walton). One of Piscator's lectures to Venator describes the many fishermen in the Old Testament. Walton, through the voice of Piscator, makes the New Testament parallels clear: Most of the Apostles, after all, were fishermen, whom Christ proposed to make fishers of men. The brother that Piscator meets at the inn (it is unclear whether Walton uses the term "brother" in its genealogic sense or in the wider sense of belonging to what he calls "the brotherhood of the angle") is named Peter.

Walton's themes are not purely religious, however; he also expresses very definite political views. For example, the social class of Piscator and Venator is deliberately left undefined. It seems clear that they are neither very rich nor very poor; however, they are definitely not snobbish or class-conscious. When they meet the lowly milkmaid and her mother, Piscator and Venator do not talk down to them or treat them as inferiors; instead they jovially offer the trade of fish for songs and milk. It is interesting to note Walton's choice of songs for the milkmaid and her mother. The milkmaid sings Christopher Marlowe's "The Passionate Shepherd to His Love" ("Come live with me and be my love"), a romantic verse about idealistic pastoral love. Her mother replies by singing Sir Walter Ralegh's "The Nymph's Reply to the Shepherd" ("If all the world and love were young"). Once again, Walton contrasts opposing views, this time extreme romanticism and cynicism about love, suggesting that extreme views can tell only part of the story.

Piscator's story of his meeting with the Gypsies and beggars is illustrative of his political view. Piscator describes how the Gypsies got into an argument over how to divide a sum of money. Likewise, the beggars argued over the answer to a riddle about whether it was easier to rip or to "unrip" a cloak. In each case, the dispute was resolved peacefully and diplomatically by the "government" of each group. Instead of looking down on these traditional outcasts as inferiors, Piscator seems to admire the democracy of their way of life, using the favorable terms "commonwealth," "government," and "corporation" to describe their social organization. In Piscator's other encounters with men who may be his social superiors, equals, or inferiors (the hunter, innkeeper, brother, and friend), all are treated with exactly the same courtesy and frankness.

No study of Walton's work could be complete without a discussion of his style. By choosing a dialogue as the structure of his work, Walton is able to maintain an informal, conversational tone. He constantly lightens the lengthy technical passages with humorous verses or observations, and his philosophical and theological observations are neither pedantic nor belabored. Walton uses devices such as Piscator's seeming to lose his train of thought or wander from the subject, and his crediting things like recipes and bits of fishing lore to friends (who are sometimes named and sometimes not), to make the dialogue seem as if it were really spoken by a living person rather than formally composed by an author. This apparent artlessness is a very careful construction used by Walton to give the dialogue a warm, intimate, and often humorous tone. It is this easy and pleasant tone, along with Walton's intelligent observations on a wide variety of political and religious subjects, that makes *The Compleat Angler* more than a sportsman's handbook. It is also a finely crafted work of literature that for centuries has been enjoyed by fishermen and lovers of literature alike.

Catherine Swanson

Further Reading

Bevan, Jonquil. *Izaak Walton's "The Compleat Angler."* New York: St. Martin's Press, 1988. Provides a thorough discussion of the religious and political underpinnings of *The Compleat Angler*, placing the work in its social and historical context. Demonstrates the relation of *The Compleat Angler* to other literature of its time. Includes an extensive bibliography.

Bottrall, Margaret. *Izaak Walton*. London: Longmans, Green, 1955. Discusses Walton's religious and political beliefs and offers some general criticism on *The Compleat Angler*. Examines Walton's biographical works.

Cooper, John R. *The Art of "The Compleat Angler."* Durham, N.C.: Duke University Press, 1968. Cooper's study of Walton's technique focuses on his form, style, and sources. Provides a good discussion of the different traditions that influenced Walton's work as well as an interesting section detailing Walton's borrowings from other authors.

Keynes, Geoffrey. *The Compleat Angler*. New York: Random House, 1945. This edition of Walton's work is of interest for its textual variations section, which shows some of the major differences between successive editions of the work. It also contains a biography of Walton and detailed bibliographical notes.

Semenza, Gregory M. Colón. "The Danger of 'Innocent, Harmless Mirth': Walton's *Compleat Angler* in the Interregnum." In *Sport, Politics, and Literature in the English Renaissance*. Newark: University of Delaware Press, 2003. Examines the significance of sports in sixteenth and seventeenth century England, where educators, physicians, and military scientists praised participation in athletic events as beneficial to the individual, vital to military preparedness, and necessary to maintain the class hierarchy. Analyzes *The Compleat Angler* and other books about sports, placing them within the political and literary context of their time.

Stanwood, P. G. *Izaak Walton*. New York: Twayne, 1998. Critical introduction to Walton's life and writings. Analyzes *The Compleat Angler* and his other works, discussing their interrelationship. Examines the events of his life and his ideas within the context of his times.

Walton, Izaak. *The Compleat Angler*. Edited by Jonquil Bevan. New York: Oxford University Press, 1983. Offers two different editions of *The Compleat Angler* (1653 and 1676) in their entirety, along with an extensive introduction covering Walton's life, his literary sources, and a comprehensive discussion of the many different editions of *The Compleat Angler*. Includes reproductions of the original illustrations.

The Complete Poems of Emily Dickinson

Author: Emily Dickinson (1830-1886)
First published: 1960
Type of work: Poetry

After Emily Dickinson's death in 1886, her sister Lavinia found forty-nine fascicles, or packets, of poems that Dickinson had sewn together during the late 1850's and early 1860's. Lavinia enlisted the help of Mabel Loomis Todd, the wife of an Amherst professor, to transcribe them. With the assistance of the literary editor Thomas Wentworth, they altered the rhyme scheme, regularized the meter, and revised unconventional metaphors for the 115 poems they published in 1890. These were well received and led to the publication in 1891 of 161 additional poems and, in 1896, of 168 more.

In 1914, Dickinson's niece and literary heir, Martha Dickinson Bianchi, compiled other poems. She kept alterations to the verse to a minimum, as was also the case with additional volumes in 1929 and 1935. Millicent Todd Bingham in 1945 published the remaining 688 poems and fragments. When Dickinson's literary estate was transferred to Harvard University in 1950, Thomas H. Johnson began to arrange the unreconstructed and comprehensive body of Dickinson's poetry chronologically. *The Poems of Emily Dickinson* appeared in 1955, and *The Complete Poems of Emily Dickinson* appeared in 1960. Aside from correcting misspellings and misplaced apostrophes, Johnson let Dickinson's original punctuation and capitalization stand. To the previously editorialized publications, Johnson restored the original dashes and other nonconformist usage, listing for each poem both the approximate date of the earliest known manuscript and the date of first publication. There is also a helpful "Index of First Lines" (Dickinson did not title her poems) and a fairly comprehensive subject index based on key words or images in the poems, the three most prominent being life, death, and love.

Of those poems that celebrate life, a substantial number are about nature, the inhabitants of which Dickinson frequently praises. Dickinson describes her mission to reveal nature in #441: "This is my letter to the World/ That never wrote to me—/ The simple News that Nature told—/ With tender majesty." In #111, "The Bee is not afraid of me," butterflies, brooks, and breezes are among her dearest friends. She often pays tribute to these friends, nature's creatures, as in "A fuzzy fellow, without feet" (#173), which catalogs the glorious transformation of a caterpillar into a butterfly, or "A narrow Fellow in the Grass" (#986), a multisensory description of a sleek but frightening snake. In "An awful Tempest mashed the air" (#198), nature is personified. In #214, nature is a "liquor never brewed" that inebriates the speaker with joy. The sunset is a "Housewife" who has swept the west with color in "She sweeps with many-colored Brooms" (#219). Nature assumes the role of "Gentlest Mother" in #790, bestowing "infinite Affection—/ And infiniter Care" on all the world. Likewise the "Juggler of Day," the sun, blazes in gold and quenches in purple (#228). In "These are the days when Birds come back" (#130), Dickinson uses sacred—Sacrament, Last Communion—diction to welcome the holy return of spring. In "An altered look about the hill" (#140), she likens the return of spring to the resurrection with a biblical allusion to Nicodemus.

Nature is the focus of Dickinson's spiritual life as well. Her play with custom is seen in her subverting of religious ceremonies. In "The Gentian weaves her fringes" (#18), Dickinson reveres nature, which pools her resources to memorialize "departing blossoms." She joins with Bobolink and Bee, Gentian and Maple in this commemoration service, which she closes with a sacrilegious play on the Trinity: "In

the name of the Bee—/ And of the Butterfly—/ And of the Breeze—Amen!" Refreshingly, these are the entities with which Dickinson is most comfortable: In #19, the Bee and the Breeze enable her transformation into a Rose; and in #111, the reader learns that her reverence of them is not based in fear, nor is it founded upon not knowing the Other. Rather, they share a mutual knowledge and comfortable relationship:

> The Bee is not afraid of me.
> I know the Butterfly.
> The pretty people in the Woods
> Receive me cordially—
>
> The Brooks laugh louder when I come—
> The Breezes madder play;
> Wherefore mine eye thy silver mists,
> Wherefore, Oh Summer's Day?

Her communion with nature is a voluntary ritual, a genuine connection that makes her misty-eyed. Equally significant, she implies that it is a reciprocally nurturing relationship.

Dickinson resents the dominance of nature by predominantly male scientists and is "mad" about its co-optation, as she writes in #70:

> "Arcturus" is his other name—
> I'd rather call him "Star."
> It's very mean of Science
> To go and interfere!
> . . . .
> I pull a flower from the woods—
> A monster with a glass
> Computes the stamens in a breath—
> And has her in a "class"!
>
> Whereas I took the Butterfly
> Aforetime in my hat—
> He sits erect in "Cabinets"—
> The Clover bells forgot.

She has contempt for the scientists, whom she mocks for thinking they can objectively know nature through detached analysis. She fears that such objectification of an entity that she reverences will destroy or endanger its spiritual aspect, "What once was 'Heaven'." Poems #97, #108, and #185 are among others that indict science's "advances" and its preoccupation with subduing nature, suppressing its playfulness, and interfering with its course.

Dickinson likewise makes a farce of militarism and its threat to life and the world; in #73 she criticizes the hypocrisy of militarism, first camouflaging her satire with the interrogative form, then affirming her disgusted sarcasm with exclamation points.

> Who never lost, are unprepared
> A Coronet to find!
> . . . .
> How many Legions overcome—
> The Emperor will say?
> How many *Colors* taken
> On Revolution Day?
>
> How many *Bullets* bearest?
> Hast Thou the Royal scar?
> Angels! Write "Promoted"
> On this Soldier's brow!

She concludes that what makes "sense" to society is "Madness" (#435), whereas what society, with its undiscerning eye, would deem "mad" makes the most sense:

> Much Madness is divinest Sense—
> To a discerning Eye—
> Much Sense—the starkest Madness—
> 'Tis the Majority
> In this, as All, prevail—
> Assent—and you are sane—
> Demur—you're straightway dangerous—
> And handled with a Chain—

Dickinson knows the cost of being labeled mad yet risks it, for she can discern the value of her genius and—in a society of one—it matters not whether anyone else can discern that value. The poet understands the price exacted for nonconformity or originality, but nature allows her to balance the risk with her sense of hope, "the thing with feathers—/ That perches in the soul—" (#254). The creator in "He fumbles at your Soul" (#315) stuns "by degrees" until he "Deals-One-imperial-thunderbolt—/ That scalps your naked Soul—." Dickinson reveals her pantheism in "Some keep the Sabbath going to Church" (#324), wherein the speaker stays at home "With a Bobolink for a Chorister—/ And an Orchard, for a Dome—." Here, a choir of sextons makes for a heavenly service. Heaven is as accessible as our "Capacity" to imagine, according to poem #370, one of 366 poems written during Dickinson's marathon poetry year of 1862. This seems quite understandable if one agrees with #383 that "Exhilaration—

is within—" and is among the divine feelings "the Soul achieves—Herself—."

Two other soul poems, #303 and #306, are thematically linked: "The Soul selects her own Society," which embodies willful solitude and seclusion, and "The Soul's Superior instants." One of her best-known "soul" poems is #512, which delineates the soul's varied dimensions, such as "Bandaged moments" when healing from a blow; "moments of Escape" when it "dances like a Bomb, abroad," testing the limits of its liberty, and "retaken moments" of caution. The soul is also "an imperial friend" to itself (#683), a theme Dickinson resumes in "There is a solitude of space" (#1695), wherein the soul enjoys a "polar privacy" and, with itself, experiences the paradox of "Finite infinity." In "A Thought went up my mind today," the soul even facilitates so-called déjà-vu experiences. The integral connection between the soul and Dickinson's poetry is encapsulated in "There is no Frigate like a Book" (#1263), wherein "a Page/ Of prancing Poetry—" can bear the soul "Lands away."

This transport may be necessary when grieving the loss of loved ones to death, another of Dickinson's subjects. One of the most prominent of these poems is "I felt a Funeral, in my Brain" (#280) wherein the mourners pace and the service drones on to the point that "My Mind was going numb—." Along similar lines, in "After great pain, a formal feeling comes" (#341), grief reduces the narrator to disorientation and mechanical, routine functioning. Also mournful in tone is #258, "There's a certain Slant of light," in which "Winter Afternoons," like "Cathedral tunes," are oppressive. Even "the Landscape listens" to what is like "the Distance/ On the look of Death—."

Similarly, in #389, the House wherein "There's been a Death" has a "numb look" as it prepares for the "Dark Parade" of mourners. It is in just such a house that the speaker of "I heard a Fly buzz—when I died—" (#465) met her death. The tenuous "Stillness" that pervades the atmosphere of anticipated death is broken only by the "Blue—uncertain stumbling Buzz—" of a carrion insect, oblivious to the exhausted tears of loving relations. This deceased speaker, in turn, could inhabit "I died for Beauty" (#449) wherein she converses with a kindred "One who died for Truth," "until the Moss had reached our lips." Or, she could become one of those who are "Safe in their Alabaster Chambers" (#216), awaiting the Resurrection, unable to experience the light of day before that moment. The undercurrent of finality also surfaces in "'Twas warm—at first—like Us" (#519), a graphic and sobering delineation of the stages of rigor mortis and burial, and in "All but Death, can be Adjusted" (#749), a brief poem about death's irrevocability and incapacity for change.

Personification enables another view of death in one of Dickinson's most famous poems, "Because I could not stop for Death" (#712). In one of several lyrical poems that correspond to the rhythm and meter of the hymn "Amazing Grace," Death stops for the speaker in a carriage wherein they pass a figurative panorama of her life and her gravesite on the way to "Eternity." The redemptive quality of death also surfaces in "A Death blow is a Life blow to Some" (#816), a one-stanza paradox wherein death is described as a wake-up call, as a prerequisite to "Vitality." In #501, life on earth is merely a way station to what scholars and the faithful can only conjecture. Death, therefore, is to be welcomed rather than feared. Beyond riddle and bordering conundrum are Dickinson's poems about pain, in which Dickinson undercuts dualities by conflating opposites. Perhaps most poignant among these is #125:

> For each ecstatic instant
> We must an anguish pay
> In keen and quivering ratio
> To the ecstasy.
>
> For each beloved hour
> Sharp pittances of years—
> Bitter contested farthings—
> And Coffers heaped with Tears!

Even in her earliest poems, Dickinson demonstrates the fun she has with experimental language, particularly with wordplay that reverses meaning, as in #33:

> If recollecting were forgetting,
> Then I remember not.
> And if forgetting, recollecting,
> How near I had forgot.
> And if to miss, were merry,
> And to mourn, were gay,
> How very blithe the fingers
> That gathered this, Today!

In #67, those who can define or know a thing such as successor victory are those most removed from it: "Success is counted sweetest/ By those who ne'er succeed." Here, Dickinson again explores notions of identification through opposites and explodes the duality of language as found, for example, in the oxymoron saved for the final line of #1695:

> There is a solitude of space
> A solitude of sea
> A solitude of death, but these
> Society shall be
> Compared with that profounder site
> That polar privacy
> A soul admitted to itself—
> Finite infinity.

In society, people experience the loneliness of death and of vastness; true solitude is that found by the soul that admits only itself but, strangely, has limitless potential—infinity—within the finite bounds it sets itself. Interestingly, in #303, the soul—significantly gendered as feminine—"selects her own Society—." She "Then—shuts the Door—/ To her divine Majority—/ Present no more—." In her society of "One" (which she chooses, as readers learn in the third stanza), the poet is free to exercise any choice and free to play with the language of religion, custom, or ceremony. To demonstrate the former, Dickinson in #172 realizes that concepts and words are just that: They have no power beyond themselves. As she says in stanza 2,

> Life is but Life! And Death, but Death!
> Bliss is, but Bliss, and Breath but Breath!
> And if indeed I fail,
> At least to know the worst, is sweet!
> Defeat means nothing *but* Defeat,
> No drearier, can befall!

Even defeat and death lose their force. The only threat lies in what can be imagined, not in what simply is. Demonstrative of her play with language's dictates, too, is her use of the exclamation points in this poem and others. Having discovered the limits of language, the poet can not only (ex)claim revelatory/revolutionary discoveries but also sustain whatever degree of emphasis she wishes.

In #165 ("A *Wounded* Deer—leaps highest"), Dickinson combines these techniques to address the subject of disguising pain by suggesting the unexpected or something seemingly disparate. In another poem referring specifically to female deer (#754), Dickinson dissociates herself from those, especially women, who would defer to powerful forces. Instead, she defines her life as a "Loaded Gun" in search of the doe. Every time she speaks, "The Mountains straight reply—," thus satisfying her desires both to be heard (for she incurs an echo) and to have, like a bullet, an impact. Only then can she experience pleasure, as the reader learns in stanza 3:

And do I smile, such cordial light
Upon the Valley glow—
It is as a Vesuvian face
Had let its pleasure through—

Dickinson's persona in this poem is both madly at play and enjoying the pleasures of play.

As these poems illustrate, Dickinson's language is highly compressed and disjunctive. The compression accounts for the multiplicity of meaning and the often anomalous, riddling quality of her poems, though it is not clear whether her intention is to speak subversively, to disguise her power or pain, or to express through form her personal ethic of renunciation. Disjunction in punctuation, syntax, action, and tone disrupts the expected patterns of style and meaning. Disjunctive poetry disallows a single "correct" interpretation. Dickinson's surface features of often inexplicable punctuation, inverted and elliptical syntax, occasional metrical irregularity, off-rhyme, and ungrammaticality rest on the acceptance of an underlying regularity of meter, rhyme, and stanza forms. A similar interplay is found in the juxtaposition of singular nouns with plural verbs and vice versa, as well as in singular versions of plural reflexive pronouns (as in "ourself"). While Dickinson primarily uses the lyric present tense, the subjunctive mood often connotes conditionality or universality. In similar fashion, her figurative language reinforces the nonconventional.

Dickinson believed that language's potential for meaning exceeds the individual's control of it. She manipulates punctuation to reflect the resulting flux. Her use of the dash, for example, represents a resistance to definiteness, definition, or closure, as does her irregular vocabulary. Her use of exclamation points and question marks expresses emotional urgency and self-doubt. She also draws on an ironic tone, negation, qualification, and challenges to authority.

Dickinson was reluctant to publicize her rich, nontraditional work, and she was adamant about not selling out. "Publication—is the Auction/ Of the Mind of Man—" she contends in #709, wherein she reluctantly concedes that only poverty could justify "so foul a thing." She cautions readers not to reduce their souls "To Disgrace of Price—." Not surprisingly—as in "I'm Nobody! Who are you?" (#288)—she prefers the privacy and dignity that come from being unknown, to the dreariness of being "Somebody!/ How public—like a Frog—" a simile that captures her disdain for those who crave fame and recognition. This poem, like countless others about the subject of poetry (#1212, #1261, #754, #657), demonstrates the integrity of her philosophy and the quiet genius of her poetics, shaped as it is by her age.

As a female literary genius born into a male writing and publishing world in a region where late Calvinist and Puritan theology manifested itself in ideal conventional feminine behavior, Dickinson had few options. Her art expresses an attempt to transcend the patriarchally imposed limits on prose (#613), heaven (#947), and her own sexual identity (#908), limits that she felt deprived her of purpose or place. As she wrote early in her career, in the poem #613 of approximately 1862:

They shut me up in Prose—
As when a little Girl
They put me in a Closet—
Because they liked me "still"—

Still! Could themself have peeped—
And seen my Brain—go round—
They might as wise have lodged a Bird
For Treason—in the Pound—
Himself has but to will
And easy as a Star
Abolish his Captivity—
And laugh—No more have I—

The negative images of the first line suggest that Dickinson did not regard prose highly. In a letter, Dickinson wrote, "We please ourselves with the fancy that we're the only poets, everyone else is prose." Stating that she had the madness of a poet who would not stay shut up in convention, Dickinson will break out of this outer-imposed prison and reveal the true singer. The very fact that this inhibition is outer-imposed rather than chosen leaves the persona speechless (that is, "shut up"). Only by creating her own self-initiated and self-chosen style can she abolish her captivity, similar to the "Patriarch's bird" as female explorer in poem #48. The captive's dream of freedom found in #613 and #48 also surfaces in #661, when the bee escapes the authoritative chase of police and exclaims: "What Liberty! So Captives deem/ Who tight in Dungeons are." In another poem, #657, poetry and possibility provide more freedom than prose: "I dwell in Possibility—/ A fairer house than Prose—."

Prose, specifically as it was conventionally practiced at the time, was not a form of expression conducive to Dickinson's art, for most of its forms would have required a plot—typically a romance plot whose end restricts female characters either to marriage or death, and in any case a linear progression of events. Dickinson is aware that her mind does not follow such a path and that it is, instead, cyclic, circular, and concentric. In pursuing the nonlinear nature of her thinking and writing, Dickinson created her new aesthetic. She may also have found the prose with which she was familiar to be static, final, and lacking in affect. Its syntax and grammar represent the rational structures she wished to undercut.

The imagination can enact simultaneously both needed sequestration and escape. Dickinson hoped through words to assert autonomy and independence. She mocked social efforts to control and negate her adult liberating self-expression. Through laughter, Dickinson overcame confinement and transformed into success the futility she felt in poems such as #77:

> I never hear the word "escape"
> Without a quicker blood,
> A sudden expectation,
> A flying attitude!
>
> I never hear of prisons broad
> By soldiers battered down,
> But I tug childish at my bars
> Only to fail again!

This poem, written in 1859, during a year of self-initiated and symbolic changes that Dickinson made in her life—she began, for example, to wear white—indicates her conscious affirmation of her own emancipatory poetry and her decision to ignore external pressures and follow on her own artistic independence and convictions, as she writes in so many subsequent poems.

Dickinson became a stylistic innovator and modern experimentalist so as to voice her sense of autonomy. At the same time, she recognized the tension this innovation would necessarily entail. She discovers, for example, the inevitable discontinuity of her thought in #937:

> I felt a Cleaving in my Mind—
> As if my Brain had split—
> I tried to match it—Seam by Seam—
> But could not make them fit.
> The thought behind, I strove to join
> Unto the thought before—
> But Sequence ravelled out of Sound
> Like Balls—upon a Floor.

Perhaps the split is a result of the agonistic relation between her poetic aesthetic and conventional writing. Even though sequential thought decomposes and ruptures cognition, incoherence attests Dickinson's use of paradoxes to explode binarism and enable multiplicity and disunity.

If, therefore, Dickinson is to tell the truth, she must tell it "slant," "in circuit" (#1129):

> Tell all the Truth but tell it slant—
> Success in Circuit lies
> Too bright for our infirm Delight
> The Truth's superb surprise
>
> As Lightning to the Children eased
> With explanation kind
> The Truth must dazzle gradually
> Or every man be blind—

Dickinson reveals truth gradually, so as not to blind its recipients with its dazzling light. Dazzled by her own discoveries, she experiences a splitting that leads to loneliness and possibly even insanity, as indicated by the final two stanzas of #410:

> My Brain—begun to laugh—
> I mumbled—like a fool—
> And tho' 'tis Years ago—that Day—
> My Brain keeps giggling—still.
>
> And Something's odd—within—
> That person that I was—
> And this One—do not feel the same—
> Could it be Madness—this?

Again laughter accompanies this splitting and multiplicity, as it liberates the speaker to the space of madness in which to create and to exercise poetic license. In her attempts to dissociate self, mind, and world, Dickinson in her multiplicitous project tries to speak for those who do not have the language, to see for those who are less conscious, and to create a poetry of extreme states that allows others to go further into their awareness and consciousness.

Dickinson's poetry focuses meaning even as it scatters, disperses, undoes, and disrupts it. Dancing, spinning, and weaving, even of webs, serve as metaphors for her poesis: She is the performing artist and craftswoman in a sharply defined world. The poet artistically adopts several roles but settles for none. Dickinson believed that the female, like the male, poet would be able to dance freely and fiercely, like the lilies and daisies liberated from toil into ecstasy. Her poetry offers readers the same opportunities.

Roseanne L. Hoefel

Further Reading

Bennett, Paula. *Emily Dickinson: Woman Poet.* Iowa City: University of Iowa Press, 1990. A probing, instructive discussion of feminine creativity, sexual imagery, and themes of desire.

Ferlazzo, Paul. *Emily Dickinson.* Boston: Twayne, 1984. Written specifically for those new to Dickinson, this easy-to-understand text is a good introduction to her poetry and life.

Grabher, Gudrun, Roland Hagenbüchle, and Cristanne Miller, eds. *The Emily Dickinson Handbook.* Amherst: University of Massachusetts Press, 1998. Collection of essays discussing Dickinson's poetry from a broad range of perspectives. Includes discussions of her literary background, the themes and metaphors of her poetry, her lyrical self, and the critical reception of her work.

Juhasz, Suzanne, ed. *Feminist Critics Read Emily Dickinson.* Bloomington: Indiana University Press, 1983. This collection of essays by some of the most respected Dickinson scholars is prefaced with a piece by Juhasz providing a brief history of feminist interpretations of Dickinson's poetry.

Keane, Patrick J. *Emily Dickinson's Approving God: Divine Design and the Problem of Suffering.* Columbia: University of Missouri Press, 2008. Focuses on Dickinson's poems about God, in which she often challenges the assumption that God is omnipotent and all-loving in a world filled with pain and violence.

Martin, Wendy. *The Cambridge Introduction to Emily Dickinson.* New York: Cambridge University Press, 2007. Brief but comprehensive introduction to Dickinson, with information about her life, analyses of her work, and a discussion of the critical reception of her poetry. Places her work within the context of the religious culture, politics, and social movements of her time, as well as Transcendentalism and the Civil War.

_____, ed. *The Cambridge Companion to Emily Dickinson.* New York: Cambridge University Press, 2006. Collection of essays by Dickinson scholars discussing her life, publication history, poetic strategies and themes, and the cultural contexts of her poetry.

Pollak, Vivian R. *Dickinson: The Anxiety of Gender.* Ithaca, N.Y.: Cornell University Press, 1986. A psychobiographical, feminist study of the poetry's intensity and resonance in Dickinson's relations with family, friends, and literary acquaintances.

Sewall, Richard B. *The Life of Emily Dickinson.* 3d ed. Cambridge, Mass.: Harvard University Press, 1997. Winner of the National Book Award for biography, this interpretive biography brilliantly discusses Dickinson's poetry in the context of her life, family, region, and historical setting.

Stonum, Gary Lee. *The Dickinson Sublime.* Madison: University of Wisconsin Press, 1990. Analyzes Dickinson's idiosyncratic style. Uses literary theory to assess topics such as reading, writing, language, intention, fame, power, knowledge, imagination, the resistance to closure, and the suspension between trauma and sublimation.

Wolff, Cynthia Griffin. *Emily Dickinson.* Reading, Mass.: Perseus, 1999. This critical biography makes use of past biographies and is much more manageable and accessible than they are. The bibliography is extensive and the index helpful.

Wolosky, Shira. *Emily Dickinson: A Voice of War.* New Haven, Conn.: Yale University Press, 1984. Examines Dickinson's poetic forms and syntax, as well as martial imagery and historical and metaphysical issues.

The Complete Tales of Uncle Remus

Author: Joel Chandler Harris (1848-1908)
First published: 1880-1948; anthologized in 1955
Type of work: Short fiction

Without the efforts of Joel Chandler Harris, it is doubtful that many of the African American folktales he preserved would have survived, or that anyone other than folklorists would have any idea of who Brer Rabbit or any of his associates are. Bugs Bunny might not even exist.

Between 1880 and his death in August, 1908, Harris produced many Uncle Remus books, containing a total of 168 African American folktales: *Uncle Remus: His Songs and His Sayings* (1880) contains thirty-four tales; *Nights with Uncle Remus: Myths and Legends of the Old Plantation*

(1883), sixty-nine; *Daddy Jake the Runaway: And Short Stories Told After Dark* (1889), thirteen; *Uncle Remus and His Friends: Old Plantation Stories, Songs, and Ballads with Sketches of Negro Character* (1892), twenty-four; *Told by Uncle Remus: New Stories of the Old Plantation* (1905), sixteen; *Uncle Remus and Brer Rabbit* (1907), six; and *Uncle Remus and the Little Boy* (1910), six.

After his death, two more volumes were published: *Uncle Remus Returns* (1918), with six tales, edited by his biographer daughter-in-law, Julia Collier Harris; and *Seven Tales of Uncle Remus* (1948), edited by Thomas H. English.

The Complete Tales of Uncle Remus, edited by Richard Chase, contains all 181 of these folktales, together with the narrative frames in which they were originally presented, unbowdlerized and absent any attempt to modernize the mid-Georgia black dialect of the stories' primary raconteur, Uncle Remus, or the Gullah dialect of his friend Daddy Jack, who tells ten tales in *Nights with Uncle Remus*.

The most famous of the Uncle Remus stories is the story of Brer Rabbit and the tar-baby, told in two chapters from *Uncle Remus: His Songs and His Sayings*. In "The Wonderful Tar-Baby Story," Brer Fox fashions a small tar figure and leaves it by the side of the big road down which Brer Rabbit soon comes pacing, "lippity-clippity, clippity-lippity—dez ez sassy ez a jay-bird." When Brer Rabbit smacks the tar baby for not responding to his greeting, his paw sticks to it. Demanding to be let loose, the rabbit hits the figure three more times, getting another paw stuck each time. Then he butts it with his head, and now he is stuck in five places. Brer Fox emerges and, when he can finally stop laughing, captures the helpless Brer Rabbit.

When the story resumes, in "How Mr. Rabbit Was Too Sharp for Mr. Fox," Brer Fox first threatens to "bobbycue" Brer Rabbit, then to hang him, then to drown him. Each time, Brer Rabbit says fine, do anything you want, but please do not throw me in the briar patch. After Brer Rabbit says he would even prefer having his eye gouged out, his ears torn, and his legs cut off than to be thrown into the briar patch, the stupid fox, who "wanter hurt Brer Rabbit ez bad ez he kin," flings Brer Rabbit into the briar patch. A few minutes later, Brer Fox hears someone calling him. Looking up to the top of a hill, he sees Brer Rabbit seated on a log and combing the tar out of his fur. Brer Fox realizes he has been had, and Brer Rabbit cannot help but taunt him, hollering out, "'Bred en bawn in a brier-patch, Brer Fox—bred en bawn in a brier-patch!' en wid dat he skip out des ez lively ez a cricket in de embers."

This story is not only the most famous of the Uncle Remus stories, it is also one of the most typical. First, it is what could be termed an animal tale: The characters are sen-

tient animals who act like human beings. There are only sixteen Uncle Remus tales in which this is not the case: from *Uncle Remus: His Songs and His Stories*, "A Plantation Witch," "Jacky-My-Lantern," and "Why the Negro Is Black"; from *Nights with Uncle Remus*, "Spirits, Seen and Unseen" and "A Ghost Story"; from *Daddy Jake, the Runaway*, "How a Witch Was Caught," "The Little Boy and His Dogs," "The Foolish Woman," and "The Adventures of Simon and Susanna"; from *Uncle Remus and His Friends*, "Death and the Negro Man," "According to How the Drop Falls," "A Fool for Luck," "The Man and His Boots," and "How the King Recruited His Army"; from *Told by Uncle Remus*, "The Hard-Headed Woman"; and from *Uncle Remus Returns*, "Impty-Umpty and the Blacksmith."

Second, the tar-baby story belongs to the largest of the three primary groups of tales into which all Uncle Remus stories can be divided, without regard to the presence or absence of animals as main characters. It is a trickster tale, a tale in which one or more of the main characters seeks to dupe one or more others. There are more than 120 such Uncle Remus tales, of which all but four are animal tales, and all but twenty-nine have Brer Rabbit as their protagonist.

Sometimes, the consequences of the trickery are horrific, as in the following three examples. "The Awful Fate of Mr. Wolf," from *Uncle Remus: His Songs and His Stories*, is a variation on the story of "The Three Little Pigs." Brer Rabbit revenges himself on Brer Wolf by tricking him into getting into a large chest, then scalding him to death. In another story, from *Nights with Uncle Remus*, a bear cub uses trickery to get away with eating all of the alligator's children, while ostensibly taking care of them. In "Brother Bear Learns to Comb His Head," from *Seven Tales of Uncle Remus*, Brer Rabbit tricks Brer Bear into getting Miss Bear to cut off Brer Bear's head so she can comb it well.

At other times, the injury is less harsh. In "Brother Rabbit's Laughing-Place," from *Told by Uncle Remus*, Brer Rabbit sends Brer Fox into what Brer Rabbit says is his laughing place, and Brer Fox walks straight into a hornets' nest. As he struggles to escape the insects, Brer Fox protests that he does not see anything funny about the place, whereupon Brer Rabbit replies, "I said 'twas my laughin'-place, an' I'll say it ag'in. What you reckon I been doin' all dis time? Ain't you hear me laughin'?"

Sometimes, the injury is only to the dupe's pride. For example, in "The Moon in the Mill Pond," from *Nights with Uncle Remus*, Brer Rabbit and Terrapin trick Brer Bear, Fox, and Wolf into trying to seine for the moon in a mill pond, with the result that the latter three end up getting soaked and made to look foolish in front of Miss Meadows and her "gals."

The other two major kinds of stories in these collections are the myth and the supernatural tale. The myth seeks to explain the origin of something; it is sometimes called an etiological tale. There are twenty-three of these. Four tales representative of the myth are "Why the Negro Is Black," from *Uncle Remus: His Songs and His Sayings*; "Why the Alligator's Back Is Rough," from *Nights with Uncle Remus*; "Where the Harrycane Comes From," from *Uncle Remus and His Friends*; and "When Brother Rabbit Was King," from *Told by Uncle Remus*, which tells why dogs are always sniffing around.

In a supernatural tale, one of the main characters is a witch, a ghost, the devil, or some similar creature, or a magical object is used to significant effect. The sixteen supernatural tales in the Uncle Remus stories include two bargain-with-the-devil stories, "Jacky-My-Lantern" (from *Uncle Remus: His Songs and His Sayings*) and "Impty-Umpty and the Blacksmith" (from *Uncle Remus Returns*); a gruesome shape-shifter story, "How a Witch Was Caught" (from *Daddy Jake, the Runaway*); two golden-arm stories, "A Ghost Story" (from *Nights with Uncle Remus*) and "Taily-po" (from *Uncle Remus Returns*); and a chilling story about a demoniac changeling, "The Baby and the Punkins" (from *Seven Tales of Uncle Remus*).

One reason the Uncle Remus tales are important is that they represent the first time anyone seriously attempted to record the folktales of African Americans in the exact form, language, and style in which they existed. They not only inspired future folklorists to interest themselves in African American folklore but also encouraged them to record such material as precisely as they could.

A second reason for their significance is that these tales, together with the narrative frameworks in which they are embedded, provide an insight into the psyche of blacks in the antebellum South. It should not be surprising, Harris always maintained, that a trickster rabbit is the hero of the majority of these tales. The rabbit is among the most physically helpless wild animals in the South, lacking not only fangs and claws but also hooves and horns. Likewise, the slave was the most physically helpless person in the antebellum South, exploited almost as much by his owner as the rabbit is by the predators who rule forest and swamp. In the triumph of the prey animal over the predator, the slave could enjoy, if only vicariously, a triumph over his owner and the other predatory whites by whom he was surrounded.

This is not to say, as some have, that there is validity to the idea that Uncle Remus tells these stories in order to give a little white boy nightmares, to be Brer Rabbit to the little boy's Brer Fox. Uncle Remus says, explicitly and often, that there

is a difference between the world of the "creeturs" and the world of people: Human beings have preachers and the Bible to tell them how they should behave, whereas the creatures have no idea of the difference between right and wrong. Brer Rabbit is not an allegorical embodiment of Nat Turner. Many of the stories are told, in fact, to point out to the boy that one should not try to imitate the animals in one's behavior.

The Uncle Remus stories do not present a picture of a world that Uncle Remus, or the average reader, would want to see come into being. Instead, they present readers with a world that is already far too like their own, one that human beings should work to keep from becoming realized.

Viktor R. Kemper

Further Reading

Baer, Florence E. *Sources and Analogues of the Uncle Remus Tales*. Helsinki: Suomalainen Tiedeakatemia, 1980. Essential for cross-cultural comparison of an Uncle Remus tale with other folktales of the same type. Finds close African analogs for almost 70 percent of the Uncle Remus tales.

Bickley, R. Bruce, Jr. *Joel Chandler Harris*. Boston: Twayne, 1978. Chapters 3, 4, and 7 focus on the major critical approaches to these tales. Includes useful notes, index, and selected bibliography.

_____. "John, Brer Rabbit, and Babo: The Trickster and Cultural Power in Melville and Joel Chandler Harris." In *Trickster Lives: Culture and Myth in American Fiction*, edited by Jeanne Campbell Reesman. Athens: University of Georgia Press, 2001. Analyzes the character of the black trickster, comparing Brer Rabbit to characters created by Herman Melville.

_____, ed. *Critical Essays on Joel Chandler Harris*. Boston: G. K. Hall, 1981. A casebook for all of Harris's work. Eight of its eighteen scholarly articles address the Uncle Remus stories.

Brasch, Walter M. *Brer Rabbit, Uncle Remus, and the "Cornfield Journalist": The Tale of Joel Chandler Harris*. Macon, Ga.: Mercer University Press, 2000. A balanced examination of Harris and his stories—part biography, part analysis—aimed at an audience from whom, as children, the Uncle Remus tales had been withheld in deference to the sensitive racial issues encumbering the stories.

Brookes, Stella Brewer. *Joel Chandler Harris—Folklorist*. Athens: University of Georgia Press, 1950. Chapters 3 through 7 and the appendix are especially valuable in a study of Uncle Remus tales.

Cartwright, Keith. "Creole Self-Fashioning: Joel Chandler Harris's 'Other Fellow.'" In *Reading Africa into American Literature: Epics, Fables, and Gothic Tales*. Lexington: University Press of Kentucky, 2002. Cartwright defines Harris as a "self-fashioned Afro-Creole fabulist" and demonstrates the elements of African folklore in Harris's work.

Mixon, Wayne. "The Ultimate Irrelevance of Race: Joel Chandler Harris and Uncle Remus in Their Time." *Journal of Southern History* 56, no. 3 (August, 1990): 457-

480. By far the most reasoned discussion of the question of whether these stories are racist.

Wyatt-Brown, Bertram. "Trickster Motif and Disillusion: Uncle Remus and Mark Twain." In *Hearts of Darkness: Wellsprings of a Southern Literary Tradition*. Baton Rouge: Louisiana State University Press, 2003. This comparison of the two authors is part of Wyatt-Brown's examination of the role of melancholy and alienation in nineteenth century southern literature.

Comus

Author: John Milton (1608-1674)
First produced: 1634; first published, 1637
Type of work: Drama
Type of plot: Allegory
Time of plot: Antiquity
Locale: Kingdom of Neptune

Principal characters:
ATTENDANT SPIRIT, later disguised as Thyrsis
COMUS, an evil magician who beguiles travelers
THE LADY,
THE ELDER BROTHER, and
THE SECOND BROTHER, children traveling to meet their father Neptune
SABRINA, a river nymph

The Story:

The Attendant Spirit comes into a wild wood, far from his usual abode outside Jove's court, far above the dirt and hubbub of the world. He is on earth only to show the rare mortals before him some of the ways to godly virtue. He speaks of the plight of three children who are traveling to visit their father Neptune, ruler of many island kingdoms. Their path lies through a dark and treacherous wood where their lives would have been in danger if Jove had not sent the Spirit to protect them. The chief danger is Comus, son of Bacchus and Circe. He lives in the wood and possesses a magic wine that, when drunk by thirsty travelers, gives them the heads and inclinations of wild animals. The Spirit disguises himself as a shepherd to guide the children of Neptune. He leaves when he hears Comus and his band of bewitched travelers approaching.

Comus, invoking joy and feasting, drinking and dancing, declares that the night is made for love and should be so used before the sun reveals the revels of his band and turns them to sinfulness. His followers dance until he stops them, sensing the approach of a young woman whom he immediately wishes to enchant.

The Lady enters, drawn to the scene by the noise of the revelers. Unwilling as she is to meet such people, she nevertheless believes that they are the only hope she has of finding her way out of the wood. Because she is tired by her walking, her brothers leave her to find wild fruit for refreshment, but night falls before they can return and they are unable to find her again. Meanwhile, a dark cloud covers the stars. The Lady calls and sings to the nymph, Echo, to guide her to her brothers.

Comus, delighted with the song she sings, decides that the Lady should be his queen, and, in the disguise of a village boy, he greets her as a goddess. The Lady reproves him and says that she wants help to find her companions. After questioning her about them, he says that he saw two such young men gathering fruit and that it will be a delight to help her find them. Comus adds that he knows the woods perfectly and that he will therefore lead the Lady to her brothers. She replies that she will trust him. They leave the clearing together.

The two brothers arrive and the elder calls to heaven for the moon and stars, so that they might see their way. Failing this, he wishes to see the lights of someone's cottage. The

Second Brother, adding that even the sound of penned-up flocks will help them, expresses great fear for his sister's fate. The Elder Brother insists that the Lady's perfect virtue will protect her. The Second Brother says that beauty such as hers needs to be guarded and that she can easily be in danger in such a place. The Elder Brother repeats that he has great hope for her safety as she is armed by chastity. Nothing can violate this; the very angels in heaven will protect her.

Hearing someone approaching, the brothers call out to him. When the Attendant Spirit greets them, they think they recognize him as their father's shepherd, Thyrsis. He anxiously asks where their sister is and, hearing that she is lost, tells them that Comus dwells in the wood. He adds that he overheard Comus offer to escort a lady to her companions. Fearing that she is their sister, he leaves to find the brothers. That news plunges the Second Brother into complete despair. The Elder Brother, maintaining that virtue can be attacked but not injured, declares that they must find Comus and fight him for their sister, but the Attendant Spirit warns them that swords will not help them against Comus. He says, however, that he was given a magic herb that is effective against all enchantments. He instructs the brothers to break the glass in Comus's hand when they find him and to seize his wand.

In Comus's palace, meanwhile, the Lady refuses his wine and attempts to leave, but she is restrained by a threat to transfix her in her chair. When she declares that Comus cannot control her mind, he propounds his hedonistic philosophy, saying that she should enjoy her youth and beauty, not cruelly deny them. She replies that she will never accept anything from him, since only the good man can give good things. Comus argues that in rejecting him she is denying life and the plentiful gifts of nature by her abstinence; beauty should be enjoyed, not left to wither like a dying rose. The Lady decides that she must refute these arguments with her own. She states that nature's gifts are for the temperate to use well and that excess of luxury breeds only ingratitude in men. She fears that Comus can never understand this doctrine, and she believes that if she attempts to explain, her conviction will be so strong that his palace will tumble around him. Comus is impressed by her argument, which seems to him inspired by Jove himself, yet he determines to try again to persuade her. As he begins to speak, the brothers rush in, break his glass on the ground, and overwhelm his followers.

Comus escapes because they have not captured his wand. The Attendant Spirit despairs of freeing the Lady until he remembers that he can summon Sabrina. This river nymph will help them, since she loves the virtue that the Lady personifies. By song, he summons her in the name of Neptune and Triton to save the girl. As Sabrina rises from the river, she sings of the willows and flowers that she left. She frees the Lady by sprinkling on her the pure and precious water from her fountain. The Attendant Spirit gives Sabrina his blessing and prays that the river should always flow in good measure and that its banks will be fertile.

The Attendant Spirit then tells the Lady that he will lead them to Neptune's house, where many friends are gathered to congratulate him. In Ludlow Town, at the castle, country dancers lead the Lady and her two brothers before the Earl and the Countess, who impersonate Neptune and his Queen. There the Attendant Spirit praises the young people's beauty, patience, and honesty, and their triumph over folly; then he announces his return to his natural home in the Gardens of Hesperus, for his task is done. If any mortal would go with him, however, his way is the path of virtue.

Critical Evaluation:

John Milton's *Comus* was first published in 1637 as *A Maske Presented at Ludlow Castle*. The title *Comus*, derived from the name of the evil magician in the masque, became the normal designation during the eighteenth century and has replaced the original title. The work—written as dramatic entertainment for the installation of John Egerton, Earl of Bridgewater, as Lord President of Wales—was performed at Ludlow Castle on September 29, 1634. Written primarily in blank verse, with rhymed lyrics interspersed, the drama extends to 1,023 lines, exceptionally brief for a play but above average length for a masque. The work was a collaboration between Milton and his friend Henry Lawes, a tutor to the Egerton children. Lawes wrote the music for the songs, staged the production, and acted the part of Thyrsis.

Much critical attention has centered upon *Comus* as a masque and its resemblance to other masques of the period. A popular form of aristocratic entertainment, the masque was a relatively short drama featuring simple conflict, static characters, song and dance, and pageantry. The actors were usually amateurs, often members of a noble family, who felt free to take part in private dramatic productions but would not have ventured onto the public stage. The plot of *Comus* features a simple journey through a wood at whose end the three young actors are presented to their parents. The masque pits the three children of the Egerton family, who acted the parts of the Lady and her two brothers, against the evil magician Comus and his deformed rout of followers, whose dances form the antimasque.

Milton draws upon the classics, early English literature, and folk tradition to present an elemental conflict between good and evil. Overall, the tone of the poem, despite its philosophical speeches and theme of rigid morality, suggests a fairy tale. Spirits intervene at the appropriate times; evil magic is countered by good magic; and the creatures with supernatural powers exercise them within conventional limits. Thyrsis, the spirit who becomes a shepherd, cannot intervene directly to protect the Lady but must serve as instructor and guide to her brothers, who attack the magician with drawn swords. Their failure to carry out all of their instructions, to seize Comus's wand, means that Sabrina must be summoned to release the Lady. Spells and incantations are as much a part of the masque as is Comus's seductive, transforming chalice.

A few critics have suggested that Milton's strong ethical theme and limited use of singing and dancing mean that the work is not really a masque but a type of ethical debate. Passages like the somewhat formal speeches of the Elder Brother, the Lady's refutation of Comus's arguments in support of immediate pleasures, and the concluding speech of Thyrsis represent examples of extended moralizing. Most critical opinion, however, while acknowledging that Milton presses the limits of the genre, accepts its classification as a masque. The original title suggests that Milton believed he was writing a masque; in addition, he had earlier produced another example of the genre in Arcades, for the countess of Derby, the stepmother of the earl of Bridgewater.

Exploration of Milton's connection with the Egerton family has unearthed some hints of a scandal that had little direct effect on the family. These discoveries were sufficient, however, to fuel critical speculation that the ethical emphasis in Milton's drama was adopted as an effort to enhance their reputation.

A more likely explanation for the moral theme arises when one places the masque within the context of Milton's major poetry. Along with *Paradise Lost* (1667, 1674), *Paradise Regained* (1671), and *Samson Agonistes* (1671), it forms a fourth major poetic work on the theme of temptation. All four present an ethical conflict marked by the fundamental contrast between right and wrong, occurring within the context of a Providential view of history and human life. In *Comus*, the Lady must preserve her chastity by rejecting the sensual life that Comus urges upon her. She recognizes that the values espoused by Comus and his followers are incompatible with both temperance and chastity. Her ethical understanding and strong will enable her to overcome his arguments and defeat his purpose. While her character remains unblemished, however, her body is imprisoned by Comus, whose magical power forces her to sit immobile in an alabaster chair. Humanity's dependence upon Providence is demonstrated when Sabrina, symbolizing grace, arrives to release the Lady through sprinkling drops of water over her, an allegorical representation of Christian baptism. The Lady

emerges triumphant over evil, and her brothers demonstrate their courage in putting Comus and his followers to flight.

Among numerous poetic elements in the masque, Milton draws heavily on myth and on the pastoral tradition. He develops an ethic based upon willful choice through the speeches of the Lady, the Elder Brother, and the guardian spirit Thyrsis. As the Elder Brother explains, throughout life one rises to ever greater spirituality by making right choices, and each correct choice leads to a higher level of ethical being. Conversely, each wrong choice causes one to become progressively more immoral. In the end, evil is self-defeating, and good is triumphant. In *Comus*, as in other poems, however, Milton portrays ethical behavior as a simple choice between right and wrong, and the Lady's decision is neither complex nor subtle.

To mirror and reinforce his ethical theme, Milton makes elaborate use of the idea of metamorphosis or transformation, borrowed from the Roman poet Ovid but imbued with Christian overtones. The followers of Comus, with their animal faces, have been partially transformed to a lower life because they failed to resist his blandishments. Other transformations are self-imposed. Thyrsis is able to transform himself into the likeness of a shepherd on a mission to help the two brothers free the Lady. For the purpose of deception, Comus transforms himself into the appearance of a country person. Providence also intervenes to transform the virtuous. Sabrina, who represents grace, has been made into a river goddess that she might escape pursuit by a cruel stepmother. It remains for the Lady and the Brothers to retain the virtue they possess, not to be led astray by evil. Their most important transformation will occur at the end of life as a confirmation of their virtue.

"Critical Evaluation" by Stanley Archer

Further Reading

Burbery, Timothy J. *Milton the Dramatist*. Pittsburgh, Pa.: Duquesne University Press, 2007. Chronicles Milton's interest in the theater and analyzes his theatrical works, including *Comus*. Milton attended plays as a child, and Burbery suggests that his experiences may have influenced some of the dialogue in *Comus*.

Campbell, Gordon, and Thomas N. Corns. *John Milton: Life, Work, and Thought*. New York: Oxford University Press, 2008. Insightful and comprehensive biography written by the editors of the *Oxford Milton* that is based in part on new information about seventeenth century English history. Sheds light on Milton's ideas and the turbulent times in which he lived.

Diekhoff, John, ed. *A Mask at Ludlow: Essays on Milton's "Comus."* Cleveland, Ohio: Case Western Reserve University Press, 1968. Assembles previously published essays by eminent Milton critics. The selections deal with all major critical issues concerning the masque.

Duran, Angelica, ed. *A Concise Companion to Milton.* Malden, Mass.: Blackwell, 2007. Collection of essays analyzing Milton's works, including discussions of his legacy, a survey of more than three hundred years of Milton criticism, and Katsuhiro Engetsu's piece on *Comus*, "*A Mask*: Tradition and Innovation."

Hanford, James Holly, and James G. Taaffe. *A Milton Handbook.* New York: Meredith, 1970. A mine of information about Milton's life, works, and critical reputation, this book offers synopses of individual works and comprehensive critical assessments. An excellent beginning point for the general reader and student.

Hunter, William B., ed. *Milton's English Poetry.* Lewisburg, Pa.: Bucknell University Press, 1986. Hunter's book assembles entries on Milton's poetry. The essay on *Comus*, listed under its original title, provides an introductory overview of the masque and a detailed survey of critical opinion.

Lovelock, Julian, ed. *Milton: "Comus" and "Samson Agonistes."* New York: Macmillan, 1975. In his casebook, Lovecock reprints five significant twentieth century studies of Milton's masque. Five additional selections include significant criticism from the eighteenth and nineteenth centuries.

McGuire, Maryann Cale. *Milton's Puritan Masque.* Athens: University of Georgia Press, 1983. In an extended analysis of the masque, McGuire places *Comus* within the Puritan tradition. In a genre that was usually Royalist, she finds Puritan values reflected in its style, ethical themes, and historical contexts.

Shullenberger, William. *Lady in the Labyrinth: Milton's Comus as Initiation.* Madison, N.J.: Fairleigh Dickinson University Press, 2008. This feminist analysis of the play focuses on the character of the Lady, who is described as the first of Milton's heroes of "Christian Liberty."

The Concubine

Author: Elechi Amadi (1934-   )
First published: 1966
Type of work: Novel
Type of plot: Tragedy
Time of plot: Precolonial times, mid-nineteenth century
Locale: Eastern Nigeria

Principal characters:
EMENIKE, a fine wrestler and a favorite son of the village
IHUOMA, his young, beautiful wife, the village model of ideal womanhood
NWONNA, Ihuoma's son
NNADI, Ihuoma's brother-in-law
MADUME, the "big eyed," quarrelsome land grabber
WOLU, his unfortunate wife
EKWUEME, an accomplished singer and trapper
WIGWE and ADAKU, his parents
AHUROLE, Ekwueme's immature, moody girl bride
WODU WAKIRI, the village wag, a gifted singer and comic
ANYIKA, village medicine man (*dibia*), diviner of Omokachi
AGWOTURUMBE, a rival, powerful *dibia* from Aliji village

The Story:

Emenike dies suddenly, after a full recovery from injuries he suffered during a fight with Madume, his neighbor and adversary, over some disputed farmland. Although the villagers are uncertain about the cause of death, and even though they suspect that Madume had a hand in Emenike's death, they say Emenike died from "lock chest." Ignoring the arbitration on the land dispute that the village elders and priests made in favor of Emenike, and with Emenike out of the way, Madume decides to stake his claim on the disputed farmland. While at it, he claims Ihuoma, whom he alleges Emenike snatched from him. In a show of power, Madume embarks on assaults on Ihuoma and her brother-in-law, Nnadi, as they try to protect Emenike's land and crops from Madume's "big eyes." A series of misfortunes, brought on by personal ill will, inordinate greed, and insensitivity, befall Madume until excessive cockiness and a final act of brazenness bring him face-to-face with a spitting cobra, which blinds him as he reaches in defiantly to harvest a plantain tree on Emenike's farm. Blinded and miserable, Madume hangs himself. The villagers agree that his abominable death is retributive justice from the ever-watchful, powerful gods. Though finally rid of Madume, Ihuoma characteristically bemoans the loss of two village men in a two-year span, fearing that there will be "too few left to organize village activities."

Young, already a mother of three children, and widowed at the tender age of twenty-two, Ihuoma continues to live out her widowhood in her dead husband's compound, devoted to his memory and care of her children. More attractive than ever even in her misfortune, Ihuoma commands great respect from the village women, especially Madume's wife, Wolu. Ekwueme, the gifted song composer and singer, although betrothed to Ahurole, is irrepressibly taken by Ihuoma's exceptional beauty of character and looks. In a bind, aware of his obligation to filial obedience and to the propriety of Omokachi tradition, Ekwueme gives up his personal desires and marries Ahurole, his immature, neurotic child bride, whose unpredictable mood swings and incessant sobbing test their marriage sorely. Although Ekwueme reconciles himself to his marriage to Ahurole, he cannot repress his desire for Ihuoma, his ideal of a wife. As his halfhearted interest in Ahurole wanes, his repressed feelings for Ihuoma emerge stronger. Suspecting this, and upon her mother's advice, Ahurole seeks the help of a diviner to renew Ekwueme's diminishing conjugal interest. Unfortunately, Ahurole's effort to recapture Ekwueme's love interest, by way of a love potion, succeeds only in bewitching him and temporarily bringing on madness.

After being relieved of Ahurole, Ekwueme openly declares his intentions to marry Ihuoma, who is responsible for curing him of his madness. The diviner-priest Anyika, however, reveals to Ekwueme's parents the ill-fatedness of an Ihuoma-Ekwueme union because, contrary to physical appearances, Ihuoma is not an ordinary human being but a goddess-human, a mermaid in human form, betrothed to the powerful, malevolent Sea-King. Only the series of bizarre events toward the end of the novel reveal the truth of an identity of which she herself is unaware. Her husband's sudden death and Madume's blindness and subsequent suicide after he assaults her are all explained by her secret godlike status.

Unequivocal in his resolve, and secretly hoping that the cause of the ill-fatedness of the proposed marriage to Ihuoma

can be mediated, Ekwueme and his parents seek a second opinion from a rival diviner, the renowned Agwoturumbe of Iliji village. Unlike Anyika, Agwoturumbe, perhaps in a bid to outdivine his rival Anyika, assures Ekwueme and his parents that Agwoturumbe has the power to bind the Sea-King and render him powerless through appropriate sacrifice. Preparations for the elaborate and costly sacrificial mediation are well under way when a sudden turn of events during the search for the lizard, the final item called for on the list of items for the sacrifice, hasten the end of Ekwueme's life. Ekwueme's bizarre, premonitory dream of being lured away to the land of the dead by Emenike, Ihuoma's dead husband, comes true tragically and ironically at the hands of Nwonna, Ihuoma's son. Ekwueme instructs Nwonna in the art of lizard-shooting moments before the young man looses the arrow that, intended for the desired "big coloured male lizard," fells Ekwueme.

Critical Evaluation:

Unlike Chinua Achebe's *Things Fall Apart* (1958) and *Arrow of God* (1964), which infuse the elements of the tragic into the themes of the impact of colonialism on traditional African cultures, Elechi Amadi's lesser-known *The Concubine* focuses on the private, the social, and the supernatural. Notably lacking the fanfare of color, ritual, rhetoric, and ceremony characteristic of many West African novels of the 1960's, Amadi's novel concerns the notion of cosmic totality, the precarious nature of man's relationship to the supernatural—a relationship in which unseen forces manipulate human life and control human thought and action in the painful and tragic human drama. From its opening chapters to the end, the novel teems with omens, its pages pervaded by fatalism. Divine authority predominates; the presence of the gods is felt long before the story of Ihuoma's status begins to unfold. Its plot and structure are controlled by supernatural forces. The remarkably simple plot describes a complex situation in which the fortunes and misfortunes of four key characters are set against a background of communal peace and harmony, an idyllic setting governed by a traditional propriety. Good behavior is applauded, excessive and fanatical feelings are frowned upon, and personal feelings are controlled almost to a fault. Except for Madume, the quarrelsome and greedy land grabber, the generous villagers of Omokachi live peacefully with one another. The good-natured humor, the constant bantering, and the profuse singing and dancing that characterize this seemingly perfect community is disrupted by implacable gods. In their hands it appears humans are like puppets, goaded by fate into the gods' wily snares.

The tragedy of *The Concubine* is centered on the dual character of Ihuoma, the almost flawless embodiment of Omokachi's ideal of propriety, a goddess-human who, unbeknown to her and the villagers, is fated to be the wife of the Sea-King even before birth. Reincarnated into the Omokachi community, Ihuoma becomes a death-snare for men, the bait to lure those with amorous intentions to a deadly rivalry with the Sea-King. Given this femme fatale's winning personality and looks, it is not surprising that the cream of the village manhood is attracted to her. While the villagers readily give plausible explanations for Emenike's and Madume's deaths ("lock chest" and "big eyes" respectively), they are particularly stunned by the cruel and mysterious circumstances of Ekwueme's death on the eve of his impending marriage to Ihuoma and on the day that his life is especially sweet.

When the two rival diviners—Anyika and Agwoturumbe—enter the scene, each with his own explanation and vision of the potency of the superior power at work and how to "bind" it, the action of the tragedy shifts to a blatant contention between man and god on two counts: Ekwueme's unequivocal, often-repeated love for Ihuoma and his intentions to marry her, and Agwoturumbe's presumptuous claim to power and knowledge strong enough to fetter the Sea-King. Moreover, Ekwueme's well-intentioned but proud quip that "if Ihuoma was a sea-goddess, then he could very well be a sea-god himself," combined with Agwoturumbe's equally boastful reassurance that all will be well, even if it means making a journey to the bottom of the river himself, inevitably hasten the tragic denouement of the story.

The role of mystery, though downplayed through twenty-eight of the novel's thirty chapters, is crucial in sustaining the plot and structure of the story. For example, even the most discerning reader, though vaguely suspicious of Emenike's and Madume's sudden deaths, does not discover the mystery of Ihuoma's true identity and the nature of her unusualness until Anyika divulges it in fragments in chapter 28. Mysterious as Ihuoma's goddess-human nature might be, the reader's surprise at its revelation is short-lived because the reader recognizes the novel's implicit belief in the coexistence of the natural and supernatural worlds.

Once made in light of Ihuoma's "almost perfect" nature, Anyika's revelation makes sense and is therefore credible because no human can be "quite so right in everything, almost perfect." Emenike's "lock chest" death, Madume's "big eye" death, and Ekwueme's young lover's death are now fully explained because the jealous Sea-King husband, after highly involved rites, can be persuaded to tolerate concubinage but not marriage. For this reason, Ekwueme is marked, destined to die from the moment he expresses amorous interests in Ihuoma. Ekwueme, like the grasshoppers that Ihuoma's second son feeds limb by limb to some ants, is helpless in the web of the relentless Sea-King. He is felled by an errant arrow meant for a lizard, the final, perhaps least consequential item on the list of materials for the rite that would ensure the future Ekwueme and Ihuoma were preparing for optimistically.

Amadi's achievement in his first novel is his controlled narrative and sustained dialogue. Although not given to rendering the rhythms of traditional speech with the same flair with which Achebe captures Ibo oratory, Amadi successfully combines narrative simplicity with conversational language of everyday realities. Without being idealistic, Amadi paints an idyllic picture of village life, including the aesthetic and artistic, using the language of good-natured bantering, humor, singing and dancing. *The Concubine* ranks as one of the most successful, realistic West African village novels.

Pamela J. Olubunmi Smith

Further Reading

Banyiwa-Horne, Naana. "African Womanhood: The Contrasting Perspectives of Flora Nwapa's *Efuru* and Elechi Amadi's *The Concubine.*" In *Ngambika: Studies of Women in African Literature*, edited by Carole Boyce Davies and Anne Adams Graves. Trenton, N.J.: Africa World Press, 1986. Gives a strictly feminist reading of the writers' contrasting portrayal of their female protagonists. Concludes that Amadi's perspective is male oriented and therefore limiting.

Gikandi, Simon. "Myth, Language and Culture in Chinua Achebe's *Arrow of God* and Elechi Amadi's *The Concubine.*" In *Reading the African Novel*. London: Heinemann, 1987. Suggests a reinterpretation of the narrowly held view that, in Achebe's and Amadi's novels, myth is simply an expression of a community's fears, hopes, or expectations.

Nyamndi, George. "Elechi Amadi's Women." In *Gender, Literature, and Religion in Africa*, by Elizabeth Le Roux et al. Dakar, Senegal: Council for the Development of Social Science Research in Africa, 2005. Nyamndi examines Amadi's female characters in *The Concubine* and other novels published in the 1960's and 1970's. He maintains that Amadi saw women as a force of stability and progress in a male-dominated society.

Obiechina, Emmanuel. *Culture, Tradition, and Society in the West African Novel*. New York: Cambridge University Press, 1980. Discusses *The Concubine* as one of ten major West African novels. This classic study gives a comprehensive analysis of many aspects of the novel—characterization, setting, language, and aesthetics.

Osundare, Niyi. "As Grasshoppers to Wanton Boys: The Role of the Gods in the Novels of Elechi Amadi." *African Literature Today* 11 (1980): 97-109. An insightful essay on Amadi's preoccupation with fatalism. It examines how supernatural forces shape human action and control the plots of Amadi's novels.

Umoren, Tonia. *Literature and Society: Social Order in the Novels of Elechi Amadi*. Calabar, Nigeria: University of Calabar Press, 2004. Umoren's study of Amadi's representation of Nigerian society includes analysis of *The Concubine*. Includes bibliography and index.

_____. *Portrait of Womanhood in African Literary Tradition: Reflections on Elechi Amadi's Works*. Calabar, Nigeria: Clear Lines, 2002. Umoren analyzes the female characters in *The Concubine* and other works. Includes bibliography and index.

Confessions

Author: Saint Augustine (354-430)
First transcribed: Confessiones, 397-401 C.E. (English translation, 1620)
Type of work: Autobiography

Principal personages:
SAINT AUGUSTINE
MONICA, his mother
ADEODATUS, his son
FAUSTUS, the bishop of the Manichaean sect
AMBROSE, the bishop of Milan
ALYPIUS, a friend from Tagaste

The *Confessions* was a new form in literature. Others, like Marcus Aurelius, had set down meditations, but this was different. Others had written biographies and autobiographies, but Saint Augustine did not follow that model exactly. True, he does tell about his life, but his method is a departure from a narrative of dates and events. He is more interested in his thievery of pears than in more important actions, and he makes the fruit as meaningful in his life as the Old Testament symbolism of the apples in the Garden of Eden. Other episodes are selected because of their revelation of the grace and provision of God. "I pass over many things, hastening on to those which more strongly compel me to confess to thee," he tells the reader.

"My *Confessions*, in thirteen books," writes Saint Augustine, looking back from the age of sixty-three at his various writings, "praise the righteous and good God as they speak either of my evil or good, and they are meant to excite men's minds and affections toward him. . . . The first through the tenth books were written about myself, the other three about the Holy Scripture." In the year before his death, writing to Darius, he declared: "Take the books of my *Confessions* and use them as a good man should. Here see me as I am and do not praise me for more than I am." One may argue that it took the invention of the Christian faith to lead to the creation of the confession as a genre of literature.

In fact, Augustine's life story might be looked on as a parallel to the parable of the prodigal son, with his heart "restless till it finds its rest in God"; he brings his account to an end, after his struggles to free himself from pride and sensuality, with his return to his home at Tagaste. Half his life still lay ahead of him. Although his friends, his teachers, and his mother appear in the *Confessions*, they lack any physical details by which one may visualize them. Two lines cover the death of his father. Neither name nor description is given to his mistress and the mother of his child, nor of the friend whose death drove him from his native city. Detail is of less importance to Saint Augustine than theological meditation and interpretation.

Taking his text from the psalmist who would "confess my transgressions unto the Lord," this work is one long prayer beginning, "Great art thou, O Lord, and greatly to be praised," and ending with the hope that "thus shall thy door be opened."

From the very first, the consolation of God's mercy sustained Saint Augustine. His memories of infancy made him wonder what preceded that period, as later he theorized about what had been before the creation. His pictures of himself crying and flinging his arms about because he could not make his wants known were symbols to him of the Christian life, even as the acquisition of facts about this early period from his mother impressed on him the need for help from others to gain self-knowledge.

Though his mother Monica was a devout Christian and her son had been brought up in that faith, young Aurelius Augustinus was more interested in the hero Aeneas than in God. Once, at the point of death from a stomach ailment, he begged to be baptized, but his mother refused to have him frightened into becoming a Christian. So he went on, reading Latin and disliking Greek and taking delight in the theater. A frank but modest description of his many abilities, the gift of his God to one not yet dedicated to God, ends the first book of this revealing work.

Book 2 concentrates on the sixteenth year of lazy, lustful, and mischievous Aurelius. He and his companions robbed a pear tree, not because they wanted the fruit, since they threw it to the swine, but because it was forbidden. His confession that he loved doing wrong made him ponder his reasons for wandering from the path of good and becoming a "wasteland." When he traveled to Carthage to study, at the age of nineteen, his chief delights were his mistress and the theater. In the course of his prescribed studies he read an essay by Cicero, *Hortensius*, now lost, urging the study of philosophy. Remembering his mother's hopes that he would become a Christian, he tried to read the Scriptures; he found them inferior in style to Cicero. He did, however, become involved with a pseudo-Christian sect, founded by the Persian religious teacher Mani (c. 216-277), because he approved of their logical approach to the problems of evil and good, represented by the dualistic concept of the universe. During the nine years that he was a Manichaean, his mother, encouraged by a dream that he would eventually see his error, kept loyally by him.

Back in Tagaste, he wrote plays, taught rhetoric, and lived with a mistress. He had no patience with a bishop, sent by his mother, to instruct him in Christianity. He was equally scornful of a magician who offered to cast spells to ensure his success in a drama competition. He thought he was sufficient to himself, and by his own efforts he won a rhetoric contest. His temporary interest in astrology ended when he was unable to prove that successful divinations were more than chance. The death of a dear friend, who during his last illness becomes a Christian and denounced the life Aurelius is leading, so profoundly affected him that he returned to Carthage. There, still following the Manichaean beliefs, he wrote several essays, now lost. He was soon to be disillusioned. Fau-

stus, reputed to be the most learned of Manichaean bishops, came to Carthage, and Aurelius Augustinus went to him to clear his religious doubts. Augustinus found Faustus more eloquent than logical. Hoping to improve himself, Augustinus then went to Rome to teach rhetoric; students there were reported to be less rowdy than those in his classes in Carthage. In Rome, malaria, the teaching of the skeptics who upset his confidence in the certainty of knowledge, and, above all, the lack of classroom discipline induced him to accept the invitation of officials to resume his teaching career in Milan.

In Milan he enjoyed the companionship of two friends from Tagaste, Alypius and Nebridius. His mother, coming to live with him, persuaded Bishop Ambrose to try to convert her son. About the same time efforts to get him married and to regularize his life caused a break with his mistress, who on her departure left him with his young son Adeodatus. The group around the young rhetorician often discussed philosophy, and in Neoplatonism he found an answer to his greatest perplexity: If there is a God, what is the nature of his material existence? Finally, he was ready to study Christianity, especially the writings of Saint Paul. In book 7, which describes this period of his life, appears one of Saint Augustine's two ecstatic visions, a momentary glimpse of the One.

Book 8 recounts his conversion. Anxious to imitate those who had gained what he sought, he listened to an account of the conversion of the orator Marius Victorinus. While returning home, still upset and uncertain, he heard a child chanting: "Pick it up and read it." Taking these words as God's command, he opened the Bible at random and found himself reading Romans 13:13: "Put on the Lord Jesus Christ." Convinced, he called Alypius, and they found Monica and reported to her their newly acquired convictions.

Giving up his teaching, Saint Augustine prepared for baptism, along with his friend and Adeodatus. He was baptized by Bishop Ambrose during Easter Week, 387. Then the party set out to return to Tagaste. During their journey, and following another moment of Christian ecstasy, Monica died at Ostia on the Tiber. Her son's *Confessions* contains touching chapters of affection and admiration for her; sure of his faith at the time of her death, however, he fell into no period of abject mourning such as that which had followed the death of his friend at an earlier time.

With book 10, Saint Augustine turns from episodes of his life to self-analysis, detailing the three steps of the soul's approach to God, passing from an appreciation of the beauties of the outside world to an introspective study of itself, and ending with an inexplicable anticipation of the blessedness of the knowledge of God, the "truth-given Joy," that crowns the soul's pilgrimage.

Book 11 represents one of Saint Augustine's great contributions to Christian thought, the analysis of time. Pondering the mysteries of creation in an "eternal world," he saw it not as measured by "the motion of sun, moon, and stars," but as determined by the soul, the past being its remembrance; the present, its attention; and the future, its anticipation. He wrote: "The past increases by the diminution of the future, until by the consumption of all the future, all is past."

The last two books present speculation on the methods of creation and on the truth of the Scriptures, with most of the chapters devoted to interpretation of the opening verses of Genesis. The Old Testament account is open to many interpretations, and the final book of the *Confessions* deals with the material and allegorical possibilities of the story of the Creation. At the end, Saint Augustine acknowledges the goodness of creation, and meditates on verses describing the rest on the seventh day. He begs that God will bestow the rest and blessedness of that Sabbath in the life eternal that is to come.

Further Reading

Augustine, Saint. *Saint Augustine's Childhood: Confessiones.* Edited and translated by Garry Wills. New York: Viking, 2001. Wills's commentary draws comparison between Augustine's theory of language and that of linguist Noam Chomsky.

Brown, Peter. *Augustine of Hippo.* New ed. Berkeley: University of California Press, 2000. One of the best biographical accounts of Augustine, this book uses a chronological approach to reveal how Augustine's writings evolved during his lifetime. Heavily annotated.

_____. *Religion and Society in the Age of Augustine.* Eugene, Oreg.: Wipf and Stock, 2007. Places Saint Augustine in his historical context.

Kenney, John Peter. *The Mysticism of Saint Augustine: Rereading "The Confessions."* New York: Routledge, 2005. Examines Augustine's vision of Ostia as described in *Confessions* and examines his mysticism in relation to the ideas of ancient Platonism.

Evans, G. R. *Augustine on Evil.* New York: Cambridge University Press, 2000. Begins with Augustine's thoughts as a young pagan philosopher on the nature of humankind, then shows the changes in his thinking after his conversion to Christianity. Epilogue covers later philosophers and their interpretations of Augustine's ideas.

Gilson, Étienne. *The Christian Philosophy of Saint Augustine.* Translated by L. E. M. Lynch. New York: Octagon Books, 1988. Discusses Saint Augustine's central importance in the development of early Christian thought. Describes *Confessions* as a truly original work of literature.

Mann, William E., ed. *Augustine's "Confessions": Critical Essays.* Lanham, Md.: Rowman & Littlefield, 2006. The essays provide various interpretations of the work, including discussions of Augustine's conversion and his ideas on evil and original sin, divine nature, and suffering love.

O'Donnell, James J. *Augustine.* New York: Harper Perennial, 2006. Contains a thoughtful and clear introduction to the rich diversity of Saint Augustine's writings on grace, free will, and scripture. Chapter 5 analyzes the theological aspects of *Confessions*.

Paffenroth, Kim, and Robert P. Kennedy, eds. *A Reader's Companion to Augustine's "Confessions."* Louisville, Ky.: Westminster John Knox Press, 2003. A guide for teaching or studying *Confessions*. Following an introduction, thirteen scholars interpret one of the book's thirteen chapters, discussing the chapter within the context of the entire work and of Augustine's other writings.

Portalié, Eugène. *A Guide to the Thought of Saint Augustine.* Translated by Ralph Bastian. Westport, Conn.: Greenwood Press, 1975. Originally published in French in 1923, this work remains a clear general survey of Saint Augustine's life, works, and influence. Examines Saint Augustine's contributions to Christian theology.

Scott, T. Kermit. *Augustine: His Thought in Context.* New York: Paulist Press, 1995. Discusses the philosophies and the ideologies that influenced Augustine's early life, then traces his spiritual search and the results of that search. Interprets Augustine within the context of his own time. Good discussion of Augustine's doctrine of predestination.

Starnes, Colin. *Augustine's Conversion: A Guide to the Argument of Confessions I-IX.* Waterloo, Ont.: Wilfred Laurier University Press, 1990. Presents a clear exposition of the levels of meaning in the first nine books of *Confessions*. Describes the theological and the philosophical dimensions of the work.

Confessions

Author: Jean-Jacques Rousseau (1712-1778)
First published: Les Confessions de J.-J. Rousseau,
  1782, 1789 (English translation, 1783-1790)
Type of work: Autobiography

Jean-Jacques Rousseau undoubtedly succeeded in his effort to write an autobiography of such character that he could present himself before "the sovereign Judge with this book in my hand, and loudly proclaim, Thus have I acted; these were my thoughts; such was I. With equal freedom and veracity I have related what was laudable or wicked, I have concealed no crimes, added no virtues." Rousseau's revolutionary view of the human psyche led to the flowering of the autobiography as a form of expression. There are few examples before his. Rousseau's *Confessions* (full title: *The Confessions of J.-J. Rousseau*) has been praised as perhaps the first instance of a writer's being candid and honest with the world about the writer. The book became a model for what, paradoxically, is indeed an art form: being honest, telling all.

Only a person attempting to tell all would have revealed so frankly the sensual satisfaction he received from the spankings administered by Mlle Lambercier, the sister of the pastor at Bossey, who was his tutor. Only a writer finding satisfaction either in truth or self-abasement would have gone on to tell that his passion for being overpowered by women continued throughout his adult life: "To fall at the feet of an imperious mistress, obey her mandates, or implore pardon, were for me the most exquisite enjoyments; and the more my blood was inflamed by the efforts of a lively imagination, the more I acquired the appearance of a whining lover." Having made this confession, Rousseau probably found it easier to tell of his extended affair with Madame de Warens at Annecy and of his experiences with his mistress and common-law wife, Thérèse Levasseur.

Rousseau records that he was born at Geneva in 1712, the son of Isaac Rousseau, a watchmaker, and Suzanne Bernard. His mother died at his birth, "the first of my misfortunes." According to the son's account of his father's grief, Isaac Rousseau had mixed feelings toward his son, seeing in him an image of Suzanne and, at the same time, the cause of her death. Rousseau writes: "[N]or did he ever embrace me, but his sighs, the convulsive pressure of his arms, witnessed that a bitter regret mingled itself with his caresses. When he said to me, 'Jean Jacques, let us talk of your mother,' my usual reply was, 'Yes, father, but then you know we shall cry,' and immediately the tears started from his eyes."

Rousseau describes his first experiences with reading. He turned to the romances that his mother had loved, and he and his father sometimes spent the entire night reading aloud alternately. His response to these books was almost entirely emotional, but he finally discovered other books in his grandfather's library, works that demanded something from the intellect: Plutarch, Ovid, Molière, and others.

He describes with great affection how his Aunt Suzanne, his father's sister, moved him with her singing; and he attributes his interest in music to her influence. After his stay at Bossey with Pastor Lambercier, Rousseau was apprenticed to an engraver, Abel Ducommun, in the hope that he would succeed better in the engraver's workshop than he had with City Registrar Masseron, who had fired him after a brief trial. Ducommun is described as "a young man of a very violent and boorish character," who was something of a tyrant, punishing Rousseau if he failed to return to the city before the gates were closed. Rousseau was by this time, according to his account, a liar and a petty thief, and without reluctance he stole his master's tools in order to misplace them.

Returning from a Sunday walk with some companions, Rousseau found the city gates closing an hour before time. He ran to reach the bridge, but he was too late. Reluctant to be punished by the engraver, he suddenly decided to give up his apprenticeship.

Having left Geneva, Rousseau wandered aimlessly in the environs of the city, finally arriving at Confignon. There he was welcomed by the village curate, M. de Pontverre, who gave him a good meal and sent him on to Madame Louise de Warens at Annecy. Rousseau expected to find "a devout, forbidding old woman"; instead, he discovered "a face beaming with charms, fine blue eyes full of sweetness, a complexion whose whiteness dazzled the sight, the form of an enchanting neck." He was sixteen, she was twenty-eight. She became something of a mother to him (he called her "Maman") and something of a goddess, but within five years he was her lover, at her instigation. Her motive was to protect him and to initiate him into the mysteries of love. She explained what she intended and gave him eight days to think it over; her proposal was intellectually cool and morally motivated. Since Rousseau had long imagined the delights of making love to her, he spent the eight days enjoying thoughts more lively than ever; but when he finally found himself in her arms, he was miserable: "Was I happy? No: I felt I know not what invincible sadness which empoisoned my happiness: it seemed that I had committed an incest, and two or three times, pressing her eagerly in my arms, I deluged her bosom with my tears."

Madame de Warens was at the same time involved with Claude Anet, a young peasant with a knowledge of herbs who had become one of her domestics. Before becoming intimate with Rousseau she had confessed to him that Anet was her lover, having been upset by Anet's attempt to poison himself after a quarrel with her. Despite her generosity to the two young men, she was no wanton; her behavior was more a sign of friendship than of passion, and she was busy being an intelligent and gracious woman of the world.

Through her efforts Rousseau secured a position registering land for the king in the office at Chambery. His interest in music, however, led him to give more and more time to arranging concerts and giving music lessons; he gave up his job in the survey office. This was the turning point of his life, the decision that threw him into the society of his times and made possible his growing familiarity with the world of music and letters. His alliance with Madame de Warens continued, but the alliance was no longer of an intimate sort, for he had been supplanted by Winzenreid de Courtilles during their stay at Les Charmettes. Winzenreid came on the scene after the first idyllic summer, a period in his life that Rousseau describes as "the short happiness of my life." He tells of rising with the sun, walking through the woods, over the hills, and along the valley; his delight in nature is evident, and his theories concerning natural man become comprehensible. On his arrival Winzenreid took over physical chores and was forever walking about with a hatchet or a pickax; for all practical purposes Rousseau's close relationship with Madame de Warens was finished, even if a kind of filial affection on his part survived. He describes other adventures in love, and although some of them gave him extreme pleasure, he never found another "Maman."

Rousseau, having invented a new musical notation, went to Paris hoping to convince others of its value. The system was dismissed as unoriginal and too difficult, but Rousseau had by that time been introduced to Parisian society and was known as a young philosopher as well as a writer of poetry and operas. He received an appointment as secretary to the French ambassador at Venice, but he and M. de Montaigu irritated each other and he left his post about a year later.

Returning to Paris, Rousseau became involved with the illustrious circle containing the encyclopedist Diderot, Friedrich Melchior Grimm, and Mme Louise d'Epinay. He later became involved in a bitter quarrel with all three, stemming from a remark in a play by Diderot, but Rousseau was reconciled with Diderot and continued the novel he was writing at the time, *Julie: Ou, La Nouvelle Héloïse* (1761; *The New Héloïse*). The account of the quarrel and the letters that marked its progress are among the liveliest parts of the *Confessions*.

As important an event as any in Rousseau's life was his meeting with Thérèse Levasseur, a tailor between twenty-two and twenty-three years of age, with a "lively yet charming look." Rousseau reports, "At first, amusement was my only object," but in making love to her he found that he was happy and that she was a suitable successor to "Maman." Despite the difficulties put in his way by her mother, and despite the fact that his attempts to improve her mind were useless, he was satisfied with her as his companion. She bore him five children who were sent to the foundling hospital against Thérèse's will and to Rousseau's subsequent regret.

Rousseau describes the moment on the road to Vincennes when the question proposed by the Academy of Dijon— "Has the progress of sciences and arts contributed to corrupt or purify morals?"—so struck him that he "seemed to behold another world." The discourse that resulted from his inspired moment won him the prize and brought him fame. Yet it may be that here, as elsewhere in the *Confessions*, the actual circumstances have been considerably altered by a romantic and forgetful author.

The *Confessions* carries the account of Rousseau's life to the point when, having been asked to leave Bern by the ecclesiastical authorities as a result of the uproar over *Émile: Ou, De l'éducation* (1762; *Émile: Or, Education*, 1911), he set off for England, where David Hume had offered him asylum.

Rousseau's *Confessions* offers a personal account of the experiences of a great writer. The events that history notes are mentioned—his literary triumphs; his early conversion; his reconversion; his romance with Madame d'Houdetot; his quarrels with Voltaire, Diderot, and churchmen; his musical successes—but they are all transformed by the passionate perspective from which Rousseau, writing years after most of the events he describes, imagines his own past. *Confessions* leaves the reader with the intimate knowledge of a human being, full of faults and passions, but driven by ambition and ability to a significant position in the history of literature. *Confessions* has, since its publication, been a model for the artistic endeavor of the confession.

Further Reading

Damrosch, Leo. *Jean-Jacques Rousseau: Restless Genius*. Boston: Houghton Mifflin, 2005. This one-volume biography is a useful addition to Rousseau scholarship, providing an incisive, accessible account of Rousseau's life and contributions to philosophy and literature. Includes illustrations, time line, bibliography, and index.

De Mijolla, Elizabeth. *Autobiographical Quests: Augustine, Montaigne, Rousseau, and Wordsworth.* Charlottesville: University Press of Virginia, 1994. Stimulating study, especially for readers familiar with some of the other authors discussed.

Ellis, Madeleine M. *Rousseau's Venetian Story: An Essay upon Art and Truth in "Les Confessions."* Baltimore: Johns Hopkins University Press, 1966. Reinforces the fact that what Rousseau said about himself often is seriously inaccurate.

Gay, Peter. *The Enlightenment: An Interpretation.* 2 vols. New York: W. W. Norton, 1977. Both volumes include numerous references to Rousseau; a good source on his historical and intellectual contexts.

Kelly, Christopher. *Rousseau's Exemplary Life: The "Confessions" as Political Philosophy.* Ithaca, N.Y.: Cornell University Press, 1987. Argues that regarding the *Confessions* as primarily a political statement negates criticism of its inaccuracies.

O'Rourke, James L. *Sex, Lies, and Autobiography: The Ethics of Confession.* Charlottesville: University of Virginia Press, 2006. Traces the ethical legacy of *Confessions*, describing how the autobiographies of Rousseau and other writers depict the moral complexities of everyday life.

Riley, Patrick, ed. *The Cambridge Companion to Rousseau.* New York: Cambridge University Press, 2001. Collection of essays, including an overview of Rousseau's life and work, discussions of his philosophy, and an analysis of *Confessions* by Christopher Kelly.

Wokler, Robert. *Rousseau: A Very Short Introduction.* 2d ed. New York: Oxford University Press, 2001. A concise and lucid introduction to Rousseau's life and works, with information about his fiction, educational, and religious writings, and his theories about politics, history, and music.

Confessions of an English Opium Eater

Author: Thomas De Quincey (1785-1859)
First published: 1821
Type of work: Short fiction

The Story:

Intense stomach pains drive Thomas De Quincey, at age twenty-eight, to take opium daily for relief. He had begun taking opium almost ten years before. These stomach pains are a legacy from hardships he had endured as an adolescent. His father had died when the boy was seven years old. The young De Quincy became the responsibility of four guardians. At school, he becomes an excellent Greek scholar.

At Manchester Grammar School, he is so superior to his teachers in Greek that he soon feels a desire to leave the school. His guardians are against this plan, however, so De Quincey asks an old friend for money. He receives it and plans to make his escape from a school that he feels has nothing to offer him intellectually.

The day of De Quincey's escape comes. The groom of his hall, who is carrying De Quincey's book-laden trunk down a narrow stairway, slips and falls, and the trunk clatters noisily to the floor below. De Quincey is sure he will be caught. The noise, incredibly, does not arouse the curiosity of the resident master, and the youth is able to get away.

Seventeen-year-old De Quincey heads westward, walking through Wales, where, in Bangor, he takes a room. His landlady is the former servant of a bishop's family. On one of her regular visits to the bishop's house, she discloses that she is taking in lodgers. When she reports her disclosure to De Quincey, he takes exception to the tenor of her remarks concerning him, moves out of her house at once, and finds lodging in inns. This type of lodging is relatively expensive, so the young man soon finds himself reduced to eating only once a day—a meal of only coffee or tea. The mountain air of Wales and the walking make him abnormally hungry, so that his having to subsist off berries and charitable handouts hurts him physically. As time goes by, he manages to earn a meager living by writing letters for the illiterate and by doing odd jobs. The damage to his health, however, has been done.

De Quincey's travels take him from Wales to London, where, utterly destitute and afraid to reveal himself to any friends of his family, he lives for several months on little more than a small ration of bread. Also, he sleeps outdoors. At last, in cold weather, an acquaintance gives him shelter in a large, almost empty house; De Quincey's companion is a ten-year-old girl. Pains in his stomach prevent him from ever getting a proper night's sleep; consequently, he sleeps by fits and snatches both day and night. The master of the house is a legal representative of moneylenders, but despite the man's apparent lack of principles, De Quincey finds him generous in his way. The little girl appears to be a servant in the large house, which is situated near Soho Square.

De Quincey walks the streets and often sits all day in parks, until Ann, a sixteen-year-old streetwalker, befriends him. One night, when he has violent stomach pains, Ann spends part of her scant savings on wine and spices for him. Soon afterward, he meets an old family acquaintance who gives him money, thus ending De Quincey's period of extreme poverty. Previously, he had been afraid to appeal to family friends for help for fear that his guardians would send him back to the grammar school. It never occurs to him that he might have taken on literary work of some kind. Now, solvent for the moment, he makes arrangements to get an advance on his patrimony, which is not legally his until his twenty-first birthday.

After saying good-bye to Ann, he takes a coach to Eton to get a signature that is required for an advance on his patrimony. At Eton he calls upon an acquaintance, young Lord Desart, who invites him to breakfast. Finding that he cannot keep down the food, he takes wine to his great comfort. Lord Desart, who is only eighteen years old, is reluctant to sign for security, but he finally consents. De Quincey returns to London, where he finds that Lord Desart's signature does not impress the moneylenders with whom he is negotiating for the advance. Again, he is threatened with hardship; again, however, he is saved, for his reconciled relatives send him to Oxford University. Meanwhile, before he leaves London, he searches unsuccessfully for Ann. She is nowhere to be found, and he never sees her again.

De Quincey, now nineteen years old, makes frequent weekend trips to London from Oxford. One Sunday, while in the metropolis, he suffers greatly from neuralgic head pains, and a fellow student whom he encounters recommends opium for relief. He thereupon buys a small amount of laudanum, the tincture of opium, from an apothecary. He returns to his room and takes the prescribed amount. The result seems phenomenal to him; all his pain ceases, and he knows boundless pleasure. There is no intoxication, as from wine or

spirits; there is only a protracted sense of being utterly at peace with the world and with himself. The opium uplifts the intellect rather than the animal spirits, and when its effect wears off, there is no period of depression, such as induced by spirits.

As a college student, De Quincey's two great pleasures are to hear Grassini, an Italian soprano who often sings in London, and to take opium and join the Saturday night crowds in the London markets. Even greater than these pleasures, however, is that of withdrawing himself at the time when the opium has reached its maximum effect on his mind, so that he can get the most complete enjoyment from his opium-induced dreams and visions.

De Quincey leaves Oxford. In 1812, he takes a cottage, where he studies German metaphysics and continues to take opium once a week. His health is apparently never better. Even after eight years of taking opium, he is able to say that he has not become a slave to the drug; he is still able to control the amount taken and the intervals between doses.

A recurrence, in 1813, of his old stomach disorder leads De Quincey to take the drug every day. His partial addiction is a secondary reason for his increased use of opium. For two years he takes 320 grains of opium daily, but at last he is able to reduce the amount to 40 grains. Staying on that allowance, he experiences the happiest year of his life.

About this time a traveler on foot, a Malay sailor, stops for a night at the cottage. De Quincey is impressed by the aspect and garb of the traveler. Before the traveler leaves the next morning, De Quincey gives him enough opium, divided into three parts, to kill a person if taken all at once. The traveler claps all three pieces into his mouth and departs. De Quincey feels concern for several days, but to his relief he never hears or reads of the untimely death of a Malay man in his part of Great Britain.

In his little cottage in the mountains of northern England, De Quincey, in the winter of 1816-1817, knows complete happiness in his experience with opium. Deep snows, heavy rains, a snug cottage, a roaring fire, a large collection of good books, plenty of tea, and daily consumption of laudanum bring him idyllic happiness.

Matters soon begin to change. Addicted to the daily taking of opium, it becomes impossible for De Quincey to reduce his daily allowance without bringing on abnormal perspiration and excruciating abdominal pains. He soon loses interest in reading and the study of mathematics and philosophy. A friend sends him David Ricardo's *Principles of Political Economy and Taxation* (1817). The book arouses him from his lethargy long enough to write for publication on the popular subject. Then, unable to write a preface for his work, he shelves the project. He neglects household responsibilities. At night he lies awake in his bed, processions of visions passing through his mind. These visions consist largely of scenes from the English Civil War and from ancient Rome. Soon he finds it difficult to distinguish between the real and the unreal. Furthermore, other dreams and visions take him into frightful abysses. Constantly depressed, he loses all normal sense of space and time, and he often has the sensation of having lived through a millennium. Also, he finds himself able to recall insignificant events of his childhood, details that he had never been conscious of remembering.

The opium dreams are periodic: There are nights during which he dreams historical scenes; then there is a period of architectural dreams—vast piles of buildings and enormous cities; these are followed by dreams of water—lakes, lagoons, vast oceans. He next dreams of countless human faces presenting themselves in peculiar situations to his mind's eye.

In May, 1818, De Quincey's dream visions take on an Asian theme. At times he is in China, or in India. Where in previous dream sequences he had known only spiritual horrors, in these Asian dreams he senses physical horror from reptiles and frightful birds. In the summer of 1819, still addicted to opium, he dreams of a graveyard in his own little valley. In the dream he arises and walks out of his cottage yard to enjoy the air. He thinks he sees an Asian city and, beneath a palm tree, Ann, the streetwalker friend of his youth. She does not speak; the dream fades and he finds himself walking with her in the streets of London. In 1820, one vision is so terrifying in its profundity and breadth that he awakes and declares that he will never sleep again.

Finally, De Quincey reasons that he will surely die if he continues to take opium and that he might die in the attempt to break the habit. With so little choice, he decides to try to free himself from opium. He reduces his ration gradually and finally breaks free, thus proving to himself that an addict may end a habit of seventeen years' duration.

Critical Evaluation:

Repugnance toward opium as well as the gothic nature of De Quincey's prose style had obscured the reputation of *Confessions of an English Opium Eater* in the century after it was published. It has since been recognized as one of the most remarkable pieces of writing of the English Romantic period and as a major work of English literature. To many early readers, *Confessions of an English Opium Eater* represents the most garish aspects of English romanticism. The topic, opium eating, is sensationalist and unappealing. De Quincey's prose seems feverish and overwrought. The per-

sona of the narrator is at times self-absorbed, sentimental, erudite, digressive, and prone to Latin and literary quotations.

Modern scholars have resuscitated De Quincey's reputation. In its genre of confessional literature, *Confessions of an English Opium Eater* follows in the course of such important works as the confessions of Saint Augustine and the confessions of Jean-Jacques Rousseau. Although De Quincey is clearly an imaginative author, *Confessions of an English Opium Eater* is painfully realistic when it discusses his opium addiction. In this sense it prefigures both the psychological literature of the twentieth century and the psychedelic journalism of the 1960's, including works by authors such as Ken Kesey and William S. Burroughs.

De Quincey's book remains the most arresting and touchingly human account in English literature of the widespread phenomenon of opium addiction in the early nineteenth century. Laudanam, or tincture of opium, was readily available at pharmacies in De Quincey's time, and it was considered an effective cure for extreme headaches and depression. Writer Samuel Taylor Coleridge also took laudanam for his neuralgia, and most readers of Romantic literature are familiar with the exotic fragment "Kubla Khan," which is purported to be the result of an interrupted attempt to capture the elusive memories of an opium dream.

In his *Confessions of an English Opium Eater*, De Quincey refrains from trying to construct art, even in fragments, from his opium reveries. Instead, he is a kind of impressionistic reporter, a writer who shares, in a descriptive and evenhanded way, his visions and their sources in the experiences of his life. The result is a curious taming of the marvelous, a domestication of the horrific. Although to many readers the book may seem prolix, it is compellingly constructed. When readers first encounter the gentle and simple Ann, a child prostitute, De Quincey knows that readers will recognize her at the end of his book in the terrifying dream of "female forms" crying "everlasting farewells." This dream, one of the "Pains of Opium," recalls the agonizing inability of De Quincey to find Ann again after their separation in London. The opium dream becomes a final farewell to this pathetic adolescent experience. As terrifying as it is, the dream is also cathartic and humanizing. In a sense, the dream finally "finds" Ann.

Opium dreams might revivify haunting memories; they also might immortalize trivial moments. The chance visit of the traveling Malay sailor at De Quincey's cottage becomes the source of a series of opium dreams on Asian themes. These dreams become increasingly terrifying and fantastic; they reveal De Quincey's deep fears of the unknown and his subconscious racial prejudices. The influence of these dreamlike sequences is evident in the works of later writers such as Edgar Allan Poe, Charles Baudelaire, and Charles Dickens. Writers who explore the interior spaces of the mind, such as James Joyce, D. H. Lawrence, Virginia Woolf, and Jorge Luis Borges, have acknowledged their debt to De Quincey. The critic Patrick Bridgwater has demonstrated at length that De Quincey is a precursor of Franz Kafka in the fairytale and alienated quality of these writers' fiction.

Furthermore, De Quincey's mixing of orientalism and consumption of opium calls to mind the Opium War of 1839-1842, when British gunboats compelled Chinese markets to remain open to shipments of opium. De Quincey's decision to revise *Confessions of an English Opium Eater* in 1856 resulted in part from the British interest in things Asian and in opium in the decades of the 1840's and 1850's. In its mix of introspection, fantasy, racial investigation, and exploration of consciousness, *Confessions of an English Opium Eater* seems out of place in the Victorian era but speaks well to readers in the twenty-first century.

Revised by Howard Bromberg

Further Reading

Bridgwater, Patrick. *De Quincey's Gothic Masquerade.* Atlanta: Rodopi, 2004. Bridgwater maintains that De Quincey differs from other gothic-influenced writers because his work interweaves Germanic elements with those of the gothic genre. *Confessions of an Opium Eater* is one of De Quincey's "dream works," discussed in chapter 5. The literary relationship of De Quincey and Kafka is explored in chapter 9.

De Quincey, Thomas. *Confessions of an English Opium-Eater.* Edited by Joel Faflak. Peterborough, Ont.: Broadview Press, 2009. A critically edited edition, with extensive appendixes containing related texts, reviews, and the history, politics, psychology, and medicinal structure of opium.

Hayter, Alethea. "De Quincey (I)" and "De Quincey (II)." In *Opium and the Romantic Imagination.* Berkeley: University of California Press, 1968. Discusses De Quincey's conviction that creativity is rooted in one's dreams and his belief that opium enhances those dreams.

Levin, Susan M. *The Romantic Art of Confession: De Quin-cey, Musset, Sand, Lamb, Hogg, Frémy, Soulié, Janin.* Columbia, S.C.: Camden House, 1998. Examines *Confessions of an English Opium Eater* and other confessional works written by British and French authors during the Romantic period. Maintains that these works share common characteristics, including a resemblance to religious writing, narrators who are outcasts and with whom the authors identify, and a focus on societal problems, such as opium addiction.

Morrison, Robert. *The English Opium-Eater: A Biography of Thomas De Quincey.* London: Weidenfeld and Nicholson, 2010. Making full use of De Quincey's published and unpublished papers, Morrison argues for his enduring importance in English literature.

Morrison, Robert, and Daniel Sanjiv Roberts, eds. *Thomas De Quincey: New Theoretical and Critical Directions.* New York: Routledge, 2008. Collection of essays offering numerous interpretations of De Quincey's work: "Brunonianism, Radicalism, and 'the Pleasures of Opium'" by Barry Milligan and "'Earthquake and Eclipse': Radical Energies and De Quincey's 1821 Confessions" by Robert Morrison.

Roberts, Daniel Sanjiv. *Revisionary Gleam: De Quincey, Coleridge, and the High Romantic Argument.* Liverpool, England: Liverpool University Press, 2000. Exploration of De Quincey's relation to contemporaries such as Samuel Taylor Coleridge, William Wordsworth, Immanuel Kant, and Edmund Burke.

Rzepka, Charles J. "The Body, the Book, and 'The True Hero of the Tale': De Quincey's 1821 Confessions and Romantic Autobiography as Cultural Artifact." In *Studies in Autobiography,* edited by James Olney. New York: Oxford University Press, 1988. Argues that the person who is supposedly De Quincey in *Confessions of an English Opium Eater* is a fabrication, and that this fabrication is created anew in the mind of each reader.

Schmitt, Cannon. "De Quincey's Gothic Autobiography and the Opium Wars." In *Alien Nation: Nineteenth-Century Gothic Fictions and English Nationality.* Philadelphia: University of Pennsylvania Press, 1997. Schmitt argues that gothic fiction by De Quincey and other nineteenth century writers helped create an English national identity.

Confessions of Felix Krull, Confidence Man
The Early Years

Author: Thomas Mann (1875-1955)
First published: Bekenntnisse des Hochstaplers Felix Krull: Der Memoiren erster Teil, 1954 (English translation, 1955)
Type of work: Novel
Type of plot: Picaresque
Time of plot: Early twentieth century
Locale: Germany, Paris, and Lisbon

Principal characters:
FELIX KRULL, alias Armand, a hotel employee
ENGELBERT KRULL, his father
FRAU KRULL, his mother
OLYMPIA, his sister
HERR SCHIMMELPREESTER, his godfather
MÜLLER ROSE, an actor and a friend of Engelbert Krull
MADAME HOUPFLÉ, a sentimental novelist
DOM ANTONIO JOSÉ KUCKUCK, a Portuguese museum director
DONA MARIA PIA KUCKUCK, his wife
SUSANNA (ZOUZOU) KUCKUCK, their daughter
MARQUIS DE VENOSTA, a wealthy young nobleman
ZAZA, the marquis's mistress

The Story:

Felix Krull is born in the Rhine Valley, the son of a champagne maker named Engelbert Krull. Townspeople consider the Krull family upper class but frown on the easygoing way of life in the Krull household; Engelbert, for one thing, shows too much interest in one of his female employees. The Krulls frequently invite friends, among them Felix's godfather, Herr Schimmelpreester, for merry parties, in which Felix and his sister Olympia are allowed to take part.

The greatest experience of Felix's youth is a dramatic performance by a famous actor, Müller Rose. Since the actor is a friend of his father, Felix is allowed to visit backstage. When he sees the actor removing his makeup, he is completely disillusioned, but he marvels at the impressions an actor can create. Before long, Felix himself becomes an actor. He starts extending school vacations by falsifying his father's signature on absentee notes, but he finds even more satisfaction from feigning sickness so convincingly as to leave the family doctor completely persuaded of his illness.

The champagne business unfortunately does not prosper. Englebert's champagne is bottled exquisitely, but the wine is of such poor quality that even Herr Schimmelpreester speaks of it only with disdain. The loss of his business and, soon thereafter, his friends is too much for Engelbert, who shoots himself. Herr Schimmelpreester recommends that Frau Krull open a rooming house in Frankfurt. He arranges for Olympia to be employed in a light opera company and Felix to be apprenticed in a Paris hotel. When the prospect of military conscription prevents Felix's departure, he is free to explore city life in Frankfurt, although lack of financial means restricts his role to that of an outside observer. He studies the behavior of society at theaters and learns from window displays what is recommended for gentlemen. With equal interest, he studies the lives of prostitutes. Until now he had only one experience with one of his father's female employees. He meets Rosza and, while her procurer is in jail, becomes her lover.

If Felix wants to follow Herr Schimmelpreester's advice to seek employment in Paris, he has two alternatives: to serve his military term or to be excused entirely from service. After careful preparation, he goes to the army medical examination center. While declaring his fervent desire to serve the fatherland, he manages to convey the most unfavorable information about his background, and he crowns his performance with a pretended epileptic fit. Pretending to be heartbroken because of his military rejection, he leaves for Paris. During the confusion at customs inspection, he inadvertently, as he assures himself, slips the jewel case of a woman traveler into his suitcase.

In Paris he finds himself the lowest member of the hotel hierarchy. With the help of a roommate, he sells some of the stolen jewels. As an elevator operator in a luxury hotel, he makes every effort to please his customers, especially the women. The hotel director gives him the name Armand. One of the guests in his elevator turns out to be the original owner of the jewel case, Madame Houpflé, the wife of a rich Strasbourg merchant. When Armand realizes that the woman does not suspect him of the theft, he is very considerate toward her and is rewarded with an invitation to visit her during off-duty hours.

Armand becomes her lover. Madame Houpflé especially enjoys the humiliating aspect of the affair and talks about her need to be humiliated. Armand considers the moment appropriate for confessing the theft of the jewel case. Madame Houpflé enjoys the confession because it increases her abasement, and she suggests that he should rob her of all her valuables. He gladly obliges.

After he sells the valuables, he rents a room in town. A dual life begins: During the day, he is Armand the hotel employee; during the night, he is Felix, man about town. Thanks to his excellent manners, he is soon promoted to the post of waiter. Difficulties, however, arise when the sixteen-year-old daughter of a wealthy family falls hopelessly in love with him, and when the Scottish Lord Strathbogie is determined to have Armand as his valet. Armand says no to all offers; freedom to do as he pleases seems to him the most valuable goal in life.

His favorite customer is the young Marquis de Venosta, who enjoys the witty remarks of the waiter Armand. The nobleman's mistress, a Parisian dancing girl named Zaza, also approves of him because he does not fail to call her Madame la Marquise. It is de Venosta who finally discovers Armand's double life when he comes across Felix dining in a famous restaurant.

A great dilemma develops for de Venosta. His parents do not approve of his relationship with Zaza and plan to send him on a trip around the world. Because he finds the thought of parting from Zaza unbearable, the marquis is happy to find in Felix a sympathetic listener. Felix explains that the only way for him to stay with Zaza would be to let someone else assume his identity and travel under his name. Delighted with the idea, de Venosta decides that Felix is the best candidate.

After elaborate preparations and much coaching, Felix receives a letter of credit and takes the train to Lisbon. On the way, he meets Dom Antonio José Kuckuck, director of the Museum of Natural History in Lisbon. Impressed by the high social standing of his fellow traveler, the professor explains the outline of his philosophy. Felix finds in the professor's theories an explanation of his own being; all developments of natural history seem to him only steps toward himself. The professor's opinion that all phases of development are still with them and around them give Felix a clue to the stagelike appearance of the world. He gladly accepts an invitation to visit Kuckuck in Lisbon.

When he meets Dona Maria Pia Kuckuck and her daughter Susanna, who is called Zouzou, Felix is struck by the beauty of the two women, who are in turn equally impressed with the handsome "marquis." Determined to kiss Zouzou before his departure but finding his time in Lisbon running short, Felix writes a letter to "his parents," presenting his stay in Lisbon in such a favorable light that they agree to the postponement of the scheduled trip to South America. Under the pretext of wanting to show some of his drawings to Zouzou, Felix meets her secretly in Kuckuck's garden. The incident results in a kiss, which is suddenly interrupted by Dona Maria, who sternly asks "the marquis" to come into the house and reprimands him for abusing her hospitality. Outspoken Dona Maria wants to know why Felix cannot appreciate maturity instead of asking satisfaction from childishness. Dona Maria throws herself into his arms, and he realizes that his attempted seduction of the daughter ends with the unforeseen conquest of the mother.

Critical Evaluation:

Confessions of Felix Krull, Confidence Man, the last work by Thomas Mann and the only one that can be categorized as humorous, is a twentieth century version of the classic picaresque novel. The picaresque approach, in which social criticism is made more palatable by a liberal application of humor, reveals the discrepancy between what people are and what they think they are. Yet because the picaresque approach aims at vice, not at the person who has it, the protagonist or picaro becomes a hero—or, to be more precise, an antihero. Appropriately, picaresque fiction is often categorized as black humor; the picaro is earthbound and filled with angst and with an existential, if comically portrayed, anguish. He is the perpetual outsider gazing into the light but forever condemned to the dark side of reality; he epitomizes the individual who is a member of society but is alienated from and isolated by it. The picaro is forced to survive by whatever means he finds available, most commonly chicanery and illusion. Thus, he projects a respectable illusion onto a receptive world, already enmeshed in delusion. Readers of picaresque fiction must be constantly aware that the presentation is subjective, the perception superficial and the point of view (generally first person) dominated by illusion, disguise, and literal and figurative masks.

Pretense, role-playing, mask-wearing, and disguise are thus traditional elements in the picaresque novel; however, in *Confessions of Felix Krull, Confidence Man*, Mann takes the pretense one step further, for in this work the mask eventually replaces the man. Felix Krull is a chameleon, constantly altering his color to fit his environment. He hides behind multiple personae until "the real I, could not be identified because it actually did not exist." Felix personifies the twentieth century picaro—a hero one step beyond rebellion with no viable religion or creed, a lost soul who is floating on an island of his own imagination. It is ironic that, for perhaps the first time in the picaresque genre, the reader is allowed to penetrate the inner dimensions of a rounded character only to find that, too, is a disguise. Felix sculpts himself and those around him to support his role-playing. From his childhood dress-up and pretend games to feigning epilepsy at his military induction examination, Felix is so adept an actor that he is lost in the impersonations, separated not only from society but also from himself.

Although he is more sophisticated than his fellow picaros and his criminal behavior is the byproduct of chance and not contrivance, Felix demonstrates that survival with style still takes precedence over morality. He moves through initiation fully aware that the person who loves the world shapes himself to please it and that, in turn, he who loves himself shapes the world to suit himself. Despite his dealings in illusion and verbal magic, the character is a realist, knowing well the darkness beyond, of which he is a product. He is also aware that regardless of how thoroughly he may succeed in deceiving his fellows, the darkness still waits, ready to topple him from his temporary pedestal of success and suck him back into obscurity. Felix subsists in a dual struggle with the illusion he creates to survive and the reality that it is an illusion.

Felix, alias Armand, alias the marquis, proposes a theory of interchangeability according to which the sole difference between people is monetary; with a change of clothes, the servant can become the master. This theory becomes the controlling factor in the work and in the protagonist himself, who becomes so adept at it that the real Felix, if there ever was one, disappears and the character becomes no more than a sponge, soaking up each new identity in turn and altering his shape at will.

Through his association with the professor of natural history, Professor Kuckuck, Felix grasps that all humanity is created from raw material much as he has created himself. Mann dedicates long passages of the work to anthropological discussions of the rationalization that if evolution created humans from primeval slime, humans should be able to re-create themselves from whatever material is available. The professor explains evolutionary theory as stages of three spontaneous generations, and it is not inconceivable to relate this hierarchy to the three stages of Felix's life, which culminate in his rebirth as a marquis.

Given his century's overpopulation and zealous mass media, the twentieth century picaro, in contrast to the picaro of previous ages, is forced inward into the chaotic world of the unconscious. Mann does not use the character Felix to castigate the potential disintegration of society, for he sees it as already complete. Rather, it becomes Felix's chore to symbolize the disintegration of the individual.

Confessions of Felix Krull, Confidence Man, Mann's last work, remained uncompleted at his death. Although readers of picaresque fiction are accustomed to episodic wanderings and the unresolved cessation of action, this novel cries out for additional details to dispel the impression of the unfinished. All the easier, however, is it for the reader able to agree with Mann that "life is an episode, on the scale of aeons, a very fleeting one."

"Critical Evaluation" by Joyce Duncan

Further Reading

Alter, Robert. *Rogue's Progress: Studies in the Picaresque Novel*. Cambridge, Mass.: Harvard University Press, 1965. One of the better-known works on the picaresque novel, the book discusses changes in the genre as it moved across generations and national borders. The book treats several novels considered picaresque, including *Confessions of Felix Krull, Confidence Man*.

Hatfield, Henry. *From the Magic Mountain: Mann's Later Masterpieces*. Ithaca, N.Y.: Cornell University Press, 1979. A critical look at Mann's novels based, in part, on his correspondence. Addresses Mann's increasing political awareness, his use of myth and comedy, and how he was viewed by his contemporaries.

Kurzke, Hermann. *Thomas Mann: Life as a Work of Art, a Biography*. Translated by Leslie Willson. Princeton, N.J.: Princeton University Press, 2002. An English translation of a work that was celebrated upon its publication in Germany. Kurzke provides a balanced approach to Mann's life and work, and he addresses Mann's homosexuality and relationship to Judaism.

Lehnert, Herbert, and Eva Wessell, eds. *A Companion to the Works of Thomas Mann*. Rochester, N.Y.: Camden House, 2004. A collection of essays about the range of Mann's work, including discussions of his late politics, female identities and autobiographical impulses in his writings, and *"Felix Krull"* by Egon Schwarz.

Lewis, R. W. B. *The Picaresque Saint*. Philadelphia: J. B. Lippincott, 1961. A critical survey of the picaresque genre with a primary concentration on other novelists but many references to Mann. *Confessions of Felix Krull, Confidence Man* is judged to be one of Mann's masterpieces and the "logical hero" of the age.

Mundt, Hannelore. *Understanding Thomas Mann*. Columbia: University of South Carolina Press, 2004. Mundt discusses the themes, concerns, presentation, and meanings of many of Mann's works, using her later published diaries as one of the sources for her analysis. *Confessions of Felix Krull, Confidence Man* is analyzed in chapter 12.

Robertson, Ritchie, ed. *The Cambridge Companion to Thomas Mann.* New York: Cambridge University Press, 2002. A collection of essays, some analyzing individual works and others discussing Mann's intellectual world, Mann and history, his literary techniques, and his representation of gender and sexuality. *The Confessions of Felix Krull, Confidence Man* is examined in chapter 13.

Schonfield, Ernest. *Art and Its Uses in Thomas Mann's "Felix Krull."* London: Maney Publishing for the Modern Humanities Research Association, 2008. A detailed analysis of the novel, discussing its importance in Mann's development as a writer and placing it within the context of his oeuvre.

Torrance, Robert M. *The Comic Hero.* Cambridge, Mass.: Harvard University Press, 1979. Traces the origin of the comic hero from his mythological antecedents through the modern novel. Contains an extended discussion of *Confessions of Felix Krull, Confidence Man* as representative of the picaresque.

The Confessions of Nat Turner

Author: William Styron (1925-2006)
First published: 1967
Type of work: Novel
Type of plot: Psychological realism
Time of plot: c. 1810-1831
Locale: Southampton County, Virginia

Principal characters:
NAT TURNER, slave leader of an insurrection
SAMUEL TURNER, one of Nat's owners
MARGARET WHITEHEAD, white woman acquaintance of Nat
HARK, a slave
THOMAS GRAY, a lawyer
JEREMIAH COBB, a judge
WILL, a runaway slave

The Story:

Nat Turner joins with at least sixty other slaves and free blacks to kill fifty-seven whites in Southampton County, Virginia, in 1831. Armed with guns, axes, and other weapons, Turner and his men aim to leave no whites alive. At least forty-six of the victims are women, children, or teenagers. After two days of violence, whites succeed in defeating Turner's group in a battle. Turner initially evades capture but soon finds himself in the Southampton jail awaiting execution. A self-proclaimed preacher, Turner is unable to pray and feels abandoned by his God.

On November 1, 1831, an elderly white man by the name of Thomas Ruffin Gray enters Turner's cell. Gray defended some of the insurgent slaves in court. He explains to Turner that Southampton whites simply cannot understand why their slaves revolted. Gray wants to publish a full confession by Turner that will tell the public the facts about the revolt. Gray's concept of his job is to prove that Turner is not a typical slave but a fanatic whose revolt is an isolated event and therefore no threat to the institution of slavery. He tries to

convince Turner that the major reason for his defeat is that most of the slaves defended their owners.

While Gray talks about the rebellion, Turner thinks back to his various owners, from Benjamin and Samuel Turner to Joseph Travis. The memory that dominates from the Travis years concerns Jeremiah Cobb, the man who eventually sentences Nat Turner to death. Cobb was impressed with the slave's intelligence while listening to him explain that Hark, a fellow slave, was disoriented because of the sale of his wife and children. After the conversation with Cobb, Turner decided that Cobb would "be among the few spared the sword." Turner's memory shifts to Cobb's voice in the courtroom warning him to stay awake. Gray, agreeing with the prosecution's call for "swift retribution," states in court that a slave rebellion is not likely to happen again because of "the basic weakness and inferiority, the moral deficiency of the Negro character." It is a rationalization of slavery that the public wants to hear. During the trial, Turner thinks of Margaret Whitehead. Although she is the only person he kills, she was also one of the whites that he was close to. He recalls the day when she read her poem to him and told him that he was the only person at home whom she could confide in.

Turner's reverie is interrupted by Cobb's voice sentencing him to death by hanging. Back in jail after the trial, Gray arrives and attacks Christianity, saying that it accomplished nothing but "misery and suffering for untold generations." Pondering Gray's words, Turner has doubts about being called by God for his "divine mission." The condemned man recalls trying to escape from his dilemma by thinking about his youth at Turner's Mill. Turner learned to read by smuggling a book out of the Turner library. When Samuel Turner discovered his slave's ability to read, he was delighted. It validated his belief that "slaves were capable of intellectual enlightenment." While Samuel argued with his brother Benjamin over the potential of slaves, Turner became aware as never before that he was indeed a slave himself, a piece of property. The conservative Benjamin soon died. Nat became a pet of the family and was encouraged to read and to learn. Samuel Turner apprenticed him as a carpenter and eventually promoted Nat to a position of authority on the plantation. This led to the promise of emancipation at the age of twenty-five, a promise that was not kept when the plantation began to decline. Four slaves were sold. Although Turner had sexual fantasies of golden-haired white girls, his only sexual experience was an encounter with another slave, Willis. Samuel Turner eventually lost the plantation, and Turner became the property of the Reverend Alexander Eppes who, after unsuccessfully trying to rape Turner, relegated him to hard labor as the only slave in the village of Shiloh. Turner's loneliness and frustration continued when he was sold to Thomas Moore. Moore's response to Turner's ability to read was to whip him.

The prisoner next contemplates his developing hatred, the obsession he has to kill all whites in Southampton County. During his almost ten-year tenure with Moore, Turner nursed his hatred and planned his insurrection. He became a preacher and the subjects of his sermons were black pride and the necessity of rebellion. He created objectives and recruited members of his army. The plan included the destruction of local farms and plantations, the killing of all whites, the conquest of the village of Jerusalem for the purpose of possessing its armory, and the establishment of headquarters in the Dismal Swamp. When Moore died, Turner became the property of Joseph Travis. Despite better living conditions, Turner remained determined to fulfill his mission. He convinced himself that he heard a mandate from God. Independence Day of 1831 was chosen as the beginning of the rebellion, but the plan was canceled when Will, a slave on a nearby plantation, assaulted his master and ran away, creating a general atmosphere of suspicion. Turner interrupts his reflection on the insurrection to recall an episode with Margaret. She sympathized with Will for attacking his cruel master. She wondered "why darkies stay the way they do." Margaret asked Turner about a biblical passage that he identified as: "There is no fear in love; but perfect love casteth out fear." Turner remembers his lust for her, but at the time, he converted it into hatred for the "godless white bitch" who was attempting to distract him from his mission of vengeance. Turner turns his thoughts to the Sunday night when the rebellion was launched with an attack on the Travis farm. When Turner was unable to kill Travis with the first blow, Will, the runaway who joined the rebel group, killed Travis and his wife. He taunted Turner for being a weak leader.

Gray intrudes into the prisoner's reveries by asking if Turner feels any remorse. When Nat admits to none, Gray gives his analysis of the defeat of the insurrection, stressing the role played by the faithful retainers, the slaves who defended their masters. After Gray's visit, Turner "was affected by fear and uneasiness." Except for the slaying of Margaret, however, he knows that he did what was necessary. Turner's memory returns to the conflict with Will during the beginning of the rebellion. To regain control, Turner killed Margaret. After the act, he circled the body aimlessly and envisioned Margaret rising from the blazing field. After recovering from the killing, Turner returned to the battle. At the Harris farm, Turner saw a white girl escape, but he made no attempt to stop her. Once the girl sounded the alarm, the insurrection was doomed. Turner let himself be doomed. Turner awakens in his cell on the morning of his execution. He speaks to Hark in the neighboring cell, but he can find no consolation for his despair, no sign of redemption. Gray appears and gives him a Bible, but Turner does not open it. He observes the morning star and thinks of Margaret. He remembers their discussion about "the perfect Christian love of God, and of one another." He feels redeemed. As the executioner arrives, he hears a voice say, "Come, my son," and he surrenders to the morning star.

"The Story" by Noel Schraufnagel;
revised by Caryn E. Neumann

Critical Evaluation:

In 1968, *The Confessions of Nat Turner*, a book based upon the most significant slave revolt in American history, won the Pulitzer Prize in fiction. William Styron's novel about Turner continues to provoke discussion in the decades since its publication because it addresses the complicated relationship between black versus white, fact versus fiction, and art versus history. *The Confessions of Nat Turner* has been a controversial novel, but it is also a book that can stand on its artistic merits. To create a rounded character, Styron expanded upon the limited material of the slave's life presented in the actual confession. The result is a fictional character who is credible. The negative side of Styron's approach is that it left him vulnerable to charges of racism and historical falsification.

Nine months after publication of *The Confessions of Nat Turner*, a book of vehement disapproval appeared. *William Styron's Nat Turner: Ten Black Writers Respond* attacked the novelist for distorting the image of a black hero. They complained that Styron turned a strong black man into an indecisive and emasculated figure. In reality, Turner's revolt had far-reaching effects because of the strength of its leader. Most slave revolts never got as far as Turner's Rebellion. The significance of the revolt is easily seen in the reaction to it. Turner undermined the theory that slaves were docile and happy, intensified the always-present fear of slave revolts, provoked the tightening of slave regulations, sparked the enactment of harsher policies toward slaves and free blacks, sped the decline of abolitionism in the South and its rise in the North, and influenced John Brown's ill-fated 1859 raid on Harpers Ferry. The reception of the novel, especially the ferocity of attacks from black readers, shocked Styron. He mistakenly assumed that Turner's "heroic" deeds were erased from the historical memory of African Americans.

Styron's work appeared in print in 1967 as the United States experienced a round of riots and other forms of rebellion by blacks who protested their second-class citizenship. The social and political context of the Civil Rights movement and the Black Power movement shaped the public response to *The Confessions of Nat Turner*. At the time, some black revolutionaries embraced black philosopher Frantz Fanon's belief that oppressed peoples could liberate themselves psychologically as well as politically only through murderous violence. Styron convicted Turner of moral blindness and sent him, a penitent, to Judgment. Styron's critics challenged the presumption that Turner's actions lacked morality. Vincent Harding, in *William Styron's Nat Turner: Ten Black Writers Respond*, also faulted the novelist for entering into a black man's skin and mind. As the other writers in the book also declared, Styron took away Turner's voice. The voice in the confession is that of Styron. The images are those of Styron. The confession is that of Styron. Rather than meditating on history, as he aimed to do, Styron in the eyes of his critics simply repeated history by erasing the black man from the record of the past.

Additionally, Harding argued that Styron mistakenly believed that he had the right to judge black rebels in the past as well as the present. The charge touched on the issue of whether it is proper for a white writer to use a black character. Styron initially responded to his critics, then chose to back off and let others, such as historian Eugene Genovese, defend him. In 1992, however, Styron broke his silence by penning an essay, "Nat Turner Revisited," that continued to defend his right to write about the black experience.

Styron also defended his right to use Margaret Whitehead. In reality, this young woman was the only person killed by Turner. She hid in her home as six members of her family died at the hands of the rebelling slaves, then attempted to flee before being beaten to death in a field with a fence post. In Styron's novel, Turner lusts after white women, particularly Margaret. Black critics faulted Styron for neglecting black women and for supposing that Turner would destroy his movement because of his weakness for white flesh in the form of the escaping white girl at the Harris farm. It seemed that Styron assumed that black women were less desirable than white women, which prompted critics such as Harding to ask whether Styron related Turner's sexual fantasies or his own. The presumption that black women were second rate deeply offended African Americans. Underlying these criticisms of the black-white romance is the historical fact that many of the thousands of lynchings of black men were justified on the grounds of protecting white women from lustful black men. Styron seemed to support this racist assumption, thereby touching on an extremely sensitive issue to the African American community.

The historical community was a bit kinder to *The Confessions of Nat Turner*. Genovese, a prominent historian of the slave experience, stated that Styron properly took liberties with historical details. Genovese faulted Styron's critics for confusing history with fiction and, worse, for demanding that both serve political and ideological agendas. He challenged the white academic community for seeing Turner as a sainted figure because he happened to be on the right side of history. Genovese argued that oppressed people do not have the right to use "any means necessary." He theorized that Turner may well have been a religious fanatic who not only shed blood but also acknowledged the sin of doing so and sought redemption.

Styron's major fault appears to be that he did not create the Turner that the revolutionaries of the 1960's wanted. He aimed for a Turner who is an admirable but necessarily flawed hero who strikes a blow for liberty. As he later stated, a man bedeviled by bloody visions who leads a drunken band of followers to butcher unarmed women and children is not in the same category as a Spartacus or a Toussaint L'Ouverture. Styron intended for his book to shed light on slavery in America and on the modern condition of race relations by showing how the present is bound to the past. Like countless other novelists, he took literary liberties with the historical record to create a recognizably human figure with conflicted but rational motives. To do so, he crossed racial lines, which inflamed racial tensions.

The controversy over *The Confessions of Nat Turner* essentially imposed an informal boycott on the novel, though this condemnation has weakened in the twenty-first century. The book is useful as much for its literary merit as for its place in the history of censorship and race relations. It illuminates the confrontation between fiction and fact.

"Critical Evaluation" by Caryn E. Neumann

Further Reading

Clarke, John Henrik, ed. *The Second Crucifixion of Nat Turner.* 2d ed. Baltimore: Black Classic Press, 1997. A new edition, with a new introduction by Clarke, of the book originally published in 1968 as *William Styron's Nat Turner: Ten Black Writers Respond.* Styron is charged with misrepresenting Turner's life.

Cologne-Brookes, Gavin. *The Novels of William Styron: From Harmony to History.* Baton Rouge: Louisiana State University Press, 1995. Examines the influence of the modernist movement on Styron's novels, exploring his psychological themes and analyzing his shifting patterns of discourse.

Davis, Mary Kemp. *Nat Turner Before the Bar of Judgment: Fictional Treatments of the Southampton Slave Insurrection.* Baton Rouge: Louisiana State University Press, 1999. Surveys four nineteenth century novels and two twentieth century novels about Nat Turner's Rebellion, including Styron's work.

Friedman, Melvin J., and Irving Malin, eds. *William Styron's The Confessions of Nat Turner: A Critical Handbook.* Belmont, Calif.: Wadsworth, 1970. Contains background materials on the revolt, including the original confession of Turner as well as an autobiography of Styron and three interviews with Styron after the publication of his novel.

Hadaller, David. *Gynicide: Women in the Novels of William Styron.* Madison, N.J.: Fairleigh Dickinson University Press, 1996. Explores the treatment of women in Styron's fiction, with special emphasis on his handling of women's deaths and the meaning of these deaths. Styron's depictions force readers to question a society that victimizes women.

Oates, Stephen B. *The Fires of Jubilee: Nat Turner's Fierce Rebellion.* New York: HarperCollins, 1990. This is the standard historical account of Nat Turner's rebellion.

Ross, Daniel W., ed. *The Critical Response to William Styron.* Westport, Conn.: Greenwood Press, 1995. A collection of previously printed reviews and articles, as well as original essays, which chronologically trace the critical reception of Styron's novels.

Stone, Albert E. *The Return of Nat Turner: History, Literature, and Cultural Politics in Sixties America.* Athens: University of Georgia Press, 1992. Focuses on Styron's novel, the cultural landscape that produced it, and the cultural politics that engulfed it.

West, James L. W., III, ed. *William Styron: A Life.* New York: Random House, 1998. An essential biography about Styron that connects events in his life to his fiction.

The Confidence Man
His Masquerade

Author: Herman Melville (1819-1891)
First published: 1857
Type of work: Novel
Type of plot: Satire
Time of plot: Nineteenth century, before the Civil War
Locale: Mississippi River

Principal characters:
THE CONFIDENCE MAN, referred to as such only in the title
THE MAN IN CREAM COLORS, a deaf-mute, a guise of the Confidence Man
DER BLACK GUINEA, a lame beggar, a guise of the Confidence Man
JOHN RINGMAN, an unfortunate gentleman, a guise of the Confidence Man
THE MAN IN THE GRAY COAT AND WHITE TIE, a collector for charities, a guise of the Confidence Man
JOHN TRUMAN, the president and transfer agent of the Black Rapids Coal Company, a guise of the Confidence Man
THE HERB-DOCTOR, a dealer in herbal medicine, a guise of the Confidence Man
A REPRESENTATIVE OF THE PHILOSOPHICAL INTELLIGENCE OFFICE, a guise of the Confidence Man
FRANCIS GOODMAN, a cosmopolitan, a guise of the Confidence Man
ROBERTS, a country merchant
THE COLLEGE SOPHOMORE, a young man reading Tacitus
THE MISER, a wealthy but sickly old man
PITCH, a Missourian
CHARLIE NOBLE, an amiable passenger
MARK WINSOME, a mystic
EGBERT, his practical disciple
WILLIAM CREAM, the ship's barber

The Story:

On an April morning in St. Louis, a deaf-mute boards the steamer *Fidèle* (faith). Many passengers gather around a placard advertising a reward for the capture of a mysterious impostor, and some take this opportunity to purchase money belts or biographies of famous criminals. The deaf-mute approaches the placard, writes platitudes about charity on a slate, and displays them to the crowd. Meanwhile, a barber opens his shop and hangs a sign that reads "No Trust." Rebuffed, the mute walks to the forecastle and falls asleep at the foot of a ladder.

After the ship leaves dock, a group of passengers amuse themselves by tossing pennies (or, more cruelly, buttons) to a lame black man who catches them in his mouth. He identifies himself as Der Black Guinea, but he is confronted by a man with a wooden leg who accuses him of being a sham. An Episcopalian minister intercedes and, when the beggar

describes several people on the ship who will vouch for him, goes to find them. The wooden-legged man renews his attack, but a Methodist minister rebukes him until he withdraws. Although the Methodist apparently triumphs, he immediately demonstrates similar suspicion. Further complications are averted when a kind merchant offers the beggar alms, in the process accidentally dropping a business card, which the beggar surreptitiously covers with his stump.

Roberts, the merchant, is soon accosted by a man with a weed in his hat who identifies himself as John Ringman and claims to be an old acquaintance. When Roberts protests he has no recollection of their meeting, Ringman presses him to admit he had a fever at about that time that might have erased his memory. Ringman relates a story of profound personal misfortune, until the merchant offers him a banknote and then a larger one. In return, Ringman tells Roberts that the president of the Black Rapids Coal Company, which represents a rare investment opportunity, is on board.

Ringman next encounters a college sophomore reading Tacitus. In impassioned rhetoric, he urges the student to toss the volume overboard before he loses confidence in his fellows. Nonplussed, the young man departs.

The Episcopalian minister's search for someone who knows Der Black Guinea concludes when he encounters a man in a gray coat and white tie, exactly as the beggar described. The unnamed man bears witness to Der Black Guinea's authenticity. The wooden-legged man reappears and amusedly ridicules human credulity. Wanting to distance himself from this cynicism, the minister gives the stranger money for the beggar. The stranger then extracts an additional contribution for the Seminole Widow and Orphan Asylum.

This unnamed man manages to compel a donation for this charity from another gentleman, then a further contribution to support an ambitious plan to unite all of the world's charities under one organization. The man concludes his operations by obtaining a donation for the asylum from a woman reading the Bible. Quoting the New Testament, he then departs.

The sophomore is approached by John Truman, the president and transfer agent of the Black Rapids Coal Company. Truman claims to be searching for Ringman in order to give him money and to have just spoken with the man in the gray coat. The sophomore invests an undisclosed amount in the company. The hapless Roberts follows suit, and in the process informs Truman of the existence of an old miser onboard. The miser, sickly and confused, invests one hundred dollars. He immediately regrets his decision but is too weak to pursue Truman.

Not all of the financial transactions aboard the *Fidèle* involve large sums. After Truman's departure, an herb-doctor moves about the ship selling his wares, alternately called Omni-Balsamic Reinvigorator and Samaritan Pain Dissuader. Several passengers, including the miser, make purchases for two or three dollars. Only a Missourian, professing universal distrust of people and nature, resists.

Pitch, the Missourian, tells of a succession of untrustworthy boys he employed on his farm. Shortly after the herb-doctor's departure, however, a representative of the Philosophical Intelligence Office, an employment agency, persuades him to try another, sight unseen. Pitch gives the stranger a small fee and passage money. He later has second thoughts but is interrupted by a man describing himself as a cosmopolitan who argues against a solitary life. Despite the cosmopolitan's protests, Pitch welcomes him as a fellow misanthrope, which compels him to leave.

Francis Goodman, the cosmopolitan, next meets a talkative passenger calling himself Charlie Noble. Noble relates a long tale about an Indian-hater named Colonel John Moredock. Finding that they share a low opinion of misanthropy, Noble and Goodman strike up an immediate friendship over wine, though Noble seems determined to drink less than his companion. All goes well until Goodman claims to need money and asserts that Noble will lend him fifty dollars. Noble erupts, and Goodman insists he was joking. Goodman tells a story about a young merchant, Charlemont, who without warning turned away from his friends. Noble claims fatigue and leaves.

Mark Winsome, a mystic philosopher who overhears the previous conversation, introduces himself to Goodman. Using obscure references to ancient Egypt and Greece, Winsome warns that Noble is out to cheat him. Goodman thanks the mystic but insists that he sees no reason to lack confidence in Noble's nature. Winsome introduces Goodman to his disciple, Egbert, and departs.

Egbert proves to be as practical as his mentor has been abstruse. Apparently interested in understanding Winsome's philosophy, Goodman asks Egbert to act out a scenario involving a man in need who begs a loan of a friend. The two men do so at great length, with Goodman requesting the loan and Egbert justifying his refusal. To support his argument, Egbert tells of China Aster, who came to ruin and death through a friendly loan. Defeated, the cosmopolitan withdraws.

Goodman goes to the ship's barbershop with its "No Trust" sign displayed. After great effort, he convinces the barber to give him a shave on credit and continue the policy for the rest of the voyage for other passengers. He signs an agreement to compensate the barber for any losses. After Goodman leaves, however, the barber rehangs his sign and tears up the agreement.

Goodman retires to the cabin, where he encounters a well-to-do old man reading the Bible by lamplight. The two men agree on the importance of having confidence in one's fellow. Afterward, the old man brings a traveler's lock and money belt from a young peddler. Goodman refuses to purchase anything. Extinguishing the light, he leads the man, holding his money belt and a life preserver, into the darkness.

"The Story" revised by Richard A. Nanian

Critical Evaluation:

Herman Melville's work was largely forgotten during his own lifetime, and it was only in the 1920's that this author began to receive his due, for the first time, as one of the most important writers the United States has ever produced. *The Confidence Man: His Masquerade* was still not appreciated, however, until some thirty years later. As *Moby Dick* (1851) appealed to modernists in the 1920's because of its symbolic investigations of human evil and its experimental form, so *The Confidence Man*, the last of Melville's novels published in his lifetime (*Billy Budd, Foretopman* was published posthumously in 1924), found its audience in the post-World War II readership's cynicism, sense of the absurd, and interest in language play. Its dense structure, paradoxes, and puns remind the reader less of Melville's contemporaries than of such postmodern authors as Vladimir Nabokov and Jorge Luis Borges.

Yet *The Confidence Man* is a work deeply rooted in its own time. Gertrude Stein once wrote that no writer is ahead of his or her time, but a unique writer's understanding of his or her own time may not be understood by others also living in that moment: The writer may be living in the present while all others are still living in the past. This is certainly true of Melville in *The Confidence Man*. For while the United States remained obsessed with its own promises of freedom and democracy, Melville was interested in showing how the manipulation of the language of freedom and democracy could become the true discourse of the nation. Incidental historical references make clear to the reader the historical correlative of ruse, swindle, and appearance that Melville is interested in exposing. The hoaxes of circus showman P. T. Barnum and the financial panics and wildcat banking of the nineteenth century manipulated public trust for profit. In *The Confidence Man*, hucksters and con artists try to sell one another bogus stock, swindle one another out of services, and rob one another of whatever property they might have. The masquerade in the title suggests that the novel is not interested in describing a single individual but rather a type. The American confidence man dons any number of masks, but one thing always remains the same: He is trying to sell something, and to do so he must gain the trust of his potential victim. As one character says: "Confidence is the indispensable basis of all sorts of business transactions. Without it, commerce between man and man, between country and country, would, like a watch, run down and stop." No character can steer clear of potential swindles, for to do so would mean distrust of an entire system: capitalism and the American project. Nearly every character in the novel is practicing his own type of shell game, so mutual wariness abounds. The implicit criticism of business and capitalism is clear.

The idea of the masquerade also leads to a very unconventional novel. There is no plot per se. Rather, the novel relies on an intricate plan to structure its narrative. It is forty-five chapters in length: Twenty-two of these occur before twilight, and twenty-two after, in the darkness of night. The characters' actions, as well, grow gradually darker, ending with the planned robbery and murder of an old man whose lantern (symbolizing the light of God) has been extinguished moments before, after midnight. The action takes place aboard a steamship traveling down the Mississippi River, during the period of tension between the North and South prior to the Civil War. In chapter twenty-three, the book's middle chapter, the boat sits still in Cairo, at the southern tip of Illinois. From there on, the characters enter slave territory, which Melville suggests is a state of moral darkness. Thereafter, too, the various guises of the confidence man coalesce into one figure, the cosmopolitan.

In the first half of the novel, transactions have taken place in the light of day. People have been swindled, but the stakes have been low and the consequences not altogether severe. Things take a decidedly more serious turn in the second half of the novel, after the pivotal twenty-third chapter. A chapter concerning "the metaphysics of Indian hating" makes clear that biases against Native Americans have not been based so much upon reality as on the stories that have been built up over the years characterizing Indians as deceitful, treacherous, and bloodthirsty. It is not the truth of a situation upon which people act, but its appearance. As any student of American history knows, massacres resulted on the basis of such fictions. The masks that truth wears are thus of great concern to all if people intend to have anything resembling justice in the world.

The difficulty of ascertaining what is true in a world of appearances makes for a hazardous existence. At the beginning of the novel, a mute man with a chalkboard inscribes various messages, about the virtue of charity, from Corinthians. In a world where what purports to be charity may be villainy in disguise, however, it is not easy to recognize charity when it appears. This is the dark world that Melville describes, a world in which the light of God fades and is replaced by the confusions of evil. The virtues of trust in one's fellow human being, including geniality, philanthropy, fidelity, and consistency, are all, at various times in the novel, manipulated for personal gain. Behind all cons, moreover, is the threat of violence. When, at the end of the novel, the cosmopolitan "kindly" leads the old man to his stateroom, the reader has no doubt that murder and robbery await the old man. The old man, suspicious of the world, having bought a lock for his room and a money belt in which to hide his valuables, is nevertheless trusting of the cosmopolitan, who has spent time with him discussing the Bible. The true (or at least the more successful) criminals of the world, Melville suggests, are those who seem to be benefactors and who know how to use a language that will make themselves attractive.

"Critical Evaluation" by Ted Pelton

Further Reading

Bloom, Harold, ed. *Herman Melville*. New ed. New York: Bloom's Literary Criticism, 2008. Collection of critical essays analyzing Melville's work, including John Bryant's piece "Allegory and Breakdown in *The Confidence Man*: Melville's Comedy of Doubt."

Cook, Jonathan. *Satirical Apocalypse: An Anatomy of Melville's "The Confidence Man."* Westport, Conn.: Greenwood Press, 1996. Analyzes how Melville uses characters and scenes in the novel to satirize political, religious, social, literary, and familial issues and events.

Delbanco, Andrew. *Melville: His World and Work*. New York: Knopf, 2005. Delbanco's critically acclaimed biography places Melville in his time, including information about the debate over slavery and details of life in 1840's New York. Delbanco also discusses the significance of Melville's works at the time they were published and in the twenty-first century.

Levine, Robert S., ed. *The Cambridge Companion to Herman Melville*. New York: Cambridge University Press, 1998. An indispensable tool for the student of Melville, this collection of essays includes discussions of Melville and sexuality, his "traveling god," and an analysis of *The Confidence Man* by Elizabeth Renker.

Lindberg, Gary. *The Confidence-Man in American Literature*. New York: Oxford University Press, 1982. A discussion of Melville's novel frames this investigation of the confidence man in American literature and history. Includes discussions of Huckleberry Finn, P. T. Barnum, Walt Whitman, and Thomas Jefferson, among others.

Melville, Herman. *The Confidence-Man: His Masquerade—An Authoritative Text, Contemporary Reviews, Biographical Overviews, Sources, Backgrounds, and Criticism*. Edited by Hershel Parker and Mark Niemeyer. 2d ed. New York: W. W. Norton, 2006. In addition to the text of the novel, this edition includes explanatory annotations, nineteen reviews and commentaries about the book, an overview of biographical information about Melville that was obtained in the past three decades, and information about social developments and popular culture that are pertinent to the novel.

_____. *Journals*. Edited by Howard C. Horsford and Lynn Horth. Evanston, Ill.: Northwestern University Press, 1989. Includes entries and passages written soon after Melville finished *The Confidence Man*.

Rogin, Michael Paul. *Subversive Genealogy: The Politics and Art of Herman Melville*. Berkeley: University of California Press, 1985. Incisive psychological and Marxist reading of Melville's life and work, arguing that Melville was one of the leading thinkers of his age. The reading of Melville's family's place in the historical context of the 1840's is unparalleled. Includes an excellent discussion of *The Confidence Man*.

Rollyson, Carl E., and Lisa Paddock. *Herman Melville A to Z: The Essential Reference to His Life and Work*. New York: Checkmark Books, 2001. A comprehensive and encyclopedic coverage of Melville's life, works, and times; the 675 detailed entries provide information on the characters, settings, allusions, and references in his fiction, his friends and associates, and the critics and scholars who have studied his work.

Spanos, William V. "Cavilers and Con Men: *The Confidence Man: His Masquerade*." In *Herman Melville and the American Calling: Fiction After "Moby-Dick," 1851-1857*. Albany: State University of New York Press, 2008. Analyzes the major works that appeared after the publication of *Moby Dick*. Argues that these works shared the metaphor of the orphanage: a place that represents both estrangement from a symbolic fatherland, as well as the myth of American exceptionalism.

The Confidential Clerk

Author: T. S. Eliot (1888-1965)
First produced: 1953; first published, 1954
Type of work: Drama
Type of plot: Comedy of manners
Time of plot: Mid-twentieth century
Locale: London

Principal characters:
SIR CLAUDE MULHAMMER, a successful financier
EGGERSON, his former confidential clerk
COLBY SIMPKINS, his new confidential clerk
B. KAGHAN, a businessman and Lucasta's fiancé
LUCASTA ANGEL, Sir Claude's illegitimate daughter
LADY ELIZABETH MULHAMMER, Sir Claude's wife
MRS. GUZZARD, Colby's aunt

The Story:

Sir Claude Mulhammer, a successful middle-aged financier, invites his retired confidential clerk, Eggerson, down to London from his home in the suburbs. He asks Eggerson for the specific purpose of meeting Lady Elizabeth's plane on her return from a trip to Switzerland and telling her that he was replaced in his position by a young man named Colby Simpkins. Sir Claude and Eggerson are apprehensive that Lady Elizabeth will be suspicious and disapproving, and Sir Claude wants to keep from her the fact that Colby is his illegitimate son until she comes to like him and accepts him in the household. Sir Claude and Eggerson hope that Lady Elizabeth might even decide that she likes him enough to want to adopt him, to take the place of a son she gave up in her youth.

Before Eggerson can leave for the airport, Lady Elizabeth returns unexpectedly and has to be introduced to Colby without any preparation. Lady Elizabeth, however, preoccupied by her spiritual life and convinced that she is the one who recommended Colby to begin with, eagerly takes him under her wing. Colby makes a favorable impression on all the members of the household, including Sir Claude's daughter Lucasta and her fiancé B. Kaghan.

An unsuccessful musician, Colby agrees to introduce Lucasta to the pleasures of music. During a long introspective conversation in Colby's new flat, which Sir Claude acquires for him and Lady Elizabeth enthusiastically offers to decorate, Colby and Lucasta discover a mutual liking. Lucasta, who begins to question her feelings for Kaghan, confides to Colby that she is Sir Claude's daughter. Colby is shocked to learn that she is his half sister, a fact he is, however, unable to reveal to her. Lucasta is disappointed in Colby's reaction, which she misunderstands, and reclaims Kaghan as her fiancé when he arrives to see Colby's new flat.

Lady Elizabeth appears soon after, and once she nudges Lucasta and Kaghan on their way, she begins to question Colby closely about his background. Upon discovering that

he was raised by an aunt, Mrs. Guzzard, in Teddington, just outside London, she becomes convinced that he is the son she had as a very young woman. She relinquished the baby to his father and knows that the child was adopted by a couple with an unusual name from a place she now recalls is Teddington. Because she does not tell Colby what she suspects, he cannot understand her interest in his background and tries to turn the conversation. When they are joined by Sir Claude, Lady Elizabeth announces her belief that Colby is her lost son.

Sir Claude decides she must be told the truth about Colby's relationship with him, but Lady Elizabeth remains convinced that he is mistaken. Colby is frustrated to have both a mother and a father claiming him as their own, and he demands that his real identity be determined. All agree that Mrs. Guzzard must be summoned and questioned.

Sir Claude arranges a meeting in his business room. While waiting for the arrival of Eggerson, who is to chair the meeting, Sir Claude and Lady Elizabeth speak honestly and gain a deeper understanding of each other. When Eggerson arrives, he is accompanied by an uninvited guest, Lucasta, who is looking for Colby. When Sir Claude informs her that Colby is her half brother, Lucasta understands the reason for Colby's shock at her earlier disclosure and she thereupon formally announces her marriage to Kaghan.

Mrs. Guzzard is shown in by Kaghan, and when Eggerson begins to question her, she reveals that Kaghan is the son Lady Elizabeth had given up; the child remained with the Guzzards for a while before being adopted by the Kaghans, formerly of Teddington. Mrs. Guzzard also reveals that her sister, who was expecting Sir Claude's baby, died before giving birth and that Colby is actually her own son. She was recently widowed when Sir Claude sought them out and played along with his belief that Colby is his illegitimate son so that she would receive some financial help for his upbringing. When Colby learns that he is the son of Herbert Guzzard, a disappointed musician, he resolves on music as a career, even if he lacks great talent. Colby refuses Sir Claude's offer that he continue to think of him as at least a father figure and to stay at the Mulhammer home. Instead, he decides to apply for the post of organist at the parish church in Eggerson's neighborhood. Sir Claude, inclined to doubt Mrs. Guzzard's revelation about Colby's lineage, dolefully accepts it when he sees that Eggerson, whom he trusts explicitly, believes her. Bereft, the Mulhammers turn for consolation to Sir Claude's daughter Lucasta and Lady Elizabeth's son Kaghan, who promises that their relationship will help stabilize the newly established family.

Critical Evaluation:

T. S. Eliot, best known as one of the greatest English poets of the modern age, also produced several poetic dramas, of which *The Confidential Clerk*, first staged in Edinburgh in 1953, is perhaps the least known and appreciated. Eliot is reported to have said at a press conference after the play's first stage production that "if one wanted to say something serious nowadays it was easier to say it in comedy"; this play can be considered both a serious tale conveyed comically and a high farce dramatized in serious tones. Certainly Eliot was inspired by Greek tragicomedies. The plot of *The Confidential Clerk* is based on Euripides' *Iōn* (c. 411 B.C.E.; *Ion*; 1781). With its lost children, searching parents, and mistaken identities, Eliot's play also resembles the kind of comedy of manners made famous by Oscar Wilde. Despite the appearance of frivolity, however, a serious undertone is integrated into the pattern of events, and behind the farcical interchange of parents and children lies the spiritual revelation that all earthly relationships are swallowed up in one's relation to God.

Eliot explored the worlds of spirituality and religion widely and deeply in all his writing. In this play, the central concept is Colby's search for a way to integrate the outer world of action with the world of spiritual being, the two aspects of reality. He discovers, in the course of the play, that the path lies through the fulfillment of his true relationships to others, especially to his dead father (the failed musician Herbert Guzzard) and to God, and it is hinted that he may finally find his true vocation in the church. The other characters in the play find their spiritual peace in their own way. Eggerson, for example, finds physical and spiritual solace in retiring regularly to his "secret garden," where he tends vegetables to bring back to his wife.

The play exists simultaneously at two levels: There is the comic, farcical world, in which long-lost relatives, parents, and children are revealed and reunited, and there is the world of spiritual discovery, in which self-knowledge is the goal.

The play's ultimate revelation is that the only way to unite the outer (public) and inner (private) worlds is through love and communion with another human being and/or with God. As in much of Eliot's other work, especially the plays *The Family Reunion* (1939) and *The Cocktail Party* (1949), a choice is made between normal family life and a dedicated life that leads away from family, probably to God. Lucasta wisely discovers that though she feels an attraction to Colby, he does not really need another human being and that her family-oriented future lies with Kaghan and the Mulhammers. Sir Claude, who craves human closeness and desires Colby for a son, has to learn the hard lesson that he must let Colby go. Eliot emphasizes the need for people to try to understand each other's needs and motivations. Even Lady Elizabeth, who despite her idiosyncratic nature is wiser at the end of the play, expresses the hope that she and Sir Claude may try to understand each other better "and perhaps that will help us to understand other people."

Colby's brief presence among them inspires these new attempts at understanding; his departure does not split the family but reinforces their newfound solidarity. This allows Eliot to end the play on a note of hope. Although Colby's departure saddens the Mulhammers, it makes clear to them the need for self-knowledge and mutual understanding, which are the two prominent themes of *The Confidential Clerk*.

The play is structured in three acts: Act 1 introduces and explains, act 2 develops, and act 3 provides revelations and closure. A preliminary dialogue between Sir Claude and Eggerson clarifies the situation for the reader/audience, after which the rest of the characters are introduced slowly. Eliot carefully leads up to Lady Elizabeth's entrance and then gives the actual moment dramatic flair: Sir Claude, Eggerson, and Lucasta have all talked about her and raised suspense about how she will react to Colby; her unexpected arrival quickly becomes a comic anticlimax when she declares that it was she who had interviewed and recommended Colby.

Act 2 begins with another exploratory dialogue, which, however, approaches the level of intensity associated with poetry. The poetry is not sustained in this play but appears in passages in which Eliot highlights religious and spiritual experience. At other moments, the tone is conversational, with only a touch of poetic language giving it elegance or depth at moments when the characters are expressing their innermost thoughts and feelings.

Act 3 unravels the mysteries and provides closure. In the course of the play, a sense of unity is established among the characters, each of whom seems equally important and involved in the play's development. A weakness in the play may be that there is no compelling, central episode, no passage of heightened poetic beauty. Instead, Eliot's message is in the design of the entire plot and in the relationships of all the characters to one another. Eliot is considered a writer of poetic drama, but *The Confidential Clerk* exists at the borders of prose, where the dramatist, instead of confining the focus to a single revelation, has concentrated on overall plot development and the experiences of an entire group.

Brinda Bose

Further Reading

Browne, Elliot Martin. *The Making of T. S. Eliot's Plays*. London: Cambridge University Press, 1970. The classic testament to the writing and production of Eliot's plays from the man who collaborated in their staging and provided invaluable help and criticism to the dramatist at every stage.

Däumer, Elisabeth. "Vipers, Viragos, and Spiritual Rebels: Women in T. S. Eliot's Christian Society Plays." In *Gender, Desire, and Sexuality in T. S. Eliot*, edited by Cassandra Laity and Nancy K. Gish. New York: Cambridge University Press, 2004. Däumer analyzes Eliot's depiction of women in *The Confidential Clerk* and several other plays.

Gordon, Lyndall. *T. S. Eliot: An Imperfect Life*. New York: W. W. Norton, 1999. An authoritative, thoroughly researched biography that concedes Eliot's many personal flaws as well as describing his poetic genius.

Jones, David Edwards. *The Plays of T. S. Eliot*. London: Routledge & Kegan Paul, 1960. Provides a useful chapter-length analysis of *The Confidential Clerk*, as well as an introductory discussion of the genre of poetic drama.

Moody, A. David, ed. *The Cambridge Companion to T. S. Eliot*. New York: Cambridge University Press, 1994. Collection of essays, including discussions of Eliot's life; Eliot as a philosopher, a social critic, and a product of America; and religion, literature, and society in Eliot's work. Also features the essay "Pereira and After: The Cures of Eliot's Theater" by Robin Grove.

Raine, Craig. *T. S. Eliot*. New York: Oxford University Press, 2006. In this examination of Eliot's work, Raine maintains that "the buried life," or the failure of feeling, is a consistent theme in the poetry and plays. Chapter 5 focuses on Eliot's plays.

Smith, Carol H. *T. S. Eliot's Dramatic Theory and Practice*. New York: Gordian Press, 1977. A good basic account of Eliot's ideas of dramatic theory and practice, which gives the reader a sense of what Eliot intended to achieve in his work.

Smith, Grover. *T. S. Eliot's Poetry and Plays: A Study in Sources and Meanings*. 2d ed. Chicago: University of Chicago Press, 1974. An essential reference guide for any interested reader of Eliot's work, which provides details of his sources and inspirations, as well as a comprehensive analysis of the explicit and implicit meanings.

Ward, David. *T. S. Eliot Between Two Worlds: A Reading of T. S. Eliot's Poetry and Plays*. London: Routledge & Kegan Paul, 1973. Provides a useful reading of the conflicts and complexities in Eliot's thinking, a discussion that is relevant to an understanding of the play.